Official
Nationa e

Record & Fact Book

A National Football League Book.
Workman Publishing Co., New York.

National Football League, 1987

410 Park Avenue, New York, N.Y. 10022 (212) 758-1500

Commissioner: Pete Rozelle
Executive Vice President & League Counsel: Jay Moyer
Treasurer: John Schoemer
Executive Director: Don Weiss
Director of Administration: Joe Rhein
Director of Communications: Joe Browne
Director of Operations: Jan Van Duser
Director of Broadcasting: Val Pinchbeck, Jr.
Director of Public Relations: Jim Heffernan
Director of Security: Warren Welsh
Assistant Director of Security: Charles R. Jackson
Director of Player Personnel: Joel Bussert
Supervisor of Officials: Art McNally
Assistant Supervisors of Officials: Jack Reader, Nick Skorich, Joe Gardi, Tony Veteri
Director of Special Events: Jim Steeg
Assistant Director of Special Events: Susan McCann
Assistant Counsel: Jim Noel
Controller: Tom Sullivan
Director of Player Relations: Mel Blount

American Football Conference

President: Lamar Hunt, Kansas City Chiefs
Assistant to President: Al Ward
Director of Information: Pete Abitante

National Football Conference

President: Wellington Mara, New York Giants
Assistant to President: Bill Granholm
Director of Information: Dick Maxwell

Cover Photograph by Jim Turner.

Printed in the United States of America.

A National Football League Book.
Compiled by the NFL Public Relations Department and Seymour Siwoff, Elias Sports Bureau.
Edited by Pete Abitante, NFL Public Relations and Chuck Garrity, Jr., NFLP Creative Services.
Statistics by Elias Sports Bureau.
Produced by NFL Properties, Inc., Creative Services Division.

Workman Publishing Co.
1 West 39th Street, New York, N.Y. 10018
Manufactured in the United States of America.
First printing, July 1987.

10 9 8 7 6 5 4 3 2 1

Contents

1987 SCHEDULE AND NOTE CALENDAR

All times P.M. local daylight.
Nationally televised games in parentheses. CBS and NBC television doubleheader games in the regular season to be announced.

Preseason/First Week

Saturday, August 8	Hall of Fame Game at Canton, Ohio Kansas City ___ vs. San Francisco ___	(ABC) 12:00
Sunday, August 9	American Bowl '87 at London, England Los Angeles Rams ___ vs. Denver ___	(NBC) 6:00
Thursday, August 13	Kansas City ___ at Houston ___	7:00
	Seattle ___ at Los Angeles Rams ___	7:30
Friday, August 14	Pittsburgh ___ at Washington ___	8:00
Saturday, August 15	Buffalo ___ at Atlanta ___	8:00
	Cincinnati ___ at Tampa Bay ___	7:00
	Dallas ___ at San Diego ___	6:00
	Denver ___ vs. Green Bay ___ at Tempe, Ariz.	7:00
	Indianapolis ___ at Detroit ___	8:00
	Minnesota ___ at New Orleans ___	7:00
	Philadelphia ___ at New York Jets ___	8:00
	St. Louis ___ at Cleveland ___	7:30
	San Francisco ___ at Los Angeles Raiders ___	7:00
Sunday, August 16	Chicago ___ at Miami ___	(ESPN) 8:00
	New York Giants ___ at New England ___	(ABC) 1:30

Preseason/Second Week

Saturday, August 22	Atlanta ___ at Kansas City ___	7:30
	Buffalo ___ at Los Angeles Raiders ___	6:00
	Cincinnati ___ at Detroit ___	8:00
	Cleveland ___ at New York Giants ___	8:00
	Dallas ___ at San Francisco ___	(CBS) 6:00
	Houston ___ at New Orleans ___	7:00
	Indianapolis ___ at Minnesota ___	7:00
	New York Jets ___ at Tampa Bay ___	7:00
	Pittsburgh ___ at Chicago ___	6:00
	Seattle ___ at St. Louis ___	7:00
	Washington ___ vs. Green Bay ___ at Madison, Wis.	1:00
Sunday, August 23	Los Angeles Rams ___ at San Diego ___	(ESPN) 5:00
	Philadelphia ___ at New England ___	7:00
Monday, August 24	Miami ___ at Denver ___	(ABC) 6:00

Preseason/Third Week

Thursday, August 27	San Diego ___ at San Francisco ___	6:00
Friday, August 28	Detroit ___ at Seattle ___	7:30
Saturday, August 29	Buffalo ___ at Kansas City ___	7:30
	Cincinnati ___ at Green Bay ___	7:00
	Cleveland ___ at Atlanta ___	8:00
	Denver ___ at Los Angeles Rams ___	7:00
	Houston ___ at Indianapolis ___	7:30
	Miami ___ at Philadelphia ___	7:30
	New England ___ at Minnesota ___	(CBS) 2:00
	New York Jets ___ at New York Giants ___	(NBC) 9:00
	Pittsburgh ___ at New Orleans ___	7:00
	Washington ___ at Tampa Bay ___	7:00
Sunday, August 30	Los Angeles Raiders ___ at Dallas ___	(ESPN) 7:00
Monday, August 31	St. Louis ___ at Chicago ___	(ABC) 7:00

Preseason/Fourth Week

Thursday, September 3	Minnesota ___ at Denver ___	(ESPN) 6:00
	Detroit ___ at Philadelphia ___	7:30
Friday, September 4	Buffalo ___ at Miami ___	8:00
	New England ___ vs. Atlanta ___ at Jacksonville, Florida	8:00
	New Orleans ___ at Cincinnati ___	7:35
	New York Jets ___ at San Diego ___	7:00
	San Francisco ___ at Seattle ___	(NBC) 5:00
Saturday, September 5	Chicago ___ at Los Angeles Raiders ___	1:00
	Cleveland ___ vs. Green Bay ___ at Milwaukee	7:00
	Houston ___ at Dallas ___	8:00
	New York Giants ___ at Pittsburgh ___	(CBS) 9:00
	Tampa Bay ___ at Indianapolis ___	7:30
	Washington ___ at Los Angeles Rams ___	6:00
Sunday, September 6	Kansas City ___ vs. St. Louis ___ at Memphis, Tennessee	1:30

First Week

Sunday, September 13 (NBC-TV doubleheader)	Atlanta ___ at Tampa Bay ___	1:00
	Cincinnati ___ at Indianapolis ___	12:00
	Cleveland ___ at New Orleans ___	12:00
	Dallas ___ at St. Louis ___	12:00
	Detroit ___ at Minnesota ___	12:00
	Los Angeles Raiders ___ at Green Bay ___	3:00
	Los Angeles Rams ___ at Houston ___	12:00
	Miami ___ at New England ___	1:00
	New York Jets ___ at Buffalo ___	1:00
	Philadelphia ___ at Washington ___	1:00
	San Diego ___ at Kansas City ___	12:00
	San Francisco ___ at Pittsburgh ___	1:00
	Seattle ___ at Denver ___	2:00
Monday, September 14	New York Giants ___ at Chicago ___	(ABC) 8:00

Second Week

Sunday, September 20 (CBS-TV doubleheader)	Dallas ___ at New York Giants ___	4:00
	Denver ___ vs. Green Bay ___ at Milwaukee	12:00
	Detroit ___ at Los Angeles Raiders ___	1:00
	Houston ___ at Buffalo ___	1:00
	Kansas City ___ at Seattle ___	1:00
	Miami ___ at Indianapolis ___	12:00
	Minnesota ___ at Los Angeles Rams ___	1:00
	New Orleans ___ at Philadelphia ___	1:00
	Pittsburgh ___ at Cleveland ___	1:00
	St. Louis ___ at San Diego ___	1:00
	San Francisco ___ at Cincinnati ___	1:00
	Tampa Bay ___ at Chicago ___	12:00
	Washington ___ at Atlanta ___	1:00
Monday, September 21	New England ___ at New York Jets ___	(ABC) 9:00

Third Week

Sunday, September 27 (NBC-TV doubleheader)	Atlanta ___ at New Orleans ___	12:00
	Buffalo ___ at Dallas ___	12:00
	Chicago ___ at Detroit ___	1:00
	Cincinnati ___ at Los Angeles Rams ___	1:00
	Green Bay ___ at Tampa Bay ___	1:00
	Indianapolis ___ at St. Louis ___	12:00
	Los Angeles Raiders ___ at Houston ___	12:00
	Minnesota ___ at Kansas City ___	12:00
	New England ___ at Washington ___	1:00
	New York Giants ___ at Miami ___	1:00
	New York Jets ___ at Pittsburgh ___	4:00
	Philadelphia ___ at San Francisco ___	1:00
	Seattle ___ at San Diego ___	1:00
Monday, September 28	Denver ___ at Cleveland ___	(ABC) 9:00

Fourth Week

Sunday, October 4	Chicago ___ at Philadelphia ___	1:00
(CBS-TV doubleheader)	Cleveland ___ at New England ___	1:00
	Dallas ___ at New York Jets ___	4:00
	Green Bay ___ at Minnesota ___	12:00
	Houston ___ at Denver ___	2:00
	Indianapolis ___ at Buffalo ___	1:00
	Kansas City ___ at Los Angeles Raiders ___	1:00
	Los Angeles Rams ___ at New Orleans ___	12:00
	Miami ___ at Seattle ___	1:00
	Pittsburgh ___ at Atlanta ___	1:00
	St. Louis ___ at Washington ___	1:00
	San Diego ___ at Cincinnati ___	1:00
	Tampa Bay ___ at Detroit ___	1:00
Monday, October 5	San Francisco ___ at New York Giants ___	(ABC) 9:00

Fifth Week

Sunday, October 11	Atlanta ___ at San Francisco ___	1:00
(CBS-TV doubleheader)	Buffalo ___ at New England ___	1:00
	Cincinnati ___ at Seattle ___	1:00
	Detroit ___ at Green Bay ___	12:00
	Houston ___ at Cleveland ___	1:00
	Kansas City ___ at Miami ___	1:00
	Minnesota ___ at Chicago ___	12:00
	New Orleans ___ at St. Louis ___	12:00
	New York Jets ___ at Indianapolis ___	12:00
	Philadelphia ___ at Dallas ___	12:00
	Pittsburgh ___ at Los Angeles Rams ___	1:00
	San Diego ___ at Tampa Bay ___	1:00
	Washington ___ at New York Giants ___	4:00
Monday, October 12	Los Angeles Raiders ___ at Denver ___	(ABC) 7:00

Sixth Week

Sunday, October 18	Cleveland ___ at Cincinnati ___	1:00
(NBC-TV doubleheader)	Denver ___ at Kansas City ___	3:00
	Indianapolis ___ at Pittsburgh ___	1:00
	Los Angeles Rams ___ at Atlanta ___	1:00
	Miami ___ at New York Jets ___	1:00
	New England ___ at Houston ___	12:00
	New Orleans ___ at Chicago ___	12:00
	New York Giants ___ at Buffalo ___	4:00
	Philadelphia ___ at Green Bay ___	12:00
	St. Louis ___ at San Francisco ___	1:00
	San Diego ___ at Los Angeles Raiders ___	1:00
	Seattle ___ at Detroit ___	1:00
	Tampa Bay ___ at Minnesota ___	12:00
Monday, October 19	Washington ___ at Dallas ___	(ABC) 8:00

Seventh Week

Sunday, October 25	Atlanta ___ at Houston ___	12:00
(NBC-TV doubleheader)	Buffalo ___ at Miami ___	1:00
	Chicago ___ at Tampa Bay ___	1:00
	Cincinnati ___ at Pittsburgh ___	1:00
	Dallas ___ at Philadelphia ___	1:00
	Denver ___ at Minnesota ___	12:00
	Green Bay ___ at Detroit ___	1:00
	Kansas City ___ at San Diego ___	1:00
	New England ___ at Indianapolis ___	1:00
	New York Jets ___ at Washington ___	1:00
	St. Louis ___ at New York Giants ___	4:00
	San Francisco ___ at New Orleans ___	12:00
	Seattle ___ at Los Angeles Raiders ___	1:00
Monday, October 26	Los Angeles Rams ___ at Cleveland ___	(ABC) 9:00

Eighth Week

Sunday, November 1	Cleveland ___ at San Diego ___	1:00
(CBS-TV doubleheader)	Detroit ___ at Denver ___	2:00
	Houston ___ at Cincinnati ___	1:00
	Indianapolis ___ at New York Jets ___	1:00
	Kansas City ___ at Chicago ___	12:00
	Los Angeles Raiders ___ at New England ___	1:00
	Minnesota ___ at Seattle ___	1:00
	New Orleans ___ at Atlanta ___	1:00
	Philadelphia ___ at St. Louis ___	12:00
	Pittsburgh ___ at Miami ___	1:00
	San Francisco ___ at Los Angeles Rams ___	1:00
	Tampa Bay ___ vs. Green Bay ___ at Milwaukee	12:00
	Washington ___ at Buffalo ___	1:00
Monday, November 2	New York Giants ___ at Dallas ___	(ABC) 8:00

Ninth Week

Sunday, November 8	Atlanta ___ at Cleveland ___	1:00
(NBC-TV doubleheader)	Chicago ___ at Green Bay ___	12:00
	Dallas ___ at Detroit ___	1:00
	Denver ___ at Buffalo ___	1:00
	Houston ___ at San Francisco ___	1:00
	Los Angeles Raiders ___ at Minnesota ___	12:00
	Miami ___ at Cincinnati ___	4:00
	New Orleans ___ at Los Angeles Rams ___	1:00
	Pittsburgh ___ at Kansas City ___	12:00
	San Diego ___ at Indianapolis ___	1:00
	Tampa Bay ___ at St. Louis ___	12:00
	Washington ___ at Philadelphia ___	1:00
Sunday Night	New England ___ at New York Giants ___	(ESPN) 8:00
Monday, November 9	Seattle ___ at New York Jets ___	(ABC) 9:00

Tenth Week

Sunday, November 15	Buffalo ___ at Cleveland ___	1:00
(CBS-TV doubleheader)	Cincinnati ___ at Atlanta ___	4:00
	Dallas ___ at New England ___	1:00
	Detroit ___ at Washington ___	1:00
	Green Bay ___ at Seattle ___	1:00
	Houston ___ at Pittsburgh ___	1:00
	Indianapolis ___ at Miami ___	1:00
	Los Angeles Rams ___ at St. Louis ___	12:00
	Minnesota ___ at Tampa Bay ___	1:00
	New Orleans ___ at San Francisco ___	1:00
	New York Giants ___ at Philadelphia ___	4:00
	New York Jets ___ at Kansas City ___	12:00
Sunday Night	Los Angeles Raiders ___ at San Diego ___	(ESPN) 5:00
Monday, November 16	Chicago ___ at Denver ___	(ABC) 7:00

Eleventh Week

Sunday, November 22	Atlanta ___ at Minnesota ___	12:00
(NBC-TV doubleheader)	Buffalo ___ at New York Jets ___	1:00
	Cleveland ___ at Houston ___	12:00
	Denver ___ at Los Angeles Raiders ___	1:00
	Detroit ___ at Chicago ___	12:00
	Green Bay ___ at Kansas City ___	12:00
	Indianapolis ___ at New England ___	1:00
	New York Giants ___ at New Orleans ___	3:00
	Pittsburgh ___ at Cincinnati ___	1:00
	St. Louis ___ at Philadelphia ___	1:00
	San Diego ___ at Seattle ___	1:00
	San Francisco ___ at Tampa Bay ___	1:00
Sunday Night	Miami ___ at Dallas ___	(ESPN) 7:00
Monday, November 23	Los Angeles Rams ___ at Washington ___	(ABC) 9:00

Twelfth Week

Thursday, November 26 (Thanksgiving Day)	Kansas City ___ at Detroit ___	(NBC)	12:30
	Minnesota ___ at Dallas ___	(CBS)	3:00
Sunday, November 29 (CBS-TV doubleheader)	Cincinnati ___ at New York Jets ___		1:00
	Denver ___ at San Diego ___		1:00
	Green Bay ___ at Chicago ___		12:00
	Houston ___ at Indianapolis ___		1:00
	Miami ___ at Buffalo ___		1:00
	New Orleans ___ at Pittsburgh ___		1:00
	New York Giants ___ at Washington ___		4:00
	Philadelphia ___ at New England ___		1:00
	St. Louis ___ at Atlanta ___		1:00
	Tampa Bay ___ at Los Angeles Rams ___		1:00
Sunday Night	Cleveland ___ at San Francisco ___	(ESPN)	5:00
Monday, November 30	Los Angeles Raiders ___ at Seattle ___	(ABC)	6:00

Thirteenth Week

Sunday, December 6 (NBC-TV doubleheader)	Atlanta ___ at Dallas ___		12:00
	Buffalo ___ at Los Angeles Raiders ___		1:00
	Indianapolis ___ at Cleveland ___		1:00
	Kansas City ___ at Cincinnati ___		1:00
	Los Angeles Rams ___ at Detroit ___		1:00
	New England ___ at Denver ___		2:00
	Philadelphia ___ at New York Giants ___		1:00
	San Diego ___ at Houston ___		12:00
	San Francisco ___ at Green Bay ___		12:00
	Seattle ___ at Pittsburgh ___		1:00
	Tampa Bay ___ at New Orleans ___		3:00
	Washington ___ at St. Louis ___		12:00
Sunday Night	Chicago ___ at Minnesota ___	(ESPN)	7:00
Monday, December 7	New York Jets ___ at Miami ___	(ABC)	9:00

Fourteenth Week

Sunday, December 13 (CBS-TV doubleheader)	Atlanta ___ at Los Angeles Rams ___		1:00
	Buffalo ___ at Indianapolis ___		1:00
	Cincinnati ___ at Cleveland ___		1:00
	Dallas ___ at Washington ___		1:00
	Detroit ___ at Tampa Bay ___		4:00
	Houston ___ at New Orleans ___		12:00
	Los Angeles Raiders ___ at Kansas City ___		3:00
	Miami ___ at Philadelphia ___		1:00
	Minnesota ___ vs. Green Bay ___ at Milwaukee		12:00
	New York Giants ___ at St. Louis ___		3:00
	New York Jets ___ at New England ___		1:00
	Pittsburgh ___ at San Diego ___		1:00
Sunday Night	Denver ___ at Seattle ___	(ESPN)	5:00
Monday, December 14	Chicago ___ at San Francisco ___	(ABC)	6:00

Fifteenth Week

Saturday, December 19	Green Bay ___ at New York Giants ___	(CBS)	12:30
	Kansas City ___ at Denver ___	(NBC)	2:00
Sunday, December 20 (NBC-TV doubleheader)	Cleveland ___ at Los Angeles Raiders ___		1:00
	Indianapolis ___ at San Diego ___		1:00
	Minnesota ___ at Detroit ___		1:00
	New England ___ at Buffalo ___		1:00
	New Orleans ___ at Cincinnati ___		1:00
	Philadelphia ___ at New York Jets ___		1:00
	Pittsburgh ___ at Houston ___		12:00
	St. Louis ___ at Tampa Bay ___		4:00
	San Francisco ___ at Atlanta ___		1:00
	Seattle ___ at Chicago ___		12:00
Sunday Night	Washington ___ at Miami ___	(ESPN)	8:00
Monday, December 21	Dallas ___ at Los Angeles Rams ___	(ABC)	6:00

Sixteenth Week

Saturday, December 26	Cleveland ___ at Pittsburgh ___	(NBC)	12:30
	Washington ___ at Minnesota ___	(CBS)	3:00
Sunday, December 27 (CBS-TV doubleheader)	Buffalo ___ at Philadelphia ___		1:00
	Chicago ___ at Los Angeles Raiders ___		1:00
	Cincinnati ___ at Houston ___		12:00
	Detroit ___ at Atlanta ___		1:00
	Green Bay ___ at New Orleans ___		12:00
	New York Jets ___ at New York Giants ___		1:00
	St. Louis ___ at Dallas ___		12:00
	San Diego ___ at Denver ___		2:00
	Seattle ___ at Kansas City ___		12:00
	Tampa Bay ___ at Indianapolis ___		1:00
Sunday Night	Los Angeles Rams ___ at San Francisco ___	(ESPN)	5:00
Monday, December 28	New England ___ at Miami ___	(ABC)	9:00

First-Round Playoff Games

Site Priorities
Two wild card teams (fourth- and fifth-best records) from each conference will enter the first round of the playoffs. The wild cards from the same conference will play each other. Home clubs will be the clubs with the best won-lost-tied percentage in the regular season. If tied in record, the tie will be broken by the tie-breaking procedures already in effect.

Sunday, January 3, 1988

American Football Conference

___ at ___ (NBC)

National Football Conference

___ at ___ (CBS)

Divisional Playoff Games

Site Priorities
In each conference, the two division winners with the highest won-lost-tied percentage during the regular season will be the home teams. The division winner with the best percentage will be host to the wild card winner from the first-round playoff, and the division winner with the second-best percentage will be host to the third division winner, unless the wild card team is from the same division as the winner with the highest percentage. In that case, the division winner with the best percentage will be host to the third division winner and the second highest division winner will be host to the wild card.

Saturday, January 9, 1988

American Football Conference

___ at ___ (NBC)

National Football Conference

___ at ___ (CBS)

Sunday, January 10, 1988

American Football Conference

___ at ___ (NBC)

National Football Conference

___ at ___ (CBS)

Conference Championship Games, Super Bowl XXII, and AFC-NFC Pro Bowl

Site Priorities for Championship Games
The home teams will be the surviving divisional playoff winners with the best won-lost-tied percentage during the regular season. The wild card team will never be the home team, in either the divisional playoffs or the championship games. Any ties in won-lost-tied percentage will be broken by the tie-breaking procedures already in effect.

Sunday, January 17, 1988

American Football Conference Championship Game

___ at ___ (NBC)

National Football Conference Championship Game

___ at ___ (CBS)

Sunday, January 31, 1988

Super Bowl XXII at San Diego Jack Murphy Stadium, San Diego, California

___ vs. ___ (ABC)

Sunday, February 7, 1988

AFC-NFC Pro Bowl at Honolulu, Hawaii

AFC ___ vs. NFC ___ (ESPN)

Postseason Games

Sunday, January 3, 1988	AFC and NFC First-Round Playoffs (NBC and CBS)
Saturday, January 9, 1988	AFC and NFC Divisional Playoffs (NBC and CBS)
Sunday, January 10, 1988	AFC and NFC Divisional Playoffs (NBC and CBS)
Sunday, January 17, 1988	AFC and NFC Championship Games (NBC and CBS)
Sunday, January 31, 1988	Super Bowl XXII at San Diego Jack Murphy Stadium, San Diego, California (ABC)
Sunday, February 7, 1988	AFC-NFC Pro Bowl at Honolulu, Hawaii (ESPN)

1987 Nationally Televised Games

(All games carried on CBS Radio Network.)

Regular Season

Monday, September 14	New York Giants at Chicago (night, ABC)
Monday, September 21	New England at New York Jets (night, ABC)
Monday, September 28	Denver at Cleveland (night, ABC)
Monday, October 5	San Francisco at New York Giants (night, ABC)
Monday, October 12	Los Angeles Raiders at Denver (night, ABC)
Monday, October 19	Washington at Dallas (night, ABC)
Monday, October 26	Los Angeles Rams at Cleveland (night, ABC)
Monday, November 2	New York Giants at Dallas (night, ABC)
Sunday, November 8	New England at New York Giants (night, ESPN)
Monday, November 9	Seattle at New York Jets (night, ABC)
Sunday, November 15	Los Angeles Raiders at San Diego (night, ESPN)
Monday, November 16	Chicago at Denver (night, ABC)
Sunday, November 22	Miami at Dallas (night, ESPN)
Monday, November 23	Los Angeles Rams at Washington (night, ABC)
Thursday, November 26 (Thanksgiving)	Kansas City at Detroit (day, NBC) Minnesota at Dallas (day, CBS)
Sunday, November 29	Cleveland at San Francisco (night, ESPN)
Monday, November 30	Los Angeles Raiders at Seattle (night, ABC)
Sunday, December 6	Chicago at Minnesota (night, ESPN)
Monday, December 7	New York Jets at Miami (night, ABC)
Sunday, December 13	Denver at Seattle (night, ESPN)
Monday, December 14	Chicago at San Francisco (night, ABC)
Saturday, December 19	Green Bay at New York Giants (day, CBS) Kansas City at Denver (day, NBC)
Sunday, December 20	Washington at Miami (night, ESPN)
Monday, December 21	Dallas at Los Angeles Rams (night, ABC)
Saturday, December 26	Cleveland at Pittsburgh (day, NBC) Washington at Minnesota (day, CBS)
Sunday, December 27	Los Angeles Rams at San Francisco (night, ESPN)
Monday, December 28	New England at Miami (night, ABC)

1987 AFC-NFC Interconference Games

(Sunday unless noted; all times local)

September 13	Cleveland at New Orleans	12:00
	Los Angeles Raiders at Green Bay	3:00
	Los Angeles Rams at Houston	12:00
	San Francisco at Pittsburgh	1:00
September 20	Denver vs. Green Bay at Milwaukee	12:00
	Detroit at Los Angeles Raiders	1:00
	St. Louis at San Diego	1:00
	San Francisco at Cincinnati	1:00
September 27	Buffalo at Dallas	12:00
	Cincinnati at Los Angeles Rams	1:00
	Indianapolis at St. Louis	12:00
	Minnesota at Kansas City	12:00
	New York Giants at Miami	1:00
	New England at Washington	1:00
October 4	Dallas at New York Jets	4:00
	Pittsburgh at Atlanta	1:00
October 11	Pittsburgh at Los Angeles Rams	1:00
	San Diego at Tampa Bay	1:00
October 18	New York Giants at Buffalo	4:00
	Seattle at Detroit	1:00
October 25	Atlanta at Houston	12:00
	Denver at Minnesota	12:00
	New York Jets at Washington	1:00
October 26	Los Angeles Rams at Cleveland (Monday)	9:00
November 1	Detroit at Denver	2:00
	Kansas City at Chicago	12:00
	Minnesota at Seattle	1:00
	Washington at Buffalo	1:00
November 8	Atlanta at Cleveland	1:00
	Houston at San Francisco	1:00
	Los Angeles Raiders at Minnesota	12:00
	New England at New York Giants (night)	8:00
November 15	Cincinnati at Atlanta	4:00
	Dallas at New England	1:00
	Green Bay at Seattle	1:00
November 16	Chicago at Denver (Monday)	7:00
November 22	Green Bay at Kansas City	12:00
	Miami at Dallas (night)	7:00
November 26	Kansas City at Detroit (Thanksgiving)	12:30
November 29	New Orleans at Pittsburgh	1:00
	Philadelphia at New England	1:00
	Cleveland at San Francisco (night)	5:00
December 13	Houston at New Orleans	12:00
	Miami at Philadelphia	1:00
December 20	New Orleans at Cincinnati	1:00
	Philadelphia at New York Jets	1:00
	Seattle at Chicago	12:00
	Washington at Miami (night)	8:00
December 27	Buffalo at Philadelphia	1:00
	Chicago at Los Angeles Raiders	1:00
	New York Jets at New York Giants	1:00
	Tampa Bay at Indianapolis	1:00

Sunday and Monday Night Games at a Glance

(All times local; Sunday on ESPN, Monday on ABC-TV; all on CBS Radio Network)

Monday, September 14	New York Giants at Chicago (ABC)	8:00
Monday, September 21	New England at New York Jets (ABC)	9:00
Monday, September 28	Denver at Cleveland (ABC)	9:00
Monday, October 5	San Francisco at New York Giants (ABC)	9:00
Monday, October 12	Los Angeles Raiders at Denver (ABC)	7:00
Monday, October 19	Washington at Dallas (ABC)	8:00
Monday, October 26	Los Angeles Rams at Cleveland (ABC)	9:00
Monday, November 2	New York Giants at Dallas (ABC)	8:00
Sunday, November 8	New England at New York Giants (ESPN)	8:00
Monday, November 9	Seattle at New York Jets (ABC)	9:00
Sunday, November 15	Los Angeles Raiders at San Diego (ESPN)	5:00
Monday, November 16	Chicago at Denver (ABC)	7:00
Sunday, November 22	Miami at Dallas (ESPN)	7:00
Monday, November 23	Los Angeles Rams at Washington (ABC)	9:00
Sunday, November 29	Cleveland at San Francisco (ESPN)	5:00
Monday, November 30	Los Angeles Raiders at Seattle (ABC)	6:00
Sunday, December 6	Chicago at Minnesota (ESPN)	7:00
Monday, December 7	New York Jets at Miami (ABC)	9:00
Sunday, December 13	Denver at Seattle (ESPN)	5:00
Monday, December 14	Chicago at San Francisco (ABC)	6:00
Sunday, December 20	Washington at Miami (ESPN)	8:00
Monday, December 21	Dallas at Los Angeles Rams (ABC)	6:00
Sunday, December 27	Los Angeles Rams at San Francisco (ESPN)	5:00
Monday, December 28	New England at Miami (ABC)	9:00

Important Dates

1987

July 6	Claiming period of 24 hours begins in waiver system. All waivers for the year are no-recall and no-withdrawal.
Mid-July	Team training camps open.
August 8	Hall of Fame Game, Canton, Ohio: Kansas City vs. San Francisco.
August 9	American Bowl '87, London, England: Denver vs. Los Angeles Rams.
August 13-16	First preseason weekend.
August 22-24	Second preseason weekend.
August 27-31	Third preseason weekend.
September 1	Roster cutdown to maximum of 60 players.
September 3-6	Fourth preseason weekend.
September 7	Roster cutdown to maximum of 45 players.
September 13-14	Regular season opens.
September 29	Priority on multiple waiver claims is now based on the current season's standings.
October 20	Clubs may begin signing free agents for the 1988 season.
October 20	Trading of player contracts/rights ends at 4:00 p.m., New York Time.
October 27-28	NFL Meeting, Kansas City, Missouri.
November 28	Deadline for reinstatement of players in Reserve List categories of Retired, Did Not Report, and Veteran Free Agents Asked to Re-Sign.
December 21-22	Balloting for AFC-NFC Pro Bowl.
December 25	Deadline for waiver requests in 1987.
December 30	Deadline for postseason participants to sign free agents for playoffs, except punters or kickers.

1988

January 3	AFC and NFC First-Round Playoff Games.
January 9-10	AFC and NFC Divisional Playoff Games.
January 17	AFC and NFC Championship Games.
January 31	Super Bowl XXII at San Diego Jack Murphy Stadium, San Diego, California.
February 7	AFC-NFC Pro Bowl at Aloha Stadium, Honolulu, Hawaii.
February 8	Waiver system begins for 1988.
February 8	Trading period begins.
March 14-18	NFL Annual Meeting, Phoenix, Arizona.
April-May	53rd annual NFL Selection Meeting, New York, New York.
July 30	Hall of Fame Game, Canton, Ohio: Cincinnati vs. Los Angeles Rams.
August 5-7	First preseason weekend.
September 4-5	Regular season opens.
December 18-19	Regular season closes.
December 24 and/or 26	AFC and NFC First-Round Playoff Games.
December 31	AFC and NFC Divisional Playoff Games.

1989

January 1	AFC and NFC Divisional Playoff Games.
January 8	AFC and NFC Championship Games.
January 22	Super Bowl XXIII at Joe Robbie Stadium, Miami, Florida.
January 29	AFC-NFC Pro Bowl.
March 20-24	NFL Annual Meeting at Desert Springs, California.

1990

January 28	Super Bowl XXIV at Louisiana Superdome, New Orleans, Louisiana.
February 4	AFC-NFC Pro Bowl.
March 12-16	NFL Annual Meeting at Orlando, Florida.

Future Super Bowl Dates and Sites

Super Bowl XXII	Jan. 31, 1988	San Diego Jack Murphy Stadium, San Diego, California
Super Bowl XXIII	Jan. 22, 1989	Joe Robbie Stadium, Miami, Florida
Super Bowl XXIV	Jan. 28, 1990	Louisiana Superdome, New Orleans, Louisiana

Waivers

The waiver system is a procedure by which player contracts or NFL rights to players are made available by a club to other clubs in the League. During the procedure the 27 other clubs either file claims to obtain the players or waive the opportunity to do so—thus the term "waiver." Claiming clubs are assigned players on a priority based on the inverse of won-and-lost standing. The claiming period normally is 10 days during the offseason and 24 hours from early July through December. In some circumstances another 24 hours is added on to allow the original club to rescind its action (known as a recall of a waiver request) and/or the claiming club to do the same (known as withdrawal of a claim). If a player passes through waivers unclaimed and is not recalled by the original club, he becomes a free agent. All waivers from July through December are no-recall and no withdrawal. Under the Collective Bargaining Agreement, from February 1 through October 20, any veteran who has acquired four years of pension credit may, if about to be assigned to another club through the waiver system, reject such assignment and become a free agent.

Active List

The Active List is the principal status for players participating for a club. It consists of all players under contract, including option, who are eligible for preseason, regular season, and postseason games. Clubs are allowed to open training camp with an unlimited number of players but thereafter must meet a series of mandatory roster reductions prior to the season opener. Teams will be permitted to dress up to 45 players for each regular season and postseason game during the 1987 season. The Active List maximums and dates for 1987 are:

September 1 .... 60 players
September 7 .... 45 players

Reserve List

The Reserve List is a status for players who, for reasons of injury, retirement, military service, or other circumstances, are not immediately available for participation with a club. Those players in the category of Reserve/Injured who were physically unable to play football for a minimum of four weeks from the date of going onto Reserve may be re-activated by their clubs upon clearing procedural recall waivers; in addition, each club will have eight free re-activations for players meeting the four-week requirement, but no more than three can be used for players who were placed on Reserve/Injured prior to or concurrent with the final cutdown on September 7. Clubs participating in postseason competition will be granted an additional re-activation. Players not meeting the four-week requirement may return to their club if they are released, re-signed, and subsequently clear procedural recall waivers. Players in the category of Reserve/Retired, Reserve/Did Not Report, or Reserve/Veteran Free Agent Asked to Re-sign, may not be reinstated during the period from 30 days before the end of the regular season on through the postseason.

Trades

Unrestricted trading between the AFC and NFC is allowed in 1987 through October 20, after which trading of player contracts/rights will end until February 8, 1988.

Annual Player Limits

NFL

Year(s)	Limit
1985-87	45
1983-84	49
1982	45†–49
1978–81	45
1975–77	43
1974	47
1964–73	40
1963	37
1961–62	36
1960	38
1959	36
1957–58	35
1951–56	33
1949–50	32
1948	35
1947	35*–34
1945–46	33
1943–44	28
1940–42	33
1938–39	30
1936–37	25
1935	24
1930–34	20
1926–29	18
1925	16

†45 for first two games
*35 for first three games

AFL

Year(s)	Limit
1966–69	40
1965	38
1964	34
1962–63	33
1960–61	35

Tie-Breaking Procedures

The following procedures will be used to break standings ties for postseason playoffs and to determine regular season schedules.

To Break a Tie Within a Division

If, at the end of the regular season, two or more clubs in the same division finish with identical won-lost-tied percentages, the following steps will be taken until a champion is determined.

Two Clubs

1. Head-to-head (best won-lost-tied percentage in games between the clubs).
2. Best won-lost-tied percentage in games played within the division.
3. Best won-lost-tied percentage in games played within the conference.
4. Best won-lost-tied percentage in common games, if applicable.
5. Best net points in division games.
6. Best net points in all games.
7. Strength of schedule.
8. Best net touchdowns in all games.
9. Coin toss.

Three or More Clubs

(Note: If two clubs remain tied after a third club is eliminated during any step, tie-breaker reverts to step 1 of two-club format.)

1. Head-to-head (best won-lost-tied percentage in games among the clubs).
2. Best won-lost-tied percentage in games played within the division.
3. Best won-lost-tied percentage in games played within the conference.
4. Best won-lost-tied percentage in common games.
5. Best net points in division games.
6. Best net points in all games.
7. Strength of schedule.
8. Best net touchdowns in all games.
9. Coin toss.

To Break a Tie for the Wild Card Team

If it is necessary to break ties to determine the two Wild Card clubs from each conference, the following steps will be taken.

1. If the tied clubs are from the same division, apply division tie-breaker.
2. If the tied clubs are from different divisions, apply the following steps.

Two Clubs

1. Head-to-head, if applicable.
2. Best won-lost-tied percentage in games played within the conference.
3. Best won-lost-tied percentage in common games, minimum of four.
4. Best average net points in conference games.
5. Best net points in all games.
6. Strength of schedule.
7. Best net touchdowns in all games.
8. Coin toss.

Three or More Clubs

(Note: If two clubs remain tied after other clubs are eliminated, tie-breaker reverts to step 1 of applicable two-club format.)

1. Head-to-head sweep. (Applicable only if one club has defeated each of the others, or if one club has lost to each of the others.)
2. Best won-lost-tied percentage in games played within the conference.
3. Best won-lost-tied percentage in common games, minimum of four.
4. Best average net points in conference games.
5. Best net points in all games.
6. Strength of schedule.
7. Best net touchdowns in all games.
8. Coin toss.

Tie-Breaking Procedure for Selection Meeting

If two or more clubs are tied for selection order, the conventional strength of schedule tie-breaker will be applied, subject to the following exceptions for playoff teams.

1. The Super Bowl winner will be last and the Super Bowl loser will be next-to-last.
2. Any non-Super Bowl playoff team involved in a tie moves down in drafting priority as follows:
   A. Participation by a club in the playoffs without a victory adds one-half victory to the club's regular season won-lost-tied record.
   B. For each victory in the playoffs, one full victory will be added to the club's regular season won-lost-tied record.
3. Clubs with the best won-lost-tied records after these steps are applied will drop to their appropriate spots at the bottom of the tied segment. In no case will the above process move a club lower than the segment in which it was initially tied.
4. Tied clubs will alternate priority throughout the 12 rounds of the draft. In case of a tie involving three or more teams, the club with priority in the first round will drop to the bottom of the tied segment in the second round and move its way back to the top of the segment in each succeeding round.

Figuring the 1988 NFL Schedule

As soon as the final game of the 1987 NFL regular season (New England at Miami, December 28) has been completed, it will be possible to determine the 1988 opponents of the 28 teams.

Each 1988 team schedule is based on a "common opponent" formula initiated for the 1978 season and most recently modified in 1987. Under the common opponent format, the first- through fourth-place teams in a division play at least 12 of their 16 games the following season against common opponents, and the fifth-place team in the division plays at least 10 common opponent games. It is not a position scheduling format in which the strong play the strong and the weak play the weak.

For years the NFL had been seeking a more easily understood and balanced schedule that would provide both competitive equality and a variety of opponents. Under the old rotation scheduling system in effect from 1970–77, non-division opponents were determined by a pre-set formula. This often resulted in competitive imbalances.

With "common opponents" the basis for scheduling, a more competitive and equitable method of determining division champions and postseason playoff representatives has developed. Teams battling for a division title are playing at least 75 percent of their games against common opponents.

At their 1987 annual meeting in March, NFL owners passed two by-law proposals designed to modify the common opponent scheduling format in the hopes of creating even more equity. The first concerns pairings with non-division opponents:

Prior Year's Finish in Division	Pairings in Non-Division Games Within Conference	Previous Pairings 1978-86
1	1-1-2-3	1-1-4-4
2	1-2-2-4	2-2-3-3
3	1-3-3-4	2-2-3-3
4	2-3-4-4	1-1-4-4

The second change, recommended by the NFL's Competition Committee, states: "For the 1987, 1988, and 1989 seasons, site locations for the interconference games of teams which finish 1 through 4 in a division and fifth-place teams where possible, will be assigned so that, where possible by formula, teams do not play a second consecutive regular-season home or road game with an opponent."

Under the common opponent format, schedules of any NFL team are figured according to one of the following three formulas. (The reference point for the figuring is the team's final division standing. Ties for a position in divisions are broken according to the tie-breaking procedures outlined on page 13. The chart on the following page is included for use as you go through each step.)

A. First- through fourth-place teams in a five-team division (AFC East, AFC West, NFC East, NFC Central).

1. Home-and-home round-robin within the division (8 games).
2. One game each with the first- through fourth-place teams in a division of the other conference (4 games). In 1988, AFC East will play the NFC Central, AFC Central will play the NFC East, and the AFC West will play the NFC West.
3. The first-place team plays the first-place teams in the other divisions within the conference plus a second- and third-place team within the conference. The second-place team plays the second-place teams in the other divisions within the conference plus a first- and fourth-place team within the conference. The third-place team plays the third-place teams in the other divisions within the conference plus a first- and fourth-place team within the conference. The fourth-place team plays the fourth-place teams in the other divisions within the conference plus a second- and third-place team within the conference (4 games).

This completes the 16-game schedule.

B. First- through fourth-place teams in a four-team division (AFC Central, NFC West).

1. Home-and-home round-robin within the division (6 games).
2. One game with each of the fifth-place teams in the conference (2 games).
3. The same procedure that is listed in step A2 (4 games).
4. The same procedure that is listed in step A3 (4 games).

This completes the 16-game schedule.

C. The fifth-place teams in a division (AFC East, AFC West, NFC East, NFC Central).

1. Home-and-home round-robin within the division (8 games).
2. One game with each team in the four-team division of the conference (4 games).
3. A home-and-home with the other fifth-place team in the conference (2 games).
4. One game each with the fifth-place teams in the other conference (2 games).

This completes the 16-game schedule.

The 1988 Opponent Breakdown chart on the following page does not include the round-robin games within the division. Those are automatically on a home-and-away basis.

1987 NFL Standings

AFC

EAST AE
1 ______
2 ______
3 ______
4 ______
5 ______

CENTRAL AC
1 ______
2 ______
3 ______
4 ______

WEST AW
1 ______
2 ______
3 ______
4 ______
5 ______

NFC

EAST NE
1 ______
2 ______
3 ______
4 ______
5 ______

WEST NW
1 ______
2 ______
3 ______
4 ______

CENTRAL NC
1 ______
2 ______
3 ______
4 ______
5 ______

A Team's 1988 Schedule

Team Name ______

1988 Opponent Breakdown

*Game Site to be Determined by Formula

AE AFC East Home Away	AC AFC Central Home Away	AW AFC West Home Away	NE NFC East Home Away	NC NFC Central Home Away	NW NFC West Home Away
AE-1 AW-1 AC-1 AC-2 AW-3 *NC-1 *NC-2 *NC-3 *NC-4	**AC-1** AE-1 AW-1 AW-2 AE-3 *NE-1 *NE-2 *NE-3 *NE-4 *AE-5 *AW-5	**AW-1** AC-1 AE-1 AE-2 AC-3 *NW-1 *NW-2 *NW-3 *NW-4	**NE-1** NC-1 NW-1 NW-2 NC-3 *AC-1 *AC-2 *AC-3 *AC-4	**NC-1** NW-1 NE-1 NE-2 NW-3 *AE-1 *AE-2 *AE-3 *AE-4	**NW-1** NE-1 NC-1 NC-2 NE-3 *AW-1 *AW-2 *AW-3 *AW-4 *NE-5 *NW-5
AE-2 AW-2 AC-2 AC-4 AW-4 *NC-1 *NC-2 *NC-3 *NC-4	**AC-2** AE-2 AW-2 AW-4 AE-1 *NE-1 *NE-2 *NE-3 *NE-4 *AE-5 *AW-5	**AW-2** AC-2 AE-2 AE-4 AC-1 *NW-1 *NW-2 *NW-3 *NW-4	**NE-2** NC-2 NW-2 NW-4 NC-1 *AC-1 *AC-2 *AC-3 *AC-4	**NC-2** NW-2 NE-2 NE-4 NW-1 *AE-1 *AE-2 *AE-3 *AE-4	**NW-2** NE-2 NC-2 NC-4 NE-1 *AW-1 *AW-2 *AW-3 *AW-4 *NE-5 *NW-5
AE-3 AW-3 AC-3 AC-1 AW-4 *NC-1 *NC-2 *NC-3 *NC-4	**AC-3** AE-2 AW-3 AW-1 AE-4 *NE-1 *NE-2 *NE-3 *NE-4 *AE-5 *AW-5	**AW-3** AC-3 AE-3 AE-1 AC-4 *NW-1 *NW-2 *NW-3 *NW-4	**NE-3** NC-3 NW-3 NW-1 NC-4 *AC-1 *AC-2 *AC-3 *AC-4	**NC-3** NW-3 NE-3 NE-1 NW-4 *AE-1 *AE-2 *AE-3 *AE-4	**NW-3** NE-3 NC-3 NC-1 NE-4 *AW-1 *AW-2 *AW-3 *AW-4 *NE-5 *NW-5
AE-4 AW-4 AC-4 AC-3 AW-2 *NC-1 *NC-2 *NC-3 *NC-4	**AC-4** AE-4 AW-4 AW-3 AE-2 *NE-1 *NE-2 *NE-3 *NE-4 *AE-5 *AW-5	**AW-4** AC-4 AE-4 AE-3 AC-2 *NW-1 *NW-2 *NW-3 *NW-4	**NE-4** NC-4 NW-4 NW-3 NC-2 *AC-1 *AC-2 *AC-3 *AC-4	**NC-4** NW-4 NE-4 NE-3 NW-2 *AE-1 *AE-2 *AE-3 *AE-4	**NW-4** NE-4 NC-4 NC-3 NE-2 *AW-1 *AW-2 *AW-3 *AW-4 *NE-5 *NW-5
AE-5 AW-5 AW-5 *NE-5 *NC-5 *AC-1 *AC-2 *AC-3 *AC-4		**AW-5** AE-5 AE-5 *NE-5 *NC-5 *AC-1 *AC-2 *AC-3 *AC-4	**NE-5** NC-5 NC-5 *AE-5 *AW-5 *NW-1 *NW-2 *NW-3 *NW-4	**NC-5** NE-5 NE-5 *AE-5 *AW-5 *NW-1 *NW-2 *NW-3 *NW-4	

Instant Replay Approved for 1987

For the second year in a row, NFL clubs have approved a limited system of Instant Replay on a one-year basis.

The system basically stays the same as in 1986 with the exception that larger monitors (12 inch) will be used by Replay Officials. In 1986, there were 374 plays closely reviewed (defined as a contact to the field, but not necessarily stoppage of play). There were 38 reversals for an average of one reversal in each six games. There were three other rulings (clarifications of rules) by Replay Officials.

In 1986, the system was approved by a 23-4-1 vote. In 1987, the vote was 21-7.

The NFL has discussed Instant Replay in some degree or other since the early 1970s. The League experimented in 1976 and 1978 using two basic frameworks—an independent system using cameras, replay machines, and technicians separate from the network covering the game and a "no-frills" approach using existing TV coverage.

The NFL in 1985 used the network feed of the nine nationally-televised preseason games to experiment with the basic system which later was adopted for 1986 and 1987. A total of 28 plays (17 confirmed calls, 4 inconclusive, 1 reversed, and 6 no replay shown) were closely examined in the 1985 experiment.

Q—What is the objective of this system?

A—The clubs feel that on certain plays the telecast viewed by the general public should be used to correct an indisputable error. The system will be used to reverse an on-field decision only when the Replay Official has **indisputable visual evidence** available to him that warrants the change.

Q—Who will be involved?

A—The Replay Official (a veteran former NFL official or a member of the League's officiating supervisory staff) will be positioned in a sideline Replay Booth, which will house two TV monitors and two high-speed VCRs plus radio communications to the on-field officials. The Replay Official makes the decision although a Communicator (normally a member of the League Office staff) and a Technician also will be there to lend logistical help.

Q—Why is the system referred to as "limited" Instant Replay?

A—This system will concentrate on plays of **possession** or **touching** (e.g. fumbles, receptions, interceptions, muffs) and most plays governed by the **sidelines, goal lines, end lines,** and **line of scrimmage** (e.g. receiver or runner in or out of bounds, forward or backward passes, breaking the plane of the goal line). It also will be used to determine whether there are more than 11 men on the field.

Q—Why aren't most fouls included in this system?

A—It is recognized that in most circumstances the on-field officials have the best vantage points involving fouls. It is for this reason that Instant Replay **will not review** a list of the following 26 fouls:

1. Clipping
2. Encroachment and offsides
3. Grasp of facemask
4. False start
5. Defensive pass interference
6. Offensive pass interference
7. Offensive holding and illegal use of hands
8. Illegal batting or punching ball
9. Illegal block on free kick or scrimmage kick
10. Illegal crackback
11. Illegal motion
12. Illegal use of forearm or elbow
13. Illegal use of hands by defense
14. Illegally kicking ball
15. Illegally snapping ball
16. Intentional grounding
17. Member of punting team downfield early
18. Illegal formation
19. Palpably unfair act
20. Piling on
21. Roughing the passer
22. Running into/roughing kicker
23. Striking, kicking, or kneeing
24. Unnecessary roughness
25. Unsportsmanlike conduct
26. Use of helmet as a weapon

Q—Is the television network carrying the game part of the review process?

A—No. Although the Replay Official will be viewing the live network feed, there is no communication to television personnel as to what plays to show or not to show.

Q—What is the step-by-step procedure of a play review?

A—The Replay Official will view game action and a play will be replayed immediately on one of the two monitors, while the other one continues to record the live feed.

The Replay Official makes a determination if further study of the play is needed. If not, there is no contact with the field and play continues without interruption.

If the Replay Official believes an error may have been made the Umpire will be contacted via a headset.

The Replay Official will watch replay(s) on one or both monitors and complete his review within a reasonable period after the play is over.

The Replay Official will inform the Umpire of his decision, and the Referee will make the appropriate announcement on the wireless microphone.

Active Coaches' Career Records

Start of 1987 Season

Coach	Team(s)	Regular Season Yrs.	Won	Lost	Tied	Pct.	Postseason Won	Lost	Tied	Pct.	Career Won	Lost	Tied	Pct.
Don Shula	Baltimore Colts, Miami Dolphins	24	247	94	6	.720	16	13	0	.552	263	107	6	.707
Tom Landry	Dallas Cowboys	27	240	141	6	.628	20	16	0	.556	260	157	6	.622
Chuck Noll	Pittsburgh Steelers	18	155	107	1	.591	15	7	0	.682	170	114	1	.598
Chuck Knox	Los Angeles Rams, Buffalo Bills, Seattle Seahawks	14	130	76	1	.630	7	9	0	.438	137	85	1	.617
Tom Flores	Los Angeles Raiders	8	78	43	0	.645	8	3	0	.727	86	46	0	.652
Bill Walsh	San Francisco 49ers	8	69	51	1	.574	7	3	0	.700	76	54	1	.584
Forrest Gregg	Cleveland Browns, Cincinnati Bengals, Green Bay Packers	10	70	76	0	.479	2	2	0	.500	72	78	0	.480
Joe Gibbs	Washington Redskins	6	63	26	0	.708	8	3	0	.727	71	29	0	.710
Dan Reeves	Denver Broncos	6	56	33	0	.629	2	3	0	.400	58	36	0	.617
Mike Ditka	Chicago Bears	5	50	23	0	.685	4	2	0	.667	54	25	0	.684
John Robinson	Los Angeles Rams	4	40	24	0	.625	2	4	0	.333	42	28	0	.600
Bill Parcells	New York Giants	4	36	27	1	.570	5	2	0	.714	41	29	1	.585
Joe Walton	New York Jets	4	35	29	0	.547	1	2	0	.333	36	31	0	.537
Marv Levy	Kansas City Chiefs, Buffalo Bills	6	33	47	0	.413	0	0	0	.000	33	47	0	.413
Raymond Berry	New England Patriots	3	26	14	0	.650	3	2	0	.600	29	16	0	.644
Marty Schottenheimer	Cleveland Browns	3	24	16	0	.600	1	2	0	.333	25	18	0	.581
Sam Wyche	Cincinnati Bengals	3	25	23	0	.521	0	0	0	.000	25	23	0	.521
Ray Perkins	New York Giants, Tampa Bay Buccaneers	4	23	34	0	.404	1	1	0	.500	24	35	0	.407
Marion Campbell	Atlanta Falcons, Philadelphia Eagles	6	23	48	1	.326	0	0	0	.000	23	48	1	.326
Ron Meyer	New England Patriots, Indianapolis Colts	4	21	15	0	.583	0	1	0	.000	21	16	0	.568
Darryl Rogers	Detroit Lions	2	12	20	0	.375	0	0	0	.000	12	20	0	.375
Jerry Burns	Minnesota Vikings	1	9	7	0	.563	0	0	0	.000	9	7	0	.563
Jim Mora	New Orleans Saints	1	7	9	0	.438	0	0	0	.000	7	9	0	.438
Jerry Glanville	Houston Oilers	2	5	13	0	.278	0	0	0	.000	5	13	0	.278
Buddy Ryan	Philadelphia Eagles	1	5	10	1	.344	0	0	0	.000	5	10	1	.344
Gene Stallings	St. Louis Cardinals	1	4	11	1	.281	0	0	0	.000	4	11	1	.281
Al Saunders	San Diego Chargers	1	3	5	0	.375	0	0	0	.000	3	5	0	.375
Frank Gansz	Kansas City Chiefs	0	0	0	0	.000	0	0	0	.000	0	0	0	.000

Coaches With 100 Career Victories

Start of 1987 Season

Coach	Team(s)	Regular Season Yrs.	Won	Lost	Tied	Pct.	Postseason Won	Lost	Tied	Pct.	Career Won	Lost	Tied	Pct.
George Halas	Chicago Bears	40	319	148	31	.672	6	3	0	.667	325	151	31	.672
Don Shula	Baltimore Colts, Miami Dolphins	24	247	94	6	.720	16	13	0	.552	263	107	6	.707
Tom Landry	Dallas Cowboys	27	240	141	6	.628	20	16	0	.556	260	157	6	.622
Earl (Curly) Lambeau	Green Bay Packers, Chicago Cardinals, Washington Redskins	33	226	132	22	.624	3	2	0	.600	229	134	22	.623
Paul Brown	Cleveland Browns, Cincinnati Bengals	21	166	100	6	.621	4	8	0	.333	170	108	6	.609
Chuck Noll	Pittsburgh Steelers	18	155	107	1	.591	15	7	0	.682	170	114	1	.598
Bud Grant	Minnesota Vikings	18	158	96	5	.620	10	12	0	.455	168	108	5	.607
Steve Owen	New York Giants	23	151	100	17	.595	2	8	0	.200	153	108	17	.581
Chuck Knox	Los Angeles Rams, Buffalo Bills, Seattle Seahawks	14	130	76	1	.630	7	9	0	.438	137	85	1	.617
Hank Stram	Kansas City Chiefs, New Orleans Saints	17	131	97	10	.571	5	3	0	.625	136	100	10	.573
Weeb Ewbank	Baltimore Colts, New York Jets	20	130	129	7	.502	4	1	0	.800	134	130	7	.507
Sid Gillman	Los Angeles Rams, San Diego Chargers, Houston Oilers	18	122	99	7	.550	1	5	0	.167	123	104	7	.541
George Allen	Los Angeles Rams, Washington Redskins	12	116	47	5	.705	2	7	0	.222	118	54	5	.681
Don Coryell	St. Louis Cardinals, San Diego Chargers	14	111	83	1	.572	3	6	0	.333	114	89	1	.561
John Madden	Oakland Raiders	10	103	32	7	.750	9	7	0	.563	112	39	7	.731
Ray (Buddy) Parker	Chicago Cardinals, Detroit Lions, Pittsburgh Steelers	15	104	75	9	.577	3	1	0	.750	107	76	9	.581
Vince Lombardi	Green Bay Packers, Washington Redskins	10	96	34	6	.728	9	1	0	.900	105	35	6	.740

AFC ACTIVE STATISTICAL LEADERS

LEADING ACTIVE PASSERS, AMERICAN FOOTBALL CONFERENCE
1,000 or more attempts

	Yrs.	Att.	Comp.	Pct. Comp.	Yards	Avg. Gain	TD	Pct. TD	Had Int.	Pct. Int.	Rate Pts.
Dan Marino, Mia.	4	2050	1249	60.9	16177	7.89	142	6.9	67	3.3	95.2
Ken O'Brien, N.Y.J.	3	1173	713	60.8	8980	7.66	56	4.8	35	3.0	88.1
Boomer Esiason, Cin.	3	1002	575	57.4	7932	7.92	54	5.4	32	3.2	87.5
Dave Krieg, Sea.	7	1822	1046	57.4	13677	7.51	107	5.9	73	4.0	84.1
Tony Eason, N.E.	4	1273	749	58.8	9269	7.28	54	4.2	40	3.1	82.5
Ken Anderson, Cin.	16	4475	2654	59.3	32838	7.34	197	4.4	160	3.6	81.9
Dan Fouts, S.D.	14	5240	3091	59.0	40523	7.73	244	4.7	227	4.3	80.9
Bill Kenney, K.C.	7	2043	1118	54.7	14621	7.16	90	4.4	72	3.5	77.5
Gary Danielson, Clev.	9	1847	1049	56.8	13159	7.12	77	4.2	77	4.2	75.6
John Elway, Den.	4	1748	944	54.0	11637	6.66	66	3.8	65	3.7	71.9
Steve Grogan, N.E.	12	2939	1536	52.3	22557	7.68	155	5.3	169	5.8	71.2
Warren Moon, Hou.	3	1315	715	54.4	9536	7.25	40	3.0	59	4.5	69.1
Mark Malone, Pitt.	6	1038	534	51.4	6686	6.44	48	4.6	49	4.7	67.5
Jim Plunkett, Raiders	15	3701	1943	52.5	25882	6.99	164	4.4	198	5.3	67.5
Marc Wilson, Raiders	7	1400	719	51.4	9690	6.92	65	4.6	78	5.6	66.0
Mike Pagel, Clev.	5	1157	589	50.9	7527	6.51	39	3.4	47	4.1	65.9

TOP 10 ACTIVE RUSHERS, AFC
2,000 or more yards

	Yrs.	Att.	Yards	TD
1. Mike Pruitt, K.C.	11	1844	7378	51
2. Marcus Allen, Raiders	5	1289	5397	49
3. Freeman McNeil, N.Y.J.	6	1185	5320	22
4. Tony Collins, N.E.	6	1044	4173	29
5. Curt Warner, Sea.	4	955	4064	34
6. Curtis Dickey, Clev.	7	937	4019	32
7. James Brooks, Cin.	6	823	3883	26
8. Randy McMillan, Ind.	6	990	3876	24
9. Sammy Winder, Den.	5	998	3672	25
10. Tony Nathan, Mia.	8	728	3523	16

Other Leading Rushers

Frank Pollard, Pitt.	7	794	3360	17
Earnest Jackson, Pitt.	4	805	3156	18
Walter Abercrombie, Pitt.	5	719	2884	20
Wayne Wilson, Raiders	8	666	2476	16
Craig James, N.E.	3	577	2444	10
Greg Bell, Buff.	3	575	2360	19
Ken Anderson, Cin.	16	397	2220	20
Steve Grogan, N.E.	12	406	2113	32
Larry Kinnebrew, Cin.	4	494	2012	29

TOP 10 ACTIVE PASS RECEIVERS, AFC
250 or more receptions

	Yrs.	No.	Yards	TD
1. Steve Largent, Sea.	11	694	11129	87
2. Ozzie Newsome, Clev.	9	541	6698	42
3. James Lofton, Raiders	9	530	9656	49
4. Wes Chandler, S.D.	9	516	8316	54
5. Nat Moore, Mia.	13	510	7546	74
6. John Stallworth, Pitt.	13	496	8202	61
7. Kellen Winslow, S.D.	8	488	6222	42
8. Stanley Morgan, N.E.	10	435	8692	57
9. Henry Marshall, K.C.	11	406	6419	33
10. Todd Christensen, Raid.	8	399	5019	39

Other Leading Receivers

Wesley Walker, N.Y.J.	10	395	7476	63
Cris Collinsworth, Cin.	6	373	5977	35
Tony Nathan, Mia.	8	373	3515	16
Steve Watson, Den.	8	342	5945	35
Paul Coffman, K.C.	9	334	4298	41
Mickey Shuler, N.Y.J.	9	296	3258	29
Marcus Allen, Raiders	5	283	2757	15
Jerry Butler, Buff.	7	278	4301	29
Mike Pruitt, K.C.	11	270	1860	5

TOP 10 ACTIVE SCORERS, AFC
250 or more points

	Yrs.	TD	FG	PAT	TP
1. Pat Leahy, N.Y.J.	13	0	200	393	993
2. Chris Bahr, Raiders	11	0	187	397	958
3. Tony Franklin, N.E.	8	0	158	298	772
4. Rolf Benirschke, S.D.	10	0	146	328	766
5. Nick Lowery, K.C.	8	0	155	255	720
6. Jim Breech, Cin.	8	0	137	300	711
7. Matt Bahr, Clev.	8	0	138	268	682
8. Steve Largent, Sea.	11	88	0	1	529
9. Gary Anderson, Pitt.	5	0	115	177	522
10. Rich Karlis, Den.	5	0	96	171	459

Other Leading Scorers

Nat Moore, Mia.	13	75	0	0	450
Norm Johnson, Sea.	5	0	84	194	446
Marcus Allen, Raiders	5	65	0	0	390
Wesley Walker, N.Y.J.	10	63	0	0	*380
John Stallworth, Pitt.	13	62	0	0	372
Stanley Morgan, N.E.	10	58	0	0	348
Mike Pruitt, K.C.	11	56	0	0	336
Wes Chandler, S.D.	9	54	0	0	324
James Lofton, Raiders	9	50	0	0	300
Ozzie Newsome, Clev.	9	44	0	0	264
Kellen Winslow, S.D.	8	42	0	0	252

**total includes safety scored*

TOP 10 ACTIVE INTERCEPTORS, AFC
20 or more interceptions

	Yrs.	No.	Yards	TD
1. Dave Brown, Sea.	12	50	643	5
Donnie Shell, Pitt.	13	50	440	1
3. Steve Foley, Den.	11	44	622	1
4. Mike Haynes, Raiders	11	41	649	2
5. Lester Hayes, Raiders	10	39	572	4
6. Dwight Hicks, Ind.	8	32	602	3
7. Louis Breeden, Cin.	9	31	509	2
Deron Cherry, K.C.	6	31	481	1
9. Ray Clayborn, N.E.	10	29	466	1
10. Charles Romes, Buff.	10	28	493	1
Kenny Easley, Sea.	6	28	491	3

Other Leading Interceptors

Glenn Blackwood, Mia.	8	26	381	1
Louis Wright, Den.	12	26	360	1
Mike Harden, Den.	7	25	522	4
Roland James, N.E.	7	22	276	0
Vann McElroy, Raiders	5	22	238	0
Woodrow Lowe, S.D.	11	21	343	4
Dwayne Woodruff, Pitt.	7	21	322	1
Steve Wilson, Den.	8	21	257	0
Hanford Dixon, Clev.	6	20	194	0
Albert Lewis, K.C.	4	20	176	0
Brad Van Pelt, Clev.	14	20	135	0

TOP 10 ACTIVE QUARTERBACK SACKERS, AFC
Official statistic since 1982

	No.
1. Mark Gastineau, N.Y.J.	62.5
2. Jacob Green, Sea.	57.5
3. Andre Tippett, N.E.	53.0
4. Howie Long, Raiders	48.0
5. Doug Betters, Mia.	43.5
6. Eddie Edwards, Cin.	43.0
7. Bill Pickel, Raiders	42.5
8. Rulon Jones, Den.	40.5
9. Greg Townsend, Raiders	39.0
10. Jeff Bryant, Sea.	38.0

TOP 10 ACTIVE PUNT RETURNERS, AFC
40 or more punt returns

	Yrs.	No.	Yards	Avg.	TD
1. Louis Lipps, Pitt.	3	92	1109	12.1	3
2. Irving Fryar, N.E.	3	108	1233	11.4	3
3. James Brooks, Cin.	6	52	565	10.9	0
4. Gerald Willhite, Den.	5	84	900	10.7	1
5. Mike Martin, Cin.	4	92	967	10.5	0
Kirk Springs, Ind.	5	65	681	10.5	1
7. Mike Haynes, Raiders	11	112	1168	10.4	2
Stanley Morgan, N.E.	10	92	960	10.4	1
9. Fulton Walker, Raiders	6	145	1437	9.9	1
10. Robbie Martin, Ind.	6	175	1670	9.5	3
Tony Nathan, Mia.	8	51	484	9.5	1
Roland James, N.E.	7	42	400	9.5	1

Other Leading Punt Returners

Mark Clayton, Mia.	4	52	485	9.3	1
Paul Skansi, Sea.	4	95	858	9.0	0
Gerald McNeil, Clev.	1	40	348	8.7	1
Nesby Glasgow, Ind.	8	79	651	8.2	1
Willie Drewrey, Hou.	2	58	477	8.2	0
Rick Woods, Pitt.	5	70	568	8.1	0
Lionel James, S.D.	3	64	515	8.0	1
Brian Brennan, Clev.	3	44	352	8.0	1
Kurt Sohn, N.Y.J.	5	64	504	7.9	0
Dwight Hicks, Ind.	8	54	403	7.5	0
Wes Chandler, S.D.	9	61	400	6.6	0
Robb Riddick, Buff.	4	46	289	6.3	0

TOP 10 ACTIVE KICKOFF RETURNERS, AFC
40 or more kickoff returns

	Yrs.	No.	Yards	Avg.	TD
1. Ray Clayborn, N.E.	10	57	1538	27.0	3
2. Bobby Humphery, N.Y.J.	3	67	1693	25.3	2
3. Tim McGee, Cin.	1	43	1007	23.4	0
4. Albert Bentley, Ind.	2	59	1361	23.1	0
5. Wayne Wilson, Raiders	8	70	1598	22.8	0
6. Nesby Glasgow, Ind.	8	84	1904	22.7	0
Carlos Carson, K.C.	7	57	1296	22.7	0
Kirk Springs, Ind.	5	49	1112	22.7	0
9. Fulton Walker, Raiders	6	167	3779	22.6	1
10. Willie Drewrey, Hou.	2	51	1142	22.4	0

Other Leading Kickoff Returners

Lorenzo Hampton, Mia.	2	54	1202	22.3	0
Mike Martin, Cin.	4	72	1592	22.1	0
Willie Tullis, Ind.	6	63	1384	22.0	1
Gene Lang, Den.	3	57	1245	21.8	0
James Brooks, Cin.	6	115	2487	21.6	0
Stephen Starring, N.E.	4	84	1814	21.6	0
Wes Chandler, S.D.	9	48	1032	21.5	0
Tony Nathan, Mia.	8	53	1133	21.4	0
Lionel James, S.D.	3	97	2053	21.2	0
Gerald McNeil, Clev.	1	47	997	21.2	1
Rich Erenberg, Pitt.	3	49	1016	20.7	0
Tony Collins, N.E.	6	64	1317	20.6	0
Robb Riddick, Buff.	4	50	1025	20.5	0
Randall Morris, Sea.	3	62	1254	20.2	0
Drew Hill, Hou.	7	172	3460	20.1	1
Anthony Hancock, K.C.	5	64	1281	20.0	0
Stanford Jennings, Cin.	3	47	927	19.7	0
Jeff Smith, K.C.	2	62	1211	19.5	0
Steve Wilson, Den.	8	58	1107	19.1	0
Kurt Sohn, N.Y.J.	5	51	958	18.8	0
Robbie Martin, Ind.	6	112	2084	18.6	0

TOP 10 ACTIVE PUNTERS, AFC
50 or more punts

	Yrs.	No.	Avg.	LG
1. Rohn Stark, Ind.	5	389	45.2	72
2. Reggie Roby, Mia.	4	240	43.8	73
3. Rich Camarillo, N.E.	6	406	42.9	76
4. Ray Guy, Raiders	14	1049	42.4	74
5. Ralf Mojsiejenko, S.D.	2	140	42.2	67
6. Mike Horan, Den.	3	204	41.8	75
7. Dave Jennings, N.Y.J.	13	1090	41.4	73
John Kidd, Buff.	3	255	41.4	67
Lee Johnson, Hou.	2	171	41.4	66
10. Jeff Gossett, Clev.	5	296	40.7	64
Lewis Colbert, K.C.	1	99	40.7	56

Other Leading Punters

Harry Newsome, Pitt.	2	164	39.8	64
Vince Gamache, Sea.	1	79	38.6	55
Jeff Hayes, S.D.	5	267	38.2	59

NFC ACTIVE STATISTICAL LEADERS

LEADING ACTIVE PASSERS, NATIONAL FOOTBALL CONFERENCE

1,000 or more attempts

	Yrs.	Att.	Comp.	Pct. Comp.	Yards	Avg. Gain	TD	Pct. TD	Had Int.	Pct. Int.	Rate Pts.
Joe Montana, S.F.	8	2878	1818	63.2	21498	7.47	141	4.9	76	2.6	91.2
Danny White, Dall.	11	2546	1517	59.6	19068	7.49	142	5.6	112	4.4	83.2
Neil Lomax, St.L.	6	2247	1287	57.3	15989	7.12	92	4.1	67	3.0	80.7
Jim McMahon, Chi.	5	1111	635	57.2	8218	7.40	49	4.4	41	3.7	79.9
Tommy Kramer, Minn.	10	3258	1811	55.6	22153	6.80	143	4.4	138	4.2	73.7
Phil Simms, N.Y.G.	7	2492	1326	53.2	17585	7.06	104	4.2	103	4.1	72.5
Steve Fuller, Chi.	7	1066	605	56.8	7156	6.71	28	2.6	41	3.8	70.1
Eric Hipple, Det.	7	1501	811	54.0	10463	6.97	55	3.7	67	4.5	69.8
Joe Ferguson, Det.	14	4375	2292	52.4	28895	6.60	190	4.3	200	4.6	68.7
Steve DeBerg, T.B.	9	2722	1539	56.5	17691	6.50	102	3.7	132	4.8	68.6
Doug Williams, Wash.	6	1891	895	47.3	12648	6.69	73	3.9	73	3.9	66.2

TOP 10 ACTIVE RUSHERS, NFC

2,000 or more yards

	Yrs.	Att.	Yards	TD
1. Walter Payton, Chi.	12	3692	16193	106
2. Tony Dorsett, Dall.	10	2625	11580	71
3. Ottis Anderson, N.Y.G.	8	1882	8080	47
4. Eric Dickerson, Rams	4	1465	6968	55
5. George Rogers, Wash.	6	1529	6563	48
6. William Andrews, Atl.	6	1315	5986	30
7. Gerald Riggs, Atl.	5	1271	5268	45
8. Joe Cribbs, S.F.	6	1234	5035	26
9. James Wilder, T.B.	6	1313	4882	36
10. Ted Brown, Minn.	8	1117	4546	40

Other Leading Rushers

	Yrs.	Att.	Yards	TD
Tony Galbreath, N.Y.G.	11	1021	3998	34
Gerry Ellis, G.B.	7	836	3826	25
Joe Morris, N.Y.G.	5	818	3555	40
Roger Craig, S.F.	4	749	3254	31
Stump Mitchell, St.L.	6	576	2977	25
Eddie Lee Ivery, G.B.	8	667	2933	23
Darrin Nelson, Minn.	5	669	2870	13
James Jones, Det.	4	768	2796	23
Matt Suhey, Chi.	7	714	2618	17

TOP 10 ACTIVE PASS RECEIVERS, NFC

250 or more receptions

	Yrs.	No.	Yards	TD
1. Dwight Clark, S.F.	8	482	6460	43
2. Tony Hill, Dall.	10	479	7988	51
3. Pat Tilley, St.L.	11	468	7005	37
4. Art Monk, Wash.	7	466	6550	28
5. Tony Galbreath, N.Y.G.	11	464	3818	9
6. Walter Payton, Chi.	12	459	4321	14
7. Tony Dorsett, Dall.	10	363	3255	12
8. Russ Francis, S.F.	11	360	4899	40
9. David Hill, Rams	11	347	4107	28
10. Ted Brown, Minn.	8	339	2850	13
James Wilder, T.B.	6	339	2705	5

Other Leading Receivers

	Yrs.	No.	Yards	TD
Billy Johnson, Atl.	12	329	4127	25
Jimmie Giles, Det.	10	315	4645	37
Roy Green, St.L.	8	314	5168	44
Ottis Anderson, N.Y.G.	8	308	2541	5
Kevin House, Rams	7	293	5106	33
Roger Craig, S.F.	4	292	2742	13
J.T. Smith, St.L.	9	290	3868	15
Dan Ross, G.B.	7	290	3419	19
Leonard Thompson, Det.	12	277	4682	35
Mike Renfro, Dall.	9	277	4046	24
William Andrews, Atl.	6	277	2647	11
Mike Quick, Phil.	5	273	4803	43
Gerry Ellis, G.B.	7	267	2514	10
Doug Cosbie, Dall.	8	252	3195	27

TOP 10 ACTIVE SCORERS, NFC

250 or more points

	Yrs.	TD	FG	PAT	TP
1. Ray Wersching, S.F.	14	0	209	412	1039
2. Walter Payton, Chi.	12	120	0	0	720
3. Ed Murray, Det.	7	0	152	228	684
4. Mick Luckhurst, Atl.	6	0	106	196	514
5. Tony Dorsett, Dall.	10	84	0	0	504
6. Morten Andersen, N.O.	5	0	97	134	425
7. Mike Lansford, Rams	5	0	79	141	378
8. Raul Allegre, N.Y.G.	4	0	81	105	348
9. Eric Dickerson, Rams	4	57	0	0	342
10. Ted Brown, Minn.	8	53	0	0	318

Other Leading Scorers

	Yrs.	TD	FG	PAT	TP
Ottis Anderson, N.Y.G.	8	52	0	0	312
Tony Hill, Dall.	10	51	0	0	306
Paul McFadden, Phil.	3	0	75	81	306
George Rogers, Wash.	6	48	0	0	288
Roy Green, St.L.	8	47	0	0	282
Gerald Riggs, Atl.	5	45	0	0	270
Tony Galbreath, N.Y.G.	11	43	2	1	265
Kevin Butler, Chi.	2	0	59	87	264
Roger Craig, S.F.	4	44	0	0	264
Dwight Clark, S.F.	8	43	0	0	258
Mike Quick, Phil.	5	43	0	0	258
Ali Haji-Sheikh, Atl.	4	0	63	66	255
Joe Morris, N.Y.G.	5	42	0	0	252

TOP 10 ACTIVE INTERCEPTORS, NFC

20 or more interceptions

	Yrs.	No.	Yards	TD
1. John Harris, Minn.	9	44	494	2
2. Gary Fencik, Chi.	11	38	488	1
3. Everson Walls, Dall.	6	37	353	0
4. Nolan Cromwell, Rams	10	35	643	4
5. Ronnie Lott, S.F.	6	33	462	5
6. Michael Downs, Dall.	6	28	374	1
7. LeRoy Irvin, Rams	7	26	539	4
8. Mark Lee, G.B.	7	24	202	0
9. Steve Freeman, Minn.	12	23	329	3
Dave Waymer, N.O.	7	23	160	0

Other Leading Interceptors

	Yrs.	No.	Yards	TD
John Anderson, G.B.	9	22	144	1
Vernon Dean, Wash.	5	21	243	2
Leslie Frazier, Chi.	5	20	343	2
Bobby Watkins, Det.	5	20	85	0
Roynell Young, Phil.	7	20	71	0

TOP 10 ACTIVE QUARTERBACK SACKERS, NFC

Official statistic since 1982

	No.
1. Dexter Manley, Wash.	64.5
2. Lawrence Taylor, N.Y.G.	61.5
3. Greg Brown, Phil.	50.5
4. Richard Dent, Chi.	49.0
5. Rickey Jackson, N.O.	48.5
6. Al Baker, St.L.	46.0
7. Curtis Greer, St.L.	44.5
Randy White, Dall.	44.5
9. Dwaine Board, S.F.	43.0
10. William Gay, Det.	42.5

TOP 10 ACTIVE PUNT RETURNERS, NFC

40 or more punt returns

	Yrs.	No.	Yards	Avg.	TD
1. Henry Ellard, Rams	4	97	1248	12.9	4
2. Billy Johnson, Atl.	12	258	3123	12.1	6
Vai Sikahema, St.L.	1	43	522	12.1	2
4. J.T. Smith, St.L.	9	247	2611	10.6	4
5. Walter Stanley, G.B.	2	47	495	10.5	1
6. Dana McLemore, N.O.	5	131	1333	10.2	3
7. LeRoy Irvin, Rams	7	144	1448	10.1	4
8. Pete Mandley, Det.	3	83	823	9.9	2
Ken Jenkins, Wash.	4	78	773	9.9	0
10. Dennis McKinnon, Chi.	3	43	422	9.8	1

Other Leading Punt Returners

	Yrs.	No.	Yards	Avg.	TD
Stump Mitchell, St.L.	6	156	1377	8.8	1
Lew Barnes, Chi.	1	57	482	8.5	0
Phillip Epps, G.B.	5	100	819	8.2	1
Rod Hill, Det.	5	51	391	7.7	0
Phil McConkey, N.Y.G.	3	131	1001	7.6	0
Evan Cooper, Phil.	3	99	753	7.6	0
Rufus Bess, Minn.	8	48	346	7.2	0
John Simmons, G.B.	6	44	302	6.9	0
Ron Fellows, Dall.	6	46	308	6.7	0

TOP 10 ACTIVE KICKOFF RETURNERS, NFC

40 or more kickoff returns

	Yrs.	No.	Yards	Avg.	TD
1. Ron Brown, Rams	3	64	1712	26.8	3
2. Buster Rhymes, Minn.	2	62	1558	25.1	0
3. Billy Johnson, Atl.	12	123	2941	23.9	2
4. Dennis Gentry, Chi.	5	65	1542	23.7	2
5. Darrin Nelson, Minn.	5	69	1624	23.5	0
6. Roy Green, St.L.	8	83	1917	23.1	1
7. Stump Mitchell, St.L.	6	167	3836	23.0	0
8. Derrick Harmon, S.F.	3	40	906	22.7	0
9. Ken Jenkins, Wash.	4	108	2427	22.5	0
10. Sylvester Stamps, Atl.	3	47	1055	22.4	0

Other Leading Kickoff Returners

	Yrs.	No.	Yards	Avg.	TD
Carl Monroe, S.F.	4	71	1569	22.1	1
Jimmy Rogers, S.F.	5	77	1678	21.8	0
Barry Redden, Rams	5	64	1390	21.7	0
Herman Hunter, Det.	2	97	2054	21.2	0
Phil Freeman, T.B.	2	79	1667	21.1	0
Dana McLemore, N.O.	5	55	1124	20.4	0
Ron Fellows, Dall.	6	73	1478	20.2	0
Cliff Austin, Atl.	4	57	1147	20.1	1
Robert Lavette, Dall.	2	70	1381	19.7	0
Phil McConkey, N.Y.G.	3	64	1246	19.5	0
Mark Lee, G.B.	7	45	859	19.1	0
Charles White, Rams	6	47	859	18.3	0

TOP 10 ACTIVE PUNTERS, NFC

50 or more punts

	Yrs.	No.	Avg.	LG
1. Sean Landeta, N.Y.G.	2	160	43.8	68
Rick Donnelly, Atl.	2	137	43.8	71
3. Brian Hansen, N.O.	3	239	42.8	66
4. Steve Cox, Wash.	6	317	42.3	69
5. Maury Buford, Chi.	5	287	42.2	71
6. Jim Arnold, Det.	4	320	42.1	64
7. John Teltschik, Phil.	1	108	41.6	62
8. Frank Garcia, T.B.	5	319	41.5	64
9. Mike Saxon, Dall.	2	167	41.3	58
10. Mike Black, Minn.	4	266	41.2	63

Other Leading Punters

	Yrs.	No.	Avg.	LG
Greg Coleman, Minn.	10	736	40.8	73
Dale Hatcher, Rams	2	184	40.8	67
Max Runager, S.F.	8	540	40.6	64
Don Bracken, G.B.	2	81	40.2	63
Danny White, Dall.	11	610	40.2	73
Greg Cater, St.L.	5	338	38.9	71

DRAFT LIST FOR 1987

52nd Annual NFL Draft, April 28-29, 1987

Atlanta Falcons

1. Chris Miller—13, QB, Oregon
2. Kenny Flowers—31, RB, Clemson, from Green Bay
   Choice to Green Bay
3. Choice to Green Bay
4. Ralph Van Dyke—97, T, Southern Illinois
5. Mark Mraz—125, DE, Utah State
6. Paul Kiser—153, G, Wake Forest
7. Michael Reid—181, LB, Wisconsin
8. Curtis Taliaferro—208, LB, Virginia Tech
9. Terrence Anthony—236, DB, Iowa State
10. Jerry Reese—264, TE, Illinois
11. Elbert Shelley—292, DB, Arkansas State
12. Larry Emery—320, RB, Wisconsin

Buffalo Bills

1. Choice to Houston
   Shane Conlan—8, LB, Penn State, from Houston
2. Nathaniel Odomes—29, DB, Wisconsin, from Tampa Bay
   Roland Mitchell—33, DB, Texas Tech
3. David Brandon—60, LB, Memphis State
   Jamie Mueller—78, RB, Benedictine, from San Francisco
4. Choice to Tampa Bay
   Leon Seals—109, DE, Jackson State, from Washington
5. Choice to Washington
6. Choice to Washington
7. Kerry Porter—171, RB, Washington State
8. Choice to Indianapolis
   Bruce Mesner—209, DE, Maryland, from L.A. Raiders
9. Keith McKeller—227, TE, Jacksonville State
10. Choice to L.A. Raiders
11. Howard Ballard—283, T, Alabama A&M
12. Joe McGrail—311, DT, Delaware

Chicago Bears

1. Jim Harbaugh—26, QB, Michigan
2. Ron Morris—54, WR, Southern Methodist
3. Choice to Cleveland through L.A. Rams
4. Sean Smith—101, DE, Grambling, from L.A. Rams
   Choice to L.A. Raiders
5. Steve Bryan—120, DE, Oklahoma, from Houston through Washington and L.A. Raiders
   Will Johnson—138, LB, Northeast Louisiana
6. John Adickes—154, C, Baylor, from L.A. Raiders
   Choice to L.A. Rams
7. Archie Harris—193, T, William & Mary
8. Paul Migliazzo—221, LB, Oklahoma
9. Lakei Heimuli—249, RB, Brigham Young
10. Dick Chapura—277, DT, Missouri
11. Tim Jessie—305, RB, Auburn
12. Eric Jeffries—333, DB, Texas

Cincinnati Bengals

1. Jason Buck—17, DE, Brigham Young
2. Eric Thomas—49, DB, Tulane
3. Leonard Bell—76, DB, Indiana
   Skip McClendon—77, DE, Arizona State, from Seattle
4. Jim Riggs—103, TE, Clemson
5. Marc Logan—130, RB, Kentucky
   Greg Horne—139, P, Arkansas, from Denver
6. Sonny Gordon—157, DB, Ohio State
7. Chris Thatcher—188, G, Lafayette
8. Solomon Wilcots—215, DB, Colorado
9. Craig Raddatz—242, LB, Wisconsin
10. David McCluskey—269, RB, Georgia
11. Jim Warne—296, T, Arizona State
12. John Holifield—328, RB, West Virginia

Cleveland Browns

1. Mike Junkin—5, LB, Duke, from San Diego
   Choice to San Diego
2. Gregg Rakoczy—32, C, Miami, from San Diego
   Choice to San Diego
3. Tim Manoa—80, RB, Penn State
   Jeff Jaeger—82, K, Washington, from Chicago through L.A. Rams
4. Choice to L.A. Rams
5. Choice to L.A. Rams
6. Stephen Braggs—165, DB, Texas
7. Choice to Green Bay
8. Steve Bullitt—220, LB, Texas A&M
9. Choice to Indianapolis
10. Frank Winters—276, C, Western Illinois
11. Larry Brewton—303, DB, Temple
12. Choice to L.A. Rams

Dallas Cowboys

1. Danny Noonan—12, DT, Nebraska
2. Ron Francis—39, DB, Baylor
3. Jeff Zimmerman—68, G, Florida
4. Kelvin Martin—95,WR, Boston College
5. Everett Gay—124, WR, Texas
6. Joe Onosai—151, G, Hawaii
7. Kevin Sweeney—180, QB, Fresno State
8. Kevin Gogan—206, T, Washington
9. Alvin Blount—235, RB, Maryland
10. Dale Jones—262, LB, Tennessee
11. Jeff Ward—291, K, Texas
12. Scott Armstrong—318, LB, Florida

Denver Broncos

1. Ricky Nattiel—27, WR, Florida
2. Choice to N.Y. Giants
3. Michael Brooks—86, LB, Louisiana State
4. Marc Munford—111, LB, Nebraska
5. Choice to Cincinnati
6. Warren Marshall—167, RB, James Madison
7. Wilbur Strozier—194, TE, Georgia
8. Dan Morgan—222, G, Penn State
9. Bruce Plummer—250, DB, Mississippi State
10. Rafe Wilkinson—278, LB, Richmond
11. Steve Roberts—299, DE, Washington, from L.A. Rams
    Tommy Neal—306, RB, Maryland
12. Tyrone Braxton—334, DB, North Dakota State

Detroit Lions

1. Reggie Rogers—7, DE, Washington
2. Choice to Tampa Bay through Houston and Buffalo
3. Jerry Ball—63, NT, Southern Methodist
4. Garland Rivers—92, DB, Michigan
5. Choice to Seattle
6. Danny Lockett—148, LB, Arizona
7. Dan Saleaumua—175, DT, Arizona State
8. Dennis Gibson—203, LB, Iowa State
9. Rick Calhoun—230, RB, Cal State-Fullerton
10. Raynard Brown—259, WR, South Carolina
11. Brian Siverling—286, TE, Penn State
12. Gary Lee—315, WR, Georgia Tech

Green Bay Packers

1. Brent Fullwood—4, RB, Auburn
2. Choice to Atlanta
   Johnny Holland—41, LB, Texas A&M, from Atlanta
3. Dave Croston—61, T, Iowa
   Scott Stephen—69, LB, Arizona State, from Atlanta
   Frankie Neal—71, WR, Fort Hays State, from L.A. Raiders
4. Lorenzo Freeman—89, DT, Pittsburgh
5. Choice to San Diego
6. Willie Marshall—145, WR, Temple
7. Tony Leiker—172, DT, Stanford
   Bill Smith—191, P, Mississippi, from Cleveland
8. Jeff Drost—198, DT, Iowa
9. Gregg Harris—228, G, Wake Forest
10. Don Majkowski—255, QB, Virginia
11. Patrick Scott—282, WR, Grambling
12. Choice to Seattle
    Norman Jefferson—335, DB, Louisiana State, from N.Y. Giants

Houston Oilers

1. Alonzo Highsmith—3, RB, Miami, from Buffalo
   Choice to Buffalo
   Haywood Jeffires—20, WR, North Carolina State, from L.A. Rams
2. Choice to Kansas City
   Walter Johnson—46, LB, Louisiana Tech, from Kansas City
3. Cody Carlson—64, QB, Baylor
4. Choice to L.A. Rams
   Mark Dusbabek—105, LB, Minnesota, from Kansas City
5. Choice to Chicago through Washington and L.A. Raiders
   Spencer Tillman—133, RB, Oklahoma, from L.A. Rams
6. Al Smith—147, LB, Utah State
   Toby Caston—159, LB, Louisiana State, from Kansas City
7. Robert Banks—176, DT, Notre Dame
8. Michel James—202, WR, Washington State
9. Wes Neighbors—231, C, Alabama
10. Curtis Duncan—258, WR, Northwestern
11. John Davis—287, G, Georgia Tech
12. Ira Valentine—314, RB, Texas A&M

Indianapolis Colts

1. Cornelius Bennett—2, LB, Alabama
2. Choice to Washington
3. Chris Gambol—58, T, Iowa
4. Randy Dixon—85, T, Pittsburgh
5. Roy Banks—114, WR, Eastern Illinois
6. Freddie Robinson—142, DB, Alabama
7. Mark Bellini—170, WR, Brigham Young
8. Choice to Tampa Bay
   Chuckie Miller—200, DB, UCLA, from Buffalo
9. Choice to N.Y. Giants
   Bob Ontko—247, LB, Penn State, from Cleveland
10. Chris Goode—253, DB, Alabama
11. Jim Reynosa—281, DE, Arizona State
12. David Adams—309, RB, Arizona

Kansas City Chiefs

1. Paul Palmer—19, RB, Temple
2. Christian Okoye—35, RB, Azusa Pacific, from Houston
   Choice to Houston
3. Todd Howard—73, LB, Texas A&M
4. Choice to Houston
5. Kitrick Taylor—128, WR, Washington State, from Minnesota through Miami
   Choice to Miami
6. Choice to Houston
7. Doug Hudson—186, QB, Nicholls State
8. Choice to Miami
   Michael Clemons—218, RB, William & Mary, from New England
9. Randy Watts—244, DE, Catawba
10. James Evans—271, RB, Southern
11. Craig Richardson—298, WR, Eastern Washington
12. Bruce Holmes—325, LB, Minnesota

Los Angeles Raiders

1. John Clay—15, T, Missouri
2. Choice to N.Y. Jets
   Bruce Wilkerson—52, T, Tennessee, from Washington
3. Choice to Green Bay
   Steve Smith—81, RB, Penn State, from Washington through New England
4. Choice to New England
   Steve Beuerlein—110, QB, Notre Dame, from Chicago
5. Choice to St. Louis
6. Choice to Chicago
7. Bo Jackson—183, RB, Auburn
8. Choice to Buffalo
9. Scott Eccles—238, TE, Eastern New Mexico
10. Rob Harrison—254, DB, Cal State-Sacramento, from Buffalo
    John Gesek—265, G, Cal State-Sacramento
    Jim Ellis—273, LB, Boise State, from San Francisco through Buffalo
11. Chris McLemore—288, RB, Arizona, from Philadelphia through San Francisco
    Mario Perry—294, TE, Mississippi
12. Choice to N.Y. Giants

Los Angeles Rams

1. Choice to Houston
2. Donald Evans—47, DE, Winston-Salem
3. Cliff Hicks—74, DB, Oregon
4. Doug Bartlett—91, NT, Northern Illinois, from Houston
   Choice to Chicago
   Larry Kelm—108, LB, Texas A&M, from Cleveland
5. Choice to Houston
   Scott Mersereau—136, DT, Southern Connecticut, from Cleveland
6. Choice to N.Y. Giants
   Jon Embree—166, TE, Colorado, from Chicago
7. Choice exercised in 1986 Supplemental Draft by Philadelphia for Charles Crawford, RB, Oklahoma
8. Michael Stewart—213, DB, Fresno State
9. Tracy Ham—240, RB, Georgia Southern
10. David Smith—272, LB, Northern Arizona
11. Choice to Denver
12. Alonzo Williams—326, RB, Mesa, Colorado
    Fred Stokes—332, DE, Georgia Southern, from Cleveland

Miami Dolphins

1. Choice to Minnesota
   John Bosa—16, DE, Boston College, from Minnesota
2. Rick Graf—43, LB, Wisconsin
   Scott Schwedes—56, WR, Syracuse, from N.Y. Giants through St. Louis
3. Choice to St. Louis
4. Troy Stradford—99, RB, Boston College
5. Choice to St. Louis
   Chris Conlin—132, T, Penn State, from Kansas City
6. Lance Sellers—155, LB, Boise State
7. Tom Brown—182, RB, Pittsburgh
8. Joel Williams—210, TE, Notre Dame
   Mark Dennis—212, T, Illinois, from Kansas City
9. Tim Pidgeon—237, LB, Syracuse
10. Bobby Taylor—266, DB, Wisconsin
11. Terence Mann—293, NT, Southern Methodist
12. Jim Karsatos—322, QB, Ohio State

Minnesota Vikings

1. D.J. Dozier—14, RB, Penn State, from Miami
   Choice to Miami
2. Ray Berry—44, LB, Baylor
3. Henry Thomas—72, NT, Louisiana State
4. Reggie Rutland—100, DB, Georgia Tech
5. Choice to Kansas City through Miami
6. Greg Richardson—156, WR, Alabama
7. Choice to Seattle
8. Rick Fenney—211, RB, Washington
9. Leonard Jones—239, DB, Texas Tech
10. Bob Riley—267, T, Indiana
11. Brent Pease—295, QB, Montana
12. Keith Williams—323, DT, Florida

New England Patriots

1. Bruce Armstrong—23, T, Louisville
2. Choice to Tampa Bay
3. Bob Perryman—79, RB, Michigan
4. Rich Gannon—98, QB, Delaware, from L.A. Raiders
   Derrick Beasley—102, DB, Winston-Salem, from N.Y. Jets through L.A. Raiders
   Tim Jordan—107, LB, Wisconsin
5. Danny Villa—113, T, Arizona State, from Tampa Bay
   Tom Gibson—116, DE, Northern Arizona, from San Diego
   Choice to Tampa Bay
6. Gene Taylor—163, WR, Fresno State
7. Choice to Tampa Bay
8. Choice to Kansas City
9. Choice to Tampa Bay
10. Choice to San Francisco through Buffalo
11. Carlos Reveiz—302, K, Tennessee
12. Elgin Davis—330, RB, Central Florida

New Orleans Saints

1. Shawn Knight—11, DT, Brigham Young
2. Lonzell Hill—40, WR, Washington
3. Mike Adams—67, DB, Arkansas State
4. Steve Trapilo—96, G, Boston College
5. Milton Mack—123, DB, Alcorn State
6. Thomas Henley—152, WR, Stanford
7. Gene Atkins—179, DB, Florida A&M
8. Toi Cook—207, DB, Stanford
9. Scott Leach—234, LB, Ohio State
10. Robert Clark—263, WR, North Carolina Central
11. Arthur Wells—290, TE, Grambling
12. Tyrone Sorrells—319, G, Georgia Tech

New York Giants

1. Mark Ingram—28, WR, Michigan State
2. Adrian White—55, DB, Florida, from Denver
   Choice to Miami through St. Louis
3. Stephen Baker—83, WR, Fresno State
4. Odessa Turner—112, WR, Northwestern State, La.
5. Paul O'Connor—140, G, Miami
6. Tim Richardson—160, RB, Pacific, from L.A. Rams
   Doug Riesenberg—168, T, California
7. Choice to St. Louis
8. Rod Jones—223, TE, Washington
9. Stan Parker—225, G, Nebraska, from Indianapolis
   Dana Wright—251, RB, Findlay
10. Chuck Faucette—279, LB, Maryland
11. Dave Walter—307, QB, Michigan Tech
12. Bill Berthusen—321, DT, Iowa State, from L.A. Raiders
    Chad Stark—329, RB, North Dakota State, from San Francisco through L.A. Raiders
    Choice to Green Bay

New York Jets

1. Roger Vick—21, RB, Texas A&M
2. Alex Gordon—42, LB, Cincinnati, from L.A. Raiders
   Choice to Washington through L.A. Raiders
3. Onzy Elam—75, LB, Tennessee State
4. Choice to New England through L.A. Raiders
5. Kirby Jackson—129, DB, Mississippi State
6. Tracy Martin—161, WR, North Dakota
7. Gerald Nichols—187, NT, Florida State
8. Eddie Hunter—196, RB, Virginia Tech, from Tampa Bay
   Mike Rice—214, P, Montana
9. Ron McLean—241, DE, Cal State-Fullerton
10. Sid Lewis—268, DB, Penn State
11. Kirk Timmer—300, LB, Montana State
12. Bill Ransdell—327, QB, Kentucky

Philadelphia Eagles

1. Jerome Brown—9, DT, Miami
2. Choice to San Francisco
3. Ben Tamburello—65, C, Auburn
4. Byron Evans—93, LB, Arizona
5. David Alexander—121, G, Tulsa
6. Ron Moten—149, LB, Florida
   Chris Pike—158, DT, Tulsa, from Seattle
7. Brian Williams—177, T, Central Michigan
   Choice from L.A. Rams, exercised in 1986 Supplemental Draft for Charles Crawford, RB, Oklahoma State
8. Choice to San Diego
9. Ken Lambiotte—232, QB, William & Mary
10. Paul Carberry—260, DT, Oregon State
11. Choice to L.A. Raiders through San Francisco
12. Bobby Morse—316, RB, Michigan State

Pittsburgh Steelers

1. Rod Woodson—10, DB, Purdue
2. Delton Hall—38, DB, Clemson
3. Charles Lockett—66, WR, Long Beach State
4. Thomas Everett—94, DB, Baylor
5. Hardy Nickerson—122, LB, California
6. Tim Johnson—141, NT, Penn State, from Tampa Bay
   Greg Lloyd—150, LB, Fort Valley State
7. Chris Kelley—178, TE, Akron
8. Charles Buchanan—205, DE, Tennessee State
9. Joey Clinkscales—233, WR, Tennessee
10. Merril Hoge—261, RB, Idaho State
11. Paul Oswald—289, C, Kansas
12. Theo Young—317, TE, Arkansas

St. Louis Cardinals

1. Kelly Stouffer—6, QB, Colorado State
2. Tim McDonald—34, DB, Southern California
3. Robert Awalt—62, TE, San Diego State
   Colin Scotts—70, DT, Hawaii, from Miami
4. Rod Saddler—90, DT, Texas A&M
5. George Swarn—118, RB, Miami, Ohio
   John Bruno—126, P, Penn State, from Miami
   Ilia Jarostchuk—127, LB, New Hampshire, from L.A. Raiders
6. Mark Garalczyk—146, DT, Western Michigan
7. Tim Peoples—174, DB, Washington
   William Harris—195, TE, Bishop College, from N.Y. Giants
8. Steve Alvord—201, DT, Washington
9. Wayne Davis—229, LB, Alabama
10. Charles Wright—257, DB, Tulsa
11. Todd Peat—285, G, Northern Illinois
12. Choice to Tampa Bay

San Diego Chargers

1. Choice to Cleveland
   Rod Bernstine—24, TE, Texas A&M, from Cleveland
2. Choice to Cleveland
   Louis Brock—53, DB, Southern California, from Cleveland
3. Karl Wilson—59, DE, Louisiana State
4. Mark Vlasic—88, QB, Iowa
5. Nelson Jones—115, DB, North Carolina State, from Green Bay
   Choice to New England
6. Choice to Tampa Bay
7. Jamie Holland—173, WR, Ohio State
8. Joe MacEsker—199, T, Texas-El Paso
   Ron Brown—204, LB, Southern California, from Philadelphia
9. Thomas Wilcher—226, RB, Michigan
10. Anthony Anderson—256, DB, Grambling
11. Joe Goebel—284, C, UCLA
12. Marcus Greenwood—310, RB, UCLA

San Francisco 49ers

1. Harris Barton—22, T, North Carolina
   Terrence Flagler—25, RB, Clemson, from Washington
2. Jeff Bregel—37, G, Southern California, from Philadelphia
   Choice to Tampa Bay
3. Choice to Buffalo
4. Choice to Tampa Bay
5. Paul Jokisch—134, WR, Michigan
6. Bob White—162, LB, Penn State
7. Steve DeLine—189, K, Colorado State
8. Dave Grayson—217, LB, Fresno State
9. Jonathan Shelley—245, DB, Mississippi
10. Choice to L.A. Raiders through Buffalo
    John Paye—275, QB, Stanford, from New England through L.A. Raiders
11. Calvin Nicholas—301, WR, Grambling
12. Choice to N.Y. Giants through L.A. Raiders

Seattle Seahawks

1. Tony Woods—18, LB, Pittsburgh
2. Dave Wyman—45, LB, Stanford
3. Choice to Cincinnati
4. Mark Moore—104, DB, Oklahoma State
5. Tommie Agee—119, RB, Auburn, from Detroit
   Ruben Rodriguez—131, P, Arizona
6. Choice to Philadelphia
7. Roland Barbay—184, NT, Louisiana State, from Minnesota
   Derek Tennell—[illegible]5, TE, UCLA
8. Sammy Garza—216, QB, Texas-El Paso
9. M.L. Johnson—243, LB, Hawaii
10. Louis Clark—270, WR, Mississippi State
11. Darryl Oliver—297, RB, Miami
12. Wes Dove—312, DE, Syracuse, from Green Bay
    Tony Burse—324, RB, Middle Tennessee State

Tampa Bay Buccaneers

1. Vinny Testaverde—1, QB, Miami
2. Choice to Buffalo
   Ricky Reynolds—36, DB, Washington State, from Detroit through Houston and Buffalo
   Winston Moss—50, LB, Miami, from San Francisco
   Don Smith—51, RB, Mississippi State, from New England
3. Mark Carrier—57, WR, Nicholls State
4. Don Graham—84, LB, Penn State
   Ron Hall—87, TE, Hawaii, from Buffalo
   Bruce Hill—106, WR, Arizona State, from San Francisco
5. Choice to New England
   Henry Rolling—135, LB, Nevada-Reno, from New England
   Tony Mayes—137, DB, Kentucky, from Washington
6. Choice to Pittsburgh
   Steve Bartalo—143, RB, Colorado State, from San Diego
7. Curt Jarvis—169, NT, Alabama
   Harry Swayne—190, DE, Rutgers, from New England
8. Choice to N.Y. Jets
   Stan Mataele—197, NT, Arizona, from Indianapolis
9. Joe Armentrout—224, RB, Wisconsin
   Greg Davis—246, P, Citadel, from New England
10. Mike Simmonds—252, G, Indiana State
11. Reggie Taylor—280, RB, Cincinnati
12. Scott Cooper—308, DT, Kearney State
    Mike Shula—313, QB, Alabama, from St. Louis

Washington Redskins

1. Choice to San Francisco
2. Brian Davis—30, DB, Nebraska, from Indianapolis
   Wally Kleine—48, T, Notre Dame, from N.Y. Jets through L.A. Raiders
   Choice to L.A. Raiders
3. Choice to L.A. Raiders through New England
4. Choice to Buffalo
5. Timmy Smith—117, RB, Texas Tech, from Buffalo
   Choice to Tampa Bay
6. Steve Gage—144, DB, Tulsa, from Buffalo
   Ed Simmons—164, T, Eastern Washington
7. Johnny Thomas—192, DB, Baylor
8. Clarence Vaughn—219, DB, Northern Illinois
9. Alfred Jenkins—248, RB, Arizona
10. Ted Wilson—274, WR, Central Florida
11. Laron Brown—304, WR, Texas
12. Ray Hitchcock—331, C, Minnesota

Look for in 1987

Things that could happen in 1987:

• **Steve Largent,** Seattle, needs six receptions to become the second player in NFL history with 700 career catches. He starts the 1987 season 56 receptions short of the all-time record of 750, held by Charlie Joiner.

• Largent starts 1987 with 11,129 yards on receptions, and needs 1,018 yards to supplant Joiner (12,146) as the NFL record holder in that category.

• Largent's next touchdown reception will be the eighty-eighth of his NFL career, and will tie him with Don Maynard for second place on the all-time list. The NFL record of 99 is held by Don Hutson.

• Largent also needs three 100-yard receiving games to pass Lance Alworth for second on the all-time list. Largent has 39 100-yard games, Alworth 41, and Don Maynard leads with 50. **Stanley Morgan,** New England, has 35 100-yard receiving games and can also move up on the list.

• Largent and **Tony Dorsett,** Dallas, are both within reach of their ninetieth career touchdown, a mark achieved by only 10 players in NFL history. Dorsett starts the season with 84 touchdowns; Largent has 88.

• Dorsett needs 132 yards via rushing, receiving, or returns to become the third player in NFL history to reach 15,000 combined yards. Only Walter Payton (21,053) and Jim Brown (15,459) stand ahead of Dorsett, who starts the 1987 season with 14,868.

• Dorsett has 11,580 yards rushing, and needs 541 to pass Franco Harris (12,120) into third place on the all-time list. He needs 733 yards rushing to pass Jim Brown (12,312) into second place.

• **Walter Payton,** Chicago, needs one rushing touchdown to break the NFL record of 106 that he currently shares with Jim Brown. Payton has scored 120 total touchdowns in his career, second all-time to Brown's 126.

• **Dan Fouts,** San Diego, needs one touchdown pass to break a fourth-place tie with John Hadl at 244. With 12 scoring passes, Fouts would also pass Sonny Jurgensen (255) into third place all-time, behind Fran Tarkenton (342) and Johnny Unitas (290).

• **Dan Marino,** Miami, has thrown at least one touchdown pass in 23 straight games and needs a touchdown pass in his first six games to surpass Daryle Lamonica (25 consecutive games) and **Dave Krieg,** Seattle, (28) and move into second place behind Johnny Unitas (47).

• **Ottis Anderson,** New York Giants, needs two yards rushing to pass Larry Csonka into tenth place on the all-time NFL rushing list. Anderson starts the season with 8,080 yards in eight seasons; Csonka had 8,081 in eleven years.

• **Eric Dickerson,** Los Angeles Rams, starts the 1987 season with 6,968 yards rushing, and needs 1,032 to become the first player to accumulate 8,000 yards rushing in his first five seasons in the NFL.

• **Ozzie Newsome,** Cleveland, starts the season with 541 receptions, just one short of Lance Alworth's 542, which ranks tenth in NFL history.

• **James Lofton,** Los Angeles Raiders, needs 344 yards on receptions to reach 10,000 career yards, a total achieved by only five players in NFL history.

• **John Stallworth,** Pittsburgh, needs four receptions to become the eighteenth player in NFL history to have 500 career receptions.

• **Pat Leahy,** New York Jets, and **Chris Bahr,** Los Angeles Raiders, are within reach of 1,000 career points, a total achieved by only 12 players in NFL history. Leahy starts 1987 with 993 points; Bahr has 958.

• **Morten Andersen,** New Orleans, needs three field goals to reach 100 for his NFL career, the minimum number needed for inclusion in the career ranking for field goal percentage. At that time, he could become the NFL's all-time leader in the category. Andersen starts the season with a career percentage of 80.2; the qualifying leader is **Gary Anderson,** Pittsburgh, with 77.2 percent.

• Anderson, looks to continue his current NFL-leading streak of 153 consecutive extra point attempts made.

• **Rohn Stark,** Indianapolis, needs to average over 45 yards per punt to maintain his status as the record holder for career punting average. Stark begins 1987 with an average of 45.16 yards per punt. Sammy Baugh stands second at 45.10.

• **Henry Ellard,** Los Angeles Rams, needs to average nearly 13 yards per punt return to maintain his status as the record holder for career punt-return average. Ellard begins 1987 with an average of 12.87 yards per return. George McAfee stands second at 12.78.

• **Billy Johnson,** Atlanta, needs one punt return to become the record holder for career punt returns. Johnson and Emlen Tunnell are tied with 258.

• **J. T. Smith,** St. Louis, needs seven punt returns to pass Alvin Haymond for third on the all-time career list. Smith begins the 1987 season with 247 career returns.

• Smith also starts the season with 2,611 career punt return yards, 50 shy of moving into third place on the all-time list. He trails Mike Fuller, who had 2,660 career yards.

• **Chuck Noll,** Pittsburgh, needs one victory to become the fifth-winningest coach in NFL history. Entering the 1987 season, he is tied for fifth with Paul Brown with 170 wins.

THE AFC

American Football Conference Eastern Division

Team Colors: Royal Blue, Scarlet Red, and White

One Bills Drive
Orchard Park, New York 14127
Telephone: (716) 648-1800

Club Officials

President: Ralph C. Wilson, Jr.
Executive Vice President: David N. Olsen
General Manager and Vice President-Administration: Bill Polian
Assistant General Manager: Bill Munson
Treasurer: Jeff Littmann
Vice President-Head Coach: Marv Levy
Director of College Scouting: John Butler
Director of Pro Personnel: Bob Ferguson
Director of Media Relations: Dave Senko
Director of Public and Community Relations: Denny Lynch
Director of Marketing and Sales: Jerry Foran
Ticket Director: TBA
Director of Stadium Operations and Security: Ed Stillwell
Manager of Stadium Operations and Engineering: Steve Champlin
Trainers: Ed Abramoski, Bud Carpenter
Equipment Manager: Dave Hojnowski
Assistant Equipment Manager: Randy Ribbeck
Strength and Conditioning Coordinator: Rusty Jones

Stadium: Rich Stadium • **Capacity:** 80,290
One Bills Drive
Orchard Park, New York 14127

Playing Surface: AstroTurf

Training Camp: Fredonia State University
Fredonia, New York 14063

1987 Schedule

Preseason

Aug. 15	at Atlanta	8:00
Aug. 22	at Los Angeles Raiders	6:00
Aug. 29	at Kansas City	7:30
Sept. 4	at Miami	8:00

Regular Season

Sept. 13	**New York Jets**	1:00
Sept. 20	**Houston**	1:00
Sept. 27	at Dallas	12:00
Oct. 4	**Indianapolis**	1:00
Oct. 11	at New England	1:00
Oct. 18	**New York Giants**	4:00
Oct. 25	at Miami	1:00
Nov. 1	**Washington**	1:00
Nov. 8	**Denver**	1:00
Nov. 15	at Cleveland	1:00
Nov. 22	at New York Jets	1:00
Nov. 29	**Miami**	1:00
Dec. 6	at Los Angeles Raiders	1:00
Dec. 13	at Indianapolis	1:00
Dec. 20	**New England**	1:00
Dec. 27	at Philadelphia	1:00

Bills Coaching History

(160-229-8)

1960-61	Buster Ramsey	11-16-1
1962-65	Lou Saban	38-18-3
1966-68	Joe Collier*	13-17-1
1968	Harvey Johnson	1-10-1
1969-70	John Rauch	7-20-1
1971	Harvey Johnson	1-13-0
1972-76	Lou Saban**	32-29-1
1976-77	Jim Ringo	3-20-0
1978-82	Chuck Knox	38-38-0
1983-84	Kay Stephenson***	10-26-0
1985-86	Hank Bullough****	4-17-0
1986	Marv Levy	2-5-0

*Released after two games in 1968
**Resigned after five games in 1976
***Released after four games in 1985
****Released after nine games in 1986

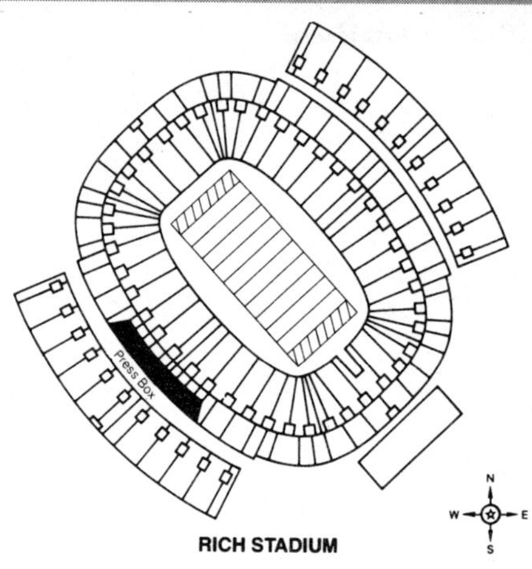

RICH STADIUM

Record Holders

Individual Records—Career

Category	Name	Performance
Rushing (Yds.)	O.J. Simpson, 1969-1977	10,183
Passing (Yds.)	Joe Ferguson, 1973-1984	27,590
Passing (TDs)	Joe Ferguson, 1973-1984	181
Receiving (No.)	Elbert Dubenion, 1960-67	296
Receiving (Yds.)	Elbert Dubenion, 1960-67	5,304
Interceptions	George (Butch) Byrd, 1964-1970	40
Punting (Avg.)	Paul Maguire, 1964-1970	42.1
Punt Return (Avg.)	Keith Moody, 1976-79	10.5
Kickoff Return (Avg.)	Wallace Francis, 1973-74	27.2
Field Goals	John Leypoldt, 1971-76	74
Touchdowns (Tot.)	O.J. Simpson, 1969-1977	70
Points	O.J. Simpson, 1969-1977	420

Individual Records—Single Season

Category	Name	Performance
Rushing (Yds.)	O.J. Simpson, 1973	2,003
Passing (Yds.)	Joe Ferguson, 1981	3,652
Passing (TDs)	Joe Ferguson, 1983	26
Receiving (No.)	Frank Lewis, 1981	70
Receiving (Yds.)	Frank Lewis, 1981	1,244
Interceptions	Billy Atkins, 1961	10
	Tom Janik, 1967	10
Punting (Avg.)	Billy Atkins, 1961	44.5
Punt Return (Avg.)	Keith Moody, 1977	13.1
Kickoff Return (Avg.)	Ed Rutkowski, 1963	30.2
Field Goals	Pete Gogolak, 1965	28
Touchdowns (Tot.)	O.J. Simpson, 1975	23
Points	O.J. Simpson, 1975	138

Individual Records—Single Game

Category	Name	Performance
Rushing (Yds.)	O.J. Simpson, 11-25-76	273
Passing (Yds.)	Joe Ferguson, 10-9-83	419
Passing (TDs)	Joe Ferguson, 9-23-79	5
	Joe Ferguson, 10-9-83	5
Receiving (No.)	Greg Bell, 9-8-85	13
Receiving (Yds.)	Jerry Butler, 9-23-79	255
Interceptions	Many times	3
	Last time by Jeff Nixon, 9-7-80	
Field Goals	Pete Gogolak, 12-5-65	5
Touchdowns (Tot.)	Cookie Gilchrist, 12-8-63	5
Points	Cookie Gilchrist, 12-8-63	30

1986 Team Statistics

	Bills	Opp.
Total First Downs	291	334
Rushing	101	100
Passing	152	204
Penalty	38	30
Third Down: Made/Att.	60/185	79/218
Fourth Down: Made/Att.	8/14	12/18
Total Net Yards	5017	5523
Avg. Per Game	313.6	345.2
Total Plays	963	1071
Avg. Per Play	5.2	5.2
Net Yards Rushing	1654	1721
Avg. Per Game	103.4	107.6
Total Rushes	419	465
Net Yards Passing	3363	3802
Avg. Per Game	210.2	237.6
Tackled/Yards Lost	45/334	36/267
Gross Yards	3697	4069
Att./Completions	499/294	570/343
Completion Pct.	58.9	60.2
Had Intercepted	19	10
Punts/Avg.	75/40.4	83/38.1
Net Punting Avg.	34.5	33.4
Penalties/Yards Lost	121/878	128/1098
Fumbles/Ball Lost	40/20	19/8
Touchdowns	34	40
Rushing	9	18
Passing	22	21
Returns	3	1
Avg. Time of Possession	28:02	31:58

1986 Team Record

Preseason (1-3)

Date	Result		Opponents
8/9	L	17-19	at Cleveland
8/16	L	20-23	at Houston
8/23	W	13- 6	at Kansas City
8/30	L	17-31	Chicago
		67-79	

Regular Season (4-12)

Date	Result		Opponents	Att.
9/7	L	24-28	N.Y. Jets	79,951
9/14	L	33-36	at Cincinnati (OT)	52,714
9/21	W	17-10	St. Louis	65,762
9/28	L	17-20	Kansas City	67,555
10/5	L	13-14	at N.Y. Jets	69,504
10/12	L	14-27	at Miami	49,467
10/19	W	24-13	Indianapolis	50,050
10/26	L	3-23	New England	77,808
11/2	L	28-34	at Tampa Bay	32,806
11/9	W	16-12	Pittsburgh	72,000
11/16	L	24-34	Miami	76,474
11/23	L	19-22	at New England	60,455
11/30	W	17-14	at Kansas City	31,492
12/7	L	17-21	Cleveland	42,213
12/14	L	14-24	at Indianapolis	52,783
12/21	L	7-16	at Houston	31,409

(OT) Overtime

Score by Periods

Bills	51	87	71	78	0	—	287
Opponents	70	91	69	115	3	—	348

Attendance

Home 531,813 Away 349,221 Total 881,034
Single game home record, 79,951 (9-7-86)
Single season home record, 601,712 (1981)

1986 Individual Statistics

Scoring	TD R	TD P	TD Rt	PAT	FG	Saf	TP
Norwood	0	0	0	32/34	17/27	0	83
Reed	0	7	0	0/0	0/0	0	42
Bell	4	2	0	0/0	0/0	0	36
Riddick	4	1	0	0/0	0/0	0	30
Burkett	0	4	0	0/0	0/0	0	24
Metzelaars	0	3	1	0/0	0/0	0	24
Butler	0	2	0	0/0	0/0	0	12
Bellinger	0	0	1	0/0	0/0	0	6
Byrum	0	1	0	0/0	0/0	0	6
Harmon	0	1	0	0/0	0/0	0	6
Moore	1	0	0	0/0	0/0	0	6
Pitts	0	0	1	0/0	0/0	0	6
Teal	0	1	0	0/0	0/0	0	6
Bills	9	22	3	32/34	17/27	0	287
Opponents	18	21	1	38/40	22/33	2	348

Passing	Att.	Comp.	Yds.	Pct.	TD	Int.	Tkld.	Rate
Kelly	480	285	3593	59.4	22	17	43/330	83.3
Reich	19	9	104	47.4	0	2	2/4	24.8
Bills	499	294	3697	58.9	22	19	45/334	80.9
Opponents	570	343	4069	60.2	21	10	36/267	86.9

Rushing	Att.	Yds.	Avg.	LG	TD
Riddick	150	632	4.2	41t	4
Bell	90	377	4.2	42	4
Kelly	41	199	4.9	20	0
Harmon	54	172	3.2	38	0
Byrum	38	156	4.1	18	0
Moore	33	104	3.2	14	1
Wilkins	3	18	6.0	11	0
King	4	10	2.5	7	0
Kidd	1	0	0.0	0	0
Reich	1	0	0.0	0	0
Broughton	1	−6	−6.0	−6	0
Reed	3	−8	−2.7	4	0
Bills	419	1654	3.9	42	9
Opponents	465	1721	3.7	45t	18

Receiving	No.	Yds.	Avg.	LG	TD
Reed	53	739	13.9	55t	7
Metzelaars	49	485	9.9	44t	3
Riddick	49	468	9.6	31t	1
Burkett	34	778	22.9	84t	4
Moore	23	184	8.0	27	0
Harmon	22	185	8.4	27	1
Butler	15	302	20.1	53	2
Byrum	13	104	8.0	17	1
Bell	12	142	11.8	40t	2
Wilkins	8	74	9.3	26	0
Teal	6	60	10.0	20	1
Rolle	4	56	14.0	20	0
Broughton	3	71	23.7	57	0
Richardson	3	49	16.3	32	0
Bills	294	3697	12.6	84t	22
Opponents	343	4069	11.9	71t	21

Interceptions	No.	Yds.	Avg.	LG	TD
Romes	4	23	5.8	23	0
Burroughs	2	49	24.5	41	0
Bellinger	1	14	14.0	14	0
Smerlas	1	3	3.0	3	0
Bayless	1	0	0.0	0	0
Freeman	1	0	0.0	0	0
Bills	10	89	8.9	41	0
Opponents	19	284	14.9	69	0

Punting	No.	Yds.	Avg.	In 20	LG
Kidd	75	3031	40.4	14	57
Bills	75	3031	40.4	14	57
Opponents	83	3162	38.1	31	64

Punt Returns	No.	FC	Yds.	Avg.	LG	TD
Pitts	18	11	194	10.8	49t	1
Broughton	12	2	53	4.4	13	0
Hill	1	0	0	0.0	0	0
Richardson	1	0	0	0.0	0	0
Bills	32	13	247	7.7	49t	1
Opponents	32	12	260	8.1	17	0

Kickoff Returns	No.	Yds.	Avg.	LG	TD
Harmon	18	321	17.8	32	0
Tasker, Hou.-Buff.	12	213	17.8	24	0
Tasker, Buff.	9	148	16.4	24	0
Broughton	11	243	22.1	39	0
Riddick	8	200	25.0	49	0
Richardson	6	123	20.5	28	0
Bellinger	2	32	16.0	16	0
Pitts	1	7	7.0	7	0
Bills	55	1074	19.5	49	0
Opponents	56	1157	20.7	44	0

Sacks	No.
B. Smith	15.0
McNanie	6.5
Talley	3.0
Marve	2.5
Smerlas	2.0
Bayless	1.0
Cumby	1.0
Drane	1.0
Frazier	1.0
Hamby	1.0
Prater	1.0
Sanford	1.0
Bills	36.0
Opponents	45.0

FIRST-ROUND SELECTIONS

(If club had no first-round selection, first player drafted is listed with round in parentheses.)

Year	Player, College, Position
1960	Richie Lucas, Penn State, QB
1961	Ken Rice, Auburn, T
1962	Ernie Davis, Syracuse, RB
1963	Dave Behrman, Michigan State, C
1964	Carl Eller, Minnesota, DE
1965	Jim Davidson, Ohio State, T
1966	Mike Dennis, Mississippi, RB
1967	John Pitts, Arizona State, S
1968	Haven Moses, San Diego State, WR
1969	O.J. Simpson, Southern California, RB
1970	Al Cowlings, Southern California, DE
1971	J. D. Hill, Arizona State, WR
1972	Walt Patulski, Notre Dame, DE
1973	Paul Seymour, Michigan, TE
	Joe DeLamielleure, Michigan State, G
1974	Reuben Gant, Oklahoma State, TE
1975	Tom Ruud, Nebraska, LB
1976	Mario Clark, Oregon, DB
1977	Phil Dokes, Oklahoma State, DT
1978	Terry Miller, Oklahoma State, RB
1979	Tom Cousineau, Ohio State, LB
	Jerry Butler, Clemson, WR
1980	Jim Ritcher, North Carolina State, C
1981	Booker Moore, Penn State, RB
1982	Perry Tuttle, Clemson, WR
1983	Tony Hunter, Notre Dame, TE
	Jim Kelly, Miami, QB
1984	Greg Bell, Notre Dame, RB
1985	Bruce Smith, Virginia Tech, DE
	Derrick Burroughs, Memphis State, DB
1986	Ronnie Harmon, Iowa, RB
	Will Wolford, Vanderbilt, T
1987	Shane Conlan, Penn State, LB

Buffalo Bills 1987 Veteran Roster

No.	Name	Pos.	Ht.	Wt.	Birth-date	NFL Exp.	College	Hometown	How Acq.	'86 Games/ Starts
43	†Bayless, Martin	S	6-2	195	10/11/62	4	Bowling Green	Dayton, Ohio	W(StL)-'84	16/15
28	Bell, Greg	RB	5-10	210	8/1/62	4	Notre Dame	Columbus, Ohio	D1-'84	6/6
36	Bellinger, Rodney	CB	5-8	189	6/4/62	4	Miami	Coral Gables, Fla.	D3a-'84	16/9
50	Bentley, Ray	LB	6-2	250	11/25/60	2	Central Michigan	Grand Rapids, Mich.	FA-'86	13/7
81	Brookins, Mitchell	WR	5-11	196	12/10/60	3	Illinois	Chicago, Ill.	D4-'84	0*
29	Broughton, Walter	WR	5-10	180	10/20/62	2	Jacksonville State	Weaver, Ala.	FA-'86	8/0
85	Burkett, Chris	WR	6-4	198	8/21/62	3	Jackson State	Collins, Miss.	D2b-'85	14/10
29	Burroughs, Derrick	CB	6-1	180	5/18/62	3	Memphis State	Mobile, Ala.	D1b-'85	15/5
61	Burton, Leonard	C	6-3	265	6/18/64	2	South Carolina	Memphis, Tenn.	D3-'86	14/0
80	†Butler, Jerry	WR	6-0	178	10/2/57	8	Clemson	Ware Shoals, S.C.	D1b-'79	11/6
35	Byrum, Carl	RB	6-0	232	6/29/63	2	Mississippi Valley State	Southaven, Miss.	D5-'86	13/3
68	t-Caron, Roger	T	6-5	292	6/3/62	3	Harvard	Norwell, Mass.	T(Ind)-'87	3/0
69	Christy, Greg	G	6-4	285	4/29/62	2	Pittsburgh	Freeport, Pa.	FA-'85	0*
63	†Cross, Justin	T	6-6	265	4/29/59	6	Western State, Colo.	Portsmouth, N.H.	D10-'81	10/1
70	Devlin, Joe	T	6-5	280	2/23/54	11	Iowa	Frazer, Pa.	D2b-'76	16/16
45	Drane, Dwight	S	6-1	200	5/6/62	2	Oklahoma	Miami, Fla.	SD1-'84	13/1
53	Furjanic, Tony	LB	6-1	228	2/26/64	2	Notre Dame	Chicago, Ill.	D8-'86	14/1
99	Garner, Hal	LB	6-4	225	1/18/62	3	Utah State	Logan, Utah	D3b-'85	16/1
8	Gelbaugh, Stan	QB	6-3	207	12/4/62	2	Maryland	Carlisle, Pa.	FA-'86	0*
75	Hamby, Mike	DE	6-4	270	11/2/62	2	Utah State	Lehi, Utah	D6-'85	16/1
33	Harmon, Ronnie	RB	5-11	192	5/7/64	2	Iowa	Queens, N.Y.	D1a-'86	14/2
55	Haslett, Jim	LB	6-3	236	12/9/56	8	Indiana, Pa.	Pittsburgh, Pa.	D2b-'79	0*
71	Hellestrae, Dale	T	6-5	275	7/11/62	3	Southern Methodist	Scottsdale, Ariz.	D4b-'85	8/0
67	Hull, Kent	C	6-4	262	1/13/61	2	Mississippi State	Greenwood, Miss.	FA-'86	16/16
48	†Johnson, Lawrence	S	5-11	202	9/11/57	7	Wisconsin	Gary, Ind.	T(Clev)-'84	0*
93	Jolly, Ken	LB	6-2	220	2/28/62	3	Mid-America Nazarene	Dallas, Tex.	FA-'87	0*
72	Jones, Ken	T	6-5	285	12/1/52	12	Arkansas State	Bridgeton, Mo.	D2a-'76	12/12
12	Kelly, Jim	QB	6-3	215	2/14/60	2	Miami	East Brady, Pa.	D1b-'83	16/16
38	Kelso, Mark	S	5-11	177	7/23/63	2	William & Mary	Pittsburgh, Pa.	FA-'86	3/0
84	Kern, Don	TE	6-4	235	8/25/62	3	Arizona State	Los Gatos, Calif.	FA-'86	1/0
4	Kidd, John	P	6-3	208	8/22/61	4	Northwestern	Findlay, Ohio	D5-'84	16/0
49	King, Bruce	RB	6-1	219	1/7/63	3	Purdue	Lincoln City, Ind.	FA-'86	10/1*
54	Marve, Eugene	LB	6-2	240	8/14/60	6	Saginaw Valley State	Flint, Mich.	D3-'82	16/10
95	McNanie, Sean	DE	6-5	270	9/9/61	4	San Diego State	Mundelein, Ill.	D3b-'84	16/16
88	†Metzelaars, Pete	TE	6-7	243	5/24/60	6	Wabash	Portage, Mich.	T(Sea)-'85	16/16
11	Norwood, Scott	K	6-0	207	7/17/60	3	James Madison	Alexandria, Va.	FA-'85	16/0
27	Pitts, Ron	CB-S	5-10	175	10/14/62	2	UCLA	Orchard Park, N.Y.	D7-'85	10/0
68	Ploeger, Kurt	DE	6-5	260	12/1/62	2	Gustavus Adolphus	LeSuer, Minn.	FA-'86	4/0*
79	Prater, Dean	DE	6-4	256	9/28/58	6	Oklahoma State	Wichita Falls, Tex.	FA-'85	16/0
83	Reed, Andre	WR	6-0	186	1/29/64	3	Kutztown State	Allentown, Pa.	D4a-'85	15/15
14	Reich, Frank	QB	6-3	208	12/4/61	3	Maryland	Lebanon, Pa.	D3a-'85	3/0
82	Richardson, Eric	WR	6-1	185	4/18/62	3	San Jose State	Novato, Calif.	D2-'84	14/1
40	Riddick, Robb	RB	6-0	195	4/26/57	5	Millersville State	Perkasie, Pa.	D9-'81	15/8
51	Ritcher, Jim	G	6-3	265	5/21/58	8	North Carolina State	Medina, Ohio	D1-'80	16/16
87	Rolle, Butch	TE	6-3	242	8/19/64	2	Michigan State	Hallandale, Fla.	D7c-'86	16/1
26	†Romes, Charles	CB	6-1	190	12/16/54	11	North Carolina Central	Durham, N.C.	D12-'77	16/16
76	Smerlas, Fred	NT	6-3	280	4/8/57	9	Boston College	Waltham, Mass.	D2a-'79	16/16
78	Smith, Bruce	DE	6-4	280	6/18/63	3	Virginia Tech	Norfolk, Va.	D1a-'85	16/15
74	Smith, Don	NT	6-5	262	5/9/57	9	Miami	Tarpon Springs, Fla.	T(Atl)-'85	5/0
56	†Talley, Darryl	LB	6-4	227	7/10/60	5	West Virginia	Cleveland, Ohio	D2-'83	16/16
89	Tasker, Steve	WR-KR	5-9	185	4/10/62	3	Northwestern	Leoti, Kan.	W(Hou)-'86	9/0*
86	Teal, Jimmy	WR	5-10	170	8/18/62	3	Texas A&M	Diboll, Tex.	D5-'85	5/1
62	Traynowicz, Mark	G	6-5	275	11/20/62	3	Nebraska	Omaha, Neb.	D2-'85	16/0
65	†Vogler, Tim	G-T-C	6-3	285	10/2/56	9	Ohio State	Covington, Ohio	FA-'79	9/3
34	Wilkins, Gary	RB	6-1	235	11/23/63	2	Georgia Tech	Riviera Beach, Fla.	FA-'86	16/2
23	Williams, Kevin	CB	5-9	170	11/28/61	2	Iowa State	San Diego, Calif.	FA-'86	1/0
73	Wolford, Will	G	6-5	276	5/18/64	2	Vanderbilt	Louisville, Ky.	D1b-'86	16/16

* Brookins, Christy, Haslett, and Johnson missed '86 season due to injury; Gelbaugh active for 5 games with Buffalo but did not play; Jolly last active with Kansas City in '85; King played 5 games with Kansas City, 5 with Buffalo in '86; Ploeger played 3 games with Dallas, 1 with Green Bay; Tasker played 2 games with Houston, 7 with Buffalo.

†Option playout; subject to developments.

t-Bills traded for Caron (Indianapolis).

Traded—Safety Steve Freeman to Minnesota.

Also played with Bills in '86—NT Jerry Boyarsky (10 games), NT Mark Catano (1), LB George Cumby (11), LB Guy Frazier (7), CB Rod Hill (6), RB Ricky Moore (11), Lucius Sanford (10).

Coaching Staff

Head Coach, Marv Levy

Pro Career: Begins first full season as Bills head coach. Replaced Hank Bullough on November 3, 1986, and compiled a 2-5 record over final seven weeks of season. Previously served as head coach of the Kansas City Chiefs from 1978-82, producing a 31-42 mark. Levy began pro coaching career in 1969 as an assistant with the Philadelphia Eagles. He joined George Allen and the Los Angeles Rams as an assistant one year later and followed Allen to Washington, where he remained with the Redskins through the 1972 season when the Redskins played in Super Bowl VII. He was named head coach of the Montreal Alouettes (CFL) in 1973 and posted a 50-34-4 record and two Grey Cup victories (1974, 1977) in five seasons in Canada. After two seasons away from football, he became head coach of the Chicago Blitz of the USFL for 1984, the team's only year in existence. No pro playing experience. Career record: 33-47.

Background: Running back Coe College 1948-50. Coached high school for two years before returning to alma mater from 1953-55. Joined New Mexico staff in 1956 where he served as head coach from 1958-59. Head coach at California from 1960-63 before becoming head coach at William & Mary from 1964-68.

Personal: Born August 3, 1928, Chicago, Ill. Levy was Phi Beta Kappa at Coe College and earned master's degree in English history from Harvard. Marv and his wife, Dorothy, live in Orchard Park, N.Y.

Assistant Coaches

Walt Corey, defensive coordinator, linebackers; born May 9, 1938, Latrobe, Pa., lives in Orchard Park, N.Y. Defensive end Miami 1957-59. Pro linebacker Kansas City Chiefs 1960-66. College coach: Utah State 1967-69, Miami 1970-71. Pro coach: Kansas City Chiefs 1971-74, 1978-86, Cleveland Browns 1975-77, first year with Bills.

Ted Cottrell, defensive line; born June 13, 1947, Chester, Pa., lives in Orchard Park, N.Y. Linebacker Delaware Valley College 1966-68. Pro linebacker Atlanta Falcons 1969-70, Winnipeg Blue Bombers (CFL) 1971. College coach: Rutgers 1973-80, 1983. Pro coach: Kansas City Chiefs 1981-82, New Jersey Generals (USFL) 1983-84, joined Bills in 1986.

Bruce DeHaven, special teams; born September 6, 1948, Trousdale, Kan., lives in Orchard Park, N.Y. No college or pro playing experience. College coach: Kansas 1979-81, New Mexico State 1982. Pro coach: New Jersey Generals (USFL) 1983, Pittsburgh Maulers (USFL) 1984, Orlando Renegades (USFL) 1985, first year with Bills.

Chuck Dickerson, special assistant to head coach; born August 1, 1937, Hammond, Ind., lives in Orchard Park, N.Y. Defensive tackle Florida 1955-56, Illinois 1961. Pro defensive lineman Montreal Alouettes (CFL) 1962-64. College coach: Eastern Illinois 1967-70, 1981-82, Minnesota 1983. Pro coach: Toronto Rifles (Continental League) 1964-66, Chicago Fire (WFL) 1974-75, Toronto Argonauts (CFL) 1976-79, Memphis Showboats (USFL) 1984-86, first year with Bills.

Rusty Jones, strength and conditioning; born August 14, 1953, Berwick, Maine, lives in Orchard Park, N.Y. No college or pro playing experience. College coach: Springfield 1978-79. Pro coach: Pittsburgh Maulers (USFL) 1983-84, joined Bills in 1985.

Chuck Lester, defensive assistant; born May 18, 1955, lives in Orchard Park, N.Y. Linebacker Oklahoma 1974. No pro playing experience. College coach: Iowa State 1980-81, Oklahoma 1982-84. Pro coach: First year with Bills.

Buffalo Bills 1987 First-Year Roster

Name	Pos.	Ht.	Wt.	Birth-date	College	Hometown	How Acq.
Armstrong, John	CB-KR	5-9	185	7/7/63	Richmond	Pittsboro, Miss.	FA
Ballard, Howard	T	6-6	300	11/3/63	Alabama A&M	Ashland, Ala.	D11
Brandon, David	LB	6-4	225	2/9/65	Memphis State	Memphis, Tenn.	D3a
Brown, Marc	WR	6-2	195	5/7/61	Towson State	Central Nyack, N.Y.	FA
Bynum, Reggie (1)	WR	6-1	185	2/10/64	Oregon State	San Jose, Calif.	D9-'86
Christian, Derek (1)	LB	6-2	240	4/30/63	West Virginia	St. Albans, W. Va.	D12b-'86
Clark, Steve	S	6-3	185	12/14/62	Liberty University	Falls Church, Va.	FA
Conlan, Shane	LB	6-3	230	4/3/64	Penn State	Frewsburg, N.Y.	D1
Hammond, Steve	LB	6-4	225	2/25/60	Wake Forest	Merrick, N.Y.	FA
Howard, Joe	WR	5-9	165	12/21/62	Notre Dame	Clinton, Md.	FA
Jones, Glenn	CB	6-0	175	12/4/61	Norfolk State	Norfolk, Va.	FA
Kenealy, Mike	S	6-1	190	4/3/63	Central Michigan	Royal Oak, Mich.	FA
McClure, Brian (1)	QB	6-6	222	12/28/63	Bowling Green	Rootstown, Ohio	D12a-'86
McGrail, Joe	NT	6-3	280	6/6/64	Delaware	Glendora, N.J.	D12
McKeller, Keith	TE	6-6	230	7/9/64	Jacksonville State	Fairfield, Ala.	D9
Melka, Jim	LB	6-1	228	1/15/62	Wisconsin	West Allis, Wis.	FA
Mesner, Bruce	NT	6-4	280	3/21/64	Maryland	Harrison, N.Y.	D8b
Mitchell, Roland	CB-KR	5-11	180	3/15/64	Texas Tech	Bay City, Tex.	D2b
Mueller, Jamie	RB	6-1	225	10/4/64	Benedictine College	Fairview Park, Ohio	D3b
Odomes, Nate	CB-KR	5-9	188	8/25/65	Wisconsin	Columbus, Ga.	D2a
Olson, Ken	K	6-0	195	9/15/60	Salisbury State	Camp Springs, Md.	FA
Pike, Mark (1)	LB	6-4	257	12/27/63	Georgia Tech	Villa Hills, Ky.	D7b-'86
Porter, Kerry	RB	6-1	210	9/23/64	Washington State	Great Falls, Mont.	D7
Rush, Mark	RB	6-2	215	3/31/59	Miami	Ft. Lauderdale, Fla.	FA
Schankweiler, Scott	LB	6-0	230	10/15/63	Maryland	Camp Hill, Pa.	FA
Schlopy, Todd	K	5-10	165	6/17/61	Michigan	Orchard Park, N.Y.	FA
Seals, Leon	DE	6-4	265	1/30/64	Jackson State	Baton Rouge, La.	D4b
Seawright, James (1)	LB	6-2	220	3/30/62	South Carolina	Simpsonville, S.C.	D11-'85
Sommer, Donnie	T	6-4	290	2/1/64	Texas-El Paso	Houston, Tex.	FA
Williams, Bob (1)	TE	6-3	240	9/22/63	Penn State	Easton, Pa.	D7a-'86
Witt, Billy (1)	DE	6-5	265	4/15/64	North Alabama	Russellville, Ala.	D11b-'86

The term NFL Rookie is defined as a player who is in his first season of professional football and has not been on the roster of another professional football team for any regular-season or postseason games. A Rookie is designated by an "R" on NFL rosters. Players who have been active in another professional football league or players who have NFL experience, including either preseason training camp or being on an active roster for fewer than three regular-season or postseason games, are termed NFL First-Year Players. An NFL First-Year Player is designated by a "1" on NFL rosters. Thereafter, a player on an NFL active roster for at least three regular-season or postseason games is credited with an additional year of NFL playing experience.

NOTES

Ted Marchibroda, quarterbacks, passing-game coordinator; born March 15, 1931, Franklin, Pa., lives in Orchard Park, N.Y. Quarterback St. Bonaventure 1950-51, Detroit 1952. Pro quarterback Pittsburgh Steelers 1953, 1955-56, Chicago Cardinals 1957. Pro coach: Washington Redskins 1961-65, 1971-74, Los Angeles Rams 1966-70, Baltimore Colts 1975-79 (head coach), Chicago Bears 1981, Detroit Lions 1982-83, Philadelphia Eagles 1984-85, first year with Bills.

Elijah Pitts, running backs; born February 3, 1938, Mayflower, Ark., lives in Orchard Park, N.Y. Running back Philander Smith 1957-60. Pro running back Green Bay Packers 1961-69, 1971, Los Angeles Rams 1970, Chicago Bears 1970, New Orleans Saints 1970. Pro coach: Los Angeles Rams 1974-77, Buffalo Bills 1978-80, Houston Oilers 1981-83, Hamilton Tiger-Cats (CFL) 1984, rejoined Bills in 1985.

Jim Ringo, offensive coordinator, running-game coordinator, offensive line; born November 21, 1932, Orange, N.J., lives in Orchard Park, N.Y. Center Syracuse 1950-52. Pro center Green Bay Packers 1953-63, Philadelphia Eagles 1964-66. Pro coach: Chicago Bears 1969-71, Buffalo Bills 1972-77 (1976-77 head coach), New England Patriots 1978-81, Los Angeles Rams 1982, New York Jets 1983-84, rejoined Bills in 1985. Member of Pro Football Hall of Fame.

Dick Roach, defensive backs, born August 23, 1937, Rapid City, S.D., lives in Orchard Park, N.Y. Defensive back Black Hills State 1952-55. No pro playing experience. College coach: Montana State 1966-69, Oregon State 1970, Wyoming 1971-72, Fresno State 1973, Washington State 1974-75. Pro coach: Montreal Alouettes (CFL) 1976-77, Kansas City Chiefs 1978-80, New England Patriots 1981, Michigan Panthers (USFL) 1983-84, Tampa Bay Buccaneers 1985-86, first year with Bills.

Ted Tollner, receivers; born May 29, 1940, San Francisco, Calif., lives in Orchard Park, N.Y. Quarterback Cal Poly-SLO 1959-61. No pro playing experience. College coach: College of San Mateo 1971-72 (head coach), San Diego State 1973-80, Brigham Young 1981, Southern California 1982-86 (head coach 1983-86). Pro coach: First year with Bills.

CINCINNATI BENGALS

American Football Conference Central Division

Team Colors: Black, Orange, and White

200 Riverfront Stadium
Cincinnati, Ohio 45202
Telephone: (513) 621-3550

Club Officials

President: John Sawyer
General Manager: Paul E. Brown
Assistant General Manager: Michael Brown
Business Manager: Bill Connelly
Director of Public Relations: Allan Heim
Director of Player Personnel: Pete Brown
Accountant: Jay Reis
Ticket Manager: Paul Kelly
Consultant: John Murdough
Trainer: Marv Pollins
Equipment Manager: Tom Gray
Video Director: Al Davis

Stadium: Riverfront Stadium • **Capacity:** 59,754
200 Riverfront Stadium
Cincinnati, Ohio 45202

Playing Surface: AstroTurf

Training Camp: Wilmington College
Wilmington, Ohio 45177

1987 Schedule

Preseason

Aug. 15	at Tampa Bay	7:00
Aug. 22	at Detroit	8:00
Aug. 29	at Green Bay	7:00
Sept. 4	**New Orleans**	7:35

Regular Season

Sept. 13	at Indianapolis	12:00
Sept. 20	**San Francisco**	1:00
Sept. 27	at Los Angeles Rams	1:00
Oct. 4	**San Diego**	1:00
Oct. 11	at Seattle	1:00
Oct. 18	**Cleveland**	1:00
Oct. 25	at Pittsburgh	1:00
Nov. 1	**Houston**	1:00
Nov. 8	**Miami**	4:00
Nov. 15	at Atlanta	4:00
Nov. 22	**Pittsburgh**	1:00
Nov. 29	at New York Jets	1:00
Dec. 6	**Kansas City**	1:00
Dec. 13	at Cleveland	1:00
Dec. 20	**New Orleans**	1:00
Dec. 27	at Houston	12:00

Bengals Coaching History

(140-143-1)

1968-75	Paul Brown	55-59-1
1976-78	Bill Johnson*	18-15-0
1978-79	Homer Rice	8-19-0
1980-83	Forrest Gregg	34-27-0
1984-86	Sam Wyche	25-23-0

*Resigned after five games in 1978

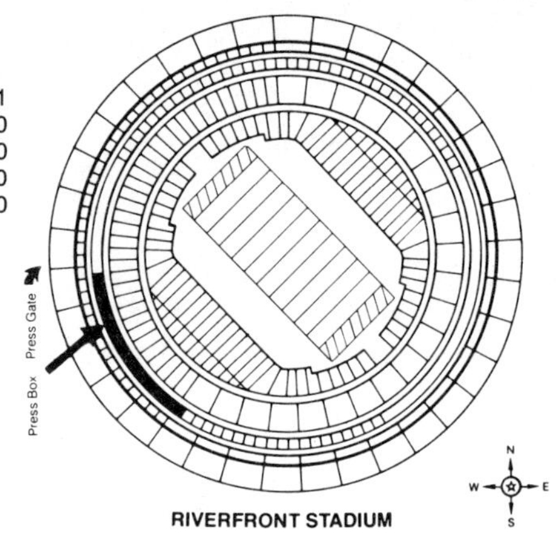

RIVERFRONT STADIUM

Record Holders

Individual Records—Career

Category	Name	Performance
Rushing (Yds.)	Pete Johnson, 1977-1983	5,421
Passing (Yds.)	Ken Anderson, 1973-1986	32,838
Passing (TDs)	Ken Anderson, 1973-1986	197
Receiving (No.)	Isaac Curtis, 1973-1984	420
Receiving (Yds.)	Isaac Curtis, 1973-1984	7,106
Interceptions (No.)	Ken Riley, 1969-1983	63
Punting (Avg.)	Dave Lewis, 1970-73	43.9
Punt Return (Avg.)	Mike Martin, 1983-86	10.5
Kickoff Return (Avg.)	Lemar Parrish, 1970-78	24.7
Field Goals	Horst Muhlmann, 1969-1974	120
Touchdowns (Tot.)	Pete Johnson, 1977-1983	70
Points	Jim Breech, 1981-86	616

Individual Records—Single Season

Category	Name	Performance
Rushing (Yds.)	James Brooks, 1986	1,087
Passing (Yds.)	Boomer Esiason, 1986	3,959
Passing (TDs)	Ken Anderson, 1981	29
Receiving (No.)	Dan Ross, 1981	71
Receiving (Yds.)	Cris Collinsworth, 1983	1,130
Interceptions	Ken Riley, 1976	9
Punting (Avg.)	Dave Lewis, 1970	46.2
Punt Return (Avg.)	Mike Martin, 1984	15.7
Kickoff Return (Avg.)	Lemar Parrish, 1980	30.2
Field Goals	Horst Muhlmann, 1972	27
Touchdowns (Tot.)	Pete Johnson, 1981	16
Points	Jim Breech, 1985	120

Individual Records—Single Game

Category	Name	Performance
Rushing (Yds.)	James Brooks, 12-7-86	163
Passing (Yds.)	Ken Anderson, 11-17-75	447
Passing (TDs)	Boomer Esiason, 12-21-86	5
Receiving (No.)	Many times	10
	Last time by Cris Collinsworth, 9-22-85	
Receiving (Yds.)	Cris Collinsworth, 10-2-83	216
Interceptions	Many times	3
	Last time by Ken Riley, 11-28-83	
Field Goals	Horst Muhlmann, 11-8-70	5
	Horst Muhlmann, 9-24-72	5
Touchdowns (Tot.)	Larry Kinnebrew, 10-28-84	4
Points	Larry Kinnebrew, 10-28-84	24

1986 Team Statistics

	Bengals	Opp.
Total First Downs	348	336
Rushing	134	134
Passing	183	171
Penalty	31	31
Third Down: Made/Att.	79/199	84/218
Fourth Down: Made/Att.	9/16	12/16
Total Net Yards	6490	5274
Avg. Per Game	405.6	329.6
Total Plays	1046	1051
Avg. Per Play	6.2	5.0
Net Yards Rushing	2533	2122
Avg. Per Game	158.3	132.6
Total Rushes	521	514
Net Yards Passing	3957	3152
Avg. Per Game	247.3	197.0
Tackled/Yards Lost	28/203	42/368
Gross Yards	4160	3520
Att./Completions	497/287	495/278
Completion Pct.	57.7	56.2
Had Intercepted	20	17
Punts/Avg.	59/33.8	77/39.8
Net Punting Avg.	29.7	34.5
Penalties/Yards Lost	111/847	93/840
Fumbles/Ball Lost	31/16	30/11
Touchdowns	51	47
Rushing	24	23
Passing	25	17
Returns	2	7
Avg. Time of Possession	28:48	31:12

1986 Team Record

Preseason (1-3)

Date	Result		Opponents
8/9	L	0-20	at Kansas City
8/16	L	17-28	at N.Y. Jets
8/23	W	34-12	Green Bay
8/29	L	20-30	Detroit
		71-90	

Regular Season (10-6)

Date	Result		Opponents	Att.
9/7	L	14-24	at Kansas City	43,430
9/14	W	36-33	Buffalo (OT)	52,714
9/18	W	30-13	at Cleveland	78,779
9/28	L	7-44	Chicago	55,146
10/5	W	34-28	at Green Bay	51,230
10/13	W	24-22	Pittsburgh	54,283
10/19	W	31-28	Houston	53,844
10/26	L	9-30	at Pittsburgh	50,815
11/2	W	24-17	at Detroit	52,423
11/9	L	28-32	at Houston	32,130
11/16	W	34- 7	Seattle	54,410
11/23	W	24-20	Minnesota	53,003
11/30	L	28-34	at Denver	58,705
12/7	W	31- 7	at New England	60,633
12/14	L	3-34	Cleveland	58,062
12/21	W	52-21	N.Y. Jets	51,619

(OT) Overtime

Score by Periods

Bengals	69	126	72	139	3	—	409
Opponents	113	92	122	67	0	—	394

Attendance

Home 433,081 Away 428,145 Total 861,226
Single game home record, 60,284 (10-17-71)
Single season home record, 433,081 (1986)

1986 Individual Statistics

Scoring

	TD R	TD P	TD Rt	PAT	FG	Saf	TP
Breech	0	0	0	50/51	17/32	0	101
Collinsworth	0	10	0	0/0	0/0	0	60
Brooks	5	4	0	0/0	0/0	0	54
Kinnebrew	8	1	0	0/0	0/0	0	54
Wilson	8	0	0	0/0	0/0	0	48
Brown	0	4	0	0/0	0/0	0	24
Holman	0	2	0	0/0	0/0	0	12
Muñoz	0	2	0	0/0	0/0	0	12
Breeden	0	0	1	0/0	0/0	0	6
Edwards	0	0	1	0/0	0/0	0	6
Esiason	1	0	0	0/0	0/0	0	6
Hayes	1	0	0	0/0	0/0	0	6
Jennings	1	0	0	0/0	0/0	0	6
Kattus	0	1	0	0/0	0/0	0	6
McGee	0	1	0	0/0	0/0	0	6
White	0	0	0	0/0	0/0	1	2
Bengals	24	25	2	50/51	17/32	1	409
Opponents	23	17	7	44/47	22/30	1	394

Passing

	Att.	Comp.	Yds.	Pct.	TD	Int.	Tkld.	Rate
Esiason	469	273	3959	58.2	24	17	26/194	87.7
Anderson	23	11	171	47.8	1	2	1/4	51.2
Gaynor	3	3	30	100.0	0	0	1/5	108.3
Brooks	1	0	0	0.0	0	0	0/0	39.6
Kreider	1	0	0	0.0	0	1	0/0	0.0
Bengals	497	287	4160	57.7	25	20	28/203	85.1
Opponents	495	278	3520	56.2	17	17	42/368	75.7

Rushing

	Att.	Yds.	Avg.	LG	TD
Brooks	205	1087	5.3	56t	5
Kinnebrew	131	519	4.0	39	8
Wilson	68	379	5.6	58t	8
Johnson	39	226	5.8	34	0
Esiason	44	146	3.3	23	1
Hayes	3	92	30.7	61t	1
Jennings	16	54	3.4	10	1
Brown	8	32	4.0	17	0
McGee	4	10	2.5	8	0
Gaynor	1	4	4.0	4	0
Collinsworth	2	−16	−8.0	−6	0
Bengals	521	2533	4.9	61t	24
Opponents	514	2122	4.1	75t	23

Receiving

	No.	Yds.	Avg.	LG	TD
Collinsworth	62	1024	16.5	46t	10
Brown	58	964	16.6	57	4
Brooks	54	686	12.7	54	4
Holman	40	570	14.3	34t	2
McGee	16	276	17.3	51	1
Kinnebrew	13	136	10.5	31	1
Johnson	13	103	7.9	17	0
Kattus	11	99	9.0	28	1
Jennings	6	86	14.3	34	0
Kreider	5	96	19.2	23	0
Wilson	4	45	11.3	34	0
Martin	3	68	22.7	51	0
Muñoz	2	7	3.5	5t	2
Bengals	287	4160	14.5	57	25
Opponents	278	3520	12.7	84t	17

Interceptions

	No.	Yds.	Avg.	LG	TD
Breeden	7	72	10.3	36t	1
Fulcher	4	20	5.0	15	0
Barker	2	7	3.5	7	0
Bussey	1	19	19.0	19	0
Zander	1	18	18.0	18	0
Kelly	1	6	6.0	6	0
Horton	1	4	4.0	4	0
Bengals	17	146	8.6	36t	1
Opponents	20	189	9.5	49	0

Punting

	No.	Yds.	Avg.	In 20	LG
Hayes	56	1965	35.1	11	52
Esiason	1	31	31.0	1	31
Bengals	59	1996	33.8	12	52
Opponents	77	3068	39.8	14	66

Punt Returns

	No.	FC	Yds.	Avg.	LG	TD
Martin	13	6	96	7.4	14	0
Horton	11	3	111	10.1	25	0
McGee	3	4	21	7.0	9	0
Simmons	2	4	7	3.5	6	0
Bengals	29	17	235	8.1	25	0
Opponents	19	14	182	9.6	54	0

Kickoff Returns

	No.	Yds.	Avg.	LG	TD
McGee	43	1007	23.4	94	0
Jennings	12	257	21.4	41	0
Martin	4	83	20.8	21	0
Simpkins	2	24	12.0	15	0
Holman	1	18	18.0	18	0
Simmons	1	0	0.0	0	0
Bengals	63	1389	22.0	94	0
Opponents	80	1611	20.1	96t	1

Sacks

	No.
King	9.0
Browner	6.5
Edwards	6.5
Williams	4.5
Zander	3.5
Skow	3.0
Fulcher	2.0
Billups	1.0
Bussey	1.0
DeAyala	1.0
Hammerstein	1.0
Kelly	1.0
Krumrie	1.0
Simmons	1.0
Bengals	42.0
Opponents	28.0

FIRST-ROUND SELECTIONS

(If club had no first-round selection, first player drafted is listed with round in parentheses.)

Year	Player, College, Position
1968	Bob Johnson, Tennessee, C
1969	Greg Cook, Cincinnati, QB
1970	Mike Reid, Penn State, DT
1971	Vernon Holland, Tennessee State, T
1972	Sherman White, California, DE
1973	Isaac Curtis, San Diego State, WR
1974	Bill Kollar, Montana State, DT
1975	Glenn Cameron, Florida, LB
1976	Billy Brooks, Oklahoma, WR
	Archie Griffin, Ohio State, RB
1977	Eddie Edwards, Miami, DT
	Wilson Whitley, Houston, DT
	Mike Cobb, Michigan State, TE
1978	Ross Browner, Notre Dame, DT
	Blair Bush, Washington, C
1979	Jack Thompson, Washington State, QB
	Charles Alexander, Louisiana State, RB
1980	Anthony Muñoz, Southern California, T
1981	David Verser, Kansas, WR
1982	Glen Collins, Mississippi State, DE
1983	Dave Rimington, Nebraska, C
1984	Ricky Hunley, Arizona, LB
	Pete Koch, Maryland, DE
	Brian Blados, North Carolina, T
1985	Eddie Brown, Miami, WR
	Emanuel King, Alabama, LB
1986	Joe Kelly, Washington, LB
	Tim McGee, Tennessee, WR
1987	Jason Buck, Brigham Young, DE

Cincinnati Bengals 1987 Veteran Roster

No.	Name	Pos.	Ht.	Wt.	Birth-date	NFL Exp.	College	Hometown	How Acq.	'86 Games/ Starts
	Arapostathis, Evan	P-K	5-10	175	10/30/63	2	Eastern Illinois	La Mesa, Calif.	FA-'87	5/0*
53	Barker, Leo	LB	6-2	227	11/7/59	4	New Mexico State	Cristobal, Panama	D7-'84	16/9
24	Billups, Lewis	CB	5-11	190	10/10/63	2	North Alabama	Ft. Walton Beach, Fla.	D2-'86	12/12
74	Blados, Brian	G	6-5	295	1/11/62	4	North Carolina	Arlington, Va.	D1b-'84	16/8
55	Brady, Ed	LB	6-2	235	6/17/60	4	Illinois	Morris, Ill.	D8-'84	16/0
3	Breech, Jim	K	5-6	161	4/11/56	9	California	Sacramento, Calif.	FA-'80	16/0
34	Breeden, Louis	CB	5-11	185	10/26/53	10	North Carolina Central	Hamlet, N.C.	D7-'77	16/16
21	Brooks, James	RB	5-10	182	12/28/58	7	Auburn	Warner Robins, Ga.	T(SD)-'84	16/16
81	Brown, Eddie	WR	6-0	185	12/17/62	3	Miami	Miami, Fla.	D1-'85	16/16
79	Browner, Ross	DE	6-3	265	3/22/54	10	Notre Dame	Warren, Ohio	D1-'78	16/15
27	Bussey, Barney	S	6-0	195	5/20/62	2	South Carolina State	Lincolnton, Ga.	D5-'84	16/0
80	Collinsworth, Cris	WR	6-5	192	1/27/59	7	Florida	Titusville, Fla.	D2-'81	16/15
93	DeAyala, Kiki	LB	6-1	225	10/23/61	2	Texas	Miami, Fla.	D6-'83	16/0
67	Douglas, David	T	6-4	280	3/20/63	2	Tennessee	Evansville, Tenn.	D8-'86	14/0
73	Edwards, Eddie	DE	6-5	256	4/25/54	11	Miami	Sumter, S.C.	D1-'77	16/16
7	Esiason, Boomer	QB	6-4	220	4/17/61	4	Maryland	East Islip, N.Y.	D2-'84	16/16
33	Fulcher, David	S	6-3	228	9/28/64	2	Arizona State	Los Angeles, Calif.	D3b-'86	16/16
11	Gaynor, Doug	QB	6-2	205	7/5/63	2	Long Beach State	Fresno, Calif.	D4a-'86	1/0
71	Hammerstein, Mike	DE	6-4	270	3/29/63	2	Michigan	Wapakoneta, Ohio	D3a-'86	15/0
82	Holman, Rodney	TE	6-3	238	4/20/60	6	Tulane	Ypsilanti, Mich.	D3-'82	16/16
20	†Horton, Ray	CB	5-11	190	4/12/60	5	Washington	Tacoma, Wash.	D2-'83	16/4
37	Jackson, Robert	S	5-10	186	10/10/58	6	Central Michigan	Allendale, Mich.	D11-'81	7/6
36	Jennings, Stanford	RB	6-1	205	3/12/62	4	Furman	Summerville, S.C.	D3-'84	16/0
30	Johnson, Bill	RB	6-2	230	10/31/60	3	Arkansas State	Millerton, N.Y.	SD2-'85	14/4
84	Kattus, Eric	TE	6-5	235	3/4/63	2	Michigan	Cincinnati, Ohio	D4-'86	16/1
58	Kelly, Joe	LB	6-2	227	12/11/64	2	Washington	Los Angeles, Calif.	D1-'86	16/7
90	King, Emanuel	LB	6-4	251	8/15/63	3	Alabama	Leroy, Ala.	D1a-'85	16/16
28	Kinnebrew, Larry	RB	6-1	258	6/11/59	5	Tennessee State	Rome, Ga.	D6a-'83	16/9
64	Kozerski, Bruce	C	6-4	275	4/2/62	4	Holy Cross	Plains, Pa.	D9-'84	16/15
86	Kreider, Steve	WR	6-3	192	5/12/58	9	Lehigh	Reading, Pa.	D6-'79	10/0
69	Krumrie, Tim	NT	6-2	262	5/20/60	5	Wisconsin	Eau Claire, Wis.	D10-'83	16/16
88	Martin, Mike	WR	5-10	186	11/18/60	5	Illinois	Washington, D.C.	D8-'83	7/0
85	McGee, Tim	WR	5-10	175	8/7/64	2	Tennessee	Cleveland, Ohio	D1a-'86	16/0
65	Montoya, Max	G	6-5	275	5/12/56	9	UCLA	La Puente, Calif.	D7-'79	16/16
78	†Muñoz, Anthony	T	6-6	278	8/19/58	8	Southern California	Ontario, Calif.	D1-'80	16/16
75	Reimers, Bruce	T	6-7	280	9/18/60	4	Iowa State	Humboldt, Iowa	D8-'84	16/5
60	Rimington, Dave	C	6-3	288	8/13/62	5	Nebraska	Omaha, Neb.	D1-'83	12/12
56	†Simpkins, Ron	LB	6-1	235	4/2/58	7	Michigan	Detroit, Mich.	D7-'80	16/0
70	Skow, Jim	DE	6-3	250	6/29/63	2	Nebraska	Omaha, Neb.	D3-'86	16/1
63	Walter, Joe	T	6-6	290	6/18/63	3	Texas Tech	Dallas, Tex.	D7a-'85	15/8
51	White, Leon	LB	6-2	236	10/4/63	2	Brigham Young	La Mesa, Calif.	D5-'86	16/0
57	Williams, Reggie	LB	6-0	228	9/19/54	12	Dartmouth	Flint, Mich.	D3a-'76	16/16
32	Wilson, Stanley	RB	5-10	210	8/23/61	3	Oklahoma	Carson, Calif.	D9-'83	10/3
91	Zander, Carl	LB	6-2	235	3/23/63	3	Tennessee	Mendham, N.J.	D2-'85	16/16

* Araposthatis played 5 games with St. Louis in '86.

†Option playout; subject to developments.

Retired—Ken Anderson, 16-year quarterback, 8 games in '86.

Also played with Bengals in '86—P Jeff Hayes (16 games), S Bobby Kemp (16), CB-KR John Simmons (10), CB Jimmy Turner (8).

COACHING STAFF

Head Coach, Sam Wyche

Pro Career: Became the fifth head coach in Cincinnati history when he was named to lead the Bengals on December 28, 1983. Played quarterback with Bengals 1968-70, Washington Redskins 1971-73, Detroit Lions 1974-75, St. Louis Cardinals 1976, and Buffalo Bills 1977. Quarterback coach with the San Francisco 49ers 1979-82. Career record: 25-23.

Background: Attended North Fulton High School in Atlanta and Furman University where he was the quarterback from 1962-66. Assistant coach at South Carolina in 1967. Head coach at Indiana University in 1983.

Personal: Born January 5, 1945, in Atlanta, Ga. Sam and his wife, Jane, have two children—Zak and Kerry. They live in Cincinnati.

Assistant Coaches

Jim Anderson, running backs; born March 27, 1948, Harrisburg, Pa., lives in Cincinnati. Linebacker-defensive end Cal Western (U.S. International) 1969-70. No pro playing experience. College coach: Cal Western 1970-71, Scottsdale Community College 1973, Nevada-Las Vegas 1974-75, Southern Methodist 1977-80, Stanford 1981-83. Pro coach: Joined Bengals in 1984.'

Bruce Coslet, offensive coordinator; born August 5, 1946, Oakdale, Calif., lives in Cincinnati. Tight end University of the Pacific 1965-67. Pro tight end Cincinnati Bengals 1969-76. Pro coach: San Francisco 49ers 1980, joined Bengals in 1981.

Bill Johnson, tight ends; born July 14, 1926, Tyler, Tex., lives in Cincinnati. Center Texas A&M 1944-46. Pro center San Francisco 49ers 1948-55. Pro coach: San Francisco 49ers 1956-67, Cincinnati Bengals 1968-78 (head coach 1976-78), Tampa Bay Buccaneers 1979-82, Detroit Lions 1983-84, rejoined Bengals in 1985.

Dick LeBeau, defensive coordinator-defensive backs; born September 9, 1937, London, Ohio, lives in Cincinnati. Halfback Ohio State 1957-59. Pro defensive back Detroit Lions 1959-72. Pro coach: Philadelphia Eagles 1973-75, Green Bay Packers 1976-79, joined Bengals in 1980.

Jim McNally, offensive line-running game; born December 13, 1943, Buffalo, N.Y., lives in Cincinnati. Guard Buffalo 1961-65. No pro playing experience. College coach: Buffalo 1966-69, Marshall 1973-75, Boston College 1976-78, Wake Forest 1979. Pro coach: Joined Bengals in 1980.

Dick Selcer, linebackers; born August 22, 1937, Cincinnati, Ohio, lives in Cincinnati. Running back Notre Dame 1955-58. No pro playing experience. College coach: Xavier, Ohio 1962-64, 1970-71 (head coach), Cincinnati 1965-66, Brown 1967-69, Wisconsin 1972-74, Kansas State 1975-77, Southwestern Louisiana 1978-80. Pro coach: Houston Oilers 1981-83, joined Bengals in 1984.

Mike Stock, special teams; born September 29, 1939, Barberton, Ohio, lives in Cincinnati. Fullback Northwestern 1958-60. No pro playing experience. College coach: Northwestern 1961, Buffalo 1966-67, Navy 1968, Notre Dame 1969-75, Wisconsin 1976-77, Eastern Michigan 1978-82 (head coach), Notre Dame 1983-86. Pro coach: first year with Bengals.

Bill Urbanik, defensive line; born December 27, 1946, Donora, Pa., lives in Cincinnati. Lineman Ohio State 1965-68. No pro playing experience. College coach: Marshall 1971-73, 1975, Northern Illinois 1976-78, Wake Forest 1979-83. Pro coach: Joined Bengals in 1984.

Kim Wood, strength; born July 12, 1945, Barrington, Ill., lives in Cincinnati. Running back Wisconsin 1965-68. No pro playing experience. Pro coach: Joined Bengals in 1975.

Cincinnati Bengals 1987 First-Year Roster

Name	Pos.	Ht.	Wt.	Birth-date	College	Hometown	How Acq.
Aronson, Doug	G	6-3	290	8/14/64	San Diego State	San Francisco, Calif.	FA
Banks, Michael	WR	5-9	180	4/17/64	Utah State	Logan, Utah	FA
Bell, Leonard	S	5-11	201	3/14/64	Indiana	Rockford, Ill.	D3a
Berry, Shannon	DE	6-2	260	10/27/64	Western Illinois	Wichita, Kan.	FA
Brown, Tom	WR	6-4	190	12/24/63	Augustana, S.D.	Sioux Falls, S.D.	FA
Buck, Jason	DE	6-5	264	7/27/63	Brigham Young	St. Anthony, Idaho	D1
Burrow, Curtis	K	5-11	185	12/11/62	Central Arkansas	Brinkley, Ark.	FA
Butler, David	LB	6-3	225	7/17/65	Notre Dame	Toledo, Ohio	FA
Carney, John	K	5-10	170	4/20/64	Notre Dame	West Palm Beach, Fla.	FA
Cupp, Keith	T	6-6	305	6/20/64	Findlay College	Bowling Green, Ohio	FA
Ehrhardt, Thomas	QB	6-3	205	10/11/63	Rhode Island	Flushing, N.Y.	FA
Fehr, Steve	K	6-0	185	9/24/59	Navy	Louisville, Ky.	FA
Fulhage, Scott	P	5-11	185	11/17/61	Kansas State	Beloit, Kan.	FA
Gordon, Sonny	S	5-11	192	7/30/65	Ohio State	Middletown, Ohio	D6
Harris, R.L.	CB-S	5-11	190	12/13/61	Stephen F. Austin	Aurora, Colo.	FA
Holifield, John	RB	6-0	193	7/14/64	West Virginia	Romulus, Mich.	D12
Horne, Greg	P	6-0	188	11/22/64	Arkansas	Russellville, Ark.	D5b
Inglis, Tim	LB	6-3	241	3/10/64	Toledo	Toledo, Ohio	FA
Logan, Marc	RB	5-11	207	5/9/65	Kentucky	Lexington, Ky.	D5a
McClendon, Skip	DE	6-6	270	4/9/64	Arizona State	Detroit, Mich.	D3b
McCluskey, David	RB	6-1	220	11/5/63	Georgia	Rome, Ga.	D10
Meehan, Greg	WR	6-0	192	4/27/63	Bowling Green	Phoenix, Ariz.	FA
Morrison, Tim	T-G	6-3	261	8/23/64	Wake Forest	Wilmington, N.C.	FA
Quaites, James	WR	6-1	186	5/1/64	Nebraska-Omaha	Omaha, Neb.	FA
Raddatz, Craig	LB	6-3	242	2/4/64	Wisconsin	Cedarburg, Wis.	D9
Riggs, Jim	TE	6-5	245	9/29/63	Clemson	Laurinburg, N.C.	D4
Sawyer, Robert	P	6-1	205	11/18/62	Texas A&M	Joshua, Tex.	FA
Schwanke, Chul (1)	RB	5-11	200	4/2/63	South Dakota	Hutchinson, Minn.	FA
Smith, Daryl	CB	5-9	185	5/8/63	North Alabama	Hopkins, S.C.	FA
Smith, Jeffrey	DE	6-4	246	5/4/62	Earlham College	Lexington, Ky.	FA
Starnes, John	P	5-11	185	12/25/62	North Texas State	Tulsa, Okla.	FA
Thatcher, Chris	G-C	6-4	275	10/10/64	Lafayette	Kings Park, N.Y.	D7
Thomas, Dennis	TE	6-3	245	11/7/63	South Dakota State	DePere, Wis.	FA
Thomas, Eric	CB	5-11	175	9/11/64	Tulane	Sacramento, Calif.	D2
Tigges, Mark	T	6-3	290	2/5/64	Western Illinois	Fenton, Iowa	FA
Tweet, Rodney	WR	6-1	195	2/20/64	South Dakota	Austin, Minn.	FA
Ward, Rick	P	6-2	210	4/5/62	Eastern Oregon State	Lake Oswego, Ore.	FA
Warne, Jim	T	6-7	315	11/11/64	Arizona State	Tempe, Ariz.	D11
Wilcots, Solomon	CB	5-11	180	10/9/64	Colorado	Rubidoux, Calif.	D8
Zimmer, Doug	S	6-1	192	6/27/65	Dayton	Tipp City, Ohio	FA

The term NFL Rookie is defined as a player who is in his first season of professional football and has not been on the roster of another professional football team for any regular-season or postseason games. A Rookie is designated by an "R" on NFL rosters. Players who have been active in another professional football league or players who have NFL experience, including either preseason training camp or being on an active roster for fewer than three regular-season or postseason games, are termed NFL First-Year Players. An NFL First-Year Player is designated by a "1" on NFL rosters. Thereafter, a player on an NFL active roster for at least three regular-season or postseason games is credited with an additional year of NFL playing experience.

NOTES

CLEVELAND BROWNS

American Football Conference
Central Division

Team Colors: Seal Brown, Orange, and White

Tower B
Cleveland Stadium
Cleveland, Ohio 44114
Telephone: (216) 696-5555

Club Officials

President and Owner: Arthur B. Modell
Executive Vice President/Legal and Administrative: Jim Bailey
Executive Vice President/Football Operations: Ernie Accorsi
Vice President/Public Relations: Kevin Byrne
Vice President/Finance: Mike Poplar
Director of Player Personnel: Chip Falivene
Director of Player Relations: Ricky Feacher
Director of Marketing: David Modell
Director of Security: Ted Chappelle
Assistant Directors of Public Relations: Bob Eller, Francine Lubera
Area Scouts: Dom Anile, Tom Dimitroff, Tom Heckert, Tom Miner
Head Trainer: Bill Tessendorf
Equipment Manager: Charley Cusick

Stadium: Cleveland Stadium • **Capacity:** 80,098
West 3rd Street
Cleveland, Ohio 44114

Playing Surface: Grass

Training Camp: Lakeland Community College
Mentor, Ohio 44060

1987 Schedule

Preseason

Aug. 15	**St. Louis**	7:30
Aug. 22	at New York Giants	8:00
Aug. 29	at Atlanta	8:00
Sept. 5	vs. Green Bay at Milw.	7:00

Regular Season

Sept. 13	at New Orleans	12:00
Sept. 20	**Pittsburgh**	1:00
Sept. 28	**Denver** (Monday)	9:00
Oct. 4	at New England	1:00
Oct. 11	**Houston**	1:00
Oct. 18	at Cincinnati	1:00
Oct. 26	**L.A. Rams** (Monday)	9:00
Nov. 1	at San Diego	1:00
Nov. 8	**Atlanta**	1:00
Nov. 15	**Buffalo**	1:00
Nov. 22	at Houston	12:00
Nov. 29	at San Francisco	5:00
Dec. 6	**Indianapolis**	1:00
Dec. 13	**Cincinnati**	1:00
Dec. 20	at Los Angeles Raiders	1:00
Dec. 26	at Pittsburgh (Saturday)	12:30

Browns Coaching History

(314-207-9)

1950-62	Paul Brown	115-49-5
1963-70	Blanton Collier	79-38-2
1971-74	Nick Skorich	30-26-2
1975-77	Forrest Gregg*	18-23-0
1977	Dick Modzelewski	0-1-0
1978-84	Sam Rutigliano**	47-52-0
1984-86	Marty Schottenheimer	25-18-0

*Resigned after 13 games in 1977
**Released after eight games in 1984

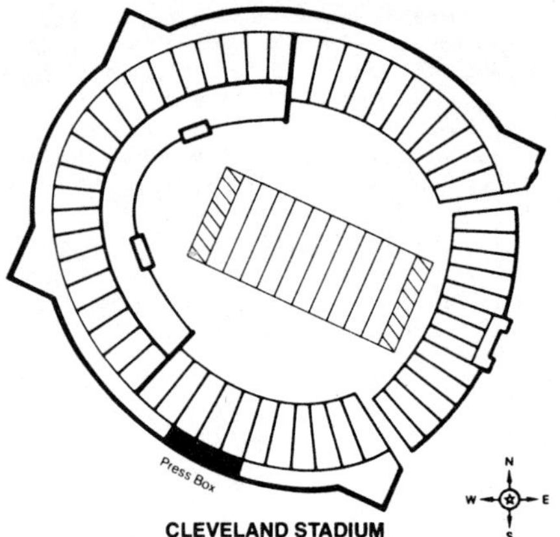

CLEVELAND STADIUM

Record Holders

Individual Records—Career

Category	Name	Performance
Rushing (Yds.)	Jim Brown, 1957-1965	12,312
Passing (Yds.)	Brian Sipe, 1974-1983	23,713
Passing (TDs)	Brian Sipe, 1974-1983	154
Receiving (No.)	Ozzie Newsome, 1978-1986	541
Receiving (Yds.)	Ozzie Newsome, 1978-1986	6,698
Interceptions	Thom Darden, 1972-74, 1976-1981	45
Punting (Avg.)	Horace Gillom, 1950-56	43.8
Punt Return (Avg.)	Greg Pruitt, 1973-1981	11.8
Kickoff Return (Avg.)	Greg Pruitt, 1973-1981	26.3
Field Goals	Lou Groza, 1950-59, 1961-67	234
Touchdowns (Tot.)	Jim Brown, 1957-1965	126
Points	Lou Groza, 1950-59, 1961-67	1,349

Individual Records—Single Season

Category	Name	Performance
Rushing (Yds.)	Jim Brown, 1963	1,863
Passing (Yds.)	Brian Sipe, 1980	4,132
Passing (TDs)	Brian Sipe, 1980	30
Receiving (No.)	Ozzie Newsome, 1983	89
	Ozzie Newsome, 1984	89
Receiving (Yds.)	Paul Warfield, 1968	1,067
Interceptions	Thom Darden, 1978	10
Punting (Avg.)	Gary Collins, 1965	46.7
Punt Return (Avg.)	Leroy Kelly, 1965	15.6
Kickoff Return (Avg.)	Billy Reynolds, 1954	29.5
Field Goals	Matt Bahr, 1984	24
Touchdowns (Tot.)	Jim Brown, 1965	21
Points	Jim Brown, 1965	126

Individual Records—Single Game

Category	Name	Performance
Rushing (Yds.)	Jim Brown, 11-24-57	237
	Jim Brown, 11-19-61	237
Passing (Yds.)	Bernie Kosar, 1-3-87	489
Passing (TDs)	Frank Ryan, 12-12-64	5
	Bill Nelsen, 11-2-69	5
	Brian Sipe, 10-7-79	5
Receiving (No.)	Ozzie Newsome, 10-14-84	14
Receiving (Yds.)	Ozzie Newsome, 10-14-84	191
Interceptions	Many times	3
	Last time by Hanford Dixon, 12-19-82	
Field Goals	Don Cockroft, 10-19-75	5
Touchdowns (Tot.)	Dub Jones, 11-25-51	6
Points	Dub Jones, 11-25-51	36

1986 Team Statistics

	Browns	Opp.
Total First Downs	302	302
Rushing	102	113
Passing	175	171
Penalty	25	18
Third Down: Made/Att.	81/220	82/219
Fourth Down: Made/Att.	7/15	10/18
Total Net Yards	5394	5269
Avg. Per Game	337.1	329.3
Total Plays	1047	1047
Avg. Per Play	5.2	5.0
Net Yards Rushing	1650	1981
Avg. Per Game	103.1	123.8
Total Rushes	470	494
Net Yards Passing	3744	3288
Avg. Per Game	234.0	205.5
Tackled/Yards Lost	39/274	35/258
Gross Yards	4018	3546
Att./Completions	538/315	518/291
Completion Pct.	58.6	56.2
Had Intercepted	11	18
Punts/Avg.	83/41.2	80/37.9
Net Punting Avg.	35.6	31.5
Penalties/Yards Lost	101/807	101/754
Fumbles/Ball Lost	31/13	36/19
Touchdowns	45	36
Rushing	20	12
Passing	18	21
Returns	7	3
Avg. Time of Possession	29:42	30:18

1986 Team Record

Preseason (4-0)

Date	Result		Opponents
8/9	W	19-17	Buffalo
8/15	W	17-10	at Miami
8/23	W	27-21	at Atlanta
8/28	W	25-22	at L.A. Raiders
		88-70	

Regular Season (12-4)

Date	Result		Opponents	Att.
9/7	L	31-41	at Chicago	66,030
9/14	W	23-20	at Houston	46,049
9/18	L	13-30	Cincinnati	78,779
9/28	W	24-21	Detroit	72,029
10/5	W	27-24	at Pittsburgh	57,327
10/12	W	20- 7	Kansas City	71,278
10/19	L	14-17	Green Bay	76,438
10/26	W	23-20	at Minnesota	59,133
11/2	W	24- 9	at Indianapolis	57,962
11/10	W	26-16	Miami	77,949
11/16	L	14-27	at L.A. Raiders	65,461
11/23	W	37-31	Pittsburgh (OT)	76,452
11/30	W	13-10	Houston (OT)	62,309
12/7	W	21-17	at Buffalo	42,213
12/14	W	34- 3	at Cincinnati	58,062
12/21	W	47-17	San Diego	68,505

Postseason (1-1)

Date	Result		Opponents	Att.
1/3/87	W	23-20	N.Y. Jets (OT)	75,262
1/11/87	L	20-23	Denver (OT)	79,973

(OT) Overtime

Score by Periods

Browns	82	102	112	86	9	—	391
Opponents	54	98	62	96	0	—	310

Attendance

Home 583,739 Away 452,237 Total 1,035,976
Single game home record, 85,703 (9-21-70)
Single season home record, 620,496 (1980)

1986 Individual Statistics

Scoring	TD R	TD P	TD Rt	PAT	FG	Saf	TP
Bahr	0	0	0	30/30	20/26	0	90
Moseley, Wash.-Clev.	0	0	0	25/28	12/19	0	61
Moseley, Clev.	0	0	0	13/14	6/7	0	31
Mack	10	0	0	0/0	0/0	0	60
Brennan	0	6	1	0/0	0/0	0	42
Dickey	6	0	0	0/0	0/0	0	36
Slaughter	0	4	1	0/0	0/0	0	30
Byner	2	2	0	0/0	0/0	0	24
Newsome	0	3	0	0/0	0/0	0	18
Fontenot	1	1	0	0/0	0/0	0	12
Holt	1	1	0	0/0	0/0	0	12
McNeil	0	0	2	0/0	0/0	0	12
Gross	0	0	1	0/0	0/0	0	6
Langhorne	0	1	0	0/0	0/0	0	6
Minnifield	0	0	1	0/0	0/0	0	6
Wright	0	0	1	0/0	0/0	0	6
Browns	20	18	7	43/44	26/33	0	391
Opponents	12	21	3	34/36	20/29	0	310

Passing	Att.	Comp.	Yds.	Pct.	TD	Int.	Tkld.	Rate
Kosar	531	310	3854	58.4	17	10	39/274	83.8
Pagel	3	2	53	66.7	0	0	0/0	109.7
Gossett	2	1	30	50.0	0	1	0/0	56.3
Brennan	1	1	35	100.0	0	0	0/0	118.8
Fontenot	1	1	46	100.0	1	0	0/0	158.3
Browns	538	315	4018	58.6	18	11	39/274	84.6
Opponents	518	291	3546	56.2	21	18	35/258	76.5

Rushing	Att.	Yds.	Avg.	LG	TD
Mack	174	665	3.8	20	10
Dickey	135	523	3.9	47	6
Byner	94	277	2.9	37	2
Fontenot	25	105	4.2	16	1
Everett	12	43	3.6	8	0
Kosar	24	19	0.8	17	0
Holt	1	16	16.0	16t	1
McNeil	1	12	12.0	12	0
Baker, Atl.-Clev.	1	3	3.0	3	0
Slaughter	1	1	1.0	1	0
Pagel	2	0	0.0	0	0
Langhorne	1	−11	−11.0	−11	0
Browns	470	1650	3.5	47	20
Opponents	494	1981	4.0	53	12

Receiving	No.	Yds.	Avg.	LG	TD
Brennan	55	838	15.2	57t	6
Fontenot	47	559	11.9	72t	1
Slaughter	40	577	14.4	47t	4
Langhorne	39	678	17.4	66	1
Newsome	39	417	10.7	31	3
Byner	37	328	8.9	40	2
Mack	28	292	10.4	44	0
Dickey	10	78	7.8	12	0
Weathers	9	100	11.1	16	0
Holt	4	61	15.3	34	1
Greer	3	51	17.0	22	0
Tucker	2	29	14.5	16	0
McNeil	1	9	9.0	9	0
Kosar	1	1	1.0	1	0
Browns	315	4018	12.8	72t	18
Opponents	291	3546	12.2	75t	21

Interceptions	No.	Yds.	Avg.	LG	TD
Dixon	5	35	7.0	19	0
Wright	3	33	11.0	33	0
Minnifield	3	20	6.7	20	0
Rockins	2	41	20.5	24	0
Ellis	2	12	6.0	7	0
Matthews	2	12	6.0	8	0
Harper	1	31	31.0	31	0
Browns	18	184	10.2	33	0
Opponents	11	135	12.3	58t	1

Punting	No.	Yds.	Avg.	In 20	LG
Gossett	83	3423	41.2	21	61
Browns	83	3423	41.2	21	61
Opponents	80	3033	37.9	14	57

Punt Returns	No.	FC	Yds.	Avg.	LG	TD
McNeil	40	10	348	8.7	84t	1
Slaughter	1	0	2	2.0	2	0
Browns	41	10	350	8.5	84t	1
Opponents	44	11	268	6.1	20	0

Kickoff Returns	No.	Yds.	Avg.	LG	TD
McNeil	47	997	21.2	100t	1
Fontenot	7	99	14.1	19	0
Langhorne	4	57	14.3	20	0
Nicolas	3	28	9.3	13	0
Puzzuoli	1	32	32.0	32	0
Browns	62	1213	19.6	100t	1
Opponents	78	1476	18.9	91t	1

Sacks	No.
Hairston	9.0
Camp	7.0
Clancy	6.5
Puzzuoli	6.0
Banks	4.5
Ellis	1.0
Matthews	1.0
Browns	35.0
Opponents	39.0

FIRST-ROUND SELECTIONS

(If club had no first-round selection, first player drafted is listed with round in parentheses.)

Year	Player, College, Position
1950	Ken Carpenter, Oregon State, B
1951	Ken Konz, Louisiana State, B
1952	Bert Rechichar, Tennessee, DB
	Harry Agganis, Boston U., QB
1953	Doug Atkins, Tennessee, DE
1954	Bobby Garrett, Stanford, QB
	John Bauer, Illinois, G
1955	Kurt Burris, Oklahoma, C
1956	Preston Carpenter, Arkansas, B
1957	Jim Brown, Syracuse, B
1958	Jim Shofner, Texas Christian, DB
1959	Rich Kreitling, Illinois, DE
1960	Jim Houston, Ohio State, DE
1961	Bobby Crespino, Mississippi, TE
1962	Gary Collins, Maryland, WR
	Leroy Jackson, Western Illinois, RB
1963	Tom Hutchinson, Kentucky, WR
1964	Paul Warfield, Ohio State, WR
1965	James Garcia, Purdue, T (2)
1966	Milt Morin, Massachusetts, TE
1967	Bob Matheson, Duke, LB
1968	Marvin Upshaw, Trinity, Texas, DT-DE
1969	Ron Johnson, Michigan, RB
1970	Mike Phipps, Purdue, QB
	Bob McKay, Texas, T
1971	Clarence Scott, Kansas State, CB
1972	Thom Darden, Michigan, DB
1973	Steve Holden, Arizona State, WR
	Pete Adams, Southern California, T
1974	Billy Corbett, Johnson C. Smith, T (2)
1975	Mack Mitchell, Houston, DE
1976	Mike Pruitt, Purdue, RB
1977	Robert Jackson, Texas A&M, LB
1978	Clay Matthews, Southern California, LB
	Ozzie Newsome, Alabama, TE
1979	Willis Adams, Houston, WR
1980	Charles White, Southern California, RB
1981	Hanford Dixon, Southern Mississippi, DB
1982	Chip Banks, Southern California, LB
1983	Ron Brown, Arizona State, WR (2)
1984	Don Rogers, UCLA, DB
1985	Greg Allen, Florida State, RB (2)
1986	Webster Slaughter, San Diego State, WR (2)
1987	Mike Junkin, Duke, LB

Cleveland Browns 1987 Veteran Roster

No.	Name	Pos.	Ht.	Wt.	Birth-date	NFL Exp.	College	Hometown	How Acq.	'86 Games/ Starts
66	Andrews, Tom	G	6-4	267	1/11/62	3	Louisville	Parma, Ohio	FA-'87	0*
61	†Baab, Mike	C	6-4	270	12/6/59	6	Texas	Euless, Tex.	D5-'82	16/16
9	Bahr, Matt	K	5-10	175	7/6/56	9	Penn State	Neshaminy, Pa.	T(SF)-'81	12/0
41	Baker, Tony	RB	5-10	175	6/11/64	2	East Carolina	High Point, N.C.	FA-'87	6/0*
99	†Baldwin, Keith	DE	6-4	270	10/13/60	5	Texas A&M	Houston, Tex.	D2-'82	0*
77	†Bolden, Rickey	T	6-6	280	9/8/61	4	Southern Methodist	Dallas, Tex.	D4a-'84	7/5
54	Bowser, Charles	LB	6-3	235	10/2/59	5	Duke	Plymouth, N.C.	W(Mia)-'87	0*
86	†Brennan, Brian	WR	5-9	178	2/15/62	4	Boston College	Bloomfield, Mich.	D4b-'84	16/0
44	Byner, Earnest	RB	5-10	215	9/15/62	4	East Carolina	Milledgeville, Ga.	D10-'84	7/7
96	Camp, Reggie	DE	6-4	280	2/28/61	5	California	San Francisco, Calif.	D3-'83	16/16
91	†Clancy, Sam	DE	6-7	260	5/29/58	4	Pittsburgh	Pittsburgh, Pa.	T(Sea)-'85	16/1
18	Danielson, Gary	QB	6-2	196	9/10/51	10	Purdue	Dearborn, Mich.	T(Det)-'85	0*
38	Davis, Johnny	RB	6-1	235	7/17/56	10	Alabama	Montgomery, Ala.	FA-'82	6/0
60	Dennard, Mark	C	6-4	260	11/2/56	8	Texas A&M	Bay City, Tex.	FA-'86	0*
33	Dickey, Curtis	RB	6-1	220	11/27/56	8	Texas A&M	Bryan, Tex.	W(Ind)-'85	14/10
29	Dixon, Hanford	CB	5-11	186	12/25/58	7	Southern Mississippi	Theodore, Ala.	D1-'81	16/16
26	Duncan, Clyde	WR	6-2	211	2/5/61	3	Tennessee	Oxon Hill, Md.	FA-'87	0*
24	Ellis, Ray	S	6-1	196	4/27/59	7	Ohio State	Philadelphia, Pa.	FA-'86	15/15
39	Everett, Major	RB	5-10	218	1/4/60	5	Mississippi College	Jackson, Miss.	FA-'86	9/0
74	Farren, Paul	T-G	6-5	280	12/24/60	5	Boston University	Cohasset, Mass.	D12-'83	16/16
69	Fike, Dan	G	6-7	280	6/16/61	3	Florida	Pensacola, Fla.	FA-'85	16/16
28	Fontenot, Herman	RB-KR	6-0	206	9/12/63	3	Louisiana State	Beaumont, Tex.	FA-'85	16/3
79	Golic, Bob	NT	6-2	270	10/26/57	8	Notre Dame	Cleveland, Ohio	W(NE)-'82	16/16
7	†Gossett, Jeff	P	6-2	200	1/25/57	6	Eastern Illinois	Charleston, Ill.	FA-'85	16/0
80	Greer, Terry	WR	6-2	197	9/27/57	2	Alabama State	Memphis, Tenn.	T(Rams)-'86	11/1
53	Griggs, Anthony	LB	6-3	230	2/12/60	6	Ohio State	Somerville, N.J.	T(Phil)-'86	16/15
27	Gross, Al	S	6-3	195	1/4/61	5	Arizona	Stockton, Calif.	W(Dall)-'83	4/1
78	Hairston, Carl	DE	6-4	260	12/15/52	12	Maryland-East. Shore	Martinsville, Va.	T(Phil)-'84	16/16
23	Harper, Mark	CB	5-9	174	11/5/61	2	Alcorn State	Memphis, Tenn.	FA-'86	16/1
48	Hoggard, D.D.	CB	6-0	188	5/20/61	2	North Carolina State	Falls Church, Va.	FA-'86	16/0
81	Holt, Harry	TE	6-4	240	12/29/57	5	Arizona	Harlingen, Tex.	FA-'83	14/0
51	Johnson, Eddie	LB	6-1	225	2/3/59	7	Louisville	Albany, Ga.	D7-'81	16/16
59	Johnson, Mike	LB	6-1	228	11/26/62	2	Virginia Tech	Hyattsville, Md.	SD1b-'84	16/0
92	Kab, Vyto	TE	6-5	240	12/23/59	5	Penn State	Wayne, N.J.	FA-'87	0*
19	Kosar, Bernie	QB	6-5	210	11/25/63	3	Miami	Boardman, Ohio	SD1-'85	16/16
88	†Langhorne, Reggie	WR	6-2	195	4/7/63	3	Elizabeth City State	Smithfield, Va.	D7-'85	16/15
62	†Lilja, George	G-C	6-4	270	3/3/58	6	Michigan	Orland Park, Ill.	FA-'84	16/0
34	Mack, Kevin	RB	6-0	212	8/9/62	3	Clemson	King Mountain, N.C.	SD1a-'84	12/12
90	Malone, Ralph	DE	6-5	225	1/12/64	2	Georgia Tech	Atlanta, Ga.	FA-'86	16/0
57	Matthews, Clay	LB	6-2	235	3/15/56	10	Southern California	Los Angeles, Calif.	D1a-'78	16/16
89	McNeil, Gerald	WR-KR	5-7	140	3/27/62	2	Baylor	Killeen, Tex.	SD2a-'84	16/0
31	Minnifield, Frank	CB	5-9	180	1/1/60	4	Louisville	Lexington, Ky.	FA-'84	16/15
82	Newsome, Ozzie	TE	6-2	232	3/16/56	10	Alabama	Muscle Shoals, Ala.	D1b-'78	16/16
58	Nicolas, Scott	LB	6-3	226	8/7/60	6	Miami	Clearwater, Fla.	D12-'82	16/0
10	†Pagel, Mike	QB	6-2	200	9/13/60	6	Arizona State	Phoenix, Ariz.	T(Ind)-'86	1/0
72	Puzzuoli, Dave	NT	6-3	260	1/12/61	5	Pittsburgh	Stamford, Conn.	D6b-'83	16/0
63	†Risien, Cody	T	6-7	280	3/22/57	8	Texas A&M	Cypress, Tex.	D7-'79	16/16
37	Rockins, Chris	S	6-0	195	5/18/62	4	Oklahoma State	Sherman, Tex.	D2a-'84	16/16
84	Slaughter, Webster	WR	6-0	170	10/19/64	2	San Diego State	El Cajon, Calif.	D2-'86	16/16
87	†Tucker, Travis	TE	6-3	240	9/19/63	3	So. Connecticut State	Brooklyn, N.Y.	D11-'85	16/0
50	†Van Pelt, Brad	LB	6-5	235	4/5/51	15	Michigan State	Torrance, Calif.	W(Raiders)-'86	16/0
85	†Weathers, Clarence	WR-KR	5-9	170	1/10/62	5	Delaware State	Fort Pierce, Fla.	W(NE)-'85	16/0
55	†Weathers, Curtis	LB	6-5	230	9/16/56	8	Mississippi	Memphis, Tenn.	D9b-'79	0*
70	†Williams, Larry	G	6-5	290	7/3/63	2	Notre Dame	Olmsted Twnsp., Ohio	D10-'85	16/11
22	Wright, Felix	CB-S	6-2	190	6/22/59	3	Drake	Carthage, Mo.	FA-'85	16/0
83	Young, Glen	WR	6-2	205	10/11/60	4	Mississippi State	Greenwood, Miss.	FA-'87	0*

* Andrews last active with Chicago in '85; Baker played 4 games with Atlanta in '86, 2 with Cleveland; Baldwin, Danielson, Curtis Weathers missed entire '86 season due to injury; Bowser last active with Miami in '85; Dennard last active with Philadelphia in '85; Duncan last active with St. Louis in '85; Kab last active with N.Y. Giants in '85; Young last active with Cleveland in '85.

†Option playout; subject to developments.

Traded—Linebacker Chip Banks to San Diego.

Also played with Browns in '86—T Bill Contz (1 game), T Bob Gruber (active for 9 games, but did not play), K Mark Moseley (10), G Jeff Wiska (1).

COACHING STAFF

Head Coach, Marty Schottenheimer

Pro Career: Begins third full season as head coach. Became sixth head coach in Cleveland history on October 22, 1984, after Browns' 1-7 start under Sam Rutigliano, and led Browns to a 4-4 finish. In first two full seasons, has led Browns to consecutive AFC Central championships. Joined the Cleveland staff in 1980 as defensive coordinator. Served as an assistant coach with Portland Storm (WFL) in 1974, was linebacker coach and defensive coordinator with New York Giants 1975-77, and linebacker coach with Detroit Lions 1978-79. Drafted in the seventh round of the 1965 draft by the Buffalo Bills. Played linebacker for Bills 1965-68 and for Boston Patriots 1969-70. Career record: 25-18.

Background: All-America linebacker at University of Pittsburgh 1962-64. Following retirement from pro football, worked as a real estate developer in both Miami and Denver from 1971-74.

Personal: Born September 23, 1943, Canonsburg, Pa. Marty and his wife, Patricia, live in Strongsville, Ohio, and have two children—Kristen and Brian.

Assistant Coaches

Dave Adolph, defensive coordinator; born June 6, 1937, Akron, Ohio, lives in Berea, Ohio. Guard-linebacker Akron 1955-58. No pro playing experience. College coach: Akron 1963-64, Connecticut 1965-68, Kentucky 1969-72, Illinois 1973-76, Ohio State 1977-78. Pro coach: Cleveland Browns 1979-84, San Diego Chargers 1985, rejoined Browns in 1986.

Bill Cowher, secondary; born May 8, 1957, Pittsburgh, Pa., lives in Strongsville, Ohio. Linebacker North Carolina State 1975-78. Pro linebacker Cleveland Browns 1980-82, Philadelphia Eagles 1983-84. Pro coach: Joined Browns in 1985 (special teams coach 1985-86).

Charlie Davis, tight ends; born August 7, 1944, San Diego, Calif., lives in Middleburg Heights, Ohio. Linebacker UCLA 1962-64. No pro playing experience. College coach: San Françisco State 1967-70, Xavier 1971-73, Ball State 1974-75, Tulane 1976-80. Pro coach: Jacksonville Bulls (USFL) 1984-85, joined Browns in 1986.

Lindy Infante, offensive coordinator-quarterbacks; born May 27, 1940, Miami, Fla., lives in Berea, Ohio. Running back-defensive back Florida 1960-62. Pro running back Hamilton Tiger-Cats (CFL) 1963. College coach: Florida 1966-71, Memphis State 1972-73, Tulane 1976, 1979. Pro coach: Charlotte Hornets (WFL) 1975, New York Giants 1977-78, Cincinnati Bengals 1980-82, Jacksonville Bulls (USFL, head coach) 1984-85, joined Browns in 1986.

Richard Mann, receivers; born April 20, 1947, Aliquippa, Pa., lives in Strongsville, Ohio. Wide receiver Arizona State 1966-68. No pro playing experience. College coach: Arizona State 1974-79, Louisville 1980-81. Pro coach: Indianapolis Colts 1982-84, joined Browns in 1985.

Howard Mudd, offensive line; born February 10, 1942, Midland, Mich., lives in Medina, Ohio. Guard Hillsdale 1961-63. Pro guard San Francisco 49ers 1964-69, Chicago Bears 1970-71. College coach: California 1972-73. Pro coach: San Diego Chargers 1974-76, San Francisco 49ers 1977, Seattle Seahawks 1978-82, joined Browns in 1983.

Joe Pendry, running backs; born August 5, 1947, Matheny, W. Va., lives in Strongsville, Ohio. Tight end West Virginia 1966-67. No pro playing experience. College coach: West Virginia 1967-74, 1976-77, Kansas State 1975, Pittsburgh 1978-79, Michigan State 1980-81. Pro coach: Philadelphia Stars (USFL) 1983, Pittsburgh Maulers (USFL, head coach) 1984, joined Browns in 1985.

Tom Pratt, defensive line; born June 21, 1935, Edgerton, Wis., lives in Medina, Ohio. Linebacker Miami 1954-56. No pro playing experience. College coach: Miami 1957-59, Southern Mississippi 1960-62. Pro coach: Kansas City Chiefs 1963-77, New Orleans Saints 1978-80, joined Browns in 1981.

Dave Redding, strength and conditioning; born June 14, 1952, North Platte, Neb., lives in Medina, Ohio. Defensive end Nebraska 1972-75. No pro playing experience. College coach: Nebraska 1976, Washington State 1977, Missouri 1978-81. Pro coach: Joined Browns in 1982.

Kurt Schottenheimer, special teams; born October 1, 1949, McDonald, Pa., lives in Medina, Ohio. Defensive back Miami 1969-70. No pro playing experience. College coach: William Patterson 1974, Michigan State 1978-82, Tulane 1983, Louisiana State 1984-85, Notre Dame 1986. Pro coach: First year with Browns.

Darvin Wallis, special assistant-defense; born February 14, 1949, Ft. Branch, Ind., lives in Middleburg Heights, Ohio. Defensive end Arizona 1970-71. No pro playing experience. College coach: Adams State 1976-77, Tulane 1978-79, Mississippi 1980-81. Pro coach: Joined Browns in 1982.

Cleveland Browns 1987 First-Year Roster

Name	Pos.	Ht.	Wt.	Birth-date	College	Hometown	How Acq.
Anderson, Greg (1)	WR	5-10	170	5/20/59	Alabama State	North Olmsted, Ohio	FA-'86
Battaglia, Matt	LB	6-2	225	9/25/65	Louisville	Lithonia, Ga.	FA
Bayless, Gerald	TE	6-3	235	7/5/64	Bowling Green	Dayton, Ohio	FA
Bell, Albert	WR	6-0	170	4/23/64	Alabama	Los Angeles, Calif.	FA
Braggs, Stephen	CB-S	5-9	175	8/29/65	Texas	Houston, Tex.	D6
Brewton, Larry	CB-S	5-9	180	4/23/64	Temple	New Castle, Pa.	D11
Bullitt, Steve	LB	6-2	222	4/21/65	Texas A&M	El Paso, Tex.	D8
Cullity, Dave	T-G-C	6-7	275	6/15/64	Utah	La Mirada, Calif.	FA
Degnan, Mike	DE	6-4	248	4/25/64	Boston College	Norwood, Mass.	FA
Eddins, Tony	WR	6-1	210	3/9/63	Mississippi College	Columbus, Miss.	FA
Fletcher, John	G	6-3	280	8/22/65	Texas A&I	Corpus Christi, Tex.	FA
Heffern, Shawn	T-G-C	6-5	277	3/15/64	Notre Dame	Carmel, Ind.	FA
Hill, Will	CB-S	5-11	170	3/5/63	Bishop College	Vero Beach, Fla.	FA
Holloway, Anthony	LB	6-3	224	4/21/64	Nebraska	Bellevue, Neb.	FA
Jackson, Enis (1)	CB	5-9	180	5/16/63	Memphis State	Helena, Ark.	FA-'86
Jackson, Milton	WR	5-10	178	12/10/63	Notre Dame	Fairfield, Iowa	FA
Jaeger, Jeff	K	5-11	189	11/24/64	Washington	Kent, Wash.	D3b
Johnson, Nate	RB	6-1	213	10/25/63	Texas Southern	Ft. Worth, Tex.	FA
Johnson, Samuel	WR	5-11	180	9/7/64	Prairie View	Lynwood, Calif.	FA
Junkin, Mike	LB	6-3	235	11/24/64	Duke	Belvidere, Ill.	D1
Kehoe, Scott	T-G-C	6-4	275	9/20/64	Illinois	Oak Lawn, Ill.	FA
Kemp, Perry (1)	WR	5-11	170	12/31/61	California, Pa.	McDonald, Pa.	FA
Kidd, Billy	C	6-4	280	11/28/59	Houston	Keller, Tex.	FA
Lawrence, Steve	CB-S	5-11	190	5/9/65	Notre Dame	Ypsilanti, Mich.	FA
Manoa, Tim	RB	6-1	227	9/9/64	Penn State	Pittsburgh, Pa.	D3a
McBride, Richard (1)	CB-S	6-0	195	3/23/63	Missouri	Zanesville, Ohio	FA
McLees, Matt	LB	6-2	235	6/7/64	So. Connecticut State	West Islip, N.Y.	FA
Meyer, Jim (1)	T	6-5	295	6/9/63	Illinois State	Normal, Ill.	D7a-'86
Miller, Nick (1)	LB	6-2	238	10/26/63	Arkansas	Fayetteville, Ark.	D5-'86
Norseth, Mike (1)	QB	6-2	200	8/22/64	Kansas	Lawrence, Kan.	D7b-'86
Palumbis, Gary	NT	6-1	265	4/28/63	Portland State	Lake Oswego, Ore.	FA
Pasquale, Ron	G	6-3	270	2/28/64	Akron	Akron, Ohio	FA
Pauciello, Jim	DE-NT	6-3	255	1/14/64	Utah State	Trumbull, Conn.	FA
Pegues, Jeff (1)	LB	6-2	241	1/19/62	East Carolina	Laurinburg, N.C.	FA
Poole, Shelley	RB	5-9	222	12/3/64	Temple	Norcross, Ga.	FA
Pyles, Robert (1)	T	6-5	275	9/3/60	Miami, Ohio	Wheelersburg, Ohio	FA
Rakoczy, Gregg	C-T	6-6	290	5/18/65	Miami	Medford, N.J.	D2
Remo, Roger	LB	6-3	235	8/7/64	Syracuse	Mahwah, N.J.	FA
Sam, Aaron	RB	5-9	196	1/17/66	Florida Central	Glen Mills, Pa.	FA
Shepas, Richard	WR	5-11	200	3/16/65	Youngstown State	Youngstown, Ohio	FA
Simmons, King (1)	S	6-2	200	2/12/63	Texas Tech	Atlanta, Ga.	D12-'86
Smythe, Mark (1)	DE-NT	6-3	285	12/12/59	Indiana	Bloomington, Ind.	FA
Thomas, Danny	TE	6-5	232	5/30/64	Louisville	Aliquippa, Pa.	FA
Tiller, Bruce	WR	6-2	188	5/10/63	Kutztown	Downington, Pa.	FA
Turpin, Miles (1)	LB	6-4	230	5/15/64	California	Fremont, Calif.	FA
Watson, Remi	S	6-0	174	9/8/64	Bethune-Cookman	Plant City, Fla.	FA
Watters, Scott	LB	6-2	228	1/1/65	Wittenberg	Gahanna, Ohio	FA
West, Doug (1)	LB	6-4	225	11/2/60	UCLA	Del Mar, Calif.	FA
White, James (1)	DE	6-3	245	7/5/62	Louisiana State	Rayville, La.	FA-'86
Wiggins, Stephen	CB-S	6-0	182	7/25/63	Prairie View	San Antonio, Tex.	FA
Wilson, Troy	CB-S	5-10	170	9/19/65	Notre Dame	Frederick, Md.	FA
Winslow, George	P	6-4	205	7/28/63	Villanova	Wyndmour, Pa.	FA
Winters, Frank	C	6-3	290	1/23/64	Western Illinois	Union City, N.J.	D10
Wright, Terry	S	5-11	182	7/15/64	Temple	Miami, Fla.	FA

The term NFL Rookie is defined as a player who is in his first season of professional football and has not been on the roster of another professional football team for any regular-season or postseason games. A Rookie is designated by an "R" on NFL rosters. Players who have been active in another professional football league or players who have NFL experience, including either preseason training camp or being on an active roster for fewer than three regular-season or postseason games, are termed NFL First-Year Players. An NFL First-Year Player is designated by a "1" on NFL rosters. Thereafter, a player on an NFL active roster for at least three regular-season or postseason games is credited with an additional year of NFL playing experience.

NOTES

American Football Conference Western Division

Team Colors: Orange, Royal Blue, and White

5700 Logan Street
Denver, Colorado 80216
Telephone: (303) 296-1982

Club Officials

President-Chief Executive Officer: Patrick D. Bowlen
Vice President-Head Coach: Dan Reeves
General Manager: John Beake
Chief Financial Officer-Treasurer: Robert M. Hurley
Director of Administration: Sandy Waters
Director of Player Personnel: Reed Johnson
Director of Pro Personnel: Carroll Hardy
Director of Media Relations: Jim Saccomano
Ticket Manager: Gail Stuckey
Marketing Director: Bill Harpole
Video Director: Rusty Nail
Director of Player and Community Relations: Charlie Lee
Equipment Manager: Dan Bill
Trainer: Steve Antonopulos

Stadium: Denver Mile High Stadium • **Capacity:** 76,274
1900 West Eliot
Denver, Colorado 80204

Playing Surface: Grass (PAT)

Training Camp: University of Northern Colorado
Greeley, Colorado 80639

1987 Schedule

Preseason

Aug. 9	vs. L.A. Rams at London	6:00
Aug. 15	vs. G.B. at Tempe, Ariz.	7:00
Aug. 24	**Miami**	6:00
Aug. 29	at Los Angeles Rams	7:00
Sept. 3	**Minnesota**	6:00

Regular Season

Sept. 13	**Seattle**	2:00
Sept. 20	vs. Green Bay at Milw.	12:00
Sept. 28	at Cleveland (Monday)	9:00
Oct. 4	**Houston**	2:00
Oct. 12	**L.A. Raiders** (Monday)	7:00
Oct. 18	at Kansas City	3:00
Oct. 25	at Minnesota	12:00
Nov. 1	**Detroit**	2:00
Nov. 8	at Buffalo	1:00
Nov. 16	**Chicago** (Monday)	7:00
Nov. 22	at Los Angeles Raiders	1:00
Nov. 29	at San Diego	1:00
Dec. 6	**New England**	2:00
Dec. 13	at Seattle	5:00
Dec. 19	**Kansas City** (Saturday)	2:00
Dec. 27	**San Diego**	2:00

Broncos Coaching History

(182-208-9)

1960-61	Frank Filchock	7-20-1
1962-64	Jack Faulkner*	9-22-1
1964-66	Mac Speedie**	6-19-1
1966	Ray Malavasi	4-8-0
1967-71	Lou Saban***	20-42-3
1971	Jerry Smith	2-3-0
1972-76	John Ralston	34-33-3
1977-80	Robert (Red) Miller	42-25-0
1981-86	Dan Reeves	58-36-0

*Released after four games in 1964
**Resigned after two games in 1966
***Resigned after nine games in 1971

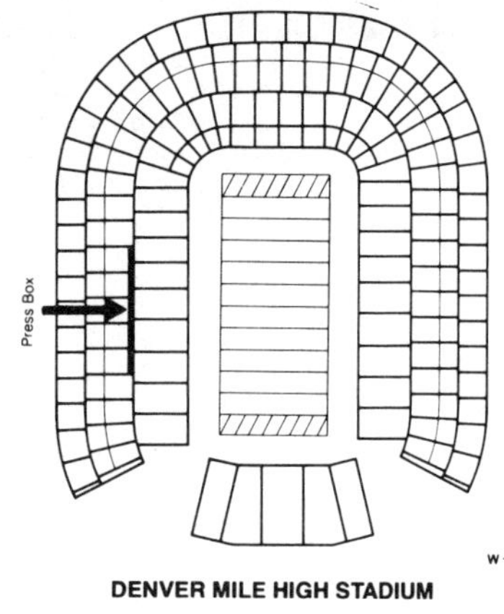

DENVER MILE HIGH STADIUM

Record Holders

Individual Records—Career

Category	Name	Performance
Rushing (Yds.)	Floyd Little, 1967-1975	6,323
Passing (Yds.)	Craig Morton, 1977-1982	11,895
Passing (TDs)	Craig Morton, 1977-1982	74
Receiving (No.)	Lionel Taylor, 1960-66	543
Receiving (Yds.)	Lionel Taylor, 1960-66	6,872
Interceptions	Steve Foley, 1976-1986	44
Punting (Avg.)	Jim Fraser, 1962-64	45.2
Punt Return (Avg.)	Rick Upchurch, 1975-1983	12.1
Kickoff Return (Avg.)	Abner Haynes, 1965-66	26.3
Field Goals	Jim Turner, 1971-79	151
Touchdowns (Tot.)	Floyd Little, 1967-1975	54
Points	Jim Turner, 1971-79	742

Individual Records—Single Season

Category	Name	Performance
Rushing (Yds.)	Otis Armstrong, 1974	1,407
Passing (Yds.)	John Elway, 1985	3,891
Passing (TDs)	Frank Tripucka, 1960	24
Receiving (No.)	Lionel Taylor, 1961	100
Receiving (Yds.)	Steve Watson, 1981	1,244
Interceptions	Goose Gonsoulin, 1960	11
Punting (Avg.)	Jim Fraser, 1963	46.1
Punt Return (Avg.)	Floyd Little, 1967	16.9
Kickoff Return (Avg.)	Bill Thompson, 1969	28.5
Field Goals	Gene Mingo, 1962	27
Touchdowns (Tot.)	Sammy Winder, 1986	14
Points	Gene Mingo, 1962	137

Individual Records—Single Game

Category	Name	Performance
Rushing (Yds.)	Otis Armstrong, 12-8-74	183
Passing (Yds.)	Frank Tripucka, 9-15-62	447
Passing (TDs)	Frank Tripucka, 10-28-62	5
	John Elway, 11-18-84	5
Receiving (No.)	Lionel Taylor, 11-29-64	13
	Bobby Anderson, 9-30-73	13
Receiving (Yds.)	Lionel Taylor, 11-27-60	199
Interceptions	Goose Gonsoulin, 9-18-60	4
	Willie Brown, 11-15-64	4
Field Goals	Gene Mingo, 10-6-63	5
	Rich Karlis, 11-20-83	5
Touchdowns (Tot.)	Many times	3
	Last time by Gerald Willhite, 11-16-86	
Points	Gene Mingo, 12-10-60	21

1986 Team Statistics

	Broncos	Opp.
Total First Downs	319	291
Rushing	94	93
Passing	184	177
Penalty	41	21
Third Down: Made/Att.	93/223	76/222
Fourth Down: Made/Att.	2/5	7/15
Total Net Yards	5216	4947
Avg. Per Game	326.0	309.2
Total Plays	1042	1026
Avg. Per Play	5.0	4.8
Net Yards Rushing	1678	1651
Avg. Per Game	104.9	103.2
Total Rushes	455	432
Net Yards Passing	3538	3296
Avg. Per Game	221.1	206.0
Tackled/Yards Lost	38/273	49/459
Gross Yards	3811	3755
Att./Completions	549/306	545/301
Completion Pct.	55.7	55.2
Had Intercepted	16	18
Punts/Avg.	86/39.3	86/42.9
Net Punting Avg.	33.0	34.2
Penalties/Yards Lost	104/910	127/1034
Fumbles/Ball Lost	24/13	32/17
Touchdowns	45	36
Rushing	17	13
Passing	22	21
Returns	6	2
Avg. Time of Possession	30:30	29:30

1986 Team Record

Preseason (2-2)

Date	Result		Opponents
8/9	L	7-10	New Orleans
8/16	L	27-29	at Minnesota
8/23	W	14- 9	San Francisco
8/29	W	19-10	L.A. Rams
		67-48	

Regular Season (11-5)

Date	Result		Opponents	Att.
9/7	W	38-36	L.A. Raiders	75,695
9/15	W	21-10	at Pittsburgh	57,305
9/21	W	33- 7	at Philadelphia	63,839
9/28	W	27-20	New England	75,804
10/5	W	29-14	Dallas	76,082
10/12	W	31-14	at San Diego	55,662
10/20	L	10-22	at N.Y. Jets	73,759
10/26	W	20-13	Seattle	76,089
11/2	W	21-10	at L.A. Raiders	90,153
11/9	L	3- 9	San Diego	75,012
11/16	W	38-17	Kansas City	75,745
11/23	L	16-19	at N.Y. Giants	75,116
11/30	W	34-28	Cincinnati	58,705
12/7	L	10-37	at Kansas City	47,019
12/13	W	31-30	Washington	75,905
12/20	L	16-41	at Seattle	63,697

Postseason (2-1)

Date	Result		Opponents	Att.
1/4/87	W	22-17	New England	76,105
1/11/87	W	23-20	at Cleveland (OT)	79,973
1/25/87	L	20-39	at N.Y. Giants	101,063

(OT) Overtime

Score by Periods

Broncos	69	131	89	89	0	—	378
Opponents	58	92	61	116	0	—	327

Attendance

Home 589,037 Away 531,256 Total 1,178,074
Single game home record, 76,105 (1-4-87)
Single season home record, 598,224 (1981)

1986 Individual Statistics

Scoring	TD R	TD P	TD Rt	PAT	FG	Saf	TP
Karlis	0	0	0	44/45	20/28	0	104
Winder	9	5	0	0/0	0/0	0	84
Willhite	5	3	1	0/0	0/0	0	54
Harden	0	0	3	0/0	0/0	0	18
Lang	1	2	0	0/0	0/0	0	18
Watson	0	3	0	0/0	0/0	0	18
Elway	1	1	0	0/0	0/0	0	12
Johnson	0	2	0	0/0	0/0	0	12
Sewell	1	1	0	0/0	0/0	0	12
M. Jackson	0	1	0	0/0	0/0	0	6
Kay	0	1	0	0/0	0/0	0	6
Mobley	0	1	0	0/0	0/0	0	6
Studdard	0	1	0	0/0	0/0	0	6
Townsend	0	0	1	0/0	0/0	0	6
Wilson	0	1	0	0/0	0/0	0	6
Woodard	0	0	1	0/0	0/0	0	6
Jones	0	0	0	0/0	0/0	1	2
Broncos	17	22	6	44/45	20/28	2	378
Opponents	13	21	2	35/36	24/32	2	327

Passing	Att.	Comp.	Yds.	Pct.	TD	Int.	Tkld.	Rate
Elway	504	280	3485	55.6	19	13	32/233	79.0
Kubiak	38	23	249	60.5	1	3	3/23	55.7
Willhite	4	1	11	25.0	0	0	0/0	39.6
Johnson	1	0	0	0.0	0	0	0/0	39.6
Norman	1	1	43	100.0	1	0	0/0	158.3
Sewell	1	1	23	100.0	1	0	3/17	158.3
Broncos	549	306	3811	55.7	22	16	38/273	78.7
Opponents	545	301	3755	55.2	21	18	49/459	75.9

Rushing	Att.	Yds.	Avg.	LG	TD
Winder	240	789	3.3	31	9
Willhite	85	365	4.3	42	5
Elway	52	257	4.9	24	1
Sewell	23	123	5.3	15	1
Lang	29	94	3.2	14	1
Kubiak	6	22	3.7	10	0
Bell	9	17	1.9	12	0
Johnson	5	15	3.0	6	0
M. Jackson	2	6	3.0	5	0
Boddie	1	2	2.0	2	0
Horan	1	0	0.0	0	0
Mobley	1	−1	−1.0	−1	0
Norman	1	−11	−11.0	−11	0
Broncos	455	1678	3.7	42	17
Opponents	432	1651	3.8	60t	13

Receiving	No.	Yds.	Avg.	LG	TD
Willhite	64	529	8.3	31	3
Watson	45	699	15.5	46	3
M. Jackson	38	738	19.4	53	1
Johnson	31	363	11.7	34t	2
Winder	26	171	6.6	20t	5
Sewell	23	294	12.8	40	1
Mobley	22	332	15.1	32	1
Sampson	21	259	12.3	43	0
Kay	15	195	13.0	34	1
Lang	13	105	8.1	26	2
Hackett	3	48	16.0	19	0
Bell	2	10	5.0	7	0
Wilson	1	43	43.0	43t	1
Elway	1	23	23.0	23t	1
Studdard	1	2	2.0	2t	1
Broncos	306	3811	12.5	53	22
Opponents	301	3755	12.5	57t	21

Interceptions	No.	Yds.	Avg.	LG	TD
Harden	6	179	29.8	52	2
Wright	3	56	18.7	56	0
Lilly	3	22	7.3	15	0
Foley	2	39	19.5	24	0
Hunley	1	22	22.0	22	0
Dennison	1	5	5.0	5	0
D. Smith	1	0	0.0	0	0
Wilson	1	−5	−5.0	−5	0
Broncos	18	318	17.7	56	2
Opponents	16	363	22.7	78t	2

Punting	No.	Yds.	Avg.	In 20	LG
Horan	21	864	41.1	8	50
Weil	34	1344	39.5	5	55
Norman	30	1168	38.9	2	57
Broncos	86	3376	39.3	15	57
Opponents	86	3689	42.9	18	59

Punt Returns	No.	FC	Yds.	Avg.	LG	TD
Willhite	42	8	468	11.1	70t	1
Johnson	3	0	36	12.0	19	0
M. Jackson	2	0	7	3.5	6	0
Harden	1	0	41	41.0	41t	1
Broncos	48	8	552	11.5	70t	2
Opponents	40	16	362	9.1	30	0

Kickoff Returns	No.	Yds.	Avg.	LG	TD
Bell	23	531	23.1	42	0
Lang	21	480	22.9	42	0
Willhite	3	35	11.7	23	0
Hunley	2	11	5.5	6	0
Johnson	2	21	10.5	21	0
M. Jackson	1	16	16.0	16	0
Ryan	1	0	0.0	0	0
Broncos	53	1094	20.6	42	0
Opponents	65	1299	20.0	51	0

Sacks	No.
Jones	13.5
Mecklenburg	9.5
Fletcher	5.5
Gilbert	4.0
Robbins	4.0
Woodard	3.0
Townsend	2.5
Comeaux	1.0
Dennison	1.0
Lilly	1.0
Ryan	1.0
D. Smith	1.0
Hunley	0.5
T. Jackson	0.5
Broncos	49.0
Opponents	38.0

FIRST-ROUND SELECTIONS

(If club had no first-round selection, first player drafted is listed with round in parentheses.)

Year	Player, College, Position
1960	Roger LeClerc, Trinity, Connecticut, C
1961	Bob Gaiters, New Mexico State, RB
1962	Merlin Olsen, Utah State, DT
1963	Kermit Alexander, UCLA, CB
1964	Bob Brown, Nebraska, T
1965	Dick Butkus, Illinois, LB (2)
1966	Jerry Shay, Purdue, DT
1967	Floyd Little, Syracuse, RB
1968	Curley Culp, Arizona State, DE (2)
1969	Grady Cavness, Texas-El Paso, DB (2)
1970	Bob Anderson, Colorado, RB
1971	Marv Montgomery, Southern California, T
1972	Riley Odoms, Houston, TE
1973	Otis Armstrong, Purdue, RB
1974	Randy Gradishar, Ohio State, LB
1975	Louis Wright, San Jose State, DB
1976	Tom Glassic, Virginia, G
1977	Steve Schindler, Boston College, G
1978	Don Latimer, Miami, DT
1979	Kelvin Clark, Nebraska, T
1980	Rulon Jones, Utah State, DE (2)
1981	Dennis Smith, Southern California, DB
1982	Gerald Willhite, San Jose State, RB
1983	Chris Hinton, Northwestern, G
1984	Andre Townsend, Mississippi, DE (2)
1985	Steve Sewell, Oklahoma, RB
1986	Jim Juriga, Illinois, T (4)
1987	Ricky Nattiel, Florida, WR

Denver Broncos 1987 Veteran Roster

No.	Name	Pos.	Ht.	Wt.	Birth-date	NFL Exp.	College	Hometown	How Acq.	'86 Games/ Starts
35	Bell, Ken	RB-KR	5-10	190	11/16/64	2	Boston College	Greenwich, Conn.	FA-'86	16/0
54	Bishop, Keith	C-G	6-3	265	3/10/57	7	Baylor	La Jolla, Calif.	D6-'80	16/14
64	Bryan, Billy	C	6-2	255	9/21/55	10	Duke	Burlington, N.C.	D4-'77	16/16
69	Colorito, Tony	NT	6-5	260	9/8/64	2	Southern California	Brooklyn, N.Y.	D5-'86	15/0
59	Comeaux, Darren	LB	6-1	227	4/15/60	6	Arizona State	San Diego, Calif.	FA-'82	16/0
63	†Cooper, Mark	G	6-5	267	2/14/60	5	Miami	Miami, Fla.	D2-'83	8/4
55	Dennison, Rick	LB	6-3	220	6/22/58	6	Colorado State	Kalispel, Mont.	FA-'82	16/2
7	Elway, John	QB	6-3	210	6/28/60	5	Stanford	Port Angeles, Wash.	T(Ind)-'83	16/16
73	Fletcher, Simon	DE	6-5	240	2/18/62	3	Houston	Bay City, Tex.	D2b-'85	16/2
43	Foley, Steve	S	6-3	190	11/11/53	11	Tulane	New Orleans, La.	D8-'75	16/15
62	Freeman, Mike	G	6-3	256	10/13/61	3	Arizona	Mt. Holly, N.J.	FA-'84	3/0
90	Gilbert, Freddie	DE	6-4	275	4/8/62	2	Georgia	Griffin, Ga.	SD1-'84	15/0
85	Hackett, Joey	TE	6-5	267	9/29/58	2	Elon College	Greensboro, N.C.	FA-'86	16/4
31	Harden, Mike	CB	6-1	192	2/16/59	8	Michigan	Memphis, Tenn.	D5a-'80	16/16
36	Haynes, Mark	CB	5-11	195	11/6/58	8	Colorado	Kansas City, Kan.	T(NYG)-'86	11/0
2	Horan, Mike	P	5-11	190	2/1/59	4	Long Beach State	Orange, Calif.	FA-'86	4/0
60	Howard, Paul	G	6-3	260	9/12/50	14	Brigham Young	San Jose, Calif.	D3a-'73	15/13
98	Hunley, Ricky	LB	6-2	238	11/11/61	4	Arizona	Petersburg, Va.	T(Cin)-'84	16/15
80	Jackson, Mark	WR	5-9	174	7/23/63	2	Purdue	Chicago, Ill.	D6b-'86	16/1
82	Johnson, Vance	WR	5-11	174	3/13/63	3	Arizona	Trenton, N.J.	D2a-'85	12/7
75	Jones, Rulon	DE	6-6	260	3/25/58	8	Utah State	Salt Lake City, Utah	D2-'80	16/16
3	†Karlis, Rich	K	6-0	180	5/23/59	6	Cincinnati	Salem, Ohio	FA-'82	16/0
88	Kay, Clarence	TE	6-2	237	7/30/61	4	Georgia	Seneca, S.C.	D7-'84	13/12
71	†Kragen, Greg	NT	6-3	245	3/4/62	3	Utah State	Chicago, Ill.	FA-'85	16/14
8	Kubiak, Gary	QB	6-0	192	8/15/61	5	Texas A&M	Houston, Tex.	D8-'83	16/0
33	Lang, Gene	RB	5-10	196	3/15/62	4	Louisiana State	Pass Christian, Miss.	D11-'84	15/2
76	Lanier, Ken	T	6-3	269	7/8/59	7	Florida State	Columbus, Ohio	D5-'81	16/16
22	Lilly, Tony	S	6-0	199	2/16/62	4	Florida	Alexandria, Va.	D3-'84	16/1
77	Mecklenburg, Karl	DE-LB	6-3	230	9/1/60	5	Minnesota	Edina, Minn.	D12-'83	16/16
87	†Micho, Bobby	TE	6-3	240	3/7/62	3	Texas	Omaha, Neb.	W(SD)-'86	4/0
89	Mobley, Orson	TE	6-5	256	3/4/63	2	Salem College	Brooksville, Fla.	D6a-'86	15/3
74	Remsberg, Dan	T	6-6	275	4/7/62	2	Abilene Christian	Temple, Tex.	FA-'86	16/1
48	Robbins, Randy	S	6-2	189	9/14/62	4	Arizona	Casa Grande, Ariz.	D4-'84	16/1
50	Ryan, Jim	LB	6-1	218	5/18/57	9	William & Mary	Bellmawr, N.J.	FA-'79	16/14
84	†Sampson, Clint	WR	5-11	183	1/4/61	5	San Diego State	Los Angeles, Calif.	D3-'83	15/5
30	Sewell, Steve	RB-WR	6-3	210	4/2/63	3	Oklahoma	San Francisco, Calif.	D1-'85	11/2
49	Smith, Dennis	S	6-3	200	2/3/59	7	Southern California	Santa Monica, Calif.	D1-'81	14/14
70	Studdard, Dave	T	6-4	260	11/22/55	9	Texas	San Antonio, Tex.	FA-'79	15/15
61	Townsend, Andre	DE-NT	6-3	265	10/8/62	4	Mississippi	Chicago, Ill.	D2-'84	16/16
81	Watson, Steve	WR	6-4	195	5/28/57	9	Temple	Baltimore, Md.	FA-'79	16/16
47	†Willhite, Gerald	RB	5-10	200	5/30/59	6	San Jose State	Sacramento, Calif.	D1-'82	16/12
45	Wilson, Steve	CB	5-10	195	8/25/57	9	Howard	Los Angeles, Calif.	FA-'82	16/0
23	Winder, Sammy	RB	5-11	203	7/15/59	6	Southern Mississippi	Madison, Miss.	D5-'82	16/15
52	Woodard, Ken	LB	6-1	218	1/22/60	6	Tuskegee Institute	Detroit, Mich.	D10-'82	16/1
20	Wright, Louis	CB	6-3	200	1/31/53	13	San Jose State	Gilmer, Tex.	D1-'75	16/16

†Option playout; subject to developments.

Retired—Rubin Carter, 12-year nose tackle, 5 games in '86; Tom Jackson, 14-year linebacker, 16 games in '86.

Also played with the Broncos in '86—RB Tony Boddie (1 game), T Winford Hood (9), S Daniel Hunter (10), P Chris Norman (6), QB Scott Stankavage (active for 1 game but did not play), P Jack Weil (6).

COACHING STAFF

Head Coach, Dan Reeves

Pro Career: Became ninth head coach in Broncos history on February 28, 1981, after spending entire pro career as both player and coach with Dallas Cowboys. Reeves's Broncos won the AFC Western Division title and AFC championship in 1986 after going 11-5 in the regular season. Led Denver to an 11-5 record in 1985, barely missing a playoff berth. Guided Broncos to AFC West championship with a 13-3 record in 1984, and a 9-7 mark and playoff berth in 1983. His teams were 10-6 in 1981 and 2-7 in 1982. He joined the Cowboys as a free agent running back in 1965 and became a member of the coaching staff in 1970 when he undertook the dual role of player-coach for two seasons. Was Cowboys offensive backfield coach from 1972-76 and became offensive coordinator in 1977. Was an all-purpose running back during his eight seasons as a player, rushing for 1,990 yards and catching 129 passes for 1,693. Career record: 58-36.

Background: Quarterback at South Carolina from 1962-64 and was inducted into the school's Hall of Fame in 1978.

Personal: Born January 19, 1944, Rome, Ga. Dan and his wife, Pam, live in Denver and have three children—Dana, Laura, and Lee.

Assistant Coaches

Marvin Bass, special assistant; born August 28, 1919, Norfolk, Va., lives in Denver. Tackle William & Mary 1940-42. No pro playing experience. College coach: William & Mary 1944-48, 1950-51 (head coach), North Carolina 1949, 1953-55, South Carolina 1956-59, 1961-65, Georgia Tech 1960, Richmond 1973. Pro coach: Washington Redskins 1952, Montreal Beavers (Continental League) 1966-67, Montreal Alouettes (CFL) 1968, Buffalo Bills 1969-71, Birmingham Americans (WFL) 1974-75, joined Broncos in 1982.

Rubin Carter, assistant defensive line; born December 12, 1952, Pompano Beach, Fla., lives in Aurora, Colo. Nose tackle Miami 1972-74. Pro nose tackle Denver Broncos 1975-86. Pro coach: First year with Broncos.

Joe Collier, assistant head coach, defense; born June 7, 1932, Rock Island, Ill., lives in Denver. End Northwestern 1950-53. No pro playing experience. College coach: Western Illinois 1957-59. Pro coach: Boston Patriots 1960-62, Buffalo Bills 1963-68 (head coach 1966-68), joined Broncos in 1969.

Chan Gailey, tight ends, wide receivers; born January 5, 1952, Americus, Ga., lives in Denver. Quarterback Florida 1971-74. No pro playing experience. College coach: Troy State 1976-77, 1983-84 (head coach), Air Force Academy 1978-82. Pro coach: Joined Broncos in 1985.

Alex Gibbs, head offensive line, running game; born February 11, 1941, Morganton, N.C., lives in Denver. Running back-defensive back Davidson 1959-63. No pro playing experience. College coach: Duke 1969-70, Kentucky 1971-72, West Virginia 1973-74, Ohio State 1975-78, Auburn 1979-81, Georgia 1982-83. Pro coach: Joined Broncos in 1984.

Stan Jones, defensive line; born November 24, 1931, Altoona, Pa., lives in Denver. Tackle Maryland 1950-53. Pro lineman Chicago Bears 1954-65, Washington Redskins 1966. Pro coach: Denver Broncos 1967-71, Buffalo Bills 1972-75, rejoined Broncos in 1976.

Al Miller, strength and conditioning; born August 29, 1947, El Dorado, Ark., lives in Denver. Wide receiver Northeast Louisiana 1966-69. No pro playing experience. College coach: Northwestern Louisiana 1974-78, Mississippi State 1980, Northeast Louisiana 1981, Alabama 1982-84. Pro coach: Joined Broncos in 1985.

Myrel Moore, linebackers; born March 9, 1934, Sebastopol, Calif., lives in Denver. Receiver California-Davis 1955-57. Pro defensive back Washington Redskins 1958. College coach: Santa Ana, Calif., J.C. 1959-62, California 1963-71. Pro coach: Denver Broncos 1972-77, Oakland Raiders 1978-79, rejoined Broncos in 1982.

Nick Nicolau, running backs, play-action passing game; born May 5, 1933, New York, N.Y., lives in Denver. Running back Southern Connecticut 1957-59. No pro playing experience. College coach: Southern Connecticut 1960, Springfield 1961, Bridgeport 1962-69 (head coach 1965-69), Massachusetts 1970, Connecticut 1971-72, Kentucky 1973-75, Kent State 1976. Pro coach: Hamilton Tiger-Cats (CFL) 1977, Montreal Alouettes (CFL) 1978-79, New Orleans Saints 1980, joined Broncos in 1981.

Mike Nolan, special teams; born March 7, 1959, Baltimore, Md., lives in Denver. Safety Oregon 1977-80. No pro playing experience. College coach: Stanford 1982-83, Rice 1984-85, Louisiana State 1986. Pro coach: First year with Broncos.

Mike Shanahan, offensive coordinator, quarterbacks; born August 24, 1952, Oak Park, Ill., lives in Denver. Quarterback Eastern Illinois 1970-73. No pro playing experience. College coach: Oklahoma 1975-76, Northern Arizona 1977, Eastern Illinois 1978, Minnesota 1979, Florida 1980-83. Pro coach: Joined Broncos in 1984.

Charlie West, defensive backs; born August 31, 1946, Big Spring, Tex., lives in Denver. Defensive back Texas-El Paso 1963-67. Pro defensive back Minnesota Vikings 1968-73, Detroit Lions 1974-77, Denver Broncos 1978-79. College coach: MacAlister 1981, California 1982. Pro coach: Joined Broncos in 1983.

Denver Broncos 1987 First-Year Roster

Name	Pos.	Ht.	Wt.	Birth-date	College	Hometown	How Acq.
Andrews, Mitch (1)	TE	6-1	240	3/4/64	Louisiana State	Monroe, La.	FA
Babyar, Chris (1)	T-G	6-4	265	6/1/62	Illinois	Schaumburg, Ill.	FA
Baran, Dave (1)	T-G	6-5	280	6/28/63	UCLA	Vineland, N.J.	FA
Belcher, Kevin (1)	T	6-6	300	11/9/61	Wisconsin	Torrance, Calif.	FA
Bell, Mickey (1)	WR	5-9	195	8/6/62	Utah State	Glendale, Ariz.	FA
Benson, Jeff (1)	T	6-6	290	8/22/63	Southern California	Costa Mesa, Calif.	FA
Braxton, Tyrone	CB	5-11	174	12/17/64	North Dakota State	Madison, Wis.	D12
Brooks, Michael	LB	6-1	235	10/2/64	Louisiana State	Rustin, La.	D3
Caldwell, Scott (1)	RB	5-11	200	2/8/63	Texas-Arlington	Grand Prairie, Tex.	FA
Cameron, Dallas (1)	LB	6-2	242	11/6/63	Miami	Melbourne, Fla.	FA-'86
Christensen, Jeff (1)	QB	6-3	195	1/8/61	Eastern Illinois	Saybrook, Ill.	FA
Clendenen, Mike (1)	K	5-11	190	6/12/63	Houston	Houston, Tex.	FA
Demerritt, James (1)	RB	6-0	225	5/31/63	Jackson State	Miami, Fla.	FA
Dudek, Joe (1)	RB	6-0	181	1/22/64	Plymouth State	Worcester, Mass.	FA-'86
Fairbanks, Don (1)	LB	6-3	250	2/13/64	Colorado	Wheat Ridge, Colo.	FA
Foggie, Gerald (1)	RB	6-0	225	1/28/64	South Carolina State	Greenville, S.C.	FA
Johnson, Tracy (1)	LB	6-1	235	4/3/62	Morningside College	Omaha, Neb.	FA
Juriga, Jim (1)	G-T	6-6	269	9/12/64	Illinois	Fort Wayne, Ind.	D4-'86
Kartz, Keith (1)	T-G-C	6-4	260	5/5/63	California	Las Vegas, Nev.	FA
King, David (1)	CB-S	5-9	175	5/19/63	Auburn	Mobile, Ala.	FA
Klostermann, Bruce (1)	LB	6-4	225	4/17/63	South Dakota State	Dubuque, Iowa	D8-'86
Marshall, Warren	RB	6-0	216	7/24/64	James Madison	High Point, N.C.	D6
Massie, Rick (1)	WR	6-1	185	1/16/60	Kentucky	Paris, Ky.	FA
May, Dean (1)	QB	6-5	225	5/26/62	Louisville	Orlando, Fla.	FA
Miles, Paul (1)	RB	5-10	200	7/11/63	Nebraska	Orange, N.J.	FA
Morgan, Dan	G	6-6	285	2/2/64	Penn State	Wheeling, W. Va.	D8
Munford, Marc	LB	6-2	231	2/14/65	Nebraska	Lincoln, Neb.	D4
Nattiel, Ricky	WR	5-9	180	1/25/66	Florida	Gainesville, Fla.	D1
Neal, Tommy	RB	5-10	210	6/5/65	Maryland	Olney, Md.	D11b
O'Brien, Chris (1)	K	6-0	180	8/5/64	San Diego State	Menlo Park, Calif.	FA
Olderman, Bob (1)	T	6-5	270	6/5/62	Virginia	Atlanta, Ga.	FA
O'Malley, Steve (1)	NT-DE	6-3	260	12/7/62	Northern Illinois	Chicago, Ill.	FA
Pickens, Lyle (1)	CB-S	5-10	165	9/5/64	Colorado	Van Nuys, Calif.	FA
Pieper, John (1)	P	6-1	200	5/3/61	Concordia	Minneapolis, Minn.	FA
Plummer, Bruce	S	6-1	197	9/1/64	Mississippi State	Bogalusa, La.	D9
Roberts, Steve	DE	6-5	238	12/8/63	Washington	Detroit, Mich.	D11a
Rolle, Gary (1)	WR	5-11	174	2/16/62	Florida	Augsburg, Germany	FA-'86
Short, Stan (1)	G-T	6-4	269	9/20/63	Penn State	Fort Riley, Kan.	FA-'86
Strozier, Wilbur	T-TE	6-4	264	11/12/64	Georgia	La Grange, Ga.	D7
Swanson, Shane (1)	WR	5-9	200	10/4/62	Nebraska	Hershey, Neb.	FA
Wagner, Bryan (1)	K	6-1	190	3/28/62	Cal State-Northridge	Chula Vista, Calif.	FA
Weiler, Andrew (1)	K	5-11	185	11/25/62	New Mexico State	Temple City, Calif.	FA
Wilkinson, Rafe	LB	6-3	235	12/28/65	Richmond	Redwood City, Calif.	D10
Winn, Bryant (1)	LB	6-4	240	11/7/62	Houston	Memphis, Tenn.	FA
Woodard, Raymond (1)	DE	6-6	290	8/20/61	Texas	Lufkin, Tex.	FA-'86

The term NFL Rookie is defined as a player who is in his first season of professional football and has not been on the roster of another professional football team for any regular-season or postseason games. A Rookie is designated by an "R" on NFL rosters. Players who have been active in another professional football league or players who have NFL experience, including either preseason training camp or being on an active roster for fewer than three regular-season or postseason games, are termed NFL First-Year Players. An NFL First-Year Player is designated by a "1" on NFL rosters. Thereafter, a player on an NFL active roster for at least three regular-season or postseason games is credited with an additional year of NFL playing experience.

NOTES

American Football Conference Central Division

Team Colors: Columbia Blue, Scarlet, and White

Post Office Box 1516
Houston, Texas 77001
Telephone: (713) 797-9111

Club Officials

President: K. S. (Bud) Adams, Jr.
Executive Vice President-General Manager: Ladd K. Herzeg
Vice President-Player Personnel: Mike Holovak
Director of Administration: Rick Nichols
Director of Media Relations: Chip Namias
Director of Public Relations: Gregg Stengel
Ticket Manager: Mike Mullis
Head Trainer: Brad Brown
Assistant Trainer: Don Moseley
Equipment Manager: Gordon Batty

Stadium: Astrodome • **Capacity:** 50,599
Loop 610, Kirby and Fannin Streets
Houston, Texas 77054

Playing Surface: AstroTurf

Training Camp: Angelo State University
San Angelo, Texas 76901

1987 Schedule

Preseason

Aug. 13	**Kansas City**	7:00
Aug. 22	at New Orleans	7:00
Aug. 29	at Indianapolis	7:30
Sept. 5	at Dallas	8:00

Regular Season

Sept. 13	**Los Angeles Rams**	12:00
Sept. 20	at Buffalo	1:00
Sept. 27	**Los Angeles Raiders**	12:00
Oct. 4	at Denver	2:00
Oct. 11	at Cleveland	1:00
Oct. 18	**New England**	12:00
Oct. 25	**Atlanta**	12:00
Nov. 1	at Cincinnati	1:00
Nov. 8	at San Francisco	1:00
Nov. 15	at Pittsburgh	1:00
Nov. 22	**Cleveland**	12:00
Nov. 29	at Indianapolis	1:00
Dec. 6	**San Diego**	12:00
Dec. 13	at New Orleans	12:00
Dec. 20	**Pittsburgh**	12:00
Dec. 27	**Cincinnati**	12:00

Oilers Coaching History

(170-225-6)

1960-61	Lou Rymkus*	12-7-1
1961	Wally Lemm	10-0-0
1962-63	Frank (Pop) Ivy	17-12-0
1964	Sammy Baugh	4-10-0
1965	Hugh Taylor	4-10-0
1966-70	Wally Lemm	28-40-4
1971	Ed Hughes	4-9-1
1972-73	Bill Peterson**	1-18-0
1973-74	Sid Gillman	8-15-0
1975-80	O.A. (Bum) Phillips	59-38-0
1981-83	Ed Biles***	8-23-0
1983	Chuck Studley	2-8-0
1984-85	Hugh Campbell****	8-22-0
1985-86	Jerry Glanville	5-13-0

*Released after five games in 1961
**Released after five games in 1973
***Resigned after six games in 1983
****Released after 14 games in 1985

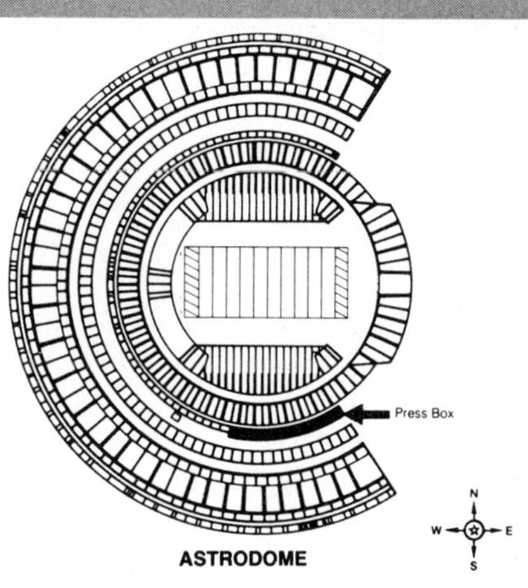

ASTRODOME

Record Holders

Individual Records—Career

Category	Name	Performance
Rushing (Yds.)	Earl Campbell, 1978-1984	8,574
Passing (Yds.)	George Blanda, 1960-66	19,149
Passing (TDs)	George Blanda, 1960-66	165
Receiving (No.)	Charley Hennigan, 1960-66	410
Receiving (Yds.)	Ken Burrough, 1971-1981	6,907
Interceptions	Jim Norton, 1960-68	45
Punting (Avg.)	Jim Norton, 1960-68	42.3
Punt Return (Avg.)	Billy Johnson, 1974-1980	13.2
Kickoff Return (Avg.)	Bobby Jancik, 1962-67	26.4
Field Goals	George Blanda, 1960-66	91
Touchdowns (Tot.)	Earl Campbell, 1978-1984	73
Points	George Blanda, 1960-66	596

Individual Records—Single Season

Category	Name	Performance
Rushing (Yds.)	Earl Campbell, 1980	1,934
Passing (Yds.)	Warren Moon, 1986	3,489
Passing (TDs)	George Blanda, 1961	36
Receiving (No.)	Charley Hennigan, 1964	101
Receiving (Yds.)	Charley Hennigan, 1961	1,746
Interceptions	Fred Glick, 1963	12
	Mike Reinfeldt, 1979	12
Punting (Avg.)	Jim Norton, 1965	44.2
Punt Return (Avg.)	Billy Johnson, 1977	15.4
Kickoff Return (Avg.)	Ken Hall, 1960	31.2
Field Goals	Tony Zendejas, 1986	22
Touchdowns (Tot.)	Earl Campbell, 1979	19
Points	George Blanda, 1960	115

Individual Records—Single Game

Category	Name	Performance
Rushing (Yds.)	Billy Cannon, 12-10-61	216
Passing (Yds.)	George Blanda, 10-29-61	464
Passing (TDs)	George Blanda, 11-19-61	7
Receiving (No.)	Charley Hennigan, 10-13-61	13
Receiving (Yds.)	Charley Hennigan, 10-13-61	272
Interceptions	Many times	3
	Last time by Willie Alexander, 11-14-71	
Field Goals	Skip Butler, 10-12-75	6
Touchdowns (Tot.)	Billy Cannon, 12-10-61	5
Points	Billy Cannon, 12-10-61	30

1986 Team Statistics

	Oilers	Opp.
Total First Downs	299	285
Rushing	101	102
Passing	179	137
Penalty	19	46
Third Down: Made/Att.	88/233	79/223
Fourth Down: Made/Att.	4/13	6/12
Total Net Yards	5149	5034
Avg. Per Game	321.8	314.6
Total Plays	1089	1054
Avg. Per Play	4.7	4.8
Net Yards Rushing	1700	2035
Avg. Per Game	106.3	127.2
Total Rushes	490	532
Net Yards Passing	3449	2999
Avg. Per Game	215.6	187.4
Tackled/Yards Lost	48/394	32/201
Gross Yards	3843	3200
Att./Completions	551/288	490/228
Completion Pct.	52.3	46.5
Had Intercepted	31	16
Punts/Avg.	89/41.1	94/39.5
Net Punting Avg.	35.7	33.3
Penalties/Yards Lost	121/1018	85/674
Fumbles/Ball Lost	28/12	31/16
Touchdowns	30	39
Rushing	13	13
Passing	14	25
Returns	3	1
Avg. Time of Possession	30:33	29:27

1986 Team Record

Preseason (4-0)

Date	Result		Opponents
8/5	W	17-14	at L.A. Rams
8/16	W	23-20	Buffalo
8/23	W	24-13	New Orleans
8/30	W	17-14	at Dallas
		81-61	

Regular Season (5-11)

Date	Result		Opponents	Att.
9/7	W	31- 3	at Green Bay	54,065
9/14	L	20-23	Cleveland	46,049
9/21	L	13-27	at Kansas City	43,699
9/28	L	16-22	Pittsburgh (OT)	42,001
10/5	L	13-24	at Detroit	41,960
10/12	L	7-20	Chicago	46,026
10/19	L	28-31	at Cincinnati	53,844
10/26	L	17-28	L.A. Raiders	41,641
11/2	L	7-28	at Miami	43,804
11/9	W	32-28	Cincinnati	32,130
11/16	L	10-21	at Pittsburgh	49,724
11/23	W	31-17	Indianapolis	31,792
11/30	L	10-13	at Cleveland (OT)	62,309
12/7	L	0-27	at San Diego	40,103
12/14	W	23-10	Minnesota	32,738
12/21	W	16- 7	Buffalo	31,409

(OT) Overtime

Score by Periods

Oilers	57	70	71	76	0	—	274
Opponents	37	131	71	81	9	—	329

Attendance

Home 303,786 Away 389,508 Total 693,294
Single game home record, 55,452 (12-4-80)
Single season home record, 400,156 (1980)

1986 Individual Statistics

Scoring	TD R	TD P	TD Rt	PAT	FG	Saf	TP
Zendejas	0	0	0	28/29	22/27	0	94
D. Hill	0	5	0	0/0	0/0	0	30
Wallace	3	2	0	0/0	0/0	0	30
Givins	1	3	0	0/0	0/0	0	24
Rozier	4	0	0	0/0	0/0	0	24
Pinkett	2	1	0	0/0	0/0	0	18
Moon	2	0	0	0/0	0/0	0	12
Woolfolk	0	2	0	0/0	0/0	0	12
Donaldson	0	0	1	0/0	0/0	0	6
Lyles	0	0	1	0/0	0/0	0	6
Moriarty	1	0	0	0/0	0/0	0	6
Munchak	0	0	1	0/0	0/0	0	6
J. Williams	0	1	0	0/0	0/0	0	6
Oilers	13	14	3	28/30	22/27	0	274
Opponents	13	25	1	38/38	19/29	0	329

Passing	Att.	Comp.	Yds.	Pct.	TD	Int.	Tkld.	Rate
Moon	488	256	3489	52.5	13	26	41/332	62.3
Luck	60	31	341	51.7	1	5	7/62	39.7
Givins	2	0	0	0.0	0	0	0/0	39.6
Rozier	1	1	13	100.0	0	0	0/0	118.8
Oilers	551	288	3843	52.3	14	31	48/394	59.7
Opponents	490	228	3200	46.5	25	16	32/201	71.5

Rushing	Att.	Yds.	Avg.	LG	TD
Rozier	199	662	3.3	19t	4
Pinkett	77	225	2.9	14	2
Wallace	52	218	4.2	19	3
Moon	42	157	3.7	19	2
Givins	9	148	16.4	43t	1
Moriarty	55	137	2.5	9	1
Banks	29	80	2.8	9	0
Woolfolk	23	57	2.5	15	0
Luck	2	12	6.0	8	0
Edwards	1	3	3.0	3	0
Oliver	1	1	1.0	1	0
Oilers	490	1700	3.5	43t	13
Opponents	532	2035	3.8	45	13

Receiving	No.	Yds.	Avg.	LG	TD
D. Hill	65	1112	17.1	81t	5
Givins	61	1062	17.4	60	3
Pinkett	35	248	7.1	20	1
Woolfolk	28	314	11.2	30	2
Rozier	24	180	7.5	23	0
J. Williams	22	227	10.3	33	1
Drewrey	18	299	16.6	31	0
Wallace	17	177	10.4	35t	2
Banks	7	71	10.1	17	0
T. Smith	4	72	18.0	25	0
Akiu	4	67	16.8	27	0
Moriarty	2	16	8.0	17	0
Oliver	1	−2	−2.0	−2	0
Oilers	288	3843	13.3	81t	14
Opponents	228	3200	14.0	85t	25

Interceptions	No.	Yds.	Avg.	LG	TD
Lyday	3	24	8.0	24	0
Allen	3	20	6.7	18	0
Brown	2	34	17.0	38	0
Eason	2	16	8.0	11	0
R. Johnson	2	6	3.0	6	0
Lyles	2	0	0.0	0	0
Bostic	1	0	0.0	0	0
Donaldson	1	0	0.0	0	0
Oilers	16	100	6.3	38	0
Opponents	31	325	10.5	36	1

Punting	No.	Yds.	Avg.	In 20	LG
L. Johnson	88	3623	41.2	26	66
Zendejas	1	36	36.0	1	36
Oilers	89	3659	41.1	27	66
Opponents	94	3713	39.5	16	61

Punt Returns	No.	FC	Yds.	Avg.	LG	TD
Drewrey	34	13	262	7.7	25	0
Givins	8	0	80	10.0	17	0
Pinkett	1	2	−1	−1.0	−1	0
Oilers	43	15	341	7.9	25	0
Opponents	40	21	303	7.6	41	0

Kickoff Returns	No.	Yds.	Avg.	LG	TD
Drewrey	25	500	20.0	32	0
Pinkett	26	519	20.0	48	0
Tasker	3	65	21.7	24	0
Riley	2	17	8.5	10	0
Woolfolk	2	38	19.0	21	0
Madsen	1	0	0.0	0	0
Oilers	59	1139	19.3	48	0
Opponents	32	695	21.7	44	0

Sacks	No.
Childress	5.0
Meads	3.5
Baker, Dall.-Hou.	3.0
Baker, Hou.	2.0
Byrd	3.0
Lyles	3.0
Abraham	2.0
Bostic	2.0
D. Smith	2.0
Donaldson	1.5
Brown	1.0
Bush	1.0
Fuller	1.0
Golic	1.0
Grimsley	1.0
R. Johnson	1.0
Madsen	1.0
Taylor	1.0
Oilers	32.0
Opponents	48.0

FIRST-ROUND SELECTIONS

(If club had no first-round selection, first player drafted is listed with round in parentheses.)

Year	Player, College, Position
1960	Billy Cannon, Louisiana State, RB
1961	Mike Ditka, Pittsburgh, E
1962	Ray Jacobs, Howard Payne, DT
1963	Danny Brabham, Arkansas, LB
1964	Scott Appleton, Texas, DT
1965	Lawrence Elkins, Baylor, WR
1966	Tommy Nobis, Texas, LB
1967	George Webster, Michigan State, LB
	Tom Regner, Notre Dame, G
1968	Mac Haik, Mississippi, WR (2)
1969	Ron Pritchard, Arizona State, LB
1970	Doug Wilkerson, N. Carolina Central, G
1971	Dan Pastorini, Santa Clara, QB
1972	Greg Sampson, Stanford, DE
1973	John Matuszak, Tampa, DE
	George Amundson, Iowa State, RB
1974	Steve Manstedt, Nebraska, LB (4)
1975	Robert Brazile, Jackson State, LB
	Don Hardeman, Texas A&I, RB
1976	Mike Barber, Louisiana Tech, TE (2)
1977	Morris Towns, Missouri, T
1978	Earl Campbell, Texas, RB
1979	Mike Stensrud, Iowa State, DE (2)
1980	Angelo Fields, Michigan State, T (2)
1981	Michael Holston, Morgan State, WR (3)
1982	Mike Munchak, Penn State, G
1983	Bruce Matthews, Southern California, T
1984	Dean Steinkuhler, Nebraska, T
1985	Ray Childress, Texas A&M, DE
	Richard Johnson, Wisconsin, DB
1986	Jim Everett, Purdue, QB
1987	Alonzo Highsmith, Miami, RB
	Haywood Jeffires, North Carolina St., WR

Houston Oilers 1987 Veteran Roster

No.	Name	Pos.	Ht.	Wt.	Birth-date	NFL Exp.	College	Hometown	How Acq.	'86 Games/Starts
56	Abraham, Robert	LB	6-1	236	7/13/60	6	North Carolina State	Myrtle Beach, S.C.	D3c-'82	16/16
86	†Akiu, Mike	WR	5-9	182	2/12/62	3	Hawaii	Kailua, Hawaii	D7-'85	11/1
29	Allen, Patrick	CB	5-10	179	8/26/61	4	Utah State	Seattle, Wash.	D4b-'84	16/16
75	†Baker, Jesse	DE	6-5	271	7/10/57	9	Jacksonville State	Conyers, Ga.	FA-'86	14/0*
36	Banks, Chuck	RB	6-2	225	1/4/64	2	West Virginia Tech	Baltimore, Md.	D12-'86	13/3
25	†Bostic, Keith	S	6-1	223	1/17/61	5	Michigan	Ann Arbor, Mich.	D2b-'83	16/16
92	†Briehl, Tom	LB	6-3	246	9/8/62	2	Stanford	Phoenix, Ariz.	D4-'85	0*
24	Brown, Steve	CB	5-11	187	3/20/60	5	Oregon	Sacramento, Calif.	D3c-'83	16/16
94	Bush, Frank	LB	6-1	228	1/10/63	3	North Carolina State	Athens, Ga.	D5b-'85	3/3
71	Byrd, Richard	DE	6-3	264	3/20/62	3	Southern Mississippi	Jackson, Miss.	D2b-'85	16/16
79	Childress, Ray	DE	6-6	276	10/20/62	3	Texas A&M	Richardson, Tex.	D1a-'85	16/16
50	Dodge, Kirk	LB	6-1	231	6/4/62	3	Nevada-Las Vegas	San Francisco, Calif.	FA-'86	9/0
31	Donaldson, Jeff	S	6-0	194	4/19/62	4	Colorado	Ft. Collins, Colo.	D9a-'84	16/7
88	†Dressel, Chris	TE	6-4	239	2/7/61	5	Stanford	Placentia, Calif.	D3b-'83	16/0
82	Drewrey, Willie	WR-KR	5-7	164	4/28/63	3	West Virginia	Columbus, N.J.	D11b-'85	15/0
21	Eason, Bo	S	6-2	204	3/10/61	4	California-Davis	Walnut Grove, Calif.	D2b-'84	9/9
51	Fairs, Eric	LB	6-3	235	2/17/64	2	Memphis State	Memphis, Tenn.	FA-'86	12/0
95	Fuller, William	DE	6-3	255	3/8/62	2	North Carolina	Chesapeake, Va.	T(Rams)-'86	13/0
81	Givins, Ernest	WR	5-9	175	9/3/64	2	Louisville	St. Petersburg, Fla.	D2-'86	15/15
68	†Golic, Mike	NT	6-5	272	12/12/62	2	Notre Dame	Cleveland, Ohio	D10-'85	16/9
59	†Grimsley, John	LB	6-2	236	2/25/62	4	Kentucky	Canton, Ohio	D6a-'83	16/10
85	Hill, Drew	WR	5-9	168	2/5/56	8	Georgia Tech	Newman, Ga.	T(Rams)-'85	16/16
72	†Hill, Kent	G	6-5	260	3/7/57	9	Georgia Tech	Americus, Ga.	T(Rams)-'86	15/15*
22	Johnson, Kenny	S	5-11	172	1/7/58	8	Mississippi State	Moss Point, Miss.	W(Atl)-'86	8/2*
11	Johnson, Lee	P	6-1	199	11/2/61	3	Brigham Young	The Woodlands, Tex.	D5c-'85	16/0
23	Johnson, Richard	CB	6-1	190	9/16/63	3	Wisconsin	Harvey, Ill.	D1b-'85	16/0
38	Jordan, Donald	RB	6-0	215	2/9/62	2	Houston	Houston, Tex.	FA-'87	0*
58	Kelley, Mike	C-G	6-5	281	2/27/62	2	Notre Dame	Westfield, Mass.	D3c-'85	0*
37	Kush, Rod	S	6-1	198	12/29/56	7	Nebraska-Omaha	Gretna, Neb.	FA-'85	0*
10	Luck, Oliver	QB	6-2	196	4/5/60	6	West Virginia	Cleveland, Ohio	D2b-'82	4/1
28	Lyday, Allen	S	5-10	197	9/16/60	4	Nebraska	Wichita, Kan.	FA-'84	12/0
93	Lyles, Robert	LB	6-1	225	3/21/61	4	Texas Christian	Los Angeles, Calif.	D5-'84	16/16
98	Madsen, Lynn	DE	6-4	260	8/8/60	2	Washington	Vista, Calif.	SD3-'84	15/0
78	Maggs, Don	T-G	6-5	279	11/1/61	2	Tulane	Youngstown, Ohio	SD2-'84	14/2
47	Maidlow, Steve	LB	6-2	240	6/6/60	4	Michigan State	East Lansing, Mich.	FA-'87	0*
74	†Matthews, Bruce	T	6-4	283	8/8/61	5	Southern California	Arcadia, Calif.	D1-'83	16/16
26	McMillian, Audrey	CB	6-0	190	8/13/62	3	Houston	Carthage, Tex.	W(NE)-'85	16/0
91	Meads, Johnny	LB	6-2	235	6/25/61	4	Nicholls State	Napoleonville, La.	D3-'84	16/13
1	Moon, Warren	QB	6-3	210	11/18/56	4	Washington	Los Angeles, Calif.	FA-'84	15/15
76	†Moran, Eric	T-G	6-5	294	6/10/60	4	Washington	Pleasanton, Calif.	FA-'84	14/4
67	†Morgan, Karl	NT	6-1	255	2/23/61	4	UCLA	Houma, La.	FA-'86	13/0*
63	Munchak, Mike	G	6-3	278	3/5/60	6	Penn State	Scranton, Pa.	D1-'82	6/6
39	Oliver, Hubert	RB	5-10	230	11/12/57	5	Arizona	Elyria, Ohio	FA-'86	6/0*
89	Parks, Jeff	TE	6-4	236	9/14/64	2	Auburn	Gardendale, Ala.	D5-'86	5/0
52	Pennison, Jay	C	6-1	265	9/9/61	2	Nicholls State	Bourg, La.	FA-'86	16/12
20	Pinkett, Allen	RB	5-9	185	1/25/64	2	Notre Dame	Sterling, Va.	D3-'86	16/3
53	Riley, Avon	LB	6-3	240	2/10/58	7	UCLA	Savannah, Ga.	D9-'81	16/6
55	†Romano, Jim	C	6-3	264	9/7/59	6	Penn State	Glen Cove, N.Y.	T(Raiders)-'84	9/9
33	Rozier, Mike	RB	5-10	211	3/1/61	3	Nebraska	Camden, N.J.	SD1-'84	13/13
99	Smith, Doug	NT	6-4	287	6/6/60	3	Auburn	Bayboro, N.C.	D2a-'84	13/7
70	Steinkuhler, Dean	T-G	6-3	275	1/27/61	4	Nebraska	Burr, Neb.	D1-'84	16/16
35	Wallace, Ray	RB	6-0	221	12/3/63	2	Purdue	Indianapolis, Ind.	D6-'86	8/4
69	Williams, Doug	T-G	6-5	285	10/1/62	2	Texas A&M	Cincinnati, Ohio	W(NYJ)-'86	15/2
87	Williams, Jamie	TE	6-4	245	2/25/60	5	Nebraska	Davenport, Iowa	W(TB)-'84	16/16
80	Williams, Oliver	WR	6-2	195	10/17/62	2	Illinois	Gardena, Calif.	FA-'87	0*
12	Witkowski, John	QB	6-1	205	6/18/62	3	Columbia	New York, N.Y.	FA-'86	0*
40	Woolfolk, Butch	RB	6-1	215	3/1/60	6	Michigan	Westfield, N.J.	T(NYG)-'85	10/5
7	Zendejas, Tony	K	5-8	165	5/15/60	3	Nevada-Reno	Chino, Calif.	T(Wash)-'85	15/0

* Baker played 3 games with Dallas, 11 with Houston in '86; Briehl, Kelley, and Kush missed '86 season due to injury; K. Hill played 2 games with L.A. Rams, 13 with Houston; K. Johnson played 7 games with Atlanta, 1 with Houston; Jordan last active with Chicago in '84; Maidlow last active with Buffalo in '85; Morgan played 12 games with Tampa Bay, 1 with Houston; Oliver played 4 games with Indianapolis, 2 with Houston; O. Williams last active with Indianapolis in '85; Witkowski active for 7 games, but did not play.

†Option playout; subject to developments.

Traded—Wide receiver Tim Smith to San Diego.

Also played with Oilers in '86—RB Stan Edwards (3 games), S Larry Griffin (3), RB Larry Moriarty (5), T Harvey Salem (1), WR Steve Tasker (2), DE Malcolm Taylor (3).

COACHING STAFF

Head Coach, Jerry Glanville

Pro Career: Named Houston's head coach on January 20, 1986, after serving as interim coach for last two games of 1985 season. Glanville was the Oilers' defensive coordinator in 1984-85, and has 23 years of coaching experience. He initially coached in the NFL for the Detroit Lions from 1974-76 as the special teams/defense coach. His next NFL position was with the Atlanta Falcons from 1977-82, first serving as defensive backfield/special teams coach before being elevated to defensive coordinator. In 1983, Glanville joined the Buffalo Bills as defensive backfield coach before assuming his duties with the Oilers. Career record: 5-13.

Background: Attended Montana State in 1960 before transferring to Northern Michigan, where he played linebacker from 1961-63. He coached in the Ohio high school system from 1964-66 before accepting an assistant coaching post at Western Kentucky in 1967. From 1968-73, he was an assistant at Georgia Tech, helping the Yellow Jackets to three bowl games.

Personal: Born October 14, 1941, in Detroit, Mich. Jerry and his wife, Brenda, live in Sugar Land, Tex., with their son, Justin.

Assistant Coaches

Tom Bettis, defensive backfield; born March 17, 1933, Chicago, Ill., lives in Sugar Land, Tex. Linebacker-offensive guard Purdue 1951-54. Pro linebacker Green Bay Packers 1955-61, Pittsburgh Steelers 1962, Chicago Bears 1963. Pro coach: Kansas City Chiefs 1966-77 (head coach for final seven games, 1977), St. Louis Cardinals 1978-84, Cleveland Browns 1985, joined Oilers in 1986.

Kim Helton, offensive line; born July 28, 1948, Pensacola, Fla., lives in Sugar Land, Tex. Center Florida 1967-69. No pro playing experience. College coach: Florida 1972-78, Miami 1979-82. Pro coach: Tampa Bay Buccaneers 1983-86, first year with Oilers.

Milt Jackson, receivers; born October 16, 1943, Groesbeck, Tex., lives in Missouri City, Tex. Defensive back Tulsa 1965-66. Pro defensive back San Francisco 49ers 1967. College coach: Oregon State 1973, Rice 1974, California 1975-76, Oregon 1977-78, UCLA 1979. Pro coach: San Francisco 49ers 1980-82, Buffalo Bills 1983-84, Philadelphia Eagles 1985, joined Oilers in 1986.

Dick Jamieson, offensive coordinator-running backs; born November 13, 1937, Streator, Ill., lives in Missouri City, Tex. Quarterback Bradley 1955-58. Pro quarterback Baltimore Colts 1959, New York Titans (AFL) 1960. College coach: Bradley 1962-64, Missouri 1972-77, Indiana State 1978-79. Pro coach: St. Louis Cardinals 1980-85, joined Oilers in 1986.

June Jones, quarterbacks; born February 19, 1953, Portland, Ore., lives in Sugar Land, Tex. Quarterback Hawaii 1973-74, Portland State 1975-76. Pro quarterback Atlanta Falcons 1977-81, Toronto Argonauts (CFL) 1982. College coach: Hawaii 1983. Pro coach: Toronto Argonauts (CFL) 1982, Houston Gamblers (USFL) 1984, Denver Gold (USFL) 1985, first year with Oilers.

Miller McCalmon, special teams-tight ends; born January 9, 1947, Denver, Colo., lives in Missouri City, Tex. Defensive back Tulsa 1967-69. No pro playing experience. College coach: Colorado State 1971-73. Pro coach: Baltimore Colts 1978-79, Buffalo Bills 1980-84, joined Oilers in 1986.

Floyd Reese, linebackers; born August 8, 1948, Springfield, Mo., lives in Sugar Land, Tex. Linebacker UCLA 1967-69. Pro defensive lineman Montreal Alouettes (CFL) 1970. College coach: UCLA 1971-73, Georgia Tech 1974. Pro coach: Detroit Lions 1975-77, San Francisco 49ers 1978, Minnesota Vikings 1979-85, joined Oilers in 1986.

Doug Shively, defensive line; born March 18, 1938, Lexington, Ky., lives in Sugar Land, Tex. End Kentucky 1955-58. No pro playing experience. College coach: Virginia Tech 1960-66, Kentucky 1967-70, Clemson 1971-72, North Carolina 1973. Pro coach: New Orleans Saints 1974-76, Atlanta Falcons 1977-82, Arizona Wranglers (USFL, head coach) 1983, San Diego Chargers 1984, Tampa Bay Buccaneers 1985, joined Oilers in 1986.

Houston Oilers 1987 First-Year Roster

Name	Pos.	Ht.	Wt.	Birth-date	College	Hometown	How Acq.
Banks, Robert	DE-NT-LB	6-5	254	12/10/63	Notre Dame	Hampton, Va.	D7
Bryant, Domingo	S	6-3	176	12/8/63	Texas A&M	Garrison, Tex.	FA
Caldwell, Ralph	LB	6-2	242	1/18/61	Indiana	Los Angeles, Calif.	FA
Carlson, Cody	QB	6-3	203	11/5/63	Baylor	San Antonio, Tex.	D3
Caston, Toby	LB	6-1	235	7/17/65	Louisiana State	Monroe, La.	D6b
Davis, John	T-G	6-4	304	8/22/65	Georgia Tech	Ellijay, Ga.	D11
Dellocono, Neal (1)	LB	6-1	225	6/1/63	UCLA	Baton Rouge, La.	FA
Dixon, Willie	NT	6-2	275	1/8/64	Tulsa	Pocola, Okla.	FA
Duncan, Curtis	WR-KR	5-11	180	1/26/65	Northwestern	Detroit, Mich.	D10
Dusbabek, Mark	LB	6-3	232	6/23/64	Minnesota	Fairbault, Minn.	D4
Fitzpatrick, Tony	NT	6-0	260	4/10/61	Miami	Seminole, Fla.	FA
Gerhart, Todd	RB	5-11	240	12/8/62	Cal State-Fullerton	Norco, Calif.	FA
Highsmith, Alonzo	RB	6-1	235	2/26/65	Miami	Miami, Fla.	D1a
James, Michel	WR	6-0	188	11/19/63	Washington State	Tacoma, Wash.	D8
Jeffires, Haywood	WR	6-2	198	12/12/64	North Carolina State	Greensboro, N.C.	D1b
Johnson, Walter	LB	6-0	241	11/13/63	Louisiana Tech	Ferriday, La.	D2
Jones, Joe	TE	6-4	250	6/26/62	Virginia Tech	Sidman, Va.	FA
Neighbors, Wes	C	6-2	250	2/28/64	Alabama	Huntsville, Ala.	D9
Pettyjohn, Barry	T-G	6-5	285	3/29/64	Pittsburgh	Cincinnati, Ohio	FA
Smith, Al	LB	6-1	230	11/26/64	Utah State	Los Angeles, Calif.	D6a
Stagliano, Victor	RB	6-0	225	7/21/63	Texas-El Paso	Thornwood, N.Y.	FA
Stanberry, Keith	S	6-0	208	9/3/61	Oklahoma	Mt. Pleasant, Tex.	FA
Stroud, Horace	RB	6-1	221	6/1/59	Texas Southern	Tampa, Fla.	FA
Superick, Steve	P	6-0	204	8/9/63	West Virginia	North Brunswick, N.J.	FA
Tillman, Spencer	RB	5-11	206	4/21/64	Oklahoma	Tulsa, Okla.	D5
Valentine, Ira	RB	5-11	212	6/4/63	Texas A&M	Marshall, Tex.	D12
White, Robert	CB-S	6-2	180	11/24/62	Lamar	Warren, Tex.	FA

The term NFL Rookie is defined as a player who is in his first season of professional football and has not been on the roster of another professional football team for any regular-season or postseason games. A Rookie is designated by an "R" on NFL rosters. Players who have been active in another professional football league or players who have NFL experience, including either preseason training camp or being on an active roster for fewer than three regular-season or postseason games, are termed NFL First-Year Players. An NFL First-Year Player is designated by a "1" on NFL rosters. Thereafter, a player on an NFL active roster for at least three regular-season or postseason games is credited with an additional year of NFL playing experience.

NOTES

American Football Conference Eastern Division

Team Colors: Royal Blue, White, and Silver

P.O. Box 24100
Indianapolis, Indiana 46224-0100
Telephone: (317) 297-2658

Club Officials

President-Treasurer: Robert Irsay
Vice President-General Manager: James Irsay
Vice President-General Counsel: Michael G. Chernoff
Assistant General Manager: Bob Terpening
Director of Player Personnel: Jack Bushofsky
Director of Pro Personnel: Clyde Powers
Controller: Kurt Humphrey
Director of Operations: Pete Ward
Director of Public Relations: Craig Kelley
Ticket Manager: Larry Hall
Public Relations Assistant: Anne Phillips
Purchasing Administrator: David Filar
Equipment Manager: Jon Scott
Assistant Equipment Manager: Chris Matlock
Video Director: Marty Heckscher
Assistant Video Director: John Starliper
Head Trainer: Hunter Smith
Assistant Trainer: Dave Hammer

Stadium: Hoosier Dome • **Capacity:** 60,127
100 South Capitol Avenue
Indianapolis, Indiana 46225

Playing Surface: AstroTurf

Training Camp: Anderson College
Anderson, Indiana 46011

1987 Schedule

Preseason

Aug. 15	at Detroit	8:00
Aug. 22	at Minnesota	7:00
Aug. 29	**Houston**	7:30
Sept. 5	**Tampa Bay**	7:30

Regular Season

Sept. 13	**Cincinnati**	12:00
Sept. 20	**Miami**	12:00
Sept. 27	at St. Louis	12:00
Oct. 4	at Buffalo	1:00
Oct. 11	**New York Jets**	12:00
Oct. 18	at Pittsburgh	1:00
Oct. 25	**New England**	1:00
Nov. 1	at New York Jets	1:00
Nov. 8	**San Diego**	1:00
Nov. 15	at Miami	1:00
Nov. 22	at New England	1:00
Nov. 29	**Houston**	1:00
Dec. 6	at Cleveland	1:00
Dec. 13	**Buffalo**	1:00
Dec. 20	at San Diego	1:00
Dec. 27	**Tampa Bay**	1:00

Colts Coaching History

Baltimore 1953-83
(242-237-7)

1953	Keith Molesworth	3-9-0
1954-62	Weeb Ewbank	61-52-1
1963-69	Don Shula	73-26-4
1970-72	Don McCafferty*	26-11-1
1972	John Sandusky	4-5-0
1973-74	Howard Schnellenberger**	4-13-0
1974	Joe Thomas	2-9-0
1975-79	Ted Marchibroda	41-36-0
1980-81	Mike McCormack	9-23-0
1982-84	Frank Kush***	11-28-1
1984	Hal Hunter	0-1-0
1985-86	Rod Dowhower****	5-24-0
1986	Ron Meyer	3-0-0

*Released after five games in 1972
**Released after three games in 1974
***Resigned after 15 games in 1984
****Released after 13 games in 1986

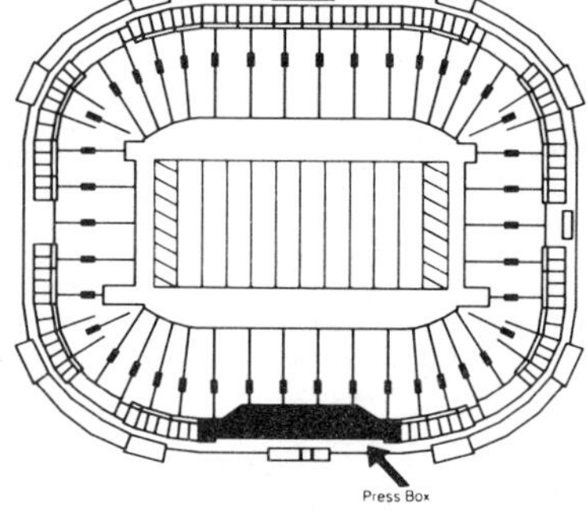

HOOSIER DOME

Record Holders

Individual Records—Career

Category	Name	Performance
Rushing (Yds.)	Lydell Mitchell, 1972-77	5,487
Passing (Yds.)	Johnny Unitas, 1956-1972	39,768
Passing (TDs)	Johnny Unitas, 1956-1972	287
Receiving (No.)	Raymond Berry, 1955-1967	631
Receiving (Yds.)	Raymond Berry, 1955-1967	9,275
Interceptions	Bob Boyd, 1960-68	57
Punting (Avg.)	Rohn Stark, 1982-86	45.2
Punt Return (Avg.)	Wendell Harris, 1964	12.6
Kickoff Return (Avg.)	Jim Duncan, 1969-1971	32.5
Field Goals	Lou Michaels, 1964-69	107
Touchdowns (Tot.)	Lenny Moore, 1956-1967	113
Points	Lenny Moore, 1956-1967	678

Individual Records—Single Season

Category	Name	Performance
Rushing (Yds.)	Lydell Mitchell, 1976	1,200
Passing (Yds.)	Johnny Unitas, 1963	3,481
Passing (TDs)	Johnny Unitas, 1959	32
Receiving (No.)	Joe Washington, 1979	82
Receiving (Yds.)	Raymond Berry, 1960	1,298
Interceptions	Tom Keane, 1953	11
Punting (Avg.)	Rohn Stark, 1985	45.9
Punt Return (Avg.)	Wendell Harris, 1964	12.6
Kickoff Return (Avg.)	Jim Duncan, 1970	35.4
Field Goals	Raul Allegre, 1983	30
Touchdowns (Tot.)	Lenny Moore, 1964	20
Points	Lenny Moore, 1964	120

Individual Records—Single Game

Category	Name	Performance
Rushing (Yds.)	Norm Bulaich, 9-19-71	198
Passing (Yds.)	Johnny Unitas, 9-17-67	401
Passing (TDs)	Gary Cuozzo, 11-14-65	5
Receiving (No.)	Lydell Mitchell, 12-15-74	13
	Joe Washington, 9-2-79	13
Receiving (Yds.)	Raymond Berry, 11-10-57	224
Interceptions	Many times	3
	Last time by Leonard Coleman, 10-12-86	
Field Goals	Many times	5
	Last time by Raul Allegre, 10-30-83	
Touchdowns (Tot.)	Many times	4
	Last time by Lydell Mitchell, 10-12-75	
Points	Many times	24
	Last time by Lydell Mitchell, 10-12-75	

1986 Team Statistics

	Colts	Opp.
Total First Downs	278	334
Rushing	77	123
Passing	173	185
Penalty	28	26
Third Down: Made/Att.	78/225	86/206
Fourth Down: Made/Att.	10/28	1/5
Total Net Yards	4700	5701
Avg. Per Game	293.8	356.3
Total Plays	1046	1051
Avg. Per Play	4.5	5.4
Net Yards Rushing	1491	1962
Avg. Per Game	93.2	122.6
Total Rushes	407	517
Net Yards Passing	3209	3739
Avg. Per Game	200.6	233.7
Tackled/Yards Lost	53/406	24/194
Gross Yards	3615	3933
Att./Completions	586/300	510/306
Completion Pct.	51.2	60.0
Had Intercepted	24	16
Punts/Avg.	81/44.7	67/40.7
Net Punting Avg.	36.9	35.7
Penalties/Yards Lost	99/880	100/728
Fumbles/Ball Lost	41/20	41/19
Touchdowns	27	47
Rushing	10	14
Passing	16	28
Returns	1	5
Avg. Time of Possession	29:12	30:48

1986 Team Record

Preseason (1-3)

Date	Result		Opponents
8/8	L	14-21	at Seattle
8/16	L	21-38	at Chicago
8/23	W	20-13	Detroit
8/30	L	20-23	Minnesota (OT)
		75-95	

Regular Season (3-13)

Date	Result		Opponents	Att.
9/7	L	3-33	at New England	55,208
9/14	L	10-30	at Miami	51,848
9/21	L	7-24	L.A. Rams	59,012
9/28	L	7-26	N.Y. Jets	56,075
10/5	L	14-35	at San Francisco	57,252
10/12	L	14-17	New Orleans	53,512
10/19	L	13-24	at Buffalo	50,050
10/26	L	13-17	Miami	58,350
11/2	L	9-24	Cleveland	57,962
11/9	L	21-30	New England	56,890
11/16	L	16-31	at N.Y. Jets	65,149
11/23	L	17-31	at Houston	31,792
11/30	L	3-17	San Diego	47,950
12/7	W	28-23	at Atlanta	30,397
12/14	W	24-14	Buffalo	52,783
12/21	W	30-24	at L.A. Raiders	41,349

(OT) Overtime

Score by Periods

Colts	51	41	55	82	0	—	229
Opponents	123	101	106	70	0	—	400

Attendance

Home 442,534 Away 383,045 Total 825,579
Single game home record, 61,479 (11-13-83)
Single season home record, 481,305 (1984)

1986 Individual Statistics

Scoring	TD R	TD P	TD Rt	PAT	FG	Saf	TP
Biasucci	0	0	0	26/27	13/25	0	65
Brooks	0	8	0	0/0	0/0	0	48
Bouza	0	5	0	0/0	0/0	0	30
Bentley	3	0	0	0/0	0/0	0	18
McMillan	3	0	0	0/0	0/0	0	18
Beach	0	1	0	0/0	0/0	0	6
Boyer	0	1	0	0/0	0/0	0	6
E. Daniel	0	0	1	0/0	0/0	0	6
Gill	1	0	0	0/0	0/0	0	6
Hogeboom	1	0	0	0/0	0/0	0	6
Sherwin	0	1	0	0/0	0/0	0	6
Trudeau	1	0	0	0/0	0/0	0	6
Wonsley	1	0	0	0/0	0/0	0	6
Leiding	0	0	0	0/0	0/0	1	2
Colts	10	16	1	26/27	13/25	1	229
Opponents	14	28	5	46/47	24/35	0	400

Passing	Att.	Comp.	Yds.	Pct.	TD	Int.	Tkld.	Rate
Trudeau	417	204	2225	48.9	8	18	29/213	53.5
Hogeboom	144	85	1154	59.0	6	6	18/144	81.2
Kiel	25	11	236	44.0	2	0	5/42	104.8
Bentley	0	0	0	—	0	0	1/7	0.0
Colts	586	300	3615	51.2	16	24	53/406	62.5
Opponents	510	306	3933	60.0	28	16	24/194	89.4

Rushing	Att.	Yds.	Avg.	LG	TD
McMillan	189	609	3.2	28	3
Bentley	73	351	4.8	70t	3
Gill	53	228	4.3	18	1
Wonsley	60	214	3.6	46	1
Trudeau	13	21	1.6	8	1
Hogeboom	10	20	2.0	6	1
Kiel	3	20	6.7	9	0
Bouza	1	12	12.0	12	0
Capers	1	11	11.0	11	0
Brooks	4	5	1.3	12	0
Colts	407	1491	3.7	70t	10
Opponents	517	1962	3.8	40	14

Receiving	No.	Yds.	Avg.	LG	TD
Bouza	71	830	11.7	33	5
Brooks	65	1131	17.4	84t	8
McMillan	34	289	8.5	45	0
Beach	25	265	10.6	26	1
Bentley	25	230	9.2	38	0
Boyer	22	237	10.8	38	1
Wonsley	16	175	10.9	60	0
Gill	16	137	8.6	15	0
Capers	9	118	13.1	27	0
LaFleur	7	56	8.0	11	0
Harbour	4	46	11.5	28	0
Sherwin	3	26	8.7	15	1
Murray	2	34	17.0	24	0
Martin	1	41	41.0	41	0
Colts	300	3615	12.1	84t	16
Opponents	306	3933	12.9	72t	28

Interceptions	No.	Yds.	Avg.	LG	TD
Coleman	4	36	9.0	31	0
E. Daniel	3	11	3.7	5	0
Hicks	2	16	8.0	16	0
Bickett	2	10	5.0	10	0
Holt	1	80	80.0	80	0
Hand	1	8	8.0	8	0
Armstrong	1	4	4.0	4	0
Cooks	1	1	1.0	1	0
K. Daniel	1	0	0.0	0	0
Colts	16	166	10.4	80	0
Opponents	24	310	12.9	40	2

Punting	No.	Yds.	Avg.	In 20	LG
Stark	76	3432	45.2	22	63
Kiel	5	190	38.0	0	43
Colts	81	3622	44.7	22	63
Opponents	67	2725	40.7	20	60

Punt Returns	No.	FC	Yds.	Avg.	LG	TD
Brooks	18	7	141	7.8	18	0
Martin	17	5	109	6.4	25	0
Jackson	0	1	0	—	0	0
Colts	35	13	250	7.1	25	0
Opponents	52	6	533	10.3	71t	1

Kickoff Returns	No.	Yds.	Avg.	LG	TD
Bentley	32	687	21.5	37	0
Martin	21	385	18.3	27	0
Brooks	8	143	17.9	24	0
K. Daniel	5	109	21.8	30	0
Gill	5	73	14.6	28	0
Wonsley	2	31	15.5	20	0
Williams	1	15	15.0	15	0
Colts	74	1443	19.5	37	0
Opponents	43	827	19.2	41	0

Sacks	No.
Bickett	5.0
Hand	5.0
Thompson	4.0
Armstrong	3.5
Ahrens	2.0
Broughton	1.0
Cooks	1.0
Kellar	1.0
Odom	1.0
Holt	0.5
Colts	24.0
Opponents	53.0

FIRST-ROUND SELECTIONS

(If club had no first-round selection, first player drafted is listed with round in parentheses.)

Year	Player, College, Position
1953	Billy Vessels, Oklahoma, B
1954	Cotton Davidson, Baylor, B
1955	George Shaw, Oregon, B
	Alan Ameche, Wisconsin, FB
1956	Lenny Moore, Penn State, B
1957	Jim Parker, Ohio State, G
1958	Lenny Lyles, Louisville, B
1959	Jackie Burkett, Auburn, C
1960	Ron Mix, Southern California, T
1961	Tom Matte, Ohio State, RB
1962	Wendell Harris, Louisiana State, S
1963	Bob Vogel, Ohio State, T
1964	Marv Woodson, Indiana, CB
1965	Mike Curtis, Duke, LB
1966	Sam Ball, Kentucky, T
1967	Bubba Smith, Michigan State, DT
	Jim Detwiler, Michigan, RB
1968	John Williams, Minnesota, G
1969	Eddie Hinton, Oklahoma, WR
1970	Norman Bulaich, Texas Christian, RB
1971	Don McCauley, North Carolina, RB
	Leonard Dunlap, North Texas State, DB
1972	Tom Drougas, Oregon, T
1973	Bert Jones, Louisiana State, QB
	Joe Ehrmann, DT, Syracuse
1974	John Dutton, Nebraska, DE
	Roger Carr, Louisiana Tech, WR
1975	Ken Huff, North Carolina, G
1976	Ken Novak, Purdue, DT
1977	Randy Burke, Kentucky, WR
1978	Reese McCall, Auburn, TE
1979	Barry Krauss, Alabama, LB
1980	Curtis Dickey, Texas A&M, RB
	Derrick Hatchett, Texas, DB
1981	Randy McMillan, Pittsburgh, RB
	Donnell Thompson, North Carolina, DT
1982	Johnie Cooks, Mississippi State, LB
	Art Schlichter, Ohio State, QB
1983	John Elway, Stanford, QB
1984	Leonard Coleman, Vanderbilt, DB
	Ron Solt, Maryland, G
1985	Duane Bickett, Southern California, LB
1986	Jon Hand, Alabama, DE
1987	Cornelius Bennett, Alabama, LB

Indianapolis Colts 1987 Veteran Roster

No.	Name	Pos.	Ht.	Wt.	Birth-date	NFL Exp.	College	Hometown	How Acq.	'86 Games/ Starts
57	Ahrens, Dave	LB	6-3	245	12/5/58	7	Wisconsin	Oregon, Wis.	T(StL)-'85	16/10
79	Armstrong, Harvey	NT	6-3	261	12/29/59	5	Southern Methodist	Houston, Tex.	FA-'86	16/1
72	Baldischwiler, Karl	T	6-5	276	1/19/56	9	Oklahoma	Okmulgee, Okla.	T(Det)-'83	15/2
81	Beach, Pat	TE	6-4	244	12/28/59	5	Washington State	Pullman, Wash.	D6-'82	16/16
20	Bentley, Albert	RB	5-11	215	8/15/60	3	Miami	Immokalee, Fla.	SD2-'84	12/3
4	Biasucci, Dean	K	6-0	198	7/25/62	3	Western Carolina	Niagara Falls, N.Y.	FA-'86	16/0
50	Bickett, Duane	LB	6-5	244	12/1/62	3	Southern California	Los Angeles, Calif.	D1-'85	16/16
85	Bouza, Matt	WR	6-3	215	4/8/59	6	California	Sacramento, Calif.	FA-'82	16/14
84	Boyer, Mark	TE	6-4	232	9/16/62	3	Southern California	Huntington Beach, Calif.	D9-'85	16/7
80	Brooks, Bill	WR	5-11	190	4/6/64	2	Boston University	Milton, Mass.	D4-'86	16/12
68	Broughton, Willie	DE	6-5	282	9/9/64	3	Miami	Fort Pierce, Fla.	D4-'85	15/8
71	Call, Kevin	T	6-7	288	11/13/61	4	Colorado State	Boulder, Colo.	D5b-'84	16/16
47	Clinkscale, Dextor	S	5-11	195	4/13/58	7	South Carolina State	Greenville, S.C.	FA-'86	5/0
31	Coleman, Leonard	S	6-2	211	1/30/62	3	Vanderbilt	Boynton Beach, Fla.	D1-'84	16/16
98	Cooks, Johnie	LB	6-4	243	11/23/58	6	Mississippi State	Leland, Miss.	D1a-'82	15/15
38	Daniel, Eugene	CB	5-11	184	5/4/61	4	Louisiana State	Baton Rouge, La.	D8-'84	15/15
23	†Daniel, Kenny	CB	5-10	180	6/1/60	3	San Jose State	Martinez, Calif.	T(Wash)-'86	15/2
53	Donaldson, Ray	C	6-4	281	5/17/58	8	Georgia	Rome, Ga.	D2a-'80	16/16
44	Gill, Owen	RB	6-1	230	2/19/62	3	Iowa	Brooklyn, N.Y.	W(Sea)-'85	16/1
25	Glasgow, Nesby	S	5-10	191	4/15/57	9	Washington	Los Angeles, Calif.	D8a-'79	14/14
90	Haines, John	NT-DE	6-7	266	12/16/61	3	Texas	Fort Worth, Tex.	FA-'86	11/0
78	Hand, Jon	DE	6-6	280	11/13/63	2	Alabama	Sylacauga, Ala.	D1-'86	15/15
87	Harbour, James	WR	6-0	192	11/10/62	2	Mississippi	Meridian, Miss.	D7-'85	9/0
29	Hicks, Dwight	S	6-1	192	4/5/56	9	Michigan	Mount Holly, N.J.	FA-'86	9/6
75	Hinton, Chris	G	6-4	285	7/31/61	5	Northwestern	Chicago, Ill.	T(Den)-'83	16/16
7	Hogeboom, Gary	QB	6-4	200	8/21/58	8	Central Michigan	Grand Rapids, Mich.	T(Dall)-'86	5/5
21	†Holt, John	CB	5-11	180	5/14/59	7	West Texas State	Lawton, Okla.	T(TB)-'86	16/4
56	†Hunley, Lamonte	LB	6-2	238	1/31/63	3	Arizona	Petersburg, Va.	FA-'85	6/2
94	Kellar, Scott	NT	6-3	278	12/31/63	2	Northern Illinois	Elgin, Ill.	D5a-'86	14/8
5	Kiel, Blair	QB	6-0	200	11/29/61	3	Notre Dame	Columbus, Ind.	FA-'86	3/0
55	Krauss, Barry	LB	6-3	253	3/17/57	9	Alabama	Pompano Beach, Fla.	D1-'79	4/4
92	Leiding, Jeff	LB	6-3	232	10/28/61	2	Texas	Kansas City, Mo.	FA-'86	12/0
59	†Lowry, Orlando	LB	6-4	238	8/14/61	3	Ohio State	Shaker Heights, Ohio	FA-'85	16/1
88	†Martin, Robbie	WR-KR	5-8	187	12/3/58	7	Cal Poly-SLO	Villa Park, Calif.	T(Det)-'85	7/0
32	McMillan, Randy	RB	6-0	220	12/17/58	7	Pittsburgh	Jarrettsville, Md.	D1a-'81	16/16
86	Murray, Walter	WR	6-4	200	12/13/62	2	Hawaii	Berkeley, Calif.	T(Wash)-'86	5/0
93	Odom, Cliff	LB	6-2	241	9/15/58	7	Texas-Arlington	Beaumont, Tex.	W(Raiders)-'82	16/16
35	†Randle, Tate	CB-S	6-0	204	8/15/59	6	Texas Tech	Fort Stockton, Tex.	FA-'83	15/6
58	†Redd, Glen	LB	6-1	232	6/17/58	6	Brigham Young	Ogden, Utah	FA-'86	12/0*
83	Sherwin, Tim	TE	6-6	246	5/4/58	7	Boston College	Watervliet, N.Y.	D4-'81	7/2
66	Solt, Ron	G	6-3	283	5/19/62	4	Maryland	Wilkes-Barre, Pa.	D1b-'84	16/16
26	t-Springs, Kirk	S	6-0	197	8/10/58	6	Miami, Ohio	Cincinnati, Ohio	T(NYJ)-'87	0*
3	Stark, Rohn	P	6-3	212	6/4/59	6	Florida State	Minneapolis, Minn.	D2b-'82	16/0
99	Thompson, Donnell	DE	6-5	269	10/27/58	7	North Carolina	Lumberton, N.C.	D1b-'81	16/16
10	Trudeau, Jack	QB	6-3	211	9/9/62	2	Illinois	Livermore, Calif.	D2-'86	12/11
64	Utt, Ben	G	6-5	281	6/13/59	6	Georgia Tech	Visalia, Calif.	FA-'82	9/9
34	Wonsley, George	RB	6-0	221	11/23/60	4	Mississippi State	Moss Point, Miss.	D4b-'84	16/6

* Redd played 4 games with New Orleans, 8 with Indianapolis in '86; Springs missed '86 season due to injury.

†Option playout; subject to developments.

t-Colts traded for Springs (N.Y. Jets)

Traded—Tackle Roger Caron to Buffalo.

Retired—Mark Kirchner, 4-year tackle, 13 games in '86.

Also played with Colts in '86—CB-S Pat Ballage (2 games), WR Wayne Capers (6), CB Preston Davis (8), CB-S Victor Jackson (2), TE Greg LaFleur (9), S Mike Lush (4), QB Ed Luther (active for 10 games, but did not play), RB Hubert Oliver (4), CB-S Tommy Sims (1), WR Oliver Williams (3).

COACHING STAFF

Head Coach, Ron Meyer

Pro Career: Named Colts' twelfth head coach on December 1, 1986. Led Colts to 3-0 mark to close the regular season. Served as head coach with New England Patriots from 1982-84. Compiled 18-15 regular-season record with one playoff game following the 1982 season. Career record: 21-16.

Background: Entered coaching ranks at Penn High School in Mishawauka, Indiana, in 1964. Joined staff at Purdue (where he played defensive back 1959-62) in 1965 in charge of the offensive backfield, receivers, and the overall passing game. Remained at Purdue until becoming a scout with Dallas Cowboys for the 1971 and 1972 seasons. Named head coach at Nevada-Las Vegas in 1973, directing the Rebels to a three-year 27-8 mark, including an undefeated (11-0) regular season in 1974 before losing in the national semifinals in the NCAA Division II playoffs. Named head coach at Southern Methodist in 1976, where he coached until 1981. The Mustangs had a 34-31-1 record during Meyer's tenure and won the Southwestern Conference championship his final year.

Personal: Born February 17, 1941, in Westerville, Ohio. Ron and his wife, Cindy, live in Indianapolis with their daughters Kathryn and Elizabeth. Ron's sons, Ron, Jr., and Ralph, reside in Dallas.

Assistant Coaches

John Becker, offensive coordinator; born February 16, 1943, Alexandria, Va., lives in Indianapolis. Cal State-Northridge 1965. No college or pro playing experience. College coach: UCLA 1970, New Mexico State 1971, New Mexico 1972-73, Los Angeles Valley Jr. College 1974-76 (head coach), Oregon 1977-79. Pro coach: Philadelphia Eagles 1980-83, Buffalo Bills 1984, joined Colts in 1985.

Greg Briner, research and development; born December 28, 1950, Los Angeles, Calif., lives in Indianapolis. Quarterback-defensive back Southern California 1968-71. No pro playing experience. College coach: Portland State 1981-82, Oregon State 1983-84. Pro coach: First year with Colts.

Leon Burtnett, running backs; born May 30, 1943, Fresno, Calif., lives in Indianapolis. Fullback Southwestern (Kansas) University 1961-65. No pro playing experience. College coach: Montana State 1970, Washington State 1971, Wyoming 1972-73, San Jose State 1974-75, Michigan State 1976, Purdue 1977-86 (head coach 1982-86). Pro coach: First year with Colts.

George Catavolos, secondary; born May 8, 1945, Chicago, Ill., lives in Indianapolis. Defensive back Purdue 1964-66. No pro playing experience. College coach: Purdue 1967-68, 1971-76, Middle Tennessee State 1969, Louisville 1970, Kentucky 1977-81, Tennessee 1982-83. Pro coach: Joined Colts in 1984.

George Hill, defensive coordinator; born April 28, 1933, Bay Village, Ohio, lives in Indianapolis. Tackle-fullback Denison 1954-57. No pro playing experience. College coach: Findlay 1959, Denison 1960-64, Cornell 1965, Duke 1966-70, Ohio State 1971-78. Pro coach: Philadelphia Eagles 1979-84, joined Colts in 1985.

Tom Lovat, assistant head coach-offensive line; born December 28, 1938, Bingham, Utah, lives in Indianapolis. Guard-linebacker Utah 1958-60. No pro playing experience. College coach: Utah 1967, 1972-76 (head coach 1974-76), Idaho State 1968-70, Stanford 1977-79. Pro coach: Saskatchewan Roughriders (CFL) 1971, Green Bay Packers 1980, St. Louis Cardinals 1981-84, joined Colts in 1985.

John Marshall, defensive line; born October 2, 1945, Arroyo Grande, Calif., lives in Indianapolis. Linebacker Washington State 1964. No pro playing experience. College coach: Oregon 1970-76, Southern California 1977-79. Pro coach: Green Bay Packers 1980-82, Atlanta Falcons 1983-85, joined Colts in 1986.

Indianapolis Colts 1987 First-Year Roster

Name	Pos.	Ht.	Wt.	Birth-date	College	Hometown	How Acq.
Adams, David	RB	5-6	163	6/24/64	Arizona	Tucson, Ariz.	D12
Banks, Roy	WR	5-10	188	11/29/65	Eastern Illinois	Detroit, Mich.	D5
Bennett, Cornelius	LB	6-2	235	8/25/65	Alabama	Birmingham, Ala.	D1
Bellini, Mark	WR	5-11	185	1/19/64	Brigham Young	San Leandro, Calif.	D7
Blankenship, Brian (1)	T-G	6-2	280	4/7/63	Nebraska	Omaha, Neb.	FA
Colson, Edward (1)	RB	6-0	230	9/8/63	North Carolina	Maple Hill, N.C.	FA
Dixon, Randy	T	6-4	292	3/12/65	Pittsburgh	Clewiston, Fla.	D4
Gambol, Chris	T	6-6	291	9/14/64	Iowa	Pittsburgh, Pa.	D3
Goode, Chris	CB-S	6-0	194	9/17/63	Alabama	Town Creek, Ala.	D10
Grimsley, Ed (1)	LB	6-1	235	3/22/63	Akron	Massillon, Ohio	FA
Ledenko, Robert (1)	CB-S	6-2	198	5/28/63	Brigham Young	Blue Springs, Mo.	FA
Lester, Keith (1)	TE	6-5	235	5/28/62	Murray State	Lake Panasoffkee, Fla.	FA
Miller, Chuckie	CB-S	5-8	178	5/9/65	UCLA	Anniston, Ala.	D8
Noble, James (1)	WR	6-0	193	8/14/63	Stephen F. Austin	Humble, Tex.	FA
Ontke, Bob	LB	6-3	233	3/21/64	Penn State	Swoyersville, Pa.	D9
Osswald, Chris (1)	G	6-4	270	11/13/62	Wisconsin	Reston, Va.	FA
Reynosa, Jim	DE	6-4	256	5/19/64	Arizona State	Glendale, Calif.	D11
Robinson, Freddie	CB-S	6-0	184	2/1/64	Alabama	Mobile, Ala.	D6
Sims, Freddie (1)	RB	5-10	212	1/4/63	Oklahoma	Tucson, Ariz.	FA
Spivey, Lee (1)	T-G	6-3	285	12/17/58	Southern Methodist	Houston, Tex.	FA
Williams, Isaac (1)	NT	6-2	275	10/9/64	Florida State	Tallahassee, Fla.	FA

The term NFL Rookie is defined as a player who is in his first season of professional football and has not been on the roster of another professional football team for any regular-season or postseason games. A Rookie is designated by an "R" on NFL rosters. Players who have been active in another professional football league or players who have NFL experience, including either preseason training camp or being on an active roster for fewer than three regular-season or postseason games, are termed NFL First-Year Players. An NFL First-Year Player is designated by a "1" on NFL rosters. Thereafter, a player on an NFL active roster for at least three regular-season or postseason games is credited with an additional year of NFL playing experience.

NOTES

Chip Myers, receivers; born July 9, 1945, Panama City, Fla., lives in Indianapolis. Receiver Northwest Oklahoma 1964-66. Pro receiver San Francisco 49ers 1967, Cincinnati Bengals 1969-76. College coach: Illinois 1980-82. Pro coach: Tampa Bay Buccaneers 1983-84, joined Colts in 1985.

Keith Rowen, special teams-assistant offensive line; born September 2, 1952, New York, N.Y., lives in Indianapolis. Offensive tackle Stanford 1972-74. No pro playing experience. College coach: Stanford 1975-76, Long Beach State 1977-78, Arizona 1979-82. Pro coach: Boston/New Orleans Breakers (USFL) 1983-84, Cleveland Browns 1984, joined Colts in 1985.

Rick Venturi, linebackers; born February 23, 1946, Taylorville, Ill., lives in Indianapolis. Quarterback Northwestern 1965-67. No pro playing experience. College coach: Northwestern 1968-72, 1978-80 (head coach), Purdue 1973-76, Illinois 1977. Pro coach: Joined Colts in 1982.

Tom Zupancic, strength and conditioning; born September 14, 1955, Indianapolis, Ind., lives in Indianapolis. Defensive tackle-offensive tackle Indiana Central 1975-78. No pro playing experience. Pro coach: Joined Colts in 1984.

American Football Conference Western Division

Team Colors: Red, Gold, and White

One Arrowhead Drive
Kansas City, Missouri 64129
Telephone: (816) 924-9300

Club Officials

Owner: Lamar Hunt
President: Jack Steadman
Vice President-General Manager: Jim Schaaf
Assistant to General Manager: Dennis Thum
Vice President-Administration: Don Steadman
Treasurer: Bob Tamasi
Secretary: Jim Seigfreid
College Personnel Director: Les Miller
Director of Public Relations and Community Relations: Gary Heise
Community Relations Manager: Brenda Boatright
Director of Sales and Promotions: Mitch Wheeler
Director of Marketing: Ken Blume
Manager of Ticket Operations: Phil Youtsey
Stadium Operations: Bob Wachter
Trainer: Dave Kendall
Equipment Coordinator: Jon Phillips
Video Coordinator: Mike Dennis

Stadium: Arrowhead Stadium • **Capacity:** 78,067
One Arrowhead Drive
Kansas City, Missouri 64129

Playing Surface: AstroTurf-8

Training Camp: William Jewell College
Liberty, Missouri 64068

1987 Schedule

Preseason

Aug. 8	vs. S.F. at Canton, Ohio	12:00
Aug. 13	at Houston	7:00
Aug. 22	**Atlanta**	7:30
Aug. 29	**Buffalo**	7:30
Sept. 4	at Miami	8:00

Regular Season

Sept. 13	**San Diego**	12:00
Sept. 20	at Seattle	1:00
Sept. 27	**Minnesota**	12:00
Oct. 4	at Los Angeles Raiders	1:00
Oct. 11	at Miami	1:00
Oct. 18	**Denver**	3:00
Oct. 25	at San Diego	1:00
Nov. 1	at Chicago	12:00
Nov. 8	**Pittsburgh**	12:00
Nov. 15	**New York Jets**	12:00
Nov. 22	**Green Bay**	12:00
Nov. 26	at Detroit (Thanksgiving)	12:30
Dec. 6	at Cincinnati	1:00
Dec. 13	**Los Angeles Raiders**	3:00
Dec. 19	at Denver (Saturday)	2:00
Dec. 27	**Seattle**	12:00

Chiefs Coaching History

Dallas Texans 1960-62
(202-186-10)

1960-74	Hank Stram	129-79-10
1975-77	Paul Wiggin*	11-24-0
1977	Tom Bettis	1-6-0
1978-82	Marv Levy	31-42-0
1983-86	John Mackovic	30-35-0

*Released after seven games in 1977

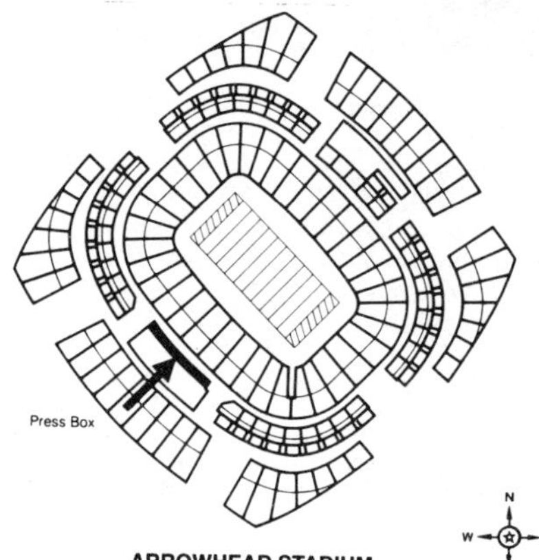

ARROWHEAD STADIUM

Record Holders

Individual Records—Career

Category	Name	Performance
Rushing (Yds.)	Ed Podolak, 1969-1977	4,451
Passing (Yds.)	Len Dawson, 1962-1975	28,507
Passing (TDs)	Len Dawson, 1962-1975	237
Receiving (No.)	Otis Taylor, 1965-1975	410
Receiving (Yds.)	Otis Taylor, 1965-1975	7,306
Interceptions	Emmitt Thomas, 1966-1978	58
Punting (Avg.)	Jerrel Wilson, 1963-1977	43.5
Punt Return (Avg.)	J.T. Smith, 1979-1984	10.6
Kickoff Return (Avg.)	Noland Smith, 1967-69	26.8
Field Goals	Jan Stenerud, 1967-1979	279
Touchdowns (Tot.)	Otis Taylor, 1965-1975	60
Points	Jan Stenerud, 1967-1979	1,231

Individual Records—Single Season

Category	Name	Performance
Rushing (Yds.)	Joe Delaney, 1981	1,121
Passing (Yds.)	Bill Kenney, 1983	4,348
Passing (TDs)	Len Dawson, 1964	30
Receiving (No.)	Carlos Carson, 1983	80
Receiving (Yds.)	Carlos Carson, 1983	1,351
Interceptions	Emmitt Thomas, 1974	12
Punting (Avg.)	Jerrel Wilson, 1965	46.0
Punt Return (Avg.)	Abner Haynes, 1960	15.4
Kickoff Return (Avg.)	Dave Grayson, 1962	29.7
Field Goals	Jan Stenerud, 1968	30
	Jan Stenerud, 1970	30
Touchdowns (Tot.)	Abner Haynes, 1962	19
Points	Jan Stenerud, 1968	129

Individual Records—Single Game

Category	Name	Performance
Rushing (Yds.)	Joe Delaney, 11-15-81	193
Passing (Yds.)	Len Dawson, 11-1-64	435
Passing (TDs)	Len Dawson, 11-1-64	6
Receiving (No.)	Ed Podolak, 10-7-73	12
Receiving (Yds.)	Stephone Paige, 12-22-85	309
Interceptions	Bobby Ply, 12-16-62	4
	Bobby Hunt, 12-4-64	4
	Deron Cherry, 9-29-85	4
Field Goals	Jan Stenerud, 11-2-69	5
	Jan Stenerud, 12-7-69	5
	Jan Stenerud, 12-19-71	5
Touchdowns (Tot.)	Abner Haynes, 11-26-61	5
Points	Abner Haynes, 11-26-61	30

1986 Team Statistics

	Chiefs	Opp.
Total First Downs	264	310
Rushing	83	111
Passing	152	173
Penalty	29	26
Third Down: Made/Att.	74/220	80/224
Fourth Down: Made/Att.	5/9	7/16
Total Net Yards	4218	4934
Avg. Per Game	263.6	308.4
Total Plays	1003	1098
Avg. Per Play	4.2	4.5
Net Yards Rushing	1468	1739
Avg. Per Game	91.8	108.7
Total Rushes	432	485
Net Yards Passing	2750	3195
Avg. Per Game	171.9	199.7
Tackled/Yards Lost	50/372	44/360
Gross Yards	3122	3555
Att./Completions	521/257	569/303
Completion Pct.	49.3	53.3
Had Intercepted	18	31
Punts/Avg.	99/40.7	83/37.0
Net Punting Avg.	33.7	30.9
Penalties/Yards Lost	97/829	114/965
Fumbles/Ball Lost	27/17	26/18
Touchdowns	43	38
Rushing	10	13
Passing	23	21
Returns	10	4
Avg. Time of Possession	28:29	31:31

1986 Team Record

Preseason (2-2)

Date	Result		Opponents
8/9	W	20- 0	Cincinnati
8/16	W	27-26	at St. Louis
8/23	L	6-13	Buffalo
8/30	L	10-13	at New Orleans
		63-52	

Regular Season (10-6)

Date	Result		Opponents	Att.
9/7	W	24-14	Cincinnati	43,430
9/14	L	17-23	at Seattle	61,068
9/21	W	27-13	Houston	43,699
9/28	W	20-17	at Buffalo	67,555
10/5	L	17-24	L.A. Raiders	74,430
10/12	L	7-20	at Cleveland	71,278
10/19	W	42-41	San Diego	55,767
10/26	W	27-20	Tampa Bay	36,230
11/2	W	24-23	at San Diego	48,518
11/9	W	27- 7	Seattle	53,268
11/16	L	17-38	at Denver	75,745
11/23	L	14-23	at St. Louis	29,680
11/30	L	14-17	Buffalo	31,492
12/7	W	37-10	Denver	47,019
12/14	W	20-17	at L.A. Raiders	60,952
12/21	W	24-19	at Pittsburgh	47,150

Postseason (0-1)

Date	Result		Opponent	Att.
12/28	L	15-35	at N.Y. Jets	75,210

Score by Periods

Chiefs	67	113	83	95	0	—	358
Opponents	49	121	90	66	0	—	326

Attendance

Home 385,335 Away 470,670 Total 856,005
Single game home record, 82,094 (11-5-72)
Single season home record, 509,291 (1972)

1986 Individual Statistics

Scoring	TD R	TD P	TD Rt	PAT	FG	Saf	TP
Lowery	0	0	0	43/43	19/26	0	100
Paige	0	11	0	0/0	0/0	0	66
J. Smith	3	3	0	0/0	0/0	0	36
Burruss	0	0	4	0/0	0/0	0	24
Carson	0	4	0	0/0	0/0	0	24
Green	3	0	1	0/0	0/0	0	24
Arnold	0	1	1	0/0	0/0	0	12
Cherry	0	0	2	0/0	0/0	0	12
Coffman	0	2	0	0/0	0/0	0	12
Heard	2	0	0	0/0	0/0	0	12
Pruitt	2	0	0	0/0	0/0	0	12
Harry	0	1	0	0/0	0/0	0	6
Hill	0	0	1	0/0	0/0	0	6
Marshall	0	1	0	0/0	0/0	0	6
Moriarty, Hou.-K.C.	1	0	0	0/0	0/0	0	6
Ross	0	0	1	0/0	0/0	0	6
Chiefs	10	23	10	43/43	19/26	0	358
Opponents	13	21	4	36/38	20/31	1	326

Passing	Att.	Comp.	Yds.	Pct.	TD	Int.	Tkld.	Rate
Kenney	308	161	1922	52.3	13	11	25/180	70.8
Blackledge	211	96	1200	45.5	10	6	25/192	67.6
Green	1	0	0	0.0	0	1	0/0	0.0
Marshall	1	0	0	0.0	0	0	0/0	39.6
Chiefs	521	257	3122	49.3	23	18	50/372	68.5
Opponents	569	303	3555	53.3	21	31	44/360	62.1

Rushing	Att.	Yds.	Avg.	LG	TD
Pruitt	139	448	3.2	16	2
Green	90	314	3.5	27	3
Heard	71	295	4.2	40	2
Moriarty, Hou.-K.C.	90	252	2.8	11	1
Moriarty, K.C.	35	115	3.3	11	0
J. Smith	54	238	4.4	32t	3
Blackledge	23	60	2.6	14	0
Kenney	18	0	0.0	9	0
Paige	2	−2	−1.0	12	0
Chiefs	432	1468	3.4	40	10
Opponents	485	1739	3.6	41t	13

Receiving	No.	Yds.	Avg.	LG	TD
Paige	52	829	15.9	51	11
Marshall	46	652	14.2	31	1
J. Smith	33	230	7.0	18	3
Carson	21	497	23.7	70t	4
Arnold	20	169	8.5	27	1
Green	19	137	7.2	17	0
Heard	17	83	4.9	13	0
Coffman	12	75	6.3	10	2
Harry	9	211	23.4	53	1
Moriarty, Hou.-K.C.	9	67	7.4	19	0
Moriarty, K.C.	7	51	7.3	19	0
Hayes	8	69	8.6	16	0
Pruitt	8	56	7.0	13	0
Hancock	4	63	15.8	25	0
Kenney	1	0	0.0	0	0
Chiefs	257	3122	12.1	70t	23
Opponents	303	3555	11.7	51	21

Interceptions	No.	Yds.	Avg.	LG	TD
Cherry	9	150	16.7	49	0
Burruss	5	193	38.6	72t	3
Ross	4	66	16.5	35	0
Lewis	4	18	4.5	13	0
Hill	3	64	21.3	26t	1
Cocroft	3	32	10.7	13	0
Spani	1	24	24.0	24	0
Radecic	1	20	20.0	20	0
Hackett	1	0	0.0	0	0
Chiefs	31	567	18.3	72t	4
Opponents	18	181	10.1	32	1

Punting	No.	Yds.	Avg.	In 20	LG
Colbert	99	4033	40.7	23	56
Chiefs	99	4033	40.7	23	56
Opponents	83	3067	37.0	11	62

Punt Returns	No.	FC	Yds.	Avg.	LG	TD
J. Smith	29	11	245	8.4	48	0
Harry	6	7	20	3.3	7	0
Chiefs	35	18	265	7.6	48	0
Opponents	52	19	572	11.0	70t	1

Kickoff Returns	No.	Yds.	Avg.	LG	TD
J. Smith	29	557	19.2	29	0
Green	10	254	25.4	97t	1
Harry	6	115	19.2	26	0
Carson	5	88	17.6	29	0
Moriarty	4	80	20.0	23	0
Cocroft	1	23	23.0	23	0
A. Pearson	1	0	0.0	0	0
Chiefs	56	1117	19.9	97t	1
Opponents	71	1278	18.0	58	0

Sacks	No.
Still	10.5
Maas	7.0
Koch	5.5
Cofield	5.0
Cooper	4.5
Griffin	2.0
Ross	2.0
Paul	1.5
Cherry	1.0
Holle	1.0
Lewis	1.0
McAlister	1.0
J. Pearson	1.0
Radecic	1.0
Chiefs	44.0
Opponents	50.0

FIRST-ROUND SELECTIONS

(If club had no first-round selection, first player drafted is listed with round in parentheses.)

Year	Player, College, Position
1960	Don Meredith, Southern Methodist, QB
1961	E.J. Holub, Texas Tech, C
1962	Ronnie Bull, Baylor, RB
1963	Buck Buchanan, Grambling, DT
	Ed Budde, Michigan State, G
1964	Pete Beathard, Southern California, QB
1965	Gale Sayers, Kansas, RB
1966	Aaron Brown, Minnesota, DE
1967	Gene Trosch, Miami, DE-DT
1968	Mo Moorman, Texas A&M, G
	George Daney, Texas-El Paso, G
1969	Jim Marsalis, Tennessee State, CB
1970	Sid Smith, Southern California, T
1971	Elmo Wright, Houston, WR
1972	Jeff Kinney, Nebraska, RB
1973	Gary Butler, Rice, TE (2)
1974	Woody Green, Arizona State, RB
1975	Elmore Stephens, Kentucky, TE (2)
1976	Rod Walters, Iowa, G
1977	Gary Green, Baylor, DB
1978	Art Still, Kentucky, DE
1979	Mike Bell, Colorado State, DE
	Steve Fuller, Clemson, QB
1980	Brad Budde, Southern California, G
1981	Willie Scott, South Carolina, TE
1982	Anthony Hancock, Tennessee, WR
1983	Todd Blackledge, Penn State, QB
1984	Bill Maas, Pittsburgh, DT
	John Alt, Iowa, T
1985	Ethan Horton, North Carolina, RB
1986	Brian Jozwiak, West Virginia, T
1987	Paul Palmer, Temple, RB

Kansas City Chiefs 1987 Veteran Roster

No.	Name	Pos.	Ht.	Wt.	Birth-date	NFL Exp.	College	Hometown	How Acq.	'86 Games/ Starts
61	Adickes, Mark	G	6-4	274	4/22/61	2	Baylor	Waco, Tex.	SD1-'84	15/15
76	Alt, John	T	6-7	282	5/30/62	4	Iowa	Columbia Heights, Minn.	D1b-'84	7/0
87	Arnold, Walt	TE	6-3	224	8/31/58	8	New Mexico	Los Alamos, N.M.	FA-'84	16/16
91	Baldinger, Gary	DE	6-3	265	10/4/63	2	Wake Forest	Long Island, N.Y.	D9-'86	5/0
77	†Baldinger, Rich	G-T	6-4	285	12/31/59	5	Wake Forest	Long Island, N.Y.	FA-'83	16/8
58	Baugh, Tom	C	6-3	274	12/1/63	2	Southern Illinois	North Riverside, Ill.	D4a-'86	5/0
99	Bell, Mike	DE	6-4	250	8/30/57	7	Colorado State	Wichita, Kan.	D1a-'79	0*
14	†Blackledge, Todd	QB	6-3	223	2/25/61	5	Penn State	Canton, Ohio	D1-'83	10/8
71	Budde, Brad	G	6-4	271	5/9/58	8	Southern California	Kansas City, Mo.	D1-'80	16/16
34	Burruss, Lloyd	S	6-0	209	10/31/57	7	Maryland	Charlottesville, N.C.	D3c-'81	15/13
88	Carson, Carlos	WR	5-11	184	12/28/58	8	Louisiana State	Lake Worth, Fla.	D5a-'80	10/7
20	Cherry, Deron	S	5-11	196	9/12/59	7	Rutgers	Palmyra, N.J.	FA-'81	16/16
22	†Cocroft, Sherman	S-CB	6-1	195	8/29/61	3	San Jose State	Mobile, Ala.	FA-'85	16/0
84	Coffman, Paul	TE	6-3	225	3/29/56	10	Kansas State	Chase, Kan.	FA-'86	15/0
54	Cofield, Tim	LB	6-2	245	5/18/63	2	Elizabeth City State	Murfreesboro, N.C.	FA-'86	15/15
5	Colbert, Lewis	P	5-11	180	8/23/63	2	Auburn	Phenix City, Ala.	D8-'86	16/0
55	Cooper, Louis	LB	6-2	235	8/5/63	3	Western Carolina	Marion, S.C.	FA-'85	16/13
51	Donnalley, Rick	C	6-2	270	12/11/58	7	North Carolina	Wilmington, Del.	T(Wash)-'86	16/16
75	Eatman, Irv	T	6-7	293	1/1/61	2	UCLA	Dayton, Ohio	D8-'83	16/16
80	Fox, Chas	WR	5-11	180	10/3/63	2	Furman	Rapid City, S.D.	D4b-'86	4/3*
40	†Green, Boyce	RB	5-11	215	6/24/60	5	Carson-Newman	Beaufort, S.C.	T(Clev)-'86	16/7
98	Griffin, Leonard	DE	6-4	252	9/22/62	2	Grambling	Lake Providence, La.	D3-'86	9/0
56	Hackett, Dino	LB	6-3	225	6/28/64	2	Appalachian State	Greensboro, N.C.	D2-'86	16/16
82	†Hancock, Anthony	WR-KR	6-0	204	6/10/60	6	Tennessee	Cleveland, Ohio	D1-'82	4/0
92	Harris, Bob	LB	6-2	223	11/11/60	4	Auburn	Ellenwood, Ga.	FA-'87	0*
86	Harry, Emile	WR	5-11	175	4/5/63	2	Stanford	Los Angeles, Calif.	FA-'86	12/0
85	Hayes, Jonathan	TE	6-5	236	8/11/62	3	Iowa	Pittsburgh, Pa.	D2-'85	16/4
44	Heard, Herman	RB	5-10	190	11/24/61	4	Southern Colorado	Denver, Colo.	D3-'84	15/7
23	†Hill, Greg	CB	6-1	199	2/12/61	5	Oklahoma State	Orange, Tex.	W(Hou)-'84	13/1
93	†Holle, Eric	DE-NT	6-5	265	9/5/60	4	Texas	Austin, Tex.	D5a-'84	16/0
73	Jozwiak, Brian	T	6-5	308	6/20/63	2	West Virginia	Baltimore, Md.	D1-'86	15/1
9	Kenney, Bill	QB	6-4	211	1/20/55	9	Northern Colorado	San Clemente, Calif.	FA-'79	15/8
74	†Koch, Pete	DE	6-6	275	1/23/62	4	Maryland	Manhasset, N.Y.	FA-'85	16/16
70	Lathrop, Kit	DE	6-5	261	8/10/56	4	Arizona State	San Jose, Calif.	FA-'86	16/0
29	Lewis, Albert	CB	6-2	192	10/6/60	5	Grambling	Mansfield, La.	D3-'83	15/15
8	Lowery, Nick	K	6-4	189	5/27/56	8	Dartmouth	Washington, D.C.	FA-'80	16/0
72	Lutz, David	T	6-6	295	12/30/59	5	Georgia Tech	Peachland, N.C.	D2-'83	9/8
63	Maas, Bill	NT	6-5	268	3/2/62	4	Pittsburgh	Newtown Square, Pa.	D1-'84	16/16
89	Marshall, Henry	WR	6-2	216	8/9/54	12	Missouri	Dalzell, S.C.	D3d-'76	16/9
94	†McAlister, Ken	LB	6-5	230	4/15/60	6	San Francisco	Oakland, Calif.	FA-'84	3/3
32	Moriarty, Larry	RB	6-1	237	4/24/58	5	Notre Dame	Santa Barbara, Calif.	T(Hou)-'86	15/5*
83	Paige, Stephone	WR	6-2	183	10/15/61	5	Fresno State	Long Beach, Calif.	FA-'83	16/15
96	Pearson, Aaron	LB	6-0	236	8/22/64	2	Mississippi State	Gadsden, Ala.	D11-'86	15/0
24	Pearson, J.C.	CB	5-11	183	8/17/63	2	Washington	Oceanside, Calif.	FA-'86	8/0
43	Pruitt, Mike	RB	6-0	235	4/3/54	12	Purdue	Chicago, Ill.	FA-'85	15/15
97	†Radecic, Scott	LB	6-3	242	6/14/62	4	Penn State	Pittsburgh, Pa.	D2-'84	16/13
30	†Robinson, Mark	S	5-11	206	9/13/62	4	Penn State	Pittsburgh, Pa.	D4-'84	9/3
31	Ross, Kevin	CB	5-9	182	1/16/62	4	Temple	Paulsboro, N.J.	D7-'84	16/16
10	Seurer, Frank	QB	6-1	195	8/16/62	2	Kansas	Huntington Beach, Calif.	FA-'86	1/0
42	Smith, Jeff	RB-KR	5-9	201	3/22/62	3	Nebraska	Wichita, Kan.	D10-'85	15/0
59	†Spani, Gary	LB	6-2	229	1/9/56	10	Kansas State	Manhattan, Kan.	D3-'78	16/3
67	Still, Art	DE	6-7	255	12/5/55	10	Kentucky	Camden, N.J.	D1-'78	16/16

* Bell missed '86 season due to suspension; Fox played 4 games with St. Louis in '86; Harris last active with St. Louis in '85; Moriarty played 5 games with Houston, 10 with Kansas City.

†Option playout; subject to developments.

Also played with Chiefs in '86—RB Bruce King (4 games), C-G Adam Lingner (12), T Matt Moran (active for 2 games, but did not play), LB Whitney Paul (13), G-T Jim Rourke (4).

COACHING STAFF

Head Coach, Frank Gansz

Pro Career: Was named sixth head coach in Chiefs history on January 10, 1987. Had been NFL assistant coach previous nine years, including two different stints in Kansas City. Coached Chiefs special teams and tight ends in 1981-82 under Marv Levy, then rejoined club in 1986 under John Mackovic as assistant head coach and special teams coach. Led special teams to NFL-high and team-record 10 blocked kicks and five touchdowns. Entered NFL in 1978 as special teams coach for San Francisco 49ers. Also, held special teams and tight ends coaching duties with Cincinnati Bengals (1979-80) and Philadelphia Eagles (1983-85). No pro playing experience.

Background: Began coaching career in 1964 as general assistant coach at the Air Force Academy while serving as a military officer. Spent three years at Air Force, then was commercial airline pilot for two years. Returned to coaching in 1968 as head freshman coach at Colgate. Spent three years as assistant at U.S. Naval Academy (1969-72), then became receivers coach at Oklahoma State (1973, 1975), offensive coordinator at West Point (1974), and offensive assistant at UCLA (1976-77). Played center and linebacker for Naval Academy, graduating in 1960.

Personal: Born November 22, 1938, Altoona, Pa. Frank and wife, Barbara, live in Kansas City, and have two children—Frank, Jr., and Jennifer Anne.

Assistant Coaches

Ed Beckman, special teams; born January 2, 1955, Key West, Fla., lives in Kansas City. Tight end Florida State 1970-73. Pro tight end Kansas City Chiefs 1977-84. Pro coach: First year with Chiefs.

David Brazil, defensive backs; born March 25, 1936, Detroit, Mich., lives in Kansas City. No college or pro playing experience. College coach: Holy Cross 1968-69, Tulsa 1970-71, Eastern Michigan 1972-74, Boston College 1978-79. Pro coach: Detroit Wheels (WFL) 1975, Chicago Fire (WFL) 1976, joined Chiefs in 1984.

Mark Hatley, defensive quality control, linebackers; born September 19, 1949, Bolger, Tex., lives in Kansas City. Linebacker Oklahoma State 1968-72. No pro playing experience. College coach: Oklahoma State 1973-76, Texas Christian 1977-82, Baylor 1983. Pro coach: New Orleans Saints 1984-85, first year with Chiefs.

J.D. Helm, offensive quality control, tight ends; born December 27, 1940, El Dorado Springs, Mo., lives in Overland Park, Kan. Running back Kansas 1959-60. No pro playing experience. College coach: Brigham Young 1969-75. Pro coach: Joined Chiefs in 1976.

C.T. Hewgley, strength and conditioning coordinator, linemen; born August 22, 1925, Nashville, Tenn., lives in Kansas City. Tackle Wyoming 1947-50. No pro playing experience. College coach: Miami 1968-70, Wyoming 1971-73, Nebraska-Omaha 1974 (head coach), Michigan State 1976-79, Arizona State 1980-82. Pro coach: Joined Chiefs in 1983.

Don Lawrence, defensive line; born June 4, 1937, Cleveland, Ohio, lives in Kansas City. Tackle Notre Dame 1953-55. Pro tackle Washington Redskins 1956-61. College coach: Notre Dame 1963-67, Kansas State 1968-69, Cincinnati 1970, Virginia 1971-73 (head coach), Texas Christian 1974-75, Missouri 1976-77. Pro coach: British Columbia Lions (CFL) 1978-79, Kansas City Chiefs 1980-82, Buffalo Bills 1983-84, Tampa Bay Buccaneers 1985-86, rejoined Chiefs in 1987.

Billie Matthews, running backs; born March 15, 1930, Houston, Tex., lives in Kansas City. Quarterback Southern University 1948-51. No pro playing experience. College coach: Kansas 1970, UCLA 1971-78. Pro coach: San Francisco 49ers 1979-82, Philadelphia Eagles 1983-84, Indianapolis Colts 1985-86, first year with Chiefs.

Kansas City Chiefs 1987 First-Year Roster

Name	Pos.	Ht.	Wt.	Birth-date	College	Hometown	How Acq.
Bergmann, Paul (1)	TE	6-2	235	3/30/61	UCLA	Carlsbad, Calif.	FA-'86
Clemons, Michael	RB-KR	5-5	166	1/15/65	William & Mary	Clearwater, Fla.	D8
Coffey, Wayne	WR	5-7	161	5/30/64	Southwest Texas State	Abilene, Tex.	FA
Evans, James	RB	6-0	220	8/17/63	Southern	Mobile, Ala.	D10
Freeman, Ron	LB	6-2	230	1/21/60	Pittsburgh State	Booneville, Mo.	FA
Garron, Andre (1)	RB	5-11	193	2/6/64	New Hampshire	Framingham, Mass.	FA-'86
Goodburn, Kelly	P	6-2	205	4/14/62	Emporia State	Cherokee, Iowa	FA
Holmes, Bruce	LB	6-2	220	10/24/64	Minnesota	Detroit, Mich.	D12
Howard, Todd	LB	6-2	235	2/18/65	Texas A&M	Bryan, Tex.	D3
Hudson, Doug	QB	6-2	201	9/11/64	Nicholls State	Gulf Breeze, Fla.	D7
Hulberg, Robert	P	6-0	182	12/10/64	Nevada-Las Vegas	San Jacinto, Calif.	FA
Koss, Stein	TE	6-3	230	8/21/63	Arizona State	Durango, Colo.	FA
Merritt, Charles	LB	6-2	225	1/13/63	Carson-Newman	Valdosta, Ga.	FA
Okoye, Christian	RB	6-1	253	8/16/61	Azusa Pacific	Enugu, Nigeria	D2
Palmer, Paul	RB	5-9	184	10/14/64	Temple	Potomac, Md.	D1
Petersen, George	LB	6-2	220	9/9/62	Fresno State	Fresno, Calif.	FA
Pontiakos, Stephen	TE	6-5	237	4/23/63	Delaware	Orange, N.J.	FA
Richardson, Craig	WR-KR	5-11	189	11/11/63	Eastern Washington	Seattle, Wash.	D11
Smith, Chris (1)	RB	6-0	222	6/1/63	Notre Dame	Cincinnati, Ohio	FA-'86
Stockemer, Ralph	RB	6-1	215	12/20/62	Baylor	Shreveport, La.	FA
Stone, Timothy	C	6-5	290	11/24/60	Kansas State	Elmira, N.Y.	FA
Stroth, Vincent	G	6-4	270	11/25/60	Brigham Young	San Jose, Calif.	FA
Taylor, Kitrick	WR-KR	5-10	183	7/22/64	Washington State	Claremont, Calif.	D5
Thomas, Carlton	CB	6-0	195	11/25/63	Elizabeth City State	Portsmouth, Va.	FA
Trahan, John	WR	5-9	165	4/19/62	Southern Colorado	Denver, Colo.	FA
Ware, Willie	WR-KR	5-7	162	9/9/63	Mississippi Valley	Carrollton, Miss.	FA
Watts, Randy	DE	6-6	279	6/22/63	Catawba	Sandersville, Ga.	D9

The term NFL Rookie is defined as a player who is in his first season of professional football and has not been on the roster of another professional football team for any regular-season or postseason games. A Rookie is designated by an "R" on NFL rosters. Players who have been active in another professional football league or players who have NFL experience, including either preseason training camp or being on an active roster for fewer than three regular-season or postseason games, are termed NFL First-Year Players. An NFL First-Year Player is designated by a "1" on NFL rosters. Thereafter, a player on an NFL active roster for at least three regular-season or postseason games is credited with an additional year of NFL playing experience.

NOTES

Carl Mauck, offensive line; born July 7, 1947, McLeansboro, Ill., lives in Kansas City. Center Southern Illinois 1965-68. Pro center San Diego Chargers 1969-74, Houston Oilers 1975-80. Pro coach: New Orleans Saints 1982-85, joined Chiefs in 1986.

Homer Smith, offensive coordinator, quarterbacks; born October 9, 1931, Omaha, Neb., lives in Kansas City. Running back Princeton 1951-53. No pro playing experience. College coach: Stanford 1958-60, Air Force 1961-64, Davidson 1965-69 (head coach), University of the Pacific 1970-71 (head coach), UCLA 1972-73, 1980-86, Army 1974-78 (head coach). Pro coach: First year with Chiefs.

Richard Wood, receivers; born February 2, 1936, Lanett, Ala., lives in Kansas City. Quarterback Auburn 1956-59. Pro quarterback Baltimore Colts 1960-61, San Diego Chargers 1962, Denver Broncos 1962, New York Jets 1963-64, Oakland Raiders 1965, Miami Dolphins 1966. College coach: Georgia 1967-68, Mississippi 1971-73, Auburn 1986. Pro coach: Oakland Raiders 1969-70, Cleveland Browns 1974, New Orleans Saints 1976-77, Atlanta Falcons 1978-82, Philadelphia Eagles 1983, first year with Chiefs.

John Paul Young, defensive coordinator, linebackers; born December 31, 1939, Dallas, Tex., lives in Kansas City. Linebacker Texas-El Paso 1959-61. No pro playing experience. College coach: Texas-El Paso 1962-63, Southern Methodist 1967-68, Oklahoma State 1969, Texas A&M 1970-77. Pro coach: Houston Oilers 1978-80, New Orleans Saints 1981-85, joined Chiefs in 1986.

American Football Conference Western Division

Team Colors: Silver and Black

332 Center Street
El Segundo, California 90245
Telephone: (213) 322-3451

Club Officials

Managing General Partner: Al Davis
Executive Assistant: Al LoCasale
Player Personnel: Ron Wolf
Business Manager: Ken LaRue
Finance: Michael Reinfeldt
Senior Administrators: Irv Kaze, John Herrera, Mike Ornstein
Pro Football Scout: George Karras
Community Relations: Gil Hernandez, Calvin Peterson
Publications: Steve Hartman
Ticket Operations: Peter Eiges
Trainers: George Anderson, H. Rod Martin
Equipment Manager: Richard Romanski

Stadium: Los Angeles Memorial Coliseum • **Capacity:** 92,516
3911 South Figueroa Street
Los Angeles, California 90037

Playing Surface: Grass

Training Camp: Radisson Hotel
Oxnard, California 93030

1987 Schedule

Preseason

Aug. 15	**San Francisco**	7:00
Aug. 22	**Buffalo**	6:00
Aug. 30	at Dallas	7:00
Sept. 5	**Chicago**	1:00

Regular Season

Sept. 13	at Green Bay	3:00
Sept. 20	**Detroit**	1:00
Sept. 27	at Houston	12:00
Oct. 4	**Kansas City**	1:00
Oct. 12	at Denver (Monday)	7:00
Oct. 18	**San Diego**	1:00
Oct. 25	**Seattle**	1:00
Nov. 1	at New England	1:00
Nov. 8	at Minnesota	12:00
Nov. 15	at San Diego	5:00
Nov. 22	**Denver**	1:00
Nov. 30	at Seattle (Monday)	6:00
Dec. 6	**Buffalo**	1:00
Dec. 13	at Kansas City	3:00
Dec. 20	**Cleveland**	1:00
Dec. 27	**Chicago**	1:00

Raiders Coaching History

Oakland 1960-81
(265-144-11)

1960-61	Eddie Erdelatz*	6-10-0
1961-62	Marty Feldman**	2-15-0
1962	Red Conkright	1-8-0
1963-65	Al Davis	23-16-3
1966-68	John Rauch	35-10-1
1969-78	John Madden	112-39-7
1979-86	Tom Flores	86-46-0

*Released after two games in 1961
**Released after five games in 1962

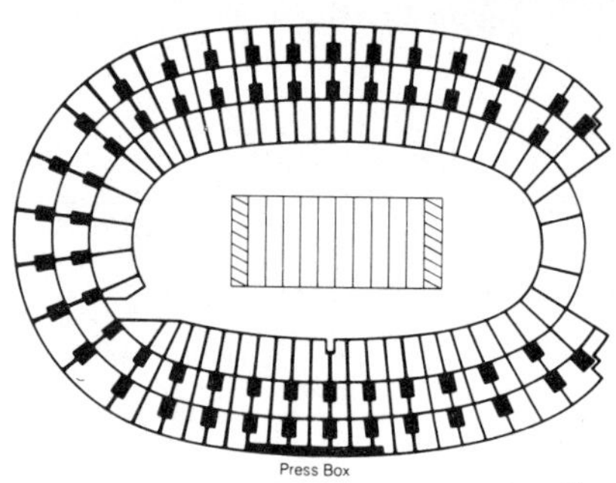

MEMORIAL COLISEUM

Record Holders

Individual Records—Career

Category	Name	Performance
Rushing (Yds.)	Mark van Eeghen, 1974-1981	5,907
Passing (Yds.)	Ken Stabler, 1970-79	19,078
Passing (TDs)	Ken Stabler, 1970-79	150
Receiving (No.)	Fred Biletnikoff, 1965-1978	589
Receiving (Yds.)	Fred Biletnikoff, 1965-1978	8,974
Interceptions	Willie Brown, 1967-1978	39
	Lester Hayes, 1977-1986	39
Punting (Avg.)	Ray Guy, 1973-1986	42.5
Punt Return (Avg.)	Claude Gibson, 1963-65	12.6
Kickoff Return (Avg.)	Jack Larscheid, 1960-61	28.4
Field Goals	George Blanda, 1967-1975	156
Touchdowns (Tot.)	Fred Biletnikoff, 1965-1978	77
Points	George Blanda, 1967-1975	863

Individual Records—Single Season

Category	Name	Performance
Rushing (Yds.)	Marcus Allen, 1985	1,759
Passing (Yds.)	Ken Stabler, 1979	3,615
Passing (TDs)	Daryle Lamonica, 1969	34
Receiving (No.)	Todd Christensen, 1986	95
Receiving (Yds.)	Art Powell, 1964	1,361
Interceptions	Lester Hayes, 1980	13
Punting (Avg.)	Ray Guy, 1973	45.3
Punt Return (Avg.)	Claude Gibson, 1964	14.4
Kickoff Return (Avg.)	Harold Hart, 1975	30.5
Field Goals	George Blanda, 1973	23
Touchdowns (Tot.)	Marcus Allen, 1984	18
Points	George Blanda, 1968	117

Individual Records—Single Game

Category	Name	Performance
Rushing (Yds.)	Clem Daniels, 10-20-63	200
Passing (Yds.)	Cotton Davidson, 10-25-64	427
Passing (TDs)	Tom Flores, 12-22-63	6
	Daryle Lamonica, 10-19-69	6
Receiving (No.)	Dave Casper, 10-3-76	12
Receiving (Yds.)	Art Powell, 12-22-63	247
Interceptions	Many times	3
	Last time by Charles Phillips, 12-8-75	
Field Goals	Many times	4
	Last time by Chris Bahr, 10-6-85	
Touchdowns (Tot.)	Art Powell, 12-22-63	4
	Marcus Allen, 9-24-84	4
Points	Art Powell, 12-22-63	24
	Marcus Allen, 9-24-84	24

1986 Team Statistics

	Raiders	Opp.
Total First Downs	302	283
Rushing	97	85
Passing	186	168
Penalty	19	30
Third Down: Made/Att.	86/221	81/215
Fourth Down: Made/Att.	2/6	2/7
Total Net Yards	5299	4804
Avg. Per Game	331.2	300.3
Total Plays	1069	1003
Avg. Per Play	5.0	4.8
Net Yards Rushing	1790	1728
Avg. Per Game	111.9	108.0
Total Rushes	475	439
Net Yards Passing	3509	3076
Avg. Per Game	219.3	192.3
Tackled/Yards Lost	64/464	63/463
Gross Yards	3973	3539
Att./Completions	530/281	501/271
Completion Pct.	53.0	54.1
Had Intercepted	25	26
Punts/Avg.	90/40.2	97/42.1
Net Punting Avg.	33.8	35.1
Penalties/Yards Lost	114/951	118/868
Fumbles/Ball Lost	36/24	33/12
Touchdowns	37	43
Rushing	6	19
Passing	27	21
Returns	4	3
Avg. Time of Possession	30:40	29:20

1986 Team Record

Preseason (2-2)

Date	Result		Opponents
8/10	L	0-32	at San Francisco
8/16	W	24-19	Dallas
8/22	W	24-10	New England
8/28	L	22-25	Cleveland
		70-86	

Regular Season (8-8)

Date	Result		Opponents	Att.
9/7	L	36-38	at Denver	75,695
9/14	L	6-10	at Washington	55,235
9/21	L	9-14	N.Y. Giants	71,164
9/28	W	17-13	San Diego	63,153
10/5	W	24-17	at Kansas City	74,430
10/12	W	14-10	Seattle	70,635
10/19	W	30-28	at Miami	53,421
10/26	W	28-17	at Houston	41,641
11/2	L	10-21	Denver	90,153
11/9	W	17-13	at Dallas	61,706
11/16	W	27-14	Cleveland	65,461
11/20	W	37-31	at San Diego (OT)	56,031
11/30	L	27-33	Philadelphia (OT)	53,338
12/8	L	0-37	at Seattle	62,923
12/14	L	17-20	Kansas City	60,952
12/21	L	24-30	Indianapolis	41,349

(OT) Overtime

Score by Periods

Raiders	96	88	90	43	6	—	323
Opponents	69	99	92	80	6	—	346

Attendance

Home 516,205 Away 481,082 Total 997,287
Single game home record, 90,334 (1-1-84)
Single season home record, 516,205 (1986)

1986 Individual Statistics

Scoring

	TD R	TD P	TD Rt	PAT	FG	Saf	TP
Bahr	0	0	0	36/36	21/28	0	99
Christensen	0	8	0	0/0	0/0	0	48
Williams	0	8	0	0/0	0/0	0	48
Allen	5	2	0	0/0	0/0	0	42
Hester	0	6	0	0/0	0/0	0	36
Barksdale	0	2	0	0/0	0/0	0	12
Robinson	0	0	2	0/0	0/0	0	12
Hayes	0	0	1	0/0	0/0	0	6
McCallum	1	0	0	0/0	0/0	0	6
Parker	0	1	0	0/0	0/0	0	6
Walker	0	0	1	0/0	0/0	0	6
Townsend	0	0	0	0/0	0/0	1	2
Raiders	6	27	4	36/36	21/28	1	323
Opponents	19	21	3	40/42	16/21	0	346

Passing

	Att.	Comp.	Yds.	Pct.	TD	Int.	Tkld.	Rate
Plunkett	252	133	1986	52.8	14	9	27/215	82.5
Wilson	240	129	1721	53.8	12	15	34/227	67.4
Hilger	38	19	266	50.0	1	1	3/22	70.7
Raiders	530	281	3973	53.0	27	25	64/464	74.8
Opponents	501	271	3539	54.1	21	26	63/463	68.9

Rushing

	Att.	Yds.	Avg.	LG	TD
Allen	208	759	3.6	28t	5
McCallum	142	536	3.8	18	1
Hawkins	58	245	4.2	15	0
Strachan	18	53	2.9	10	0
Hilger	6	48	8.0	16	0
Plunkett	12	47	3.9	11	0
Wilson	14	45	3.2	13	0
Mueller	13	30	2.3	8	0
Williams	3	27	9.0	19	0
Guy	1	0	0.0	0	0
Raiders	475	1790	3.8	28t	6
Opponents	439	1728	3.9	70t	19

Receiving

	No.	Yds.	Avg.	LG	TD
Christensen	95	1153	12.1	35	8
Allen	46	453	9.8	36	2
Williams	43	843	19.6	53	8
Hawkins	25	166	6.6	16	0
Hester	23	632	27.5	81t	6
Barksdale	18	434	24.1	57t	2
McCallum	13	103	7.9	22	0
Moffitt	6	77	12.8	17	0
Mueller	6	54	9.0	20	0
Junkin	2	38	19.0	19	0
Pattison	2	12	6.0	6	0
Parker	2	8	4.0	6	1
Raiders	281	3973	14.1	81t	27
Opponents	271	3539	13.1	68t	21

Interceptions

	No.	Yds.	Avg.	LG	TD
McElroy	7	105	15.0	28	0
Robinson	4	42	10.5	32t	1
Seale	4	2	0.5	2	0
Haynes	2	28	14.0	22	0
Toran	2	28	14.0	19	0
Barnes	2	7	3.5	7	0
Hayes	2	7	3.5	7	0
Adams	1	32	32.0	32	0
Martin	1	15	15.0	15	0
McKenzie	1	9	9.0	9	0
Raiders	26	275	10.6	32t	1
Opponents	25	282	11.3	40t	1

Punting

	No.	Yds.	Avg.	In 20	LG
Guy	90	3620	40.2	20	64
Raiders	90	3620	40.2	20	64
Opponents	97	4087	42.1	15	63

Punt Returns

	No.	FC	Yds.	Avg.	LG	TD
Walker	49	15	440	9.0	70t	1
McCallum	7	1	44	6.3	13	0
Raiders	56	16	484	8.6	70t	1
Opponents	42	19	357	8.5	76t	1

Kickoff Returns

	No.	Yds.	Avg.	LG	TD
Adams	27	573	21.2	51	0
Walker	23	368	16.0	27	0
McCallum	8	183	22.9	59	0
Millen	3	40	13.3	19	0
Mueller	2	73	36.5	46	0
Hawkins	1	15	15.0	15	0
Raiders	64	1252	19.6	59	0
Opponents	63	1064	16.9	37	0

Sacks

	No.
Jones	15.5
Pickel	11.5
Townsend	11.5
Long	7.5
Toran	6.0
Martin	5.0
Barnes	2.0
Robinson	2.0
Franks, Jets-Raiders	1.0
McKenzie	1.0
Millen	1.0
Raiders	63.0
Opponents	64.0

FIRST-ROUND SELECTIONS

(If club had no first-round selection, first player drafted is listed with round in parentheses.)

Year	Player, College, Position
1960	Dale Hackbart, Wisconsin, CB
1961	Joe Rutgens, Illinois, DT
1962	Roman Gabriel, North Carolina State, QB
1963	George Wilson, Alabama, RB (6)
1964	Tony Lorick, Arizona State, RB
1965	Harry Schuh, Memphis State, T
1966	Rodger Bird, Kentucky, S
1967	Gene Upshaw, Texas A&I, G
1968	Eldridge Dickey, Tennessee State, QB
1969	Art Thoms, Syracuse, DT
1970	Raymond Chester, Morgan State, TE
1971	Jack Tatum, Ohio State, S
1972	Mike Siani, Villanova, WR
1973	Ray Guy, Southern Mississippi, K-P
1974	Henry Lawrence, Florida A&M, T
1975	Neal Colzie, Ohio State, DB
1976	Charles Philyaw, Texas Southern, DT (2)
1977	Mike Davis, Colorado, DB (2)
1978	Dave Browning, Washington, DE (2)
1979	Willie Jones, Florida State, DE (2)
1980	Marc Wilson, Brigham Young, QB
1981	Ted Watts, Texas Tech, DB
	Curt Marsh, Washington, T
1982	Marcus Allen, Southern California, RB
1983	Don Mosebar, Southern California, T
1984	Sean Jones, Northeastern, DE (2)
1985	Jessie Hester, Florida State, WR
1986	Bob Buczkowski, Pittsburgh, DE
1987	John Clay, Missouri, T

Los Angeles Raiders 1987 Veteran Roster

No.	Name	Pos.	Ht.	Wt.	Birth-date	NFL Exp.	College	Hometown	How Acq.	'86 Games/ Starts
44	Adams, Stefon	S	5-10	185	8/11/63	2	East Carolina	High Point, N.C.	D3-'85	16/0
32	Allen, Marcus	RB	6-2	205	3/22/60	6	Southern California	San Diego, Calif.	D1-'82	13/10
10	Bahr, Chris	K	5-10	170	2/3/53	12	Penn State	Feasterville, Pa.	FA-'80	16/0
88	Barksdale, Rod	WR	6-1	180	9/8/62	2	Arizona	Compton, Calif.	FA-'85	16/15
56	Barnes, Jeff	LB	6-2	230	3/1/55	11	California	Hayward, Calif.	D5-'77	16/0
82	Branton, Gene	TE	6-5	245	11/23/60	2	Texas Southern	Tampa, Fla.	FA-'86	0*
50	Byrd, Darryl	LB	6-1	220	9/3/60	3	Illinois	Union City, Calif.	FA-'87	0*
46	Christensen, Todd	TE	6-3	230	8/3/56	9	Brigham Young	Eugene, Ore.	FA-'79	16/16
79	†Davis, Bruce	T	6-6	280	6/21/56	9	UCLA	Marbury, Md.	D11-'79	16/16
45	Davis, James	S	6-0	190	6/12/57	6	Southern	Los Angeles, Calif.	D5-'81	16/0
36	Davis, Mike	S	6-3	200	4/15/56	9	Colorado	Los Angeles, Calif.	D2-'77	0*
94	Franks, Elvis	DE	6-4	265	7/9/57	8	Morgan State	Woodville, Tex.	FA-'86	7/0*
73	Hannah, Charley	G	6-5	265	7/26/55	11	Alabama	Chattanooga, Tenn.	T(TB)-'83	12/12
27	Hawkins, Frank	RB	5-9	210	7/3/59	7	Nevada-Reno	Las Vegas, Nev.	D10-'81	16/15
37	Hayes, Lester	CB	6-0	200	1/22/56	11	Texas A&M	Houston, Tex.	D5-'77	14/14
22	Haynes, Mike	CB	6-0	190	7/1/53	12	Arizona State	Los Angeles, Calif.	T(NE)-'83	13/13
84	Hester, Jessie	WR	5-11	170	1/21/63	3	Florida State	Belle Glade, Fla.	D1-'85	13/1
12	Hilger, Rusty	QB	6-4	205	5/9/62	3	Oklahoma State	Oklahoma City, Okla.	D6-'85	2/0
23	Horton, Ethan	RB	6-4	220	12/19/62	2	North Carolina	Kannapolis, N.C.	FA-'87	0*
99	Jones, Sean	DE	6-7	265	12/19/62	4	Northeastern	Montclair, N.J.	D2-'84	16/16
74	†Jordan, Shelby	T	6-7	280	1/23/52	12	Washington, Mo.	East St. Louis, Ill.	T(NE)-'83	16/2
87	Junkin, Trey	TE	6-2	225	1/23/61	5	Louisiana Tech	Winnfield, La.	FA-'85	3/0
59	Kimmel, Jamie	LB	6-3	235	3/28/61	2	Syracuse	Conklin, N.Y.	D4-'85	16/0
33	King, Kenny	RB	5-11	205	3/7/57	8	Oklahoma	Clarendon, Tex.	FA-'87	0*
52	King, Linden	LB	6-4	245	6/28/55	10	Colorado State	Colorado Springs, Colo.	FA-'86	16/0
70	Lawrence, Henry	T	6-4	270	9/26/51	14	Florida A&M	Palmetto, Fla.	D1-'74	16/14
51	Lewis, Bill	C	6-7	275	7/12/63	2	Nebraska	Sioux City, Iowa	D7-'86	4/0
80	t-Lofton, James	WR	6-3	197	7/5/56	10	Stanford	Los Angeles, Calif.	T(GB)-'87	15/15
75	Long, Howie	DE	6-5	270	1/6/60	7	Villanova	Charlestown, Mass.	D2-'81	13/12
11	Luther, Ed	QB	6-2	205	1/2/57	7	San Jose State	La Mirada, Calif.	FA-'87	10/0*
60	Marsh, Curt	G	6-5	270	8/25/59	5	Washington	Snohomish, Wash.	D1-'81	2/2
53	Martin, Rod	LB	6-2	225	4/7/54	11	Southern California	Los Angeles, Calif.	D12-'77	16/16
65	Marvin, Mickey	G	6-4	265	10/5/55	11	Tennessee	Hendersonville, N.C.	D4-'77	16/16
7	Mathison, Bruce	QB	6-3	210	4/25/59	4	Nebraska	Superior, Wis.	FA-'87	2/0*
34	McCallum, Napoleon	RB	6-2	215	10/6/63	2	Navy	Milford, Ohio	D4c-'86	15/5
47	McCloskey, Mike	TE	6-6	240	2/2/61	4	Penn State	Philadelphia, Pa.	FA-'87	0*
26	McElroy, Vann	S	6-0	195	1/13/60	6	Baylor	Uvalde, Tex.	D3-'82	16/16
54	McKenzie, Reggie	LB	6-1	240	2/8/63	3	Tennessee	Knoxville, Tenn.	D10-'85	16/16
55	Millen, Matt	LB	6-2	245	3/12/58	8	Penn State	Hokendauqua, Pa.	D2-'80	16/16
64	Miraldi, Dean	T	6-5	285	4/5/58	4	Utah	Rosemead, Calif.	FA-'87	0*
83	Moffett, Tim	WR	6-2	180	2/28/62	3	Mississippi	Taylorsville, Miss.	D3-'85	16/1
72	†Mosebar, Don	C	6-6	275	9/11/61	5	Southern California	Visalia, Calif.	D1-'83	16/16
42	Mueller, Vance	RB	6-0	210	5/5/64	2	Occidental	Jackson, Calif.	D4b-'86	15/1
81	Parker, Andy	TE	6-5	240	9/8/61	4	Utah	Ramona, Calif.	D5-'84	13/0
89	Pattison, Mark	WR	6-2	190	12/13/61	2	Washington	Seattle, Wash.	FA-'86	3/0*
71	Pickel, Bill	DT-NT	6-5	260	11/5/59	5	Rutgers	Brooklyn, N.Y.	D2-'83	15/15
16	†Plunkett, Jim	QB	6-2	220	12/5/47	17	Stanford	San Jose, Calif.	FA-'78	10/8
77	Riehm, Chris	G	6-6	275	4/14/61	2	Ohio State	Toledo, Ohio	FA-'86	12/2
57	Robinson, Jerry	LB	6-2	225	12/18/56	9	UCLA	Santa Rosa, Calif.	T(Phil)-'85	16/16
69	Russell, Rusty	T	6-5	275	8/16/63	2	South Carolina	Orangeburg, S.C.	FA-'86	0*
43	Seale, Sam	CB	5-9	180	10/6/62	4	Western State, Colo.	East Orange, N.J.	D8-'84	16/5
39	Strachan, Steve	RB	6-1	215	3/22/63	3	Boston College	Burlington, Mass.	D11-'85	16/1
30	Toran, Stacey	S	6-2	200	10/11/61	4	Notre Dame	Indianapolis, Ind.	D6-'84	16/16
93	†Townsend, Greg	DE	6-3	250	11/3/61	5	Texas Christian	Compton, Calif.	D4-'83	15/4
41	Walker, Fulton	S-KR	5-11	195	4/30/58	7	West Virginia	Martinsburg, W. Va.	FA-'85	14/0
48	t-Washington, Lionel	CB	6-0	185	10/21/60	5	Tulane	New Orleans, La.	T(StL)-'87	16/12
67	Wheeler, Dwight	C-G	6-3	285	1/3/55	7	Tennessee State	Memphis, Tenn.	FA-'87	0*
85	Williams, Dokie	WR	5-11	180	8/25/60	5	UCLA	Oceanside, Calif.	D5-'83	15/15
24	Williams, Gardner	CB	6-3	200	12/11/61	2	St. Mary's, Calif.	Oakland, Calif.	FA-'86	0*
98	Willis, Mitch	DT-NT	6-8	275	3/16/62	3	Southern Methodist	Arlington, Tex.	D7-'84	16/1
6	Wilson, Marc	QB	6-6	205	2/15/57	8	Brigham Young	Seattle, Wash.	D1-'80	16/8
31	Wilson, Wayne	RB	6-3	225	9/4/57	9	Shepard	Ellicott City, Md.	FA-'87	12/0*
90	Wise, Mike	DE	6-6	260	6/5/64	2	California-Davis	Novato, Calif.	D4a-'86	6/0

* Branton, M. Davis, G. Williams missed '86 season due to injury; Byrd last active with L.A. Raiders in '84; Franks played 4 games with L.A. Raiders in '86, 3 with N.Y. Jets; Horton last active with Kansas City in '86; K. King last active with L.A. Raiders in '85; Luther active for 10 games with Indianapolis in '86; Mathison played 2 games with San Diego; McCloskey last active with Houston in '85; Miraldi last active with Denver in '85; Pattison played 1 game with L.A. Rams, 2 with L.A. Raiders; Russell last active with Philadelphia in '84; Wheeler last active with L.A. Raiders in '84; W. Wilson played 7 games with Minnesota, 5 with New Orleans.

†Option playout; subject to developments.

t-Raiders traded for Lofton (Green Bay), Washington (St. Louis).

Retired—Ray Guy, 14-year punter, 16 games in '86; Derrick Jensen, 7-year tight end, 1 game in '86; Odis McKinney, 8-year safety, 2 games in '86.

Also played with Raiders in '86—TE Earl Cooper (5 games).

COACHING STAFF

Head Coach, Tom Flores

Pro Career: Begins ninth year as head coach. Guided Raiders to 38-9 victory over Redskins in Super Bowl XVIII and 27-10 win over Eagles in Super Bowl XV. Has been with Raiders' organization as either a player or coach for 22 years. Played six years at quarterback for Raiders 1960-61, 1963-66. After spending two years (1967-68) with the Buffalo Bills and two seasons (1969-70) with the Kansas City Chiefs, Flores returned to Oakland as receivers coach in February, 1972. Ranks as Raiders number-four all-time passer with 11,635 yards and 92 touchdowns. He also passed for a club-record six touchdowns in one game in 1963. Career record: 86-46.

Background: Quarterback at Fresno, Calif., J.C. 1954-55 and Pacific 1956-57. Coached at his alma mater in 1959 before joining Raiders as a quarterback in 1960.

Personal: Born March 21, 1937, in Fresno, Calif. Tom and his wife, Barbara, live in Manhattan Beach, Calif. They have twin sons, Mark and Scott, and a daughter, Kimberly.

Assistant Coaches

Sam Boghosian, offensive line; born December 22, 1931, Fresno, Calif., lives in Manhattan Beach, Calif. Guard UCLA 1951-54. No pro playing experience. College coach: UCLA 1955-64, Oregon State 1965-73. Pro coach: Houston Oilers 1974-75, Seattle Seahawks 1976-77, joined Raiders in 1979.

Willie Brown, defensive backfield; born December 2, 1940, Yazoo City, Miss., lives in Rancho Palos Verdes, Calif. Defensive back Grambling 1959-62. Pro cornerback Denver Broncos 1963-66, Oakland Raiders 1967-78. Pro coach: Joined Raiders in 1979.

Sam Gruneisen, linebackers; born January 16, 1941, Louisville, Ky., lives in El Segundo, Calif. Tight end, linebacker, kicker Villanova 1959-61. Pro center San Diego Chargers 1962-72, Houston Oilers 1973. College coach: Grossmont, Calif., J.C. 1981, California 1982-83, San Jose State 1986. Pro coach: Los Angeles Express (USFL) 1984-85, first year with Raiders.

Larry Kennan, quarterbacks; born June 13, 1944, Pomona, Calif., lives in Rancho Palos Verdes, Calif. Quarterback LaVerne College 1962-65. College coach: Colorado 1969-72, Nevada-Las Vegas 1973-75, Southern Methodist 1976-78, Lamar 1979-81. Pro coach: Joined Raiders in 1982.

Earl Leggett, defensive line; born May 5, 1933, Jacksonville, Fla., lives in Fountain Valley, Calif. Tackle Hinds J.C. 1953-54, Louisiana State 1955-56. Pro defensive tackle Chicago Bears 1957-65, Los Angeles Rams 1966, New Orleans Saints 1967-68. College coach: Nicholls State 1971, Texas Christian 1972-73. Pro coach: Southern California Sun (WFL) 1974-75, Seattle Seahawks 1976-77, San Francisco 49ers 1978, joined Raiders in 1980.

Terry Robiskie, coaches assistant; born November 12, 1954, New Orleans, La., lives in Beverly Hills, Calif. Running back Louisiana State 1973-76. Pro running back Oakland Raiders 1971-79, Miami Dolphins 1980-81. Pro coach: Joined Raiders in '82.

Joe Scannella, offensive backfield; born May 22, 1932, Passaic, N.J., lives in El Segundo, Calif. Quarterback Lehigh 1947-50. Pro safety Saskatchewan Roughriders (CFL) 1951-52. College coach: Cornell 1960, C.W. Post 1963-68 (head coach 1964-68), Vermont 1970-71. Pro coach: Montreal Alouettes (CFL) 1969, Oakland Raiders 1972-77, Montreal Alouettes (CFL) (head coach) 1978-81, Cleveland Browns 1982-84, rejoined Raiders in 1987.

Art Shell, offensive line; born November 26, 1946, Charleston, S.C., lives in Rancho Palos Verdes, Calif. Tackle Maryland State 1965-67. Pro offensive tackle Oakland Raiders 1968-81, Los Angeles Raiders 1982. Pro coach: Joined Raiders in 1983.

Los Angeles Raiders 1987 First-Year Roster

Name	Pos.	Ht.	Wt.	Birth-date	College	Hometown	How Acq.
Beuerlein, Steve	QB	6-2	205	3/7/65	Notre Dame	Fullerton, Calif.	D4
Blalock, Stanley (1)	WR	5-8	160	3/18/64	Georgia	Atlanta, Ga.	FA
Buczkowski, Bob (1)	DE	6-5	270	5/5/64	Pittsburgh	Monroeville, Pa.	D1-'86
Carter, Jeff (1)	P	5-11	205	7/25/63	Cal State-Fullerton	Merced, Calif.	FA
Clay, John	T	6-5	305	5/1/64	Missouri	St. Louis, Mo.	D1
Cochran, Brad (1)	CB	6-3	200	6/17/63	Michigan	Royal Oak, Mich.	D3-'86
Criswell, Ray (1)	P	6-0	185	8/16/63	Florida	Orange Park, Fla.	FA
Davis, Lee (1)	CB	5-11	190	12/18/62	Mississippi State	Amory, Miss.	FA
Eccles, Scott	TE	6-4	250	6/28/63	Eastern New Mexico	San Jose, Calif.	D9
Ellis, Jim	LB	6-2	240	3/25/64	Boise State	Redondo Beach, Calif.	D10c
Fernandez, Mervyn (1)	WR	6-3	205	12/29/59	San Jose State	San Jose, Calif.	D10-'83
Foster, Ron	S	6-1	200	11/25/63	Cal State-Northridge	Los Angeles, Calif.	FA
Gesek, John	G	6-5	275	2/18/63	Cal State-Sacramento	Danville, Calif.	D10b
Gilmore, Jim (1)	G	6-4	265	12/19/62	Ohio State	Philadelphia, Pa.	FA
Hall, Joe	LB	6-1	245	12/18/61	Cal State-Sacramento	Lombard, Ill.	FA
Harrison, Rob	RB	6-1	205	8/31/63	Cal State-Sacramento	Eureka, Calif.	D10a
Hess, Collins	S	6-3	200	7/9/64	Southern Mississippi	Huntsville, Tex.	FA
Hutson, Brian	CB	6-1	195	2/20/65	Mississippi State	Brandon, Miss.	FA
Johnson, Pat	RB	5-10	220	4/25/64	Cal State-Humboldt	Riverdale, Calif.	FA
Knapp, Greg (1)	QB	6-4	200	3/5/63	Cal State-Sacramento	Seal Beach, Calif.	FA
Lee, Zeph (1)	RB	6-3	215	6/17/63	Southern California	San Francisco, Calif.	D9-'86
Livingston, Scott (1)	P-K	6-1	205	6/1/62	Nebraska	Lakewood, Calif.	FA
Lockett, Wade	WR	6-1	195	2/13/64	Cal State-Fullerton	San Diego, Calif.	FA
McKinnerny, Deryl	LB	6-2	230	8/31/64	Mesa, Colo.	Weslaco, Tex.	FA
McLemore, Chris	RB	6-1	225	12/31/63	Arizona	Las Vegas, Nev.	D11a
McMillan, Dan (1)	LB	6-4	230	2/23/64	Colorado	Colorado Springs, Colo.	FA
Miller, Mike	DE	6-4	245	9/8/64	California Lutheran	Altadena, Calif.	FA
Miller, Patrick (1)	LB	6-1	215	6/24/64	Florida	Panama City, Fla.	FA
Owens, Jack	TE	6-4	230	9/10/64	Wichita State	Los Angeles, Calif.	FA
Perkins, Claude (1)	WR	5-11	175	5/28/62	Tarkio	Waterloo, Iowa	FA
Perry, Mario	TE	6-5	240	12/20/63	Mississippi	Memphis, Tenn.	D11b
Peterson, Bill	LB	6-1	230	12/4/64	Lock Haven State	Lock Haven, Pa.	FA
Regent, Shawn (1)	C	6-5	270	4/14/63	Boston College	Cheektowaga, N.Y.	FA
Reinke, Jeff (1)	DE	6-5	270	9/12/62	Mankato State	Sacred Heart, Minn.	D10-'86
Sartin, Martin (1)	RB	5-10	195	3/9/63	Long Beach State	Camden, N.J.	FA-'86
Smith, Steve	RB	6-1	235	8/30/64	Penn State	Clinton, Md.	D3
Stinson, Elliston (1)	WR	5-9	170	10/3/62	Rice	Galveston, Tex.	FA
Talley, Stan (1)	P	6-5	225	9/5/58	Texas Christian	Dana Point, Calif.	FA
Tillman, Tony	CB	5-9	170	9/12/63	Texas	Borger, Tex.	FA
Tubbs, Brad (1)	WR	6-4	200	3/14/63	St. Mary's, Calif.	Pleasant Hill, Calif.	FA-'86
White, Chris (1)	K	5-11	170	6/17/62	Illinois	Champaign, Ill.	FA
Walters, Rex	LB	6-2	215	1/29/61	Boise State	Aurora, Colo.	FA
Wilkerson, Bruce	T	6-5	290	7/28/64	Tennessee	Philadelphia, Tenn.	D2
Williams, Demise	S	6-1	215	7/9/64	Oklahoma State	Oxon Hill, Md.	FA
Williams, Keith (1)	LB	6-4	240	4/30/64	Clemson	St. Matthews, S.C.	FA
Williams, Lynn (1)	RB	6-0	210	12/19/62	Kansas	Carson, Calif.	FA
Woods, Chris (1)	WR	5-11	185	7/19/62	Auburn	Birmingham, Ala.	SD1-'84
Woolf, Scott (1)	QB	6-1	200	12/26/61	Mt. Union	Beloit, Ohio	FA

The term NFL Rookie is defined as a player who is in his first season of professional football and has not been on the roster of another professional football team for any regular-season or postseason games. A Rookie is designated by an "R" on NFL rosters. Players who have been active in another professional football league or players who have NFL experience, including either preseason training camp or being on an active roster for fewer than three regular-season or postseason games, are termed NFL First-Year Players. An NFL First-Year Player is designated by a "1" on NFL rosters. Thereafter, a player on an NFL active roster for at least three regular-season or postseason games is credited with an additional year of NFL playing experience.

NOTES

Charley Sumner, linebackers; born October 19, 1930, Radford, Va., lives in El Segundo, Calif. Back William & Mary 1952-54. Pro defensive back Chicago Bears 1955-60, Minnesota Vikings 1961-62. Pro coach: Oakland Raiders 1963-68, 1979-81, Los Angeles Raiders 1982-83, Pittsburgh Steelers 1969-72, New England Patriots 1973-78, Oakland Invaders (USFL) (head coach) 1985, rejoined Raiders in 1987.

Tom Walsh, receivers; born April 16, 1949, Vallejo, Calif., lives in Manhattan Beach, Calif. UC-Santa Barbara 1971. No college or pro playing experience. College coach: University of San Diego 1972-76, U.S. International 1979, Murray State 1980, Cincinnati 1981. Pro coach: Joined Raiders in 1982.

Ray Willsey, special teams; born September 30, 1929, Regina, Saskatchewan, lives in Playa del Rey, Calif. Quarterback-defensive back California 1951-52. Pro back Edmonton Eskimos (CFL) 1953. College coach: California 1954-55, 1964-71 (head coach), Washington 1956, Texas 1957-59. Pro coach: St. Louis Cardinals 1960-61, 1973-77, Washington Redskins 1962-63, joined Raiders in 1978.

American Football Conference Eastern Division

Team Colors: Aqua, Coral, and White

4770 Biscayne Boulevard
Suite 1440
Miami, Florida 33137
Telephone: (305) 576-1000

Club Officials

President: Joseph Robbie
Executive Vice President/General Manager: J. Michael Robbie
Vice President/Head Coach: Don Shula
Director of Pro Scouting: Charley Winner
Director of Player Personnel: Chuck Connor
Director of Publicity: Eddie White
Ticket Director: Kevin Fitzgerald
Controller: Howard Rieman
Traveling Secretary: Bryan Wiedmeier
Trainer: Bob Lundy
Equipment Manager: Bob Monica

Stadium: Joe Robbie Stadium • **Capacity:** 75,500
N.W. 27th Ave. & N.W. 199th St.
Miami, Florida 33125

Playing Surface: Grass

Training Camp: St. Thomas University
16400-D N.W. 32nd Avenue
Miami, Florida 33054

1987 Schedule

Preseason

Aug. 16	**Chicago**	8:00
Aug. 24	at Denver	6:00
Aug. 29	at Philadelphia	7:30
Sept. 4	**Buffalo**	8:00

Regular Season

Sept. 13	at New England	1:00
Sept. 20	at Indianapolis	12:00
Sept. 27	**New York Giants**	1:00
Oct. 4	at Seattle	1:00
Oct. 11	**Kansas City**	1:00
Oct. 18	at New York Jets	1:00
Oct. 25	**Buffalo**	1:00
Nov. 1	**Pittsburgh**	1:00
Nov. 8	at Cincinnati	4:00
Nov. 15	**Indianapolis**	1:00
Nov. 22	at Dallas	7:00
Nov. 29	at Buffalo	1:00
Dec. 7	**New York Jets** (Monday)	9:00
Dec. 13	at Philadelphia	1:00
Dec. 20	**Washington**	8:00
Dec. 28	**New England** (Monday)	9:00

Dolphins Coaching History

(205-120-4)

1966-69	George Wilson	15-39-2
1970-86	Don Shula	190-81-2

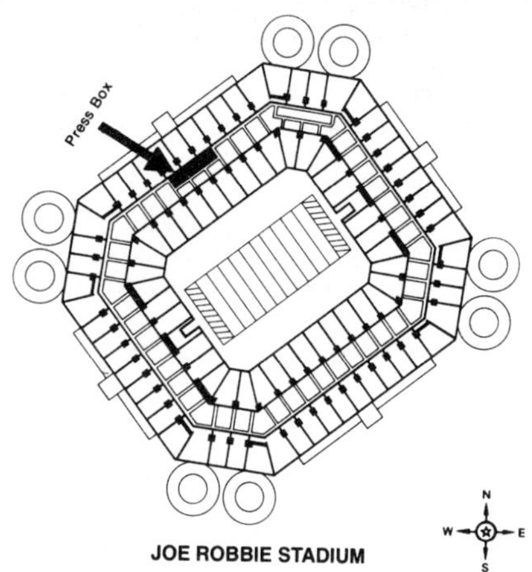

JOE ROBBIE STADIUM

Record Holders

Individual Records—Career

Category	Name	Performance
Rushing (Yds.)	Larry Csonka, 1968-1974, 1979	6,737
Passing (Yds.)	Bob Griese, 1967-1980	25,092
Passing (TDs)	Bob Griese, 1967-1980	192
Receiving (No.)	Nat Moore, 1974-1986	510
Receiving (Yds.)	Nat Moore, 1974-1986	7,547
Interceptions	Jake Scott, 1970-75	35
Punting (Avg.)	Reggie Roby, 1983-86	43.8
Punt Return (Avg.)	Freddie Solomon, 1975-77	11.4
Kickoff Return (Avg.)	Mercury Morris, 1969-1975	26.5
Field Goals	Garo Yepremian, 1970-78	165
Touchdowns (Tot.)	Nat Moore, 1974-1986	75
Points	Garo Yepremian, 1970-78	830

Individual Records—Single Season

Category	Name	Performance
Rushing (Yds.)	Delvin Williams, 1978	1,258
Passing (Yds.)	Dan Marino, 1984	5,084
Passing (TDs)	Dan Marino, 1984	48
Receiving (No.)	Mark Clayton, 1984	73
Receiving (Yds.)	Mark Clayton, 1984	1,389
Interceptions	Dick Westmoreland, 1967	10
Punting (Avg.)	Reggie Roby, 1984	44.7
Punt Return (Avg.)	Freddie Solomon, 1975	12.3
Kickoff Return (Avg.)	Duriel Harris, 1976	32.9
Field Goals	Garo Yepremian, 1971	28
Touchdowns (Tot.)	Mark Clayton, 1984	18
Points	Garo Yepremian, 1971	117

Individual Records—Single Game

Category	Name	Performance
Rushing (Yds.)	Mercury Morris, 9-30-73	197
Passing (Yds.)	Dan Marino, 12-2-84	470
Passing (TDs)	Bob Griese, 11-24-77	6
	Dan Marino, 9-21-86	6
Receiving (No.)	Duriel Harris, 10-28-79	10
	Tony Nathan, 9-29-85	10
	Tony Nathan, 9-28-86	10
Receiving (Yds.)	Mark Duper, 11-10-85	217
Interceptions	Dick Anderson, 12-3-73	4
Field Goals	Garo Yepremian, 9-26-71	5
Touchdowns (Tot.)	Paul Warfield, 12-15-73	4
Points	Paul Warfield, 12-15-73	24

1986 Team Statistics

	Dolphins	Opp.
Total First Downs	351	337
Rushing	84	144
Passing	250	177
Penalty	17	16
Third Down: Made/Att.	97/191	86/209
Fourth Down: Made/Att.	2/10	10/18
Total Net Yards	6324	6050
Avg. Per Game	395.3	378.1
Total Plays	1011	1058
Avg. Per Play	6.3	5.7
Net Yards Rushing	1545	2493
Avg. Per Game	96.6	155.8
Total Rushes	349	540
Net Yards Passing	4779	3557
Avg. Per Game	298.7	222.3
Tackled/Yards Lost	17/119	33/268
Gross Yards	4898	3825
Att./Completions	645/392	485/290
Completion Pct.	60.8	59.8
Had Intercepted	23	13
Punts/Avg.	56/44.2	64/41.4
Net Punting Avg.	37.4	36.1
Penalties/Yards Lost	72/609	82/596
Fumbles/Ball Lost	37/14	32/14
Touchdowns	56	47
Rushing	9	23
Passing	46	22
Returns	1	2
Avg. Time of Possession	29:24	30:26

1986 Team Record

Preseason (2-2)

Date	Result		Opponents
8/9	L	16-30	at Minnesota
8/15	L	10-17	Cleveland
8/23	W	20-15	at Philadelphia
8/29	W	21- 3	Tampa Bay
		67-65	

Regular Season (8-8)

Date	Result		Opponents	Att.
9/7	L	28-50	at San Diego	57,726
9/14	W	30-10	Indianapolis	51,848
9/21	L	45-51	at N.Y. Jets (OT)	71,025
9/28	L	16-31	San Francisco	70,264
10/5	L	7-34	at New England	60,689
10/12	W	27-14	Buffalo	49,467
10/19	L	28-30	L.A. Raiders	53,421
10/26	W	17-13	at Indianapolis	58,350
11/2	W	28- 7	Houston	43,804
11/10	L	16-26	at Cleveland	77,949
11/16	W	34-24	at Buffalo	76,474
11/24	W	45- 3	N.Y. Jets	70,206
11/30	L	14-20	Atlanta	53,762
12/7	W	31-27	at New Orleans	64,761
12/14	W	37-31	at L.A. Rams (OT)	62,629
12/22	L	27-34	New England	74,516

(OT) Overtime

Score by Periods

Dolphins	45	177	102	100	6	—	430
Opponents	101	127	58	113	6	—	405

Attendance

Home 467,288 Away 529,603 Total 996,891
Single game home record, 78,939 (1-2-72; Orange Bowl)
Single season home record, 542,951 (1985; Orange Bowl)

1986 Individual Statistics

Scoring	TD R	TD P	TD Rt	PAT	FG	Saf	TP
Reveiz	0	0	0	52/55	14/22	0	94
Hampton	9	3	0	0/0	0/0	0	72
Duper	0	11	0	0/0	0/0	0	66
Clayton	0	10	0	0/0	0/0	0	60
N. Moore	0	7	0	0/0	0/0	0	42
Hardy	0	5	0	0/0	0/0	0	30
Johnson	0	4	0	0/0	0/0	0	24
Pruitt	0	2	1	0/0	0/0	0	18
Nathan	0	2	0	0/0	0/0	0	12
Davenport	0	1	0	0/0	0/0	0	6
Jensen	0	1	0	0/0	0/0	0	6
Dolphins	9	46	1	52/55	14/22	0	430
Opponents	23	22	2	45/46	26/31	0	405

Passing	Att.	Comp.	Yds.	Pct.	TD	Int.	Tkld.	Rate
Marino	623	378	4746	60.7	44	23	17/119	92.5
Strock	20	14	152	70.0	2	0	0/0	125.4
Jensen	2	0	0	0.0	0	0	0/0	39.6
Dolphins	645	392	4898	60.8	46	23	17/119	93.3
Opponents	485	290	3825	59.8	22	13	33/268	88.7

Rushing	Att.	Yds.	Avg.	LG	TD
Hampton	186	830	4.5	54t	9
Davenport	75	314	4.2	35	0
Nathan	27	203	7.5	20	0
Bennett	36	162	4.5	16	0
Clayton	2	33	16.5	22	0
Carter	4	18	4.5	9	0
Ellis	3	6	2.0	2	0
Strock	1	0	0.0	0	0
Marino	12	−3	−0.3	13	0
Roby	2	−8	−4.0	0	0
Duper	1	−10	−10.0	−10	0
Dolphins	349	1545	4.4	54t	9
Opponents	540	2493	4.6	47	23

Receiving	No.	Yds.	Avg.	LG	TD
Duper	67	1313	19.6	85t	11
Hampton	61	446	7.3	19	3
Clayton	60	1150	19.2	68t	10
Hardy	54	430	8.0	18t	5
Nathan	48	457	9.5	23t	2
N. Moore	38	431	11.3	38t	7
Davenport	20	177	8.9	27	1
Johnson	19	170	8.9	20	4
Pruitt	15	235	15.7	27	2
Jensen	5	50	10.0	20t	1
Bennett	4	33	8.3	13	0
Carter	1	6	6.0	6	0
Dolphins	392	4898	12.5	85t	46
Opponents	290	3825	13.2	65t	22

Interceptions	No.	Yds.	Avg.	LG	TD
Rose	2	63	31.5	36	0
McNeal	2	46	23.0	29	0
G. Blackwood	2	10	5.0	7	0
Judson	2	0	0.0	0	0
D. Brown, S.D.-Mia	1	23	23.0	23	0
L. Blackwood	1	14	14.0	14	0
Offerdahl	1	14	14.0	14	0
B. Brown	1	3	3.0	3	0
Charles	1	2	2.0	2	0
Kozlowski	1	0	0.0	0	0
Dolphins	13	152	11.7	36	0
Opponents	23	221	9.6	70t	1

Punting	No.	Yds.	Avg.	In 20	LG
Roby	56	2476	44.2	13	73
Dolphins	56	2476	44.2	13	73
Opponents	64	2648	41.4	16	64

Punt Returns	No.	FC	Yds.	Avg.	LG	TD
Ellis	24	1	149	6.2	17	0
Pruitt	11	1	150	13.6	71t	1
G. Blackwood	1	0	0	0.0	0	0
L. Blackwood	1	0	0	0.0	0	0
Clayton	1	0	0	0.0	0	0
N. Moore	1	6	−2	−2.0	0	0
Thompson	1	0	0	0.0	0	0
Kozlowski	0	3	0	—	0	0
Dolphins	40	11	297	7.4	71t	1
Opponents	23	15	200	8.7	34	0

Kickoff Returns	No.	Yds.	Avg.	LG	TD
Ellis	25	541	21.6	41	0
Davenport	16	285	17.8	37	0
Hampton	9	182	20.2	25	0
Carter	9	133	14.8	22	0
Hardy	3	39	13.0	16	0
L. Lee	1	5	5.0	5	0
Johnson	1	0	0.0	0	0
Toth	1	0	0.0	0	0
Dolphins	65	1185	18.2	41	0
Opponents	53	997	18.8	40	0

Sacks	No.
M. Brown	5.0
Betters	4.0
H. Green	4.0
Little	4.0
J. Foster	3.0
Robinson, S.D.-Mia.	3.0
Robinson, Mia.	2.0
Brudzinski	2.0
Offerdahl	2.0
Turner	2.0
Baumhower	1.0
Frazier, Buff.-Mia	1.0
M. Moore	1.0
Shipp	1.0
Smith	1.0
Sochia	1.0
Dolphins	33.0
Opponents	17.0

FIRST-ROUND SELECTIONS

(If club had no first-round selection, first player drafted is listed with round in parentheses.)

Year	Player, College, Position
1966	Jim Grabowski, Illinois, RB
	Rick Norton, Kentucky, QB
1967	Bob Griese, Purdue, QB
1968	Larry Csonka, Syracuse, RB
	Doug Crusan, Indiana, T
1969	Bill Stanfill, Georgia, DE
1970	Jim Mandich, Michigan, TE (2)
1971	Otto Stowe, Iowa State, WR (2)
1972	Mike Kadish, Notre Dame, DT
1973	Chuck Bradley, Oregon, C (2)
1974	Donald Reese, Jackson State, DE
1975	Darryl Carlton, Tampa, T
1976	Larry Gordon, Arizona State, LB
	Kim Bokamper, San Jose State, LB
1977	A.J. Duhe, Louisiana State, DT
1978	Guy Benjamin, Stanford, QB (2)
1979	Jon Giesler, Michigan, T
1980	Don McNeal, Alabama, DB
1981	David Overstreet, Oklahoma, RB
1982	Roy Foster, Southern California, G
1983	Dan Marino, Pittsburgh, QB
1984	Jackie Shipp, Oklahoma, LB
1985	Lorenzo Hampton, Florida, RB
1986	John Offerdahl, Western Michigan, LB (2)
1987	John Bosa, Boston College, DE

Miami Dolphins 1987 Veteran Roster

No.	Name	Pos.	Ht.	Wt.	Birth-date	NFL Exp.	College	Hometown	How Acq.	'86 Games/ Starts
1	Banks, Fred	WR-KR	5-10	165	5/26/62	2	Liberty University	Columbus, Ga.	FA-'87	0*
73	†Baumhower, Bob	NT	6-5	265	8/4/55	10	Alabama	Palm Beach Gardens, Fla.	D2-'77	12/12
34	†Bennett, Woody	RB	6-2	225	3/24/56	9	Miami	York, Pa.	W(NYJ)-'80	16/14
75	Betters, Doug	DE	6-7	265	6/11/56	10	Nevada-Reno	Arlington Heights, Ill.	D6-'78	16/1
47	Blackwood, Glenn	S	6-0	190	2/23/57	9	Texas	San Antonio, Tex.	D8b-'79	10/10
43	†Brown, Bud	S	6-0	194	4/19/61	4	Southern Mississippi	DeKalb, Miss.	D11-'84	16/15
32	Brown, Donald	CB	5-11	189	11/28/63	2	Maryland	Annapolis, Md.	FA-'86	15/7*
51	†Brown, Mark	LB	6-2	230	7/18/61	5	Purdue	Inglewood, Calif.	D9-'83	14/11
59	Brudzinski, Bob	LB	6-4	223	1/1/55	11	Ohio State	Fremont, Ohio	T(Rams)-'81	16/16
71	Charles, Mike	NT	6-4	287	9/23/62	5	Syracuse	Newark, N.J.	D2-'83	9/4
	Clark, Steve	G	6-4	260	8/2/60	5	Utah	Salt Lake City, Utah	D9a-'82	0*
83	Clayton, Mark	WR	5-9	175	4/8/61	5	Louisville	Indianapolis, Ind.	D8b-'83	15/14
30	Davenport, Ron	RB	6-2	230	12/22/62	3	Louisville	Atlanta, Ga.	D6b-'85	16/2
65	Dellenbach, Jeff	T	6-6	280	2/14/63	3	Wisconsin	Wausau, Wis.	D4b-'85	13/6
85	Duper, Mark	WR	5-9	187	1/25/59	6	Northwestern State, La.	Moreauville, La.	D2-'82	16/16
61	Foster, Roy	G	6-4	275	5/24/60	6	Southern California	Shawnee Mission, Kan.	D1-'82	16/16
53	Frye, David	LB	6-2	227	6/21/61	5	Purdue	Cincinnati, Ohio	FA-'86	9/2
79	Giesler, Jon	T	6-5	265	12/23/56	9	Michigan	Woodville, Ohio	D1-'79	7/7
74	Green, Cleveland	T	6-3	262	9/11/57	9	Southern	Utica, Miss.	FA-'87	11/5
55	Green, Hugh	LB	6-2	225	7/27/59	7	Pittsburgh	Natchez, Miss.	T(TB)-'85	3/3
21	Griffin, Larry	CB-S	6-0	203	1/11/63	2	North Carolina	Chesapeake, Va.	FA-'87	3/0*
27	Hampton, Lorenzo	RB	6-0	212	3/12/62	3	Florida	Lake Wales, Fla.	D1-'85	16/16
84	Hardy, Bruce	TE	6-5	232	6/1/56	10	Arizona State	Bingham, Utah	D9-'78	16/16
90	Hendel, Andy	LB	6-1	230	3/4/61	2	North Carolina State	Rochester, N.Y.	FA-'86	16/1
29	Hobley, Liffort	CB-S	6-1	199	5/12/62	2	Louisiana State	Shreveport, La.	FA-'87	0*
11	Jensen, Jim	WR-QB	6-4	215	11/14/58	7	Boston University	Doylestown, Pa.	D11-'81	16/0
87	Johnson, Dan	TE	6-3	240	5/17/60	5	Iowa State	New Hope, Minn.	D7a-'82	15/1
49	Judson, William	CB	6-2	190	3/26/59	6	South Carolina State	Atlanta, Ga.	D8-'81	16/16
68	†Koch, Greg	T	6-4	276	6/14/55	11	Arkansas	Houston, Tex.	FA-'86	16/16
54	Kolic, Larry	LB	6-1	242	8/31/63	2	Ohio State	Smithville, Ohio	D7-'86	2/2
40	Kozlowski, Mike	S	6-1	198	2/24/56	8	Colorado	Encinitas, Calif.	D10b-'79	15/0
44	Lankford, Paul	CB	6-2	184	6/15/58	6	Penn State	Farmingdale, N.Y.	D3-'82	12/12
66	†Lee, Larry	G-C	6-2	263	9/10/59	7	UCLA	Dayton, Ohio	W(Det)-'85	16/5
72	Lee, Ronnie	G	6-4	265	12/24/56	9	Baylor	Tyler, Tex.	T(Atl)-'84	10/9
99	Little, George	DE	6-4	278	6/27/63	3	Iowa	Duquesne, Pa.	D3a-'85	16/16
13	Marino, Dan	QB	6-4	214	9/15/61	5	Pittsburgh	Pittsburgh, Pa.	D1-'83	16/16
96	Marshall, David	LB	6-2	220	1/31/61	2	Eastern Michigan	Cleveland, Ohio	FA-'87	0*
28	†McNeal, Don	CB	5-11	192	5/6/58	7	Alabama	Atmore, Ala.	D1-'80	15/1
69	Mendoza, Ruben	G	6-3	278	5/10/63	2	Wayne State	Milwaukee, Wis.	FA-'87	6/0*
89	†Moore, Nat	WR	5-9	188	9/19/51	14	Florida	Miami, Fla.	D3-'74	16/1
22	Nathan, Tony	RB	6-0	206	12/14/56	9	Alabama	Birmingham, Ala.	D3a-'79	16/0
56	Offerdahl, John	LB	6-2	232	8/17/64	2	Western Michigan	Fort Atkinson, Wis.	D2-'86	15/15
82	Pruitt, James	WR	6-2	199	1/29/64	2	Cal State-Fullerton	Los Angeles, Calif.	D4-'86	16/0
7	Reveiz, Fuad	K	5-11	222	2/24/63	3	Tennessee	Miami, Fla.	D7-'85	16/0
4	Roby, Reggie	P	6-2	243	7/30/61	5	Iowa	East Waterloo, Iowa	D6-'83	15/0
26	Rose, Donovan	S	6-1	190	3/9/57	3	Hampton Institute	Norfolk, Va.	FA-'86	12/2
80	Rose, Joe	TE	6-3	230	6/24/57	7	California	Marysville, Calif.	D7-'80	0*
52	Sendlein, Robin	LB	6-3	225	12/1/58	6	Texas	Las Vegas, Nev.	T(Minn)-'85	0*
50	Shipp, Jackie	LB	6-2	236	3/19/62	4	Oklahoma	Stillwater, Okla.	D1-'84	16/14
25	Smith, Mike	CB	6-0	171	10/24/62	3	Texas-El Paso	Houston, Tex.	D4a-'85	14/0
70	Sochia, Brian	NT-DE	6-3	274	7/21/61	5	N.W. Oklahoma State	Brasher Falls, N.Y.	FA-'86	6/0
57	Stephenson, Dwight	C	6-2	255	11/20/57	8	Alabama	Hampton, Va.	D2-'80	16/16
10	†Strock, Don	QB	6-5	225	11/27/50	14	Virginia Tech	Pottstown, Pa.	D5-'73	16/0
24	Thompson, Reyna	CB	5-11	194	8/28/63	2	Baylor	Dallas, Tex.	D9-'86	16/4
76	Toth, Tom	T	6-5	275	5/23/62	2	Western Michigan	Orland Park, Ill.	FA-'86	13/0
95	Turner, T.J.	DE	6-4	265	5/16/63	2	Houston	Lufkin, Tex.	D3-'86	16/15

* Banks last active with Cleveland in '85; D. Brown played 13 games with San Diego in '86, 2 with Miami; Clark, J. Rose, and Sendlein missed '86 season due to injury; Griffin played 3 games with Houston; Hobley last active with St. Louis in '85; Marshall last active with Cleveland in '84; Mendoza played 6 games with Green Bay.

†Option playout; subject to developments.

Also played with Dolphins in '86—S Lyle Blackwood (5 games), LB Jay Brophy (4), RB Joe Carter (7), RB-KR Craig Ellis (9), NT Jerome Foster (14), DE Mack Moore (7), LB Alex Moyer (3), LB Fred Robinson (15), LB Jack Squirek (2), LB Johnny Taylor (1), T Chris Ward (active for 1 game, but did not play).

COACHING STAFF

Head Coach, Don Shula

Pro Career: Begins his twenty-fifth season as an NFL head coach, and eighteenth with the Dolphins. Miami has won or shared first place in the AFC East in 13 of his 17 years. Has highest overall winning percentage (.707) among active NFL coaches with 75 or more wins. Captured back-to-back NFL championships, defeating Washington 14-7 in Super Bowl VII and Minnesota 24-7 in Super Bowl VIII. Lost to Dallas 24-3 in Super Bowl VI, to Washington 27-17 in Super Bowl XVII, and to San Francisco 38-16 in Super Bowl XIX. His 1972 17-0 club is the only team in NFL history to go undefeated throughout the regular season and postseason. Started his pro playing career with Cleveland Browns as defensive back in 1951. After two seasons with Browns, spent 1953-56 with Baltimore Colts and 1957 with Washington Redskins. Joined Detroit Lions as defensive coach in 1960 and was named head coach of the Colts in 1963. Baltimore had a 13-1 record in 1968 and captured NFL championship before losing to New York Jets in Super Bowl III. Career record: 263-107-6.

Background: Outstanding offensive player at John Carroll University in Cleveland before becoming defensive specialist as a pro. His alma mater gave him doctorate in humanities, May 1973. Served as assistant coach at Virginia in 1958 and at Kentucky in 1959.

Personal: Born January 4, 1930, in Painesville, Ohio. Don and his wife, Dorothy, live in Miami Lakes and have five children—David, Donna, Sharon, Annie, and Mike.

Assistant Coaches

Tom Olivadotti, defense; born September 22, 1945, Long Branch, N.J., lives in Miami. Defensive end-wide receiver Upsala 1963-66. No pro playing experience. College coach: Princeton 1975-77, Boston College 1978-79, Miami 1980-83. Pro coach: Cleveland Browns 1985-86, first year with Dolphins.

Mel Phillips, defensive backfield; born January 6, 1942, Shelby, N.C., lives in Miami Lakes. Defensive back-running back North Carolina A&T 1964-65. Pro defensive back San Francisco 49ers 1966-77. Pro coach: Detroit Lions 1980-84, joined Dolphins in 1985.

John Sandusky, offense-offensive line; born December 28, 1925, Philadelphia, Pa., lives in Cooper City, Fla. Tackle Villanova 1946-49. Pro tackle Cleveland Browns 1950-55, Green Bay Packers 1956. College coach: Villanova 1957-58. Pro coach: Baltimore Colts 1959-72 (head coach 1972), Philadelphia Eagles 1973-75, joined Dolphins in 1976.

Dan Sekanovich, defensive line; born July 27, 1933, West Hazleton, Pa., lives in Miami. End Tennessee 1951-53. Pro defensive end Montreal Alouettes (CFL) 1954. College coach: Susquehanna 1961-63, Connecticut 1964-67, Pittsburgh 1968, Navy 1969-70, Kentucky 1971-72. Pro coach: Montreal Alouettes (CFL) 1973-76, New York Jets 1977-82, Atlanta Falcons 1983-85, joined Dolphins in 1986.

David Shula, assistant head coach-receivers and quarterbacks; born May 28, 1959, Lexington, Ky., lives in Miami Lakes. Wide receiver Dartmouth 1978-80. Pro receiver Baltimore Colts 1981. Pro coach: Joined Dolphins in 1982.

Chuck Studley, linebackers; born January 17, 1929, Maywood, Ill., lives in Miami Lakes. Guard Illinois 1949-51. No pro playing experience. College coach: Illinois 1955-59, Massachusetts 1960 (head coach), Cincinnati 1961-68 (head coach). Pro coach: Cincinnati Bengals 1969-78, San Francisco 49ers 1979-82, Houston Oilers 1983 (interim head coach for last 10 games), joined Dolphins in 1984.

Carl Taseff, offensive backfield; born September 28, 1928, Cleveland, Ohio, lives in Pembroke Pines, Fla. Back John Carroll 1947-50. Pro defensive back Cleveland Browns 1951, Baltimore Colts 1953-61, Philadelphia Eagles 1961, Buffalo Bills 1962. Pro coach: Boston Patriots 1964, Detroit Lions 1965-66, joined Dolphins in 1970.

Miami Dolphins 1987 First-Year Roster

Name	Pos.	Ht.	Wt.	Birth-date	College	Hometown	How Acq.
Bennett, Charles (1)	DE	6-5	257	2/9/63	S.W. Louisiana	Clarksdale, Miss.	FA
Bosa, John	DE	6-4	263	1/10/64	Boston College	Keene, N.H.	D1
Brown, Tom	RB	6-1	218	11/20/64	Pittsburgh	Burrell, Pa.	D7
Browne, Jim (1)	RB	6-1	216	3/16/62	Boston College	Pontiac, Mich.	FA
Carter, Alex (1)	DE	6-3	255	9/6/63	Tennessee State	Miami, Fla.	FA
Casale, Mark (1)	QB	6-2	217	9/17/62	Montclair State	Union, N.J.	FA
Chavez, Laz (1)	LB	6-0	220	12/20/63	Iona	Port Chester, N.Y.	FA
Chavis, Eddie	WR	6-0	182	7/12/63	Montclair State	Plainfield, N.J.	FA
Conlin, Chris	T-G	6-4	290	6/7/65	Penn State	Glenside, Pa.	D5
Corsetti, Enrico	LB	6-1	225	1/13/63	Bates College	Belmont, Mass.	FA
Dennis, Mark	T	6-6	291	4/15/65	Illinois	Washington, Ill.	D8b
Douglas, Leland	WR	6-0	179	9/23/63	Baylor	Beaumont, Tex.	FA
Dycus, Lanny (1)	QB	6-2	219	11/29/62	Sam Houston State	Abilene, Tex.	FA
Gabrish, Jim (1)	G-T	6-3	258	6/12/63	Citadel	Canfield, Ohio	FA
Gieselman, Scott (1)	TE	6-6	247	4/3/63	Boston College	Belmont, Mass.	FA
Graf, Rick	LB	6-5	239	8/29/63	Wisconsin	Madison, Wis.	D2a
Guth, Chris	LB	6-2	219	6/14/64	Columbia	Woodbridge, N.J.	FA
Hooper, Trell (1)	CB-S	5-11	182	12/22/61	Memphis State	Jackson, Tenn.	FA
Isom, Rickey (1)	RB	6-0	224	11/30/63	North Carolina State	Harrisburg, Pa.	FA
Jenkins, DeShon	CB-S	6-1	198	12/19/64	Northwestern St., La.	Jena, La.	FA
Karsatos, Jim	QB	6-4	238	5/26/63	Ohio State	Fullerton, Calif.	D12
Katolin, Mike (1)	C	6-3	270	1/30/58	San Jose State	Whittier, Calif.	FA
Konecny, Mark (1)	RB	5-11	197	4/2/63	Alma College	Muskegon, Mich.	FA
Lambrecht, Mike	NT	6-1	271	5/2/63	St. Cloud State	Watertown, Minn.	FA
Lilja, David	TE	6-4	230	8/14/64	Indiana	Orland Park, Ill.	FA
Little, John	CB-S	6-2	196	6/12/64	Georgia	Panama, Fla.	FA
MacDonald, Danny (1)	LB	6-3	244	9/2/63	Idaho State	Kennewick, Wash.	FA
Mann, Terance	NT	6-4	295	9/29/64	Southern Methodist	Detroit, Mich.	D11
Marrone, Doug (1)	T	6-5	269	7/25/64	Syracuse	New York, N.Y.	FA
Nuffer, Brian	RB	5-10	184	6/12/63	Northwestern	Boise, Idaho	FA
O'Neill, Brian (1)	DE	6-4	266	12/31/62	New Hampshire	Waterville, Maine	FA
Ours, Greg (1)	G	6-5	279	10/29/63	Muskingum College	Hebron, Ohio	FA
Pidgeon, Tim	LB	5-11	237	9/20/64	Syracuse	Oneonta, N.Y.	D9
Rosado, Dan (1)	G	6-4	275	7/6/59	Northern Illinois	Canton, Ga.	FA
Schwedes, Scott	WR-KR	6-0	174	6/30/65	Syracuse	Jamesville, N.Y.	D2b
Sellers, Lance	LB	6-1	231	2/24/63	Boise State	Twin Falls, Idaho	D6
Shakespeare, Stanley (1)	WR	5-11	180	2/5/63	Miami	Boynton Beach, Fla.	FA
Slater, Elton	CB-S	5-10	193	3/10/64	S.W. Louisiana	Port Arthur, Tex.	FA
Smith, Ken (1)	G	6-1	285	10/16/60	Miami, Ohio	Indianapolis, Ind.	FA
Smith, Vernice	G	6-2	256	10/24/65	Florida A&M	Orlando, Fla.	FA
Stradford, Troy	RB	5-9	191	9/11/64	Boston College	Linden, N.J.	D4
Taylor, Bobby	CB-S	5-9	179	2/24/65	Wisconsin	Columbus, Ga.	D10
Walling, Brian	RB	5-8	188	9/16/63	Acadia U., Canada	Mississauga, Ontario	FA
Washington, Keith	WR	5-11	162	5/10/65	Virginia Military	Pomfret, Md.	FA
Williams, Joel	TE	6-3	242	3/16/65	Notre Dame	Monroeville, Pa.	D8a
Wise, Daryl	WR	6-2	197	7/7/64	Georgia Tech	Vidalia, Ga.	FA

The term NFL Rookie is defined as a player who is in his first season of professional football and has not been on the roster of another professional football team for any regular-season or postseason games. A Rookie is designated by an "R" on NFL rosters. Players who have been active in another professional football league or players who have NFL experience, including either preseason training camp or being on an active roster for fewer than three regular-season or postseason games, are termed NFL First-Year Players. An NFL First-Year Player is designated by a "1" on NFL rosters. Thereafter, a player on an NFL active roster for at least three regular-season or postseason games is credited with an additional year of NFL playing experience.

NOTES

Junior Wade, strength-conditioning; born February 2, 1947, Bath, S.C., lives in Miami. South Carolina State 1969. No college or pro playing experience. Pro coach: Joined Dolphins in 1975, coach since 1983.

Mike Westhoff, special teams-tight ends; born January 10, 1948, Pittsburgh, Pa., lives in Miami. Center-linebacker Wichita State 1967-69. No pro playing experience. College coach: Indiana 1974-75, Dayton 1976, Indiana State 1977, Northwestern 1978-80, Texas Christian 1981. Pro coach: Baltimore/Indianapolis Colts 1982-84, Arizona Outlaws (USFL) 1985, joined Dolphins in 1986.

American Football Conference
Eastern Division

Team Colors: Red, White, and Blue

Sullivan Stadium
Route 1
Foxboro, Massachusetts 02035
Telephone: (617) 543-7911

Club Officials

President: William H. Sullivan, Jr.
Executive Vice President: Charles W. Sullivan
Vice President: Francis J. (Bucko) Kilroy
General Manager: Patrick J. Sullivan
Director of Player Development: Dick Steinberg
Director of Pro Scouting: Bill McPeak
Director of College Scouting: Joe Mendes
Executive Director of Player Personnel: Darryl Stingley
Personnel Scouts: George Blackburn, Larry Cook, Charles Garcia, Pat Naughton, Bob Teahan
Director of Public Relations and Sales: Dave Wintergrass
Director of Publicity: Jim Greenidge
Assistant Publicity Director: Jimmy Oldham
Box Office Manager: Ken Sternfeld
Trainer: Ron O'Neil
Equipment Manager: George Luongo
Video Manager: Ken Deininger

Stadium: Sullivan Stadium • **Capacity:** 61,000
Route 1
Foxboro, Massachusetts 02035

Playing Surface: SuperTurf

Training Camp: Bryant College
Smithfield, Rhode Island 02917

1987 Schedule

Preseason

Aug. 16	**New York Giants**	1:30
Aug. 23	**Philadelphia**	7:00
Aug. 29	at Minnesota	2:00
Sept. 4	vs. Atl. at Jacksonville, Fla.	8:00

Regular Season

Sept. 13	**Miami**	1:00
Sept. 21	at N.Y. Jets (Monday)	9:00
Sept. 27	at Washington	1:00
Oct. 4	**Cleveland**	1:00
Oct. 11	**Buffalo**	1:00
Oct. 18	at Houston	12:00
Oct. 25	at Indianapolis	1:00
Nov. 1	**Los Angeles Raiders**	1:00
Nov. 8	at New York Giants	8:00
Nov. 15	**Dallas**	1:00
Nov. 22	**Indianapolis**	1:00
Nov. 29	**Philadelphia**	1:00
Dec. 6	at Denver	2:00
Dec. 13	**New York Jets**	1:00
Dec. 20	at Buffalo	1:00
Dec. 28	at Miami (Monday)	9:00

Patriots Coaching History

Boston 1960-70
(189-201-9)

1960-61	Lou Saban*	7-12-0
1961-68	Mike Holovak	53-47-9
1969-70	Clive Rush**	5-16-0
1970-72	John Mazur***	9-21-0
1972	Phil Bengtson	1-4-0
1973-78	Chuck Fairbanks****	46-41-0
1978	Hank Bullough-Ron Erhardt#	0-1-0
1979-81	Ron Erhardt	21-27-0
1982-84	Ron Meyer##	18-16-0
1984-86	Raymond Berry	29-16-0

*Released after five games in 1961
**Released after seven games in 1970
***Resigned after nine games in 1972
****Resigned after 15 games in 1978
#Co-coaches
##Released after eight games in 1984

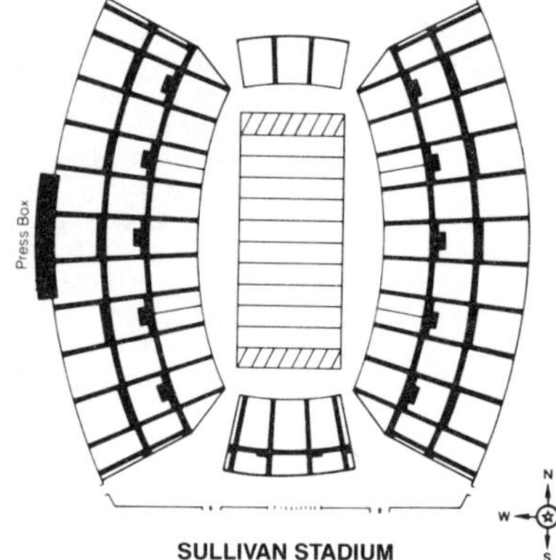

SULLIVAN STADIUM

Record Holders

Individual Records—Career

Category	Name	Performance
Rushing (Yds.)	Sam Cunningham, 1973-79, 1981-82	5,453
Passing (Yds.)	Steve Grogan, 1975-1986	22,557
Passing (TDs)	Steve Grogan, 1975-1986	155
Receiving (No.)	Stanley Morgan, 1977-1986	435
Receiving (Yds.)	Stanley Morgan, 1977-1986	8,692
Interceptions	Ron Hall, 1961-67	29
	Raymond Clayborn, 1977-1986	29
Punting (Avg.)	Rich Camarillo, 1981-86	42.9
Punt Return (Avg.)	Mack Herron, 1973-75	12.0
Kickoff Return (Avg.)	Horace Ivory, 1977-1981	27.6
Field Goals	Gino Cappelletti, 1960-1970	176
Touchdowns (Tot.)	Stanley Morgan, 1977-1986	58
Points	Gino Cappelletti, 1960-1970	1,130

Individual Records—Single Season

Category	Name	Performance
Rushing (Yds.)	Jim Nance, 1966	1,458
Passing (Yds.)	Vito (Babe) Parilli, 1964	3,465
Passing (TDs)	Vito (Babe) Parilli, 1964	31
Receiving (No.)	Stanley Morgan, 1986	84
Receiving (Yds.)	Stanley Morgan, 1986	1,491
Interceptions	Ron Hall, 1964	11
Punting (Avg.)	Rich Camarillo, 1983	44.6
Punt Return (Avg.)	Mack Herron, 1974	14.8
Kickoff Return (Avg.)	Raymond Clayborn, 1977	31.0
Field Goals	Tony Franklin, 1986	32
Touchdowns (Tot.)	Steve Grogan, 1976	13
	Stanley Morgan, 1979	13
Points	Gino Cappelletti, 1964	155

Individual Records—Single Game

Category	Name	Performance
Rushing (Yds.)	Tony Collins, 9-18-83	212
Passing (Yds.)	Tony Eason, 9-21-86	414
Passing (TDs)	Vito (Babe) Parilli, 11-15-64	5
	Vito (Babe) Parilli, 10-15-67	5
	Steve Grogan, 9-9-79	5
Receiving (No.)	Art Graham, 11-20-66	11
Receiving (Yds.)	Stanley Morgan, 11-8-81	182
Interceptions	Many times	3
	Last time by Roland James, 10-23-83	
Field Goals	Gino Cappelletti, 10-4-64	6
Touchdowns (Tot.)	Many times	3
	Last time by Stanley Morgan, 9-21-86	
Points	Gino Cappelletti, 12-18-65	28

1986 Team Statistics

	Patriots	Opp.
Total First Downs	314	286
Rushing	77	118
Passing	202	153
Penalty	35	15
Third Down: Made/Att.	77/227	78/219
Fourth Down: Made/Att.	8/11	7/12
Total Net Yards	5327	5181
Avg. Per Game	332.9	323.8
Total Plays	1073	1031
Avg. Per Play	5.0	5.0
Net Yards Rushing	1373	2203
Avg. Per Game	85.8	137.7
Total Rushes	469	510
Net Yards Passing	3954	2978
Avg. Per Game	247.1	186.1
Tackled/Yards Lost	47/367	48/346
Gross Yards	4321	3324
Att./Completions	557/340	473/255
Completion Pct.	61.0	53.9
Had Intercepted	13	21
Punts/Avg.	92/40.7	90/39.8
Net Punting Avg.	33.1	33.4
Penalties/Yards Lost	87/672	106/866
Fumbles/Ball Lost	27/11	38/19
Touchdowns	45	35
Rushing	10	19
Passing	29	15
Returns	6	1
Avg. Time of Possession	30:29	29:31

1986 Team Record

Preseason (4-1)

Date	Result		Opponents
8/2	W	21-16	St. Louis
8/10	W	18- 7	Washington
8/16	W	38-34	at New Orleans
8/22	L	10-24	at L.A. Raiders
8/30	W	16- 9	at Green Bay
		103-90	

Regular Season (11-5)

Date	Result		Opponents	Att.
9/7	W	33- 3	Indianapolis	55,208
9/11	W	20- 6	at N.Y. Jets	72,422
9/21	L	31-38	Seattle	58,977
9/28	L	20-27	at Denver	75,804
10/5	W	34- 7	Miami	60,689
10/12	L	24-31	N.Y. Jets	60,342
10/19	W	34- 0	at Pittsburgh	54,743
10/26	W	23- 3	at Buffalo	77,808
11/2	W	25-17	Atlanta	60,597
11/9	W	30-21	at Indianapolis	56,890
11/16	W	30-28	at L.A. Rams	64,339
11/23	W	22-19	Buffalo	60,455
11/30	W	21-20	at New Orleans	58,259
12/7	L	7-31	Cincinnati	60,633
12/14	L	24-29	San Francisco	60,787
12/22	W	34-27	at Miami	74,516

Postseason (0-1)

Date	Result		Opponent	Att.
1/4/87	L	17-22	Denver	76,105

Score by Periods

Patriots	82	102	99	129	0	—	412
Opponents	34	83	64	126	0	—	307

Attendance

Home 482,572 Away 558,763 Total 1,041,335
Single game home record, 61,457 (12-5-71)
Single season home record, 482,572 (1986)

1986 Individual Statistics

Scoring	TD R	TD P	TD Rt	PAT	FG	Saf	TP
Franklin	0	0	0	44/45	32/41	0	140
Morgan	0	10	0	0/0	0/0	0	60
Collins	3	5	0	0/0	0/0	0	48
Fryar	0	6	1	0/0	0/0	0	42
C. James	4	0	0	0/0	0/0	0	24
Scott	0	3	0	0/0	0/0	0	18
Baty	0	2	0	0/0	0/0	0	12
Starring	0	2	0	0/0	0/0	0	12
Tatupu	1	0	1	0/0	0/0	0	12
Grogan	1	0	0	0/0	0/0	0	6
Jones	0	1	0	0/0	0/0	0	6
Marion	0	0	1	0/0	0/0	0	6
McSwain	0	0	1	0/0	0/0	0	6
Rembert	0	0	1	0/0	0/0	0	6
B. Williams	0	0	1	0/0	0/0	0	6
Weathers	1	0	0	0/0	0/0	0	6
Patriots	10	29	6	44/45	32/41	1	412
Opponents	19	15	1	34/35	21/28	0	307

Passing	Att.	Comp.	Yds.	Pct.	TD	Int.	Tkld.	Rate
Eason	448	276	3328	61.6	19	10	43/336	89.2
Grogan	102	62	976	60.8	9	2	4/31	113.8
C. James	4	1	10	25.0	1	1	0/0	39.6
Ramsey	3	1	7	33.3	0	0	0/0	42.4
Patriots	557	340	4321	61.0	29	13	47/367	92.9
Opponents	473	255	3324	53.9	15	21	48/346	68.4

Rushing	Att.	Yds.	Avg.	LG	TD
C. James	154	427	2.8	16	4
Collins	156	412	2.6	17	3
Tatupu	71	172	2.4	13	1
Eason	35	170	4.9	26	0
Fryar	4	80	20.0	31	0
Weathers	21	58	2.8	16t	1
Dupard	15	39	2.6	11	0
Grogan	9	23	2.6	10	1
Hawthorne	1	5	5.0	5	0
Starring	1	0	0.0	0	0
Ramsey	1	−6	−6.0	−6	0
Jones	1	−7	−7.0	−7	0
Patriots	469	1373	2.9	31	10
Opponents	510	2203	4.3	58t	19

Receiving	No.	Yds.	Avg.	LG	TD
Morgan	84	1491	17.8	44t	10
Collins	77	684	8.9	49	5
Fryar	43	737	17.1	69t	6
Baty	37	331	8.9	22	2
Hawthorne	24	192	8.0	17	0
C. James	18	129	7.2	17	0
Starring	16	295	18.4	47	2
Tatupu	15	145	9.7	25	0
Jones	14	222	15.9	28	1
Scott	8	41	5.1	8t	3
D. Williams	2	35	17.5	26	0
Weathers	1	14	14.0	14	0
Holloway	1	5	5.0	5	0
Patriots	340	4321	12.7	69t	29
Opponents	255	3324	13.0	67t	15

Interceptions	No.	Yds.	Avg.	LG	TD
Lippett	8	76	9.5	43	0
Clayborn	3	4	1.3	4	0
Marion	2	56	28.0	37t	1
McGrew	2	44	22.0	27	0
R. James	2	39	19.5	21	0
Nelson	2	21	10.5	17	0
Rembert	1	37	37.0	37	0
McSwain	1	3	3.0	3	0
Tippett	0	32	—	32	0
Patriots	21	312	14.9	69	1
Opponents	13	151	11.6	26	0

Punting	No.	Yds.	Avg.	In 20	LG
Camarillo	89	3746	42.1	16	64
Patriots	92	3746	40.7	16	64
Opponents	90	3585	39.8	21	73

Punt Returns	No.	FC	Yds.	Avg.	LG	TD
Fryar	35	10	366	10.5	59t	1
Starring	6	0	18	3.0	12	0
Marion	1	1	12	12.0	12	0
R. James	0	1	0	—	0	0
Patriots	42	12	396	9.4	59t	1
Opponents	60	4	565	9.4	39	0

Kickoff Returns	No.	Yds.	Avg.	LG	TD
Starring	36	802	22.3	52	0
Fryar	10	192	19.2	33	0
Jones	4	63	15.8	20	0
Dupard	3	50	16.7	21	0
Rembert	3	27	9.0	14	0
Hawthorne	2	13	6.5	13	0
Patriots	58	1147	19.8	52	0
Opponents	81	1480	18.3	39	0

Sacks	No.
Veris	11.0
Tippett	9.5
Blackmon	7.5
B. Williams	7.0
Rembert	4.0
Hodge	1.0
R. James	1.0
McGrew	1.0
Nelson	1.0
Owens	1.0
Reynolds	1.0
Ruth	1.0
Thomas	1.0
Sims	0.5
T. Williams	0.5
Patriots	48.0
Opponents	47.0

FIRST-ROUND SELECTIONS

(If club had no first-round selection, first player drafted is listed with round in parentheses.)

Year	Player, College, Position
1960	Ron Burton, Northwestern, RB
1961	Tommy Mason, Tulane, RB
1962	Gary Collins, Maryland, WR
1963	Art Graham, Boston College, WR
1964	Jack Concannon, Boston College, QB
1965	Jerry Rush, Michigan State, DE
1966	Karl Singer, Purdue, T
1967	John Charles, Purdue, S
1968	Dennis Byrd, North Carolina State, DE
1969	Ron Sellers, Florida State, WR
1970	Phil Olsen, Utah State, DE
1971	Jim Plunkett, Stanford, QB
1972	Tom Reynolds, San Diego State, WR (2)
1973	John Hannah, Alabama, G
	Sam Cunningham, Southern California, RB
	Darryl Stingley, Purdue, WR
1974	Steve Corbett, Boston College, G (2)
1975	Russ Francis, Oregon, TE
1976	Mike Haynes, Arizona State, DB
	Pete Brock, Colorado, C
	Tim Fox, Ohio State, DB
1977	Raymond Clayborn, Texas, DB
	Stanley Morgan, Tennessee, WR
1978	Bob Cryder, Alabama, G
1979	Rick Sanford, South Carolina, DB
1980	Roland James, Tennessee, DB
	Vagas Ferguson, Notre Dame, RB
1981	Brian Holloway, Stanford, T
1982	Kenneth Sims, Texas, DT
	Lester Williams, Miami, DT
1983	Tony Eason, Illinois, QB
1984	Irving Fryar, Nebraska, WR
1985	Trevor Matich, Brigham Young, C
1986	Reggie Dupard, Southern Methodist, RB
1987	Bruce Armstrong, Louisville, T

New England Patriots 1987 Veteran Roster

No.	Name	Pos.	Ht.	Wt.	Birth-date	NFL Exp.	College	Hometown	How Acq.	'86 Games/ Starts
62	†Bain, Bill	T	6-4	290	8/9/52	13	Southern California	Los Angeles, Calif.	FA-'86	7/0*
48	Baty, Greg	TE	6-5	241	8/28/64	2	Stanford	Sparta, N.J.	D8-'86	16/7
94	Black, Mel	LB	6-2	228	2/2/62	2	Eastern Illinois	West Haven, Conn.	FA-'86	3/0
55	Blackmon, Don	LB	6-3	235	3/14/58	7	Tulsa	Land-O-Lakes, Fla.	D4-'81	15/15
28	Bowman, Jim	S	6-2	210	10/26/63	3	Central Michigan	Cadillac, Mich.	D2b-'85	16/1
58	†Brock, Pete	C	6-5	275	7/14/54	12	Colorado	Portland, Ore.	D1b-'76	16/16
3	†Camarillo, Rich	P	5-11	185	11/29/59	7	Washington	Pico Rivera, Calif.	FA-'81	16/0
26	Clayborn, Raymond	CB	6-0	186	1/2/55	11	Texas	Ft. Worth, Tex.	D1a-'77	16/16
33	Collins, Tony	RB	5-11	222	5/27/59	7	East Carolina	Penn Yan, N.Y.	D2-'81	16/15
87	†Dawson, Lin	TE	6-3	240	6/24/59	6	North Carolina State	Kinston, N.C.	D8b-'81	0*
49	Dennison, Glenn	TE	6-3	225	11/17/61	2	Miami	Beaver Falls, Pa.	FA-'87	0*
59	Doig, Steve	LB	6-2	240	3/28/60	5	New Hampshire	North Reading, Mass.	FA-'86	5/0
21	Dupard, Reggie	RB	5-11	205	10/30/63	2	Southern Methodist	New Orleans, La.	D1-'86	6/0
11	†Eason, Tony	QB	6-4	212	10/8/59	5	Illinois	Walnut Grove, Calif.	D1-'83	15/14
66	†Fairchild, Paul	G	6-4	270	9/14/61	4	Kansas	Glidden, Iowa	D5-'84	15/15
62	t-Farrell, Sean	G	6-3	260	5/25/60	6	Penn State	Westhampton, N.Y.	T(TB)-'87	16/15
1	†Franklin, Tony	K	5-8	182	11/18/56	9	Texas A&M	Big Spring, Tex.	T(Phil)-'84	16/0
80	Fryar, Irving	WR-KR	6-0	200	9/28/62	4	Nebraska	Mt. Holly, N.J.	D1-'84	14/13
43	†Gibson, Ernest	CB	5-10	185	10/3/61	4	Furman	Jacksonville, Fla.	D6-'84	15/1
14	Grogan, Steve	QB	6-4	210	7/24/53	13	Kansas State	Ottawa, Kan.	D5a-'75	4/2
68	Haley, Darryl	T	6-4	265	2/16/61	5	Utah	Los Angeles, Calif.	D2c-'82	16/6
27	Hawthorne, Greg	TE	6-2	235	9/5/56	9	Baylor	Ft. Worth, Tex.	T(Pitt)-'84	14/10
97	Hodge, Milford	DE	6-3	278	3/11/61	2	Washington State	San Francisco, Calif.	FA-'86	7/0*
76	Holloway, Brian	T	6-7	288	7/25/59	7	Stanford	Potomac, Md.	D1-'81	15/15
51	Ingram, Brian	LB	6-4	235	10/31/59	5	Tennessee	Memphis, Tenn.	D4b-'82	0*
32	†James, Craig	RB	6-0	215	1/2/61	4	Southern Methodist	Houston, Tex.	D7-'83	13/12
38	James, Roland	S	6-2	191	2/18/58	8	Tennessee	Xenia, Ohio	D1a-'80	15/15
83	Jones, Cedric	WR	6-1	184	6/1/60	6	Duke	Weldon, N.C.	D3a-'82	16/0
42	†Lippett, Ronnie	CB	5-11	180	12/10/60	5	Miami	Sebring, Fla.	D8-'83	15/15
31	Marion, Fred	S	6-2	191	8/2/59	6	Miami	Gainesville, Fla.	D5-'82	16/16
64	Matich, Trevor	C	6-4	270	10/9/61	3	Brigham Young	Sacramento, Calif.	D1-'85	11/1
50	McGrew, Lawrence	LB	6-5	233	7/23/57	7	Southern California	Berkeley, Calif.	D2-'80	14/14
23	McSwain, Rod	CB	6-1	198	1/28/62	4	Clemson	Caroleen, N.C.	T(Atl)-'84	9/0
67	Moore, Steve	T	6-5	305	10/1/60	5	Tennessee State	Memphis, Tenn.	D3b-'83	11/11
75	Morriss, Guy	C-G	6-4	275	5/13/51	15	Texas Christian	Arlington, Tex.	FA-'84	16/0
86	Morgan, Stanley	WR	5-11	181	2/17/55	11	Tennessee	Easley, S.C.	D1b-'77	16/16
57	Nelson, Steve	LB	6-2	230	4/26/51	14	North Dakota State	Anoka, Minn.	D2b-'74	10/10
98	Owens, Dennis	NT	6-1	258	2/24/60	6	North Carolina State	Clinton, N.C.	FA-'82	16/1
70	†Plunkett, Art	T	6-8	282	3/8/59	6	Nevada-Las Vegas	Salt Lake City, Utah	FA-'85	0*
22	Profit, Eugene	CB	5-10	165	11/11/64	2	Yale	Baton Rouge, La.	FA-'86	4/0
12	†Ramsey, Tom	QB	6-1	189	7/9/61	3	UCLA	Encino, Calif.	D10c-'83	5/0
52	Rembert, Johnny	LB	6-3	234	1/19/61	5	Clemson	Arcadia, Fla.	D4-'83	16/10
95	Reynolds, Ed	LB	6-5	242	9/23/61	5	Virginia	Ridgeway, Va.	FA-'83	16/3
65	Ruth, Mike	NT	6-1	266	2/25/64	2	Boston College	Norristown, Pa.	D2a-'86	6/0
88	t-Scott, Willie	TE	6-4	245	2/13/59	7	South Carolina	Newberry, S.C.	T(KC)-'86	14/0
77	†Sims, Kenneth	DE	6-5	271	10/31/59	6	Texas	Kosse, Tex.	D1a-'82	3/0
81	Starring, Stephen	WR-KR	5-10	172	7/30/61	5	McNeese State	Vinton, La.	D3a-'83	14/2
30	†Tatupu, Mosi	RB	6-0	227	4/26/55	10	Southern California	Honolulu, Hawaii	D8b-'78	16/5
56	Tippett, Andre	LB	6-3	241	12/27/59	6	Iowa	Newark, N.J.	D2b-'82	11/11
60	Veris, Garin	DE	6-4	255	2/27/63	3	Stanford	Chillicothe, Ohio	D2a-'85	16/15
24	†Weathers, Robert	RB	6-2	225	9/13/60	6	Arizona State	Ft. Pierce, Fla.	D2a-'82	5/0
53	Weishuhn, Clayton	LB	6-1	218	10/7/59	4	Angelo State	San Angelo, Tex.	D3b-'82	4/0
96	Williams, Brent	DE	6-3	278	10/23/64	2	Toledo	Flint, Mich.	D7b-'86	16/16
82	†Williams, Derwin	WR	6-1	185	5/6/61	3	New Mexico	Brownwood, Tex.	D7b-'84	16/0
54	Williams, Ed	LB	6-4	244	9/8/61	4	Texas	Ector, Tex.	D2-'84	8/0
90	Williams, Toby	NT	6-4	270	11/19/59	5	Nebraska	Washington, D.C.	D10b-'83	16/16
61	Wooten, Ron	G	6-4	273	6/28/59	6	North Carolina	Kinston, N.C.	D6-'81	16/16

* Bain played 4 games with N.Y. Jets, 3 games with New England in '86; Hodge played 1 game with New Orleans, 6 games with New England; Dawson, Ingram, and Plunkett missed '86 season due to injury; Dennison last active with N.Y. Jets in '84.

†Option playout; subject to developments.

t-Patriots traded for Farrell (Tampa Bay), Scott (Kansas City).

Also played with Patriots in '86—G Adam Lingner (active for 1 game, but did not play).

COACHING STAFF

Head Coach, Raymond Berry

Pro Career: Has led the Patriots to two playoff appearances in two full years as the team's head coach (came to club midway through 1984 season). New England has gone 11-5 in each of the last two regular seasons. In 1986, the Patriots won the AFC East title and then lost to the host Denver Broncos in a divisional playoff game. The previous season saw the Patriots reach Super Bowl XX after gaining entry into the playoffs as a wild-card team. New England reached the Super Bowl by winning three straight road games, the only time it has been done in NFL history. Became the ninth head coach in Patriots history when he was named to replace Ron Meyer on October 25, 1984, after the eighth game of the season. Played receiver for the Baltimore Colts 1955-67. Made 631 catches for 9,275 yards and 68 touchdowns in his playing career. His number of career catches is presently fifth-best ever in the NFL, while his receiving yardage is seventh-best and his career touchdown catches fifteenth. Helped Colts to two world championships (1958 and 1959) and to NFL Championship Game (1964). Named all-pro three times (1958-60) and played in five Pro Bowl games. Led NFL in receiving 1958-60. Holds NFL Championship Game records for yardage (178) and receptions (12), set in 1958 sudden-death title game vs. New York Giants. Was inducted into Pro Football Hall of Fame on July 29, 1973, five years after his retirement. Was receivers coach with Dallas Cowboys in 1968-69, Detroit Lions 1973-75, Cleveland Browns 1976-77, and New England Patriots 1978-81. Career record: 29-16.

Background: Attended Paris (Tex.) High School and Southern Methodist 1951-54, where he played receiver. Receivers coach at Arkansas 1970-72.

Personal: Born February 27, 1933, in Corpus Christi, Tex. Raymond and his wife, Sally, live in Medfield, Mass., with their children—Mark, Suzanne, and Ashley.

Assistant Coaches

Dean Brittenham, strength-conditioning; born June 25, 1931, Brady, Neb., lives in Smithfield, R.I. 1957 graduate of Nebraska. No college or pro playing experience. College coach: Kansas 1962-64, Occidental 1965-67, Nebraska 1968-71, Colorado 1972-81. Pro coach: Kansas City Chiefs 1969-70, New Orleans Saints 1977-78, Denver Broncos 1982-83, Minnesota Vikings 1984, joined Patriots in 1985.

Jim Carr, defensive backs; born March 25, 1933, Kayford, W. Va., lives in North Attleboro, Mass. Running back-defensive back-linebacker Morris Harvey (now Univ. of Charleston, W. Va.) 1951-54. Pro running back-defensive back-linebacker Chicago Cardinals 1955-57, Montreal Alouettes (CFL) 1958, Philadelphia Eagles 1959-63, Washington Redskins 1964-65. Pro coach: Minnesota Vikings 1966-68, 1979-81, Chicago Bears 1969, 1973-74, Philadelphia Eagles 1970-72, Detroit Lions 1975-76, Buffalo Bills 1977, San Francisco 49ers 1978, Denver Gold (USFL) 1983-84, joined Patriots in 1985.

Ray Hamilton, assistant defensive line; born January 20, 1951, Omaha, Neb., lives in Sharon, Mass. Defensive tackle Oklahoma 1970-72. Nose tackle New England Patriots 1973-81. Pro coach: Joined Patriots in 1985.

Rod Humenuik, assistant head coach-offense, offensive coordinator; born June 17, 1938, Detroit, Mich., lives in Mansfield, Mass. Guard Southern California 1956-58. Pro guard Winnipeg Blue Bombers (CFL) 1960-62. College coach: Fullerton, Calif., J.C. 1964-65, Southern California 1966-70, Cal State-Northridge 1971-72 (head coach). Pro coach: Toronto Argonauts (CFL) 1973-74, Cleveland Browns 1975-82, Kansas City Chiefs 1983-84, joined Patriots in 1985.

Harold Jackson, receivers; born January 6, 1946, Quincy, Miss., lives in Foxboro, Mass. Wide receiver Jackson State 1964-67. Pro wide receiver Los Angeles Rams 1968, 1973-77, Philadelphia Eagles 1969-72, New England Patriots 1978-81, Seattle Seahawks 1983. Pro coach: Joined Patriots in 1985.

New England Patriots 1987 First-Year Roster

Name	Pos.	Ht.	Wt.	Birth-date	College	Hometown	How Acq.
Armstrong, Bruce	T	6-4	284	9/7/65	Louisville	Miami, Fla.	D1
Beasley, Derrick	CB-S	6-1	205	7/13/65	Winston-Salem	Detroit, Mich.	D4b
Chapman, David (1)	TE	6-4	245	5/8/62	West Virginia Tech	New Martinsville, W.Va.	FA
Colton, George (1)	G	6-3	279	7/28/63	Maryland	Lindenhurst, N.Y.	FA
Davis, Elgin	RB	5-10	192	10/23/65	Central Florida	Jacksonville, Fla.	D12
Gannon, Rich	QB-RB	6-2	197	12/20/65	Delaware	Philadelphia, Pa.	D4a
Gibson, Tom	DE	6-7	250	12/20/63	Northern Arizona	Saugus, Calif.	D5b
Jones, Cletis (1)	RB	5-10	217	8/6/64	Florida State	Tallahassee, Fla.	FA
Jordan, Eric (1)	RB-KR	6-0	190	11/17/61	Purdue	Las Vegas, Nev.	SD2-'84
Jordan, Tim	LB	6-3	226	4/26/64	Wisconsin	Madison, Wis.	D4c
Keel, Mark (1)	TE	6-3	242	10/1/62	Arizona	Tacoma, Wash.	D9-'83
Linne, Larry (1)	WR	6-1	185	7/20/62	Texas-El Paso	Midland, Tex.	FA
Perryman, Bob	RB	6-2	233	10/16/64	Michigan	Bourne, Mass.	D3
Reed, Benton (1)	DE	6-5	262	5/7/63	Mississippi	Baton Rouge, La.	FA
Reveiz, Carlos	K	5-8	189	4/20/64	Tennessee	Miami, Fla.	D11
Shegog, Ron (1)	CB-S	6-0	185	3/2/64	Austin-Peay	Batesville, Miss.	FA
Taylor, Gene	WR	6-2	189	11/12/62	Fresno State	Oakland, Calif.	D6
Thomas, Gene (1)	WR	5-10	157	6/7/62	Pacific	San Diego, Calif.	FA
Villa, Danny	T	6-5	305	9/21/64	Arizona	Nogales, Ariz.	D5a

The term NFL Rookie is defined as a player who is in his first season of professional football and has not been on the roster of another professional football team for any regular-season or postseason games. A Rookie is designated by an "R" on NFL rosters. Players who have been active in another professional football league or players who have NFL experience, including either preseason training camp or being on an active roster for fewer than three regular-season or postseason games, are termed NFL First-Year Players. An NFL First-Year Player is designated by a "1" on NFL rosters. Thereafter, a player on an NFL active roster for at least three regular-season or postseason games is credited with an additional year of NFL playing experience.

NOTES

Ed Khayat, defensive line; born September 14, 1935, Moss Point, Miss., lives in Quincy, Mass. Offensive-defensive end Millsaps 1953, Perkinston J.C. 1954, Tulane 1955-56. Pro defensive end-defensive tackle Washington Redskins 1957, 1962-63, Philadelphia Eagles 1958-61, 1964-65, Boston Patriots 1966. Pro coach: New Orleans Saints 1967-70, Philadelphia Eagles 1971-72 (head coach), Detroit Lions 1973-74, Atlanta Falcons 1975-76, Baltimore Colts 1977-81, Detroit Lions 1982-84, joined Patriots in 1985.

John Polonchek, special assistant to head coach; born January 1, 1928, in Granastrov, Czechoslovakia, lives in Foxboro, Mass. Running back-defensive back Michigan State 1947-49. No pro playing experience. College coach: Michigan State 1950, 1955-57, Colorado 1959-61. Pro coach: Oakland Raiders 1967-71, Green Bay Packers 1972-74, New England Patriots 1975-81, New Jersey Generals (USFL) 1982-83, rejoined Patriots in 1985.

Rod Rust, defensive coordinator; born August 2, 1928, Webster City, Iowa, lives in Foxboro, Mass. Center-linebacker Iowa State 1947-49. No pro playing experience. College coach: New Mexico 1960-62, Stanford 1963-66, North Texas State 1967-72 (head coach). Pro coach: Montreal Alouettes (CFL) 1973-75, Philadelphia Eagles 1976-77, Kansas City Chiefs 1978-82, joined Patriots in 1983.

Dante Scarnecchia, special teams-tight ends; born February 15, 1948, Los Angeles, Calif., lives in Wrentham, Mass. Center Taft, Calif., J.C. 1966-67, California Western 1968-69. No pro playing experience. College coach: California Western 1970-72, Iowa State 1973-74, Southern Methodist 1975-76, 1980-81, Pacific 1977-78, Northern Arizona 1979. Pro coach: Joined Patriots in 1982.

Don Shinnick, linebackers; born May 15, 1935, Kansas City, Mo., lives in Walpole, Mass. Guard-defensive back-running back-linebacker UCLA 1954-56. Pro linebacker Baltimore Colts 1957-69. College coach: Central Methodist College (Fayette, Missouri; head coach) 1979-81. Pro coach: Chicago Bears 1970-71, St. Louis Cardinals 1972, Oakland Raiders 1973-77, joined Patriots in 1985.

Les Steckel, quarterbacks-passing game coordinator; born July 1, 1946, Whitehall, Pa., lives in Foxboro, Mass. Running back Kansas 1964-68. No pro playing experience. College coach: Colorado 1972-76, Navy 1977. Pro coach: San Francisco 49ers 1978, Minnesota Vikings 1979-84 (head coach 1984), joined Patriots in 1985.

NEW YORK JETS

American Football Conference Eastern Division

Team Colors: Kelly Green and White

598 Madison Avenue
New York, New York 10022
Telephone: (212) 421-6600

Club Officials

Chairman of the Board: Leon Hess
President-Chief Operating Officer: Jim Kensil
Corporate Treasurer/Secretary and Administrative Manager: Steve Gutman
Director of Player Personnel: Mike Hickey
Pro Personnel Director: Jim Royer
Talent Scouts: Joe Collins, Don Grammer, Sid Hall, Marv Sunderland
Director of Public Relations: Frank Ramos
Assistant Director of Public Relations: Ron Cohen
Director of Operations: Mike Kensil
Ticket Manager: Bob Parente
Video Director: Jim Pons
Trainer: Bob Reese
Assistant Trainers: Pepper Burruss, Joe Patten
Equipment Manager: Bill Hampton

Stadium: Giants Stadium • **Capacity:** 76,891
East Rutherford, New Jersey 07073

Playing Surface: AstroTurf

Training Center: 1000 Fulton Avenue
Hempstead, New York 11550
(516) 538-6600

1987 Schedule

Preseason

Aug. 15	**Philadelphia**	8:00
Aug. 22	at Tampa Bay	7:00
Aug. 29	at New York Giants	9:00
Sept. 4	at San Diego	7:00

Regular Season

Sept. 13	at Buffalo	1:00
Sept. 21	**New England** (Monday)	9:00
Sept. 27	at Pittsburgh	4:00
Oct. 4	**Dallas**	4:00
Oct. 11	at Indianapolis	12:00
Oct. 18	**Miami**	1:00
Oct. 25	at Washington	1:00
Nov. 1	**Indianapolis**	1:00
Nov. 9	**Seattle** (Monday)	9:00
Nov. 15	at Kansas City	12:00
Nov. 22	**Buffalo**	1:00
Nov. 29	**Cincinnati**	1:00
Dec. 7	at Miami (Monday)	9:00
Dec. 13	at New England	1:00
Dec. 20	**Philadelphia**	1:00
Dec. 27	at New York Giants	1:00

Jets Coaching History

New York Titans 1960-62
(182-210-7)

1960-61	Sammy Baugh	14-14-0
1962	Clyde (Bulldog) Turner	5-9-0
1963-73	Weeb Ewbank	73-78-6
1974-75	Charley Winner*	9-14-0
1975	Ken Shipp	1-4-0
1976	Lou Holtz**	3-10-0
1976	Mike Holovak	0-1-0
1977-82	Walt Michaels	41-49-1
1983-86	Joe Walton	36-31-0

*Released after nine games in 1975
**Resigned after 13 games in 1976

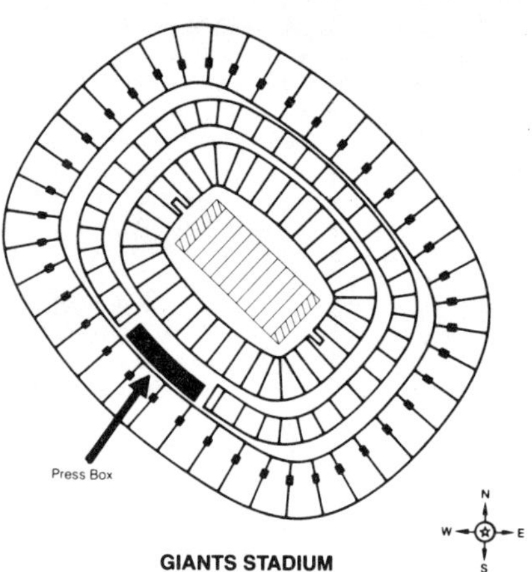

GIANTS STADIUM

Record Holders

Individual Records—Career

Category	Name	Performance
Rushing (Yds.)	Freeman McNeil,1981-86	5,320
Passing (Yds.)	Joe Namath, 1965-1976	27,057
Passing (TDs)	Joe Namath, 1965-1976	170
Receiving (No.)	Don Maynard, 1960-1972	627
Receiving (Yds.)	Don Maynard, 1960-1972	11,732
Interceptions	Bill Baird, 1963-69	34
Punting (Avg.)	Curley Johnson, 1961-68	42.8
Punt Return (Avg.)	Dick Christy, 1961-63	16.2
Kickoff Return (Avg.)	Bobby Humphery, 1984-86	25.3
Field Goals	Pat Leahy, 1974-1986	200
Touchdowns (Tot.)	Don Maynard, 1960-1972	88
Points	Pat Leahy, 1974-1986	993

Individual Records—Single Season

Category	Name	Performance
Rushing (Yds.)	Freeman McNeil, 1985	1,331
Passing (Yds.)	Joe Namath, 1967	4,007
Passing (TDs)	Al Dorow, 1960	26
	Joe Namath, 1967	26
Receiving (No.)	Al Toon, 1986	85
Receiving (Yds.)	Don Maynard, 1967	1,434
Interceptions	Dainard Paulson, 1964	12
Punting (Avg.)	Curley Johnson, 1965	45.3
Punt Return (Avg.)	Dick Christy, 1961	21.3
Kickoff Return (Avg.)	Bobby Humphery, 1984	30.7
Field Goals	Jim Turner, 1968	34
Touchdowns (Tot.)	Art Powell, 1960	14
	Don Maynard, 1965	14
	Emerson Boozer, 1972	14
Points	Jim Turner, 1968	145

Individual Records—Single Game

Category	Name	Performance
Rushing (Yds.)	Freeman McNeil, 9-15-85	192
Passing (Yds.)	Joe Namath, 9-24-72	496
Passing (TDs)	Joe Namath, 9-24-72	6
Receiving (No.)	Clark Gaines, 9-21-80	17
Receiving (Yds.)	Don Maynard, 11-17-68	228
Interceptions	Dainard Paulson, 9-28-63	3
	Bill Baird, 10-31-64	3
	Rich Sowells, 9-23-73	3
Field Goals	Jim Turner, 11-3-68	6
	Bobby Howfield, 12-3-72	6
Touchdowns (Tot.)	Wesley Walker, 9-21-86	4
Points	Jim Turner, 11-3-68	19
	Pat Leahy, 9-16-84	19

1986 Team Statistics

	Jets	Opp.
Total First Downs	319	349
Rushing	104	92
Passing	191	216
Penalty	24	41
Third Down: Made/Att.	88/227	100/233
Fourth Down: Made/Att.	7/17	7/21
Total Net Yards	5375	6050
Avg. Per Game	335.9	378.1
Total Plays	1072	1081
Avg. Per Play	5.0	5.6
Net Yards Rushing	1729	1661
Avg. Per Game	108.1	103.8
Total Rushes	490	450
Net Yards Passing	3646	4389
Avg. Per Game	227.9	274.3
Tackled/Yards Lost	45/386	28/178
Gross Yards	4032	4567
Att./Completions	537/334	603/348
Completion Pct.	62.2	57.7
Had Intercepted	21	20
Punts/Avg.	85/39.4	75/39.7
Net Punting Avg.	36.1	31.9
Penalties/Yards Lost	131/981	102/795
Fumbles/Ball Lost	37/16	48/18
Touchdowns	45	48
Rushing	16	12
Passing	27	35
Returns	2	1
Avg. Time of Possession	29:51	30:09

1986 Team Record

Preseason (2-2)

Date	Result		Opponents
8/9	L	14-38	at Green Bay
8/16	W	28-17	Cincinnati
8/23	L	16-20	at N.Y. Giants
8/28	W	37-30	at Philadelphia
		95-105	

Regular Season (10-6)

Date	Result		Opponents	Att.
9/7	W	28-24	at Buffalo	79,951
9/11	L	6-20	New England	72,422
9/21	W	51-45	Miami (OT)	71,025
9/28	W	26- 7	at Indianapolis	56,075
10/5	W	14-13	Buffalo	69,504
10/12	W	31-24	at New England	60,342
10/20	W	22-10	Denver	73,759
10/26	W	28-23	New Orleans	44,246
11/2	W	38- 7	at Seattle	62,497
11/9	W	28-14	at Atlanta	53,476
11/16	W	31-16	Indianapolis	65,149
11/24	L	3-45	at Miami	70,206
11/30	L	3-17	L.A. Rams	70,539
12/7	L	10-24	at San Francisco	58,091
12/13	L	24-45	Pittsburgh	58,044
12/21	L	21-52	at Cincinnati	51,619

Postseason (1-1)

Date	Result		Opponents	Att.
12/28	W	35-15	Kansas City	75,210
1/3/87	L	20-23	at Cleveland (OT)	79,720

(OT) Overtime

Score by Periods

Jets	54	181	30	93	6	—	364
Opponents	55	91	95	145	0	—	386

Attendance

Home 524,688 Away 492,257 Total 1,016,945
Single game home record, 74,975 (12-2-84)
Single season home record, 541,832 (1985)

1986 Individual Statistics

Scoring	TD R	TD P	TD Rt	PAT	FG	Saf	TP
Leahy	0	0	0	44/44	16/19	0	92
Walker	0	12	0	0/0	0/0	0	72
Hector	8	0	0	0/0	0/0	0	48
Toon	0	8	0	0/0	0/0	0	48
McNeil	5	1	0	0/0	0/0	0	36
Shuler	0	4	0	0/0	0/0	0	24
Paige	2	0	0	0/0	0/0	0	12
Sohn	0	2	0	0/0	0/0	0	12
Humphery	0	0	1	0/0	0/0	1	8
Bligen	1	0	0	0/0	0/0	0	6
Townsell	0	0	1	0/0	0/0	0	6
Jets	16	27	2	44/44	16/19	1	364
Opponents	12	35	1	48/48	16/27	1	386

Passing	Att.	Comp.	Yds.	Pct.	TD	Int.	Tkld.	Rate
O'Brien	482	300	3690	62.2	25	20	40/353	85.8
Ryan	55	34	342	61.8	2	1	5/33	84.1
Jets	537	334	4032	62.2	27	21	45/386	85.7
Opponents	603	348	4567	57.7	35	20	28/178	87.3

Rushing	Att.	Yds.	Avg.	LG	TD
McNeil	214	856	4.0	40	5
Hector	164	605	3.7	41	8
Paige	47	109	2.3	9	2
Bligen	20	65	3.3	10	1
O'Brien	17	46	2.7	11	0
Ryan	8	28	3.5	18	0
Barber	11	27	2.5	8	0
Faaola	3	5	1.7	2	0
Townsell	1	2	2.0	2	0
Jennings	1	0	0.0	0	0
Toon	2	−3	−1.5	2	0
Sohn	2	−11	−5.5	−3	0
Jets	490	1729	3.5	41	16
Opponents	450	1661	3.7	54t	12

Receiving	No.	Yds.	Avg.	LG	TD
Toon	85	1176	13.8	62t	8
Shuler	69	675	9.8	36t	4
Walker	49	1016	20.7	83t	12
McNeil	49	410	8.4	26	1
Hector	33	302	9.2	23	0
Paige	18	121	6.7	18	0
Klever	15	150	10.0	21	0
Sohn	8	129	16.1	24t	2
Barber	5	36	7.2	16	0
Bligen	2	6	3.0	4	0
Townsell	1	11	11.0	11	0
Jets	334	4032	12.1	83t	27
Opponents	348	4567	13.1	69t	35

Interceptions	No.	Yds.	Avg.	LG	TD
Holmes	6	29	4.8	28	0
Lyles	5	36	7.2	22	0
Lynn	5	36	7.2	26	0
Clifton	2	8	4.0	7	0
Hamilton	1	29	29.0	29	0
Crable	1	26	26.0	26	0
Jets	20	164	8.2	29	0
Opponents	21	230	11.0	67t	1

Punting	No.	Yds.	Avg.	In 20	LG
Jennings	85	3353	39.4	27	55
Jets	85	3353	39.4	27	55
Opponents	75	2977	39.7	11	71

Punt Returns	No.	FC	Yds.	Avg.	LG	TD
Sohn	35	8	289	8.3	27	0
Townsell	4	1	52	13.0	28	0
Jets	39	9	341	8.7	28	0
Opponents	36	17	165	4.6	40	0

Kickoff Returns	No.	Yds.	Avg.	LG	TD
Humphery	28	655	23.4	96t	1
Townsell	13	322	24.8	93t	1
Harper	7	71	10.1	19	0
Sohn	7	124	17.7	36	0
Rudolph	3	17	5.7	10	0
Baldwin	2	3	1.5	4	0
Shuler	2	−3	−1.5	0	0
Lynn	1	0	0.0	0	0
Jets	63	1189	18.9	96t	2
Opponents	62	1307	21.1	52	0

Sacks	No.
Humphery	4.0
Klecko	4.0
Bennett	3.5
Crable	3.5
Foster, Mia.-Jets	3.0
Lyons	3.0
Gastineau	2.0
Jackson	2.0
Baldwin	1.0
Franks	1.0
Lyles	1.0
McArthur	1.0
Mehl	1.0
Rudolph	1.0
Jets	28.0
Opponents	45.0

FIRST-ROUND SELECTIONS

(If club had no first-round selection, first player drafted is listed with round in parentheses.)

Year	Player, College, Position
1960	George Izo, Notre Dame, QB
1961	Tom Brown, Minnesota, G
1962	Sandy Stephens, Minnesota, QB
1963	Jerry Stovall, Louisiana State, S
1964	Matt Snell, Ohio State, RB
1965	Joe Namath, Alabama, QB
	Tom Nowatzke, Indiana, RB
1966	Bill Yearby, Michigan, DT
1967	Paul Seiler, Notre Dame, T
1968	Lee White, Weber State, RB
1969	Dave Foley, Ohio State, T
1970	Steve Tannen, Florida, CB
1971	John Riggins, Kansas, RB
1972	Jerome Barkum, Jackson State, WR
	Mike Taylor, Michigan, LB
1973	Burgess Owens, Miami, DB
1974	Carl Barzilauskas, Indiana, DT
1975	Anthony Davis, Southern California, RB (2)
1976	Richard Todd, Alabama, QB
1977	Marvin Powell, Southern California, T
1978	Chris Ward, Ohio State, T
1979	Marty Lyons, Alabama, DE
1980	Johnny (Lam) Jones, Texas, WR
1981	Freeman McNeil, UCLA, RB
1982	Bob Crable, Notre Dame, LB
1983	Ken O'Brien, Cal-Davis, QB
1984	Russell Carter, Southern Methodist, DB
	Ron Faurot, Arkansas, DE
1985	Al Toon, Wisconsin, WR
1986	Mike Haight, Iowa, T
1987	Roger Vick, Texas A&M, RB

New York Jets 1987 Veteran Roster

No.	Name	Pos.	Ht.	Wt.	Birth-date	NFL Exp.	College	Hometown	How Acq.	'86 Games/ Starts
60	Alexander, Dan	G	6-4	268	6/17/55	11	Louisiana State	Houston, Tex.	D8a-'77	16/16
95	Baldwin, Tom	DT	6-4	270	5/13/61	4	Tulsa	Lansing, Ill.	D9-'84	16/6
63	Banker, Ted	G-T-C	6-2	265	2/17/61	4	Southeast Missouri	Belleville, Ill.	FA-'84	15/13
31	Barber, Marion	RB	6-3	228	12/6/59	6	Minnesota	Detroit, Mich.	D2-'81	15/0
78	Bennett, Barry	DE-DT	6-4	260	12/10/55	10	Concordia	St. Paul, Minn.	W(Minn)-'82	16/15
54	Benson, Troy	LB	6-2	235	7/30/63	2	Pittsburgh	Altoona, Pa.	D5a-'85	15/1
64	Bingham, Guy	C-T-G	6-3	260	2/25/58	8	Montana	Aberdeen, Wash.	D10-'80	16/9
90	Brophy, Jay	LB	6-3	233	7/27/60	4	Miami	Akron, Ohio	FA-'87	4/0*
27	Carter, Russell	CB-S	6-2	195	2/10/62	4	Southern Methodist	Ardmore, Pa.	D1a-'84	13/13
59	Clifton, Kyle	LB	6-4	230	8/23/62	4	Texas Christian	Bridgeport, Tex.	D3-'84	16/16
50	Crable, Bob	LB	6-3	230	9/22/59	6	Notre Dame	Cincinnati, Ohio	D1-'82	16/15
30	Faaola, Nuu	RB	5-11	215	1/15/64	2	Hawaii	Honolulu, Hawaii	D9-'86	12/0
65	Fields, Joe	C	6-2	253	11/14/53	13	Widener	Deptford, N.J.	D14-'75	9/9
98	Foster, Jerome	DE	6-2	275	7/25/60	4	Ohio State	Detroit, Mich.	FA-'86	15/0*
99	Gastineau, Mark	DE	6-5	270	11/20/56	9	East Central Oklahoma	Springerville, Ariz.	D2-'79	10/7
35	Glenn, Kerry	CB	5-9	175	3/31/62	2	Minnesota	East St. Louis, Ill.	D10-'85	1/1
81	Griggs, Billy	TE	6-3	230	8/4/62	3	Virginia	Pennsauken, N.J.	D8a-'84	16/1
94	†Guilbeau, Rusty	LB	6-4	235	11/20/58	6	McNeese State	Sunset, La.	FA-'82	6/4
79	Haight, Mike	G-T	6-4	270	10/6/62	2	Iowa	Dyersville, Iowa	D1-'86	2/0
39	Hamilton, Harry	S	6-0	195	11/29/62	4	Penn State	Wilkes-Barre, Pa.	D7-'84	15/11
84	Harper, Michael	WR	5-10	180	5/11/61	2	Southern California	Kansas City, Mo.	FA-'86	16/0
34	Hector, Johnny	RB	5-11	200	11/26/60	5	Texas A&M	New Iberia, La.	D2-'83	13/6
47	†Holmes, Jerry	CB	6-2	175	12/22/57	6	West Virginia	Hampton, Va.	FA-'86	15/14
28	†Howard, Carl	CB-S	6-2	190	9/20/61	4	Rutgers	Irvington, N.J.	FA-'85	14/3
48	†Humphery, Bobby	CB-KR	5-10	180	8/23/61	4	New Mexico State	Lubbock, Tex.	D9-'83	16/1
13	Jennings, Dave	P	6-4	200	6/8/52	14	St. Lawrence	Garden City, N.Y.	W(NYG)-'85	16/0
80	Jones, Johnny (Lam)	WR	5-11	180	4/4/58	6	Texas	Lampasas, Tex.	D1-'80	0*
72	King, Gordon	T-G	6-6	270	2/3/56	9	Stanford	Fair Oaks, Calif.	W(NYG)-'86	11/9
73	Klecko, Joe	DT-DE	6-3	263	10/15/53	11	Temple	Chester, Pa.	D6-'77	11/10
89	Klever, Rocky	TE	6-3	228	7/10/59	5	Montana	Anchorage, Alaska	D9-'82	16/11
5	Leahy, Pat	K	6-0	200	3/19/51	14	St. Louis	St. Louis, Mo.	FA-'74	16/0
26	Lyles, Lester	S	6-3	218	12/27/62	3	Virginia	Washington, D.C.	D2-'85	16/14
93	Lyons, Marty	DE-DT	6-5	269	1/15/57	9	Alabama	St. Petersburg, Fla.	D1-'79	12/11
57	McArthur, Kevin	LB	6-2	230	5/11/63	2	Lamar	Lake Charles, La.	FA-'86	8/1
68	†McElroy, Reggie	T	6-6	270	3/4/60	5	West Texas State	Beaumont, Tex.	D2-'82	8/8
24	McNeil, Freeman	RB	5-11	214	4/22/59	7	UCLA	Carson, Calif.	D1-'81	12/11
56	Mehl, Lance	LB	6-3	233	2/14/58	8	Penn State	Bellaire, Ohio	D3-'80	8/7
36	Miano, Rich	S	6-0	200	9/3/62	3	Hawaii	Honolulu, Hawaii	D6b-'85	14/1
58	Monger, Matt	LB	6-1	238	11/15/61	3	Oklahoma State	Miami, Okla.	D8-'85	16/1
74	Moore, Derland	DT	6-4	273	10/7/51	15	Oklahoma	Poplar Bluff, Md.	FA-'86	1/0
7	O'Brien, Ken	QB	6-4	208	11/27/60	5	California-Davis	Sacramento, Calif.	D1-'83	15/14
49	†Paige, Tony	RB	5-10	225	10/14/62	4	Virginia Tech	Washington, D.C.	D6-'84	16/7
10	Ryan, Pat	QB	6-3	210	9/16/55	10	Tennessee	Oklahoma City, Okla.	D11-'78	16/2
82	Shuler, Mickey	TE	6-3	231	8/21/56	10	Penn State	Enola, Pa.	D3-'78	16/16
87	Sohn, Kurt	WR-KR	5-11	180	6/26/57	6	Fordham	Huntington, N.Y.	FA-'81	15/1
53	Sweeney, Jim	T	6-4	260	8/8/62	4	Pittsburgh	Pittsburgh, Pa.	D2a-'84	16/16
88	Toon, Al	WR	6-4	205	4/30/63	3	Wisconsin	Newport News, Va.	D1-'85	16/16
83	Townsell, JoJo	WR	5-9	180	11/4/60	3	UCLA	Reno, Nev.	D3-'83	14/1
85	Walker, Wesley	WR	6-0	182	5/26/55	11	California	Carson, Calif.	D2-'77	16/8

* Brophy played 4 games with Miami in '86; Foster played 14 games with Miami, 1 with N.Y. Jets; Jones missed '86 season due to injury.

†Option playout; subject to developments.

Traded—Safety Kirk Springs to Indianapolis.

Also played with Jets in '86—LB Rogers Alexander (1 game), T Bill Bain (4), RB Dennis Bligen (4), CB Robert Ducksworth (2), DE Elvis Franks (3), LB Charles Jackson (15), S Johnny Lynn (16), CB-KR Davlin Mullen (5), DE Ben Rudolph (16), G Ron Sams (active for 2 games, but did not play), DE Jim Stuckey (5), QB Richard Todd (3).

COACHING STAFF

Head Coach, Joe Walton

Pro Career: Begins fifth year as head coach of the Jets. Entered pro coaching ranks as an assistant with the New York Giants in 1969-73. Joined the Washington Redskins' staff in 1974 and became the Redskins' offensive coordinator in 1978. Originally came to the Jets as the offensive coordinator in 1981. Career record: 36-31.

Background: Played tight end for the University of Pittsburgh 1953-56, before playing professionally for the Washington Redskins 1957-60 and the New York Giants 1961-63. Walton did some radio work before joining the Giants' staff as a scout in 1967-68.

Personal: Born December 15, 1935, Beaver Falls, Pa. Joe and his wife, Ginger, have three children—Jodi, Stacy, and Joseph, Jr. They live in Long Island.

Assistant Coaches

Zeke Bratkowski, quarterbacks; born October 20, 1931, Danville, Ill., lives in Long Island. Quarterback Georgia 1951-53. Pro quarterback Chicago Bears 1954, 1957-60, Los Angeles Rams 1961-63, Green Bay Packers 1963-68, 1971. Pro coach: Green Bay Packers 1969-70, 1975-81, Chicago Bears 1972-74, Indianapolis Colts 1982-84, joined Jets in 1985.

Ray Callahan, defensive line; born April 28, 1933, Lebanon, Ky., lives in Long Island. Guard-linebacker Kentucky 1952-56. No pro playing experience. College coach: Kentucky 1963-67, Cincinnati 1968-72 (head coach 1969-72). Pro coach: Baltimore Colts 1973, Florida Blazers (WFL) 1974, Chicago Bears 1975-77, Houston Oilers 1981-82, joined Jets in 1983.

Bud Carson, defensive coordinator; born April 28, 1931, Brackenridge, Pa., lives in Long Island. Defensive back North Carolina 1948-52. No pro playing experience. College coach: North Carolina 1957-64, South Carolina 1965, Georgia Tech 1966-71 (head coach). Pro coach: Pittsburgh Steelers 1972-77, Los Angeles Rams 1978-81, Baltimore Colts 1982, Kansas City Chiefs 1983-84, joined Jets in 1985.

Mike Faulkiner, special assistant to the head coach; born March 27, 1947, Cameron, W. Va., lives in Long Island. Quarterback-defensive back West Virginia Tech 1967-70. No pro playing experience. College coach: Eastern Illinois 1981. Pro coach: Toronto Argonauts (CFL) 1979, New York Giants 1980, Montreal Alouettes (CFL) 1982, joined Jets in 1983.

Bobby Hammond, running backs; born February 20, 1952, Orangeburg, S.C., lives in New York. Running back Morgan State 1973-75. Pro running back New York Giants 1976-79, Washington Redskins 1979-80. Pro coach: Joined Jets in 1983.

Rich Kotite, offensive coordinator-receivers; born October 13, 1942, Brooklyn, N.Y., lives in Staten Island. End Wagner 1963-65. Pro tight end New York Giants 1967, 1969-72, Pittsburgh Steelers 1968. College coach: Tennessee-Chattanooga 1973-76. Pro coach: New Orleans Saints 1977, Cleveland Browns 1978-82, joined Jets in 1983.

Larry Pasquale, special teams; born April 21, 1941, Brooklyn, N.Y., lives in Long Island. Quarterback Bridgeport 1961-63. No pro playing experience. College coach: Slippery Rock State 1967, Boston University 1968, Navy 1969-70, Massachusetts 1971-75, Idaho State 1976. Pro coach: Montreal Alouettes (CFL) 1977-78, Detroit Lions 1979, joined Jets in 1980.

Dan Radakovich, linebackers; born November 27, 1935, Duquesne, Pa., lives in Long Island. Center-linebacker Penn State 1954-56. No pro playing experience. College coach: Penn State 1960-69, Cincinnati 1970, Colorado 1972-73, North Carolina State 1982. Pro coach: Pittsburgh Steelers 1971, 1974-77, San Francisco 49ers 1978, Los Angeles Rams 1979-81, Denver Broncos 1983, Minnesota Vikings 1984, joined Jets in 1985.

New York Jets 1987 First-Year Roster

Name	Pos.	Ht.	Wt.	Birth-date	College	Hometown	How Acq.
Alexander, Rogers (1)	LB	6-3	209	8/11/64	Penn State	Riverdale, Md.	D4-'86
Amoia, Vince (1)	RB	5-11	220	3/30/63	Arizona State	Buffalo, N.Y.	D11-'86
Archie, Herman (1)	WR	6-2	196	12/31/63	Georgia	Cols, Ga.	FA
Baldwin, Don (1)	DE	6-3	245	7/9/64	Purdue	St. Charles, Mo.	FA
Branaman, Lance (1)	DE	6-3	258	7/15/64	Wisconsin	Oak Creek, Wis.	FA
Briggs, Walter	QB	6-1	196	8/6/65	Montclair State	Hackensack, N.J.	FA
Caldwell, Darryl (1)	T	6-5	275	2/2/60	Tennessee State	Birmingham, Ala.	FA
Cesario, Sal (1)	G	6-5	260	7/4/63	Cal Poly-SLO	San Jose, Calif.	D12-'86
Chickillo, Tony (1)	DE	6-3	249	7/8/61	Miami	Miami, Fla.	FA
Collins, Trent (1)	CB	6-1	187	5/18/61	San Diego State	Marrero, La.	FA
Crawford, Tim (1)	DE-LB	6-4	230	12/17/62	Texas Tech	Houston, Tex.	D3-'86
Danforth, Kenneth	CB	5-11	189	12/5/62	Clemson	Aiken, S.C.	FA
Dorundo, Mike (1)	T	6-3	270	3/1/63	Pittsburgh	Greensburg, Pa.	FA
Dreiband, Eric (1)	G	6-3	270	9/23/63	Princeton	Indianapolis, Ind.	FA
Ducksworth, Robert (1)	CB	5-11	200	1/5/63	Southern Mississippi	Biloxi, Miss.	D8-'86
Dykes, Sean (1)	CB	5-10	170	8/8/64	Bowling Green	New Orleans, La.	FA
Elam, Onzy	LB	6-2	225	12/1/64	Tennessee State	Miami, Fla.	D3
Farr, James (1)	G	6-2	249	8/10/62	Clemson	Thomson, Ga.	FA
Flanagan, Tom (1)	TE	6-2	224	5/18/63	New Hampshire	Leominster, N.H.	FA
Giaquinto, Joseph	WR	5-11	190	9/11/63	Boston College	Winthrop, Mass.	FA
Gordon, Alex	LB	6-5	245	9/14/63	Cincinnati	Jacksonville, Fla.	D2
Heffernan, Dave (1)	G	6-4	255	10/28/62	Miami	Miami, Fla.	FA
Horn, Marty (1)	QB	6-2	206	3/27/63	Lehigh	Millburn, N.J.	FA
Hunter, Eddie	RB-KR	5-10	205	1/20/65	Virginia Tech	Oxen Hill, Md.	D8a
Hunter, Stan	WR	6-1	184	11/29/63	Bowling Green	Clayton, Ohio	FA
Jackson, Kirby	CB	5-10	180	2/2/65	Mississippi State	Sturgis, Miss.	D5
Jensen, Greg	T	6-3	275	1/23/62	No College	Sauk City, Wis.	FA
Johnson, Morris (1)	T	6-3	321	6/25/62	Alabama A&M	Detroit, Mich.	FA
Kearney, Robert (1)	CB-S	5-11	195	4/10/63	No. Carolina Central	Norfolk, Va.	FA
Lewis, Gary (1)	DE-DT	6-3	261	1/14/61	Oklahoma State	Oklahoma City, Okla.	FA
Lewis, Sid	CB	5-11	180	5/30/64	Penn State	Canton, Ohio	D10
Martin, Tracy	WR	6-3	205	12/4/64	North Dakota	Minneapolis, Minn.	D6
McClean, Ron	DE-DT	6-4	270	4/13/63	Cal State-Fullerton	Santa Maria, Calif.	D9
McCullough, Jim (1)	T-G	6-4	263	7/21/64	UCLA	Hemet, Calif.	FA
McSwain, Chuck (1)	RB	5-11	190	2/21/61	Clemson	Forest City, N.C.	FA
Nichols, Gerald	NT	6-1	270	2/10/64	Florida State	St. Louis, Mo.	D7
Mimbs, Robert (1)	RB	5-10	207	8/6/64	Kansas	Kansas City, Kan.	FA
Norrie, David (1)	QB	6-4	228	11/30/63	UCLA	Portland, Ore.	FA
O'Malley, Sean (1)	LB	6-1	215	3/9/64	Northeastern	Lansdale, Pa.	FA
Peete, Willie III (1)	WR	5-11	191	1/30/63	Kansas	Tucson, Ariz.	FA
Plantz, Ron (1)	G	6-3	253	1/27/64	Notre Dame	Chicago, Ill.	FA
Price, Jeffrey (1)	WR	5-11	197	4/18/63	Purdue	Newport News, Va.	FA
Ransdell, Bill	QB	6-2	205	4/15/63	Kentucky	Elizabeth, Ky.	D12
Rice, Mike	P	5-11	196	8/12/65	Montana	Twin Falls, Idaho	D8b
Robinson, Larry (1)	CB	5-9	194	4/30/62	Northwestern	Match, La.	FA
Rose, Ken (1)	WR	6-1	219	6/9/61	Nevada-Las Vegas	Sacramento, Calif.	FA
Russo, Tony (1)	G-T	6-4	277	3/16/64	Texas-El Paso	Mahopac, N.Y.	FA
Sagnella, Tony (1)	DE-DT	6-5	250	2/28/64	Rutgers	Hamden, Conn.	FA
Saranovitz, Brian	G	6-3	260	2/18/63	New Hampshire	Lunenburg, Mass.	FA
Saylor, Scott	T	6-4	275	2/10/64	West Virginia	Whitehall, Pa.	FA
Scott, Carlos (1)	T	6-2	293	7/2/60	Texas-El Paso	Waller, Tex.	FA
Scott, James (1)	DE	6-4	255	4/14/62	Clemson	Alexandria, Va.	FA
Smith, Jeffrey	WR	6-3	175	5/28/63	Cal Poly-SLO	Poway, Calif.	FA
Tagart, Mark (1)	LB	6-3	226	11/15/63	Illinois	San Jose, Calif.	FA
Thomas, Curtland (1)	WR	5-11	189	2/11/62	Missouri	St. Louis, Mo.	FA
Thorp, Don (1)	DE	6-4	252	7/10/62	Illinois	Buffalo Grove, Ill.	FA
Timmer, Kirk	LB	6-3	242	12/18/63	Montana State	Boulder, Mont.	D11
Turner, Maurice (1)	RB	5-11	200	9/10/60	Utah State	Layton, Utah	FA
Vick, Roger	RB	6-3	230	8/11/64	Texas A&M	Tomball, Tex.	D1
Villani, James (1)	P	5-10	185	3/27/60	East Stroudsburg	Bethlehem, Pa.	FA
Vittium, Craig	T	6-5	266	5/29/64	Norwich	Marlboro, Mass.	FA
Zordich, Mike (1)	CB	5-11	207	10/12/63	Penn State	Youngstown, Ohio	FA

The term NFL Rookie is defined as a player who is in his first season of professional football and has not been on the roster of another professional football team for any regular-season or postseason games. A Rookie is designated by an "R" on NFL rosters. Players who have been active in another professional football league or players who have NFL experience, including either preseason training camp or being on an active roster for fewer than three regular-season or postseason games, are termed NFL First-Year Players. An NFL First-Year Player is designated by a "1" on NFL rosters. Thereafter, a player on an NFL active roster for at least three regular-season or postseason games is credited with an additional year of NFL playing experience.

NOTES

Jim Vechiarella, linebackers; born February 20, 1937, Youngstown, Ohio, lives in Long Island. Linebacker Youngstown State 1955-57. No pro playing experience. College coach: Youngstown State 1964-74, Southern Illinois 1976-77, Tulane 1978-80. Pro coach: Charlotte Hornets (WFL) 1975, Los Angeles Rams 1981-82, Kansas City Chiefs 1983-85, joined Jets in 1986.

PITTSBURGH STEELERS

American Football Conference Central Division

Team Colors: Black and Gold

Three Rivers Stadium
300 Stadium Circle
Pittsburgh, Pennsylvania 15212
Telephone: (412) 323-1200

Club Officials

Chairman of the Board: Arthur J. Rooney, Sr.
President: Daniel M. Rooney
Vice President: John R. McGinley
Vice President: Arthur J. Rooney, Jr.
Treasurer: Dennis P. Thimons
Business Manager: Joe Gordon
Chief Negotiator: James A. Boston
Office Manager-Stadium: Dan Ferens
Publicity Director: Dan Edwards
Assistant Publicity Director: Pat Hanlon
Director of Player Personnel: Dick Haley
Director of Pro Scouting: Tom Modrak
Talent Scout-West Coast: Bob Schmitz
Talent Scout-East: Tom Donahoe
Talent Scout-Midwest: Jesse Kaye
Director of Ticket Sales: Geraldine R. Glenn
Computer Director-Accounting: Jim Ellenberger
Trainers: Ralph Berlin, Francis Feld
Equipment Manager: Anthony Parisi

Stadium: Three Rivers Stadium • **Capacity:** 59,000
300 Stadium Circle
Pittsburgh, Pennsylvania 15212

Playing Surface: AstroTurf

Training Camp: St. Vincent College
Latrobe, Pennsylvania 15650

1987 Schedule

Preseason

Aug. 14	at Washington	8:00
Aug. 22	at Chicago	6:00
Aug. 29	at New Orleans	7:00
Sept. 5	**New York Giants**	9:00

Regular Season

Sept. 13	**San Francisco**	1:00
Sept. 20	at Cleveland	1:00
Sept. 27	**New York Jets**	4:00
Oct. 4	at Atlanta	1:00
Oct. 11	at Los Angeles Rams	1:00
Oct. 18	**Indianapolis**	1:00
Oct. 25	**Cincinnati**	1:00
Nov. 1	at Miami	1:00
Nov. 8	at Kansas City	12:00
Nov. 15	**Houston**	1:00
Nov. 22	at Cincinnati	1:00
Nov. 29	**New Orleans**	1:00
Dec. 6	**Seattle**	1:00
Dec. 13	at San Diego	1:00
Dec. 20	at Houston	12:00
Dec. 26	**Cleveland** (Saturday)	12:30

Steelers Coaching History

Pittsburgh Pirates 1933-40
(331-369-20)

1933	Forrest (Jap) Douds	3-6-2
1934	Luby DiMelio	2-10-0
1935-36	Joe Bach	10-14-0
1937-39	Johnny Blood (McNally)*	6-19-0
1939-40	Walt Kiesling	3-13-3
1941	Bert Bell**	0-2-0
	Aldo (Buff) Donelli***	0-5-0
1941-44	Walt Kiesling****	13-20-2
1945	Jim Leonard	2-8-0
1946-47	Jock Sutherland	13-10-1
1948-51	Johnny Michelosen	20-26-2
1952-53	Joe Bach	11-13-0
1954-56	Walt Kiesling	14-22-0
1957-64	Raymond (Buddy) Parker	51-47-6
1965	Mike Nixon	2-12-0
1966-68	Bill Austin	11-28-3
1969-86	Chuck Noll	170-114-1

*Released after three games in 1939
**Resigned after two games in 1941
***Released after five games in 1941
****Co-coach with Earle (Greasy) Neale in Philadelphia-Pittsburgh merger in 1943 and with Phil Handler in Chicago Cardinals-Pittsburgh merger in 1944

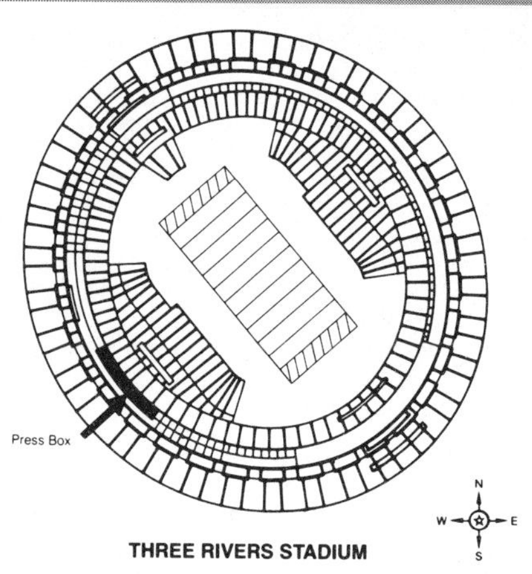

THREE RIVERS STADIUM

Record Holders

Individual Records—Career

Category	Name	Performance
Rushing (Yds.)	Franco Harris, 1972-1983	11,950
Passing (Yds.)	Terry Bradshaw, 1970-1983	27,989
Passing (TDs)	Terry Bradshaw, 1970-1983	212
Receiving (No.)	John Stallworth, 1974-1986	496
Receiving (Yds.)	John Stallworth, 1974-1986	8,202
Interceptions	Mel Blount, 1970-1983	57
Punting (Avg.)	Bobby Joe Green, 1960-61	45.7
Punt Return (Avg.)	Bobby Gage, 1949-1950	14.9
Kickoff Return (Avg.)	Lynn Chandnois, 1950-56	29.6
Field Goals	Roy Gerela, 1971-78	146
Touchdowns (Tot.)	Franco Harris, 1972-1983	100
Points	Roy Gerela, 1971-78	731

Individual Records—Single Season

Category	Name	Performance
Rushing (Yds.)	Franco Harris, 1975	1,246
Passing (Yds.)	Terry Bradshaw, 1979	3,724
Passing (TDs)	Terry Bradshaw, 1978	28
Receiving (No.)	John Stallworth, 1984	80
Receiving (Yds.)	John Stallworth, 1984	1,395
Interceptions	Mel Blount, 1975	11
Punting (Avg.)	Bobby Joe Green, 1961	47.0
Punt Return (Avg.)	Bobby Gage, 1949	16.0
Kickoff Return (Avg.)	Lynn Chandnois, 1952	35.2
Field Goals	Gary Anderson, 1985	33
Touchdowns (Tot.)	Louis Lipps, 1985	15
Points	Gary Anderson, 1985	139

Individual Records—Single Game

Category	Name	Performance
Rushing (Yds.)	John Fuqua, 12-20-70	218
Passing (Yds.)	Bobby Layne, 12-3-58	409
Passing (TDs)	Terry Bradshaw, 11-15-81	5
	Mark Malone, 9-8-85	5
Receiving (No.)	J.R. Wilburn, 10-22-67	12
Receiving (Yds.)	Buddy Dial, 10-22-61	235
Interceptions	Jack Butler, 12-13-53	4
Field Goals	Gary Anderson, 11-10-85	5
Touchdowns (Tot.)	Ray Mathews, 10-17-54	4
	Roy Jefferson, 11-3-68	4
Points	Ray Mathews, 10-17-54	24
	Roy Jefferson, 11-3-68	24

1986 Team Statistics

	Steelers	Opp.
Total First Downs	292	303
Rushing	125	97
Passing	140	176
Penalty	27	30
Third Down: Made/Att.	86/232	81/228
Fourth Down: Made/Att.	11/18	7/13
Total Net Yards	4811	5252
Avg. Per Game	300.7	328.3
Total Plays	1075	1050
Avg. Per Play	4.5	5.0
Net Yards Rushing	2223	1872
Avg. Per Game	138.9	117.0
Total Rushes	564	471
Net Yards Passing	2588	3380
Avg. Per Game	161.8	211.3
Tackled/Yards Lost	20/159	43/289
Gross Yards	2747	3669
Att./Completions	491/238	536/311
Completion Pct.	48.5	58.0
Had Intercepted	20	20
Punts/Avg.	89/38.7	82/39.0
Net Punting Avg.	32.2	33.5
Penalties/Yards Lost	104/853	109/904
Fumbles/Ball Lost	27/16	31/13
Touchdowns	35	39
Rushing	18	10
Passing	16	22
Returns	1	7
Avg. Time of Possession	29:45	30:15

1986 Team Record

Preseason (1-3)

Date	Result		Opponents
8/9	L	13-33	Chicago
8/15	L	24-27	at Washington
8/22	W	41-28	at Dallas
8/30	L	3-17	at N.Y. Giants
		81-105	

Regular Season (6-10)

Date	Result		Opponents	Att.
9/7	L	0-30	at Seattle	61,461
9/15	L	10-21	Denver	57,305
9/21	L	7-31	at Minnesota	56,795
9/28	W	22-16	at Houston (OT)	42,001
10/5	L	24-27	Cleveland	57,327
10/13	L	22-24	at Cincinnati	54,283
10/19	L	0-34	New England	54,743
10/26	W	30- 9	Cincinnati	50,815
11/2	W	27- 3	Green Bay	52,831
11/9	L	12-16	at Buffalo	72,000
11/16	W	21-10	Houston	49,724
11/23	L	31-37	at Cleveland (OT)	76,452
11/30	L	10-13	at Chicago (OT)	61,425
12/7	W	27-17	Detroit	45,042
12/13	W	45-24	at N.Y. Jets	58,044
12/21	L	19-24	Kansas City	47,150

(OT) Overtime

Score by Periods

Steelers	51	83	90	77	6	—	307
Opponents	67	129	54	77	9	—	336

Attendance

Home 414,937 Away 482,461 Total 897,398
Single game home record, 59,541 (9-30-85)
Single season home record, 462,567 (1983)

1986 Individual Statistics

Scoring	TD R	TD P	TD Rt	PAT	FG	Saf	TP
Anderson	0	0	0	32/32	21/32	0	95
Abercrombie	6	2	0	0/0	0/0	0	48
Jackson	5	0	0	0/0	0/0	0	30
Malone	5	0	0	0/0	0/0	0	30
Thompson	0	5	0	0/0	0/0	0	30
Erenberg	1	3	0	0/0	0/0	0	24
Lipps	0	3	0	0/0	0/0	0	18
Brister	1	0	0	0/0	0/0	0	6
Gothard	0	1	0	0/0	0/0	0	6
Sanchez	0	0	1	0/0	0/0	0	6
Stallworth	0	1	0	0/0	0/0	0	6
Sweeney	0	1	0	0/0	0/0	0	6
Edwards	0	0	0	0/0	0/0	1	2
Steelers	18	16	1	32/34	21/32	1	307
Opponents	10	22	7	36/38	22/39	0	336

Passing	Att.	Comp.	Yds.	Pct.	TD	Int.	Tkld.	Rate
Malone	425	216	2444	50.8	15	18	13/97	62.5
Brister	60	21	291	35.0	0	2	6/57	37.6
Campbell	4	0	0	0.0	0	0	1/5	39.6
Newsome	2	1	12	50.0	1	0	0/0	108.3
Steelers	491	238	2747	48.5	16	20	20/159	59.7
Opponents	536	311	3669	58.0	22	20	43/289	77.1

Rushing	Att.	Yds.	Avg.	LG	TD
Jackson	216	910	4.2	31	5
Abercrombie	214	877	4.1	38t	6
Erenberg	42	170	4.0	17	1
Malone	31	107	3.5	45	5
Pollard	24	86	3.6	12	0
Hughes	14	32	2.3	8	0
Reeder	6	20	3.3	6	0
Sanders	4	12	3.0	13	0
Brister	6	10	1.7	9	1
Seitz	3	2	0.7	2	0
Lipps	4	−3	−0.8	8	0
Steelers	564	2223	3.9	45	18
Opponents	471	1872	4.0	61t	10

Receiving	No.	Yds.	Avg.	LG	TD
Abercrombie	47	395	8.4	27	2
Lipps	38	590	15.5	48	3
Stallworth	34	466	13.7	40t	1
Erenberg	27	217	8.0	19	3
Sweeney	21	337	16.0	58	1
Gothard	21	246	11.7	34	1
Thompson	17	191	11.2	20	5
Jackson	17	169	9.9	28	0
Hughes	10	98	9.8	22	0
Sanders	2	19	9.5	10	0
Pollard	2	15	7.5	10	0
Reeder	2	4	2.0	3	0
Steelers	238	2747	11.5	58	16
Opponents	311	3669	11.8	55t	22

Interceptions	No.	Yds.	Avg.	LG	TD
Sanchez	3	71	23.7	67t	1
E. Williams	3	44	14.7	25	0
Shell	3	29	9.7	17	0
Woods	3	26	8.7	23	0
Clayton	3	18	6.0	14	0
Hinkle	3	7	2.3	6	0
Merriweather	2	14	7.0	11	0
Swain	0	9	—	9	0
Steelers	20	218	10.9	67t	1
Opponents	20	244	12.2	37t	2

Punting	No.	Yds.	Avg.	In 20	LG
Newsome	86	3447	40.1	18	64
Steelers	89	3447	38.7	18	64
Opponents	82	3194	39.0	17	69

Punt Returns	No.	FC	Yds.	Avg.	LG	TD
Woods	33	12	294	8.9	41	0
Lipps	3	1	16	5.3	10	0
Steelers	36	13	310	8.6	41	0
Opponents	34	14	364	10.7	44	0

Kickoff Returns	No.	Yds.	Avg.	LG	TD
Sanchez	25	591	23.6	64	0
Elder	21	425	20.2	36	0
Sanders	8	148	18.5	29	0
Reeder	4	52	13.0	17	0
Hughes	2	16	8.0	16	0
Seitz	2	25	12.5	14	0
Merriweather	1	27	27.0	27	0
Rostosky	1	3	3.0	3	0
Sweeney	1	0	0.0	0	0
Woods	1	17	17.0	17	0
Steelers	66	1304	19.8	64	0
Opponents	56	1362	24.3	100t	3

Sacks	No.
Willis	12.0
Gary	6.5
Merriweather	6.0
Nelson	5.0
Hinkle	4.5
G. Williams	3.5
Dunn	2.5
Sims	1.0
Cole	0.5
Little	0.5
Steelers	43.0
Opponents	20.0

FIRST-ROUND SELECTIONS

(If club had no first-round selection, first player drafted is listed with round in parentheses.)

Year	Player, College, Position
1936	Bill Shakespeare, Notre Dame, B
1937	Mike Basrak, Duquesne, C
1938	Byron (Whizzer) White, Colorado, B
1939	Bill Patterson, Baylor, B (3)
1940	Kay Eakin, Arkansas, B
1941	Chet Gladchuk, Boston College, C (2)
1942	Bill Dudley, Virginia, B
1943	Bill Daley, Minnesota, B
1944	Johnny Podesto, St. Mary's, California, B
1945	Paul Duhart, Florida, B
1946	Felix (Doc) Blanchard, Army, B
1947	Hub Bechtol, Texas, E
1948	Dan Edwards, Georgia, E
1949	Bobby Gage, Clemson, B
1950	Lynn Chandnois, Michigan State, B
1951	Butch Avinger, Alabama, B
1952	Ed Modzelewski, Maryland, B
1953	Ted Marchibroda, St. Bonaventure, B
1954	Johnny Lattner, Notre Dame, B
1955	Frank Varrichione, Notre Dame, T
1956	Gary Glick, Colorado A&M, B
	Art Davis, Mississippi State, B
1957	Len Dawson, Purdue, B
1958	Larry Krutko, West Virginia, B (2)
1959	Tom Barnett, Purdue, B (8)
1960	Jack Spikes, Texas Christian, RB
1961	Myron Pottios, Notre Dame, LB (2)
1962	Bob Ferguson, Ohio State, RB
1963	Frank Atkinson, Stanford, T (8)
1964	Paul Martha, Pittsburgh, S
1965	Roy Jefferson, Utah, WR (2)
1966	Dick Leftridge, West Virginia, RB
1967	Don Shy, San Diego State, RB (2)
1968	Mike Taylor, Southern California, T
1969	Joe Greene, North Texas State, DT
1970	Terry Bradshaw, Louisiana Tech, QB
1971	Frank Lewis, Grambling, WR
1972	Franco Harris, Penn State, RB
1973	J.T. Thomas, Florida State, DB
1974	Lynn Swann, Southern California, WR
1975	Dave Brown, Michigan, DB
1976	Bennie Cunningham, Clemson, TE
1977	Robin Cole, New Mexico, LB
1978	Ron Johnson, Eastern Michigan, DB
1979	Greg Hawthorne, Baylor, RB
1980	Mark Malone, Arizona State, QB
1981	Keith Gary, Oklahoma, DE
1982	Walter Abercrombie, Baylor, RB
1983	Gabriel Rivera, Texas Tech, DT
1984	Louis Lipps, Southern Mississippi, WR
1985	Darryl Sims, Wisconsin, DE
1986	John Rienstra, Temple, G
1987	Rod Woodson, Purdue, DB

Pittsburgh Steelers 1987 Veteran Roster

No.	Name	Pos.	Ht.	Wt.	Birth-date	NFL Exp.	College	Hometown	How Acq.	'86 Games/ Starts
34	Abercrombie, Walter	RB	6-0	210	9/26/59	6	Baylor	Waco, Tex.	D1-'82	16/16
1	Anderson, Gary	K	5-11	179	7/16/59	6	Syracuse	Durban, South Africa	W(Buff)-'82	16/0
66	Behning, Mark	T	6-6	285	9/26/61	2	Nebraska	Denton, Tex.	D2-'85	16/1
6	Brister, Bubby	QB	6-2	192	8/15/62	2	Northeast Louisiana	Monroe, La.	D3-'86	2/2
88	Britt, Jessie	WR	6-4	200	3/3/63	2	North Carolina A&T	Greensboro, N.C.	FA-'86	8/0
91	Carr, Gregg	LB	6-1	220	3/31/62	3	Auburn	Birmingham, Ala.	D6-'85	16/0
33	Clayton, Harvey	CB	5-9	186	4/4/61	5	Florida State	Florida City, Fla.	FA-'83	15/12
56	Cole, Robin	LB	6-2	225	9/11/55	11	New Mexico	Compton, Calif.	D1-'77	16/16
67	Dunn, Gary	NT	6-3	275	8/24/53	11	Miami	Coral Gables, Fla.	D6-'76	16/16
42	Edwards, Dave	S	6-0	198	3/31/62	3	Illinois	Decatur, Ga.	FA-'85	16/1
24	Erenberg, Rich	RB	5-10	205	4/17/62	4	Colgate	Chappaqua, N.Y.	D9-'84	16/0
92	Gary, Keith	DE	6-3	269	9/14/59	5	Oklahoma	Fairfax, Va.	D1-'81	16/0
86	Gothard, Preston	TE	6-4	242	2/23/62	3	Alabama	Montgomery, Ala.	FA-'85	16/16
96	Henton, Anthony	LB	6-1	218	7/27/63	2	Troy State	Bessemer, Ala.	D9-'86	16/0
53	Hinkle, Bryan	LB	6-2	220	6/4/59	6	Oregon	Silverdale, Wash.	D6-'81	16/16
36	Hughes, David	RB	6-0	220	6/1/59	7	Boise State	Honolulu, Hawaii	FA-'86	5/0
62	Ilkin, Tunch	T	6-3	265	9/23/57	8	Indiana State	Highland Park, Ill.	D6-'80	15/15
43	Jackson, Earnest	RB	5-9	218	12/18/59	5	Texas A&M	Rosenberg, Tex.	FA-'86	13/13*
83	Lipps, Louis	WR-KR	5-10	187	8/9/62	4	Southern Mississippi	Reserve, La.	D1-'84	13/12
50	Little, David	LB	6-1	242	1/3/59	7	Florida	Miami, Fla.	D7-'81	16/16
74	Long, Terry	G	5-11	270	7/21/59	4	East Carolina	Columbia, S.C.	D4-'84	16/16
16	Malone, Mark	QB	6-4	222	11/22/58	8	Arizona State	El Cajon, Calif.	D1-'80	14/14
57	Merriweather, Mike	LB	6-2	219	11/26/60	6	Pacific	Vallejo, Calif.	D3-'82	16/16
64	Nelson, Edmund	DE-NT	6-3	271	4/30/60	6	Auburn	Tampa, Fla.	D7-'82	16/16
18	Newsome, Harry	P	6-0	186	1/25/63	3	Wake Forest	Cheraw, S.C.	D8-'85	16/0
65	Pinney, Ray	T	6-4	274	6/29/54	9	Washington	Seattle, Wash.	D2-'76	16/15
30	Pollard, Frank	RB	5-10	230	6/15/57	8	Baylor	Meridian, Tex.	D11-'80	3/3
60	Rasmussen, Randy	C-G	6-1	254	9/27/60	4	Minnesota	Minneapolis, Minn.	D8-'84	4/3
40	Reeder, Dan	RB	5-11	235	3/18/61	2	Delaware	Newark, Del.	FA-'86	11/0
79	Rienstra, John	G	6-4	275	3/22/63	2	Temple	Colorado Springs, Colo.	D1-'86	4/4
63	Rostosky, Pete	T	6-4	265	7/29/61	4	Connecticut	Monongahela, Pa.	FA-'83	11/1
28	Sanchez, Lupe	CB-KR	5-10	192	10/28/61	2	UCLA	Visalia, Calif.	FA-'86	11/4
45	Sanders, Chuck	RB	6-1	233	4/24/64	2	Slippery Rock	Penn Hills, Pa.	FA-'86	14/0
80	Seitz, Warren	TE	6-4	223	9/29/62	2	Missouri	Topeka, Kan.	D10-'86	16/0
41	Sheffield, Chris	CB	6-1	188	1/9/63	2	Albany State	Cairo, Ga.	FA-'86	10/6
31	Shell, Donnie	S	5-11	198	8/26/52	14	South Carolina State	Whitmire, S.C.	FA-'74	15/15
99	Sims, Darryl	DE-DT	6-3	284	7/23/61	3	Wisconsin	Bridgeport, Conn.	D1-'85	16/0
82	Stallworth, John	WR	6-2	202	7/15/52	14	Alabama A&M	Tuscaloosa, Ala.	D4-'74	11/9
90	Station, Larry	LB	5-11	232	12/5/63	2	Iowa	Omaha, Neb.	D11-'86	6/0
85	Sweeney, Calvin	WR	6-2	192	1/12/55	8	Southern California	Santa Monica, Calif.	D4-'79	16/7
87	Thompson, Weegie	WR	6-6	210	3/21/61	4	Florida State	Midlothian, Va.	D4-'84	16/4
52	Webster, Mike	C	6-1	257	3/18/52	14	Wisconsin	Tomahawk, Wis.	D5-'74	12/12
21	Williams, Eric	S	6-1	190	2/21/60	5	North Carolina State	Garner, N.C.	D6-'83	16/16
98	Williams, Gerald	NT	6-3	280	9/3/63	2	Auburn	Lanett, Ala.	D2-'86	16/0
93	Willis, Keith	DE	6-1	263	7/29/59	6	Northeastern	Newark, N.J.	FA-'82	16/16
55	Winston, Dennis	LB	6-0	224	10/25/55	11	Arkansas	Marianna, Ark.	FA-'85	16/0
73	Wolfley, Craig	G	6-1	268	5/19/58	8	Syracuse	Orchard Park, N.Y.	D5-'80	9/9
49	Woodruff, Dwayne	CB	6-0	198	2/18/57	8	Louisville	New Richmond, Ohio	D6-'79	0*
22	Woods, Rick	S-CB	6-0	195	11/16/59	6	Boise State	Boise, Idaho	D4-'82	15/0

* Jackson active for 2 games with Philadelphia in '86 but did not play, played 13 games with Pittsburgh; Woodruff missed '86 season due to injury.

†Option playout; subject to developments.

Traded—Center Dan Turk to Tampa Bay.

Also played with Steelers in '86—G Emil Boures (1 game), QB Scott Campbell (3), CB Donnie Elder (9), CB John Swain (11).

COACHING STAFF

Head Coach, Chuck Noll

Pro Career: Became only NFL coach to win four Super Bowls when Steelers defeated Los Angeles Rams 31-19 in Super Bowl XIV. Put together 13 consecutive non-losing seasons and has guided Steelers into postseason play 11 of last 15 years. Led Pittsburgh to consecutive NFL championships twice (1974-75, 1978-79). With 170 career wins, is third among active NFL coaches behind Don Shula (263) and Tom Landry (260). Has tenth-highest winning percentage (.594) among active coaches and is tied for fifth among the NFL's all-time winningest coaches with a 170-114-1 career record. Noll is one of only four all-time NFL head coaches to lead a team for 19 consecutive seasons—Curly Lambeau (29), Landry (26), and Steve Owen (23) are the others. Played pro ball as guard-linebacker for Cleveland Browns from 1953-59. At age 28, he started coaching career as defensive coach with Los Angeles (San Diego) Chargers in 1960. Left after 1965 season to become Don Shula's defensive backfield assistant in Baltimore. Remained with Colts until taking over Pittsburgh reins as head coach in 1969. Career record: 170-114-1.

Background: Was an all-state star at Benedictine High in Cleveland. Captained the University of Dayton team, playing both tackle and linebacker. He was drafted by the Browns in 1953.

Personal: Born in Cleveland on January 5, 1932. He and his wife, Marianne, live in Pittsburgh and have one son—Chris.

Assistant Coaches

Ron Blackledge, offensive line-tackles/tight ends; born April 15, 1938, Canton, Ohio, lives in Pittsburgh. Tight end-defensive end Bowling Green 1957-59. No pro playing experience. College coach: Ashland 1968-69, Cincinnati 1970-72, Kentucky 1973-75, Princeton 1976, Kent State 1977-81 (head coach 1979-81). Pro coach: Joined Steelers in 1982.

Tony Dungy, defensive coordinator; born October 6, 1955, Jackson, Mich., lives in Pittsburgh. Quarterback Minnesota 1973-76. Pro safety Pittsburgh Steelers 1977-78, San Francisco 49ers 1979. College coach: Minnesota 1980. Pro coach: Joined Steelers in 1981.

Walt Evans, conditioning and training; born May 15, 1951, Pittsburgh, Pa., lives in Pittsburgh. Marietta College 1974. No college or pro playing experience. Pro coach: Joined Steelers in 1983.

Dennis Fitzgerald, computer and special teams; born March 13, 1936, Ann Arbor, Mich., lives in Pittsburgh. Running back Michigan 1958-60. No pro playing experience. College coach: Michigan 1961-68, Kentucky 1969-70, Kent State 1971-77 (head coach 1975-77), Syracuse 1978-80, Tulane 1981. Pro coach: Joined Steelers in 1982.

Joe Greene, defensive line; born September 24, 1946, Temple, Tex., lives in Pittsburgh. Defensive tackle North Texas State 1966-68. Pro defensive tackle Pittsburgh Steelers 1969-81. Pro coach: First year with Steelers.

Dick Hoak, offensive backfield; born December 8, 1939, Jeannette, Pa., lives in Greenburg, Pa. Halfback-quarterback Penn State 1958-60. Pro running back Pittsburgh Steelers 1961-70. Pro coach: Joined Steelers in 1972.

Jed Hughes, linebackers; born November 14, 1947, New York, N.Y., lives in Pittsburgh. Linebacker Springfield 1966-68, tight end Gettysburg 1969-70. No pro playing experience. College coach: Stanford 1971-72, Michigan 1973-75, UCLA 1976-81. Pro coach: Minnesota Vikings 1982-83, joined Steelers in 1984.

Hal Hunter, offensive line-guards/centers; born June 3, 1934, Canonsburg, Pa., lives in Pittsburgh. Linebacker-guard Pittsburgh 1955-57. No pro playing experience. College coach: Richmond 1958-61, West Virginia 1962-63, Maryland 1964-65, Duke 1966-70, Kentucky 1971-72, Indiana 1973-76, California State (Pa.) 1977-80 (head coach). Pro coach: Hamilton Tiger-Cats (CFL) 1981, Indianapolis Colts 1982-84, joined Steelers in 1985.

Pittsburgh Steelers 1987 First-Year Roster

Name	Pos.	Ht.	Wt.	Birth-date	College	Hometown	How Acq.
Apke, Stephen	LB	6-1	218	8/3/65	Pittsburgh	Pittsburgh, Pa.	FA
Baker, Andrew (1)	WR	6-1	195	12/17/62	Rutgers	Trenton, N.J.	FA-'86
Bone, Warren	DE	6-0	242	11/4/64	Texas Southern	Houston, Tex.	FA
Bosselmann, Richard	LB	6-2	225	5/11/64	Cal Poly-SLO	San Luis Obispo, Calif.	FA
Brown, Gordon (1)	RB	5-10	225	3/19/63	Tulsa	Tulsa, Okla.	FA
Buchanan, Charles	DE	6-2	232	9/20/64	Tennessee State	Memphis, Tenn.	D8
Carter, Rodney (1)	RB	5-11	213	10/30/64	Purdue	Elizabeth, N.J.	D7-'86
Clinkscales, Joey	WR	6-0	199	5/21/64	Tennessee	Knoxville, Tenn.	D9
Everett, Thomas	S	5-9	177	11/21/64	Baylor	Daingerfield, Tex.	D4
Hall, Delton	CB	6-1	195	1/16/65	Clemson	Greensboro, N.C.	D2
Herron, Donald (1)	LB	6-2	225	6/7/64	North Carolina State	Kansas City, Kan.	FA-'86
Hoge, Merril	RB	6-2	221	1/26/65	Idaho State	Pocatello, Idaho	D10
Johnson, Tim	DE-NT	6-3	251	1/29/65	Penn State	Sarasota, Fla.	D6a
Jones, Bruce (1)	CB-S	6-1	195	12/26/62	North Alabama	Courtland, Ala.	FA
Kelley, Chris	TE	6-3	236	11/13/64	Akron	Lorain, Ohio	D7
Kimmel, Jerry (1)	LB	6-2	240	7/18/63	Syracuse	Kirkwood, N.Y.	FA
Lloyd, Greg	LB	6-2	224	5/26/65	Fort Valley State	Fort Valley, Ga.	D6b
Lockett, Charles	WR	6-0	175	10/1/65	Long Beach State	Los Angeles, Calif.	D3
Mancini, Michael (1)	P	5-10	173	4/3/63	Fresno State	San Mateo, Calif.	FA
McCombs, Glenn (1)	TE	6-4	225	2/11/63	Central Florida	Altemonte Springs, Fla.	FA-'86
Middleton, Kelvin (1)	S	6-0	188	9/8/61	Wichita State	Macon, Ga.	FA
Mosely, Anthony	RB	5-10	210	6/17/65	Fresno State	Selma, Calif.	FA
Nickerson, Hardy	LB	6-2	230	9/1/65	California	Los Angeles, Calif.	D5
Opfar, David (1)	NT	6-4	270	1/16/60	Penn State	Elizabeth, Pa.	FA
Oswald, Paul	C	6-3	273	4/9/64	Kansas	Topeka, Kan.	D11
Pizzo, Joe	QB	6-2	220	6/25/65	Mars Hill College	Quartz Hill, Calif.	FA
Quick, Jerry (1)	T	6-5	270	12/30/63	Wichita State	Anthony, Kan.	FA-'86
Stewart, Vernon	WR	6-2	176	3/1/64	Akron	Farrell, Pa.	FA
Tucker, Erroll (1)	CB-KR	5-7	170	7/5/64	Utah	Long Beach, Calif.	D5a-'86
Wiederkehr, Hans (1)	G	6-4	275	2/11/63	Syracuse	Ballston Lake, N.Y.	FA-'86
Williams, Albert	LB	6-3	229	9/7/64	Texas-El Paso	San Antonio, Tex.	FA
Woodson, Rod	CB	6-0	195	3/10/65	Purdue	Ft. Wayne, Ind.	D1
Young, Theo	TE	6-2	228	4/25/65	Arkansas	Newport, Ark.	D12

The term NFL Rookie is defined as a player who is in his first season of professional football and has not been on the roster of another professional football team for any regular-season or postseason games. A Rookie is designated by an "R" on NFL rosters. Players who have been active in another professional football league or players who have NFL experience, including either preseason training camp or being on an active roster for fewer than three regular-season or postseason games, are termed NFL First-Year Players. An NFL First-Year Player is designated by a "1" on NFL rosters. Thereafter, a player on an NFL active roster for at least three regular-season or postseason games is credited with an additional year of NFL playing experience.

NOTES

Jon Kolb, computer and special teams; born August 30, 1947, Ponca City, Okla., lives in Pittsburgh. Center-linebacker Oklahoma State 1966-68. Pro tackle Pittsburgh Steelers 1969-81. Pro coach: Joined Steelers in 1982.

Tom Moore, offensive coordinator; born November 7, 1938, Owatonna, Minn., lives in Pittsburgh. Quarterback Iowa 1957-60. No pro playing experience. College coach: Iowa 1961-62, Dayton 1965-68, Wake Forest 1969, Georgia Tech 1970-71, Minnesota 1972-73, 1975-76. Pro coach: New York Stars (WFL) 1974, joined Steelers in 1977.

SAN DIEGO CHARGERS

American Football Conference Western Division

Team Colors: Blue, White, and Gold

San Diego Jack Murphy Stadium
P.O. Box 20666
San Diego, California 92120
Telephone: (619) 280-2111

Club Officials

Chairman of the Board/President: Alex G. Spanos
Director of Football Operations: Steve Ortmayer
Asst. Director of Football Operations: John Sanders
Director of Administration: Jack Teele
Director of Player Personnel: Chet Franklin
Pro Scouting: Rudy Feldman
Director of Public Relations: Rick Smith
Business Manager: Pat Curran
Director of Marketing: Rich Israel
Director of Ticket Operations: Joe Scott
Assistant Director of Public Relations: Bill Johnston
Chief Financial Officer: Jerry Murphy
Head Trainer: Mark Howard
Equipment Manager: Sid Brooks

Stadium: San Diego Jack Murphy Stadium • **Capacity:** 60,750
9449 Friars Road
San Diego, California 92108

Playing Surface: Grass

Training Camp: University of California-San Diego
Third College
La Jolla, California 92037

1987 Schedule

Preseason

Aug. 15	**Dallas**	6:00
Aug. 23	**Los Angeles Rams**	5:00
Aug. 27	at San Francisco	6:00
Sept. 4	**New York Jets**	7:00

Regular Season

Sept. 13	at Kansas City	12:00
Sept. 20	**St. Louis**	1:00
Sept. 27	**Seattle**	1:00
Oct. 4	at Cincinnati	1:00
Oct. 11	at Tampa Bay	1:00
Oct. 18	at Los Angeles Raiders	1:00
Oct. 25	**Kansas City**	1:00
Nov. 1	**Cleveland**	1:00
Nov. 8	at Indianapolis	1:00
Nov. 15	**Los Angeles Raiders**	5:00
Nov. 22	at Seattle	1:00
Nov. 29	**Denver**	1:00
Dec. 6	at Houston	12:00
Dec. 13	**Pittsburgh**	1:00
Dec. 20	**Indianapolis**	1:00
Dec. 27	at Denver	2:00

Chargers Coaching History

Los Angeles 1960 (200-190-11)

1960-69	Sid Gillman*	83-51-6
1969-70	Charlie Waller	9-7-3
1971	Sid Gillman**	4-6-0
1971-73	Harland Svare***	7-17-2
1973	Ron Waller	1-5-0
1974-78	Tommy Prothro****	21-39-0
1978-86	Don Coryell#	72-60-0
1986	Al Saunders	3-5-0

*Retired after nine games in 1969
**Resigned after 10 games in 1971
***Resigned after eight games in 1973
****Resigned after four games in 1978
#Resigned after eight games in 1986

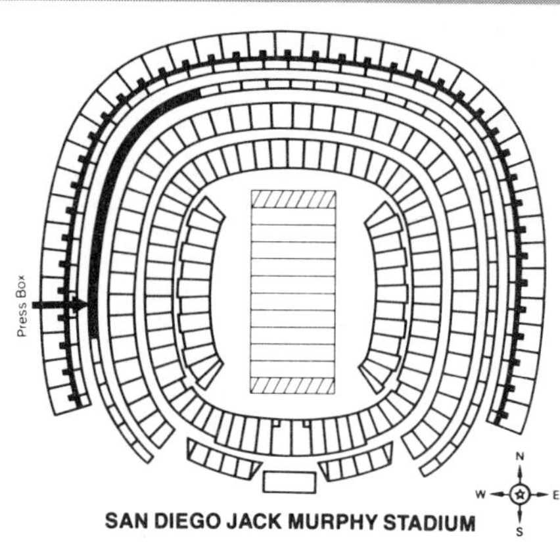

SAN DIEGO JACK MURPHY STADIUM

Record Holders

Individual Records—Career

Category	Name	Performance
Rushing (Yds.)	Paul Lowe, 1960-67	4,963
Passing (Yds.)	Dan Fouts, 1973-1986	40,425
Passing (TDs)	Dan Fouts, 1973-1986	244
Receiving (No.)	Charlie Joiner, 1976-1986	586
Receiving (Yds.)	Lance Alworth, 1962-1970	9,585
Interceptions	Dick Harris, 1960-65	29
Punting (Avg.)	Maury Buford, 1982-84	42.7
Punt Return (Avg.)	Leslie (Speedy) Duncan, 1964-1970	12.3
Kickoff Return (Avg.)	Leslie (Speedy) Duncan, 1964-1970	25.2
Field Goals	Rolf Benirschke, 1977-1986	146
Touchdowns	Lance Alworth, 1962-1970	83
Points	Rolf Benirschke, 1977-1986	766

Individual Records—Single Season

Category	Name	Performance
Rushing (Yds.)	Earnest Jackson, 1984	1,179
Passing (Yds.)	Dan Fouts, 1981	4,802
Passing (TDs)	Dan Fouts, 1981	33
Receiving (No.)	Kellen Winslow, 1980	89
Receiving (Yds.)	Lance Alworth, 1965	1,602
Interceptions	Charlie McNeil, 1961	9
Punting (Avg.)	Dennis Partee, 1969	44.6
Punt Return (Avg.)	Leslie (Speedy) Duncan, 1965	15.5
Kickoff Return (Avg.)	Keith Lincoln, 1962	28.4
Field Goals	Rolf Benirschke, 1980	24
Touchdowns	Chuck Muncie, 1981	19
Points	Rolf Benirschke, 1980	118

Individual Records—Single Game

Category	Name	Performance
Rushing (Yds.)	Keith Lincoln, 1-5-64	206
Passing (Yds.)	Dan Fouts, 10-19-80	444
	Dan Fouts, 12-11-82	444
Passing (TDs)	Dan Fouts, 11-22-81	6
Receiving (No.)	Kellen Winslow, 10-7-84	15
Receiving (Yds.)	Wes Chandler, 12-20-82	260
Interceptions	Many times	3
	Last time by Pete Shaw, 11-2-80	
Field Goals	Many times	4
	Last time by Rolf Benirschke, 12-22-80	
Touchdowns (Tot.)	Kellen Winslow, 11-22-81	5
Points	Kellen Winslow, 11-22-81	30

1986 Team Statistics

	Chargers	Opp.
Total First Downs	334	308
Rushing	98	104
Passing	212	182
Penalty	24	22
Third Down: Made/Att.	98/231	95/221
Fourth Down: Made/Att.	6/13	1/5
Total Net Yards	5356	5366
Avg. Per Game	334.8	335.4
Total Plays	1107	1046
Avg. Per Play	4.8	5.1
Net Yards Rushing	1576	1678
Avg. Per Game	98.5	104.9
Total Rushes	471	475
Net Yards Passing	3780	3688
Avg. Per Game	236.3	230.5
Tackled/Yards Lost	32/265	62/440
Gross Yards	4045	4128
Att./Completions	604/339	509/288
Completion Pct.	56.1	56.6
Had Intercepted	33	15
Punts/Avg.	79/40.4	81/40.8
Net Punting Avg.	32.9	34.9
Penalties/Yards Lost	119/977	108/918
Fumbles/Ball Lost	29/16	42/22
Touchdowns	41	47
Rushing	19	14
Passing	21	27
Returns	1	6
Avg. Time of Possession	30:32	29:28

1986 Team Record

Preseason (3-1)

Date	Result		Opponents
8/9	W	20- 0	Dallas
8/16	W	45-38	Philadelphia
8/23	L	17-20	at L.A. Rams (OT)
8/29	W	24-17	St. Louis
		106-75	

Regular Season (4-12)

Date	Result		Opponents	Att.
9/7	W	50-28	Miami	57,726
9/14	L	7-20	at N.Y. Giants	74,921
9/21	L	27-30	Washington	57,853
9/28	L	13-17	at L.A. Raiders	63,153
10/6	L	7-33	at Seattle	63,207
10/12	L	14-31	Denver	55,662
10/19	L	41-42	at Kansas City	55,767
10/26	L	7-23	at Philadelphia	41,469
11/2	L	23-24	Kansas City	44,518
11/9	W	9- 3	at Denver	75,012
11/16	L	21-24	Dallas	55,622
11/20	L	31-37	L.A. Raiders (OT)	56,031
11/30	W	17- 3	at Indianapolis	47,950
12/7	W	27- 0	Houston	40,103
12/14	L	24-34	Seattle	47,096
12/21	L	17-47	at Cleveland	68,505

(OT) Overtime

Score by Periods

Chargers	73	125	48	89	0	—	335
Opponents	64	98	101	127	6	—	396

Attendance

Home 414,611 Away 489,984 Total 904,595
Single game home record, 58,566 (11-10-85)
Single season home record, 415,626 (1985)

1986 Individual Statistics

Scoring

	TD R	TD P	TD Rt	PAT	FG	Saf	TP
Benirschke	0	0	0	39/41	16/25	0	87
Anderson	1	8	0	0/0	0/0	0	54
McGee	7	0	0	0/0	0/0	0	42
Spencer	6	0	0	0/0	0/0	0	36
Winslow	0	5	0	0/0	0/0	0	30
Adams	4	0	0	0/0	0/0	0	24
Chandler	0	4	0	0/0	0/0	0	24
Joiner	0	2	0	0/0	0/0	0	12
Flick	1	0	0	0/0	0/0	0	6
Holohan	0	1	0	0/0	0/0	0	6
Johnson	0	1	0	0/0	0/0	0	6
O'Neal	0	0	1	0/0	0/0	0	6
Chargers	19	21	1	39/41	16/25	1	335
Opponents	14	27	6	45/46	23/31	0	396

Passing

	Att.	Comp.	Yds.	Pct.	TD	Int.	Tkld.	Rate
Fouts	430	252	3031	58.6	16	22	21/173	71.4
Herrmann	97	51	627	52.6	2	3	5/43	66.8
Flick	73	33	361	45.2	2	8	6/49	29.9
Holohan	2	1	21	50.0	0	0	0/0	87.5
Anderson	1	1	4	100.0	1	0	0/0	122.9
McGee	1	1	1	100.0	0	0	0/0	79.2
Chargers	604	339	4045	56.1	21	33	32/265	65.6
Opponents	509	288	4128	56.6	27	15	62/440	88.4

Rushing

	Att.	Yds.	Avg.	LG	TD
Anderson	127	442	3.5	17	1
Adams	118	366	3.1	22	4
Spencer	99	350	3.5	23	6
James	51	224	4.4	24	0
McGee	63	187	3.0	20	7
Herrmann	2	6	3.0	6	0
Flick	6	5	0.8	7	1
Mathison	1	−1	−1.0	−1	0
Fouts	4	−3	−0.8	0	0
Chargers	471	1576	3.3	24	19
Opponents	475	1678	3.5	28t	14

Receiving

	No.	Yds.	Avg.	LG	TD
Anderson	80	871	10.9	65t	8
Winslow	64	728	11.4	28t	5
Chandler	56	874	15.6	40	4
Joiner	34	440	12.9	33	2
Johnson	30	399	13.3	30	1
Holohan	29	356	12.3	34	1
James	23	173	7.5	18	0
McGee	10	105	10.5	18	0
Spencer	6	48	8.0	15	0
Adams	4	26	6.5	10	0
Sievers	2	14	7.0	9	0
Ware	1	11	11.0	11	0
Chargers	339	4045	11.9	65t	21
Opponents	288	4128	14.3	72t	27

Interceptions

	No.	Yds.	Avg.	LG	TD
Byrd	5	45	9.0	18	0
Dale	4	153	38.3	50	0
Glenn	2	31	15.5	31	0
O'Neal	2	22	11.0	17	1
Brown	1	23	23.0	23	0
Taylor	1	0	0.0	0	0
Chargers	15	274	18.3	50	1
Opponents	33	421	12.8	80	2

Punting

	No.	Yds.	Avg.	In 20	LG
Mojsiejenko	72	3026	42.0	15	62
Chandler	5	167	33.4	0	38
Chargers	79	3193	40.4	15	62
Opponents	81	3304	40.8	15	59

Punt Returns

	No.	FC	Yds.	Avg.	LG	TD
Anderson	25	10	227	9.1	30	0
James	9	6	94	10.4	21	0
Chandler	3	0	13	4.3	10	0
Chargers	37	16	334	9.0	30	0
Opponents	43	5	370	8.6	48	1

Kickoff Returns

	No.	Yds.	Avg.	LG	TD
Anderson	24	482	20.1	35	0
James	18	315	17.5	31	0
Adams	5	100	20.0	25	0
Spencer	5	81	16.2	21	0
Wyatt	5	74	14.8	23	0
Johnson	3	48	16.0	21	0
Winslow	2	11	5.5	8	0
McGee	1	15	15.0	15	0
Chandler	1	11	11.0	11	0
Plummer	1	0	0.0	0	0
Chargers	65	1137	17.5	35	0
Opponents	60	1088	18.1	46	0

Sacks

	No.
Williams	15.0
O'Neal	12.5
Smith	11.0
Hardison	6.5
Wilson	5.5
Benson	5.0
Ehin	2.5
Plummer	2.5
Snipes, Wash.-S.D.	2.0
Moore, Mia.-S.D.	1.0
Robinson	1.0
Unrein	0.5
Chargers	62.0
Opponents	32.0

FIRST-ROUND SELECTIONS

(If club had no first-round selection, first player drafted is listed with round in parentheses.)

Year	Player, College, Position
1960	Monty Stickles, Notre Dame, E
1961	Earl Faison, Indiana, DE
1962	Bob Ferguson, Ohio State, RB
1963	Walt Sweeney, Syracuse, G
1964	Ted Davis, Georgia Tech, LB
1965	Steve DeLong, Tennessee, DE
1966	Don Davis, Cal State-Los Angeles, DT
1967	Ron Billingsley, Wyoming, DE
1968	Russ Washington, Missouri, DT Jimmy Hill, Texas A&I, DB
1969	Marty Domres, Columbia, QB Bob Babich, Miami, Ohio, LB
1970	Walker Gillette, Richmond, WR
1971	Leon Burns, Long Beach State, RB
1972	Pete Lazetich, Stanford, DE (2)
1973	Johnny Rodgers, Nebraska, WR
1974	Bo Matthews, Colorado, RB Don Goode, Kansas, LB
1975	Gary Johnson, Grambling, DT Mike Williams, Louisiana State, DB
1976	Joe Washington, Oklahoma, RB
1977	Bob Rush, Memphis State, C
1978	John Jefferson, Arizona State, WR
1979	Kellen Winslow, Missouri, TE
1980	Ed Luther, San Jose State, QB (4)
1981	James Brooks, Auburn, RB
1982	Hollis Hall, Clemson, DB (7)
1983	Billy Ray Smith, Arkansas, LB Gary Anderson, Arkansas, WR Gill Byrd, San Jose State, DB
1984	Mossy Cade, Texas, DB
1985	Jim Lachey, Ohio State, G
1986	Leslie O'Neal, Oklahoma State, DE James FitzPatrick, Southern California, T
1987	Rod Bernstine, Texas A&M, TE

San Diego Chargers 1987 Veteran Roster

No.	Name	Pos.	Ht.	Wt.	Birth-date	NFL Exp.	College	Hometown	How Acq.	'86 Games/ Starts
42	Adams, Curtis	RB	5-11	194	4/30/62	2	Central Michigan	Muskegon, Ill.	D8-'85	7/2
56	Allert, Ty	LB	6-2	233	7/7/63	2	Texas	Houston, Tex.	D4-'86	16/3
40	Anderson, Gary	RB-WR	6-0	180	4/18/61	3	Arkansas	Columbia, Mo.	D1b-'83	16/12
	t-Banks, Chip	LB	6-4	233	9/18/59	6	Southern California	Augusta, Ga.	T(Clev)-'86	16/16
6	Benirschke, Rolf	K	6-1	180	2/7/55	10	California-Davis	La Jolla, Calif.	W(Raiders)-'77	16/0
57	†Benson, Thomas	LB	6-2	235	9/6/61	4	Oklahoma	Ardmore, Tex.	T(Atl)-'86	16/16
22	Byrd, Gill	CB-S	5-11	194	2/20/61	5	San Jose State	San Francisco, Calif.	D1c-'85	15/14
89	Chandler, Wes	WR	6-0	188	8/22/56	10	Florida	New Smyrna Beach, Fla.	T(NO)-'81	16/14
77	Claphan, Sam	T	6-6	288	10/10/56	7	Oklahoma	Stillwell, Okla.	FA-'81	16/14
37	Dale, Jeffrey	S	6-3	213	10/6/62	3	Louisiana State	Winnfield, La.	D2b-'85	16/16
61	Dallafior, Ken	G	6-4	277	8/26/59	3	Minnesota	Madison Heights, Mich.	FA-'85	12/1
20	Davis, Wayne	CB	5-11	175	7/17/63	3	Indiana State	Mt. Healthy, Ohio	D2a-'85	16/5
75	DiGiacomo, Curt	G	6-4	275	10/24/63	2	Arizona	Citrus Heights, Calif.	FA-'86	3/0
78	†Ehin, Chuck	NT	6-4	257	7/1/61	5	Brigham Young	Leyton, Utah	D12b-'83	12/9
70	FitzPatrick, James	T	6-7	302	2/1/64	2	Southern California	Beaverton, Ore.	D1b-'86	4/0
12	Flick, Tom	QB	6-3	191	8/30/58	5	Washington	Seattle, Wash.	FA-'86	11/3
14	Fouts, Dan	QB	6-3	204	6/10/51	15	Oregon	Rancho Santa Fe, Calif.	D3-'73	12/12
25	Glenn, Vencie	S	6-0	183	10/26/64	2	Indiana State	Terre Haute, Ind.	T(NE)-'86	16/7
92	Hardison, Dee	DE	6-4	274	5/2/56	10	North Carolina	Fayetteville, N.C.	W(NYG)-'86	15/0
59	Hawkins, Andy	LB	6-2	230	3/31/58	6	Texas A&I	Bay City, Tex.	T(TB)-'86	10/0
29	Hendy, John	CB-S	5-11	199	10/9/62	2	Long Beach State	Santa Clara, Calif.	D3-'85	0*
9	†Herrmann, Mark	QB	6-4	199	1/8/59	7	Purdue	Carmel, Ind.	T(Ind)-'85	6/1
88	Holohan, Pete	TE	6-4	232	7/25/59	7	Notre Dame	Liverpool, N.Y.	D7-'81	16/6
27	Hunter, Daniel	CB	5-11	180	9/1/62	3	Henderson State, Ark.	Arkadelphia, Ark.	FA-'86	15/2*
26	James, Lionel	RB-WR	5-6	170	5/25/62	4	Auburn	Albany, Ga.	D5-'84	7/1
83	Johnson, Trumaine	WR	6-1	191	1/16/60	3	Grambling	Baker, La.	D6-'83	16/4
68	Kowalski, Gary	G-T	6-6	280	7/2/60	4	Boston College	Clinton, Conn.	T(Rams)-'85	16/16
74	Lachey, Jim	T	6-6	284	6/4/63	3	Ohio State	St. Henry, Ohio	D1-'85	16/15
63	†Leonard, Jim	C-G	6-3	270	10/19/57	7	Santa Clara	Santa Cruz, Calif.	FA-'85	15/5
51	Lowe, Woodrow	LB	6-0	229	6/9/54	12	Alabama	Phenix City, Ala.	D5-'76	16/10
62	†Macek, Don	C	6-2	270	7/2/54	12	Boston College	Manchester, N.H.	D2-'76	13/13
21	†McGee, Buford	RB	6-0	206	8/16/60	4	Mississippi	Durant, Miss.	D11-'84	9/3
60	†McKnight, Dennis	C-G	6-3	270	9/12/59	6	Drake	Staten Island, N.Y.	FA-'82	16/16
2	Mojsiejenko, Ralf	P-K	6-2	210	1/28/63	3	Michigan State	Bridgman, Mich.	D4-'85	16/0
90	Moore, Mack	DE	6-4	258	3/4/59	3	Texas A&M	Pembrook Pines, Fla.	FA-'86	10/0*
55	Nelson, Derrie	LB	6-2	239	2/8/58	5	Nebraska	Fairmont, Neb.	FA-'82	11/0
91	O'Neal, Leslie	DE	6-4	255	5/7/64	2	Oklahoma State	Little Rock, Ark.	D1a-'86	13/13
50	Plummer, Gary	LB	6-2	230	1/26/60	2	California	Fremont, Calif.	FA-'86	15/13
85	Sievers, Eric	TE	6-4	235	11/9/58	7	Maryland	Arlington, Va.	D4b-'81	9/1
97	Simmons, Tony	DE	6-4	268	12/18/62	2	Tennessee	Oakland, Calif.	D12a-'85	0*
54	†Smith, Billy Ray	LB	6-3	236	8/10/61	5	Arkansas	Plano, Tex.	D1a-'83	16/15
86	t-Smith, Tim	WR	6-2	206	3/20/57	8	Nebraska	San Diego, Calif.	T(Hou)-'86	13/0
52	Snipes, Angelo	LB	6-0	215	1/11/63	2	West Georgia	Reston, Va.	FA-'86	16/0*
43	Spencer, Tim	RB	6-1	227	12/10/60	3	Ohio State	St. Clairsville, Ohio	D11b-'83	14/12
33	Sullivan, John	CB-S	6-1	190	10/15/61	2	California	Oakland, Calif.	FA-'86	15/0*
24	Taylor, Ken	CB	6-1	186	9/2/63	3	Oregon State	San Jose, Calif.	FA-'86	14/11
98	Unrein, Terry	NT	6-5	283	10/24/62	2	Colorado State	Ft. Lupton, Colo.	D3a-'86	12/7
72	Walker, Jeff	G	6-4	295	1/22/63	2	Memphis State	Olive Branch, Miss.	D3b-'86	16/0
23	Walters, Danny	CB	6-1	200	11/4/60	4	Arkansas	Chicago, Ill.	D4-'83	2/2
81	Ware, Timmie	WR	5-10	171	4/2/63	2	Southern California	Compton, Calif.	FA-'86	9/0
99	Williams, Lee	DE	6-5	263	10/15/62	4	Bethune-Cookman	Ft. Lauderdale, Fla.	SD1-'84	16/16
93	†Wilson, Earl	DE	6-4	280	9/13/58	3	Kentucky	Atlantic City, N.J.	FA-'85	16/6
80	Winslow, Kellen	TE	6-5	250	11/5/57	9	Missouri	St. Louis, Mo.	D1-'79	16/16
96	Winter, Blaise	DE	6-3	274	1/31/62	3	Syracuse	Blauvelt, N.Y.	FA-'86	4/0
30	Wyatt, Kevin	CB	5-10	190	3/14/64	2	Arkansas	Kansas City, Mo.	W(Mia)-'86	16/0

* Hendy and Simmons missed '86 season due to injury; Hunter played 10 games with Denver in '86, 5 with San Diego; Moore played 7 games with Miami, 3 with San Diego; Snipes played 10 games with Washington, 6 with San Diego; Sullivan played 6 games with Green Bay, 9 with San Diego.

†Option playout; subject to developments.

t-Chargers traded for Banks (Cleveland), T. Smith (Houston).

Retired—Charlie Joiner, 18-year wide receiver, 15 games in '86.

Also played with Chargers in '86—CB Don Brown (13 games), LB Mike Douglass (7), LB Mark Fellows (1), CB David Martin (4), QB Bruce Mathison (2), LB Fred Robinson (10), NT Lester Williams (4).

COACHING STAFF

Head Coach, Al Saunders

Pro Career: Begins first full season as San Diego's head coach. Named seventh head coach in Chargers history on October 29, 1986, and led team to a 3-5 record in his first head coaching assignment. Came to Chargers and the NFL in 1983 as receivers coach and was named assistant head coach/receivers at the start of the 1986 season. Career record: 3-5.

Background: Academic All-America defensive back and team captain at San Jose State 1969. Graduate assistant at Southern California 1970-71. Receivers coach at Missouri 1972. Offensive backfield coach at Utah State 1973-75. Assistant head coach and offensive coordinator at California from 1976-81. Offensive coordinator and quarterbacks coach at Tennessee 1982.

Personal: Born February 1, 1947, in London, England. Attended St. Ignatius High School in San Francisco. Graduated with honors from San Jose State 1969. Received masters degree in education and physical education from Stanford in 1970 before moving to Southern California, where he is completing his doctorate in sports administration. Saunders and his wife, Karen, live in Scripps Ranch, Calif., and have three children—Robert, William, and Korrin.

Assistant Coaches

Gunther Cunningham, defensive line; born June 19, 1946, Munich, Germany, lives in San Diego. Linebacker Oregon 1965-67. No pro playing experience. College coach: Oregon 1969-71, Arkansas 1972, Stanford 1973-76, California 1977-80. Pro coach: Hamilton Tiger-Cats (CFL) 1981, Indianapolis Colts 1982-84, joined Chargers in 1985.

Mike Haluchak, linebackers; born November 28, 1949, Concord, Calif., lives in San Diego. Linebacker Southern California 1967-70. No pro playing experience. College coach: Southern California 1976-77, Cal State-Fullerton 1978, Pacific 1979-80, California 1981, North Carolina State 1982. Pro coach: Oakland Invaders (USFL) 1983-85, joined Chargers in 1986.

Bobby Jackson, running backs; born February 16, 1940, Forsyth, Ga., lives in San Diego. Linebacker-running back Samford, Ga., 1959-62. No pro playing experience. College coach: Florida State 1965-69, Kansas State 1970-74, Louisville 1975-76, Tennessee 1977-82. Pro coach: Atlanta Falcons 1983-86, first year with Chargers.

Charlie Joiner, receivers; born October 14, 1947, Many, La., lives in San Diego. Wide receiver Grambling 1965-68. Defensive back-wide receiver Houston Oilers 1969-72, wide receiver Cincinnati Bengals 1972-75, San Diego Chargers 1976-86. Pro coach: first year with Chargers.

Dave Levy, offensive coordinator; born October 25, 1932, Carrollton, Mo., lives in Solana Beach, Calif. Guard UCLA 1952-53. No pro playing experience. College coach: UCLA 1954, Long Beach City College 1955, Southern California 1960-75. Pro coach: Joined Chargers in 1980.

Ron Lynn, defensive coordinator; born December 6, 1944, Youngstown, Ohio, lives in San Diego. Quarterback-defensive back Mount Union (Ohio) 1963-65. College coach: Toledo 1966, Mount Union 1967-73, Kent State 1974-76, San Jose State 1977-78, Pacific 1979, California 1980-82. Pro coach: Oakland Invaders (USFL) 1983-85, joined Chargers in 1986.

Wayne Sevier, special teams; born July 3, 1941, San Diego, Calif., lives in San Diego. Quarterback Chaffey, Calif., J.C. 1960, San Diego State 1961-62. No pro playing experience. College coach: California Western 1968-69. Pro coach: St. Louis Cardinals 1974-75, Atlanta Falcons 1976, San Diego Chargers 1979-80, Washington Redskins 1981-86, rejoined Chargers in 1987.

Roger Theder, quarterbacks; born September 22, 1939, Watertown, Wis., lives in San Diego. Quarterback Western Michigan 1960-62. No pro playing experience. College coach: Bowling Green 1963, Northern Illinois 1964-67, Stanford 1968-71, California 1972-81. Pro coach: Baltimore/Indianapolis Colts 1982-84, Arizona Outlaws (USFL) 1985-86, first year with Chargers.

San Diego Chargers 1987 First-Year Roster

Name	Pos.	Ht.	Wt.	Birth-date	College	Hometown	How Acq.
Abbott, Vincent (1)	K	5-11	200	5/31/58	Cal State-Fullerton	Vancouver, Canada	FA
Anderson, Anthony	CB-S	6-2	205	10/24/64	Grambling	Jonesboro, Ark.	D10
Bernstine, Rod	TE	6-3	235	2/8/65	Texas A&M	Bryan, Tex.	D1
Brock, Lou	CB	5-10	175	5/8/64	Southern California	St. Louis, Mo.	D2
Brown, Ron	LB	6-4	235	4/28/64	Southern California	La Puente, Calif.	D8b
Catan, Pete (1)	DE	6-3	245	11/12/57	Eastern Illinois	Penfield, N.Y.	FA
Champion, Tony (1)	WR	6-1	180	3/19/63	Tennessee-Martin	Humboldt, Tenn.	FA
Collins, Clarence (1)	WR	6-1	180	2/1/62	Illinois State	St. Louis, Mo.	FA
Goebel, Joe	C	6-5	268	12/12/63	UCLA	Midland, Tex.	D11
Greenwood, Marcus	RB	6-0	210	3/7/63	UCLA	Bakersfield, Calif.	D12
Holland, Jamie	WR	6-1	186	2/1/64	Ohio State	Wake Forest, N.C.	D7
Jackson, Jeffrey (1)	LB	6-1	230	10/9/61	Auburn	Griffin, Ga.	FA
Jones, Nelson	CB	6-1	190	2/13/64	North Carolina State	Woodbury, N.J.	D5
MacEster, Joe	T	6-7	307	9/21/65	Texas-El Paso	Mahopac, N.Y.	D8a
Moore, Malcolm (1)	TE	6-3	236	6/24/61	Southern California	Los Angeles, Calif.	FA-'86
Powell, Jeff (1)	WR	5-10	185	2/27/63	Tennessee	White Creek, Tenn.	FA
Rogers, Chuck	T	6-9	335	11/30/62	Dayton	Pittsburgh, Pa.	FA
Rome, Tag (1)	WR	5-9	175	8/13/61	Northeast Louisiana	Ruston, La.	FA
Shepherd, Larry (1)	WR	6-3	204	4/9/63	Houston	Kilgore, Tex.	FA
Stadnik, John	T	6-4	275	2/18/60	Western Illinois	Blue Island, Ill.	FA
Vlasic, Mark	QB	6-3	206	10/25/63	Iowa	Monaca, Pa.	D4
Wilcher, Tom	RB	5-10	188	4/11/64	Michigan	Detroit, Mich.	D9
Wilson, Karl	DE	6-4	268	9/10/64	Louisiana State	Baton Rouge, La.	D3
Williams, Al (1)	WR	5-10	180	10/5/61	Nevada-Reno	Long Beach, Calif.	FA

The term NFL Rookie is defined as a player who is in his first season of professional football and has not been on the roster of another professional football team for any regular-season or postseason games. A Rookie is designated by an "R" on NFL rosters. Players who have been active in another professional football league or players who have NFL experience, including either preseason training camp or being on an active roster for fewer than three regular-season or postseason games, are termed NFL First-Year Players. An NFL First-Year Player is designated by a "1" on NFL rosters. Thereafter, a player on an NFL active roster for at least three regular-season or postseason games is credited with an additional year of NFL playing experience.

NOTES

American Football Conference Western Division

Team Colors: Blue, Green, and Silver

11220 N.E. 53rd Street
Kirkland, Washington 98033
Telephone: (206) 827-9777

Club Officials

President-General Manager: Mike McCormack
Assistant General Manager: Chuck Allen
Player Personnel Director: Mike Allman
Public Relations Director: Gary Wright
Assistant Public Relations Director: Dave Neubert
Administrative Assistant: Sandy Gregory
Sales and Marketing Coordinator: Lowell Perry
Sales and Marketing Assistant: Reggie McKenzie
Business Manager: Mickey Loomis
Data Processing Director: Tom Monroe
Ticket Manager: James Nagaoka
Trainer: Jim Whitesel
Equipment Manager: Walt Loeffler

Stadium: Kingdome • **Capacity:** 64,984
201 South King Street
Seattle, Washington 98104

Playing Surface: AstroTurf

Training Camp: 11220 N.E. 53rd Street
Kirkland, Washington 98033

1987 Schedule

Preseason

Aug. 13	at Los Angeles Rams	7:30
Aug. 22	at St. Louis	7:00
Aug. 28	**Detroit**	7:30
Sept. 4	**New York Jets**	5:00

Regular Season

Sept. 13	at Denver	2:00
Sept. 20	**Kansas City**	1:00
Sept. 27	at San Diego	1:00
Oct. 4	**Miami**	1:00
Oct. 11	**Cincinnati**	1:00
Oct. 18	at Detroit	1:00
Oct. 25	at Los Angeles Raiders	1:00
Nov. 1	**Minnesota**	1:00
Nov. 9	at N.Y. Jets (Monday)	9:00
Nov. 15	**Green Bay**	1:00
Nov. 22	**San Diego**	1:00
Nov. 30	**L.A. Raiders** (Monday)	6:00
Dec. 6	at Pittsburgh	1:00
Dec. 13	**Denver**	5:00
Dec. 20	at Chicago	12:00
Dec. 27	at Kansas City	12:00

Seahawks Coaching History

(81-89-0)

1976-82	Jack Patera*	35-59-0
1982	Mike McCormack	4-3-0
1983-86	Chuck Knox	42-27-0

*Released after two games in 1982

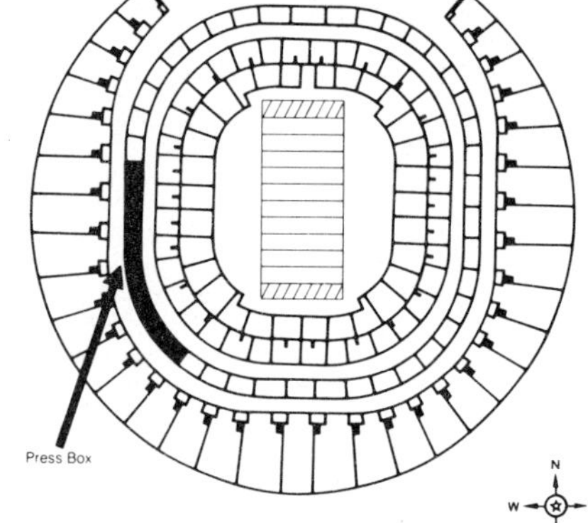

KINGDOME

Record Holders

Individual Records—Career

Category	Name	Performance
Rushing (Yds.)	Curt Warner, 1983-86	4,064
Passing (Yds.)	Jim Zorn, 1976-1984	20,042
Passing (TDs)	Jim Zorn, 1976-1984	107
	Dave Krieg, 1980-86	107
Receiving (No.)	Steve Largent, 1976-1986	694
Receiving (Yds.)	Steve Largent, 1976-1986	11,129
Interceptions	Dave Brown, 1976-1986	50
Punting (Avg.)	Herman Weaver, 1977-1980	40.0
Punt Return (Avg.)	Paul Johns, 1981-84	11.4
Kickoff Return (Avg.)	Zachary Dixon, 1983-84	23.4
Field Goals	Norm Johnson, 1982-86	84
Touchdowns (Tot.)	Steve Largent, 1976-1986	88
Points	Steve Largent, 1976-1986	529

Individual Records—Single Season

Category	Name	Performance
Rushing (Yds.)	Curt Warner, 1986	1,481
Passing (Yds.)	Dave Krieg, 1984	3,671
Passing (TDs)	Dave Krieg, 1984	32
Receiving (No.)	Steve Largent, 1985	79
Receiving (Yds.)	Steve Largent, 1985	1,287
Interceptions	John Harris, 1981	10
	Kenny Easley, 1984	10
Punting (Avg.)	Herman Weaver, 1980	41.8
Punt Return (Avg.)	Bobby Joe Edmonds, 1986	12.3
Kickoff Return (Avg.)	Al Hunter, 1978	24.1
Field Goals	Norm Johnson, 1986	22
Touchdowns (Tot.)	David Sims, 1978	15
	Sherman Smith, 1979	15
Points	Norm Johnson, 1984	110

Individual Records—Single Game

Category	Name	Performance
Rushing (Yds.)	Curt Warner, 11-27-83	207
Passing (Yds.)	Dave Krieg, 11-20-83	418
Passing (TDs)	Dave Krieg, 12-2-84	5
	Dave Krieg, 9-15-85	5
Receiving (No.)	David Hughes, 9-27-81	12
	Steve Largent, 11-25-84	12
Receiving (Yds.)	Steve Largent, 11-25-84	191
Interceptions	Kenny Easley, 9-3-84	3
Field Goals	Efren Herrera, 10-5-80	4
	Norm Johnson, 9-3-84	4
	Norm Johnson, 10-6-86	4
Touchdowns (Tot.)	Daryl Turner, 9-15-85	4
Points	Daryl Turner, 9-15-85	24

1986 Team Statistics

	Seahawks	Opp.
Total First Downs	291	310
Rushing	123	93
Passing	158	192
Penalty	10	25
Third Down: Made/Att.	96/221	84/225
Fourth Down: Made/Att.	0/6	6/18
Total Net Yards	5409	5341
Avg. Per Game	338.1	333.8
Total Plays	1005	1053
Avg. Per Play	5.4	5.1
Net Yards Rushing	2300	1759
Avg. Per Game	143.8	109.9
Total Rushes	513	471
Net Yards Passing	3109	3582
Avg. Per Game	194.3	223.9
Tackled/Yards Lost	39/315	47/306
Gross Yards	3424	3888
Att./Completions	453/268	535/301
Completion Pct.	59.2	56.3
Had Intercepted	14	22
Punts/Avg.	79/38.6	81/40.4
Net Punting Avg.	33.0	33.7
Penalties/Yards Lost	98/813	81/652
Fumbles/Ball Lost	29/13	26/14
Touchdowns	43	34
Rushing	15	12
Passing	24	20
Returns	4	2
Avg. Time of Possession	29:47	30:13

1986 Team Record

Preseason (2-2)

Date	Result		Opponents
8/8	W	21-14	Indianapolis
8/15	L	27-30	at Detroit (OT)
8/22	W	27-17	Minnesota
8/29	L	10-21	at San Francisco
		85-82	

Regular Season (10-6)

Date	Result		Opponents	Att.
9/7	W	30- 0	Pittsburgh	61,461
9/14	W	23-17	Kansas City	61,068
9/21	W	38-31	at New England	58,977
9/28	L	14-19	at Washington	54,157
10/6	W	33- 7	San Diego	63,207
10/12	L	10-14	at L.A. Raiders	70,635
10/19	W	17-12	N.Y. Giants	62,282
10/26	L	13-20	at Denver	76,089
11/2	L	7-38	N.Y. Jets	62,497
11/9	L	7-27	at Kansas City	53,268
11/16	L	7-34	at Cincinnati	54,410
11/23	W	24-20	Philadelphia	55,786
11/27	W	31-14	at Dallas	58,020
12/8	W	37- 0	L.A. Raiders	62,923
12/14	W	34-24	at San Diego	47,096
12/20	W	41-16	Denver	63,697

(OT) Overtime

Score by Periods

Seahawks	69	96	80	121	0	—	366
Opponents	60	103	52	78	0	—	293

Attendance

Home 492,921 Away 476,652 Total 969,573
Single game home record, 64,411 (12-15-84)
Single season home record, 493,657 (1985)

1986 Individual Statistics

Scoring	TD R	TD P	TD Rt	PAT	FG	Saf	TP
N. Johnson	0	0	0	42/42	22/35	0	108
Warner	13	0	0	0/0	0/0	0	78
Largent	0	9	0	0/0	0/0	0	54
Turner	0	7	0	0/0	0/0	0	42
R. Butler	0	4	0	0/0	0/0	0	24
Franklin	0	2	0	0/0	0/0	0	12
Lane	0	1	1	0/0	0/0	0	12
Brown	0	0	1	0/0	0/0	0	6
Edmonds	0	0	1	0/0	0/0	0	6
Hudson	0	1	0	0/0	0/0	0	6
Krieg	1	0	0	0/0	0/0	0	6
Morris	1	0	0	0/0	0/0	0	6
Moyer	0	0	1	0/0	0/0	0	6
Seahawks	15	24	4	42/43	22/35	0	366
Opponents	12	20	2	32/34	19/28	0	293

Passing	Att.	Comp.	Yds.	Pct.	TD	Int.	Tkld.	Rate
Krieg	375	225	2921	60.0	21	11	35/281	91.0
Gilbert	76	42	485	55.3	3	3	4/34	71.4
Largent	1	1	18	100.0	0	0	0/0	118.8
Morris	1	0	0	0.0	0	0	0/0	39.6
Seahawks	453	268	3424	59.2	24	14	39/315	87.7
Opponents	535	301	3888	56.3	20	22	47/306	74.6

Rushing	Att.	Yds.	Avg.	LG	TD
Warner	319	1481	4.6	60t	13
Williams	129	538	4.2	36	0
Morris	19	149	7.8	49t	1
Krieg	35	122	3.5	19	1
Lane	6	11	1.8	4	0
Gilbert	3	8	2.7	12	0
Franklin	1	2	2.0	2	0
Edmonds	1	−11	−11.0	−11	0
Seahawks	513	2300	4.5	60t	15
Opponents	471	1759	3.7	25	12

Receiving	No.	Yds.	Avg.	LG	TD
Largent	70	1070	15.3	38t	9
Warner	41	342	8.3	26	0
Franklin	33	547	16.6	49	2
Williams	33	219	6.6	23	0
Skansi	22	271	12.3	30	0
R. Butler	19	351	18.5	67t	4
Turner	18	334	18.6	72t	7
Tice	15	150	10.0	25	0
Hudson	13	131	10.1	30	1
Lane	3	6	2.0	4	1
Bailey	1	3	3.0	3	0
Seahawks	268	3424	12.8	72t	24
Opponents	301	3888	12.9	83t	20

Interceptions	No.	Yds.	Avg.	LG	TD
Brown	5	58	11.6	24	1
Justin	4	29	7.3	18	0
Robinson	3	39	13.0	25	0
Moyer	3	38	12.7	20	0
Easley	2	34	17.0	24	0
Scholtz	2	10	5.0	10	0
Taylor	2	0	0.0	0	0
Gaines	1	8	8.0	8	0
Seahawks	22	216	9.8	25	1
Opponents	14	216	15.4	36t	1

Punting	No.	Yds.	Avg.	In 20	LG
Gamache	79	3048	38.6	10	55
Seahawks	79	3048	38.6	10	55
Opponents	81	3270	40.4	20	60

Punt Returns	No.	FC	Yds.	Avg.	LG	TD
Edmonds	34	14	419	12.3	75t	1
Skansi	5	0	38	7.6	14	0
Seahawks	39	14	457	11.7	75t	1
Opponents	38	21	298	7.8	28	0

Kickoff Returns	No.	Yds.	Avg.	LG	TD
Edmonds	34	764	22.5	46	0
Morris	23	465	20.2	38	0
Scholtz	3	39	13.0	16	0
Skansi	1	21	21.0	21	0
Tice	1	17	17.0	17	0
Edwards	1	13	13.0	13	0
Lane	1	3	3.0	3	0
Seahawks	64	1322	20.7	46	0
Opponents	59	1002	17.0	42	0

Sacks	No.
Green	12.0
Young	6.0
Gaines	5.0
Nash	5.0
Bryant	4.0
Edwards	4.0
Scholtz	3.0
Merriman	2.0
K. Butler	1.0
Easley	1.0
G. Johnson	1.0
Mitz	1.0
Moyer	1.0
Seahawks	47.0
Opponents	39.0

FIRST-ROUND SELECTIONS

(If club had no first-round selection, first player drafted is listed with round in parentheses.)

Year	Player, College, Position
1976	Steve Niehaus, Notre Dame, DT
1977	Steve August, Tulsa, G
1978	Keith Simpson, Memphis State, DB
1979	Manu Tuiasosopo, UCLA, DT
1980	Jacob Green, Texas A&M, DE
1981	Ken Easley, UCLA, DB
1982	Jeff Bryant, Clemson, DE
1983	Curt Warner, Penn State, RB
1984	Terry Taylor, Southern Illinois, DB
1985	Owen Gill, Iowa, RB (2)
1986	John L. Williams, Florida, RB
1987	Tony Woods, Pittsburgh, LB

Seattle Seahawks 1987 Veteran Roster

No.	Name	Pos.	Ht.	Wt.	Birth-date	NFL Exp.	College	Hometown	How Acq.	'86 Games/ Starts
47	Anderson, Eddie	S	6-1	199	7/22/63	2	Fort Valley State	Warner Robins, Ga.	D6-'86	5/0
65	Bailey, Edwin	G	6-4	276	5/15/59	7	South Carolina State	Savannah, Ga.	D5-'81	12/12
76	†Borchardt, Jon	G	6-5	272	8/13/57	9	Montana State	Minneapolis, Minn.	FA-'86	16/4
22	Brown, Dave	CB	6-1	197	1/16/53	13	Michigan	Akron, Ohio	VA-'76	16/16
77	Bryant, Jeff	DE	6-5	272	5/22/60	6	Clemson	Decatur, Ga.	D1-'82	12/12
59	Bush, Blair	C	6-3	272	11/25/56	10	Washington	Palos Verdes, Calif.	T(Cin)-'83	7/7
53	Butler, Keith	LB	6-4	238	5/16/56	10	Memphis State	Huntsville, Ala.	D2-'78	16/16
83	Butler, Ray	WR	6-3	203	6/28/57	8	Southern California	Sweeny, Tex.	FA-'85	16/0
45	Easley, Kenny	S	6-3	206	1/15/59	7	UCLA	Chesapeake, Va.	D1-'81	10/10
30	Edmonds, Bobby Joe	RB-KR	5-11	186	9/26/64	2	Arkansas	Nashville, Tenn.	D5-'86	15/0
68	Edwards, Randy	DE	6-4	266	3/9/61	4	Alabama	Atlanta, Ga.	FA-'84	16/4
64	Essink, Ron	T	6-6	282	7/30/58	7	Grand Valley State	Zeeland, Mich.	D10-'80	0*
97	Feasel, Grant	C	6-7	280	6/28/60	3	Abilene Christian	Barstow, Calif.	FA-'87	0*
88	Franklin, Byron	WR	6-1	183	9/4/58	6	Auburn	Sheffield, Ala.	T(Buff)-'85	14/1
56	†Gaines, Greg	LB	6-3	222	10/16/58	6	Tennessee	Heritage, Tex.	FA-'81	16/15
2	Gamache, Vince	P	5-11	176	11/18/61	2	Cal State-Fullerton	Los Angeles, Calif.	FA-'86	16/0
7	†Gilbert, Gale	QB	6-3	206	12/20/61	3	California	Red Bluff, Calif.	FA-'85	16/2
52	†Grant, Will	C	6-3	268	3/7/54	10	Kentucky	Milton, Mass.	FA-'86	7/6
79	Green, Jacob	DE	6-3	252	1/21/57	8	Texas A&M	Houston, Tex.	D1-'80	16/16
84	†Greene, Danny	WR	5-11	197	12/26/61	2	Washington	Compton, Calif.	D3-'85	0*
85	Hudson, Gordon	TE	6-4	241	6/22/62	2	Brigham Young	Kennewick, Wash.	FA-'86	16/4
23	Hunter, Patrick	CB	5-11	185	10/24/64	2	Nevada-Reno	San Francisco, Calif.	D3-'86	16/0
27	Johnson, Greggory	S	6-1	197	10/20/58	5	Oklahoma State	Houston, Tex.	FA-'86	15/0
9	†Johnson, Norm	K	6-2	194	5/31/60	6	UCLA	Garden Grove, Calif.	FA-'82	16/0
26	Justin, Kerry	CB	5-11	175	5/3/55	8	Oregon State	New Orleans, La.	FA-'86	16/1
54	†Kaiser, John	LB	6-3	227	6/6/62	4	Arizona	Hartland, Wis.	D6-'84	16/0
62	†Kauahi, Kani	C	6-2	254	9/6/59	6	Hawaii	Honolulu, Hawaii	FA-'86	16/3
15	t-Kemp, Jeff	QB	6-0	201	7/11/59	7	Dartmouth	Bethesda, Md.	T(SF)-'87	10/6
63	Kinlaw, Reggie	NT	6-2	249	1/9/57	8	Oklahoma	Miami, Fla.	W(Raiders)-'85	14/5
17	†Krieg, Dave	QB	6-1	196	10/20/58	8	Milton	Schofield, Wis.	FA-'80	15/14
37	†Lane, Eric	RB	6-0	201	1/6/59	7	Brigham Young	Hayward, Calif.	D8-'81	15/0
80	Largent, Steve	WR	5-11	191	9/28/54	12	Tulsa	Oklahoma City, Okla.	T(Hou)-'76	16/16
70	Mattes, Ron	T	6-6	306	8/8/63	2	Virginia	Shenandoah, Pa.	D7-'85	16/16
51	Merriman, Sam	LB	6-3	232	5/5/61	5	Idaho	Tucson, Ariz.	D7-'83	16/1
71	Millard, Bryan	G	6-5	284	12/2/60	4	Texas	Dumas, Tex.	FA-'84	16/16
61	Mitz, Alonzo	DE	6-3	273	6/5/63	2	Florida	Henderson, N.C.	D8-'86	6/0
43	Morris, Randall	RB	6-0	200	4/22/61	4	Tennessee	Long Beach, Calif.	D10-'84	16/0
21	Moyer, Paul	S	6-1	203	7/26/61	5	Arizona State	Villa Park, Calif.	FA-'83	16/6
72	†Nash, Joe	NT	6-2	257	10/11/60	6	Boston College	Boston, Mass.	FA-'82	16/11
41	†Robinson, Eugene	S	6-0	186	5/28/63	3	Colgate	Hartford, Conn.	FA-'85	16/16
8	Salisbury, Sean	QB	6-5	215	3/9/63	2	Southern California	Long Beach, Calif.	FA-'86	0*
58	Scholtz, Bruce	LB	6-6	244	9/26/58	6	Texas	Austin, Tex.	D2-'82	16/16
74	Singer, Curt	T	6-5	279	11/4/64	2	Tennessee	Aliquippa, Pa.	FA-'86	11/0
82	Skansi, Paul	WR	5-11	183	1/11/61	5	Washington	Gig Harbor, Wash.	FA-'85	16/0
20	Taylor, Terry	CB	5-10	191	7/18/61	4	Southern Illinois	Youngstown, Ohio	D1-'84	16/15
86	Tice, Mike	TE	6-7	247	2/2/59	7	Maryland	Central Islip, N.Y.	FA-'81	16/15
81	Turner, Daryl	WR	6-3	194	12/15/61	4	Michigan	Flint, Mich.	D2-'84	15/12
89	Walker, Byron	WR	6-4	188	7/28/60	5	Citadel	Warner Robins, Ga.	FA-'86	1/0
28	Warner, Curt	RB	5-11	204	3/18/61	4	Penn State	Pineville, W. Va.	D1-'83	16/16
32	Williams, John L.	RB	5-11	226	11/23/64	2	Florida	Palatka, Fla.	D1-'86	16/16
75	†Wilson, Mike	T	6-5	280	5/28/55	10	Georgia	Norfolk, Va.	T(Cin)-'86	16/16
50	†Young, Fredd	LB	6-1	233	11/14/61	4	New Mexico State	Dallas, Tex.	D3-'84	15/15

* Essink and Greene missed '86 season due to injury; Feasel active for 1 game with Minnesota in '86, but did not play; Salisbury active for 7 games with Seattle, but did not play.

†Option playout; subject to developments.

Retired—Michael Jackson, 8-year linebacker, 16 games in '86.

t-Seahawks traded for Kemp (San Francisco).

Also played with Seahawks in '86—T Bob Cryder (1 game), C Glenn Hyde (3), TE Jim Laughton (6).

COACHING STAFF

Head Coach, Chuck Knox

Pro Career: Named head coach of Seahawks on January 26, 1983, after five seasons as head coach at Buffalo, where he led Bills to AFC East title in 1980. Led Los Angeles Rams to five straight NFC West titles before taking over Bills in 1978. Pro assistant with New York Jets 1963-66, coaching offensive line, before moving to Detroit in 1967. Served Lions in same capacity until named head coach of Rams in 1973. No pro playing experience. Career record: 137-85-1.

Background: Played tackle for Juniata College in Huntingdon, Pa., 1950-53. Was assistant coach at his alma mater in 1954, then spent 1955 season as line coach at Ellwood City High School in Pennsylvania. Moved to Wake Forest as an assistant coach in 1959-60, then Kentucky in 1961-62.

Personal: Born April 27, 1932, Sewickley, Pa. Chuck and his wife, Shirley, live in Bellevue, Wash., and have four children—Chris, Kathy, Colleen, and Chuck.

Assistant Coaches

Tom Catlin, assistant head coach-defensive coordinator; born September 8, 1931, Ponca City, Okla., lives in Redmond, Wash. Center-linebacker Oklahoma 1950-52. Pro linebacker Cleveland Browns 1953-54, 1957-58, Philadelphia Eagles 1959. College coach: Army 1956. Pro coach: Dallas Texans-Kansas City Chiefs 1960-65, Los Angeles Rams 1966-77, Buffalo Bills 1978-82, joined Seahawks in 1983.

George Dyer, defensive line; born May 4, 1940, Alhambra, Calif., lives in Redmond, Wash. Center-linebacker U.C. Santa Barbara 1961-63. No pro playing experience. College coach: Humboldt State 1964-66, Coalinga, Calif., J.C. 1967 (head coach), Portland State 1968-71, Idaho 1972, San Jose State 1973, Michigan State 1977-79, Arizona State 1980-81. Pro coach: Winnipeg Blue Bombers (CFL) 1974-76, Buffalo Bills 1982, joined Seahawks in 1983.

Chick Harris, offensive backfield; born September 21, 1945, Durham, N.C., lives in Redmond, Wash. Running back Northern Arizona 1966-69. No pro playing experience. College coach: Colorado State 1970-72, Long Beach State 1973-74, Washington 1975-80. Pro coach: Buffalo Bills 1981-82, joined Seahawks in 1983.

Ralph Hawkins, defensive backfield; born May 4, 1935, Washington, D.C., lives in Redmond, Wash. Quarterback-defensive back Maryland 1953-55. Pro defensive back New York Titans (AFL) 1960. College coach: Maryland 1959, 1967, Southern Methodist 1961, Kentucky 1962-65, Army 1966, Cincinnati 1968. Pro coach: Buffalo Bills 1969-71, 1981-82, Washington Redskins 1973-77, Baltimore Colts 1978, New York Giants 1979-80, joined Seahawks in 1983.

Ken Meyer, quarterbacks; born July 14, 1926, Erie, Pa., lives in Bellevue, Wash. Quarterback Denison 1947-50. No pro playing experience. College coach: Denison 1952-57, Wake Forest 1958-59, Florida State 1960-62, Alabama 1963-67, Tulane 1981-82. Pro coach: San Francisco 49ers 1968, 1977 (head coach), New York Jets 1969-72, Los Angeles Rams 1973-76, Chicago Bears 1978-80, joined Seahawks in 1983.

Steve Moore, offensive coordinator-receivers; born August 19, 1947, Los Angeles, Calif., lives in Bellevue, Wash. Wide receiver U.C. Santa Barbara 1968-69. No pro playing experience. College coach: U.C. Santa Barbara 1970-71, Army 1975, Rice 1976-77. Pro coach: Buffalo Bills 1978-82, joined Seahawks in 1983.

Russ Purnell, tight ends-assistant special teams; born June 12, 1948, Chicago, Ill., lives in Bellevue, Wash. Center Orange Coast College and Whittier College 1966-70. No pro playing experience. College coach: Whittier 1970-71, Southern California 1982-85. Pro coach: Joined Seahawks in 1986.

Seattle Seahawks 1987 First-Year Roster

Name	Pos.	Ht.	Wt.	Birth-date	College	Hometown	How Acq.
Agee, Tommy	RB	6-0	220	2/22/64	Auburn	Maplesville, Ala.	D5a
Barbay, Roland	NT	6-4	260	10/1/64	Louisiana State	New Orleans, La.	D7a
Burse, Tony	RB	6-0	220	4/4/65	Middle Tennessee St.	Lafayette, Ga.	D12b
Clark, Louis	WR	6-0	206	7/3/64	Mississippi State	Shannon, Miss.	D10
Davis, Tony (1)	TE	6-5	239	2/11/62	Missouri	Colorado Springs, Colo.	D4-'85
Dove, Wes	DE	6-7	270	2/9/64	Syracuse	Tonawanda, N.Y.	D12a
Eisenhooth, Stan (1)	C	6-6	291	7/8/63	Towson State	Harrisburg, Pa.	FA-'86
Garza, Sammy	QB	6-1	184	7/10/65	Texas-El Paso	Harlingen, Tex.	D8
Graves, Rory (1)	T	6-6	290	7/21/63	Ohio State	Atlanta, Ga.	FA-'86
Johnson, M.L.	LB	6-3	220	1/26/64	Hawaii	Los Angeles, Calif.	D8
Moore, Mark	S	6-0	194	9/3/64	Oklahoma State	Nacogdoches, Tex.	D4
Oliver, Daryl	RB	5-11	195	7/13/64	Miami	Palatka, Fla.	D11
Powell, Alvin (1)	G	6-5	296	11/19/59	Winston-Salem	Fayetteville, N.C.	FA
Rodriguez, Ruben	P	6-2	220	3/3/65	Arizona	Woodlake, Calif.	D5b
Tennell, Derek	TE	6-5	245	2/12/64	UCLA	West Covina, Calif.	D7b
Woods, Tony	LB	6-4	244	9/11/65	Pittsburgh	Newark, N.J.	D1
Wyman, Dave	LB	6-2	229	3/31/64	Stanford	Reno, Nev.	D2

The term NFL Rookie is defined as a player who is in his first season of professional football and has not been on the roster of another professional football team for any regular-season or postseason games. A Rookie is designated by an "R" on NFL rosters. Players who have been active in another professional football league or players who have NFL experience, including either preseason training camp or being on an active roster for fewer than three regular-season or postseason games, are termed NFL First-Year Players. An NFL First-Year Player is designated by a "1" on NFL rosters. Thereafter, a player on an NFL active roster for at least three regular-season or postseason games is credited with an additional year of NFL playing experience.

NOTES

Kent Stephenson, offensive line; born February 4, 1942, Anita, Iowa, lives in Redmond, Wash. Guard-nose tackle Northern Iowa 1962-64. No pro playing experience. College coach: Wayne State 1965-68, North Dakota 1969-71, Southern Methodist 1972-73, Iowa 1974-76, Oklahoma State 1977-78, Kansas 1979-82. Pro coach: Michigan Panthers (USFL) 1983-84, joined Seahawks in 1985.

Rusty Tillman, special teams, assistant linebackers; born February 27, 1948, Beloit, Wis., lives in Bellevue, Wash. Linebacker Northern Arizona 1967-69. Pro linebacker Washington Redskins 1970-77. Pro coach: Joined Seahawks in 1979.

Joe Vitt, special assignments; born August 23, 1954, Camden, N.J., lives in Redmond, Wash. Linebacker Towson State 1973-75. No pro playing experience. Pro coach: Baltimore Colts 1979-81, joined Seahawks in 1982.

THE NFC

ATLANTA FALCONS

National Football Conference Western Division

Team Colors: Red, Black, White, and Silver

Suwanee Road at I-85
Suwanee, Georgia 30174
Telephone: (404) 945-1111

Club Officials

Chairman of the Board: Rankin M. Smith, Sr.
President: Rankin Smith, Jr.
Executive Vice President: Taylor Smith
Vice President & Chief Financial Officer: Jim Hay
Director of College Player Personnel: Ken Herock
Director of Pro Personnel: Bill Jobko
Scouts: Elbert Dubenion, Bill Groman, Joe Mack, Tom Miner
Director of Marketing: Tommy Nobis
Marketing/Community Affairs: Carol Breeding
Director of Public Relations: Charlie Taylor
Assistant Director of Public Relations: Frank Kleha
Ticket Manager: Jack Ragsdale
Assistant Ticket Manager: Luci Bailey
Director of Video Operations: Tom Atcheson
Assistant Director of Video Operations: Danny Mock
Head Trainer: Jerry Rhea
Assistant Trainer: Billy Brooks
Equipment Manager: Whitey Zimmerman
Assistant Equipment Manager: Horace Daniel

Stadium: Atlanta-Fulton County Stadium • **Capacity:** 59,643
521 Capitol Avenue, S.W.
Atlanta, Georgia 30312

Playing Surface: Grass

Training Camp: Suwanee Road at I-85
Suwanee, Georgia 30174

1987 Schedule

Preseason

Aug. 15	**Buffalo**	8:00
Aug. 22	at Kansas City	7:30
Aug. 29	**Cleveland**	8:00
Sept. 4	vs. N.E. at Jacksonville, Fla.	8:00

Regular Season

Sept. 13	at Tampa Bay	1:00
Sept. 20	**Washington**	1:00
Sept. 27	at New Orleans	12:00
Oct. 4	**Pittsburgh**	1:00
Oct. 11	at San Francisco	1:00
Oct. 18	**Los Angeles Rams**	1:00
Oct. 25	at Houston	12:00
Nov. 1	**New Orleans**	1:00
Nov. 8	at Cleveland	1:00
Nov. 15	**Cincinnati**	4:00
Nov. 22	at Minnesota	12:00
Nov. 29	**St. Louis**	1:00
Dec. 6	at Dallas	12:00
Dec. 13	at Los Angeles Rams	1:00
Dec. 20	**San Francisco**	1:00
Dec. 27	**Detroit**	1:00

Falcons Coaching History

(119-185-5)

1966-68	Norb Hecker*	4-26-1
1968-74	Norm Van Brocklin**	37-49-3
1974-76	Marion Campbell***	6-19-0
1976	Pat Peppler	3-6-0
1977-82	Leeman Bennett	47-44-0
1983-86	Dan Henning	22-41-1

*Released after three games in 1968
**Released after eight games in 1974
***Released after five games in 1976

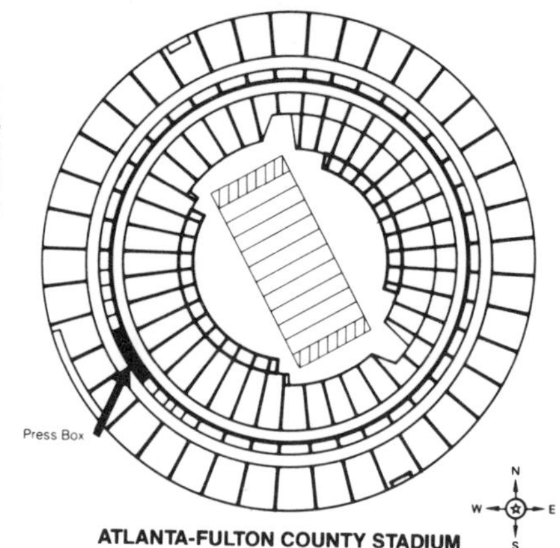

ATLANTA-FULTON COUNTY STADIUM

Record Holders

Individual Records—Career

Category	Name	Performance
Rushing (Yds.)	William Andrews, 1979-1986	5,986
Passing (Yds.)	Steve Bartkowski, 1975-1985	23,468
Passing (TDs)	Steve Bartkowski, 1975-1985	154
Receiving (No.)	Alfred Jenkins, 1975-1983	359
Receiving (Yds.)	Alfred Jenkins, 1975-1983	6,257
Interceptions	Rolland Lawrence, 1973-1980	39
Punting (Avg.)	Rick Donnelly, 1985-86	43.6
Punt Return (Avg.)	Al Dodd, 1973-74	11.8
Kickoff Return (Avg.)	Ron Smith, 1966-67	24.3
Field Goals	Mick Luckhurst, 1981-86	106
Touchdowns (Tot.)	Gerald Riggs, 1982-86	45
Points	Mick Luckhurst, 1981-86	514

Individual Records—Single Season

Category	Name	Performance
Rushing (Yds.)	Gerald Riggs, 1985	1,719
Passing (Yds.)	Steve Bartkowski, 1981	3,830
Passing (TDs)	Steve Bartkowski, 1980	31
Receiving (No.)	William Andrews, 1981	81
Receiving (Yds.)	Alfred Jenkins, 1981	1,358
Interceptions	Rolland Lawrence, 1975	9
Punting (Avg.)	Billy Lothridge, 1968	44.3
Punt Return (Avg.)	Gerald Tinker, 1974	13.9
Kickoff Return (Avg.)	Dennis Pearson, 1978	26.7
Field Goals	Nick Mike-Mayer, 1973	26
Touchdowns (Tot.)	Alfred Jenkins, 1981	13
	Gerald Riggs, 1984	13
Points	Mick Luckhurst, 1981	114

Individual Records—Single Game

Category	Name	Performance
Rushing (Yds.)	Gerald Riggs, 9-2-84	202
Passing (Yds.)	Steve Bartkowski, 11-15-81	416
Passing (TDs)	Randy Johnson, 11-16-69	4
	Steve Bartkowski, 10-19-80	4
	Steve Bartkowski, 10-18-81	4
Receiving (No.)	William Andrews, 11-15-81	15
Receiving (Yds.)	Alfred Jackson, 12-2-84	193
Interceptions	Many times	2
	Last time by Dennis Woodberry, 11-30-86	
Field Goals	Nick Mike-Mayer, 11-4-73	5
	Tim Mazzetti, 10-30-78	5
Touchdowns (Tot.)	Many times	3
	Last time by Gerald Riggs, 11-17-85	
Points	Many times	18
	Last time by Gerald Riggs, 11-17-85	

1986 Team Statistics

	Falcons	Opp.
Total First Downs	305	268
Rushing	149	111
Passing	137	139
Penalty	19	18
Third Down: Made/Att.	85/235	74/207
Fourth Down: Made/Att.	15/25	6/11
Total Net Yards	5106	4908
Avg. Per Game	319.1	306.8
Total Plays	1086	964
Avg. Per Play	4.7	5.1
Net Yards Rushing	2524	1916
Avg. Per Game	157.8	119.8
Total Rushes	578	485
Net Yards Passing	2582	2992
Avg. Per Game	161.4	187.0
Tackled/Yards Lost	56/464	26/177
Gross Yards	3046	3169
Att./Completions	452/246	453/241
Completion Pct.	54.4	53.2
Had Intercepted	17	22
Punts/Avg.	79/43.3	83/41.4
Net Punting Avg.	35.0	35.7
Penalties/Yards Lost	99/763	106/834
Fumbles/Ball Lost	31/16	30/14
Touchdowns	30	34
Rushing	12	10
Passing	14	19
Returns	4	5
Avg. Time of Possession	32:35	27:25

1986 Team Record

Preseason (2-2)

Date	Result		Opponents
8/6	W	31-24	N.Y. Giants
8/16	W	20-17	at Tampa Bay
8/23	L	21-27	Cleveland
8/29	L	21-29	at Washington
		93-97	

Regular Season (7-8-1)

Date	Result		Opponents	Att.
9/7	W	31-10	at New Orleans	67,950
9/14	W	33-13	St. Louis	46,463
9/21	W	37-35	at Dallas	62,880
9/28	W	23-20	at Tampa Bay (OT)	38,950
10/5	L	0-16	Philadelphia	57,104
10/12	W	26-14	L.A. Rams	51,662
10/19	T	10-10	San Fran. (OT)	55,306
10/26	L	7-14	at L.A. Rams	56,993
11/2	L	17-25	at New England	60,597
11/9	L	14-28	N.Y. Jets	53,476
11/16	L	10-13	Chicago	55,520
11/23	L	0-20	at San Francisco	58,747
11/30	W	20-14	at Miami	53,762
12/7	L	23-28	Indianapolis	30,397
12/14	L	9-14	New Orleans	39,994
12/21	W	20- 6	at Detroit	35,255

(OT) Overtime

Score by Periods

Falcons	74	51	64	88	3	—	280
Opponents	34	131	48	67	0	—	280

Attendance

Home 389,922 Away 435,134 Total 825,056
Single game home record, 59,257 (10-30-77)
Single season home record, 442,457 (1980)

1986 Individual Statistics

Scoring	TD R	TD P	TD Rt	PAT	FG	Saf	TP
Luckhurst	0	0	0	21/21	14/24	0	63
Riggs	9	0	0	0/0	0/0	0	54
Haji-Sheikh	0	0	0	7/8	9/12	0	34
C. Brown	0	4	0	0/0	0/0	0	24
Whisenhunt	0	3	0	0/0	0/0	0	18
Allen	0	2	0	0/0	0/0	0	12
Dixon	0	2	0	0/0	0/0	0	12
Andrews	1	0	0	0/0	0/0	0	6
Austin	1	0	0	0/0	0/0	0	6
Britt	0	0	1	0/0	0/0	0	6
Butler	0	0	1	0/0	0/0	0	6
Cox	0	1	0	0/0	0/0	0	6
Pitts	0	0	1	0/0	0/0	0	6
Schonert	1	0	0	0/0	0/0	0	6
Stamps	0	1	0	0/0	0/0	0	6
J. Williams	0	0	1	0/0	0/0	0	6
K. Williams	0	1	0	0/0	0/0	0	6
Gann	0	0	0	0/0	0/0	1	2
Donnelly	0	0	0	1/1	0/0	0	1
Falcons	12	14	4	29/30	23/36	1	280
Opponents	10	19	5	31/34	15/26	0	280

Passing	Att.	Comp.	Yds.	Pct.	TD	Int.	Tkld.	Rate
Archer	294	150	2007	51.0	10	9	34/249	71.6
Schonert	154	95	1032	61.7	4	8	21/206	68.4
Campbell, Pitt.-Atl.	7	1	7	14.3	0	0	2/14	39.6
Campbell, Atl.	3	1	7	33.3	0	0	1/9	42.4
Riggs	1	0	0	0.0	0	0	0/0	39.6
Falcons	452	246	3046	54.4	14	17	56/464	70.2
Opponents	453	241	3169	53.2	19	22	26/177	69.3

Rushing	Att.	Yds.	Avg.	LG	TD
Riggs	343	1327	3.9	31	9
Archer	52	298	5.7	22	0
Austin	62	280	4.5	22	1
Stamps	30	220	7.3	48	0
Andrews	52	214	4.1	13	1
Dixon	11	67	6.1	23	0
B. Johnson	6	25	4.2	10	0
Whisenhunt	1	20	20.0	20	0
K. Williams	3	18	6.0	8	0
Au. Matthews	1	12	12.0	12	0
Schonert	11	12	1.1	7	1
Clark	2	8	4.0	6	0
Campbell	1	7	7.0	7	0
Jones	1	7	7.0	7	0
Bailey	1	6	6.0	6	0
Baker	1	3	3.0	3	0
Falcons	578	2524	4.4	48	12
Opponents	485	1916	4.0	28	10

Receiving	No.	Yds.	Avg.	LG	TD
C. Brown	63	918	14.6	42	4
Dixon	42	617	14.7	65	2
Cox	24	301	12.5	49	1
Riggs	24	136	5.7	11	0
Stamps	20	221	11.1	39t	1
Whisenhunt	20	184	9.2	23t	3
K. Williams	12	164	13.7	32t	1
Allen	10	156	15.6	32	2
Jones	7	141	20.1	41	0
B. Johnson	6	57	9.5	27	0
Middleton	6	31	5.2	8	0
Andrews	5	35	7.0	14	0
Bailey	3	39	13.0	21	0
Austin	3	21	7.0	9	0
Au. Matthews	1	25	25.0	25	0
Falcons	246	3046	12.4	65	14
Opponents	241	3169	13.1	85	19

Interceptions	No.	Yds.	Avg.	LG	TD
Clark	5	94	18.8	34	0
Case	4	41	10.3	41	0
Croudip	2	35	17.5	29	0
J. Williams	2	18	9.0	14t	1
Woodberry	2	14	7.0	9	0
Wilkes	2	11	5.5	10	0
Butler	1	33	33.0	33t	1
Curry	1	32	32.0	32	0
Cason	1	10	10.0	10	0
Rade	1	6	6.0	6	0
Moore	1	0	0.0	0	0
Falcons	22	294	13.4	41	2
Opponents	17	198	11.6	30	1

Punting	No.	Yds.	Avg.	In 20	LG
Donnelly	78	3421	43.9	19	71
Falcons	79	3421	43.3	19	71
Opponents	83	3436	41.4	22	61

Punt Returns	No.	FC	Yds.	Avg.	LG	TD
Dixon	26	3	151	5.8	16	0
B. Johnson	8	8	87	10.9	30	0
Jones	7	1	36	5.1	14	0
Allen	2	0	10	5.0	9	0
Stamps	1	0	8	8.0	8	0
Falcons	44	12	292	6.6	30	0
Opponents	47	12	477	10.1	81t	3

Kickoff Returns	No.	Yds.	Avg.	LG	TD
Stamps	24	514	21.4	35	0
K. Williams	14	255	18.2	32	0
Austin	7	120	17.1	25	0
Andrews	4	71	17.8	22	0
Au. Matthews	3	42	14.0	20	0
Croudip	1	20	20.0	20	0
Dixon	1	13	13.0	13	0
Falcons	54	1035	19.2	35	0
Opponents	59	1190	20.2	48	0

Sacks	No.
Bryan	7.0
Gann	5.5
Pitts	5.5
Costello	2.0
Casillas	1.0
Clark	1.0
Harrison	1.0
Moore	1.0
Rade	1.0
Falcons	26.0
Opponents	56.0

FIRST-ROUND SELECTIONS

(If club had no first-round selection, first player drafted is listed with round in parentheses.)

Year	Player, College, Position
1966	Tommy Nobis, Texas, LB
	Randy Johnson, Texas A&I, QB
1967	Leo Carroll, San Diego State, DE (2)
1968	Claude Humphrey, Tennessee State, DE
1969	George Kunz, Notre Dame, T
1970	John Small, Citadel, LB
1971	Joe Profit, Northeast Louisiana, RB
1972	Clarence Ellis, Notre Dame, DB
1973	Greg Marx, Notre Dame, DT (2)
1974	Gerald Tinker, Kent State, WR (2)
1975	Steve Bartkowski, California, QB
1976	Bubba Bean, Texas A&M, RB
1977	Warren Bryant, Kentucky, T
	Wilson Faumuina, San Jose State, DT
1978	Mike Kenn, Michigan, T
1979	Don Smith, Miami, DE
1980	Junior Miller, Nebraska, TE
1981	Bobby Butler, Florida State, DB
1982	Gerald Riggs, Arizona State, RB
1983	Mike Pitts, Alabama, DE
1984	Rick Bryan, Oklahoma, DT
1985	Bill Fralic, Pittsburgh, T
1986	Tony Casillas, Oklahoma, NT
	Tim Green, Syracuse, LB
1987	Chris Miller, Oregon, QB

Atlanta Falcons 1987 Veteran Roster

No.	Name	Pos.	Ht.	Wt.	Birth-date	NFL Exp.	College	Hometown	How Acq.	'86 Games/ Starts
85	†Allen, Anthony	WR	5-11	182	6/29/59	3	Washington	Seattle, Wash.	D6-'85	5/2
31	Andrews, William	RB	6-0	220	12/25/55	7	Auburn	Thomasville, Ga.	D3b-'79	15/0
16	†Archer, Dave	QB	6-2	208	2/15/62	4	Iowa State	Soda Springs, Idaho	FA-'84	11/11
39	†Austin, Cliff	RB	6-1	213	3/2/60	5	Clemson	Avondale, Ga.	FA-'84	15/1
82	Bailey, Stacey	WR	6-0	157	2/10/60	6	San Jose State	San Rafael, Calif.	D3-'82	6/1
26	Britt, James	CB	6-0	185	9/12/60	4	Louisiana State	Minden, La.	D2-'83	16/2
52	Brown, Aaron	LB	6-2	238	1/13/56	5	Ohio State	Warren, Ohio	FA-'86	16/0
89	†Brown, Charlie	WR	5-10	184	10/29/58	6	South Carolina State	St. John's Island, S.C.	T(Wash)-'85	16/15
77	Bryan, Rick	DE	6-4	265	3/20/62	4	Oklahoma	Coweta, Okla.	D1-'84	16/16
23	Butler, Bobby	CB	5-11	182	5/28/59	7	Florida State	Delray Beach, Fla.	D1-'81	7/7
10	Campbell, Scott	QB	6-0	195	4/15/62	4	Purdue	Hershey, Pa.	FA-'86	4/0*
25	Case, Scott	CB	6-0	178	5/17/62	4	Oklahoma	Edmond, Okla.	D2a-'84	16/15
75	Casillas, Tony	NT	6-3	280	10/26/63	2	Oklahoma	Norman, Okla.	D1a-'86	16/16
20	†Cason, Wendell	CB	5-11	197	1/22/63	3	Oregon	Carson, Calif.	FA-'85	16/6
28	Clark, Bret	S	6-3	198	2/24/61	2	Nebraska	Nebraska City, Neb.	T(Raiders)-'86	16/16
56	Costello, Joe	LB	6-3	250	6/1/60	2	Cent. Connecticut St.	New York, N.Y.	FA-'86	14/0
88	Cox, Arthur	TE	6-2	262	2/5/61	5	Texas Southern	Plant City, Fla.	FA-'83	16/15
30	Croudip, David	CB	5-8	185	1/25/59	4	San Diego State	Compton, Calif.	FA-'85	15/7
50	Curry, Buddy	LB	6-4	222	6/4/58	8	North Carolina	Danville, Va.	D2-'80	16/16
86	Dixon, Floyd	WR	5-9	170	4/9/64	2	Stephen F. Austin	Beaumont, Tex.	D6a-'86	16/12
3	Donnelly, Rick	P	6-0	190	5/17/62	3	Wyoming	Long Island, N.Y.	FA-'85	16/0
73	Dukes, Jamie	G	6-1	270	6/14/64	2	Florida State	Orlando, Fla.	FA-'86	14/4
79	Fralic, Bill	T-G	6-5	280	10/31/62	3	Pittsburgh	Penn Hills, Pa.	D1-'85	16/16
76	Gann, Mike	DE	6-5	265	10/19/63	3	Notre Dame	Lakewood, Colo.	D2-'85	16/16
99	Green, Tim	LB	6-2	249	12/16/63	2	Syracuse	Liverpool, N.Y.	D1b-'86	11/1
6	†Haji-Sheikh, Ali	K	6-0	172	1/11/61	4	Michigan	Ann Arbor, Mich.	FA-'86	6/0
68	Harrison, Dennis	DE	6-8	280	7/31/56	10	Vanderbilt	Cleveland, Ohio	W(SF)-'86	15/0*
71	†Howe, Glen	T	6-7	298	10/18/61	3	Southern Mississippi	New Albany, Miss.	FA-'85	7/3
81	Johnson, Billy	WR	5-9	170	1/27/52	12	Widener	Chichester, Pa.	FA-'82	4/0
43	Jones, Daryll	CB-S	6-1	195	3/23/62	4	Georgia	Columbus, Ga.	FA-'87	0*
84	Jones, Joey	WR	5-8	165	10/29/62	2	Alabama	Mobile, Ala.	SD1-'84	11/2
78	Kenn, Mike	T	6-7	277	2/9/56	10	Michigan	Evanston, Ill.	D1-'78	16/16
63	†Kiewel, Jeff	G	6-3	277	9/27/60	2	Arizona	Tucson, Ariz.	FA-'85	0*
80	†Landrum, Mike	TE	6-2	231	11/6/61	2	Southern Mississippi	Columbia, Miss.	FA-'84	0*
18	Luckhurst, Mick	K	6-1	178	3/31/58	7	California	Redbourn, England	FA-'81	10/0
83	Matthews, Aubrey	WR	5-7	165	9/15/62	2	Delta State	Pascagoula, Miss.	FA-'86	4/0
87	Middleton, Ron	TE	6-2	252	7/17/65	2	Auburn	Atmore, Ala.	FA-'86	16/3
62	Miller, Brett	T	6-7	300	10/2/58	5	Iowa	Glendale, Calif.	D5-'83	8/7
34	Moore, Robert	S	5-11	190	8/15/64	2	Northwestern State, La.	Shreveport, La.	FA-'86	16/9
64	†Pellegrini, Joe	G-C	6-4	265	4/8/57	6	Harvard	Braintree, Mass.	FA-'84	8/1
74	†Pitts, Mike	DE	6-5	277	9/25/60	5	Alabama	Baltimore, Md.	D1-'83	16/0
72	Provence, Andrew	DE	6-3	267	3/8/61	5	South Carolina	Savannah, Ga.	D3-'83	16/0
59	Rade, John	LB	6-1	240	8/31/60	5	Boise State	Sierra Vista, Ariz.	D8-'83	15/15
55	†Radloff, Wayne	C-G	6-5	277	5/17/61	3	Georgia	Winter Park, Fla.	FA-'85	16/16
42	Riggs, Gerald	RB	6-1	232	11/6/60	6	Arizona State	Las Vegas, Nev.	D1-'82	16/15
14	Schonert, Turk	QB	6-1	196	1/15/57	8	Stanford	Placentia, Calif.	T(Cin)-'86	8/5
61	Scully, John	G	6-6	270	8/2/58	7	Notre Dame	Huntington, N.Y.	D4-'81	14/14
29	†Stamps, Sylvester	RB	5-7	175	2/24/61	3	Jackson State	Vicksburg, Miss.	FA-'85	14/0
21	†Turner, Jimmy	CB	6-0	187	6/15/59	5	UCLA	Sherman, Tex.	FA-'86	14/0*
45	†Whisenhunt, Ken	TE	6-2	233	2/28/62	3	Georgia Tech	Augusta, Ga.	D12-'85	16/14
51	Wilkes, Reggie	LB	6-4	242	5/27/56	10	Georgia Tech	Atlanta, Ga.	T(Phil)-'86	16/16
54	Williams, Joel	LB	6-1	227	12/13/56	9	Wisconsin-LaCrosse	Miami, Fla.	T(Phil)-'86	15/14
35	Williams, Keith	WR-RB	5-10	173	9/30/64	2	Southwest Missouri	Springfield, Mo.	D6b-'86	12/0
22	Woodberry, Dennis	CB	5-10	183	4/22/61	2	Southern Arkansas	Texarkana, Ark.	SD3-'84	7/0

* Campbell played 3 games with Pittsburgh in '86, 1 with Atlanta; Harrison played 4 games with San Francisco, 11 with Atlanta; Jones last active with Green Bay in '85; Kiewel and Landrum missed '86 season due to injury; Turner played 8 games with Cincinnati, 6 games with Atlanta.

†Option playout; subject to developments.

Retired—Jeff Van Note, 18-year center, 15 games in '86.

Also played with Falcons in '86—RB Tony Baker (2 games), DT Dan Benish (5), CB Herman Edwards (3), S Kenny Johnson (7), LB Ray Phillips (1), T Eric Sanders (8), LB Johnny Taylor (5), RB Tim Tyrrell (3).

COACHING STAFF

Head Coach and Director of Football Operations, Marion Campbell

Pro Career: Begins first season as Falcons head coach after rejoining and serving as defensive coordinator in 1986. Served as an assistant coach with the Boston Patriots 1962-63, Minnesota Vikings 1964-66, Los Angeles Rams 1967-68, Atlanta Falcons 1969-76 (head coach 1974-76), Philadelphia Eagles 1977-85 (head coach 1983-85). Campbell was a defensive tackle in the NFL with San Francisco 49ers 1954-55 and Philadelphia Eagles 1956-61. Career record: 23-48-1.

Background: Campbell is serving as head coach with the Falcons for the second time. During his first stint with the Falcons in 1974-76, his overall record was 6-19-0. Campbell was an All-America defensive tackle at Georgia 1948-51.

Personal: Born May 25, 1929, Chester, S.C. Marion and his wife, June, have two children—Scott, 25, administrative assistant for the Falcons, and Alicia, 22.

Assistant Coaches

Tommy Brasher, defensive line; born December 30, 1940, El Dorado, Ark., lives in Dunwoody, Ga. Linebacker Arkansas 1961-63. No pro playing experience. College coach: Arkansas 1970, Virginia Tech 1971-73, Northeast Louisiana 1974, 1976, Southern Methodist 1977-81. Pro coach: Shreveport Steamer (WFL) 1975, New England Patriots 1982-84, Philadelphia Eagles 1985, joined Falcons in 1986.

Fred Bruney, assistant head coach/defense; born December 30, 1931, Martins Ferry, Ohio, lives in Atlanta. Back Ohio State 1949-52. Pro defensive back San Francisco 49ers 1953-56, Pittsburgh Steelers 1957, Washington Redskins 1958, Boston Patriots 1960-62. College coach: Ohio State 1959. Pro coach: Boston Patriots 1963, Philadelphia Eagles 1964-68, 1977-85, Atlanta Falcons 1969-76, rejoined Falcons in 1986.

Scott Campbell, administrative assistant, born August 16, 1961, Philadelphia, Pa., lives in Duluth, Ga. Tackle Georgia 1982-84. No pro playing experience. College coach: Auburn 1985-86. Pro coach: First year with Falcons.

Chuck Clausen, linebackers; born June 23, 1940, Anamosa, Iowa, lives in Roswell, Ga. Defensive lineman New Mexico 1961-63. No pro playing experience. College coach: William & Mary 1969-70, Ohio State 1971-75. Pro coach: Philadelphia Eagles 1976-85, joined Falcons in 1986.

Steve Crosby, running backs; born July 3, 1950, Great Bend, Kan., lives in Norcross, Ga. Running back Fort Hays (Kansas) State 1969-72. Pro running back New York Giants 1974-76. Pro coach: Miami Dolphins 1977-82, Atlanta Falcons 1983-84, Cleveland Browns 1985, rejoined Falcons in 1986.

Rod Dowhower, offensive coordinator; born April 15, 1943, Ord, Neb., lives in Atlanta. Quarterback San Diego State 1963-64. No pro playing experience. College coach: San Diego State 1966-72, UCLA 1974-75, Boise State 1976, Stanford 1977-79 (head coach 1979). Pro coach: St. Louis Cardinals 1973, 1982-84, Denver Broncos 1980-81, Indianapolis Colts 1985-86 (head coach), first year with Falcons.

Al Groh, special teams-tight ends; born July 13, 1944, New York, N.Y., lives in Atlanta. Defensive end Virginia 1964-67. No pro playing experience. College coach: Army 1968-69, Virginia 1970-72, North Carolina 1973-77, Air Force 1978-79, Texas Tech 1980, Wake Forest 1981-86 (head coach). Pro coach: First year with Falcons.

Jim Hanifan, assistant head coach-offense; born September 21, 1933, Compton, Calif., lives in Atlanta. Tight end California 1952-54. Pro tight end Toronto Argonauts (CFL) 1955. College coach: Glendale, Calif., J.C. 1964-66, Utah 1967-70, California 1971-72, San Diego State 1972-73. Pro coach: St. Louis Cardinals 1974-85 (head coach 1980-85), first year with Falcons.

Atlanta Falcons 1987 First-Year Roster

Name	Pos.	Ht.	Wt.	Birth-date	College	Hometown	How Acq.
Anthony, Terrence	CB	5-10	183	1/17/65	Iowa State	East St. Louis, Ill.	D9
Barney, Milton	WR	5-9	157	12/23/63	Alcorn State	Gulfport, Miss.	FA
Belk, Veno (1)	TE	6-3	229	3/7/63	Michigan State	Flint, Mich.	FA
Burnette, Dave (1)	T	6-6	285	3/24/61	Central Arkansas	Parkin, Ark.	FA
Caravello, Joe (1)	NT	6-3	270	6/6/63	Tulane	El Segundo, Calif.	FA
Emery, Larry	RB	5-9	195	7/13/64	Wisconsin	Macon, Ga.	D12
Flowers, Kenny	RB	6-0	210	3/14/64	Clemson	Daytona Beach, Fla.	D2
Frank, Rick	P	6-0	205	10/15/64	Iowa State	Cypress, Calif.	FA
Gordon, Tim	CB	6-0	188	5/7/65	Tulsa	Ardmore, Okla.	FA
Hood, Howard	G	6-3	281	3/21/63	Fort Hays State	Kerryville, Tex.	FA
Jordan, Kenneth	LB	6-2	230	4/29/64	Tuskegee Institute	Birmingham, Ala.	FA
Kiser, Paul	G	6-2	272	11/19/63	Wake Forest	Connelly Springs, N.C.	D6
Meyers, Eddie (1)	RB	5-9	210	1/7/59	Navy	Pemberton, N.J.	FA
Miller, Chris	QB	6-2	195	8/9/65	Oregon	Eugene, Ore.	D1
Moor, Buddy (1)	DT	6-5	250	12/1/58	Eastern Kentucky	Valdosta, Ga.	FA
Morris, Dwaine (1)	DT	6-2	260	8/24/63	Southeast Louisiana	Greensburg, La.	FA
Mraz, Mark	DE	6-4	255	2/9/65	Utah State	Glendora, Calif.	D5
Norris, Jerome	S	6-0	187	1/31/64	Furman	Anderson, S.C.	FA
Phillips, Ray (1)	LB	6-3	245	7/24/64	North Carolina State	Huntersville, N.C.	FA
Porell, Tom	NT	6-3	258	9/23/64	Boston College	Winchester, Mass.	FA
Redd, John	RB	5-8	205	10/5/63	Missouri	Mayfield, Ky.	FA
Reese, Jerry	TE	6-2	230	8/17/63	Illinois	Citrus Heights, Calif.	D10
Reid, Michael	LB	6-2	226	6/25/64	Wisconsin	Albany, Ga.	D7
Riley, Bobby	WR	5-8	168	10/17/64	Oklahoma State	Casa Grande, Ariz.	FA
Roulhac, Terrance	WR	5-9	208	8/9/65	Clemson	West Jacksonville, Fla.	FA
Settle, John	RB	5-9	207	6/2/65	Appalachian State	Ruffin, N.C.	FA
Sharp, Dan (1)	TE	6-2	235	2/5/62	Texas Christian	Ft. Worth, Tex.	FA
Shelley, Elbert	S	5-11	180	12/24/64	Arkansas State	Trumann, Ark.	D11
Shibest, James	WR	5-10	187	10/31/64	Arkansas	Houston, Tex.	FA
Taliaferro, Curtis	LB	6-2	226	11/24/62	Virginia Tech	Salem, Va.	D8
Tiefenthaler, Jeff	WR	6-1	181	6/6/63	South Dakota State	Armor, S.D.	FA
Upchurch, Andy (1)	C	6-2	257	9/11/62	Arkansas	Ft. Smith, Ark.	FA
Van Dyke, Ralph	T	6-6	260	1/19/64	Southern Illinois	Chicago Heights, Ill.	D4
Walker, Bruce	WR	5-11	190	10/15/63	Prairie View	Los Angeles, Calif.	FA
Wallace, Calvin	DE	6-2	235	4/17/65	West Virginia Tech	Boomer, W. Va.	FA
Willis, Steve (1)	K	6-2	196	4/28/62	Kansas State	Shawnee Mission, Kan.	FA
Ziegler, Wayne	S	5-11	192	11/4/63	Kansas	Hutchinson, Kan.	FA

The term NFL Rookie is defined as a player who is in his first season of professional football and has not been on the roster of another professional football team for any regular-season or postseason games. A Rookie is designated by an "R" on NFL rosters. Players who have been active in another professional football league or players who have NFL experience, including either preseason training camp or being on an active roster for fewer than three regular-season or postseason games, are termed NFL First-Year Players. An NFL First-Year Player is designated by a "1" on NFL rosters. Thereafter, a player on an NFL active roster for at least three regular-season or postseason games is credited with an additional year of NFL playing experience.

NOTES

Claude Humphrey, defensive assistant; born November 19, 1947, Memphis, Tenn., lives in Atlanta. Defensive end Tennessee State 1965-67. Pro defensive end Atlanta Falcons 1968-77, Philadelphia Eagles 1977-81. Pro coach: First year with Falcons.

Tim Jorgensen, strength and conditioning; born April 21, 1955, St. Louis, Mo., lives in Atlanta. Guard Southwest Missouri State 1974-76. No pro playing experience. College coach: Southwest Missouri State 1977-79, Alabama 1979-80, Louisiana State 1980-83. Pro coach: Philadelphia Eagles 1984-86, first year with Falcons.

Jimmy Raye, receivers, born July 3, 1945, Fayetteville, N.C., lives in Atlanta. Quarterback Michigan State 1965-67. Pro defensive back Philadelphia Eagles 1969. College coach: Michigan State 1971-75, Wyoming 1976. Pro coach: San Francisco 49ers 1977, Detroit Lions 1978-79, Atlanta Falcons 1980-82, Los Angeles Rams 1983-84, Tampa Bay Buccaneers 1985-86, rejoined Falcons in 1987.

National Football Conference Central Division

Team Colors: Navy Blue, Orange, and White

Corporate Headquarters:
Halas Hall
250 North Washington
Lake Forest, Illinois 60045
Telephone: (312) 295-6600

Club Officials

Chairman of the Board: Edward W. McCaskey
President and Chief Executive Officer: Michael B. McCaskey
Vice President: Charles A. Brizzolara
Secretary: Virginia H. McCaskey
Vice President-Player Personnel: Bill Tobin
Director of Administration: Bill McGrane
Director of Community Involvement: Pat McCaskey
Director of Finance: Ted Phillips
Director of Public Relations: Ken Valdiserri
Assistant, Public Relations: Bryan Harlan
Ticket Manager: Gary Christenson
Trainer: Fred Caito
Assistant Trainer: Brian McCaskey
Strength Coordinator: Clyde Emrich
Equipment Manager: Ray Earley
Assistant Equipment Manager: Gary Haeger
Scouts: Jim Parmer, Rod Graves, Don King

Stadium: Soldier Field • **Capacity:** 66,030
425 McFetridge Place
Chicago, Illinois 60605

Playing Surface: AstroTurf

Training Camp: Wisconsin-Platteville
Platteville, Wisconsin 53818

1987 Schedule

Preseason

Aug. 16	at Miami	8:00
Aug. 22	**Pittsburgh**	6:00
Aug. 31	**St. Louis**	7:00
Sept. 5	at Los Angeles Raiders	1:00

Regular Season

Sept. 14	**N.Y. Giants** (Monday)	8:00
Sept. 20	**Tampa Bay**	12:00
Sept. 27	at Detroit	1:00
Oct. 4	at Philadelphia	1:00
Oct. 11	**Minnesota**	12:00
Oct. 18	**New Orleans**	12:00
Oct. 25	at Tampa Bay	1:00
Nov. 1	**Kansas City**	12:00
Nov. 8	at Green Bay	12:00
Nov. 16	at Denver (Monday)	7:00
Nov. 22	**Detroit**	12:00
Nov. 29	**Green Bay**	12:00
Dec. 6	at Minnesota	7:00
Dec. 14	at San Francisco (Monday)	6:00
Dec. 20	**Seattle**	12:00
Dec. 27	at Los Angeles Raiders	1:00

Bears Coaching History

Decatur Staleys 1920
Chicago Staleys 1921
(521-332-42)

1920-29	George Halas	84-31-19
1930-32	Ralph Jones	24-10-7
1933-42	George Halas*	89-24-4
1942-45	Hunk Anderson-Luke Johnsos**	23-12-2
1946-55	George Halas	76-43-2
1956-57	John (Paddy) Driscoll	14-10-1
1958-67	George Halas	76-53-6
1968-71	Jim Dooley	20-36-0
1972-74	Abe Gibron	11-30-1
1975-77	Jack Pardee	20-23-0
1978-81	Neill Armstrong	30-35-0
1982-86	Mike Ditka	54-25-0

*Retired after six games to enter U.S. Navy
**Co-coaches

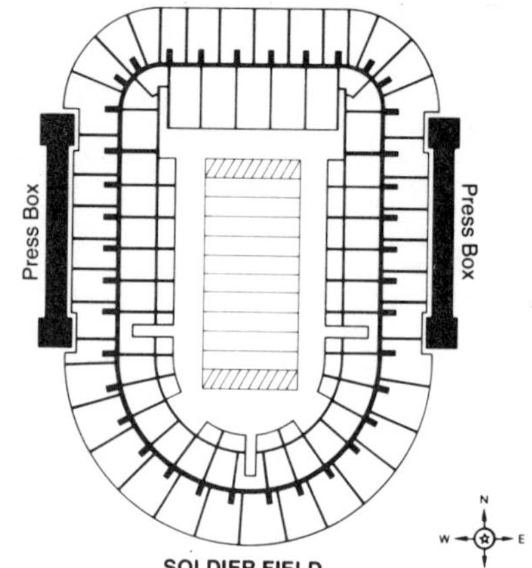

SOLDIER FIELD

Record Holders

Individual Records—Career

Category	Name	Performance
Rushing (Yds.)	Walter Payton, 1975-1986	16,193
Passing (Yds.)	Sid Luckman, 1939-1950	14,686
Passing (TDs)	Sid Luckman, 1939-1950	137
Receiving (No.)	Walter Payton, 1975-1986	459
Receiving (Yds.)	Walter Payton, 1975-1986	5,481
Interceptions	Gary Fencik, 1976-1986	38
Punting (Avg.)	George Gulyanics, 1947-1952	44.5
Punt Return (Avg.)	Ray (Scooter) McLean, 1940-47	14.8
Kickoff Return (Avg.)	Gale Sayers, 1965-1971	30.6
Field Goals	Bob Thomas, 1975-1984	128
Touchdowns (Tot.)	Walter Payton, 1975-1986	120
Points	Walter Payton, 1975-1986	720

Individual Records—Single Season

Category	Name	Performance
Rushing (Yds.)	Walter Payton, 1977	1,852
Passing (Yds.)	Bill Wade, 1962	3,172
Passing (TDs)	Sid Luckman, 1943	28
Receiving (No.)	Johnny Morris, 1964	93
Receiving (Yds.)	Johnny Morris, 1964	1,200
Interceptions	Roosevelt Taylor, 1963	9
Punting (Avg.)	Bobby Joe Green, 1963	46.5
Punt Return (Avg.)	Harry Clark, 1943	15.8
Kickoff Return (Avg.)	Gale Sayers, 1967	37.7
Field Goals	Kevin Butler, 1985	31
Touchdowns (Tot.)	Gale Sayers, 1965	22
Points	Kevin Butler, 1985	144

Individual Records—Single Game

Category	Name	Performance
Rushing (Yds.)	Walter Payton, 11-20-77	275
Passing (Yds.)	Johnny Lujack, 12-11-49	468
Passing (TDs)	Sid Luckman, 11-14-43	7
Receiving (No.)	Jim Keane, 10-23-49	14
Receiving (Yds.)	Harlon Hill, 10-31-54	214
Interceptions	Many times	3
	Last time by Ross Brupbacher, 12-12-76	
Field Goals	Roger LeClerc, 12-3-61	5
	Mac Percival, 10-20-68	5
Touchdowns (Tot.)	Gale Sayers, 12-12-65	6
Points	Gale Sayers, 12-12-65	36

1986 Team Statistics

	Bears	Opp.
Total First Downs	305	241
Rushing	166	67
Passing	118	151
Penalty	21	23
Third Down: Made/Att.	77/207	74/228
Fourth Down: Made/Att.	5/12	11/21
Total Net Yards	5459	4130
Avg. Per Game	341.2	258.1
Total Plays	1045	1002
Avg. Per Play	5.2	4.1
Net Yards Rushing	2700	1463
Avg. Per Game	168.8	91.4
Total Rushes	606	427
Net Yards Passing	2759	2667
Avg. Per Game	172.4	166.7
Tackled/Yards Lost	24/153	62/503
Gross Yards	2912	3170
Att./Completions	415/208	513/243
Completion Pct.	50.1	47.4
Had Intercepted	25	31
Punts/Avg.	70/40.7	100/40.9
Net Punting Avg.	36.9	33.5
Penalties/Yards Lost	98/765	111/866
Fumbles/Ball Lost	36/22	27/16
Touchdowns	38	20
Rushing	21	4
Passing	12	12
Returns	5	4
Avg. Time of Possession	32:21	27:39

1986 Team Record

Preseason (4-1)

Date	Result		Opponents
8/3	W	17- 6	Dallas
8/9	W	33-13	at Pittsburgh
8/16	W	38-21	Indianapolis
8/23	L	7-14	St. Louis
8/30	W	31-17	at Buffalo
		126-71	

Regular Season (14-2)

Date	Result		Opponents	Att.
9/7	W	41-31	Cleveland	66,030
9/14	W	13-10	Philadelphia (OT)	65,130
9/22	W	25-12	at Green Bay	55,527
9/28	W	44- 7	at Cincinnati	55,146
10/5	W	23- 0	Minnesota	63,921
10/12	W	20- 7	at Houston	46,026
10/19	L	7-23	at Minnesota	62,851
10/26	W	13- 7	Detroit	62,064
11/3	L	17-20	L.A. Rams	64,877
11/9	W	23- 3	at Tampa Bay	70,097
11/16	W	13-10	at Atlanta	55,520
11/23	W	12-10	Green Bay	59,291
11/30	W	13-10	Pittsburgh (OT)	61,425
12/7	W	48-14	Tampa Bay	52,746
12/15	W	16-13	at Detroit	75,602
12/21	W	24-10	at Dallas	57,256

Postseason (0-1)

Date	Result		Opponent	Att.
1/3/87	L	13-27	Washington	65,524

(OT) Overtime

Score by Periods

Bears	88	84	82	92	6	—	352
Opponents	35	36	65	51	0	—	187

Attendance

Home 495,484 Away 478,025 Total 973,509
Single game home record, 80,259 (11-24-66)
Single season home record, 495,484 (1986)

1986 Individual Statistics

Scoring	TD R	TD P	TD Rt	PAT	FG	Saf	TP
Butler	0	0	0	36/37	28/41	0	120
Payton	8	3	0	0/0	0/0	0	66
Gault	0	5	0	0/0	0/0	0	30
Sanders	5	0	0	0/0	0/0	0	30
Gentry	1	0	2	0/0	0/0	0	18
Tomczak	3	0	0	0/0	0/0	0	18
Marshall	0	0	2	0/0	0/0	0	12
Ortego	0	2	0	0/0	0/0	0	12
Suhey	2	0	0	0/0	0/0	0	12
Anderson	0	1	0	0/0	0/0	0	6
Barnes	0	0	1	0/0	0/0	0	6
Flutie	1	0	0	0/0	0/0	0	6
McMahon	1	0	0	0/0	0/0	0	6
Moorehead	0	1	0	0/0	0/0	0	6
Hampton	0	0	0	0/0	0/0	1	2
McMichael	0	0	0	0/0	0/0	1	2
Bears	21	12	5	36/38	28/41	2	352
Opponents	4	12	4	19/20	16/22	0	187

Passing	Att.	Comp.	Yds.	Pct.	TD	Int.	Tkld.	Rate
Tomczak	151	74	1105	49.0	2	10	4/30	50.2
McMahon	150	77	995	51.3	5	8	6/40	61.4
Fuller	64	34	451	53.1	2	4	8/53	60.1
Flutie	46	23	361	50.0	3	2	6/30	80.1
Payton	4	0	0	0.0	0	1	0/0	0.0
Bears	415	208	2912	50.1	12	25	24/153	57.6
Opponents	513	243	3170	47.4	12	31	62/503	49.9

Rushing	Att.	Yds.	Avg.	LG	TD
Payton	321	1333	4.2	41	8
Suhey	84	270	3.2	17	2
Sanders	27	224	8.3	75t	5
Thomas	56	224	4.0	23	0
McMahon	22	152	6.9	23	1
Anderson	35	146	4.2	23	0
Tomczak	23	117	5.1	16	3
Gentry	11	103	9.4	29	1
Gault	8	79	9.9	33	0
Flutie	9	36	4.0	19	1
Fuller	8	30	3.8	10	0
Perry	1	−1	−1.0	−1	0
Buford	1	−13	−13.0	−13	0
Bears	606	2700	4.5	75t	21
Opponents	427	1463	3.4	33	4

Receiving	No.	Yds.	Avg.	LG	TD
Gault	42	818	19.5	53t	5
Payton	37	382	10.3	57	3
Moorehead	26	390	15.0	85	1
Suhey	24	235	9.8	58	0
Ortego	23	430	18.7	58t	2
Wrightman	22	241	11.0	29	0
Gentry	19	238	12.5	41	0
Anderson	4	80	20.0	58t	1
Barnes	4	54	13.5	14	0
Thomas	4	18	4.5	18	0
Sanders	2	18	9.0	18	0
Bortz	1	8	8.0	8	0
Bears	208	2912	14.0	85	12
Opponents	243	3170	13.0	65t	12

Interceptions	No.	Yds.	Avg.	LG	TD
Richardson	7	69	9.9	32	0
Duerson	6	139	23.2	38	0
Marshall	5	68	13.6	58t	1
Fencik	3	37	12.3	24	0
Jackson	3	0	0.0	0	0
Wilson	2	31	15.5	21	0
Gayle	1	13	13.0	13	0
Phillips	1	6	6.0	6	0
McMichael	1	5	5.0	5	0
Singletary	1	3	3.0	3	0
Bell	1	−1	−1.0	−1	0
Bears	31	370	11.9	58t	1
Opponents	25	115	4.6	22	1

Punting	No.	Yds.	Avg.	In 20	LG
Buford	69	2850	41.3	20	59
Bears	70	2850	40.7	20	59
Opponents	100	4090	40.9	17	65

Punt Returns	No.	FC	Yds.	Avg.	LG	TD
Barnes	57	9	482	8.5	35	0
Bears	57	9	482	8.5	35	0
Opponents	23	14	110	4.8	15	0

Kickoff Returns	No.	Yds.	Avg.	LG	TD
Gentry	20	576	28.8	91t	1
Sanders	22	399	18.1	44	0
Anderson	4	26	6.5	13	0
Barnes	3	94	31.3	85t	1
Gault	1	20	20.0	20	0
Bears	50	1115	22.3	91t	2
Opponents	64	1376	21.5	55	0

Sacks	No.
Dent	11.5
Hampton	10.0
McMichael	8.0
Wilson	8.0
Duerson	7.0
Marshall	5.5
Perry	5.0
Harris	2.0
Singletary	2.0
Fencik	1.0
Hartenstine	1.0
Rivera	1.0
Bears	62.0
Opponents	24.0

FIRST-ROUND SELECTIONS

(If club had no first-round selection, first player drafted is listed with round in parentheses.)

Since 1953

Year	Player, College, Position
1953	Billy Anderson, Compton (Calif.) JC, B
1954	Stan Wallace, Illinois, B
1955	Ron Drzewiecki, Marquette, B
1956	Menan (Tex) Schriewer, Texas, E
1957	Earl Leggett, Louisiana State, T
1958	Chuck Howley, West Virginia, G
1959	Don Clark, Ohio State, B
1960	Roger Davis, Syracuse, G
1961	Mike Ditka, Pittsburgh, E
1962	Ronnie Bull, Baylor, RB
1963	Dave Behrman, Michigan State, C
1964	Dick Evey, Tennessee, DT
1965	Dick Butkus, Illinois, LB
	Gale Sayers, Kansas, RB
	Steve DeLong, Tennessee, T
1966	George Rice, Louisiana State, DT
1967	Loyd Phillips, Arkansas, DE
1968	Mike Hull, Southern California, RB
1969	Rufus Mayes, Ohio State, T
1970	George Farmer, UCLA, WR (3)
1971	Joe Moore, Missouri, RB
1972	Lionel Antoine, Southern Illinois, T
	Craig Clemons, Iowa, DB
1973	Wally Chambers, Eastern Kentucky, DE
1974	Waymond Bryant, Tennessee State, LB
	Dave Gallagher, Michigan, DT
1975	Walter Payton, Jackson State, RB
1976	Dennis Lick, Wisconsin, T
1977	Ted Albrecht, California, T
1978	Brad Shearer, Texas, DT (3)
1979	Dan Hampton, Arkansas, DT
	Al Harris, Arizona State, DE
1980	Otis Wilson, Louisville, LB
1981	Keith Van Horne, Southern California, T
1982	Jim McMahon, Brigham Young, QB
1983	Jimbo Covert, Pittsburgh, T
	Willie Gault, Tennessee, WR
1984	Wilber Marshall, Florida, LB
1985	William Perry, Clemson, DT
1986	Neal Anderson, Florida, RB
1987	Jim Harbaugh, Michigan, QB

Chicago Bears 1987 Veteran Roster

No.	Name	Pos.	Ht.	Wt.	Birth-date	NFL Exp.	College	Hometown	How Acq.	'86 Games/ Starts
35	Anderson, Neal	RB	5-11	210	8/14/64	2	Florida	Graceville, Fla.	D1-'86	14/1
81	Barnes, Lew	WR-KR	5-8	163	12/27/62	2	Oregon	Long Beach, Calif.	D5-'86	16/0
79	Becker, Kurt	G	6-5	270	12/22/58	6	Michigan	Aurora, Ill.	D6-'82	14/1
25	Bell, Todd	S	6-1	205	11/28/58	6	Ohio State	Middletown, Ohio	D4-'81	14/0
68	Blair, Paul	T	6-4	295	3/8/63	2	Oklahoma State	Edmund, Okla.	D4-'86	14/0
62	Bortz, Mark	G	6-6	269	2/12/61	5	Iowa	Pardeeville, Wis.	D8-'83	15/15
8	Buford, Maury	P	6-1	191	2/18/60	6	Texas Tech	Port Arthur, Tex.	T(SD)-'85	16/16
6	Butler, Kevin	K	6-1	204	7/24/62	3	Georgia	Atlanta, Ga.	D4-'85	16/16
74	Covert, Jim	T	6-4	271	3/22/60	5	Pittsburgh	Conway, Pa.	D1-'83	16/16
95	Dent, Richard	DE	6-5	263	12/13/60	5	Tennessee State	Atlanta, Ga.	D8-'83	15/14
36	Douglass, Maurice	CB-S	5-11	200	2/12/64	2	Kentucky	Trotwood, Ohio	FA-'86	4/0
22	Duerson, Dave	S	6-1	203	11/28/60	5	Notre Dame	Muncie, Ind.	D3-'83	16/16
45	Fencik, Gary	S	6-1	196	6/11/54	12	Yale	Chicago, Ill.	FA-'76	16/16
2	Flutie, Doug	QB	5-9	176	10/23/62	2	Boston College	Manchester, Md.	T(Rams)-'86	4/1
21	Frazier, Leslie	CB	6-0	187	4/3/59	6	Alcorn State	Columbus, Miss.	FA-'81	0*
4	Fuller, Steve	QB	6-4	195	1/5/57	9	Clemson	Enid, Okla.	T(Rams)-'84	16/2
83	Gault, Willie	WR	6-1	183	9/5/60	5	Tennessee	Griffin, Ga.	D1-'83	16/16
23	†Gayle, Shaun	CB	5-11	193	3/8/62	4	Ohio State	Hampton, Va.	D10-'84	16/0
29	Gentry, Dennis	WR	5-8	181	2/10/59	6	Baylor	Lubbock, Tex.	D4-'82	15/2
99	Hampton, Dan	DE	6-5	267	9/19/57	9	Arkansas	Oklahoma City, Okla.	D1a-'79	16/16
90	Harris, Al	LB	6-5	253	12/31/56	8	Arizona State	Bangor, Maine	D1b-'79	16/3
73	†Hartenstine, Mike	DE	6-3	254	7/27/53	13	Penn State	Allentown, Pa.	D2-'75	16/2
63	Hilgenberg, Jay	C	6-3	258	3/21/60	7	Iowa	Iowa City, Iowa	FA-'81	16/16
75	Humphries, Stefan	G	6-3	263	1/20/62	4	Michigan	Broward, Fla.	D3-'84	4/0
24	Jackson, Vestee	CB	6-0	186	8/14/63	2	Washington	Fresno, Calif.	D2-'86	16/8
58	Marshall, Wilber	LB	6-1	225	4/18/62	4	Florida	Titusville, Fla.	D1-'84	16/15
85	McKinnon, Dennis	WR	6-1	185	8/22/61	4	Florida State	Quitman, Ga.	FA-'83	0*
9	McMahon, Jim	QB	6-1	190	8/21/59	6	Brigham Young	Jersey City, N.J.	FA-'82	6/6
76	McMichael, Steve	DT	6-2	260	10/17/57	8	Texas	Houston, Tex.	FA-'81	16/16
87	†Moorehead, Emery	TE	6-2	220	3/22/54	11	Colorado	Evanston, Ill.	FA-'81	16/16
51	Morrissey, Jim	LB	6-3	215	12/24/62	3	Michigan State	Flint, Mich.	D11-'85	16/0
89	†Ortego, Keith	WR	6-0	180	8/30/63	3	McNeese State	Eunice, Tex.	FA-'85	16/13
34	†Payton, Walter	RB	5-10	202	7/25/54	13	Jackson State	Columbia, Miss.	D1-'75	16/16
72	Perry, William	DT	6-2	325	12/16/62	3	Clemson	Aiken, S.C.	D1-'85	16/16
48	Phillips, Reggie	CB	5-10	170	12/12/60	3	Southern Methodist	Houston, Tex.	D2-'85	16/8
86	Pickering, Clay	WR	6-5	215	6/2/61	3	Maine	Orange Park, Fla.	FA-'87	4/0
53	Rains, Dan	LB	6-1	229	4/26/56	4	Cincinnati	Rochester, Pa.	FA-'82	9/0
27	†Richardson, Mike	CB	6-0	188	5/23/61	5	Arizona State	Compton, Calif.	D2-'83	16/16
59	Rivera, Ron	LB	6-3	239	1/7/62	4	California	Monterey, Calif.	D2-'84	16/2
52	Rubens, Larry	C	6-2	262	1/25/59	4	Montana State	Spokane, Wash.	FA-'86	16/0
20	Sanders, Thomas	RB	5-11	203	1/4/62	3	Texas A&M	Giddings, Tex.	D9-'85	16/1
50	Singletary, Mike	LB	6-0	228	10/9/58	7	Baylor	Houston, Tex.	D2-'81	14/14
26	Suhey, Matt	RB	5-11	216	7/7/58	8	Penn State	State College, Pa.	D2-'80	16/14
57	†Thayer, Tom	G	6-4	261	8/16/61	3	Notre Dame	Joliet, Ill.	FA-'85	16/16
33	Thomas, Calvin	RB	5-11	245	1/7/60	6	Illinois	St. Louis, Mo.	FA-'80	16/0
18	Tomczak, Mike	QB	6-1	195	10/23/62	3	Ohio State	Calumet City, Ill.	FA-'85	13/7
78	Van Horne, Keith	T	6-6	280	11/6/57	7	Southern California	Mt. Lebanon, Pa.	D1-'81	16/16
70	Waechter, Henry	DT	6-5	275	2/13/59	6	Nebraska	Dubuque, Iowa	FA-'84	16/0
55	Wilson, Otis	LB	6-2	232	9/15/57	8	Louisville	New York, N.Y.	D1-'80	15/14
80	Wrightman, Tim	TE	6-3	237	3/27/60	3	UCLA	Harbor City, Calif.	FA-'85	16/0

* Frazier and McKinnon missed '86 season due to injury.

†Option playout; subject to developments.

Also played with Bears in '86—LB Brian Cabral (3 games), WR Ken Margerum (1).

COACHING STAFF

Head Coach, Mike Ditka

Pro Career: Became tenth head coach of Bears on January 20, 1982, after serving nine years as an offensive assistant with Dallas. Led Bears to first Super Bowl title following 15-1 1985 season. Bears shut out New York Giants and Los Angeles Rams in playoffs before routing New England, 46-10 in Super Bowl XX. Under Ditka, Chicago has won three straight NFC Central titles and posted a 14-2 record in 1986, best in NFL history for a defending Super Bowl champion. His 11-7 1984 record included a trip to NFC Championship Game at San Francisco (23-0 loss). The 46-year-old Ditka owns a 54-25 record since taking over the coaching reins and has won 48 of his last 60 games. Ditka is a 25-year veteran of the NFL as both a player and a coach. Had 12-year playing career as a tight end with Chicago (1961-66), Philadelphia (1967-68), and Dallas (1969-72). A first-round draft choice by Chicago in 1961, Ditka was NFL rookie of the year, all-NFL (1961-64), and played in five Pro Bowls (1962-66). He joined Cowboys coaching staff in 1973. In addition to working with Dallas special teams, Ditka coached Cowboys' receivers. During his NFL career, he has been in the playoffs 14 seasons and been a member of five NFC champions and three NFL champions. Career record: 54-25.

Background: Played at Pittsburgh from 1958-60 and was a unanimous All-America his senior year. A two-way performer, he played both tight end and linebacker. He also was one of the nation's leading punters with a 40-plus-yard average over three years.

Personal: Born October 18, 1939, Carnegie, Pa. Mike and his wife, Diana, live in Grayslake, Ill., and have four children—Michael, Mark, Megan, and Matt.

Assistant Coaches

Jim Dooley, research and quality control; born February 8, 1930, Stoutsville, Mo., lives in Chicago. End Miami 1949-51. Pro receiver Chicago Bears 1952-61. Pro coach: Chicago Bears 1962-71 (head coach 1968-71), Buffalo Bills 1972, rejoined Bears in 1981.

Ed Hughes, offensive coordinator; born October 23, 1927, Buffalo, N.Y., lives in Libertyville, Ill. Halfback Tulsa 1952-53. Pro defensive back Los Angeles Rams 1954-55, New York Giants 1956-58. Pro coach: Dallas Texans 1960-62, Denver Broncos 1963, Washington Redskins 1964-67, San Francisco 49ers 1968-70, Houston Oilers 1971 (head coach), St. Louis Cardinals 1972, Dallas Cowboys 1973-76, Detroit Lions 1977, New Orleans Saints 1978-80, Philadelphia Eagles 1981, joined Bears in 1982.

Steve Kazor, special teams; born February 24, 1948, New Kensington, Pa., lives in Vernon Hills, Ill. Nose tackle Westminister College 1967-70. No pro playing experience. College coach: Colorado State 1975, Wyoming 1976, Texas-El Paso 1979-80, Emporia State 1981 (head coach). Pro coach: Joined Bears in 1983.

Greg Landry, quarterbacks-receivers; born December 18, 1946, Nashua, N.H., lives in Libertyville, Ill. Quarterback Massachusetts 1965-67. Pro quarterback Detroit Lions 1968-78, Baltimore Colts 1979-81, Arizona Wranglers/Chicago Blitz (USFL) 1983-84, Chicago Bears 1984. Pro coach: Cleveland Browns 1985, joined Bears in 1986.

Jim LaRue, defensive backfield; born August 11, 1925, Clinton, Okla., lives in Libertyville, Ill. Halfback Carson-Newman 1943, Duke 1944-45, Maryland 1947-49. No pro playing experience. College coach: Maryland 1950, Kansas State 1951-54, Houston 1955-56, Southern Methodist 1957-58, Arizona 1959-66 (head coach), Utah 1967-73, Wake Forest 1974-75. Pro coach: Buffalo Bills 1976-77, joined Bears in 1978.

Chicago Bears 1987 First-Year Roster

Name	Pos.	Ht.	Wt.	Birth-date	College	Hometown	How Acq.
Adickes, John	C	6-3	266	6/29/64	Baylor	Killeen, Tex.	D6
Bryan, Steve	DE	6-3	250	5/6/64	Oklahoma	Coweta, Okla.	D5a
Chapura, Dick	DT	6-3	275	6/15/64	Missouri	Sarasota, Fla.	D10
Harbaugh, Jim	QB	6-3	202	12/23/64	Michigan	Kalamazoo, Mich.	D1
Harris, Archie	T	6-6	270	11/17/64	William & Mary	Orange, N.J.	D7
Heimuli, Lakei	RB	5-11	219	6/24/65	Brigham Young	Laie, Hawaii	D9
Jeffries, Eric	CB-S	5-10	161	7/25/64	Texas	Austin, Tex.	D12
Jessie, Tim	RB	5-11	190	3/1/63	Auburn	Opp, Ala.	D11
Johnson, Will	DE	6-4	232	12/4/64	Northeast Louisiana	Monroe, La.	D5b
Migliazzo, Paul	LB	6-1	228	3/11/64	Oklahoma	Kansas City, Mo.	D8
Morris, Ron	WR	6-1	187	11/14/64	Southern Methodist	Cooper, Tex.	D2
Popp, Jim (1)	TE	6-5	245	11/13/63	Vanderbilt	Arlington Heights, Ill.	FA
Smith, Sean	DE	6-4	256	3/27/65	Grambling	Bogalusa, La.	D4
Sowell, Brent (1)	T-G	6-5	288	3/27/63	Alabama	Clearwater, Fla.	FA

The term NFL Rookie is defined as a player who is in his first season of professional football and has not been on the roster of another professional football team for any regular-season or postseason games. A Rookie is designated by an "R" on NFL rosters. Players who have been active in another professional football league or players who have NFL experience, including either preseason training camp or being on an active roster for fewer than three regular-season or postseason games, are termed NFL First-Year Players. An NFL First-Year Player is designated by a "1" on NFL rosters. Thereafter, a player on an NFL active roster for at least three regular-season or postseason games is credited with an additional year of NFL playing experience.

NOTES

John Levra, defensive line; born October 2, 1937, Arma, Kan., lives in Libertyville, Ill. Guard-linebacker Pittsburgh (Kan.) State 1963-65. No pro playing experience. College coach: Stephen F. Austin 1971-74, Kansas 1975-78, North Texas State 1979. Pro coach: British Columbia Lions (CFL) 1980, New Orleans Saints 1981-85, joined Bears in 1986.

David McGinnis, defensive assistant; born August 7, 1951, Independence, Kan., lives in Lake Forest, Ill. Defensive back Texas Christian 1970-72. No pro playing experience. College coach: Texas Christian 1973-74, 1982, Missouri 1975-77, Indiana State 1978-81, Kansas State 1983-85. Pro coach: Joined Bears in 1986.

Johnny Roland, offensive backs; born May 21, 1943, Corpus Christi, Tex., lives in Vernon Hills, Ill. Running back Missouri 1963-65. Pro running back St. Louis Cardinals 1966-72, New York Giants 1973. College coach: Notre Dame 1975. Pro coach: Green Bay Packers 1974, Philadelphia Eagles 1976-78, joined Bears in 1983.

Dick Stanfel, offensive line; born July 20, 1927, San Francisco, Calif., lives in Libertyville, Ill. Guard San Francisco 1948-51. Pro guard Detroit Lions 1952-55, Washington Redskins 1956-58. College coach: Notre Dame 1959-62, California 1963. Pro coach: Philadelphia Eagles 1964-70, San Francisco 49ers 1971-75, New Orleans Saints 1976-80 (head coach, 4 games in 1980), joined Bears in 1981.

Vince Tobin, defensive coordinator; born September 29, 1943, in Burlington Junction, Mo., lives in Libertyville, Ill. Defensive back-running back Missouri 1961-64. No pro playing experience. College coach: Missouri 1967-76. Pro coach: British Columbia Lions (CFL) 1977-82, Philadelphia/Baltimore Stars (USFL) 1983-85, joined Bears in 1986.

National Football Conference
Eastern Division

Team Colors: Royal Blue, Metallic Silver Blue, and White

Cowboys Center
One Cowboys Parkway
Irving, Texas 75063
Telephone: (214) 556-9900

Club Officials

General Partner: H.R. Bright
President-General Manager: Texas E. Schramm
Vice President-Personnel Development: Gil Brandt
Vice President-Treasurer: Don Wilson
Vice President-Administration: Joe Bailey
Vice President-Pro Personnel: Bob Ackles
Public Relations Director: Doug Todd
Media Relations-Marketing: Greg Aiello
Business Manager: Dan Werner
Director of Counseling Services: Larry Wansley
Ticket Manager: Steve Orsini
Trainers: Don Cochren, Ken Locker
Equipment Manager: William T. (Buck) Buchanan
Cheerleaders Director: Suzanne Mitchell

Stadium: Texas Stadium • **Capacity:** 63,855
Irving, Texas 75062

Playing Surface: Texas Turf

Training Camp: California Lutheran University
Thousand Oaks, California 91360

1987 Schedule

Preseason

Aug. 15	at San Diego	6:00
Aug. 22	at San Francisco	6:00
Aug. 30	**Los Angeles Raiders**	7:00
Sept. 5	**Houston**	8:00

Regular Season

Sept. 13	at St. Louis	12:00
Sept. 20	at New York Giants	4:00
Sept. 27	**Buffalo**	12:00
Oct. 4	at New York Jets	4:00
Oct. 11	**Philadelphia**	12:00
Oct. 19	**Washington** (Monday)	8:00
Oct. 25	at Philadelphia	1:00
Nov. 2	**New York Giants** (Monday)	8:00
Nov. 8	at Detroit	1:00
Nov. 15	at New England	1:00
Nov. 22	**Miami**	7:00
Nov. 26	**Minnesota** (Thanksgiving)	3:00
Dec. 6	**Atlanta**	12:00
Dec. 13	at Washington	1:00
Dec. 21	at L.A. Rams (Monday)	6:00
Dec. 27	**St. Louis**	12:00

Cowboys Coaching History

(260-157-6)

1960-86 Tom Landry 260-157-6

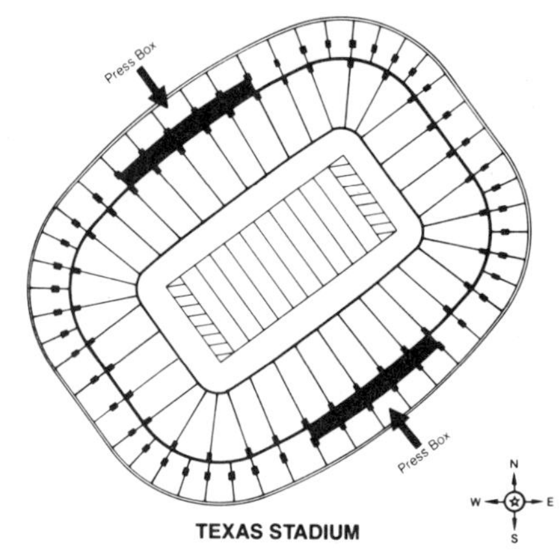

TEXAS STADIUM

Record Holders

Individual Records—Career

Category	Name	Performance
Rushing (Yds.)	Tony Dorsett, 1977-1986	11,580
Passing (Yds.)	Roger Staubach, 1969-1979	22,700
Passing (TDs)	Roger Staubach, 1969-1979	153
Receiving (No.)	Drew Pearson, 1973-1983	489
Receiving (Yds.)	Tony Hill, 1977-1986	7,988
Interceptions	Mel Renfro, 1964-1977	52
Punting (Avg.)	Sam Baker, 1962-63	45.1
Punt Return (Avg.)	Bob Hayes, 1965-1974	11.1
Kickoff Return (Avg.)	Mel Renfro, 1964-1977	26.4
Field Goals	Rafael Septien, 1978-1986	162
Touchdowns (Tot.)	Tony Dorsett, 1977-1986	85
Points	Rafael Septien, 1978-1986	874

Individual Records—Single Season

Category	Name	Performance
Rushing (Yds.)	Tony Dorsett, 1981	1,646
Passing (Yds.)	Danny White, 1983	3,980
Passing (TDs)	Danny White, 1983	29
Receiving (No.)	Herschel Walker, 1985	76
Receiving (Yds.)	Bob Hayes, 1966	1,232
Interceptions	Everson Walls, 1981	11
Punting (Avg.)	Sam Baker, 1962	45.4
Punt Return (Avg.)	Bob Hayes, 1968	20.8
Kickoff Return (Avg.)	Mel Renfro, 1965	30.0
Field Goals	Rafael Septien, 1981	27
Touchdowns (Tot.)	Dan Reeves, 1966	16
Points	Rafael Septien, 1983	123

Individual Records—Single Game

Category	Name	Performance
Rushing (Yds.)	Tony Dorsett, 12-4-77	206
Passing (Yds.)	Don Meredith, 11-10-63	460
Passing (TDs)	Many times	5
	Last time by Danny White, 10-30-83	
Receiving (No.)	Lance Rentzel, 11-19-67	13
Receiving (Yds.)	Bob Hayes, 11-13-66	246
Interceptions	Herb Adderley, 9-26-71	3
	Lee Roy Jordan, 11-4-73	3
	Dennis Thurman, 12-13-81	3
Field Goals	Many times	4
	Last time by Rafael Septien, 9-21-81	
Touchdowns (Tot.)	Many times	4
	Last time by Duane Thomas, 12-18-71	
Points	Many times	24
	Last time by Duane Thomas, 12-18-71	

1986 Team Statistics

	Cowboys	Opp.
Total First Downs	325	286
Rushing	98	118
Passing	199	148
Penalty	28	20
Third Down: Made/Att.	80/213	89/226
Fourth Down: Made/Att.	6/14	4/7
Total Net Yards	5474	4985
Avg. Per Game	342.1	311.6
Total Plays	1054	1017
Avg. Per Play	5.2	4.9
Net Yards Rushing	1969	2200
Avg. Per Game	123.1	137.5
Total Rushes	447	500
Net Yards Passing	3505	2785
Avg. Per Game	219.1	174.1
Tackled/Yards Lost	60/498	53/364
Gross Yards	4003	3149
Att./Completions	547/319	464/226
Completion Pct.	58.3	48.7
Had Intercepted	24	17
Punts/Avg.	87/40.2	87/41.6
Net Punting Avg.	34.4	36.6
Penalties/Yards Lost	112/936	91/822
Fumbles/Ball Lost	44/17	29/18
Touchdowns	43	41
Rushing	21	17
Passing	21	21
Returns	1	3
Avg. Time of Possession	31:14	28:46

1986 Team Record

Preseason (0-5)

Date	Result		Opponents
8/3	L	6-17	Chicago
8/9	L	0-20	at San Diego
8/16	L	19-24	at L.A. Raiders
8/22	L	28-41	Pittsburgh
8/30	L	14-17	Houston
		67-119	

Regular Season (7-9)

Date	Result		Opponents	Att.
9/8	W	31-28	N.Y. Giants	59,804
9/14	W	31- 7	at Detroit	73,812
9/21	L	35-37	Atlanta	62,880
9/29	W	31- 7	at St. Louis	49,077
10/5	L	14-29	at Denver	76,082
10/12	W	30- 6	Washington	63,264
10/19	W	17-14	at Philadelphia	68,572
10/26	W	37- 6	St. Louis	60,756
11/2	L	14-17	at N.Y. Giants	74,871
11/9	L	13-17	L.A. Raiders	61,706
11/16	W	24-21	at San Diego	55,622
11/23	L	14-41	at Washington	55,642
11/27	L	14-31	Seattle	58,023
12/7	L	10-29	at L.A. Rams	64,949
12/14	L	21-23	Philadelphia	46,117
12/21	L	10-24	Chicago	57,256

Score by Periods

Cowboys	61	105	62	118	0	—	346
Opponents	44	136	74	83	0	—	337

Attendance

Home 469,806 Away 518,627 Total 988,433
Single game home record, 80,259 (11-24-66)
Single season home record, 511,541 (1981)

1986 Individual Statistics

Scoring	TD R	TD P	TD Rt	PAT	FG	Saf	TP
Septien	0	0	0	43/43	15/21	0	88
Walker	12	2	0	0/0	0/0	0	84
Dorsett	5	1	0	0/0	0/0	0	36
Newsome	2	3	0	0/0	0/0	0	30
Sherrard	0	5	0	0/0	0/0	0	30
Hill	0	3	0	0/0	0/0	0	18
Renfro	0	3	0	0/0	0/0	0	18
Chandler	0	2	0	0/0	0/0	0	12
Cosbie	0	1	0	0/0	0/0	0	6
Fellows	0	0	1	0/0	0/0	0	6
Lavette	0	1	0	0/0	0/0	0	6
Pelluer	1	0	0	0/0	0/0	0	6
D. White	1	0	0	0/0	0/0	0	6
Cowboys	21	21	1	43/43	15/21	0	346
Opponents	17	21	3	39/41	16/30	2	337

Passing	Att.	Comp.	Yds.	Pct.	TD	Int.	Tkld.	Rate
Pelluer	378	215	2727	56.9	8	17	47/362	67.9
D. White	153	95	1157	62.1	12	5	10/98	97.9
Collier	15	8	96	53.3	1	2	3/38	55.8
Renfro	1	1	23	100.0	0	0	0/0	118.8
Cowboys	547	319	4003	58.3	21	24	60/498	75.7
Opponents	464	226	3149	48.7	21	17	53/364	70.8

Rushing	Att.	Yds.	Avg.	LG	TD
Dorsett	184	748	4.1	33	5
Walker	151	737	4.9	84t	12
Pelluer	41	255	6.2	21	1
Newsome	34	110	3.2	13	2
Collier	6	53	8.8	21	0
Clack	4	19	4.8	8	0
D. White	8	16	2.0	10	1
Sherrard	2	11	5.5	8	0
Cosbie	1	9	9.0	9	0
Lavette	10	6	0.6	5	0
Fowler	6	5	0.8	2	0
Cowboys	447	1969	4.4	84t	21
Opponents	500	2200	4.4	50	17

Receiving	No.	Yds.	Avg.	LG	TD
Walker	76	837	11.0	84t	2
Hill	49	770	15.7	63	3
Newsome	48	421	8.8	30	3
Sherrard	41	744	18.1	68t	5
Cosbie	28	312	11.1	22t	1
Dorsett	25	267	10.7	36t	1
Renfro	22	325	14.8	30t	3
Banks	17	202	11.9	23	0
Chandler	6	57	9.5	15	2
Lavette	5	31	6.2	9	1
Fowler	1	19	19.0	19	0
Clack	1	18	18.0	18	0
Cowboys	319	4003	12.5	84t	21
Opponents	226	3149	13.9	71t	21

Interceptions	No.	Yds.	Avg.	LG	TD
Downs	6	54	9.0	31	0
Fellows	5	46	9.2	34t	1
Walls	3	46	15.3	24	0
Scott	1	31	31.0	31	0
Lockhart	1	5	5.0	5	0
Holloway	1	1	1.0	1	0
Cowboys	17	183	10.8	34t	1
Opponents	24	331	13.8	56	2

Punting	No.	Yds.	Avg.	In 20	LG
Saxon	86	3498	40.7	28	58
Cowboys	87	3498	40.2	28	58
Opponents	87	3620	41.6	18	62

Punt Returns	No.	FC	Yds.	Avg.	LG	TD
Banks	27	14	160	5.9	20	0
Lavette	18	3	92	5.1	28	0
Holloway	1	0	0	0.0	0	0
Cowboys	46	17	252	5.5	28	0
Opponents	41	15	301	7.3	26	0

Kickoff Returns	No.	Yds.	Avg.	LG	TD
Lavette	36	699	19.4	37	0
Clack	19	421	22.2	51	0
Newsome	2	32	16.0	18	0
Banks	1	56	56.0	56	0
Tuinei	1	0	0.0	0	0
Cowboys	59	1208	20.5	56	0
Opponents	66	1358	20.6	38	0

Sacks	No.
Jeffcoat	14.0
R. White	6.5
Jones	5.5
Dutton	5.0
Lockhart	5.0
Smerek	4.5
Bates	2.5
Brooks	2.5
Penn	2.5
Rohrer	2.0
Baker	1.0
Downs	1.0
Hegman	1.0
Cowboys	53.0
Opponents	60.0

FIRST-ROUND SELECTIONS

(If club had no first-round selection, first player drafted is listed with round in parentheses.)

Year	Player, College, Position
1960	None
1961	Bob Lilly, Texas Christian, DT
1962	Sonny Gibbs, Texas Christian, QB (2)
1963	Lee Roy Jordan, Alabama, LB
1964	Scott Appleton, Texas, DT
1965	Craig Morton, California, QB
1966	John Niland, Iowa, G
1967	Phil Clark, Northwestern, DB (3)
1968	Dennis Homan, Alabama, WR
1969	Calvin Hill, Yale, RB
1970	Duane Thomas, West Texas State, RB
1971	Tody Smith, Southern California, DE
1972	Bill Thomas, Boston College, RB
1973	Billy Joe DuPree, Michigan State, TE
1974	Ed (Too Tall) Jones, Tennessee State, DE
	Charley Young, North Carolina State, RB
1975	Randy White, Maryland, LB
	Thomas Henderson, Langston, LB
1976	Aaron Kyle, Wyoming, DB
1977	Tony Dorsett, Pittsburgh, RB
1978	Larry Bethea, Michigan State, DE
1979	Robert Shaw, Tennessee, C
1980	Bill Roe, Colorado, LB (3)
1981	Howard Richards, Missouri, T
1982	Rod Hill, Kentucky State, DB
1983	Jim Jeffcoat, Arizona State, DE
1984	Billy Cannon, Jr., Texas A&M, LB
1985	Kevin Brooks, Michigan, DE
1986	Mike Sherrard, UCLA, WR
1987	Danny Noonan, Nebraska, DT

Dallas Cowboys 1987 Veteran Roster

No.	Name	Pos.	Ht.	Wt.	Birth-date	NFL Exp.	College	Hometown	How Acq.	'86 Games/ Starts
36	Albritton, Vince	S	6-2	210	7/23/62	4	Washington	Oakland, Calif.	FA-'84	16/1
62	Baldinger, Brian	G	6-4	261	1/7/59	5	Duke	Massapequa, N.Y.	FA-'82	16/0
87	Banks, Gordon	WR	5-10	173	3/12/58	5	Stanford	Los Angeles, Calif.	FA-'85	16/5
40	Bates, Bill	S	6-1	204	6/6/61	5	Tennessee	Knoxville, Tenn.	FA-'83	15/15
99	Brooks, Kevin	DE	6-6	273	2/9/63	3	Michigan	Detroit, Mich.	D1-'85	9/0
85	Chandler, Thornton	TE	6-5	245	11/27/63	2	Alabama	Jacksonville, Fla.	D6a-'86	15/1
42	Clack, Darryl	RB	5-10	218	10/29/63	2	Arizona State	Security, Colo.	D2-'86	16/0
10	Collier, Reggie	QB	6-3	207	5/14/61	2	Southern Mississippi	Biloxi, Miss.	D6-'83	4/1
84	Cosbie, Doug	TE	6-6	238	2/27/56	9	Santa Clara	Mountain View, Calif.	D3-'79	16/15
55	DeOssie, Steve	LB	6-2	245	11/22/62	4	Boston College	Roslindale, Mass.	D4-'84	16/0
33	Dorsett, Tony	RB	5-11	189	4/7/54	11	Pittsburgh	Aliquippa, Pa.	D1-'77	13/12
26	Downs, Michael	S	6-3	204	6/9/59	7	Rice	Dallas, Tex.	FA-'81	16/16
78	Dutton, John	DT	6-7	261	2/6/51	14	Nebraska	Rapid City, S.D.	T(Balt)-'79	16/16
27	†Fellows, Ron	CB	6-0	173	11/7/58	7	Missouri	South Bend, Ind.	D7a-'81	16/16
46	Fowler, Todd	RB	6-3	221	6/9/62	3	Stephen F. Austin	Van, Tex.	SD1-'84	16/0
58	Hegman, Mike	LB	6-1	227	1/17/53	12	Tennessee State	Memphis, Tenn.	D7-'75	16/16
45	Hendrix, Manny	CB-S	5-10	178	10/20/64	2	Utah	Phoenix, Ariz.	FA-'86	13/0
80	Hill, Tony	WR	6-2	205	6/23/56	11	Stanford	Long Beach, Calif.	D3a-'77	16/16
23	Holloway, Johnny	CB	5-11	182	11/8/63	2	Kansas	Houston, Tex.	D7-'86	16/0
53	Jax, Garth	LB	6-2	225	9/16/63	2	Florida State	Houston, Tex.	D11-'86	16/0
77	Jeffcoat, Jim	DE	6-5	260	4/1/61	5	Arizona State	Cliffwood, N.J.	D1-'83	16/16
72	Jones, Ed	DE	6-9	273	2/23/51	13	Tennessee State	Jackson, Tenn.	D1a-'74	16/16
68	Ker, Crawford	G	6-3	285	5/5/62	3	Florida	Dunedin, Fla.	D3-'85	16/16
29	Lavette, Robert	RB	5-11	190	9/8/63	3	Georgia Tech	Cartersville, Ga.	D4-'85	16/0
56	Lockhart, Eugene	LB	6-2	235	3/8/61	4	Houston	Crockett, Tex.	D6a-'84	16/16
14	McDonald, Paul	QB	6-2	185	2/23/58	8	Southern California	Montebello, Calif.	FA-'86	1/0
30	Newsome, Timmy	RB	6-1	237	5/17/58	8	Winston-Salem State	Ahoskie, N.C.	D6-'80	16/12
67	Newton, Nate	G	6-3	317	12/20/61	2	Florida A&M	Orlando, Fla.	FA-'86	11/0
16	Pelluer, Steve	QB	6-4	208	7/29/62	4	Washington	Bellevue, Wash.	D5a-'84	16/9
59	Penn, Jesse	LB	6-3	218	9/6/62	3	Virginia Tech	Martinsville, Va.	D2-'85	15/0
65	Petersen, Kurt	G	6-4	272	6/17/57	7	Missouri	St. Louis, Mo.	D4-'80	0*
81	Powe, Karl	WR	6-2	178	1/17/62	2	Alabama State	Mobile, Ala.	D7a-'85	1/0
75	Pozderac, Phil	T	6-9	283	12/19/59	6	Notre Dame	Garfield Heights, Ohio	D5-'82	16/10
64	Rafferty, Tom	C	6-3	262	8/2/54	12	Penn State	Fayetteville, N.Y.	D4-'76	16/16
82	Renfro, Mike	WR	6-0	187	6/19/55	10	Texas Christian	Fort Worth, Tex.	T(Hou)-'84	12/6
70	Richards, Howard	T	6-6	269	8/7/59	7	Missouri	St. Louis, Mo.	D1-'81	9/2
50	Rohrer, Jeff	LB	6-2	227	12/25/58	6	Yale	Manhattan Beach, Calif.	D2-'82	16/16
76	Rudolph, Ben	DT	6-5	271	8/29/58	5	Long Beach State	Evergreen, Ala.	FA-'87	16/3*
89	Salonen, Brian	LB	6-3	223	7/29/61	3	Montana	Great Falls, Mont.	D10-'84	0*
4	Saxon, Mike	P	6-3	188	7/10/62	3	San Diego State	Arcadia, Calif.	FA-'85	16/0
22	Scott, Victor	CB-S	6-0	203	6/1/62	4	Colorado	East St. Louis, Ill.	D2-'84	5/0
86	Sherrard, Mike	WR	6-2	187	6/21/63	2	UCLA	Chico, Calif.	D1-'86	16/4
60	†Smerek, Don	DT	6-7	262	12/10/57	6	Nevada-Reno	Henderson, Nev.	FA-'80	11/0
63	Titensor, Glen	G	6-4	270	2/21/58	7	Brigham Young	Garden Grove, Calif.	D3-'81	16/16
71	Tuinei, Mark	C	6-5	283	3/31/60	5	Hawaii	Honolulu, Hawaii	FA-'83	16/11
34	Walker, Herschel	RB	6-1	223	3/3/62	2	Georgia	Wrightsville, Ga.	D5a-'85	16/9
24	Walls, Everson	CB	6-1	193	12/28/59	7	Grambling	Dallas, Tex.	FA-'81	16/16
11	White, Danny	QB	6-3	197	2/9/52	12	Arizona State	Mesa, Ariz.	D3a-'74	7/6
54	White, Randy	DT	6-4	265	1/15/53	13	Maryland	Wilmington, Del.	D1a-'75	16/16

* Petersen and Salonen missed '86 season due to injury; Rudolph last active with N.Y. Jets in '86.

†Option playout; subject to developments.

Retired—Jim Cooper, 10-year tackle, 12 games in '86.

Also played with Cowboys in '86—DE Jesse Baker (3 games), CB-S Cornell Gowdy (3), DT-DE Bob Otto (4), DE Kurt Ploeger (3), K Rafael Septien (16).

COACHING STAFF

Head Coach, Tom Landry

Pro Career: Landry, the Cowboys' only head coach in their 27-year history, compiled 20 consecutive winning seasons from 1966 through 1985, and his overall record of 260-157-6 is second only to Don Shula among active coaches. Cowboys became the fourth team in NFL to win a second Super Bowl. They defeated Denver 27-10 in Super Bowl XII on January 15, 1978, at Louisiana Superdome. Dallas has played in four other Super Bowls (V, VI, X, and XIII), winning Game VI 24-3 over Miami. Pro defensive back with New York Yanks (AAFC) 1949, New York Giants 1950-55. Player-coach with Giants 1954-55, named all-pro in 1954. Defensive assistant coach with Giants 1956-59 before moving to Dallas as head coach in 1960. Career record: 260-157-6.

Background: Fullback and defensive back, University of Texas 1947-48, and played in Longhorns' victories over Alabama in 1948 Sugar Bowl and Georgia in 1949 Orange Bowl.

Personal: Born September 11, 1924, Mission, Tex. A World War II bomber pilot. Tom and his wife, Alicia, live in Dallas and have three children—Tom Jr., Kitty, and Lisa.

Assistant Coaches

Neill Armstrong, research and development; born March 9, 1926, Tishomingo, Okla., lives in Roanoke, Tex. End Oklahoma State 1943-46. Pro end-defensive back Philadelphia Eagles 1947-51, Winnipeg Blue Bombers (CFL) 1951, 1953-54. College coach: Oklahoma State 1955-61. Pro coach: Houston Oilers 1962-63, Edmonton Eskimos (CFL) 1964-69 (head coach), Minnesota Vikings 1970-77, Chicago Bears 1978-81 (head coach), joined Cowboys in 1982.

Jim Erkenbeck, offensive line; born September 10, 1931, Los Angeles, Calif., lives in Roanoke, Tex. Fullback San Diego State 1949-52. No pro playing experience. College coach: San Diego State 1960-63, Grossmont, Calif., J.C. 1964-67, Utah State 1968, Washington State 1969-71, California 1972-76. Pro coach: Winnipeg Blue Bombers (CFL) 1977, Montreal Alouettes (CFL) 1978-81, Calgary Stampeders (CFL) 1982, Philadelphia/Baltimore Stars (USFL) 1983-85, New Orleans Saints 1986, first year with Cowboys.

Paul Hackett, pass offense coordinator; born July 5, 1947, Burlington, Vt., lives in Southlake, Tex. Quarterback Cal-Davis 1965-68. No pro playing experience. College coach: Cal-Davis 1970-71, California 1972-75, Southern California 1976-80. Pro coach: Cleveland Browns 1981-82, San Francisco 49ers 1983-85, joined Cowboys in 1986.

Al Lavan, running backs; born September 13, 1946, Pierce, Fla., lives in Plano, Tex. Defensive back Colorado State 1965-67. Pro defensive back Philadelphia Eagles 1968, Atlanta Falcons 1969-70. College coach: Colorado State 1972, Louisville 1973, Iowa State 1974, Georgia Tech 1977-78, Stanford 1979. Pro coach: Atlanta Falcons 1975-76, joined Cowboys in 1980.

Alan Lowry, receivers; born November 21, 1950, Irving, Tex., lives in Dallas. Defensive back-quarterback Texas 1970-72. No pro playing experience. College coach: Virginia Tech 1974, Wyoming 1975, Texas 1976-81. Pro coach: Joined Cowboys in 1982.

Dick Nolan, defensive backs; born March 26, 1932, Pittsburgh, Pa., lives in Roanoke, Tex. Offensive-defensive back Maryland 1951-53. Pro defensive back New York Giants 1954-57, 1959-61, St. Louis Cardinals 1958, Dallas 1962 (player-coach). Pro coach: Dallas Cowboys 1963-67, San Francisco 49ers 1968-75 (head coach), New Orleans Saints 1977-80 (head coach), Houston Oilers 1981, re-joined Cowboys in 1982.

Mike Solari, special teams; born January 16, 1955, Daly City, Calif., lives in Grapevine, Tex. Offensive lineman San Diego State 1975-76. No pro playing experience. College coach: Mira Vista, Calif., J.C. 1977-78, U.S. International 1979, Boise State 1980, Cincinnati 1981-82, Kansas 1983-85, Pittsburgh 1986. Pro coach: First year with Cowboys.

Dallas Cowboys 1987 First-Year Roster

Name	Pos.	Ht.	Wt.	Birth-date	College	Hometown	How Acq.
Aikens, Carl (1)	WR	6-0	183	6/5/62	Northern Illinois	Chicago, Ill.	FA
Alexander, Ray (1)	WR	6-4	190	1/8/62	Florida A&M	Mobile, Ala.	FA
Armstrong, Scott	LB	6-1	230	12/17/63	Florida	Ocala, Fla.	D12
Blount, Alvin	RB	5-9	197	2/12/65	Maryland	Greenbelt, Md.	D9
Brady, Kerry	K	6-1	205	8/27/63	Hawaii	Vancouver, Wash.	FA
Burke, Joe	RB	6-0	200	2/9/61	Rutgers	Albany, N.Y.	FA
Cisowski, Steve (1)	T	6-5	275	1/23/63	Santa Clara	Campbell, Calif.	FA
Courville, Vince (1)	WR	5-9	170	12/5/59	Rice	Galveston, Tex.	FA
Duliban, Chris (1)	LB	6-2	216	1/9/63	Texas	Houston, Tex.	D12a-'86
Dwyer, Mike (1)	DT	6-3	280	6/13/63	Massachusetts	Hyannis, Mass.	FA
Folsom, Steve (1)	TE	6-5	245	3/21/58	Utah	Sante Fe Springs, Calif.	FA
Francis, Ron	CB-S	5-9	201	4/7/64	Baylor	La Marque, Tex.	D2
Franco, Brian (1)	K	5-8	165	12/3/59	Penn State	Altoona, Pa.	FA
Gay, Everett	WR	6-2	204	10/23/64	Texas	Houston, Tex.	D5
Gogan, Kevin	T	6-7	295	11/2/64	Washington	Pacifica, Calif.	D8
Holland, Rodney (1)	CB-S	5-10	184	12/29/62	Montana State	Longview, Wash.	FA-'86
Jones, Dale	LB	6-1	234	3/8/63	Tennessee	Cleveland, Tenn.	D10
Kagey, William	K	5-9	172	10/22/61	Liberty	Lynchburg, Va.	FA
LeBlanc, Bob	LB	6-1	238	11/5/62	Elon	Kansas City, Mo.	FA
McDermott, Fran (1)	CB-S	5-10	182	4/3/60	St. Mary's, Calif.	Davis, Calif.	FA
McDonald, Ray (1)	WR	5-11	181	8/24/64	Florida	Belle Glade, Fla.	FA
Martin, Kelvin	WR	5-9	161	5/14/65	Boston College	Jacksonville, Fla.	D4
Melvin, Leland (1)	WR	5-11	178	2/15/64	Richmond	Lynchburg, Va.	FA
Miller, Carl (1)	RB	5-10	204	11/18/63	Arkansas	Pine Bluff, Ark.	FA-'86
Noonan, Danny	DT	6-4	282	7/14/65	Nebraska	Lincoln, Neb.	D1
Onosai, Joe	G	6-3	283	12/10/65	Hawaii	Honolulu, Hawaii	D6
Roby, Wayne (1)	WR	6-2	190	1/10/62	Wisconsin	Sycamore, Ill.	FA-'86
Ruzek, Roger (1)	K	6-1	185	12/17/60	Weber State	San Francisco, Calif.	FA
Savard, Steve (1)	LB	6-1	222	11/23/63	Northwest Missouri	St. Louis, Mo.	FA
Schoppe, Todd (1)	C	6-5	265	6/4/63	Houston	Deer Park, Tex.	FA
Smith, Reggie (1)	T	6-4	291	8/29/61	Kansas	Chicago, Ill.	FA
Smith, Robert (1)	DE	6-7	270	12/3/62	Grambling	Bogalusa, La.	FA
Sweeney, Kevin	QB	6-0	191	11/16/63	Fresno State	Fresno, Calif.	D7
Trout, David (1)	K	5-6	175	11/12/57	Pittsburgh	Alverton, Pa.	FA
Walen, Mark (1)	DT	6-5	265	3/10/63	UCLA	Burlingame, Calif.	D3-'86
Ward, Jeff	K	5-9	169	12/4/64	Texas	Austin, Tex.	D11
Warren, John (1)	CB-S	5-10	180	4/25/63	Virginia Union	Washington, D.C.	FA
White, Bob (1)	T	6-5	270	4/9/63	Rhode Island	Lunenburg, Mass.	FA
Williams, Robert (1)	CB-S	5-10	195	10/2/62	Baylor	Galveston, Tex.	FA
Yancey, Lloyd (1)	G	6-4	275	12/8/62	Temple	Philadelphia, Pa.	D6c-'86
Zendejas, Luis (1)	K	5-9	190	10/22/61	Arizona State	Chino, Calif.	FA
Zimmerman, Jeff	G-T-C	6-3	310	1/10/65	Florida	Orlando, Fla.	D3

The term NFL Rookie is defined as a player who is in his first season of professional football and has not been on the roster of another professional football team for any regular-season or postseason games. A Rookie is designated by an "R" on NFL rosters. Players who have been active in another professional football league or players who have NFL experience, including either preseason training camp or being on an active roster for fewer than three regular-season or postseason games, are termed NFL First-Year Players. An NFL First-Year Player is designated by a "1" on NFL rosters. Thereafter, a player on an NFL active roster for at least three regular-season or postseason games is credited with an additional year of NFL playing experience.

NOTES

Ernie Stautner, defensive coordinator-defensive line; born April 2, 1925, Cham, Bavaria, lives in Dallas. Tackle Boston College 1946-49. Pro defensive tackle Pittsburgh Steelers 1950-63. Pro coach: Pittsburgh Steelers 1963-64, Washington Redskins 1965, joined Cowboys in 1966.

Jerry Tubbs, linebackers; born January 23, 1935, Breckenridge, Tex., lives in Dallas. Center-linebacker Oklahoma 1954-56. Pro linebacker Chicago Cardinals 1957, San Francisco 49ers 1958-59, Dallas Cowboys 1960-67. Pro coach: Joined Cowboys in 1966 (player-coach 1966-67).

Bob Ward, conditioning; born July 4, 1933, Huntington Park, Calif., lives in Dallas. Fullback-quarterback Whitworth College 1952-54. Doctorate in physical education, Indiana University. No pro playing experience. College coach: Fullerton, Calif., J.C. (track) 1965-75. Pro coach: Joined Cowboys in 1975.

National Football Conference Central Division

Team Colors: Honolulu Blue and Silver

Pontiac Silverdome
1200 Featherstone Road — Box 4200
Pontiac, Michigan 48057
Telephone: (313) 335-4131

Club Officials

President-Owner: William Clay Ford
Executive Vice President-General Manager: Russell Thomas
Director of Football Operations-Head Coach: Darryl Rogers
Director of Player Personnel: Joe Bushofsky
Controller: Charles Schmidt
In-House Counsel: Jerome R. Vainisi
Scouts: Dirk Dierking, Ron Hughes, Jim Owens, Jerry Neri, John Trump
Director of Public Relations: Bill Keenist
Director of Communications: Tim Pendell
Ticket Manager: Fred Otto
Trainer: Kent Falb
Strength and Conditioning: Don Clemons
Equipment Manager: Dan Jaroshewich

Stadium: Pontiac Silverdome • **Capacity:** 80,638
1200 Featherstone Road
Pontiac, Michigan 48057

Playing Surface: AstroTurf

Training Camp: Oakland University
Rochester, Michigan 48063

1987 Schedule

Preseason

Aug. 15	**Indianapolis**	8:00
Aug. 22	**Cincinnati**	8:00
Aug. 28	at Seattle	7:30
Sept. 3	at Philadelphia	7:30

Regular Season

Sept. 13	at Minnesota	12:00
Sept. 20	at Los Angeles Raiders	1:00
Sept. 27	**Chicago**	1:00
Oct. 4	**Tampa Bay**	1:00
Oct. 11	at Green Bay	12:00
Oct. 18	**Seattle**	1:00
Oct. 25	**Green Bay**	1:00
Nov. 1	at Denver	2:00
Nov. 8	**Dallas**	1:00
Nov. 15	at Washington	1:00
Nov. 22	at Chicago	12:00
Nov. 26	**Kansas City** (Thanks.)	12:30
Dec. 6	**Los Angeles Rams**	1:00
Dec. 13	at Tampa Bay	4:00
Dec. 20	**Minnesota**	1:00
Dec. 27	at Atlanta	1:00

Lions Coaching History

Portsmouth Spartans 1930-33
(360-356-32)

1930-36	George (Potsy) Clark	54-26-9
1937-38	Earl (Dutch) Clark	14-8-0
1939	Elmer (Gus) Henderson	6-5-0
1940	George (Potsy) Clark	5-5-1
1941-42	Bill Edwards*	4-9-1
1942	John Karcis	0-8-0
1943-47	Charles (Gus) Dorais	20-31-2
1948-50	Alvin (Bo) McMillin	12-24-0
1951-56	Raymond (Buddy) Parker	50-24-2
1957-64	George Wilson	55-45-6
1965-66	Harry Gilmer	10-16-2
1967-72	Joe Schmidt	43-35-7
1973	Don McCafferty	6-7-1
1974-76	Rick Forzano**	15-17-0
1976-77	Tommy Hudspeth	11-13-0
1978-84	Monte Clark	43-63-1
1985-86	Darryl Rogers	12-20-0

*Released after three games in 1942
**Resigned after four games in 1976

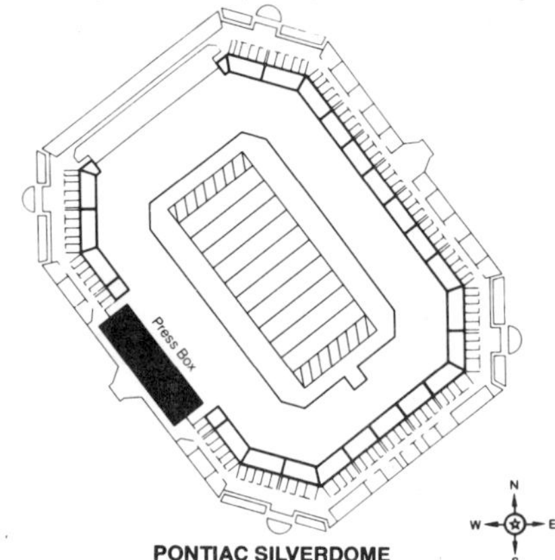

PONTIAC SILVERDOME

Record Holders

Individual Records—Career

Category	Name	Performance
Rushing (Yds.)	Billy Sims, 1980-1984	5,106
Passing (Yds.)	Bobby Layne, 1950-58	15,710
Passing (TDs)	Bobby Layne, 1950-58	118
Receiving (No.)	Charlie Sanders, 1968-1977	336
Receiving (Yds.)	Gail Cogdill, 1960-68	5,220
Interceptions	Dick LeBeau, 1959-1972	62
Punting (Avg.)	Yale Lary, 1952-53, 1956-1964	44.3
Punt Return (Avg.)	Jack Christiansen, 1951-58	12.8
Kickoff Return (Avg.)	Pat Studstill, 1961-67	25.7
Field Goals	Eddie Murray, 1980-86	152
Touchdowns (Tot.)	Billy Sims, 1980-84	47
Points	Eddie Murray, 1980-86	684

Individual Records—Single Season

Category	Name	Performance
Rushing (Yds.)	Billy Sims, 1981	1,437
Passing (Yds.)	Gary Danielson, 1980	3,223
Passing (TDs)	Bobby Layne, 1951	26
Receiving (No.)	James Jones, 1984	77
Receiving (Yds.)	Pat Studstill, 1966	1,266
Interceptions	Don Doll, 1950	12
	Jack Christiansen, 1953	12
Punting (Avg.)	Yale Lary, 1963	48.9
Punt Return (Avg.)	Jack Christiansen, 1952	21.5
Kickoff Return (Avg.)	Tom Watkins, 1965	34.4
Field Goals	Eddie Murray, 1980	27
Touchdowns (Tot.)	Billy Sims, 1980	16
Points	Doak Walker, 1950	128

Individual Records—Single Game

Category	Name	Performance
Rushing (Yds.)	Bob Hoernschemeyer, 11-23-50	198
Passing (Yds.)	Bobby Layne, 11-5-50	374
Passing (TDs)	Gary Danielson, 12-9-78	5
Receiving (No.)	Cloyce Box, 12-5-50	12
	James Jones, 9-28-86	12
Receiving (Yds.)	Cloyce Box, 12-3-50	302
Interceptions	Don Doll, 10-23-49	4
Field Goals	Garo Yepremian, 11-13-66	6
Touchdowns (Tot.)	Cloyce Box, 12-3-50	4
Points	Cloyce Box, 12-3-50	24

1986 Team Statistics

	Lions	Opp.
Total First Downs	287	298
Rushing	100	134
Passing	156	148
Penalty	31	16
Third Down: Made/Att.	85/222	88/213
Fourth Down: Made/Att.	7/14	5/8
Total Net Yards	4555	5149
Avg. Per Game	284.7	321.8
Total Plays	1009	1028
Avg. Per Play	4.5	5.0
Net Yards Rushing	1771	2349
Avg. Per Game	110.7	146.8
Total Rushes	470	519
Net Yards Passing	2784	2800
Avg. Per Game	174.0	175.0
Tackled/Yards Lost	39/323	41/290
Gross Yards	3107	3090
Att./Completions	500/286	468/279
Completion Pct.	57.2	59.6
Had Intercepted	20	22
Punts/Avg.	85/39.9	68/41.7
Net Punting Avg.	31.4	33.8
Penalties/Yards Lost	84/658	99/781
Fumbles/Ball Lost	30/17	36/19
Touchdowns	32	36
Rushing	13	15
Passing	18	14
Returns	1	7
Avg. Time of Possession	29:42	30:18

1986 Team Record

Preseason (2-2)

Date	Result		Opponents
8/8	L	9-17	Philadelphia
8/15	W	30-27	Seattle (OT)
8/23	L	13-20	at Indianapolis
8/29	W	30-20	at Cincinnati
		82-84	

Regular Season (5-11)

Date	Result		Opponents	Att.
9/7	W	13-10	at Minnesota	54,851
9/14	L	7-31	Dallas	73,812
9/21	L	20-24	Tampa Bay	38,453
9/28	L	21-24	at Cleveland	72,029
10/5	W	24-13	Houston	41,960
10/12	W	21-14	at Green Bay	52,290
10/19	L	10-14	at L.A. Rams	50,992
10/26	L	7-13	at Chicago	62,064
11/2	L	17-24	Cincinnati	52,423
11/9	L	10-24	Minnesota	53,725
11/16	W	13-11	at Philadelphia	54,568
11/23	W	38-17	at Tampa Bay	30,029
11/27	L	40-44	Green Bay	61,199
12/7	L	17-27	at Pittsburgh	45,042
12/15	L	13-16	Chicago	75,602
12/21	L	6-20	Atlanta	35,255

(OT) Overtime

Score by Periods

Lions	34	82	71	90	0	—	277
Opponents	63	100	62	101	0	—	326

Attendance

Home 432,429 Away 421,865 Total 854,294
Single game home record, 80,444 (12-20-81)
Single season home record, 622,593 (1980)

1986 Individual Statistics

Scoring	TD R	TD P	TD Rt	PAT	FG	Saf	TP
Murray	0	0	0	31/32	18/25	0	85
Jones	8	1	0	0/0	0/0	0	54
Chadwick	0	5	0	0/0	0/0	0	30
Thompson	0	5	0	0/0	0/0	0	30
Giles, T.B.-Det.	0	4	0	0/0	0/0	0	24
Giles, Det.	0	3	0	0/0	0/0	0	18
James	3	0	0	0/0	0/0	0	18
Bland	0	2	0	0/0	0/0	0	12
S. Williams	2	0	0	0/0	0/0	0	12
Hunter	0	1	0	0/0	0/0	0	6
Lewis	0	1	0	0/0	0/0	0	6
Mandley	0	0	1	0/0	0/0	0	6
Lions	13	18	1	31/32	18/25	0	277
Opponents	15	14	7	36/36	24/35	1	326

Passing	Att.	Comp.	Yds.	Pct.	TD	Int.	Tkld.	Rate
Hipple	305	192	1919	63.0	9	11	21/153	75.6
J. Ferguson	155	73	941	47.1	7	7	10/101	62.9
Long	40	21	247	52.5	2	2	8/69	67.4
Lions	500	286	3107	57.2	18	20	39/323	71.0
Opponents	468	279	3090	59.6	14	22	41/290	69.7

Rushing	Att.	Yds.	Avg.	LG	TD
Jones	252	903	3.6	39	8
James	159	688	4.3	60t	3
Moore	19	73	3.8	18	0
Hipple	16	46	2.9	13	0
J. Ferguson	5	25	5.0	14	0
Hunter	3	22	7.3	18	0
S. Williams	13	22	1.7	5	2
Long	2	0	0.0	0	0
Black	1	−8	−8.0	−8	0
Lions	470	1771	3.8	60t	13
Opponents	519	2349	4.5	55t	15

Receiving	No.	Yds.	Avg.	LG	TD
Jones	54	334	6.2	21	1
Chadwick	53	995	18.8	73	5
Bland	44	511	11.6	34	2
Giles, T.B.-Det.	37	376	10.2	30	4
Giles, Det.	19	198	10.4	30	3
James	34	219	6.4	26	0
Thompson	25	320	12.8	36t	5
Hunter	25	218	8.7	18t	1
Lewis	10	88	8.8	16	1
Moore	8	47	5.9	8	0
Mandley	7	106	15.1	51	0
Rubick	5	62	12.4	27	0
S. Williams	2	9	4.5	6	0
Lions	286	3107	10.9	73	18
Opponents	279	3090	11.1	81t	14

Interceptions	No.	Yds.	Avg.	LG	TD
Mitchell	5	41	8.2	17	0
Galloway	4	58	14.5	36	0
McNorton	4	10	2.5	10	0
Griffin	2	34	17.0	21	0
D. Johnson	2	18	9.0	18	0
J. Williams	2	12	6.0	11	0
Bostic	1	8	8.0	8	0
K. Ferguson	1	7	7.0	7	0
E. Williams	1	2	2.0	2	0
Lions	22	190	8.6	36	0
Opponents	20	311	15.6	80t	2

Punting	No.	Yds.	Avg.	In 20	LG
Arnold	36	1533	42.6	7	60
Black	46	1819	39.5	11	57
Murray	1	37	37.0	0	37
Lions	85	3389	39.9	18	60
Opponents	68	2836	41.7	16	58

Punt Returns	No.	FC	Yds.	Avg.	LG	TD
Mandley	43	9	420	9.8	81t	1
Hill, Buff.-Det.	1	0	0	0.0	0	0
Lions	43	9	420	9.8	81t	1
Opponents	39	14	517	13.3	84t	2

Kickoff Returns	No.	Yds.	Avg.	LG	TD
Hunter	49	1007	20.6	54	0
Elder, Pitt.-Det.	22	435	19.8	36	0
Elder, Det.	1	10	10.0	10	0
Bland	6	114	19.0	24	0
Smith	5	81	16.2	30	0
Graham	3	72	24.0	27	0
Mandley	2	37	18.5	37	0
Evans	1	0	0.0	0	0
Lions	67	1321	19.7	54	0
Opponents	56	1096	19.6	36	0

Sacks	No.
K. Ferguson	9.5
Cofer	7.5
Gay	6.5
E. Williams	4.0
Green	3.5
Griffin	2.0
King	2.0
Maxwell	2.0
J. Williams	2.0
Harrell	0.5
Robinson	0.5
Lions	41.0
Opponents	39.0

FIRST-ROUND SELECTIONS

(If club had no first-round selection, first player drafted is listed with round in parentheses.)

Since 1940

Year	Player, College, Position
1940	Doyle Nave, Southern California, B
1941	Jim Thomason, Texas A&M, B
1942	Bob Westfall, Michigan, B
1943	Frank Sinkwich, Georgia, B
1944	Otto Graham, Northwestern, B
1945	Frank Szymanski, Notre Dame, C
1946	Bill Dellastatious, Missouri, B
1947	Glenn Davis, Army, B
1948	Y.A. Tittle, Louisiana State, B
1949	John Rauch, Georgia, B
1950	Leon Hart, Notre Dame, E
	Joe Watson, Rice, C
1951	Dick Stanfel, San Francisco, G (2)
1952	Yale Lary, Texas A&M, B (3)
1953	Harley Sewell, Texas, G
1954	Dick Chapman, Rice, T
1955	Dave Middleton, Auburn, B
1956	Hopalong Cassady, Ohio State, B
1957	Bill Glass, Baylor, G
1958	Alex Karras, Iowa, T
1959	Nick Pietrosante, Notre Dame, B
1960	John Robinson, Louisiana State, S
1961	Danny LaRose, Missouri, T (2)
1962	John Hadl, Kansas, QB
1963	Daryl Sanders, Ohio State, T
1964	Pete Beathard, Southern California, QB
1965	Tom Nowatzke, Indiana, RB
1966	Nick Eddy, Notre Dame, RB (2)
1967	Mel Farr, UCLA, RB
1968	Greg Landry, Massachusetts, QB
	Earl McCullouch, Southern California, WR
1969	Altie Taylor, Utah State, RB (2)
1970	Steve Owens, Oklahoma, RB
1971	Bob Bell, Cincinnati, DT
1972	Herb Orvis, Colorado, DE
1973	Ernie Price, Texas A&I, DE
1974	Ed O'Neil, Penn State, LB
1975	Lynn Boden, South Dakota State, G
1976	James Hunter, Grambling, DB
	Lawrence Gaines, Wyoming, RB
1977	Walt Williams, New Mexico State, DB (2)
1978	Luther Bradley, Notre Dame, DB
1979	Keith Dorney, Penn State, T
1980	Billy Sims, Oklahoma, RB
1981	Mark Nichols, San Jose State, WR
1982	Jimmy Williams, Nebraska, LB
1983	James Jones, Florida, RB
1984	David Lewis, California, TE
1985	Lomas Brown, Florida, T
1986	Chuck Long, Iowa, QB
1987	Reggie Rogers, Washington, DE

Detroit Lions 1987 Veteran Roster

No.	Name	Pos.	Ht.	Wt.	Birth-date	NFL Exp.	College	Hometown	How Acq.	'86 Games/ Starts
6	Arnold, Jim	P	6-3	211	1/31/61	5	Vanderbilt	Dalton, Ga.	FA-'86	7/0
68	Baack, Steve	G	6-4	265	11/16/60	4	Oregon	John Day, Ore.	D3c-'84	16/0
61	Barrows, Scott	G-C	6-2	278	3/31/63	2	West Virginia	Marietta, Ohio	FA-'86	16/4
80	Bland, Carl	WR	5-11	182	8/17/61	4	Virginia Union	Richmond, Va.	FA-'85	16/16
42	†Bostic, John	CB	5-10	178	10/6/62	3	Bethune-Cookman	Titusville, Fla.	FA-'85	13/0
23	†Brown, Arnold	CB	5-10	185	8/27/62	2	North Carolina Central	Wilmington, N.C.	FA-'85	0*
75	Brown, Lomas	T	6-4	282	3/30/63	3	Florida	Miami, Fla.	D1-'85	16/16
96	Butcher, Paul	LB	6-0	219	11/8/63	2	Wayne State	Dearborn, Mich.	FA-'86	12/0
89	†Chadwick, Jeff	WR	6-3	190	12/16/60	5	Grand Valley State	Dearborn, Mich.	FA-'83	15/15
55	†Cofer, Michael	LB	6-5	245	4/7/60	5	Tennessee	Knoxville, Tenn.	D3-'83	16/15
44	D'Addio, Dave	RB	6-2	229	7/13/61	2	Maryland	Union, N.J.	FA-'87	0*
72	Dieterich, Chris	G-T	6-3	275	7/27/58	7	North Carolina State	Raleigh, N.C.	D6-'80	3/3
70	Dorney, Keith	G-T	6-5	285	12/3/57	9	Penn State	Emmaus, Pa.	D1-'79	12/12
94	Drake, Joe	NT	6-3	290	5/28/63	2	Arizona	San Francisco, Calif.	FA-'87	0*
43	Elder, Donnie	CB	5-9	175	12/13/62	3	Memphis State	Chattanooga, Tenn.	FA-'86	12/0*
15	Erxleben, Russell	P	6-4	238	1/13/57	5	Texas	Seguin, Tex.	FA-'87	0*
66	Evans, Leon	DE	6-5	282	10/12/61	3	Miami	Silver Spring, Md.	FA-'85	16/0
12	Ferguson, Joe	QB	6-1	195	4/23/50	15	Arkansas	Shreveport, La.	T(Buff)-'85	6/4
77	Ferguson, Keith	DE	6-5	260	4/3/59	7	Ohio State	Miami, Fla.	W(SD)-'85	16/15
40	†Galloway, Duane	CB-S	5-8	181	11/7/61	2	Arizona State	Los Angeles, Calif.	FA-'85	16/12
79	Gay, William	DE	6-5	260	5/28/55	10	Southern California	San Diego, Calif.	T(Den)-'78	16/16
81	†Giles, Jimmie	TE	6-3	240	11/8/54	11	Alcorn State	Greenville, Miss.	FA-'86	16/15*
53	Glover, Kevin	C-G	6-2	267	6/17/63	3	Maryland	Upper Marlboro, Md.	D2-'85	4/1
33	Graham, William	S	5-11	191	9/27/59	6	Texas	Silsbee, Tex.	D5-'82	16/0
62	†Green, Curtis	DE-NT	6-3	265	6/3/57	7	Alabama State	Quincy, Fla.	D2-'81	16/1
34	Griffin, James	S	6-2	197	9/7/61	5	Middle Tennessee State	Camilla, Ga.	FA-'86	16/0
58	†Harrell, James	LB	6-1	230	7/19/57	8	Florida	Tampa, Fla.	FA-'85	16/15
47	Hill, Rod	CB	6-0	188	3/14/59	5	Kentucky State	Detroit, Mich.	FA-'86	9/2*
17	†Hipple, Eric	QB	6-2	198	9/16/57	8	Utah State	Downey, Calif.	D4-'80	16/10
36	Hunter, Herman	RB-KR	6-1	193	2/14/61	3	Tennessee State	Columbus, Ga.	FA-'86	16/0
32	James, Garry	RB	5-10	214	9/4/63	2	Louisiana State	Gretna, La.	D2-'86	16/15
21	Johnson, Demetrious	S	5-11	190	7/21/61	5	Missouri	St. Louis, Mo.	D5a-'83	16/16
54	Johnson, James	LB	6-2	236	6/21/62	2	San Diego State	Lake Elsinore, Calif.	FA-'86	11/0
30	Jones, James	RB	6-2	229	3/21/61	5	Florida	Pompano Beach, Fla.	D1-'83	16/16
63	Kenney, Steve	G	6-4	262	12/26/55	8	Clemson	Raleigh, N.C.	FA-'86	9/1
92	King, Angelo	LB	6-1	222	2/10/58	7	South Carolina State	Columbia, S.C.	T(Dall)-'84	11/5
87	Lewis, David	TE	6-3	235	6/8/61	4	California	Portland, Ore.	D1-'84	11/7
16	Long, Chuck	QB	6-4	211	2/18/63	2	Iowa	Wheaton, Ill.	D1-'86	3/2
82	Mandley, Pete	WR-KR	5-10	191	7/29/61	4	Northern Arizona	Mesa, Ariz.	D2-'84	16/0
57	†Maxwell, Vernon	LB	6-2	235	10/25/61	5	Arizona State	Los Angeles, Calif.	FA-'85	15/15
29	†McNorton, Bruce	CB	5-11	175	2/28/59	6	Georgetown, Ky.	Daytona Beach, Fla.	D4-'82	16/16
31	Mitchell, Devon	S	6-1	194	12/30/62	2	Iowa	Brooklyn, N.Y.	D4-'86	16/16
24	Moore, Alvin	RB	6-0	194	5/3/59	5	Arizona State	Coolidge, Ariz.	T(Ind)-'85	13/0
52	Mott, Steve	C	6-3	270	3/24/61	5	Alabama	New Orleans, La.	D5-'83	14/14
3	Murray, Eddie	K	5-10	175	8/29/56	8	Tulane	Victoria, British Columbia	D7-'80	16/0
86	Nichols, Mark	WR	6-2	208	10/29/59	6	San Jose State	Bakersfield, Calif.	D1-'81	0*
51	†Robinson, Shelton	LB	6-2	236	9/16/60	6	North Carolina	Pikeville, N.C.	T(Sea)-'86	16/4
84	Rubick, Rob	TE	6-3	234	9/27/60	6	Grand Valley State	Newberry, Mich.	D12b-'82	16/2
73	†Salem, Harvey	T-G	6-6	285	1/15/61	5	California	El Cerrito, Calif.	T(Hou)-'86	14/13*
64	Sanders, Eric	T-G	6-7	280	10/22/58	7	Nevada-Reno	Reno, Nev.	W(Atl)-'86	3/0*
71	Strenger, Rich	T	6-7	285	3/10/60	4	Michigan	Grafton, Wis.	D2-'83	16/16
39	†Thompson, Leonard	WR	5-11	192	7/28/52	13	Oklahoma State	Tucson, Ariz.	D8-'75	16/1
27	Watkins, Bobby	CB	5-10	184	5/31/60	6	Southwest Texas State	Dallas, Tex.	D2-'82	5/4
76	†Williams, Eric	NT	6-4	280	2/24/62	4	Washington State	Stockton, Calif.	D3a-'84	16/16
59	Williams, Jimmy	LB	6-3	230	11/15/60	6	Nebraska	Washington, D.C.	D1-'82	10/10
38	Williams, Scott	RB	6-2	234	7/21/62	2	Georgia	Charlotte, N.C.	FA-'86	16/0

* A. Brown, D'Addio, and Nichols missed '86 season due to injury; Drake last active with Philadelphia in '85; Erxleben last active with New Orleans in '83; Elder played 9 games with Pittsburgh, 3 with Detroit in '86; Giles played 7 games with Tampa Bay, 9 with Detroit; Hill played 6 games with Buffalo, 3 with Detroit; Salem played 1 game with Houston, 13 with Detroit; Sanders played 8 games with Atlanta, 3 with Detroit.

†Option playout; subject to developments.

Also played with Lions in '86—P Mike Black (9 games), LB August Curley (4), WR Tim Kearse (active for 1 game, but did not play), RB-KR Oscar Smith (2), G-C Tom Turnure (13).

COACHING STAFF

Head Coach, Darryl Rogers

Pro Career: Became Lions' sixteenth head coach and director of football operations on February 6, 1985. No pro playing experience. Career record: 12-20.

Background: Wide receiver who gained all-West Coast honors while playing at Fresno State. Served in U.S. Marine Corps and later earned his master's degree in physical education from Fresno State. Spent twenty years coaching in the collegiate ranks at Hayward State 1965, Fresno State 1966-72, San Jose State 1973-75 (head coach), Michigan State 1976-79 (head coach), Arizona State 1980-84 (head coach). Named national college coach of the year in 1978 while at Michigan State. Ranked as one of the winningest coaches in the college ranks with a 129-84-7 mark.

Personal: Born May 28, 1935, Los Angeles, Calif. Darryl and his wife, Marsha, live in Bloomfield Hills, Mich., and have three daughters—Jamie, Keely, and Stacy.

Assistant Coaches

Bob Baker, offensive coordinator; born November 28, 1927, Lima, Ohio, lives in Rochester Hills, Mich. Quarterback Ball State 1947-51. No pro playing experience. College coach: Indiana 1966-73, Michigan State 1977-79, Arizona State 1980-82. Pro coach: Calgary Stampeders (CFL) 1974-76 (head coach 1976), Los Angeles Rams 1983-84, joined Lions in 1985.

Carl Battershell, special teams-secondary; born November 5, 1948, Alliance, Ohio, lives in Rochester, Mich. Offensive tackle Bowling Green 1966-69. No pro playing experience. College coach: Bowling Green 1973-76, Syracuse 1977-79, West Virginia 1980-82, Arizona State 1983-84. Pro coach: Joined Lions in 1985.

Lew Carpenter, receivers; born January 12, 1932, Hayti, Mo., lives in Rochester, Mich. Running back-end Arkansas 1950-52. Pro running back-defensive back-end Detroit Lions 1953-55, Cleveland Browns 1957-58, Green Bay Packers 1959-63. Pro coach: Minnesota Vikings 1964-66, Atlanta Falcons 1967-68, Washington Redskins 1969-70, St. Louis Cardinals 1971-72, Houston Oilers 1973-74, Green Bay Packers 1975-85, first year with Lions.

Don Doll, administrative assistant to coaching staff-tight ends; born August 29, 1926, Los Angeles, Calif., lives in Birmingham, Mich. Defensive back Southern California 1944, 1946-48. Pro defensive back Detroit Lions 1949-52, Washington Redskins 1953, Los Angeles Rams 1954. College coach: Washington 1955, Contra Costa, Calif., J.C. 1956, Southern California 1957-58, Notre Dame 1959-62. Pro coach: Detroit Lions 1963-64, Los Angeles Rams 1965, Washington Redskins 1966-70, Green Bay Packers 1971-73, Baltimore Colts 1974, Miami Dolphins 1975-76, rejoined Lions in 1978.

Wayne Fontes, defensive coordinator; born February 17, 1940, New Bedford, Mass., lives in Rochester, Mich. Defensive back Michigan State 1959-62. Pro defensive back New York Titans (AFL) 1962. College coach: Dayton 1967-68, Iowa 1969-70, Southern California 1971-75. Pro coach: Tampa Bay Buccaneers 1976-84, joined Lions in 1985.

Bill Muir, offensive line; born October 26, 1942, Pittsburgh, Pa., lives in Rochester Hills, Mich. Tackle Susquehanna 1962-64. No pro playing experience. College coach: Susquehanna 1965, Delaware Valley 1966-67, Rhode Island 1970-71, Idaho State 1972-73, Southern Methodist 1976-77. Pro coach: Orlando (Continental Football League) 1968-69, Houston-Shreveport Steamer (WFL) 1975, New England Patriots 1982-84, joined Lions in 1985.

Mike Murphy, linebackers; born September 25, 1944, New York, N.Y., lives in Rochester, Mich. Guard-linebacker Huron, S.D., College 1962-65. No pro playing experience. College coach: Vermont 1970-73, Idaho State 1974-76, Western Illinois 1977-78. Pro coach: Saskatchewan Roughriders (CFL) 1979-83, Chicago Blitz (USFL) 1984, joined Lions in 1985.

Detroit Lions 1987 First-Year Roster

Name	Pos.	Ht.	Wt.	Birth-date	College	Hometown	How Acq.
Ball, Jerry	NT	6-0	296	12/15/64	Southern Methodist	Beaumont, Tex.	D3
Brown, Raynard	WR-KR	5-9	185	7/25/65	South Carolina	Greensboro, S.C.	D10
Brown, Tony (1)	T	6-5	295	7/11/64	Pittsburgh	Stamford, Conn.	FA
Calhoun, Rick	WR-KR	5-7	185	5/30/63	Cal State-Fullerton	Riverside, Calif.	D9
Coleman, Ed	WR	5-11	180	3/31/64	Bluffton	Toledo, Ohio	FA
Garbarczyk, Tony (1)	NT	6-3	275	1/20/64	Wake Forest	Hauppauge, N.Y.	FA
Gibson, Dennis	LB	6-2	240	2/8/64	Iowa State	Ankeny, Iowa	D8
Grymes, Darrell (1)	WR	6-2	186	12/4/62	Central State, Ohio	Washington, D.C.	FA
Hines, Todd (1)	WR	5-11	180	7/6/64	Hanover	Portland, Ind.	FA
Hughes, Allen (1)	DE	6-3	254	9/8/59	Western Michigan	Detroit, Mich.	FA-'86
Jamison, George (1)	LB	6-1	226	9/30/62	Cincinnati	Bridgeton, N.J.	FA-'86
Ledbetter, Weldon (1)	RB	6-0	223	10/23/60	Oklahoma	Clayton, Mo.	FA
Lee, Gary	WR-KR	6-1	202	2/12/65	Georgia Tech	Albany, Ga.	D12
Lockett, Danny	LB	6-2	228	7/11/64	Arizona	Ft. Valley, Ga.	D6
Mattiace, Frank (1)	NT	6-1	270	1/20/61	Holy Cross	Montville, N.J.	FA
Milinichik, Joe (1)	G-T	6-5	300	3/30/63	North Carolina State	Macungie, Pa.	D3-'86
Oliver, Jack (1)	G	6-4	285	2/3/62	Memphis State	Pensacola, Fla.	FA
Pearson, Bret (1)	TE	6-4	240	3/31/62	Wisconsin	Menominee, Wis.	FA
Rivers, Garland	S	6-1	181	11/3/64	Michigan	Canton, Ohio	D4
Rogers, Reggie	DE	6-6	272	1/21/64	Washington	Sacramento, Calif.	D1
Saleaumua, Dan	NT	6-0	285	11/11/64	Arizona State	San Diego, Calif.	D7
Sebring, Bob (1)	LB	6-2	238	4/10/63	Illinois	Villa Park, Calif.	FA
Siverling, Brian	TE	6-7	253	9/3/63	Penn State	North East, Pa.	D11
Smith, Oscar (1)	RB	5-9	203	4/5/63	Nicholls State	Tampa, Fla.	D5-'86
Smith, Steve (1)	S	6-0	200	12/19/62	Michigan	Grand Blanc, Mich.	FA
Snyder, Don (1)	T	6-5	290	5/24/63	Tennessee Tech	Scott City, Kan.	FA
Truvillion, Eric (1)	WR	6-4	205	6/18/59	Florida A&M	Queens, N.Y.	FA

The term NFL Rookie is defined as a player who is in his first season of professional football and has not been on the roster of another professional football team for any regular-season or postseason games. A Rookie is designated by an "R" on NFL rosters. Players who have been active in another professional football league or players who have NFL experience, including either preseason training camp or being on an active roster for fewer than three regular-season or postseason games, are termed NFL First-Year Players. An NFL First-Year Player is designated by a "1" on NFL rosters. Thereafter, a player on an NFL active roster for at least three regular-season or postseason games is credited with an additional year of NFL playing experience.

NOTES

Rex Norris, defensive line; born December 10, 1939, Tipton, Ind., lives in Bloomfield Hills, Mich. Linebacker East Texas State 1964. No pro playing experience. College coach: Navarro, Tex., J.C. 1970-71, Texas A&M 1972, Oklahoma 1973-83, Arizona State 1984. Pro coach: Joined Lions in 1985.

Vic Rapp, running backs; born December 23, 1935, Marionville, Mo., lives in Rochester, Mich. Running back Southwest Missouri State 1954-57. No pro playing experience. College coach: Arizona 1965-66, Missouri 1967-71. Pro coach: Edmonton Eskimos (CFL) 1972-76, British Columbia Lions (CFL) 1977-82 (head coach), Houston Oilers 1983, Los Angeles Rams 1984, Tampa Bay Buccaneers 1985-86, first year with Lions.

Willie Shaw, defensive backs; born January 11, 1944, Glenmora, La., lives in Rochester, Mich. Defensive back New Mexico 1966-68. No pro playing experience. College coach: San Diego City College 1970-72, Stanford 1973-76, Long Beach State 1977-78, Oregon 1979, Arizona State 1980-84. Pro coach: Joined Lions in 1985.

National Football Conference Central Division

Team Colors: Dark Green, Gold, and White

1265 Lombardi Avenue
Green Bay, Wisconsin 54307-0628
Telephone: (414) 494-2351

Club Officials

Chairman of the Board: Dominic Olejniczak
President, CEO: Robert Parins
Vice President: Tony Canadeo
Secretary: Peter M. Platten III
Treasurer: Phil Hendrickson
Assistant to the President: Bob Harlan
Assistant to the President: Tom Miller
Executive Vice President, Football Operations: Tom Braatz
Public Relations Director: Lee Remmel
Assistant Director of Public Relations: Scott Berchtold
Green Bay Ticket Director: Mark Wagner
Director of College Scouting: Dick Corrick
Pro Scout: Chuck Hutchison
Video Director: Al Treml
Trainer: Domenic Gentile
Equipment Manager: Bob Noel

Stadium: Lambeau Field • **Capacity:** 57,091
P.O. Box 10628
1265 Lombardi Avenue
Green Bay, Wisconsin 54307-0628
Milwaukee County Stadium • **Capacity:** 56,051
Highway I-94
Milwaukee, Wisconsin 53214

Playing Surfaces: Grass

Training Camp: St. Norbert College
DePere, Wisconsin 54115

1987 Schedule

Preseason

Aug. 15	vs. Denver at Tempe, Ariz.	7:00
Aug. 22	vs. Wash. at Madison, Wis.	1:00
Aug. 29	**Cincinnati**	7:00
Sept. 5	vs. Cleveland at Milw.	7:00

Regular Season

Sept. 13	**Los Angeles Raiders**	3:00
Sept. 20	**Denver** at Milwaukee	12:00
Sept. 27	at Tampa Bay	1:00
Oct. 4	at Minnesota	12:00
Oct. 11	**Detroit**	12:00
Oct. 18	**Philadelphia**	12:00
Oct. 25	at Detroit	1:00
Nov. 1	**Tampa Bay** at Milwaukee	12:00
Nov. 8	**Chicago**	12:00
Nov. 15	at Seattle	1:00
Nov. 22	at Kansas City	12:00
Nov. 29	at Chicago	12:00
Dec. 6	**San Francisco**	12:00
Dec. 13	**Minnesota** at Milwaukee	12:00
Dec. 19	at N.Y. Giants (Saturday)	12:30
Dec. 27	at New Orleans	12:00

Packers Coaching History

(460-364-35)

1921-49	Earl (Curly) Lambeau	212-106-21
1950-53	Gene Ronzani*	14-31-1
1953	Hugh Devore-Ray (Scooter) McLean**	0-2-0
1954-57	Lisle Blackbourn	17-31-0
1958	Ray (Scooter) McLean	1-10-1
1959-67	Vince Lombardi	98-30-4
1968-70	Phil Bengtson	20-21-1
1971-74	Dan Devine	25-28-4
1975-83	Bart Starr	53-77-3
1984-86	Forrest Gregg	20-28-0

*Released after 10 games in 1953
**Co-coaches

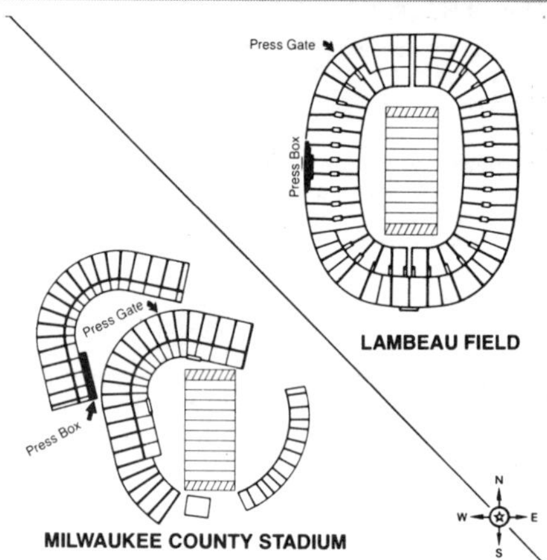

Record Holders

Individual Records—Career

Category	Name	Performance
Rushing (Yds.)	Jim Taylor, 1958-1966	8,207
Passing (Yds.)	Bart Starr, 1956-1971	23,718
Passing (TDs)	Bart Starr, 1956-1971	152
Receiving (No.)	James Lofton, 1978-1986	530
Receiving (Yds.)	James Lofton, 1978-1986	9,656
Interceptions	Bobby Dillon, 1952-59	52
Punting (Avg.)	Dick Deschaine, 1955-57	42.6
Punt Return (Avg.)	Billy Grimes, 1950-52	13.2
Kickoff Return (Avg.)	Travis Williams, 1967-1970	26.7
Field Goals	Chester Marcol, 1972-1980	120
Touchdowns (Tot.)	Don Hutson, 1935-1945	105
Points	Don Hutson, 1935-1945	823

Individual Records—Single Season

Category	Name	Performance
Rushing (Yds.)	Jim Taylor, 1962	1,407
Passing (Yds.)	Lynn Dickey, 1983	4,458
Passing (TDs)	Lynn Dickey, 1983	32
Receiving (No.)	Don Hutson, 1942	74
Receiving (Yds.)	James Lofton, 1984	1,361
Interceptions	Irv Comp, 1943	10
Punting (Avg.)	Jerry Norton, 1963	44.7
Punt Return (Avg.)	Billy Grimes, 1950	19.1
Kickoff Return (Avg.)	Travis Williams, 1967	41.1
Field Goals	Chester Marcol, 1972	33
Touchdowns (Tot.)	Jim Taylor, 1962	19
Points	Paul Hornung, 1960	176

Individual Records—Single Game

Category	Name	Performance
Rushing (Yds.)	Jim Taylor, 12-3-61	186
Passing (Yds.)	Lynn Dickey, 10-12-80	418
Passing (TDs)	Many times	5
	Last time by Lynn Dickey, 9-4-83	
Receiving (No.)	Don Hutson, 11-22-42	14
Receiving (Yds.)	Bill Howton, 10-21-56	257
Interceptions	Bobby Dillon, 11-26-53	4
	Willie Buchanon, 9-24-78	4
Field Goals	Many times	4
	Last time by Al Del Greco, 9-22-86	
Touchdowns (Tot.)	Paul Hornung, 12-12-65	5
Points	Paul Hornung, 10-8-61	33

1986 Team Statistics

	Packers	Opp.
Total First Downs	286	313
Rushing	96	135
Passing	172	151
Penalty	18	27
Third Down: Made/Att.	79/222	94/217
Fourth Down: Made/Att.	13/25	7/14
Total Net Yards	5061	5015
Avg. Per Game	316.3	313.4
Total Plays	1026	1041
Avg. Per Play	4.9	4.8
Net Yards Rushing	1614	2095
Avg. Per Game	100.9	130.9
Total Rushes	424	565
Net Yards Passing	3447	2920
Avg. Per Game	215.4	182.5
Tackled/Yards Lost	37/261	28/222
Gross Yards	3708	3142
Att./Completions	565/305	448/267
Completion Pct.	54.0	59.6
Had Intercepted	27	20
Punts/Avg.	75/37.7	70/39.6
Net Punting Avg.	32.2	31.3
Penalties/Yards Lost	128/949	79/657
Fumbles/Ball Lost	35/18	32/12
Touchdowns	29	52
Rushing	8	16
Passing	18	31
Returns	3	5
Avg. Time of Possession	28:11	31:49

1986 Team Record

Preseason (1-3)

Date	Result		Opponents
8/9	W	38-14	N.Y. Jets
8/16	L	14-22	N.Y. Giants
8/23	L	12-34	at Cincinnati
8/30	L	9-16	New England
		73-86	

Regular Season (4-12)

Date	Result		Opponents	Att.
9/7	L	3-31	Houston	54,065
9/14	L	10-24	at New Orleans	46,383
9/22	L	12-25	Chicago	55,527
9/28	L	7-42	at Minnesota	60,478
10/5	L	28-34	Cincinnati	51,230
10/12	L	14-21	Detroit	52,290
10/19	W	17-14	at Cleveland	76,438
10/26	L	17-31	San Francisco	50,557
11/2	L	3-27	at Pittsburgh	52,831
11/9	L	7-16	Washington	47,728
11/16	W	31- 7	Tampa Bay	48,271
11/23	L	10-12	at Chicago	59,291
11/27	W	44-40	at Detroit	61,199
12/7	L	6-32	Minnesota	47,637
12/14	W	21- 7	at Tampa Bay	30,099
12/20	L	24-55	at N.Y. Giants	71,351

Score by Periods

Packers	57	80	65	52	0	—	254
Opponents	124	106	78	110	0	—	418

Attendance

Home 407,305 Away 458,070 Total 865,375
Single game home record, 56,895 (11-3-85; Lambeau Field) 56,258 (9-28-80; Milwaukee County Stadium)
Single season home record, 435,521 (1980)

1986 Individual Statistics

Scoring	TD R	TD P	TD Rt	PAT	FG	Saf	TP
Del Greco	0	0	0	29/29	17/27	0	80
Carruth	2	2	0	0/0	0/0	0	24
Epps	0	4	0	0/0	0/0	0	24
Lofton	0	4	0	0/0	0/0	0	24
Ellerson	3	0	0	0/0	0/0	0	18
Stanley	0	2	1	0/0	0/0	0	18
Ellis	2	0	0	0/0	0/0	0	12
M. Lewis	0	2	0	0/0	0/0	0	12
Davis	0	1	0	0/0	0/0	0	6
Ivery	0	1	0	0/0	0/0	0	6
Ross	0	1	0	0/0	0/0	0	6
Simmons	0	0	1	0/0	0/0	0	6
Stills	0	0	1	0/0	0/0	0	6
West	0	1	0	0/0	0/0	0	6
Wright	1	0	0	0/0	0/0	0	6
Packers	8	18	3	29/29	17/27	0	254
Opponents	16	31	5	48/52	18/25	2	418

Passing	Att.	Comp.	Yds.	Pct.	TD	Int.	Tkld.	Rate
Wright	492	263	3247	53.5	17	23	33/243	66.2
Ferragamo	40	23	283	57.5	1	3	3/15	56.6
Fusina	32	19	178	59.4	0	1	1/3	61.7
Lofton	1	0	0	0.0	0	0	0/0	39.6
Packers	565	305	3708	54.0	18	27	37/261	65.1
Opponents	448	267	3142	59.6	31	20	28/222	85.4

Rushing	Att.	Yds.	Avg.	LG	TD
Davis	114	519	4.6	50	0
Ellis	84	345	4.1	24	2
Carruth	81	308	3.8	42	2
Ellerson	90	287	3.2	18	3
Clark	18	41	2.3	9	0
Wright	18	41	2.3	18	1
Ivery	4	25	6.3	15	0
Stanley	1	19	19.0	19	0
Epps	4	18	4.5	20	0
Fusina	7	11	1.6	6	0
Ferragamo	1	0	0.0	0	0
Renner	1	0	0.0	0	0
Swanke	1	0	0.0	0	0
Packers	424	1614	3.8	50	8
Opponents	565	2095	3.7	41t	16

Receiving	No.	Yds.	Avg.	LG	TD
Lofton	64	840	13.1	36	4
Epps	49	612	12.5	53t	4
Stanley	35	723	20.7	62	2
Ivery	31	385	12.4	42	1
Ellis	24	258	10.8	29	0
Carruth	24	134	5.6	19	2
Davis	21	142	6.8	18	1
Ross	17	143	8.4	16	1
West	15	199	13.3	46t	1
Ellerson	12	130	10.8	32	0
Clark	6	41	6.8	12	0
Moffitt	4	87	21.8	34	0
M. Lewis	2	7	3.5	4t	2
Franz	1	7	7.0	7	0
Packers	305	3708	12.2	62	18
Opponents	267	3142	11.8	84	31

Interceptions	No.	Yds.	Avg.	LG	TD
Lee	9	33	3.7	11	0
Cade	4	26	6.5	18	0
Greene	2	0	0.0	0	0
Stills	1	58	58.0	58t	1
Leopold	1	21	21.0	21	0
Watts	1	6	6.0	6	0
Anderson	1	3	3.0	3	0
Flynn	1	0	0.0	0	0
Packers	20	147	7.4	58t	1
Opponents	27	357	13.2	88t	3

Punting	No.	Yds.	Avg.	In 20	LG
Renner	15	622	41.5	2	50
Bracken	55	2203	40.1	6	63
Packers	75	2825	37.7	8	63
Opponents	70	2769	39.6	16	61

Punt Returns	No.	FC	Yds.	Avg.	LG	TD
Stanley	33	7	316	9.6	83t	1
Simmons, Cin.-G.B.	2	4	7	3.5	6	0
Packers	33	7	316	9.6	83t	1
Opponents	44	5	287	6.5	17	0

Kickoff Returns	No.	Yds.	Avg.	LG	TD
Stanley	28	559	20.0	55	0
Davis	12	231	19.3	35	0
Watts	12	239	19.9	40	0
Stills	10	209	20.9	38	0
Ellerson	7	154	22.0	57	0
Carruth	4	40	10.0	20	0
Berry	1	16	16.0	16	0
Epps	1	21	21.0	21	0
Noble	1	1	1.0	1	0
Simmons, Cin.-G.B.	1	0	0.0	0	0
Packers	76	1470	19.3	57	0
Opponents	62	1181	19.0	64	0

Sacks	No.
Harris	8.0
Greenwood	3.0
Johnson	3.0
Carreker	2.5
Brown	2.0
Noble	2.0
Thomas, N.E.-G.B.	2.0
Thomas, G.B.	1.0
Leopold	1.5
Cade	1.0
Greene	1.0
Martin	1.0
Scott	1.0
Simmons, Cin.-G.B.	1.0
Watts	1.0
Packers	28.0
Opponents	37.0

FIRST-ROUND SELECTIONS

(If club had no first-round selection, first player drafted is listed with round in parentheses.)

Since 1958

Year	Player, College, Position
1958	Dan Currie, Michigan State, C
1959	Randy Duncan, Iowa, B
1960	Tom Moore, Vanderbilt, RB
1961	Herb Adderley, Michigan State, CB
1962	Earl Gros, Louisiana State, RB
1963	Dave Robinson, Penn State, LB
1964	Lloyd Voss, Nebraska, DT
1965	Donny Anderson, Texas Tech, RB
	Larry Elkins, Baylor, E
1966	Jim Grabowski, Illinois, RB
	Gale Gillingham, Minnesota, T
1967	Bob Hyland, Boston College, C
	Don Horn, San Diego State, QB
1968	Fred Carr, Texas-El Paso, LB
	Bill Lueck, Arizona, G
1969	Rich Moore, Villanova, DT
1970	Mike McCoy, Notre Dame, DT
	Rich McGeorge, Elon, TE
1971	John Brockington, Ohio State, RB
1972	Willie Buchanon, San Diego State, DB
	Jerry Tagge, Nebraska, QB
1973	Barry Smith, Florida State, WR
1974	Barty Smith, Richmond, RB
1975	Bill Bain, Southern California, G (2)
1976	Mark Koncar, Colorado, T
1977	Mike Butler, Kansas, DE
	Ezra Johnson, Morris Brown, DE
1978	James Lofton, Stanford, WR
	John Anderson, Michigan, LB
1979	Eddie Lee Ivery, Georgia Tech, RB
1980	Bruce Clark, Penn State, DE
	George Cumby, Oklahoma, LB
1981	Rich Campbell, California, QB
1982	Ron Hallstrom, Iowa, G
1983	Tim Lewis, Pittsburgh, DB
1984	Alphonso Carreker, Florida State, DE
1985	Ken Ruettgers, Southern California, T
1986	Kenneth Davis, Texas Christian, RB (2)
1987	Brent Fullwood, Auburn, RB

Green Bay Packers 1987 Veteran Roster

No.	Name	Pos.	Ht.	Wt.	Birth-date	NFL Exp.	College	Hometown	How Acq.	'86 Games/ Starts
59	Anderson, John	LB	6-3	228	2/14/56	10	Michigan	Waukesha, Wis.	D1b-'78	4/4
20	Berry, Ed	CB-S	5-10	183	9/28/63	2	Utah State	Belmont, Calif.	D7-'86	16/10
17	†Bracken, Don	P	6-0	211	2/16/62	3	Michigan	Thermopolis, Wyo.	FA-'85	13/0
93	Brown, Robert	DE	6-2	267	5/21/60	6	Virginia Tech	Edenton, N.C.	D4-'82	16/16
24	Cade, Mossy	CB	6-1	198	12/26/61	3	Texas	Eloy, Ariz.	T(SD)-'85	16/16
58	Cannon, Mark	C	6-3	258	6/14/62	4	Texas-Arlington	Austin, Tex.	D11-'84	7/7
76	Carreker, Alphonso	DE	6-6	271	5/25/62	4	Florida State	Columbus, Ohio	D1-'84	16/16
30	Carruth, Paul Ott	RB	6-1	220	7/22/61	2	Alabama	McComb, Miss.	FA-'86	16/12
69	Cherry, Bill	C-G	6-4	277	1/5/61	2	Middle Tennessee State	Dover, Tenn.	FA-'86	16/1
33	†Clark, Jessie	RB	6-0	228	1/3/60	5	Arkansas	Crossett, Ark.	D7-'83	5/1
36	Davis, Kenneth	RB	5-10	209	4/16/62	2	Texas Christian	Temple, Tex.	D2-'86	16/6
10	Del Greco, Al	K	5-10	191	3/2/62	4	Auburn	Coral Gables, Fla.	FA-'84	16/0
56	Dent, Burnell	LB	6-1	236	3/16/63	2	Tulane	St. Rose, La.	D6-'86	16/1
99	Dorsey, John	LB	6-2	243	8/31/60	4	Connecticut	Leonardtown, Md.	D4-'84	16/9
42	Ellerson, Gary	RB	5-11	219	7/17/63	3	Wisconsin	Albany, Ga.	D7b-'85	16/6
31	†Ellis, Gerry	RB	5-11	235	11/12/57	8	Missouri	Columbia, Mo.	FA-'80	16/6
85	Epps, Phillip	WR	5-10	165	11/11/59	5	Texas Christian	Atlanta, Tex.	D12-'82	12/12
77	Feasel, Greg	T	6-7	301	11/7/58	2	Abilene Christian	Barstow, Calif.	FA-'86	15/0
84	Franz, Nolan	WR	6-2	183	9/11/59	2	Tulane	Metairie, La.	FA-'86	1/0
4	Fusina, Chuck	QB	6-1	195	5/31/57	5	Penn State	McKees Rock, Pa.	FA-'86	7/0
23	Greene, George	CB-S	6-0	194	2/15/62	3	Western Carolina	Hendersonville, N.C.	FA-'86	13/10
49	Greenwood, David	S	6-3	210	3/25/60	3	Wisconsin	Park Falls, Wis.	FA-'86	9/0
65	Hallstrom, Ron	G	6-6	290	6/11/59	6	Iowa	Moline, Ill.	D1-'82	16/16
97	Harris, Tim	LB	6-5	235	9/10/64	2	Memphis State	Birmingham, Ala.	D4a-'86	16/10
79	Humphrey, Donnie	DE	6-3	295	4/20/61	4	Auburn	Huntsville, Ala.	D3-'84	16/5
40	Ivery, Eddie Lee	WR-RB	6-0	206	7/30/57	8	Georgia Tech	Thomson, Ga.	D1-'79	12/1
90	Johnson, Ezra	DE	6-4	264	10/2/55	11	Morris Brown	Shreveport, La.	D1b-'77	16/0
22	†Lee, Mark	CB	5-11	189	3/20/58	8	Washington	Hanford, Calif.	D2-'80	16/16
53	Leopold, Bobby	LB	6-1	224	10/18/57	6	Notre Dame	Port Arthur, Tex.	FA-'86	12/7
89	Lewis, Mark	TE	6-2	237	5/5/61	3	Texas A&M	Houston, Tex.	D6-'85	16/1
94	Martin, Charles	DE	6-4	280	8/31/59	4	Livingston	Canton, Ga.	FA-'84	14/11
82	Moffitt, Mike	TE	6-4	211	7/28/63	2	Fresno State	Los Angeles, Calif.	FA-'86	4/0
57	Moran, Rich	C-G	6-2	275	3/19/62	3	San Diego State	Pleasanton, Calif.	D3-'85	5/1
37	Murphy, Mark	S	6-2	201	4/22/58	6	West Liberty	Canton, Ohio	FA-'84	0*
72	Neville, Tom	T-G	6-5	306	9/4/61	2	Fresno State	Salcha, Ark.	FA-'86	16/15
91	Noble, Brian	LB	6-3	252	9/6/62	3	Arizona State	Anaheim, Calif.	D5-'85	16/16
13	Renner, Bill	P	6-0	198	5/23/59	2	Virginia Tech	Springfield, Va.	FA-'86	3/0
81	Ross, Dan	TE	6-4	240	2/9/57	8	Northeastern	Everett, Mass.	T(Sea)-'86	15/10
75	Ruettgers, Ken	T	6-5	280	8/20/62	3	Southern California	Bakersfield, Calif.	D1-'85	16/16
55	Scott, Randy	LB	6-1	228	1/31/59	6	Alabama	Decatur, Ga.	FA-'81	15/15
18	Shield, Joe	QB	6-1	185	6/26/62	2	Trinity College	Brattleboro, Vt.	FA-'86	3/0
32	Simmons, John	CB-KR	5-11	192	12/1/58	7	Southern Methodist	Little Rock, Ark.	W(Cin)-'86	16/0*
87	Stanley, Walter	WR-KR	5-9	179	11/5/62	3	Mesa, Colo.	Chicago, Ill.	D4-'85	16/4
29	†Stills, Ken	CB-S	5-10	186	9/6/63	3	Wisconsin	Oceanside, Calif.	D8-'85	16/10
67	Swanke, Karl	T-C	6-6	262	12/29/57	8	Boston College	Newington, Conn.	D6-'80	10/8
92	Thomas, Ben	DE-NT	6-4	275	7/2/61	3	Auburn	Ashburn, Ga.	W(NE)-'86	13/0*
70	Uecker, Keith	G-T	6-5	284	6/29/60	5	Auburn	Hollywood, Fla.	W(Den)-'84	0*
73	Veingrad, Alan	T-G	6-5	277	7/24/63	2	East Texas State	Miami, Fla.	FA-'86	16/16
28	Watts, Elbert	CB	6-1	205	3/20/63	2	Southern California	Carson, Calif.	W(Rams)-'86	9/0
52	Weddington, Mike	LB	6-4	245	10/9/60	2	Oklahoma	Temple, Tex.	FA-'86	3/0
86	West, Ed	TE	6-1	243	8/2/61	4	Auburn	Leighton, Ala.	FA-'84	16/6
16	†Wright, Randy	QB	6-2	203	1/12/61	4	Wisconsin	St. Charles, Ill.	D6-'84	16/16

* Murphy and Uecker missed '86 season due to injury; Simmons played 10 games with Cincinnati in '86, 6 with Green Bay; Thomas played four games with New England, 9 with Green Bay.

†Option playout; subject to developments.

Traded—Wide receiver James Lofton to L.A. Raiders.

Also played with Packers in '86—NT Jerry Boyarsky (2 games), QB Vince Ferragamo (3), S Tom Flynn (7), CB-S Gary Hayes (10), DE Matt Koart (6), CB Tim Lewis (3), WR Phil McConkey (4), G Ruben Mendoza (6), DE Kurt Ploeger (1), LB Jeff Schuh (12), S John Sullivan (6), LB Mike Turpin (1).

COACHING STAFF

Head Coach, Forrest Gregg

Pro Career: Named Packers head coach on December 26, 1983, after compiling 34-27 record as Cincinnati's coach from 1980-83, including 1981 AFC Central title and Super Bowl XVI appearance. Was previously head coach of Cleveland Browns, where he compiled an 18-23 record from 1975-77, including 9-5 record in 1976. Also was head coach of Toronto Argonauts (CFL) in 1979 before signing to take over Bengals. Served as an NFL assistant coach from 1972-74. He was offensive line coach with San Diego Chargers in 1972-73 before joining Cleveland Browns in same capacity in 1974. Had outstanding 15-year playing career in NFL as a guard-tackle with Green Bay Packers 1956-70 (he played in the Packers' two Super Bowl wins) and as a player-coach with Dallas Cowboys in Super Bowl championship season of 1971. Inducted into the Pro Football Hall of Fame in 1977. Career record: 72-78.

Background: Tackle at Southern Methodist 1953-55. Twice named to the All-Southwest Conference team. Captain of the SMU team his senior year. Spent 1957 in military service.

Personal: Born October 18, 1933, in Birthright, Tex. Attended Sulphur Springs (Tex.) High School. He and his wife, Barbara, live in Green Bay and have two children—Forrest, Jr., and Karen.

Assistant Coaches

Tom Coughlin, passing game-wide receivers; born August 31, 1946, Waterloo, N.Y., lives in Green Bay. Halfback Syracuse 1965-67. No pro playing experience. College coach: Rochester Tech (head coach) 1969-73, Syracuse 1974-80, Boston College 1981-83. Pro coach: Philadelphia Eagles 1984-85, joined Packers in 1986.

Forrest Gregg, Jr., administrative assistant-defense; born February 23, 1962, Dallas, Tex., lives in Green Bay. Center Southern Methodist 1984. No pro playing experience. Pro coach: Joined Packers in 1986.

Dick Jauron, defensive backfield; born October 7, 1950, Swampscott, Mass., lives in Green Bay. Defensive back Yale 1970-72. Pro defensive back Detroit Lions 1973-77, Cincinnati Bengals 1978-80. Pro coach: Buffalo Bills 1985, joined Packers in 1986.

Virgil Knight, strength-conditioning; born January 30, 1948, Clarksville, Ark., lives in Green Bay. Tight end Northeastern Oklahoma 1968-70. No pro playing experience. College coach: Arkansas Tech 1975-78, Florida 1979-80, Auburn 1981-83. Pro coach: Joined Packers in 1985.

Dale Lindsey, linebackers; born January 18, 1943, Bowling Green, Ky., lives in Green Bay. Linebacker Western Kentucky 1961-64. Pro linebacker Cleveland Browns 1965-73. Pro coach: Cleveland Browns 1974, Portland Storm (WFL) 1975, Toronto Argonauts (CFL) 1979-82, Boston Breakers (USFL) 1983, New Jersey Generals (USFL) 1984-85, joined Packers in 1986.

Dick Modzelewski, defensive coordinator-defensive line; born January 16, 1931, West Natrona, Pa., lives in Green Bay. Tackle Maryland 1950-52. Pro defensive tackle Washington Redskins 1953-54, Pittsburgh Steelers 1955, New York Giants 1956-63, Cleveland Browns 1964-66. Pro coach: Cleveland Browns 1968-77, New York Giants 1978, Cincinnati Bengals 1979-83, joined Packers in 1984.

Willie Peete, offensive backfield-special teams coordinator; born July 14, 1937, Mesa, Ariz., lives in Green Bay. Tight end-defensive end Arizona 1956-59. No pro playing experience. College coach: Arizona 1960-62, 1971-82. Pro coach: Kansas City Chiefs 1983-86, first year with Packers.

George Sefcik, quarterbacks; born December 27, 1939, Cleveland, Ohio, lives in Green Bay. Halfback Notre Dame 1959-61. No pro playing experience. College coach: Notre Dame 1963-68, Kentucky 1969-72. Pro coach: Baltimore Colts 1973-74, Cleveland Browns 1975-77, Cincinnati Bengals 1978-83, joined Packers in 1984.

Jerry Wampfler, offensive line; born August 6, 1932, New Philadelphia, Ohio, lives in Green Bay. Tackle Miami, Ohio 1951-54. No pro playing experience. College coach: Presbyterian 1955, Miami, Ohio 1963-65, Notre Dame 1966-69, Colorado State 1970-72 (head coach). Pro coach: Philadelphia Eagles 1973-75, 1979-83, Buffalo Bills 1976-77, New York Giants 1978, joined Packers in 1984.

Green Bay Packers 1987 First-Year Roster

Name	Pos.	Ht.	Wt.	Birth-date	College	Hometown	How Acq.
Byrd, Sylvester (1)	TE-LB	6-2	240	5/1/63	Kansas	Kansas City, Kan.	FA
Carr, Carl (1)	LB	6-4	232	3/26/64	North Carolina	Alexandria, Va.	FA
Carter, Thomas (1)	LB	6-2	240	2/5/61	San Diego State	San Fernando, Calif.	FA
Croston, Dave	T	6-5	280	11/10/63	Iowa	Sioux City, Iowa	D3a
Drost, Jeff	DT	6-5	286	1/27/64	Iowa	Indianola, Iowa	D8
Fitzgerald, Patrick (1)	WR	6-3	197	10/13/63	Boise State	Boise, Idaho	FA
Freeman, Lorenzo	DT	6-5	255	5/23/64	Pittsburgh	East Camden, N.J.	D4
Fullwood, Brent	RB	5-11	209	10/10/63	Auburn	St. Cloud, Fla.	D1
Garrett, Curtis (1)	DE-NT	6-6	270	6/9/62	Illinois State	Harvey, Ill.	FA
Harris, Gregg	G	6-4	279	4/8/66	Wake Forest	Norfolk, Va.	D9
Holland, Johnny	LB	6-2	221	3/11/65	Texas A&M	Hempstead, Tex.	D2
Jefferson, Norman	CB-S	5-10	183	8/7/64	Louisiana State	Marrero, La.	D12
Johnson, Kenneth	CB	6-0	185	12/28/63	Mississippi State	Weir, Miss.	FA
Leiker, Tony	NT	6-5	250	9/26/64	Stanford	Silver Lake, Kan.	D7a
Marshall, Willie	WR	6-1	190	5/23/64	Temple	Browns Mill, N.J.	D6
Majkowski, Don	QB	6-2	197	2/25/64	Virginia	Depew, N.Y.	D10
Neal, Frankie	WR	6-1	202	10/1/65	Fort Hays State	Okeechobee, Fla.	D3c
Robison, Tommy	T	6-4	290	11/17/61	Texas A&M	Gregory, Tex.	T(Clev)-'85
Scott, Pat	WR	5-10	170	9/13/64	Grambling	Ringgold, La.	D11
Stephen, Scott	LB	6-2	232	6/18/64	Arizona State	Los Angeles, Calif.	D3b
Smith, Bill	P	6-3	222	6/9/65	Mississippi	Little Rock, Ark.	D7b
Sullivan, Carl (1)	DE	6-4	248	4/30/62	San Jose State	San Jose, Calif.	FA
Thomas, Lavale (1)	RB	6-0	205	12/12/63	Fresno State	Tulare, Calif.	FA

The term NFL Rookie is defined as a player who is in his first season of professional football and has not been on the roster of another professional football team for any regular-season or postseason games. A Rookie is designated by an "R" on NFL rosters. Players who have been active in another professional football league or players who have NFL experience, including either preseason training camp or being on an active roster for fewer than three regular-season or postseason games, are termed NFL First-Year Players. An NFL First-Year Player is designated by a "1" on NFL rosters. Thereafter, a player on an NFL active roster for at least three regular-season or postseason games is credited with an additional year of NFL playing experience.

NOTES

LOS ANGELES RAMS

National Football Conference
Western Division

Team Colors: Royal Blue, Gold, and White

Business Address:
2327 West Lincoln Avenue
Anaheim, California 92801

Ticket Office:
Anaheim Stadium
1900 State College Boulevard
Anaheim, California 92806
Telephone: (714) 535-7267
or (213) 585-5400

Club Officials

President: Georgia Frontiere
Vice President, Finance: John Shaw
General Counsel: Jay Zygmunt
Administrator, Football Operations: Jack Faulkner
Director of Operations: Dick Beam
Director of Player Personnel: John Math
Administrative Assistant/Consultant: Paul (Tank) Younger
Administration: Jack Youngblood
Director of Community Relations: Marshall Klein
Director of Administration: Barbara Robinson
Director of Promotions/Sales: Pete Donovan
Directors of Public Relations: John Oswald, Jerry Wilcox
Public Relations Assistant: Doug Ward
Trainers: George Menefee, Jim Anderson, Garrett Giemont
Equipment Manager: Don Hewitt
Assistant Equipment Manager: Todd Hewitt

Stadium: Anaheim Stadium • **Capacity:** 69,007
Anaheim, California 92806

Playing Surface: Grass

Training Camp: California State University
Fullerton, California 92634

1987 Schedule

Preseason

Aug. 9	vs. Denver at London, Eng.	6:00
Aug. 13	**Seattle**	7:30
Aug. 23	at San Diego	5:00
Aug. 29	**Denver**	7:00
Sept. 3	Minnesota	6:00

Regular Season

Sept. 13	at Houston	12:00
Sept. 20	**Minnesota**	1:00
Sept. 27	**Cincinnati**	1:00
Oct. 4	at New Orleans	12:00
Oct. 11	**Pittsburgh**	1:00
Oct. 18	at Atlanta	1:00
Oct. 26	at Cleveland (Monday)	9:00
Nov. 1	**San Francisco**	1:00
Nov. 8	**New Orleans**	1:00
Nov. 15	at St. Louis	12:00
Nov. 23	at Washington (Monday)	9:00
Nov. 29	**Tampa Bay**	1:00
Dec. 6	at Detroit	1:00
Dec. 13	**Atlanta**	1:00
Dec. 21	**Dallas** (Monday)	6:00
Dec. 27	at San Francisco	5:00

Rams Coaching History

Cleveland 1937-45
(359-290-20)

1937-38	Hugo Bezdek*	1-13-0
1938	Art Lewis	4-4-0
1939-42	Earl (Dutch) Clark	16-26-2
1944	Aldo (Buff) Donelli	4-6-0
1945-46	Adam Walsh	16-5-1
1947	Bob Snyder	6-6-0
1948-49	Clark Shaughnessy	14-8-3
1950-52	Joe Stydahar**	19-9-0
1952-54	Hamp Pool	23-11-2
1955-59	Sid Gillman	28-32-1
1960-62	Bob Waterfield***	9-24-1
1962-65	Harland Svare	14-31-3
1966-70	George Allen	49-19-4
1971-72	Tommy Prothro	14-12-2
1973-77	Chuck Knox	57-20-1
1978-82	Ray Malavasi	43-36-0
1983-86	John Robinson	42-28-0

*Released after three games in 1938
**Resigned after one game in 1952
***Resigned after eight games in 1962

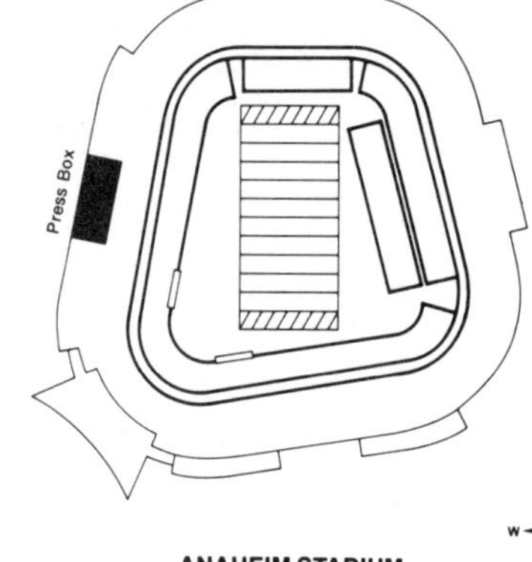

ANAHEIM STADIUM

Record Holders

Individual Records—Career

Category	Name	Performance
Rushing (Yds.)	Eric Dickerson, 1983-86	6,968
Passing (Yds.)	Roman Gabriel, 1962-1972	22,223
Passing (TDs)	Roman Gabriel, 1962-1972	154
Receiving (No.)	Tom Fears, 1948-1956	400
Receiving (Yds.)	Elroy (Crazylegs) Hirsch, 1949-1957	6,289
Interceptions	Ed Meador, 1959-1970	46
Punting (Avg.)	Danny Villanueva, 1960-64	44.2
Punt Return (Avg.)	Henry Ellard, 1983-86	12.9
Kickoff Return (Avg.)	Tom Wilson, 1956-1961	27.1
Field Goals	Bruce Gossett, 1964-69	120
Touchdowns (Tot.)	Eric Dickerson, 1983-86	57
Points	Bob Waterfield, 1946-1952	573

Individual Records—Single Season

Category	Name	Performance
Rushing (Yds.)	Eric Dickerson, 1984	2,105
Passing (Yds.)	Vince Ferragamo, 1983	3,276
Passing (TDs)	Vince Ferragamo, 1980	30
Receiving (No.)	Tom Fears, 1950	84
Receiving (Yds.)	Elroy (Crazylegs) Hirsch, 1951	1,425
Interceptions	Dick (Night Train) Lane, 1952	14
Punting (Avg.)	Danny Villanueva, 1962	45.5
Punt Return (Avg.)	Woodley Lewis, 1952	18.5
Kickoff Return (Avg.)	Verda (Vitamin T) Smith, 1950	33.7
Field Goals	David Ray, 1973	30
Touchdowns (Tot.)	Eric Dickerson, 1983	20
Points	David Ray, 1973	130

Individual Records—Single Game

Category	Name	Performance
Rushing (Yds.)	Eric Dickerson, 1-4-86	248
Passing (Yds.)	Norm Van Brocklin, 9-28-51	554
Passing (TDs)	Many times	5
	Last time by Vince Ferragamo, 10-23-83	
Receiving (No.)	Tom Fears, 12-3-50	18
Receiving (Yds.)	Jim Benton, 11-22-45	303
Interceptions	Many times	3
	Last time by Pat Thomas, 10-7-79	
Field Goals	Bob Waterfield, 12-9-51	5
Touchdowns (Tot.)	Bob Shaw, 12-11-49	4
	Elroy (Crazylegs) Hirsch, 9-28-51	4
	Harold Jackson, 10-14-73	4
Points	Bob Shaw, 12-11-49	24
	Elroy (Crazylegs) Hirsch, 9-28-51	24
	Harold Jackson, 10-14-73	24

1986 Team Statistics

	Rams	Opp.
Total First Downs	269	272
Rushing	139	93
Passing	105	169
Penalty	25	10
Third Down: Made/Att.	74/222	70/226
Fourth Down: Made/Att.	3/8	8/17
Total Net Yards	4653	4871
Avg. Per Game	290.8	304.4
Total Plays	1008	1038
Avg. Per Play	4.6	4.7
Net Yards Rushing	2457	1681
Avg. Per Game	153.6	105.1
Total Rushes	578	460
Net Yards Passing	2196	3190
Avg. Per Game	137.3	199.4
Tackled/Yards Lost	27/184	39/292
Gross Yards	2380	3482
Att./Completions	403/194	539/313
Completion Pct.	48.1	58.1
Had Intercepted	15	28
Punts/Avg.	98/38.2	96/41.4
Net Punting Avg.	32.9	36.2
Penalties/Yards Lost	84/603	92/804
Fumbles/Ball Lost	39/22	25/15
Touchdowns	37	28
Rushing	16	9
Passing	15	17
Returns	6	2
Avg. Time of Possession	29:41	30:19

1986 Team Record

Preseason (2-2)

Date	Result		Opponents
8/5	L	14-17	Houston
8/18	W	31-17	San Francisco
8/23	W	20-17	San Diego (OT)
8/29	L	10-19	at Denver
		75-70	

Regular Season (10-6)

Date	Result		Opponents	Att.
9/7	W	16-10	at St. Louis	40,347
9/14	W	16-13	San Francisco	65,195
9/21	W	27- 7	at Indianapolis	59,012
9/28	L	20-34	at Philadelphia	65,646
10/5	W	26-20	Tampa Bay (OT)	50,585
10/12	L	14-26	at Atlanta	51,662
10/19	W	14-10	Detroit	50,992
10/26	W	14- 7	Atlanta	56,993
11/3	W	20-17	at Chicago	64,877
11/9	L	0- 6	at New Orleans	62,352
11/16	L	28-30	New England	64,339
11/23	W	26-13	New Orleans	58,600
11/30	W	17- 3	at N.Y. Jets	70,539
12/7	W	29-10	Dallas	64,949
12/14	L	31-37	Miami (OT)	62,629
12/19	L	14-24	at San Francisco	60,366

Postseason (0-1)

Date	Result		Opponents	Att.
12/28	L	7-19	at Washington	54,567

(OT) Overtime

Score by Periods

Rams	59	98	72	74	6	—	309
Opponents	46	87	72	56	6	—	267

Attendance

Home 474,282 Away 474,801 Total 949,083
Single game home record, 102,368 (11-10-57; L.A. Coliseum), 67,037 (12-23-84; Anaheim Stadium)
Single season home record, 519,175 (1973; L.A. Coliseum), 500,403 (1980; Anaheim Stadium)

1986 Individual Statistics

Scoring	TD R	TD P	TD Rt	PAT	FG	Saf	TP
Lansford	0	0	0	34/35	17/24	0	85
Dickerson	11	0	0	0/0	0/0	0	66
Redden	4	1	0	0/0	0/0	0	30
Ellard	0	4	0	0/0	0/0	0	24
Brown	0	3	0	0/0	0/0	0	18
Irvin	0	0	3	0/0	0/0	0	18
Young	0	3	0	0/0	0/0	0	18
House	0	2	0	0/0	0/0	0	12
Cromwell	0	0	1	0/0	0/0	0	6
Duckworth	0	1	0	0/0	0/0	0	6
Everett	1	0	0	0/0	0/0	0	6
D. Hill	0	1	0	0/0	0/0	0	6
Jerue	0	0	1	0/0	0/0	0	6
Newberry	0	0	1	0/0	0/0	0	6
Jeter	0	0	0	0/0	0/0	1	2
Rams	16	15	6	34/36	17/24	1	309
Opponents	9	17	2	27/27	24/31	0	267

Passing	Att.	Comp.	Yds.	Pct.	TD	Int.	Tkld.	Rate
Everett	147	73	1018	49.7	8	8	8/50	67.8
Dils	129	59	693	45.7	4	4	7/44	60.0
Bartkowski	126	61	654	48.4	2	3	11/84	59.4
Dickerson	1	1	15	100.0	1	0	0/0	158.3
House	0	0	0	—	0	0	1/6	0.0
Rams	403	194	2380	48.1	15	15	27/184	63.7
Opponents	539	313	3482	58.1	17	28	39/292	66.3

Rushing	Att.	Yds.	Avg.	LG	TD
Dickerson	404	1821	4.5	42t	11
Redden	110	467	4.2	41t	4
White	22	126	5.7	19	0
Everett	16	46	2.9	14	1
Brown	4	5	1.3	11	0
Dils	10	5	0.5	5	0
House, T.B.-Rams	2	5	2.5	4	0
Bartkowski	6	3	0.5	7	0
Carpenter	2	3	1.5	3	0
Guman	2	2	1.0	3	0
Hunter	1	−6	−6.0	−6	0
Ellard	1	−15	−15.0	−15	0
Rams	578	2457	4.3	42t	16
Opponents	460	1681	3.7	59t	9

Receiving	No.	Yds.	Avg.	LG	TD
Ellard	34	447	13.1	34t	4
Redden	28	217	7.8	24t	1
Dickerson	26	205	7.9	28	0
Brown	25	396	15.8	65t	3
House, T.B.-Rams	18	384	21.3	60t	2
House, Rams	7	178	25.4	60t	2
Hunter	15	206	13.7	42	0
Young	15	181	12.1	21	3
D. Hill	14	202	14.4	33	1
Duckworth	9	141	15.7	32	1
Guman	9	68	7.6	13	0
Scott	5	76	15.2	21	0
Long	5	47	9.4	13	0
Tyrrell	1	9	9.0	9	0
White	1	7	7.0	7	0
Rams	194	2380	12.3	65t	15
Opponents	313	3482	11.1	69t	17

Interceptions	No.	Yds.	Avg.	LG	TD
Gray	8	101	12.6	28	0
Irvin	6	150	25.0	50t	1
Cromwell	5	101	20.2	80t	1
Newsome	3	45	15.0	34	0
Sutton	2	25	12.5	20	0
Jerue	2	23	11.5	22t	1
J. Johnson	1	13	13.0	13	0
Wilcher	1	0	0.0	0	0
Rams	28	458	16.4	80t	3
Opponents	15	128	8.5	34	0

Punting	No.	Yds.	Avg.	In 20	LG
Hatcher	97	3740	38.6	26	57
Rams	98	3740	38.2	26	57
Opponents	96	3975	41.4	26	59

Punt Returns	No.	FC	Yds.	Avg.	LG	TD
Sutton	28	5	234	8.4	32	0
Ellard	14	10	127	9.1	20	0
J. Johnson	0	7	0	—	0	0
Rams	42	22	361	8.6	32	0
Opponents	47	30	416	8.9	32	0

Kickoff Returns	No.	Yds.	Avg.	LG	TD
Brown	36	794	22.1	55	0
White	12	216	18.0	28	0
Sutton	5	91	18.2	22	0
Carpenter	2	19	9.5	11	0
Guman	2	28	14.0	16	0
Ellard	1	18	18.0	18	0
Love	1	−6	−6.0	−6	0
Rams	59	1160	19.7	55	0
Opponents	64	1282	20.0	84	0

Sacks	No.
Jeter	8.0
Greene	7.0
Reed	6.5
Wilcher	5.5
Miller	5.0
Owens	4.0
Meisner	2.0
Ekern	1.0
Rams	39.0
Opponents	27.0

FIRST-ROUND SELECTIONS

(If club had no first-round selection, first player drafted is listed with round in parentheses.)

Since 1954

Year	Player, College, Position
1954	Ed Beatty, Cincinnati, C
1955	Larry Morris, Georgia Tech, C
1956	Joe Marconi, West Virginia, B
	Charles Horton, Vanderbilt, B
1957	Jon Arnett, Southern California, B
	Del Shofner, Baylor, E
1958	Lou Michaels, Kentucky, T
	Jim Phillips, Auburn, E
1959	Dick Bass, Pacific, B
	Paul Dickson, Baylor, T
1960	Billy Cannon, Louisiana State, RB
1961	Marlin McKeever, Southern California, E-LB
1962	Roman Gabriel, North Carolina State, QB
	Merlin Olsen, Utah State, DT
1963	Terry Baker, Oregon State, QB
	Rufus Guthrie, Georgia Tech, G
1964	Bill Munson, Utah State, QB
1965	Clancy Williams, Washington State, CB
1966	Tom Mack, Michigan, G
1967	Willie Ellison, Texas Southern, RB (2)
1968	Gary Beban, UCLA, QB (2)
1969	Larry Smith, Florida, RB
	Jim Seymour, Notre Dame, WR
	Bob Klein, Southern California, TE
1970	Jack Reynolds, Tennessee, LB
1971	Isiah Robertson, Southern, LB
	Jack Youngblood, Florida, DE
1972	Jim Bertelsen, Texas, RB (2)
1973	Cullen Bryant, Colorado, DB (2)
1974	John Cappelletti, Penn State, RB
1975	Mike Fanning, Notre Dame, DT
	Dennis Harrah, Miami, T
	Doug France, Ohio State, T
1976	Kevin McLain, Colorado State, LB
1977	Bob Brudzinski, Ohio State, LB
1978	Elvis Peacock, Oklahoma, RB
1979	George Andrews, Nebraska, LB
	Kent Hill, Georgia Tech, T
1980	Johnnie Johnson, Texas, DB
1981	Mel Owens, Michigan, LB
1982	Barry Redden, Richmond, RB
1983	Eric Dickerson, Southern Methodist, RB
1984	Hal Stephens, East Carolina, DE (5)
1985	Jerry Gray, Texas, DB
1986	Mike Schad, Queen's University, Canada, T
1987	Donald Evans, Winston-Salem, DE (2)

Los Angeles Rams 1987 Veteran Roster

No.	Name	Pos.	Ht.	Wt.	Birth-date	NFL Exp.	College	Hometown	How Acq.	'86 Games/ Starts
89	Brown, Ron	WR	5-11	181	3/31/61	4	Arizona State	Baldwin Park, Calif.	T(Clev)-'84	14/12
53	Busick, Steve	LB	6-4	227	12/10/58	7	Southern California	Temple City, Calif.	T(Den)-'86	4/1
50	†Collins, Jim	LB	6-2	230	6/11/58	6	Syracuse	Mendham, N.J.	D2-'81	0*
21	Cromwell, Nolan	S	6-1	200	1/30/55	11	Kansas	Ransom, Kan.	D2-'77	16/16
29	Dickerson, Eric	RB	6-3	220	9/2/60	5	Southern Methodist	Sealy, Tex.	D1-'83	16/16
8	Dils, Steve	QB	6-1	191	12/8/55	8	Stanford	Vancouver, Wash.	T(Minn)-'84	15/5
71	Doss, Reggie	DE	6-4	263	12/7/56	10	Hampton Institute	San Antonio, Tex.	D7-'78	16/16
55	Ekern, Carl	LB	6-3	230	5/27/54	11	San Jose State	Sunnyvale, Calif.	D5-'76	13/13
80	†Ellard, Henry	WR-KR	5-11	175	7/21/61	5	Fresno State	Fresno, Calif.	D2-'83	9/8
11	Everett, Jim	QB	6-5	212	1/3/63	2	Purdue	Albuquerque, N.M.	T(Hou)-'86	6/5
25	Gray, Jerry	CB	6-0	185	12/2/62	3	Texas	Lubbock, Tex.	D1-'85	16/16
91	Greene, Kevin	LB	6-3	238	7/31/62	3	Auburn	Anderson, Ala.	D5-'85	16/0
44	†Guman, Mike	RB	6-2	218	4/21/58	8	Penn State	Bethlehem, Pa.	D6-'80	12/3
60	Harrah, Dennis	G	6-5	265	3/9/53	13	Miami	Charleston, W. Va.	D1b-'75	16/16
3	Hatcher, Dale	P	6-2	200	4/5/63	3	Clemson	Cheraw, S.C.	D3-'85	16/0
81	Hill, David	TE	6-2	240	1/1/54	12	Texas A&I	San Antonio, Tex.	T(Det)-'83	16/15
83	House, Kevin	WR	6-1	185	12/20/57	8	Southern Illinois	St. Louis, Mo.	W(TB)-'86	15/10*
87	†Hunter, Tony	TE	6-4	237	5/22/60	5	Notre Dame	Cincinnati, Ohio	T(Buff)-'85	7/1
47	Irvin, LeRoy	CB	5-11	184	9/15/57	8	Kansas	Augusta, Ga.	D5-'80	16/15
59	Jerue, Mark	LB	6-3	232	1/15/60	5	Washington	Seattle, Wash.	T(Ind)-'83	16/16
77	Jeter, Gary	DE	6-4	260	3/24/55	11	Southern California	Cleveland, Ohio	T(NYG)-'83	15/0
86	Johnson, Damone	TE	6-4	230	3/2/62	2	Cal Poly-SLO	Santa Monica, Calif.	D6-'85	5/0
20	†Johnson, Johnnie	S	6-1	183	10/8/56	8	Texas	LaGrange, Tex.	D1-'80	16/5
1	†Lansford, Mike	K	6-0	183	7/20/58	6	Washington	Arcadia, Calif.	FA-'82	16/0
45	Long, Darren	TE	6-3	240	7/12/59	2	Long Beach State	Exeter, Calif.	FA-'86	4/0
67	†Love, Duval	G	6-3	263	6/24/63	3	UCLA	Fountain Valley, Calif.	D10-'85	16/0
14	McIvor, Rick	WR-RB	6-4	210	9/26/60	3	Texas	Ft. Davis, Tex.	FA-'87	0*
69	Meisner, Greg	NT	6-3	253	4/23/59	7	Pittsburgh	New Kensington, Pa.	D3-'81	15/0
98	Miller, Shawn	NT	6-4	255	3/14/61	4	Utah State	Ogden, Utah	FA-'84	16/16
66	Newberry, Tom	G	6-2	279	12/20/62	2	Wisconsin-LaCrosse	Onalaska, Wis.	D2-'86	16/14
22	†Newsome, Vince	S	6-1	179	1/22/61	5	Washington	Vacaville, Calif.	D4-'83	16/12
58	Owens, Mel	LB	6-2	224	12/7/58	7	Michigan	Detroit, Mich.	D1-'81	16/16
75	†Pankey, Irv	T	6-4	267	12/15/58	7	Penn State	Aberdeen, Pa.	D2-'80	16/16
30	†Redden, Barry	RB	5-10	205	7/21/60	6	Richmond	Sarasota, Fla.	D1-'82	15/14
93	Reed, Doug	DE	6-3	262	7/16/60	4	San Diego State	San Diego, Calif.	D4-'83	16/10
84	Scott, Chuck	WR	6-2	202	5/24/63	2	Vanderbilt	Maitland, Fla.	D2-'85	9/0
78	Slater, Jackie	T	6-4	271	5/27/54	12	Jackson State	Meridian, Miss.	D3-'76	16/16
61	Slaton, Tony	C	6-3	265	4/12/61	4	Southern California	Merced, Calif.	FA-'84	14/0
56	Smith, Doug	C	6-3	260	11/25/56	10	Bowling Green	Columbus, Ohio	FA-'78	16/16
49	Sutton, Mickey	CB	5-8	165	8/28/60	2	Montana	Union City, Calif.	FA-'86	16/0
52	Thrift, Cliff	LB	6-2	235	5/3/56	9	East Central Oklahoma	Dallas, Tex.	FA-'86	12/0
32	Tyrrell, Tim	RB	6-1	201	2/19/61	4	Northern Illinois	Hoffman Estates, Ill.	FA-'86	9/1*
51	†Vann, Norwood	LB	6-2	225	2/18/62	4	East Carolina	Magnolia, S.C.	D10-'84	16/0
33	White, Charles	RB	5-10	190	1/22/58	7	Southern California	San Fernando, Calif.	FA-'85	16/0
54	†Wilcher, Mike	LB	6-3	240	3/20/60	5	North Carolina	Washington, D.C.	D2-'83	16/16
99	Wright, Alvin	NT	6-2	285	2/5/61	2	Jacksonville State	Nedonee, Ala.	FA-'86	4/0
88	†Young, Michael	WR	6-1	185	2/2/62	3	UCLA	Visalia, Calif.	D6-'85	16/1

* Collins missed '86 season due to injury; House played 7 games with Tampa Bay in '86, 8 with Rams; McIvor last active with St. Louis in '85; Tyrrell played 3 games with Atlanta, 6 with Rams.

†Option playout; subject to developments.

Retired—Quarterback Steve Bartkowski, 12-year veteran, 6 games in '86.

Also played with Rams in '86— RB Rob Carpenter (6 games), NT Charles DeJurnett (7), WR Bobby Duckworth (7), CB Herman Edwards (4), S Tim Fox (14), G Kent Hill (2), LB Jim Laughlin (16), LB Mike McDonald (13), WR Mark Pattison (1).

COACHING STAFF

Head Coach, John Robinson

Pro Career: Enters fifth season as Rams head coach. Guided Rams to a 10-6 record and berth in NFC Wild Card Game in 1986. Has taken Rams to playoffs four straight years. Became seventeenth head coach in Rams history on February 14, 1983. Arrived with 23 years of coaching experience, including one on professional level with the Raiders in 1975. No pro playing experience. Career record: 42-28.

Background: Played end at Oregon 1955-58. Began coaching career with his alma mater from 1960-71. Became an assistant at Southern California from 1972-74. Returned as head coach in 1976 before resigning after the 1982 season. Compiled seven-year .819 winning percentage at Southern California with 67 wins, 14 losses, and 2 ties.

Personal: Born July 25, 1935, in Chicago, Ill. John and his wife, Barbara, live in Fullerton, Calif., and have four children—Teresa, Lynn, David, and Christopher.

Assistant Coaches

Larry Brooks, assistant defensive line; born June 10, 1950, Prince George, Va., lives in Fountain Valley, Calif. Defensive tackle Virginia State 1968-71. Pro defensive tackle Los Angeles Rams 1972-82. Pro coach: Joined Rams in 1983.

Dick Coury, quarterbacks; born September 29, 1929, Athens, Ohio, lives in Anaheim, Calif. No college or pro playing experience. College coach: Southern California 1965-67, Cal State-Fullerton 1968-70 (head coach). Pro coach: Denver Broncos 1971-73, Portland Storm (WFL) 1974 (head coach), San Diego Chargers 1975, Philadelphia Eagles 1976-81, Boston/Portland Breakers (USFL) 1983-85 (head coach), joined Rams in 1986.

Artie Gigantino, special teams; born June 14, 1951, Edison, N.J., lives in Long Beach, Calif. Linebacker Bridgeport 1969-72. College coach: California 1973-78, Southern California 1979-86. Pro coach: First year with Rams.

Marv Goux, defensive line; born September 8, 1932, Santa Barbara, Calif., lives in Long Beach, Calif. Linebacker Southern California 1952, 1954-55. No pro playing experience. College coach: Southern California 1957-82. Pro coach: Joined Rams in 1983.

Gil Haskell, running backs; born September 24, 1943, San Francisco, Calif., lives in Diamond Bar, Calif. Defensive back San Francisco State 1961, 1963-65. No pro playing experience. College coach: Southern California 1978-82. Pro coach: Joined Rams in 1983.

Hudson Houck, offensive line; born January 7, 1943, Los Angeles, Calif., lives in Long Beach, Calif. Center Southern California 1962-64. No pro playing experience. College coach: Southern California 1970-72, 1976-82, Stanford 1973-75. Pro coach: Joined Rams in 1983.

Steve Shafer, defensive backs; born December 8, 1940, Glendale, Calif., lives in Anaheim, Calif. Quarterback-defensive back Utah State 1961-62. Pro defensive back British Columbia Lions (CFL) 1963-67. College coach: San Mateo, Calif., J.C. 1968-74 (head coach 1973-74), San Diego State 1975-82. Pro coach: Joined Rams in 1983.

Fritz Shurmur, defensive coordinator-inside linebackers; born July 15, 1932, Riverview, Mich., lives in Diamond Bar, Calif. Center Albion 1951-53. No pro playing experience. College coach: Albion 1956-61, Wyoming 1962-74 (head coach 1971-74). Pro coach: Detroit Lions 1975-77, New England Patriots 1978-81, joined Rams in 1982.

Norval Turner, tight ends-wide receivers; born May 17, 1952, Martinez, Calif., lives in Long Beach, Calif. Quarterback Oregon 1972-74. No pro playing experience. College coach: Oregon 1975, Southern California 1976-84. Pro coach: Joined Rams in 1985.

Los Angeles Rams 1987 First-Year Roster

Name	Pos.	Ht.	Wt.	Birth-date	College	Hometown	How Acq.
Bartlett, Doug	LB	6-2	257	2/22/57	Northern Illinois	Springfield, Ill.	D4a
Bowman, Barry	P	6-0	185	12/18/64	Louisiana Tech	Longview, Tex.	FA
Borland, Kyle	LB	6-3	232	7/5/61	Wisconsin	Fort Atkinson, Wis.	FA
Brown, Kevin	QB	6-2	208	7/7/64	California	Glendale, Calif.	FA
Brown, Lloyd	T	6-8	305	12/7/62	St. Mary's, Calif.	Vallejo, Calif.	FA
Byrne, James (1)	T	6-3	280	12/30/59	Wisconsin-LaCrosse	Gloversville, N.Y.	FA
Cox, Robert (1)	T	6-5	258	12/30/63	UCLA	Dublin, Calif.	D6a-'86
Embree, Jon	TE	6-2	230	10/15/65	Colorado	Cherry Creek, Colo.	D6
Emery, Rod	RB	5-9	175	2/9/64	Nevada-Las Vegas	Fountain Valley, Calif.	FA
Evans, Donald	DE	6-2	262	3/14/64	Winston-Salem	Raleigh, N.C.	D2
Goebel, Hank (1)	T	6-7	270	11/1/64	Cal State-Fullerton	Newport Beach, Calif.	D8b-'85
Ham, Tracy	RB	5-11	187	1/5/64	Georgia Southern	High Springs, Fla.	D9
Hampton, Kwante	WR	6-1	178	12/11/63	Long Beach State	Van Nuys, Calif.	FA
Hannemann, Clifford	LB	6-2	230	10/21/64	Fresno State	Fresno, Calif.	FA
Haynes, Tommy	CB-S	6-1	200	2/6/63	Southern California	Covina, Calif.	FA
Hicks, Cliff	CB	5-10	188	8/18/64	Oregon	San Diego, Calif.	D3
Kelm, Larry	LB	6-4	226	11/29/64	Texas A&M	Corpus Christi, Tex.	D4
Laughton, James	LB	6-5	230	1/18/60	San Diego State	Salinas, Calif.	FA
Marks, Steve	WR	5-10	175	7/5/64	U.C. Santa Barbara	Woodland, Calif.	FA
Mersereau, Scott	NT	6-4	275	4/8/65	So. Connecticut State	Riverhead, N.Y.	D5
Millen, Hugh (1)	QB	6-4	216	11/22/63	Washington	Seattle, Wash.	D3-'86
Power, Jim (1)	K	6-0	180	8/7/60	Southern California	Palos Verdes, Calif.	FA
Richardson, Reggie (1)	S	6-0	170	4/13/63	Utah	Gardena, Calif.	FA
Riley, Eric	CB	6-0	177	8/15/62	Florida State	Fort Myers, Fla.	FA
Schad, Mike (1)	G	6-5	290	10/4/63	Queen's U., Canada	Belleville, Ontario	D1-'86
Schamel, Duke (1)	LB	6-2	220	11/3/63	South Dakota	Tulelake, Calif.	FA
Smith, David	LB	6-6	235	3/14/65	Northern Arizona	Yerington, Nev.	D10
Stewart, Michael	S	5-11	195	7/12/65	Fresno State	Bakersfield, Calif.	D8
Stokes, Fred	DE	6-3	253	3/14/64	Georgia Southern	Vidalia, Ga.	D12b
Templeton, Mark	RB	6-1	205	8/29/63	Long Beach State	Santa Ana, Calif.	FA
Tinsley, Keith	WR	5-9	190	3/31/65	Pittsburgh	Detroit, Mich.	FA
Williams, Alonzo	RB	5-9	190	8/9/63	Mesa, Colo.	Inglewood, Calif.	D12a

The term NFL Rookie is defined as a player who is in his first season of professional football and has not been on the roster of another professional football team for any regular-season or postseason games. A Rookie is designated by an "R" on NFL rosters. Players who have been active in another professional football league or players who have NFL experience, including either preseason training camp or being on an active roster for fewer than three regular-season or postseason games, are termed NFL First-Year Players. An NFL First-Year Player is designated by a "1" on NFL rosters. Thereafter, a player on an NFL active roster for at least three regular-season or postseason games is credited with an additional year of NFL playing experience.

NOTES

Fred Whittingham, outside linebackers; born February 4, 1942, Boston, Mass., lives in Anaheim, Calif. Linebacker Cal Poly-SLO 1960-62. Pro linebacker Los Angeles Rams 1964, Philadelphia Eagles 1965-66, 1971, New Orleans Saints 1967-68, Dallas Cowboys 1969-70. College coach: Brigham Young 1973-81. Pro coach: Joined Rams in 1982.

Ernie Zampese, offensive coordinator; born March 12, 1936, Santa Barbara, Calif., lives in Anaheim, Calif. Halfback Southern California 1956-58. No pro playing experience. College coach: Hancock, Calif., J.C. 1962-65, Cal Poly-SLO 1966, San Diego State 1967-75. Pro coach: San Diego Chargers 1976, 1979-86, first year with Rams.

National Football Conference
Central Division

Team Colors: Purple, Gold, and White

9520 Viking Drive
Eden Prairie, Minnesota 55344
Telephone: (612) 828-6500

Club Officials

Chairman of the Board: John Skoglund
President: Max Winter
Senior Vice President: Jack Steele
Secretary/Treasurer: Sheldon Kaplan
Executive Vice President/General Manager: Mike Lynn
Assistant to the General Manager/Director of Operations: Jeff Diamond
Director of Administration: Harley Peterson
Ticket Manager: Harry Randolph
Director of Football Operations: Jerry Reichow
Director of Player Personnel: Frank Gilliam
Director of Pro Personnel: Bob Hollway
Head Scout: Ralph Kohl
Assistant Head Scout: Don Deisch
Regional Scout: John Carson
Director of Public Relations: Merrill Swanson
Director of Communications and Community Relations: Kernal Buhler
Public Relations Assistant: Katie Hogan
Public Relations Assistant: Daniel Endy
Trainer: Fred Zamberletti
Equipment Manager: Dennis Ryan

Stadium: Hubert H. Humphrey Metrodome • **Capacity:** 63,000
500 11th Avenue So.
Minneapolis, Minnesota 55415

Playing Surface: AstroTurf

Training Camp: Mankato State University
Mankato, Minnesota 56001

1987 Schedule

Preseason

Aug. 15	at New Orleans	7:00
Aug. 22	**Indianapolis**	7:00
Aug. 29	**New England**	2:00
Sept. 3	at Denver	6:00

Regular Season

Sept. 13	**Detroit**	12:00
Sept. 20	at Los Angeles Rams	1:00
Sept. 27	at Kansas City	12:00
Oct. 4	**Green Bay**	12:00
Oct. 11	at Chicago	12:00
Oct. 18	**Tampa Bay**	12:00
Oct. 25	**Denver**	12:00
Nov. 1	at Seattle	1:00
Nov. 8	**Los Angeles Raiders**	12:00
Nov. 15	at Tampa Bay	1:00
Nov. 22	**Atlanta**	12:00
Nov. 26	at Dallas (Thanksgiving)	3:00
Dec. 6	**Chicago**	7:00
Dec. 13	vs. Green Bay at Milw.	12:00
Dec. 20	at Detroit	1:00
Dec. 26	**Washington** (Saturday)	3:00

Vikings Coaching History

(209-179-9)

1961-66	Norm Van Brocklin	29-51-4
1967-83	Bud Grant	161-99-5
1984	Les Steckel	3-13-0
1985	Bud Grant	7-9-0
1986	Jerry Burns	9-7-0

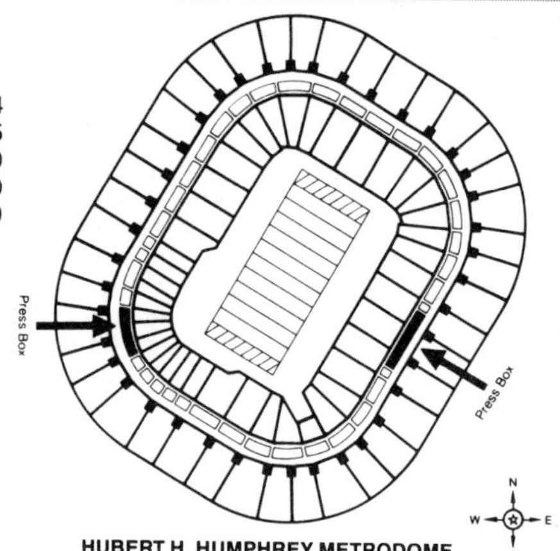

HUBERT H. HUMPHREY METRODOME

Record Holders

Individual Records—Career

Category	Name	Performance
Rushing (Yds.)	Chuck Foreman, 1973-79	5,879
Passing (Yds.)	Fran Tarkenton, 1961-66, 1972-78	33,098
Passing (TDs)	Fran Tarkenton, 1961-66, 1972-78	239
Receiving (No.)	Ahmad Rashad, 1976-1982	400
Receiving (Yds.)	Sammy White, 1976-1985	5,925
Interceptions	Paul Krause, 1968-1979	53
Punting (Avg.)	Bobby Walden, 1964-67	42.9
Punt Return (Avg.)	Tommy Mason, 1961-66	10.5
Kickoff Return (Avg.)	Bob Reed, 1962-63	27.1
Field Goals	Fred Cox, 1963-1977	282
Touchdowns (Tot.)	Bill Brown, 1962-1974	76
Points	Fred Cox, 1963-1977	1,365

Individual Records—Single Season

Category	Name	Performance
Rushing (Yds.)	Chuck Foreman, 1976	1,155
Passing (Yds.)	Tommy Kramer, 1981	3,912
Passing (TDs)	Tommy Kramer, 1981	26
Receiving (No.)	Rickey Young, 1978	88
Receiving (Yds.)	Ahmad Rashad, 1979	1,156
Interceptions	Paul Krause, 1975	10
Punting (Avg.)	Bobby Walden, 1964	46.4
Punt Return (Avg.)	Billy Butler, 1963	10.5
Kickoff Return (Avg.)	John Gilliam, 1972	26.3
Field Goals	Fred Cox, 1970	30
Touchdowns (Tot.)	Chuck Foreman, 1975	22
Points	Chuck Foreman, 1975	132

Individual Records—Single Game

Category	Name	Performance
Rushing (Yds.)	Chuck Foreman, 10-24-76	200
Passing (Yds.)	Tommy Kramer, 11-2-86	490
Passing (TDs)	Joe Kapp, 9-28-69	7
Receiving (No.)	Rickey Young, 12-16-79	15
Receiving (Yds.)	Sammy White, 11-7-76	210
Interceptions	Many times	3
	Last time by Willie Teal, 11-28-82	
Field Goals	Fred Cox, 9-23-73	5
	Jan Stenerud, 9-23-84	5
Touchdowns (Tot.)	Chuck Foreman, 12-20-75	4
	Ahmad Rashad, 9-2-79	4
Points	Chuck Foreman, 12-20-75	24
	Ahmad Rashad, 9-2-79	24

1986 Team Statistics

	Vikings	Opp.
Total First Downs	321	286
Rushing	114	106
Passing	186	155
Penalty	21	25
Third Down: Made/Att.	89/212	80/217
Fourth Down: Made/Att.	12/15	8/17
Total Net Yards	5651	5012
Avg. Per Game	353.2	313.3
Total Plays	1024	1013
Avg. Per Play	5.5	4.9
Net Yards Rushing	1738	1796
Avg. Per Game	108.6	112.3
Total Rushes	461	481
Net Yards Passing	3913	3216
Avg. Per Game	244.6	201.0
Tackled/Yards Lost	44/272	38/259
Gross Yards	4185	3475
Att./Completions	519/290	494/276
Completion Pct.	55.9	55.9
Had Intercepted	15	24
Punts/Avg.	73/40.0	75/40.3
Net Punting Avg.	34.1	36.6
Penalties/Yards Lost	96/890	99/806
Fumbles/Ball Lost	31/14	32/18
Touchdowns	48	28
Rushing	14	10
Passing	31	16
Returns	3	2
Avg. Time of Possession	30:15	29:45

1986 Team Record

Preseason (3-1)

Date	Result		Opponents
8/9	W	30-16	Miami
8/16	W	29-27	Denver
8/22	L	17-27	at Seattle
8/30	W	23-20	at Indianapolis
		99-90	

Regular Season (9-7)

Date	Result		Opponents	Att.
9/7	L	10-13	Detroit	54,851
9/14	W	23-10	at Tampa Bay	34,579
9/21	W	31- 7	Pittsburgh	56,795
9/28	W	42- 7	Green Bay	60,478
10/5	L	0-23	at Chicago	63,921
10/12	W	27-24	at San Fran. (OT)	58,637
10/19	W	23- 7	Chicago	62,851
10/26	L	20-23	Cleveland	59,133
11/2	L	38-44	at Wash. (OT)	51,928
11/9	W	24-10	at Detroit	53,725
11/16	L	20-22	N.Y. Giants	62,003
11/23	L	20-24	at Cincinnati	53,003
11/30	W	45-13	Tampa Bay	56,235
12/7	W	32- 6	at Green Bay	47,637
12/14	L	10-23	at Houston	32,738
12/21	W	33-17	New Orleans	51,209

(OT) Overtime

Score by Periods

Vikings	151	85	71	88	3	—	398
Opponents	60	75	43	89	6	—	273

Attendance

Home 463,555 Away 396,168 Total 859,723
Single game home record, 62,851 (10-19-86)
Single season home record, 464,902 (1983)

1986 Individual Statistics

Scoring	TD R	TD P	TD Rt	PAT	FG	Saf	TP
C. Nelson	0	0	0	44/47	22/28	0	110
Carter	0	7	0	0/0	0/0	0	42
D. Nelson	4	3	0	0/0	0/0	0	42
Jordan	0	6	0	0/0	0/0	0	36
Rice	2	3	0	0/0	0/0	0	30
Anderson	2	2	0	0/0	0/0	0	24
Brown	4	0	0	0/0	0/0	0	24
Jones	0	4	0	0/0	0/0	0	24
Gustafson	0	2	0	0/0	0/0	0	12
Lewis	0	2	0	0/0	0/0	0	12
Mularkey	0	2	0	0/0	0/0	0	12
Browner	0	0	1	0/0	0/0	0	6
Doleman	0	0	1	0/0	0/0	0	6
Holt	0	0	1	0/0	0/0	0	6
Kramer	1	0	0	0/0	0/0	0	6
Wad. Wilson	1	0	0	0/0	0/0	0	6
Vikings	14	31	3	44/48	22/28	0	398
Opponents	10	16	2	24/27	27/33	0	273

Passing	Att.	Comp.	Yds.	Pct.	TD	Int.	Tkld.	Rate
Kramer	372	208	3000	55.9	24	10	31/178	92.6
Wad. Wilson	143	80	1165	55.9	7	5	13/94	84.4
Anderson	2	1	17	50.0	0	0	0/0	79.2
Bono	1	1	3	100.0	0	0	0/0	79.2
Rice	1	0	0	0.0	0	0	0/0	39.6
Vikings	519	290	4185	55.9	31	15	44/272	90.1
Opponents	494	276	3475	55.9	16	24	38/259	68.5

Rushing	Att.	Yds.	Avg.	LG	TD
D. Nelson	191	793	4.2	42	4
Anderson	83	347	4.2	29	2
Brown	63	251	4.0	60	4
Rice	73	220	3.0	19	2
Kramer	23	48	2.1	13	1
Coleman	2	46	23.0	30	0
Jones	1	14	14.0	14	0
Way. Wilson	8	14	1.8	6	0
Carter	1	12	12.0	12	0
Wad. Wilson	13	9	0.7	13	1
Lewis	3	−16	−5.3	−2	0
Vikings	461	1738	3.8	60	14
Opponents	481	1796	3.7	41	10

Receiving	No.	Yds.	Avg.	LG	TD
Jordan	58	859	14.8	68t	6
D. Nelson	53	593	11.2	34	3
Carter	38	686	18.1	60t	7
Lewis	32	600	18.8	76t	2
Rice	30	391	13.0	32t	3
Jones	28	570	20.4	55t	4
Anderson	17	179	10.5	37t	2
Brown	15	132	8.8	20	0
Mularkey	11	89	8.1	20	2
Gustafson	5	61	12.2	18	2
Rhymes	3	25	8.3	12	0
Vikings	290	4185	14.4	76t	31
Opponents	276	3475	12.6	59	16

Interceptions	No.	Yds.	Avg.	LG	TD
Holt	8	54	6.8	27	0
Browner	4	62	15.5	39t	1
Harris	3	69	23.0	28	0
Lee	3	10	3.3	10	0
Solomon	2	34	17.0	18	0
Doleman	1	59	59.0	59t	1
Millard	1	17	17.0	17	0
Bess	1	12	12.0	12	0
Studwell	1	2	2.0	2	0
Vikings	24	319	13.3	59t	2
Opponents	15	88	5.9	24	0

Punting	No.	Yds.	Avg.	In 20	LG
Coleman	67	2774	41.4	15	69
Wad. Wilson	2	76	38.0	0	46
C. Nelson	3	72	24.0	0	31
Vikings	73	2922	40.0	15	69
Opponents	75	3021	40.3	27	61

Punt Returns	No.	FC	Yds.	Avg.	LG	TD
Bess	23	10	162	7.0	15	0
Lewis	7	4	53	7.6	13	0
Rice	1	0	0	0.0	0	0
Carter	0	1	0	—	0	0
Morrell	0	2	0	—	0	0
Vikings	31	17	215	6.9	15	0
Opponents	40	10	356	8.9	25	0

Kickoff Returns	No.	Yds.	Avg.	LG	TD
Bess	31	705	22.7	43	0
Rhymes	9	213	23.7	34	0
Rice	5	88	17.6	23	0
Anderson	3	38	12.7	17	0
D. Nelson	3	105	35.0	40	0
Brown	2	18	9.0	17	0
Way. Wilson	2	33	16.5	26	0
Irwin	1	0	0.0	0	0
Vikings	56	1200	21.4	43	0
Opponents	79	1532	19.4	94	0

Sacks	No.
Millard	10.5
D. Martin	9.0
Newton	5.0
Robinson	3.5
Doleman	3.0
Howard	2.5
Mullaney	2.0
Stensrud	1.0
Studwell	1.0
Browner	0.5
Vikings	38.0
Opponents	44.0

FIRST-ROUND SELECTIONS

(If club had no first-round selection, first player drafted is listed with round in parentheses.)

Year	Player, College, Position
1961	Tommy Mason, Tulane, RB
1962	Bill Miller, Miami, WR (3)
1963	Jim Dunaway, Mississippi, T
1964	Carl Eller, Minnesota, DE
1965	Jack Snow, Notre Dame, WR
1966	Jerry Shay, Purdue, DT
1967	Clinton Jones, Michigan State, RB
	Gene Washington, Michigan State, WR
	Alan Page, Notre Dame, DT
1968	Ron Yary, Southern California, T
1969	Ed White, California, G (2)
1970	John Ward, Oklahoma State, DT
1971	Leo Hayden, Ohio State, RB
1972	Jeff Siemon, Stanford, LB
1973	Chuck Foreman, Miami, RB
1974	Fred McNeill, UCLA, LB
	Steve Riley, Southern California, T
1975	Mark Mullaney, Colorado State, DE
1976	James White, Oklahoma State, DT
1977	Tommy Kramer, Rice, QB
1978	Randy Holloway, Pittsburgh, DE
1979	Ted Brown, North Carolina State, RB
1980	Doug Martin, Washington, DT
1981	Mardye McDole, Mississippi State, WR (2)
1982	Darrin Nelson, Stanford, RB
1983	Joey Browner, Southern California, DB
1984	Keith Millard, Washington State, DE
1985	Chris Doleman, Pittsburgh, LB
1986	Gerald Robinson, Auburn, DE
1987	D.J. Dozier, Penn State, RB

Minnesota Vikings 1987 Veteran Roster

No.	Name	Pos.	Ht.	Wt.	Birth-date	NFL Exp.	College	Hometown	How Acq.	'86 Games/ Starts
46	Anderson, Alfred	RB	6-1	219	8/4/61	4	Baylor	Waco, Tex.	D3-'84	16/8
58	Ashley, Walker Lee	LB	6-0	240	7/28/60	4	Penn State	Jersey City, N.J.	D3-'83	16/0
21	Bess, Rufus	CB	5-9	187	3/13/56	9	South Carolina State	Hartsville, S.C.	W(Buff)-'82	16/0
23	Brown, Ted	RB	5-10	212	2/2/57	9	North Carolina State	High Point, N.C.	D1-'79	13/0
47	Browner, Joey	S	6-2	212	5/15/60	5	Southern California	Warren, Ohio	D1-'83	16/16
81	Carter, Anthony	WR	5-11	166	9/17/60	3	Michigan	Riviera Beach, Fla.	T(Mia)-'85	12/10
8	Coleman, Greg	P	6-0	181	9/9/54	11	Florida A&M	Jacksonville, Fla.	FA-'78	16/0
56	Doleman, Chris	DE	6-5	250	10/16/61	3	Pittsburgh	York, Pa.	D1-'85	16/9
26	Evans, David	CB	6-0	178	5/1/59	2	Central Arkansas	Naples, Tex.	FA-'86	16/1
41	Guggemos, Neal	S	6-0	187	6/14/64	2	St. Thomas	Winsted, Minn.	FA-'86	4/0
80	†Gustafson, Jim	WR	6-1	181	3/16/61	2	St. Thomas	Minneapolis, Minn.	FA-'85	14/0
44	Harris, John	S	6-2	198	6/13/56	10	Arizona State	Miami, Fla.	T(Sea)-'86	16/15
82	Hilton, Carl	TE	6-3	232	2/28/64	2	Houston	Galveston, Tex.	D7-'86	16/0
30	Holt, Issiac	CB	6-1	197	10/4/62	3	Alcorn State	Birmingham, Ala.	D2-'85	16/15
51	Hough, Jim	G	6-2	276	8/4/56	10	Utah State	La Mirada, Calif.	D4-'78	16/15
99	Howard, David	LB	6-2	228	12/8/61	3	Long Beach State	Long Beach, Calif.	SD3-'84	14/13
72	†Huffman, David	G	6-6	283	4/4/57	8	Notre Dame	Dallas, Tex.	FA-'85	16/1
76	Irwin, Tim	T	6-6	289	12/13/58	7	Tennessee	Knoxville, Tenn.	D3-'81	16/16
84	Jones, Hassan	WR	6-0	195	7/2/64	2	Florida State	Clearwater, Fla.	D5-'86	16/6
83	Jordan, Steve	TE	6-3	236	1/10/61	6	Brown	Phoenix, Ariz.	D7-'82	16/16
9	Kramer, Tommy	QB	6-2	207	3/7/55	11	Rice	San Antonio, Tex.	D1-'77	13/13
39	Lee, Carl	CB	5-11	184	4/6/61	5	Marshall	South Charleston, W. Va.	D7-'83	16/16
87	Lewis, Leo	WR	5-8	171	9/17/56	7	Missouri	Columbia, Mo.	FA-'81	16/16
63	Lowdermilk, Kirk	C	6-3	263	4/10/63	3	Ohio State	Salem, Ohio	D3a-'85	11/11
27	Lush, Mike	S	6-2	195	4/18/58	2	East Stroudsburg State	Allentown, Pa.	W(Ind)-'86	10/0*
71	MacDonald, Mark	G	6-4	267	4/30/61	3	Boston College	West Roxbury, Mass.	D5-'85	10/0
56	Martin, Chris	LB	6-2	233	12/19/60	5	Auburn	Huntsville, Ala.	W(NO)-'84	16/10
79	Martin, Doug	DE	6-3	270	5/22/57	8	Washington	Fairfield, Calif.	D1-'80	15/15
75	Millard, Keith	DT	6-6	260	3/18/62	3	Washington State	Pullman, Wash.	D1-'84	15/15
86	Mularkey, Mike	TE	6-4	238	11/19/61	5	Florida	Ft. Lauderdale, Fla.	W(SF)-'83	16/1
77	Mullaney, Mark	DE	6-6	246	4/30/53	13	Colorado State	Denver, Colo.	D1-'75	11/9
1	†Nelson, Chuck	K	5-11	172	2/23/60	4	Washington	Seattle, Wash.	FA-'86	16/0
20	Nelson, Darrin	RB	5-9	183	1/2/59	6	Stanford	Downey, Calif.	D1-'82	16/16
96	Newton, Tim	DT	6-0	283	3/23/63	3	Florida	Orlando, Fla.	D6b-'85	15/9
91	Phillips, Joe	DT	6-4	278	7/15/63	2	Southern Methodist	Vancouver, Wash.	D4-'86	16/1
88	Rhymes, Buster	WR	6-1	216	1/27/62	3	Oklahoma	Miami, Fla.	D4a-'85	5/0
36	Rice, Allen	RB	5-10	203	4/5/62	4	Baylor	Houston, Tex.	D5-'84	14/8
95	Robinson, Gerald	DE	6-3	256	5/4/63	2	Auburn	Notasulga, Ala.	D1-'86	12/4
68	Rouse, Curtis	G	6-3	322	7/13/60	6	Tenn.-Chattanooga	Augusta, Ga.	D11-'82	5/0
53	†Schuh, Jeff	LB	6-3	234	5/22/58	7	Minnesota	Minneapolis, Minn.	FA-'86	14/2*
54	Solomon, Jesse	LB	6-0	235	11/4/63	2	Florida State	Madison, Fla.	D12-'86	13/4
74	†Stensrud, Mike	DT	6-5	280	2/19/56	9	Iowa State	Lake Mills, Iowa	FA-'86	11/4
55	Studwell, Scott	LB	6-2	228	8/27/54	11	Illinois	Evansville, Ind.	D9-'77	15/15
67	Swilley, Dennis	C	6-3	257	6/28/55	10	Texas A&M	Pine Bluff, Ark.	D2-'77	16/16
66	Tausch, Terry	T	6-5	275	2/5/59	6	Texas	New Braunfels, Tex.	D2-'82	16/16
37	†Teal, Willie	CB	5-10	190	12/20/57	7	Louisiana State	Texarkana, Tex.	D2-'80	11/0
11	Wilson, Wade	QB	6-3	208	2/1/59	7	East Texas State	Commerce, Tex.	D8-'81	9/3
65	Zimmerman, Gary	T	6-6	277	12/13/61	2	Oregon	Fullerton, Calif.	T(NYG)-'86	16/16

* Lush played 4 games with Indianapolis in '86, 6 with Minnesota; Schuh played 12 games with Green Bay, 2 with Minnesota.

†Option playout; subject to developments.

Retired—Sammy White, 11-year wide receiver, 0 games in '86.

Also played with Vikings in '86—QB Steve Bono (1 game), G Brent Boyd (4), DE Neil Elshire (11), T Grant Feasel (active for 1 game, but did not play), P Mike Horan (active for 1 game, but did not play), DE Leroy Howell (active for 2 games, but did not play), S Kyle Morrell (5), RB Wayne Wilson (7).

COACHING STAFF

Head Coach, Jerry Burns

Pro Career: Named fourth head coach in Vikings' history on January 6, 1986. Served as Vikings' assistant head coach and offensive coordinator under Bud Grant in 1985. Since his arrival in Minnesota as offensive coordinator in 1968, became known as an innovator and was credited with popularizing such changes as the one-back offense and short passing game. Has coached in six Super Bowls. Directed Vikings offense in Super Bowls IV, VIII, IX, and XI, and coached defensive backs for Vince Lombardi on Green Bay's Super Bowl champions in Super Bowls I and II. Career record: 9-7.

Background: Quarterback at Michigan 1949-50. No pro playing experience. Began coaching career at Hawaii in 1951 as backfield coach for football team and head baseball coach. Moved to Whittier (Calif.) College in 1952 as backfield coach before returning to native Detroit in 1953 as head football coach at St. Mary's of Redford High School. Assistant coach at Iowa from 1954-60 before being named Hawkeyes head coach in 1961. Iowa was 16-27-2 in five seasons under Burns. He coached with the Packers in 1966-67 before joining the Vikings in 1968.

Personal: Born January 24, 1927, in Detroit, Mich. Graduated from Michigan with bachelor of science degree in physical education. Jerry and his wife, Marlyn, live in Eden Prairie, Minn., and have five children—Michael, Erin, Kelly, Kathy, and Kerry.

Assistant Coaches

Tom Batta, tight ends-special teams; born October 6, 1942, Youngstown, Ohio, lives in Bloomington, Minn. Offensive-defensive lineman Kent State 1961-63. No pro playing experience. College coach: Akron 1973, Colorado 1974-78, Kansas 1979-82, North Carolina State 1983. Pro coach: Joined Vikings in 1984.

Pete Carroll, secondary; born September 15, 1951, San Francisco, Calif., lives in Bloomington, Minn. Defensive back Pacific 1969-72. No pro playing experience. College coach: Arkansas 1977, Iowa State 1978, Ohio State 1979, North Carolina State 1980-82, Pacific 1983. Pro coach: Buffalo Bills 1984, joined Vikings in 1985.

Rollie Dotsch, running backs; born February 14, 1933, Garden, Mich. Guard Michigan State 1951-54. No pro playing experience. College coach: Northern Michigan 1958-60, 1966-70 (head coach), Colorado 1961, Missouri 1962-65. Pro coach: Green Bay Packers 1971-74, New England Patriots 1975-76, Detroit Lions 1977, Pittsburgh Steelers 1978-82, Birmingham Stallions (USFL) 1983-85 (head coach), first year with Vikings.

Monte Kiffin, linebackers; born February 29, 1940, Lexington, Neb., lives in Bloomington, Minn. Defensive end Nebraska 1961-63. Pro defensive end Winnipeg Blue Bombers (CFL) 1965-66. College coach: Nebraska 1966-76, Arkansas 1977-79, North Carolina State 1980-82 (head coach). Pro coach: Green Bay Packers 1983, Buffalo Bills 1984-85, joined Vikings in 1986.

John Michels, offensive line; born February 15, 1931, Philadelphia, Pa., lives in Bloomington, Minn. Guard Tennessee 1949-52. Pro guard Philadelphia Eagles 1953, 1956, Winnipeg Blue Bombers (CFL) 1957. College coach: Texas A&M 1958. Pro coach: Winnipeg Blue Bombers (CFL) 1959-66, joined Vikings in 1967.

Floyd Peters, defensive coordinator; born May 21, 1936, Council Bluffs, Iowa, lives in Bloomington, Minn. Defensive tackle-guard San Francisco State 1954-57. Pro defensive lineman Baltimore Colts 1958, Cleveland Browns 1959-62, Detroit Lions 1963, Philadelphia Eagles 1964-69, Washington Redskins 1970 (player/coach). Pro scout: Miami Dolphins 1971-73. Pro coach: New York Giants 1974-75, San Francisco 49ers 1976-77, Detroit Lions 1978-81, St. Louis Cardinals 1982-85, joined Vikings in 1986.

Minnesota Vikings 1987 First-Year Roster

Name	Pos.	Ht.	Wt.	Birth-date	College	Hometown	How Acq.
Berry, Ray	LB	6-2	225	10/28/63	Baylor	Abilene, Tex.	D2
Bunch, Derek	LB	6-3	215	10/28/61	Michigan State	Dayton, Ohio	FA
Dozier, D.J.	RB	6-0	203	9/21/65	Penn State	Norfolk, Va.	D1
Fenney, Rick	RB	6-1	245	12/7/64	Washington	Seattle, Wash.	D8
Johnson, Juan (1)	WR	6-0	195	2/21/62	Langston	Okmulgee, Okla.	FA
Jones, Leonard	S	6-1	187	10/28/64	Texas Tech	Ft. Worth, Tex.	D9
Jones, Wayne	G	6-4	270	2/10/60	Utah	Grand Island, Neb.	FA
Kelley, Ken	LB	6-2	228	6/20/60	Penn State	Somerdale, N.J.	FA
Lindholm, Matti	LB	6-2	230	10/28/62	Kapylan Iltapooikoulu	Helsinki, Finland	FA
McFadden, Thad	WR-KR	6-2	193	8/14/62	Wisconsin	Flint, Mich.	FA
Najarian, Peter (1)	LB	6-2	233	12/22/63	Minnesota	Minneapolis, Minn.	FA
Pease, Brent	QB	6-2	201	10/8/64	Montana	Mt. Home, Idaho	D11
Richardson, Greg	WR-KR	5-7	159	10/6/64	Alabama	Mobile, Ala.	D6
Riley, Bob	T	6-5	276	6/23/64	Indiana	Wexford, Pa.	D10
Robinson, Michael	NT	6-1	265	9/1/62	Tennessee State	Ocala, Fla.	FA
Rutland, Reggie	S	6-1	195	6/20/64	Georgia Tech	East Point, Ga.	D4
Schippang, Gary (1)	T	6-4	254	4/16/63	West Chester	Bethlehem, Pa.	D8-'86
Thomas, Henry	NT	6-2	263	1/12/65	Louisiana State	Houston, Tex.	D3
Williams, Keith	DT	6-4	267	10/9/63	Florida	Milton, Fla.	D12

The term NFL Rookie is defined as a player who is in his first season of professional football and has not been on the roster of another professional football team for any regular-season or postseason games. A Rookie is designated by an "R" on NFL rosters. Players who have been active in another professional football league or players who have NFL experience, including either preseason training camp or being on an active roster for fewer than three regular-season or postseason games, are termed NFL First-Year Players. An NFL First-Year Player is designated by a "1" on NFL rosters. Thereafter, a player on an NFL active roster for at least three regular-season or postseason games is credited with an additional year of NFL playing experience.

NOTES

Dick Rehbein, receivers; born November 22, 1955, Green Bay, Wis., lives in Edina, Minn. Center Ripon 1973-77. No pro playing experience. Pro coach: Green Bay Packers 1979-83, Los Angeles Express (USFL) 1984, joined Vikings in 1984.

Bob Schnelker, offensive coordinator; born October 17, 1928, Galion, Ohio, lives in Bloomington, Minn. Tight end Bowling Green 1946-49. Pro tight end Cleveland Browns 1953, New York Giants 1954-59, Minnesota Vikings 1961, Pittsburgh Steelers 1961. Pro coach: Los Angeles Rams 1963-65, Green Bay Packers 1966-71, 1982-85, San Diego Chargers 1972-73, Miami Dolphins 1974, Kansas City Chiefs 1975-77, Detroit Lions 1978-81, joined Vikings in 1986.

Paul Wiggin, defensive line; born November 18, 1934, Modesto, Calif., lives in Eden Prairie, Minn. Offensive-defensive tackle Stanford 1953-56. Pro defensive end Cleveland Browns 1957-67. College coach: Stanford 1980-83 (head coach). Pro coach: San Francisco 49ers 1968-74, Kansas City Chiefs 1975-77 (head coach), New Orleans Saints 1978-79, joined Vikings in 1985.

NEW ORLEANS SAINTS

National Football Conference Western Division

Team Colors: Old Gold, Black, and White

1500 Poydras Street
New Orleans, Louisiana 70112
Telephone: (504) 522-1500

Club Officials

Owner/General Partner: Tom Benson
President/General Manager: Jim Finks
Vice President/Administration: Jim Miller
Business Manager/Controller: Bruce Broussard
Director of Player Personnel: Bill Kuharich
Director of Public Relations/Marketing: Greg Suit
Director of Media Services: Rusty Kasmiersky
Director of Travel/Entertainment: Barra Birrcher
Assistant Director of Marketing: Bill Ferrante
Public Relations/Marketing Assistant: Sylvia Alfortish
Player Personnel Scouts: Bill Baker, Hamp Cook, Tom Marino, Carmen Piccone
Ticket Manager: Sandy King
Trainer: Dean Kleinschmidt
Equipment Manager: Dan Simmons

Stadium: Louisiana Superdome • **Capacity:** 69,723
1500 Poydras Street
New Orleans, Louisiana 70112

Playing Surface: AstroTurf

Training Camp: Southeastern Louisiana University
Hammond, Louisiana 70402

1987 Schedule

Preseason

Aug. 15	**Minnesota**	7:00
Aug. 22	**Houston**	7:00
Aug. 29	**Pittsburgh**	7:00
Sept. 4	at Cincinnati	7:35

Regular Season

Sept. 13	**Cleveland**	12:00
Sept. 20	at Philadelphia	1:00
Sept. 27	**Atlanta**	12:00
Oct. 4	**Los Angeles Rams**	12:00
Oct. 11	at St. Louis	12:00
Oct. 18	at Chicago	12:00
Oct. 25	**San Francisco**	12:00
Nov. 1	at Atlanta	1:00
Nov. 8	at Los Angeles Rams	1:00
Nov. 15	at San Francisco	1:00
Nov. 22	**New York Giants**	3:00
Nov. 29	at Pittsburgh	1:00
Dec. 6	**Tampa Bay**	3:00
Dec. 13	**Houston**	12:00
Dec. 20	at Cincinnati	1:00
Dec. 27	**Green Bay**	12:00

Saints Coaching History

(90-196-5)

1967-70	Tom Fears*	13-34-2
1970-72	J.D. Roberts	7-25-3
1973-75	John North**	11-23-0
1975	Ernie Hefferle	1-7-0
1976-77	Hank Stram	7-21-0
1978-80	Dick Nolan***	15-29-0
1980	Dick Stanfel	1-3-0
1981-85	O.A. (Bum) Phillips****	27-42-0
1985	Wade Phillips	1-3-0
1986	Jim Mora	7-9-0

*Released after seven games in 1970
**Released after six games in 1975
***Released after 12 games in 1980
****Resigned after 12 games in 1985

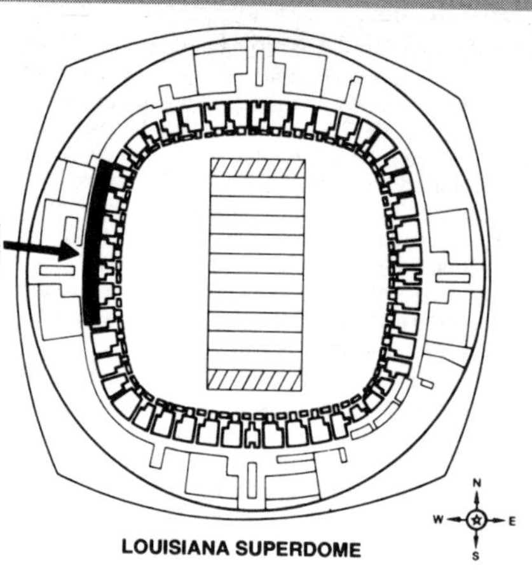

LOUISIANA SUPERDOME

Record Holders

Individual Records—Career

Category	Name	Performance
Rushing (Yds.)	George Rogers, 1981-84	4,267
Passing (Yds.)	Archie Manning, 1971-1982	21,734
Passing (TDs)	Archie Manning, 1971-1982	115
Receiving (No.)	Dan Abramowicz, 1967-1973	309
Receiving (Yds.)	Dan Abramowicz, 1967-1973	4,875
Interceptions	Tommy Myers, 1972-1982	36
Punting (Avg.)	Brian Hansen, 1984-86	42.8
Punt Return (Avg.)	Gil Chapman, 1975	12.2
Kickoff Return (Avg.)	Mel Gray, 1986	27.7
Field Goals	Morten Andersen, 1982-86	97
Touchdowns (Tot.)	Dan Abramowicz, 1967-1973	37
Points	Morten Andersen, 1982-86	425

Individual Records—Single Season

Category	Name	Performance
Rushing (Yds.)	George Rogers, 1981	1,674
Passing (Yds.)	Archie Manning, 1980	3,716
Passing (TDs)	Archie Manning, 1980	23
Receiving (No.)	Tony Galbreath, 1978	74
Receiving (Yds.)	Wes Chandler, 1979	1,069
Interceptions	Dave Whitsell, 1967	10
Punting (Avg.)	Brian Hansen, 1984	43.8
Punt Return (Avg.)	Gil Chapman, 1975	12.2
Kickoff Return (Avg.)	Don Shy, 1969	27.9
Field Goals	Morten Andersen, 1985	31
Touchdowns (Tot.)	George Rogers, 1981	13
Points	Morten Andersen, 1985	120

Individual Records—Single Game

Category	Name	Performance
Rushing (Yds.)	George Rogers, 9-4-83	206
Passing (Yds.)	Archie Manning, 12-7-80	377
Passing (TDs)	Billy Kilmer, 11-2-69	6
Receiving (No.)	Tony Galbreath, 9-10-78	14
Receiving (Yds.)	Wes Chandler, 9-2-79	205
Interceptions	Tommy Myers, 9-3-78	3
	Dave Waymer, 10-6-85	3
Field Goals	Morten Andersen, 12-1-85	5
Touchdowns (Tot.)	Many times Last time by Wayne Wilson, 1-2-83	3
Points	Many times Last time by Wayne Wilson, 1-2-83	18

1986 Team Statistics

	Saints	Opp.
Total First Downs	275	331
Rushing	109	104
Passing	137	197
Penalty	29	30
Third Down: Made/Att.	59/197	97/230
Fourth Down: Made/Att.	7/13	7/14
Total Net Yards	4742	5102
Avg. Per Game	296.4	318.9
Total Plays	957	1109
Avg. Per Play	5.0	4.6
Net Yards Rushing	2074	1559
Avg. Per Game	129.6	97.4
Total Rushes	505	486
Net Yards Passing	2668	3543
Avg. Per Game	166.8	221.4
Tackled/Yards Lost	27/225	47/343
Gross Yards	2893	3886
Att./Completions	425/232	576/331
Completion Pct.	54.6	57.5
Had Intercepted	25	26
Punts/Avg.	82/42.1	78/42.5
Net Punting Avg.	36.6	35.6
Penalties/Yards Lost	109/855	104/791
Fumbles/Ball Lost	33/18	37/17
Touchdowns	30	34
Rushing	15	11
Passing	13	21
Returns	2	2
Avg. Time of Possession	27:59	32:01

1986 Team Record

Preseason (2-2)

Date	Result		Opponents
8/9	W	10- 7	at Denver
8/16	L	34-38	New England
8/23	L	13-24	at Houston
8/30	W	13-10	Kansas City
		70-79	

Regular Season (7-9)

Date	Result		Opponents	Att.
9/7	L	10-31	Atlanta	67,950
9/14	W	24-10	Green Bay	46,383
9/21	L	17-26	at San Francisco	58,297
9/28	L	17-20	at N.Y. Giants	72,769
10/5	L	6-14	Washington	57,378
10/12	W	17-14	at Indianapolis	53,512
10/19	W	38- 7	Tampa Bay	43,355
10/26	L	23-28	at N.Y. Jets	44,246
11/2	W	23-10	San Francisco	53,234
11/9	W	6- 0	L.A. Rams	62,352
11/16	W	16- 7	at St. Louis	32,069
11/23	L	13-26	at L.A. Rams	58,600
11/30	L	20-21	New England	58,259
12/7	L	27-31	Miami	64,761
12/14	W	14- 9	at Atlanta	39,994
12/21	L	17-33	at Minnesota	51,209

Score by Periods

Saints	81	62	47	98	0	—	288
Opponents	64	92	71	60	0	—	287

Attendance

Home 463,611 Away 410,692 Total 874,303
Single game home record, 70,940 (11-4-79)
Single season home record, 529,878 (1979)

1986 Individual Statistics

Scoring	TD R	TD P	TD Rt	PAT	FG	Saf	TP
Andersen	0	0	0	30/30	26/30	0	108
Mayes	8	0	0	0/0	0/0	0	48
Hilliard	5	0	0	0/0	0/0	0	30
Martin	0	5	0	0/0	0/0	0	30
Jones	0	3	0	0/0	0/0	0	18
Tice	0	3	0	0/0	0/0	0	18
Goodlow	0	2	0	0/0	0/0	0	12
Gray	0	0	1	0/0	0/0	0	6
Haynes	0	0	1	0/0	0/0	0	6
Jordan	1	0	0	0/0	0/0	0	6
D. Wilson	1	0	0	0/0	0/0	0	6
Saints	15	13	2	30/30	26/30	0	288
Opponents	11	21	2	32/34	17/27	0	287

Passing	Att.	Comp.	Yds.	Pct.	TD	Int.	Tkld.	Rate
D. Wilson	342	189	2353	55.3	10	17	22/191	65.8
Hebert	79	41	498	51.9	2	8	5/34	40.5
Hilliard	3	1	29	33.3	1	0	0/0	109.7
Wattelet	1	1	13	100.0	0	0	0/0	118.8
Saints	425	232	2893	54.6	13	25	27/225	61.6
Opponents	576	331	3886	57.5	21	26	47/343	71.4

Rushing	Att.	Yds.	Avg.	LG	TD
Mayes	286	1353	4.7	50	8
Hilliard	121	425	3.5	36	5
Jordan	68	207	3.0	10	1
Gray	6	29	4.8	11	0
D. Wilson	14	19	1.4	14	1
W. Wilson, Minn.-N.O.	10	19	1.9	6	0
W. Wilson, N.O.	2	5	2.5	3	0
Del Rio	1	16	16.0	16	0
Hebert	5	14	2.8	7	0
Edwards	1	6	6.0	6	0
Hansen	1	0	0.0	0	0
Saints	505	2074	4.1	50	15
Opponents	486	1559	3.2	27	11

Receiving	No.	Yds.	Avg.	LG	TD
Jones	48	625	13.0	45	3
Martin	37	675	18.2	84	5
Tice	37	330	8.9	29t	3
Goodlow	20	306	15.3	29t	2
Brenner	18	286	15.9	34	0
Hilliard	17	107	6.3	17	0
Mayes	17	96	5.6	18	0
Harris	11	148	13.5	27	0
Jordan	11	127	11.5	37	0
Edwards	10	132	13.2	24	0
Gray	2	45	22.5	38	0
Waymer	1	13	13.0	13	0
J. Williams	1	5	5.0	5	0
Hebert	1	1	1.0	1	0
W. Wilson	1	−3	−3.0	−3	0
Saints	232	2893	12.5	84	13
Opponents	331	3886	11.7	62t	21

Interceptions	No.	Yds.	Avg.	LG	TD
Waymer	9	48	5.3	17	0
Poe	4	42	10.5	30	0
Wattelet	3	34	11.3	22	0
Gibson	2	43	21.5	43	0
Maxie	2	15	7.5	15	0
Jakes	2	6	3.0	4	0
Haynes	1	17	17.0	17t	1
V. Johnson	1	15	15.0	15	0
Gary	1	14	14.0	14	0
Jackson	1	1	1.0	1	0
Saints	26	235	9.0	43	1
Opponents	25	362	14.5	46	0

Punting	No.	Yds.	Avg.	In 20	LG
Hansen	81	3456	42.7	17	66
Saints	82	3456	42.1	17	66
Opponents	78	3315	42.5	23	62

Punt Returns	No.	FC	Yds.	Avg.	LG	TD
Martin	24	9	227	9.5	39	0
McLemore	10	3	67	6.7	23	0
Poe	8	3	71	8.9	17	0
Edwards	3	0	2	0.7	5	0
Tullis	2	0	10	5.0	7	0
Saints	47	15	377	8.0	39	0
Opponents	37	11	234	6.3	20	0

Kickoff Returns	No.	Yds.	Avg.	LG	TD
Gray	31	866	27.9	101t	1
Mayes	10	213	21.3	34	0
Harris	7	122	17.4	22	0
Martin	3	64	21.3	27	0
McLemore	2	39	19.5	22	0
Tullis	2	28	14.0	19	0
W. Wilson, Minn.-N.O.	2	33	16.5	26	0
Saints	55	1332	24.2	101t	1
Opponents	35	662	18.9	55	0

Sacks	No.
Geathers	9.0
Jackson	9.0
Warren	7.5
Clark	6.0
Swilling	4.0
Elliott	3.5
Gibson	3.0
Haynes	2.0
V. Johnson	1.0
Poe	1.0
Wilks	1.0
Saints	47.0
Opponents	27.0

FIRST-ROUND SELECTIONS

(If club had no first-round selection, first player drafted is listed with round in parentheses.)

Year	Player, College, Position
1967	Les Kelley, Alabama, RB
1968	Kevin Hardy, Notre Dame, DE
1969	John Shinners, Xavier, G
1970	Ken Burrough, Texas Southern, WR
1971	Archie Manning, Mississippi, QB
1972	Royce Smith, Georgia, G
1973	Derland Moore, Oklahoma, DE (2)
1974	Rick Middleton, Ohio State, LB
1975	Larry Burton, Purdue, WR
	Kurt Schumacher, Ohio State, T
1976	Chuck Muncie, California, RB
1977	Joe Campbell, Maryland, DE
1978	Wes Chandler, Florida, WR
1979	Russell Erxleben, Texas, P-K
1980	Stan Brock, Colorado, T
1981	George Rogers, South Carolina, RB
1982	Lindsay Scott, Georgia, WR
1983	Steve Korte, Arkansas, G (2)
1984	James Geathers, Wichita State, DE
1985	Alvin Toles, Tennessee, LB
1986	Jim Dombrowski, Virginia, T
1987	Shawn Knight, Brigham Young, DT

New Orleans Saints 1987 Veteran Roster

No.	Name	Pos.	Ht.	Wt.	Birth-date	NFL Exp.	College	Hometown	How Acq.	'86 Games/ Starts
7	Andersen, Morten	K	6-2	205	8/19/60	6	Michigan State	Indianapolis, Ind.	D4-'82	16/0
85	Brenner, Hoby	TE	6-4	245	6/2/59	7	Southern California	Fullerton, Calif.	D3b-'81	15/12
67	†Brock, Stan	T	6-6	292	6/8/58	8	Colorado	Beaverton, Ore.	D1-'81	16/16
75	Clark, Bruce	DE	6-3	274	3/31/58	6	Penn State	New Castle, Pa.	T(GB)-'82	16/16
66	Commiskey, Chuck	G	6-4	290	3/2/58	2	Mississippi	Pascagoula, Miss.	FA-'86	16/10
70	†Contz, Bill	T	6-5	270	5/12/61	5	Penn State	Belle Vernon, Pa.	FA-'86	14/13*
50	†Del Rio, Jack	LB	6-4	238	4/4/63	3	Southern California	Castro Valley, Calif.	D3-'85	16/1
72	Dombrowski, Jim	T	6-5	298	10/19/63	2	Virginia	Williamsville, N.Y.	D1-'86	3/3
95	Dumbauld, Jonathan	NT	6-4	256	2/14/63	2	Kentucky	Lexington, Ky.	D10-'86	9/0
63	†Edelman, Brad	G	6-6	270	9/3/60	6	Missouri	Creve Coeur, Mo.	D2-'82	13/13
83	Edwards, Kelvin	WR	6-2	197	7/19/64	2	Liberty Baptist	Lynchburg, Va.	D4-'86	14/3
99	†Elliott, Tony	NT	6-2	295	4/23/59	6	North Texas State	Bridgeport, Conn.	D5-'82	16/16
43	Fowler, Bobby	RB	6-2	225	9/11/60	2	Louisiana Tech	Angleton, Tex.	FA-'85	0*
46	Gajan, Hokie	RB	5-11	230	9/6/59	5	Louisiana State	Baker, La.	D10-'81	0*
97	†Geathers, James	DE	6-7	290	6/26/60	4	Wichita State	Georgetown, S.C.	D2-'84	16/2
27	Gibson, Antonio	S	6-3	204	7/5/62	2	Cincinnati	Jackson, Miss.	FA-'86	16/13
77	Gilbert, Daren	T	6-6	295	10/3/63	3	Cal State-Fullerton	Compton, Calif.	D2-'85	10/0
88	Goodlow, Eugene	WR	6-2	186	12/19/58	5	Kansas State	Rochester, N.Y.	D3b-'82	16/6
37	Gray, Mel	RB	5-9	166	3/16/61	2	Purdue	Williamsburg, Va.	SD2-'84	16/0
10	Hansen, Brian	P	6-3	209	10/18/60	4	Sioux Falls	Hawarden, Iowa	D9-'84	16/0
80	Harris, Herbert	WR	6-1	206	5/4/61	2	Lamar	Houston, Tex.	FA-'86	7/1
92	Haynes, James	LB	6-2	233	8/9/60	4	Mississippi Valley	Tallulah, La.	FA-'84	16/16
3	Hebert, Bobby	QB	6-4	214	8/19/60	3	Northwestern State, La.	Cut Off, La.	FA-'85	4/3
61	†Hilgenberg, Joel	C-G	6-3	252	7/10/62	4	Iowa	Iowa City, Iowa	D4-'84	16/2
40	Hilliard, Dalton	RB	5-8	204	1/21/64	2	Louisiana State	Patterson, La.	D2-'86	16/5
57	†Jackson, Rickey	LB	6-2	243	3/20/58	7	Pittsburgh	Pahokee, Fla.	D2b-'81	16/16
32	Jakes, Van	CB-S	6-0	190	5/10/61	4	Kent State	Buffalo, N.Y.	FA-'86	12/0
24	Johnson, Bobby	CB-S	6-0	187	9/1/60	5	Texas	LaGrange, Tex.	FA-'86	11/0*
53	Johnson, Vaughan	LB	6-3	235	3/24/62	2	North Carolina State	Morehead City, N.C.	SD1-'84	16/0
86	Jones, Mike	WR	5-11	183	4/14/60	5	Tennessee	Chattanooga, Tenn.	T(Minn)-'86	16/8
23	Jordan, Buford	RB	6-0	223	6/26/62	2	McNeese State	Iota, La.	FA-'86	16/9
55	†Kohlbrand, Joe	LB	6-4	242	3/18/63	3	Miami	Merritt Island, Fla.	D8-'85	16/0
60	Korte, Steve	C	6-2	269	1/15/60	5	Arkansas	Littleton, Colo.	D2-'83	16/16
84	†Martin, Eric	WR	6-1	207	11/8/61	3	Louisiana State	Van Vleck, Tex.	D7-'85	16/11
39	†Maxie, Brett	CB-S	6-2	194	1/13/62	3	Texas Southern	Dallas, Tex.	FA-'85	15/0
36	Mayes, Rueben	RB	5-11	200	6/16/63	2	Washington State	N. Battleford, Saskatchewan	D3a-'86	16/12
43	McLemore, Dana	CB-S	5-10	183	7/1/60	6	Hawaii	Los Angeles, Calif.	FA-'86	6/0*
51	Mills, Sam	LB	5-9	225	6/3/59	2	Montclair State	Long Branch, N.J.	FA-'86	16/13
25	Poe, Johnnie	CB	6-1	194	8/29/59	7	Missouri	East St. Louis, Ill.	D6b-'81	16/16
68	Saindon, Pat	G	6-3	273	3/3/61	2	Vanderbilt	Jacksonville, Fla.	FA-'86	9/1
56	Swilling, Pat	LB	6-2	242	10/25/64	2	Georgia Tech	Toccoa, Ga.	D3b-'86	16/0
82	Tice, John	TE	6-5	249	6/22/60	5	Maryland	Central Islip, N.Y.	D3a-'83	16/13
54	†Toles, Alvin	LB	6-1	227	3/23/63	3	Tennessee	Forsythe, Ga.	D1-'85	16/15
73	†Warren, Frank	DE	6-4	290	9/14/59	7	Auburn	Birmingham, Ala.	D3a-'81	16/0
33	Waters, Mike	RB	6-2	230	3/15/62	2	San Diego State	Ridgecrest, Calif.	FA-'87	5/1*
49	†Wattelet, Frank	S	6-0	186	10/25/58	7	Kansas	Abilene, Kan.	FA-'81	16/16
44	†Waymer, Dave	CB	6-1	188	7/1/58	8	Notre Dame	Charlotte, N.C.	D2-'80	16/15
69	Weaver, Emanuel	NT	6-5	285	6/28/60	2	South Carolina	New Orleans, La.	FA-'87	0*
94	†Wilks, Jim	DE	6-5	266	3/12/58	7	San Diego State	Pasadena, Calif.	D12-'81	16/15
45	Williams, John	RB	5-11	205	10/26/60	3	Wisconsin	Muskegan, Mich.	FA-'86	7/0
79	Williams, Ralph	G	6-3	298	3/27/58	5	Southern	West Monroe, La.	FA-'85	6/6
18	†Wilson, Dave	QB	6-3	206	4/27/59	6	Illinois	Anaheim, Calif.	SD1-'81	14/13

* Contz played 1 game with Cleveland in '86, 13 with New Orleans; Fowler and Gajan missed '86 season due to injury; B. Johnson played 3 games with St. Louis, 8 with New Orleans; McLemore played 3 games with San Francisco, 3 with New Orleans; Waters played 5 games with Philadelphia; Weaver last active with Cincinnati in '82.

†Option playout; subject to developments.

Also played with Saints in '86—S Russell Gary (8 games), DE Milford Hodge (1), QB Babe Laufenberg (active for 5 games, played in 1), DE Casey Merrill (1), LB Glen Redd (4), CB Willie Tullis (7), RB Wayne Wilson (5).

COACHING STAFF

Head Coach, Jim Mora

Pro Career: Begins second year as NFL coach, after leading Saints to 7-9 record in 1986. Came to New Orleans following a three-year career as the winningest coach in USFL history as head coach of the Philadelphia/Baltimore Stars. Directed Stars to championship game in each of his three seasons and won league championship in 1984 and 1985. He won coach of the year honors following the 1984 season. Mora began his pro coaching career in 1978 as defensive line coach of the Seattle Seahawks. In 1982, he became defensive coordinator of the New England Patriots and played a vital role in the Patriots' march to the playoffs that year. No pro playing experience. Career record: 7-9

Background: Played tight end and defensive end at Occidental College. Assistant coach at Occidental 1960-63 and head coach 1964-67. Linebacker coach at Stanford on a staff that included former Eagles head coach Dick Vermeil. Defensive assistant at Colorado 1968-73. Linebacker coach under Vermeil at UCLA 1974. Defensive coordinator at Washington 1975-77. Received bachelor's degree in physical education from Occidental in 1957. Also holds master's degree in education from Southern California.

Personal: Born May 24, 1935, in Glendale, Calif. Jim and his wife, Connie, live in Metairie, La., and have three sons—Michael, Stephen, and Jim, a defensive assistant for the San Diego Chargers.

Assistant Coaches

Paul Boudreau, offensive line; born December 30, 1949, Somerville, Mass., lives in Metairie, La. Guard Boston College 1971-73. No pro playing experience. College coach: Boston College 1974-76, Maine 1977-78, Dartmouth 1979-81, Navy 1983. Pro coach: Edmonton Eskimos (CFL) 1983-86, first year with Saints.

Dom Capers, defensive backs; born August 7, 1950, Cambridge, Ohio, lives in Metairie, La. Defensive back Mount Union College 1968-71. No pro playing experience. College coach: Hawaii 1975-76, San Jose State 1977, California 1978-79, Tennessee 1980-81, Ohio State 1982-83. Pro coach: Philadelphia/Baltimore Stars (USFL) 1984-85, joined Saints in 1986.

Vic Fangio, outside linebackers; born August 22, 1958, Dunmore, Pa., lives in Destrehan, La. Defensive back East Stroudsburg 1976-78. No pro playing experience. College coach: North Carolina 1983. Pro coach: Philadelphia/Baltimore Stars (USFL) 1983-85, joined Saints in 1986.

Joe Marciano, tight ends-special teams; born February 10, 1954, Scranton, Pa., lives in Metairie, La. Quarterback Temple 1972-75. No pro playing experience. College coach: East Stroudsburg 1977, Rhode Island 1978-79, Villanova 1980, Penn State 1981, Temple 1982. Pro coach: Philadelphia/Baltimore Stars (USFL) 1983-85, joined Saints in 1986.

Russell Paternostro, strength and conditioning; born July 21, 1940, New Orleans, La., lives in Jefferson, La. San Diego State. No college or pro playing experience. Pro coach: Joined Saints in 1981.

John Pease, defensive line; born October 14, 1943, Pittsburgh, Pa., lives in Kenner, La. Wingback Utah 1963-64. No pro playing experience. College coach: Fullerton, Calif., J.C. 1970-73, Long Beach State 1974-76, Utah 1977, Washington 1978-83. Pro coach: Philadelphia/Baltimore Stars (USFL) 1983-85, joined Saints in 1986.

Steve Sidwell, defensive coordinator-inside linebackers; born August 30, 1944, Winfield, Kan., lives in Destrehan, La. Linebacker Colorado 1962-65. No pro playing experience. College coach: Colorado 1966-73, Nevada-Las Vegas 1974-75, Southern Methodist 1976-81. Pro coach: New England Patriots 1982-84, Indianapolis Colts 1985, joined Saints in 1986.

Jim Skipper, running backs; born January 23, 1949, Breaux Bridge, La., lives in Metairie, La. Defensive back Whittier College 1971-72. No pro playing experience. College coach: Cal Poly-Pomona 1974-76, San Jose State 1977-78, Pacific 1979, Oregon 1980-82. Pro coach: Philadelphia/Baltimore Stars (USFL) 1983-85, joined Saints in 1986.

Carl Smith, offensive coordinator-quarterbacks; born April 26, 1948, Wasco, Calif., lives in Metairie, La. Defensive back Cal Poly-SLO 1968-70. No pro playing experience. College coach: Cal Poly-SLO 1971, Colorado 1972-73, Southwestern Louisiana 1974-78, Lamar 1979-81, North Carolina State 1982. Pro coach: Philadelphia/Baltimore Stars (USFL) 1983-85, joined Saints in 1986.

Steve Walters, wide receivers; born June 16, 1948, Jonesboro, Ark., lives in Metairie, La. Quarterback-defensive back Arkansas 1967-70. No pro playing experience. College coach: Tampa 1973, Northeast Louisiana 1974-75, Morehead State 1976, Tulsa 1977-78, Memphis State 1979, Southern Methodist 1980-81, Alabama 1985. Pro coach: New England Patriots 1982-84, joined Saints in 1986.

New Orleans Saints 1987 First-Year Roster

Name	Pos.	Ht.	Wt.	Birth-date	College	Hometown	How Acq.
Adams, Michael	CB	5-10	195	4/5/64	Arkansas State	Cleveland, Miss.	D3
Atkins, Gene	CB-S	6-1	200	8/31/64	Florida A&M	Tallahassee, Fla.	D7
Bealles, Bill	T	6-7	285	6/11/63	Northern Iowa	Tinley Park, Ill.	FA
Campen, James	C	6-2	255	6/11/64	Tulane	Sacramento, Calif.	FA
Clark, Robert	WR	5-11	175	8/6/65	No. Carolina Central	Richmond, Va.	D10
Cook, Toi	CB-S	5-11	188	12/3/64	Stanford	Canoga Park, Calif.	D8
Evans, Vince	RB	5-10	216	9/8/63	North Carolina State	Fayetteville, N.C.	FA
Hill, Lonzell	WR	5-11	189	9/25/65	Washington	Stockton, Calif.	D2
Jones, Merlon	LB	6-2	232	9/25/64	Florida A&M	Gainesville, Fla.	FA
Karcher, Ken	QB	6-2	200	7/1/63	Tulane	Glenshaw, Pa.	FA
Knight, Shawn	DE	6-6	288	6/4/64	Brigham Young	Sparks, Nev.	D1
Leach, Scott	LB	6-2	221	9/18/63	Ohio State	Bridgeport, Conn.	D9
Mack, Milton	CB-S	5-11	182	9/20/63	Alcorn State	Jackson, Miss.	D5
Sorrells, Tyrone	G	6-3	265	5/8/63	Georgia Tech	Buford, Ga.	D12
Sutton, Reggie (1)	CB	5-10	180	2/16/65	Miami	Miami, Fla.	D5-'86
Thompson, Robert (1)	WR	5-9	170	9/9/62	Youngstown State	Hollywood, Fla.	D6-'86
Trapilo, Steve	G	6-5	281	9/20/64	Boston College	Milton, Mass.	D4
Tuggle, Anthony	CB-S	6-2	210	9/13/63	Nicholls State	Baker, La.	FA
Wells, Arthur	TE	6-4	236	2/1/63	Grambling	Mansfield, La.	D11

The term NFL Rookie is defined as a player who is in his first season of professional football and has not been on the roster of another professional football team for any regular-season or postseason games. A Rookie is designated by an "R" on NFL rosters. Players who have been active in another professional football league or players who have NFL experience, including either preseason training camp or being on an active roster for fewer than three regular-season or postseason games, are termed NFL First-Year Players. An NFL First-Year Player is designated by a "1" on NFL rosters. Thereafter, a player on an NFL active roster for at least three regular-season or postseason games is credited with an additional year of NFL playing experience.

NOTES

National Football Conference Eastern Division

Team Colors: Blue, Red, and White

Giants Stadium
East Rutherford, New Jersey 07073
Telephone: (201) 935-8111

Club Officials

President: Wellington T. Mara
Vice President-Treasurer: Timothy J. Mara
Vice President-Secretary: Raymond J. Walsh
Vice President-General Manager: George Young
Assistant General Manager: Harry Hulmes
Controller: John Pasquali
Director of Player Personnel: Tom Boisture
Director of Pro Personnel: Tim Rooney
Director of Media Services: Ed Croke
Director of Promotions: Tom Power
Director of Special Projects: Victor Del Guercio
Box Office Treasurer: Jim Gleason
Trainer Emeritus: John Dziegiel
Head Trainer: Ronnie Barnes
Assistant Trainers: John Johnson, Jim Madaleno
Equipment Manager: Ed Wagner, Jr.

Stadium: Giants Stadium • **Capacity:** 76,891
East Rutherford, New Jersey 07073

Playing Surface: AstroTurf

Training Camp: Pace University
Pleasantville, New York 10570

1987 Schedule

Preseason

Aug. 16	at New England	1:30
Aug. 22	**Cleveland**	8:00
Aug. 29	**New York Jets**	9:00
Sept. 4	at Cincinnati	7:35

Regular Season

Sept. 14	at Chicago (Monday)	8:00
Sept. 20	**Dallas**	4:00
Sept. 27	at Miami	1:00
Oct. 5	**San Francisco** (Monday)	9:00
Oct. 11	**Washington**	4:00
Oct. 18	at Buffalo	4:00
Oct. 25	**St. Louis**	4:00
Nov. 2	at Dallas (Monday)	8:00
Nov. 8	**New England**	8:00
Nov. 15	at Philadelphia	4:00
Nov. 22	at New Orleans	3:00
Nov. 29	at Washington	4:00
Dec. 6	**Philadelphia**	1:00
Dec. 13	at St. Louis	3:00
Dec. 19	**Green Bay** (Saturday)	12:30
Dec. 27	**New York Jets**	1:00

Giants Coaching History

(436-367-32)

1925	Bob Folwell	8-4-0
1926	Joe Alexander	8-4-1
1927-28	Earl Potteiger	15-8-3
1929-30	LeRoy Andrews	26-5-1
1931-53	Steve Owen	153-108-17
1954-60	Jim Lee Howell	54-29-4
1961-68	Allie Sherman	57-54-4
1969-73	Alex Webster	29-40-1
1974-76	Bill Arnsparger*	7-28-0
1976-78	John McVay	14-23-0
1979-82	Ray Perkins	24-35-0
1983-86	Bill Parcells	41-29-1

*Released after seven games in 1976

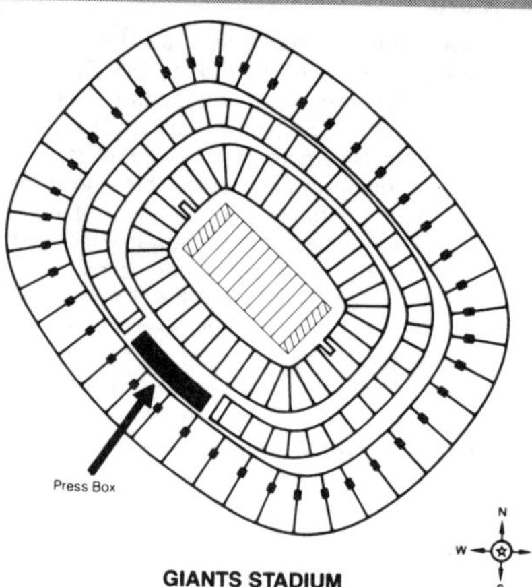

GIANTS STADIUM

Record Holders

Individual Records—Career

Category	Name	Performance
Rushing (Yds.)	Alex Webster, 1955-1964	4,638
Passing (Yds.)	Charlie Conerly, 1948-1961	19,488
Passing (TDs)	Charlie Conerly, 1948-1961	173
Receiving (No.)	Joe Morrison, 1959-1972	395
Receiving (Yds.)	Frank Gifford, 1952-1960, 1962-64	5,434
Interceptions	Emlen Tunnell, 1948-1958	74
Punting (Avg.)	Don Chandler, 1956-1964	43.8
	Sean Landeta, 1985-86	43.8
Punt Return (Avg.)	Bob Hammond, 1976-78	9.1
Kickoff Return (Avg.)	Rocky Thompson, 1971-72	27.2
Field Goals	Pete Gogolak, 1966-1974	126
Touchdowns (Tot.)	Frank Gifford, 1952-1960, 1962-64	78
Points	Pete Gogolak, 1966-1974	646

Individual Records—Single Season

Category	Name	Performance
Rushing (Yds.)	Joe Morris, 1986	1,516
Passing (Yds.)	Phil Simms, 1984	4,044
Passing (TDs)	Y.A. Tittle, 1963	36
Receiving (No.)	Earnest Gray, 1983	78
Receiving (Yds.)	Homer Jones, 1967	1,209
Interceptions	Otto Schnellbacher, 1951	11
	Jim Patton, 1958	11
Punting (Avg.)	Don Chandler, 1959	46.6
Punt Return (Avg.)	Merle Hapes, 1942	15.5
Kickoff Return (Avg.)	John Salscheider, 1949	31.6
Field Goals	Ali Haji-Sheikh, 1983	35
Touchdowns (Tot.)	Joe Morris, 1985	21
Points	Ali Haji-Sheikh, 1983	127

Individual Records—Single Game

Category	Name	Performance
Rushing (Yds.)	Gene Roberts, 11-12-50	218
Passing (Yds.)	Phil Simms, 10-13-85	513
Passing (TDs)	Y.A. Tittle, 10-28-62	7
Receiving (No.)	Mark Bavaro, 10-13-85	12
Receiving (Yds.)	Del Shofner, 10-28-62	269
Interceptions	Many times	3
	Last time by Carl Lockhart, 12-4-66	
Field Goals	Joe Danelo, 10-18-81	6
Touchdowns (Tot.)	Ron Johnson, 10-2-72	4
	Earnest Gray, 9-7-80	4
Points	Ron Johnson, 10-2-72	24
	Earnest Gray, 9-7-80	24

1986 Team Statistics

	Giants	Opp.
Total First Downs	324	284
Rushing	127	78
Passing	171	177
Penalty	26	29
Third Down: Made/Att.	85/228	75/212
Fourth Down: Made/Att.	10/14	2/11
Total Net Yards	5378	4757
Avg. Per Game	336.1	297.3
Total Plays	1076	996
Avg. Per Play	5.0	4.8
Net Yards Rushing	2245	1284
Avg. Per Game	140.3	80.3
Total Rushes	558	350
Net Yards Passing	3133	3473
Avg. Per Game	195.8	217.1
Tackled/Yards Lost	46/367	59/414
Gross Yards	3500	3887
Att./Completions	472/260	587/334
Completion Pct.	55.1	56.9
Had Intercepted	22	24
Punts/Avg.	79/44.8	89/39.3
Net Punting Avg.	37.1	34.5
Penalties/Yards Lost	96/738	119/988
Fumbles/Ball Lost	31/10	36/19
Touchdowns	42	26
Rushing	18	10
Passing	22	15
Returns	2	1
Avg. Time of Possession	31:50	28:10

1986 Team Record

Preseason (3-1)

Date	Result		Opponents
8/6	L	24-31	at Atlanta
8/16	W	22-14	at Green Bay
8/23	W	20-16	N.Y. Jets
8/30	W	17- 3	Pittsburgh
		83-64	

Regular Season (14-2)

Date	Result		Opponents	Att.
9/8	L	28-31	at Dallas	59,804
9/14	W	20- 7	San Diego	74,921
9/21	W	14- 9	at L.A. Raiders	71,164
9/28	W	20-17	New Orleans	72,769
10/5	W	13- 6	at St. Louis	40,562
10/12	W	35- 3	Philadelphia	74,221
10/19	L	12-17	at Seattle	62,282
10/27	W	27-20	Washington	75,923
11/2	W	17-14	Dallas	74,871
11/9	W	17-14	at Philadelphia	60,601
11/16	W	22-20	at Minnesota	62,003
11/23	W	19-16	Denver	75,116
12/1	W	21-17	at San Francisco	59,777
12/7	W	24-14	at Washington	55,642
12/14	W	27- 7	St. Louis	75,261
12/20	W	55-24	Green Bay	71,351

Postseason (3-0)

Date	Result		Opponents	Att.
1/4/87	W	49- 3	San Francisco	75,691
1/11/87	W	17- 0	Washington	76,633
1/25/87	W	39-20	Denver	101,063

Score by Periods

Giants	40	130	106	95	0	—	371
Opponents	39	84	37	76	0	—	236

Attendance

Home 594,433 Away 471,835 Total 1,066,268
Single game home record, 76,633 (1-11-87)
Single season home record, 594,433 (1986)

1986 Individual Statistics

Scoring	TD R	TD P	TD Rt	PAT	FG	Saf	TP
Allegre	0	0	0	33/33	24/32	0	105
Morris	14	1	0	0/0	0/0	0	90
B. Johnson	0	5	0	0/0	0/0	0	30
Bavaro	0	4	0	0/0	0/0	0	24
Anderson, StL-Giants	3	0	0	0/0	0/0	0	18
Anderson, Giants	1	0	0	0/0	0/0	0	6
Manuel	0	3	0	0/0	0/0	0	18
Rouson	2	1	0	0/0	0/0	0	18
Miller	0	2	0	0/0	0/0	0	12
Mowatt	0	2	0	0/0	0/0	0	12
Robinson	0	2	0	0/0	0/0	0	12
Cooper	0	0	0	4/4	2/4	0	10
Carson	0	1	0	0/0	0/0	0	6
Flynn	0	0	1	0/0	0/0	0	6
Martin	0	0	1	0/0	0/0	0	6
McConkey	0	1	0	0/0	0/0	0	6
Simms	1	0	0	0/0	0/0	0	6
Thomas	0	0	0	4/4	0/1	0	4
Giants	18	22	2	41/42	26/37	0	371
Opponents	10	15	1	26/26	18/25	0	236

Passing	Att.	Comp.	Yds.	Pct.	TD	Int.	Tkld.	Rate
Simms	468	259	3487	55.3	21	22	45/359	74.6
Rutledge	3	1	13	33.3	1	0	0/0	87.5
Galbreath	1	0	0	0.0	0	0	1/8	39.6
Giants	472	260	3500	55.1	22	22	46/367	75.0
Opponents	587	334	3887	56.9	15	24	59/414	68.6

Rushing	Att.	Yds.	Avg.	LG	TD
Morris	341	1516	4.4	54	14
Carthon	72	260	3.6	12	0
Anderson, StL-Giants	75	237	3.2	16	3
Anderson, Giants	24	81	3.4	16	1
Rouson	54	179	3.3	21t	2
Simms	43	72	1.7	18	1
Galbreath	16	61	3.8	10	0
B. Johnson	2	28	14.0	22	0
Manuel	1	25	25.0	25	0
Rutledge	3	19	6.3	18	0
Miller	1	3	3.0	3	0
Hostetler	1	1	1.0	1	0
Giants	558	2245	4.0	54	18
Opponents	350	1284	3.7	50	10

Receiving	No.	Yds.	Avg.	LG	TD
Bavaro	66	1001	15.2	41	4
Galbreath	33	268	8.1	19	0
B. Johnson	31	534	17.2	44t	5
Robinson	29	494	17.0	49	2
Morris	21	233	11.1	23	1
Anderson, StL-Giants	19	137	7.2	19	0
Anderson, Giants	9	46	5.1	12	0
McConkey	16	279	17.4	46	1
Carthon	16	67	4.2	10	0
Manuel	11	181	16.5	35	3
Mowatt	10	119	11.9	30	2
Miller	9	144	16.0	32t	2
Rouson	8	121	15.1	37t	1
Carson	1	13	13.0	13t	1
Giants	260	3500	13.5	49	22
Opponents	334	3887	11.6	75t	15

Interceptions	No.	Yds.	Avg.	LG	TD
Kinard	4	52	13.0	25	0
Williams	4	31	7.8	15	0
Hill	3	25	8.3	23	0
Reasons	2	28	14.0	18	0
Patterson	2	26	13.0	26	0
Welch	2	22	11.0	16	0
Martin	1	78	78.0	78t	1
Carson	1	20	20.0	20	0
P. Johnson	1	13	13.0	13	0
Headen	1	1	1.0	1	0
Collins	1	0	0.0	0	0
Flynn, G.B.-Giants	1	0	0.0	0	0
Lasker	1	0	0.0	0	0
Marshall	1	0	0.0	0	0
Giants	24	296	12.3	78t	1
Opponents	22	218	9.9	58t	1

Punting	No.	Yds.	Avg.	In 20	LG
Landeta	79	3539	44.8	24	61
Giants	79	3539	44.8	24	61
Opponents	89	3499	39.3	15	59

Punt Returns	No.	FC	Yds.	Avg.	LG	TD
McConkey	32	12	253	7.9	22	0
Collins	3	1	11	3.7	6	0
Galbreath	3	1	1	0.3	1	0
Manuel	3	6	22	7.3	12	0
Giants	41	20	287	7.0	22	0
Opponents	41	14	386	9.4	61	0

Kickoff Returns	No.	Yds.	Avg.	LG	TD
McConkey	24	471	19.6	27	0
Collins	11	204	18.5	26	0
Miller	7	111	15.9	23	0
Hill	5	61	12.2	30	0
Rouson	2	21	10.5	12	0
Lasker	1	0	0.0	0	0
Giants	50	868	17.4	30	0
Opponents	70	1362	19.5	57	0

Sacks	No.
Taylor	20.5
Marshall	12.0
Banks	6.5
Sally	3.5
Martin	3.0
Headen	2.5
Carson	2.0
Howard	2.0
P. Johnson	2.0
Burt	1.0
Hill	1.0
Kinard	1.0
Lasker	1.0
Williams	1.0
Giants	59.0
Opponents	46.0

FIRST-ROUND SELECTIONS

(If club had no first-round selection, first player drafted is listed with round in parentheses.)

Since 1962

Year	Player, College, Position
1962	Jerry Hillebrand, Colorado, LB
1963	Frank Lasky, Florida, T (2)
1964	Joe Don Looney, Oklahoma, RB
1965	Tucker Frederickson, Auburn, RB
1966	Francis Peay, Missouri, T
1967	Louis Thompson, Alabama, DT (4)
1968	Dick Buzin, Penn State, T (2)
1969	Fred Dryer, San Diego State, DE
1970	Jim Files, Oklahoma, LB
1971	Rocky Thompson, West Texas State, WR
1972	Eldridge Small, Texas A&I, DB
	Larry Jacobson, Nebraska, DE
1973	Brad Van Pelt, Michigan State, LB (2)
1974	John Hicks, Ohio State, G
1975	Al Simpson, Colorado State, T (2)
1976	Troy Archer, Colorado, DE
1977	Gary Jeter, Southern California, DT
1978	Gordon King, Stanford, T
1979	Phil Simms, Morehead State, QB
1980	Mark Haynes, Colorado, DB
1981	Lawrence Taylor, North Carolina, LB
1982	Butch Woolfolk, Michigan, RB
1983	Terry Kinard, Clemson, DB
1984	Carl Banks, Michigan State, LB
	Bill Roberts, Ohio State, T
1985	George Adams, Kentucky, RB
1986	Eric Dorsey, Notre Dame, DE
1987	Mark Ingram, Michigan State, WR

New York Giants 1987 Veteran Roster

No.	Name	Pos.	Ht.	Wt.	Birth-date	NFL Exp.	College	Hometown	How Acq.	'86 Games/ Starts
33	Adams, George	RB	6-1	225	12/22/62	2	Kentucky	Lexington, Ky.	D1-'85	0*
2	Allegre, Raul	K	5-10	167	6/15/59	5	Texas	Torreon, Mexico	FA-'86	13/0
24	Anderson, Ottis	RB	6-2	225	11/19/57	9	Miami	West Palm Beach, Fla.	T(StL)-'86	12/0*
67	Ard, Billy	G	6-3	270	3/12/59	7	Wake Forest	Watchung, N.J.	D8c-'81	16/16
58	Banks, Carl	LB	6-4	235	8/29/62	4	Michigan State	Flint, Mich.	D1-'84	16/16
89	Bavaro, Mark	TE	6-4	245	4/28/63	3	Notre Dame	Danvers, Mass.	D4-'85	16/15
60	Benson, Brad	T	6-3	270	11/25/55	10	Penn State	Altoona, Pa.	FA-'77	16/16
64	†Burt, Jim	NT	6-1	260	6/7/59	7	Miami	Orchard Park, N.Y.	FA-'81	13/13
53	Carson, Harry	LB	6-2	240	11/26/53	12	South Carolina State	Florence, S.C.	D4-'76	16/16
44	Carthon, Maurice	RB	6-1	225	4/24/61	3	Arkansas State	Osceola, Ark.	FA-'85	16/16
25	Collins, Mark	CB	5-10	190	1/16/64	2	Cal State-Fullerton	San Bernardino, Calif.	D2a-'86	15/9
39	Davis, Tyrone	CB	6-1	190	11/16/61	2	Clemson	Athens, Ga.	D3-'85	0*
77	Dorsey, Eric	DE	6-5	280	8/5/64	2	Notre Dame	McLean, Va.	D1-'86	16/0
28	Flynn, Tom	S	6-0	195	3/24/62	4	Pittsburgh	Verona, Pa.	FA-'86	9/0*
30	Galbreath, Tony	RB	6-0	228	1/29/54	12	Missouri	Fulton, Mo.	T(Minn)-'84	16/0
61	Godfrey, Chris	G	6-3	265	5/17/58	5	Michigan	Detroit, Mich.	FA-'84	16/16
54	Headen, Andy	LB	6-5	242	7/8/60	5	Clemson	Asheboro, N.C.	D8-'83	15/0
48	Hill, Kenny	S	6-0	195	7/25/58	7	Yale	Oak Grove, La.	T(Raiders)-'84	16/16
15	†Hostetler, Jeff	QB	6-3	212	4/22/61	4	West Virginia	Johnstown, Pa.	D3-'84	13/0
74	Howard, Erik	NT	6-4	268	11/12/64	2	Washington State	San Jose, Calif.	D2b-'86	8/2
57	Hunt, Byron	LB	6-5	242	12/17/58	7	Southern Methodist	Longview, Tex.	D9-'81	16/0
88	Johnson, Bob	WR	5-11	171	12/14/61	4	Kansas	East St. Louis, Ill.	FA-'84	16/12
68	Johnson, Damian	T	6-5	290	12/18/62	2	Kansas State	Great Bend, Kan.	FA-'85	16/0
52	Johnson, Thomas	LB	6-3	248	7/29/64	2	Ohio State	Detroit, Mich.	D2c-'86	16/0
59	Johnston, Brian	C	6-3	275	11/26/62	2	North Carolina	Highland, Md.	D3a-'85	4/0
51	Jones, Robbie	LB	6-2	230	12/25/59	4	Alabama	Demopolis, Ala.	D12-'83	16/0
69	†Jordan, David	G	6-6	276	7/14/62	3	Auburn	Vestavia Hills, Ala.	D10-'84	0*
43	Kinard, Terry	S	6-1	200	11/24/59	5	Clemson	Sumter, S.C.	D1-'83	14/14
5	Landeta, Sean	P	6-0	200	1/6/62	3	Towson State	Baltimore, Md.	FA-'85	16/0
46	Lasker, Greg	S	6-0	200	9/28/64	2	Arkansas	Conway, Ark.	D2d-'86	16/0
86	†Manuel, Lionel	WR	5-11	175	4/13/62	4	Pacific	La Puente, Calif.	D7-'84	4/4
70	Marshall, Leonard	DE	6-3	285	10/22/61	5	Louisiana State	Franklin, La.	D2-'83	16/16
75	†Martin, George	DE	6-4	255	2/16/53	13	Oregon	Fairfield, Calif.	D11-'75	16/16
80	McConkey, Phil	WR	5-10	170	2/24/57	4	Navy	Buffalo, N.Y.	FA-'84	16/0*
76	†McGriff, Curtis	DE	6-5	276	5/17/58	7	Alabama	Cottonwood, Ala.	FA-'80	0*
87	Miller, Solomon	WR	6-1	185	12/6/64	2	Utah State	Los Angeles, Calif.	D6b-'86	16/2
20	Morris, Joe	RB	5-7	195	9/15/60	6	Syracuse	Ayer, Mass.	D2-'82	15/15
84	Mowatt, Zeke	TE	6-3	240	3/5/61	4	Florida State	Wauchula, Fla.	FA-'83	16/5
63	Nelson, Karl	T	6-6	285	6/14/60	4	Iowa State	Dekalb, Ill.	D3-'83	16/16
65	Oates, Bart	C	6-3	265	12/16/58	3	Brigham Young	Albany, Ga.	FA-'85	16/16
34	Patterson, Elvis	CB	5-11	188	10/21/60	4	Kansas	Houston, Tex.	FA-'84	15/7
55	†Reasons, Gary	LB	6-4	234	2/18/62	4	Northwestern State, La.	Crowley, Tex.	D4a-'84	16/16
66	Roberts, William	T	6-5	280	8/5/62	3	Ohio State	Miami, Fla.	D1a-'84	16/0
81	Robinson, Stacy	WR	5-11	186	2/19/62	3	North Dakota State	St. Paul, Minn.	D2-'85	12/10
22	†Rouson, Lee	RB	6-1	222	10/18/62	3	Colorado	Greensboro, N.C.	D8-'85	14/1
17	†Rutledge, Jeff	QB	6-1	195	1/22/57	9	Alabama	Birmingham, Ala.	T(Rams)-'82	16/0
78	†Sally, Jerome	NT	6-3	270	2/24/59	6	Missouri	Maywood, Ill.	FA-'82	16/1
11	Simms, Phil	QB	6-3	214	11/3/56	8	Morehead State	Louisville, Ky.	D1-'79	16/16
56	Taylor, Lawrence	LB	6-3	243	2/4/59	7	North Carolina	Williamsburg, Va.	D1-'81	16/16
83	Warren, Vince	WR	6-0	180	2/18/63	2	San Diego State	Albuquerque, N.M.	D5-'86	4/0
73	Washington, John	DE	6-4	275	2/20/63	2	Oklahoma State	Houston, Tex.	D3-'86	16/0
27	Welch, Herb	S	5-11	180	1/12/61	3	UCLA	Downey, Calif.	D12-'85	16/2
23	Williams, Perry	CB	6-2	203	5/12/61	4	North Carolina State	Hamlet, N.C.	D7-'83	16/16

* Adams, Davis, Jordan, and McGriff missed '86 season due to injury; Anderson played 4 games with St. Louis in '86, 8 with N.Y. Giants; Flynn played 7 games with Green Bay, 2 with N.Y. Giants; McConkey played 4 games with Green Bay, 12 with N.Y. Giants.

†Option playout; subject to developments.

Also played with Giants in '86—K Bob Thomas (1 game), K Joe Cooper (2).

COACHING STAFF

Head Coach, Bill Parcells

Pro Career: Became twelfth head coach in New York Giants history on December 15, 1982. Parcells begins fifth campaign as head coach after spending two seasons as the Giants' defensive coordinator and linebacker coach. Led Giants to Super Bowl XXI victory over Denver 39-20 after Wild Card playoff berths in both 1984 and 1985. Started pro coaching career in 1980 as linebacker coach with New England Patriots. Career record: 41-29-1.

Background: Linebacker at Wichita State 1961-63. College assistant Hastings (Neb.) 1964, Wichita State 1965, Army 1966-69, Florida State 1970-72, Vanderbilt 1973-74, Texas Tech 1975-77, Air Force 1978 (head coach).

Personal: Born August 22, 1941, Englewood, N.J. Bill and his wife, Judy, live in Upper Saddle River, N.J., and have three daughters—Suzy, Jill, and Dallas.

Assistant Coaches

Bill Belichick, defensive coordinator; born April 16, 1952, Nashville, Tenn., lives in Chatham, N.J. Center-tight end Wesleyan 1972-74. No pro playing experience. Pro coach: Baltimore Colts 1975, Detroit Lions 1976-77, Denver Broncos 1978, joined Giants in 1979.

Romeo Crennell, special teams; born June 18, 1947, Lynchburg, Va., lives in Montvale, N.J. Defensive lineman Western Kentucky 1966-69. No pro playing experience. College coach: Western Kentucky 1970-74, Texas Tech 1975-77, Mississippi 1978-79, Georgia Tech 1980. Pro coach: Joined Giants in 1981.

Ron Erhardt, offensive coordinator; born February 27, 1932, Mandan, N.D., lives in Wykoff, N.J. Quarterback Jamestown (N.D.) College 1951-54. No pro playing experience. College coach: North Dakota State 1963-72 (head coach 1966-72). Pro coach: New England Patriots 1973-81 (head coach 1979-81), joined Giants in 1982.

Len Fontes, defensive backfield; born March 8, 1938, New Bedford, Mass., lives in Dover, N.J. Defensive back Ohio State 1958-59. No pro playing experience. College coach: Eastern Michigan 1968, Dayton 1969-72, Navy 1973-76, Miami 1977-79. Pro coach: Cleveland Browns 1980-82, joined Giants in 1983.

Ray Handley, running backs; born October 8, 1944, Artesia, N.M., lives in West Orange, N.J. Running back Stanford 1963-65. No pro playing experience. College coach: Stanford 1967, 1971-74, 1979-83, Army 1968-69, Air Force 1975-78. Pro coach: Joined Giants in 1984.

Fred Hoaglin, offensive line; born January 28, 1944, Alliance, Ohio, lives in Sparta, N.J. Center Pittsburgh 1962-65. Pro center Cleveland Browns 1966-72, Baltimore Colts 1973, Houston Oilers 1974-75, Seattle Seahawks 1976. Pro coach: Detroit Lions 1978-84, joined Giants in 1985.

Pat Hodgson, receivers; born January 30, 1944, Columbus, Ga., lives in East Rutherford, N.J. Tight end Georgia 1963-65. Pro tight end Washington Redskins 1966, Minnesota Vikings 1967. College coach: Georgia 1968-70, 1972-77, Florida State 1971, Texas Tech 1978. Pro coach: San Diego Chargers 1978, joined Giants in 1979.

Lamar Leachman, defensive line; born August 7, 1934, Cartersville, Ga., lives in Ridgewood, N.J. Center-linebacker Tennessee 1952-55. No pro playing experience. College coach: Richmond 1966-67, Georgia Tech 1968-71, Memphis State 1972, South Carolina 1973. Pro coach: New York Stars (WFL) 1974, Toronto Argonauts (CFL) 1975-77, Montreal Alouettes (CFL) 1978-79, joined Giants in 1980.

Johnny Parker, strength and conditioning; born February 1, 1947, Greenville, S.C., lives in Montvale, N.J. No pro playing experience. Graduate of Mississippi, master's degree from Delta State University. College coach: South Carolina 1974-76, Indiana 1977-79, Louisiana State 1980, Mississippi 1981-83. Pro coach: Joined Giants in 1984.

Mike Pope, tight ends; born March 15, 1942, Monroe, N.C., lives in River Vale, N.J. Quarterback Lenoir Rhyne 1962-64. No pro playing experience. College coach: Florida State 1970-74, Texas Tech 1975-77, Mississippi 1978-82. Pro coach: Joined Giants in 1983.

Mike Sweatman, assistant special teams; born October 23, 1946, Kansas City, Mo., lives in Wayne, N.J. Linebacker Kansas 1964-67. No pro playing experience. College coach: Kansas 1973-74, 1979-82, Tulsa 1977-78, Tennessee 1983. Pro coach: Minnesota Vikings 1984, joined Giants in 1985.

New York Giants 1987 First-Year Roster

Name	Pos.	Ht.	Wt.	Birth-date	College	Hometown	How Acq.
Baker, Stephen	WR	5-7	160	8/30/64	Fresno State	Los Angeles, Calif.	D3
Berthusen, Bill	NT	6-5	286	6/26/64	Iowa State	Marshalltown, Iowa	D12a
Faucette, Chuck	LB	6-2	238	10/7/63	Maryland	Willingboro, N.J.	D10
Ingram, Mark	WR	5-11	188	8/23/65	Michigan State	Flint, Mich.	D1
Jones, Rod	TE	6-4	240	3/3/64	Washington	Richmond, Calif.	D8
O'Connor, Paul	G	6-3	274	11/7/62	Miami	Berkeley Heights, N.J.	D5
Parker, Stan	G	6-5	276	3/19/64	Nebraska	Bellevue, Neb.	D9a
Riesenberg, Doug	T	6-5	270	7/22/65	California	Moscow, Idaho	D6b
Richardson, Tim	RB	6-0	210	2/23/64	Pacific	Springfield, Ill.	D6a
Stark, Chad	RB	6-2	230	4/4/65	North Dakota State	Brookings, S.D.	D12b
Turner, Odessa	WR	6-3	205	10/12/64	Northwestern St., La.	Monroe, La.	D4
Walter, Dave	QB	6-3	218	12/9/64	Michigan Tech	Sanford, Mich.	D11
White, Adrian	CB-S	6-0	200	4/6/64	Florida	Orange Park, Fla.	D2
Wright, Dana	RB	6-2	214	6/2/63	Findlay	Kent, Ohio	D9b

The term NFL Rookie is defined as a player who is in his first season of professional football and has not been on the roster of another professional football team for any regular-season or postseason games. A Rookie is designated by an "R" on NFL rosters. Players who have been active in another professional football league or players who have NFL experience, including either preseason training camp or being on an active roster for fewer than three regular-season or postseason games, are termed NFL First-Year Players. An NFL First-Year Player is designated by a "1" on NFL rosters. Thereafter, a player on an NFL active roster for at least three regular-season or postseason games is credited with an additional year of NFL playing experience.

NOTES

National Football Conference
Eastern Division

Team Colors: Kelly Green, Silver, and White

Veterans Stadium
Broad Street and Pattison Avenue
Philadelphia, Pennsylvania 19148
Telephone: (215) 463-2500

Club Officials

Owner: Norman Braman
President-Chief Operating Officer: Harry Gamble
Vice President-Chief Financial Officer: Mimi Box
Vice President-Marketing and Development: Decker Uhlhorn
Assistants to the President: George Azar and Patrick Forte
Director of Player Personnel: Joe Woolley
Talent Scouts: Bill Baker, Lou Blumling
Director of Communications: Ed Wisneski
Assistant Director of Communications: Ron Howard
Associate Directors of Sales and Marketing: Jim Gallagher and Leslie Stephenson
Ticket Manager: Leo Carlin
Director of Penthouse Sales: Lou Scheinfeld
Trainer: Otho Davis
Assistant Trainer: David Price
Equipment Manager: Rusty Sweeney
Video Director: Mike Dougherty

Stadium: Veterans Stadium •
Capacity: 66,592
Broad Street and Pattison Avenue
Philadelphia, Pennsylvania 19148

Playing Surface: AstroTurf

Training Camp: West Chester University
West Chester, Pennsylvania 19382

1987 Schedule

Preseason

Aug. 15	at New York Jets	8:00
Aug. 23	at New England	7:00
Aug. 29	**Miami**	7:30
Sept. 3	**Detroit**	7:30

Regular Season

Sept. 13	at Washington	1:00
Sept. 20	**New Orleans**	1:00
Sept. 27	at San Francisco	1:00
Oct. 4	**Chicago**	1:00
Oct. 11	at Dallas	12:00
Oct. 18	at Green Bay	12:00
Oct. 25	**Dallas**	1:00
Nov. 1	at St. Louis	12:00
Nov. 8	**Washington**	1:00
Nov. 15	**New York Giants**	4:00
Nov. 22	**St. Louis**	1:00
Nov. 29	at New England	1:00
Dec. 6	at New York Giants	1:00
Dec. 13	**Miami**	1:00
Dec. 20	at New York Jets	1:00
Dec. 27	**Buffalo**	1:00

Eagles Coaching History

(295-386-24)

1933-35	Lud Wray	9-21-1
1936-40	Bert Bell	10-44-2
1941-50	Earle (Greasy) Neale*	66-44-5
1951	Alvin (Bo) McMillin**	2-0-0
1951	Wayne Millner	2-8-0
1952-55	Jim Trimble	25-20-3
1956-57	Hugh Devore	7-16-1
1958-60	Lawrence (Buck) Shaw	20-16-1
1961-63	Nick Skorich	15-24-3
1964-68	Joe Kuharich	28-41-1
1969-71	Jerry Williams***	7-22-2
1971-72	Ed Khayat	8-15-2
1973-75	Mike McCormack	16-25-1
1976-82	Dick Vermeil	57-51-0
1983-85	Marion Campbell****	17-29-1
1985	Fred Bruney	1-0-0
1986	Buddy Ryan	5-10-1

*Co-coach with Walt Kiesling in Philadelphia-Pittsburgh merger in 1943
**Retired after two games in 1951
***Released after three games in 1971
****Released after 15 games in 1985

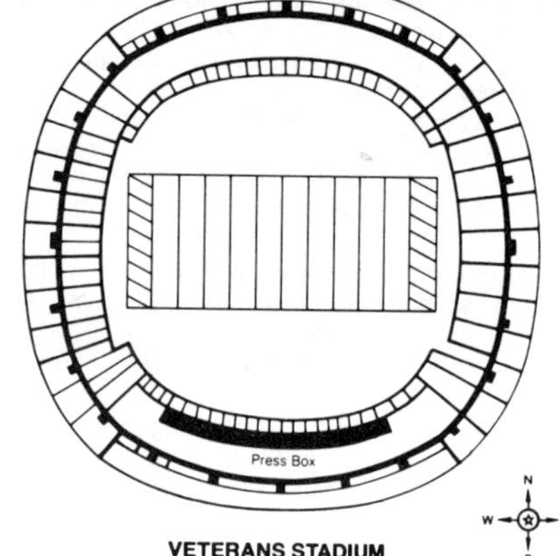

VETERANS STADIUM

Record Holders

Individual Records—Career

Category	Name	Performance
Rushing (Yds.)	Wilbert Montgomery, 1977-1984	6,538
Passing (Yds.)	Ron Jaworski, 1977-1986	26,963
Passing (TDs)	Ron Jaworski, 1977-1986	175
Receiving (No.)	Harold Carmichael, 1971-1983	589
Receiving (Yds.)	Harold Carmichael, 1971-1983	8,978
Interceptions	Bill Bradley, 1969-1976	34
Field Goals	Sam Baker, 1964-69	90
Touchdowns (Tot.)	Harold Carmichael, 1971-1983	79
Points	Bobby Walston, 1951-1962	881

Individual Records—Single Season

Category	Name	Performance
Rushing (Yds.)	Wilbert Montgomery, 1979	1,512
Passing (Yds.)	Sonny Jurgensen, 1961	3,723
Passing (TDs)	Sonny Jurgensen, 1961	32
Receiving (No.)	Mike Quick, 1985	71
Receiving (Yds.)	Mike Quick, 1983	1,409
Interceptions	Bill Bradley, 1971	11
Field Goals	Paul McFadden, 1984	30
Touchdowns (Tot.)	Steve Van Buren, 1945	18
Points	Paul McFadden, 1984	116

Individual Records—Single Game

Category	Name	Performance
Rushing (Yds.)	Steve Van Buren, 11-27-49	205
Passing (Yds.)	Bobby Thomason, 11-18-53	437
Passing (TDs)	Adrian Burk, 10-17-54	7
Receiving (No.)	Don Looney, 12-1-40	14
Receiving (Yds.)	Tommy McDonald, 12-10-60	237
Interceptions	Russ Craft, 9-24-50	4
Field Goals	Tom Dempsey, 11-12-72	6
Touchdowns (Tot.)	Many times Last time by Wilbert Montgomery, 10-7-79	4
Points	Bobby Walston, 10-17-54	25

1986 Team Statistics

	Eagles	Opp.
Total First Downs	287	278
Rushing	113	97
Passing	150	156
Penalty	24	25
Third Down: Made/Att.	105/273	79/230
Fourth Down: Made/Att.	5/12	9/16
Total Net Yards	4542	5224
Avg. Per Game	283.9	326.5
Total Plays	1117	1043
Avg. Per Play	4.1	5.0
Net Yards Rushing	2002	1989
Avg. Per Game	125.1	124.3
Total Rushes	499	458
Net Yards Passing	2540	3235
Avg. Per Game	158.8	202.2
Tackled/Yards Lost	104/708	53/406
Gross Yards	3248	3641
Att./Completions	514/268	532/260
Completion Pct.	52.1	48.9
Had Intercepted	17	23
Punts/Avg.	111/41.0	97/38.7
Net Punting Avg.	33.5	32.3
Penalties/Yards Lost	102/901	115/884
Fumbles/Ball Lost	34/10	30/13
Touchdowns	28	39
Rushing	8	14
Passing	19	21
Returns	1	4
Avg. Time of Possession	31:57	28:03

1986 Team Record

Preseason (1-3)

Date	Result		Opponents
8/8	W	17- 9	at Detroit
8/16	L	38-45	at San Diego
8/23	L	15-20	Miami
8/28	L	30-37	N.Y. Jets
		100-111	

Regular Season (5-10-1)

Date	Result		Opponents	Att.
9/7	L	14-41	at Washington	53,982
9/14	L	10-13	at Chicago (OT)	65,130
9/21	L	7-33	Denver	63,839
9/28	W	34-20	L.A. Rams	65,646
10/5	W	16- 0	at Atlanta	57,104
10/12	L	3-35	at N.Y. Giants	74,221
10/19	L	14-17	Dallas	68,572
10/26	W	23- 7	San Diego	41,469
11/2	L	10-13	at St. Louis	33,051
11/9	L	14-17	N.Y. Giants	60,601
11/16	L	11-13	Detroit	54,568
11/23	L	20-24	at Seattle	55,786
11/30	W	33-27	at L.A. Raid. (OT)	53,338
12/7	T	10-10	St. Louis (OT)	50,148
12/14	W	23-21	at Dallas	46,117
12/21	L	14-21	Washington	61,816

(OT) Overtime

Score by Periods

Eagles	66	51	48	85	6	—	256
Opponents	50	75	86	98	3	—	312

Attendance

Home 466,659   Away 438,729   Total 905,388
Single game home record, 72,111 (11-1-81)
Single season home record, 557,325 (1980)

1986 Individual Statistics

Scoring	TD R	TD P	TD Rt	PAT	FG	Saf	TP
McFadden	0	0	0	26/27	20/31	0	86
Quick	0	9	0	0/0	0/0	0	54
K. Jackson	0	6	0	0/0	0/0	0	36
Cunningham	5	0	0	0/0	0/0	0	30
Tautalatasi	0	2	0	0/0	0/0	0	12
Byars	1	0	0	0/0	0/0	0	6
Crawford	1	0	0	0/0	0/0	0	6
Duckworth, Rams-Phil.	0	1	0	0/0	0/0	0	6
Garrity	0	0	1	0/0	0/0	0	6
R. Johnson	0	1	0	0/0	0/0	0	6
Spagnola	0	1	0	0/0	0/0	0	6
Toney	1	0	0	0/0	0/0	0	6
Brown	0	0	0	0/0	0/0	1	2
Eagles	8	19	1	26/27	20/31	1	256
Opponents	14	21	4	37/39	13/26	1	312

Passing	Att.	Comp.	Yds.	Pct.	TD	Int.	Tkld.	Rate
Jaworski	245	128	1405	52.2	8	6	22/156	70.2
Cunning-ham	209	111	1391	53.1	8	7	72/489	72.9
Cavanaugh	58	28	397	48.3	2	4	9/56	53.6
Byars	2	1	55	50.0	1	0	1/7	135.4
Eagles	514	268	3248	52.1	19	17	104/708	70.4
Opponents	532	260	3641	48.9	21	23	53/406	66.5

Rushing	Att.	Yds.	Avg.	LG	TD
Byars	177	577	3.3	32	1
Cunningham	66	540	8.2	20	5
Toney	69	285	4.1	43	1
Haddix	79	276	3.5	18	0
Tautalatasi	51	163	3.2	50	0
Crawford	28	88	3.1	15	1
Jaworski	13	33	2.5	10	0
Cavanaugh	9	26	2.9	11	0
M. Waters	5	8	1.6	5	0
K. Jackson	1	6	6.0	6	0
Teltschik	1	0	0.0	0	0
Eagles	499	2002	4.0	50	8
Opponents	458	1989	4.3	84t	14

Receiving	No.	Yds.	Avg.	LG	TD
Quick	60	939	15.7	75t	9
Tautalatasi	41	325	7.9	56	2
Spagnola	39	397	10.2	38	1
K. Jackson	30	506	16.9	49	6
Haddix	26	150	5.8	29	0
Little	14	132	9.4	26	0
Toney	13	177	13.6	47	0
Garrity	12	227	18.9	34	0
R. Johnson	11	207	18.8	39	1
Byars	11	44	4.0	17	0
Duckworth, Rams-Phil.	10	148	14.8	32	1
Duckworth, Phil.	1	7	7.0	7	0
Smith	6	94	15.7	36	0
M. Waters	2	27	13.5	19	0
Darby	2	16	8.0	13	0
Eagles	268	3248	12.1	75t	19
Opponents	260	3641	14.0	84t	21

Interceptions	No.	Yds.	Avg.	LG	TD
A. Waters	6	39	6.5	21	0
Young	6	9	1.5	9	0
Cooper	3	20	6.7	20	0
A. Johnson	3	6	2.0	9	0
Hoage	1	18	18.0	18	0
Foules	1	14	14.0	14	0
Gary, N.O.-Phil.	1	14	14.0	14	0
Schulz	1	11	11.0	11	0
Joyner	1	4	4.0	4	0
Cobb	1	3	3.0	3	0
Eagles	23	124	5.4	21	0
Opponents	17	192	11.3	32t	1

Punting	No.	Yds.	Avg.	In 20	LG
Teltschik	108	4493	41.6	20	62
Cunningham	2	54	27.0	0	39
Eagles	111	4547	41.0	20	62
Opponents	97	3751	38.7	23	68

Punt Returns	No.	FC	Yds.	Avg.	LG	TD
Garrity	17	7	187	11.0	76t	1
Cooper	16	7	139	8.7	58	0
M. Waters	7	1	30	4.3	13	0
Smith	4	1	18	4.5	7	0
Eagles	44	16	374	8.5	76t	1
Opponents	63	13	634	10.1	75t	2

Kickoff Returns	No.	Yds.	Avg.	LG	TD
Crawford	27	497	18.4	36	0
Tautalatasi	18	344	19.1	51	0
Byars	2	47	23.5	31	0
Cooper	2	42	21.0	24	0
Quick	2	6	3.0	6	0
Schulz	1	9	9.0	9	0
Simmons	1	0	0.0	0	0
Eagles	53	945	17.8	51	0
Opponents	62	1261	20.3	40	0

Sacks	No.
White	18.0
Brown	9.0
Clarke	8.0
Cobb	6.0
Jiles	2.0
Joyner	2.0
Simmons	2.0
A. Waters	2.0
Cooper	1.0
Darby	1.0
A. Johnson	1.0
Singletary	1.0
Eagles	53.0
Opponents	104.0

FIRST-ROUND SELECTIONS

(If club had no first-round selection, first player drafted is listed with round in parentheses.)

Since 1953

Year	Player, College, Position
1953	Al Conway, Army, B (2)
1954	Neil Worden, Notre Dame, B
1955	Dick Bielski, Maryland, B
1956	Bob Pellegrini, Maryland, C
1957	Clarence Peaks, Michigan State, B
1958	Walt Kowalczyk, Michigan State, B
1959	J.D. Smith, Rice, T (2)
1960	Ron Burton, Northwestern, RB
1961	Art Baker, Syracuse, RB
1962	Pete Case, Georgia, G (2)
1963	Ed Budde, Michigan State, G
1964	Bob Brown, Nebraska, T
1965	Ray Rissmiller, Georgia, T (2)
1966	Randy Beisler, Indiana, DE
1967	Harry Jones, Arkansas, RB
1968	Tim Rossovich, Southern California, DE
1969	Leroy Keyes, Purdue, RB
1970	Steve Zabel, Oklahoma, TE
1971	Richard Harris, Grambling, DE
1972	John Reaves, Florida, QB
1973	Jerry Sisemore, Texas, T
	Charle Young, Southern California, TE
1974	Mitch Sutton, Kansas, DT (3)
1975	Bill Capraun, Miami, T (7)
1976	Mike Smith, Florida, DE (4)
1977	Skip Sharp, Kansas, DB (5)
1978	Reggie Wilkes, Georgia Tech, LB (3)
1979	Jerry Robinson, UCLA, LB
1980	Roynell Young, Alcorn State, DB
1981	Leonard Mitchell, Houston, DE
1982	Mike Quick, North Carolina State, WR
1983	Michael Haddix, Mississippi State, RB
1984	Kenny Jackson, Penn State, WR
1985	Kevin Allen, Indiana, T
1986	Keith Byars, Ohio State, RB
1987	Jerome Brown, Miami, DT

Philadelphia Eagles 1987 Veteran Roster

No.	Name	Pos.	Ht.	Wt.	Birth-date	NFL Exp.	College	Hometown	How Acq.	'86 Games/ Starts
63	Baker, Ron	G	6-4	274	11/19/54	10	Oklahoma State	Emerson, Ind.	T(Ind)-'80	16/16
77	Black, Mike	T-G	6-4	290	8/24/64	2	Sacramento State	Loomis, Calif.	FA-'86	1/0
98	Brown, Greg	DE	6-5	265	1/5/57	7	Kansas State	Washington, D.C.	FA-'81	16/15
41	Byars, Keith	RB	6-1	230	10/14/63	2	Ohio State	Dayton, Ohio	D1-'86	16/8
6	Cavanaugh, Matt	QB	6-2	212	10/27/56	10	Pittsburgh	Youngstown, Ohio	T(SF)-'86	10/2
71	Clarke, Ken	DT	6-2	275	8/28/56	10	Syracuse	Boston, Mass.	FA-'78	16/16
50	Cobb, Garry	LB	6-2	230	3/16/57	9	Southern California	Stamford, Conn.	T(Det)-'85	16/16
79	Conwell, Joe	T	6-5	275	2/24/61	2	North Carolina	Ardmore, Pa.	T(SF)-'86	16/9
21	†Cooper, Evan	CB-KR	5-11	184	6/28/62	4	Michigan	Miami, Fla.	D4-'84	16/13
45	Crawford, Charles	RB-KR	6-2	235	3/8/64	2	Oklahoma State	Bristow, Okla.	SD7-'86	16/5
12	Cunningham, Randall	QB	6-4	192	3/27/63	3	Nevada-Las Vegas	Santa Barbara, Calif.	D2-'85	15/5
84	†Darby, Byron	TE	6-4	262	6/4/60	5	Southern California	Inglewood, Calif.	D5-'83	16/7
78	Darwin, Matt	C	6-4	260	3/11/63	2	Texas A&M	Spring, Tex.	D4-'86	16/10
67	Feehery, Gerry	C	6-2	270	3/9/60	5	Syracuse	Springfield, Pa.	FA-'83	6/6
29	†Foules, Elbert	CB	5-11	185	7/4/61	5	Alcorn State	Greenville, Miss.	FA-'83	16/3
33	†Frizzell, William	S	6-3	198	9/8/62	4	North Carolina Central	Greenville, N.C.	FA-'86	8/0
86	Garrity, Gregg	WR-KR	5-10	169	11/24/61	5	Penn State	Bradford Woods, Pa.	FA-'84	12/0
26	Haddix, Michael	RB	6-2	227	12/27/61	5	Mississippi State	Walnut, Miss.	D1-'83	16/9
62	Haden, Nick	G-C	6-2	270	11/7/62	2	Penn State	McKees Rocks, Pa.	W(Raiders)-'86	8/6
34	†Hoage, Terry	S	6-3	199	4/11/62	4	Georgia	Huntsville, Tex.	FA-'86	16/12
48	Hopkins, Wes	S	6-1	212	9/26/61	5	Southern Methodist	Birmingham, Ala.	D2a-'83	4/4
81	Jackson, Kenny	WR	6-0	180	2/15/62	4	Penn State	South River, N.J.	D1-'84	16/14
53	†Jiles, Dwayne	LB	6-4	242	11/23/61	3	Texas Tech	Linden, Tex.	D5-'85	16/3
54	Johnson, Alonzo	LB	6-3	222	4/4/63	2	Florida	Panama City, Fla.	D2b-'86	15/9
85	†Johnson, Ron	WR	6-3	186	9/21/58	3	Long Beach State	Monterey, Calif.	FA-'85	12/0
59	Joyner, Seth	LB	6-2	241	11/18/64	2	Texas-El Paso	Spring Valley, N.Y.	D8-'86	14/7
52	Kraynak, Rich	LB	6-1	230	1/20/61	5	Pittsburgh	Phoenixville, Pa.	D8-'83	6/0
65	Landsee, Bob	G-C	6-4	273	3/21/64	2	Wisconsin	Iron Mountain, Mich.	D6-'86	7/1
58	Lee, Byron	LB	6-2	230	9/8/64	2	Ohio State	Columbus, Ohio	D7b-'86	3/0
89	Little, Dave	TE	6-2	236	4/18/61	4	Middle Tennessee State	Fresno, Calif.	FA-'85	16/5
8	†McFadden, Paul	K	5-11	163	9/24/61	4	Youngstown State	Euclid, Ohio	D12-'84	16/0
74	Mitchell, Leonard	T	6-7	295	10/12/58	7	Houston	Houston, Tex.	D1-'81	10/10
82	Quick, Mike	WR	6-2	190	5/14/59	6	North Carolina State	Richmond, N.C.	D1-'82	16/16
66	Reeves, Ken	T-G	6-5	275	10/4/61	3	Texas A&M	Pittsburg, Tex.	D6b-'85	15/15
55	Reichenbach, Mike	LB	6-2	238	9/14/61	4	East Stroudsburg	Bethlehem, Pa.	FA-'84	16/16
76	Schreiber, Adam	G-C	6-4	270	2/20/62	4	Texas	Huntsville, Ala.	FA-'86	9/0
95	†Schulz, Jody	LB	6-3	235	8/17/60	4	East Carolina	Centreville, Md.	D2b-'83	16/0
96	Simmons, Clyde	DT-DE	6-6	258	8/4/64	2	Western Carolina	Wilmington, N.C.	D9-'86	16/0
68	Singletary, Reggie	G-T	6-3	272	1/17/64	2	North Carolina State	Whiteville, N.C.	D12a-'86	16/6
83	Smith, Phil	WR	6-3	188	4/28/60	4	San Diego State	Gardena, Calif.	FA-'86	3/2
88	Spagnola, John	TE	6-4	242	8/1/57	8	Yale	Bethlehem, Pa.	FA-'79	15/12
93	†Strauthers, Tom	DT-DE	6-4	264	4/6/61	5	Jackson State	Brookhaven, Miss.	D10-'83	11/1
37	Tautalatasi, Junior	RB	5-10	205	3/24/62	2	Washington State	Alameda, Calif.	D10-'86	16/2
10	Teltschik, John	P	6-2	215	3/8/64	2	Texas	Floresville, Tex.	W(Chi)-'86	16/0
25	Toney, Anthony	RB	6-0	227	9/23/62	2	Texas A&M	Salinas, Calif.	D2a-'86	12/5
69	Tupper, Jeff	DE	6-5	269	12/26/62	2	Oklahoma	Joplin, Mo.	FA-'86	3/0
20	†Waters, Andre	S	5-11	185	3/10/62	4	Cheyney State	Pahokee, Fla.	FA-'84	16/16
92	White, Reggie	DE-DT	6-5	285	12/19/61	3	Tennessee	Chattanooga, Tenn.	SD1-'84	16/16
22	Wilson, Brenard	S	6-0	185	8/15/55	9	Vanderbilt	Daytona Beach, Fla.	FA-'79	16/0
43	†Young, Roynell	CB	6-1	185	12/1/57	8	Alcorn State	New Orleans, La.	D1-'80	16/16

†Option playout; subject to developments.

Also played with Eagles in '86—WR Bobby Duckworth (4 games), S Russell Gary (6), G-C Jim Gilmore (2), RB Earnest Jackson (active for 2 games, but did not play), QB Ron Jaworski (10), T Tom Jelesky (9), QB Kyle Mackey (active for 2 games, but did not play), RB Mike Waters (5).

COACHING STAFF

Head Coach, Buddy Ryan

Pro Career: Ryan was named head coach of the Eagles on January 29, 1986, after eight seasons as the defensive coordinator of the Chicago Bears. An NFL assistant coach for 18 years, Ryan has been on the staffs of three Super Bowl teams: Jets, 1968; Vikings, 1976; Bears, 1985. He served as defensive line coach under Bud Grant with the Minnesota Vikings in 1976 and 1977 before joining Chicago. From 1968-75, he was on the defensive staff of the New York Jets under coach Weeb Ewbank. In Ryan's eight seasons as defensive coordinator with Chicago, his defenses ranked among the NFL's top 10 six times. He devised the "46 defense" with its multiple variations of alignments and coverages. Career record: 5-10-1.

Background: Ryan was a four-year letterman at Oklahoma State from 1952-55 as an offensive guard. While serving in the U.S. Army in Korea, Ryan played on the Fourth Army championship team in Japan. He served as an assistant at the University of Buffalo from 1961-65, Vanderbilt 1966, and the University of the Pacific 1967. Ryan has a master's degree in education from Middle Tennessee State.

Personal: Born James Ryan on February 17, 1934, in Frederick, Okla. Buddy and his wife, Joan, live in Cherry Hill, N.J., and have three sons: Jimmy, Jr., Rex, and Robert.

Assistant Coaches

Dave Atkins, offensive backfield; born May 18, 1949, Victoria, Tex., lives in Marlton, N.J. Running back Texas-El Paso 1970-72. Pro running back San Francisco 49ers 1973, Honolulu Hawaiians (WFL) 1974, San Diego Chargers 1975. College coach: Texas-El Paso 1979-80, San Diego State 1981-85. Pro coach: Joined Eagles in 1986.

Jeff Fisher, defensive backs; born February 25, 1958, Culver City, Calif., lives in Voorhees, N.J. Defensive back Southern California 1978-80. Pro defensive back-punt returner Chicago Bears 1981-85. Pro coach: Joined Eagles in 1986.

Dale Haupt, defensive line; born April 12, 1929, Manitowoc, Wis., lives in Cherry Hill, N.J. Defensive lineman-linebacker Wyoming 1950-53. No pro playing experience. College coach: Tennessee 1960-63, Iowa State 1964-65, Richmond 1966-71, North Carolina State 1972-76, Duke 1977. Pro coach: Chicago Bears 1978-85, joined Eagles in 1986.

Ronnie Jones, strength and conditioning; born October 17, 1955, Dumas, Tex., lives in Cherry Hill, N.J. Running back Northwestern State (Okla.) 1974-77. College coach: Northeastern State (Okla.) 1979-83, Tulsa 1984, Arizona State 1985-86. Pro coach: First year with Eagles.

Dan Neal, special teams; born August 30, 1949, Corbin, Ky., lives in Cherry Hill, N.J. Center Kentucky 1970-72. Pro center Baltimore Colts 1973-74, Chicago Bears 1975-83. Pro coach: Joined Eagles in 1986.

Wade Phillips, defensive coordinator-linebackers; born June 21, 1947, Orange, Tex., lives in Mt. Laurel, N.J. Linebacker Houston 1966-68. No pro playing experience. College coach: Houston 1969, Oklahoma State 1973-74, Kansas 1975. Pro coach: Houston Oilers 1976-80, New Orleans Saints 1981-85 (head coach last four games of 1985), joined Eagles in 1986.

Ted Plumb, assistant head coach-offense; born August 20, 1939, Reno, Nev., lives in Cherry Hill, N.J. Wide receiver Baylor 1960-61. Pro wide receiver Buffalo Bills 1962. College coach: Cerritos, Calif., J.C. 1966-67, Texas Christian 1968-70, Tulsa 1971, Kansas 1972-73. Pro coach: New York Giants 1974-76, Atlanta Falcons 1977-79, Chicago Bears 1980-85, joined Eagles in 1986.

Philadelphia Eagles 1987 First-Year Roster

Name	Pos.	Ht.	Wt.	Birth-date	College	Hometown	How Acq.
Alexander, David	G	6-3	279	7/28/64	Tulsa	Broken Arrow, Okla.	D5
Booker, Martin (1)	WR	6-1	183	3/8/63	Villanova	Camden, N.J.	FA-'86
Brown, Cedrick (1)	CB	5-10	178	9/6/64	Washington State	Compton, Calif.	FA-'86
Brown, Jerome	DT	6-2	292	2/4/65	Miami	Brooksville, Fla.	D1
Carberry, Paul	DT-DE	6-3	262	8/1/64	Oregon State	Oak Lawn, Ill.	D10
Dunn, David	DE-TE	6-8	240	12/1/64	Georgia	Mobleton, Ga.	FA
Evans, Byron	LB	6-2	228	2/23/64	Arizona	Phoenix, Ariz.	D4
Fricke, Rusty	K	6-1	195	9/1/64	Lycoming College	Willow Grove, Pa.	FA
Gorecki, Chuck (1)	LB	6-4	237	4/7/64	Boston College	Berwyn, Pa.	FA
Klingel, John	DE	6-3	260	12/21/63	Eastern Kentucky	Lincoln, Ohio	FA
Lambiotte, Ken	QB	6-3	187	10/17/63	William & Mary	Woodstock, Va.	D9
Lingmerth, Goran	K	5-8	170	11/11/64	Northern Arizona	Kingsburg, Calif.	FA
Mitchell, Randall	DE-DT	6-1	275	9/19/63	Tenn.-Chattanooga	Savannah, Ga.	FA
Moore, Irvin	RB	6-0	225	11/2/64	Nevada-Las Vegas	Pasadena, Calif.	FA
Morse, Bobby	RB	5-10	201	10/3/65	Michigan State	Muskegon, Mich.	D12
Moten, Ron	LB	6-1	230	9/15/64	Florida	Clearwater, Fla.	D6a
Pike, Chris	DT	6-7	291	1/13/64	Tulsa	Washington, D.C.	D6b
Redick, Cornelius (1)	WR-KR	5-11	185	1/7/64	Cal State-Fullerton	Los Angeles, Calif.	D7a-'86
Reid, Alan (1)	RB	5-8	190	9/6/60	Minnesota	El Paso, Tex.	FA
Tamburello, Ben	G-C	6-3	278	9/9/64	Auburn	Birmingham, Ala.	D3
Turral, Willie	RB-KR	5-10	190	2/1/64	New Mexico	Tallahassee, Fla.	FA
Williams, Brian (1)	T	6-7	293	3/30/64	Central Michigan	Haslett, Mich.	FA-'86

The term NFL Rookie is defined as a player who is in his first season of professional football and has not been on the roster of another professional football team for any regular-season or postseason games. A Rookie is designated by an "R" on NFL rosters. Players who have been active in another professional football league or players who have NFL experience, including either preseason training camp or being on an active roster for fewer than three regular-season or postseason games, are termed NFL First-Year Players. An NFL First-Year Player is designated by a "1" on NFL rosters. Thereafter, a player on an NFL active roster for at least three regular-season or postseason games is credited with an additional year of NFL playing experience.

NOTES

Doug Scovil, quarterbacks; born July 1, 1927, Anacortes, Wash., lives in Voorhees, N.J. Quarterback Stockton, Calif., J.C. and Pacific 1948-51. No pro playing experience. College coach: San Mateo, Calif., J.C. 1958-62 (head coach), Navy 1963-65, Pacific 1966-69 (head coach), Brigham Young 1976-77, 1979-80, San Diego State 1981-85 (head coach). Pro coach: San Francisco 49ers 1970-75, Chicago Bears 1978, joined Eagles in 1986.

Bill Walsh, offensive line; born September 8, 1927, Phillipsburg, N.J., lives in Marlton, N.J. Center Notre Dame 1945-48. Pro center Pittsburgh Steelers 1949-54. College coach: Notre Dame 1955-58, Kansas State 1959. Pro coach: Dallas Texans-Kansas City Chiefs 1960-74, Atlanta Falcons 1975-82, Houston Oilers 1983-86, first year with Eagles.

ST. LOUIS CARDINALS

National Football Conference Eastern Division

Team Colors: Cardinal Red, Black, and White

Busch Stadium, Box 888
St. Louis, Missouri 63188
Telephone: (314) 421-0777

Club Officials

Chairman/President: William V. Bidwill
Vice President/Administration: Curt Mosher
Secretary and General Counsel: Thomas J. Guilfoil
Treasurer: Charley Schlegel
Director of Pro Personnel: Larry Wilson
Director of Player Personnel: George Boone
Public Relations Director: Bob Rose
Media Coordinator: Greg Gladysiewski
Director of Community Relations: Adele Harris
Ticket Manager: Steve Walsh
Trainer: John Omohundro
Assistant Trainers: Jim Shearer, Jeff Herndon
Equipment Manager: Mark Ahlemeier

Stadium: Busch Stadium •
Capacity: 54,392
200 Stadium Plaza
St. Louis, Missouri 63102

Playing Surface: AstroTurf-8

Training Camp: Eastern Illinois University
Charleston, Illinois 61920

1987 Schedule

Preseason

Aug. 15	at Cleveland	7:30
Aug. 22	**Seattle**	7:00
Aug. 31	at Chicago	7:00
Sept. 6	vs. K.C. at Memphis, Tenn.	1:30

Regular Season

Sept. 13	**Dallas**	12:00
Sept. 20	at San Diego	1:00
Sept. 27	**Indianapolis**	12:00
Oct. 4	at Washington	1:00
Oct. 11	**New Orleans**	12:00
Oct. 18	at San Francisco	1:00
Oct. 25	at New York Giants	4:00
Nov. 1	**Philadelphia**	12:00
Nov. 8	**Tampa Bay**	12:00
Nov. 15	**Los Angeles Rams**	12:00
Nov. 22	at Philadelphia	1:00
Nov. 29	at Atlanta	1:00
Dec. 6	**Washington**	12:00
Dec. 13	**New York Giants**	3:00
Dec. 20	at Tampa Bay	4:00
Dec. 27	at Dallas	12:00

Cardinals Coaching History

Chicago 1920-59 (347-454-39)

1920-22	John (Paddy) Driscoll	17-8-4
1923-24	Arnold Horween	13-8-1
1925-26	Norman Barry	16-8-2
1927	Guy Chamberlin	3-7-1
1928	Fred Gillies	1-5-0
1929	Dewey Scanlon	6-6-1
1930	Ernie Nevers	5-6-2
1931	LeRoy Andrews*	0-2-0
1931	Ernie Nevers	5-2-0
1932	Jack Chevigny	2-6-2
1933-34	Paul Schissler	6-15-1
1935-38	Milan Creighton	16-26-4
1939	Ernie Nevers	1-10-0
1940-42	Jimmy Conzelman	8-22-3
1943-45	Phil Handler**	1-29-0
1946-48	Jimmy Conzelman	27-10-0
1949	Phil Handler-Buddy Parker***	2-4-0
	Raymond (Buddy) Parker	4-1-1
1950-51	Earl (Curly) Lambeau****	7-15-0
	Phil Handler-Cecil Isbell#	1-1-0
1952	Joe Kuharich	4-8-0
1953-54	Joe Stydahar	3-20-1
1955-57	Ray Richards	14-21-1
1958-61	Frank (Pop) Ivy##	17-29-2
1961	Chuck Drulis-Ray Prochaska-Ray Willsey###	2-0-0
1962-65	Wally Lemm	27-26-3
1966-70	Charley Winner	35-30-5
1971-72	Bob Hollway	8-18-2
1973-77	Don Coryell	42-29-1
1978-79	Bud Wilkinson####	9-20-0
1979	Larry Wilson	2-1-0
1980-85	Jim Hanifan	39-50-1
1986	Gene Stallings	4-11-1

*Resigned after two games in 1931
**Co-coach with Walt Kiesling in Chicago Cardinals-Pittsburgh merger in 1944
***Co-coaches for first six games in 1949
****Resigned after 10 games in 1951
#Co-coaches
##Resigned after 12 games in 1961
###Co-coaches
####Released after 13 games in 1979

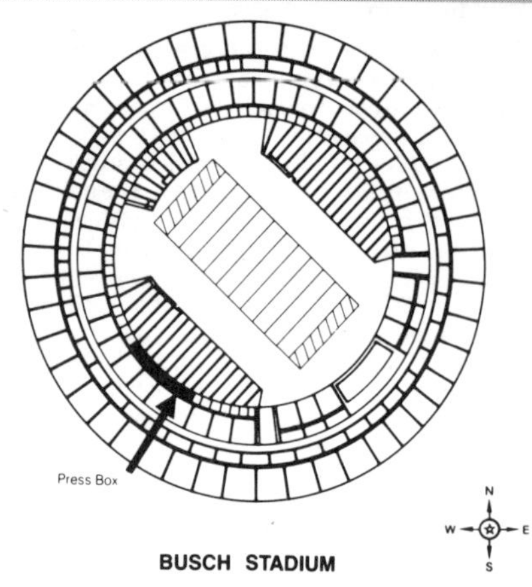

BUSCH STADIUM

Record Holders

Individual Records—Career

Category	Name	Performance
Rushing (Yds.)	Ottis Anderson, 1979-1986	7,999
Passing (Yds.)	Jim Hart, 1966-1983	34,639
Passing (TDs)	Jim Hart, 1966-1983	209
Receiving (No.)	Jackie Smith, 1963-1977	480
Receiving (Yds.)	Jackie Smith, 1963-1977	7,918
Interceptions	Larry Wilson, 1960-1972	52
Punting (Avg.)	Jerry Norton, 1959-1961	44.9
Punt Return (Avg.)	Charley Trippi, 1947-1955	13.7
Kickoff Return (Avg.)	Ollie Matson, 1952, 1954-58	28.5
Field Goals	Jim Bakken, 1962-1978	282
Touchdowns (Tot.)	Sonny Randle, 1959-1966	60
Points	Jim Bakken, 1962-1978	1,380

Individual Records—Single Season

Category	Name	Performance
Rushing (Yds.)	Ottis Anderson, 1979	1,605
Passing (Yds.)	Neil Lomax, 1984	4,614
Passing (TDs)	Charley Johnson, 1963	28
	Neil Lomax, 1984	28
Receiving (No.)	J. T. Smith, 1986	80
Receiving (Yds.)	Roy Green, 1984	1,555
Interceptions	Bob Nussbaumer, 1949	12
Punting (Avg.)	Jerry Norton, 1960	45.6
Punt Return (Avg.)	John (Red) Cochran, 1949	20.9
Kickoff Return (Avg.)	Ollie Matson, 1958	35.5
Field Goals	Jim Bakken, 1967	27
Touchdowns (Tot.)	John David Crow, 1962	17
Points	Jim Bakken, 1967	117
	Neil O'Donoghue, 1984	117

Individual Records—Single Game

Category	Name	Performance
Rushing (Yds.)	John David Crow, 12-18-60	203
Passing (Yds.)	Neil Lomax, 12-16-84	468
Passing (TDs)	Jim Hardy, 10-2-50	6
	Charley Johnson, 9-26-65	6
	Charley Johnson, 11-2-69	6
Receiving (No.)	Sonny Randle, 11-4-62	16
Receiving (Yds.)	Sonny Randle, 11-4-62	256
Interceptions	Bob Nussbaumer, 11-13-49	4
	Jerry Norton, 11-20-60	4
Field Goals	Jim Bakken, 9-24-67	7
Touchdowns (Tot.)	Ernie Nevers, 11-28-29	6
Points	Ernie Nevers, 11-28-29	40

1986 Team Statistics

	Cardinals	Opp.
Total First Downs	273	304
Rushing	102	125
Passing	149	149
Penalty	22	30
Third Down: Made/Att.	70/214	80/220
Fourth Down: Made/Att.	8/15	8/14
Total Net Yards	4503	4864
Avg. Per Game	281.4	304.0
Total Plays	994	1037
Avg. Per Play	4.5	4.7
Net Yards Rushing	1787	2227
Avg. Per Game	111.7	139.2
Total Rushes	419	560
Net Yards Passing	2716	2637
Avg. Per Game	169.8	164.8
Tackled/Yards Lost	59/424	41/355
Gross Yards	3140	2992
Att./Completions	516/293	436/215
Completion Pct.	56.8	49.3
Had Intercepted	19	10
Punts/Avg.	92/37.1	83/42.3
Net Punting Avg.	33.0	33.6
Penalties/Yards Lost	116/932	86/682
Fumbles/Ball Lost	25/10	40/12
Touchdowns	27	40
Rushing	8	17
Passing	17	21
Returns	2	2
Avg. Time of Possession	29:18	30:42

1986 Team Record

Preseason (2-3)

Date	Result		Opponents
8/2	L	16-21	New England
8/9	W	26-10	at Tampa Bay
8/16	L	26-27	Kansas City
8/23	W	14- 7	at Chicago
8/29	W	17-24	at San Diego
		99-89	

Regular Season (4-11-1)

Date	Result		Opponents	Att.
9/7	L	10-16	L.A. Rams	40,347
9/14	L	13-33	at Atlanta	46,463
9/21	L	10-17	at Buffalo	65,762
9/29	L	7-31	Dallas	49,077
10/5	L	6-13	N.Y. Giants	40,562
10/12	W	30-19	at Tampa Bay	33,307
10/19	L	21-28	at Washington	53,494
10/26	L	6-37	at Dallas	60,756
11/2	W	13-10	Philadelphia	33,051
11/9	L	17-43	at San Francisco	59,172
11/16	L	7-16	New Orleans	32,069
11/23	W	23-14	Kansas City	29,680
11/30	L	17-20	Washington	35,637
12/7	T	10-10	at Phil. (OT)	50,148
12/14	L	7-27	at N.Y. Giants	75,261
12/21	W	21-17	Tampa Bay	23,957

(OT) Overtime

Score by Periods

Cardinals	15	79	41	83	0	—	218
Opponents	82	106	64	99	0	—	351

Attendance

Home 284,380 Away 444,363 Total 728,743
Single game home record, 72,033 (1-6-80)
Single season home record, 545,980 (1979)

1986 Individual Statistics

Scoring	TD R	TD P	TD Rt	PAT	FG	Saf	TP
Lee	0	0	0	14/17	8/13	0	38
Green	0	6	0	0/0	0/0	0	36
J. Smith	0	6	0	0/0	0/0	0	36
Mitchell	5	0	0	0/0	0/0	0	30
Ferrell	0	3	0	0/0	0/0	0	18
Schubert	0	0	0	9/9	3/11	0	18
Sikahema	0	1	2	0/0	0/0	0	18
Anderson	2	0	0	0/0	0/0	0	12
Fox	0	1	0	0/0	0/0	0	6
Lomax	1	0	0	0/0	0/0	0	6
Cardinals	8	17	2	23/27	11/24	0	218
Opponents	17	21	2	37/40	24/32	1	351

Passing	Att.	Comp.	Yds.	Pct.	TD	Int.	Tkld.	Rate
Lomax	421	240	2583	57.0	13	12	52/381	73.6
Stoudt	91	52	542	57.1	3	7	7/43	53.5
Mitchell	3	1	15	33.3	1	0	0/0	90.3
Arapostathis	1	0	0	0.0	0	0	0/0	39.6
Cardinals	516	293	3140	56.8	17	19	59/424	70.4
Opponents	436	215	2992	49.3	21	10	41/355	78.3

Rushing	Att.	Yds.	Avg.	LG	TD
Mitchell	174	800	4.6	44	5
Ferrell	124	548	4.4	25	0
Anderson	51	156	3.1	14	2
Lomax	35	148	4.2	18	1
Sikahema	16	62	3.9	23	0
Stoudt	7	53	7.6	17	0
Wolfley	8	19	2.4	8	0
Marsh	1	5	5.0	5	0
Austin	1	0	0.0	0	0
Green	2	−4	−2.0	1	0
Cardinals	419	1787	4.3	44	8
Opponents	560	2227	4.0	54	17

Receiving	No.	Yds.	Avg.	LG	TD
J. Smith	80	1014	12.7	45	6
Ferrell	56	434	7.8	30t	3
Green	42	517	12.3	48t	6
Mitchell	41	276	6.7	24	0
Marsh	25	313	12.5	27	0
T. Johnson	14	203	14.5	39	0
Sikahema	10	99	9.9	27	1
Anderson	10	91	9.1	19	0
Fox	5	59	11.8	38t	1
Tilley	3	51	17.0	18	0
Holman	3	41	13.7	18	0
Wolfley	2	32	16.0	28	0
Sargent	1	8	8.0	8	0
Novacek	1	2	2.0	2	0
Cardinals	293	3140	10.7	48t	17
Opponents	215	2992	13.9	51	21

Interceptions	No.	Yds.	Avg.	LG	TD
Mack	4	42	10.5	24	0
Washington	2	19	9.5	19	0
Carter	2	12	6.0	11	0
W. Smith	1	35	35.0	35	0
Le. Smith	1	13	13.0	13	0
Cardinals	10	121	12.1	35	0
Opponents	19	271	14.3	78t	2

Punting	No.	Yds.	Avg.	In 20	LG
Arapostathis	30	1140	38.0	5	50
Carter	61	2271	37.2	16	52
Cardinals	92	3411	37.1	21	52
Opponents	83	3514	42.3	24	60

Punt Returns	No.	FC	Yds.	Avg.	LG	TD
Sikahema	43	16	522	12.1	71t	2
Carter	1	0	0	0.0	0	0
J. Smith	1	0	6	6.0	6	0
Cardinals	45	16	528	11.7	71t	2
Opponents	44	20	296	6.7	22	0

Kickoff Returns	No.	Yds.	Avg.	LG	TD
Sikahema	37	847	22.9	44	0
Swanson	10	206	20.6	40	0
Fox	6	161	26.8	38	0
Mitchell	6	203	33.8	53	0
Ferrell	3	41	13.7	27	0
T. Johnson	3	46	15.3	25	0
Carter	2	21	10.5	14	0
Sargent	2	27	13.5	14	0
Holmes	1	2	2.0	2	0
Wolfley	0	−6	—	−6	0
Cardinals	70	1548	22.1	53	0
Opponents	50	886	17.7	56	0

Sacks	No.
A. Baker	10.5
Nunn	7.0
Galloway	4.5
Bell	4.0
C. Baker	3.5
Clasby	3.0
Le. Smith	3.0
Noga	2.0
La. Smith	2.0
Young	1.5
Cardinals	41.0
Opponents	59.0

FIRST-ROUND SELECTIONS

(If club had no first-round selection, first player drafted is listed with round in parentheses.)

Since 1942

Year	Player, College, Position
1942	Steve Lach, Duke, B
1943	Glenn Dobbs, Tulsa, B
1944	Pat Harder, Wisconsin, B
1945	Charley Trippi, Georgia, B
1946	Dub Jones, Louisiana State, B
1947	DeWitt (Tex) Coulter, Army, T
1948	Jim Spavital, Oklahoma A&M, B
1949	Bill Fischer, Notre Dame, G
1950	Jack Jennings, Ohio State, T (2)
1951	Jerry Groom, Notre Dame, C
1952	Ollie Matson, San Francisco, B
1953	Johnny Olszewski, California, B
1954	Lamar McHan, Arkansas, B
1955	Max Boydston, Oklahoma, E
1956	Joe Childress, Auburn, B
1957	Jerry Tubbs, Oklahoma, C
1958	King Hill, Rice, B
	John David Crow, Texas A&M, B
1959	Bill Stacy, Mississippi State, B
1960	George Izo, Notre Dame, QB
1961	Ken Rice, Auburn, T
1962	Fate Echols, Northwestern, DT
	Irv Goode, Kentucky, C
1963	Jerry Stovall, Louisiana State, S
	Don Brumm, Purdue, DE
1964	Ken Kortas, Louisville, DT
1965	Joe Namath, Alabama, QB
1966	Carl McAdams, Oklahoma, LB
1967	Dave Williams, Washington, WR
1968	MacArthur Lane, Utah State, RB
1969	Roger Wehrli, Missouri, DB
1970	Larry Stegent, Texas A&M, RB
1971	Norm Thompson, Utah, CB
1972	Bobby Moore, Oregon, RB-WR
1973	Dave Butz, Purdue, DT
1974	J.V. Cain, Colorado, TE
1975	Tim Gray, Texas A&M, DB
1976	Mike Dawson, Arizona, DT
1977	Steve Pisarkiewicz, Missouri, QB
1978	Steve Little, Arkansas, K
	Ken Greene, Washington State, DB
1979	Ottis Anderson, Miami, RB
1980	Curtis Greer, Michigan, DE
1981	E. J. Junior, Alabama, LB
1982	Luis Sharpe, UCLA, T
1983	Leonard Smith, McNeese State, DB
1984	Clyde Duncan, Tennessee, WR
1985	Freddie Joe Nunn, Mississippi, LB
1986	Anthony Bell, Michigan State, LB
1987	Kelly Stouffer, Colorado State, QB

St. Louis Cardinals 1987 Veteran Roster

No.	Name	Pos.	Ht.	Wt.	Birth-date	NFL Exp.	College	Hometown	How Acq.	'86 Games/ Starts
16	Austin, Kent	QB	6-1	195	6/25/63	2	Mississippi	Natick, Miss.	D12-'86	16/0
60	†Baker, Al	DE	6-6	270	12/9/56	10	Colorado State	Newark, N.J.	T(Det)-'83	16/13
52	†Baker, Charlie	LB	6-2	234	9/26/57	8	New Mexico	Odessa, Tex.	D3-'80	16/16
55	Bell, Anthony	LB	6-3	231	7/2/64	2	Michigan State	Miami, Fla.	D1-'86	16/1
72	Bergold, Scott	DE	6-7	263	11/19/61	2	Wisconsin	Wauwatosa, Wis.	D2-'85	0*
71	†Bostic, Joe	G	6-3	268	4/20/57	9	Clemson	Greensboro, N.C.	D3-'79	13/13
62	Brown, Ray	T-G	6-5	257	12/12/62	2	Arkansas State	Marion, Ark.	D8-'86	11/4
41	Carter, Carl	CB	5-11	180	3/7/64	2	Texas Tech	Fort Worth, Tex.	D4-'86	14/4
14	†Cater, Greg	P	6-0	191	4/17/57	6	Tenn.-Chattanooga	La Grange, Ga.	FA-'86	11/0
58	Chilton, Gene	C	6-3	271	3/27/64	2	Texas	Houston, Tex.	D3-'86	16/7
79	Clasby, Bob	DE	6-5	260	9/28/60	2	Notre Dame	Milton, Mass.	FA-'86	16/10
66	Dawson, Doug	G	6-3	267	12/27/61	3	Texas	Houston, Tex.	D2-'84	1/1
56	DiBernardo, Rick	LB	6-3	225	6/12/64	2	Notre Dame	Redondo Beach, Calif.	T(TB)-'86	16/0
73	†Duda, Mark	NT	6-3	279	2/4/61	5	Maryland	Plymouth, Pa.	D4-'83	14/3
31	Ferrell, Earl	RB	6-0	224	3/27/58	6	East Tennessee State	Halifax, Va.	D5-'82	16/15
65	Galloway, David	NT	6-3	279	2/16/59	6	Florida	Brandon, Fla.	D2-'82	14/13
81	Green, Roy	WR	6-0	195	6/30/57	9	Henderson State	Magnolia, Ark.	D4-'79	11/10
75	Greer, Curtis	DE	6-4	258	11/10/57	7	Michigan	Detroit, Mich.	D1-'80	0*
82	Holmes, Don	WR	5-10	180	4/1/61	2	Mesa, Colo.	Grand Junction, Colo.	W(Ind)-'86	12/0
78	Hughes, Van	DE	6-3	280	11/14/60	2	Southwest Texas State	Waco, Tex.	FA-'86	8/0
87	Johnson, Troy	WR	6-1	175	10/20/62	2	Southern	Houma, La.	FA-'86	13/2
54	Junior, E.J.	LB	6-3	235	12/8/59	7	Alabama	Nashville, Tenn.	D1-'81	13/13
70	Kennard, Derek	G	6-3	285	9/9/62	2	Nevada-Reno	Stockton, Calif.	SD2-'84	15/10
10	Lee, John	K	5-11	182	5/19/64	2	UCLA	Downey, Calif.	D2-'86	11/0
15	Lomax, Neil	QB	6-3	215	2/17/59	7	Portland State	Portland, Ore.	D2-'81	14/14
47	†Mack, Cedric	CB	6-0	194	9/14/60	5	Baylor	Freeport, Tex.	D2-'83	15/9
80	†Marsh, Doug	TE	6-3	238	6/18/58	8	Michigan	Akron, Ohio	D2-'80	16/15
76	†Mays, Stafford	DE	6-2	255	3/13/58	8	Washington	Tacoma, Wash.	D9-'80	16/6
30	Mitchell, Stump	RB	5-9	188	3/15/59	7	Citadel	St. Mary's, Ga.	D9-'81	15/13
59	Monaco, Ron	LB	6-1	225	5/3/63	2	South Carolina	Hamden, Conn.	FA-'86	15/2
57	†Noga, Niko	LB	6-1	235	3/2/62	4	Hawaii	Honolulu, Hawaii	D8-'84	16/16
85	Novacek, Jay	TE	6-4	217	10/24/62	3	Wyoming	Gothenburg, Neb.	D6-'85	8/0
53	Nunn, Freddie Joe	LB	6-4	228	4/9/62	3	Mississippi	Louisville, Miss.	D1-'85	16/16
63	†Robbins, Tootie	T	6-5	302	6/2/58	6	East Carolina	Windsor, N.C.	D4-'82	13/5
51	Ruether, Mike	C	6-4	275	9/20/62	2	Texas	Inglewood, Calif.	SD1-'86	10/1
39	Sargent, Broderick	RB	5-10	215	9/16/62	2	Baylor	Waxahachie, Tex.	FA-'86	16/0
11	Schubert, Eric	K	5-8	193	5/28/62	3	Pittsburgh	Greenwood, N.J.	FA-'86	5/0
67	Sharpe, Luis	T	6-4	260	6/16/60	6	UCLA	Detroit, Mich.	D1-'82	16/16
36	Sikahema, Vai	RB-KR	5-9	191	8/29/62	2	Brigham Young	American Samoa	D10a-'86	16/0
84	Smith, J.T.	WR	6-2	185	10/29/55	10	North Texas State	Leonard, Tex.	FA-'85	16/16
61	Smith, Lance	T	6-2	262	1/1/63	3	Louisiana State	Kannapolis, N.C.	D3-'85	15/13
45	Smith, Leonard	S	5-11	202	9/2/60	5	McNeese State	Baton Rouge, La.	D1-'83	16/16
44	Smith, Wayne	CB	6-0	170	5/9/57	8	Purdue	Chicago, Ill.	FA-'82	16/7
18	Stoudt, Cliff	QB	6-4	215	3/27/55	9	Youngstown State	Oberlin, Ohio	T(Pitt)-'86	16/7
86	Swanson, Eric	WR	5-11	186	8/25/63	2	Tennessee	San Bernardino, Calif.	D7-'86	16/0
83	Tilley, Pat	WR	5-10	178	2/15/53	11	Louisiana Tech	Shreveport, La.	D4-'76	1/1
24	Wolfley, Ron	RB	6-0	222	10/14/62	3	West Virginia	Orchard Park, N.Y.	D4-'85	16/1
43	Young, Lonnie	S	6-1	182	7/18/63	3	Michigan State	Flint, Mich.	D12-'85	16/13

* Bergold and Greer missed entire '86 season due to injury.

†Option playout; subject to developments.

Traded—Cornerback Lionel Washington to L.A. Raiders.

Also played with Cardinals in '86—RB Ottis Anderson (4 games), P-K Evan Arapostathis (5), C Randy Clark (12), DE Gary Dulin (3), WR Chas Fox (4), WR Scott Holman (3), CB-S Bobby Johnson (3), TE Greg LaFleur (4), TE Robert Stallings (3), S Dennis Thurman (16).

Coaching Staff

Head Coach, Gene Stallings

Pro Career: Named head coach on February 10, 1986. Became the ninth head coach since the team's move to St. Louis in 1960, and thirtieth in the history of the franchise dating back to 1920. Defensive backfield coach with Dallas from 1972-85. Career record: 4-11-1.

Background: End Texas A&M 1954-57. No pro playing experience. College coach: Texas A&M 1957, 1965-71 (head coach), Alabama 1958-64. Assistant under just two coaches in career: Paul "Bear" Bryant at Alabama, and Tom Landry at Dallas. Was All-Southwest Conference receiver at Texas A&M under Bryant and tri-captain on undefeated 1956 team.

Personal: Born March 2, 1935, in Paris, Tex. Gene and his wife, Ruth Ann, live in St. Louis and have five children: Anna Lee, Laurie, John Mark, Jacklyn, and Martha Kate.

Assistant Coaches

Marv Braden, special teams; born January 25, 1938, Kansas City, Mo., lives in Manchester, Mo. Linebacker Southwest Missouri State 1956-59. No pro playing experience. College coach: Parsons 1963-66, Northeast Missouri State 1967-68 (head coach), U.S. International 1969-72, Iowa State 1973, Southern Methodist 1974-75, Michigan State 1976. Pro coach: Denver Broncos 1977-80, San Diego Chargers 1981-85, joined Cardinals in 1986.

Tom Bresnahan, offensive line; born January 21, 1935, Springfield, Mass., lives in St. Louis. Tackle Holy Cross 1953-55. No pro playing experience. College coach: Williams 1963-67, Columbia 1968-72, Navy 1973-80. Pro coach: Kansas City Chiefs 1981-82, New York Giants 1983-84, joined Cardinals in 1986.

LeBaron Caruthers, strength and conditioning; born April 20, 1954, Nashville, Tenn., lives in St. Louis. Tackle East Carolina 1972-73. No pro playing experience. College coach: Auburn 1978-79, Southern Methodist 1980-81. Pro coach: New England Patriots 1982-84, joined Cardinals in 1986.

Jim Johnson, defensive line; born May 26, 1941, Maywood, Ill., lives in St. Louis. Quarterback Missouri 1959-62. Pro tight end Buffalo Bills 1963-64. College coach: Missouri Southern 1967-68 (head coach), Drake 1969-72, Indiana 1973-76, Notre Dame 1977-80. Pro coach: Oklahoma Outlaws (USFL) 1984, Jacksonville Bulls (USFL) 1985, joined Cardinals in 1986.

Hank Kuhlmann, running backs; born October 6, 1937, St. Louis, Mo., lives in St. Louis. Running back Missouri 1956-59. No pro playing experience. College coach: Missouri 1963-71, Notre Dame 1975-77. Pro coach: Green Bay Packers 1972-74, Chicago Bears 1978-82, Birmingham Stallions (USFL) 1983-85, joined Cardinals in 1986.

Leon McLaughlin, special assistant-quality control; born May 30, 1925, San Diego, Calif., lives in St. Louis. Center-linebacker UCLA 1946-49. Pro center Los Angeles Rams 1951-55. College coach: Washington State 1956, Stanford 1959-65, San Fernando Valley State 1969-70 (head coach). Pro coach: Pittsburgh Steelers 1966-68, Los Angeles Rams 1971-72, Detroit Lions 1973-74, Green Bay Packers 1975-76, New England Patriots 1977, joined Cardinals in 1978.

Mal Moore, receivers; born December 19, 1939, Dozier, Ala., lives in St. Louis. Quarterback-defensive back Alabama 1958-62. No pro playing experience. College coach: Montana State 1963, Alabama 1964-82, Notre Dame 1983-85. Pro coach: Joined Cardinals in 1986.

Joe Pascale, linebackers; born April 4, 1946, New York, N.Y., lives in St. Louis. Linebacker Connecticut 1963-66. No pro playing experience. College coach: Connecticut 1967-68, Rhode Island 1969-73, Idaho State 1974-76 (head coach 1976), Princeton 1977-79. Pro coach: Montreal Alouettes (CFL) 1980-81, Ottawa Rough Riders (CFL) 1982-83, New Jersey Generals (USFL) 1984-85, joined Cardinals in 1986.

St. Louis Cardinals 1987 First-Year Roster

Name	Pos.	Ht.	Wt.	Birth-date	College	Hometown	How Acq.
Alvord, Steve	DT	6-4	272	10/2/64	Washington	Bellingham, Wash.	D8
Awalt, Robert	TE	6-5	258	4/9/64	San Diego State	Sacramento, Calif.	D3a
Bruno, John	P	6-1	200	9/10/64	Penn State	Upper St. Clair, Pa.	D5b
Davis, Wayne	LB	6-1	213	3/10/64	Alabama	Gordo, Ala.	D9
Garalczyk, Mark	DT	6-5	272	8/12/65	Western Michigan	Roseville, Mich.	D6
Harris, William	TE	6-4	243	2/10/65	Bishop College	Houston, Tex.	D7b
Jarostchuk, Ilia	LB	6-3	231	8/1/64	New Hampshire	Utica, N.Y.	D5c
Massey, Tim	CB-S	5-11	190	1/22/64	Valdosta State	Woodbine, Ga.	FA
McDonald, Tim	CB-S	6-2	207	1/6/65	Southern California	Fresno, Calif.	D2
Peat, Todd	G	6-2	294	5/20/64	Northern Illinois	Champaign, Ill.	D11
Peoples, Tim	CB-S	6-0	200	7/26/64	Washington	San Jose, Calif.	D7a
Saddler, Rod	DT	6-5	276	9/26/65	Texas A&M	Columbia, Ga.	D4
Scotts, Colin	DE	6-5	263	4/26/63	Hawaii	Sydney, Australia	D3
Stouffer, Kelly	QB	6-3	212	7/6/64	Colorado State	Rushville, Neb.	D1
Swarn, George	RB	5-10	205	2/15/64	Miami, Ohio	Cincinnati, Ohio	D5a
Wright, Charles	CB-S	5-9	178	4/5/64	Tulsa	Carthage, Mo.	D10

The term NFL Rookie is defined as a player who is in his first season of professional football and has not been on the roster of another professional football team for any regular-season or postseason games. A Rookie is designated by an "R" on NFL rosters. Players who have been active in another professional football league or players who have NFL experience, including either preseason training camp or being on an active roster for fewer than three regular-season or postseason games, are termed NFL First-Year Players. An NFL First-Year Player is designated by a "1" on NFL rosters. Thereafter, a player on an NFL active roster for at least three regular-season or postseason games is credited with an additional year of NFL playing experience.

NOTES

Mel Renfro, defensive backs; born December 30, 1941, Houston, Tex., lives in St. Louis. Running back Oregon 1961-63. Pro defensive back Dallas Cowboys 1964-77. Pro coach: Los Angeles Express (USFL) 1984, joined Cardinals in 1986.

Jim Shofner, offensive coordinator; born December 18, 1935, Grapevine, Tex., lives in Chesterfield, Mo. Running back Texas Christian 1955-57. Pro defensive back Cleveland Browns 1958-63. College coach: Texas Christian 1964-66, 1974-76 (head coach). Pro coach: San Francisco 49ers 1967-73, 1977, Cleveland Browns 1978-80, Houston Oilers 1981-82, Dallas Cowboys 1983-85, joined Cardinals in 1986.

SAN FRANCISCO 49ERS

National Football Conference Western Division

Team Colors: Forty Niners Gold and Scarlet

711 Nevada Street
Redwood City, California 94061
Telephone (415) 365-3420

Club Officials

Owner, Chairman of the Board: Edward J. DeBartolo, Jr.
President, Head Coach: Bill Walsh
Vice President, General Manager: John McVay
Business Manager: Keith Simon
Executive Administrative Assistant: Norb Hecker
Director of Pro Scouting: Alan Webb
Director of College Scouting: Tony Razzano
Director of Public Relations: Jerry Walker
Publications Coordinator: Rodney Knox
Coordinator of Football Operations: Neal Dahlen
Ticket Manager: Ken Dargel
Marketing/Promotions Coordinator: Laurie Welling
Trainer: Lindsy McLean
Equipment Manager: Bronco Hinek
Equipment Manager Emeritus: Chico Norton

Stadium: Candlestick Park • **Capacity:** 61,891
San Francisco, California 94124

Playing Surface: Grass

Training Camp: Sierra Community College
Rocklin, California 95677

1987 Schedule

Preseason

Aug. 8	vs. K.C. at Canton, Ohio	12:00
Aug. 15	at Los Angeles Raiders	7:00
Aug. 22	**Dallas**	6:00
Aug. 27	**San Diego**	6:00
Sept. 4	at Seattle	5:00

Regular Season

Sept. 13	at Pittsburgh	1:00
Sept. 20	at Cincinnati	1:00
Sept. 27	**Philadelphia**	1:00
Oct. 5	at N.Y. Giants (Monday)	9:00
Oct. 11	**Atlanta**	1:00
Oct. 18	**St. Louis**	1:00
Oct. 25	at New Orleans	12:00
Nov. 1	at Los Angeles Rams	1:00
Nov. 8	**Houston**	1:00
Nov. 15	**New Orleans**	1:00
Nov. 22	at Tampa Bay	1:00
Nov. 29	**Cleveland**	5:00
Dec. 6	at Green Bay	12:00
Dec. 14	**Chicago** (Monday)	6:00
Dec. 20	at Atlanta	1:00
Dec. 27	**Los Angeles Rams**	5:00

49ers Coaching History

(256-254-13)

1950-54	Lawrence (Buck) Shaw	33-25-2
1955	Norman (Red) Strader	4-8-0
1956-58	Frankie Albert	19-17-1
1959-63	Howard (Red) Hickey*	27-27-1
1963-67	Jack Christiansen	26-38-3
1968-75	Dick Nolan	56-56-5
1976	Monte Clark	8-6-0
1977	Ken Meyer	5-9-0
1978	Pete McCulley**	1-8-0
1978	Fred O'Connor	1-6-0
1979-86	Bill Walsh	76-54-1

*Resigned after three games in 1963
**Released after nine games in 1978

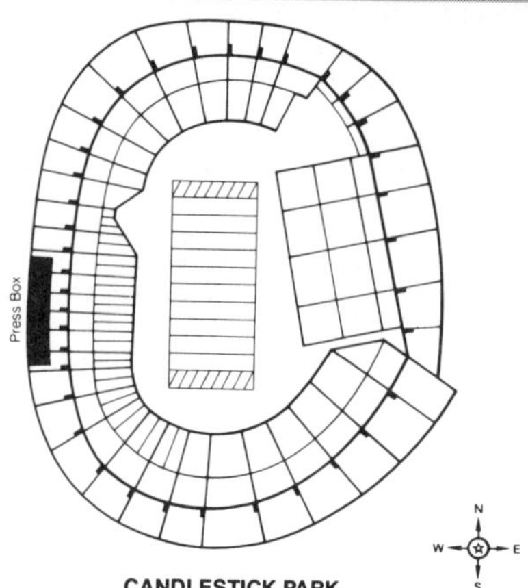

CANDLESTICK PARK

Record Holders

Individual Records—Career

Category	Name	Performance
Rushing (Yds.)	Joe Perry, 1950-1960, 1963	7,344
Passing (Yds.)	John Brodie, 1957-1973	31,548
Passing (TDs)	John Brodie, 1957-1973	214
Receiving (No.)	Dwight Clark, 1979-1986	482
Receiving (Yds.)	Gene Washington, 1969-1977	6,664
Interceptions	Jimmy Johnson, 1961-1976	47
Punting (Avg.)	Tommy Davis, 1959-1969	44.7
Punt Return (Avg.)	Manfred Moore, 1974-75	14.7
Kickoff Return (Avg.)	Abe Woodson, 1958-1964	29.4
Field Goals	Ray Wersching, 1977-1986	185
Touchdowns (Tot.)	Ken Willard, 1965-1973	61
Points	Ray Wersching, 1977-1986	896

Individual Records—Single Season

Category	Name	Performance
Rushing (Yds.)	Wendell Tyler, 1984	1,262
Passing (Yds.)	Joe Montana, 1983	3,910
Passing (TDs)	John Brodie, 1965	30
Receiving (No.)	Roger Craig, 1985	92
Receiving (Yds.)	Jerry Rice, 1986	1,570
Interceptions	Dave Baker, 1960	10
	Ronnie Lott, 1986	10
Punting (Avg.)	Tommy Davis, 1965	45.8
Punt Return (Avg.)	Dana McLemore, 1982	22.3
Kickoff Return (Avg.)	Joe Arenas, 1953	34.4
Field Goals	Bruce Gossett, 1973	26
Touchdowns (Tot.)	Jerry Rice, 1986	16
Points	Ray Wersching, 1984	131

Individual Records—Single Game

Category	Name	Performance
Rushing (Yds.)	Delvin Williams, 10-31-76	194
Passing (Yds.)	Joe Montana, 11-17-86	441
Passing (TDs)	John Brodie, 11-23-65	5
	Steve Spurrier, 11-19-72	5
	Joe Montana, 10-6-85	5
Receiving (No.)	Many times	12
	Last time by Roger Craig, 12-1-86	
Receiving (Yds.)	Jerry Rice, 12-9-85	241
Interceptions	Dave Baker, 12-4-60	4
Field Goals	Ray Wersching, 10-16-83	6
Touchdowns (Tot.)	Billy Kilmer, 10-15-61	4
Points	Gordy Soltau, 10-27-51	26

1986 Team Statistics

	49ers	Opp.
Total First Downs	346	285
Rushing	114	97
Passing	213	169
Penalty	19	19
Third Down: Made/Att.	80/224	67/221
Fourth Down: Made/Att.	6/12	9/20
Total Net Yards	6082	4880
Avg. Per Game	380.1	305.0
Total Plays	1118	1061
Avg. Per Play	5.4	4.6
Net Yards Rushing	1986	1555
Avg. Per Game	124.1	97.2
Total Rushes	510	406
Net Yards Passing	4096	3325
Avg. Per Game	256.0	207.8
Tackled/Yards Lost	26/203	51/448
Gross Yards	4299	3773
Att./Completions	582/353	604/324
Completion Pct.	60.7	53.6
Had Intercepted	20	39
Punts/Avg.	85/40.6	91/41.4
Net Punting Avg.	34.3	35.0
Penalties/Yards Lost	95/691	89/653
Fumbles/Ball Lost	32/9	31/10
Touchdowns	43	29
Rushing	16	8
Passing	21	18
Returns	6	3
Avg. Time of Possession	30:28	29:32

1986 Team Record

Preseason (2-2)

Date	Result		Opponents
8/10	W	32- 0	L.A. Raiders
8/18	L	17-31	at L.A. Rams
8/23	L	9-14	at Denver
8/29	W	21-10	Seattle
		79-55	

Regular Season (10-5-1)

Date	Result		Opponents	Att.
9/7	W	31- 7	at Tampa Bay	50,780
9/14	L	13-16	at L.A. Rams	65,195
9/21	W	26-17	New Orleans	58,297
9/28	W	31-16	at Miami	70,264
10/5	W	35-14	Indianapolis	57,252
10/12	L	24-27	Minnesota (OT)	58,637
10/19	T	10-10	at Atlanta (OT)	55,306
10/26	W	31-17	at Green Bay	50,557
11/2	L	10-23	at New Orleans	53,234
11/9	W	43-17	St. Louis	59,172
11/17	L	6-14	at Washington	54,774
11/23	W	20- 0	Atlanta	58,747
12/1	L	17-21	N.Y. Giants	59,777
12/7	W	24-10	N.Y. Jets	58,091
12/14	W	29-24	at New England	60,787
12/19	W	24-14	L.A. Rams	60,366

Postseason (0-1)

Date	Result		Opponents	Att.
1/4/87	L	49- 3	at N.Y. Giants	75,691

(OT) Overtime

Score by Periods

49ers	92	123	72	87	0	—	374
Opponents	64	61	58	61	3	—	247

Attendance

Home 470,339 Away 460,897 Total 931,236
Single game home record, 61,040 (1-6-85)
Single season home record, 470,506 (1985)

1986 Individual Statistics

Scoring

	TD R	TD P	TD Rt	PAT	FG	Saf	TP
Wersching	0	0	0	41/42	25/35	0	116
Rice	1	15	0	0/0	0/0	0	96
Craig	7	0	0	0/0	0/0	0	42
Cribbs	5	0	0	0/0	0/0	0	30
Clark	0	2	0	0/0	0/0	0	12
Frank	0	2	0	0/0	0/0	0	12
Holmoe	0	0	2	0/0	0/0	0	12
Francis	0	1	0	0/0	0/0	0	6
Griffin	0	0	1	0/0	0/0	0	6
Harmon	1	0	0	0/0	0/0	0	6
Lott	0	0	1	0/0	0/0	0	6
McKyer	0	0	1	0/0	0/0	0	6
Moroski	1	0	0	0/0	0/0	0	6
Nixon	0	0	1	0/0	0/0	0	6
Rathman	1	0	0	0/0	0/0	0	6
Wilson	0	1	0	0/0	0/0	0	6
49ers	16	21	6	41/43	25/35	0	374
Opponents	8	18	3	28/29	15/25	0	247

Passing

	Att.	Comp.	Yds.	Pct.	TD	Int.	Tkld.	Rate
Montana	307	191	2236	62.2	8	9	12/95	80.7
Kemp	200	119	1554	59.5	11	8	8/56	85.7
Moroski	73	42	493	57.5	2	3	6/52	70.2
Rice	2	1	16	50.0	0	0	0/0	77.1
49ers	582	353	4299	60.7	21	20	26/203	81.1
Opponents	604	324	3773	53.6	18	39	51/448	55.8

Rushing

	Att.	Yds.	Avg.	LG	TD
Craig	204	830	4.1	25	7
Cribbs	152	590	3.9	19	5
Rathman	33	138	4.2	29t	1
Tyler	31	127	4.1	14	0
Harmon	27	77	2.9	15	1
Rice	10	72	7.2	18	1
Kemp	15	49	3.3	12	0
Cherry	11	42	3.8	10	0
Montana	17	38	2.2	17	0
Moroski	6	22	3.7	12	1
Ring	3	4	1.3	4	0
Frank	1	−3	−3.0	−3	0
49ers	510	1986	3.9	29t	16
Opponents	406	1555	3.8	36	8

Receiving

	No.	Yds.	Avg.	LG	TD
Rice	86	1570	18.3	66t	15
Craig	81	624	7.7	48	0
Clark	61	794	13.0	45t	2
Francis	41	505	12.3	52	1
Cribbs	35	346	9.9	33	0
Rathman	13	121	9.3	14	0
Wilson	9	104	11.6	18	1
Frank	9	61	6.8	17	2
Harmon	8	78	9.8	15	0
Crawford	5	70	14.0	42	0
Margerum	2	12	6.0	6	0
Monroe	2	6	3.0	5	0
Ring	1	8	8.0	8	0
49ers	353	4299	12.2	66t	21
Opponents	324	3773	11.6	84t	18

Interceptions

	No.	Yds.	Avg.	LG	TD
Lott	10	134	13.4	57t	1
McKyer	6	33	5.5	21t	1
J. Fahnhorst	4	52	13.0	46	0
Fuller	4	44	11.0	26	0
Holmoe	3	149	49.7	78t	2
Williamson	3	3	1.0	2	0
Griffin	3	0	0.0	0	0
Nixon	2	106	53.0	88t	1
Tuiasosopo	1	22	22.0	22	0
Cousineau	1	18	18.0	18	0
Turner	1	9	9.0	9	0
Haley	1	8	8.0	8	0
49ers	39	578	14.8	88t	5
Opponents	20	205	10.3	57	0

Punting

	No.	Yds.	Avg.	In 20	LG
Runager	83	3450	41.6	23	62
49ers	85	3450	40.6	23	62
Opponents	91	3765	41.4	20	73

Punt Returns

	No.	FC	Yds.	Avg.	LG	TD
Griffin	38	18	377	9.9	76t	1
Crawford	4	0	15	3.8	9	0
McKyer	1	1	5	5.0	5	0
49ers	43	19	397	9.2	76t	1
Opponents	49	12	373	7.6	39	0

Kickoff Returns

	No.	Yds.	Avg.	LG	TD
Crawford	15	280	18.7	34	0
Monroe	8	139	17.4	25	0
Griffin	5	97	19.4	28	0
Harmon	4	82	20.5	28	0
Rathman	3	66	22.0	22	0
Cherry	2	29	14.5	17	0
Frank	2	24	12.0	16	0
McKyer	1	15	15.0	15	0
Ring	1	15	15.0	15	0
Wilson	1	10	10.0	10	0
49ers	42	757	18.0	34	0
Opponents	71	1598	22.5	101t	1

Sacks

	No.
Haley	12.0
Stover	11.0
Board	8.0
Roberts	5.5
Turner	3.0
Fuller	2.5
Carter	2.0
Lott	2.0
McColl	2.0
J. Fahnhorst	1.0
Griffin	1.0
Walter	1.0
49ers	51.0
Opponents	26.0

FIRST-ROUND SELECTIONS

(If club had no first-round selection, first player drafted is listed with round in parentheses.)

Since 1962

Year	Player, College, Position
1962	Lance Alworth, Arkansas, WR
1963	Kermit Alexander, UCLA, CB
1964	Dave Parks, Texas Tech, WR
1965	Ken Willard, North Carolina, RB
	George Donnelly, Illinois, DB
1966	Stan Hindman, Mississippi, DE
1967	Steve Spurrier, Florida, QB
	Cas Banaszek, Northwestern, T
1968	Forrest Blue, Auburn, C
1969	Ted Kwalick, Penn State, TE
	Gene Washington, Stanford, WR
1970	Cedrick Hardman, North Texas State, DE
	Bruce Taylor, Boston U., DB
1971	Tim Anderson, Ohio State, DB
1972	Terry Beasley, Auburn, WR
1973	Mike Holmes, Texas Southern, DB
1974	Wilbur Jackson, Alabama, RB
	Bill Sandifer, UCLA, DT
1975	Jimmy Webb, Mississippi State, DT
1976	Randy Cross, UCLA, C (2)
1977	Elmo Boyd, Eastern Kentucky, WR (3)
1978	Ken MacAfee, Notre Dame, TE
	Dan Bunz, Cal State-Long Beach, LB
1979	James Owens, UCLA, WR (2)
1980	Earl Cooper, Rice, RB
	Jim Stuckey, Clemson, DT
1981	Ronnie Lott, Southern California, DB
1982	Bubba Paris, Michigan, T (2)
1983	Roger Craig, Nebraska, RB (2)
1984	Todd Shell, Brigham Young, LB
1985	Jerry Rice, Mississippi Valley State, WR
1986	Larry Roberts, Alabama, DE (2)
1987	Harris Barton, North Carolina, T
	Terrence Flagler, Clemson, RB

San Francisco 49ers 1987 Veteran Roster

No.	Name	Pos.	Ht.	Wt.	Birth-date	NFL Exp.	College	Hometown	How Acq.	'86 Games/ Starts
68	Ayers, John	G	6-5	265	4/14/53	11	West Texas State	Carrizo Springs, Tex.	D8-'76	14/14
76	Board, Dwaine	DE	6-5	248	11/29/56	8	North Carolina A&T	Rocky Mount, Va.	FA-'79	16/15
59	t-Browner, Keith	LB	6-6	245	1/24/62	4	Southern California	Atlanta, Ga.	T(TB)-'87	15/13
95	Carter, Michael	NT	6-2	285	10/29/60	4	Southern Methodist	Dallas, Tex.	D5a-'84	15/13
87	Clark, Dwight	WR	6-4	215	1/8/57	9	Clemson	Charlotte, N.C.	D10a-'79	16/14
69	Collie, Bruce	T-G	6-6	275	6/27/62	3	Texas-Arlington	San Antonio, Tex.	D5-'85	16/7
57	Cousineau, Tom	LB	6-3	225	5/6/57	6	Ohio State	Lakewood, Ohio	FA-'86	5/0
33	Craig, Roger	RB	6-0	224	7/10/60	5	Nebraska	Davenport, Iowa	D2-'83	16/15
83	Crawford, Derrick	WR-KR	5-10	185	9/3/60	2	Memphis State	Memphis, Tenn.	FA-'86	10/0
28	Cribbs, Joe	RB	5-11	193	1/5/58	7	Auburn	Sulligent, Ala.	T(Buff)-'86	14/10
51	Cross, Randy	G	6-3	265	4/25/54	12	UCLA	Encino, Calif.	D2-'76	16/16
64	Durrette, Michael	G	6-4	280	8/11/57	2	West Virginia	Charlottesville, Va.	FA-'86	9/0
50	Ellison, Riki	LB	6-2	225	8/15/60	5	Southern California	Tucson, Ariz.	D5-'83	16/16
55	Fahnhorst, Jim	LB	6-4	230	11/8/58	4	Minnesota	St. Cloud, Minn.	FA-'84	16/14
71	Fahnhorst, Keith	T	6-6	273	2/6/52	14	Minnesota	St. Cloud, Minn.	D2a-'74	16/16
54	†Ferrari, Ron	LB	6-0	215	7/30/59	6	Illinois	Moweaqua, Ill.	D7-'82	16/0
81	Francis, Russ	TE	6-6	242	4/3/53	12	Oregon	Pleasant Hill, Ore.	T(NE)-'82	16/14
86	†Frank, John	TE	6-3	225	4/17/62	4	Ohio State	Mt. Lebanon, Pa.	D2-'84	16/6
49	Fuller, Jeff	S-LB	6-2	216	8/8/62	4	Texas A&M	Dallas, Tex.	D5b-'84	6/0
11	Gagliano, Bob	QB	6-3	205	9/5/58	4	Utah State	Glendale, Calif.	FA-'87	0*
29	Griffin, Don	CB	6-0	176	3/17/64	2	Middle Tennessee State	Pelham, Ga.	D6-'86	16/15
94	Haley, Charles	DE-LB	6-5	230	1/6/64	2	James Madison	Campbell County, Va.	D4a-'86	16/1
24	†Harmon, Derrick	RB-KR	5-10	202	4/26/63	4	Cornell	Queens, N.Y.	D9b-'84	8/2
75	Harty, John	DE	6-4	260	12/17/58	6	Iowa	Sioux City, Iowa	D2a-'81	7/5
46	†Holmoe, Tom	S	6-2	195	3/7/60	4	Brigham Young	La Crescenta, Calif.	D4-'83	16/2
67	Kugler, Pete	NT-DE	6-4	255	8/9/59	5	Penn State	Cherry Hill, N.J.	FA-'86	3/0
42	Lott, Ronnie	S	6-0	200	5/8/59	7	Southern California	Rialto, Calif.	D1-'81	14/14
84	Margerum, Ken	WR	6-0	180	10/5/58	6	Stanford	Fountain Valley, Calif.	FA-'86	6/0*
53	McColl, Milt	LB	6-6	230	8/28/59	7	Stanford	Covina, Calif.	FA-'81	16/15
62	McIntyre, Guy	G	6-3	264	2/17/61	4	Georgia	Thomasville, Ga.	D3-'84	16/2
22	McKyer, Tim	CB	6-0	174	9/5/63	2	Texas-Arlington	Port Arthur, Tex.	D3b-'86	16/16
32	Monroe, Carl	RB-KR	5-8	180	2/20/60	5	Utah	San Jose, Calif.	FA-'83	5/0
16	Montana, Joe	QB	6-2	195	6/11/56	9	Notre Dame	Monongahela, Pa.	D3-'79	8/8
20	Nixon, Tory	CB	5-11	186	2/24/62	3	San Diego State	Phoenix, Ariz.	T(Wash)-'85	16/0
77	Paris, Bubba	T	6-6	299	10/6/60	5	Michigan	Louisville, Ky.	D2-'82	10/9
56	†Quillan, Fred	C	6-5	266	1/27/56	10	Oregon	Portland, Ore.	D7-'78	16/16
44	Rathman, Tom	RB	6-1	232	10/7/62	2	Nebraska	Grand Island, Neb.	D3a-'86	16/1
80	Rice, Jerry	WR	6-2	200	10/13/62	3	Mississippi Valley State	Crawford, Miss.	D1-'85	16/15
30	Ring, Bill	RB	5-10	205	12/13/56	7	Brigham Young	Belmont, Calif.	FA-'81	7/0
91	Roberts, Larry	DE	6-3	264	6/2/63	2	Alabama	Dothan, Ala.	D2-'86	16/2
65	Rogers, Doug	DE	6-5	280	6/23/60	5	Stanford	Bakersfield, Calif.	FA-'86	8/0
25	Rogers, Jimmy	RB	5-10	190	6/29/55	6	Oklahoma	Forrest City, Ark.	FA-'86	0*
4	Runager, Max	P	6-1	189	3/24/56	9	South Carolina	Orangeburg, S.C.	FA-'84	16/0
61	Sapolu, Jesse	G-C	6-4	260	3/10/61	2	Hawaii	Honolulu, Hawaii	D11-'83	0*
90	Shell, Todd	LB	6-4	225	6/24/62	3	Brigham Young	Mesa, Ariz.	D1-'84	1/0
72	†Stover, Jeff	DE	6-5	275	5/22/58	6	Oregon	Corning, Calif.	FA-'82	15/6
78	†Tuiasosopo, Manu	NT	6-3	262	8/30/57	9	UCLA	Long Beach, Calif.	T(Sea)-'84	15/7
58	Turner, Keena	LB	6-2	222	10/22/58	8	Purdue	Chicago, Ill.	D2-'80	16/16
74	Wallace, Steve	T	6-5	276	12/27/64	2	Auburn	Atlanta, Ga.	D4b-'86	16/0
99	Walter, Michael	LB	6-3	238	11/30/60	5	Oregon	Eugene, Ore.	FA-'84	16/2
14	Wersching, Ray	K	5-11	215	8/21/50	15	California	Downey, Calif.	FA-'77	16/0
27	Williamson, Carlton	S	6-0	204	6/12/58	7	Pittsburgh	Atlanta, Ga.	D3-'81	16/16
85	Wilson, Mike	WR	6-3	215	12/19/58	7	Washington State	Carson, Calif.	FA-'81	11/1
21	Wright, Eric	CB	6-1	185	4/18/59	7	Missouri	East St. Louis, Ill.	D2b-'81	2/1
8	t-Young, Steve	QB	6-2	200	10/11/61	3	Brigham Young	Greenwich, Conn.	T(TB)-'87	14/14

* Gagliano active for 1 game in '86, but did not play; Margerum played 1 game with Chicago in '86, 5 with San Francisco; J. Rogers and Sapolu missed '86 season due to injury.

†Option playout; subject to developments.

t-49ers traded for Browner (Tampa Bay), Young (Tampa Bay).

Retired—Wendell Tyler, 9-year running back, 5 games in '86.

Traded—Quarterback Jeff Kemp to Seattle.

Also played with 49ers in '86—RB Tony Cherry (5 games), DT Dennis Harrison (5), CB Dana McLemore (3), QB Mike Moroski (15), DE Jim Stuckey (1).

COACHING STAFF

Head Coach, Bill Walsh

Pro Career: Begins ninth season as an NFL head coach. Directed 49ers to NFC championship in 1981 and 1984 and to victories in Super Bowl XVI (26-21 over Cincinnati) and Super Bowl XIX (38-16 over Miami). Started pro coaching career in 1966 as offensive backfield coach for the Oakland Raiders. He then spent eight seasons (1968-75) in Cincinnati, where he was responsible for coaching the Bengals' quarterbacks and receivers. His tenure in Cincinnati was followed by a season with the San Diego Chargers as offensive coordinator. While at Cincinnati he tutored Ken Anderson, who became the first NFL quarterback to lead the league in passing two straight years. At San Diego, he helped develop the talents of quarterback Dan Fouts. No pro playing experience. Career record: 76-54-1.

Background: End at San Jose State in 1953-54. Started college coaching career at California, where he served under Marv Levy from 1960-62. In 1963, he joined John Ralston's Stanford staff and worked with the defensive backfield for three seasons. Returned to Stanford as head coach in 1977 and directed Cardinals to a two-year record of 17-7, including wins in the Sun and Bluebonnet Bowls. Received his master's degree in history from San Jose State in 1959.

Personal: Born November 30, 1931, in Los Angeles, Calif. He and his wife, Geri, live in Menlo Park, Calif., and have three children—Steve, Craig, and Elizabeth.

Assistant Coaches

Jerry Attaway, conditioning; born January 3, 1946, Susanville, Calif., lives in San Carlos, Calif. Defensive back Yuba, Calif., J.C. 1964-65, Cal-Davis 1967. No pro playing experience. College coach: Cal-Davis 1970-71, Idaho 1972-74, Utah State 1975-77, Southern California 1978-82. Pro coach: Joined 49ers in 1983.

Dennis Green, receivers; born February 17, 1949, Harrisburg, Pa., lives in Santa Cruz, Calif. Running back Iowa 1968-70. Pro running back British Columbia Lions (CFL) 1971. College coach: Iowa 1972, 1974-76, Dayton 1973, Stanford 1977-78, 1980, Northwestern 1981-85 (head coach). Pro coach: San Francisco 49ers 1979, rejoined 49ers in 1987.

Mike Holmgren, quarterbacks; born June 15, 1948, San Francisco, Calif., lives in San Jose, Calif. Quarterback Southern California 1966-69. No pro playing experience. College coach: San Francisco State 1981, Brigham Young 1982-85. Pro coach: First year with 49ers.

Sherman Lewis, running backs, born June 29, 1942, Louisville, Ky., lives in Redwood City, Calif. Running back Michigan State 1961-63. Pro running back Toronto Argonauts (CFL) 1964-65, New York Jets 1966. College coach: Michigan State 1969-82. Pro coach: Joined 49ers in 1983.

Bobb McKittrick, offensive line; born December 29, 1935, Baker, Ore., lives in San Mateo, Calif. Guard Oregon State 1955-57. No pro playing experience. College coach: Oregon State 1961-64, UCLA 1965-70. Pro coach: Los Angeles Rams 1971-72, San Diego Chargers 1974-78, joined 49ers in 1979.

Bill McPherson, linebackers; born October 24, 1931, Santa Clara, Calif., lives in San Jose, Calif. Tackle Santa Clara 1950-52. No pro playing experience. College coach: Santa Clara 1963-74, UCLA 1975-77. Pro coach: Philadelphia Eagles 1978, joined 49ers in 1979.

Ray Rhodes, defensive backfield; born October 20, 1950, Mexia, Tex., lives in Fremont, Calif. Running back-wide receiver Texas Christian 1969-70, Tulsa 1972-73. Pro defensive back New York Giants 1974-79, San Francisco 49ers 1980. Pro coach: Joined 49ers in 1981.

San Francisco 49ers 1987 First-Year Roster

Name	Pos.	Ht.	Wt.	Birth-date	College	Hometown	How Acq.
Asmus, Jim (1)	K	6-1	190	12/2/58	Hawaii	La Puente, Calif.	FA
Barton, Harris	T	6-3	280	4/19/64	North Carolina	Atlanta, Ga.	D1a
Benn, Rennie (1)	WR	6-3	198	3/3/63	Lehigh	Millburn, N.J.	FA
Bregel, Jeff	G	6-4	279	5/1/64	Southern California	Granada Hills, Calif.	D2a
Brockhaus, Jeff (1)	K	6-2	212	4/15/59	Missouri	St. Louis, Mo.	FA
Butler, Elvis	DE	6-5	295	10/26/64	Mississippi State	Clermont, Fla.	FA
Cochran, Mark (1)	T	6-5	285	5/6/63	Baylor	Pasadena, Tex.	FA
Cormier, Joe (1)	WR	6-6	235	5/3/63	Southern California	Gardena, Calif.	FA
Courtney, Matt (1)	CB-S	5-11	194	12/12/61	Idaho State	Littleton, Colo.	FA
Cox, Tom	C	6-5	268	12/4/62	Southern California	Xenia, Ohio	FA
Dailey, John (1)	LB	6-3	232	10/5/62	Auburn	Birmingham, Ala.	FA
DeLine, Steve	K	5-11	180	8/19/61	Colorado State	Rand, Colo.	D7
Fagan, Kevin	DT	6-3	260	4/25/63	Miami	Lake Worth, Fla.	D4c
Flagler, Terrence	RB	6-0	200	9/24/64	Clemson	Fernandia Beach, Fla.	D1b
Franz, Tracy (1)	G	6-5	270	3/26/60	San Jose State	Sacramento, Calif.	FA
Glover, Clyde (1)	DE	6-6	280	7/16/60	Fresno State	Las Vegas, Nev.	FA
Grayson, David	LB	6-2	220	2/27/64	Fresno State	San Diego, Calif.	D8
Hall, Victor (1)	TE	6-2	238	11/8/63	Jackson State	Columbus, Miss.	FA
Heller, Ron	TE	6-3	235	9/18/63	Oregon State	Clarkfork, Idaho	FA
Holyfield, Anthony (1)	DE	6-3	275	11/22/60	Hawaii	San Francisco, Calif.	FA
Jokisch, Paul	WR	6-7	230	1/4/64	Michigan	Birmingham, Mich.	D5
Jones, Brent (1)	TE	6-4	230	2/12/63	Santa Clara	San Jose, Calif.	FA
Justin, Tyrone (1)	CB	5-10	173	1/17/59	Cal State-Fullerton	Los Angeles, Calif.	FA
Keeble, Jerry (1)	LB	6-3	230	8/19/63	Minnesota	St. Louis, Mo.	FA
Lilly, Kevin (1)	DE	6-4	265	5/14/63	Tulsa	Tulsa, Okla.	FA
Long, Tim (1)	C	6-6	295	4/20/63	Memphis State	Cleveland, Tenn.	FA
Mikolas, Doug (1)	NT	6-1	270	6/7/62	Portland State	Scio, Ore.	FA
Nicholas, Calvin	WR	6-4	208	6/11/64	Grambling	Baton Rouge, La.	D11b
Paye, John	QB	6-3	205	3/30/65	Stanford	Atherton, Calif.	D10
Pike, Vance	T-C	6-4	220	1/7/63	Georgia Southern	Warner Robins, Ga.	FA
Reach, Kevin (1)	C-G	6-3	270	10/24/63	Utah	Stockbridge, Ga.	FA
Ridgle, Elston (1)	DE	6-6	260	8/24/63	Nevada-Reno	Woodland Hills, Calif.	FA
Shelley, Jo-Nathan	CB	6-0	176	8/6/64	Mississippi	Vicksburg, Miss.	D9
Spelman, Rich	K	5-8	177	11/19/61	Hawaii	Honolulu, Hawaii	FA
Standifer, Bob (1)	DT	6-5	265	6/3/63	Tenn.-Chattanooga	Chattanooga, Tenn.	FA
Stokes, Eric (1)	T	6-4	275	1/13/62	Northeastern	Ansonia, Conn.	FA
Sydney, Harry (1)	RB	6-0	217	6/26/59	Kansas	Fay, N.C.	FA
Taylor, John	WR	6-1	185	3/31/62	Delaware State	Pensauken, N.J.	D3c
Thomas, Sean (1)	CB	5-11	192	4/12/62	Texas Christian	Sacramento, Calif.	FA
Webster, Randall (1)	LB	6-3	225	8/22/63	S.W. Oklahoma State	Durant, Miss.	FA
White, Bob	LB	6-2	246	7/1/64	Penn State	Freeport, Pa.	D6
Young, Almon (1)	G	6-3	270	7/3/62	Bethune-Cookman	Umatilla, Fla.	FA

The term NFL Rookie is defined as a player who is in his first season of professional football and has not been on the roster of another professional football team for any regular-season or postseason games. A Rookie is designated by an "R" on NFL rosters. Players who have been active in another professional football league or players who have NFL experience, including either preseason training camp or being on an active roster for fewer than three regular-season or postseason games, are termed NFL First-Year Players. An NFL First-Year Player is designated by a "1" on NFL rosters. Thereafter, a player on an NFL active roster for at least three regular-season or postseason games is credited with an additional year of NFL playing experience.

NOTES

George Seifert, defensive coordinator; born January 22, 1940, San Francisco, Calif., lives in Sunnyvale, Calif. Linebacker Utah 1960-62. No pro playing experience. College coach: Westminster 1965 (head coach), Iowa 1966, Oregon 1967-71, Stanford 1972-74, 1977-79, Cornell 1975-76 (head coach). Pro coach: Joined 49ers in 1980.

Lynn Stiles, special teams; born April 12, 1941, Kermit, Tex., lives in Redwood City, Calif. Guard Utah 1961-62. No pro playing experience. College coach: Utah 1963-65, Iowa 1966-70, UCLA 1971-75, San Jose State 1976-78 (head coach). Pro coach: Philadelphia Eagles 1979-85, first year with 49ers.

Fred von Appen, defensive line; born March 22, 1942, Eugene, Ore., lives in Cupertino, Calif. Lineman Linfield College 1960-63. No pro playing experience. College coach: Linfield 1967-68, Arkansas 1969, 1981, UCLA 1970, Virginia Tech 1971, Oregon 1972-76, Stanford 1977-78, 1982. Pro coach: Green Bay Packers 1979-80, joined 49ers in 1983.

National Football Conference Central Division

Team Colors: Florida Orange, White, and Red

One Buccaneer Place
Tampa, Florida 33607
Telephone: (813) 870-2700

Club Officials

Owner-President: Hugh F. Culverhouse
Vice President: Joy Culverhouse
Vice President-Head Coach: Ray Perkins
Vice President-Community Relations: Gay Culverhouse
Secretary-Treasurer: Ward Holland
Director of Administration: Jim McVay
Assistant to the President: Phil Krueger
Director of Player Personnel: Jerry Angelo
Director of Pro Personnel: Erik Widmark
Director of Ticket Operations: Terry Wooten
Director of Public Relations: Rick Odioso
Director of Marketing & Advertising: Fred Doremus
Assistant Director-Community Relations: Jill Massicotte
Assistant Director-Media Relations: John Gerdes
College Personnel: Gary Horton, Leland Kendall, Dean Rossi
Controller: Ed Easom
Trainer: Chris Smith
Assistant Trainer: Joe Joe Petrone
Equipment Manager: Frank Pupello
Assistant Equipment Manager: Carl Melchior
Video Director: Marvin Scott

Stadium: Tampa Stadium • **Capacity:** 74,315
North Dale Mabry
Tampa, Florida 33607

Playing Surface: Grass

Training Camp: University of Tampa
401 W. Kennedy Boulevard
Tampa, Florida 33606

1987 Schedule

Preseason

Aug. 15	**Cincinnati**	7:00
Aug. 22	**New York Jets**	7:00
Aug. 29	**Washington**	7:00
Sept. 5	at Indianapolis	7:30

Regular Season

Sept. 13	**Atlanta**	1:00
Sept. 20	at Chicago	12:00
Sept. 27	**Green Bay**	1:00
Oct. 4	at Detroit	1:00
Oct. 11	**San Diego**	1:00
Oct. 18	at Minnesota	12:00
Oct. 25	**Chicago**	1:00
Nov. 1	vs. Green Bay at Milw.	12:00
Nov. 8	at St. Louis	12:00
Nov. 15	**Minnesota**	1:00
Nov. 22	**San Francisco**	1:00
Nov. 29	at Los Angeles Rams	1:00
Dec. 6	at New Orleans	3:00
Dec. 13	**Detroit**	4:00
Dec. 20	**St. Louis**	4:00
Dec. 27	at Indianapolis	1:00

Buccaneers Coaching History

(49-119-1)

1976-84	John McKay	45-91-1
1985-86	Leeman Bennett	4-28-0

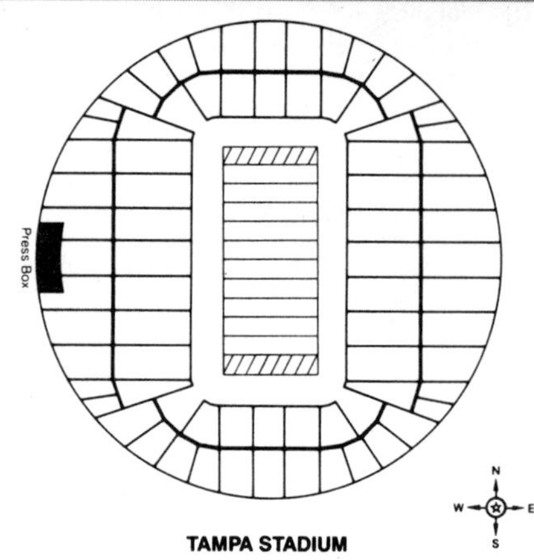

TAMPA STADIUM

Record Holders

Individual Records—Career

Category	Name	Performance
Rushing (Yds.)	James Wilder, 1981-86	4,882
Passing (Yds.)	Doug Williams, 1978-1982	12,648
Passing (TDs)	Doug Williams, 1978-1982	73
Receiving (No.)	James Wilder, 1981-86	339
Receiving (Yds.)	Kevin House, 1980-86	4,928
Interceptions	Cedric Brown, 1977-1984	29
Punting (Avg.)	Frank Garcia, 1983-86	41.6
Punt Return (Avg.)	John Holt, 1981-83	7.5
Kickoff Ret. (Avg.)	Isaac Hagins, 1976-1980	21.9
Field Goals	Bill Capece, 1981-83	43
Touchdowns (Tot.)	James Wilder, 1981-86	41
Points	James Wilder, 1981-86	246

Individual Records—Single Season

Category	Name	Performance
Rushing (Yds.)	James Wilder, 1984	1,544
Passing (Yds.)	Doug Williams, 1981	3,563
Passing (TDs)	Doug Williams, 1980	20
Receiving (No.)	James Wilder, 1984	85
Receiving (Yds.)	Kevin House, 1981	1,176
Interceptions	Cedric Brown, 1981	9
Punting (Avg.)	Larry Swider, 1981	42.7
Punt Return (Avg.)	Leon Bright, 1985	10.3
Kickoff Return (Avg.)	Isaac Hagins, 1977	23.5
Field Goals	Donald Igwebuike, 1985	22
Touchdowns (Tot.)	James Wilder, 1984	13
Points	Donald Igwebuike, 1985	96

Individual Records—Single Game

Category	Name	Performance
Rushing (Yds.)	James Wilder, 11-6-83	219
Passing (Yds.)	Doug Williams, 11-16-80	486
Passing (TDs)	Many times	4
	Last time by Steve DeBerg, 10-20-85	
Receiving (No.)	James Wilder, 9-15-85	13
Receiving (Yds.)	Kevin House, 10-18-81	178
Interceptions	Many times	2
	Last time by Vito McKeever, 11-16-86	
Field Goals	Bill Capece, 10-30-83	4
	Bill Capece, 1-2-83	4
	Donald Igwebuike, 11-24-85	4
Touchdowns	Jimmie Giles, 10-20-85	4
Points	Jimmie Giles, 10-20-85	24

1986 Team Statistics

	Buccaneers	Opp.
Total First Downs	273	362
Rushing	100	162
Passing	142	177
Penalty	31	23
Third Down: Made/Att.	59/193	90/193
Fourth Down: Made/Att.	8/19	6/10
Total Net Yards	4361	6333
Avg. Per Game	272.6	395.8
Total Plays	970	1061
Avg. Per Play	4.5	6.0
Net Yards Rushing	1863	2648
Avg. Per Game	116.4	165.5
Total Rushes	455	558
Net Yards Passing	2498	3685
Avg. Per Game	156.1	230.3
Tackled/Yards Lost	56/394	19/153
Gross Yards	2892	3838
Att./Completions	459/245	484/289
Completion Pct.	53.4	59.7
Had Intercepted	25	13
Punts/Avg.	78/40.2	59/41.3
Net Punting Avg.	32.8	37.4
Penalties/Yards Lost	83/661	116/941
Fumbles/Ball Lost	36/17	39/19
Touchdowns	27	59
Rushing	12	31
Passing	13	23
Returns	2	5
Avg. Time of Possession	28:40	31:20

1986 Team Record

Preseason (0-4)

Date	Result		Opponents
8/9	L	10-26	St. Louis
8/16	L	17-20	Atlanta
8/23	L	13-21	Washington
8/29	L	3-21	at Miami
		43-88	

Regular Season (2-14)

Date	Result		Opponents	Att.
9/7	L	7-31	San Francisco	50,780
9/14	L	10-23	Minnesota	34,579
9/21	W	24-20	at Detroit	38,453
9/28	L	20-23	Atlanta (OT)	38,950
10/5	L	20-26	at L.A. Rams (OT)	50,585
10/12	L	19-30	St. Louis	33,307
10/19	L	7-38	at New Orleans	43,355
10/26	L	20-27	at Kansas City	36,230
11/2	W	34-28	Buffalo	32,806
11/9	L	3-23	Chicago	70,097
11/16	L	7-31	at Green Bay	48,271
11/23	L	17-38	Detroit	30,029
11/30	L	13-45	at Minnesota	56,235
12/7	L	14-48	at Chicago	52,746
12/14	L	7-21	Green Bay	30,099
12/21	L	17-21	at St. Louis	23,957

(OT) Overtime

Score by Periods

Buccaneers	39	74	41	85	0	—	239
Opponents	111	105	103	145	9	—	473

Attendance

Home 320,646 Away 349,832 Total 670,478
Single game home record, 72,033 (1-6-80)
Single season home record, 545,980 (1979)

1986 Individual Statistics

Scoring	TD R	TD P	TD Rt	PAT	FG	Saf	TP
Igwebuike	0	0	0	26/27	17/24	0	77
Magee	0	5	0	0/0	0/0	0	30
Young	5	0	0	0/0	0/0	0	30
Wilder	2	1	0	0/0	0/0	0	18
Wonsley	3	0	0	0/0	0/0	0	18
Carter	0	2	0	0/0	0/0	0	12
Franklin	0	1	1	0/0	0/0	0	12
Freeman	0	2	0	0/0	0/0	0	12
Bligen, Jets-T.B.	1	0	0	0/0	0/0	0	6
DeBerg	1	0	0	0/0	0/0	0	6
Giles	0	1	0	0/0	0/0	0	6
Heflin	0	0	1	0/0	0/0	0	6
Heller	0	1	0	0/0	0/0	0	6
Howard	1	0	0	0/0	0/0	0	6
Buccaneers	12	13	2	26/27	17/24	0	239
Opponents	31	23	5	56/58	21/30	0	473

Passing	Att.	Comp.	Yds.	Pct.	TD	Int.	Tkld.	Rate
Young	363	195	2282	53.7	8	13	47/326	65.5
DeBerg	96	50	610	52.1	5	12	9/68	49.7
Buccaneers	459	245	2892	53.4	13	25	56/394	59.6
Opponents	484	289	3838	59.7	23	13	19/153	89.5

Rushing	Att.	Yds.	Avg.	LG	TD
Wilder	190	704	3.7	45t	2
Young	74	425	5.7	31	5
Wonsley	73	339	4.6	59t	3
Springs	74	285	3.9	40	0
Howard	30	110	3.7	16	1
Bligen, Jets-T.B.	20	65	3.3	10	1
Franklin	7	7	1.0	4	0
House	2	5	2.5	4	0
Allen	1	3	3.0	3	0
DeBerg	2	1	0.5	1t	1
Carter	1	−5	−5.0	−5	0
Garcia	1	−11	−11.0	−11	0
Buccaneers	455	1863	4.1	59t	12
Opponents	558	2648	4.7	60	31

Receiving	No.	Yds.	Avg.	LG	TD
Magee	45	564	12.5	45	5
Wilder	43	326	7.6	25	1
Carter	42	640	15.2	46	2
Springs	24	187	7.8	46	0
Giles	18	178	9.9	20	1
Freeman	14	229	16.4	33t	2
House	11	206	18.7	40	0
Bell	10	120	12.0	25	0
Wonsley	8	57	7.1	11	0
Franklin	7	29	4.1	9	1
Williams	6	91	15.2	25	0
Howard	5	60	12.0	29	0
Dunn	3	83	27.7	38	0
Harris	3	52	17.3	23	0
Heflin	3	42	14.0	15	0
Bligen, Jets-T.B.	2	6	3.0	4	0
Gillespie	1	18	18.0	18	0
Mallory	1	9	9.0	9	0
Heller	1	1	1.0	1t	1
Buccaneers	245	2892	11.8	46	13
Opponents	289	3838	13.3	73	23

Interceptions	No.	Yds.	Avg.	LG	TD
McKeever	3	12	4.0	10	0
Brantley	2	65	32.5	57	0
Curry	2	0	0.0	0	0
Swoope	1	23	23.0	23	0
Browner	1	16	16.0	16	0
Washington	1	12	12.0	12	0
Davis	1	0	0.0	0	0
Easmon	1	0	0.0	0	0
Jones	1	0	0.0	0	0
Buccaneers	13	128	9.8	57	0
Opponents	25	236	9.4	59t	1

Punting	No.	Yds.	Avg.	In 20	LG
Springs	1	43	43.0	0	43
Garcia	77	3089	40.1	19	60
Buccaneers	78	3132	40.2	19	60
Opponents	59	2438	41.3	24	57

Punt Returns	No.	FC	Yds.	Avg.	LG	TD
Futrell	14	5	67	4.8	12	0
K. Walker	9	0	27	3.0	10	0
Harris	3	0	16	5.3	8	0
Buccaneers	26	5	110	4.2	12	0
Opponents	39	15	414	10.6	71t	3

Kickoff Returns	No.	Yds.	Avg.	LG	TD
Freeman	31	582	18.8	33	0
Wonsley	10	208	20.8	29	0
K. Walker	8	146	18.3	26	0
Futrell	5	115	23.0	30	0
Harris	4	63	15.8	23	0
Howard	4	71	17.8	24	0
Franklin	3	23	7.7	18	0
Magee	2	21	10.5	11	0
Williams	2	29	14.5	15	0
Allen	1	21	21.0	21	0
Boatner	1	2	2.0	2	0
Curry	1	6	6.0	6	0
Dunn	1	0	0.0	0	0
Heflin	1	15	15.0	15	0
Randle	1	0	0.0	0	0
Buccaneers	75	1302	17.4	33	0
Opponents	46	1009	21.9	85t	1

Sacks	No.
Browner	4.0
Washington	4.0
Holmes	2.5
Cannon	2.0
Kellin	2.0
Logan	2.0
Nelson	1.0
Swoope	1.0
Randle	0.5
Buccaneers	19.0
Opponents	56.0

FIRST-ROUND SELECTIONS

(If club had no first-round selection, first player drafted is listed with round in parentheses.)

Year	Player, College, Position
1976	Lee Roy Selmon, Oklahoma, DT
1977	Ricky Bell, Southern California, RB
1978	Doug Williams, Grambling, QB
1979	Greg Roberts, Oklahoma, G (2)
1980	Ray Snell, Wisconsin, G
1981	Hugh Green, Pittsburgh, LB
1982	Sean Farrell, Penn State, G
1983	Randy Grimes, Baylor, C (2)
1984	Keith Browner, Southern California, LB (2)
1985	Ron Holmes, Washington, DE
1986	Bo Jackson, Auburn, RB
	Roderick Jones, Southern Methodist, DB
1987	Vinny Testaverde, Miami, QB

Tampa Bay Buccaneers 1987 Veteran Roster

No.	Name	Pos.	Ht.	Wt.	Birth-date	NFL Exp.	College	Hometown	How Acq.	'86 Games/ Starts
82	†Bell, Jerry	TE	6-5	230	3/7/59	6	Arizona State	Richmond, Calif.	D3-'82	10/3
38	Bligen, Dennis	RB	5-11	215	3/6/62	4	St. John's	Queens Village, N.Y.	W(NYJ)-'86	5/0*
34	Boatner, Mack	RB	6-0	220	10/4/63	2	Southeast Louisiana	White Castle, La.	FA-'86	7/0
52	Brantley, Scot	LB	6-1	230	2/24/58	8	Florida	Ocala, Fla.	D3-'80	16/16
78	†Cannon, John	DE	6-5	260	7/30/60	6	William & Mary	Long Branch, N.J.	D3-'82	9/8
87	Carter, Gerald	WR	6-1	190	6/19/57	8	Texas A&M	Bryan, Tex.	D9-'80	15/15
23	†Castille, Jeremiah	CB-S	5-10	175	1/15/61	5	Alabama	Phenix City, Ala.	D3-'83	13/6
31	†Curry, Craig	CB-S	6-1	190	7/20/61	4	Texas	Houston, Tex.	FA-'84	16/10
58	†Davis, Jeff	LB	6-0	230	1/26/60	6	Clemson	Greensboro, N.C.	D5-'82	16/16
17	DeBerg, Steve	QB	6-3	210	1/19/54	11	San Jose State	Anaheim, Calif.	T(SF)-'84	16/2
85	Dunn, K.D.	TE	6-3	235	4/28/63	3	Clemson	Decatur, Ga.	FA-'86	7/0
26	Easmon, Ricky	CB-S	5-10	160	7/20/63	3	Florida	Dunnellon, Fla.	FA-'85	9/2
95	Faulkner, Chris	TE	6-4	250	4/13/60	3	Florida	Atlanta, Ind.	FA-'86	0*
35	Franklin, Pat	RB	6-1	230	8/16/63	2	Southwest Texas State	Bay City, Tex.	FA-'86	8/1
81	Freeman, Phil	WR	5-11	185	12/9/62	3	Arizona	Los Angeles, Calif.	D8-'85	15/6
36	Futrell, Bobby	CB-S	5-11	190	8/4/62	2	Elizabeth City State	Ahoskie, N.C.	FA-'86	16/0
5	†Garcia, Frank	P	6-0	210	6/5/57	5	Arizona	Tucson, Ariz.	FA-'83	16/0
83	Gillespie, Willie	WR	5-9	170	10/24/61	2	Tenn.-Chattanooga	Starkeville, Miss.	FA-'86	2/0
4	Gonzalez, Leon	WR	5-11	165	9/21/63	2	Bethune-Cookman	Jacksonville, Fla.	FA-'87	0*
92	Goode, Conrad	T	6-6	285	1/9/62	3	Missouri	Creve Coeur, Mo.	FA-'87	0*
60	Grimes, Randy	C	6-4	270	7/20/60	5	Baylor	Tyler, Tex.	D2-'83	16/16
84	Harris, Leonard	WR	5-8	155	11/17/60	2	Texas Tech	McKinney, Tex.	FA-'86	6/1
89	†Heflin, Vince	WR	6-0	185	7/7/59	6	Central State, Ohio	Dayton, Ohio	FA-'86	6/3
73	Heller, Ron	T	6-6	280	8/25/62	4	Penn State	Farmingdale, N.Y.	D4-'84	16/16
90	Holmes, Ron	DE	6-4	255	8/26/63	3	Washington	Lacey, Wash.	D1-'85	14/12
25	Howard, Bobby	RB	6-0	210	6/1/64	2	Indiana	Pittsburgh, Pa.	FA-'86	7/2
1	†Igwebuike, Donald	K	5-9	185	12/27/60	3	Clemson	Anambra, Nigeria	D10-'85	16/0
22	Jones, Rod	CB-S	6-0	175	3/31/64	2	Southern Methodist	Dallas, Tex.	D1-'86	16/16
75	Kellin, Kevin	DE	6-6	265	11/16/59	2	Minnesota	Grand Rapids, Minn.	FA-'86	9/0
33	Kemp, Bobby	S	6-0	191	5/29/59	7	Cal State-Fullerton	Pomona, Calif.	W(Cin)-'87	16/0
98	†Keys, Tyrone	DE	6-7	270	10/24/59	5	Mississippi State	Jackson, Miss.	W(Chi)-'86	14/2
76	†Logan, David	NT	6-2	250	10/25/62	9	Pittsburgh	Pittsburgh, Pa.	D12-'79	16/16
77	Maarleveld, J.D.	T	6-6	300	10/24/61	2	Maryland	Rutherford, N.J.	D5-'86	14/0
86	Magee, Calvin	TE	6-3	240	4/23/63	3	Southern	New Orleans, La.	FA-'85	16/13
68	Mallory, Rick	G	6-2	265	10/21/60	3	Washington	Renton, Wash.	D9-'84	16/1
21	McKeever, Vito	CB-S	6-0	180	10/8/61	2	Florida	Dunnellon, Fla.	FA-'86	16/8
59	Murphy, Kevin	LB	6-2	230	9/8/63	2	Oklahoma	Plano, Tex.	D2-'86	16/0
71	Nelson, Bob	NT-DE	6-3	265	3/3/59	2	Miami	Patapsco, Md.	FA-'86	16/10
74	Powell, Marvin	T	6-5	270	8/30/55	11	Southern California	Fayetteville, N.C.	T(NYJ)-'86	3/3
54	Randle, Ervin	LB	6-1	250	10/12/62	3	Baylor	Hearne, Tex.	D3-'85	16/0
64	Robinson, Greg	T	6-5	285	12/25/62	2	Cal State-Sacramento	Sacramento, Calif.	FA-'86	3/0
41	Swoope, Craig	CB-S	6-1	200	2/3/64	2	Illinois	Ft. Pierce, Fla.	D4-'86	15/13
72	Taylor, Rob	T	6-6	290	11/14/60	2	Northwestern	St. Charles, Ill.	FA-'86	16/13
50	t-Turk, Dan	C	6-4	270	6/25/62	2	Wisconsin	Milwaukee, Wis.	T(Pitt)-'87	16/4
56	Walker, Jackie	LB	6-5	245	11/3/62	2	Jackson State	Monroe, La.	D2-'86	15/3
37	Walker, Kevin	CB-S	5-11	180	10/20/63	2	East Carolina	Greensboro, N.C.	D6-'86	4/0
27	Walker, Quentin	RB	6-0	205	8/27/61	2	Virginia	Teaneck, N.J.	FA-'87	0*
10	Walls, Herkie	WR-KR	5-8	160	7/18/61	4	Texas	Garland, Tex.	FA-'87	0*
51	†Washington, Chris	LB	6-4	230	3/6/62	4	Iowa State	Chicago, Ill.	D6-'84	16/16
32	Wilder, James	RB	6-3	225	5/12/58	7	Missouri	Sikeston, Mo.	D2-'82	12/12
80	Williams, David	WR	6-3	190	6/10/63	2	Illinois	Los Angeles, Calif.	W(Chi)-'86	15/0
46	Wonsley, Nathan	RB	5-10	190	12/7/63	2	Mississippi	Moss Point, Miss.	FA-'86	10/2
66	Yarno, George	G-T	6-2	265	8/12/57	8	Washington State	Spokane, Wash.	FA-'79	16/16

* Bligen played 4 games with N.Y. Jets in '86, 1 with Tampa Bay; Faulkner, Gonzalez, Goode, Q. Walker, and Walls missed '86 season due to injury; Kemp played 16 games with Cincinnati; Turk played 16 games with Pittsburgh.

†Option playout; subject to developments.

Traded—Linebacker Keith Browner to San Francisco, guard Sean Farrell to New England, quarterback Steve Young to San Francisco.

t-Buccaneers traded for Turk (Pittsburgh).

Also played with Buccaneers in '86—RB Greg Allen (2 games), TE Jimmie Giles (7), WR Kevin House (7), NT Karl Morgan (12), LB Jeff Spek (2), RB Ron Springs (12), CB-S Ivory Sully (16).

COACHING STAFF

Head Coach, Ray Perkins

Pro Career: Named third head coach in Tampa Bay Buccaneers history on December 31, 1986. Previous head coaching experience in the NFL came with New York Giants when he compiled a 24-35 record between 1979 and 1982. Perkins built the Giants into a playoff team by 1981, his third season. It marked the Giants' first playoff appearance in 18 years. Worked five years as an assistant in the NFL, spending 1974-77 as receivers coach with New England Patriots and 1978 as offensive coordinator with San Diego Chargers. Drafted by Baltimore Colts in seventh round of 1967, and played five seasons there. Career record: 24-35.

Background: Bear Bryant's hand-picked successor at University of Alabama, where he compiled a 32-15-1 record between 1983-86, including three bowl game victories. College receiver at Alabama 1964-66 and All-America as a senior. College assistant at Mississippi State (1973).

Personal: Born November 6, 1941, in Mt. Olive, Mississippi. Ray and his wife, Carolyn, live in Tampa and have two sons—Tony and Mike.

Assistant Coaches

Larry Beightol, offensive line; born November 21, 1942, Morrisdale, Pa., lives in Tampa. Guard-linebacker Catawba College 1961-63. No pro playing experience. College coach: William & Mary 1968-71, North Carolina State 1972-75, Auburn 1976, Arkansas 1977-78, Louisiana Tech 1979, Missouri 1980-84. Pro coach: Atlanta Falcons 1985-86, first year with Buccaneers.

John Bobo, offensive assistant; born February 18, 1958, Alapaha, Ga., lives in Tampa. Tight end-defensive end Maryville 1976-79. No pro playing experience. College coach: Alabama 1985-86. Pro coach: First year with Buccaneers.

Bill Clay, defensive assistant; born September 5, 1941, Marianna, Ark., lives in Tampa. Tackle Arkansas 1960-62. No pro playing experience. College coach: Virginia, 1969-71, 1975, Virginia Tech 1972, South Carolina 1973-74, Southern Mississippi 1976-81, Southern Methodist 1982-86. Pro coach: First year with Buccaneers.

Sylvester Croom, running backs; born September 25, 1954, Tuscaloosa, Ala., lives in Tampa. Center Alabama 1971-74. Pro center New Orleans Saints 1975. College coach: Alabama 1976-86. Pro coach: First year with Buccaneers.

Mike DuBose, defensive line; born January 5, 1953, Opp, Ala., lives in Tampa. Defensive lineman Alabama 1971-73. No pro playing experience. College coach: Alabama 1974-75, 1983-86, Tennessee-Chattanooga 1980-81, Southern Mississippi 1982. Pro coach: First year with Buccaneers.

Doug Graber, defensive coordinator-secondary; born September 26, 1944, Detroit, Mich., lives in Tampa. Defensive back Wayne State 1963-66. No pro playing experience. College coach: Michigan Tech 1969-71, Eastern Michigan 1972-75, Ball State 1976-77, Wisconsin 1978-81, Montana State 1982 (head coach). Pro coach: Kansas City Chiefs 1983-86, first year with Buccaneers.

Kent Johnston, strength and conditioning; born February 21, 1956, Mexia, Tex., lives in Tampa. Defensive back Stephen F. Austin 1974-77. No pro playing experience. College coach: Northeast Louisiana 1979, Northwestern State (La.) 1980-81, Alabama 1983-86. Pro coach: First year with Buccaneers.

Joe Kines, outside linebackers; born July 13, 1944, Piedmont, Ala., lives in Tampa. Linebacker Jacksonville (Ala.) State 1963-65. No pro playing experience. College coach: Jacksonville State 1966, 1972-76, Clemson 1977-78, Florida 1979-84, Alabama 1985-86. Pro coach: First year with Buccaneers.

Tampa Bay Buccaneers 1987 First-Year Roster

Name	Pos.	Ht.	Wt.	Birth-date	College	Hometown	How Acq.
Anderson, Dwayne (1)	CB-S	6-0	205	12/7/61	Southern Methodist	St. Louis, Mo.	FA
Armentrout, Joe	RB	6-0	230	11/4/64	Wisconsin	Elgin, Ill.	D9a
Barnhardt, Tommy (1)	P	6-3	205	6/11/63	North Carolina	China Grove, N.C.	FA
Bartalo, Steve	RB	5-9	200	7/15/64	Colorado State	Colorado Springs, Colo.	D6
Carrier, Mark	WR	6-0	182	10/28/65	Nicholls State	Church Point, La.	D3
Carter, Stephen	WR	5-10	170	9/12/62	Albany State	Detroit, Mich.	FA
Cooper, Scott	DE	6-5	275	6/20/64	Kearney State	Oshkosh, Neb.	D12a
Davis, Greg	P	5-11	190	10/29/65	Citadel	Atlanta, Ga.	D9b
Fonoti, David (1)	T	6-4	280	8/17/63	Arizona State	Aiea, Hawaii	FA
Graham, Don	LB	6-2	244	1/31/64	Penn State	Pittsburgh, Pa.	D4a
Hall, Ron	TE	6-4	238	3/15/64	Hawaii	Escondido, Calif.	D4b
Hill, Bruce	WR	6-0	175	2/29/64	Arizona State	Lancaster, Calif.	D4c
Huddleston, James (1)	G	6-4	280	9/2/62	Virginia	Alexandria, Va.	FA
Hunt, Gary (1)	CB-S	5-11	180	10/28/63	Memphis State	Texarkana, Tex.	FA
Jacobs, Cam (1)	LB	6-2	230	3/10/62	Kentucky	Coral Gables, Fla.	FA
Jarvis, Curt	NT	6-2	266	1/28/65	Alabama	Gardendale, Ala.	D7a
Mayes, Tony	CB-S	6-0	200	5/19/64	Kentucky	Paintsville, Ky.	D5b
McCallister, Fred (1)	LB	6-1	250	2/17/62	Florida	Palm Bay, Fla.	FA
Moss, Winston	LB	6-3	235	12/24/65	Miami	Miami, Fla.	D2b
Mataele, Stan	NT	6-2	277	6/24/63	Arizona	Lale, Hawaii	D8
Nelson, Jeff (1)	WR	5-9	170	9/25/64	Texas A&M	Beaumont, Tex.	FA
Perrino, Michael (1)	T	6-5	285	3/2/64	Notre Dame	Elmhurst, Ill.	FA
Pumphrey, Donald	G	6-4	275	11/22/63	Valdosta State	Tallahassee, Fla.	FA
Reynolds, Ricky	CB-S	5-11	182	1/19/65	Washington State	Sacramento, Calif.	D2a
Rolling, Henry	LB	6-2	220	9/8/65	Nevada-Reno	Henderson, Nev.	D5a
Scott, Ed (1)	WR	6-0	190	12/29/62	Idaho State	San Diego, Calif.	FA
Shula, Mike	QB	6-2	200	6/3/65	Alabama	Miami, Fla.	D12b
Simmonds, Mike	T-G	6-4	281	8/12/64	Indiana State	West Belleville, Ill.	D10
Smith, Don	RB	5-11	200	10/30/63	Mississippi State	Hamilton, Miss.	D2c
Spek, Jeff (1)	TE	6-3	240	10/1/60	San Diego State	Orange, Calif.	FA-'86
Swayne, Harry	DE	6-5	268	2/2/65	Rutgers	Philadelphia, Pa.	D7b
Taylor, Reggie	RB	5-5	170	2/8/64	Cincinnati	Los Angeles, Calif.	D11
Testaverde, Vinny	QB	6-5	220	11/13/63	Miami	Elmont, N.Y.	D1
Turner, Craig	RB	5-11	220	2/19/63	Alabama	Damascus, Md.	FA

The term NFL Rookie is defined as a player who is in his first season of professional football and has not been on the roster of another professional football team for any regular-season or postseason games. A Rookie is designated by an "R" on NFL rosters. Players who have been active in another professional football league or players who have NFL experience, including either preseason training camp or being on an active roster for fewer than three regular-season or postseason games, are termed NFL First-Year Players. An NFL First-Year Player is designated by a "1" on NFL rosters. Thereafter, a player on an NFL active roster for at least three regular-season or postseason games is credited with an additional year of NFL playing experience.

NOTES

Herb Paterra, inside linebackers; born November 8, 1940, Glassport, Pa., lives in Tampa. Offensive guard-linebacker Michigan State 1960-62. Pro linebacker Buffalo Bills 1963-64, Hamilton Tiger-Cats (CFL) 1965-68. College coach: Michigan State 1969-71, Wyoming 1972-74. Pro coach: Charlotte Hornets (WFL) 1975, Hamilton Tiger-Cats (CFL) 1978-79, Los Angeles Rams 1980-82, Edmonton Eskimos (CFL) 1983, Green Bay Packers 1984-85, Buffalo Bills 1986, first year with Buccaneers.

Rodney Stokes, special teams; born February 3, 1953, Brookhaven, Mass., lives in Tampa. Linebacker Delta State 1976-77. No pro playing experience. College coach: Alabama 1983-86. Pro coach: First year with Buccaneers.

Marc Trestman, quarterbacks; born January 15, 1956, Minneapolis, Minn., lives in Tampa. Quarterback Minnesota 1976-78. No pro playing experience. College coach: Miami 1981-84. Pro coach: Minnesota Vikings 1985-86, first year with Buccaneers.

Richard Williamson, receivers; born April 13, 1941, Fort Deposit, Ala., lives in Tampa. Receiver Alabama 1959-62. No pro playing experience. College coach: Alabama 1963-67, 1970-71, Arkansas 1968-69, 1972-74, Memphis State 1975-80 (head coach). Pro coach: Kansas City Chiefs 1983-86, first year with Buccaneers.

National Football Conference Eastern Division

Team Colors: Burgundy and Gold

Redskin Park
P.O. Box 17247
Dulles International Airport
Washington, D.C. 20041
Telephone: (703) 471-9100

Club Officials

Chairman of the Board-Chief Operating Executive: Jack Kent Cooke
Executive Vice President: John Kent Cooke
Secretary: Robert N. Eisman
Controller: Doug Porter
Board of Directors: Jack Kent Cooke, John Kent Cooke, James Lacher, William A. Shea, Esq., The Honorable John W. Warner
General Manager: Bobby Beathard
Assistant General Managers: Bobby Mitchell, Charles Casserly
Director of Player Personnel: Dick Daniels
Director of Pro Scouting: Kirk Mee
Talent Scouts: Billy Devaney, George Saimes, Jerry Fauls
Director of Media Relations: John C. Konoza
Director of Publications: Ronn Levine
Director of Marketing: Paul Denfeld
Director of Photography: Nate Fine
Ticket Manager: Sue Barton
Head Trainer: Lamar (Bubba) Tyer
Assistant Trainers: Joe Kuczo, Keoki Kamau
Equipment Manager: Jay Brunetti

Stadium: Robert F. Kennedy Stadium • **Capacity:** 55,750
East Capitol Street
Washington, D.C. 20003

Playing Surface: Grass (PAT)

Training Camp: Dickinson College
Carlisle, Pennsylvania 17013

1987 Schedule

Preseason

Aug. 14	**Pittsburgh**	8:00
Aug. 22	vs. G.B. at Madison, Wis.	1:00
Aug. 29	at Tampa Bay	7:00
Sept. 5	at Los Angeles Rams	6:00

Regular Season

Sept. 13	**Philadelphia**	1:00
Sept. 20	at Atlanta	1:00
Sept. 27	**New England**	1:00
Oct. 4	**St. Louis**	1:00
Oct. 11	at New York Giants	4:00
Oct. 19	at Dallas (Monday)	8:00
Oct. 25	**New York Jets**	1:00
Nov. 1	at Buffalo	1:00
Nov. 8	at Philadelphia	1:00
Nov. 15	**Detroit**	1:00
Nov. 23	**L.A. Rams** (Monday)	9:00
Nov. 29	**New York Giants**	4:00
Dec. 6	at St. Louis	12:00
Dec. 13	**Dallas**	1:00
Dec. 20	at Miami	8:00
Dec. 26	at Minnesota (Saturday)	3:00

Redskins Coaching History

Boston 1932-36
(377-329-26)

1932	Lud Wray	4-4-2
1933-34	William (Lone Star) Dietz	11-11-2
1935	Eddie Casey	2-8-1
1936-42	Ray Flaherty	56-23-3
1943	Arthur (Dutch) Bergman	7-4-1
1944-45	Dudley DeGroot	14-6-1
1946-48	Glen (Turk) Edwards	16-18-1
1949	John Whelchel*	3-3-1
1949-51	Herman Ball**	4-16-0
1951	Dick Todd	5-4-0
1952-53	Earl (Curly) Lambeau	10-13-1
1954-58	Joe Kuharich	26-32-2
1959-60	Mike Nixon	4-18-2
1961-65	Bill McPeak	21-46-3
1966-68	Otto Graham	17-22-3
1969	Vince Lombardi	7-5-2
1970	Bill Austin	6-8-0
1971-77	George Allen	69-35-1
1978-80	Jack Pardee	24-24-0
1981-86	Joe Gibbs	71-29-0

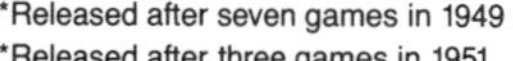

*Released after seven games in 1949
**Released after three games in 1951

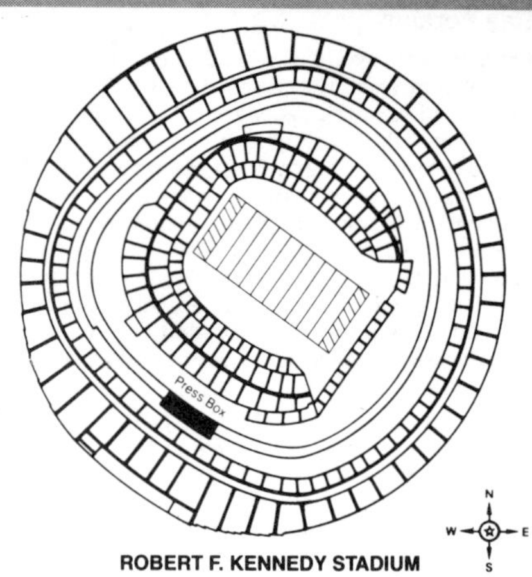

ROBERT F. KENNEDY STADIUM

Record Holders

Individual Records—Career

Category	Name	Performance
Rushing (Yds.)	John Riggins, 1976-79, 1981-85	7,472
Passing (Yds.)	Joe Theismann, 1974-1985	25,206
Passing (TDs)	Sonny Jurgensen, 1964-1974	209
Receiving (No.)	Charley Taylor, 1964-1977	649
Receiving (Yds.)	Charley Taylor, 1964-1977	9,140
Interceptions	Brig Owens, 1966-1977	36
Punting (Avg.)	Sammy Baugh, 1937-1952	45.1
Punt Return (Avg.)	Johnny Williams, 1952-53	12.8
Kickoff Return (Avg.)	Bobby Mitchell, 1962-68	28.5
Field Goals	Mark Moseley, 1974-1986	263
Touchdowns (Tot.)	Charley Taylor, 1964-1977	90
Points	Mark Moseley, 1974-1986	1,206

Individual Records—Single Season

Category	Name	Performance
Rushing (Yds.)	John Riggins, 1983	1,347
Passing (Yds.)	Jay Schroeder, 1986	4,109
Passing (TDs)	Sonny Jurgensen, 1967	31
Receiving (No.)	Art Monk, 1984	106
Receiving (Yds.)	Bobby Mitchell, 1963	1,436
Interceptions	Dan Sandifer, 1948	13
Punting (Avg.)	Sammy Baugh, 1940	51.4
Punt Return (Avg.)	Johnny Williams, 1952	15.3
Kickoff Return (Avg.)	Mike Nelms, 1981	29.7
Field Goals	Mark Moseley, 1983	33
Touchdowns (Tot.)	John Riggins, 1983	24
Points	Mark Moseley, 1983	161

Individual Records—Single Game

Category	Name	Performance
Rushing (Yds.)	George Rogers, 12-21-85	206
Passing (Yds.)	Sammy Baugh, 10-31-48	446
Passing (TDs)	Sammy Baugh, 10-31-43	6
	Sammy Baugh, 11-23-47	6
Receiving (No.)	Art Monk, 12-15-85	13
	Kelvin Bryant, 12-7-86	13
Receiving (Yds.)	Gary Clark, 10-27-86	241
Interceptions	Sammy Baugh, 11-14-43	4
	Dan Sandifer, 10-31-48	4
Field Goals	Many times	5
	Last time by Mark Moseley, 10-26-80	
Touchdowns (Tot.)	Dick James, 12-17-61	4
	Larry Brown, 12-4-73	4
Points	Dick James, 12-17-61	24
	Larry Brown, 12-4-73	24

1986 Team Statistics

	Redskins	Opp.
Total First Downs	312	316
Rushing	112	103
Passing	177	181
Penalty	23	32
Third Down: Made/Att.	92/220	72/217
Fourth Down: Made/Att.	5/9	6/14
Total Net Yards	5601	5297
Avg. Per Game	350.1	331.1
Total Plays	1044	1046
Avg. Per Play	5.4	5.1
Net Yards Rushing	1732	1805
Avg. Per Game	108.3	112.8
Total Rushes	474	459
Net Yards Passing	3869	3492
Avg. Per Game	241.8	218.3
Tackled/Yards Lost	28/240	55/424
Gross Yards	4109	3916
Att./Completions	542/276	532/302
Completion Pct.	50.9	56.8
Had Intercepted	22	19
Punts/Avg.	75/43.6	95/41.3
Net Punting Avg.	36.4	33.8
Penalties/Yards Lost	94/860	115/1026
Fumbles/Ball Lost	29/10	21/9
Touchdowns	46	35
Rushing	23	14
Passing	22	21
Returns	1	0
Avg. Time of Possession	29:56	30:04

1986 Team Record

Preseason (3-1)

Date	Result		Opponents
8/10	L	7-18	at New England
8/15	W	27-24	Pittsburgh (OT)
8/23	W	21-13	at Tampa Bay
8/29	W	29-21	Atlanta
		84-76	

Regular Season (12-4)

Date	Result		Opponents	Att.
9/7	W	41-14	Philadelphia	53,982
9/14	W	10- 6	L.A. Raiders	55,235
9/21	W	30-27	at San Diego	57,853
9/28	W	19-14	Seattle	54,157
10/5	W	14- 6	at New Orleans	57,378
10/12	L	6-30	at Dallas	63,264
10/19	W	28-21	St. Louis	53,494
10/27	L	20-27	at N.Y. Giants	75,923
11/2	W	44-38	Minnesota (OT)	51,928
11/9	W	16- 7	at Green Bay	47,728
11/17	W	14- 6	San Francisco	54,774
11/23	W	41-14	Dallas	55,642
11/30	W	20-17	at St. Louis	35,637
12/7	L	14-24	N.Y. Giants	55,642
12/13	L	30-31	at Denver	75,905
12/21	W	21-14	at Philadelphia	61,816

Postseason (2-1)

Date	Result		Opponents	Att.
12/28	W	19- 7	L.A. Rams	54,567
1/3/87	W	27-13	at Chicago	65,524
1/11/87	L	0-17	at N.Y. Giants	76,891

(OT) Overtime

Score by Periods

Redskins	79	101	92	90	6	—	368
Opponents	82	77	68	69	0	—	296

Attendance

Home 434,854 Away 475,504 Total 910,358
Single game home record, 55,750 (11-10-85)
Single season home record, 434,854 (1986)

1986 Individual Statistics

Scoring	TD R	TD P	TD Rt	PAT	FG	Saf	TP
Rogers	18	0	0	0/0	0/0	0	108
Zendejas	0	0	0	23/28	9/14	0	50
Bryant	4	3	0	0/0	0/0	0	42
Clark	0	7	0	0/0	0/0	0	42
Moseley	0	0	0	12/14	6/12	0	30
Didier	0	4	0	0/0	0/0	0	24
Monk	0	4	0	0/0	0/0	0	24
Sanders	0	2	0	0/0	0/0	0	12
Cox	0	0	0	0/0	3/5	0	9
Manley	0	0	1	0/0	0/0	0	6
Orr	0	1	0	0/0	0/0	0	6
Schroeder	1	0	0	0/0	0/0	0	6
Warren	0	1	0	0/0	0/0	0	6
Atkinson	0	0	0	3/3	0/0	0	3
Redskins	23	22	1	38/45	18/32	0	368
Opponents	14	21	0	35/35	17/24	0	296

Passing	Att.	Comp.	Yds.	Pct.	TD	Int.	Tkld.	Rate
Schroeder	541	276	4109	51.0	22	22	28/240	72.9
Williams	1	0	0	0.0	0	0	0/0	39.6
Redskins	542	276	4109	50.9	22	22	28/240	72.7
Opponents	532	302	3916	56.8	21	19	55/424	78.3

Rushing	Att.	Yds.	Avg.	LG	TD
Rogers	303	1203	4.0	42	18
Bryant	69	258	3.7	22t	4
Griffin	62	197	3.2	12	0
Schroeder	36	47	1.3	20	1
Monk	4	27	6.8	21	0
Redskins	474	1732	3.7	42	23
Opponents	459	1805	3.9	39	14

Receiving	No.	Yds.	Avg.	LG	TD
Clark	74	1265	17.1	55	7
Monk	73	1068	14.6	69	4
Bryant	43	449	10.4	40	3
Didier	34	691	20.3	71t	4
Warren	20	164	8.2	20	1
Sanders	14	286	20.4	71	2
Griffin	11	110	10.0	28	0
Orr	3	45	15.0	22t	1
Rogers	3	24	8.0	13	0
Holloway	1	7	7.0	7	0
Redskins	276	4109	14.9	71t	22
Opponents	302	3916	13.0	76t	21

Interceptions	No.	Yds.	Avg.	LG	TD
Green	5	9	1.8	7	0
Jordan	3	46	15.3	20	0
Milot	2	33	16.5	31	0
Wilburn	2	14	7.0	14	0
Bowles	2	0	0.0	0	0
Coffey	2	0	0.0	0	0
Olkewicz	1	15	15.0	15	0
Dean	1	5	5.0	5	0
Daniels	1	4	4.0	4	0
Redskins	19	126	6.6	31	0
Opponents	22	186	8.5	35	0

Punting	No.	Yds.	Avg.	In 20	LG
Cox	75	3271	43.6	21	58
Redskins	75	3271	43.6	21	58
Opponents	95	3923	41.3	22	55

Punt Returns	No.	FC	Yds.	Avg.	LG	TD
Jenkins	28	11	270	9.6	39	0
Green	12	2	120	10.0	23	0
Yarber	9	4	143	15.9	44	0
Clark	1	3	14	14.0	14	0
Milot	1	0	3	3.0	3	0
Redskins	51	20	550	10.8	44	0
Opponents	36	10	220	6.1	24	0

Kickoff Returns	No.	Yds.	Avg.	LG	TD
Jenkins	27	554	20.5	37	0
Verdin	12	240	20.0	29	0
Griffin	8	156	19.5	35	0
Garner	7	142	20.3	26	0
Holloway	3	44	14.7	18	0
Orr	2	31	15.5	16	0
Krakoski	1	8	8.0	8	0
Redskins	60	1175	19.6	37	0
Opponents	50	1005	20.1	59	0

Sacks	No.
Manley	18.5
Mann	10.0
Butz	6.0
Hamilton	4.5
Coleman	3.0
Kaufman	3.0
Grant	2.0
Milot	2.0
Olkewicz	2.0
Snipes	2.0
Daniels	1.0
Walton	1.0
Redskins	55.0
Opponents	28.0

FIRST-ROUND SELECTIONS

(If club had no first-round selection, first player drafted is listed with round in parentheses.)

Since 1940

Year	Player, College, Position
1940	Ed Boell, New York U., B
1941	Forest Evashevski, Michigan, B
1942	Orban (Spec) Sanders, Texas, B
1943	Jack Jenkins, Missouri, B
1944	Mike Micka, Colgate, B
1945	Jim Hardy, Southern California, B
1946	Cal Rossi, UCLA, B*
1947	Cal Rossi, UCLA, B
1948	Harry Gilmer, Alabama, B
	Lowell Tew, Alabama, B
1949	Rob Goode, Texas A&M, B
1950	George Thomas, Oklahoma, B
1951	Leon Heath, Oklahoma, B
1952	Larry Isbell, Baylor, B
1953	Jack Scarbath, Maryland, B
1954	Steve Meilinger, Kentucky, E
1955	Ralph Guglielmi, Notre Dame, B
1956	Ed Vereb, Maryland, B
1957	Don Bosseler, Miami, B
1958	M. Sommer, George Washington, B (2)
1959	Don Allard, Boston College, B
1960	Richie Lucas, Penn State, QB
1961	Norman Snead, Wake Forest, QB
	Joe Rutgens, Illinois, DT
1962	Ernie Davis, Syracuse, RB
1963	Pat Richter, Wisconsin, TE
1964	Charley Taylor, Arizona State, RB-WR
1965	Bob Breitenstein, Tulsa, T (2)
1966	Charlie Gogolak, Princeton, K
1967	Ray McDonald, Idaho, RB
1968	Jim Smith, Oregon, DB
1969	Eugene Epps, Texas-El Paso, DB (2)
1970	Bill Brundige, Colorado, DT (2)
1971	Cotton Speyrer, Texas, WR (2)
1972	Moses Denson, Maryland State, RB (8)
1973	Charles Cantrell, Lamar, G (5)
1974	Jon Keyworth, Colorado, TE (6)
1975	Mike Thomas, Nevada-Las Vegas, RB (6)
1976	Mike Hughes, Baylor, G (5)
1977	Duncan McColl, Stanford, DE (4)
1978	Tony Green, Florida, RB (6)
1979	Don Warren, San Diego State, TE (4)
1980	Art Monk, Syracuse, WR
1981	Mark May, Pittsburgh, T
1982	Vernon Dean, San Diego State, DB (2)
1983	Darrell Green, Texas A&I, DB
1984	Bob Slater, Oklahoma, DT (2)
1985	Tory Nixon, San Diego State, DB (2)
1986	Markus Koch, Boise State, DE (2)
1987	Brian Davis, Nebraska, DB (2)

**Choice lost due to ineligibility.*

Washington Redskins 1987 Veteran Roster

No.	Name	Pos.	Ht.	Wt.	Birth-date	NFL Exp.	College	Hometown	How Acq.	'86 Games/ Starts
4	Atkinson, Jess	K	5-9	168	12/11/61	3	Maryland	Temple Hills, Md.	FA-'86	1/0
26	Badanjek, Rick	RB	5-8	217	3/25/62	2	Maryland	West Farmington, Ohio	D7-'86	6/0
53	†Bostic, Jeff	C	6-2	260	9/18/58	8	Clemson	Greensboro, N.C.	FA-'80	16/16
23	Bowles, Todd	S	6-2	203	11/18/63	2	Temple	Elizabeth, N.J.	FA-'86	15/2
29	Branch, Reggie	RB	5-11	227	10/22/62	3	East Carolina	Sanford, Fla.	FA-'86	1/0
24	Bryant, Kelvin	RB	6-2	195	9/26/60	2	North Carolina	Tarboro, N.C.	FA-'86	10/0
58	Burks, Shawn	LB	6-1	230	2/10/63	2	Louisiana State	Baton Rouge, La.	FA-'86	15/0
65	†Butz, Dave	DT	6-7	295	6/23/50	14	Purdue	Park Ridge, Ill.	FA-'75	16/16
84	Clark, Gary	WR	5-9	173	5/1/62	3	James Madison	Dublin, Va.	FA-'85	15/5
48	†Coffey, Ken	S	6-0	198	11/7/60	4	Southwest Texas State	Big Spring, Tex.	D9-'82	16/9
51	Coleman, Monte	LB	6-2	230	11/4/57	9	Central Arkansas	Pine Bluff, Ark.	D11-'79	11/4
12	†Cox, Steve	P	6-4	195	5/11/58	7	Arkansas	Charleston, Ark.	FA-'85	16/0
32	Dean, Vernon	CB	5-11	178	5/5/59	6	San Diego State	Los Angeles, Calif.	D2-'82	16/8
86	Didier, Clint	TE	6-5	240	4/4/59	6	Portland State	Pasco, Wash.	D12-'81	14/11
30	Garner, Dwight	RB	5-8	183	10/25/64	2	California	Oakland, Calif.	FA-'86	2/0
77	Grant, Darryl	DT	6-1	275	11/22/59	7	Rice	San Antonio, Tex.	D9-'81	16/8
28	Green, Darrell	CB	5-8	170	2/15/60	5	Texas A&I	Houston, Tex.	D1-'83	16/15
35	†Griffin, Keith	RB	5-8	185	10/26/61	4	Miami	Eastmoor, Ohio	D10-'84	16/1
68	Grimm, Russ	G	6-3	275	5/2/59	7	Pittsburgh	Southmoreland, Pa.	D3-'81	15/14
78	Hamel, Dean	DT	6-3	280	7/7/61	3	Tulsa	Warren, Mich.	D12-'85	16/8
64	Hamilton, Steve	DE-DT	6-4	255	9/28/61	3	East Carolina	Williamsville, N.Y.	D2-'84	12/2
88	Holloway, Derek	WR	5-7	166	8/17/61	2	Arkansas	Palmyra, N.J.	FA-'86	9/1
66	†Jacoby, Joe	T	6-7	305	7/6/59	7	Louisville	Louisville, Ky.	FA-'81	16/16
31	Jenkins, Ken	RB-KR	5-8	185	5/8/59	5	Bucknell	Bethesda, Md.	FA-'86	12/0
82	†Jones, Anthony	TE	6-3	248	5/16/60	4	Wichita State	Baltimore, Md.	D11-'84	15/1
22	Jordan, Curtis	S	6-2	205	1/25/54	11	Texas Tech	Lubbock, Tex.	FA-'81	16/16
55	†Kaufman, Mel	LB	6-2	218	2/24/58	6	Cal Poly-SLO	Santa Monica, Calif.	FA-'81	2/2
74	Koch, Markus	DE	6-5	275	2/13/63	2	Boise State	Ontario, Canada	D2a-'86	16/0
54	Krakoski, Joe	LB	6-1	224	11/11/62	2	Washington	San Jose, Calif.	FA-'86	8/0
72	Manley, Dexter	DE	6-3	257	2/2/59	7	Oklahoma State	Houston, Tex.	D5-'81	16/16
71	Mann, Charles	DE	6-6	270	4/12/61	5	Nevada-Reno	Sacramento, Calif.	D3-'83	15/15
73	May, Mark	T	6-6	295	11/2/59	7	Pittsburgh	Oneonta, N.Y.	D1-'81	16/16
63	McKenzie, Raleigh	G	6-2	262	2/8/63	3	Tennessee	Knoxville, Tenn.	D11-'85	15/5
60	†McQuaid, Dan	T	6-7	278	10/4/60	3	Nevada-Las Vegas	Clarksburg, Calif.	T(Rams)-'85	13/0
57	†Milot, Rich	LB	6-4	237	5/28/57	9	Penn State	Coraopolis, Pa.	D7-'79	16/15
81	Monk, Art	WR	6-3	209	12/5/57	8	Syracuse	White Plains, N.Y.	D1-'80	16/16
41	Morrison, Tim	CB	6-1	195	4/3/63	2	North Carolina	Fayetteville, N.C.	FA-'86	16/5
52	Olkewicz, Neal	LB	6-0	233	1/30/57	9	Maryland	Phoenixville, Pa.	FA-'79	16/16
87	†Orr, Terry	TE	6-3	227	9/27/61	2	Texas	Abilene, Tex.	D10-'85	16/1
38	Rogers, George	RB	6-2	229	12/8/58	7	South Carolina	Duluth, Ga.	T(NO)-'85	15/15
46	Sanders, Ricky	RB	5-11	180	8/30/62	2	Southwest Texas State	Temple, Tex.	T(NE)-'86	10/3
10	†Schroeder, Jay	QB	6-4	215	6/28/61	4	UCLA	Pacific Palisades, Calif.	D3-'84	16/16
69	Thielemann, R.C.	G	6-4	262	8/12/55	11	Arkansas	Houston, Tex.	T(Atl)-'85	14/13
76	Tilton, Ron	G	6-4	250	8/9/63	2	Tulane	Tampa, Fla.	FA-'86	7/0
89	Verdin, Clarence	WR-KR	5-8	160	6/14/63	2	Southwestern Louisiana	Houma, La.	FA-'86	8/0
40	Walton, Alvin	S	6-0	180	3/14/64	2	Kansas	Banning, Calif.	D3-'86	16/4
85	Warren, Don	TE	6-4	242	5/5/56	9	San Diego State	Covina, Calif.	D4-'79	16/16
45	†Wilburn, Barry	CB	6-3	186	12/9/63	3	Mississippi	Memphis, Tenn.	D8-'85	16/5
17	Williams, Doug	QB	6-4	220	8/9/55	7	Grambling	Zachary, La.	T(TB)-'86	1/0
80	Yarber, Eric	WR-KR	5-8	156	9/22/63	2	Idaho	Los Angeles, Calif.	D12-'86	2/0
14	Zendejas, Max	K	5-11	184	9/2/63	2	Arizona	Chino, Calif.	FA-'86	9/0

†Option playout; subject to developments.

Also played with Redskins in '86—DE Tom Beasley (1 game), LB Calvin Daniels (13), K Mark Moseley (6), WR James Noble (6), LB Jeff Paine (2), LB Angelo Snipes (10).

COACHING STAFF

Head Coach, Joe Gibbs

Pro Career: Enters seventh year as Redskins coach. Led Washington to a 12-4 record in 1986, and fourth playoff appearance in five years. Team has now played in three of last five NFC Championship Games. Named head coach on January 13, 1981, after spending eight years as an NFL assistant coach and nine years on the college level. Came to Redskins from the San Diego Chargers where he was offensive coordinator in 1979 and 1980. Prior to that, he was offensive coordinator for the Tampa Bay Buccaneers in 1978 and offensive backfield coach for the St. Louis Cardinals from 1973-77. While he was with San Diego, the Chargers won the AFC West title and led the NFL in passing two straight years. No pro playing experience. Career record: 71-29.

Background: Played tight end, linebacker, and guard under Don Coryell at San Diego State in 1961 and 1962 after spending two years at Cerritos, Calif., J.C. 1959-60. Started his college coaching career at San Diego State 1964-66, followed by stints at Florida State 1967-68, Southern California 1969-70, and Arkansas 1971-72.

Personal: Born November 25, 1940, in Mocksville, N.C. Graduated from Santa Fe Springs, Calif., High School. Two-time national racquetball champion and ranked second in the over-35 category in 1978. He and his wife, Pat, live in Vienna, Va., and have two sons—J.D. and Coy.

Assistant Coaches

Chuck Banker, special teams; born March 12, 1941, Prescott, Ariz. Linebacker-tight end Pasadena C.C. 1959-60. No pro playing experience. College coach: Glendale, Calif., J.C. 1962-65, Utah 1966-67, 1974-75, Westminster 1968-70, Boise State 1976-79, Iowa State 1986. Pro coach: St. Louis Cardinals 1980-85, first year with Redskins.

Don Breaux, offensive backs; born August 3, 1940, Jennings, La., lives in Centerville, Va. Quarterback McNeese State 1959-61. Pro quarterback Denver Broncos 1963, San Diego Chargers 1964-65. College coach: Florida State 1966-67, Arkansas 1968-71, 1977-80, Florida 1973-74, Texas 1975-76. Pro coach: Joined Redskins in 1981.

Joe Bugel, assistant head coach-offense; born March 10, 1940, Pittsburgh, Pa., lives in Oakton, Va. Guard Western Kentucky 1960-62. No pro playing experience. College coach: Western Kentucky 1964-68, Navy 1969-72, Iowa State 1973, Ohio State 1974. Pro coach: Detroit Lions 1975-76, Houston Oilers 1977-80, joined Redskins in 1981.

Joe Diange, strength; born April 24, 1956, Massapequa, N.Y. Linebacker Penn State 1976-77. No pro playing experience. College coach: Penn State 1978-81, Navy 1982-83. Pro coach: Tampa Bay Buccaneers 1984-86, first year with Redskins.

Dan Henning, offensive assistant-receivers, born June 21, 1942, Bronx, N.Y. Quarterback William & Mary 1960-63. Pro quarterback San Diego Chargers 1964-67. College coach: Florida State 1968-70, 1974, Virginia Tech 1971, 1973. Pro coach: Houston Oilers 1972, New York Jets 1976-78, Miami Dolphins 1979-80, Washington Redskins 1981-82, Atlanta Falcons 1983-86 (head coach), rejoined Redskins in 1987.

Bill Hickman, administrative assistant; born June 21, 1923, Baltimore, Md., lives in Leesburg, Va. Halfback Virginia 1946-48. No pro playing experience. College coach: Virginia 1949, Duke 1950, North Carolina State 1951, Vanderbilt 1953, North Carolina 1966-72. Pro coach: Washington Redskins 1973-77, Los Angeles Rams 1978-80, rejoined Redskins in 1981.

Larry Peccatiello, defensive coordinator; born December 21, 1935, Newark, N.J., lives in Warrenton, Va. Receiver William & Mary 1955-58. No pro playing experience. College coach: William & Mary 1961-68, Navy 1969-70, Rice 1971. Pro coach: Houston Oilers 1972-75, Seattle Seahawks 1976-80, joined Redskins in 1981.

Washington Redskins 1987 First-Year Roster

Name	Pos.	Ht.	Wt.	Birth-date	College	Hometown	How Acq.
Armstrong, Otha	RB	6-2	231	5/28/65	E. Central Oklahoma	Altus, Okla.	FA
Brilz, Darrick	T	6-3	264	2/14/64	Oregon State	Richmond, Calif.	FA
Brown, Laron	WR	5-10	175	11/10/63	Texas	Dayton, Ohio	D11
Burgess, Marvell	CB	6-2	210	10/7/65	Henderson State	Miami, Fla.	FA
Caldwell, Ravin (1)	LB	6-3	229	8/4/63	Arkansas	Ft. Smith, Ark.	D5-'86
Carlson, Mark	T	6-6	284	6/6/63	So. Connecticut St.	Milford, Conn.	FA
Chapman, Ted	DT	6-3	260	4/5/64	Maryland	Philadelphia, Pa.	FA
Copeland, Anthony (1)	LB	6-2	230	4/14/63	Louisville	East Point, Ga.	FA-'86
Coyle, Eric	C	6-3	260	10/26/63	Colorado	Longmont, Colo.	FA
Davis, Brian	CB	6-2	190	8/31/63	Nebraska	Phoenix, Ariz.	D2a
Fells, Kenny (1)	RB	6-0	190	1/9/64	Henderson State	Little Rock, Ark.	D11-'86
Frain, Todd (1)	TE	6-2	235	1/31/62	Nebraska	Treynor, Iowa	FA-'86
Gage, Steve	S	6-3	210	5/10/64	Tulsa	Tulsa, Okla.	D6a
Gouveia, Kurt (1)	LB	6-1	227	9/14/64	Brigham Young	Waianae, Hawaii	D8-'86
Grooms, Greg	RB	6-2	193	10/16/64	Richmond	Richmond, Va.	FA
Guardi, Andre	K	6-2	200	4/23/65	Utah	La Mirada, Calif.	FA
Hitchcock, Ray	C	6-2	289	6/20/65	Minnesota	Pine Bluff, Ark.	D12
Jackson, Charles (1)	S	6-4	210	3/12/63	Texas Tech	Ft. Gaines, Fla.	FA
Jemison, Rickey	RB	5-10	214	10/15/64	Arkansas State	Earle, Ark.	FA
Jenkins, Alfred	TE	6-4	230	4/1/64	Arizona	Lynwood, Calif.	D9
Kehr, Rick (1)	G	6-3	285	6/18/59	Carthage	Phoenixville, Pa.	FA
Kleine, Wally	T	6-9	300	10/22/64	Notre Dame	Midland, Tex.	D2b
Kmet, James	DT	6-3	250	1/16/64	Wisconsin	Chicago, Ill.	FA
McEwen, Craig	TE	6-1	220	12/16/65	Utah	Queens, N.Y.	FA
Mitchell, Michael (1)	CB	5-10	180	10/18/61	Howard Payne	Waco, Tex.	FA
Nave,Stevan	LB	6-2	252	8/29/63	Kansas	Nowata, Okla.	FA
Radecic, Keith	C	6-1	260	12/24/63	Penn State	Pittsburgh, Pa.	FA
Reese, Albert	TE	6-4	245	2/15/65	Southern Methodist	Temple, Tex.	FA
Robinson, Kenneth	LB	6-1	234	12/4/63	South Carolina	Charleston, S.C.	FA
Romney, Theodore	T	6-4	268	3/13/64	Missouri	Paterson, N.J.	FA
Rubbert, Ed	QB	6-5	225	5/28/65	Louisville	New City, N.Y.	FA
Rypien, Mark (1)	QB	6-4	234	10/2/62	Washington State	Spokane, Wash.	D6a-'86
Shepard, Derrick	WR	5-11	183	1/22/64	Oklahoma	Odessa, Tex.	FA
Simmons, Ed	T	6-5	275	12/31/63	Eastern Washington	Stockton, Calif.	D6b
Smith, Timmy	RB	5-11	216	1/21/64	Texas Tech	Hobbs, N.M.	D5
Spachman, Chris	DT	6-4	265	12/25/63	Nebraska	Kansas City, Mo.	FA
Thomas, Johnny	CB	5-9	190	7/3/64	Baylor	Houston, Tex.	D7
Truitt, Dave	TE	6-4	232	2/18/64	North Carolina	Somerset, N.J.	FA
Vaughn, Clarence	S	6-0	202	7/17/64	Northern Illinois	Chicago, Ill.	D8
Wills, Ladell (1)	LB	6-3	239	5/30/62	Jackson State	Flint, Mich.	FA
Wilson, Norries	T	6-5	295	6/24/65	Minnesota	Chicago, Ill.	FA
Wilson, Ted	WR	5-9	170	7/14/64	Central Florida	Dade City, Fla.	D10

The term NFL Rookie is defined as a player who is in his first season of professional football and has not been on the roster of another professional football team for any regular-season or postseason games. A Rookie is designated by an "R" on NFL rosters. Players who have been active in another professional football league or players who have NFL experience, including either preseason training camp or being on an active roster for fewer than three regular-season or postseason games, are termed NFL First-Year Players. An NFL First-Year Player is designated by a "1" on NFL rosters. Thereafter, a player on an NFL active roster for at least three regular-season or postseason games is credited with an additional year of NFL playing experience.

NOTES

Richie Petitbon, assistant head coach-defense; born April 18, 1938, New Orleans, La., lives in Vienna, Va. Back Tulane 1955-58. Pro defensive back Chicago Bears 1959-67, Los Angeles Rams 1969-70, Washington Redskins 1971-73. Pro coach: Houston Oilers 1974-77, joined Redskins in 1978.

Jerry Rhome, quarterbacks; born March 6, 1942, Dallas, Tex., lives in Herndon, Va. Quarterback Southern Methodist 1960-61, Tulsa 1963-64. Pro quarterback Dallas Cowboys 1965-68, Cleveland Browns 1969, Houston Oilers 1970, Los Angeles Rams 1971-72. College coach: Tulsa 1973-75. Pro coach: Seattle Seahawks 1976-82, joined Redskins in 1983.

Dan Riley, conditioning; born October 19, 1949, Syracuse, N.Y., lives in Herndon, Va. No college or pro playing experience. College coach: Army 1973-76, Penn State 1977-81. Pro coach: Joined Redskins in 1982.

Warren Simmons, tight ends; born February 25, 1942, Poughkeepsie, N.Y., lives in Centerville, Va. Center San Diego State 1963-65. No pro playing experience. College coach: Cal State-Fullerton 1972-75, Cerritos, Calif., J.C. 1976-80. Pro coach: Joined Redskins in 1981.

Charley Taylor, wide receivers; born September 28, 1942, Grand Prairie, Tex., lives in Sterling, Va. Running back Arizona State 1961-63. Pro running back-wide receiver Washington Redskins 1964-76. Pro coach: Joined Redskins in 1982.

Emmitt Thomas, defensive assistant; born June 4, 1943, Angleton, Tex., lives in Reston, Va. Quarterback-wide receiver Bishop (Tex.) College 1963-65. Pro defensive back Kansas City Chiefs 1966-78. College coach: Central Missouri State 1979-80. Pro coach: St. Louis Cardinals 1981-85, joined Redskins in 1986.

LaVern Torgeson, defensive line; born February 28, 1929, LaCrosse, Wash., lives in Fairfax, Va. Center-linebacker Washington State 1948-50. Pro linebacker Detroit Lions 1951-54, Washington Redskins 1955-58. Pro coach: Washington Redskins 1959-61, 1971-77, Pittsburgh Steelers 1962-68, Los Angeles Rams 1969-70, 1978-80, rejoined Redskins in 1981.

1986 SEASON IN REVIEW

Trades

1986 Interconference Trades

Defensive end **Glen Collins** from Cincinnati to Green Bay for a draft choice (5/12).

Wide receiver **Jesse Bendross** from San Diego to Tampa Bay for a draft choice (5/13).

Tight end **Earl Cooper** from San Francisco to the Los Angeles Raiders for a draft choice (5/14).

Tackle **Marvin Powell** from the New York Jets to Tampa Bay for a draft choice (5/19).

Linebacker **Roosevelt Barnes** from Detroit to Indianapolis for a draft choice (5/22).

Linebacker **Thomas Benson** from Atlanta to San Diego for a draft choice (7/25).

Guard **Greg Naron** from Philadelphia to Seattle for a draft choice (8/9).

Rights to wide receiver **Ricky Sanders** from New England to Washington for a draft choice (8/11).

Cornerback **John Holt** from Tampa Bay to Indianapolis for a draft choice (8/13).

Quarterback **Ed Luther** from San Diego to Atlanta for linebacker **Ronnie Washington** and a draft choice (8/14).

Running back **Joe Cribbs** from Buffalo to San Francisco for draft choices (8/19).

Punter **Jeff Hayes** from Washington to Cincinnati for cash (8/19).

Tight end **Dan Ross** from Seattle to Green Bay for a draft choice (8/19).

Linebacker **Andy Hawkins** from Tampa Bay to San Diego for a draft choice (8/20).

Defensive end **Casey Merrill** from the New York Giants to Cleveland for a draft choice (8/22).

Cornerback **Kenny Daniel** from the New York Giants to Indianapolis for a draft choice (8/26).

Linebacker **Shelton Robinson** from Seattle to Detroit for a draft choice (9/1).

Quarterback **Cliff Stoudt** from Pittsburgh to St. Louis for a draft choice (9/2).

Linebacker **Steve Busick** from Denver to the Los Angeles Rams for draft choices (9/2).

Safety **John Harris** from Seattle to Minnesota for a draft choice (9/3).

Selection rights to quarterback **Jim Everett** from Houston to the Los Angeles Rams for defensive end **William Fuller,** guard **Kent Hill,** and draft choices (9/19).

Tackle **Harvey Salem** from Houston to Detroit for a draft choice (9/23).

Wide receiver **Walter Murray** from Washington to Indianapolis for a draft choice (10/7).

1987 Interconference Trades

Tampa Bay traded guard **Sean Farrell** to New England for the Patriots' second-, seventh-, and ninth-round choices in 1987 (2/20).

Buffalo traded safety **Steve Freeman** to Minnesota for a past consideration (3/12).

St. Louis traded cornerback **Lionel Washington** to the Los Angeles Raiders for the Raiders' fifth-round choice in 1987 (3/18).

Pittsburgh traded center **Dan Turk** to Tampa Bay for the Buccaneers' sixth-round choice in 1987 (4/14).

Green Bay traded wide receiver **James Lofton** to the Los Angeles Raiders for the Raiders' third-round choice in 1987 and a future choice (4/14).

Minnesota traded its first- and fifth-round choices in 1987 to Miami for the Dolphins' first choice in 1987. Minnesota selected running back **D.J. Dozier** (Penn State). Miami selected defensive end **John Bosa** (Boston College) and traded Minnesota's fifth-round choice to Kansas City (4/28).

Buffalo traded Detroit's second-round choice (acquired by Buffalo) and its fourth-round choice in 1987 to Tampa Bay for the Buccaneers' second-round choice in 1987. Buffalo selected cornerback-safety **Nate Odomes** (Wisconsin). Tampa Bay selected cornerback-safety **Ricky Reynolds** (Washington State) and tight end **Ron Hall** (Hawaii) (4/28).

Washington traded its second-round choice and Houston's fifth-round choice (acquired by Washington) in 1987 to the Los Angeles Raiders for the New York Jets' second-round choice in 1987 (acquired by the Raiders). Washington selected tackle **Wally Kleine** (Notre Dame). The Raiders selected tackle **Bruce Wilkerson** (Tennessee) and traded Houston's fifth-round choice to Chicago (4/28).

Miami traded its third- and fifth-round choices in 1987 to St. Louis for the New York Giants' second-round choice in 1987 (acquired by St. Louis). Miami selected wide receiver **Scott Schwedes** (Syracuse). St. Louis selected defensive tackle **Colin Scotts** (Hawaii) and punter **John Bruno** (Penn State) (4/28).

Cleveland traded its fourth-, fifth-, and twelfth-round choices in 1987 to the Los Angeles Rams for Chicago's third-round choice in 1987 (acquired by the Rams). Cleveland selected kicker **Jeff Jaeger** (Washington). The Rams selected linebacker **Larry Kelm** (Texas A&M), tackle **Scott Mersereau** (Southern Connecticut State), and defensive end **Fred Stokes** (Georgia Southern) (4/28).

Washington traded its fourth-round choice in 1987 to Buffalo for the Bills' fifth- and sixth-round choices in 1987. Washington selected running back **Tim Smith** (Texas Tech) and cornerback-safety **Steve Gage** (Tulsa). Buffalo selected defensive end **Leon Seals** (Jackson State) (4/28).

The Los Angeles Raiders traded Houston's fifth-round choice (acquired by the Raiders) and their sixth-round choice in 1987 to Chicago for the Bears' fourth-round choice in 1987. The Raiders selected quarterback **Steve Beuerlein** (Notre Dame). Chicago selected defensive end **Steve Bryan** (Oklahoma) and center **John Adickes** (Baylor) (4/28).

Tampa Bay traded a 1988 draft choice to New England for the Patriots' fifth-round choice in 1987. Tampa Bay selected linebacker **Henry Rolling** (Nevada-Reno) (4/28).

San Francisco traded Philadelphia's eleventh-round choice (acquired by San Francisco) and its twelfth-round choice in 1987 to the Los Angeles Raiders for New England's tenth-round choice in 1987 (acquired by the Raiders). San Francisco selected quarterback **John Paye** (Stanford). The Raiders selected running back **Chris McLemore** (Arizona) and traded San Francisco's choice to the New York Giants (4/28).

The New York Giants traded a future draft choice to the Los Angeles Raiders for the Raiders' twelfth-round choice and San Francisco's twelfth-round choice (acquired by the Raiders) in 1987. The Giants selected defensive tackle **Bill Berthusen** (Iowa State) and running back **Chad Stark** (North Dakota State) (4/28).

1986 AFC Trades

Tackle **Jim Mills** from Indianapolis to Denver for a draft choice (5/19).

Running back **Mark Schellen** from San Diego to Houston for a draft choice (5/21).

Quarterback **Mike Pagel** from Indianapolis to Cleveland for a draft choice (5/23).

Tight end **Willie Scott** from Kansas City to New England for a draft choice (7/22).

Tackle **Mike Wilson** from Cincinnati to Seattle for a draft choice (8/28).

Cornerback-safety **Vencie Glenn** from New England to San Diego for a draft choice (9/29).

Running back **Larry Moriarty** from Houston to Kansas City for a draft choice (10/14).

1987 AFC Trades

The New York Jets traded safety **Kirk Springs** to Indianapolis for a future draft choice (4/1).

Indianapolis traded guard **Roger Caron** to Buffalo for the Bills' eighth-round choice in 1987 (4/15).

Houston traded wide receiver **Tim Smith** to San Diego for a future draft choice (4/27).

Houston traded its first-round choice in 1987 and Detroit's second-round choice in 1987 (owned by Houston) to Buffalo for the Bills' first-round choice in 1987. Houston selected running back **Alonzo Highsmith** (Miami). Buffalo selected linebacker **Shane Conlan** (Penn State) and traded Detroit's second-round choice to Tampa Bay (4/28).

Cleveland traded its first- and second-round choices in 1987 and linebacker **Chip Banks** to San Diego for the Chargers' first- and second-round choices in 1987. Cleveland selected linebacker **Mike Junkin** (Duke) and center **Gregg Rakoczy** (Miami). San Diego selected tight end **Rod Bernstine** (Texas A&M) and cornerback **Louis Brock** (Southern California) (4/28).

Kansas City traded its second- and fourth-round choices in 1987 to Houston for the Oilers' second-round choice in 1987. Kansas City selected running back **Christian Okoye** (Azusa Pacific). Houston selected linebacker **Walter Johnson** (Louisiana Tech) and linebacker **Mark Dusbabek** (Minnesota) (4/28).

The New York Jets traded their second- and fourth-round choices in 1987 to the Los Angeles Raiders for the Raiders' second-round choice in 1987. The Jets selected linebacker **Alex Gordon** (Cincinnati). The Raiders traded the Jets' second choice to Washington and traded the Jets' fourth-round choice to New England (4/28).

The Los Angeles Raiders traded their fourth-round choice and the New York Jets' fourth-round choice in 1987 (acquired by the Raiders) to New England for Washington's third-round choice (acquired by New England) and the Patriots' tenth-round choice in 1987. The Raiders selected running back **Steve Smith** (Penn State) and traded New England's tenth-round choice to San Francisco. New England selected quarterback **Rich Gannon** (Delaware) and cornerback-safety **Derrick Beasley** (Winston-Salem) (4/28).

Buffalo traded its tenth-round choice and San Francisco's tenth-round choice in 1987 (acquired by Buffalo) to the Los Angeles Raiders for the Raiders' eighth-round choice in 1987. Buffalo selected defensive end **Bruce Mesner** (Maryland). The Raiders selected cornerback-safety **Rob Harrison** (Cal State-Sacramento) and linebacker **Jim Ellis** (Boise State) (4/28).

Kansas City traded its fifth- and eighth-round draft choices in 1987 to Miami for Minnesota's fifth-round choice in 1987 (acquired by Miami). Kansas City selected wide receiver **Kitrick Taylor** (Washington State). Miami selected tackle **Chris Conlin** (Penn State) and tackle **Mark Dennis** (Illinois) (4/28).

1986 NFC Trades

Quarterback **Jeff Kemp** from the Los Angeles Rams to San Francisco for a past consideration (5/17).

Running back **Rob Carpenter** from the New York Giants to the Los Angeles Rams for a draft choice (6/13).

Guard **Del Wilkes** from Tampa Bay to Atlanta for a past consideration (7/2).

Quarterback **Doug Williams** from Tampa Bay to Washington for a draft choice (8/13).

Linebacker **Rick DiBernardo** from Tampa Bay to St. Louis for a draft choice (8/18).

Rights to tackle **Joe Conwell** from San Francisco to Philadelphia for a draft choice (8/19).

Running back **Wayne Wilson** from New Orleans to Minnesota for wide receiver **Mike Jones** (9/3).

Wide receiver **Phil McConkey** from Green Bay to the New York Giants for a draft choice (9/30).

Running back **Ottis Anderson** from St. Louis to the New York Giants for draft choices (10/9).

Selection rights to quarterback **Doug Flutie** and a draft choice from the Los Angeles Rams to Chicago for draft choices (10/14).

1987 NFC Trades

Tampa Bay traded linebacker **Keith Browner** to San Francisco for a future draft choice (3/2).

Tampa Bay traded quarterback **Steve Young** to San Francisco for the 49ers' second- and fourth-round choices in 1987 (4/27).

Atlanta traded its second- and third-round choices in 1987 to Green Bay for the Packers' second-round choice in 1987. Atlanta selected running back **Kenny Flowers** (Clemson). Green Bay selected linebacker **Johnny Holland** (Texas A&M) and linebacker **Scott Stephen** (Arizona State) (4/28).

1986 PRESEASON STANDINGS

American Football Conference

Eastern Division

	W	L	T	Pct.	Pts.	OP
New England*	4	1	0	.800	103	90
Miami	2	2	0	.500	67	65
N.Y. Jets	2	2	0	.500	95	105
Buffalo	1	3	0	.250	67	79
Indianapolis	1	3	0	.250	75	95

Central Division

	W	L	T	Pct.	Pts.	OP
Cleveland	4	0	0	1.000	88	70
Houston	4	0	0	1.000	81	61
Cincinnati	1	3	0	.250	71	90
Pittsburgh	1	3	0	.250	81	105

Western Division

	W	L	T	Pct.	Pts.	OP
San Diego	3	1	0	.750	106	75
Denver	2	2	0	.500	67	58
Kansas City	2	2	0	.500	63	52
L.A. Raiders	2	2	0	.500	70	86
Seattle	2	2	0	.500	85	82

National Football Conference

Eastern Division

	W	L	T	Pct.	Pts.	OP
N.Y. Giants	3	1	0	.750	83	64
Washington	3	1	0	.750	84	76
St. Louis*	2	3	0	.400	99	89
Philadelphia	1	3	0	.250	100	111
Dallas**	0	5	0	.000	67	119

Central Division

	W	L	T	Pct.	Pts.	OP
Chicago**	4	1	0	.800	126	71
Minnesota	3	1	0	.750	99	90
Detroit	2	2	0	.500	82	84
Green Bay	1	3	0	.250	73	86
Tampa Bay	0	4	0	.000	43	88

Western Division

	W	L	T	Pct.	Pts.	OP
Atlanta	2	2	0	.500	93	97
L.A. Rams	2	2	0	.500	75	70
New Orleans	2	2	0	.500	70	79
San Francisco	2	2	0	.500	79	55

**Includes Hall of Fame Game*
***Includes American Bowl '86 Game in London, England*

AFC Preseason Standings—Team By Team

Eastern Division

BUFFALO (1-3)

17	Cleveland	19
20	Houston	23
13	Kansas City	6
17	*Chicago	31
67		79

INDIANAPOLIS (1-3)

14	Seattle	21
21	Chicago	38
20	*Detroit	13
20	*Minnesota (OT)	23
75		95

MIAMI (2-2)

16	Minnesota	30
10	*Cleveland	17
20	Philadelphia	15
21	*Tampa Bay	3
67		65

NEW ENGLAND (4-1)

21	St. Louis (HOF)	16
18	*Washington	7
38	New Orleans	34
10	L.A. Raiders	24
16	Green Bay	9
103		90

N.Y. JETS (2-2)

14	Green Bay	38
28	*Cincinnati	17
16	N.Y. Giants	20
37	Philadelphia	30
95		105

Central Division

CINCINNATI (1-3)

0	Kansas City	20
17	N.Y. Jets	28
34	*Green Bay	12
20	*Detroit	30
71		90

CLEVELAND (4-0)

19	*Buffalo	17
17	Miami	10
27	Atlanta	21
25	L.A. Raiders	22
88		70

HOUSTON (4-0)

17	L.A. Rams	14
23	*Buffalo	20
24	*New Orleans	13
17	Dallas	14
81		61

PITTSBURGH (1-3)

13	*Chicago	33
24	Washington (OT)	27
41	Dallas	28
3	N.Y. Giants	17
81		105

Western Division

DENVER (2-2)

7	*New Orleans	10
27	Minnesota	29
14	*San Francisco	9
19	*L.A. Rams	10
67		58

KANSAS CITY (2-2)

20	*Cincinnati	0
27	St. Louis	26
6	*Buffalo	13
10	New Orleans	13
63		52

L.A. RAIDERS (2-2)

0	San Francisco	32
24	*Dallas	19
24	*New England	10
22	*Cleveland	25
70		86

SAN DIEGO (3-1)

20	*Dallas	0
45	*Philadelphia	38
17	L.A. Rams (OT)	20
24	*St. Louis	17
106		75

SEATTLE (2-2)

21	*Indianapolis	14
27	Detroit (OT)	30
27	*Minnesota	17
10	San Francisco	21
85		82

NFC Preseason Standings—Team By Team

Eastern Division

DALLAS (0-5)

6	Chicago (AB)	17
0	San Diego	20
19	L.A. Raiders	24
28	*Pittsburgh	41
14	*Houston	17
67		119

N.Y. GIANTS (3-1)

24	Atlanta	31
22	Green Bay	14
20	*N.Y. Jets	16
17	*Pittsburgh	3
83		64

PHILADELPHIA (1-3)

17	Detroit	9
38	San Diego	45
15	*Miami	20
30	*N.Y. Jets	37
100		111

ST. LOUIS (2-3)

16	*New Eng. (HOF)	21
26	Tampa Bay	10
26	*Kansas City	27
14	Chicago	7
17	San Diego	24
99		89

WASHINGTON (3-1)

7	New England	18
27	*Pittsburgh (OT)	24
21	Tampa Bay	13
29	*Atlanta	21
84		76

Central Division

CHICAGO (4-1)

17	*Dallas (AB)	6
33	Pittsburgh	13
38	*Indianapolis	21
7	*St. Louis	14
31	Buffalo	17
126		71

DETROIT (2-2)

9	*Philadelphia	17
30	*Seattle (OT)	27
13	Indianapolis	20
30	Cincinnati	20
82		84

GREEN BAY (1-3)

38	*N.Y. Jets	14
14	*N.Y. Giants	22
12	Cincinnati	34
9	*New England	16
73		86

MINNESOTA (3-1)

30	*Miami	16
29	*Denver	27
17	Seattle	27
23	Indianapolis	20
99		90

TAMPA BAY (0-4)

10	*St. Louis	26
17	*Atlanta	20
13	*Tampa Bay	21
3	Miami	21
43		88

Western Division

ATLANTA (2-2)

31	*N.Y. Giants	24
20	Tampa Bay	17
21	*Cleveland	27
21	Washington	29
93		97

L.A. RAMS (2-2)

14	*Houston	17
31	*San Francisco	17
20	*San Diego (OT)	17
10	Denver	19
75		70

NEW ORLEANS (2-2)

10	Denver	7
34	*New England	38
13	Houston	24
13	*Kansas City	10
70		79

SAN FRANCISCO (2-2)

32	*L.A. Raiders	0
17	L.A. Rams	31
9	Denver	14
21	*Seattle	10
79		55

**denotes home game*
(OT) denotes overtime
(HOF) denotes Hall of Fame Game
(AB) denotes American Bowl '86 Game

1986 NFL STANDINGS

American Football Conference

Eastern Division

	W	L	T	Pct.	Pts.	OP
New England	11	5	0	.688	412	307
N.Y. Jets*	10	6	0	.625	364	386
Miami	8	8	0	.500	430	405
Buffalo	4	12	0	.250	287	348
Indianapolis	3	13	0	.188	229	400

Central Division

	W	L	T	Pct.	Pts.	OP
Cleveland	12	4	0	.750	391	310
Cincinnati	10	6	0	.625	409	394
Pittsburgh	6	10	0	.375	307	336
Houston	5	11	0	.313	274	329

Western Division

	W	L	T	Pct.	Pts.	OP
Denver	11	5	0	.688	378	327
Kansas City*	10	6	0	.625	358	326
Seattle	10	6	0	.625	366	293
L.A. Raiders	8	8	0	.500	323	346
San Diego	4	12	0	.250	335	396

National Football Conference

Eastern Division

	W	L	T	Pct.	Pts.	OP
N.Y. Giants	14	2	0	.875	371	236
Washington*	12	4	0	.750	368	296
Dallas	7	9	0	.438	346	337
Philadelphia	5	10	1	.344	256	312
St. Louis	4	11	1	.281	218	351

Central Division

	W	L	T	Pct.	Pts.	OP
Chicago	14	2	0	.875	352	187
Minnesota	9	7	0	.563	398	273
Detroit	5	11	0	.313	277	326
Green Bay	4	12	0	.250	254	418
Tampa Bay	2	14	0	.125	239	473

Western Division

	W	L	T	Pct.	Pts.	OP
San Francisco	10	5	1	.656	374	247
L.A. Rams*	10	6	0	.625	309	267
Atlanta	7	8	1	.469	280	280
New Orleans	7	9	0	.438	288	287

*Wild Card qualifiers for playoffs

New York Jets gained first AFC Wild Card position based on better conference record (8-4) over Kansas City (9-5), Seattle (7-5), and Cincinnati (7-5). Kansas City gained second Wild Card based on better conference record (9-5) over Seattle (7-5) and Cincinnati (7-5).

First-Round Playoffs

AFC .... New York Jets 35, Kansas City 15, December 28, at East Rutherford

NFC .... Washington 19, Los Angeles Rams 7, December 28, at Washington

Divisional Playoffs

AFC .... Cleveland 23, New York Jets 20 (OT), January 3, at Cleveland
Denver 22, New England 17, January 4, at Denver

NFC .... Washington 27, Chicago 13, January 3, at Chicago
New York Giants 49, San Francisco 3, January 4, at East Rutherford

Championship Games

AFC.......................... Denver 23, Cleveland 20 (OT), January 11, at Cleveland

NFC................. New York Giants 17, Washington 0, January 11, at East Rutherford

SUPER BOWL XXI .... New York Giants 39, Denver 20, January 25, at Rose Bowl, Pasadena, California

AFC-NFC PRO BOWL .. AFC 10, NFC 6, February 1, at Aloha Stadium, Honolulu, Hawaii

AFC Season Records—Team by Team

BUFFALO (4-12)

24	*N.Y. Jets	28
33	at Cincinnati (OT)	36
17	*St. Louis	10
17	*Kansas City	20
13	at N.Y. Jets	14
14	at Miami	27
24	*Indianapolis	13
3	*New England	23
28	at Tampa Bay	34
16	*Pittsburgh	12
24	*Miami	34
19	at New England	22
17	at Kansas City	14
17	*Cleveland	21
14	at Indianapolis	24
7	at Houston	16
287		348

CINCINNATI (10-6)

14	at Kansas City	24
36	*Buffalo (OT)	33
30	at Cleveland	13
7	*Chicago	44
34	at Green Bay	28
24	*Pittsburgh	22
31	*Houston	28
9	at Pittsburgh	30
24	at Detroit	17
28	at Houston	32
34	*Seattle	7
24	*Minnesota	20
28	at Denver	34
31	at New England	7
3	*Cleveland	34
52	*N.Y. Jets	21
409		394

CLEVELAND (12-4)

31	at Chicago	41
23	at Houston	20
13	*Cincinnati	30
24	*Detroit	21
27	at Pittsburgh	24
20	*Kansas City	7
14	*Green Bay	17
23	at Minnesota	20
24	at Indianapolis	9
26	*Miami	16
14	at L.A. Raiders	27
37	*Pittsburgh (OT)	31
13	*Houston (OT)	10
21	at Buffalo	17
34	at Cincinnati	3
47	*San Diego	17
391		310

DENVER (11-5)

38	*L.A. Raiders	36
21	at Pittsburgh	10
33	at Philadelphia	7
27	*New England	20
29	*Dallas	14
31	at San Diego	14
10	at N.Y. Jets	22
20	*Seattle	13
21	at L.A. Raiders	10
3	*San Diego	9
38	*Kansas City	17
16	at N.Y. Giants	19
34	*Cincinnati	28
10	at Kansas City	37
31	*Washington	30
16	at Seattle	41
378		327

HOUSTON (5-11)

31	at Green Bay	3
20	*Cleveland	23
13	at Kansas City	27
16	*Pittsburgh (OT)	22
13	at Detroit	24
7	*Chicago	20
28	at Cincinnati	31
17	*L.A. Raiders	28
7	at Miami	28
32	*Cincinnati	28
10	at Pittsburgh	21
31	*Indianapolis	17
10	at Cleveland (OT)	13
0	at San Diego	27
23	*Minnesota	10
16	*Buffalo	7
274		329

INDIANAPOLIS (3-13)

3	at New England	33
10	at Miami	30
7	*L.A. Rams	24
7	*N.Y. Jets	26
14	at San Francisco	35
14	*New Orleans	17
13	at Buffalo	24
13	*Miami	17
9	*Cleveland	24
21	*New England	30
16	at N.Y. Jets	31
17	at Houston	31
3	*San Diego	17
28	at Atlanta	23
24	*Buffalo	14
30	at L.A. Raiders	24
229		400

KANSAS CITY (10-6)

24	*Cincinnati	14
17	at Seattle	23
27	*Houston	13
20	at Buffalo	17
17	*L.A. Raiders	24
7	at Cleveland	20
42	*San Diego	41
27	*Tampa Bay	20
24	at San Diego	23
27	*Seattle	7
17	at Denver	38
14	at St. Louis	23
14	*Buffalo	17
37	*Denver	10
20	at L.A. Raiders	17
24	at Pittsburgh	19
358		326

L.A. RAIDERS (8-8)

36	at Denver	38
6	at Washington	10
9	*N.Y. Giants	14
17	*San Diego	13
24	at Kansas City	17
14	*Seattle	10
30	at Miami	28
28	at Houston	17
10	*Denver	21
17	at Dallas	13
27	*Cleveland	14
37	at San Diego (OT)	31
27	*Philadelphia (OT)	33
0	at Seattle	37
17	*Kansas City	20
24	*Indianapolis	30
323		346

MIAMI (8-8)

28	at San Diego	50
30	*Indianapolis	10
45	at N.Y. Jets (OT)	51
16	*San Francisco	31
7	at New England	34
27	*Buffalo	14
28	*L.A. Raiders	30
17	at Indianapolis	13
28	*Houston	7
16	at Cleveland	26
34	at Buffalo	24
45	*N.Y. Jets	3
14	*Atlanta	20
31	at New Orleans	27
37	at L.A. Rams (OT)	31
27	*New England	34
430		405

NEW ENGLAND (11-5)

33	*Indianapolis	3
20	at N.Y. Jets	6
31	*Seattle	38
20	at Denver	27
34	*Miami	7
24	*N.Y. Jets	31
34	at Pittsburgh	0
23	at Buffalo	3
25	*Atlanta	17
30	at Indianapolis	21
30	at L.A. Rams	28
22	*Buffalo	19
21	at New Orleans	20
7	*Cincinnati	31
24	*San Francisco	29
34	at Miami	27
412		307

N.Y. JETS (10-6)

28	at Buffalo	24
6	*New England	20
51	*Miami (OT)	45
26	at Indianapolis	7
14	*Buffalo	13
31	at New England	24
22	*Denver	10
28	*New Orleans	23
38	at Seattle	7
28	at Atlanta	14
31	*Indianapolis	16
3	at Miami	45
3	*L.A. Rams	17
10	at San Francisco	24
24	*Pittsburgh	45
21	at Cincinnati	52
364		386

PITTSBURGH (6-10)

0	at Seattle	30
10	*Denver	21
7	at Minnesota	31
22	at Houston (OT)	16
24	*Cleveland	27
22	at Cincinnati	24
0	*New England	34
30	*Cincinnati	9
27	*Green Bay	3
12	at Buffalo	16
21	*Houston	10
31	at Cleveland (OT)	37
10	at Chicago (OT)	13
27	*Detroit	17
45	at N.Y. Jets	24
19	*Kansas City	24
307		336

SAN DIEGO (4-12)

50	*Miami	28
7	at N.Y. Giants	20
27	*Washington	30
13	at L.A. Raiders	17
7	at Seattle	33
14	*Denver	31
41	at Kansas City	42
7	at Philadelphia	23
23	*Kansas City	24
9	at Denver	3
21	*Dallas	24
31	*L.A. Raiders (OT)	37
17	at Indianapolis	3
27	*Houston	0
24	*Seattle	34
17	at Cleveland	47
335		396

SEATTLE (10-6)

30	*Pittsburgh	0
23	*Kansas City	17
38	at New England	31
14	at Washington	19
33	*San Diego	7
10	at L.A. Raiders	14
17	*N.Y. Giants	12
13	at Denver	20
7	*N.Y. Jets	38
7	at Kansas City	27
7	at Cincinnati	34
24	*Philadelphia	20
31	at Dallas	14
37	*L.A. Raiders	0
34	at San Diego	24
41	*Denver	16
366		293

**Denotes Home Game*
(OT) Denotes Overtime

NFC Season Records—Team by Team

ATLANTA (7-8-1)		
31	at New Orleans	10
33	*St. Louis	13
37	at Dallas	35
23	at Tampa Bay (OT)	20
0	*Philadelphia	16
26	*L.A. Rams	14
10	*San Fran. (OT)	10
7	at L.A. Rams	14
17	at New England	25
14	*N.Y. Jets	28
10	*Chicago	13
0	at San Francisco	20
20	at Miami	14
23	*Indianapolis	28
9	*New Orleans	14
20	at Detroit	6
280		280

CHICAGO (14-2)		
41	*Cleveland	31
13	*Philadelphia (OT)	10
25	at Green Bay	12
44	at Cincinnati	7
23	*Minnesota	0
20	at Houston	7
7	at Minnesota	23
13	*Detroit	7
17	*L.A. Rams	20
23	at Tampa Bay	3
13	at Atlanta	10
12	*Green Bay	10
13	*Pittsburgh (OT)	10
48	*Tampa Bay	14
16	at Detroit	13
24	at Dallas	10
352		187

DALLAS (7-9)		
31	*N.Y. Giants	28
31	at Detroit	7
35	*Atlanta	37
31	at St. Louis	7
14	at Denver	29
30	*Washington	6
17	at Philadelphia	14
37	*St. Louis	6
14	at N.Y. Giants	17
13	*L.A. Raiders	17
24	at San Diego	21
14	at Washington	41
14	*Seattle	31
10	at L.A. Rams	29
21	*Philadelphia	23
10	*Chicago	24
346		337

DETROIT (5-11)		
13	at Minnesota	10
7	*Dallas	31
20	*Tampa Bay	24
21	at Cleveland	24
24	*Houston	13
21	at Green Bay	14
10	at L.A. Rams	14
7	at Chicago	13
17	*Cincinnati	24
10	*Minnesota	24
13	at Philadelphia	11
38	at Tampa Bay	17
40	*Green Bay	44
17	at Pittsburgh	27
13	*Chicago	16
6	*Atlanta	20
277		326

GREEN BAY (4-12)		
3	*Houston	31
10	at New Orleans	24
12	*Chicago	25
7	at Minnesota	42
28	*Cincinnati	34
14	*Detroit	21
17	at Cleveland	14
17	*San Francisco	31
3	at Pittsburgh	27
7	*Washington	16
31	*Tampa Bay	7
10	at Chicago	12
44	at Detroit	40
6	*Minnesota	32
21	at Tampa Bay	7
24	at N.Y. Giants	55
254		418

L.A. RAMS (10-6)		
16	at St. Louis	10
16	*San Francisco	13
24	at Indianapolis	7
20	at Philadelphia	34
26	*Tampa Bay (OT)	20
14	at Atlanta	26
14	*Detroit	10
14	*Atlanta	7
20	at Chicago	17
0	at New Orleans	6
28	*New England	30
26	*New Orleans	13
17	at N.Y. Jets	3
29	*Dallas	10
31	*Miami (OT)	37
14	at San Francisco	24
309		267

MINNESOTA (9-7)		
10	*Detroit	13
23	at Tampa Bay	10
31	*Pittsburgh	7
42	*Green Bay	7
0	at Chicago	23
27	at San Fran. (OT)	24
23	*Chicago	7
20	*Cleveland	23
38	at Wash. (OT)	44
24	at Detroit	10
20	*N.Y. Giants	22
20	at Cincinnati	24
45	*Tampa Bay	13
32	at Green Bay	6
10	at Houston	23
33	*New Orleans	17
398		273

NEW ORLEANS (7-9)		
10	*Atlanta	31
24	*Green Bay	10
17	at San Francisco	26
17	at N.Y. Giants	20
6	*Washington	14
17	at Indianapolis	14
38	*Tampa Bay	7
23	at N.Y. Jets	28
23	*San Francisco	10
6	*L.A. Rams	0
16	at St. Louis	7
13	at L.A. Rams	26
20	*New England	21
27	*Miami	31
14	at Atlanta	9
17	at Minnesota	33
288		287

N.Y. GIANTS (14-2)		
28	at Dallas	31
20	*San Diego	7
14	at L.A. Raiders	9
20	*New Orleans	17
13	at St. Louis	6
35	*Philadelphia	3
12	at Seattle	17
27	*Washington	20
17	*Dallas	14
17	at Philadelphia	14
22	at Minnesota	20
19	*Denver	16
21	at San Francisco	17
24	at Washington	14
27	*St. Louis	7
55	*Green Bay	24
371		236

PHILADELPHIA (5-10-1)		
14	at Washington	41
10	at Chicago (OT)	13
7	*Denver	33
34	*L.A. Rams	20
16	at Atlanta	0
3	at N.Y. Giants	35
14	*Dallas	17
23	*San Diego	7
10	at St. Louis	13
14	*N.Y. Giants	17
11	*Detroit	13
20	at Seattle	24
33	at L.A. Raid. (OT)	27
10	*St. Louis (OT)	10
23	at Dallas	21
14	*Washington	21
256		312

ST. LOUIS (4-11-1)		
10	*L.A. Rams	16
13	at Atlanta	33
10	at Buffalo	17
7	*Dallas	31
6	*N.Y. Giants	13
30	at Tampa Bay	19
21	at Washington	28
6	at Dallas	37
13	*Philadelphia	10
17	at San Francisco	43
7	*New Orleans	16
23	*Kansas City	14
17	*Washington	20
10	at Phil. (OT)	10
7	at N.Y. Giants	27
21	*Tampa Bay	17
218		351

SAN FRANCISCO (10-5-1)		
31	at Tampa Bay	7
13	at L.A. Rams	16
26	*New Orleans	17
31	at Miami	16
35	*Indianapolis	14
24	*Minnesota (OT)	27
10	at Atlanta (OT)	10
31	at Green Bay	17
10	at New Orleans	23
43	*St. Louis	17
6	at Washington	14
20	*Atlanta	0
17	*N.Y. Giants	21
24	*N.Y. Jets	10
29	at New England	24
24	*L.A. Rams	14
374		247

TAMPA BAY (2-14)		
7	*San Francisco	31
10	*Minnesota	23
24	at Detroit	20
20	*Atlanta (OT)	23
20	at L.A. Rams (OT)	26
19	*St. Louis	30
7	at New Orleans	38
20	at Kansas City	27
34	*Buffalo	28
3	*Chicago	23
7	at Green Bay	31
17	*Detroit	38
13	at Minnesota	45
14	at Chicago	48
7	*Green Bay	21
17	at St. Louis	21
239		473

WASHINGTON (12-4)		
41	*Philadelphia	14
10	*L.A. Raiders	6
30	at San Diego	27
19	*Seattle	14
14	at New Orleans	6
6	at Dallas	30
28	*St. Louis	21
20	at N.Y. Giants	27
44	*Minnesota (OT)	38
16	at Green Bay	7
14	*San Francisco	6
41	*Dallas	14
20	at St. Louis	17
14	*N.Y. Giants	24
30	at Denver	31
21	at Philadelphia	14
368		296

**Denotes Home Game*
(OT) Denotes Overtime

Attendances as they appear in the following, and in the club-by-club sections starting on page 24, are turnstile counts and not paid attendance. Paid attendance totals are on page 167.

First Week Summaries

Standings

American Football Conference

Eastern Division

	W	L	T	Pct.	Pts.	OP
New England	1	0	0	1.000	33	3
N.Y. Jets	1	0	0	1.000	28	24
Buffalo	0	1	0	.000	24	28
Indianapolis	0	1	0	.000	3	33
Miami	0	1	0	.000	28	50
Central Division						
Houston	1	0	0	1.000	31	3
Cincinnati	0	1	0	.000	14	24
Cleveland	0	1	0	.000	31	41
Pittsburgh	0	1	0	.000	0	30
Western Division						
Denver	1	0	0	1.000	38	36
Kansas City	1	0	0	1.000	24	14
San Diego	1	0	0	1.000	50	28
Seattle	1	0	0	1.000	30	0
L.A. Raiders	0	1	0	.000	36	38

National Football Conference

Eastern Division

	W	L	T	Pct.	Pts.	OP
Dallas	1	0	0	1.000	31	28
Washington	1	0	0	1.000	41	14
N.Y. Giants	0	1	0	.000	28	31
Philadelphia	0	1	0	.000	14	41
St. Louis	0	1	0	.000	10	16
Central Division						
Chicago	1	0	0	1.000	41	31
Detroit	1	0	0	1.000	13	10
Green Bay	0	1	0	.000	3	31
Minnesota	0	1	0	.000	10	13
Tampa Bay	0	1	0	.000	7	31
Western Division						
Atlanta	1	0	0	1.000	31	10
L.A. Rams	1	0	0	1.000	16	10
San Francisco	1	0	0	1.000	31	7
New Orleans	0	1	0	.000	10	31

Sunday, September 7

Atlanta 31, New Orleans 10—At Louisiana Superdome, attendance 67,950. David Archer threw for two touchdowns and Cliff Austin rushed for his first NFL 100-yard game as the Falcons rolled over the Saints. Austin, who gained 104 yards on 27 carries, had a one-yard touchdown run in the second quarter. Atlanta's Charlie Brown led all receivers with seven catches for 119 yards, including a 17-yard touchdown from Archer. Archer's other scoring pass was a 19-yarder to Anthony Allen. Paced by 245 rushing yards, the Falcons outgained the Saints 442 yards to 176 and maintained a 37:58 to 22:02 time of possession advantage.

Atlanta	7	7	7	10	— 31
New Orleans	0	3	0	7	— 10

Atl —Brown 17 pass from Archer (Luckhurst kick)
Atl —Austin 1 run (Luckhurst kick)
NO —FG Andersen 47
Atl —Riggs 1 run (Luckhurst kick)
Atl —Allen 19 pass from Archer (Luckhurst kick)
Atl —FG Luckhurst 32
NO —Hilliard 1 run (Andersen kick)

Kansas City 24, Cincinnati 14—At Arrowhead Stadium, attendance 43,430. Deron Cherry recovered a blocked punt for one touchdown and the Chiefs capitalized on two Bengals turnovers for two more scores en route to the victory. Todd Blackledge's 15-yard scoring pass to Jeff Smith gave Kansas City a 14-7 third-quarter edge. The Chiefs' Art Still and Bill Maas each recovered fumbles by Boomer Esiason to set up scores by tight end Walt Arnold, who fell on teammate Herman Heard's fumble in the end zone, and Nick Lowery's 18-yard field goal. Cincinnati's Cris Collinsworth caught six passes for 75 yards, including both of the Bengals' touchdowns (15 and 28 yards).

Cincinnati	0	7	0	7	— 14
Kansas City	7	0	14	3	— 24

KC —Cherry recovered blocked punt in end zone (Lowery kick)
Cin —Collinsworth 15 pass from Esiason (Breech kick)
KC —J. Smith 15 pass from Blackledge (Lowery kick)
KC —Arnold fumble recovery in end zone (Lowery kick)
Cin —Collinsworth 28 pass from Esiason (Breech kick)
KC —FG Lowery 18

Chicago 41, Cleveland 31—At Soldier Field, attendance 61,975. Dennis Gentry returned a kickoff 91 yards for one touchdown and Walter Payton scored two more as the Bears downed the Browns. Following a first-quarter Cleveland touchdown, Chicago took the lead for good scoring 21 unanswered points on Gentry's return, Payton's two-yard run, and Wilber Marshall's 58-yard interception return. Payton, who rushed for 113 yards on 22 carries, also caught an 11-yard touchdown pass from Jim McMahon. Kevin Butler kicked a 19-yard field goal and Matt Suhey scored on a six-yard run with 2:01 left in the game to thwart Cleveland's second-half rally.

Cleveland	7	7	7	10	— 31
Chicago	21	3	7	10	— 41

Clev —Gross fumble recovery in end zone (Bahr kick)
Chi —Gentry 91 kickoff return (Butler kick)
Chi —Payton 2 run (Butler kick)
Chi —Marshall 58 interception return (Butler kick)
Clev —Mack 3 run (Bahr kick)
Chi —FG Butler 47
Clev —Mack 14 run (Bahr kick)
Chi —Payton 11 pass from McMahon (Butler kick)
Clev —FG Bahr 22
Chi —FG Butler 19
Clev —Brennan 15 pass from Kosar (Bahr kick)
Chi —Suhey 6 run (Butler kick)

Detroit 13, Minnesota 10—At Metrodome, attendance 54,851. James Jones ran for a career-high 174 yards on 36 carries and Eddie Murray kicked a pair of field goals to lead the Lions past the Vikings. Jones, who scored Detroit's only touchdown on a two-yard run, tied Billy Sims's club record for rushing attempts. Murray's kicks were from distances of 33 and 44 yards. The Lions outrushed the Vikings 224 yards to 62 to contribute to their 37:41 to 22:19 time of possession advantage.

Detroit	0	7	3	3	— 13
Minnesota	3	0	0	7	— 10

Minn —FG C. Nelson 35
Det —J. Jones 2 run (Murray kick)
Det —FG Murray 33
Det —FG Murray 44
Minn —Gustafson 5 pass from Kramer (C. Nelson kick)

Houston 31, Green Bay 3—At Lambeau Field, attendance 54,065. Warren Moon passed for two touchdowns and ran for another to lead the Oilers over the Packers. Larry Moriarty opened Houston's scoring with a three-yard run in the first quarter. Moon, who completed 14 of 21 passes for 218 yards, threw scoring passes to Butch Woolfolk (29 yards) and Drew Hill (44). Moon also scored on a three-yard run in the third period. The Oilers outgained the Packers 375 yards to 224. Houston's 28-point margin of victory was its largest since a 47-0 win over the Bears on November 6, 1977.

Houston	7	7	10	7	— 31
Green Bay	3	0	0	0	— 3

GB —FG Del Greco 26
Hou —Moriarty 3 run (Zendejas kick)
Hou —Woolfolk 29 pass from Moon (Zendejas kick)
Hou —FG Zendejas 20
Hou —Moon 3 run (Zendejas kick)
Hou —Hill 44 pass from Moon (Zendejas kick)

New England 33, Indianapolis 3—At Sullivan Stadium, attendance 55,208. Tony Franklin kicked four field goals and Craig James ran for one touchdown to lead the Patriots over the Colts. New England took a 10-3 first-half advantage on Franklin's 38-yard field goal and James's three-yard scoring run. Highlighting the win for New England were wide receivers Stephen Starring and Stanley Morgan, who became the first pair of Patriots since 1979 to each total over 100 yards receiving. Starring had five catches for 102 yards, while Morgan had seven for 116, including a 43-yard touchdown from Tony Eason. Linebacker Don Blackmon had three of New England's six sacks to pace the defense.

Indianapolis	0	3	0	0	— 3
New England	3	7	10	13	— 33

NE —FG Franklin 38
NE —James 3 run (Franklin kick)
Ind —FG Biasucci 25
NE —Morgan 43 pass from Eason (Franklin kick)
NE —FG Franklin 39
NE —FG Franklin 49
NE —FG Franklin 25
NE —Rembert fumble recovery in end zone (Franklin kick)

Denver 38, Los Angeles Raiders 36—At Mile High Stadium, attendance 75,695. Quarterback John Elway passed for two touchdowns and caught another to help the Broncos register their 100th victory at Mile High Stadium. Elway kept the Broncos close in the first half by firing a 35-yard touchdown pass to Steve Watson and catching another from Steve Sewell (23 yards). Rich Karlis's 51-yard field goal, along with Elway's seven-yard scoring pass to Gene Lang, rallied the Broncos from an eight-point fourth-quarter deficit. Raiders running back Marcus Allen broke Walter Payton's NFL record for consecutive 100-yard games with his tenth by gaining 102 yards on 28 carries. Teammate Marc Wilson completed 20 of 33 passes for a career-high 346 yards and three touchdowns. Allen caught six for 102 yards.

L.A. Raiders	16	6	14	0	— 36
Denver	7	14	7	10	— 38

Den —Watson 35 pass from Elway (Karlis kick)
Raiders —Allen 24 pass from Wilson (Bahr kick)
Raiders —Christensen 16 pass from Wilson (Bahr kick)
Raiders —Safety, Townsend tackled Elway in end zone
Raiders —FG Bahr 43
Den —Elway 23 pass from Sewell (Karlis kick)
Raiders —FG Bahr 42
Den —Lang 1 run (Karlis kick)
Raiders —Allen 2 run (Bahr kick)
Den —Woodard 16 fumble recovery return (Karlis kick)
Raiders —Barksdale 57 pass from Wilson (Bahr kick)
Den —FG Karlis 51
Den —Lang 7 pass from Elway (Karlis kick)

Los Angeles Rams 16, St. Louis 10—At Busch Memorial Stadium, attendance 40,347. Eric Dickerson gained 193 yards rushing on a career-high 38 attempts to help the Rams down the Cardinals. Los Angeles took a 16-3 third-quarter lead on Dickerson touchdown runs of 1 and 16 yards and Mike Lansford's 26-yard field goal. St. Louis rallied in the fourth period to trim the deficit to 16-10 on Ottis Anderson's four-yard scoring run. However, the Cardinals' final drive ended as time expired at the Rams' 1-yard line. Mike Wilcher had two of the Rams' five sacks to pace the defense.

L.A. Rams	0	6	10	0	— 16
St. Louis	0	3	0	7	— 10

Rams —Dickerson 1 run (kick failed)
StL —FG Lee 28
Rams —Dickerson 16 run (Lansford kick)
Rams —FG Lansford 26
StL —Anderson 4 run (Lee kick)

San Diego 50, Miami 28—At San Diego Jack Murphy Stadium, attendance 57,726. Dan Fouts passed for three touchdowns and Rolf Benirschke kicked three field goals to lead the Chargers' 50-28 rout of the Dolphins. San Diego took a 17-0 first-quarter lead on Fouts's 18-yard scoring pass to Gary Anderson, Benirschke's 26-yard field goal, and Tim Spencer's 17-yard touchdown run. Fouts added touchdown passes of seven yards to Wes Chandler and 17 yards to Pete Holohan, while Benirschke also converted a pair of 36-yarders. Miami's Mark Clayton caught five passes for 143 yards and two touchdowns.

Miami	0	14	7	7	— 28
San Diego	17	9	14	10	— 50

SD —Anderson 18 pass from Fouts (Benirschke kick)
SD —FG Benirschke 26
SD —Spencer 17 run (Benirschke kick)
Mia —Clayton 22 pass from Marino (Reveiz kick)
SD —McGee 4 run (kick blocked)
Mia —Clayton 49 pass from Marino (Reveiz kick)
SD —FG Benirschke 36
SD —Chandler 7 pass from Fouts (Benirschke kick)
Mia —N. Moore 6 pass from Marino (Reveiz kick)
SD —Holohan 17 pass from Fouts (Benirschke kick)
SD —McGee 4 run (Benirschke kick)
SD —FG Benirschke 36
Mia —N. Moore 17 pass from Strock (Reveiz kick)

New York Jets 28, Buffalo 24—At Rich Stadium, attendance 79,951. Ken O'Brien completed 18 of 25 passes for 318 yards and a pair of touchdowns to help the Jets down the Bills. Buffalo took an early fourth-quarter lead, 17-14, on Jim Kelly's 55-yard scoring pass to Andre Reed. However, New York countered with Johnny Hector's one-yard touchdown dive and O'Brien's 71-yard scoring pass to Wesley Walker to take the lead for good, 28-17. Kelly completed 20 of 33 passes for 292 yards and three touchdowns in his NFL debut. New York's Al Toon led all receivers with six catches for 119 yards, including a 46-yard touchdown reception.

N.Y Jets	7	7	0	14	— 28
Buffalo	7	3	0	14	— 24

Buff —Bell 2 pass from Kelly (Norwood kick)
NYJ —Paige 2 run (Leahy kick)
NYJ —Toon 46 pass from O'Brien (Leahy kick)
Buff —FG Norwood 19
Buff —Reed 55 pass from Kelly (Norwood kick)
NYJ —Hector 1 run (Leahy kick)
NYJ —Walker 71 pass from O'Brien (Leahy kick)
Buff —Metzelaars 4 pass from Kelly (Norwood kick)

Washington 41, Philadelphia 14—At Robert F. Kennedy Stadium, attendance 53,982. George Rogers rushed for 104 yards and Jay Schroeder completed a pair of touchdown passes as the Redskins defeated the Eagles. Washington opened a 20-14 halftime lead with a 17-point second-quarter explosion, as Schroeder ran one yard for a score and passed 36 yards to Kelvin Bryant for another, and Steve Cox kicked a club-record 55-yard field goal. Schroeder completed a 36-yard touchdown pass to Clint

Didier, and Bryant and Rogers added runs of 16 and 5 yards, respectively, to finish the Redskins' scoring. Dave Butz and Steve Hamilton each recorded a pair of sacks to lead Washington's defense.

Philadelphia	7	7	0	0	— 14
Washington	3	17	14	7	— 41

Wash — FG Moseley 19
Phil — Johnson 17 pass from Jaworski (McFadden kick)
Wash — Bryant 36 pass from Schroeder (Moseley kick)
Wash — Schroeder 1 run (Moseley kick)
Phil — Tautalatasi 3 pass from Jaworski (McFadden kick)
Wash — FG Cox 55
Wash — Didier 36 pass from Schroeder (Moseley kick)
Wash — Bryant 16 run (Moseley kick)
Wash — Rogers 5 run (Moseley kick)

Seattle 30, Pittsburgh 0—At Kingdome, attendance 61,461. Curt Warner rushed for 114 yards on 21 carries and Dave Krieg threw a pair of touchdown passes as the Seahawks handed Pittsburgh its first opening-day shutout in its 54-year history. Seattle opened a 16-0 third-period lead on Krieg's four-yard scoring pass to Daryl Turner, Dave Brown's 18-yard interception return for a touchdown, and Norm Johnson's 24-yard field goal. Steve Largent caught seven passes for 65 yards, including a 10-yard touchdown, to extend his consecutive games streak with a reception to 124. Rookie kick returner Bobby Joe Edmonds returned four punts for a club-record 101 yards.

Pittsburgh	0	0	0	0	— 0
Seattle	0	6	10	14	— 30

Sea — Turner 4 pass from Krieg (kick failed)
Sea — Brown 18 interception return (Johnson kick)
Sea — FG Johnson 24
Sea — Largent 10 pass from Krieg (Johnson kick)
Sea — Morris 49 run (Johnson kick)

San Francisco 31, Tampa Bay 7—At Tampa Stadium, attendance 50,780. San Francisco's defense intercepted a club-record seven passes and Roger Craig ran for two touchdowns as the 49ers easily beat the Buccaneers. Joe Montana completed 32 of 46 passes for 356 yards, including a four-yard touchdown to Mike Wilson. Craig scored on a pair of one-yard runs. Dwight Clark's seven catches for 100 yards led all receivers. Ronnie Lott's two interceptions and Jeff Stover's career-high three sacks highlighted the defense's record-setting afternoon.

San Francisco	14	0	3	14	— 31
Tampa Bay	0	0	7	0	— 7

SF — Craig 1 run (Wersching kick)
SF — Wilson 4 pass from Montana (Wersching kick)
TB — G. Carter 31 pass from DeBerg (Igwebuike kick)
SF — FG Wersching 30
SF — Craig 1 run (Wersching kick)
SF — Frank 10 pass from Kemp (Wersching kick)

Monday, September 8

Dallas 31, New York Giants 28—At Texas Stadium, attendance 59,804. Herschel Walker, making his NFL debut, ran 10 yards for the game-winning touchdown with 1:16 left to help the Cowboys squeak past the Giants. Dallas took a 17-14 halftime lead on Danny White's 36-yard scoring pass to Tony Dorsett, Walker's one-yard run, and Rafael Septien's 35-yard field goal. New York rallied in the second half to take a 28-24 advantage by scoring a pair of touchdowns around White's one-yard touchdown pass to Thornton Chandler. White connected on 23 of 39 passes for 265 yards, including five to Tony Hill for 107 yards. The Giants' Bobby Johnson had eight catches for 115 yards and two touchdowns to pace all receivers.

N.Y. Giants	0	14	7	7	— 28
Dallas	0	17	0	14	— 31

Dall — Dorsett 36 pass from D. White (Septien kick)
Dall — Walker 1 run (Septien kick)
NYG — B. Johnson 13 pass from Simms (Thomas kick)
NYG — Robinson 3 pass from Simms (Thomas kick)
Dall — FG Septien 35
NYG — Morris 2 run (Thomas kick)
Dall — Chandler 1 pass from D. White (Septien kick)
NYG — B. Johnson 44 pass from Simms (Thomas kick)
Dall — Walker 10 run (Septien kick)

Second Week Summaries

Standings

American Football Conference

Eastern Division	W	L	T	Pct.	Pts.	OP
New England	2	0	0	1.000	53	9
Miami	1	1	0	.500	58	60
N.Y. Jets	1	1	0	.500	34	44
Buffalo	0	2	0	.000	57	64
Indianapolis	0	2	0	.000	13	63
Central Division						
Cincinnati	1	1	0	.500	50	57
Cleveland	1	1	0	.500	54	61
Houston	1	1	0	.500	51	26
Pittsburgh	0	2	0	.000	10	51
Western Division						
Denver	2	0	0	1.000	59	46
Seattle	2	0	0	1.000	53	17
Kansas City	1	1	0	.500	41	37
San Diego	1	1	0	.500	57	48
L.A. Raiders	0	2	0	.000	42	48

National Football Conference

Eastern Division	W	L	T	Pct.	Pts.	OP
Dallas	2	0	0	1.000	62	35
Washington	2	0	0	1.000	51	20
N.Y. Giants	1	1	0	.500	48	38
Philadelphia	0	2	0	.000	24	54
St. Louis	0	2	0	.000	23	49
Central Division						
Chicago	2	0	0	1.000	54	41
Detroit	1	1	0	.500	20	41
Minnesota	1	1	0	.500	33	23
Green Bay	0	2	0	.000	13	55
Tampa Bay	0	2	0	.000	17	54
Western Division						
Atlanta	2	0	0	1.000	64	23
L.A. Rams	2	0	0	1.000	32	23
New Orleans	1	1	0	.500	34	41
San Francisco	1	1	0	.500	44	23

Thursday, September 11

New England 20, New York Jets 6—At Giants Stadium, attendance 72,422. Tony Collins scored a pair of touchdowns and Tony Franklin kicked two field goals to highlight the Patriots' victory. Tony Eason's first-quarter six-yard scoring pass to Collins, plus Franklin's extra point provided all the points New England needed as the Patriots' defense limited New York to two field goals. Collins also caught a 10-yard scoring pass from running back Craig James in the third quarter. Franklin converted field goals of 45 and 42 yards to complete the Patriots' scoring. Stanley Morgan registered his second straight 100-yard receiving game with 104 yards on eight catches.

New England	7	0	10	3	— 20
N.Y. Jets	0	6	0	0	— 6

NE — Collins 6 pass from Eason (Franklin kick)
NYJ — FG Leahy 33
NYJ — FG Leahy 47
NE — Collins 10 pass from C. James (Franklin kick)
NE — FG Franklin 45
NE — FG Franklin 42

Sunday, September 14

Cincinnati 36, Buffalo 33—At Riverfront Stadium, attendance 52,714. Jim Breech kicked a 20-yard field goal 56 seconds into overtime to give the Bengals a 36-33 win over the Bills. Trailing 33-23 with 6:27 left, Cincinnati rallied to force the extra period on Breech's 51-yard field goal and Boomer Esiason's two-yard touchdown run. Linebacker Carl Zander's 18-yard interception return to the Buffalo 17-yard line set up Breech's decisive kick. Esiason completed second-quarter touchdown passes of 35 and 17 yards to Eddie Brown to help the Bengals to a 21-9 halftime advantage.

Buffalo	3	6	17	7	0	— 33
Cincinnati	7	14	0	12	3	— 36

Cin — Kinnebrew 11 run (Breech kick)
Buff — FG Norwood 20
Cin — Brown 35 pass from Esiason (Breech kick)
Buff — Riddick 6 run (kick failed)
Cin — Brown 17 pass from Esiason (Breech kick)
Buff — FG Norwood 44
Buff — Bell 9 run (Norwood kick)
Buff — Burkett 84 pass from Kelly (Norwood kick)
Cin — Safety, White tackled Kidd in end zone
Buff — Metzelaars fumble recovery in end zone (Norwood kick)
Cin — FG Breech 51
Cin — Esiason 2 run (Breech kick)
Cin — FG Breech 20

Cleveland 23, Houston 20—At Astrodome, attendance 46,049. Earnest Byner's one-yard touchdown run with 1:30 remaining lifted the Browns over the Oilers. Trailing 13-9 with 2:10 left, Cleveland quarterback Bernie Kosar tossed a 55-yard scoring pass to Reggie Langhorne to give Cleveland a 16-13 advantage. D.D. Hoggard recovered the ensuing kickoff at the Houston 20-yard line and five plays later Byner scored the decisive touchdown. Langhorne registered his first career 100-yard receiving game with 115 yards on three receptions. Cornerback Hanford Dixon had two (one interception and one fumble recovery) of the Browns' five takeaways.

Cleveland	0	3	6	14	— 23
Houston	7	0	0	13	— 20

Hou — Moriarty 8 run (Zendejas kick)
Clev — FG Bahr 34
Clev — FG Bahr 29
Clev — FG Bahr 45
Hou — FG Zendejas 35
Hou — FG Zendejas 36
Clev — Langhorne 55 pass from Kosar (Bahr kick)
Clev — Byner 1 run (Bahr kick)
Hou — Woolfolk 20 pass from Moon (Zendejas kick)

Dallas 31, Detroit 7—At Pontiac Silverdome, attendance 73,812. Danny White ran for one touchdown and passed for another to highlight the Cowboys' 31-7 win over the Lions. Dallas opened a 17-0 halftime lead on Tony Dorsett's five-yard scoring run, White's 15-yard touchdown pass to Timmy Newsome, and Rafael Septien's 27-yard field goal. White and Herschel Walker added one- and seven-yard scoring runs, respectively, in the final quarter to complete the Cowboys' scoring. Dorsett had 117 yards on 23 carries as Dallas outgained Detroit 388 total yards to 184.

Dallas	0	17	0	14	— 31
Detroit	0	0	0	7	— 7

Dall — Dorsett 5 run (Septien kick)
Dall — Newsome 15 pass from D. White (Septien kick)
Dall — FG Septien 27
Dall — D. White 1 run (Septien kick)
Dall — Walker 7 run (Septien kick)
Det — J. Jones 1 run (Murray kick)

New Orleans 24, Green Bay 10—At Louisiana Superdome, attendance 46,383. The Saints' defense set a club record with seven interceptions and quarterback Bobby Hebert passed for one touchdown to help Jim Mora register his first NFL head coaching victory. Eric Martin caught a 72-yard scoring pass from Hebert and set up Morten Andersen's 20-yard field goal with an 84-yard reception to give New Orleans a 10-0 first-quarter lead. Dalton Hilliard's three-yard run and James Haynes's 17-yard interception return for a score capped the Saints' scoring. Martin finished with three catches for 164 yards. Dave Waymer had two of the defense's seven interceptions.

Green Bay	0	3	7	0	— 10
New Orleans	17	7	0	0	— 24

NO — Martin 72 pass from Hebert (Andersen kick)
NO — FG Andersen 20
NO — Hilliard 3 run (Andersen kick)
GB — FG Del Greco 50
NO — Haynes 17 interception return (Andersen kick)
GB — Lofton 8 pass from Wright (Del Greco kick)

Miami 30, Indianapolis 10—At Orange Bowl, attendance 51,848. Lorenzo Hampton ran for two touchdowns and rookie James Pruitt scored another on a 71-yard punt return to help the Dolphins past the Colts. Miami trailed 7-0 in the first quarter, but the Dolphins exploded for 20 unanswered points to put the game away. Hampton's first-quarter five-yard run was followed by Dan Marino's four-yard pass to Nat Moore and Pruitt's return. Hampton (21-yard run) and Fuad Reveiz (27-yard field goal) added scores in the second half. Hugh Green and Doug Betters each had two of Miami's seven sacks.

Indianapolis	7	3	0	0	— 10
Miami	7	13	10	0	— 30

Ind — Bentley 1 run (Biasucci kick)
Mia — Hampton 5 run (Reveiz kick)
Mia — N. Moore 4 pass from Marino (kick failed)
Mia — Pruitt 71 punt return (Reveiz kick)
Ind — FG Biasucci 23
Mia — Hampton 21 run (Reveiz kick)
Mia — FG Reveiz 27

Seattle 23, Kansas City 17—At Kingdome, attendance 61,068. Norm Johnson kicked three field goals and Curt Warner ran for one touchdown to lead the Seahawks over the Chiefs. Johnson's third field goal, a 53-yarder, gave Seattle a 16-10 third-quarter edge. Two minutes later, Kenny Easley set up the Seahawks' decisive score (Warner's one-yard touchdown run) by returning an interception 18 yards to the Chiefs' 5-yard line. Steve Largent, who caught five passes for 62 yards to increase his career reception total to 636, moved ahead of Don Maynard (633) into third place on the all-time list. Johnson also converted field goals from 35 and 34 yards.

Kansas City	3	0	7	7	— 17
Seattle	0	13	10	0	— 23

KC — FG Lowery 42
Sea — FG Johnson 35
Sea — FG Johnson 34
Sea — Turner 6 pass from Krieg (Johnson kick)
KC — Carson 70 pass from Blackledge (Lowery kick)
Sea — FG Johnson 53
Sea — Warner 1 run (Johnson kick)
KC — Smith 1 run (Lowery kick)

Washington 10, Los Angeles Raiders 6—At Robert F. Kennedy Stadium, attendance 55,235. George Rogers ran three yards for the game-winning touchdown midway through the fourth quarter to highlight the Redskins' win. Trailing 6-3 in the final period, Jay Schroeder hooked up with Clint Didier on a 59-yard bomb to the Raiders' 9-yard line. Two plays later, Rogers scored Washington's decisive touchdown. Los Angeles's Marcus Allen gained 104 yards on 23 carries to extend his NFL record for consecutive 100-yard rushing games to 11.

L.A. Raiders	3	0	3	0	— 6
Washington	3	0	0	7	— 10

Raiders — FG Bahr 28
Wash — FG Moseley 45
Raiders — FG Bahr 23
Wash — Rogers 3 run (Moseley kick)

Minnesota 23, Tampa Bay 10—At Tampa Stadium, attendance 34,579. Chuck Nelson kicked three field goals and Tommy Kramer passed for one touchdown to give Jerry Burns his first NFL win. Minnesota scored early on linebacker Chris Doleman's 59-yard interception return for a touchdown and Nelson's 31-yard field goal to take a 10-0 first-quarter lead. Following a Tampa Bay field goal, Kramer completed a 10-yard scoring pass to Mike Mularkey to put the game out-of-reach. Nelson also kicked field goals from 35 and 27 yards.

Minnesota	10	7	0	6	— 23
Tampa Bay	3	7	0	0	— 10

Minn — Doleman 59 interception return (C. Nelson kick)
Minn — FG C. Nelson 31
TB — FG Igwebuike 37
Minn — Mularkey 10 pass from Kramer (C. Nelson kick)
TB — Giles 1 pass from DeBerg (Igwebuike kick)
Minn — FG C. Nelson 35
Minn — FG C. Nelson 27

Chicago 13, Philadelphia 10—At Soldier Field, attendance 65,130. Kevin Butler's 23-yard field goal 5:56 into overtime lifted the defending Super Bowl champion Bears over the Eagles. Chicago took a 10-3 third-quarter lead on Walter Payton's 100th career rushing touchdown (from one yard) and Butler's 23-yard field goal. Philadelphia forced the extra period when Ron Jaworski completed a 26-yard scoring pass to Mike Quick early in the fourth quarter. Payton gained 177 of Chicago's 244 rushing yards to pace all rushers. Safety Dave Duerson led Chicago's defense with one sack, one interception, and a forced fumble that set up Butler's winning field goal.

Philadelphia	3	0	0	7	0	— 10
Chicago	0	0	10	0	3	— 13

Phil — FG McFadden 49
Chi — Payton 1 run (Butler kick)
Chi — FG Butler 23
Phil — Quick 26 pass from Jaworski (McFadden kick)
Chi — FG Butler 23

Atlanta 33, St. Louis 13—At Atlanta-Fulton County Stadium, attendance 46,463. Gerald Riggs ran for 111 yards on 29 carries and David Archer threw for two touchdowns as the Falcons defeated the Cardinals. Atlanta broke open a 17-13 game with 16 fourth-quarter points on Archer's 22-yard scoring pass to Anthony Allen, William Andrews's one-yard touchdown run, and a safety by defensive end Mike Gann. Riggs's one-yard dive and Archer's 17-yard completion to Charlie Brown opened the Falcons' scoring. Gann also had two sacks to lead the Atlanta defense.

St. Louis	0	13	0	0	— 13
Atlanta	14	3	0	16	— 33

Atl — Riggs 1 run (Luckhurst kick)
Atl — C. Brown 17 pass from Archer (Luckhurst kick)
StL — Mitchell 1 run (Lee kick)
Atl — FG Luckhurst 42
StL — Green 45 pass from Lomax (kick failed)
Atl — Allen 22 pass from Archer (Luckhurst kick)
Atl — Safety, Gann tackled Lomax in end zone
Atl — Andrews 1 run (Luckhurst kick)

New York Giants 20, San Diego 7—At Giants Stadium, attendance 74,921. Joe Cooper kicked a pair of field goals and the Giants' defense forced seven turnovers en route to the victory. Terry Kinard's first-half fumble recovery set up Joe Morris's one-yard scoring run to give New York a 10-7 halftime lead. Phil Simms's 12-yard touchdown pass to Lionel Manuel, following an interception by Kenny Hill, increased the Giants' lead to 17-7. Cooper's field goals came from 21 and 20 yards. Six of San Diego's second-half possessions ended in turnovers as Hill and Kinard each finished with two interceptions apiece.

San Diego	0	7	0	0	— 7
N.Y. Giants	3	7	0	10	— 20

NYG — FG Cooper 21
NYG — Morris 1 run (Cooper kick)
SD — Anderson 29 pass from Fouts (Benirschke kick)
NYG — Manuel 12 pass from Simms (Cooper kick)
NYG — FG Cooper 20

Los Angeles Rams 16, San Francisco 13—At Anaheim Stadium, attendance 65,195. Mike Lansford's third field goal, an 18-yarder with two seconds left, helped the Rams edge the 49ers. Los Angeles took a 13-3 lead early in the third quarter on two Lansford field goals (24 and 32 yards) and LeRoy Irvin's 65-yard return for a touchdown of a blocked field goal. Lansford's winning kick capped a 12-play, 92-yard drive. San Francisco's Jerry Rice caught six passes for 167 yards, including a 66-yard touchdown from former Rams quarterback Jeff Kemp.

San Francisco	0	3	10	0	— 13
L.A. Rams	3	7	3	3	— 16

Rams — FG Lansford 24
Rams — Irvin 65 blocked field goal return (Lansford kick)
SF — FG Wersching 46
Rams — FG Lansford 32
SF — Rice 66 pass from Kemp (Wersching kick)
SF — FG Wersching 29
Rams — FG Lansford 18

Monday, September 15

Denver 21, Pittsburgh 10—At Three Rivers Stadium, attendance 57,305. John Elway completed 21 of 39 passes for 243 yards and three touchdowns to help the Broncos defeat the Steelers. Elway threw touchdown passes in each of the final three quarters to Steve Watson (21 yards), Steve Sewell (34), and Sammy Winder (13) to account for all of Denver's scoring. Watson's six receptions for 71 yards increased his career total to 305 and moved him ahead of Haven Moses (303) as the third-leading receiver in Broncos history. Safety Steve Foley tied Goose Gonsoulin's club record with his forty-third career interception.

Denver	0	7	7	7	— 21
Pittsburgh	0	0	3	7	— 10

Den — Watson 21 pass from Elway (Karlis kick)
Pitt — FG Anderson 42
Den — Sewell 34 pass from Elway (Karlis kick)
Pitt — Erenberg 7 run (Anderson kick)
Den — Winder 13 pass from Elway (Karlis kick)

Third Week Summaries

Standings

American Football Conference

Eastern Division	W	L	T	Pct.	Pts.	OP
New England	2	1	0	.667	84	47
N.Y. Jets	2	1	0	.667	85	89
Buffalo	1	2	0	.333	74	74
Miami	1	2	0	.333	103	111
Indianapolis	0	3	0	.000	20	87
Central Division						
Cincinnati	2	1	0	.667	80	70
Cleveland	1	2	0	.333	67	91
Houston	1	2	0	.333	64	53
Pittsburgh	0	3	0	.000	17	82
Western Division						
Denver	3	0	0	1.000	92	53
Seattle	3	0	0	1.000	91	48
Kansas City	2	1	0	.667	68	50
San Diego	1	2	0	.333	84	78
L.A. Raiders	0	3	0	.000	51	62

National Football Conference

Eastern Division	W	L	T	Pct.	Pts.	OP
Washington	3	0	0	1.000	81	47
Dallas	2	1	0	.667	97	72
N.Y. Giants	2	1	0	.667	62	47
Philadelphia	0	3	0	.000	31	87
St. Louis	0	3	0	.000	33	66
Central Division						
Chicago	3	0	0	1.000	79	53
Minnesota	2	1	0	.667	64	30
Detroit	1	2	0	.333	40	65
Tampa Bay	1	2	0	.333	41	74
Green Bay	0	3	0	.000	25	80
Western Division						
Atlanta	3	0	0	1.000	101	58
L.A. Rams	3	0	0	1.000	56	30
San Francisco	2	1	0	.667	70	40
New Orleans	1	2	0	.333	51	67

Thursday, September 18

Cincinnati 30, Cleveland 13—At Cleveland Stadium, attendance 78,779. James Brooks and Larry Kinnebrew combined for 212 yards rushing to help the Bengals defeat the Browns. Kinnebrew, who gained 94 yards on 25 carries, upped Cincinnati's 13-10 halftime lead to 27-13 with second-half touchdown runs of two and four yards. Brooks's 118 yards on 14 attempts led all rushers. Jim Breech's pair of field goals (49 and 33 yards) and Kinnebrew's first score completed the Bengals' first-half scoring.

Cincinnati	3	10	7	10	— 30
Cleveland	7	3	3	0	— 13

Cin — FG Breech 49
Clev — Minnifield recovered blocked punt in end zone (Bahr kick)
Cin — Kinnebrew 2 run (Breech kick)
Cin — FG Breech 33
Clev — FG Bahr 19
Clev — FG Bahr 34
Cin — Kinnebrew 2 run (Breech kick)
Cin — Kinnebrew 4 run (Breech kick)
Cin — FG Breech 25

Sunday, September 21

Atlanta 37, Dallas 35—At Texas Stadium, attendance 62,880. Mick Luckhurst's third field goal, an 18-yarder with 20 seconds left in the game, lifted the Falcons over the Cowboys. Atlanta overcame a 35-27 deficit in the final 3:30 as Gerald Riggs scored on a two-yard run and David Archer completed a 65-yard pass to Floyd Dixon to set up Luckhurst's winning kick. Riggs led all rushers with 109 yards on 25 carries. Dallas's Tony Hill paced all receivers with four catches for 104 yards. Luckhurst's other field goals were from 47 and 33 yards.

Atlanta	3	10	14	10	— 37
Dallas	0	21	7	7	— 35

Atl — FG Luckhurst 47
Dall — Chandler 4 pass from D. White (Septien kick)
Atl — FG Luckhurst 33
Atl — Pitts 22 fumble recovery return (Luckhurst kick)
Dall — Newsome 2 run (Septien kick)
Dall — Newsome 2 pass from D. White (Septien kick)
Atl — Whisenhunt 18 pass from Archer (Luckhurst kick)
Atl — Butler 33 interception return (Luckhurst kick)
Dall — Hill 7 pass from D. White (Septien kick)
Dall — Sherrard 22 pass from D. White (Septien kick)
Atl — Riggs 2 run (Luckhurst kick)
Atl — FG Luckhurst 18

Denver 33, Philadelphia 7—At Veterans Stadium, attendance 63,839. Sammy Winder ran for two touchdowns and John Elway passed for another as the Broncos overpowered the Eagles. Mike Harden's 32-yard interception return for a touchdown and Rich Karlis's 30-yard field goal helped Denver to a 12-0 first-quarter lead. Dave Studdard caught a two-yard pass from Elway on a tackle eligible play and Winder ran four yards to add to the Broncos' scoring. Winder gained 104 yards on 20 carries, including touchdown runs of 4 and 17 yards.

Denver	12	14	7	0	— 33
Philadelphia	0	0	7	0	— 7

Den — Safety, Tautalatasi fumbled out of end zone
Den — FG Karlis 30
Den — Harden 32 interception return (Karlis kick)
Den — Studdard 2 pass from Elway (Karlis kick)
Den — Winder 4 run (Karlis kick)
Den — Winder 17 run (Karlis kick)
Phil — K. Jackson 29 pass from Jaworski (McFadden kick)

Kansas City 27, Houston 13—At Arrowhead Stadium, attendance 43,699. Nick Lowery kicked two field goals (47 and 45 yards) and Greg Hill returned an interception 26 yards for a touchdown to lead the Chiefs over the Oilers. Herman Heard's 11-yard scoring run and Hill's touchdown, within the first five minutes of the second half, gave Kansas City a commanding 27-10 lead. Carlos Carson caught three passes for 98 yards, including a 29-yard touchdown from Todd Blackledge. Bill Maas and Art Still each had two of the Chiefs' seven sacks.

Houston	0	0	7	6	— 13
Kansas City	3	10	14	0	— 27

KC — FG Lowery 47
KC — Carson 29 pass from Blackledge (Lowery kick)
KC — FG Lowery 45
KC — Heard 11 run (Lowery kick)
KC — G. Hill 26 interception return (Lowery kick)
Hou — Donaldson fumble recovery in end zone (Zendejas kick)
Hou — Moon 1 run (kick blocked)

Los Angeles Rams 24, Indianapolis 7—At Hoosier Dome, attendance 59,012. Eric Dickerson ran for 121 yards on 25 carries and one touchdown to highlight the Rams' win. Los Angeles followed the Colts' lone touchdown with a pair of one-yard scoring runs by Barry Redden and Dickerson, and Steve Bartkowski's 10-yard touchdown pass to Ron Brown. Gary Jeter and Mike Wilcher each had two of the Rams' seven sacks as Los Angeles's defense held Indianapolis to 55 yards rushing.

L.A. Rams	14	7	0	3	— 24
Indianapolis	7	0	0	0	— 7

Ind — Wonsley 10 run (Biasucci kick)
Rams — Redden 1 run (Lansford kick)
Rams — Brown 10 pass from Bartkowski (Lansford kick)
Rams — Dickerson 1 run (Lansford kick)
Rams — FG Lansford 46

New York Jets 51, Miami 45—At Giants Stadium, attendance 71,025. Wesley Walker set a club record with four touchdown receptions, including a 43-yarder 2:35 into overtime to lift the Jets over the Dolphins. Trailing 45-38 with 1:04 remaining, Ken O'Brien completed a seven-play, 80-yard drive with a 21-yard scoring pass to Walker on the final play in regulation time to tie the score 45-45. Walker finished with six receptions for a career-high 194 yards, including second-quarter touchdown catches of 65 and 50 yards which helped New York to a 31-21 halftime lead. O'Brien completed 29 of 43 passes for 479 yards, while Miami's Dan Marino connected on 30 of 50 for 448 yards, including a team-record six touchdowns. The combined 884 total yards of both teams bettered the NFL record (883) set by San Diego and Denver on December 20, 1982.

Miami	7	14	17	7	0	— 45
N.Y. Jets	3	28	0	14	6	— 51

NYJ — FG Leahy 32
Mia — Pruitt 6 pass from Marino (Reveiz kick)
NYJ — Hector 1 run (Leahy kick)
NYJ — Hector 8 run (Leahy kick)
Mia — Johnson 1 pass from Marino (Reveiz kick)
Mia — Duper 13 pass from Marino (Reveiz kick)
NYJ — Walker 65 pass from O'Brien (Leahy kick)
NYJ — Walker 50 pass from O'Brien (Leahy kick)
Mia — Duper 46 pass from Marino (Reveiz kick)
Mia — FG Reveiz 44
Mia — Hardy 1 pass from Marino (Reveiz kick)
NYJ — Bligen 7 run (Leahy kick)
Mia — Clayton 4 pass from Marino (Reveiz kick)
NYJ — Walker 21 pass from O'Brien (Leahy kick)
NYJ — Walker 43 pass from O'Brien (no kick)

San Francisco 26, New Orleans 17—At Candlestick Park, attendance 58,927. Ray Wersching kicked four field goals to lead the 49ers past the Saints. Wersching's field goals of 30 and 40 yards and Jeff Kemp's four-yard scoring pass to Dwight Clark gave San Francisco a 13-10 halftime edge. Kemp completed a personal-best 29 of 44 passes for 332 of the 49ers' 461 total yards, while the defense held the Saints to 229. Clark and Jerry Rice each had seven receptions for 100 and 120 yards, respectively. Wersching added field goals of 28 and 32 yards to finish the 49ers' scoring.

New Orleans	3	7	7	0	— 17
San Francisco	10	3	7	6	— 26

SF — FG Wersching 30
SF — Clark 4 pass from Kemp (Wersching kick)
NO — FG Andersen 44
NO — Goodlow 29 pass from Hilliard (Andersen kick)
SF — FG Wersching 40
NO — Gray 101 kickoff return (Andersen kick)
SF — Harmon 5 run (Wersching kick)
SF — FG Wersching 28
SF — FG Wersching 32

New York Giants 14, Los Angeles Raiders 9—At Memorial Coliseum, attendance 71,164. Phil Simms completed a pair of second-half touchdown passes to Lionel Manuel to help the Giants defeat the winless Raiders. Simms's scoring passes of 18 and 11 yards to Manuel brought New York back from a 6-0 halftime deficit. Simms completed 18 of 30 passes for 239 yards. Mark Bavaro and Manuel paced all receivers with six catches for 106 and 81 yards, respectively. Joe Morris rushed for 110 yards to become the first player to gain 100 yards rushing against the Raiders since the Steelers' Walter Abercrombie ran for 111 on December 16, 1984.

N.Y. Giants	0	0	7	7	— 14
L.A. Raiders	6	0	0	3	— 9

Raiders — FG Bahr 22
Raiders — FG Bahr 25
NYG — Manuel 18 pass from Simms (Cooper kick)
NYG — Manuel 11 pass from Simms (Cooper kick)
Raiders — FG Bahr 33

Minnesota 31, Pittsburgh 7—At Metrodome, attendance 56,795. Tommy Kramer completed 19 of 27 passes for 257 yards and three touchdowns to lead the Vikings to victory. Kramer's scoring passes of 55 and 16 yards to Hassan Jones helped Minnesota to a 14-7 first-quarter lead. The Vikings capitalized on three interceptions to set up Chuck Nelson's 48-yard field goal, Allen Rice's 12-yard run, and Kramer's 9-yard pass to Jim Gustafson. Jones had six catches for 140 of the Vikings' 412 total yards.

Pittsburgh	7	0	0	0	— 7
Minnesota	14	3	7	7	— 31

Minn — Jones 55 pass from Kramer (C. Nelson kick)
Pitt — Abercrombie 18 pass from Malone (Anderson kick)
Minn — Jones 16 pass from Kramer (C. Nelson kick)
Minn — FG C. Nelson 48
Minn — Rice 12 run (C. Nelson kick)
Minn — Gustafson 9 pass from Kramer (C. Nelson kick)

Buffalo 17, St. Louis 10—At Rich Stadium, attendance 65,762. The Bills won their first game of the season as Greg Bell and Booker Moore ran for touchdowns and Scott Norwood kicked a field goal. Buffalo took a 10-0 halftime lead as Norwood connected on a 35-yard field goal and Moore ran two yards for a score after Guy Frazier recovered Neil Lomax's fumble at the St. Louis 26-yard line. Bell's six-yard touchdown run early in the fourth quarter capped a nine-play, 72-yard drive.

St. Louis	0	0	3	7	— 10
Buffalo	0	10	0	7	— 17

Buff — FG Norwood 35
Buff — Moore 2 run (Norwood kick)
StL — FG Lee 27
Buff — Bell 6 run (Norwood kick)
StL — Sikahema 19 pass from Lomax (Lee kick)

Seattle 38, New England 31—At Sullivan Stadium, attendance 58,977. Dave Krieg completed a 67-yard touchdown pass to Ray Butler with 1:14 left in the game to rally the Seahawks to a 38-31 win. Seattle erased a 31-21 deficit within a 41-second span of the fourth quarter when Norm Johnson kicked a 33-yard field goal and Paul Moyer recovered a blocked punt in the end zone. Butler, who finished with three catches for 128 yards, also caught a 54-yard scoring pass. New England's Tony Eason completed 26 of 45 passes for a club-record 414 yards. Stanley Morgan caught seven passes for 161 yards and had touchdown receptions of 27, 44, and 30 yards for the Patriots.

Seattle	7	0	7	24	— 38
New England	7	10	0	14	— 31

Sea — Warner 13 run (Johnson kick)
NE — Collins 6 run (Franklin kick)
NE — FG Franklin 26
NE — Morgan 27 pass from Eason (Franklin kick)
Sea — R. Butler 54 pass from Krieg (Johnson kick)
NE — Morgan 44 pass from Eason (Franklin kick)
Sea — Warner 1 run (Johnson kick)
NE — Morgan 30 pass from Eason (Franklin kick)
Sea — FG Johnson 33
Sea — Moyer recovered blocked punt in end zone (Johnson kick)
Sea — R. Butler 67 pass from Krieg (Johnson kick)

Tampa Bay 24, Detroit 20—At Pontiac Silverdome, attendance 38,453. Rookie running back Nathan Wonsley ran for 138 yards and two touchdowns to help the Buccaneers snap a 19-game road losing streak. Tampa Bay scored first on runs of 22 and 9 yards by Wonsley and quarterback Steve Young, respectively, and never trailed. Wonsley, replacing an injured James Wilder, closed Tampa Bay's scoring with a 55-yard run. The Buccaneers outrushed the Lions 229 to 93. Linebacker-defensive end Chris Washington had a sack and an interception to lead Tampa Bay's defense.

Tampa Bay	0	14	10	0	— 24
Detroit	0	3	3	14	— 20

TB — Wonsley 22 run (Igwebuike kick)
TB — Young 9 run (Igwebuike kick)
Det — FG Murray 41
TB — FG Igwebuike 33
Det — FG Murray 51
TB — Wonsley 55 run (Igwebuike kick)
Det — Jones 1 run (Murray kick)
Det — Jones 2 run (Murray kick)

Washington 30, San Diego 27—At San Diego Jack Murphy Stadium, attendance 57,853. Jay Schroeder completed 16 of 36 passes for 341 yards, including a game-winning 14-yard touchdown to Gary Clark with 1:16 left as the Redskins remained undefeated. Trailing 21-10 at halftime, Washington rallied on a pair of Mark Moseley field goals (24 and 26 yards) and George Rogers's 10-yard touchdown run. The Redskins' defense limited the Chargers to two field goals in the second half. Clark finished with six catches for 144 yards, while teammate Art Monk led all receivers with seven for 174.

Washington	3	7	13	7	— 30
San Diego	14	7	3	3	— 27

Wash — FG Moseley 29
SD — Anderson 13 pass from Fouts (Benirschke kick)
SD — McGee 1 run (Benirschke kick)
SD — McGee 1 run (Benirschke kick)
Wash — Rogers 2 run (Moseley kick)
Wash — FG Moseley 24
Wash — FG Moseley 26
SD — FG Benirschke 50
Wash — Rogers 10 run (Moseley kick)
SD — FG Benirschke 31
Wash — Clark 14 pass from Schroeder (Moseley kick)

Monday, September 22

Chicago 25, Green Bay 12—At Lambeau Field, attendance 55,527. Kevin Butler kicked three field goals and Steve Fuller came off the bench to pass for a touchdown to lead the Bears over the Packers. Chicago erased a 12-10 fourth-quarter deficit on Butler field goals of 52 and 27 yards, Fuller's 42-yard scoring pass to Keith Ortego, and a safety by defensive tackle Steve McMichael. McMichael and Richard Dent each had a pair of sacks to lead the Bears' defense.

Chicago	3	7	0	15	— 25
Green Bay	3	6	3	0	— 12

GB — FG Del Greco 22
Chi — FG Butler 34
Chi — Payton 2 run (Butler kick)
GB — FG Del Greco 46
GB — FG Del Greco 45
GB — FG Del Greco 50
Chi — FG Butler 52
Chi — Safety, McMichael tackled Wright in end zone
Chi — Ortego 42 pass from Fuller (Butler kick)
Chi — FG Butler 27

Fourth Week Summaries

Standings

American Football Conference

Eastern Division	W	L	T	Pct.	Pts.	OP
N.Y. Jets	3	1	0	.750	111	96
New England	2	2	0	.500	104	74
Buffalo	1	3	0	.250	91	94
Miami	1	3	0	.250	119	142
Indianapolis	0	4	0	.000	27	113
Central Division						
Cincinnati	2	2	0	.500	87	114
Cleveland	2	2	0	.500	91	112
Houston	1	3	0	.250	80	75
Pittsburgh	1	3	0	.250	39	98
Western Division						
Denver	4	0	0	1.000	119	73
Kansas City	3	1	0	.750	88	67
Seattle	3	1	0	.750	105	67
L.A. Raiders	1	3	0	.250	68	75
San Diego	1	3	0	.250	97	95

National Football Conference

Eastern Division	W	L	T	Pct.	Pts.	OP
Washington	4	0	0	1.000	100	61
Dallas	3	1	0	.750	128	79
N.Y. Giants	3	1	0	.750	82	64
Philadelphia	1	3	0	.250	65	107
St. Louis	0	4	0	.000	40	97
Central Division						
Chicago	4	0	0	1.000	123	60
Minnesota	3	1	0	.750	106	37
Detroit	1	3	0	.250	61	89
Tampa Bay	1	3	0	.250	61	97
Green Bay	0	4	0	.000	32	122
Western Division						
Atlanta	4	0	0	1.000	124	78
L.A. Rams	3	1	0	.750	76	64
San Francisco	3	1	0	.750	101	56
New Orleans	1	3	0	.250	68	87

Sunday, September 28

Atlanta 23, Tampa Bay 20—At Tampa Stadium, attendance 38,950. Mick Luckhurst's 34-yard field goal with 2:25 remaining in overtime helped the undefeated Falcons down the Buccaneers. Tampa Bay, which trailed 20-7 at halftime, closed the advantage to 20-17 on Gerald Riggs's one-yard touchdown run and Luckhurst's 43-yard field goal. Following an interception by Wendell Cason, Luckhurst kicked a 34-yard field goal with one second left in the game to force the overtime period. Riggs carried 27 times for 129 yards and Charlie Brown caught seven passes for 110 yards. The Falcons outgained the Buccaneers 490 to 322 total yards, including 300 to 67 in the second half.

Atlanta	7	0	7	6	3	— 23
Tampa Bay	3	17	0	0	0	— 20

TB — FG Igwebuike 26
Atl — Dixon 27 pass from Archer (Luckhurst kick)
TB — FG Igwebuike 24
TB — Magee 11 pass from Young (Igwebuike kick)
TB — Young 21 run (Igwebuike kick)
Atl — Riggs 1 run (Luckhurst kick)
Atl — FG Luckhurst 43
Atl — FG Luckhurst 34
Atl — FG Luckhurst 34

Chicago 44, Cincinnati 7—At Riverfront Stadium, attendance 55,146. Jim McMahon passed for three touchdowns and ran for another to power the Bears past the Bengals. Chicago took a commanding 24-7 halftime lead on McMahon's one-yard scoring run and touchdown passes to Walter Payton (two yards) and Willie Gault (53), and Kevin Butler's 41-yard field goal. Thomas Sanders added touchdown runs of 1 and 75 yards and McMahon threw a 20-yarder to Emery Moorehead to complete the Bears' scoring. Gault had his best day in the NFL, catching seven passes for 174 of Chicago's 476 total yards. The Chicago defense, which limited Cincinnati to 338 total yards, had four sacks and six interceptions.

Chicago	21	3	14	6	— 44
Cincinnati	0	7	0	0	— 7

Chi — McMahon 1 run (Butler kick)
Chi — Payton 2 pass from McMahon (Butler kick)
Chi — Gault 53 pass from McMahon (Butler kick)
Cin — Brooks 5 pass from Esiason (Breech kick)
Chi — FG Butler 41
Chi — Moorehead 20 pass from McMahon (Butler kick)
Chi — Sanders 1 run (Butler kick)
Chi — Sanders 75 run (kick failed)

Cleveland 24, Detroit 21—At Cleveland Stadium, attendance 72,029. Gerald McNeil returned a punt 84 yards for a touchdown and set up another score with a 34-yard return to lead the Browns past the Lions. McNeil's third-quarter touchdown return broke a 7-7 tie. After Chris Bahr kicked a 24-yard field goal, McNeil's second long return of the game set up Curtis Dickey's decisive one-yard score. Eric Hipple completed 33 of 48 passes for 251 yards and three touchdowns for the Lions.

Detroit	0	7	0	14	— 21
Cleveland	0	7	7	10	— 24

Clev — Brennan recovered fumble in end zone (Bahr kick)
Det — Thompson 3 pass from Hipple (Murray kick)
Clev — McNeil 84 punt return (Bahr kick)
Det — Jones 6 pass from Hipple (Murray kick)
Clev — FG Bahr 24
Clev — Dickey 1 run (Bahr kick)
Det — Bland 3 pass from Hipple (Murray kick)

Minnesota 42, Green Bay 7—At Metrodome, attendance 60,478. Tommy Kramer completed 16 of 25 passes for 241 yards and a career-high six touchdowns as the Vikings rolled over the Packers. Kramer fired a pair of touchdowns to both Steve Jordan (23 and 2 yards) and Hassan Jones (36 and 17), and a 13-yarder to Darrin Nelson to put the game away in the first half. Kramer's final scoring pass traveled seven yards to Mike Mularkey in the third quarter. Jordan and Jones each finished with six catches for 112 and 106 yards, respectively.

Green Bay	0	7	0	0	— 7
Minnesota	28	7	7	0	— 42

Minn — Jordan 23 pass from Kramer (C. Nelson kick)
Minn — D. Nelson 13 pass from Kramer (C. Nelson kick)
Minn — Jones 36 pass from Kramer (C. Nelson kick)
Minn — Jordan 2 pass from Kramer (C. Nelson kick)
GB — M. Lewis 4 pass from Ferragamo (Del Greco kick)
Minn — Jones 17 pass from Kramer (C. Nelson kick)
Minn — Mularkey 7 pass from Kramer (C. Nelson kick)

Kansas City 20, Buffalo 17—At Rich Stadium, attendance 67,555. Todd Blackledge threw two touchdown passes and Nick Lowery kicked a 46-yard field goal with 1:07 left to lead the Chiefs' 20-17 comeback win. Blackledge's one-yard touchdown pass to Paul Coffman midway through the final quarter completed a 13-play, 72-yard drive which tied the score, 17-17. Lowery's decisive kick followed an interception by safety Deron Cherry. Rookie linebacker Dino Hackett led the defense with one sack and an interception, which set up Blackledge's 26-yard scoring pass to Stephone Paige in the second quarter.

Kansas City	3	7	0	10	— 20
Buffalo	7	0	7	3	— 17

Buff — Riddick 41 run (Norwood kick)
KC — FG Lowery 24
KC — Paige 26 pass from Blackledge (Lowery kick)
Buff — Harmon 14 pass from Kelly (Norwood kick)
Buff — FG Norwood 32
KC — Coffman 1 pass from Blackledge (Lowery kick)
KC — FG Lowery 46

Philadelphia 34, Los Angeles Rams 20—At Veterans Stadium, attendance 65,646. Ron Jaworski passed for three touchdowns and Paul McFadden added two field goals as the Eagles handed the Rams their first loss of the season. Philadelphia dominated the first half as McFadden converted field goals of 22 and 41 yards and Jaworski completed scoring passes to John Spagnola (15 yards) and Kenny Jackson (27). Rookie running back Keith Byars threw a 55-yard touchdown pass to Mike Quick to give the Eagles a 27-6 halftime edge. Jaworski connected on 17 of 27 passes for 213 yards, including a 16-yard touchdown to Junior Tautalatasi in the third quarter to give the Eagles an insurmountable 34-6 lead.

L.A. Rams	0	0	6	14	— 20
Philadelphia	10	17	7	0	— 34

Phil — FG McFadden 22
Phil — Spagnola 15 pass from Jaworski (McFadden kick)
Phil — Quick 55 pass from Byars (McFadden kick)
Phil — FG McFadden 41
Phil — Jackson 27 pass from Jaworski (McFadden kick)
Phil — Tautalatasi 16 pass from Jaworski (McFadden kick)
Rams — Brown 15 pass from Dils (kick failed)
Rams — Duckworth 28 pass from Dils (Lansford kick)
Rams — Young 5 pass from Dils (Lansford kick)

Denver 27, New England 20—At Mile High Stadium, attendance 75,804. Sammy Winder and Gerald Willhite each ran for a touchdown to rally the Broncos over the Patriots. Trailing 13-3 at halftime, Denver scored 24 unanswered points on John Elway's one-yard pass to Clarence Kay, Winder's 12-yard run, Willhite's one-yard blast, and Rich Karlis's 34-yard field goal. Linebacker Karl Mecklenburg had two sacks to lead the Broncos' defense, which held the Patriots to 38 total yards in the second half.

New England	0	13	0	7	— 20
Denver	3	0	14	10	— 27

Den — FG Karlis 44
NE — FG Franklin 34
NE — Morgan 5 pass from Eason (Franklin kick)
NE — FG Franklin 37
Den — Kay 1 pass from Elway (Karlis kick)
Den — Winder 12 run (Karlis kick)
Den — Willhite 1 run (Karlis kick)
Den — FG Karlis 34
NE — Fryar 10 pass from Eason (Franklin kick)

New York Giants 20, New Orleans 17—At Louisiana Superdome, attendance 72,765. Phil Simms completed 24 of 41 passes for 286 yards and two touchdowns to highlight the Giants' come-from-behind win. New York cut a 17-0 second-quarter deficit to 17-10 at the half on Simms's 19-yard scoring pass to Mark Bavaro and Raul Allegre's 29-yard field goal. Simms completed a four-yard pass to Zeke Mowatt for the go-ahead score midway through the final period. Bavaro had seven catches for 110 yards to lead all receivers. New York outgained New Orleans 388 to 196 total yards, while maintaining a time-of-possession advantage of 38:47 to 21:13.

New Orleans	14	3	0	0	— 17
N.Y. Giants	0	10	3	7	— 20

NO — Martin 63 pass from Wilson (Andersen kick)
NO — Hilliard 1 run (Andersen kick)
NO — FG Andersen 27
NYG — FG Allegre 29
NYG — Bavaro 19 pass from Simms (Allegre kick)
NYG — FG Allegre 28
NYG — Mowatt 4 pass from Simms (Allegre kick)

New York Jets 26, Indianapolis 7—At Hoosier Dome, attendance 56,075. Pat Leahy converted all four of his field-goal attempts and Tony Paige ran for one touchdown to lead the Jets over the Colts. Leahy's field goals of 34 and 48 yards and Paige's three-yard scoring run gave New York a 13-0 halftime lead. Ken O'Brien completed a 17-yard touchdown pass to Kurt Sohn and Leahy added field goals of 47 and 24 yards to account for the Jets' second-half scoring. The Colts avoided a shutout when rookie quarterback Jack Trudeau threw a three-yard scoring pass to Bill Brooks with 14 seconds left.

N.Y. Jets	3	10	0	13	— 26
Indianapolis	0	0	0	7	— 7

NYJ — FG Leahy 34
NYJ — Paige 3 run (Leahy kick)
NYJ — FG Leahy 48
NYJ — FG Leahy 47
NYJ — Sohn 17 pass from O'Brien (Leahy kick)
NYJ — FG Leahy 24
Ind — Brooks 3 pass from Trudeau (Biasucci kick)

Pittsburgh 22, Houston 16—At Astrodome, attendance 42,001. Walter Abercrombie's three-yard touchdown run 2:35 into overtime lifted the Steelers over the Oilers. Pittsburgh rebounded from a 10-3 halftime deficit on Mark Malone's 19-yard scoring pass to Calvin Sweeney and a pair of Gary Anderson field goals (45 and 28 yards) to take a 13-10 third-quarter lead. Houston's Tony Zendejas kicked a 23-yard field goal to force the extra period. Abercrombie's decisive score was set up by Rick Woods's 41-yard punt return. Edmund Nelson had three sacks to pace the Steelers' defense.

Pittsburgh	0	3	10	3	6	— 22
Houston	3	7	0	6	0	— 16

Hou — FG Zendejas 45
Pitt — FG Anderson 42
Hou — Givins 35 pass from Moon (Zendejas kick)
Pitt — Sweeney 19 pass from Malone (Anderson kick)
Pitt — FG Anderson 45
Hou — FG Zendejas 29
Pitt — FG Anderson 28
Hou — FG Zendejas 23
Pitt — Abercrombie 3 run (no kick)

Los Angeles Raiders 17, San Diego 13—At Memorial Coliseum, attendance 63,153. Marc Wilson completed 19 of 28 passes for 314 yards and two touchdowns to help the Raiders register their first win of the season. Los Angeles overcame a 13-7 halftime deficit on Wilson's 40-yard scoring pass to Jessie Hester. Dokie Williams caught eight passes for 143 yards, including a 12-yard touchdown from Wilson. Todd Christensen recorded his tenth 100-yard receiving game with eight receptions for 105 yards. The defeat was the Chargers' eighth straight on the road.

San Diego	6	7	0	0	— 13
L.A. Raiders	0	7	7	3	— 17

SD — Winslow 9 pass from Fouts (kick failed)
SD — Johnson 9 pass from Fouts (Benirschke kick)
Raiders — Williams 12 pass from Wilson (Bahr kick)
Raiders — Hester 40 pass from Wilson (Bahr kick)
Raiders — FG Bahr 18

San Francisco 31, Miami 16—At Orange Bowl, attendance 70,264. Jeff Kemp passed for two touchdowns and the 49ers' defense intercepted four passes to defeat the Dolphins. Kemp threw touchdown passes of 18 and 50 yards to Jerry Rice to help San Francisco take a 17-9 halftime lead. Roger Craig scored on a five-yard run and Tom Holmoe ran 66 yards for a touchdown after taking a lateral from Ronnie Lott (on an interception) to complete San Francisco's scoring. Lott had two interceptions and Dwaine Board a pair of sacks to lead the defense.

San Francisco	7	10	0	14	— 31
Miami	0	9	0	7	— 16

SF — Rice 18 pass from Kemp (Wersching kick)
SF — FG Wersching 36
Mia — FG Reveiz 34
Mia — Clayton 14 pass from Marino (kick failed)
SF — Rice 50 pass from Kemp (Wersching kick)
SF — Craig 5 run (Wersching kick)
SF — Holmoe 66 interception return after lateral from Lott (Wersching kick)
Mia — Moore 9 pass from Strock (Reveiz kick)

Washington 19, Seattle 14—At Robert F. Kennedy Stadium, attendance 54,157. George Rogers ran for 115 yards and two touchdowns to help the Redskins squeak past the Seahawks. Washington took a 9-7 first-half lead on Rogers's 24-yard scoring run and Steve Cox's club-record 57-yard field goal. Rogers added a seven-yard touchdown run and Mark Moseley kicked a 36-yard field goal to complete the Redskins' scoring. Art Monk had five receptions for 103 yards. Seattle's Curt Warner carried 16 times for 106 yards and a touchdown.

Seattle	7	0	0	7	— 14
Washington	6	3	7	3	— 19

Sea — Warner 2 run (Johnson kick)
Wash — Rogers 24 run (kick blocked)
Wash — FG Cox 57
Wash — Rogers 7 run (Moseley kick)
Wash — FG Moseley 36
Sea — Largent 11 pass from Krieg (Johnson kick)

Monday, September 29

Dallas 31, St. Louis 7—At Busch Memorial Stadium, attendance 49,077. Danny White passed for three touchdowns and Ron Fellows returned an interception 34 yards for another score as the Cowboys rolled over the Cardinals. Dallas opened a 10-0 first-half lead on White's 39-yard scoring pass to Mike Sherrard and Rafael Septien's 32-yard field goal. White's other touchdown passes were to Tony Hill (13 yards) and Herschel Walker (8). The Cowboys had four interceptions, including Fellows's return for a touchdown.

Dallas	7	3	7	14	— 31
St. Louis	0	0	7	0	— 7

Dall — Sherrard 39 pass from D. White (Septien kick)
Dall — FG Septien 32
StL — Anderson 10 run (Lee kick)
Dall — Hill 13 pass from D. White (Septien kick)
Dall — Walker 8 pass from D. White (Septien kick)
Dall — Fellows 34 interception return (Septien kick)

Fifth Week Summaries

Standings

American Football Conference

Eastern Division	W	L	T	Pct.	Pts.	OP
N.Y. Jets	4	1	0	.800	125	109
New England	3	2	0	.600	138	81
Buffalo	1	4	0	.200	104	108
Miami	1	4	0	.200	126	176
Indianapolis	0	5	0	.000	41	148
Central Division						
Cincinnati	3	2	0	.600	121	142
Cleveland	3	2	0	.600	118	136
Houston	1	4	0	.200	93	99
Pittsburgh	1	4	0	.200	63	125
Western Division						
Denver	5	0	0	1.000	148	87
Seattle	4	1	0	.800	138	74
Kansas City	3	2	0	.600	105	91
L.A. Raiders	2	3	0	.400	92	92
San Diego	1	4	0	.200	104	128

National Football Conference

Eastern Division	W	L	T	Pct.	Pts.	OP
Washington	5	0	0	1.000	114	67
N.Y. Giants	4	1	0	.800	95	70
Dallas	3	2	0	.600	142	108
Philadelphia	2	3	0	.400	81	107
St. Louis	0	5	0	.000	46	110
Central Division						
Chicago	5	0	0	1.000	146	60
Minnesota	3	2	0	.600	106	60
Detroit	2	3	0	.400	85	102
Tampa Bay	1	4	0	.200	81	123
Green Bay	0	5	0	.000	60	156
Western Division						
Atlanta	4	1	0	.800	124	94
L.A. Rams	4	1	0	.800	102	84
San Francisco	4	1	0	.800	136	70
New Orleans	1	4	0	.200	74	101

Sunday, October 5

New York Jets 14, Buffalo 13—At Giants Stadium, attendance 69,504. Ken O'Brien's 36-yard touchdown pass to Mickey Shuler with 57 seconds left in the game helped the Jets squeak past the Bills. O'Brien, who tied Joe Namath's club record with 15 straight completions, opened New York's scoring with a four-yard toss to Al Toon late in the second quarter. His winning completion to Shuler capped a five-play, 80-yard drive. Johnny Hector became the first Jets player to gain 100 yards rushing and receiving in the same game with 117 (on 18 attempts) and 100 (on 9 catches), respectively.

Buffalo	0	7	3	3	— 13
N.Y. Jets	0	7	0	7	— 14

NYJ — Toon 4 pass from O'Brien (Leahy kick)
Buff — Bell 40 pass from Kelly (Norwood kick)
Buff — FG Norwood 23
Buff — FG Norwood 32
NYJ — Shuler 36 pass from O'Brien (Leahy kick)

Cincinnati 34, Green Bay 28—At Milwaukee County Stadium, attendance 51,230. Boomer Esiason completed 15 of 24 passes for 207 yards and three touchdowns to guide the Bengals over the winless Packers. Cincinnati erupted for 27 points in the second quarter on a pair of touchdowns by James Brooks and two Esiason scoring passes to Cris Collinsworth (13 and 7 yards). Brooks led all rushers with 94 yards on 20 carries. Green Bay's James Lofton caught seven passes (for 109 yards) to give him 489 career catches, breaking Don Hutson's club record of 488.

Cincinnati	0	27	0	7	— 34
Green Bay	7	0	7	14	— 28

GB — Ellerson 2 run (Del Greco kick)
Cin — Collinsworth 13 pass from Esiason (Breech kick)
Cin — Brooks 9 run (kick failed)
Cin — Brooks 8 run (Breech kick)
Cin — Collinsworth 7 pass from Esiason (Breech kick)
GB — Carruth 3 pass from Wright (Del Greco kick)
Cin — Brown 15 pass from Esiason (Breech kick)
GB — Lofton 15 pass from Wright (Del Greco kick)
GB — Ellerson 1 run (Del Greco kick)

Cleveland 27, Pittsburgh 24—At Three Rivers Stadium, attendance 57,327. Gerald McNeil returned a kickoff 100 yards for a touchdown and Matt Bahr kicked a pair of field goals to lead the Browns to their first win ever in Pittsburgh's Three Rivers Stadium. McNeil's kickoff return, the first by a Cleveland player since 1974, helped the Browns take a 17-14 halftime advantage. Following Pittsburgh's 10-point rally, Chris Rockins recovered a Mark Malone fumble, which set up Earnest Byner's four-yard touchdown run and gave the Browns the lead for good. Reggie Langhorne had four catches for 108 yards in his first 100-yard receiving performance. The win was Cleveland's first in 18 trips to Three Rivers Stadium.

Cleveland	10	7	3	7	— 27
Pittsburgh	0	14	7	3	— 24

Clev — Slaughter 15 pass from Kosar (Bahr kick)
Clev — FG Bahr 22
Pitt — Malone 1 run (Anderson kick)
Pitt — Erenberg 5 pass from Malone (Anderson kick)
Clev — McNeil 100 kickoff return (Bahr kick)
Pitt — Lipps 6 pass from Malone (Anderson kick)
Clev — FG Bahr 39
Pitt — FG Anderson 45
Clev — Byner 4 run (Bahr kick)

Denver 29, Dallas 14—At Mile High Stadium, attendance 76,082. Rulon Jones and Louis Wright led a tenacious Broncos defense that limited the Cowboys to 41 rushing yards en route to victory. Denver struck first on John Elway's nine-yard touchdown pass to Gerald Willhite following a Wright interception. Jones then added a safety when he tackled Cowboys quarterback Steve Pelluer in the end zone. Pelluer was making his first NFL start in place of an injured Danny White. Willhite capped the Broncos' 22-point second-quarter explosion with a one-yard touchdown run and a 15-yard scoring catch from Elway. Jones had two of Denver's five sacks and Wright finished with two of its three interceptions.

Dallas	0	0	7	7	— 14
Denver	0	22	0	7	— 29

Den — Willhite 9 pass from Elway (Karlis kick)
Den — Safety, Jones tackled Pelluer in end zone
Den — Willhite 1 run (Karlis kick)
Den — Willhite 15 pass from Elway (kick failed)
Dall — Walker 3 run (Septien kick)
Den — Lang 12 pass from Elway (Karlis kick)
Dall — Newsome 4 pass from Pelluer (Septien kick)

Detroit 24, Houston 13—At Pontiac Silverdome, attendance 41,960. James Jones ran for two touchdowns and Eric Hipple passed for another to help the Lions down the Oilers. Detroit opened a 21-13 halftime lead on a pair of one-yard scoring runs by Jones and Hipple's fiftieth career touchdown pass, an 18-yarder to Herman Hunter. Houston's Warren Moon, who completed 21 of 38 passes for a career-high 398 yards and a touchdown, was intercepted by the Detroit defense three times. The victory ended the Lions' four-game home losing streak.

Houston	3	10	0	0	— 13
Detroit	0	21	0	3	— 24

Hou — FG Zendejas 25
Det — Jones 1 run (Murray kick)
Det — Jones 1 run (Murray kick)
Hou — Hill 81 pass from Moon (Zendejas kick)
Det — Hunter 18 pass from Hipple (Murray kick)
Hou — FG Zendejas 19
Det — FG Murray 48

San Francisco 35, Indianapolis 14—At Candlestick Park, attendance 57,252. Jeff Kemp threw three second-half touchdown passes to Jerry Rice as the 49ers rolled over the Colts to maintain a share of first place in the NFC West. San Francisco broke open a 14-14 halftime tie with Kemp scoring completions of 45, 16, and 58 yards to Rice. San Francisco capitalized on three of Indianapolis's five turnovers (two fumbles and three interceptions) to set up three touchdowns. Rookie cornerback Tim McKyer returned an interception 21 yards for his first NFL score. Kemp connected on 18 of 27 passes for 274 yards, including six to Rice for 172 yards.

Indianapolis	0	14	0	0	— 14
San Francisco	7	7	14	7	— 35

SF — McKyer 21 interception return (Wersching kick)
Ind — Gill 1 run (Biasucci kick)
Ind — Brooks 84 pass from Trudeau (Biasucci kick)
SF — Cribbs 9 run (Wersching kick)
SF — Rice 45 pass from Kemp (Wersching kick)
SF — Rice 16 pass from Kemp (Wersching kick)
SF — Rice 58 pass from Kemp (Wersching kick)

Los Angeles Raiders 24, Kansas City 17—At Arrowhead Stadium, attendance 74,430. Jim Plunkett came off the bench to lead the Raiders to a come-from-behind victory over the Chiefs. Trailing 17-14 in the third quarter, Plunkett fired an 18-yard scoring pass to Jessie Hester to give Los Angeles its first lead of the game, 21-17. Chris Bahr added a 19-yard field goal to secure the win. Dokie Williams led all receivers with six catches for 90 yards, including a 12-yard touchdown in the second period from Marc Wilson. Rod Martin, who had two sacks, led a fierce Raiders defense that limited the Chiefs to 60 total yards and only three first downs in the second half.

L.A. Raiders	0	7	14	3	— 24
Kansas City	10	7	0	0	— 17

KC — FG Lowery 24
KC — Green 18 run (Lowery kick)
KC — Coffman 1 pass from Blackledge (Lowery kick)
Raiders — Williams 12 pass from Wilson (Bahr kick)
Raiders — McCallum 12 run (Bahr kick)
Raiders — Hester 18 pass from Plunkett (Bahr kick)
Raiders — FG Bahr 19

New England 34, Miami 7—At Sullivan Stadium, attendance 60,689. Tony Eason threw two touchdown passes and Ronnie Lippett made two interceptions as the Patriots easily beat the Dolphins, 34-7. New England took a 27-0 halftime lead by scoring on four of its first six possessions. Tony Franklin kicked a 31-yard field goal, Craig James scored on a seven-yard run, and Eason completed scoring passes to Willie Scott (2 yards) and Irving Fryar (38). Steve Grogan, who replaced Eason in the second quarter (bruised ribs), fired a 27-yard pass to Stanley Morgan in the final period to close out the Patriots' scoring. Morgan finished with six catches for 125 yards, his fourth 100-yard game of the season.

Miami	0	0	0	7	— 7
New England	10	17	0	7	— 34

NE — FG Franklin 31
NE — Scott 2 pass from Eason (Franklin kick)
NE — James 7 run (Franklin kick)
NE — Fryar 38 pass from Eason (Franklin kick)
NE — FG Franklin 21
NE — Morgan 27 pass from Grogan (Franklin kick)
Mia — Hampton 4 pass from Marino (Reveiz kick)

Chicago 23, Minnesota 0—At Soldier Field, attendance 63,921. Walter Payton rushed for one touchdown and Kevin Butler kicked three field goals as the Bears shut out the Vikings. Payton, who registered his seventy-sixth career 100-yard rushing game with 108 yards on 26 carries, opened Chicago's scoring with a two-yard run in the second quarter. Keith Ortego caught six passes for 157 yards, including a 58-yard score from Jim McMahon. Steve McMichael paced the defense with two-and-a-half of the Bears' seven sacks. Chicago outgained Minnesota 370 total yards to 159.

Minnesota	0	0	0	0	— 0
Chicago	0	10	3	10	— 23

Chi — Payton 2 run (Butler kick)
Chi — FG Butler 24
Chi — FG Butler 42
Chi — Ortego 58 pass from McMahon (Butler kick)
Chi — FG Butler 32

New York Giants 13, St. Louis 6—At Busch Memorial Stadium, attendance 40,562. Carl Banks, Leonard Marshall, and Lawrence Taylor led an aggressive Giants defense and Raul Allegre kicked a pair of field goals to help the Giants defeat the Cardinals. Allegre (field goals of 31 and 44 yards) and Joe Morris (one-yard run) gave the Giants all the points they needed to win. The Cardinals maintained a 36:45 to 23:15 time-of-possession advantage, but were limited to two field goals by rookie John Lee (from 31 and 47 yards). Banks, Marshall, and Taylor each recorded a pair of sacks for New York.

N.Y. Giants	0	6	7	0	— 13
St. Louis	3	0	3	0	— 6

StL — FG Lee 31
NYG — FG Allegre 44
NYG — FG Allegre 31
NYG — Morris 1 run (Allegre kick)
StL — FG Lee 47

Philadelphia 16, Atlanta 0—At Atlanta-Fulton County Stadium, attendance 57,104. Ron Jaworski passed for one touchdown and Paul McFadden added three field goals (31, 33, and 21 yards) as the Eagles knocked the Falcons from the unbeaten ranks. Jaworski completed 14 of 26 passes for 237 yards, including an eight-yarder to Mike Quick for Philadelphia's initial score. The Eagles' defense held Gerald Riggs and the Falcons' high-powered rushing attack to only 55 yards. Garry Cobb had four of the Eagles' seven sacks to earn NFC defensive player of the week honors.

Philadelphia	0	10	0	6	— 16
Atlanta	0	0	0	0	— 0

Phil — Quick 8 pass from Jaworski (McFadden kick)
Phil — FG McFadden 31
Phil — FG McFadden 33
Phil — FG McFadden 21

Los Angeles Rams 26, Tampa Bay 20—At Anaheim Stadium, attendance 50,585. Eric Dickerson ran for 207 yards on 30 carries, including a 42-yard touchdown 2:16 into overtime, as the Rams defeated the Buccaneers. Los Angeles took a 17-10 halftime advantage on Mike Lansford's 34-yard field goal and scoring runs by Dickerson (40 yards) and Barry Redden (1). Following a Tampa Bay touchdown, the Rams regained the lead, 20-17, on Lansford's 40-yard field goal. Donald Igwebuike's 37-yard field goal with one second left in regulation forced the extra period. Tampa Bay's Nathan Wonsley gained 108 yards rushing on 18 attempts, including a 59-yard touchdown.

Tampa Bay	0	10	7	3	0	— 20
L.A. Rams	14	3	0	3	6	— 26

Rams — Redden 1 run (Lansford kick)
Rams — Dickerson 40 run (Lansford kick)
TB — Young 4 run (Igwebuike kick)
Rams — FG Lansford 34
TB — FG Igwebuike 26
TB — Wonsley 59 run (Igwebuike kick)
Rams — FG Lansford 40
TB — FG Igwebuike 37
Rams — Dickerson 42 run (no kick)

Washington 14, New Orleans 6—At Louisiana Superdome, attendance 57,317. George Rogers ran for one touchdown and Jay Schroeder threw for another as the Redskins downed the Saints to remain undefeated. Rogers, who netted his twenty-third career 100-yard game with 110 yards on 31 carries, opened Washington's scoring with a four-yard run. Schroeder followed a pair of field goals by the Saints' Morten Andersen with a two-yard touchdown throw to Art Monk. Andersen later missed a third attempt from 51 yards to end his consecutive field goal streak at 20, the second-longest in NFL history.

Washington	7	7	0	0	— 14
New Orleans	3	3	0	0	— 6

Wash — Rogers 4 run (Moseley kick)
NO — FG Andersen 34
NO — FG Andersen 45
Wash — Monk 2 pass from Schroeder (Moseley kick)

Monday, October 6

Seattle 33, San Diego 7—At Kingdome, attendance 63,207. Dave Krieg completed 21 of 35 passes for 284 yards and three touchdowns to lead the Seahawks over the Chargers. Krieg increased Seattle's 9-7 third-quarter edge by completing touchdown passes to Byron Franklin (46 yards), Steve Largent (15), and Eric Lane (2). Largent had four catches for 78 yards to set an NFL record by catching a pass in his 128th consecutive game, breaking the previous mark of 127. San Diego's Charlie Joiner became the NFL's all-time receiving yardage leader by catching four passes for 39 yards to total 11,834. Led by Curt Warner's 142 rushing yards (28 carries) and Franklin's 118 receiving (five receptions), Seattle outgained San Diego 512 total yards to 271.

San Diego	7	0	0	0	— 7
Seattle	0	6	17	10	— 33

SD — McGee 1 run (Benirschke kick)
Sea — FG Johnson 29
Sea — FG Johnson 30
Sea — FG Johnson 54
Sea — Franklin 46 pass from Krieg (Johnson kick)
Sea — Largent 15 pass from Krieg (Johnson kick)
Sea — Lane 2 pass from Krieg (Johnson kick)
Sea — FG Johnson 20

Sixth Week Summaries

Standings

American Football Conference

Eastern Division

	W	L	T	Pct.	Pts.	OP
N.Y. Jets	5	1	0	.833	156	133
New England	3	3	0	.500	162	112
Miami	2	4	0	.333	153	190
Buffalo	1	5	0	.167	118	135
Indianapolis	0	6	0	.000	55	165

Central Division

	W	L	T	Pct.	Pts.	OP
Cincinnati	4	2	0	.667	145	164
Cleveland	4	2	0	.667	138	143
Houston	1	5	0	.167	100	119
Pittsburgh	1	5	0	.167	85	149

Western Division

	W	L	T	Pct.	Pts.	OP
Denver	6	0	0	1.000	179	101
Seattle	4	2	0	.667	148	88
Kansas City	3	3	0	.500	112	111
L.A. Raiders	3	3	0	.500	106	102
San Diego	1	5	0	.167	118	159

National Football Conference

Eastern Division

	W	L	T	Pct.	Pts.	OP
N.Y. Giants	5	1	0	.833	130	73
Washington	5	1	0	.833	120	97
Dallas	4	2	0	.667	172	114
Philadelphia	2	4	0	.333	84	142
St. Louis	1	5	0	.167	76	129

Central Division

	W	L	T	Pct.	Pts.	OP
Chicago	6	0	0	1.000	166	67
Minnesota	4	2	0	.667	133	84
Detroit	3	3	0	.500	106	116
Tampa Bay	1	5	0	.167	100	153
Green Bay	0	6	0	.000	74	177

Western Division

	W	L	T	Pct.	Pts.	OP
Atlanta	5	1	0	.833	150	108
L.A. Rams	4	2	0	.667	116	110
San Francisco	4	2	0	.667	160	97
New Orleans	2	4	0	.333	91	115

Sunday, October 12

Miami 27, Buffalo 14—At Orange Bowl, attendance 49,467. Dan Marino completed 24 of 41 passes for 337 yards and one touchdown to help the Dolphins snap a three-game losing streak. Miami extended a 10-7 halftime edge to 27-7 midway through the fourth quarter on two scoring runs by Lorenzo Hampton (one and four yards) and Fuad Reveiz's 36-yard field goal. Twenty-four of Miami's 27 points were set up by four takeaways, including Jerome Foster's fumble recovery, which led to Marino's 30-yard touchdown pass to Mark Duper in the second quarter. The defeat was Buffalo's twentieth consecutive on the road.

Buffalo	7	0	0	7	— 14
Miami	3	7	10	7	— 27

Mia — FG Reveiz 22
Buff — Bell 1 run (Norwood kick)
Mia — Duper 30 pass from Marino (Reveiz kick)
Mia — FG Reveiz 36
Mia — Hampton 4 run (Reveiz kick)
Mia — Hampton 1 run (Reveiz kick)
Buff — Reed 6 pass from Kelly (Norwood kick)

Chicago 20, Houston 7—At Astrodome, attendance 46,026. Walter Payton became the first player in NFL history to gain 20,000 yards rushing, receiving, and on kick returns as the Bears downed the Oilers. Payton's one-yard touchdown run gave Chicago a 14-0 third-quarter edge. Following a Houston touchdown, Kevin Butler added two field goals (31 and 27 yards) to secure the victory. Payton gained 76 yards rushing and 30 receiving to total 20,045 combined yards during his 12-year career.

Chicago	0	7	7	6 —	20
Houston	0	0	7	0 —	7

Chi —Gentry 21 run (Butler kick)
Chi —Payton 1 run (Butler kick)
Hou —Hill 18 pass from Moon (Zendejas kick)
Chi —FG Butler 31
Chi —FG Butler 27

Denver 31, San Diego 14—At San Diego Jack Murphy Stadium, attendance 55,662. Gerald Willhite scored two touchdowns and Tony Lilly came up with two interceptions as the undefeated Broncos rolled over the Chargers. Lilly's two interceptions halted one San Diego scoring threat and set up Willhite's one-yard touchdown run to give Denver an insurmountable 24-7 advantage. Willhite also scored on a three-yard pass from John Elway. The Broncos outrushed the Chargers 156 to 42 and maintained a time-of-possession advantage of 38:47 to 21:13.

Denver	7	3	7	14 —	31
San Diego	7	0	0	7 —	14

SD —Anderson 7 pass from Fouts (Benirschke kick)
Den —Winder 1 run (Karlis kick)
Den —FG Karlis 21
Den —Willhite 3 pass from Elway (Karlis kick)
Den —Willhite 1 run (Karlis kick)
Den —Harden 41 punt return (Karlis kick)
SD —McGee 4 run (Benirschke kick)

Detroit 21, Green Bay 14—At Lambeau Field, attendance 52,290. Rookie running back Garry James carried 20 times for 140 yards and one touchdown to power the Lions over the Packers. James's first NFL touchdown on a 41-yard run, coupled with Scott Williams's one-yard scoring dive, gave Detroit a 14-0 second-quarter advantage. Eric Hipple's two-yard touchdown pass to David Lewis proved decisive as the Packers rallied for two touchdowns. James's first 100-yard game led the Lions' rushing attack, which outgained the Packers 236 to 44.

Detroit	0	14	0	7 —	21
Green Bay	0	7	0	7 —	14

Det —James 41 run (Murray kick)
Det —S. Williams 1 run (Murray kick)
GB —Lofton 5 pass from Wright (Del Greco kick)
Det —Lewis 2 pass from Hipple (Murray kick)
GB —Ross 6 pass from Wright (Del Greco kick)

Cleveland 20, Kansas City 7—At Cleveland Stadium, attendance 71,278. Bernie Kosar completed 22 of 35 passes for 287 yards and two touchdowns to help the Browns to their third straight win. Cleveland broke open a 7-7 halftime deadlock with Kosar's six-yard scoring pass to Ozzie Newsome. Matt Bahr's field goals from 34 and 36 yards sealed the win. Kosar's other touchdown pass was a 16-yarder to running back Earnest Byner in the second quarter. Cleveland outgained Kansas City 356 total yards to 126.

Kansas City	0	7	0	0 —	7
Cleveland	0	7	10	3 —	20

KC —Paige 26 pass from Blackledge (Lowery kick)
Clev —Byner 16 pass from Kosar (Bahr kick)
Clev —Newsome 6 pass from Kosar (Bahr kick)
Clev —FG Bahr 34
Clev —FG Bahr 36

Atlanta 26, Los Angeles Rams 14—At Atlanta-Fulton County Stadium, attendance 58,637. Gerald Riggs ran for 141 yards and Mick Luckhurst kicked four field goals as the Falcons upended the Rams to take sole possession of first place in the NFC West. Luckhurst's 23-yard field goal and Riggs's four-yard run in the second quarter gave Atlanta the lead for good, 10-7. David Archer completed a 22-yard touchdown pass to Charlie Brown and Luckhurst added kicks of 32, 49, and 41 yards to finish the Falcons' scoring. Riggs's 100-yard effort was the eighteenth of his career.

L.A. Rams	0	7	0	7 —	14
Atlanta	3	7	10	6 —	26

Atl —FG Luckhurst 23
Rams —Young 18 pass from Bartkowski (Lansford kick)
Atl —Riggs 4 run (Luckhurst kick)
Atl —FG Luckhurst 32
Atl —Brown 22 pass from Archer (Luckhurst kick)
Atl —FG Luckhurst 49
Rams —Dickerson 1 run (Lansford kick)
Atl —FG Luckhurst 41

Minnesota, 27, San Francisco 24—At Candlestick Park, attendance 58,637. Chuck Nelson's 28-yard field goal 4:27 into overtime lifted the Vikings over the 49ers. Minnesota rallied from a 24-14 third-quarter deficit to force the extra period on Nelson's 26-yard field goal and Tommy Kramer's 35-yard touchdown pass to Anthony Carter. Kramer completed 26 of 41 passes for 326 yards, including a six-yard scoring pass to Carter for the Vikings' initial score. Jeff Kemp connected on 23 of 42 passes for 359 yards and three touchdowns for the 49ers, including seven for 144 yards to Jerry Rice.

Minnesota	14	0	3	7	3 —	27
San Francisco	7	10	7	0	0 —	24

Minn —Carter 6 pass from Kramer (C. Nelson kick)
SF —Clark 45 pass from Kemp (Wersching kick)
Minn —Holt fumble recovery in end zone (C. Nelson kick)
SF —FG Wersching 39
SF —Rice 34 pass from Kemp (Wersching kick)
SF —Rice 17 pass from Kemp (Wersching kick)
Minn —FG C. Nelson 26
Minn —Carter 35 pass from Kramer (C. Nelson kick)
Minn —FG Nelson 28

New Orleans 17, Indianapolis 14—At Hoosier Dome, attendance 53,512. Buford Jordan ran nine yards for one touchdown and the Saints' defense forced four turnovers in a 17-14 win over Indianapolis. New Orleans opened a 17-0 lead when Jordan scored following a fumble recovery deep in Colts' territory. After Indianapolis scored a pair of touchdowns, Johnnie Poe recovered a fumble on the Saints' 12-yard line to seal the win. Rookie Rueben Mayes gained 108 yards on 22 carries. Jack Trudeau completed 24 of 44 passes for 315 yards to become the first Colts player to go over the 300-yard mark since Bert Jones threw for 310 against Cincinnati on October 11, 1981.

New Orleans	0	10	7	0 —	17
Indianapolis	0	0	7	7 —	14

NO —Jones 18 pass from Wilson (Andersen kick)
NO —FG Andersen 46
NO —Jordan 9 run (Andersen kick)
Ind —Bouza 24 pass from Trudeau (Biasucci kick)
Ind —Bouza 16 pass from Trudeau (Biasucci kick)

New York Jets 31, New England 24—At Sullivan Stadium, attendance 60,342. Johnny Hector gained a career-high 143 yards on a club-record 40 attempts as the Jets downed the Patriots to take a two-game lead in the AFC East. New York took a commanding 24-0 halftime lead on a pair of Hector one-yard touchdown runs, Pat Leahy's 46-yard field goal, and Pat Ryan's one-yard scoring pass to Mickey Shuler. New England scored 17 unanswered points in the third quarter before Hector plowed one yard for the game-winning touchdown.

N.Y. Jets	7	17	0	7 —	31
New England	0	0	17	7 —	24

NYJ —Hector 1 run (Leahy kick)
NYJ —Hector 1 run (Leahy kick)
NYJ —FG Leahy 46
NYJ —Shuler 1 pass from Ryan (Leahy kick)
NE —FG Franklin 26
NE —Morgan 44 pass from Grogan (Franklin kick)
NE —Fryar 69 pass from Grogan (Franklin kick)
NYJ —Hector 1 run (Leahy kick)
NE —Jones 18 pass from Grogan (Franklin kick)

New York Giants 35, Philadelphia 3—At Giants Stadium, attendance 74,221. Phil Simms passed for two touchdowns and ran for another to lead the Giants past the Eagles. Simms's four-yard touchdown run and 10-yard completion to Solomon Miller helped New York take a 21-3 third-quarter lead. Linebacker Harry Carson caught a 13-yard pass from Jeff Rutledge on a fake field-goal attempt, and Simms fired a 37-yarder to Lee Rouson to finish the Giants' scoring. Lawrence Taylor had four sacks to lead the defense. New York outgained Philadelphia in total yards 394 to 117.

Philadelphia	0	3	0	0 —	3
N.Y. Giants	0	14	14	7 —	35

NYG —Morris 30 run (Allegre kick)
Phil —FG McFadden 29
NYG —Simms 4 run (Allegre kick)
NYG —Miller 10 pass from Simms (Allegre kick)
NYG —Carson 13 pass from Rutledge (Allegre kick)
NYG —Rouson 37 pass from Simms (Allegre kick)

St. Louis 30, Tampa Bay 19—At Tampa Stadium, attendance 33,307. Stump Mitchell rushed for 126 yards and two touchdowns to lead the Cardinals to their first win of the season. St. Louis took a 9-7 halftime edge on John Lee's 38-yard field goal and Mitchell's three-yard scoring run. Neil Lomax's touchdown passes of 30 yards to Earl Ferrell and 38 yards to Charles Fox upped the lead to 23-7. Tampa Bay cut the advantage to 23-19 before Mitchell's 31-yard touchdown run clinched the victory.

St. Louis	0	9	7	14 —	30
Tampa Bay	7	0	0	12 —	19

TB —Magee 15 pass from DeBerg (Igwebuike kick)
StL —FG Lee 38
StL —Mitchell 3 run (kick blocked)
StL —Ferrell 30 pass from Lomax (Lee kick)
StL —Fox 38 pass from Lomax (Lee kick)
TB —FG Igwebuike 23
TB —Freeman 30 pass from Young (kick blocked)
TB —FG Igwebuike 46
StL —Mitchell 31 run (Lee kick)

Los Angeles Raiders 14, Seattle 10—At Memorial Coliseum, attendance 70,635. Jim Plunkett, replacing an injured Marc Wilson, passed for two touchdowns to lead the Raiders over the Seahawks. Los Angeles took a 14-3 halftime lead on Plunkett's scoring passes to Dokie Williams (nine yards) and Jessie Hester (49). Chris Bahr's club-record streak of consecutive field goals ended at 12 when he missed a 37-yarder. The Raiders outgained the Seahawks in total yards 323 to 211.

Seattle	0	3	7	0 —	10
L.A. Raiders	7	7	0	0 —	14

Raiders —Williams 9 pass from Plunkett (Bahr kick)
Raiders —Hester 49 pass from Plunkett (Bahr kick)
Sea —FG Johnson 30
Sea —Warner 1 run (Johnson kick)

Dallas 30, Washington 6—At Texas Stadium, attendance 63,264. Herschel Walker ran for two touchdowns and Rafael Septien kicked three field goals to highlight the Cowboys' 30-7 win. Walker opened and closed Dallas's scoring with a pair of one-yard runs. Septien's kicks were from 21, 38, and 36 yards. Steve Pelluer passed for 323 (on 19 of 30 attempts) of the Cowboys' 424 total yards. Dallas's defense held the Redskins to only 184 total yards. Washington's lone score came on a two-yard run by George Rogers in the third quarter.

Washington	0	0	6	0 —	6
Dallas	7	9	0	14 —	30

Dall —Walker 1 run (Septien kick)
Dall —FG Septien 21
Dall —FG Septien 38
Dall —FG Septien 36
Wash —Rogers 2 run (kick failed)
Dall —Sherrard 27 pass from Pelluer (Septien kick)
Dall —Walker 1 run (Septien kick)

Monday, October 13

Cincinnati 24, Pittsburgh 22—At Riverfront Stadium, attendance 54,283. Boomer Esiason passed for two scores and punter Jeff Hayes raced 61 yards on a fake punt for another to lead the Bengals past the Steelers. Esiason's touchdown passes to Rodney Holman (32 yards) and Tim McGee (7) gave Cincinnati a 14-9 halftime edge. Hayes's fourth-quarter scoring run was the first by a punter since Denver's Billy Van Heusen's 66-yard touchdown run on September 17, 1972. Jim Breech's game-winning 40-yard field goal gave him 550 career points to overtake Horst Muhlmann (549) as the Bengals' all-time leading scorer.

Pittsburgh	7	2	10	3 —	22
Cincinnati	7	7	0	10 —	24

Cin —Holman 32 pass from Esiason (Breech kick)
Pitt —Brister 1 run (Anderson kick)
Cin —McGee 7 pass from Esiason (Breech kick)
Pitt —Safety, Hayes forced out of end zone
Pitt —Jackson 1 run (Anderson kick)
Pitt —FG Anderson 24
Cin —Hayes 61 run (Breech kick)
Cin —FG Breech 40
Pitt —FG Anderson 44

Seventh Week Summaries

Standings

American Football Conference

Eastern Division	W	L	T	Pct.	Pts.	OP
N.Y. Jets	6	1	0	.857	178	143
New England	4	3	0	.571	196	112
Buffalo	2	5	0	.286	142	148
Miami	2	5	0	.286	181	220
Indianapolis	0	7	0	.000	68	189
Central Division						
Cincinnati	5	2	0	.714	176	192
Cleveland	4	3	0	.571	152	160
Houston	1	6	0	.143	128	150
Pittsburgh	1	6	0	.143	85	183
Western Division						
Denver	6	1	0	.857	189	123
Seattle	5	2	0	.714	165	100
Kansas City	4	3	0	.571	154	152
L.A. Raiders	4	3	0	.571	136	130
San Diego	1	6	0	.143	159	201

National Football Conference

Eastern Division	W	L	T	Pct.	Pts.	OP
Washington	6	1	0	.857	148	118
Dallas	5	2	0	.714	189	128
N.Y. Giants	5	2	0	.714	142	90
Philadelphia	2	5	0	.286	98	159
St. Louis	1	6	0	.143	97	157
Central Division						
Chicago	6	1	0	.857	173	90
Minnesota	5	2	0	.714	156	91
Detroit	3	4	0	.429	116	130
Green Bay	1	6	0	.143	91	191
Tampa Bay	1	6	0	.143	107	191
Western Division						
Atlanta	5	1	1	.786	160	118
L.A. Rams	5	2	0	.714	130	120
San Francisco	4	2	1	.643	170	107
New Orleans	3	4	0	.429	129	122

Sunday, October 19

Minnesota 23, Chicago 7—At Metrodome, attendance 62,851. Tommy Kramer passed for two touchdowns and ran for another to power the Vikings over the Bears. Minnesota took a commanding 16-0 halftime lead on Chuck Nelson's 29-yard field goal and Kramer's scoring passes of 37 yards to Alfred Anderson and 60 yards to Anthony

Carter. Kramer also scored on a five-yard run in the third quarter. Gerald Robinson had two-and-a-half of the Vikings' seven sacks. Steve Fuller hit Willie Gault with a 50-yard touchdown pass to prevent the shutout as the Bears lost their first game of the season.

Chicago	0	0	0	7	— 7
Minnesota	13	3	7	0	— 23

Minn —Anderson 37 pass from Kramer (kick blocked)
Minn —Carter 60 pass from Kramer (C. Nelson kick)
Minn —FG C. Nelson 29
Minn —Kramer 5 run (C. Nelson kick)
Chi —Gault 50 pass from Fuller (Butler kick)

Dallas 17, Philadelphia 14—At Veterans Stadium, attendance 68,572. Rafael Septien's 38-yard field goal with two seconds remaining rallied the Cowboys to a 17-14 win. Both teams were led by backup quarterbacks. Dallas's Steve Pelluer, starting his third straight game replacing Danny White (injured groin), completed a 22-yard scoring pass to Doug Cosbie to open the scoring. Philadelphia's Randall Cunningham replaced starter Matt Cavanaugh in the second half and scored on a 14-yard run to tie the score 7-7. After Tony Dorsett's 15-yard touchdown run put the Cowboys on top 14-7, Cunningham hit Mike Quick on a 15-yard touchdown pass to deadlock the game 14-14 with 7:19 left. Defensive end Jim Jeffcoat had three-and-a-half of the Cowboys' 10 sacks.

Dallas	7	0	7	3	— 17
Philadelphia	0	0	7	7	— 14

Dall —Cosbie 22 pass from Pelluer (Septien kick)
Phil —Cunningham 14 run (McFadden kick)
Dall —Dorsett 15 run (Septien kick)
Phil —Quick 15 pass from Cunningham (McFadden kick)
Dall —FG Septien 38

Los Angeles Rams 14, Detroit 10—At Anaheim Stadium, attendance 50,992. Eric Dickerson carried the ball 24 times for 130 yards and the winning touchdown as the Rams downed the Lions. Dickerson's one-yard scoring run and Nolan Cromwell's 80-yard interception return for a touchdown gave the Rams a 14-0 first-quarter edge. Cromwell's 622 career interception yards moved him ahead of Ed Meador (547) into the number-one spot on the Rams' all-time list. Eric Hipple completed 31 of 50 passes for 316 yards and one touchdown for Detroit.

Detroit	0	0	0	10	— 10
L.A. Rams	14	0	0	0	— 14

Rams —Cromwell 80 interception return (Lansford kick)
Rams —Dickerson 1 run (Lansford kick)
Det —FG Murray 47
Det —Chadwick 9 pass from Hipple (Murray kick)

Green Bay 17, Cleveland 14—At Cleveland Stadium, attendance 76,438. Randy Wright completed 21 of 27 passes for 277 yards and a touchdown to lead the Packers to their first win of the season. Wright's 47-yard scoring pass to Phillip Epps gave Green Bay a 17-14 third-quarter edge and the Packers' defense held on. Al Del Greco's 24-yard field goal and Gerry Ellis's two-yard run accounted for the rest of Green Bay's scoring. The Packers limited the Browns to only 32 yards rushing.

Green Bay	0	3	14	0	— 17
Cleveland	7	7	0	0	— 14

Clev —Byner 3 pass from Kosar (Bahr kick)
GB —FG Del Greco 24
Clev —Brennan 15 pass from Kosar (Bahr kick)
GB —Ellis 2 run (Del Greco kick)
GB —Epps 47 pass from Wright (Del Greco kick)

Cincinnati 31, Houston 28—At Riverfront Stadium, attendance 53,844. James Brooks's 21-yard touchdown run with 43 seconds left helped the Bengals down the Oilers and gain sole possession of first place in the AFC Central. Cincinnati took a 24-14 lead on Jim Breech's 51-yard field goal before Houston rallied with a pair of touchdowns in the fourth quarter. Brooks gained 133 yards on 18 carries, including a 24-yard score in the first half. David Fulcher had two interceptions to lead the Bengals' defense.

Houston	7	7	0	14	— 28
Cincinnati	7	14	3	7	— 31

Cin —Collinsworth 37 pass from Esiason (Breech kick)
Hou —Rozier 1 run (Zendejas kick)
Cin —Brooks 24 run (Breech kick)
Cin —Jennings 1 run (Breech kick)
Hou —D. Hill 4 pass from Moon (Zendejas kick)
Cin —FG Breech 51
Hou —Wallace 2 run (Zendejas kick)
Hou —Lyles 93 fumble recovery return (Zendejas kick)
Cin —Brooks 21 run (Breech kick)

Buffalo 24, Indianapolis 13—At Rich Stadium, attendance 50,050. Jim Kelly completed a pair of touchdown passes to lead the Bills over the Colts. Kelly threw a six-yard scoring pass to Andre Reed for a 17-6 halftime lead and added a 13-yarder to Reed to close out the scoring. Buffalo cornerback Rodney Bellinger returned a fumble 15 yards for a touchdown 2:54 into the game for his first NFL score.

Indianapolis	3	3	7	0	— 13
Buffalo	7	10	7	0	— 24

Buff —Bellinger 15 fumble recovery return (Norwood kick)
Ind —FG Biasucci 46
Buff —FG Norwood 37
Ind —FG Biasucci 44
Buff —Reed 6 pass from Kelly (Norwood kick)
Ind —Brooks 18 pass from Trudeau (Biasucci kick)
Buff —Reed 13 pass from Kelly (Norwood kick)

Los Angeles Raiders 30, Miami 28—At Orange Bowl, attendance 53,421. Marcus Allen ran for two touchdowns and caught another to lead the Raiders to a victory over the Dolphins. Allen's two-yard scoring run and 16-yard touchdown catch from Marc Wilson helped Los Angeles take a 23-7 halftime edge. Stefon Adams's fumble recovery early in the fourth quarter set up Allen's decisive two-yard scoring run. Chris Bahr converted all three of his field-goal attempts (32, 33, and 40 yards). Allen gained 96 yards on 21 carries as the Raiders outrushed the Dolphins 214 yards to 57 and held a time-of-possession advantage of 37:21 to 22:39.

L.A. Raiders	6	17	0	7	— 30
Miami	0	7	7	14	— 28

Raiders —FG Bahr 32
Raiders —FG Bahr 33
Mia —Hardy 18 pass from Marino (Reveiz kick)
Raiders —Allen 2 run (Bahr kick)
Raiders —Allen 16 pass from Wilson (Bahr kick)
Raiders —FG Bahr 40
Mia —Johnson 5 pass from Marino (Reveiz kick)
Raiders —Allen 2 run (Bahr kick)
Mia —Hampton 2 run (Reveiz kick)
Mia —Clayton 68 pass from Marino (Reveiz kick)

New England 34, Pittsburgh 0—At Three Rivers Stadium, attendance 54,743. Steve Grogan passed for three touchdowns as the Patriots handed the Steelers their worst loss ever in Three Rivers Stadium. Grogan's scoring passes to Stephen Starring (43 yards) and Tony Collins (10), together with Tony Franklin's 31-yard field goal and Fred Marion's 37-yard interception return for a touchdown gave New England a commanding 24-0 first-half lead. Grogan also completed a two-yard touchdown pass to Willie Scott. Andre Tippett had two of the Patriots' five sacks.

New England	10	14	7	3	— 34
Pittsburgh	0	0	0	0	— 0

NE —FG Franklin 31
NE —Starring 43 pass from Grogan (Franklin kick)
NE —Marion 37 interception return (Franklin kick)
NE —Collins 10 pass from Grogan (Franklin kick)
NE —Scott 2 pass from Grogan (Franklin kick)
NE —FG Franklin 36

Seattle 17, New York Giants 12—At Kingdome, attendance 62,282. Led by Jacob Green's four sacks and Dave Brown's two interceptions, the Seahawks held off the Giants to register their fifth win. Norm Johnson's 25-yard field goal in the third quarter gave Seattle a 10-9 edge that they never relinquished. Steve Largent caught two passes for 20 yards to improve his career total to 650 receptions and move ahead of Charley Taylor (649) into second place on the NFL's all-time chart. New York's Joe Morris led all rushers with 116 yards on 24 carries.

N.Y. Giants	0	9	0	3	— 12
Seattle	7	0	3	7	— 17

Sea —Hudson 16 pass from Krieg (Johnson kick)
NYG —Miller 32 pass from Simms (kick failed)
NYG —FG Allegre 23
Sea —FG Johnson 25
Sea —Warner 1 run (Johnson kick)
NYG —FG Allegre 31

Washington 28, St. Louis 21—At Robert F. Kennedy Stadium, attendance 53,494. George Rogers rushed for 118 yards and Jay Schroeder passed for three touchdowns to highlight the Redskins' 28-21 win. Rogers's two-yard scoring run was set up by Anthony Jones's fumble recovery. Schroeder's touchdown passes were to Art Monk (16 yards), Clint Didier (21), and Gary Clark (16). Dexter Manley had two of Washington's five sacks.

St. Louis	0	7	7	7	— 21
Washington	7	14	7	0	— 28

Wash —Rogers 2 run (Zendejas kick)
Wash —Monk 16 pass from Schroeder (Zendejas kick)
Wash —Didier 21 pass from Schroeder (Zendejas kick)
StL —Ferrell 8 pass from Lomax (Lee kick)
Wash —Clark 16 pass from Schroeder (Zendejas kick)
StL —J. T. Smith 7 pass from Lomax (Lee kick)
StL —Ferrell 15 pass from Lomax (Lee kick)

Kansas City 42, San Diego 41—At Arrowhead Stadium, attendance 55,767. Safety Lloyd Burruss became the fifteenth player in NFL history to return two interceptions for touchdowns in a game and quarterback Bill Kenney came off the bench and guided the Chiefs to a pair of second-half scores as Kansas City edged San Diego. Burruss returned second-quarter interceptions 56 and 47 yards and Kevin Ross's 21-yard fumble recovery return for a score gave the Chiefs a 28-24 halftime advantage. Kenney, who replaced ineffective starter Todd Blackledge, completed a 16-yard touchdown pass to Stephone Paige and led Kansas City on an 80-yard drive that ended with a one-yard scoring run by Boyce Green. San Diego had a chance to win the game with 28 seconds left, but Rolf Benirschke's 35-yard field-goal attempt was wide left.

San Diego	7	17	7	10	— 41
Kansas City	7	21	7	7	— 42

KC —Paige 45 pass from Blackledge (Lowery kick)
SD —Anderson 7 pass from Fouts (Benirschke kick)
KC —Burruss 56 interception return (Lowery kick)
KC —Ross 21 fumble recovery return (Lowery kick)
SD —McGee 1 run (Benirschke kick)
KC —Burruss 47 interception return (Lowery kick)
SD —FG Benirschke 30
SD —O'Neal 5 interception return (Benirschke kick)
KC —Paige 16 pass from Kenney (Lowery kick)
SD —Anderson 2 run (Benirschke kick)
SD —FG Benirschke 21
KC —Green 1 run (Lowery kick)
SD —Anderson 12 pass from Herrmann (Benirschke kick)

Atlanta 10, San Francisco 10—At Atlanta-Fulton County Stadium, attendance 55,306. David Archer's 39-yard touchdown pass to Sylvester Stamps with 1:33 left in regulation produced the Falcons' first tie since 1971 as both teams failed to score in overtime. San Francisco took a 10-3 halftime lead on Roger Craig's one-yard scoring run and Ray Wersching's 24-yard field goal. Atlanta held a 47:36 to 27:24 time-of-possession advantage but turned the ball over five times (two fumbles and three interceptions).

San Francisco	7	3	0	0	0	— 10
Atlanta	3	0	0	7	0	— 10

SF —Craig 1 run (Wersching kick)
Atl —FG Luckhurst 47
SF —FG Wersching 24
Atl —Stamps 39 pass from Archer (Luckhurst kick)

New Orleans 38, Tampa Bay 7—At Louisiana Superdome, attendance 43,355. Saints rookie Rueben Mayes rushed for 172 yards on 24 carries to help the Saints to their second straight win. Mayes scored on runs of one and nine yards. Rookie Dalton Hilliard added touchdown runs of one and seven yards. Eric Martin caught a 21-yard touchdown pass from Dave Wilson and Morten Andersen kicked a 31-yard field goal to complete New Orleans's scoring. Mayes's rushing total was the second highest in club history to George Rogers's 206 versus St. Louis on September 4, 1983. The Saints' 31-point margin of victory tied their highest in franchise history.

Tampa Bay	0	0	0	7	— 7
New Orleans	10	7	7	14	— 38

NO —Mayes 9 run (Andersen kick)
NO —FG Andersen 31
NO —Mayes 1 run (Andersen kick)
NO —Hilliard 1 run (Andersen kick)
TB —DeBerg 1 run (Igwebuike kick)
NO —Martin 21 pass from Wilson (Andersen kick)
NO —Hilliard 7 run (Andersen kick)

Monday, October 20

New York Jets 22, Denver 10—At Giants Stadium, attendance 73,759. Ken O'Brien passed for one touchdown and New York's defense held Denver to only 38 yards rushing en route to handing the Broncos their first loss. O'Brien, who replaced an injured Pat Ryan in the second quarter, fired a 23-yard scoring pass to Wesley Walker to help New York to a 22-0 halftime lead. Johnny Hector opened the Jets' scoring with a one-yard run. Pat Leahy's field goals from 27 and 25 yards moved him to within one of Mark Moseley's NFL-record for consecutive field goals (23).

Denver	0	0	3	7	— 10
N.Y. Jets	10	12	0	0	— 22

NYJ —Hector 1 run (Leahy kick)
NYJ —FG Leahy 27
NYJ —FG Leahy 25
NYJ —Walker 23 pass from O'Brien (Leahy kick)
NYJ —Safety, Humphery tackled Elway in end zone
Den —FG Karlis 47
Den —Winder 20 pass from Kubiak (Karlis kick)

Eighth Week Summaries

Standings

American Football Conference

Eastern Division

	W	L	T	Pct.	Pts.	OP
N.Y. Jets	7	1	0	.875	206	166
New England	5	3	0	.625	219	115
Miami	3	5	0	.375	198	233
Buffalo	2	6	0	.250	145	171
Indianapolis	0	8	0	.000	81	206

Central Division

	W	L	T	Pct.	Pts.	OP
Cincinnati	5	3	0	.625	185	222
Cleveland	5	3	0	.625	175	180
Pittsburgh	2	6	0	.250	115	192
Houston	1	7	0	.125	145	178

Western Division

	W	L	T	Pct.	Pts.	OP
Denver	7	1	0	.875	209	136
Kansas City	5	3	0	.625	181	172
L.A. Raiders	5	3	0	.625	164	147
Seattle	5	3	0	.625	178	120
San Diego	1	7	0	.125	166	224

National Football Conference

Eastern Division

	W	L	T	Pct.	Pts.	OP
Dallas	6	2	0	.750	226	134
N.Y. Giants	6	2	0	.750	169	110
Washington	6	2	0	.750	168	145
Philadelphia	3	5	0	.375	121	166
St. Louis	1	7	0	.125	103	194
Central Division						
Chicago	7	1	0	.875	186	97
Minnesota	5	3	0	.625	176	114
Detroit	3	5	0	.375	123	143
Green Bay	1	7	0	.125	108	222
Tampa Bay	1	7	0	.125	127	218
Western Division						
L.A. Rams	6	2	0	.750	144	127
Atlanta	5	2	1	.687	167	132
San Francisco	5	2	1	.687	201	124
New Orleans	3	5	0	.375	152	150

Sunday, October 26

Los Angeles Rams 14, Atlanta 7—At Anaheim Stadium, attendance 56,993. Eric Dickerson ran for 170 yards and passed for one touchdown to spearhead the Rams' 14-7 win. Los Angeles built a 14-0 halftime lead on linebacker Mark Jerue's 22-yard interception return for a touchdown and Dickerson's 15-yard scoring completion to David Hill on a halfback option play. Jerry Gray's interception with six minutes left thwarted the Falcons' final threat at the Rams' 30-yard line. Dickerson's rushing yardage increased his league-leading total to 1,030 yards as he recorded his fourth 1,000-yard season in as many years.

Atlanta	0	0	7	0	— 7
L.A. Rams	0	14	0	0	— 14

Rams —Jerue 22 interception return (Lansford kick)
Rams —D. Hill 15 pass from Dickerson (Lansford kick)
Atl —Britt 65 fumble recovery return (Luckhurst kick)

Pittsburgh 30, Cincinnati 9—At Three Rivers Stadium, attendance 50,816. Walter Abercrombie and Earnest Jackson each ran for 100 yards to help the Steelers notch their 100th win in Three Rivers Stadium. Mark Malone, playing in his first game in three weeks, followed Gary Anderson's 31-yard field goal with touchdown passes to Rich Erenberg (10 yards) and Weegie Thompson (9). Abercrombie carried 22 times for 109 yards, while Jackson gained 132 on 21 carries. Jackson's one-yard run completed Pittsburgh's scoring.

Cincinnati	0	3	3	3	— 9
Pittsburgh	3	14	6	7	— 30

Pitt —FG Anderson 31
Pitt —Erenberg 10 pass from Malone (Anderson kick)
Cin —FG Breech 19
Pitt —Thompson 9 pass from Malone (Anderson kick)
Pitt —FG Anderson 43
Pitt —FG Anderson 41
Cin —FG Breech 40
Pitt —Jackson 1 run (Anderson kick)
Cin —FG Breech 31

Cleveland 23, Minnesota 20—At Metrodome, attendance 59,133. Matt Bahr's third field goal of the day, a 22-yarder with 1:46 remaining in the game, lifted the Browns over the Vikings. Trailing 20-10 after three quarters, Cleveland rallied for 13 straight points when Curtis Dickey ran 17 yards for a score and Bahr kicked two field goals, including the game-winner from 22 yards. Bahr also connected on a career-long 52-yarder. Dickey finished with 106 yards on 19 carries in his first 100-yard effort for Cleveland.

Cleveland	3	0	7	13	— 23
Minnesota	3	14	3	0	— 20

Minn —FG C. Nelson 33
Clev —FG Bahr 52
Minn —D. Nelson 5 run (C. Nelson kick)
Minn —Carter 8 pass from Kramer (C. Nelson kick)
Clev —Wright 30 return of blocked punt (Bahr kick)
Minn —FG C. Nelson 32
Clev —FG Bahr 19
Clev —Dickey 17 run (Bahr kick)
Clev —FG Bahr 22

Chicago 13, Detroit 7—At Soldier Field, attendance 62,064. Wilber Marshall recovered a fumble for a touchdown and Kevin Butler kicked two field goals as the Bears defeated the Lions. Quarterback Jim McMahon threw for 141 yards and helped set up two Butler field goals from 29 and 27 yards. Marshall sacked Detroit quarterback Eric Hipple in the first quarter, causing a fumble which he recovered for Chicago's only touchdown. It was the Bears' twenty-second straight win with McMahon as the starting quarterback.

Detroit	0	0	7	0	— 7
Chicago	7	3	0	3	— 13

Chi —Marshall 12 fumble recovery return (Butler kick)
Chi —FG Butler 29
Det —F. Williams 3 run (Murray kick)
Chi —FG Butler 27

Los Angeles Raiders 28, Houston 17—At Astrodome, attendance 41,641. Marc Wilson passed for four touchdowns to power the Raiders to their fifth straight win. Los Angeles took a 21-7 halftime advantage on Wilson's scoring passes to Andy Parker (two yards) and Todd Christensen (14 and 32). His fourth scoring completion was a three-yarder to Christensen in the third quarter. Houston's Warren Moon completed 18 of 46 passes for 304 yards, but threw four interceptions and was sacked six times by the Raiders' defense. Ray Guy punted nine times to become the fourth player in NFL history to punt 1,000 times in a career (1,004).

L.A. Raiders	7	14	7	0	— 28
Houston	0	7	10	0	— 17

Raiders —Parker 2 pass from Wilson (Bahr kick)
Raiders —Christensen 14 pass from Wilson (Bahr kick)
Hou —Givens 43 run (Zendejas kick)
Raiders —Christensen 32 pass from Wilson (Bahr kick)
Raiders —Christensen 3 pass from Wilson (Bahr kick)
Hou —FG Zendejas 48
Hou —Rozier 4 run (Zendejas kick)

Miami 17, Indianapolis 13—At Hoosier Dome, attendance 58,350. Dan Marino passed for 243 yards and a touchdown and John Offerdahl made a game-saving tackle at the Miami 14-yard line in the closing seconds as the Dolphins recorded their 200th win in franchise history. Marino's seven-yard touchdown pass to Mark Duper midway through the second quarter proved to be all the points Miami needed to win. Rookie Offerdahl tackled Owen Gill two yards shy of a first down on a fourth-and-two play with 30 seconds remaining. It was the Colts' thirteenth consecutive loss to the Dolphins.

Miami	7	10	0	0	— 17
Indianapolis	7	3	0	3	— 13

Mia —Hampton 1 run (Reveiz kick)
Ind —McMillan 14 run (Biasucci kick)
Mia —FG Reveiz 29
Mia —Duper 7 pass from Marino (Reveiz kick)
Ind —FG Biasucci 39
Ind —FG Biasucci 45

New England 23, Buffalo 3—At Rich Stadium, attendance 77,808. Tony Franklin kicked three field goals and the New England defense recorded four interceptions as the Patriots cruised past the Bills. In a game in which New England never trailed, Franklin converted field goals from 31, 27, and 26 yards to up his league-best point total to 75. Leading the defense were Ronnie Lippett, who had a pair of interceptions for the second time this season, and Andre Tippett, who registered a personal-best three-and-a-half sacks.

New England	7	10	3	3	— 23
Buffalo	0	0	3	0	— 3

NE —C. James 2 run (Franklin kick)
NE —FG Franklin 31
NE —Weathers 16 run (Franklin kick)
Buff —FG Norwood 26
NE —FG Franklin 27
NE —FG Franklin 26

New York Jets 28, New Orleans 23—At Giants Stadium, attendance 44,246. Ken O'Brien connected with Al Toon for three touchdown passes and Freeman McNeil ran for another to highlight the Jets' 28-23 win. New York took a 21-6 halftime lead as O'Brien threw scoring passes of 16 and 62 yards to Toon and McNeil ran one yard for a touchdown. O'Brien, who completed 20 of 32 passes for 258 yards, added a six-yarder to Toon in the third quarter to finish the Jets' scoring. Lester Lyles had two interceptions to lead New York's defense.

New Orleans	6	0	0	17	— 23
N.Y. Jets	7	14	7	0	— 28

NO —FG Andersen 26
NO —FG Andersen 53
NYJ —Toon 16 pass from O'Brien (Leahy kick)
NYJ —McNeil 1 run (Leahy kick)
NYJ —Toon 62 pass from O'Brien (Leahy kick)
NYJ —Toon 6 pass from O'Brien (Leahy kick)
NO —Tice 1 pass from Wilson (Andersen kick)
NO —Tice 29 pass from Wilson (Andersen kick)
NO —FG Andersen 28

Dallas 37, St. Louis 6—At Texas Stadium, attendance 60,756. Danny White, starting his first game in a month, passed for two touchdowns and Herschel Walker topped the 100-yard rushing mark for the first time in his NFL career to help power the Cowboys over the Cardinals. White fired touchdown passes to rookie Mike Sherrard (36 yards) and Tony Hill (20) as Dallas built a 27-6 halftime lead. Walker, who started in place of Tony Dorsett (bruised knee), rushed for 120 yards on 25 carries, including touchdown runs of 19 and 4 yards. It was the first time a running back other than Dorsett had gained over 100 yards for the Cowboys since Robert Newhouse totaled 108 yards against the Cardinals on September 2, 1979.

St. Louis	0	6	0	0	— 6
Dallas	6	21	10	0	— 37

Dall —FG Septien 44
Dall —FG Septien 43
StL —FG Lee 45
Dall —Sherrard 36 pass from D. White (Septien kick)
Dall —Walker 19 run (Septien kick)
Dall —Hill 20 pass from D. White (Septien kick)
StL —FG Lee 36
Dall —Walker 4 run (Septien kick)
Dall —FG Septien 47

Philadelphia 23, San Diego 7—At Veterans Stadium, attendance 41,469. Paul McFadden kicked three field goals (33, 34, and 36 yards) to lead the Eagles to a 23-7 win over the Chargers. Philadelphia added a pair of fourth-quarter touchdowns on Ron Jaworski's 10-yard scoring pass to Mike Quick and Keith Byars's two-yard run. San Diego's Tom Flick completed his first NFL touchdown pass, a 20-yarder to Charlie Joiner in the fourth quarter, to avoid the shutout.

San Diego	0	0	0	7	— 7
Philadelphia	3	3	3	14	— 23

Phil —FG McFadden 33
Phil —FG McFadden 34
Phil —FG McFadden 36
Phil —Quick 10 pass from Jaworski (McFadden kick)
SD —Joiner 20 pass from Flick (Benirschke kick)
Phil —Byars 2 run (McFadden kick)

San Francisco 31, Green Bay 17—At Milwaukee County Stadium, attendance 50,557. Ronnie Lott and Tory Nixon each returned interceptions for touchdowns as the 49ers upended the Packers. Lott's 55-yard return early in the fourth quarter gave San Francisco their first lead of the game and snapped a 14-14 tie. Following a Green Bay field goal, Ray Wersching kicked a 27-yard field goal and Nixon returned an interception 88 yards for a score to seal the win. Green Bay's Randy Wright completed 30 of 54 passes for 328 yards and a touchdown.

San Francisco	0	7	7	17	— 31
Green Bay	7	7	0	3	— 17

GB —Carruth 1 run (Del Greco kick)
GB —Lewis 3 pass from Wright (Del Greco kick)
SF —Rice 4 pass from Moroski (Wersching kick)
SF —Moroski 9 run (Wersching kick)
SF —Lott 55 interception return (Wersching kick)
GB —FG Del Greco 22
SF —FG Wersching 27
SF —Nixon 88 interception return (Wersching kick)

Denver 20, Seattle 13—At Mile High Stadium, attendance 76,089. John Elway set a club record with his sixth 300-yard career game to lead the Broncos to victory. Denver took a 13-0 second-quarter lead as Rich Karlis kicked a pair of field goals (22 and 47 yards) and Sammy Winder ran one yard for a score. Following two Seattle field goals by Norm Johnson, Elway hooked up with Vance Johnson on a 34-yard flea-flicker play for the decisive score. Elway completed 18 of 32 passes for 321 yards. The Seahawks' Curt Warner led all rushers with 139 yards on 21 carries.

Seattle	0	3	3	7	— 13
Denver	10	3	0	7	— 20

Den —FG Karlis 22
Den —Winder 1 run (Karlis kick)
Den —FG Karlis 47
Sea —FG Johnson 43
Sea —FG Johnson 53
Den —Johnson 34 pass from Elway (Karlis kick)
Sea —Largent 24 pass from Gilbert (Johnson kick)

Kansas City 27, Tampa Bay 20—At Arrowhead Stadium, attendance 36,230. Jeff Smith ran 32 yards for a touchdown with 4:25 to play to help the Chiefs defeat the Buccaneers 27-20. Bill Kenney, making his first start of the season, completed 15 of 29 passes for 230 yards, including a three-yard touchdown pass to Stephone Paige to give Kansas City the lead for the first time, 20-13, late in the third quarter. James Wilder's three-yard scoring run pulled Tampa Bay even with 12:52 to play. Wilder finished the game with 25 carries for 110 yards. The Chiefs' Mike Pruitt recorded his fiftieth NFL touchdown with a one-yard run in the first quarter.

Tampa Bay	3	10	0	7	— 20
Kansas City	7	3	10	7	— 27

TB —FG Igwebuike 49
KC —Pruitt 1 run (Lowery kick)
TB —Magee 10 pass from Young (Igwebuike kick)
TB —FG Igwebuike 39
KC —FG Lowery 26
KC —FG Lowery 20
KC —Paige 3 pass from Kenney (Lowery kick)
TB —Wilder 3 run (Igwebuike kick)
KC —Smith 32 run (Lowery kick)

Monday, October 27

New York Giants 27, Washington 20—At Giants Stadium, attendance 75,923. Joe Morris carried 31 times for 181 yards and two touchdowns, including a 13-yarder with 1:38 remaining, to lift the Giants over the Redskins. New York jumped out to a 13-3 halftime advantage on a pair of field goals by Raul Allegre (37 and 44 yards) and Morris's 11-yard touchdown run. Phil Simms's 30-yard touchdown pass to Bobby Johnson extended the Giants' lead to 20-3, but the Redskins bounced back to tie the score 20-20. George Rogers scored on a one-yard run, Jay Schroeder completed a 42-yard touchdown pass to Gary Clark, and Max Zendejas kicked a 29-yard field goal with 4:06 left to play to bring Washington even. Schroeder completed 22 of 40 passes for 420 yards and a touchdown. Lawrence Taylor had three of the Giants' four sacks.

Washington	0	3	14	3	— 20
N.Y. Giants	3	10	7	7	— 27

NYG —FG Allegre 37
NYG —Morris 11 run (Allegre kick)
Wash —FG Zendejas 23
NYG —FG Allegre 44

NYG — B. Johnson 30 pass from Simms (Allegre kick)
Wash — Rogers 1 run (Zendejas kick)
Wash — Clark 42 pass from Schroeder (Zendejas kick)
Wash — FG Zendejas 29
NYG — Morris 13 run (Allegre kick)

Ninth Week Summaries

Standings

American Football Conference

Eastern Division	W	L	T	Pct.	Pts.	OP
N.Y. Jets	8	1	0	.889	244	173
New England	6	3	0	.667	244	132
Miami	4	5	0	.444	226	240
Buffalo	2	7	0	.222	173	205
Indianapolis	0	9	0	.000	90	230
Central Division						
Cincinnati	6	3	0	.667	209	239
Cleveland	6	3	0	.667	199	189
Pittsburgh	3	6	0	.333	142	195
Houston	1	8	0	.111	152	206
Western Division						
Denver	8	1	0	.889	230	146
Kansas City	6	3	0	.667	205	195
L.A. Raiders	5	4	0	.556	174	168
Seattle	5	4	0	.556	185	158
San Diego	1	8	0	.111	189	248

National Football Conference

Eastern Division	W	L	T	Pct.	Pts.	OP
N.Y. Giants	7	2	0	.778	186	124
Washington	7	2	0	.778	212	183
Dallas	6	3	0	.667	240	151
Philadelphia	3	6	0	.333	131	179
St. Louis	2	7	0	.222	116	204
Central Division						
Chicago	7	2	0	.778	203	117
Minnesota	5	4	0	.556	214	158
Detroit	3	6	0	.333	140	167
Tampa Bay	2	7	0	.222	161	246
Green Bay	1	8	0	.111	111	249
Western Division						
L.A. Rams	7	2	0	.778	164	144
Atlanta	5	3	1	.611	184	157
San Francisco	5	3	1	.611	211	147
New Orleans	4	5	0	.444	175	160

Sunday, November 2

New England 25, Atlanta 17—At Sullivan Stadium, attendance 60,597. Four field goals by Tony Franklin and Irving Fryar's 59-yard punt return for a touchdown helped the Patriots over the Falcons. Trailing 10-9 at halftime, New England scored 16 straight points to take a 25-10 lead on three Franklin field goals (33, 31, and 32 yards) and Fryar's return. Franklin's first field goal, another 32-yarder, opened the Patriots' scoring. Quarterback Tony Eason had his club-record string of 178 consecutive passes without an interception snapped by Falcons rookie safety Bret Clark in the first quarter.

Atlanta	3	7	0	7	— 17
New England	3	6	10	6	— 25

Atl — FG Luckhurst 41
NE — FG Franklin 32
Atl — Riggs 1 run (Luckhurst kick)
NE — Collins 26 pass from Eason (kick failed)
NE — FG Franklin 33
NE — Fryar 59 punt return (Franklin kick)
NE — FG Franklin 31
NE — FG Franklin 32
Atl — Riggs 1 run (Donnelly kick)

Tampa Bay 34, Buffalo 28—At Tampa Stadium, attendance 32,806. Tampa Bay opened a 20-0 halftime lead and held on to defeat Buffalo and snap a five-game losing streak. Donald Igwebuike's two field goals, Pat Franklin's fumbled kickoff recovery for a touchdown, and Rod Jones's recovery of another mishandled kickoff (which set up Steve Young's two-yard scoring run), got the Buccaneers off to a quick start. Young added a one-yard touchdown sneak, and James Wilder's 45-yard touchdown run midway through the fourth quarter proved decisive. Buffalo's Jim Kelly completed 28 of 39 passes for 343 yards, including touchdowns to Pete Metzelaars (1 and 44 yards) and Jerry Butler (9).

Buffalo	0	0	14	14	— 28
Tampa Bay	10	10	0	14	— 34

TB — FG Igwebuike 49
TB — Franklin fumble recovery in end zone (Igwebuike kick)
TB — FG Igwebuike 26
TB — Young 2 run (Igwebuike kick)
Buff — Metzelaars 1 pass from Kelly (Norwood kick)
Buff — Metzelaars 44 pass from Kelly (Norwood kick)
TB — Young 1 run (Igwebuike kick)
Buff — Pitts 49 punt return (Norwood kick)
TB — Wilder 45 run (Igwebuike kick)
Buff — Butler 9 pass from Kelly (Norwood kick)

Cincinnati 24, Detroit 17—At Pontiac Silverdome, attendance 52,423. Larry Kinnebrew's one-yard scoring run with 40 seconds left helped the Bengals upend the Lions and maintain a share of first place in the AFC Central. Stanley Wilson's second touchdown run of the game, a four-yarder, gave Cincinnati a 17-10 lead after three quarters. Following a Detroit touchdown, Cincinnati marched 77 yards in nine plays to set up Kinnebrew's decisive score. James Brooks rushed for 120 yards as the Bengals outgained the Lions 222 yards rushing to 97.

Cincinnati	0	10	7	7	— 24
Detroit	7	0	3	7	— 17

Det — Thompson 36 pass from Hipple (Murray kick)
Cin — Wilson 2 run (Breech kick)
Cin — FG Breech 38
Det — FG Murray 18
Cin — Wilson 4 run (Breech kick)
Det — Giles 5 pass from Hipple (Murray kick)
Cin — Kinnebrew 1 run (Breech kick)

Cleveland 24, Indianapolis 9—At Hoosier Dome, attendance 57,962. Bernie Kosar passed for three touchdowns, including a career-long 72-yarder to Herman Fontenot, as the Browns easily defeated the winless Colts. Cleveland took a 14-0 first-half lead on Kosar's touchdown passes to Fontenot and Brian Brennan (14 yards). Kosar added a nine-yard completion to Ozzie Newsome, and Matt Bahr kicked a 38-yard field goal to finish the Browns' scoring. Reggie Camp had four sacks to pace Cleveland's defense.

Cleveland	14	0	10	0	— 24
Indianapolis	0	3	0	6	— 9

Clev — Brennan 14 pass from Kosar (Bahr kick)
Clev — Fontenot 72 pass from Kosar (Bahr kick)
Ind — FG Biasucci 40
Clev — Newsome 9 pass from Kosar (Bahr kick)
Clev — FG Bahr 38
Ind — Bouza 6 pass from Trudeau (kick failed)

New York Giants 17, Dallas 14—At Giants Stadium, attendance 74,871. Joe Morris ran for 181 yards and two touchdowns as the Giants downed the Cowboys to maintain a share of first place in the NFC East. New York took a 10-7 halftime lead on Raul Allegre's 25-yard field goal and Morris's eight-yard scoring run. Following a six-yard punt by the Cowboys' John Saxon, Morris capped a five-play, 62-yard drive with a six-yard run for the game-winning score. Carl Banks had two sacks and a fumble recovery to spearhead the Giants' defense.

Dallas	0	7	0	7	— 14
N.Y. Giants	3	7	0	7	— 17

NYG — FG Allegre 25
Dall — Renfro 11 pass from Pelluer (Septien kick)
NYG — Morris 8 run (Allegre kick)
NYG — Morris 6 run (Allegre kick)
Dall — Dorsett 23 run (Septien kick)

Denver 21, Los Angeles Raiders 10—At Memorial Coliseum, attendance 90,153. Mike Harden returned an interception for one touchdown and John Elway passed for another as the Broncos downed the Raiders for the second time this season. Denver led 14-3 after three quarters on Steve Sewell's eight-yard scoring run and Elway's three-yard touchdown pass to Sammy Winder. Harden, who accounted for two of Denver's six takeaways with a pair of interceptions, followed a Los Angeles touchdown by returning an interception 40 yards for a score. Raiders tight end Todd Christensen caught a personal-high 11 passes for 158 yards.

Denver	0	7	7	7	— 21
L.A. Raiders	3	0	0	7	— 10

Raiders — FG Bahr 38
Den — Sewell 8 run (Karlis kick)
Den — Winder 3 pass from Elway (Karlis kick)
Raiders — Hester 20 pass from Wilson (Bahr kick)
Den — Harden 40 interception return (Karlis kick)

Pittsburgh 27, Green Bay 3—At Three Rivers Stadium, attendance 52,831. Mark Malone and Weegie Thompson combined for three touchdown passes to power the Steelers over the Packers. Thompson, starting in place of injured Louis Lipps, scored on an 18-yard pass from Malone following a fumble recovery by Gary Dunn. Thompson added scoring receptions of nine and six yards in the second half to complete the scoring. His six receptions for 78 yards and three touchdowns were all career highs. An interception by Mike Merriweather preceded Thompson's final score.

Green Bay	0	3	0	0	— 3
Pittsburgh	10	3	7	7	— 27

Pitt — FG Anderson 25
Pitt — Thompson 18 pass from Malone (Anderson kick)
Pitt — FG Anderson 40
GB — FG Del Greco 34
Pitt — Thompson 9 pass from Malone (Anderson kick)
Pitt — Thompson 6 pass from Malone (Anderson kick)

Miami 28, Houston 7—At Orange Bowl, attendance 43,804. Dan Marino threw four touchdown passes to lead the Dolphins to their second straight win for the first time this season. After a scoreless first quarter, Marino blew the game wide open by throwing three quick scoring passes in a 4:29 span of the second period. Mark Clayton began the onslaught with an eight-yard reception. Nat Moore followed with a 38-yard catch. And an interception by Donovan Rose set up Tony Nathan's three-yard score 39 seconds before halftime. Marino and Mark Duper connected on an 85-yard touchdown play to open the second half. Duper finished with 110 yards on two receptions. Houston did not penetrate Miami's 40-yard line until the fourth quarter.

Houston	0	0	0	7	— 7
Miami	0	21	7	0	— 28

Mia — Clayton 8 pass from Marino (Reveiz kick)
Mia — Moore 38 pass from Marino (Reveiz kick)
Mia — Nathan 3 pass from Marino (Reveiz kick)
Mia — Duper 85 pass from Marino (Reveiz kick)
Hou — Rozier 1 run (Zendejas kick)

Kansas City 24, San Diego 23—At San Diego Jack Murphy Stadium, attendance 48,518. Nick Lowery's 37-yard field goal with seven seconds remaining brought the Chiefs their second comeback win over the Chargers in three weeks. Kansas City rallied from a 16-0 deficit to take a 21-16 lead on a pair of Bill Kenney touchdown passes to Jeff Smith (one yard) and Emile Harry (five), and Mike Pruitt's one-yard scoring run with 1:46 to play. San Diego's Tom Flick, making his first NFL start, scored on a one-yard bootleg with 1:02 remaining to put the Chargers back on top 23-21. The Chiefs' win spoiled the NFL head coaching debut of the Chargers' Al Saunders, who replaced Don Coryell.

Kansas City	0	0	7	17	— 24
San Diego	2	14	0	7	— 23

SD — Safety, ball snapped out of end zone
SD — Chandler 7 pass from Flick (Benirschke kick)
SD — Spencer 4 run (Benirschke kick)
KC — Smith 1 pass from Kenney (Lowery kick)
KC — Harry 5 pass from Kenney (Lowery kick)
KC — Pruitt 1 run (Lowery kick)
SD — Flick 1 run (Benirschke kick)
KC — FG Lowery 37

Washington 44, Minnesota 38—At Robert F. Kennedy Stadium, attendance 51,928. Jay Schroeder's 38-yard touchdown pass to Gary Clark 1:46 into overtime clinched the Redskins' 44-38 win. The extra period was forced when Vikings' defensive end Neil Elshire blocked Max Zendejas's extra-point attempt following George Rogers's two-yard touchdown run with 13 seconds remaining in regulation time. Schroeder completed 24 of 47 passes for 378 yards, including a 34-yard scoring pass to Art Monk. Monk and Clark each had six catches for 102 and 123 yards, respectively. Minnesota's Tommy Kramer connected on 20 of 35 passes for a club-record 490 yards and four touchdowns.

Minnesota	14	3	14	7	0	— 38
Washington	10	6	10	12	6	— 44

Wash — Rogers 2 run (Zendejas kick)
Wash — FG Zendejas 25
Minn — Brown 1 run (C. Nelson kick)
Minn — Lewis 67 pass from Kramer (C. Nelson kick)
Wash — Manley 26 fumble recovery return (kick blocked)
Minn — FG C. Nelson 39
Minn — Jordan 68 pass from Kramer (C. Nelson kick)
Wash — FG Zendejas 42
Wash — Rogers 40 run (Zendejas kick)
Minn — Lewis 76 pass from Kramer (C. Nelson kick)
Minn — D. Nelson 1 pass from Kramer (C. Nelson kick)
Wash — Monk 34 pass from Schroeder (kick failed)
Wash — Rogers 2 run (kick blocked)
Wash — Clark 38 pass from Schroeder (no kick)

New York Jets 38, Seattle 7—At Kingdome, attendance 62,497. Ken O'Brien completed 26 of 32 passes for 431 yards and four touchdowns as the Jets rolled over the Seahawks to register their club-record seventh straight win. Trailing 7-3 in the second quarter, New York scored 35 unanswered points within a 2:30 span, beginning with O'Brien scoring passes of 50 yards to Al Toon and 83 yards to Wesley Walker. O'Brien added second-half touchdown completions to Toon (36 yards) and Mickey Shuler (1). Toon (nine catches for 195 yards) and Walker (six for 161) each had over 100 yards receiving for the second time this season.

N.Y. Jets	3	21	7	7	— 38
Seattle	7	0	0	0	— 7

NYJ — FG Leahy 50
Sea — Turner 27 pass from Gilbert (Johnson kick)
NYJ — Toon 50 pass from O'Brien (Leahy kick)
NYJ — Walker 83 pass from O'Brien (Leahy kick)
NYJ — McNeil 9 run (Leahy kick)
NYJ — Toon 36 pass from O'Brien (Leahy kick)
NYJ — Shuler 1 pass from O'Brien (Leahy kick)

St. Louis 13, Philadelphia 10—At Busch Memorial Stadium, attendance 33,051. The Cardinals scored two touchdowns in the final six minutes of the game to snap a four-game losing streak at home. Cliff Stoudt came off the bench to throw a 14-yard touchdown pass to Roy Green with 5:04 left and Stump Mitchell scored on a one-yard run with 36 seconds remaining to cap the comeback. The Eagles came close to pulling the game out when Ron Jaworski completed a 34-yard pass to Gregg Garrity, who was tackled at the Cardinals' 2-yard line on the game's final play. Defensive end Reggie White recorded a personal-high three-and-a-half sacks for Philadelphia.

Philadelphia	7	0	3	0	—	10
St. Louis	0	0	0	13	—	13

Phil — Crawford 1 run (McFadden kick)
Phil — FG McFadden 31
StL — Green 14 pass from Stoudt (Lee kick)
StL — Mitchell 1 run (kick blocked)

New Orleans 23, San Francisco 10—At Louisiana Superdome, attendance 53,234. Rookie running back Rueben Mayes ran for 128 yards and a pair of touchdowns to power the Saints over the 49ers. New Orleans took a 14-0 lead after its first two possessions on Mayes's scoring runs of 4 and 27 yards. Morten Andersen, who scored in his club-record forty-third straight game, kicked second-half field goals of 45, 50, and 23 yards. The Saints' defense held Roger Craig and the 49ers' rushing attack to only 52 yards.

San Francisco	3	7	0	0	—	10
New Orleans	14	0	3	6	—	23

NO — Mayes 4 run (Andersen kick)
NO — Mayes 27 run (Andersen kick)
SF — FG Wersching 50
SF — Frank 3 pass from Moroski (Wersching kick)
NO — FG Andersen 45
NO — FG Andersen 50
NO — FG Andersen 23

Monday, November 3

Los Angeles Rams 20, Chicago 17—At Soldier Field, attendance 64,877. Mike Lansford connected on a 50-yard field goal with four seconds remaining to help the Rams down the Bears. Trailing 17-10 in the third quarter, Rams quarterback Steve Dils fired a 65-yard bomb to Ron Brown to tie the score 17-17. LeRoy Irvin returned a fumble 22 yards for Los Angeles's first touchdown. Eric Dickerson led all rushers with 111 yards on 29 carries. Chicago's Kevin Butler tied his own club record with his thirteenth straight field goal in the first period.

L.A. Rams	0	0	17	3	—	20
Chicago	3	0	14	0	—	17

Chi — FG Butler 30
Rams — FG Lansford 26
Rams — Irvin 22 fumble recovery return (Lansford kick)
Chi — Sanders 10 run (Butler kick)
Chi — Sanders 34 run (Butler kick)
Rams — Brown 65 pass from Dils (Lansford kick)
Rams — FG Lansford 50

Tenth Week Summaries

Standings

American Football Conference

Eastern Division

	W	L	T	Pct.	Pts.	OP
N.Y. Jets	9	1	0	.900	272	187
New England	7	3	0	.700	274	153
Miami	4	6	0	.400	242	266
Buffalo	3	7	0	.300	189	217
Indianapolis	0	10	0	.000	111	260

Central Division

	W	L	T	Pct.	Pts.	OP
Cleveland	7	3	0	.700	225	205
Cincinnati	6	4	0	.600	237	271
Pittsburgh	3	7	0	.300	154	211
Houston	2	8	0	.200	184	234

Western Division

	W	L	T	Pct.	Pts.	OP
Denver	8	2	0	.800	233	155
Kansas City	7	3	0	.700	232	202
L.A. Raiders	6	4	0	.600	191	181
Seattle	5	5	0	.500	192	185
San Diego	2	8	0	.200	198	251

National Football Conference

Eastern Division

	W	L	T	Pct.	Pts.	OP
N.Y. Giants	8	2	0	.800	203	138
Washington	8	2	0	.800	228	190
Dallas	6	4	0	.600	253	168
Philadelphia	3	7	0	.300	145	196
St. Louis	2	8	0	.200	133	247

Central Division

	W	L	T	Pct.	Pts.	OP
Chicago	8	2	0	.800	226	120
Minnesota	6	4	0	.600	238	168
Detroit	3	7	0	.300	150	191
Tampa Bay	2	8	0	.200	164	269
Green Bay	1	9	0	.100	118	265

Western Division

	W	L	T	Pct.	Pts.	OP
L.A. Rams	7	3	0	.700	164	150
San Francisco	6	3	1	.650	254	164
Atlanta	5	4	1	.550	198	185
New Orleans	5	5	0	.500	181	160

Sunday, November 9

Chicago 23, Tampa Bay 3—At Tampa Stadium, attendance 70,097. Walter Payton ran for his seventy-seventh career 100-yard game when he gained 139 yards on 20 carries as the Bears rolled over the Buccaneers. Mike Tomczak ran one yard for a score and completed a 37-yard touchdown pass to Willie Gault to give Chicago a 14-3 first-quarter advantage. Kevin Butler added three field goals (25, 23, and 22 yards) to finish the Bears' scoring. William Perry had two sacks to pace Chicago's defense.

Chicago	14	3	0	6	—	23
Tampa Bay	3	0	0	0	—	3

Chi — Tomczak 1 run (Butler kick)
Chi — Gault 37 pass from Tomczak (Butler kick)
TB — FG Igwebuike 42
Chi — FG Butler 25
Chi — FG Butler 23
Chi — FG Butler 22

Houston 32, Cincinnati 28—At Astrodome, attendance 32,120. Rookie running back Ray Wallace scored on a pair of one-yard runs to help the Oilers snap an eight-game losing streak. Houston took a 13-0 second-quarter lead on Warren Moon's five-yard scoring pass to Jamie Williams and Tony Zendejas's 42- and 25-yard field goals. Jeff Donaldson's interception set up Wallace's second score and gave the Oilers a commanding 26-0 lead. Zendejas's other two field goals, from 30 and 46 yards, proved decisive as the Bengals rallied to score 28 points in the second half.

Cincinnati	0	0	14	14	—	28
Houston	10	9	10	3	—	32

Hou — Williams 5 pass from Moon (Zendejas kick)
Hou — FG Zendejas 42
Hou — FG Zendejas 25
Hou — Wallace 1 run (kick failed)
Hou — Wallace 1 run (Zendejas kick)
Cin — Kinnebrew 29 pass from Anderson (Breech kick)
Hou — FG Zendejas 30
Cin — Brooks 39 pass from Esiason (Breech kick)
Cin — Brooks 8 pass from Esiason (Breech kick)
Cin — Muñoz 5 pass from Esiason (Breech kick)
Hou — FG Zendejas 46

Los Angeles Raiders 17, Dallas 13—At Texas Stadium, attendance 61,706. Jim Plunkett came off the bench to throw for two touchdowns and ignite the Raiders' comeback win over the Cowboys. Trailing 10-3 at halftime, Plunkett completed second-half scoring passes of 20 and 40 yards to Dokie Williams to give Los Angeles the lead for good. Vann McElroy intercepted two passes as the Raiders victimized Cowboys' quarterback Steve Pelluer for a Dallas club-record-tying five interceptions.

L.A. Raiders	0	3	7	7	—	17
Dallas	3	7	3	0	—	13

Dall — FG Septien 20
Raiders — FG Bahr 45
Dall — Dorsett 13 run (Septien kick)
Raiders — Williams 20 pass from Plunkett (Bahr kick)
Dall — FG Septien 20
Raiders — Williams 40 pass from Plunkett (Bahr kick)

New Orleans 6, Los Angeles Rams 0—At Louisiana Superdome, attendance 62,352. Morten Andersen kicked a pair of second-half field goals and the Saints' defense held the Rams' high-powered rushing attack to 53 yards en route to a 6-0 win. Andersen's first field goal, a 20-yarder, completed a 71-yard drive that consumed 10:50 of the third quarter. Linebacker James Haynes's recovery of Eric Dickerson's fumble at the Los Angeles 21-yard line set up Andersen's 22-yard field goal 2:29 into the fourth quarter. Dickerson, the NFL's leading rusher, was held to a season-low 57 yards. Bruce Clark had two sacks and a fumble recovery to earn NFC defensive player of the week honors.

L.A. Rams	0	0	0	0	—	0
New Orleans	0	0	3	3	—	6

NO — FG Andersen 20
NO — FG Andersen 22

Minnesota 24, Detroit 10—At Pontiac Silverdome, attendance 53,725. Minnesota took advantage of three Detroit turnovers, turning all three into scores, as the Vikings easily defeated the Lions. Joey Browner opened the scoring by returning an interception 39 yards for a touchdown. Jesse Solomon's fumble recovery set up Chuck Nelson's 24-yard field goal to give Minnesota a 10-0 halftime lead. Tommy Kramer, who completed 24 of 39 for 284 yards, followed Doug Martin's fumble recovery with an 11-yard touchdown pass to Anthony Carter. Carter finished with 111 yards on five receptions.

Minnesota	10	0	7	7	—	24
Detroit	0	0	10	0	—	10

Minn — Browner 39 interception return (C. Nelson kick)
Minn — FG C. Nelson 24
Det — Giles 10 pass from Hipple (Murray kick)
Minn — Carter 11 pass from Kramer (C. Nelson kick)
Det — FG Murray 35
Minn — Rice 4 run (C. Nelson kick)

New England 30, Indianapolis 21—At Hoosier Dome, attendance 56,890. Tony Franklin kicked three field goals and Tony Eason passed for two touchdowns to guide the Patriots past the Colts. Trailing 14-6 at halftime, Eason completed scoring passes of eight yards to Willie Scott and two yards to Irving Fryar to give New England the lead for good, 20-14. Franklin, the NFL's leading scorer with 100 points, connected on field goals from 38, 31, and 24 yards. Steve Nelson and Ronnie Lippett each had a pair of interceptions.

New England	3	3	14	10	—	30
Indianapolis	7	7	0	7	—	21

Ind — McMillan 1 run (Biasucci kick)
NE — FG Franklin 38
Ind — Trudeau 1 run (Biasucci kick)
NE — FG Franklin 31
NE — Scott 8 pass from Eason (Franklin kick)
NE — Fryar 2 pass from Eason (Franklin kick)
NE — FG Franklin 24
NE — Tatupu 1 run (Franklin kick)
Ind — Bouza 19 pass from Trudeau (Biasucci kick)

New York Giants 17, Philadelphia 14—At Veterans Stadium, attendance 60,601. Joe Morris carried 27 times for 111 yards and two touchdowns to spearhead the Giants' victory. Reserve quarterback Jeff Hostetler blocked a Philadelphia punt to set up Morris's 18-yard scoring run and give New York a 7-0 lead. New York increased its lead to 17-0 on Raul Allegre's 22-yard field goal and Morris's three-yard touchdown run. Both scores were set up by interceptions by Elvis Patterson and Gary Reasons. Morris's fourth-straight 100-yard effort was a club-record. Lawrence Taylor had three of New York's seven sacks.

N.Y. Giants	0	10	7	0	—	17
Philadelphia	0	0	0	14	—	14

NYG — Morris 18 run (Allegre kick)
NYG — FG Allegre 22
NYG — Morris 3 run (Allegre kick)
Phil — Quick 75 pass from Cunningham (McFadden kick)
Phil — Cunningham 1 run (McFadden kick)

New York Jets 28, Atlanta 14—At Atlanta-Fulton County Stadium, attendance 53,476. Ken O'Brien completed 26 of 33 passes, including a club-record 17 straight, for 322 yards and three touchdowns to power the Jets over the Falcons. New York took a commanding 21-0 second-quarter lead on O'Brien's scoring strikes to Al Toon (59 yards) and Wesley Walker (46 and 16). Atlanta's David Archer connected on 21 of 36 passes for 350 yards and two touchdowns, while teammate Charlie Brown led all receivers with six catches for 112 yards.

N.Y. Jets	0	21	7	0	—	28
Atlanta	0	0	7	7	—	14

NYJ — Toon 59 pass from O'Brien (Leahy kick)
NYJ — Walker 46 pass from O'Brien (Leahy kick)
NYJ — Walker 16 pass from O'Brien (Leahy kick)
NYJ — McNeil 3 run (Leahy kick)
Atl — Cox 20 pass from Archer (Luckhurst kick)
Atl — Whisenhunt 23 pass from Archer (Luckhurst kick)

Buffalo 16, Pittsburgh 12—At Rich Stadium, attendance 72,000. Robb Riddick rushed for over 100 yards for the first time in his career to power Buffalo past Pittsburgh. The Bills led 13-0 at halftime on Jim Kelly's three-yard touchdown pass to Andre Reed and Riddick's five-yard run. The Steelers narrowed the Bills' margin to 13-12 with third-quarter touchdowns by Earnest Jackson (five-yard run) and Weegie Thompson (11-yard pass), but both extra-point attempts failed. Scott Norwood's 29-yard field goal in the fourth quarter helped Buffalo head coach Marv Levy clinch his first win with the Bills.

Pittsburgh	0	0	12	0	—	12
Buffalo	6	7	0	3	—	16

Buff — Reed 3 pass from Kelly (kicked failed)
Buff — Riddick 5 run (Norwood kick)
Pitt — Jackson 5 run (kick failed)
Pitt — Thompson 11 pass from Malone (kick failed)
Buff — FG Norwood 29

San Francisco 43, St. Louis 17—At Candlestick Park, attendance 59,172. Joe Montana completed 13 of 19 passes for 270 yards, including three touchdowns to Jerry Rice, as the 49ers demolished the Cardinals. Montana, who returned to action following a nine-week layoff after back surgery, threw scoring passes of 45, 40, and 44 yards to Rice. Rice had four catches for 156 yards to lead all receivers. Joe Cribbs carried 21 times for 105 yards. Safety Tom Holmoe's 78-yard interception return for a touchdown gave the 49ers five scoring returns for the season to tie the club record.

St. Louis	3	7	0	7	—	17
San Francicso	10	13	7	13	—	43

SF — FG Wersching 47
SF — Rice 45 pass from Montana (Wersching kick)
StL — FG Lee 37
SF — FG Wersching 35
SF — Rice 40 pass from Montana (Wersching kick)
StL — Smith 24 pass from Stoudt (Lee kick)
SF — FG Wersching 41
SF — Rice 44 pass from Montana (Wersching kick)
SF — Cribbs 3 run (kick blocked)
SF — Holmoe 78 interception return (Wersching kick)
StL — Smith 24 pass from Stoudt (Lee kick)

San Diego 9, Denver 3—At Mile High Stadium, attendance 75,012. Rolf Benirschke kicked three field goals to help the Chargers end an eight-game losing streak and give head coach Al Saunders his first NFL victory. Benirschke's field goals came from 25, 48, and 21 yards. San Diego's Jeff Dale had two interceptions to earn AFC defensive player of the week honors. The Chargers' defense forced five Broncos turnovers, including three inside San Diego's 10-yard line.

San Diego	3	3	0	3	—	9
Denver	0	3	0	0	—	3

SD — FG Benirschke 25
Den — FG Karlis 44
SD — FG Benirschke 48
SD — FG Benirschke 21

Kansas City 27, Seattle 7—At Arrowhead Stadium, attendance 53,268. Bill Kenney threw for 256 yards and three touchdowns as Kansas City overpowered Seattle 27-7. After a scoreless first quarter, Kenney completed touchdown passes to Walt Arnold (two yards) and Stephone Paige (eight). Nick Lowery's 35-yard field goal put the Chiefs ahead 17-0 at halftime. Kansas City's defense held Seattle to only 133 net yards and eight first downs in capturing its fourth victory in a row.

Seattle	0	0	0	7 —	7
Kansas City	0	17	7	3 —	27

KC —Arnold 2 pass from Kenney (Lowery kick)
KC —FG Lowery 35
KC —Paige 8 pass from Kenney (Lowery kick)
KC —Carson 25 pass from Kenney (Lowery kick)
KC —FG Lowery 37
Sea —Largent 38 pass from Gilbert (Johnson kick)

Washington 16, Green Bay 7—At Lambeau Field, attendance 47,728. Jay Schroeder passed for two touchdowns to highlight the Redskins' 16-7 victory over the Packers. Washington overcame a 7-6 deficit on Schroeder's six-yard scoring pass to Kelvin Bryant. Schroeder also completed a 26-yard strike to Ricky Sanders to give the Redskins a 13-7 halftime lead. Max Zendejas added a 30-yard field goal with 5:29 left in the game to clinch the win. George Rogers was held without a rushing touchdown to bring his string of 12 consecutive games with a rushing score to an end.

Washington	6	0	7	3 —	16
Green Bay	7	0	0	0 —	7

GB —Epps 3 pass from Wright (Del Greco kick)
Wash —Sanders 26 pass from Schroeder (kick failed)
Wash —Bryant 6 pass from Schroeder (Zendejas kick)
Wash —FG Zendejas 30

Monday, November 10

Cleveland 26, Miami 16—At Cleveland Stadium, attendance 77,949. Bernie Kosar completed 32 of 50 passes for 401 yards to lead the Browns past the Dolphins. Matt Bahr's three field goals (32, 19, and 18 yards) and tight end Harry Holt's 16-yard touchdown run gave Cleveland a 16-10 halftime advantage. Curtis Dickey, who rushed for 92 yards on 15 attempts, scored on a 13-yard run, and Bahr kicked a 21-yard field goal in the second half to complete the Browns' scoring. Kosar joined Brian Sipe (444) and Otto Graham (401) as the only quarterbacks in Cleveland history to throw for over 400 yards in a game.

Miami	0	10	0	6 —	16
Cleveland	6	10	7	3 —	26

Clev —FG Bahr 32
Clev —FG Bahr 19
Mia —FG Reveiz 20
Clev —Holt 16 run (Bahr kick)
Mia —Duper 24 pass from Marino (Reveiz kick)
Clev —FG Bahr 18
Clev —Dickey 13 run (Bahr kick)
Clev —FG Bahr 21
Mia —Clayton 22 pass from Marino (kick failed)

Eleventh Week Summaries

Standings

American Football Conference

Eastern Division

	W	L	T	Pct.	Pts.	OP
N.Y. Jets	10	1	0	.909	303	203
New England	8	3	0	.727	304	181
Miami	5	6	0	.455	276	290
Buffalo	3	8	0	.273	213	251
Indianapolis	0	11	0	.000	127	291

Central Division

	W	L	T	Pct.	Pts.	OP
Cincinnati	7	4	0	.636	271	278
Cleveland	7	4	0	.636	239	232
Pittsburgh	4	7	0	.364	175	221
Houston	2	9	0	.182	194	255

Western Division

	W	L	T	Pct.	Pts.	OP
Denver	9	2	0	.818	271	172
Kansas City	7	4	0	.636	249	240
L.A. Raiders	7	4	0	.636	218	195
Seattle	5	6	0	.455	199	219
San Diego	2	9	0	.182	219	275

National Football Conference

Eastern Division

	W	L	T	Pct.	Pts.	OP
N.Y. Giants	9	2	0	.818	225	158
Washington	9	2	0	.818	242	196
Dallas	7	4	0	.636	277	189
Philadelphia	3	8	0	.273	156	209
St. Louis	2	9	0	.182	140	263

Central Division

	W	L	T	Pct.	Pts.	OP
Chicago	9	2	0	.818	239	130
Minnesota	6	5	0	.545	258	190
Detroit	4	7	0	.364	163	202
Green Bay	2	9	0	.182	149	272
Tampa Bay	2	9	0	.182	171	300

Western Division

	W	L	T	Pct.	Pts.	OP
L.A. Rams	7	4	0	.636	192	180
San Francisco	6	4	1	.591	260	178
New Orleans	6	5	0	.545	197	167
Atlanta	5	5	1	.500	208	198

Sunday, November 16

Chicago 13, Atlanta 10—At Atlanta-Fulton County Stadium, attendance 55,520. Kevin Butler kicked two field goals and Mike Tomczak ran for one touchdown as the Bears squeaked past the Falcons. Chicago overcame a 10-3 halftime deficit when Tomczak set up his one-yard scoring run with an 85-yard pass to Emery Moorehead. Butler's decisive kick, a 44-yarder, capped a nine-play, 44-yard drive. The Chicago defense held Atlanta to two first downs and 52 total yards in the second half. Bears safety Dave Duerson had two sacks and an interception.

Chicago	0	3	10	0 —	13
Atlanta	3	7	0	0 —	10

Atl —FG Haji-Sheikh 37
Atl —Williams 14 interception return (Haji-Sheikh kick)
Chi —FG Butler 32
Chi —Tomczak 1 run (Butler kick)
Chi —FG Butler 44

Los Angeles Raiders 27, Cleveland 14—At Memorial Coliseum, attendance 65,461. Jim Plunkett passed for three touchdowns, including two to Dokie Williams, to highlight the Raiders' 27-14 victory. Los Angeles opened a 17-7 halftime lead as Plunkett completed scoring passes to Williams (46 yards) and Todd Christensen (3), and Chris Bahr kicked a 40-yard field goal. Following a pair of Cleveland touchdowns, Plunkett added a 43-yard scoring strike to Williams and Bahr kicked a 27-yard field goal to put the game away. Williams finished with three receptions for 113 yards. Greg Townsend registered three of the Raiders' six sacks.

Cleveland	0	7	7	0 —	14
L.A. Raiders	10	7	0	10 —	27

Raiders —Williams 46 pass from Plunkett (C. Bahr kick)
Raiders —FG C. Bahr 40
Raiders —Christensen 3 pass from Plunkett (C. Bahr kick)
Clev —Mack 1 run (M. Bahr kick)
Clev —Mack 2 run (M. Bahr kick)
Raiders —Williams 43 pass from Plunkett (C. Bahr kick)
Raiders —FG C. Bahr 27

Dallas 24, San Diego 21—At San Diego Jack Murphy Stadium, attendance 55,622. Steve Pelluer scored on a two-yard bootleg run with 1:37 remaining as the Cowboys scored a 24-21 comeback win. Dallas jumped out to a 10-0 lead on Rafael Septien's 33-yard field goal and Pelluer's 68-yard touchdown pass to Mike Sherrard. But San Diego came back with three unanswered touchdowns. Tim Spencer scored on a seven-yard run and Dan Fouts completed a pair of scoring passes to Kellen Winslow (28 and 4 yards) to give the Chargers a 21-10 lead. Herschel Walker's one-yard scoring run, which followed a blocked punt by Michael Downs, closed the gap to 21-17.

Dallas	10	0	0	14 —	24
San Diego	0	7	7	7 —	21

Dall —FG Septien 33
Dall —Sherrard 68 pass from Pelluer (Septien kick)
SD —Spencer 7 run (Benirschke kick)
SD —Winslow 28 pass from Fouts (Benirschke kick)
SD —Winslow 4 pass from Fouts (Benirschke kick)
Dall —Walker 1 run (Septien kick)
Dall —Pelluer 2 run (Septien kick)

Detroit 13, Philadelphia 11—At Veterans Stadium, attendance 54,568. Eddie Murray kicked a 41-yard field goal with 12 seconds left in the game to help the Lions snap a four-game losing streak. Detroit took a 7-5 halftime lead on Joe Ferguson's 72-yard touchdown pass to Jeff Chadwick. Mike Cofer recovered a Randall Cunningham fumble on the Eagles' 37-yard line with 1:44 remaining to set up Murray's winning field goal. Detroit's defense registered 11 sacks but could not contain Cunningham, who rushed for 113 yards on 14 carries. Cunningham became the first NFL quarterback to gain over 100 yards rushing since Denver's Norris Weese gained 120 on 12 carries against Chicago on December 12, 1976.

Detroit	7	0	0	6 —	13
Philadelphia	0	5	0	6 —	11

Det —Chadwick 72 pass from Ferguson (Murray kick)
Phil —FG McFadden 33
Phil —Safety, Brown tackled Ferguson in end zone
Phil —FG McFadden 28
Det —FG Murray 38
Phil —FG McFadden 25
Det —FG Murray 41

Pittsburgh 21, Houston 10—At Three Rivers Stadium, attendance 49,724. Walter Abercrombie and Earnest Jackson each ran for touchdowns and Mark Malone threw for another score to give the Steelers a 21-10 win over the Oilers. Harvey Clayton's first-quarter interception set up Abercrombie's eight-yard touchdown run. After Houston scored on a 33-yard touchdown pass from Warren Moon to Ernest Givins, Pittsburgh answered with a three-yard scoring run by Jackson. Malone capped a six-play, 74-yard drive with a 17-yard completion to Rich Erenberg with 12:04 left in the second quarter. The victory was the Steelers' eighth in their last nine meetings with the Oilers.

Houston	7	3	0	0 —	10
Pittsburgh	14	7	0	0 —	21

Pitt —Abercrombie 8 run (Anderson kick)
Hou —Givins 33 pass from Moon (Zendejas kick)
Pitt —Jackson 3 run (Anderson kick)
Pitt —Erenberg 17 pass from Malone (Anderson kick)
Hou —FG Zendejas 44

New York Jets 31, Indianapolis 16—At Giants Stadium, attendance 65,149. Wesley Walker caught five passes for 113 yards, including three touchdowns from Ken O'Brien, to lead the Jets over the Colts. Holding a slim 17-16 lead in the fourth quarter, Johnny Hector raced 17 yards for one score and O'Brien fired a five-yard strike to Walker for another to clinch the win for New York. Walker also caught touchdown passes of 19 and 5 yards. Colts rookie Billy Brooks led all receivers with nine receptions for 177 yards. Johnny Lynn had two interceptions as the Jets produced a season-high six takeaways.

Indianapolis	7	2	0	7 —	16
N.Y. Jets	7	7	3	14 —	31

NYJ —Walker 19 pass from O'Brien (Leahy kick)
Ind —McMillan 4 run (Biasucci kick)
NYJ —Walker 5 pass from O'Brien (Leahy kick)
Ind —Safety, Leiding tackled Jennings in end zone
NYJ —FG Leahy 32
Ind —Brooks 48 pass from Trudeau (Biasucci kick)
NYJ —Hector 17 run (Leahy kick)
NYJ —Walker 5 pass from O'Brien (Leahy kick)

Denver 38, Kansas City 17—At Mile High Stadium, attendance 75,745. The Broncos exploded for 31 points in the first 19:10 en route to registering their eighth win. Punter Chris Norman's 43-yard touchdown pass to Steve Wilson, Andre Townsend's seven-yard fumble recovery return for a touchdown, and Gerald Willhite's one-yard scoring run gave Denver a commanding 21-0 first-quarter lead. Willhite scored on a 70-yard punt return and Rich Karlis added a 37-yard field goal in the second quarter as the Broncos never looked back. Willhite also had a one-yard touchdown in the third quarter to complete the Broncos' scoring.

Kansas City	0	7	10	0 —	17
Denver	21	10	7	0 —	38

Den —Wilson 43 pass from Norman (Karlis kick)
Den —Townsend 7 fumble recovery return (Karlis kick)
Den —Willhite 1 run (Karlis kick)
Den —Willhite 70 punt return (Karlis kick)
Den —FG Karlis 37
KC —Marshall 15 pass from Kenney (Lowery kick)
KC —Carson 27 pass from Kenney (Lowery kick)
Den —Willhite 1 run (Karlis kick)
KC —FG Lowery 37

New England 30, Los Angeles Rams 28—At Anaheim Stadium, attendance 64,339. Irving Fryar caught a 25-yard desperation pass from Tony Eason for a touchdown with one second remaining in the game to give the Patriots a dramatic comeback win. Trailing 28-16 in the fourth quarter, Eason completed a six-yard scoring pass to Fryar to cut the Patriots' deficit to 28-23. New England began the game-winning drive on its own 13 with 1:45 remaining. Eason's pass into a crowd in the end zone was tipped by Stanley Morgan into Fryar's hands. Eason set club records with 36 completions and 52 attempts while throwing for 375 yards. Los Angeles rookie quarterback Jim Everett, making his NFL debut, completed 12 of 19 passes for 193 yards and three touchdowns. The Rams' Eric Dickerson led all rushers with 102 yards on 24 attempts.

New England	6	10	0	14 —	30
L.A. Rams	0	14	7	7 —	28

NE —FG Franklin 42
NE —FG Franklin 45
NE —McSwain 31 blocked punt return (Franklin kick)
Rams —Ellard 34 pass from Everett (Lansford kick)
Rams —Redden 24 pass from Everett (Lansford kick)
NE —FG Franklin 19
Rams —Redden 11 run (Lansford kick)
Rams —Ellard 20 pass from Everett (Lansford kick)
NE —Fryar 6 pass from Eason (Franklin kick)
NE —Fryar 25 pass from Eason (Franklin kick)

Miami 34, Buffalo 24—At Rich Stadium, attendance 76,474. Dan Marino completed a career-high 39 of 54 passes for 404 yards and four touchdowns to rally the Dolphins over the Bills. Marino threw touchdown passes to Mark Duper (27 yards), Dan Johnson (4), and Lorenzo Hampton (2) in the second half to erase a 21-10 Buffalo lead. He also fired a 19-yard strike to Ron Davenport in the second quarter. Duper finished with seven receptions for 109 yards.

Miami	0	10	10	14 —	34
Buffalo	7	14	3	0 —	24

Buff —Byrum 10 pass from Kelly (Norwood kick)
Mia —Davenport 19 pass from Marino (Reveiz kick)
Buff —Riddick 11 run (Norwood kick)
Buff —Butler 25 pass from Kelly (Norwood kick)
Mia —FG Reveiz 52
Mia —FG Reveiz 36
Mia —Duper 27 pass from Marino (Reveiz kick)
Buff —FG Norwood 39
Mia —Johnson 4 pass from Marino (Reveiz kick)
Mia —Hampton 2 pass from Marino (Reveiz kick)

New York Giants 22, Minnesota 20—At Metrodome, attendance 62,003. Raul Allegre kicked five field goals, including a game-winning 33-yarder with 12 second left, to lift the Giants over the Vikings. New York took a 9-6 first-half lead on Allegre field goals from 41, 37, and 24 yards. Minnesota came back with a pair of touchdowns, but Allegre's 37-yard field goal and Phil Simms's 25-yard touchdown pass to Bobby Johnson gave the Giants a 20-19 lead. New York marched 44 yards in nine plays to set up Allegre's decisive kick. Simms's 22-yard pass to Johnson on a fourth-and-17 was the key play in the drive.

N.Y. Giants	3	6	3	10	— 22
Minnesota	3	3	7	7	— 20

NYG —FG Allegre 41
Minn —FG C. Nelson 39
NYG —FG Allegre 37
Minn —FG C. Nelson 44
NYG —FG Allegre 24
Minn —Rice 8 pass from Kramer (C. Nelson kick)
NYG —FG Allegre 37
NYG —B. Johnson 25 pass from Simms (Allegre kick)
Minn —Carter 33 pass from Wilson (C. Nelson kick)
NYG —FG Allegre 33

New Orleans 16, St. Louis 7—At Busch Memorial Stadium, attendance 32,069. Rookie Rueben Mayes rushed for 127 yards on 24 carries and Morten Andersen kicked three field goals to lead the Saints over the Cardinals. After a scoreless first quarter, Dave Wilson completed a 10-yard scoring pass to Mike Jones and Andersen kicked a 47-yard field goal to give the Saints an insurmountable 10-0 lead at halftime. Stump Mitchell's one-yard run late in the third period ended the Saints' streak of eight straight scoreless quarters.

New Orleans	0	10	0	6	— 16
St. Louis	0	0	7	0	— 7

NO —Jones 10 pass from Wilson (Andersen kick)
NO —FG Andersen 47
StL —Mitchell 1 run (Lee kick)
NO —FG Andersen 28
NO —FG Andersen 30

Cincinnati 34, Seattle 7—At Riverfront Stadium, attendance 54,410. The Bengals' defense scored two touchdowns and forced five Seattle turnovers to spearhead Cincinnati's 34-7 win. The Bengals put the game out-of-reach in the fourth quarter by scoring 17 unanswered points on Eddie Edwards's fumble recovery in the end zone, Louis Breeden's 36-yard interception return for a touchdown, and Jim Breech's 34-yard field goal. Boomer Esiason completed 22 of 31 passes for 334 yards, including a one-yard touchdown pass to Eric Kattus.

Seattle	0	0	7	0	— 7
Cincinnati	7	3	7	17	— 34

Cin —Wilson 2 run (Breech kick)
Cin —FG Breech 37
Sea —Warner 1 run (Johnson kick)
Cin —Kattus 1 pass from Esiason (Breech kick)
Cin —Edwards fumble recovery in end zone (Breech kick)
Cin —FG Breech 34
Cin —Breeden 36 interception return (Breech kick)

Green Bay 31, Tampa Bay 7—At Milwaukee County Stadium, attendance 48,271. Randy Wright threw for 238 yards and three touchdowns to help the Packers easily defeat the Buccaneers. Green Bay opened a 21-0 halftime lead on Wright scoring passes to Phillip Epps (53 and 5 yards) and James Lofton (12). The Packers added 10 more points in the third quarter on Al Del Greco's 27-yard field goal and a one-yard run by Gary Ellerson. Tampa Bay's Steve Young completed a 10-yard touchdown pass to Gerald Carter late in the fourth quarter to prevent the shutout.

Tampa Bay	0	0	0	7	— 7
Green Bay	14	7	10	0	— 31

GB —Epps 53 pass from Wright (Del Greco kick)
GB —Lofton 12 pass from Wright (Del Greco kick)
GB —Epps 5 pass from Wright (Del Greco kick)
GB —FG Del Greco 27
GB —Ellerson 1 run (Del Greco kick)
TB —Carter 10 pass from Young (Igwebuike kick)

Monday, November 17

Washington 14, San Francisco 6—At Robert F. Kennedy Stadium, attendance 54,774. George Rogers rushed for one touchdown and Jay Schroeder passed for another to lead the Redskins over the 49ers. Rogers carried 24 times for 104 yards, including a one-yard touchdown run in the first quarter. Schroeder's scoring pass was a 27-yarder to Gary Clark in the third period. San Francisco outgained Washington 501 to 266 total yards, but turned the ball over four times. Dave Butz led the Redskins' defense with three sacks.

San Francisco	0	3	3	0	— 6
Washington	7	0	7	0	— 14

Wash —Rogers 1 run (Zendejas kick)
SF —FG Wersching 34
Wash —Clark 27 pass from Schroeder (Zendejas kick)
SF —FG Wersching 38

Twelfth Week Summaries

Standings

American Football Conference

Eastern Division

	W	L	T	Pct.	Pts.	OP
N.Y. Jets	10	2	0	.833	306	248
New England	9	3	0	.750	326	200
Miami	6	6	0	.500	321	293
Buffalo	3	9	0	.250	232	273
Indianapolis	0	12	0	.000	144	322

Central Division

	W	L	T	Pct.	Pts.	OP
Cincinnati	8	4	0	.667	295	298
Cleveland	8	4	0	.667	276	263
Pittsburgh	4	8	0	.333	206	258
Houston	3	9	0	.250	225	272

Western Division

	W	L	T	Pct.	Pts.	OP
Denver	9	3	0	.750	287	191
L.A. Raiders	8	4	0	.667	255	226
Kansas City	7	5	0	.583	263	263
Seattle	6	6	0	.500	223	239
San Diego	2	10	0	.167	250	312

National Football Conference

Eastern Division

	W	L	T	Pct.	Pts.	OP
N.Y. Giants	10	2	0	.833	244	174
Washington	10	2	0	.833	283	210
Dallas	7	5	0	.583	291	230
Philadelphia	3	9	0	.250	176	233
St. Louis	3	9	0	.250	163	277

Central Division

	W	L	T	Pct.	Pts.	OP
Chicago	10	2	0	.833	251	140
Minnesota	6	6	0	.500	278	214
Detroit	5	7	0	.417	201	219
Green Bay	2	10	0	.167	159	284
Tampa Bay	2	10	0	.167	188	338

Western Division

	W	L	T	Pct.	Pts.	OP
L.A. Rams	8	4	0	.667	218	193
San Francisco	7	4	1	.625	280	178
New Orleans	6	6	0	.500	210	193
Atlanta	5	6	1	.458	208	218

Thursday, November 20

Los Angeles Raiders 37, San Diego 31—At San Diego Jack Murphy Stadium, attendance 56,031. Marcus Allen's 28-yard touchdown run 8:33 into overtime gave the Raiders a 37-31 win. Los Angeles took a 31-7 third-quarter lead with Chris Bahr's 52-yard field goal and Lester Hayes's 39-yard fumble recovery return for a score. San Diego then rallied with a pair of touchdowns to force the extra period. Jim Plunkett completed 23 of 40 passes for 348 yards and two touchdowns. Allen's winning score gave him 48 career rushing touchdowns, breaking Pete Banaszak's club record of 47.

L.A. Raiders	14	7	10	0	6	— 37
San Diego	0	10	7	14	0	— 31

Raiders —Robinson 2 return of blocked punt (Bahr kick)
Raiders —Christensen 11 pass from Plunkett (Bahr kick)
SD —FG Benirschke 47
SD —Adams 19 run (Benirschke kick)
Raiders —Williams 10 pass from Plunkett (Bahr kick)
Raiders —FG Bahr 52
Raiders —Hayes 39 fumble recovery return (Bahr kick)
SD —Adams 1 run (Benirschke kick)
SD —Adams 13 run (Benirschke kick)
SD —Joiner 16 pass from Herrmann (Benirschke kick)
Raiders —Allen 28 run (no kick)

Sunday, November 23

San Francisco 20, Atlanta 0—At Candlestick Park, attendance 58,747. Don Griffin returned a punt 76 yards for a touchdown and Ray Wersching added two field goals as the 49ers downed the Falcons. Wersching's field goals from 36 and 26 yards and Griffin's scoring return helped San Francisco take a 20-0 halftime lead. Roger Craig had 101 yards on 17 carries for his first 100-yard rushing day of the season. Rookie defensive end Charles Haley had three of the 49ers' eight sacks.

Atlanta	0	0	0	0	— 0
San Francisco	7	13	0	0	— 20

SF —Rice 2 pass from Montana (Wersching kick)
SF —FG Wersching 36
SF —Griffin 76 punt return (Wersching kick)
SF —FG Wersching 26

New England 22, Buffalo 19—At Sullivan Stadium, attendance 60,455. Tony Eason's 13-yard touchdown pass to Greg Baty with 1:40 remaining in the game lifted the Patriots over the Bills. Buffalo rallied for 13 points in the fourth quarter to take a 19-15 lead, but Eason drove the Patriots 60 yards in five plays for the winning score. Tony Franklin added to his club-record 17 straight games with at least one field goal made when he connected from 37 and 47 yards. Buffalo's Scott Norwood was good on all four of his field-goal attempts, from 28, 33, 34, and 48 yards.

Buffalo	0	3	3	13	— 19
New England	9	6	0	7	— 22

NE —Safety, ball fumbled out of end zone
NE —James 4 run (Franklin kick)
NE —FG Franklin 37
NE —FG Franklin 47
Buff —FG Norwood 48
Buff —FG Norwood 34
Buff —FG Norwood 33
Buff —FG Norwood 28
Buff —Riddick 31 pass from Kelly (Norwood kick)
NE —Baty 13 pass from Eason (Franklin kick)

Washington 41, Dallas 14—At Robert F. Kennedy Stadium, attendance 55,642. Jay Schroeder completed 16 of 31 passes for 325 yards and two touchdowns as the Redskins routed the Cowboys for their fourth straight win. Schroeder's scoring passes to Clint Didier (71 yards) and to Gary Clark (11) highlighted Washington's 34-point first-half explosion. George Rogers gained 75 yards on 10 first-half carries to increase his season total to 1,024 and become the second Redskins player to post consecutive 1,000-yard seasons (John Riggins gained 1,000 yards in 1978-79 and 1983-84). Clark finished with eight catches for 152 yards. Dexter Manley's two sacks paced the defense.

Dallas	0	0	7	7	— 14
Washington	14	20	7	0	— 41

Wash —Rogers 14 run (Zendejas kick)
Wash —Didier 71 pass from Schroeder (Zendejas kick)
Wash —FG Zendejas 25
Wash —FG Zendejas 41
Wash —Bryant 22 run (Zendejas kick)
Wash —Clark 11 pass from Schroeder (Zendejas kick)
Dall —Walker 1 run (Septien kick)
Wash —Bryant 1 run (Zendejas kick)
Dall —Lavette 8 pass from Collier (Septien kick)

New York Giants 19, Denver 16—At Giants Stadium, attendance 75,116. Raul Allegre kicked four field goals, including the game-winner from 34 yards with 12 seconds left, to give New York its fifth straight victory. The Giants took a 10-6 halftime lead as Allegre connected on a 31-yard field goal and George Martin returned an interception 78 yards for his seventh career touchdown. Phil Simms's 46-yard pass to Phil McConkey set up Allegre's winning kick. Joe Morris registered his sixth 100-yard rushing game of the season with 106 yards on 23 carries. Allegre's other field goals were from 45 and 46 yards.

Denver	3	3	3	7	— 16
N.Y. Giants	0	10	3	6	— 19

Den —FG Karlis 40
NYG —FG Allegre 31
Den —FG Karlis 32
NYG —Martin 78 interception return (Allegre kick)
NYG —FG Allegre 45
Den —FG Karlis 42
NYG —FG Allegre 46
Den —Winder 4 run (Karlis kick)
NYG —FG Allegre 34

Detroit 38, Tampa Bay 17—At Tampa Stadium, attendance 30,029. Joe Ferguson passed for two touchdowns as Detroit defeated Tampa Bay. Touchdowns by James Jones (one-yard run) and Leonard Thompson (four-yard pass) gave the Lions a 14-10 third-quarter lead. Ferguson then hit Jeff Chadwick (18 yards) for a touchdown to cap a 10-play, 75-yard drive with 1:42 left in the third period. The Lions scored again on a 13-yard run by Garry James following Devon Mitchell's interception. Detroit quarterback Chuck Long came off the bench late in the fourth quarter and connected with Thompson on a 34-yard touchdown on his first NFL pass.

Detroit	7	7	14	10	— 38
Tampa Bay	3	0	7	7	— 17

Det —Jones 1 run (Murray kick)
TB —FG Igwebuike 31
Det —Thompson 4 pass from Ferguson (Murray kick)
TB —Wilder 11 pass from Young (Igwebuike kick)
Det —Chadwick 18 pass form Ferguson (Murray kick)
Det —James 13 run (Murray kick)
Det —FG Murray 20
TB —Franklin 2 pass from Young (Igwebuike kick)
Det —Thompson 34 pass from Long (Murray kick)

Chicago 12, Green Bay 10—At Soldier Field, attendance 59,291. Kevin Butler's 32-yard field goal with 2:37 remaining lifted the Bears over the Packers. Dave Duerson's fumble recovery at the Green Bay 34-yard line set up Butler's game-winning field goal. Walter Payton carried 17 times for 85 yards to record his tenth 1,000-yard season (1,031). Dan Hampton, who had three-and-a-half sacks and was named NFC defensive player of the week, tackled Green Bay running back Kenneth Davis in the end zone for his first career safety.

Green Bay	0	0	3	7	— 10
Chicago	2	7	0	3	— 12

Chi —Safety, Hampton tackled Davis in end zone
Chi —Gentry recovered blocked punt in end zone (Butler kick)
GB —FG Del Greco 22
GB —West 46 pass from Wright (Del Greco kick)
Chi —FG Butler 32

Houston 31, Indianapolis 17—At Astrodome, attendance 31,702. Warren Moon completed 22 of 53 passes for 294 yards and three touchdowns as the Oilers easily defeated the Colts. After both teams scored on first-quarter field goals, Moon connected on a four-yard pass to Allen Pinkett to take a 10-3 lead at halftime. Houston opened the third quarter with three touchdowns in the span of four minutes by Mike Rozier (19-yard run), Ray Wallace (35-yard reception), and Drew Hill (eight-yard pass).

Indianapolis	3	0	0	14	— 17
Houston	3	7	21	0	— 31

Ind — FG Biasucci 37
Hou — FG Zendejas 34
Hou — Pinkett 4 pass from Moon (Zendejas kick)
Hou — Rozier 19 run (Zendejas kick)
Hou — Wallace 35 pass from Moon (Zendejas kick)
Hou — Hill 8 pass from Moon (Zendejas kick)
Ind — Brooks 16 pass from Kiel (Biasucci kick)
Ind — Brooks 37 pass from Kiel (Biasucci kick)

St. Louis 23, Kansas City 14—At Busch Memorial Stadium, attendance 29,680. Neil Lomax returned to the starting lineup and passed for 185 yards and three touchdowns to lead the Cardinals past the Chiefs. St. Louis led throughout the game, scoring first on a Lomax to Roy Green pass and an Eric Schubert field goal to lead 9-0 by halftime. Lomax then connected with J.T. Smith on second-half touchdowns of 25 and 4 yards to seal the victory. The Chiefs were held scoreless until Bill Kenney threw two touchdown passes of 6 and 13 yards to Stephone Paige late in the fourth quarter.

Kansas City	0	0	0	14	— 14
St. Louis	6	3	7	7	— 23

StL — Green 5 pass from Lomax (kick failed)
StL — FG Schubert 20
StL — J.T. Smith 25 pass from Lomax (Schubert kick)
StL — J.T. Smith 4 pass from Lomax (Schubert kick)
KC — Paige 6 pass from Kenney (Lowery kick)
KC — Paige 13 pass from Kenney (Lowery kick)

Cincinnati 24, Minnesota 20—At Riverfront Stadium, attendance 53,003. Stanley Wilson ran for two touchdowns while the defense shut out the Vikings in the second half to help the Bengals maintain a share of first place in the AFC Central. Cincinnati took a 21-20 halftime lead as Wilson scored on runs of two and five yards and Boomer Esiason completed an eight-yard touchdown pass to James Brooks. Jim Breech's 40-yard field goal in the fourth quarter accounted for all the scoring in the second half.

Minnesota	10	10	0	0	— 20
Cincinnati	21	0	0	3	— 24

Cin — Brooks 8 pass from Esiason (Breech kick)
Minn — FG C. Nelson 24
Cin — Wilson 2 run (Breech kick)
Minn — D. Nelson 3 run (C. Nelson kick)
Cin — Wilson 5 run (Breech kick)
Minn — Wilson 1 run (C. Nelson kick)
Minn — FG C. Nelson 35
Cin — FG Breech 40

Los Angeles Rams 26, New Orleans 13—At Anaheim Stadium, attendance 58,600. Eric Dickerson carried 27 times for 116 yards and a touchdown to power the Rams past the Saints. Los Angeles took a 17-6 third-quarter lead on four-yard scoring runs by Dickerson and rookie quarterback Jim Everett and Mike Lansford's 32-yard field goal. Nolan Cromwell had two interceptions as the Rams' defense produced five takeaways. Lansford added second-half field goals of 47, 29, and 44 yards.

New Orleans	0	6	0	7	— 13
L.A. Rams	7	3	13	3	— 26

Rams — Dickerson 4 run (Lansford kick)
NO — FG Andersen 33
Rams — FG Lansford 32
NO — FG Andersen 18
Rams — Everett 4 run (Lansford kick)
Rams — FG Lansford 47
Rams — FG Lansford 29
Rams — FG Lansford 44
NO — Martin 7 pass from Wilson (Andersen kick)

Seattle 24, Philadelphia 20—At Kingdome, attendance 55,786. The Seahawks' special teams produced two touchdowns within a 1:02 span of the second quarter to highlight their victory over the Eagles. Leading 7-6, Eric Lane returned Kerry Justin's blocked punt 12 yards for a score. Sixty-two seconds later, rookie kick returner Bobby Joe Edmonds scored his first NFL touchdown on a 75-yard punt return. Edmonds set a club record for punt-return yardage with 103 on four returns. Seattle's defense registered a club-record nine sacks in handing Philadelphia its fourth consecutive loss.

Philadelphia	3	3	7	7	— 20
Seattle	7	14	0	3	— 24

Phil — FG McFadden 35
Sea — Turner 72 pass from Krieg (Johnson kick)
Phil — FG McFadden 32
Sea — Lane 12 blocked punt return (Johnson kick)
Sea — Edmonds 75 punt return (Johnson kick)
Phil — Jackson 7 pass from Cunningham (McFadden kick)
Phil — Jackson 9 pass from Cunningham (McFadden kick)
Sea — FG Johnson 35

Cleveland 37, Pittsburgh 31—At Cleveland Stadium, attendance 76,452. Bernie Kosar completed 28 of 46 passes for 414 yards, including a game-winning 36-yard touchdown to Webster Slaughter 6:37 into overtime, as the Browns completed a season sweep of the Steelers for the first time since 1969. Matt Bahr's 25-yard field goal with 1:51 left in regulation gave Cleveland a momentary 31-28 edge. Pittsburgh's Gary Anderson sent the game into overtime when he kicked a 40-yard field goal with seven seconds left. Slaughter caught six passes for 134 yards; his first 100-yard game. Kevin Mack's 106 yards rushing helped Cleveland maintain a 40:17 to 26:20 time-of-possession advantage. The Browns outgained the Steelers 536 to 344 total yards.

Pittsburgh	7	7	7	10	0	— 31
Cleveland	0	21	7	3	6	— 37

Pitt — Abercrombie 1 run (Anderson kick)
Clev — Dickey 2 run (Bahr kick)
Clev — Mack 1 run (Bahr kick)
Pitt — Abercrombie 38 run (Anderson kick)
Clev — Newsome 20 pass from Kosar (Bahr kick)
Pitt — Malone 1 run (Anderson kick)
Clev — Dickey 4 run (Bahr kick)
Pitt — Malone 1 run (Anderson kick)
Clev — FG Bahr 25
Pitt — FG Anderson 40
Clev — Slaughter 36 pass from Kosar (no kick)

Monday, November 24

Miami 45, New York Jets 3—At Orange Bowl, attendance 70,206. Lorenzo Hampton ran for 148 yards and Dan Marino passed for four scores as the Dolphins overpowered the Jets. Hampton scored Miami's first three touchdowns—on runs of 54 and 1 yards and a one-yard pass from Marino to give the Dolphins a 21-0 first-half lead. Marino's other scoring throws were to Nat Moore (22 and 21 yards) and Bruce Hardy (1). Hampton's rushing effort was the first 100-yard game by a Miami player since Joe Carter's 105 against Houston on November 14, 1984. Miami outgained New York 514 total yards to 280.

N.Y. Jets	0	0	3	0	— 3
Miami	7	14	10	14	— 45

Mia — Hampton 54 run (Reveiz kick)
Mia — Hampton 1 run (Reveiz kick)
Mia — Hampton 1 pass from Marino (Reveiz kick)
Mia — Moore 22 pass from Marino (Reveiz kick)
NYJ — FG Leahy 45
Mia — FG Reveiz 39
Mia — Hardy 1 pass from Marino (Reveiz kick)
Mia — Moore 21 pass from Marino (Reveiz kick)

Thirteenth Week Summaries

Standings

American Football Conference

Eastern Division	W	L	T	Pct.	Pts.	OP
New England	10	3	0	.769	347	220
N.Y. Jets	10	3	0	.769	309	265
Miami	6	7	0	.462	335	313
Buffalo	4	9	0	.308	249	287
Indianapolis	0	13	0	.000	147	339
Central Division						
Cleveland	9	4	0	.692	289	273
Cincinnati	8	5	0	.615	323	332
Pittsburgh	4	9	0	.308	216	271
Houston	3	10	0	.231	235	285
Western Division						
Denver	10	3	0	.769	321	219
L.A. Raiders	8	5	0	.615	282	259
Kansas City	7	6	0	.538	277	280
Seattle	7	6	0	.538	254	253
San Diego	3	10	0	.231	267	315

National Football Conference

Eastern Division	W	L	T	Pct.	Pts.	OP
N.Y. Giants	11	2	0	.846	265	191
Washington	11	2	0	.846	303	227
Dallas	7	6	0	.538	305	261
Philadelphia	4	9	0	.308	209	260
St. Louis	3	10	0	.231	180	297
Central Division						
Chicago	11	2	0	.846	264	150
Minnesota	7	6	0	.538	323	227
Detroit	5	8	0	.385	241	263
Green Bay	3	10	0	.231	203	324
Tampa Bay	2	11	0	.154	201	383
Western Division						
L.A. Rams	9	4	0	.692	235	196
San Francisco	7	5	1	.577	297	199
Atlanta	6	6	1	.500	228	232
New Orleans	6	7	0	.462	230	214

Thursday, November 27

Green Bay 44, Detroit 40—At Pontiac Silverdome, attendance 61,199. Walter Stanley's 83-yard punt return for a touchdown with 41 seconds remaining brought the Packers their first Thanksgiving Day win since 1961. Stanley also caught scoring passes of 21 and 36 yards and set up another score with a 62-yard reception. He compiled 287 total yards on four catches for 124 yards, three kickoff returns for 50, and two punt returns for 113. Green Bay's Randy Wright hit on 18 of 26 passes for 286 yards and three scores, and Detroit's Joe Ferguson completed 19 of 37 for 256 yards and three touchdowns. Jeff Chadwick caught six passes for 121 yards and a touchdown for the Lions.

Green Bay	13	10	7	14	— 44
Detroit	10	10	17	3	— 40

Det — FG Murray 44
Det — J. Jones 1 run (Murray kick)
GB — FG Del Greco 34
GB — Simmons recovered blocked punt in end zone (Del Greco kick)
GB — FG Del Greco 48
GB — FG Del Greco 24
Det — FG Murray 30
GB — Stanley 21 pass from Wright (Del Greco kick)
Det — Chadwick 23 pass from Ferguson (Murray kick)
Det — FG Murray 32
Det — Giles 20 pass from Ferguson (Murray kick)
Det — Bland 10 pass from Ferguson (Murray kick)
GB — Stanley 36 pass from Wright (Del Greco kick)
Det — FG Murray 19
GB — Carruth 11 pass from Wright (Del Greco kick)
GB — Stanley 83 punt return (Del Greco kick)

Seattle 31, Dallas 14—At Texas Stadium, attendance 58,023. Dave Krieg passed for two touchdowns and ran for another to lead the Seahawks over the Cowboys. Seattle scored on all four of its first-half possessions to build a commanding 24-7 lead. Krieg ran four yards for a score and completed touchdown passes to Steve Largent (11 yards) and Byron Franklin (19). Norm Johnson's 42-yard field goal completed the half. Curt Warner took over in the second half by running for 98 yards and a touchdown (nine-yard run). He finished with 122 yards to go over the 1,000-yard mark for the third time in his career. Dallas's Steve Pelluer completed a club-record 14 straight passes to open the game.

Seattle	7	17	0	7	— 31
Dallas	7	0	7	0	— 14

Dall — Dorsett 8 run (Septien kick)
Sea — Krieg 4 run (Johnson kick)
Sea — Largent 11 pass from Krieg (Johnson kick)
Sea — Franklin 19 pass from Krieg (Johnson kick)
Sea — FG Johnson 42
Dall — Walker 1 run (Septien kick)
Sea — Warner 9 run (Johnson kick)

Sunday, November 30

Atlanta 20, Miami 14—At Orange Bowl, attendance 53,762. Gerald Riggs rushed for 172 yards and a touchdown to help the Falcons snap a five-game losing streak. Riggs's one-yard touchdown run, plus Ali Haji-Sheikh's 32-yard field goal, gave Atlanta a 10-0 halftime lead. Miami's Dan Marino hit Mark Duper on a 54-yard touchdown pass in the third quarter to cut the Falcons' lead to 10-7. But Turk Schonert's four-yard run and Haji-Sheikh's 47-yard field goal early in the final period put the game away. Marino completed 20 of 40 passes for 303 yards and two touchdowns, but suffered four interceptions.

Atlanta	10	0	0	10	— 20
Miami	0	0	7	7	— 14

Atl — Riggs 1 run (Haji-Sheikh kick)
Atl — FG Haji-Sheikh 32
Mia — Duper 54 pass from Marino (Reveiz kick)
Atl — Schonert 4 run (Haji-Sheikh kick)
Atl — FG Haji-Sheikh 47
Mia — Jensen 20 pass from Marino (Reveiz kick)

Buffalo 17, Kansas City 14—At Arrowhead Stadium, attendance 31,492. Jim Kelly and Andre Reed combined for two touchdowns as the Bills defeated the Chiefs to snap a 22-game losing streak on the road. Kelly's nine-yard pass to Reed and Scott Norwood's 47-yard field goal in the second quarter gave the Bills a 10-7 halftime lead. Kelly's 10-yard completion to Reed in the third quarter increased Buffalo's advantage to 17-7. The Chiefs tried to stage a comeback but were thwarted by Charles Romes's interception in the end zone and Nick Lowery's missed 44-yard field-goal attempt with 19 seconds remaining.

Buffalo	0	10	7	0	— 17
Kansas City	7	0	0	7	— 14

KC — Paige 12 pass from Kenney (Lowery kick)
Buff — FG Norwood 47
Buff — Reed 9 pass from Kelly (Norwood kick)
Buff — Reed 10 pass from Kelly (Norwood kick)
KC — Heard 1 run (Lowery kick)

Denver 34, Cincinnati 28—At Mile High Stadium, attendance 58,705. John Elway completed 22 of 34 passes for 228 yards and three touchdowns to lead the Broncos over the Bengals. Elway's three touchdown passes ended a three-game streak without having thrown a scoring pass. The scoring completions went to Vance Johnson (4 yards), Mark Jackson (19), and Sammy Winder (8) to give Denver a 24-14 halftime lead. Winder added an 11-yard scoring run in the third period. Rich Karlis's 33-yard field goal assured the Broncos sole possession of first place in the AFC West.

Cincinnati	7	7	0	14	— 28
Denver	3	21	10	0	— 34

Den — FG Karlis 49
Cin — Wilson 20 run (Breech kick)
Den — Johnson 4 pass from Elway (Karlis kick)

Cin —Kinnebrew 5 run (Breech kick)
Den —Jackson 19 pass from Elway (Karlis kick)
Den —Winder 8 pass from Elway (Karlis kick)
Den —Winder 11 run (Karlis kick)
Den —FG Karlis 33
Cin —Collinsworth 7 pass from Esiason (Breech kick)
Cin —Collinsworth 46 pass from Esiason (Breech kick)

Cleveland 13, Houston 10—At Cleveland Stadium, attendance 62,309. Newly acquired Mark Moseley kicked a 29-yard field goal with 16 seconds remaining in overtime to lift Cleveland over Houston. After a scoreless first half, Houston scored on a 47-yard field goal by Tony Zendejas. The Browns rallied in the fourth quarter when Bernie Kosar hit Brian Brennan on a 33-yard touchdown pass and Moseley added a 23-yard field goal. Oliver Luck's 11-yard touchdown pass to Ray Wallace with 50 seconds remaining in the fourth quarter sent the game into overtime. Moseley joined the Browns as a free agent on November 26.

Houston	0	0	3	7	0	— 10
Cleveland	0	0	0	10	3	— 13

Hou —FG Zendejas 47
Clev —Brennan 33 pass from Kosar (Moseley kick)
Clev —FG Moseley 23
Hou —Wallace 11 pass from Luck (Zendejas kick)
Clev —FG Moseley 29

Los Angeles Rams 17, New York Jets 3—At Giants Stadium, attendance 70,539. Eric Dickerson carried 31 times for 107 yards and a touchdown to help the Rams over the Jets. After a scoreless first quarter, Los Angeles scored twice before halftime on Jim Everett's 60-yard touchdown pass to Kevin House and Mike Lansford's 38-yard field goal. Dickerson, who topped 100 yards rushing for the ninth time this season, tied Elroy (Crazylegs) Hirsch's club record of 55 career touchdowns when he scored on a four-yard run in the fourth quarter.

L.A. Rams	0	10	0	7	— 17
N.Y. Jets	0	0	0	3	— 3

Rams —House 60 pass from Everett (Lansford kick)
Rams —FG Lansford 38
Rams —Dickerson 4 run (Lansford kick)
NYJ —FG Leahy 25

New England 21, New Orleans 20—At Louisiana Superdome, attendance 58,259. New England scored two fourth-quarter touchdowns to post their third straight come-from-behind victory. Mosi Tatupu returned a blocked punt 17 yards for a touchdown and Brent Williams returned a fumble 21 yards for another score to give the Patriots a 21-13 lead with 1:59 remaining. New England also scored on Tony Eason's 24-yard touchdown pass to Stephen Starring in the second quarter. The win was the Patriots' club-record seventh straight, which moved them into a first-place tie with the Jets in the AFC East.

New England	0	0	7	14	— 21
New Orleans	0	0	10	10	— 20

NO —FG Andersen 28
NE —Starring 24 pass from Eason (Franklin kick)
NO —Mayes 5 run (Andersen kick)
NO —FG Andersen 38
NE —Tatupu 17 blocked punt return (Franklin kick)
NE —B. Williams 21 fumble recovery return (Franklin kick)
NO —Goodlow 10 pass from Wilson (Andersen kick)

Philadelphia 33, Los Angeles Raiders 27—At Memorial Coliseum, attendance 53,338. Randall Cunningham's one-yard touchdown run 8:07 into overtime gave the Eagles a 33-27 win over the Raiders. The touchdown run was set up by Philadelphia safety Andre Waters's 81-yard fumble-recovery return. Cunningham completed 22 of 39 passes for 298 yards and three touchdowns to Mike Quick (eight catches for 145 yards) covering 62, 5, and 10 yards. Jim Plunkett connected on 16 of 42 passes for 366 yards, including scoring bombs to Jessie Hester of 49 and 81 yards. Gregg Garrity's 76-yard punt return for a score was the first by a Philadelphia player since 1978. Fulton Walker also scored on a 70-yard punt return for the Raiders. Los Angeles sacked Cunningham 10 times, including three by Bill Pickel. Reggie White had four of the Eagles' six sacks.

Philadelphia	13	0	7	7	6	— 33
L.A. Raiders	7	3	14	3	0	— 27

Raiders —Walker 70 punt return (Bahr kick)
Phil —Quick 62 pass from Cunningham (McFadden kick)
Phil —Garrity 76 punt return (kick blocked)
Raiders —FG Bahr 38
Raiders —Hester 49 pass from Plunkett (Bahr kick)
Phil —Quick 5 pass from Cunningham (McFadden kick)
Raiders —Hester 81 pass from Plunkett (Bahr kick)
Phil —Quick 10 pass from Cunningham (McFadden kick)
Raiders —FG Bahr 27
Phil —Cunningham 1 run (no kick)

Chicago 13, Pittsburgh 10—At Soldier Field, attendance 61,425. Kevin Butler's 42-yard field goal 3:55 into overtime gave the Bears a 13-10 win over the Steelers and their third straight NFC Central Division title. The winning score was set up by Mike Tomczak's 27-yard pass to Keith Ortego that put the ball at Pittsburgh's 24-yard line. Tomczak completed 19 of 30 passes for 235 yards in his first start since Jim McMahon was sidelined for the season. Walter Payton's three-yard touchdown run in the fourth quarter tied the game 10-10. The Bears had a chance to win the game with 55 seconds remaining in regulation time but Butler missed a 28-yard field goal.

Pittsburgh	0	3	7	0	0	— 10
Chicago	3	0	0	7	3	— 13

Chi —FG Butler 39
Pitt —FG Anderson 30
Pitt —Gothard 12 pass from Newsome (Anderson kick)
Chi —Payton 3 run (Butler kick)
Chi —FG Butler 42

San Diego 17, Indianapolis 3—At Hoosier Dome, attendance 47,950. Dan Fouts returned from a one-week layoff to throw for 290 yards and a touchdown as the Chargers beat the Colts. Fouts completed 24 of 31 passes, including a 30-yard touchdown pass to Wes Chandler that was set up by a 39-yard interception return by Jeff Dale. Chandler caught five passes for 110 yards, the first 100-yard game by a San Diego receiver this season. San Diego led 10-0 at halftime on Rolf Benirschke's 19-yard field goal and Curtis Adams's one-yard touchdown run. The Chargers allowed only 177 yards, their fewest since they gave up 112 against the Bears on December 4, 1978.

San Diego	10	0	0	7	— 17
Indianapolis	0	0	3	0	— 3

SD —FG Benirschke 19
SD —Chandler 30 pass from Fouts (Benirschke kick)
Ind —FG Biasucci 27
SD —Adams 1 run (Benirschke kick)

Minnesota 45, Tampa Bay 13—At Metrodome, attendance 56,235. Wade Wilson completed 22 of 33 passes for a career-high 339 yards and three touchdowns as the Vikings overpowered the Buccaneers. Wilson's three touchdown passes to Steve Jordan (36 yards), Allen Rice (4), and Alfred Anderson (23) gave Minnesota a 21-6 lead after three quarters. The Vikings put the game away by exploding for 24 points in the fourth quarter on runs by Darren Nelson (five yards), Anderson (one), and Ted Brown (one). Minnesota's Chuck Nelson (53 yards) and Tampa Bay's Donald Igwebuike (55) each kicked career-long field goals.

Tampa Bay	0	6	0	7	— 13
Minnesota	7	7	7	24	— 45

Minn —Jordan 36 pass from Wilson (C. Nelson kick)
TB —FG Igwebuike 39
Minn —Rice 4 pass from Wilson (C. Nelson kick)
TB —FG Igwebuike 55
Minn —Anderson 23 pass from Wilson (C. Nelson kick)
Minn —D. Nelson 5 run (C. Nelson kick)
Minn —Anderson 1 run (C. Nelson kick)
Minn —FG C. Nelson 53
Minn —Brown 1 run (C. Nelson kick)
TB —Heller 1 pass from DeBerg (Igwebuike kick)

Washington 20, St. Louis 17—At Busch Memorial Stadium, attendance 35,637. Max Zendejas kicked a 27-yard field goal with four seconds remaining in the game as the Redskins edged the Cardinals to remain tied with the Giants for first place in the NFC East. Jay Schroeder, who completed 23 of 44 passes for 256 yards, had touchdown passes to Gary Clark (2 yards) and Terry Orr (22) that gave the Redskins a 17-10 halftime advantage. St. Louis's Neil Lomax tied the score 17-17 with a 35-yard pass to Roy Green, but Schroeder drove Washington 58 yards to set up Zendejas's game-winning kick.

Washington	7	10	0	3	— 20
St. Louis	3	7	0	7	— 17

StL —FG Schubert 46
Wash —Clark 2 pass from Schroeder (Zendejas kick)
StL —J.T. Smith 4 pass from Lomax (Schubert kick)
Wash —Orr 22 pass from Schroeder (Zendejas kick)
Wash —FG Zendejas 30
StL —Green 35 pass from Lomax (Schubert kick)
Wash —FG Zendejas 27

Monday, December 1

New York Giants 21, San Francisco 17—At Candlestick Park, attendance 59,777. Phil Simms completed 27 of 38 passes for 388 yards and two touchdowns to lead the Giants past the 49ers. With the 49ers leading 17-0 at halftime, Simms threw scoring passes to Joe Morris (17 yards) and Stacy Robinson (34). Ottis Anderson's one-yard run late in the third quarter put the Giants ahead to stay. New York's defense held San Francisco on two fourth-quarter drives inside the Giants' 30-yard line to assure their sixth straight win.

N.Y. Giants	0	0	21	0	— 21
San Francisco	3	14	0	0	— 17

SF —FG Wersching 30
SF —Rice 11 pass from Montana (Wersching kick)
SF —Rice 1 run (Wersching kick)
NYG —Morris 17 pass from Simms (Allegre kick)
NYG —Robinson 34 pass from Simms (Allegre kick)
NYG —Anderson 1 run (Allegre kick)

Fourteenth Week Summaries

Standings

American Football Conference

Eastern Division

	W	L	T	Pct.	Pts.	OP
New England	10	4	0	.714	354	251
N.Y. Jets	10	4	0	.714	319	289
Miami	7	7	0	.500	366	340
Buffalo	4	10	0	.286	266	308
Indianapolis	1	13	0	.071	175	362
Central Division						
Cleveland	10	4	0	.714	310	290
Cincinnati	9	5	0	.643	354	339
Pittsburgh	5	9	0	.357	243	288
Houston	3	11	0	.214	235	312
Western Division						
Denver	10	4	0	.714	331	256
Kansas City	8	6	0	.571	314	290
L.A. Raiders	8	6	0	.571	282	296
Seattle	8	6	0	.571	291	253
San Diego	4	10	0	.286	294	315

National Football Conference

Eastern Division

	W	L	T	Pct.	Pts.	OP
N.Y. Giants	12	2	0	.857	289	205
Washington	11	3	0	.786	317	251
Dallas	7	7	0	.500	315	290
Philadelphia	4	9	1	.321	219	270
St. Louis	3	10	1	.250	190	307
Central Division						
Chicago	12	2	0	.857	312	164
Minnesota	8	6	0	.571	355	233
Detroit	5	9	0	.357	258	290
Green Bay	3	11	0	.214	209	356
Tampa Bay	2	12	0	.143	215	431
Western Division						
L.A. Rams	10	4	0	.714	264	206
San Francisco	8	5	1	.607	321	209
Atlanta	6	7	1	.464	251	260
New Orleans	6	8	0	.429	257	245

Sunday, December 7

Cincinnati 31, New England 7—At Sullivan Stadium, attendance 59,639. Bengals running backs James Brooks and Stanley Wilson each rushed for over 100 yards as Cincinnati easily defeated the Patriots. Brooks gained a club-record 163 yards on 18 carries and caught six passes for 101 yards to join Essex Johnson as the only players in Bengals history to rush and receive for over 100 yards in the same game. Brooks also scored on a 56-yard run. Wilson added 120 yards on 16 carries and had a 58-yard scoring run as Cincinnati rushed for a club-record 300 yards. It was the first time this season the Patriots were held under 20 points.

Cincinnati	0	7	10	14	— 31
New England	0	0	7	0	— 7

Cin —Kinnebrew 1 run (Breech kick)
Cin —FG Breech 24
NE —Collins 1 run (Franklin kick)
Cin —Brown 23 pass from Esiason (Breech kick)
Cin —Wilson 58 run (Breech kick)
Cin —Brooks 56 run (Breech kick)

Cleveland 21, Buffalo 17—At Rich Stadium, attendance 47,488. Running back Kevin Mack scored two first-half touchdowns to lead the Browns to a 21-17 win. Mack's pair of one-yard runs and Bernie Kosar's 11-yard touchdown pass to Brian Brennan gave Cleveland a 21-10 lead entering the fourth quarter. Jim Kelly completed 20 of 39 passes for 315 yards and two touchdowns for the Bills. Buffalo's Chris Burkett caught three passes for 122 yards, including a 75-yard touchdown.

Cleveland	7	7	7	0	— 21
Buffalo	0	3	7	7	— 17

Clev —Mack 1 run (Moseley kick)
Buff —FG Norwood 22
Clev —Mack 1 run (Moseley kick)
Buff —Burkett 75 pass from Kelly (Norwood kick)
Clev —Brennan 11 pass from Kosar (Moseley kick)
Buff —Teal 4 pass from Kelly (Norwood kick)

Los Angeles Rams 29, Dallas 10—At Anaheim Stadium, attendance 67,839. Jim Everett passed for 212 yards and one touchdown to lead the Rams past the Cowboys. Los Angeles took control of the game in the second quarter on Everett's 22-yard scoring pass to Henry Ellard and Mike Lansford's 37- and 27-yard field goals. Los Angeles completed its scoring when Gary Jeter sacked Cowboys quarterback Steve Pelluer in the end zone for a safety and Barry Redden ran 41 yards for a touchdown. The Rams' defense held the Cowboys to 84 yards rushing and recorded five sacks.

Dallas	7	3	0	0	— 10
L.A. Rams	7	13	2	7	— 29

Rams —Irvin 50 interception return (Lansford kick)
Dall —Newsome 5 run (Septien kick)
Rams —FG Lansford 37
Dall —FG Septien 48

Rams — Ellard 22 pass from Everett (Lansford kick)
Rams — FG Lansford 27
Rams — Safety, Jeter tackled Pelluer in end zone
Rams — Redden 41 run (Lansford kick)

Kansas City 37, Denver 10—At Arrowhead Stadium, attendance 62,402. The Chiefs' defense recorded five sacks and five interceptions, and shut out the Broncos in the second half to snap a two-game losing streak. Kansas City exploded for 20 points in the fourth quarter on Lloyd Burruss's 72-yard interception return for a touchdown, Boyce Green's one-yard run, and Nick Lowery's two field goals from 45 and 44 yards. The Broncos outgained the Chiefs 323 total yards to 169.

Denver	3	7	0	0	— 10
Kansas City	3	7	7	20	— 37

KC — FG Lowery 30
Den — FG Karlis 26
KC — Paige 9 pass from Blackledge (Lowery kick)
Den — Winder 2 pass from Elway (Karlis kick)
KC — J. Smith 17 pass from Blackledge (Lowery kick)
KC — Green 1 run (Lowery kick)
KC — FG Lowery 45
KC — FG Lowery 44
KC — Burruss 72 interception return (Lowery kick)

Pittsburgh 27, Detroit 17—At Three Rivers Stadium, attendance 57,961. Earnest Jackson rushed for 147 yards on 28 carries and Louis Lipps caught eight passes for 150 yards and two touchdowns to lead the Steelers over the Lions. Mark Malone's scoring passes to Lipps covered 12 and 39 yards. Donnie Shell's interception made him the first safety in NFL history to record 50 in a career. Pittsburgh outgained Detroit 421 yards to 218.

Detroit	0	10	7	0	— 17
Pittsburgh	3	7	14	3	— 27

Pitt — FG Anderson 26
Pitt — Lipps 12 pass from Malone (Anderson kick)
Det — James 60 run (Murray kick)
Det — FG Murray 30
Det — Chadwick 1 pass from Ferguson (Murray kick)
Pitt — Jackson 1 run (Anderson kick)
Pitt — Lipps 39 pass from Malone (Anderson kick)
Pitt — FG Anderson 28

San Diego 27, Houston 0—At San Diego Jack Murphy Stadium, attendance 50,120. Dan Fouts became the third quarterback in NFL history to pass for over 40,000 yards, as the Chargers shut out the Oilers. After a scoreless first quarter, San Diego scored 17 points on two Houston turnovers and a 20-yard Rolf Benirschke field goal. Jeff Dale's 24-yard interception set up Tim Spencer's one-yard run. Twenty seconds later, Gary Anderson's 31-yard touchdown catch followed Angelo Snipe's fumble recovery. The Chargers' defense recorded six sacks, intercepted a pass, and held Houston to under 300 yards. It was the Chargers' first shutout in 105 games.

Houston	0	0	0	0	— 0
San Diego	0	17	3	7	— 27

SD — Spencer 1 run (Benirschke kick)
SD — Anderson 31 pass from Fouts (Benirschke kick)
SD — FG Benirschke 20
SD — FG Benirschke 35
SD — Winslow 4 pass from Anderson (Benirschke kick)

Indianapolis 28, Atlanta 23—At Atlanta-Fulton County Stadium, attendance 40,003. Eugene Daniel returned a blocked punt 13 yards for a score with 20 seconds left to play as the Colts snapped a 13-game losing streak. Indianapolis entered the fourth quarter trailing 20-14, but Bill Brooks's two-yard touchdown reception midway through the period cut the deficit to 23-21. Rookie Brooks caught two passes for 30 yards to become the third 1,000-yard receiver in Colts history with 1,001. The win was the Colts' first under new coach Ron Meyer.

Indianapolis	7	0	7	14	— 28
Atlanta	14	3	3	3	— 23

Atl — Williams 32 pass from Schonert (Haji-Sheikh kick)
Ind — Bentley 2 run (Biasucci kick)
Atl — Brown 14 pass from Schonert (Haji-Sheikh kick)
Atl — FG Haji-Sheikh 19
Ind — Bouza 7 pass from Hogeboom (Biasucci kick)
Atl — FG Haji-Sheikh 45
Atl — FG Haji-Sheikh 26
Ind — Brooks 2 pass from Hogeboom (Biasucci kick)
Ind — Daniel 13 blocked punt return (Biasucci kick)

Miami 31, New Orleans 27—At Louisiana Superdome, attendance 68,239. The Dolphins, who opened a 31-10 halftime lead on three Dan Marino touchdown passes, held on to defeat the Saints 31-27. Marino completed 27 of 41 passes for 241 yards, including touchdowns to Dan Johnson (13 yards), Bruce Hardy (4), and Tony Nathan (23). New Orleans rallied to score 17 points in the second half, but Miami's defense held the Saints on the Dolphins' 6-yard line with 41 seconds remaining to secure the win. New Orleans compiled a club-record 526 total yards against the Dolphins, as rookie Rueben Mayes rushed for 203 yards on 28 carries.

Miami	14	17	0	0	— 31
New Orleans	7	3	10	7	— 27

Mia — Hampton 4 run (Reveiz kick)
NO — Mayes 20 run (Andersen kick)
Mia — Johnson 13 pass from Marino (Reveiz kick)
Mia — Hardy 4 pass from Marino (Reveiz kick)
NO — FG Andersen 27
Mia — FG Reveiz 43
Mia — Nathan 23 pass from Marino (Reveiz kick)
NO — Mayes 34 run (Andersen kick)
NO — FG Andersen 29
NO — Tice 3 pass from D. Wilson (Andersen kick)

Minnesota 32, Green Bay 6—At Lambeau Field, attendance 47,637. Minnesota remained in playoff contention by defeating Green Bay 32-6. Quarterback Tommy Kramer returned to action after missing three weeks with a thumb injury and connected with Anthony Carter on a seven-yard touchdown pass in the first quarter. The Packers outgained the Vikings 367 to 303, but Minnesota scored 19 unanswered points in the second half to put the game out of reach.

Minnesota	13	0	9	10	— 32
Green Bay	3	3	0	0	— 6

GB — FG Del Greco 39
Minn — D. Nelson 12 run (kick failed)
Minn — Carter 7 pass from Kramer (C. Nelson kick)
GB — FG Del Greco 20
Minn — Anderson 8 run (kick failed)
Minn — FG C. Nelson 28
Minn — FG C. Nelson 31
Minn — Brown 12 run (C. Nelson kick)

New York Giants 24, Washington 14—At Robert F. Kennedy Stadium, attendance 54,651. The Giants' defense intercepted six passes and registered four sacks and Phil Simms passed for three touchdowns to lead New York over Washington. The victory gave New York sole possession of first place in the NFC East. Simms completed 15 of 29 passes for 265 yards, including five for 111 yards and a nine-yard touchdown to tight end Mark Bavaro. The Giants sealed their seventh straight win by scoring 10 points in the third quarter on a Raul Allegre 21-yard field goal and Simms's 16-yard scoring pass to Phil McConkey. Washington's Jay Schroeder completed 28 of 51 passes for 309 yards and a touchdown, while Kelvin Bryant made an NFL season-high 13 receptions for 130 yards and a score.

N.Y. Giants	0	14	10	0	— 24
Washington	0	7	0	7	— 14

NYG — Bavaro 9 pass from Simms (Allegre kick)
Wash — Bryant 4 run (Zendejas kick)
NYG — B. Johnson 7 pass from Simms (Allegre kick)
NYG — FG Allegre 21
NYG — McConkey 16 pass from Simms (Allegre kick)
Wash — Bryant 22 pass from Schroeder (Zendejas kick)

San Francisco 24, New York Jets 10—At Candlestick Park, attendance 60,946. The 49ers' defense held the Jets to 149 total yards and intercepted three passes en route to a 24-10 win. After a scoreless first quarter, Roger Craig ran for two touchdowns (one and five yards) to give San Francisco a 14-3 halftime lead. In the second half, Tom Rathman scored his first NFL touchdown on a 29-yard run and Ray Wersching kicked a 33-yard field goal to round out the scoring. The 49ers gained 432 total yards.

N.Y. Jets	0	3	0	7	— 10
San Francisco	0	14	7	3	— 24

SF — Craig 1 run (Wersching kick)
NYJ — FG Leahy 22
SF — Craig 5 run (Wersching kick)
SF — Rathman 29 run (Wersching kick)
NYJ — McNeil 10 pass from O'Brien (Leahy kick)
SF — FG Wersching 33

Philadelphia 10, St. Louis 10—At Veterans Stadium, attendance 59,074. Philadelphia and St. Louis battled to only the tenth tie game since overtime play was introduced in 1974. Both teams had chances to win the game, but missed field goals in the extra period. Randall Cunningham's two-yard touchdown run gave the Eagles a 10-3 lead early in the fourth quarter, but the Cardinals tied the score on Neil Lomax's 48-yard scoring pass to Roy Green with 2:39 left in regulation. Green finished with six catches for 100 yards, while teammate J.T. Smith caught 10 for 131. St. Louis registered 10 sacks against Philadelphia.

St. Louis	0	3	0	7	0	— 10
Philadelphia	3	0	0	7	0	— 10

Phil — FG McFadden 33
StL — FG Schubert 27
Phil — Cunningham 2 run (McFadden kick)
StL — Green 48 pass from Lomax (Schubert kick)

Chicago 48, Tampa Bay 14—At Soldier Field, attendance 65,130. Walter Payton, Mike Tomczak, and Doug Flutie each accounted for two touchdowns to lead the Bears to a 48-14 win. Payton rushed for 78 yards and had a four-yard touchdown run. He also caught three passes for 98 yards, including a 27-yard touchdown from Flutie. Tomczak opened the scoring with an eight-yard touchdown run and completed an eight-yard scoring pass to Willie Gault. Flutie, playing in his first NFL game, ran four yards for a score and threw the 27-yard touchdown pass to Payton. Rookie Lew Barnes's 85-yard kickoff return finished the Bears' scoring. Chicago generated 432 total yards to Tampa Bay's 271.

Tampa Bay	0	0	0	14	— 14
Chicago	7	21	14	6	— 48

Chi — Tomczak 8 run (Butler kick)
Chi — Sanders 9 run (Butler kick)
Chi — Flutie 4 run (Butler kick)
Chi — Payton 27 pass from Flutie (Butler kick)
Chi — Gault 8 pass from Tomczak (Butler kick)
Chi — Payton 4 run (Butler kick)
TB — Heflin 48 intercepted lateral return (Igwebuike kick)
TB — Magee 14 pass from Young (Igwebuike kick)
Chi — Barnes 85 kickoff return (kick failed)

Monday, December 8

Seattle 37, Los Angeles Raiders 0—At Kingdome, attendance 64,060. Curt Warner rushed for 116 yards and two touchdowns to power the Seahawks over the Raiders. Warner scored on runs of five and three yards, while Dave Krieg completed a pair of touchdown passes to Steve Largent (10 yards) and Ray Butler (12). Norm Johnson added three field goals (46, 51, and 53 yards) to round out the scoring. Seattle's defense recorded a club-record 11 sacks and held the Raiders to a season-low 138 total yards.

L.A. Raiders	0	0	0	0	— 0
Seattle	14	10	6	7	— 37

Sea — Largent 10 pass from Krieg (Johnson kick)
Sea — Warner 5 run (Johnson kick)
Sea — FG Johnson 46
Sea — R. Butler 12 pass from Krieg (Johnson kick)
Sea — FG Johnson 51
Sea — FG Johnson 53
Sea — Warner 3 run (Johnson kick)

Fifteenth Week Summaries

Standings

American Football Conference

Eastern Division

	W	L	T	Pct.	Pts.	OP
New England	10	5	0	.667	378	280
N.Y. Jets	10	5	0	.667	343	334
Miami	8	7	0	.533	403	371
Buffalo	4	11	0	.267	280	332
Indianapolis	2	13	0	.133	199	376
Central Division						
Cleveland	11	4	0	.733	344	293
Cincinnati	9	6	0	.600	357	373
Pittsburgh	6	9	0	.400	288	312
Houston	4	11	0	.267	258	322
Western Division						
Denver	11	4	0	.733	362	286
Kansas City	9	6	0	.600	334	307
Seattle	9	6	0	.600	325	277
L.A. Raiders	8	7	0	.533	299	316
San Diego	4	11	0	.267	318	349

National Football Conference

Eastern Division

	W	L	T	Pct.	Pts.	OP
N.Y. Giants	13	2	0	.867	316	212
Washington	11	4	0	.733	347	282
Dallas	7	8	0	.467	336	313
Philadelphia	5	9	1	.367	242	291
St. Louis	3	11	1	.233	197	334
Central Division						
Chicago	13	2	0	.867	328	177
Minnesota	8	7	0	.533	365	256
Detroit	5	10	0	.333	271	306
Green Bay	4	11	0	.267	230	363
Tampa Bay	2	13	0	.133	222	452
Western Division						
L.A. Rams	10	5	0	.667	295	243
San Francisco	9	5	1	.633	350	233
New Orleans	7	8	0	.467	271	254
Atlanta	6	8	1	.433	260	274

Saturday, December 13

Pittsburgh 45, New York Jets 24—At Giants Stadium, attendance 76,025. The Steelers scored four touchdowns in the fourth quarter to break the game open and roll past the Jets 45-24. Mark Malone started the onslaught with a one-yard touchdown run and a 40-yard scoring pass to John Stallworth. Lupe Sanchez then scored his first NFL touchdown on a 67-yard interception return. Walter Abercrombie's one-yard run completed the Steelers' outburst. Earnest Jackson gained 101 yards rushing for Pittsburgh. Freeman McNeil had 137 yards on 23 carries for the Jets to become New York's all-time rushing leader with 5,214 yards, passing Emerson Boozer (5,135).

Pittsburgh	0	17	0	28	— 45
N.Y. Jets	0	14	3	7	— 24

Pitt — Abercrombie 1 run (Anderson kick)
NYJ — Townsell 93 kickoff return (Leahy kick)
Pitt — FG Anderson 36
Pitt — Abercrombie 7 pass from Malone (Anderson kick)
NYJ — Sohn 24 pass from O'Brien (Leahy kick)
NYJ — FG Leahy 18
Pitt — Malone 1 run (Anderson kick)
Pitt — Stallworth 40 pass from Malone (Anderson kick)
Pitt — Sanchez 67 interception return (Anderson kick)

NYJ —Shuler 5 pass from Ryan (Leahy kick)
Pitt —Abercrombie 1 run (Anderson kick)

Denver 31, Washington 30—At Mile High Stadium, attendance 75,265. Rich Karlis's 32-yard field goal with 3:10 remaining in the game helped the Broncos edge the Redskins. Trailing 13-0 in the second quarter, Denver scored 21 unanswered points on touchdowns by John Elway (11-yard run), Sammy Winder (6-yard run), and Steve Watson (19-yard pass from Elway) to lead 21-13 after three periods. Cornerback Mike Harden had two interceptions, the second of which set up Karlis's decisive field goal.

Washington	6	7	0	17	— 30
Denver	0	7	14	10	— 31

Wash —Sanders 10 pass from Schroeder (kick failed)
Wash —Rogers 15 run (Zendejas kick)
Den —Elway 11 run (Karlis kick)
Den —Winder 6 run (Karlis kick)
Den —Watson 19 pass from Elway (Karlis kick)
Wash —FG Cox 48
Den —Winder 1 run (Karlis kick)
Wash —Monk 55 pass from Schroeder (Zendejas kick)
Den —FG Karlis 32
Wash —Rogers 1 run (Zendejas kick)

Sunday, December 14

Indianapolis 24, Buffalo 14—At Hoosier Dome, attendance 56,972. Gary Hogeboom accounted for three touchdowns and produced his first 300-yard passing game for the Colts, as Indianapolis rallied to beat Buffalo 24-14. Hogeboom completed 23 of 33 passes for 318 yards, including a one-yard scoring pass to Tim Sherwin to tie the score 14-14, and a 15-yarder to Pat Beach to seal the win with 30 seconds remaining. The Colts ran off 24 unanswered points in the second half. Hogeboom opened the onslaught with a one-yard run midway through the third quarter. Dean Biasucci added a career-best 52-yard field goal midway through the fourth quarter.

Buffalo	7	7	0	0	— 14
Indianapolis	0	0	14	10	— 24

Buff —Burkett 42 pass from Kelly (Norwood kick)
Buff —Bell 1 run (Norwood kick)
Ind —Hogeboom 1 run (Biasucci kick)
Ind —Sherwin 1 pass from Hogeboom (Biasucci kick)
Ind —FG Biasucci 52
Ind —Beach 15 pass from Hogeboom (Biasucci kick)

Cleveland 34, Cincinnati 3—At Riverfront Stadium, attendance 58,669. The Browns held the Bengals to their lowest scoring output in five seasons as Cleveland captured its second straight AFC Central title. The Browns took a 17-3 halftime lead on Kevin Mack's one-yard run, Webster Slaughter's 47-yard touchdown catch, and Mark Moseley's 39-yard field goal. Cleveland broke the game open in the third quarter when Slaughter recovered a fumble in the end zone and Mack scored his second touchdown of the game on a one-yard run. Cincinnati was held to its fewest points since a 21-3 loss to San Francisco in 1981.

Cleveland	14	3	14	3	— 34
Cincinnati	3	0	0	0	— 3

Clev —Mack 1 run (Moseley kick)
Cin —FG Breech 23
Clev —Slaughter 47 pass from Kosar (Moseley kick)
Clev —FG Moseley 39
Clev —Mack 1 run (Moseley kick)
Clev —Slaughter recovered fumble in end zone (Moseley kick)
Clev —FG Moseley 19

Green Bay 21, Tampa Bay 7—At Tampa Stadium, attendance 40,382. Quarterback Randy Wright and running backs Gerry Ellis and Paul Carruth each scored touchdowns to lead the Packers to a 21-7 win over the Buccaneers. Wright scrambled six yards late in the second quarter to give Green Bay a 7-0 halftime lead. Ellis and Carruth added second-half scoring runs of two and one yards, respectively, to put the game away. Wright joined Lynn Dickey as the only players in Green Bay history to throw for over 3,000 yards in a season when he threw for 190 yards. Tampa Bay's Steve DeBerg completed a nine-yard touchdown pass to Calvin Magee with 6:50 remaining to help the Buccaneers avoid being shut out.

Green Bay	0	7	7	7	— 21
Tampa Bay	0	0	0	7	— 7

GB —Wright 6 run (Del Greco kick)
GB —Ellis 2 run (Del Greco kick)
GB —Carruth 1 run (Del Greco kick)
TB —Magee 9 pass from DeBerg (Igwebuike kick)

Kansas City 20, Los Angeles Raiders 17—At Memorial Coliseum, attendance 63,145. Kansas City scored two touchdowns and two field goals in the first half and then held on to defeat Los Angeles. The Chiefs turned two recovered Raiders fumbles into scores. The first led to Nick Lowery's 40-yard field goal and the second recovery set up a 26-yard pass from Bill Kenney to Stephone Paige. The Chiefs had seven takeaways, including two in the fourth quarter to secure the win.

Kansas City	10	10	0	0	— 20
L.A. Raiders	0	10	7	0	— 17

KC —FG Lowery 40
KC —Paige 26 pass from Kenney (Lowery kick)
KC —Smith 2 run (Lowery kick)
Raiders —Barksdale 34 pass from Plunkett (Bahr kick)
Raiders —FG Bahr 19
KC —FG Lowery 20
Raiders —Allen 2 run (Bahr kick)

Miami 37, Los Angeles Rams 31—At Anaheim Stadium, attendance 67,153. Dan Marino's fifth touchdown pass of the day, a 20-yarder to Mark Duper 3:04 into overtime, gave the Dolphins a 37-31 victory over the Rams. Marino, who completed 29 of 46 passes for 403 yards, threw for his NFL-record seventh 400-yard game. Duper caught five passes for 145 yards, including two other touchdowns of 69 and 5 yards. James Pruitt (6 yards) and Mark Clayton (43) also received Marino scoring tosses. Eric Dickerson rushed for 124 yards for the Rams and scored on a one-yard run with 50 seconds remaining to send the game into overtime. Los Angeles rookie Jim Everett completed 18 of 31 passes for 251 yards and two scores.

Miami	0	21	7	3	6	— 37
L.A. Rams	0	7	14	10	0	— 31

Rams —Newberry recovered fumble in end zone (Lansford kick)
Mia —Duper 69 pass from Marino (Reveiz kick)
Mia —Pruitt 6 pass from Marino (Reveiz kick)
Mia —Clayton 43 pass from Marino (Reveiz kick)
Rams —Ellard 19 pass from Everett (Lansford kick)
Rams —House 23 pass from Everett (Lansford kick)
Mia —Duper 5 pass from Marino (Reveiz kick)
Mia —FG Reveiz 18
Rams —FG Lansford 32
Rams —Dickerson 1 run (Lansford kick)
Mia —Duper 20 pass from Marino (no kick)

Houston 23, Minnesota 10—At Astrodome, attendance 32,738. Tony Zendejas kicked three field goals and the Houston defense produced six takeaways as the Oilers eliminated the Vikings from the playoffs. Zendejas's field goals of 31 and 33 yards, plus Warren Moon's 10-yard touchdown pass to Ernest Givins, gave Houston a 13-7 halftime lead it never relinquished. Zendejas added a 36-yarder in the fourth quarter and Allen Pinkett ran one yard for a score with 1:58 remaining to put the game out-of-reach. Givins caught six passes for 108 yards to become the Oilers' first rookie to gain over 1,000 yards receiving since Bill Groman in 1960.

Minnesota	0	7	0	3	— 10
Houston	3	10	0	10	— 23

Hou —FG Zendejas 31
Minn —Rice 32 pass from Kramer (C. Nelson kick)
Hou —Givins 10 pass from Moon (Zendejas kick)
Hou —FG Zendejas 33
Hou —FG Zendejas 36
Minn —FG C. Nelson 40
Hou —Pinkett 1 run (Zendejas kick)

New Orleans 14, Atlanta 9—At Atlanta-Fulton County Stadium, attendance 55,630. Dave Wilson scored on a six-yard bootleg run with 1:55 to play to help the Saints register a 14-9 win and snap a three-game losing streak. The Falcons led 9-7 with 5:39 remaining on Ali Haji-Sheikh's 43-yard field goal, before Wilson drove New Orleans 75 yards in 12 plays for the winning score. Wilson also completed a seven-yard touchdown pass to Eric Martin in the first quarter. Rickey Jackson had four of the Saints' six sacks.

New Orleans	7	0	0	7	— 14
Atlanta	0	0	6	3	— 9

NO —Martin 7 pass from Wilson (Andersen kick)
Atl —Whisenhunt 3 pass from Schonert (kick failed)
Atl —FG Haji-Sheikh 43
NO —Wilson 6 run (Andersen kick)

Philadelphia 23, Dallas 21—At Texas Stadium, attendance 62,079. Matt Cavanaugh completed a pair of touchdown passes to Kenny Jackson, including a 31-yarder with 3:57 to play, to give the Eagles a 23-21 win and knock the Cowboys out of playoff contention. Jackson's eight-yard reception late in the third quarter gave Philadelphia a 13-7 lead, but Dallas's Steve Pelluer hit Mike Renfro on a 30-yard touchdown pass to put the Cowboys back in front 14-13. Herschel Walker, who set a Dallas combined yardage record with 292 yards, scored on an 84-yard run and an 84-yard reception. Walker had nine catches for 170 yards and gained 122 yards on six carries. The victory was the Eagles' first against an NFC East opponent this season.

Philadelphia	3	3	7	10	— 23
Dallas	7	0	7	7	— 21

Phil —FG McFadden 26
Dall —Walker 84 run (Septien kick)
Phil —FG McFadden 50
Phil —Jackson 8 pass from Cavanaugh (McFadden kick)
Dall —Renfro 30 pass from Pelluer (Septien kick)
Phil —FG McFadden 40
Dall —Walker 84 pass from Pelluer (Septien kick)
Phi —Jackson 31 pass from Cavanaugh (McFadden kick)

New York Giants 27, St. Louis 7—At Giants Stadium, attendance 75,760. Joe Morris rushed for 179 yards and three touchdowns to lead the Giants over the Cardinals. Morris scored twice in the first half on runs of two and three yards, and again late in the fourth quarter to seal the win. Raul Allegre added field goals of 26 and 23 yards to complete the Giants' scoring. St. Louis's Roy Green caught a 15-yard touchdown pass in the fourth quarter to prevent the shutout. New York's number-one ranked NFL defense against the rush held the Cardinals to 84 yards rushing.

St. Louis	0	0	0	7	— 7
N.Y. Giants	7	10	3	7	— 27

NYG —Morris 2 run (Allegre kick)
NYG —Morris 3 run (Allegre kick)
NYG —FG Allegre 26
NYG —FG Allegre 23
StL —Mitchell 15 run (Schubert kick)
NYG —Morris 1 run (Allegre kick)

San Francisco 29, New England 24—At Sullivan Stadium, attendance 59,798. Running back Joe Cribbs gained 107 yards rushing and scored two touchdowns and Ray Wersching kicked three field goals to lift the 49ers over the Patriots. Trailing 17-16 entering the fourth quarter, San Francisco's defense sealed the victory by recovering a fumble and intercepting a pass to set up 10 points. The win kept the 49ers' NFC West title hopes alive.

San Francisco	7	9	0	13	— 29
New England	10	0	7	7	— 24

NE —Baty 8 pass from Eason (Franklin kick)
SF —Cribbs 3 run (Wersching kick)
NE —FG Franklin 41
SF —Craig 1 run (kick failed)
SF —FG Wersching 46
NE —Collins 4 run (Franklin kick)
SF —FG Wersching 31
SF —FG Wersching 20
SF —Cribbs 10 run (Wersching kick)
NE —Morgan 15 pass from Eason (Franklin kick)

Seattle 34, San Diego 24—At San Diego Jack Murphy Stadium, attendance 54,804. Dave Krieg passed for 305 yards and four touchdowns to lead the Seahawks over the Chargers. With the score tied 17-17 at the half, Krieg completed all 10 of his pass attempts in the second half, including touchdowns to Steve Largent (23 yards) and Ray Butler (14). Krieg completed 15 of 21 and had no interceptions. Largent caught six passes for 96 yards to go over the 11,000-yard mark for his career (11,028). San Diego's Dan Fouts completed 21 of 38 passes for 237 yards to move past Johnny Unitas into second place on the all-time passing yardage chart with 40,287. Kellen Winslow totaled 105 yards on eight receptions in his first 100-yard effort this season.

Seattle	10	7	3	14	— 34
San Diego	0	17	0	7	— 24

Sea —FG Johnson 29
Sea —Largent 6 pass from Krieg (Johnson kick)
SD —Spencer 1 run (Benirschke kick)
Sea —Turner 72 pass from Krieg (Johnson kick)
SD —FG Benirschke 23
SD —Winslow 14 pass from Fouts (Benirschke kick)
Sea —FG Johnson 25
Sea —Largent 23 pass from Krieg (Johnson kick)
SD —Spencer 1 run (Benirschke kick)
Sea —Butler 14 pass from Krieg (Johnson kick)

Monday, December 15

Chicago 16, Detroit 13—At Pontiac Silverdome, attendance 75,602. Kevin Butler kicked three field goals, including a 22-yarder on the game's final play, to lift the Bears over the Lions. Chicago rebounded from a 13-3 third-quarter deficit by scoring 13 points in the fourth quarter on Matt Suhey's four-yard run and Butler's 32-yard and game-winning field goals. Butler also converted a 41-yard attempt. The Bears' defense held the Lions to 56 yards rushing and 160 total yards.

Chicago	0	3	0	13	— 16
Detroit	3	3	7	0	— 13

Det —FG Murray 52
Chi —FG Butler 41
Det —FG Murray 39
Det —Thompson 4 pass from Long (Murray kick)
Chi —FG Butler 32
Chi —Suhey 4 run (Butler kick)
Chi —FG Butler 22

Sixteenth Week Summaries

Standings

American Football Conference

Eastern Division	W	L	T	Pct.	Pts.	OP
New England*	11	5	0	.688	412	307
N.Y. Jets*	10	6	0	.625	364	386
Miami	8	8	0	.500	430	405
Buffalo	4	12	0	.250	287	348
Indianapolis	3	13	0	.188	229	400
Central Division						
Cleveland*	12	4	0	.750	391	310
Cincinnati	10	6	0	.625	409	394
Pittsburgh	6	10	0	.375	307	336
Houston	5	11	0	.313	274	329
Western Division						
Denver*	11	5	0	.688	378	327
Kansas City*	10	6	0	.625	358	326
Seattle	10	6	0	.625	366	293
L.A. Raiders	8	8	0	.500	323	346
San Diego	4	12	0	.250	335	396

National Football Conference

Eastern Division

	W	L	T	Pct.	Pts.	OP
N.Y. Giants*	14	2	0	.875	371	236
Washington*	12	4	0	.750	368	296
Dallas	7	9	0	.438	346	337
Philadelphia	5	10	1	.344	256	312
St. Louis	4	11	1	.281	218	351

Central Division

	W	L	T	Pct.	Pts.	OP
Chicago*	14	2	0	.875	352	187
Minnesota	9	7	0	.563	398	273
Detroit	5	11	0	.313	277	326
Green Bay	4	12	0	.250	254	418
Tampa Bay	2	14	0	.125	239	473

Western Division

	W	L	T	Pct.	Pts.	OP
San Francisco*	10	5	1	.656	374	247
L.A. Rams*	10	6	0	.625	309	267
Atlanta	7	8	1	.469	280	280
New Orleans	7	9	0	.438	288	287

**Denotes playoff team*

Friday, December 19

San Francisco 24, Los Angeles Rams 14—At Candlestick Park, attendance 60,366. Joe Montana threw a pair of touchdown passes and the 49ers' defense had three interceptions to help San Francisco clinch the NFC Western Division title. Montana teamed up with Jerry Rice (44 yards) and Russ Francis (1) for touchdowns in the first and third quarters, respectively. Montana helped the 49ers to a 17-7 second-quarter lead when he engineered a 15-play, 92-yard scoring drive in the second quarter, capped by Joe Cribbs's two-yard run. Montana completed 23 of 36 passes for 238 yards. San Francisco's defense held Los Angeles's Eric Dickerson, the NFL rushing champion, under 100 yards (68) for the sixth straight time.

L.A. Rams	0	7	0	7	— 14
San Francisco	10	7	7	0	— 24

SF —FG Wersching 30
SF —Rice 44 pass from Montana (Wersching kick)
Rams —Dickerson 15 run (Lansford kick)
SF —Cribbs 2 run (Wersching kick)
SF —Francis 1 pass from Montana (Wersching kick)
Rams —Young 13 pass from Everett (Lansford kick)

Saturday, December 20

Seattle 41, Denver 16—At Kingdome, attendance 63,697. Curt Warner rushed for 192 yards and three touchdowns to help the Seahawks defeat the Broncos. Seattle exploded for 17 points in the second quarter on Warner's two-yard run, Norm Johnson's 35-yard field goal, and Dave Krieg's 16-yard scoring pass to Daryl Turner. Seattle scored 14 points in the fourth quarter on two Warner runs of 6 and 60 yards. The Seahawks' defense held Denver to just 75 yards rushing. Warner captured his second AFC rushing title with 1,481 yards.

Denver	0	10	3	3	— 16
Seattle	3	17	7	14	— 41

Sea —FG Johnson 37
Sea —Warner 2 run (Johnson kick)
Den —FG Karlis 31
Sea —FG Johnson 35
Den —Mobley 17 pass from Elway (Karlis kick)
Sea —Turner 16 pass from Krieg (Johnson kick)
Sea —Turner 7 pass from Krieg (Johnson kick)
Den —FG Karlis 34
Den —FG Karlis 47
Sea —Warner 6 run (Johnson kick)
Sea —Warner 60 run (Johnson kick)

New York Giants 55, Green Bay 24—At Giants Stadium, attendance 71,351. Phil Simms passed for three touchdowns and Lee Rouson ran for two more to help the Giants to their biggest scoring outburst in 14 years and ensure New York the home-field advantage throughout the NFC playoffs. Simms, who completed 18 of 25 passes for 245 yards, connected with Mark Bavaro on touchdowns of 24 and 4 yards and hit Zeke Mowatt on a 22-yarder. Rouson added fourth-quarter touchdown runs of 10 and 26 yards. Joe Morris gained 115 yards on 22 carries, including a three-yard score. Former Packers safety Tom Flynn scored New York's second touchdown when he blocked a punt and returned it 36 yards for a score. The Giants' 55 points were the most they had scored since 1972, when they defeated the Eagles 62-10.

Green Bay	0	17	7	0	— 24
N.Y. Giants	21	3	14	17	— 55

NYG —Bavaro 24 pass from Simms (Allegre kick)
NYG —Flynn 36 blocked punt return (Allegre kick)
NYG —Morris 3 run (Allegre kick)
NYG —FG Allegre 46
GB —Ivery 13 pass from Wright (Del Greco kick)
GB —Stills 58 interception return (Del Greco kick)
GB —FG Del Greco 34
NYG —Bavaro 4 pass from Simms (Allegre kick)
GB —Davis 15 pass from Wright (Del Greco kick)
NYG —Mowatt 22 pass from Simms (Allegre kick)
NYG —Rouson 10 run (Allegre kick)
NYG —Rouson 26 run (Allegre kick)
NYG —FG Allegre 26

Sunday, December 21

Atlanta 20, Detroit 6—At Pontiac Silverdome, attendance 35,255. The Falcons capitalized on four Detroit turnovers to defeat the Lions 20-6. Turk Schonert threw a 21-yard touchdown pass to Floyd Dixon and Gerald Riggs scored on a one-yard run to give Atlanta a 14-0 halftime lead. Ali Haji-Sheikh added a pair of field goals from 25 and 21 yards in the second half to put the game out of reach. Pete Mandley returned a punt 84 yards for a score for the Lions' only points.

Atlanta	7	7	3	3	— 20
Detroit	0	0	0	6	— 6

Atl —Dixon 21 pass from Schonert (Haji-Sheikh kick)
Atl —Riggs 1 run (Haji-Sheikh kick)
Atl —FG Haji-Sheikh 25
Det —Mandley 84 punt return (kick failed)
Atl —FG Haji-Sheikh 21

Houston 16, Buffalo 7—At Astrodome, attendance 31,049. Tony Zendejas kicked three field goals for the second straight week to lead the Oilers over the Bills. Following a one-yard touchdown run by Allen Pinkett, Zendejas made field goals from 26, 51, and 22 yards. Drew Hill caught five passes for 114 yards to top the 1,000-yard mark for the second straight season (1,112). The Bills' loss spoiled the homecoming of Buffalo quarterback Jim Kelly, who was sacked six times.

Buffalo	0	7	0	0	— 7
Houston	7	3	3	3	— 16

Hou —Pinkett 1 run (Zendejas kick)
Hou —FG Zendejas 26
Buff —Burkett 12 pass from Kelly (Norwood kick)
Hou —FG Zendejas 51
Hou —FG Zendejas 22

Chicago 24, Dallas 10—At Texas Stadium, attendance 57,256. Walter Payton tied an NFL record by rushing for his 106th career touchdown and Doug Flutie threw for two more scores to lead the Bears over the Cowboys. Flutie completed two second-quarter scoring passes to Brad Anderson (58 yards) and Willie Gault (33). Kevin Butler's 31-yard field goal in the third quarter finished Chicago's scoring. Dallas prevented being shut out by scoring 10 points in the fourth quarter, but suffered its first losing season in 22 years.

Chicago	7	14	3	0	— 24
Dallas	0	0	0	10	— 10

Chi —Payton 1 run (Butler kick)
Chi —Anderson 58 pass from Flutie (Butler kick)
Chi —Gault 33 pass from Flutie (Butler kick)
Chi —FG Butler 31
Dall —FG Septien 50
Dall —Renfro 11 pass from Pelluer (Septien kick)

Indianapolis 30, Los Angeles Raiders 24—At Memorial Coliseum, attendance 41,349. Gary Hogeboom and Bill Brooks connected on an 11-yard touchdown pass midway through the fourth quarter as the Colts rallied to win their third straight game. Trailing 17-6 at halftime, Indianapolis reeled off 17 straight points. Albert Bentley, who rushed for 162 yards on 25 carries, opened the third-quarter outburst with a 70-yard run, the longest run in the AFC this season. Hogeboom followed with a 14-yard scoring pass to Walt Boyer, and Dean Biasucci's third field goal, a 20-yarder, gave the Colts a 23-17 lead. The Raiders regained the lead 24-23 on Rusty Hilger's 14-yard pass to Todd Christensen before Hogeboom engineered the game-winning seven-play, 80-yard drive. It was the Colts' first win over the Raiders since 1971.

Indianapolis	3	3	17	7	— 30
L.A. Raiders	17	0	7	0	— 24

Raiders —FG Bahr 20
Ind —FG Biasucci 52
Raiders —Christensen 3 pass from Plunkett (Bahr kick)
Raiders —Robinson 32 interception return (Bahr kick)
Ind —FG Biasucci 40
Ind —Bentley 70 run (Biasucci kick)
Ind —Boyer 14 pass from Hogeboom (Biasucci kick)
Ind —FG Biasucci 20
Raiders —Christensen 14 pass from Hilger (Bahr kick)
Ind —Brooks 11 pass from Hogeboom (Biasucci kick)

Kansas City 24, Pittsburgh 19—At Three Rivers Stadium, attendance 47,150. Kansas City's special teams produced three first-half touchdowns to enable the Chiefs to defeat the Steelers and advance to the playoffs for the first time since 1971. Deron Cherry gave Kansas City a 7-0 lead when he recovered a blocked punt in the end zone. Boyce Green then scored on a 97-yard kickoff return, the first by a Chiefs player since 1969. Lloyd Burruss gave Kansas City a 24-6 lead at halftime on a 78-yard blocked field goal return. Albert Lewis, who blocked the punt that Cherry recovered for the touchdown, also had two interceptions; the second came with 2:30 to play to secure the win. The Steelers outgained the Chiefs 515 total yards to 171.

Kansas City	7	17	0	0	— 24
Pittsburgh	0	6	7	6	— 19

KC —Cherry recovered blocked punt in end zone (Lowery kick)
KC —FG Lowery 47
Pitt —FG Anderson 31
KC —Green 97 kickoff return (Lowery kick)
Pitt —FG Anderson 31
KC —Burruss 78 blocked field goal return (Lowery kick)
Pitt —Malone 9 run (Anderson kick)
Pitt —FG Anderson 31
Pitt —FG Anderson 26

Minnesota 33, New Orleans 17—At Metrodome, attendance 51,209. Wade Wilson completed three touchdown passes to lead the Vikings over the Saints. Wilson, starting in place of Tommy Kramer, who had an injured elbow, completed 24 of 39 passes for a career-high 361 yards. He threw a pair of touchdown passes to Steve Jordan (1 and 14 yards), and connected with Darrin Nelson on an 18-yarder to give Minnesota a commanding 30-3 lead at the half. Jordan caught seven passes for 85 yards to become the Vikings' all-time tight end reception leader with 182 catches. Minnesota's 33 points brought their season total to a club-record 398.

New Orleans	0	3	0	14	— 17
Minnesota	9	21	0	3	— 33

Minn —Jordan 1 pass from Wilson (run failed)
Minn —FG C. Nelson 46
Minn —D. Nelson 18 pass from Wilson (C. Nelson kick)
NO —FG Andersen 39
Minn —Brown 1 run (C. Nelson kick)
Minn —Jordan 14 pass from W. Wilson (C. Nelson kick)
NO —M. Jones 10 pass from Hebert (Andersen kick)
Minn —FG C. Nelson 50
NO —Mayes 1 run (Andersen kick)

Cincinnati 52, New York Jets 21—At Riverfront Stadium, attendance 51,619. Boomer Esiason threw a team-record five touchdown passes, four in the second half, to rally the Bengals to a 52-21 win. The Jets led 21-17 at the half, but Cincinnati exploded for 21 unanswered points in the third quarter on Esiason's scoring passes to Rodney Holman (34 yards), Cris Collinsworth (42), and tackle-eligible Anthony Muñoz (2). Collinsworth also scored on passes of 12 and 21 yards. Holman caught six passes for 129 yards, while Esiason finished with 23 of 30 for a club-record 425 yards. Cincinnati outgained New York 621 total yards to 199. The Jets' Freeman McNeil gained 106 yards on 17 carries and had two touchdowns.

N.Y. Jets	7	14	0	0	— 21
Cincinnati	7	10	21	14	— 52

NYJ —Humphery 96 kickoff return (Leahy kick)
Cin —Wilson 2 run (Breech kick)
NYJ —McNeil 6 run (Leahy kick)
Cin —Collinsworth 12 pass from Esiason (Breech kick)
NYJ —McNeil 2 run (Leahy kick)
Cin —FG Breech 43
Cin —Holman 34 pass from Esiason (Breech kick)
Cin —Collinsworth 42 pass from Esiason (Breech kick)
Cin —Muñoz 2 pass from Esiason (Breech kick)
Cin —Collinsworth 21 pass from Esiason (Breech kick)
Cin —Kinnebrew 2 run (Breech kick)

Cleveland 47, San Diego 17—At Cleveland Stadium, attendance 68,505. Bernie Kosar completed 21 of 28 passes for 258 yards and two touchdowns as the Browns ensured themselves of the home-field advantage throughout the playoffs. Kosar threw a 57-yard touchdown pass to Brian Brennan in the closing seconds of the first half to take a commanding 20-10 lead. The Browns added 27 points in the second half, including 17 straight in the third quarter, on touchdowns by Harry Holt (one-yard pass) and Herman Fontenot (nine-yard run), and a 37-yard Mark Moseley field goal. Fontenot also completed a 46-yard touchdown pass to Webster Slaughter to open the scoring.

San Diego	0	10	7	0	— 17
Cleveland	7	13	17	10	— 47

Clev —Slaughter 46 pass from Fontenot (Moseley kick)
Clev —Mack 2 run (Moseley kick)
SD —Chandler 19 pass from Fouts (Benirschke kick)
SD —FG Benirschke 40
Clev —Brennan 57 pass from Kosar (kick blocked)
Clev —Holt 1 pass from Kosar (Moseley kick)
Clev —Fontenot 9 run (Moseley kick)
Clev —FG Moseley 37
SD —Anderson 65 pass from Fouts (Benirschke kick)
Clev —Dickey 2 run (Moseley kick)
Clev —FG Moseley 32

St. Louis 21, Tampa Bay 17—At Busch Memorial Stadium, attendance 23,957. Rookie Vai Sikahema became only the sixth player in NFL history to score two touchdowns in a game on punt returns as the Cardinals edged the Buccaneers 21-17. Sikahema scored on returns of 71 and 60 yards in the second quarter as St. Louis exploded for a 21-7 halftime lead. Sikahema set club records for most punt-return yardage in a game (145) and a season (502). Neil Lomax scored the Cardinals' other touchdown on a two-yard run 39 seconds before halftime.

Tampa Bay	7	0	10	0	— 17
St. Louis	0	21	0	0	— 21

TB —Howard 1 run (Igwebuike kick)
StL —Sikahema 71 punt return (Schubert kick)
StL —Sikahema 60 punt return (Schubert kick)

StL —Lomax 2 run (Schubert kick)
TB —FG Igwebuike 36
TB —Freeman 33 pass from Young (Igwebuike kick)

Washington 21, Philadelphia 14—At Veterans Stadium, attendance 61,816. Jay Schroeder threw two fourth-quarter touchdown passes to rally the Redskins to a 21-14 win. Trailing 14-0 in the final period, Schroeder completed a 26-yard pass to Clint Didier and a two-yarder to Don Warren to tie the game. George Rogers had a five-yard scoring run with less than three minutes remaining for the decisive score.

Washington	0	0	0	21	— 21
Philadelphia	14	0	0	0	— 14

Phil —Cunningham 1 run (McFadden kick)
Phil —Toney 1 run (McFadden kick)
Wash —Didier 26 pass from Schroeder (Atkinson kick)
Wash —Warren 2 pass from Schroeder (Atkinson kick)
Wash —Rogers 5 run (Atkinson kick)

Monday, December 22

New England 34, Miami 27—At Orange Bowl, attendance 74,516. Steve Grogan's game-winning 30-yard touchdown pass to Stanley Morgan with 44 seconds remaining lifted the Patriots to their first AFC East title since 1978. Morgan, who had eight receptions for 148 yards to give him nine 100-yard games for the season, also scored on a 22-yard pass from Eason in the first quarter. Grogan, who replaced Tony Eason when he injured his shoulder in the first quarter, was 15 of 24 for 226 yards. Grogan also scored on a seven-yard run and threw a 12-yard scoring pass to Tony Collins. Tony Franklin kicked field goals of 47 and 44 yards. It was the Patriots' first regular-season victory in the Orange Bowl since 1966.

New England	7	6	7	14	— 34
Miami	0	10	10	7	— 27

NE —Morgan 22 pass from Eason (Franklin kick)
NE —FG Franklin 47
Mia —FG Reveiz 42
NE —FG Franklin 44
Mia —Hardy 1 pass from Marino (Reveiz kick)
Mia —FG Reveiz 21
Mia —Clayton 32 pass from Marino (Reveiz kick)
NE —Grogan 7 run (Franklin kick)
Mia —Clayton 19 pass from Marino (Reveiz kick)
NE —Collins 12 pass from Grogan (Franklin kick)
NE —Morgan 30 pass from Grogan (Franklin kick)

Seventeenth Week Summaries

Sunday, December 28, 1986
AFC First-Round Playoff Game

New York Jets 35, Kansas City 15—At Giants Stadium, attendance 75,210. Jets quarterback Pat Ryan threw three touchdown passes and Freeman McNeil ran for 135 yards to spark the Jets' first home playoff win since a 27-23 decision over the Oakland Raiders on December 29, 1968. Ryan, starting in the first playoff game of his nine-year career, completed 16 of 23 passes for 153 yards. McNeil's one-yard touchdown run gave New York a 7-6 first-quarter lead that it never relinquished. McNeil (one yard) and wide receiver Al Toon (11) caught scoring passes from Ryan in the second quarter to give the Jets a 21-6 advantage. New York linebacker Kevin McArthur scored a touchdown on a 21-yard interception return on the first play of the second half to put the game away. It was McNeil's third straight 100-yard game and second-highest playoff total of his career. He gained 202 yards against Cincinnati in 1982. Tight end Billy Griggs's six-yard touchdown catch in the fourth quarter was his first NFL reception.

Kansas City	6	0	0	9	— 15
N.Y. Jets	7	14	7	7	— 35

KC —Smith 1 run (kick failed)
NYJ —McNeil 1 run (Leahy kick)
NYJ —McNeil 1 pass from Ryan (Leahy kick)
NYJ —Toon 11 pass from Ryan (Leahy kick)
NYJ —McArthur 21 interception return (Leahy kick)
KC —Lewis recovered blocked punt in end zone (Lowery kick)
NYJ —Griggs 6 pass from Ryan (Leahy kick)
KC —Safety, Jennings ran out of end zone

Sunday, December 28, 1986
NFC First-Round Playoff Game

Washington 19, Los Angeles Rams 7—At Robert F. Kennedy Stadium, attendance 54,567. The Washington Redskins took advantage of six Los Angeles Rams turnovers (four fumbles and two interceptions) to advance to the NFC Divisional playoffs. The Redskins' Jess Atkinson tied an NFL playoff record by kicking four field goals (25, 20, 38, and 19 yards). Washington held a 36:06 to 23:54 time-of-possession advantage over Los Angeles. Both teams had 100-yard rushers in the game. Eric Dickerson of the Rams had 26 carries for 158 yards, and George Rogers of the Redskins rushed 29 times for 115 yards. Los Angeles outgained Washington 324 yards to 228, but was plagued by the turnovers. Quarterback Jay Schroeder connected with running back Kelvin Bryant for a 14-yard touchdown 12:34 into the opening period to give the Redskins a 10-0 lead. Los Angeles's touchdown came on the first play of the fourth period when quarterback Jim Everett completed a 12-yard scoring pass to wide receiver Kevin House.

L.A. Rams	0	0	0	7	— 7
Washington	10	3	3	3	— 19

Wash —FG Atkinson 25
Wash —Bryant 14 pass from Schroeder (Atkinson kick)
Wash —FG Atkinson 20
Wash —FG Atkinson 38
Rams —House 12 pass from Everett (Lansford kick)
Wash —FG Atkinson 19

Eighteenth Week Summaries

Saturday, January 3, 1987
AFC Divisional Playoff Game

Cleveland 23, New York Jets 20—At Cleveland Stadium, attendance 79,720. Mark Moseley's 27-yard field goal 17:02 into overtime gave the AFC Central Division champion Browns their first playoff victory since 1969 in the third-longest game in NFL history. Cleveland quarterback Bernie Kosar set NFL postseason passing records for attempts (64), yards (489), and average gain per attempt (14.81 yards), and tied another by completing 33 passes to rally the Browns from a 20-10 fourth-quarter deficit. After the Jets took a 10-point lead on Freeman McNeil's 25-yard touchdown run with 4:14 remaining, Kosar drove the Browns 68 yards to set up Kevin Mack's one-yard scoring run with 1:57 left. Cleveland's defense forced New York to punt on the next series. Kosar then completed a 37-yard pass to rookie Webster Slaughter to the Jets' 5-yard line to set up Moseley's 22-yard field goal with seven seconds left in regulation and send the game into overtime. Moseley tied an NFL playoff record by attempting six field goals. Cleveland tight end Ozzie Newsome caught six passes for 114 yards. The Browns' defense held the Jets to 287 total yards and registered a playoff-record nine sacks, including three by defensive end Carl Hairston. The win was Cleveland's club-record thirteenth in 1986. New York's Dave Jennings punted a playoff-record 14 times. Russell Carter's fourth-quarter interception in the end zone snapped Kosar's streak of 133 attempts without an interception.

N.Y. Jets	7	3	3	7	0	0 — 20
Cleveland	7	3	0	10	0	3 — 23

NYJ —Walker 42 pass from Ryan (Leahy kick)
Clev —Fontenot 37 pass from Kosar (Moseley kick)
Clev —FG Moseley 38
NYJ —FG Leahy 46
NYJ —FG Leahy 37
NYJ —McNeil 25 run (Leahy kick)
Clev —Mack 1 run (Moseley kick)
Clev —FG Moseley 22
Clev —FG Moseley 27

Saturday, January 3, 1987
NFC Divisional Playoff Game

Washington 27, Chicago 13—At Soldier Field, attendance 65,524. Washington gained its third NFC Championship Game berth in the past five seasons with a 27-13 victory over the NFC Central and defending NFL champion Chicago Bears. The Redskins became the first Wild Card team to advance to the NFC Championship Game since 1980, when Dallas defeated the Los Angeles Rams and Atlanta Falcons before falling to the Philadelphia Eagles in the title game. Washington took a 14-13 lead on a 23-yard touchdown pass from quarterback Jay Schroeder to wide receiver Art Monk with 7:09 to go in the third period. Monk had opened the Redskins' scoring with a 28-yard catch with 2:15 remaining in the first period. Jess Atkinson connected on 35- and 25-yard field goals late in the fourth quarter to seal the victory. Washington's defense played a major role in the win with two fumble recoveries and two interceptions. The Redskins held Bears running back Walter Payton to 38 yards on 14 carries.

Washington	7	0	7	13	— 27
Chicago	0	13	0	0	— 13

Wash —Monk 28 pass from Schroeder (Atkinson kick)
Chi —Gault 50 pass from Flutie (Butler kick)
Chi —FG Butler 23
Chi —FG Butler 41
Wash —Monk 23 pass from Schroeder (Atkinson kick)
Wash —Rogers 1 run (Atkinson kick)
Wash —FG Atkinson 35
Wash —FG Atkinson 25

Sunday, January 4, 1987
AFC Divisional Playoff Game

Denver 22, New England 17—At Mile High Stadium, attendance 75,262. Broncos quarterback John Elway ran for one touchdown and passed for another to lead Denver to its first postseason victory in Mile High Stadium since 1977. Elway threw for a Denver playoff-record 257 yards on 13 of 32 passes, including a 48-yard touchdown pass to Vance Johnson on the final play of the third quarter to give the Broncos a 20-17 lead they never relinquished. Elway's 22-yard scoring run in the second quarter put Denver ahead 10-7. New England forged a 17-13 lead on Tony Franklin's 38-yard field goal and Tony Eason's 45-yard flea-flicker touchdown pass to Stanley Morgan in the third quarter. The Broncos' Rulon Jones's two sacks included a tackle of Eason in the end zone for a safety with less than two minutes to play. Running back Sammy Winder became the first Denver player ever to rush for over 100 yards in a playoff game with 19 carries for 102 yards. The Broncos' defense set club playoff records for sacks (six), fewest first downs allowed (12), and fewest total yards allowed (271). Morgan caught three passes for 100 yards for the Patriots. Denver's last home playoff win was a 34-21 decision over Pittsburgh in a 1977 divisional playoff game.

New England	0	10	7	0	— 17
Denver	3	7	10	2	— 22

Den —FG Karlis 27
NE —Morgan 19 pass from Eason (Franklin kick)
Den —Elway 22 run (Karlis kick)
NE —FG Franklin 38
Den —FG Karlis 22
NE —Morgan 45 pass from Eason (Franklin kick)
Den —Johnson 48 pass from Elway (Karlis kick)
Den —Safety, Jones tackled Eason in end zone

Sunday, January 4, 1987
NFC Divisional Playoff Game

New York Giants 49, San Francisco 3—At Giants Stadium, attendance 75,691. The NFC Eastern Division champion New York Giants advanced to their first NFC Championship Game with a 49-3 win over NFC Western Division titlist San Francisco. The Giants won the NFL Eastern Conference title in 1963 before losing to Chicago 14-10 in the NFL Championship Game. New York's 46-point margin of victory over the 49ers tied the third-largest in NFL playoff history behind Chicago's 73-0 win over Washington in 1940; Oakland's 56-7 win over Houston in 1969; and Cleveland's 56-10 win over Detroit in 1954. The Giants compiled 21 first downs to the 49ers' 9 and outgained their opponent 366 yards to 184. New York quarterback Phil Simms tied a club playoff record with four touchdown passes. Giants running back Joe Morris rushed 24 times for 159 yards, and had 45- and 2-yard touchdown runs. New York built a 28-3 halftime lead on two scores with less than a minute to play before halftime on wide receiver Bobby Johnson's 15-yard touchdown catch with 50 seconds left and linebacker Lawrence Taylor's 34-yard interception return for a score with 28 seconds remaining.

San Francisco	3	0	0	0	— 3
N.Y. Giants	7	21	21	0	— 49

NYG —Bavaro 24 pass from Simms (Allegre kick)
SF —FG Wersching 26
NYG —Morris 45 run (Allegre kick)
NYG —Johnson 15 pass from Simms (Allegre kick)
NYG —Taylor 34 interception return (Allegre kick)
NYG —McConkey 28 pass from Simms (Allegre kick)
NYG —Mowatt 29 pass from Simms (Allegre kick)
NYG —Morris 2 run (Allegre kick)

Nineteenth Week Summaries

Sunday, January 11, 1987
AFC Championship Game

Denver 23, Cleveland 20—At Cleveland Stadium, attendance 79,973. The AFC Western Division champion Denver Broncos advanced to their second Super Bowl in franchise history by defeating the Browns 23-20 in overtime. Quarterback John Elway capped a 15-play, 98-yard touchdown drive with a five-yard scoring pass to rookie wide receiver Mark Jackson with 37 seconds left in regulation time to tie the game, 20-20. Kicker Rich Karlis added a 33-yard field goal 5:38 into overtime to complete the comeback. Cleveland won the overtime coin toss but the Denver defense held the Browns on four plays. Elway completed a 22-yard pass to rookie tight end Orson Mobley and a 28-yarder to wide receiver Steve Watson to set up Karlis's winning kick. The Browns took an early 7-0 lead, but linebacker Jim Ryan's 26-yard interception return led to Karlis's 19-yard field goal, and Ken Woodard's fumble recovery set up running back Gerald Willhite's one-yard touchdown dive to give the Broncos a 10-7 lead in the second quarter. Following a 26-yard field goal by Karlis, the Browns rallied to take a 20-13 fourth-quarter lead on Mark Moseley's 24-yard field goal and quarterback Bernie Kosar's 48-yard touchdown pass to wide receiver Brian Brennan. Elway completed passes to 10 different receivers to finish with 22 of 38 for 244 yards, with one touchdown and one interception. He also gained 56 yards on four carries. The victory earned the Broncos their first Super Bowl appearance since Super Bowl XII, in which they lost 27-10 to the Dallas Cowboys following the 1977 season.

Denver	0	10	3	7	3 — 23
Cleveland	7	3	0	10	0 — 20

Clev —Fontenot 6 pass from Kosar (Moseley kick)
Den —FG Karlis 19
Den —Willhite 1 run (Karlis kick)
Clev —FG Moseley 29
Den —FG Karlis 26
Clev —FG Moseley 24
Clev —Brennan 48 pass from Kosar (Moseley kick)
Den —Jackson 5 pass from Elway (Karlis kick)
Den —FG Karlis 33

Sunday, January 11, 1987
NFC Championship Game

New York Giants 17, Washington 0—At Giants Stadium, attendance 76,891. The NFC Eastern Division champion New York Giants gained the right to try for their first NFL championship since 1956 by blanking the Washington Redskins, 17-0. The contest marked the third straight NFC Championship Game that was won by a shutout. The Giants gained the advantage of wind gusts up to 30 miles per hour when they won the coin toss and elected to defend the eastern goal, thus having the wind at their backs the first quarter, when they scored 10 points. The Redskins ran three plays for only four yards and were forced to punt on the first series of the game. New York took over on the Redskins' 47-yard line and six plays later Raul Allegre kicked a 47-yard field goal 3:22 into the game. After Washington punted on its next series, the Giants again got excellent field position at the Redskins' 38-yard line. On third-and-20 from the Washington 36, wide receiver Lionel Manuel caught a 25-yard pass from Phil Simms for a first down. Three plays later, Simms again connected with Manuel in the end zone for an 11-yard completion. Simms threw for 60 yards in the first quarter and ended up with seven completions in 14 attempts for 90 yards. In contrast, Washington quarterback Jay Schroeder was forced to throw 50 times—an NFC Championship Game record. He completed 20 for 195 yards. In the second half, the Giants rushed 27 times and passed only twice. The Redskins passed 34 times and rushed once in the final two periods. New York's final score came on a six-play, 49-yard drive that was sparked by a 30-yard Simms completion to tight end Mark Bavaro to Washington's 17-yard line. Two plays later, running back Joe Morris, who carried 29 times for 87 yards, scored on a one-yard run.

Washington	0	0	0	0	— 0
N.Y. Giants	10	7	0	0	— 17

NYG —FG Allegre 47
NYG —Manuel 11 pass from Simms (Allegre kick)
NYG —Morris 1 run (Allegre kick)

Twentieth Week Summary

Sunday, January 25, 1987
Super Bowl XXI
Pasadena, California

New York Giants 39, Denver 20—At the Rose Bowl, attendance 101,063. The NFC champion New York Giants captured their first NFL title since 1956 when they downed the AFC champion Denver Broncos, 39-20, in Super Bowl XXI. The victory marked the NFC's fifth NFL title in the past six seasons. The Broncos, behind the passing of quarterback John Elway, who was 13 of 20 for 187 yards in the first half, held a 10-9 lead at intermission, the narrowest halftime margin in Super Bowl history. Denver's Rich Karlis opened the scoring with a Super Bowl record-tying 48-yard field goal. New York drove 78 yards in nine plays on the next series to take a 7-3 lead on quarterback Phil Simms's six-yard touchdown pass to tight end Zeke Mowatt. The Broncos came right back with a 58-yard scoring drive in six plays capped by Elway's four-yard touchdown run. The only scoring in the second period was the sack of Elway in the end zone by Giants defensive end George Martin for a New York safety. The Giants produced a key defensive stand early in the second quarter when the Broncos had a first down at the New York one-yard line but failed to score on three running plays and Karlis's 23-yard missed field-goal attempt. The Giants took command of the game in the third period en route to a 30-point second half, the most ever scored in one half of Super Bowl play. New York took the lead for good on tight end Mark Bavaro's 13-yard touchdown catch 4:52 into the third period. The nine-play, 63-yard scoring drive included the successful conversion of a fourth-and-one play on New York's 46-yard line. Denver was limited to only two net yards on 10 offensive plays in the third period. Simms set Super Bowl records for most consecutive completions (10) and highest completion percentage (88 percent on 22 completions in 25 attempts). He also passed for 268 yards and three touchdowns and was named the game's most valuable player. New York running back Joe Morris was the game's leading rusher with 20 carries for 67 yards. Denver wide receiver Vance Johnson led all receivers with five catches for 121 yards. The Giants defeated their three playoff opponents by a cumulative total of 82 points (New York 105, opponents 23), the largest margin ever by a Super Bowl winner.

Denver	10	0	0	10	— 20
N.Y. Giants	7	2	17	13	— 39

Den —FG Karlis 48
NYG —Mowatt 6 pass from Simms (Allegre kick)
Den —Elway 4 run (Karlis kick)
NYG —Safety, Martin tackled Elway in end zone
NYG —Bavaro 13 pass from Simms (Allegre kick)
NYG —FG Allegre 21
NYG —Morris 1 run (Allegre kick)
NYG —McConkey 6 pass from Simms (Allegre kick)
Den —FG Karlis 28
NYG —Anderson 2 run (kick failed)
Den —V. Johnson 47 pass from Elway (Karlis kick)

Twenty-First Week Summary

Sunday, February 1, 1987
AFC-NFC Pro Bowl
Honolulu, Hawaii

AFC 10, NFC 6—At Aloha Stadium, attendance 50,101. The AFC defeated the NFC, 10-6, in the lowest-scoring game in AFC-NFC Pro Bowl history. The AFC took a 10-0 halftime lead on Broncos quarterback John Elway's 10-yard touchdown pass to Raiders tight end Todd Christensen and Patriots kicker Tony Franklin's 26-yard field goal. The AFC defense made the lead stand up by forcing the NFC to settle for a pair of field goals from 38 and 19 yards by Saints kicker Morten Andersen after the NFC had first downs at the AFC 31-, 7-, 16-, 15-, 5-, and 7-yard lines. Both AFC scores were set up by fumble recoveries by Seahawks linebacker Fredd Young and Dolphins linebacker John Offerdahl, respectively. Eagles defensive end Reggie White, who tied a Pro Bowl record with four sacks and also contributed seven solo tackles, was voted the game's outstanding player. The AFC victory cut the NFC's lead in the Pro Bowl series to 10-7.

AFC	7	3	0	0	— 10
NFC	0	0	3	3	— 6

AFC —Christensen 10 pass from Elway (Franklin kick)
AFC —FG Franklin 26
NFC —FG Andersen 38
NFC —FG Andersen 19

1986 ALL-PRO TEAMS

1986 PFWA All-Pro Team

Selected by the Professional Football Writers of America

Offense

Jerry Rice, San Francisco . . . . . Wide Receiver
Al Toon, New York Jets . . . . . Wide Receiver
Mark Bavaro, New York Giants . . . . . Tight End
Jim Covert, Chicago . . . . . Tackle
Anthony Muñoz, Cincinnati . . . . . Tackle
Dennis Harrah, Los Angeles Rams . . . . . Guard
Russ Grimm, Washington . . . . . Guard
Dwight Stephenson, Miami . . . . . Center
Dan Marino, Miami . . . . . Quarterback
Eric Dickerson, Los Angeles Rams . . . . . Running Back
Joe Morris, New York Giants . . . . . Running Back
Morten Andersen, New Orleans . . . . . Kicker
Dennis Gentry, Chicago . . . . . Kick Returner
Bobby Joe Edmonds, Seattle . . . . . Punt Returner

Defense

Dexter Manley, Washington . . . . . Defensive End
Rulon Jones, Denver . . . . . Defensive End
Steve McMichael, Chicago . . . . . Defensive Tackle
Reggie White, Philadelphia . . . . . Defensive Tackle
Lawrence Taylor, New York Giants . . . . . Outside Linebacker
Wilber Marshall, Chicago . . . . . Outside Linebacker
Mike Singletary, Chicago . . . . . Inside Linebacker
Karl Mecklenburg, Denver . . . . . Inside Linebacker
Hanford Dixon, Cleveland . . . . . Cornerback
LeRoy Irvin, Los Angeles Rams . . . . . Cornerback
Dave Duerson, Chicago . . . . . Safety
Ronnie Lott, San Francisco . . . . . Safety
Sean Landeta, New York Giants . . . . . Punter

1986 NEA All-Pro Team

Selected by Newspaper Enterprise Association

Offense

Jerry Rice, San Francisco . . . . . Wide Receiver
Al Toon, New York Jets . . . . . Wide Receiver
Todd Christensen, Los Angeles Raiders . . . . . Tight End
Anthony Muñoz, Cincinnati . . . . . Tackle
Brian Holloway, New England . . . . . Tackle
Russ Grimm, Washington . . . . . Guard
Bill Fralic, Atlanta . . . . . Guard
Dwight Stephenson, Miami . . . . . Center
Phil Simms, New York Giants . . . . . Quarterback
Joe Morris, New York Giants . . . . . Running Back
Eric Dickerson, Los Angeles Rams . . . . . Running Back
Morten Andersen, New Orleans . . . . . Kicker

Defense

Dexter Manley, Washington . . . . . Defensive End
Dan Hampton, Chicago . . . . . Defensive End
Reggie White, Philadelphia . . . . . Defensive Tackle
Michael Carter, San Francisco . . . . . Nose Tackle
Lawrence Taylor, New York Giants . . . . . Outside Linebacker
Rickey Jackson, New Orleans . . . . . Outside Linebacker
Karl Mecklenburg, Denver . . . . . Inside Linebacker
Mike Singletary, Chicago . . . . . Inside Linebacker
Darrell Green, Washington . . . . . Cornerback
Hanford Dixon, Cleveland . . . . . Cornerback
Dennis Smith, Denver . . . . . Safety
Ronnie Lott, San Francisco . . . . . Safety
Rohn Stark, Indianapolis . . . . . Punter

1986 Associated Press All-Pro Team

Offense

Jerry Rice, San Francisco . . . . . Wide Receiver
Al Toon, New York Jets . . . . . Wide Receiver
Mark Bavaro, New York Giants . . . . . Tight End
Anthony Muñoz, Cincinnati . . . . . Tackle
Jim Covert, Chicago . . . . . Tackle
Bill Fralic, Atlanta . . . . . Guard
Dennis Harrah, Los Angeles Rams . . . . . Guard
Dwight Stephenson, Miami . . . . . Center
Dan Marino, Miami . . . . . Quarterback
Eric Dickerson, Los Angeles Rams . . . . . Running Back
Joe Morris, New York Giants . . . . . Running Back
Morten Andersen, New Orleans . . . . . Kicker
Bobby Joe Edmonds, Seattle . . . . . Kick Returner

Defense

Dexter Manley, Washington . . . . . Defensive End
Rulon Jones, Denver . . . . . Defensive End
Reggie White, Philadelphia . . . . . Defensive Tackle
Bill Pickel, Los Angeles Raiders . . . . . Nose Tackle
Lawrence Taylor, New York Giants . . . . . Outside Linebacker
Wilber Marshall, Chicago . . . . . Outside Linebacker
Mike Singletary, Chicago . . . . . Inside Linebacker
Karl Mecklenburg, Denver . . . . . Inside Linebacker
Hanford Dixon, Cleveland . . . . . Cornerback
LeRoy Irvin, Los Angeles Rams . . . . . Cornerback
Ronnie Lott, San Francisco . . . . . Safety
Deron Cherry, Kansas City . . . . . Safety
Sean Landeta, New York Giants . . . . . Punter

1986 All-NFL Team

Selected by Associated Press, Newspaper Enterprise Association, and Professional Football Writers of America

Offense

Jerry Rice, San Francisco (AP, NEA, PFWA) . . . . . Wide Receiver
Al Toon, New York Jets (AP, NEA, PFWA) . . . . . Wide Receiver
Mark Bavaro, New York Giants (AP, PFWA) . . . . . Tight End
Todd Christensen, Los Angeles Raiders (NEA) . . . . . Tight End
Anthony Muñoz, Cincinnati (AP, NEA, PFWA) . . . . . Tackle
Jim Covert, Chicago (AP, PFWA) . . . . . Tackle
Brian Holloway, New England (NEA) . . . . . Tackle
Bill Fralic, Atlanta (AP, NEA) . . . . . Guard
Russ Grimm, Washington (NEA, PFWA) . . . . . Guard
Dennis Harrah, Los Angeles Rams (AP, PFWA) . . . . . Guard
Dwight Stephenson, Miami (AP, NEA, PFWA) . . . . . Center
Dan Marino, Miami (AP, PFWA) . . . . . Quarterback
Phil Simms, New York Giants (NEA) . . . . . Quarterback
Eric Dickerson, Los Angeles Rams (AP, NEA, PFWA) . . . . . Running Back
Joe Morris, New York Giants (AP, NEA, PFWA) . . . . . Running Back
Morten Andersen, New Orleans (AP, NEA, PFWA) . . . . . Kicker
Bobby Joe Edmonds, Seattle (AP, PFWA) . . . . . Punt Returner
Dennis Gentry, Chicago (PFWA) . . . . . Kick Returner

Defense

Dexter Manley, Washington (AP, NEA, PFWA) . . . . . Defensive End
Rulon Jones, Denver (AP, PFWA) . . . . . Defensive End
Dan Hampton, Chicago (NEA) . . . . . Defensive End
Reggie White, Philadelphia (AP, NEA, PFWA) . . . . . Defensive Tackle
Steve McMichael, Chicago (PFWA) . . . . . Defensive Tackle
Michael Carter, San Francisco (NEA) . . . . . Nose Tackle
Bill Pickel, Los Angeles Raiders (AP) . . . . . Nose Tackle
Lawrence Taylor, New York Giants (AP, NEA, PFWA) . . . . . Outside Linebacker
Wilber Marshall, Chicago (AP, PFWA) . . . . . Outside Linebacker
Rickey Jackson, New Orleans (NEA) . . . . . Outside Linebacker
Karl Mecklenburg, Denver (AP, NEA, PFWA) . . . . . Inside Linebacker
Mike Singletary, Chicago (AP, NEA, PFWA) . . . . . Inside Linebacker
Hanford Dixon, Cleveland (AP, NEA, PFWA) . . . . . Cornerback
LeRoy Irvin, Los Angeles Rams (AP, PFWA) . . . . . Cornerback
Darrell Green, Washington (NEA) . . . . . Cornerback
Ronnie Lott, San Francisco (AP, NEA, PFWA) . . . . . Safety
Deron Cherry, Kansas City (AP) . . . . . Safety
Dave Duerson, Chicago (PFWA) . . . . . Safety
Dennis Smith, Denver (NEA) . . . . . Safety
Sean Landeta, New York Giants (AP, PFWA) . . . . . Punter
Rohn Stark, Indianapolis (NEA) . . . . . Punter

1986 UPI All-AFC Team

Selected by United Press International

Offense

Al Toon, New York Jets .... Wide Receiver
Stanley Morgan, New England .... Wide Receiver
Todd Christensen, Los Angeles Raiders .... Tight End
Anthony Muñoz, Cincinnati .... Tackle
Chris Hinton, Indianapolis .... Tackle
Max Montoya, Cincinnati .... Guard
Roy Foster, Miami .... Guard
Dwight Stephenson, Miami .... Center
Dan Marino, Miami .... Quarterback
Curt Warner, Seattle .... Running Back
James Brooks, Cincinnati .... Running Back
Tony Franklin, New England .... Kicker

Defense

Rulon Jones, Denver .... Defensive End
Art Still, Kansas City .... Defensive End
Bill Pickel, Los Angeles Raiders .... Defensive Tackle
Chip Banks, Cleveland .... Outside Linebacker
Andre Tippett, New England .... Outside Linebacker
Karl Mecklenburg, Denver .... Inside Linebacker
John Offerdahl, Miami .... Inside Linebacker
Hanford Dixon, Cleveland .... Cornerback
Ronnie Lippett, New England .... Cornerback
Deron Cherry, Kansas City .... Safety
Lloyd Burruss, Kansas City .... Safety
Rohn Stark, Indianapolis .... Punter

1986 UPI All-NFC Team

Selected by United Press International

Offense

Jerry Rice, San Francisco .... Wide Receiver
Gary Clark, Washington .... Wide Receiver
Mark Bavaro, New York Giants .... Tight End
Jackie Slater, Los Angeles Rams .... Tackle
Jim Covert, Chicago .... Tackle
Dennis Harrah, Los Angeles Rams .... Guard
Russ Grimm, Washington .... Guard
Jay Hilgenberg, Chicago .... Center
Tommy Kramer, Minnesota .... Quarterback
Eric Dickerson, Los Angeles Rams .... Running Back
Joe Morris, New York Giants .... Running Back
Morten Andersen, New Orleans .... Kicker

Defense

Dexter Manley, Washington .... Defensive End
Dan Hampton, Chicago .... Defensive End
Reggie White, Philadelphia .... Defensive Tackle
Lawrence Taylor, New York Giants .... Outside Linebacker
Wilber Marshall, Chicago .... Outside Linebacker
Mike Singletary, Chicago .... Inside Linebacker
Harry Carson, New York Giants .... Inside Linebacker
LeRoy Irvin, Los Angeles Rams .... Cornerback
Jerry Gray, Los Angeles Rams .... Cornerback
Ronnie Lott, San Francisco .... Safety
Dave Duerson, Chicago .... Safety
Sean Landeta, New York Giants .... Punter

1986 PFWA All-Rookie Team

Selected by Professional Football Writers of America

Offense

Bill Brooks, Indianapolis .... Wide Receiver
Ernest Givins, Houston .... Wide Receiver
Greg Baty, New England .... Tight End
J.D. Maarleveld, Tampa Bay .... Tackle
Brian Jozwiak, Kansas City .... Tackle
Tom Newberry, Los Angeles Rams .... Guard
Will Wolford, Buffalo .... Guard
Matt Darwin, Philadelphia .... Center
Jim Everett, Los Angeles Rams .... Quarterback
Rueben Mayes, New Orleans .... Running Back
John L. Williams, Seattle .... Running Back
John Lee, St. Louis .... Kicker

Defense

Leslie O'Neal, San Diego .... Defensive End
Brent Williams, New England .... Defensive End
Tony Casillas, Atlanta .... Defensive Tackle
Reggie Singletary, Philadelphia .... Defensive Tackle
Charles Haley, San Francisco .... Outside Linebacker
Tim Cofield, Kansas City .... Outside Linebacker
John Offerdahl, Miami .... Inside Linebacker
Dino Hackett, Kansas City .... Inside Linebacker
Tim McKyer, San Francisco .... Cornerback
Don Griffin, San Francisco .... Cornerback
David Fulcher, Cincinnati .... Safety
Devon Mitchell, Detroit .... Safety
John Teltschik, Philadelphia .... Punter

1986 UPI All-Rookie Team

Selected by United Press International

Offense

Bill Brooks, Indianapolis .... Wide Receiver
Ernest Givens, Houston .... Wide Receiver
Greg Baty, New England .... Tight End
Brian Jozwiak, Kansas City .... Tackle
J.D. Maarleveld, Tampa Bay .... Tackle
Tom Newberry, Los Angeles Rams .... Guard
Will Wolford, Buffalo .... Guard
Matt Darwin, Philadelphia .... Center
Jim Everett, Los Angeles Rams .... Quarterback
Rueben Mayes, New Orleans .... Running Back
Garry James, Detroit .... Running Back
Max Zendejas, Washington .... Kicker

Defense

T.J. Turner, Miami .... Defensive End
Leslie O'Neal, San Diego .... Defensive End
Tony Casillas, Atlanta .... Defensive Tackle
Charles Haley, San Francisco .... Outside Linebacker
Alonzo Johnson, Philadelphia .... Outside Linebacker
John Offerdahl, Miami .... Inside Linebacker
Dino Hackett, Kansas City .... Inside Linebacker
Tim McKyer, San Francisco .... Cornerback
Vestee Jackson, Chicago .... Cornerback
Todd Bowles, Washington .... Free Safety
Alvin Walton, Washington .... Strong Safety
John Teltschik, Philadelphia .... Punter

1986 Professional Football Awards

	NFL	AFC	NFC
Professional Football Writers of America			
Most Valuable Player	Lawrence Taylor		
Rookie of the Year	Rueben Mayes		
Coach of the Year	Bill Parcells		
Associated Press			
Most Valuable Player	Lawrence Taylor		
Offensive Player of the Year	Eric Dickerson		
Defensive Player of the Year	Lawrence Taylor		
Rookie of the Year—Offense	Rueben Mayes		
Rookie of the Year—Defense	Leslie O'Neal		
Coach of the Year	Bill Parcells		
United Press International			
Offensive Player of the Year		Curt Warner	Eric Dickerson
Defensive Player of the Year		Rulon Jones	Lawrence Taylor
Coach of the Year		Marty Schottenheimer	Bill Parcells
Newspaper Enterprise Association			
Jim Thorpe Memorial Trophy—MVP	Phil Simms		
Rookie of the Year	Rueben Mayes		
George Halas Trophy—Defensive Player of the Year	Lawrence Taylor		
The Sporting News			
Player of the Year	Lawrence Taylor		
Rookie of the Year	Rueben Mayes		
Coach of the Year	Bill Parcells		
Football News			
Coach of the Year		Marty Schottenheimer	Bill Parcells
Player of the Year		Karl Mecklenburg	Joe Morris
Pro Football Weekly			
Offensive Player of the Year	Jerry Rice		
Defensive Player of the Year	Lawrence Taylor		
Coach of the Year	Bill Parcells		
Offensive Rookie of the Year	Rueben Mayes		
Defensive Rookies of the Year	John Offerdahl, Leslie O'Neal		
Super Bowl XXI Most Valuable Player			
(Selected by Sport Magazine)	Phil Simms		
AFC-NFC Pro Bowl			
Player of the Game (Dan McGuire Award)	Reggie White		
Maxwell Club			
Player of the Year (Bert Bell Trophy)	Lawrence Taylor		
College and Pro Football Newsweekly			
Coach of the Year	Bill Parcells		
Football Digest			
Player of the Year	Lawrence Taylor		
Coach of the Year	Bill Parcells		

AFC-NFC Players-of-the-Week

	AFC Offense	AFC Defense	NFC Offense	NFC Defense
Week 1	Ken O'Brien, NYJ	Billy Ray Smith, SD	James Jones, Det.	Dave Butz, Wash.
Week 2	Boomer Esiason, Cin.	Hanford Dixon, Clev.	Walter Payton, Chi.	Terry Kinard, NYG
Week 3	Ken O'Brien, NYJ Wesley Walker, NYJ	Art Still, KC	David Archer, Atl.	Mel Owens, Rams
Week 4	Marc Wilson, Raiders	Karl Mecklenburg, Den.	Tommy Kramer, Minn.	Ronnie Lott, SF
Week 5	Steve Largent, Sea. Charlie Joiner, SD	Ronnie Lippett, NE	Eric Dickerson, Rams	Garry Cobb, Phil.
Week 6	Johnny Hector, NYJ	Leonard Coleman, Ind.	Gerald Riggs, Atl.	Lawrence Taylor, NYG
Week 7	James Brooks, Cin.	Lloyd Burruss, KC	Rueben Mayes, NO	Gerald Robinson, Minn.
Week 8	John Elway, Den.	John Offerdahl, Mia.	Joe Morris, NYG	Ronnie Lott, SF
Week 9	Ken O'Brien, NYJ	Mike Harden, Den.	Jay Schroeder, Wash.	Rickey Jackson, NO
Week 10	Bernie Kosar, Clev.	Jeff Dale, SD	Joe Montana, SF	Bruce Clark, NO
Week 11	Tony Eason, NE	Louis Breeden, Cin.	Jerry Rice, SF	Ed Jones, Dall.
Week 12	Bernie Kosar, Clev.	Jacob Green, Sea.	Gary Clark, Wash.	Nolan Cromwell, Rams
Week 13	John Elway, Den.	Charles Romes, Buff.	Walter Stanley, GB	Andre Waters, Phil.
Week 14	James Brooks, Cin.	Art Still, KC	Brad Benson, NYG	Leonard Smith, St.L.
Week 15	Dan Marino, Mia.	Deron Cherry, KC	Roger Craig, SF	Reggie White, Phil.
Week 16	Boomer Esiason, Cin.	Harvey Armstrong, Ind.	Wade Wilson, Minn.	Otis Wilson, Chi.

AFC-NFC Players-of-the-Month

	AFC Offense	AFC Defense	NFC Offense	NFC Defense
September	Ken O'Brien, NYJ	Deron Cherry, KC	David Archer, Atl.	Doug Martin, Minn.
October	Curt Warner, Sea.	Rulon Jones, Den.	Eric Dickerson, Rams	Lawrence Taylor, NYG
November	Dan Marino, Mia.	Garin Veris, NE	Jerry Rice, SF	Dexter Manley, Wash.
December	Dave Krieg, Sea.	Art Still, KC	Phil Simms, NYG	Wilber Marshall, Chi.

1986 Paid Attendance Breakdown

	Games	Attendance	Average
AFC Preseason	9	401,921	44,658
NFC Preseason	10	488,601	48,860
AFC-NFC Preseason, Interconference	39	2,091,388	53,625
NFL Preseason Total	**58**	**2,981,910**	**51,412**
AFC Regular Season	86	5,381,839	62,580
NFC Regular Season	86	5,036,157	58,560
AFC-NFC Regular Season, Interconference	52	3,170,555	60,972
NFL Regular Season Total	**224**	**13,588,551**	**60,663**
AFC First-Round Playoff	1		
(Kansas City-New York Jets)		75,210	
AFC Divisional Playoffs	2		
(New York Jets-Cleveland)		79,720	
(New England-Denver)		75,262	
AFC Championship Game	1		
(Denver-Cleveland)		79,973	
NFC First-Round Playoff	1		
(Los Angeles Rams-Washington)		54,567	
NFC Divisional Playoffs	2		
(Washington-Chicago)		65,524	
(San Francisco-New York Giants)		75,691	
NFC Championship Game	1		
(Washington-New York Giants)		76,891	
Super Bowl XXI at Pasadena, California	1		
(Denver-New York Giants)		101,063	
AFC-NFC Pro Bowl at Honolulu, Hawaii	1	50,101	
NFL Postseason Total	**10**	**734,002**	**73,400**
NFL All Games	**292**	**17,304,463**	**59,262**

Ten Best Rushing Performances, 1986

	Attempts	Yards	TD
1. Eric Dickerson L.A. Rams vs. Tampa Bay, October 5	30	207	2
2. Rueben Mayes New Orleans vs. Miami, December 7	28	203	2
3. Eric Dickerson L.A. Rams vs. St. Louis, September 7	38	193	2
4. Curt Warner Seattle vs. Denver, December 20	25	192	3
5. Joe Morris New York Giants vs. Washington, October 27	31	181	2
Joe Morris New York Giants vs. Dallas, November 2	29	181	2
7. Joe Morris New York Giants vs. St. Louis, December 14	28	179	3
8. Walter Payton Chicago vs. Philadelphia, September 14	34	177	1
9. James Jones Detroit vs. Minnesota, September 7	36	174	1
10. Rueben Mayes New Orleans vs. Tampa Bay, October 19	24	172	2
Gerald Riggs Atlanta vs. Miami, November 30	33	172	1

100-Yard Rushing Performances, 1986

First Week

Eric Dickerson, L.A. Rams — 193 yards vs. St. Louis
James Jones, Detroit — 174 yards vs. Minnesota
Curt Warner, Seattle — 114 yards vs. Pittsburgh
Walter Payton, Chicago — 113 yards vs. Cleveland
Cliff Austin, Atlanta — 104 yards vs. New Orleans
George Rogers, Washington — 104 yards vs. Philadelphia
Marcus Allen, L.A. Raiders — 102 yards vs. Denver

Second Week

Walter Payton, Chicago — 177 yards vs. Philadelphia
Tony Dorsett, Dallas — 117 yards vs. Detroit
Gerald Riggs, Atlanta — 108 yards vs. St. Louis
Marcus Allen, L.A. Raiders — 104 yards vs. Washington

Third Week

Nathan Wonsley, Tampa Bay — 138 yards vs. Detroit
Eric Dickerson, L.A. Rams — 121 yards vs. Indianapolis
James Brooks, Cincinnati — 118 yards vs. Cleveland
Joe Morris, N.Y. Giants — 110 yards vs. L.A. Raiders
Gerald Riggs, Atlanta — 109 yards vs. Dallas
Sammy Winder, Denver — 104 yards vs. Philadelphia

Fourth Week

Gerald Riggs, Atlanta — 129 yards vs. Tampa Bay
George Rogers, Washington — 115 yards vs. Seattle
Curt Warner, Seattle — 106 yards vs. Washington

Fifth Week

Eric Dickerson, L.A. Rams — 207 yards vs. Tampa Bay
Curt Warner, Seattle — 142 yards vs. San Diego
Johnny Hector, N.Y. Jets — 117 yards vs. Buffalo
George Rogers, Washington — 110 yards vs. New Orleans
Walter Payton, Chicago — 108 yards vs. Minnesota
Nathan Wonsley, Tampa Bay — 108 yards vs. L.A. Rams

Sixth Week

Johnny Hector, N.Y. Jets — 143 yards vs. New England
Gerald Riggs, Atlanta — 141 yards vs. L.A. Rams
Garry James, Detroit — 140 yards vs. Green Bay
Stump Mitchell, St. Louis — 126 yards vs. Tampa Bay
Rueben Mayes, New Orleans — 108 yards vs. Indianapolis

Seventh Week

Rueben Mayes, New Orleans — 172 yards vs. Tampa Bay
James Brooks, Cincinnati — 133 yards vs. Houston
Eric Dickerson, L.A. Rams — 130 yards vs. Detroit
George Rogers, Washington — 118 yards vs. St. Louis
Joe Morris, N.Y. Giants — 116 yards vs. Seattle

Eighth Week

Joe Morris, N.Y. Giants — 181 yards vs. Washington
Eric Dickerson, L.A. Rams — 170 yards vs. Atlanta
Curt Warner, Seattle — 139 yards vs. Denver
Earnest Jackson, Pittsburgh — 132 yards vs. Cincinnati
Herschel Walker, Dallas — 120 yards vs. St. Louis
Darrin Nelson, Minnesota — 118 yards vs. Cleveland
James Wilder, Tampa Bay — 110 yards vs. Kansas City
Walter Abercrombie, Pittsburgh — 109 yards vs. Cincinnati
Curtis Dickey, Cleveland — 106 yards vs. Minnesota

Ninth Week

Joe Morris, N.Y. Giants — 181 yards vs. Dallas
Rueben Mayes, New Orleans — 128 yards vs. San Francisco
James Brooks, Cincinnati — 120 yards vs. Detroit
Eric Dickerson, L.A. Rams — 111 yards vs. Chicago
Gary Anderson, San Diego — 100 yards vs. Kansas City

Tenth Week

Walter Payton, Chicago — 139 yards vs. Tampa Bay
Joe Morris, N.Y. Giants — 111 yards vs. Philadelphia
Robb Riddick, Buffalo — 108 yards vs. Pittsburgh
Joe Cribbs, San Francisco — 105 yards vs. St. Louis
Tony Dorsett, Dallas — 101 yards vs. L.A. Raiders

Eleventh Week

Rueben Mayes, New Orleans — 131 yards vs. St. Louis
Randall Cunningham, Phil. — 110 yards vs. Detroit
Freeman McNeil, N.Y. Jets — 104 yards vs. Indianapolis
George Rogers, Washington — 104 yards vs. San Francisco
Eric Dickerson, L.A. Rams — 102 yards vs. New England

Twelfth Week

Lorenzo Hampton, Miami — 148 yards vs. N.Y. Jets
James Wilder, Tampa Bay — 130 yards vs. Detroit
Eric Dickerson, L.A. Rams — 116 yards vs. New Orleans
Kevin Mack, Cleveland — 106 yards vs. Pittsburgh
Joe Morris, N.Y. Giants — 106 yards vs. Denver
Roger Craig, San Francisco — 101 yards vs. Atlanta

Thirteenth Week

Gerald Riggs, Atlanta — 172 yards vs. Miami
Rueben Mayes, New Orleans — 157 yards vs. New England
Curt Warner, Seattle — 122 yards vs. Dallas
Kevin Mack, Cleveland — 121 yards vs. Houston
Robb Riddick, Buffalo — 118 yards vs. Kansas City
Eric Dickerson, L.A. Rams — 107 yards vs. N.Y. Jets

Fourteenth Week

Rueben Mayes, New Orleans — 203 yards vs. Miami
James Brooks, Cincinnati — 163 yards vs. New England
Earnest Jackson, Pittsburgh — 147 yards vs. Detroit
Gerald Riggs, Atlanta — 136 yards vs. Indianapolis
Keith Byars, Philadelphia — 127 yards vs. St. Louis
Stanley Wilson, Cincinnati — 120 yards vs. New England
Curt Warner, Seattle — 116 yards vs. L.A. Raiders
Eric Dickerson, L.A. Rams — 106 yards vs. Dallas

Fifteenth Week

Joe Morris, N.Y. Giants — 179 yards vs. St. Louis
Freeman McNeil, N.Y. Jets — 137 yards vs. Pittsburgh
Eric Dickerson, L.A. Rams — 124 yards vs. Miami
Herschel Walker, Dallas — 122 yards vs. Philadelphia
Joe Cribbs, San Francisco — 107 yards vs. New England
Earnest Jackson, Pittsburgh — 101 yards vs. N.Y. Jets

Sixteenth Week

Curt Warner, Seattle — 192 yards vs. Denver
Albert Bentley, Indianapolis — 162 yards vs. L.A. Raiders
Joe Morris, N.Y. Giants — 115 yards vs. Green Bay
Lorenzo Hampton, Miami — 109 yards vs. New England
Freeman McNeil, N.Y. Jets — 106 yards vs. Cincinnati

Times 100 or More

Dickerson 11; Morris 8; Warner 7; Mayes, Riggs 6; Rogers 5; Brooks, Payton 4; Jackson, McNeil 3; Allen, Cribbs, Dorsett, Hampton, Hector, Mack, Riddick, Walker, Wilder, Wonsley 2.

Ten Best Passing Yardage Performances, 1986

	Att.	Comp.	Yards	TD
1. Tommy Kramer Minnesota vs. Washington, November 2	35	20	490	4
2. Ken O'Brien New York Jets vs. Miami, September 21	43	29	479	4
3. Dan Marino Miami vs. New York Jets, September 21	50	30	448	6
4. Joe Montana San Francisco vs. Washington, Nov. 17	60	33	441	0
5. Ken O'Brien New York Jets vs. Seattle, November 2	32	26	431	4
6. Boomer Esiason Cincinnati vs. N.Y. Jets, December 21	30	23	425	5
7. Jay Schroeder Washington vs. N.Y. Giants, October 27	40	22	420	1
8. Tony Eason New England vs. Seattle, September 21	45	26	414	3
Bernie Kosar Cleveland vs. Pittsburgh, November 23	46	28	414	2
10. Dan Marino Miami vs. Buffalo, November 16	54	39	404	4

300-Yard Passing Performances, 1986

First Week
Joe Montana, San Francisco — 356 yards vs. Tampa Bay
Marc Wilson, L.A. Raiders — 346 yards vs. Denver
Ken O'Brien, N.Y. Jets — 318 yards vs. Buffalo
Phil Simms, N.Y. Giants — 300 yards vs. Dallas

Second Week
Phil Simms, N.Y. Giants — 300 yards vs. San Diego

Third Week
Ken O'Brien, N.Y. Jets — 479 yards vs. Miami
Dan Marino, Miami — 448 yards vs. N.Y. Jets
Tony Eason, New England — 414 yards vs. Seattle
Jay Schroeder, Washington — 341 yards vs. San Diego
Jeff Kemp, San Francisco — 332 yards vs. New Orleans
Eric Hipple, Detroit — 318 yards vs. Tampa Bay

Fourth Week
Marc Wilson, L.A. Raiders — 314 yards vs. San Diego
Dan Marino, Miami — 301 yards vs. San Francisco

Fifth Week
Warren Moon, Houston — 398 yards vs. Detroit

Sixth Week
Steve Grogan, New England — 401 yards vs. N.Y. Jets
Jeff Kemp, San Francisco — 359 yards vs. Minnesota
Dan Fouts, San Diego — 352 yards vs. Denver
Dan Marino, Miami — 337 yards vs. Buffalo
Tommy Kramer, Minnesota — 326 yards vs. San Francisco
Steve Pelluer, Dallas — 323 yards vs. Washington
Jack Trudeau, Indianapolis — 315 yards vs. New Orleans

Seventh Week
Eric Hipple, Detroit — 316 yards vs. L.A. Rams

Eighth Week
Jay Schroeder, Washington — 420 yards vs. N.Y. Giants
Randy Wright, Green Bay — 328 yards vs. San Francisco
John Elway, Denver — 321 yards vs. Seattle
Warren Moon, Houston — 304 yards vs. L.A. Raiders

Ninth Week
Tommy Kramer, Minnesota — 490 yards vs. Washington
Ken O'Brien, N.Y. Jets — 431 yards vs. Seattle
Jay Schroeder, Washington — 378 yards vs. Minnesota
Marc Wilson, L.A. Raiders — 367 yards vs. Denver
Jim Kelly, Buffalo — 342 yards vs. Tampa Bay
Steve Pelluer, Dallas — 339 yards vs. N.Y. Giants
Mike Moroski, San Francisco — 332 yards vs. New Orleans

Tenth Week
Bernie Kosar, Cleveland — 401 yards vs. Miami
Dave Archer, Atlanta — 350 yards vs. N.Y. Jets
Ken O'Brien, N.Y. Jets — 322 yards vs. Atlanta
Warren Moon, Houston — 310 yards vs. Cincinnati

Eleventh Week
Joe Montana, San Francisco — 441 yards vs. Washington
Dan Marino, Miami — 404 yards vs. Buffalo
Tony Eason, New England — 375 yards vs. L.A. Rams
Jack Trudeau, Indianapolis — 359 yards vs. N.Y. Jets
Boomer Esiason, Cincinnati — 334 yards vs. Seattle
Phil Simms, N.Y. Giants — 310 yards vs. Minnesota

Twelfth Week
Bernie Kosar, Cleveland — 414 yards vs. Pittsburgh
Jim Plunkett, L.A. Raiders — 348 yards vs. San Diego
John Elway, Denver — 336 yards vs. N.Y. Giants
Jay Schroeder, Washington — 325 yards vs. Dallas

Thirteenth Week
Phil Simms, N.Y. Giants — 388 yards vs. San Francisco
Jim Plunkett, L.A. Raiders — 366 yards vs. Philadelphia
Wade Wilson, Minnesota — 339 yards vs. Tampa Bay
Boomer Esiason, Cincinnati — 306 yards vs. Denver
Dan Marino, Miami — 303 yards vs. Atlanta

Fourteenth Week
Neil Lomax, St. Louis — 390 yards vs. Philadelphia
Jim Kelly, Buffalo — 315 yards vs. Cleveland
Jay Schroeder, Washington — 309 yards vs. N.Y. Giants

Fifteenth Week
Dan Marino, Miami — 403 yards vs. L.A. Rams
Gary Hogeboom, Indianapolis — 318 yards vs. Buffalo
Dave Krieg, Seattle — 305 yards vs. San Diego

Sixteenth Week
Boomer Esiason, Cincinnati — 425 yards vs. N.Y. Jets
Wade Wilson, Minnesota — 361 yards vs. New Orleans
Mark Malone, Pittsburgh — 351 yards vs. Kansas City

Times 300 or More
Marino 6; Schroeder 5; O'Brien, Simms 4; Esiason, Moon, M. Wilson 3; Eason, Elway, Hipple, Kelly, Kemp, Kosar, Kramer, Montana, Pelluer, Plunkett, Trudeau, W. Wilson 2.

Ten Best Receiving Yardage Performances, 1986

		Yards	No.	TD
1.	Gary Clark Washington vs. New York Giants, October 27	241	11	1
2.	Jerry Rice San Francisco vs. Washington, November 17	204	12	0
3.	Al Toon New York Jets vs. Seattle, November 2	195	9	2
4.	Wesley Walker New York Jets vs. Miami, September 21	194	6	4
5.	Jessie Hester L.A. Raiders vs. Philadelphia, November 30	193	4	2
6.	Drew Hill Houston vs. Cincinnati, November 9	185	10	0
7.	Rod Barksdale L.A. Raiders vs. Indianapolis, December 21	179	6	0
	Steve Jordan Minnesota vs. Washington, November 2	179	6	1
9.	Bill Brooks Indianapolis vs. New York Jets, November 16	177	9	1
10.	Brian Brennan Cleveland vs. San Diego, December 21	176	7	1

100-Yard Receiving Performances, 1986

(Number in parentheses is receptions.)

First Week

Mark Clayton, Miami — 143 yards (5) vs. San Diego
Charlie Brown, Atlanta — 119 yards (7) vs. New Orleans
Al Toon, N.Y. Jets — 119 yards (6) vs. Buffalo
Stanley Morgan, New England — 116 yards (7) vs. Indianapolis
Tony Hill, Dallas — 107 yards (5) vs. N.Y. Giants
Bobby Johnson, N.Y. Giants — 105 yards (8) vs. Dallas
Marcus Allen, L.A. Raiders — 102 yards (6) vs. Denver
Stephen Starring, New England — 102 yards (5) vs. Indianapolis
Dwight Clark, San Francisco — 100 yards (7) vs. Tampa Bay
Gary Clark, Washington — 100 yards (7) vs. Philadelphia

Second Week

Eric Martin, New Orleans — 164 yards (3) vs. Green Bay
Jerry Rice, San Francisco — 157 yards (6) vs. L.A. Rams
Reggie Langhorne, Cleveland — 115 yards (3) vs. Houston
Stanley Morgan, New England — 104 yards (8) vs. N.Y. Jets
James Lofton, Green Bay — 100 yards (8) vs. New Orleans

Third Week

Wesley Walker, N.Y. Jets — 194 yards (6) vs. Miami
Mark Clayton, Miami — 174 yards (8) vs. N.Y. Jets
Art Monk, Washington — 174 yards (7) vs. San Diego
Stanley Morgan, New England — 161 yards (7) vs. Seattle
Mark Duper, Miami — 154 yards (7) vs. N.Y. Jets
Gary Clark, Washington — 144 yards (6) vs. San Diego
Mike Jones, Minnesota — 140 yards (6) vs. Pittsburgh
Ray Butler, Seattle — 128 yards (3) vs. New England
Kenny Jackson, Philadelphia — 127 yards (5) vs. Denver
Jerry Rice, San Francisco — 120 yards (7) vs. New Orleans
Al Toon, N.Y. Jets — 111 yards (7) vs. Miami
Irving Fryar, New England — 110 yards (6) vs. Seattle
Mark Bavaro, N.Y. Giants — 106 yards (6) vs. L.A. Raiders
Jeff Chadwick, Detroit — 106 yards (5) vs. Tampa Bay
Tony Hill, Dallas — 104 yards (4) vs. Atlanta
Dwight Clark, San Francisco — 100 yards (7) vs. New Orleans

Fourth Week

Willie Gault, Chicago — 174 yards (7) vs. Cincinnati
Dokie Williams, L.A. Raiders — 143 yards (8) vs. San Diego
Cris Collinsworth, Cincinnati — 115 yards (6) vs. Chicago
Steve Jordan, Minnesota — 112 yards (6) vs. Green Bay
Mark Bavaro, N.Y. Giants — 110 yards (7) vs. New Orleans
Charlie Brown, Atlanta — 110 yards (7) vs. Tampa Bay
Mike Jones, Minnesota — 106 yards (6) vs. Green Bay
Todd Christensen, L.A. Raiders — 105 yards (8) vs. San Diego
Art Monk, Washington — 103 yards (5) vs. Seattle
Mark Duper, Miami — 102 yards (7) vs. San Francisco
Tony Nathan, Miami — 101 yards (10) vs. San Francisco

Fifth Week

Jerry Rice, San Francisco — 172 yards (6) vs. Indianapolis
Keith Ortego, Chicago — 157 yards (6) vs. Minnesota
Ernest Givins, Houston — 155 yards (5) vs. Detroit
Floyd Dixon, Atlanta — 146 yards (8) vs. Philadelphia
Stanley Morgan, New England — 125 yards (6) vs. Miami
Byron Franklin, Seattle — 118 yards (5) vs. San Diego
James Lofton, Green Bay — 109 yards (7) vs. Cincinnati
Reggie Langhorne, Cleveland — 108 yards (4) vs. Pittsburgh
Mark Duper, Miami — 102 yards (4) vs. New England
Johnny Hector, N.Y. Jets — 100 yards (9) vs. Buffalo

Sixth Week

Stanley Morgan, New England — 162 yards (7) vs. N.Y. Jets
Herschel Walker, Dallas — 155 yards (6) vs. Washington
Jerry Rice, San Francisco — 144 yards (7) vs. Minnesota
Irving Fryar, New England — 126 yards (3) vs. N.Y. Jets

Seventh Week

Mark Clayton, Miami — 109 yards (4) vs. L.A. Raiders
Mark Duper, Miami — 101 yards (5) vs. L.A. Raiders

Eighth Week

Gary Clark, Washington — 241 yards (11) vs. N.Y. Giants
Drew Hill, Houston — 138 yards (7) vs. L.A. Raiders
Mike Sherrard, Dallas — 111 yards (5) vs. St. Louis
Al Toon, N.Y. Jets — 101 yards (6) vs. New Orleans

Ninth Week

Al Toon, N.Y. Jets — 195 yards (9) vs. Seattle
Steve Jordan, Minnesota — 179 yards (6) vs. Washington
Wesley Walker, N.Y. Jets — 161 yards (6) vs. Seattle
Leo Lewis, Minnesota — 159 yards (3) vs. Washington
Todd Christensen, L.A. Raiders — 158 yards (11) vs. Denver
Herschel Walker, Dallas — 148 yards (9) vs. N.Y. Giants
Gary Clark, Washington — 123 yards (6) vs. Minnesota
Pete Metzelaars, Buffalo — 113 yards (7) vs. Tampa Bay
Mark Duper, Miami — 110 yards (2) vs. Houston
Steve Largent, Seattle — 108 yards (7) vs. N.Y. Jets
Art Monk, Washington — 102 yards (6) vs. Minnesota
Jeff Chadwick, Detroit — 100 yards (6) vs. Cincinnati

Tenth Week

Drew Hill, Houston — 185 yards (10) vs. Cincinnati
Jerry Rice, San Francisco — 156 yards (4) vs. St. Louis
J.T. Smith, St. Louis — 154 yards (10) vs. San Francisco
Eddie Brown, Cincinnati — 132 yards (9) vs. Houston
Willie Gault, Chicago — 116 yards (4) vs. Tampa Bay
Charlie Brown, Atlanta — 112 yards (6) vs. N.Y. Jets
Anthony Carter, Minnesota — 111 yards (5) vs. Detroit
Arthur Cox, Atlanta — 108 yards (4) vs. N.Y. Jets
Dokie Williams, L.A. Raiders — 107 yards (5) vs. Dallas

Eleventh Week

Jerry Rice, San Francisco — 204 yards (12) vs. Washington
Bill Brooks, Indianapolis — 177 yards (9) vs. N.Y. Jets
Ernest Givins, Houston — 156 yards (8) vs. Pittsburgh
Gerald Carter, Tampa Bay — 143 yards (7) vs. Green Bay
Jeff Chadwick, Detroit — 139 yards (5) vs. Philadelphia
Henry Ellard, L.A. Rams — 129 yards (8) vs. New England
Stanley Morgan, New England — 118 yards (7) vs. L.A. Rams
Mike Sherrard, Dallas — 115 yards (4) vs. San Diego
Dokie Williams, L.A. Raiders — 113 yards (3) vs. Cleveland
Wesley Walker, N.Y. Jets — 110 yards (5) vs. Indianapolis
Mark Duper, Miami — 109 yards (7) vs. Buffalo
J.T. Smith, St. Louis — 106 yards (8) vs. New Orleans
Steve Largent, Seattle — 102 yards (7) vs. Cincinnati

Twelfth Week

Todd Christensen, L.A. Raiders — 173 yards (11) vs. San Diego
Gary Clark, Washington — 152 yards (8) vs. Dallas
Webster Slaughter, Cleveland — 134 yards (6) vs. Pittsburgh
Gary Anderson, San Diego — 113 yards (7) vs. L.A. Raiders
Bill Brooks, Indianapolis — 105 yards (7) vs. Houston
Ed West, Green Bay — 103 yards (5) vs. Chicago
Ernest Givins, Houston — 102 yards (7) vs. Indianapolis

Thirteenth Week

Jessie Hester, L.A. Raiders — 193 yards (4) vs. Philadelphia
Mike Quick, Philadelphia — 145 yards (8) vs. L.A. Raiders
Cris Collinsworth, Cincinnati — 138 yards (8) vs. Denver
Walter Stanley, Green Bay — 124 yards (4) vs. Detroit
Jeff Chadwick, Detroit — 121 yards (6) vs. Green Bay
Stephone Paige, Kansas City — 119 yards (9) vs. Buffalo
Stacy Robinson, N.Y. Giants — 116 yards (5) vs. San Francisco
Mark Duper, Miami — 115 yards (4) vs. Atlanta
Wes Chandler, San Diego — 110 yards (5) vs. Indianapolis

Fourteenth Week

Louis Lipps, Pittsburgh	150 yards (8) vs. Detroit
Calvin Magee, Tampa Bay	143 yards (8) vs. Chicago
J.T. Smith, St. Louis	131 yards (10) vs. Philadelphia
Kelvin Bryant, Washington	130 yards (13) vs. N.Y. Giants
Mike Quick, Philadelphia	127 yards (5) vs. St. Louis
Chris Burkett, Buffalo	122 yards (3) vs. Cleveland
Mike Jones, New Orleans	119 yards (6) vs. Miami
Mark Bavaro, N.Y. Giants	111 yards (5) vs. Washington
Stanley Morgan, New England	107 yards (5) vs. Cincinnati
James Brooks, Cincinnati	101 yards (6) vs. New England
Ron Brown, L.A. Rams	100 yards (3) vs. Dallas
Roy Green, St. Louis	100 yards (6) vs. Philadelphia

Fifteenth Week

Herschel Walker, Dallas	170 yards (9) vs. Philadelphia
Chris Burkett, Buffalo	145 yards (5) vs. Indianapolis
Mark Duper, Miami	145 yards (5) vs. L.A. Rams
Art Monk, Washington	129 yards (6) vs. Denver
Henry Ellard, L.A. Rams	121 yards (8) vs. Miami
Stanley Morgan, New England	121 yards (8) vs. San Francisco
Ernest Givins, Houston	108 yards (6) vs. Minnesota
Kellen Winslow, San Diego	105 yards (8) vs. Seattle

Sixteenth Week

Rod Barksdale, L.A. Raiders	179 yards (6) vs. Indianapolis
Brian Brennan, Cleveland	176 yards (7) vs. San Diego
Stanley Morgan, New England	148 yards (8) vs. Miami
Rodney Holman, Cincinnati	129 yards (6) vs. N.Y. Jets
Drew Hill, Houston	114 yards (5) vs. Buffalo
Wes Chandler, San Diego	113 yards (6) vs. Cleveland
Todd Christensen, L.A. Raiders	104 yards (9) vs. Indianapolis
Steve Largent, Seattle	101 yards (6) vs. Denver
Mike Jones, Minnesota	100 yards (5) vs. New Orleans

Times 100 or More

Morgan 9; Duper 8; Rice 6; G. Clark 5; Chadwick, Christensen, Givins, Monk, Toon 4; Bavaro, Brown, Clayton, D. Hill, Jones, Largent, J.T. Smith, H. Walker, W. Walker, Williams 3; Brooks, Burkett, Chandler, D. Clark, Collinsworth, Ellard, Fryar, Gault, T. Hill, Jordan, Langhorne, Lofton, Quick, Sherrard 2.

American Football Conference Offense

	Buff.	Cin.	Clev.	Den.	Hou.	Ind.	K.C.	Raid.	Mia.	N.E.	N.Y.J.	Pitt.	S.D.	Sea.
First Downs	256	344	271	339	270	282	258	304	361	294	344	315	380	299
Rushing	101	134	102	94	101	77	83	97	84	77	104	125	98	123
Passing	152	183	175	184	179	173	152	186	250	202	191	140	212	158
Penalty	38	31	25	41	19	28	29	19	17	35	24	27	24	10
Rushes	419	521	470	455	490	407	432	475	349	469	490	564	471	513
Net Yds. Gained	1654	2533	1650	1678	1700	1491	1468	1790	1545	1373	1729	2223	1576	2300
Avg. Gain	3.9	4.9	3.5	3.7	3.5	3.7	3.4	3.8	4.4	2.9	3.5	3.9	3.3	4.5
Avg. Yds. per Game	103.4	158.3	103.1	104.9	106.3	93.2	91.8	111.9	96.6	85.8	108.1	138.9	98.5	143.8
Passes Attempted	499	497	538	549	551	586	521	530	645	557	537	491	604	453
Completed	294	287	315	306	288	300	257	281	392	340	334	238	339	268
% Completed	58.9	57.7	58.6	55.7	52.3	51.2	49.3	53.0	60.8	61.0	62.2	48.5	56.1	59.2
Total Yds. Gained	3697	4160	4018	3811	3843	3615	3122	3973	4898	4321	4032	2747	4045	3424
Times Sacked	45	28	39	38	48	53	50	64	17	47	45	20	32	39
Yds. Lost	334	203	274	273	394	406	372	464	119	367	386	159	265	315
Net Yds. Gained	3363	3957	3744	3538	3449	3209	2750	3509	4779	3954	3646	2588	3780	3109
Avg. Yds. per Game	210.2	247.3	234.0	221.1	215.6	200.6	171.9	219.3	298.7	247.1	227.9	161.8	236.3	194.3
Net Yds. per Pass Play	6.18	7.54	6.49	6.03	5.76	5.02	4.82	5.91	7.22	6.55	6.26	5.06	5.94	6.32
Yds. Gained per Comp.	12.57	14.49	12.76	12.45	13.34	12.05	12.15	14.14	12.49	12.71	12.07	11.54	11.93	12.78
Combined Net Yds. Gained	5017	6490	5394	5216	5149	4700	4218	5299	6324	5327	5375	4811	5356	5409
% Total Yds. Rushing	33.0	39.0	30.6	32.2	33.0	31.7	34.8	33.8	24.4	25.8	32.2	46.2	29.4	42.5
% Total Yds. Passing	67.0	61.0	69.4	67.8	67.0	68.3	65.2	66.2	75.6	74.2	67.8	53.8	70.6	57.5
Avg. Yds. per Game	313.6	405.6	337.1	326.0	321.8	293.8	263.6	331.2	395.3	332.9	335.9	300.7	334.8	338.1
Ball Control Plays	963	1046	1047	1042	1089	1046	1003	1069	1011	1073	1072	1075	1107	1005
Avg. Yds. per Play	5.2	6.2	5.2	5.0	4.7	4.5	4.2	5.0	6.3	5.0	5.0	4.5	4.8	5.4
Avg. Time of Poss.	28:02	28:48	29:42	30:30	30:33	29:12	28:29	30:40	29:24	30:29	29:51	29:45	30:32	29:47
Third Down Efficiency	32.4	39.7	36.8	41.7	37.8	34.7	33.6	38.9	50.8	33.9	38.8	37.1	42.4	43.4
Had Intercepted	19	20	11	16	31	24	18	25	23	13	21	20	33	14
Yds. Opp. Returned	284	189	135	363	325	310	181	282	221	151	230	244	421	216
Ret. by Opp. for TD	0	0	1	2	1	2	1	1	1	0	1	2	2	1

	Buff.	Cin.	Clev.	Den.	Hou.	Ind.	K.C.	Raid.	Mia.	N.E.	N.Y.J.	Pitt.	S.D.	Sea.
Punts	75	59	83	86	89	81	99	90	56	92	85	89	79	79
Yds. Punted	3031	1996	3423	3376	3659	3622	4033	3620	2476	3746	3353	3447	3193	3048
Avg. Yds. per Punt	40.4	33.8	41.2	39.3	41.1	44.7	40.7	40.2	44.2	40.7	39.4	38.7	40.4	38.6
Punt Returns	32	29	41	48	43	35	35	56	40	42	39	36	37	39
Yds. Returned	247	235	350	552	341	250	265	484	297	396	341	310	334	457
Avg. Yds. per Return	7.7	8.1	8.5	11.5	7.9	7.1	7.6	8.6	7.4	9.4	8.7	8.6	9.0	11.7
Returned for TD	1	0	1	2	0	0	0	1	1	1	0	0	0	1
Kickoff Returns	55	63	62	53	59	74	56	64	65	58	63	66	65	64
Yds. Returned	1074	1389	1213	1094	1139	1443	1117	1252	1185	1147	1189	1304	1137	1322
Avg. Yds. per Return	19.5	22.0	19.6	20.6	19.3	19.5	19.9	19.6	18.2	19.8	18.9	19.8	17.5	20.7
Returned for TD	0	0	1	0	0	0	1	0	0	0	2	0	0	0
Fumbles	40	31	31	24	28	41	27	36	37	27	37	27	29	29
Lost	20	16	13	13	12	20	17	24	14	11	16	16	16	13
Out of Bounds	3	4	2	2	3	3	4	1	3	4	9	2	2	4
Own Rec. for TD	1	0	2	0	1	0	1	0	0	0	0	0	0	0
Opp. Rec. by	8	11	19	17	15	19	18	12	13	19	18	13	22	14
Opp. Rec. for TD	1	1	1	2	2	0	1	1	0	2	0	0	0	0
Penalties	121	111	101	104	121	99	97	114	72	87	131	104	119	98
Yds. Penalized	878	847	807	910	1018	880	829	951	609	672	981	853	977	813
Total Points Scored	287	409	391	378	274	229	358	323	430	412	364	307	335	366
Total TDs	34	51	45	45	30	27	43	37	56	45	45	35	41	43
TDs Rushing	9	24	20	17	13	10	10	6	9	10	16	18	19	15
TDs Passing	22	25	18	22	14	16	23	27	46	29	27	16	21	24
TDs on Ret. and Rec.	3	2	7	6	3	1	10	4	1	6	2	1	1	4
Extra Points	32	50	43	44	28	26	43	36	52	44	44	32	39	42
Safeties	0	1	0	2	0	1	0	1	0	1	1	1	1	0
Field Goals Made	17	17	26	20	22	13	19	21	14	32	16	21	16	22
Field Goals Attempted	27	32	33	28	27	25	26	28	22	41	19	32	25	35
% Successful	63.0	53.1	78.8	71.4	81.5	52.0	73.1	75.0	63.6	78.0	84.2	65.6	64.0	62.9

American Football Conference Defense

	Buff.	Cin.	Clev.	Den.	Hou.	Ind.	K.C.	Raid.	Mia.	N.E.	N.Y.J.	Pitt.	S.D.	Sea.
First Downs	334	336	302	291	285	334	310	283	337	286	349	303	308	310
Rushing	100	134	113	93	102	123	111	85	144	118	92	97	104	93
Passing	204	171	171	177	137	185	173	168	177	153	216	176	182	192
Penalty	30	31	18	21	46	26	26	30	16	15	41	30	22	25
Rushes	465	514	494	432	532	517	485	439	540	510	450	471	475	471
Net Yds. Gained	1721	2122	1981	1651	2035	1962	1739	1728	2493	2203	1661	1872	1678	1759
Avg. Gain	3.7	4.1	4.0	3.8	3.8	3.8	3.6	3.9	4.6	4.3	3.7	4.0	3.5	3.7
Avg. Yds. per Game	107.6	132.6	123.8	103.2	127.2	122.6	108.7	108.0	155.8	137.7	103.8	117.0	104.9	109.9
Passes Attempted	570	495	518	545	490	510	569	501	485	473	603	536	509	535
Completed	343	278	291	301	228	306	303	271	290	255	348	311	288	301
% Completed	60.2	56.2	56.2	55.2	46.5	60.0	53.3	54.1	59.8	53.9	57.7	58.0	56.6	56.3
Total Yds. Gained	4069	3520	3546	3755	3200	3933	3555	3539	3825	3324	4567	3669	4128	3888
Times Sacked	36	42	35	49	32	24	44	63	33	48	28	43	62	47
Yds. Lost	267	368	258	459	201	194	360	463	268	346	178	289	440	306
Net Yds. Gained	3802	3152	3288	3296	2999	3739	3195	3076	3557	2978	4389	3380	3688	3582
Avg. Yds. per Game	237.6	197.0	205.5	206.0	187.4	233.7	199.7	192.3	222.3	186.1	274.3	211.3	230.5	223.9
Net Yds. per Pass Play	6.27	5.87	5.95	5.55	5.75	7.00	5.21	5.45	6.87	5.72	6.96	5.84	6.46	6.15
Yds. Gained per Comp.	11.86	12.66	12.19	12.48	14.04	12.85	11.73	13.06	13.19	13.04	13.12	11.80	14.33	12.92
Combined Net Yds. Gained	5523	5274	5269	4947	5034	5701	4934	4804	6050	5181	6050	5252	5366	5341
% Total Yds. Rushing	31.2	40.2	37.6	33.4	40.4	34.4	35.2	36.0	41.2	42.5	27.5	35.6	31.3	32.9
% Total Yds. Passing	68.8	59.8	62.4	66.6	59.6	65.6	64.8	64.0	58.8	57.5	72.5	64.4	68.7	67.1
Avg. Yds. per Game	345.2	329.6	329.3	309.2	314.6	356.3	308.4	300.3	378.1	323.8	378.1	328.3	335.4	333.8
Ball Control Plays	1071	1051	1047	1026	1054	1051	1098	1003	1058	1031	1081	1050	1046	1053
Avg. Yds. per Play	5.2	5.0	5.0	4.8	4.8	5.4	4.5	4.8	5.7	5.0	5.6	5.0	5.1	5.1
Avg. Time of Poss.	31:58	31:12	30:18	29:30	29:27	30:48	31:31	29:20	30:36	29:31	30:09	30:15	29:28	30:13
Third Down Efficiency	36.2	38.5	37.4	34.2	35.4	41.7	35.7	37.7	41.1	35.6	42.9	35.5	43.0	37.3
Intercepted by	10	17	18	18	16	16	31	26	13	21	20	20	15	22
Yds. Returned by	89	146	184	318	100	166	567	275	152	312	164	218	274	216
Returned for TD	0	1	0	2	0	0	4	1	0	1	0	1	1	1
Punts	83	77	80	86	94	67	83	97	64	90	75	82	81	81
Yds. Punted	3162	3068	3033	3689	3713	2725	3067	4087	2648	3585	2977	3194	3304	3270
Avg. Yds. per Punt	38.1	39.8	37.9	42.9	39.5	40.7	37.0	42.1	41.4	39.8	39.7	39.0	40.8	40.4
Punt Returns	32	19	44	40	40	52	52	42	23	60	36	34	43	38
Yds. Returned	260	182	268	362	303	533	572	357	200	565	165	364	370	298
Avg. Yds. per Return	8.1	9.6	6.1	9.1	7.6	10.3	11.0	8.5	8.7	9.4	4.6	10.7	8.6	7.8
Returned for TD	0	0	0	0	0	1	1	1	0	0	0	0	1	0
Kickoff Returns	56	80	78	65	32	43	71	63	53	81	62	56	60	59
Yds. Returned	1157	1611	1476	1299	695	827	1278	1064	997	1480	1307	1362	1088	1002
Avg. Yds. per Return	20.7	20.1	18.9	20.0	21.7	19.2	18.0	16.9	18.8	18.3	21.1	24.3	18.1	17.0
Returned for TD	0	1	1	0	0	0	0	0	0	0	0	3	0	0
Fumbles	19	30	36	32	31	41	26	33	32	38	48	31	42	26
Lost	8	11	19	17	16	19	18	12	14	19	18	13	22	14
Out of Bounds	2	3	3	5	4	4	1	4	3	5	2	2	5	4
Own Rec. for TD	0	3	1	0	0	0	0	0	1	0	0	0	0	0
Opp. Rec. by	20	16	12	13	12	20	17	24	14	11	16	16	16	13
Opp. Rec. for TD	1	1	0	0	0	2	2	1	0	0	0	0	2	1
Penalties	128	93	101	127	85	100	114	118	82	106	102	109	108	81
Yds. Penalized	1098	840	754	1034	674	728	965	868	596	866	795	904	918	652
Total Points Scored	348	394	310	327	329	400	326	346	405	307	386	336	396	293
Total TDs	40	47	36	36	39	47	38	43	47	35	48	39	47	34
TDs Rushing	18	23	12	13	13	14	13	19	23	19	12	10	14	12
TDs Passing	21	17	21	21	25	28	21	21	22	15	35	22	27	20
TDs on Ret. and Rec.	1	7	3	2	1	5	4	3	2	1	1	7	6	2
Extra Points	38	44	34	35	38	46	36	40	45	34	48	36	45	32
Safeties	2	1	0	2	0	0	1	0	0	0	1	0	0	0
Field Goals Made	22	22	20	24	19	24	20	16	26	21	16	22	23	19
Field Goals Attempted	33	30	29	32	29	35	31	21	31	28	27	39	31	28
% Successful	66.7	73.3	69.0	75.0	65.5	68.6	64.5	76.2	83.9	75.0	59.3	56.4	74.2	67.9

National Football Conference Offense

	Atl.	Chi.	Dall.	Det.	G.B.	Rams	Minn.	N.O.	N.Y.G.	Phil.	St.L.	S.F.	T.B.	Wash.
First Downs	305	305	325	287	286	269	321	275	324	287	273	346	273	312
Rushing	149	166	98	100	96	139	114	109	127	113	102	114	100	112
Passing	137	118	199	156	172	105	186	137	171	150	149	213	142	177
Penalty	19	21	28	31	18	25	21	29	26	24	22	19	31	23
Rushes	578	606	447	470	424	578	461	505	558	499	419	510	455	474
Net Yds. Gained	2524	2700	1969	1771	1614	2457	1738	2074	2245	2002	1787	1986	1863	1732
Avg. Gain	4.4	4.5	4.4	3.8	3.8	4.3	3.8	4.1	4.0	4.0	4.3	3.9	4.1	3.7
Avg. Yds. per Game	157.8	168.8	123.1	110.7	100.9	153.6	108.6	129.6	140.3	125.1	111.7	124.1	116.4	108.3
Passes Attempted	452	415	547	500	565	403	519	425	472	514	516	582	459	542
Completed	246	208	319	286	305	194	290	232	260	268	293	353	245	276
% Completed	54.4	50.1	58.3	57.2	54.0	48.1	55.9	54.6	55.1	52.1	56.8	60.7	53.4	50.9
Total Yds. Gained	3046	2912	4003	3107	3708	2380	4185	2893	3500	3248	3140	4299	2892	4109
Times Sacked	56	24	60	39	37	27	44	27	46	104	59	26	56	28
Yds. Lost	464	153	498	323	261	184	272	225	367	708	424	203	394	240
Net Yds. Gained	2582	2759	3505	2784	3447	2196	3913	2668	3133	2540	2716	4096	2498	3869
Avg. Yds. per Game	161.4	172.4	219.1	174.0	215.4	137.3	244.6	166.8	195.8	158.8	169.8	256.0	156.1	241.8
Net Yds. per Pass Play	5.08	6.28	5.77	5.17	5.73	5.11	6.95	5.90	6.05	4.11	4.72	6.74	4.85	6.79
Yds. Gained per Comp.	12.38	14.00	12.55	10.86	12.16	12.27	14.43	12.47	13.46	12.12	10.72	12.18	11.80	14.89
Combined Net Yds. Gained	5106	5459	5474	4555	5061	4653	5651	4742	5378	4542	4503	6082	4361	5601
% Total Yds. Rushing	49.4	49.5	36.0	38.9	31.9	52.8	30.8	43.7	41.7	44.1	39.7	32.7	42.7	30.9
% Total Yds. Passing	50.6	50.5	64.0	61.1	68.1	47.2	69.2	56.3	58.3	55.9	60.3	67.3	57.3	69.1
Avg. Yds. per Game	319.1	341.2	342.1	284.7	316.3	290.8	353.2	296.4	336.1	283.9	281.4	380.1	272.6	350.1
Ball Control Plays	1086	1045	1054	1009	1026	1008	1024	957	1076	1117	994	1118	970	1044
Avg. Yds. per Play	4.7	5.2	5.2	4.5	4.9	4.6	5.5	5.0	5.0	4.1	4.5	5.4	4.5	5.4
Avg. Time of Poss.	32:35	32:21	31:14	29:42	28:11	29:41	30:15	27:59	31:50	31:57	29:18	30:28	28:40	29:56
Third Down Efficiency	36.2	37.2	37.6	38.3	35.6	33.3	42.0	29.9	37.3	38.5	32.7	35.7	30.6	41.8
Had Intercepted	17	25	24	20	27	15	15	25	22	17	19	20	25	22
Yds. Opp. Returned	198	115	331	311	357	128	88	362	218	192	271	205	236	186
Ret. by Opp. for TD	1	1	2	2	3	0	0	0	1	1	2	0	1	0
Punts	79	70	87	85	75	98	73	82	79	111	92	85	78	75
Yds. Punted	3421	2850	3498	3389	2825	3740	2922	3456	3539	4547	3411	3450	3132	3271
Avg. Yds. per Punt	43.3	40.7	40.2	39.9	37.7	38.2	40.0	42.1	44.8	41.0	37.1	40.6	40.2	43.6
Punt Returns	44	57	46	43	33	42	31	47	41	44	45	43	26	51
Yds. Returned	292	482	252	420	316	361	215	377	287	374	528	397	110	550
Avg. Yds. per Return	6.6	8.5	5.5	9.8	9.6	8.6	6.9	8.0	7.0	8.5	11.7	9.2	4.2	10.8
Returned for TD	0	0	0	1	1	0	0	0	0	1	2	1	0	0
Kickoff Returns	54	50	59	67	76	59	56	55	50	53	70	42	75	60
Yds. Returned	1035	1115	1208	1321	1470	1160	1200	1332	868	945	1548	757	1302	1175
Avg. Yds. per Return	19.2	22.3	20.5	19.7	19.3	19.7	21.4	24.2	17.4	17.8	22.1	18.0	17.4	19.6
Returned for TD	0	2	0	0	0	0	0	1	0	0	0	0	0	0
Fumbles	31	36	44	30	35	39	31	33	31	34	25	32	36	29
Lost	16	22	17	17	18	22	14	18	10	10	10	9	17	10
Out of Bounds	0	2	4	0	3	2	1	0	3	6	2	1	4	0
Own Rec. for TD	0	0	0	0	0	1	0	0	0	0	0	0	0	0
Opp. Rec. by	14	16	18	19	12	15	18	17	19	13	12	10	19	9
Opp. Rec. for TD	2	1	0	0	0	1	0	0	0	0	0	0	2	1
Penalties	99	98	112	84	128	84	96	109	96	102	116	95	83	94
Yds. Penalized	763	765	936	658	949	603	890	855	738	901	932	691	661	860
Total Points Scored	280	352	346	277	254	309	398	288	371	256	218	374	239	368
Total TDs	30	38	43	32	29	37	48	30	42	28	27	43	27	46
TDs Rushing	12	21	21	13	8	16	14	15	18	8	8	16	12	23
TDs Passing	14	12	21	18	18	15	31	13	22	19	17	21	13	22
TDs on Ret. and Rec.	4	5	1	1	3	6	3	2	2	1	2	6	2	1
Extra Points	29	36	43	31	29	34	44	30	41	26	23	41	26	38
Safeties	1	2	0	0	0	1	0	0	0	1	0	0	0	0
Field Goals Made	23	28	15	18	17	17	22	26	26	20	11	25	17	18
Field Goals Attempted	36	41	21	25	27	24	28	30	37	31	24	35	24	32
% Successful	63.9	68.3	71.4	72.0	63.0	70.8	78.6	86.7	70.3	64.5	45.8	71.4	70.8	56.3

National Football Conference Defense

	Atl.	Chi.	Dall.	Det.	G.B.	Rams	Minn.	N.O.	N.Y.G.	Phil.	St.L.	S.F.	T.B.	Wash.
First Downs	268	241	286	298	313	272	286	331	284	278	304	285	362	316
Rushing	111	67	118	134	135	93	106	104	78	97	125	97	162	103
Passing	139	151	148	148	151	169	155	197	177	156	149	169	177	181
Penalty	18	23	20	16	27	10	25	30	29	25	30	19	23	32
Rushes	485	427	500	519	565	460	481	486	350	458	560	406	558	459
Net Yds. Gained	1916	1463	2200	2349	2095	1681	1796	1559	1284	1989	2227	1555	2648	1805
Avg. Gain	4.0	3.4	4.4	4.5	3.7	3.7	3.7	3.2	3.7	4.3	4.0	3.8	4.7	3.9
Avg. Yds. per Game	119.8	91.4	137.5	146.8	130.9	105.1	112.3	97.4	80.3	124.3	139.2	97.2	165.5	112.8
Passes Attempted	453	513	464	468	448	539	494	576	587	532	436	604	484	532
Completed	241	243	226	279	267	313	276	331	334	260	215	324	289	302
% Completed	53.2	47.4	48.7	59.6	59.6	58.1	55.9	57.5	56.9	48.9	49.3	53.6	59.7	56.8
Total Yds. Gained	3169	3170	3149	3090	3142	3482	3475	3886	3887	3641	2992	3773	3838	3916
Times Sacked	26	62	53	41	28	39	38	47	59	53	41	51	19	55
Yds. Lost	177	503	364	290	222	292	259	343	414	406	355	448	153	424
Net Yds. Gained	2992	2667	2785	2800	2920	3190	3216	3543	3473	3235	2637	3325	3685	3492
Avg. Yds. per Game	187.0	166.7	174.1	175.0	182.5	199.4	201.0	221.4	217.1	202.2	164.8	207.8	230.3	218.3
Net Yds. per Pass Play	6.25	4.64	5.39	5.50	6.13	5.52	6.05	5.69	5.38	5.53	5.53	5.08	7.33	5.95
Yds. Gained per Comp.	13.15	13.05	13.93	11.08	11.77	11.12	12.59	11.74	11.64	14.00	13.92	11.65	13.28	12.97
Combined Net Yds. Gained	4908	4130	4985	5149	5015	4871	5012	5102	4757	5224	4864	4880	6333	5297
% Total Yds. Rushing	39.0	35.4	44.1	45.6	41.8	34.5	35.8	30.6	27.0	38.1	45.8	31.9	41.8	34.1
% Total Yds. Passing	61.0	64.6	55.9	54.4	58.2	65.5	64.2	69.4	73.0	61.9	54.2	68.1	58.2	65.9
Avg. Yds. per Game	306.8	258.1	311.6	321.8	313.4	304.4	313.3	318.9	297.3	326.5	304.0	305.0	395.8	331.1
Ball Control Plays	964	1002	1017	1028	1041	1038	1013	1109	996	1043	1037	1061	1061	1046
Avg. Yds. per Play	5.1	4.1	4.9	5.0	4.8	4.7	4.9	4.6	4.8	5.0	4.7	4.6	6.0	5.1
Avg. Time of Poss.	27:25	27:39	28:46	30:18	31:49	30:19	29:45	32:01	28:10	28:03	30:42	29:32	31:20	30:04
Third Down Efficiency	35.7	32.5	39.4	41.3	43.3	31.0	36.9	42.2	35.4	34.3	36.4	30.3	46.6	33.2
Intercepted by	22	31	17	22	20	28	24	26	24	23	10	39	13	19
Yds. Returned by	294	370	183	190	147	458	319	235	296	124	121	578	128	126
Returned for TD	2	1	1	0	1	3	2	1	1	0	0	5	0	0

	Atl.	Chi.	Dall.	Det.	G.B.	Rams	Minn.	N.O.	N.Y.G.	Phil.	St.L.	S.F.	T.B.	Wash.
Punts	83	100	87	68	70	96	75	78	89	97	83	91	59	95
Yds. Punted	3436	4090	3620	2836	2769	3975	3021	3315	3499	3751	3514	3765	2438	3923
Avg. Yds. per Punt	41.4	40.9	41.6	41.7	39.6	41.4	40.3	42.5	39.3	38.7	42.3	41.4	41.3	41.3
Punt Returns	47	23	41	39	44	47	40	37	41	63	44	49	39	36
Yds. Returned	477	110	301	517	287	416	356	234	386	634	296	373	414	220
Avg. Yds. per Return	10.1	4.8	7.3	13.3	6.5	8.9	8.9	6.3	9.4	10.1	6.7	7.6	10.6	6.1
Returned for TD	3	0	0	2	0	0	0	0	0	2	0	0	3	0
Kickoff Returns	59	64	66	56	62	64	79	35	70	62	50	71	46	50
Yds. Returned	1190	1376	1358	1096	1181	1282	1532	662	1362	1261	886	1598	1009	1005
Avg. Yds. per Return	20.2	21.5	20.6	19.6	19.0	20.0	19.4	18.9	19.5	20.3	17.7	22.5	21.9	20.1
Returned for TD	0	0	0	0	0	0	0	0	0	0	0	1	1	0
Fumbles	30	27	29	36	32	25	32	37	36	30	40	31	39	21
Lost	14	16	18	19	12	15	18	17	19	13	12	10	19	9
Out of Bounds	2	2	0	3	3	0	2	3	1	2	3	3	2	1
Own Rec. for TD	0	0	0	1	0	0	0	0	0	0	0	0	0	0
Opp. Rec. by	16	22	17	16	18	22	14	18	10	10	10	9	17	10
Opp. Rec. for TD	0	3	1	1	0	1	1	1	0	0	0	0	0	0
Penalties	106	111	91	99	79	92	99	104	119	115	86	89	116	115
Yds. Penalized	834	866	822	781	657	804	806	791	988	884	682	653	941	1026
Total Points Scored	280	187	337	326	418	267	273	287	236	312	351	247	473	296
Total TDs	34	20	41	36	52	28	28	34	26	39	40	29	59	35
TDs Rushing	10	4	17	15	16	9	10	11	10	14	17	8	31	14
TDs Passing	19	12	21	14	31	17	16	21	15	21	21	18	23	21
TDs on Ret. and Rec.	5	4	3	7	5	2	2	2	1	4	2	3	5	0
Extra Points	31	19	39	36	48	27	24	32	26	37	37	28	56	35
Safeties	0	0	2	1	2	0	0	0	0	1	1	0	0	0
Field Goals Made	15	16	16	24	18	24	27	17	18	13	24	15	21	17
Field Goals Attempted	26	22	30	35	25	31	33	27	25	26	32	25	30	24
% Successful	57.7	72.7	53.3	68.6	72.0	77.4	81.8	63.0	72.0	50.0	75.0	60.0	70.0	70.8

AFC, NFC, and NFL Summary

	AFC Offense Total	AFC Offense Average	AFC Defense Total	AFC Defense Average	NFC Offense Total	NFC Offense Average	NFC Defense Total	NFC Defense Average	NFL Total	NFL Average
First Downs	4304	307.4	4368	312.0	4188	299.1	4124	294.6	8492	303.3
Rushing	1400	100.0	1509	107.8	1639	117.1	1530	109.3	3039	108.5
Passing	2537	181.2	2482	177.3	2212	158.0	2267	161.9	4749	169.6
Penalty	367	26.2	377	26.9	337	24.1	327	23.4	704	25.1
Rushes	6525	466.1	6795	485.4	6984	498.9	6714	479.6	13,509	482.5
Net Yds. Gained	24,710	1765.0	26,605	1900.4	28,462	2033.0	26,567	1897.6	53,172	1899.0
Avg. Gain	—	3.8	—	3.9	—	4.1	—	4.0	—	3.9
Avg. Yds. per Game	—	110.3	—	118.8	—	127.1	—	118.6	—	118.7
Passes Attempted	7558	539.9	7339	524.2	6911	493.6	7130	509.3	14,469	516.8
Completed	4239	302.8	4114	293.9	3775	269.6	3900	278.6	8014	286.2
% Completed	—	56.1	—	56.1	—	54.6	—	54.7	—	55.4
Total Yds. Gained	53,706	3836.1	52,518	3751.3	47,422	3387.3	48,610	3472.1	101,128	3611.7
Times Sacked	565	40.4	586	41.9	633	45.2	612	43.7	1198	42.8
Yds. Lost	4331	309.4	4397	314.1	4716	336.9	4650	332.1	9047	323.1
Net Yds. Gained	49,375	3526.8	48,121	3437.2	42,706	3050.4	43,960	3140.0	92,081	3288.6
Avg. Yds. per Game	—	220.4	—	214.8	—	190.7	—	196.3	—	205.5
Net Yds. per Pass Play	—	6.08	—	6.07	—	5.66	—	5.68	—	5.88
Yds. Gained per Comp.	—	12.67	12.77	11.70	—	12.56	12.46	11.27	—	12.62
Combined Net Yds.Gained	74,085	5291.8	74,726	5337.6	71,168	5083.4	70,527	5037.6	145,253	5187.6
% Total Yds. Rushing	—	33.4	—	35.6	—	40.0	—	37.7	—	36.6
% Total Yds. Passing	—	66.6	—	64.4	—	60.0	—	62.3	—	63.4
Avg. Yds. per Game	—	330.7	—	333.6	—	317.7	—	314.9	—	324.2
Ball Control Plays	14,648	1046.3	14,720	1051.4	14,528	1037.7	14,456	1032.6	29,176	1042.0
Avg. Yds. per Play	—	5.1	—	5.1	—	4.9	—	4.9	—	5.0
Third Down Efficiency	—	38.7	—	38.0	—	36.3	—	36.9	—	37.5

	AFC Offense Total	AFC Offense Average	AFC Defense Total	AFC Defense Average	NFC Offense Total	NFC Offense Average	NFC Defense Total	NFC Defense Average	NFL Total	NFL Average
Interceptions	263	18.8	288	20.6	318	22.7	293	20.9	581	20.8
Yds. Returned	3181	227.2	3552	253.7	3569	254.9	3198	228.4	6750	241.1
Returned for TD	12	0.9	15	1.1	17	1.2	14	1.0	29	1.0
Punts	1142	81.6	1140	81.4	1169	83.5	1171	83.6	2311	82.5
Yds. Punted	46,023	3287.4	45,522	3251.6	47,451	3389.4	47,952	3425.1	93,474	3338.4
Avg. Yds. per Punt	—	40.3	—	39.9	—	40.6	—	40.9	—	40.4
Punt Returns	552	39.4	555	39.6	593	42.4	590	42.1	1145	40.9
Yds. Returned	4859	347.1	4799	342.8	4961	354.4	5021	358.6	9820	350.7
Avg. Yds. per Return	—	8.8	—	8.6	—	8.4	—	8.5	—	8.6
Returned for TD	8	0.6	4	0.3	6	0.4	10	0.7	14	0.5
Kickoff Returns	867	61.9	859	61.4	826	59.0	834	59.6	1693	60.5
Yds. Returned	17,005	1214.6	16,643	1188.8	16,436	1174.0	16,798	1199.9	33,441	1194.3
Avg. Yds. per Return	—	19.6	—	19.4	—	19.9	—	20.1	—	19.8
Returned for TD	4	0.3	5	0.4	3	0.2	2	0.1	7	0.3
Fumbles	444	31.7	465	33.2	466	33.3	445	31.8	910	32.5
Lost	221	15.8	220	15.7	210	15.0	211	15.1	431	15.4
Out of Bounds	46	3.3	47	3.4	28	2.0	27	1.9	74	2.6
Own Rec. for TD	5	0.4	5	0.4	1	0.1	1	0.1	6	0.2
Opp. Rec.	218	15.6	220	15.7	211	15.1	209	14.9	429	15.3
Opp. Rec. for TD	11	0.8	10	0.7	7	0.5	8	0.6	18	0.6
Penalties	1479	105.6	1454	103.9	1396	99.7	1421	101.5	2875	102.7
Yds. Penalized	12,025	858.9	11,692	835.1	11,202	800.1	11,535	823.9	23,227	829.5
Total Points Scored	4863	347.4	4903	350.2	4330	309.3	4290	306.4	9193	328.3
Total TDs	577	41.2	576	41.1	500	35.7	501	35.8	1077	38.5
TDs Rushing	196	14.0	215	15.4	205	14.6	186	13.3	401	14.3
TDs Passing	330	23.6	316	22.6	256	18.3	270	19.3	586	20.9
TDs on Ret. and Rec.	51	3.6	45	3.2	39	2.8	45	3.2	90	3.2
Extra Points	555	39.6	551	39.4	471	33.6	475	33.9	1026	36.6
Safeties	9	0.6	7	0.5	5	0.4	7	0.5	14	0.5
Field Goals Made	276	19.7	294	21.0	283	20.2	265	18.9	559	20.0
Field Goals Attempted	400	28.6	424	30.3	415	29.6	391	27.9	815	29.1
% Successful	—	69.0	—	69.3	—	68.2	—	67.8	—	68.6

Club Leaders

	Offense	Defense
First Downs	Mia. 351	Chi. 241
Rushing	Chi. 166	Chi. 67
Passing	Mia. 250	Hou. 137
Penalty	Den. 41	Rams 10
Rushes	Chi. 606	N.Y.G. 350
Net Yds. Gained	Chi. 2700	N.Y.G. 1284
Avg. Gain	Cin. 4.9	N.O. 3.2
Passes Attempted	Mia. 645	St. L. 436
Completed	Mia. 392	St. L. 215
% Completed	N.Y.J. 62.2	Hou. 46.5
Total Yds. Gained	Mia. 4898	St. L. 2992
Times Sacked	Mia. 17	Raiders 63
Yds. Lost	Mia. 119	Chi. 503
Net Yds. Gained	Mia. 4779	St. L. 2637
Net Yds. per Pass Play	Cin. 7.54	Chi. 4.64
Yds. Gained per Comp.	Wash. 14.89	Det. 11.08
Combined Net Yds. Gained	Cin. 6490	Chi. 4130
% Total Yds. Rushing	Rams 52.8	N.Y.G. 27.0
% Total Yds. Passing	Mia. 75.6	St. L. 54.2
Ball Control Plays	S.F. 1118	Atl. 964
Avg. Yds. per Play	Mia. 6.3	Chi. 4.1
Avg. Time of Poss.	Atl. 32:35	—
Third Down Efficiency	Mia. 50.8	S.F. 30.3
Interceptions	—	S.F. 39
Yds. Returned	—	S.F. 578
Returned for TD	—	S.F. 5
Punts	Phil. 111	—
Yds. Punted	Phil. 4547	—
Avg. Yds. per Punt	N.Y.G. 44.8	—
Punt Returns	Chi. 57	Cin. 19
Yds. Returned	Den. 552	Chi. 110
Avg. Yds. per Return	St. L. 11.7	N.Y.J. 4.6
Returned for TD	Den. & St. L. 2	—
Kickoff Returns	G.B. 76	Hou. 32
Yds. Returned	St. L. 1548	N.O. 662
Avg. Yds. per Return	N.O. 24.2	Raiders 16.9
Returned for TD	Chi. & N.Y.J. 2	—
Total Points Scored	Mia. 430	Chi. 187
Total TDs	Mia. 56	Chi. 20
TDs Rushing	Cin. 24	Chi. 4
TDs Passing	Mia. 46	Chi. 12
TDs on Ret. and Rec.	K.C. 10	Wash. 0
Extra Points	Mia. 52	Chi. 19
Safeties	Chi. & Den. 2	—
Field Goals Made	N.E. 32	Phil. 13
Field Goals Attempted	Chi. & N.E. 41	Raiders 21
% Successful	N.O. 86.7	Phil. 50.0

Club Rankings by Yards

	Offense			Defense		
Team	Total	Rush	Pass	Total	Rush	Pass
Atlanta	17	3	25	7	16	7
Buffalo	19	21	15	24	9	27
Chicago	7	*1	20	*1	2	2
Cincinnati	*1	2	3	20	22	10
Cleveland	9	22	8	19	18	15
Dallas	6	11	12	10	23	3
Denver	15	20	10	9	5	16
Detroit	24	15	19	15	26	4
Green Bay	18	23	14	12	21	5
Houston	16	19	13	13	20	8
Indianapolis	22	26	16	25	17	26
Kansas City	28	27	21	8	11	12
Los Angeles Raiders	14	13	11	3	10	9
Los Angeles Rams	23	4	28	5	8	11
Miami	2	25	*1	26t	27	22
Minnesota	4	16	5	11	13	13
New England	13	28	4	16	24	6
New Orleans	21	8	23	14	4	21
New York Giants	10	6	17	2	*1	19
New York Jets	11	18	9	26t	6	28
Philadelphia	25	9	26	17	19	14
Pittsburgh	20	7	24	18	15	18
St. Louis	26	14	22	4	25	*1
San Diego	12	24	7	23	7	25
San Francisco	3	10	2	6	3	17
Seattle	8	5	18	22	12	23
Tampa Bay	27	12	27	28	28	24
Washington	5	17	6	21	14	20

t—Tie for position

**—League leader*

AFC Takeaways/Giveaways

	Takeaways			Giveaways			
	Int.	Fum.	Total	Int.	Fum.	Total	Net Diff.
New England	21	19	40	13	11	24	16
Kansas City	31	18	49	18	17	35	14
Cleveland	18	19	37	11	13	24	13
Seattle	22	14	36	14	13	27	9
Denver	18	17	35	16	13	29	6
New York Jets	20	18	38	21	16	37	1
Pittsburgh	20	13	33	20	16	36	−3
Cincinnati	17	11	28	20	16	36	−8
Indianapolis	16	19	35	24	20	44	−9
Miami	13	14	27	23	14	37	−10
Houston	16	16	32	31	12	43	−11
Los Angeles Raiders	26	12	38	25	24	49	−11
San Diego	15	22	37	33	16	49	−12
Buffalo	10	8	18	19	20	39	−21

NFC Takeaways/Giveaways

	Takeaways			Giveaways			
	Int.	Fum.	Total	Int.	Fum.	Total	Net Diff.
San Francisco	39	10	49	20	9	29	20
Minnesota	24	18	42	15	14	29	13
New York Giants	24	19	43	22	10	32	11
Philadelphia	23	13	36	17	10	27	9
Los Angeles Rams	28	15	43	15	22	37	6
Detroit	22	19	41	20	17	37	4
Atlanta	22	14	36	17	16	33	3
Chicago	31	16	47	25	22	47	0
New Orleans	26	17	43	25	18	43	0
Washington	19	9	28	22	10	32	−4
Dallas	17	18	35	24	17	41	−6
St. Louis	10	12	22	19	10	29	−7
Tampa Bay	13	19	32	25	17	42	−10
Green Bay	20	12	32	27	18	45	−13

1986 TEAM & INDIVIDUAL STATISTICS

Scoring

Points

Kickers

AFC: 140—Tony Franklin, New England
NFC: 120—Kevin Butler, Chicago

Non-kickers

NFC: 108—George Rogers, Washington
AFC: 84—Sammy Winder, Denver

Touchdowns

NFC: 18—George Rogers, Washington
AFC: 14—Sammy Winder, Denver

Extra Points

AFC: 52—Fuad Reveiz, Miami
NFC: 44—Chuck Nelson, Minnesota

Field Goals

AFC: 32—Tony Franklin, New England
NFC: 28—Kevin Butler, Chicago

Field Goal Attempts

AFC: 41—Tony Franklin, New England
NFC: 41—Kevin Butler, Chicago

Longest Field Goal

NFC: 57—Steve Cox, Washington vs. Seattle, September 28
AFC: 54—Norm Johnson, Seattle vs. San Diego, October 6

Most Points, Game

AFC: 24—Wesley Walker, New York Jets vs. Miami, September 21 [OT] (4 TD)
NFC: 18—Jerry Rice, San Francisco vs. Indianapolis, October 5 (3 TD)
18—Jerry Rice, San Francisco vs. St. Louis, November 9 (3 TD)
18—George Rogers, Washington vs. Minnesota, November 2 [OT] (3 TD)
18—Walter Stanley, Green Bay vs. Detroit, November 27 (3 TD)
18—Mike Quick, Philadelphia vs. Los Angeles Raiders, November 30 [OT] (3 TD)
18—Joe Morris, New York Giants vs. St. Louis, December 14 (3 TD)

Team Leaders

AFC: BUFFALO: 83, Scott Norwood; CINCINNATI: 101, Jim Breech; CLEVELAND: 90, Matt Bahr; DENVER: 104, Rich Karlis; HOUSTON: 94, Tony Zendejas; INDIANAPOLIS: 65, Dean Biasucci; KANSAS CITY: 100, Nick Lowery; LOS ANGELES RAIDERS: 99, Chris Bahr; MIAMI: 94, Fuad Reveiz; NEW ENGLAND: 140, Tony Franklin; NEW YORK JETS: 92, Pat Leahy; PITTSBURGH: 95, Gary Anderson; SAN DIEGO: 87, Rolf Benirschke; SEATTLE: 108, Norm Johnson.

NFC: ATLANTA: 63, Mick Luckhurst; CHICAGO: 120, Kevin Butler; DALLAS: 88, Rafael Septien; DETROIT: 85, Ed Murray; GREEN BAY: 80, Al Del Greco; LOS ANGELES RAMS: 85, Mike Lansford; MINNESOTA: 110, Chuck Nelson; NEW ORLEANS: 108, Morten Andersen; NEW YORK GIANTS: 105, Raul Allegre; PHILADELPHIA: 86, Paul McFadden; ST. LOUIS: 38, John Lee; SAN FRANCISCO: 116, Ray Wersching; TAMPA BAY: 77, Donald Igwebuike; WASHINGTON: 108, George Rogers.

Team Champions

AFC: 430—Miami
NFC: 398—Minnesota

AFC Scoring—Team

	TD	TDR	TDP	TD Misc.	PAT	PAT Att.	FG	FG Att.	SAF	TP
Miami	56	9	46	1	52	55	14	22	0	430
New England	45	10	29	6	44	45	32	41	1	412
Cincinnati	51	24	25	2	50	51	17	32	1	409
Cleveland	45	20	18	7	43	44	26	33	0	391
Denver	45	17	22	6	44	45	20	28	2	378
Seattle	43	15	24	4	42	43	22	35	0	366
N.Y. Jets	45	16	27	2	44	44	16	19	1	364
Kansas City	43	10	23	10	43	43	19	26	0	358
San Diego	41	19	21	1	39	41	16	25	1	335
L.A. Raiders	37	6	27	4	36	36	21	28	1	323
Pittsburgh	35	18	16	1	32	34	21	32	1	307
Buffalo	34	9	22	3	32	34	17	27	0	287
Houston	30	13	14	3	28	30	22	27	0	274
Indianapolis	27	10	16	1	26	27	13	25	1	229
AFC Total	577	196	330	51	555	572	276	400	9	4863
AFC Average	41.2	14.0	23.6	3.6	39.6	40.9	19.7	28.6	0.6	347.4

NFC Scoring—Team

	TD	TDR	TDP	TD Misc.	PAT	PAT Att.	FG	FG Att.	SAF	TP
Minnesota	48	14	31	3	44	48	22	28	0	398
San Francisco	43	16	21	6	41	43	25	35	0	374
N.Y. Giants	42	18	22	2	41	42	26	37	0	371
Washington	46	23	22	1	38	45	18	32	0	368
Chicago	38	21	12	5	36	38	28	41	2	352
Dallas	43	21	21	1	43	43	15	21	0	346
L.A. Rams	37	16	15	6	34	36	17	24	1	309
New Orleans	30	15	13	2	30	30	26	30	0	288
Atlanta	30	12	14	4	29	30	23	36	1	280
Detroit	32	13	18	1	31	32	18	25	0	277
Philadelphia	28	8	19	1	26	27	20	31	1	256
Green Bay	29	8	18	3	29	29	17	27	0	254
Tampa Bay	27	12	13	2	26	27	17	24	0	239
St. Louis	27	8	17	2	23	27	11	24	0	218
NFC Total	500	205	256	39	471	497	283	415	5	4330
NFC Average	35.7	14.6	18.3	2.8	33.6	35.5	20.2	29.6	0.4	309.3
League Total	1077	401	586	90	1026	1069	559	815	14	9193
League Avg.	38.5	14.3	20.9	3.2	36.6	38.2	20.0	29.1	0.5	328.3

NFL Top 10 Scorers—Touchdowns

	TD	TDR	TDP	TD Misc.	TP
Rogers, George, Washington	18	18	0	0	108
Rice, Jerry, San Francisco	16	1	15	0	96
Morris, Joe, N.Y. Giants	15	14	1	0	90
Walker, Herschel, Dallas	14	12	2	0	84
Winder, Sammy, Denver	14	9	5	0	84
Warner, Curt, Seattle	13	13	0	0	78
Hampton, Lorenzo, Miami	12	9	3	0	72
Walker, Wesley, N.Y. Jets	12	0	12	0	72
Dickerson, Eric, L.A. Rams	11	11	0	0	66
Duper, Mark, Miami	11	0	11	0	66
Paige, Stephone, Kansas City	11	0	11	0	66
Payton, Walter, Chicago	11	8	3	0	66

NFL Top 10 Scorers—Kicking

	PAT	PAT Att.	FG	FG Att.	TP
Franklin, Tony, New England	44	45	32	41	140
Butler, Kevin, Chicago	36	37	28	41	120
Wersching, Ray, San Francisco	41	42	25	35	116
Nelson, Chuck, Minnesota	44	47	22	28	110
Andersen, Morten, New Orleans	30	30	26	30	108
Johnson, Norm, Seattle	42	42	22	35	108
Allegre, Raul, N.Y. Giants	33	33	24	32	105
Karlis, Rich, Denver	44	45	20	28	104
Breech, Jim, Cincinnati	50	51	17	32	101
Lowery, Nick, Kansas City	43	43	19	26	100

AFC Scoring—Individual

Kickers	PAT	PAT Att.	FG	FG Att.	TP
Franklin, Tony, New England	44	45	32	41	140
Johnson, Norm, Seattle	42	42	22	35	108
Karlis, Rich, Denver	44	45	20	28	104
Breech, Jim, Cincinnati	50	51	17	32	101
Lowery, Nick, Kansas City	43	43	19	26	100
Bahr, Chris, L.A. Raiders	36	36	21	28	99
Anderson, Gary, Pittsburgh	32	32	21	32	95
Reveiz, Fuad, Miami	52	55	14	22	94
Zendejas, Tony, Houston	28	29	22	27	94
Leahy, Pat, N.Y. Jets	44	44	16	19	92
Bahr, Matt, Cleveland	30	30	20	26	90
Benirschke, Rolf, San Diego	39	41	16	25	87
Norwood, Scott, Buffalo	32	34	17	27	83
Biasucci, Dean, Indianapolis	26	27	13	25	65
Moseley, Mark, Wash.-Clev.	25	28	12	19	61

Non-Kickers	TD	TDR	TDP	TD Misc.	TP
Winder, Sammy, Denver	14	9	5	0	84
Warner, Curt, Seattle	13	13	0	0	78
Hampton, Lorenzo, Miami	12	9	3	0	72
Walker, Wesley, N.Y. Jets	12	0	12	0	72
Duper, Mark, Miami	11	0	11	0	66
Paige, Stephone, Kansas City	11	0	11	0	66
Clayton, Mark, Miami	10	0	10	0	60
Collinsworth, Cris, Cincinnati	10	0	10	0	60
Mack, Kevin, Cleveland	10	10	0	0	60
Morgan, Stanley, New England	10	0	10	0	60
Anderson, Gary, San Diego	9	1	8	0	54
Brooks, James, Cincinnati	9	5	4	0	54
Kinnebrew, Larry, Cincinnati	9	8	1	0	54
Largent, Steve, Seattle	9	0	9	0	54
Willhite, Gerald, Denver	9	5	3	1	54
Abercrombie, Walter, Pittsburgh	8	6	2	0	48
Brooks, Bill, Indianapolis	8	0	8	0	48
Christensen, Todd, L.A. Raiders	8	0	8	0	48
Collins, Tony, New England	8	3	5	0	48
Hector, Johnny, N.Y. Jets	8	8	0	0	48
Toon, Al, N.Y. Jets	8	0	8	0	48
Williams, Dokie, L.A. Raiders	8	0	8	0	48

	TD	TDR	TDP	TD Misc.	TP
Wilson, Stanley, Cincinnati	8	8	0	0	48
Allen, Marcus, L.A. Raiders	7	5	2	0	42
Brennan, Brian, Cleveland	7	0	6	1	42
Fryar, Irving, New England	7	0	6	1	42
McGee, Buford, San Diego	7	7	0	0	42
Moore, Nat, Miami	7	0	7	0	42
Reed, Andre, Buffalo	7	0	7	0	42
Turner, Daryl, Seattle	7	0	7	0	42
Bell, Greg, Buffalo	6	4	2	0	36
Dickey, Curtis, Cleveland	6	6	0	0	36
Hester, Jessie, L.A. Raiders	6	0	6	0	36
McNeil, Freeman, N.Y. Jets	6	5	1	0	36
Smith, Jeff, Kansas City	6	3	3	0	36
Spencer, Tim, San Diego	6	6	0	0	36
Bouza, Matt, Indianapolis	5	0	5	0	30
Hardy, Bruce, Miami	5	0	5	0	30
Hill, Drew, Houston	5	0	5	0	30
Jackson, Earnest, Pittsburgh	5	5	0	0	30
Malone, Mark, Pittsburgh	5	5	0	0	30
Riddick, Robb, Buffalo	5	4	1	0	30
Slaughter, Webster, Cleveland	5	0	4	1	30
Thompson, Weegie, Pittsburgh	5	0	5	0	30
Wallace, Ray, Houston	5	3	2	0	30
Winslow, Kellen, San Diego	5	0	5	0	30
Adams, Curtis, San Diego	4	4	0	0	24
Brown, Eddie, Cincinnati	4	0	4	0	24
Burkett, Chris, Buffalo	4	0	4	0	24
Burruss, Lloyd, Kansas City	4	0	0	4	24
Butler, Raymond, Seattle	4	0	4	0	24
Byner, Earnest, Cleveland	4	2	2	0	24
Carson, Carlos, Kansas City	4	0	4	0	24
Chandler, Wes, San Diego	4	0	4	0	24
Erenberg, Rich, Pittsburgh	4	1	3	0	24
Givins, Earnest, Houston	4	1	3	0	24
Green, Boyce, Kansas City	4	3	0	1	24
James, Craig, New England	4	4	0	0	24
Johnson, Dan, Miami	4	0	4	0	24
Metzelaars, Pete, Buffalo	4	0	3	1	24
Rozier, Mike, Houston	4	4	0	0	24
Shuler, Mickey, N.Y. Jets	4	0	4	0	24
Bentley, Albert, Indianapolis	3	3	0	0	18
Harden, Mike, Denver	3	0	0	3	18
Lang, Gene, Denver	3	1	2	0	18
Lipps, Louis, Pittsburgh	3	0	3	0	18
McMillan, Randy, Indianapolis	3	3	0	0	18
Newsome, Ozzie, Cleveland	3	0	3	0	18
Pinkett, Allen, Houston	3	2	1	0	18
Pruitt, James, Miami	3	0	2	1	18
Scott, Willie, New England	3	0	3	0	18
Watson, Steve, Denver	3	0	3	0	18
Arnold, Walt, Kansas City	2	0	1	1	12
Barksdale, Rod, L.A. Raiders	2	0	2	0	12
Baty, Greg, New England	2	0	2	0	12
Butler, Jerry, Buffalo	2	0	2	0	12
Cherry, Deron, Kansas City	2	0	0	2	12
Coffman, Paul, Kansas City	2	0	2	0	12
Elway, John, Denver	2	1	1	0	12
Fontenot, Herman, Cleveland	2	1	1	0	12
Franklin, Byron, Seattle	2	0	2	0	12
Heard, Herman, Kansas City	2	2	0	0	12
Holman, Rodney, Cincinnati	2	0	2	0	12
Holt, Harry, Cleveland	2	1	1	0	12
Johnson, Vance, Denver	2	0	2	0	12
Joiner, Charlie, San Diego	2	0	2	0	12
Lane, Eric, Seattle	2	0	1	1	12
McNeil, Gerald, Cleveland	2	0	0	2	12
Moon, Warren, Houston	2	2	0	0	12
Muñoz, Anthony, Cincinnati	2	0	2	0	12
Nathan, Tony, Miami	2	0	2	0	12
Paige, Tony, N.Y. Jets	2	2	0	0	12
Pruitt, Mike, Kansas City	2	2	0	0	12
Robinson, Jerry, L.A. Raiders	2	0	0	2	12
Sewell, Steve, Denver	2	1	1	0	12
Sohn, Kurt, N.Y. Jets	2	0	2	0	12
Starring, Stephen, New England	2	0	2	0	12
Tatupu, Mosi, New England	2	1	0	1	12
Woolfolk, Butch, Houston	2	0	2	0	12
Humphery, Bobby, N.Y. Jets	1	0	0	1	*8
Beach, Pat, Indianapolis	1	0	1	0	6
Bellinger, Rodney, Buffalo	1	0	0	1	6
Bligen, Dennis, N.Y. Jets	1	1	0	0	6
Boyer, Mark, Indianapolis	1	0	1	0	6
Breeden, Louis, Cincinnati	1	0	0	1	6
Brister, Bubby, Pittsburgh	1	1	0	0	6
Brown, Dave, Seattle	1	0	0	1	6
Byrum, Carl, Buffalo	1	0	1	0	6
Daniel, Eugene, Indianapolis	1	0	0	1	6
Davenport, Ron, Miami	1	0	1	0	6

	TD	TDR	TDP	TD Misc.	TP
Donaldson, Jeff, Houston	1	0	0	1	6
Edmonds, Bobby Joe, Seattle	1	0	0	1	6
Edwards, Eddie, Cincinnati	1	0	0	1	6
Esiason, Boomer, Cincinnati	1	1	0	0	6
Flick, Tom, San Diego	1	1	0	0	6
Gill, Owen, Indianapolis	1	1	0	0	6
Gothard, Preston, Pittsburgh	1	0	1	0	6
Grogan, Steve, New England	1	1	0	0	6
Gross, Al, Cleveland	1	0	0	1	6
Harmon, Ronnie, Buffalo	1	0	1	0	6
Harry, Emile, Kansas City	1	0	1	0	6
Hayes, Jeff, Cincinnati	1	1	0	0	6
Hayes, Lester, L.A. Raiders	1	0	0	1	6
Hill, Greg, Kansas City	1	0	0	1	6
Hogeboom, Gary, Indianapolis	1	1	0	0	6
Holohan, Pete, San Diego	1	0	1	0	6
Hudson, Gordon, Seattle	1	0	1	0	6
Jackson, Mark, Denver	1	0	1	0	6
Jennings, Stanford, Cincinnati	1	1	0	0	6
Jensen, Jim, Miami	1	0	1	0	6
Johnson, Trumaine, San Diego	1	0	1	0	6
Jones, Cedric, New England	1	0	1	0	6
Kattus, Eric, Cincinnati	1	0	1	0	6
Kay, Clarence, Denver	1	0	1	0	6
Krieg, Dave, Seattle	1	1	0	0	6
Langhorne, Reggie, Cleveland	1	0	1	0	6
Lyles, Robert, Houston	1	0	0	1	6
Marion, Fred, New England	1	0	0	1	6
Marshall, Henry, Kansas City	1	0	1	0	6
McCallum, Napoleon, L.A. Raiders	1	1	0	0	6
McGee, Tim, Cincinnati	1	0	1	0	6
McSwain, Rod, New England	1	0	0	1	6
Minnifield, Frank, Cleveland	1	0	0	1	6
Mobley, Orson, Denver	1	0	1	0	6
Moore, Ricky, Buffalo	1	1	0	0	6
Moriarty, Larry, Houston-K.C.	1	1	0	0	6
Morris, Randall, Seattle	1	1	0	0	6
Moyer, Paul, Seattle	1	0	0	1	6
Munchak, Mike, Houston	1	0	0	1	6
O'Neal, Leslie, San Diego	1	0	0	1	6
Parker, Andy, L.A. Raiders	1	0	1	0	6
Pitts, Ron, Buffalo	1	0	0	1	6
Rembert, Johnny, New England	1	0	0	1	6
Ross, Kevin, Kansas City	1	0	0	1	6
Sanchez, Lupe, Pittsburgh	1	0	0	1	6
Sherwin, Tim, Indianapolis	1	0	1	0	6
Stallworth, John, Pittsburgh	1	0	1	0	6
Studdard, Dave, Denver	1	0	1	0	6
Sweeney, Calvin, Pittsburgh	1	0	1	0	6
Teal, Jimmy, Buffalo	1	0	1	0	6
Townsell, JoJo, N.Y. Jets	1	0	0	1	6
Townsend, Andre, Denver	1	0	0	1	6
Trudeau, Jack, Indianapolis	1	1	0	0	6
Walker, Fulton, L.A. Raiders	1	0	0	1	6
Weathers, Robert, New England	1	1	0	0	6
Williams, Brent, New England	1	0	0	1	6
Williams, Jamie, Houston	1	0	1	0	6
Wilson, Steve, Denver	1	0	1	0	6
Wonsley, George, Indianapolis	1	1	0	0	6
Woodard, Ken, Denver	1	0	0	1	6
Wright, Felix, Cleveland	1	0	0	1	6
Edwards, David, Pittsburgh	0	0	0	0	*2
Jones, Rulon, Denver	0	0	0	0	*2
Leiding, Jeff, Indianapolis	0	0	0	0	*2
Townsend, Greg, L.A. Raiders	0	0	0	0	*2
White, Leon, Cincinnati	0	0	0	0	*2

**indicates safety scored (also team safeties for Denver, New England, San Diego)*

NFC Scoring—Individual

Kickers	PAT	PAT Att.	FG	FG Att.	TP
Butler, Kevin, Chicago	36	37	28	41	120
Wersching, Ray, San Francisco	41	42	25	35	116
Nelson, Chuck, Minnesota	44	47	22	28	110
Andersen, Morten, New Orleans	30	30	26	30	108
Allegre, Raul, N.Y. Giants	33	33	24	32	105
Septien, Rafael, Dallas	43	43	15	21	88
McFadden, Paul, Philadelphia	26	27	20	31	86
Lansford, Mike, L.A. Rams	34	35	17	24	85
Murray, Ed, Detroit	31	32	18	25	85
Del Greco, Al, Green Bay	29	29	17	27	80
Igwebuike, Donald, Tampa Bay	26	27	17	24	77
Luckhurst, Mick, Atlanta	21	21	14	24	63
Zendejas, Max, Washington	23	28	9	14	50
Lee, John, St. Louis	14	17	8	13	38
Haji-Sheikh, Ali, Atlanta	7	8	9	12	34

	PAT	PAT Att.	FG	FG Att.	TP
Schubert, Eric, St. Louis	9	9	3	11	18
Cooper, Joe, N.Y. Giants	4	4	2	4	10
Cox, Steve, Washington	0	0	3	5	9
Thomas, Bob, N.Y. Giants	4	4	0	1	4
Atkinson, Jess, Washington	3	3	0	0	3
Donnelly, Rick, Atlanta	1	1	0	0	1

Non-Kickers	TD	TDR	TDP	TD Misc.	TP
Rogers, George, Washington	18	18	0	0	108
Rice, Jerry, San Francisco	16	1	15	0	96
Morris, Joe, N.Y. Giants	15	14	1	0	90
Walker, Herschel, Dallas	14	12	2	0	84
Dickerson, Eric, L.A. Rams	11	11	0	0	66
Payton, Walter, Chicago	11	8	3	0	66
Jones, James, Detroit	9	8	1	0	54
Quick, Mike, Philadelphia	9	0	9	0	54
Riggs, Gerald, Atlanta	9	9	0	0	54
Mayes, Rueben, New Orleans	8	8	0	0	48
Bryant, Kelvin, Washington	7	4	3	0	42
Carter, Anthony, Minnesota	7	0	7	0	42
Clark, Gary, Washington	7	0	7	0	42
Craig, Roger, San Francisco	7	7	0	0	42
Nelson, Darrin, Minnesota	7	4	3	0	42
Dorsett, Tony, Dallas	6	5	1	0	36
Green, Roy, St. Louis	6	0	6	0	36
Jackson, Kenny, Philadelphia	6	0	6	0	36
Jordan, Steve, Minnesota	6	0	6	0	36
Smith, J.T., St. Louis	6	0	6	0	36
Chadwick, Jeff, Detroit	5	0	5	0	30
Cribbs, Joe, San Francisco	5	5	0	0	30
Cunningham, Randall, Phil.	5	5	0	0	30
Gault, Willie, Chicago	5	0	5	0	30
Hilliard, Dalton, New Orleans	5	5	0	0	30
Johnson, Bobby, N.Y. Giants	5	0	5	0	30
Magee, Calvin, Tampa Bay	5	0	5	0	30
Martin, Eric, New Orleans	5	0	5	0	30
Mitchell, Stump, St. Louis	5	5	0	0	30
Newsome, Tim, Dallas	5	2	3	0	30
Redden, Barry, L.A. Rams	5	4	1	0	30
Rice, Allen, Minnesota	5	2	3	0	30
Sanders, Thomas, Chicago	5	5	0	0	30
Sherrard, Mike, Dallas	5	0	5	0	30
Thompson, Leonard, Detroit	5	0	5	0	30
Young, Steve, Tampa Bay	5	5	0	0	30
Anderson, Alfred, Minnesota	4	2	2	0	24
Bavaro, Mark, N.Y. Giants	4	0	4	0	24
Brown, Charlie, Atlanta	4	0	4	0	24
Brown, Ted, Minnesota	4	4	0	0	24
Carruth, Paul Ott, Green Bay	4	2	2	0	24
Didier, Clint, Washington	4	0	4	0	24
Ellard, Henry, L.A. Rams	4	0	4	0	24
Epps, Phillip, Green Bay	4	0	4	0	24
Giles, Jimmie, Tampa Bay-Detroit	4	0	4	0	24
Jones, Hassan, Minnesota	4	0	4	0	24
Lofton, James, Green Bay	4	0	4	0	24
Monk, Art, Washington	4	0	4	0	24
Anderson, Ottis, St. Louis-N.Y.G.	3	3	0	0	18
Brown, Ron, L.A. Rams	3	0	3	0	18
Ellerson, Gary, Green Bay	3	3	0	0	18
Ferrell, Earl, St. Louis	3	0	3	0	18
Gentry, Dennis, Chicago	3	1	0	2	18
Hill, Tony, Dallas	3	0	3	0	18
Irvin, LeRoy, L.A. Rams	3	0	0	3	18
James, Garry, Detroit	3	3	0	0	18
Jones, Mike, New Orleans	3	0	3	0	18
Manuel, Lionel, N.Y. Giants	3	0	3	0	18
Renfro, Mike, Dallas	3	0	3	0	18
Rouson, Lee, N.Y. Giants	3	2	1	0	18
Sikahema, Vai, St. Louis	3	0	1	2	18
Stanley, Walter, Green Bay	3	0	2	1	18
Tice, John, New Orleans	3	0	3	0	18
Tomczak, Mike, Chicago	3	3	0	0	18
Whisenhunt, Ken, Atlanta	3	0	3	0	18
Wilder, James, Tampa Bay	3	2	1	0	18
Wonsley, Nathan, Tampa Bay	3	3	0	0	18
Young, Mike, L.A. Rams	3	0	3	0	18
Allen, Anthony, Atlanta	2	0	2	0	12
Bland, Carl, Detroit	2	0	2	0	12
Carter, Gerald, Tampa Bay	2	0	2	0	12
Chandler, Thornton, Dallas	2	0	2	0	12
Clark, Dwight, San Francisco	2	0	2	0	12
Dixon, Floyd, Atlanta	2	0	2	0	12
Ellis, Gerry, Green Bay	2	2	0	0	12
Frank, John, San Francisco	2	0	2	0	12
Franklin, Pat, Tampa Bay	2	0	1	1	12
Freeman, Phil, Tampa Bay	2	0	2	0	12
Goodlow, Eugene, New Orleans	2	0	2	0	12
Gustafson, Jim, Minnesota	2	0	2	0	12
Holmoe, Tom, San Francisco	2	0	0	2	12

	TD	TDR	TDP	TD Misc.	TP
House, Kevin, L.A. Rams	2	0	2	0	12
Lewis, Leo, Minnesota	2	0	2	0	12
Lewis, Mark, Green Bay	2	0	2	0	12
Marshall, Wilber, Chicago	2	0	0	2	12
Miller, Solomon, N.Y. Giants	2	0	2	0	12
Mowatt, Zeke, N.Y. Giants	2	0	2	0	12
Mularkey, Mike, Minnesota	2	0	2	0	12
Ortego, Keith, Chicago	2	0	2	0	12
Robinson, Stacy, N.Y. Giants	2	0	2	0	12
Sanders, Ricky, Washington	2	0	2	0	12
Suhey, Matt, Chicago	2	2	0	0	12
Tautalatasi, Junior, Philadelphia	2	0	2	0	12
Williams, Scott, Detroit	2	2	0	0	12
Anderson, Neal, Chicago	1	0	1	0	6
Andrews, William, Atlanta	1	1	0	0	6
Austin, Cliff, Atlanta	1	1	0	0	6
Barnes, Lew, Chicago	1	0	0	1	6
Britt, James, Atlanta	1	0	0	1	6
Browner, Joey, Minnesota	1	0	0	1	6
Butler, Bobby, Atlanta	1	0	0	1	6
Byars, Keith, Philadelphia	1	1	0	0	6
Carson, Harry, N.Y. Giants	1	0	1	0	6
Cosbie, Doug, Dallas	1	0	1	0	6
Cox, Arthur, Atlanta	1	0	1	0	6
Crawford, Charles, Philadelphia	1	1	0	0	6
Cromwell, Nolan, L.A. Rams	1	0	0	1	6
Davis, Kenneth, Green Bay	1	0	1	0	6
DeBerg, Steve, Tampa Bay	1	1	0	0	6
Doleman, Chris, Minnesota	1	0	0	1	6
Duckworth, Bobby, L.A. Rams	1	0	1	0	6
Everett, Jim, L.A. Rams	1	1	0	0	6
Fellows, Ron, Dallas	1	0	0	1	6
Flutie, Doug, Chicago	1	1	0	0	6
Flynn, Tom, N.Y. Giants	1	0	0	1	6
Fox, Chas, St. Louis	1	0	1	0	6
Francis, Russ, San Francisco	1	0	1	0	6
Garrity, Gregg, Philadelphia	1	0	0	1	6
Gray, Mel, New Orleans	1	0	0	1	6
Griffin, Don, San Francisco	1	0	0	1	6
Harmon, Derrick, San Francisco	1	1	0	0	6
Haynes, James, New Orleans	1	0	0	1	6
Heflin, Vince, Tampa Bay	1	0	0	1	6
Heller, Ron, Tampa Bay	1	0	1	0	6
Hill, David, L.A. Rams	1	0	1	0	6
Holt, Issiac, Minnesota	1	0	0	1	6
Howard, Bobby, Tampa Bay	1	1	0	0	6
Hunter, Herman, Detroit	1	0	1	0	6
Ivery, Eddie Lee, Green Bay	1	0	1	0	6
Jerue, Mark, L.A. Rams	1	0	0	1	6
Johnson, Ron, Philadelphia	1	0	1	0	6
Jordan, Buford, New Orleans	1	1	0	0	6
Kramer, Tommy, Minnesota	1	1	0	0	6
Lavette, Robert, Dallas	1	0	1	0	6
Lewis, David, Detroit	1	0	1	0	6
Lomax, Neil, St. Louis	1	1	0	0	6
Lott, Ronnie, San Francisco	1	0	0	1	6
Mandley, Pete, Detroit	1	0	0	1	6
Manley, Dexter, Washington	1	0	0	1	6
Martin, George, N.Y. Giants	1	0	0	1	6
McConkey, Phil, N.Y. Giants	1	0	1	0	6
McKyer, Tim, San Francisco	1	0	0	1	6
McMahon, Jim, Chicago	1	1	0	0	6
Moorehead, Emery, Chicago	1	0	1	0	6
Moroski, Mike, San Francisco	1	1	0	0	6
Newberry, Tom, L.A. Rams	1	0	0	1	6
Nixon, Tory, San Francisco	1	0	0	1	6
Orr, Terry, Washington	1	0	1	0	6
Pelluer, Steve, Dallas	1	1	0	0	6
Pitts, Mike, Atlanta	1	0	0	1	6
Rathman, Tom, San Francisco	1	1	0	0	6
Ross, Dan, Green Bay	1	0	1	0	6
Schonert, Turk, Atlanta	1	1	0	0	6
Schroeder, Jay, Washington	1	1	0	0	6
Simmons, John, Green Bay	1	0	0	1	6
Simms, Phil, N.Y. Giants	1	1	0	0	6
Spagnola, John, Philadelphia	1	0	1	0	6
Stamps, Sylvester, Atlanta	1	0	1	0	6
Stills, Ken, Green Bay	1	0	0	1	6
Toney, Anthony, Philadelphia	1	1	0	0	6
Warren, Don, Washington	1	0	1	0	6
West, Ed, Green Bay	1	0	1	0	6
White, Danny, Dallas	1	1	0	0	6
Williams, Joel, Atlanta	1	0	0	1	6
Williams, Keith, Atlanta	1	0	1	0	6
Wilson, Dave, New Orleans	1	1	0	0	6
Wilson, Mike, San Francisco	1	0	1	0	6
Wilson, Wade, Minnesota	1	1	0	0	6
Wright, Randy, Green Bay	1	1	0	0	6

	TD	TDR	TDP	TD Misc.	TP
Brown, Greg, Philadelphia	0	0	0	0	*2
Gann, Mike, Atlanta	0	0	0	0	*2
Hampton, Dan, Chicago	0	0	0	0	*2
Jeter, Gary, L.A. Rams	0	0	0	0	*2
McMichael, Steve, Chicago	0	0	0	0	*2

**Indicates safety*

Field Goals

Best Percentage
NFC: .867—Morten Andersen, New Orleans
AFC: .842—Pat Leahy, New York Jets

Made
AFC: 32—Tony Franklin, New England
NFC: 28—Kevin Butler, Chicago

Attempts
AFC: 41—Tony Franklin, New England
NFC: 41—Kevin Butler, Chicago

Longest
NFC: 57—Steve Cox, Washington vs. Seattle, September 28
AFC: 54—Norm Johnson, Seattle vs. San Diego, October 6

Average Yards Made
AFC: 37.7—Dean Biasucci, Indianapolis
NFC: 36.9—Mick Luckhurst, Atlanta

AFC Field Goals—Team

	Made	Att.	Pct.	Long
New York Jets	16	19	.842	50
Houston	22	27	.815	51
Cleveland	26	33	.788	52
New England	32	41	.780	49
Los Angeles Raiders	21	28	.750	52
Kansas City	19	26	.731	47
Denver	20	28	.714	51
Pittsburgh	21	32	.656	45
San Diego	16	25	.640	50
Miami	14	22	.636	52
Buffalo	17	27	.630	48
Seattle	22	35	.629	54
Cincinnati	17	32	.531	51
Indianapolis	13	25	.520	52
AFC Totals	276	400	—	54
AFC Average	19.7	28.6	.690	—

NFC Field Goals—Team

	Made	Att.	Pct.	Long
New Orleans	26	30	.867	53
Minnesota	22	28	.786	53
Detroit	18	25	.720	52
Dallas	15	21	.714	50
San Francisco	25	35	.714	50
Los Angeles Rams	17	24	.708	50
Tampa Bay	17	24	.708	55
New York Giants	26	37	.703	46
Chicago	28	41	.683	52
Philadelphia	20	31	.645	50
Atlanta	23	36	.639	49
Green Bay	17	27	.630	50
Washington	18	32	.563	57
St. Louis	11	24	.458	47
NFC Totals	283	415	—	57
NFC Average	20.2	29.6	.682	—
League Totals	559	815	—	57
League Average	20.0	29.1	.686	—

AFC Field Goals—Individual

	1-19	20-29	30-39	40-49	50 & Over	Totals	Avg. Yds. Att.	Avg. Yds. Made	Avg. Yds. Miss	Long
Leahy, Pat,	1-1	5-5	4-4	5-8	1-1	16-19	36.3	34.8	44.7	50
N.Y. Jets	1.000	1.000	1.000	.625	1.000	.842				
Zendejas, Tony,	1-1	7-7	7-9	6-7	1-3	22-27	36.0	34.0	44.6	51
Houston	1.000	1.000	.778	.857	.333	.815				
Franklin, Tony,	1-1	7-7	15-17	9-16	0-0	32-41	36.7	34.6	44.2	49
New England	1.000	1.000	.882	.563	—	.780				
Bahr, Matt,	4-4	7-9	7-8	1-2	1-3	20-26	31.6	29.2	39.7	52
Cleveland	1.000	.778	.875	.500	.333	.769				
Bahr, Chris,	3-3	6-6	6-9	5-8	1-2	21-28	34.8	32.1	43.0	52
L.A. Raiders	1.000	1.000	.667	.625	.500	.750				
Lowery, Nick,	1-1	5-6	5-5	8-13	0-1	19-26	37.3	34.9	43.6	47
Kansas City	1.000	.833	1.000	.615	.000	.731				
Karlis, Rich,	0-0	3-4	8-8	8-14	1-2	20-28	39.4	37.2	45.0	51
Denver	—	.750	1.000	.571	.500	.714				
Anderson, Gary,	0-1	6-7	6-7	9-14	0-3	21-32	37.1	34.7	41.7	45
Pittsburgh	.000	.857	.857	.643	.000	.656				
Benirschke, Rolf,	1-1	6-9	5-8	3-5	1-2	16-25	32.8	31.8	34.8	50
San Diego	1.000	.667	.625	.600	.500	.640				
Reveiz, Fuad,	1-1	5-5	4-6	3-8	1-2	14-22	37.4	33.1	45.0	52
Miami	1.000	1.000	.667	.375	.500	.636				
Moseley, Mark,	2-2	5-6	4-5	1-6	0-0	12-19	34.3	29.8	42.0	45
Washington-Cleveland	1.000	.833	.800	.167	—	.632				
Norwood, Scott,	1-1	6-6	7-7	3-8	0-5	17-27	38.6	32.2	49.3	48
Buffalo	1.000	1.000	1.000	.375	.000	.630				
Johnson, Norm,	0-0	6-8	8-9	3-11	5-7	22-35	39.2	37.1	42.8	54
Seattle	—	.750	.889	.273	.714	.629				
Breech, Jim,	1-2	4-5	5-7	5-14	2-4	17-32	38.3	35.2	41.8	51
Cincinnati	.500	.800	.714	.357	.500	.531				
Biasucci, Dean,	0-0	4-4	2-5	5-8	2-8	13-25	42.4	37.7	47.4	52
Indianapolis	—	1.000	.400	.625	.250	.520				
AFC Totals	16-18	79-90	92-112	73-137	16-43	276-400	37.0	34.1	43.4	54
	.889	.878	.821	.533	.372	.690				
League Totals	24-26	171-193	193-245	138-258	33-93	559-815	36.9	34.3	40.6	57
	.923	.886	.788	.535	.355	.686				

NFC Field Goals — Individual

	1-19	20-29	30-39	40-49	50 & Over	Totals	Avg. Yds. Att.	Avg. Yds. Made	Avg. Yds. Miss	Long
Andersen, Morten, New Orleans	1-1 1.000	11-11 1.000	6-7 .857	6-6 1.000	2-5 .400	26-30 .867	35.3	33.8	45.5	53
Nelson, Chuck, Minnesota	0-0 —	7-8 .875	9-10 .900	4-7 .571	2-3 .667	22-28 .786	36.8	35.3	42.3	53
Allegre, Raul, N.Y. Giants	0-0 —	10-11 .909	8-8 1.000	6-11 .545	0-2 .000	24-32 .750	35.7	32.7	44.8	46
Murray, Ed, Detroit	2-2 1.000	1-2 .500	7-8 .875	6-8 .750	2-5 .400	18-25 .720	38.6	36.8	43.4	52
Septien, Rafael, Dallas	0-0 —	4-5 .800	6-7 .857	4-7 .571	1-2 .500	15-21 .714	37.3	35.5	42.0	50
Wersching, Ray, San Francisco	0-0 —	6-6 1.000	14-18 .778	4-9 .444	1-2 .500	25-35 .714	36.2	33.9	41.9	50
Igwebuike, Donald, Tampa Bay	0-0 —	5-5 1.000	7-8 .875	3-6 .500	2-5 .400	17-24 .708	39.7	36.4	47.7	55
Lansford, Mike, L.A. Rams	1-1 1.000	5-6 .833	6-9 .667	4-6 .667	1-2 .500	17-24 .708	35.8	34.2	39.4	50
Butler, Kevin, Chicago	1-1 1.000	11-14 .786	9-12 .750	6-8 .750	1-6 .167	28-41 .683	35.1	31.9	42.1	52
McFadden, Paul, Philadelphia	0-0 —	6-6 1.000	10-12 .833	3-10 .300	1-3 .333	20-31 .645	36.5	33.1	42.6	50
Del Greco, Al, Green Bay	0-0 —	8-8 1.000	4-6 .667	3-9 .333	2-4 .500	17-27 .630	37.3	33.4	43.9	50
Luckhurst, Mick, Atlanta	1-1 1.000	1-2 .500	5-7 .714	7-11 .636	0-3 .000	14-24 .583	39.4	36.9	43.0	49
Non-Qualifiers (Fewer than 16 attempts)										
Haji-Sheikh, Ali, Atlanta	1-1 1.000	3-3 1.000	2-4 .500	3-3 1.000	0-1 .000	9-12 .750	34.8	32.8	40.7	47
Zendejas, Max, Washington	0-0 —	5-5 1.000	2-3 .667	2-4 .500	0-2 .000	9-14 .643	35.6	30.2	45.2	42
Lee, John, St. Louis	0-0 —	2-3 .667	5-6 .833	1-4 .250	0-0 —	8-13 .615	36.2	34.9	38.4	47
Cooper, Joe, N.Y. Giants	0-0 —	2-2 1.000	0-1 .000	0-1 .000	0-0 —	2-4 .500	30.8	20.5	41.0	21
Cox, Steve, Washington	0-0 —	0-0 —	0-0 —	1-1 1.000	2-5 .400	3-6 .500	51.8	53.3	50.3	57
Schubert, Eric, St. Louis	0-0 —	2-2 1.000	0-4 .000	1-5 .200	0-0 —	3-11 .273	36.5	31.0	38.6	46
Thomas, Bob, N.Y. Giants	0-0 —	0-0 —	0-1 .000	0-0 —	0-0 —	0-1 .000	36.0	0.0	36.0	0
NFC Totals	8-8 1.000	92-103 .893	101-133 .759	65-121 .537	17-50 .340	283-415 .682	36.8	34.1	42.7	57
League Totals	24-26 .923	171-193 .886	193-245 .788	138-258 .535	33-93 .355	559-815 .686	36.9	34.1	43.0	57

Rushing

Individual Champions
NFC: 1,821—Eric Dickerson, Los Angeles Rams
AFC: 1,481—Curt Warner, Seattle

Attempts
NFC: 404—Eric Dickerson, Los Angeles Rams
AFC: 319—Curt Warner, Seattle

Most Attempts, Game
AFC: 40—Johnny Hector, Jets vs. New England, October 12 (143 yards)
NFC: 38—Eric Dickerson, Los Angeles Rams vs. St. Louis, September 7 (193 yards)

Yards Per Attempt
AFC: 5.3—James Brooks, Cincinnati
NFC: 4.9—Herschel Walker, Dallas

Most Yards, Game
NFC: 207—Eric Dickerson, Los Angeles Rams vs. Tampa Bay, October 5 (30 attempts)
AFC: 192—Curt Warner, Seattle vs. Denver, December 20 (24 attempts)

Longest
NFC: 84—Herschel Walker, Dallas vs. Philadelphia, December 14—(TD)
AFC: 70—Albert Bentley, Indianapolis vs. Los Angeles Raiders, December 21—TD

Touchdowns
NFC: 18—George Rogers, Washington
AFC: 13—Curt Warner, Seattle

Team Leaders, Yards
AFC: BUFFALO: 632, Robb Riddick; CINCINNATI: 1087, James Brooks; CLEVELAND: 665, Kevin Mack; DENVER: 789, Sammy Winder; HOUSTON: 662, Mike Rozier; INDIANAPOLIS: 609, Randy McMillan; KANSAS CITY: 448, Mike Pruitt; LOS ANGELES RAIDERS: 759, Marcus Allen; MIAMI: 830, Lorenzo Hampton; NEW ENGLAND: 427, Craig James; NEW YORK JETS: 856, Freeman McNeil; PITTSBURGH: 910, Earnest Jackson; SAN DIEGO: 442, Gary Anderson; SEATTLE: 1481, Curt Warner.
NFC: ATLANTA: 1327, Gerald Riggs; CHICAGO: 1333, Walter Payton; DALLAS: 748, Tony Dorsett; DETROIT: 903, James Jones; GREEN BAY: 519, Kenneth Davis; LOS ANGELES RAMS: 1821, Eric Dickerson; MINNESOTA: 793, Darrin Nelson; NEW ORLEANS: 1353, Rueben Mayes; NEW YORK GIANTS: 1516, Joe Morris; PHILADELPHIA: 577, Keith Byars; ST. LOUIS: 800, Stump Mitchell; SAN FRANCISCO: 830, Roger Craig; TAMPA BAY: 704, James Wilder; WASHINGTON: 1203, George Rogers.

Team Champions
NFC: 2,700—Chicago
AFC: 2,533—Cincinnati

AFC Rushing—Team

	Att.	Yards	Avg.	Long	TD
Cincinnati	521	2533	4.9	61t	24
Seattle	513	2300	4.5	60t	15
Pittsburgh	564	2223	3.9	45	18
Los Angeles Raiders	475	1790	3.8	28t	6
New York Jets	490	1729	3.5	41	16
Houston	490	1700	3.5	43t	13
Denver	455	1678	3.7	42	17
Buffalo	419	1654	3.9	42	9
Cleveland	470	1650	3.5	47	20
San Diego	471	1576	3.3	24	19
Miami	349	1545	4.4	54t	9
Indianapolis	407	1491	3.7	70t	10
Kansas City	432	1468	3.4	40	10
New England	469	1373	2.9	31	10
AFC Total	6525	24,710	—	70t	196
AFC Average	466.1	1,765.0	3.8	—	14.0

NFC Rushing—Team

	Att.	Yards	Avg.	Long	TD
Chicago	606	2700	4.5	75t	21
Atlanta	578	2524	4.4	48	12
Los Angeles Rams	578	2457	4.3	42t	16
New York Giants	558	2245	4.0	54	18
New Orleans	505	2074	4.1	50	15
Philadelphia	499	2002	4.0	50	8
San Francisco	510	1986	3.9	29t	16
Dallas	447	1969	4.4	84t	21
Tampa Bay	455	1863	4.1	59t	12
St. Louis	419	1787	4.3	44	8
Detroit	470	1771	3.8	60t	13
Minnesota	461	1738	3.8	60	14
Washington	474	1732	3.7	42	23
Green Bay	424	1614	3.8	50	8
NFC Total	6,984	28,462	—	84t	205
NFC Average	498.9	2033.0	4.1	—	14.6
League Total	13,509	53,172	—	84t	401
League Average	482.5	1899.0	3.9	—	14.3

NFL Top 10 Rushers

	Att.	Yards	Avg.	Long	TD
Dickerson, Eric, L.A. Rams	404	1821	4.5	42t	11
Morris, Joe, N.Y. Giants	341	1516	4.4	54	14
Warner, Curt, Seattle	319	1481	4.6	60t	13
Mayes, Rueben, New Orleans	286	1353	4.7	50	8
Payton, Walter, Chicago	321	1333	4.2	41	8
Riggs, Gerald, Atlanta	343	1327	3.9	31	9
Rogers, George, Washington	303	1203	4.0	42	18
Brooks, James, Cincinnati	205	1087	5.3	56t	5
Jackson, Earnest, Pittsburgh	216	910	4.2	31	5
Jones, James, Detroit	252	903	3.6	39	8

AFC Rushing—Individual

	Att.	Yards	Avg.	Long	TD
Warner, Curt, Seattle	319	1481	4.6	60t	13
Brooks, James, Cincinnati	205	1087	5.3	56t	5
Jackson, Earnest, Pittsburgh	216	910	4.2	31	5
Abercrombie, Walter, Pittsburgh	214	877	4.1	38t	6
McNeil, Freeman, N.Y. Jets	214	856	4.0	40	5
Hampton, Lorenzo, Miami	186	830	4.5	54t	9
Winder, Sammy, Denver	240	789	3.3	31	9
Allen, Marcus, L.A. Raiders	208	759	3.6	28t	5
Mack, Kevin, Cleveland	174	665	3.8	20	10
Rozier, Mike, Houston	199	662	3.3	19t	4
Riddick, Robb, Buffalo	150	632	4.2	41t	4
McMillan, Randy, Indianapolis	189	609	3.2	28	3
Hector, Johnny, N.Y. Jets	164	605	3.7	41	8
Williams, John L., Seattle	129	538	4.2	36	0
McCallum, Napoleon, L.A. Raid.	142	536	3.8	18	1
Dickey, Curtis, Cleveland	135	523	3.9	47	6
Kinnebrew, Larry, Cincinnati	131	519	4.0	39	8
Pruitt, Mike, Kansas City	139	448	3.2	16	2
Anderson, Gary, San Diego	127	442	3.5	17	1
James, Craig, New England	154	427	2.8	16	4
Collins, Tony, New England	156	412	2.6	17	3
Wilson, Stanley, Cincinnati	68	379	5.6	58t	8
Bell, Greg, Buffalo	90	377	4.2	42	4
Adams, Curtis, San Diego	118	366	3.1	22	4
Willhite, Gerald, Denver	85	365	4.3	42	5
Bentley, Albert, Indianapolis	73	351	4.8	70t	3
Spencer, Tim, San Diego	99	350	3.5	23	6
Davenport, Ron, Miami	75	314	4.2	35	0
Green, Boyce, Kansas City	90	314	3.5	27	3
Heard, Herman, Kansas City	71	295	4.2	40	2
Byner, Earnest, Cleveland	94	277	2.9	37	2
Elway, John, Denver	52	257	4.9	24	1
Moriarty, Larry, Houston-K.C.	90	252	2.8	11	1
Hawkins, Frank, L.A. Raiders	58	245	4.2	15	0
Smith, Jeff, Kansas City	54	238	4.4	32t	3
Gill, Owen, Indianapolis	53	228	4.3	18	1
Johnson, Bill, Cincinnati	39	226	5.8	34	0
Pinkett, Allen, Houston	77	225	2.9	14	2
James, Lionel, San Diego	51	224	4.4	24	0
Wallace, Ray, Houston	52	218	4.2	19	3
Wonsley, George, Indianapolis	60	214	3.6	46	1
Nathan, Tony, Miami	27	203	7.5	20	0
Kelly, Jim, Buffalo	41	199	4.9	20	0
McGee, Buford, San Diego	63	187	3.0	20	7
Harmon, Ronnie, Buffalo	54	172	3.2	38	0
Tatupu, Mosi, New England	71	172	2.4	13	1
Eason, Tony, New England	35	170	4.9	26	0
Erenberg, Rich, Pittsburgh	42	170	4.0	17	1
Bennett, Woody, Miami	36	162	4.5	16	0
Moon, Warren, Houston	42	157	3.7	19	2
Byrum, Carl, Buffalo	38	156	4.1	18	0
Morris, Randall, Seattle	19	149	7.8	49t	1
Givins, Earnest, Houston	9	148	16.4	43t	1
Esiason, Boomer, Cincinnati	44	146	3.3	23	1
Sewell, Steve, Denver	23	123	5.3	15	1
Krieg, Dave, Seattle	35	122	3.5	19	1
Paige, Tony, N.Y. Jets	47	109	2.3	9	2
Malone, Mark, Pittsburgh	31	107	3.5	45	5
Fontenot, Herman, Cleveland	25	105	4.2	16	1
Moore, Ricky, Buffalo	33	104	3.2	14	1
Lang, Gene, Denver	29	94	3.2	14	1
Hayes, Jeff, Cincinnati	3	92	30.7	61t	1
Pollard, Frank, Pittsburgh	24	86	3.6	12	0
Banks, Chuck, Houston	29	80	2.8	9	0
Fryar, Irving, New England	4	80	20.0	31	0
Bligen, Dennis, N.Y. Jets	20	65	3.3	10	1
Blackledge, Todd, Kansas City	23	60	2.6	14	0
Weathers, Robert, New England	21	58	2.8	16t	1
Woolfolk, Butch, Houston	23	57	2.5	15	0
Jennings, Stanford, Cincinnati	16	54	3.4	10	1
Strachan, Steve, L.A. Raiders	18	53	2.9	10	0
Hilger, Rusty, L.A. Raiders	6	48	8.0	16	0
Plunkett, Jim, L.A. Raiders	12	47	3.9	11	0
O'Brien, Ken, N.Y. Jets	17	46	2.7	11	0
Wilson, Marc, L.A. Raiders	14	45	3.2	13	0
Everett, Major, Cleveland	12	43	3.6	8	0
Dupard, Reggie, New England	15	39	2.6	11	0
Clayton, Mark, Miami	2	33	16.5	22	0
Brown, Eddie, Cincinnati	8	32	4.0	17	0
Hughes, David, Pittsburgh	14	32	2.3	8	0
Mueller, Vance, L.A. Raiders	13	30	2.3	8	0
Ryan, Pat, N.Y. Jets	8	28	3.5	18	0
Barber, Marion, N.Y. Jets	11	27	2.5	8	0
Williams, Dokie, L.A. Raiders	3	27	9.0	19	0
Grogan, Steve, New England	9	23	2.6	10	1
Kubiak, Gary, Denver	6	22	3.7	10	0
Trudeau, Jack, Indianapolis	13	21	1.6	8	1
Hogeboom, Gary, Indianapolis	10	20	2.0	6	1
Kiel, Blair, Indianapolis	3	20	6.7	9	0
Reeder, Dan, Pittsburgh	6	20	3.3	6	0
Kosar, Bernie, Cleveland	24	19	0.8	17	0
Carter, Joe, Miami	4	18	4.5	9	0
Wilkins, Gary, Buffalo	3	18	6.0	11	0
Bell, Ken, Denver	9	17	1.9	12	0
Holt, Harry, Cleveland	1	16	16.0	16t	1
Johnson, Vance, Denver	5	15	3.0	6	0
Bouza, Matt, Indianapolis	1	12	12.0	12	0
Luck, Oliver, Houston	2	12	6.0	8	0
McNeil, Gerald, Cleveland	1	12	12.0	12	0
Sanders, Chuck, Pittsburgh	4	12	3.0	13	0
Capers, Wayne, Indianapolis	1	11	11.0	11	0
Lane, Eric, Seattle	6	11	1.8	4	0
Brister, Bubby, Pittsburgh	6	10	1.7	9	1
King, Bruce, Buffalo	4	10	2.5	7	0
McGee, Tim, Cincinnati	4	10	2.5	8	0
Gilbert, Gale, Seattle	3	8	2.7	12	0
Ellis, Craig, Miami	3	6	2.0	2	0
Herrmann, Mark, San Diego	2	6	3.0	6	0
Jackson, Mark, Denver	2	6	3.0	5	0
Brooks, Bill, Indianapolis	4	5	1.3	12	0
Faaola, Nuu, N.Y. Jets	3	5	1.7	2	0
Flick, Tom, San Diego	6	5	0.8	7	1
Hawthorne, Greg, New England	1	5	5.0	5	0
Gaynor, Doug, Cincinnati	1	4	4.0	4	0
Edwards, Stan, Houston	1	3	3.0	3	0
Boddie, Tony, Denver	1	2	2.0	2	0
Franklin, Byron, Seattle	1	2	2.0	2	0
Seitz, Warren, Pittsburgh	3	2	0.7	2	0
Townsell, JoJo, N.Y. Jets	1	2	2.0	2	0
Oliver, Hubert, Houston	1	1	1.0	1	0
Slaughter, Webster, Cleveland	1	1	1.0	1	0
Guy, Ray, L.A. Raiders	1	0	0.0	0	0
Horan, Mike, Denver	1	0	0.0	0	0
Jennings, Dave, N.Y. Jets	1	0	0.0	0	0
Kenney, Bill, Kansas City	18	0	0.0	9	0
Kidd, John, Buffalo	1	0	0.0	0	0
Pagel, Mike, Cleveland	2	0	0.0	0	0
Reich, Frank, Buffalo	1	0	0.0	0	0
Starring, Stephen, New England	1	0	0.0	0	0
Strock, Don, Miami	1	0	0.0	0	0
Mathison, Bruce, San Diego	1	−1	−1.0	−1	0
Mobley, Orson, Denver	1	−1	−1.0	−1	0
Paige, Stephone, Kansas City	2	−2	−1.0	12	0
Fouts, Dan, San Diego	4	−3	−0.8	0	0
Lipps, Louis, Pittsburgh	4	−3	−0.8	8	0
Marino, Dan, Miami	12	−3	−0.3	13	0
Toon, Al, N.Y. Jets	2	−3	−1.5	2	0
Broughton, Walter, Buffalo	1	−6	−6.0	−6	0
Ramsey, Tom, New England	1	−6	−6.0	−6	0
Jones, Cedric, New England	1	−7	−7.0	−7	0
Reed, Andre, Buffalo	3	−8	−2.7	4	0
Roby, Reggie, Miami	2	−8	−4.0	0	0
Duper, Mark, Miami	1	−10	−10.0	−10	0
Edmonds, Bobby Joe, Seattle	1	−11	−11.0	−11	0
Langhorne, Reggie, Cleveland	1	−11	−11.0	−11	0
Norman, Chris, Denver	1	−11	−11.0	−11	0
Sohn, Kurt, N.Y. Jets	2	−11	−5.5	−3	0
Collinsworth, Cris, Cincinnati	2	−16	−8.0	−6	0

t indicates touchdown
Leader based on most yards gained.

NFC Rushing—Individual

	Att.	Yards	Avg.	Long	TD
Dickerson, Eric, L.A. Rams	404	1821	4.5	42t	11
Morris, Joe, N.Y. Giants	341	1516	4.4	54	14
Mayes, Rueben, New Orleans	286	1353	4.7	50	8
Payton, Walter, Chicago	321	1333	4.2	41	8
Riggs, Gerald, Atlanta	343	1327	3.9	31	9
Rogers, George, Washington	303	1203	4.0	42	18
Jones, James, Detroit	252	903	3.6	39	8
Craig, Roger, San Francisco	204	830	4.1	25	7

	Att.	Yards	Avg.	Long	TD
Mitchell, Stump, St. Louis	174	800	4.6	44	5
Nelson, Darrin, Minnesota	191	793	4.2	42	4
Dorsett, Tony, Dallas	184	748	4.1	33	5
Walker, Herschel, Dallas	151	737	4.9	84t	12
Wilder, James, Tampa Bay	190	704	3.7	45t	2
James, Garry, Detroit	159	688	4.3	60t	3
Cribbs, Joe, San Francisco	152	590	3.9	19	5
Byars, Keith, Philadelphia	177	577	3.3	32	1
Ferrell, Earl, St. Louis	124	548	4.4	25	0
Cunningham, Randall, Phil.	66	540	8.2	20	5
Davis, Kenneth, Green Bay	114	519	4.6	50	0
Redden, Barry, L.A. Rams	110	467	4.2	41t	4
Hilliard, Dalton, New Orleans	121	425	3.5	36	5
Young, Steve, Tampa Bay	74	425	5.7	31	5
Anderson, Alfred, Minnesota	83	347	4.2	29	2
Ellis, Gerry, Green Bay	84	345	4.1	24	2
Wonsley, Nathan, Tampa Bay	73	339	4.6	59t	3
Carruth, Paul Ott, Green Bay	81	308	3.8	42	2
Archer, Dave, Atlanta	52	298	5.7	22	0
Ellerson, Gary, Green Bay	90	287	3.2	18	3
Springs, Ron, Tampa Bay	74	285	3.9	40	0
Toney, Anthony, Philadelphia	69	285	4.1	43	1
Austin, Cliff, Atlanta	62	280	4.5	22	1
Haddix, Michael, Philadelphia	79	276	3.5	18	0
Suhey, Matt, Chicago	84	270	3.2	17	2
Carthon, Maurice, N.Y. Giants	72	260	3.6	12	0
Bryant, Kelvin, Washington	69	258	3.7	22t	4
Pelluer, Steve, Dallas	41	255	6.2	21	1
Brown, Ted, Minnesota	63	251	4.0	60	4
Anderson, Ottis, St. Louis-N.Y.G.	75	237	3.2	16	3
Sanders, Thomas, Chicago	27	224	8.3	75t	5
Thomas, Calvin, Chicago	56	224	4.0	23	0
Rice, Allen, Minnesota	73	220	3.0	19	2
Stamps, Sylvester, Atlanta	30	220	7.3	48	0
Andrews, William, Atlanta	52	214	4.1	13	1
Jordan, Buford, New Orleans	68	207	3.0	10	1
Griffin, Keith, Washington	62	197	3.2	12	0
Rouson, Lee, N.Y. Giants	54	179	3.3	21t	2
Tautalatasi, Junior, Philadelphia	51	163	3.2	50	0
McMahon, Jim, Chicago	22	152	6.9	23	1
Lomax, Neil, St. Louis	35	148	4.2	18	1
Anderson, Neal, Chicago	35	146	4.2	23	0
Rathman, Tom, San Francisco	33	138	4.2	29t	1
Tyler, Wendell, San Francisco	31	127	4.1	14	0
White, Charles, L.A. Rams	22	126	5.7	19	0
Tomczak, Mike, Chicago	23	117	5.1	16	3
Howard, Bobby, Tampa Bay	30	110	3.7	16	1
Newsome, Tim, Dallas	34	110	3.2	13	2
Gentry, Dennis, Chicago	11	103	9.4	29	1
Crawford, Charles, Philadelphia	28	88	3.1	15	1
Gault, Willie, Chicago	8	79	9.9	33	0
Harmon, Derrick, San Francisco	27	77	2.9	15	1
Moore, Alvin, Detroit	19	73	3.8	18	0
Rice, Jerry, San Francisco	10	72	7.2	18	1
Simms, Phil, N.Y. Giants	43	72	1.7	18	1
Dixon, Floyd, Atlanta	11	67	6.1	23	0
Sikahema, Vai, St. Louis	16	62	3.9	23	0
Galbreath, Tony, N.Y. Giants	16	61	3.8	10	0
Collier, Reggie, Dallas	6	53	8.8	21	0
Stoudt, Cliff, St. Louis	7	53	7.6	17	0
Kemp, Jeff, San Francisco	15	49	3.3	12	0
Kramer, Tommy, Minnesota	23	48	2.1	13	1
Schroeder, Jay, Washington	36	47	1.3	20	1
Coleman, Greg, Minnesota	2	46	23.0	30	0
Everett, Jim, L.A. Rams	16	46	2.9	14	1
Hipple, Eric, Detroit	16	46	2.9	13	0
Cherry, Tony, San Francisco	11	42	3.8	10	0
Clark, Jessie, Green Bay	18	41	2.3	9	0
Wright, Randy, Green Bay	18	41	2.3	18	1
Montana, Joe, San Francisco	17	38	2.2	17	0
Flutie, Doug, Chicago	9	36	4.0	19	1
Jaworski, Ron, Philadelphia	13	33	2.5	10	0
Fuller, Steve, Chicago	8	30	3.8	10	0
Gray, Mel, New Orleans	6	29	4.8	11	0
Johnson, Bobby, N.Y. Giants	2	28	14.0	22	0
Monk, Art, Washington	4	27	6.8	21	0
Cavanaugh, Matt, Philadelphia	9	26	2.9	11	0
Ferguson, Joe, Detroit	5	25	5.0	14	0
Ivery, Eddie Lee, Green Bay	4	25	6.3	15	0
Johnson, Billy, Atlanta	6	25	4.2	10	0
Manuel, Lionel, N.Y. Giants	1	25	25.0	25	0
Hunter, Herman, Detroit	3	22	7.3	18	0
Moroski, Mike, San Francisco	6	22	3.7	12	1
Williams, Scott, Detroit	13	22	1.7	5	2
Whisenhunt, Ken, Atlanta	1	20	20.0	20	0
Clack, Darryl, Dallas	4	19	4.8	8	0
Rutledge, Jeff, N.Y. Giants	3	19	6.3	18	0
Stanley, Walter, Green Bay	1	19	19.0	19	0
Wilson, Dave, New Orleans	14	19	1.4	14	1
Wilson, Wayne, Minnesota-N.O.	10	19	1.9	6	0
Wolfley, Ron, St. Louis	8	19	2.4	8	0
Epps, Phillip, Green Bay	4	18	4.5	20	0
Williams, Keith, Atlanta	3	18	6.0	8	0
Del Rio, Jack, New Orleans	1	16	16.0	16	0
White, Danny, Dallas	8	16	2.0	10	1
Hebert, Bobby, New Orleans	5	14	2.8	7	0
Jones, Hassan, Minnesota	1	14	14.0	14	0
Carter, Anthony, Minnesota	1	12	12.0	12	0
Matthews, Aubrey, Atlanta	1	12	12.0	12	0
Schonert, Turk, Atlanta	11	12	1.1	7	1
Fusina, Chuck, Green Bay	7	11	1.6	6	0
Sherrard, Mike, Dallas	2	11	5.5	8	0
Cosbie, Doug, Dallas	1	9	9.0	9	0
Wilson, Wade, Minnesota	13	9	0.7	13	1
Clark, Bret, Atlanta	2	8	4.0	6	0
Waters, Mike, Philadelphia	5	8	1.6	5	0
Campbell, Scott, Pitt.-Atlanta	1	7	7.0	7	0
Franklin, Pat, Tampa Bay	7	7	1.0	4	0
Jones, Joey, Atlanta	1	7	7.0	7	0
Bailey, Stacey, Atlanta	1	6	6.0	6	0
Edwards, Kelvin, New Orleans	1	6	6.0	6	0
Jackson, Kenny, Philadelphia	1	6	6.0	6	0
Lavette, Robert, Dallas	10	6	0.6	5	0
Brown, Ron, L.A. Rams	4	5	1.3	11	0
Dils, Steve, L.A. Rams	10	5	0.5	5	0
Fowler, Todd, Dallas	6	5	0.8	2	0
House, Kevin, Tampa Bay	2	5	2.5	4	0
Marsh, Doug, St. Louis	1	5	5.0	5	0
Ring, Bill, San Francisco	3	4	1.3	4	0
Allen, Greg, Tampa Bay	1	3	3.0	3	0
Baker, Tony, Atlanta	1	3	3.0	3	0
Bartkowski, Steve, L.A. Rams	6	3	0.5	7	0
Carpenter, Rob, L.A. Rams	2	3	1.5	3	0
Miller, Solomon, N.Y. Giants	1	3	3.0	3	0
Guman, Mike, L.A. Rams	2	2	1.0	3	0
DeBerg, Steve, Tampa Bay	2	1	0.5	1t	1
Hostetler, Jeff, N.Y. Giants	1	1	1.0	1	0
Austin, Kent, St. Louis	1	0	0.0	0	0
Ferragamo, Vince, Green Bay	1	0	0.0	0	0
Hansen, Brian, New Orleans	1	0	0.0	0	0
Long, Chuck, Detroit	2	0	0.0	0	0
Renner, Bill, Green Bay	1	0	0.0	0	0
Swanke, Karl, Green Bay	1	0	0.0	0	0
Teltschik, John, Philadelphia	1	0	0.0	0	0
Perry, William, Chicago	1	−1	−1.0	−1	0
Frank, John, San Francisco	1	−3	−3.0	−3	0
Green, Roy, St. Louis	2	−4	−2.0	1	0
Carter, Gerald, Tampa Bay	1	−5	−5.0	−5	0
Hunter, Tony, L.A. Rams	1	−6	−6.0	−6	0
Black, Mike, Detroit	1	−8	−8.0	−8	0
Garcia, Frank, Tampa Bay	1	−11	−11.0	−11	0
Buford, Maury, Chicago	1	−13	−13.0	−13	0
Ellard, Henry, L.A. Rams	1	−15	−15.0	−15	0
Lewis, Leo, Minnesota	3	−16	−5.3	−2	0

t indicates touchdown
Leader based on most yards gained.

Passing

Individual Champions (Rating Points)
NFC: 92.6—Tommy Kramer, Minnesota
AFC: 92.5—Dan Marino, Miami

Attempts
AFC: 623—Dan Marino, Miami
NFC: 541—Jay Schroeder, Washington

Completions
AFC: 378—Dan Marino, Miami
NFC: 276—Jay Schroeder, Washington

Completion Percentage
NFC: 63.0—Eric Hipple, Detroit
AFC: 62.2—Ken O'Brien, New York Jets

Yards
AFC: 4,746—Dan Marino, Miami
NFC: 4,109—Jay Schroeder, Washington

Most Yards, Game
NFC: 490—Tommy Kramer, Minnesota vs. Washington, November 2 [OT] (35 attempts, 20 completions)
AFC: 479—Ken O'Brien, New York Jets vs. Miami, September 21 [OT] (43 attempts, 29 completions)

Yards Per Attempt
AFC: 8.44—Boomer Esiason, Cincinnati
NFC: 8.06—Tommy Kramer, Minnesota

Touchdown Passes
AFC: 44—Dan Marino, Miami
NFC: 24—Tommy Kramer, Minnesota

Most Touchdowns, Game
AFC: 6—Dan Marino, Miami vs. New York Jets, September 21 [OT]
NFC: 6—Tommy Kramer, Minnesota vs. Green Bay, September 28

Longest
AFC: 85—Dan Marino (to Mark Duper), Miami vs. Houston, November 2 (TD)
NFC: 85—Mike Tomczak (to Emery Moorehead), Chicago vs. Atlanta, November 16

Lowest Interception Percentage
AFC: 1.9—Bernie Kosar, Cleveland
NFC: 2.4—Ron Jaworski, Philadelphia

Team Champions
AFC: 4,779—Miami
NFC: 4,096—San Francisco

AFC Passing—Team

	Att.	Comp.	Pct. Comp.	Gross Yards	Tkd.	Yards Lost	Net Yards	TD	Pct. TD	Long	Int.	Pct. Int.	Avg. Yds. Att.	Avg. Yds. Comp.
Miami	645	392	60.8	4898	17	119	4779	46	7.1	85t	23	3.6	7.59	12.49
Cincinnati	497	287	57.7	4160	28	203	3957	25	5.0	57	20	4.0	8.37	14.49
New England	557	340	61.0	4321	47	367	3954	29	5.2	69t	13	2.3	7.76	12.71
San Diego	604	339	56.1	4045	32	265	3780	21	3.5	65t	33	5.5	6.70	11.93
Cleveland	538	315	58.6	4018	39	274	3744	18	3.3	72t	11	2.0	7.47	12.76
New York Jets	537	334	62.2	4032	45	386	3646	27	5.0	83t	21	3.9	7.51	12.07
Denver	549	306	55.7	3811	38	273	3538	22	4.0	53	16	2.9	6.94	12.45
Los Angeles Raiders	530	281	53.0	3973	64	464	3509	27	5.1	81t	25	4.7	7.50	14.14
Houston	551	288	52.3	3843	48	394	3449	14	2.5	81t	31	5.6	6.97	13.34
Buffalo	499	294	58.9	3697	45	334	3363	22	4.4	84t	19	3.8	7.41	12.57
Indianapolis	586	300	51.2	3615	53	406	3209	16	2.7	84t	24	4.1	6.17	12.05
Seattle	453	268	59.2	3424	39	315	3109	24	5.3	72t	14	3.1	7.56	12.78
Kansas City	521	257	49.3	3122	50	372	2750	23	4.4	70t	18	3.5	5.99	12.15
Pittsburgh	491	238	48.5	2747	20	159	2588	16	3.3	58	20	4.1	5.59	11.54
AFC Total	7,558	4,239	—	53,706	565	4,331	49,375	330	—	85t	288	—	—	—
AFC Average	539.9	302.8	56.1	3,836.1	40.4	309.4	3,526.8	23.6	4.4	—	20.6	3.8	7.11	12.67

NFC Passing—Team

	Att.	Comp.	Pct. Comp.	Gross Yards	Tkd.	Yards Lost	Net Yards	TD	Pct. TD	Long	Int.	Pct. Int.	Avg. Yds. Att.	Avg. Yds. Comp.
San Francisco	582	353	60.7	4299	26	203	4096	21	3.6	66t	20	3.4	7.39	12.18
Minnesota	519	290	55.9	4185	44	272	3913	31	6.0	76t	15	2.9	8.06	14.43
Washington	542	276	50.9	4109	28	240	3869	22	4.1	71t	22	4.1	7.58	14.89
Dallas	547	319	58.3	4003	60	498	3505	21	3.8	84t	24	4.4	7.32	12.55
Green Bay	565	305	54.0	3708	37	261	3447	18	3.2	62	27	4.8	6.56	12.16
New York Giants	472	260	55.1	3500	46	367	3133	22	4.7	49	22	4.7	7.42	13.46
Detroit	500	286	57.2	3107	39	323	2784	18	3.6	73	20	4.0	6.21	10.86
Chicago	415	208	50.1	2912	24	153	2759	12	2.9	85	25	6.0	7.02	14.00
St. Louis	516	293	56.8	3140	59	424	2716	17	3.3	48t	19	3.7	6.09	10.72
New Orleans	425	232	54.6	2893	27	225	2668	13	3.1	84	25	5.9	6.81	12.47
Atlanta	452	246	54.4	3046	56	464	2582	14	3.1	65	17	3.8	6.74	12.38
Philadelphia	514	268	52.1	3248	104	708	2540	19	3.7	75t	17	3.3	6.32	12.12
Tampa Bay	459	245	53.4	2892	56	394	2498	13	2.8	46	25	5.4	6.30	11.80
Los Angeles Rams	403	194	48.1	2380	27	184	2196	15	3.7	65t	15	3.7	5.91	12.27
NFC Total	6,911	3,775	—	47,422	633	4,716	42,706	256	—	85	293	—	—	—
NFC Average	493.6	269.6	54.6	3,387.3	45.2	336.9	3,050.4	18.3	3.7	—	20.9	4.2	6.86	12.56
League Total	14,469	8,014	—	101,128	1,198	9,047	92,081	586	—	85t	581	—	—	—
League Average	516.8	286.2	55.4	3,611.7	42.8	323.1	3,288.6	20.9	4.1	—	20.8	4.0	6.99	12.62

Leader based on net yards.

NFL Top 10 Individual Qualifiers

	Att.	Comp.	Pct. Comp.	Yards	Avg. Gain	TD	Pct. TD	Long	Int.	Pct. Int.	Rating Points
Kramer, Tommy, Minnesota	372	208	55.9	3000	8.06	24	6.5	76t	10	2.7	92.6
Marino, Dan, Miami	623	378	60.7	4746	7.62	44	7.1	85t	23	3.7	92.5
Krieg, Dave, Seattle	375	225	60.0	2921	7.79	21	5.6	72t	11	2.9	91.0
Eason, Tony, New England	448	276	61.6	3328	7.43	19	4.2	49	10	2.2	89.2
Esiason, Boomer, Cincinnati	469	273	58.2	3959	8.44	24	5.1	57	17	3.6	87.7
O'Brien, Ken, N.Y. Jets	482	300	62.2	3690	7.66	25	5.2	83t	20	4.1	85.8
Kosar, Bernie, Cleveland	531	310	58.4	3854	7.26	17	3.2	72t	10	1.9	83.8
Kelly, Jim, Buffalo	480	285	59.4	3593	7.49	22	4.6	84t	17	3.5	83.3
Plunkett, Jim, L.A. Raiders	252	133	52.8	1986	7.88	14	5.6	81t	9	3.6	82.5
Montana, Joe, San Francisco	307	191	62.2	2236	7.28	8	2.6	48	9	2.9	80.7

AFC Passing—Individual Qualifiers

	Att.	Comp.	Pct. Comp.	Yards	Avg. Gain	TD	Pct. TD	Long	Int.	Pct. Int.	Rating Points
Marino, Dan, Miami	623	378	60.7	4746	7.62	44	7.1	85t	23	3.7	92.5
Krieg, Dave, Seattle	375	225	60.0	2921	7.79	21	5.6	72	11	2.9	91.0
Eason, Tony, New England	448	276	61.6	3328	7.43	19	4.2	49	10	2.2	89.2
Esiason, Boomer, Cincinnati	469	273	58.2	3959	8.44	24	5.1	57	17	3.6	87.7
O'Brien, Ken, N.Y. Jets	482	300	62.2	3690	7.66	25	5.2	83t	20	4.1	85.8
Kosar, Bernie, Cleveland	531	310	58.4	3854	7.26	17	3.2	72t	10	1.9	83.8
Kelly, Jim, Buffalo	480	285	59.4	3593	7.49	22	4.6	84t	17	3.5	83.3
Plunkett, Jim, L.A. Raiders	252	133	52.8	1986	7.88	14	5.6	81t	9	3.6	82.5

	Att.	Comp.	Pct. Comp.	Yards	Avg. Gain	TD	Pct. TD	Long	Int.	Pct. Int.	Rating Points
Elway, John, Denver	504	280	55.6	3485	6.91	19	3.8	53	13	2.6	79.0
Fouts, Dan, San Diego	430	252	58.6	3031	7.05	16	3.7	65t	22	5.1	71.4
Kenney, Bill, Kansas City	308	161	52.3	1922	6.24	13	4.2	53	11	3.6	70.8
Wilson, Marc, L.A. Raiders	240	129	53.8	1721	7.17	12	5.0	57t	15	6.3	67.4
Malone, Mark, Pittsburgh	425	216	50.8	2444	5.75	15	3.5	48	18	4.2	62.5
Moon, Warren, Houston	488	256	52.5	3489	7.15	13	2.7	81t	26	5.3	62.3
Trudeau, Jack, Indianapolis	417	204	48.9	2225	5.34	8	1.9	84t	18	4.3	53.5

Non-Qualifiers	Att.	Comp.	Pct. Comp.	Yards	Avg. Gain	TD	Pct. TD	Long	Int.	Pct. Int.	Rating Points
Strock, Don, Miami	20	14	70.0	152	7.60	2	10.0	21	0	0.0	125.4
Grogan, Steve, New England	102	62	60.8	976	9.57	9	8.8	69t	2	2.0	113.8
Kiel, Blair, Indianapolis	25	11	44.0	236	9.44	2	8.0	50	0	0.0	104.8
Ryan, Pat, N.Y. Jets	55	34	61.8	342	6.22	2	3.6	36	1	1.8	84.1
Hogeboom, Gary, Indianapolis	144	85	59.0	1154	8.01	6	4.2	60	6	4.2	81.2
Gilbert, Gale, Seattle	76	42	55.3	485	6.38	3	3.9	38t	3	3.9	71.4
Hilger, Rusty, L.A. Raiders	38	19	50.0	266	7.00	1	2.6	54	1	2.6	70.7
Blackledge, Todd, Kansas City	211	96	45.5	1200	5.69	10	4.7	70t	6	2.8	67.6
Herrmann, Mark, San Diego	97	51	52.6	627	6.46	2	2.1	28	3	3.1	66.8
Kubiak, Gary, Denver	38	23	60.5	249	6.55	1	2.6	26	3	7.9	55.7
Anderson, Ken, Cincinnati	23	11	47.8	171	7.43	1	4.3	43	2	8.7	51.2
Luck, Oliver, Houston	60	31	51.7	341	5.68	1	1.7	27	5	8.3	39.7
Brister, Bubby, Pittsburgh	60	21	35.0	291	4.85	0	0.0	58	2	3.3	37.6
Flick, Tom, San Diego	73	33	45.2	361	4.95	2	2.7	26	8	11.0	29.9
Reich, Frank, Buffalo	19	9	47.4	104	5.47	0	0.0	37	2	10.5	24.8
Less than 10 attempts											
Anderson, Gary, San Diego	1	1	100.0	4	4.00	1	100.0	4t	0	0.0	122.9
Bentley, Albert, Indianapolis	0	0	—	0	—	0	—	0	0	—	0.0
Brennan, Brian, Cleveland	1	1	100.0	35	35.00	0	0.0	35	0	0.0	118.8
Brooks, James, Cincinnati	1	0	0.0	0	0.0	0	0.0	0	0	0.0	39.6
Fontenot, Herman, Cleveland	1	1	100.0	46	46.00	1	100.0	46t	0	0.0	158.3
Gaynor, Doug, Cincinnati	3	3	100.0	30	10.00	0	0.0	16	0	0.0	108.3
Givens, Earnest, Houston	2	0	0.0	0	0.00	0	0.0	0	0	0.0	39.6
Gossett, Jeff, Cleveland	2	1	50.0	30	15.00	0	0.0	30	1	50.0	56.3
Green, Boyce, Kansas City	1	0	0.0	0	0.00	0	0.0	0	1	100.0	0.0
Holohan, Pete, San Diego	2	1	50.0	21	10.50	0	0.0	21	0	0.0	87.5
James, Craig, New England	4	1	25.0	10	2.50	1	25.0	10t	1	25.0	39.6
Jensen, Jim, Miami	2	0	0.0	0	0.00	0	0.0	0	0	0.0	39.6
Johnson, Vance, Denver	1	0	0.0	0	0.00	0	0.0	0	0	0.0	39.6
Kreider, Steve, Cincinnati	1	0	0.0	0	0.00	0	0.0	0	1	100.0	0.0
Largent, Steve, Seattle	1	1	100.0	18	18.00	0	0.0	18	0	0.0	118.8
Marshall, Henry, Kansas City	1	0	0.0	0	0.00	0	0.0	0	0	0.0	39.6
McGee, Buford, San Diego	1	1	100.0	1	1.00	0	0.0	1	0	0.0	79.2
Morris, Randall, Seattle	1	0	0.0	0	0.00	0	0.0	0	0	0.0	39.6
Newsome, Harry, Pittsburgh	2	1	50.0	12	6.00	1	50.0	12t	0	0.0	108.3
Norman, Chris, Denver	1	1	100.0	43	43.00	1	100.0	43t	0	0.0	158.3
Pagel, Mike, Cleveland	3	2	66.7	53	17.67	0	0.0	45	0	0.0	109.7
Ramsey, Tom, New England	3	1	33.3	7	2.33	0	0.0	7	0	0.0	42.4
Rozier, Mike, Houston	1	1	100.0	13	13.00	0	0.0	13	0	0.0	118.8
Sewell, Steve, Denver	1	1	100.0	23	23.00	1	100.0	23t	0	0.0	158.3
Willhite, Gerald, Denver	4	1	25.0	11	2.75	0	0.0	11	0	0.0	39.6

t indicates touchdown.
Leader based on rating points, minimum 224 attempts.

NFC Passing—Individual Qualifiers

	Att.	Comp.	Pct. Comp.	Yards	Avg. Gain	TD	Pct. TD	Long	Int.	Pct. Int.	Rating Points
Kramer, Tommy, Minnesota	372	208	55.9	3000	8.06	24	6.5	76t	10	2.7	92.6
Montana, Joe, San Francisco	307	191	62.2	2236	7.28	8	2.6	48	9	2.9	80.7
Hipple, Eric, Detroit	305	192	63.0	1919	6.29	9	3.0	46	11	3.6	75.6
Simms, Phil, N.Y. Giants	468	259	55.3	3487	7.45	21	4.5	49	22	4.7	74.6
Lomax, Neil, St. Louis	421	240	57.0	2583	6.14	13	3.1	48t	12	2.9	73.6
Schroeder, Jay, Washington	541	276	51.0	4109	7.60	22	4.1	71t	22	4.1	72.9
Archer, Dave, Atlanta	294	150	51.0	2007	6.83	10	3.4	65	9	3.1	71.6
Jaworski, Ron, Philadelphia	245	128	52.2	1405	5.73	8	3.3	56	6	2.4	70.2
Pelluer, Steve, Dallas	378	215	56.9	2727	7.21	8	2.1	84t	17	4.5	67.9
Wright, Randy, Green Bay	492	263	53.5	3247	6.60	17	3.5	62	23	4.7	66.2
Wilson, Dave, New Orleans	342	189	55.3	2353	6.88	10	2.9	63t	17	5.0	65.8
Young, Steve, Tampa Bay	363	195	53.7	2282	6.29	8	2.2	46	13	3.6	65.5

Non-Qualifiers	Att.	Comp.	Pct. Comp.	Yards	Avg. Gain	TD	Pct. TD	Long	Int.	Pct. Int.	Rating Points
White, Danny, Dallas	153	95	62.1	1157	7.56	12	7.8	63	5	3.3	97.9
Kemp, Jeff, San Francisco	200	119	59.5	1554	7.77	11	5.5	66t	8	4.0	85.7
Wilson, Wade, Minnesota	143	80	55.9	1165	8.15	7	4.9	39	5	3.5	84.4
Flutie, Doug, Chicago	46	23	50.0	361	7.85	3	6.5	58t	2	4.3	80.1
Cunningham, Randall, Philadelphia	209	111	53.1	1391	6.66	8	3.8	75t	7	3.3	72.9
Moroski, Mike, San Francisco	73	42	57.5	493	6.75	2	2.7	52	3	4.1	70.2
Schonert, Turk, Atlanta	154	95	61.7	1032	6.70	4	2.6	41	8	5.2	68.4
Everett, Jim, L.A. Rams	147	73	49.7	1018	6.93	8	5.4	60t	8	5.4	67.8
Long, Chuck, Detroit	40	21	52.5	247	6.18	2	5.0	34t	2	5.0	67.4
Ferguson, Joe, Detroit	155	73	47.1	941	6.07	7	4.5	73	7	4.5	62.9
Fusina, Chuck, Green Bay	32	19	59.4	178	5.56	0	0.0	42	1	3.1	61.7
McMahon, Jim, Chicago	150	77	51.3	995	6.63	5	3.3	58t	8	5.3	61.4
Fuller, Steve, Chicago	64	34	53.1	451	7.05	2	3.1	50t	4	6.3	60.1
Dils, Steve, L.A. Rams	129	59	45.7	693	5.37	4	3.1	65t	4	3.1	60.0
Bartkowski, Steve, L.A. Rams	126	61	48.4	654	5.19	2	1.6	42	3	2.4	59.4
Ferragamo, Vince, Green Bay	40	23	57.5	283	7.08	1	2.5	50	3	7.5	56.6

	Att.	Comp.	Pct. Comp.	Yards	Avg. Gain	TD	Pct. TD	Long	Int.	Pct. Int.	Rating Points
Collier, Reggie, Dallas	15	8	53.3	96	6.40	1	6.7	27	2	13.3	55.8
Cavanaugh, Matt, Philadelphia	58	28	48.3	397	6.84	2	3.4	49	4	6.9	53.6
Stoudt, Cliff, St. Louis	91	52	57.1	542	5.96	3	3.3	24t	7	7.7	53.5
Tomczak, Mike, Chicago	151	74	49.0	1105	7.32	2	1.3	85	10	6.6	50.2
DeBerg, Steve, Tampa Bay	96	50	52.1	610	6.35	5	5.2	45	12	12.5	49.7
Hebert, Bobby, New Orleans	79	41	51.9	498	6.30	2	2.5	84	8	10.1	40.5
Less than 10 attempts											
Anderson, Alfred, Minnesota	2	1	50.0	17	8.50	0	0.0	17	0	0.0	79.2
Arapostathis, Evan, St. Louis	1	0	0.0	0	0.00	0	0.0	0	0	0.0	39.6
Bono, Steve, Minnesota	1	1	100.0	3	3.00	0	0.0	3	0	0.0	79.2
Byars, Keith, Philadelphia	2	1	50.0	55	27.50	1	50.0	55t	0	0.0	135.4
Campbell, Scott, Pittsburgh-Atlanta	7	1	14.3	7	1.00	0	0.0	7	0	0.0	39.6
Dickerson, Eric, L.A. Rams	1	1	100.0	15	15.00	1	100.0	15t	0	0.0	158.3
Galbreath, Tony, N.Y. Giants	1	0	0.0	0	0.00	0	0.0	0	0	0.0	39.6
Hilliard, Dalton, New Orleans	3	1	33.3	29	9.67	1	33.3	29t	0	0.0	109.7
House, Kevin, L.A. Rams	0	0	—	0	—	0	—	0	0	—	0.0
Lofton, James, Green Bay	1	0	0.0	0	0.00	0	0.0	0	0	0.0	39.6
Mitchell, Stump, St. Louis	3	1	33.3	15	5.00	1	33.3	15t	0	0.0	90.3
Payton, Walter, Chicago	4	0	0.0	0	0.00	0	0.0	0	1	25.0	0.0
Renfro, Mike, Dallas	1	1	100.0	23	23.00	0	0.0	23	0	0.0	118.8
Rice, Allen, Minnesota	1	0	0.0	0	0.00	0	0.0	0	0	0.0	39.6
Rice, Jerry, San Francisco	2	1	50.0	16	8.00	0	0.0	16	0	0.0	77.1
Riggs, Gerald, Atlanta	1	0	0.0	0	0.00	0	0.0	0	0	0.0	39.6
Rutledge, Jeff, N.Y. Giants	3	1	33.3	13	4.33	1	33.3	13t	0	0.0	87.5
Wattelet, Frank, New Orleans	1	1	100.0	13	13.00	0	0.0	13	0	0.0	118.8
Williams, Doug, Washington	1	0	0.0	0	0.00	0	0.0	0	0	0.0	39.6

t indicates touchdown.
Leader based on rating points, minimum 224 attempts.

Pass Receiving

Individual Champions
- **AFC:** 95—Todd Christensen, Los Angeles Raiders
- **NFC:** 86—Jerry Rice, San Francisco

Most Receptions, Game
- **NFC:** 13—Kelvin Bryant, Washington vs. New York Giants, December 7 (130 yards)
- **AFC:** 11—Gary Anderson, San Diego vs. Kansas City, October 19 (92 yards)
  - 11—Todd Christensen, Los Angeles Raiders vs. Denver, November 2 (158 yards)
  - 11—Todd Christensen, Los Angeles Raiders vs. San Diego, November 30 [OT] (173 yards)

Yards
- **NFC:** 1,570—Jerry Rice, San Francisco
- **AFC:** 1,491—Stanley Morgan, New England

Most Yards, Game
- **NFC:** 241—Gary Clark, Washington vs. New York Giants, October 27 (11 receptions)
- **AFC:** 195—Al Toon, New York Jets vs. Seattle, November 2 (9 receptions)

Yards Per Reception
- **AFC:** 22.9—Chris Burkett, Buffalo
- **NFC:** 20.7—Walter Stanley, Green Bay

Longest
- **AFC:** 85 yards—Mark Duper (from Dan Marino), Miami vs. Houston, November 2 (TD)
- **NFC:** 85 yards—Emery Moorehead (from Mike Tomczak), Chicago vs. Atlanta, November 16

Touchdowns
- **NFC:** 15—Jerry Rice, San Francisco
- **AFC:** 12—Wesley Walker, New York Jets

Team Leaders, Receptions
- **AFC:** BUFFALO: 53, Andre Reed; CINCINNATI: 62, Cris Collinsworth; CLEVELAND: 55, Brian Brennan; DENVER: 64, Gerald Willhite; HOUSTON: 65, Drew Hill; INDIANAPOLIS: 71, Matt Bouza; KANSAS CITY: 52, Stephone Paige; LOS ANGELES RAIDERS: 95, Todd Christensen; MIAMI: 67, Mark Duper; NEW ENGLAND: 84, Stanley Morgan; NEW YORK JETS: 85, Al Toon; PITTSBURGH: 47, Walter Abercrombie; SAN DIEGO: 80, Gary Anderson; SEATTLE: 70, Steve Largent.
- **NFC:** ATLANTA: 63, Charlie Brown; CHICAGO: 42, Willie Gault; DALLAS: 76, Herschel Walker; DETROIT: 54, James Jones; GREEN BAY: 64, James Lofton; LOS ANGELES RAMS: 34, Henry Ellard; MINNESOTA: 58, Steve Jordan; NEW ORLEANS: 48, Mike Jones; NEW YORK GIANTS: 66, Mark Bavaro; PHILADELPHIA: 60, Mike Quick; ST. LOUIS: 80, J.T. Smith; SAN FRANCISCO: 86, Jerry Rice; TAMPA BAY: 45, Calvin Magee; WASHINGTON: 74, Gary Clark.

NFL Top 10 Pass Receivers

	No.	Yards	Avg.	Long	TD
Christensen, Todd, L.A. Raiders	95	1153	12.1	35	8
Rice, Jerry, San Francisco	86	1570	18.3	66t	15
Toon, Al, N.Y. Jets	85	1176	13.8	62t	8
Morgan, Stanley, New England	84	1491	17.8	44t	10
Craig, Roger, San Francisco	81	624	7.7	48	0
Smith, J.T., St. Louis	80	1014	12.7	45	6
Anderson, Gary, San Diego	80	871	10.9	65t	8
Collins, Tony, New England	77	684	8.9	49	5
Walker, Herschel, Dallas	76	837	11.0	84t	2
Clark, Gary, Washington	74	1265	17.1	55	7

NFL Top 10 Pass Receivers By Yards

	Yards	No.	Avg.	Long	TD
Rice, Jerry, San Francisco	1570	86	18.3	66t	15
Morgan, Stanley, New England	1491	84	17.8	44t	10
Duper, Mark, Miami	1313	67	19.6	85t	11
Clark, Gary, Washington	1265	74	17.1	55	7
Toon, Al, N.Y. Jets	1176	85	13.8	62t	8
Christensen, Todd, L.A. Raiders	1153	95	12.1	35	8
Clayton, Mark, Miami	1150	60	19.2	68t	10
Brooks, Bill, Indianapolis	1131	65	17.4	84t	8
Hill, Drew, Houston	1112	65	17.1	81t	5
Largent, Steve, Seattle	1070	70	15.3	38t	9

AFC Pass Receiving—Individual

	No.	Yards	Avg.	Long	TD
Christensen, Todd, L.A. Raiders	95	1153	12.1	35	8
Toon, Al, N.Y. Jets	85	1176	13.8	62t	8
Morgan, Stanley, New England	84	1491	17.8	44t	10
Anderson, Gary, San Diego	80	871	10.9	65t	8
Collins, Tony, New England	77	684	8.9	49	5
Bouza, Matt, Indianapolis	71	830	11.7	33	5
Largent, Steve, Seattle	70	1070	15.3	38t	9
Shuler, Mickey, N.Y. Jets	69	675	9.8	36t	4
Duper, Mark, Miami	67	1313	19.6	85t	11
Brooks, Bill, Indianapolis	65	1131	17.4	84t	8
Hill, Drew, Houston	65	1112	17.1	81t	5
Winslow, Kellen, San Diego	64	728	11.4	28t	5
Willhite, Gerald, Denver	64	529	8.3	31	3
Collinsworth, Cris, Cincinnati	62	1024	16.5	46t	10
Givins, Earnest, Houston	61	1062	17.4	60	3
Hampton, Lorenzo, Miami	61	446	7.3	19	3
Clayton, Mark, Miami	60	1150	19.2	68t	10
Brown, Eddie, Cincinnati	58	964	16.6	57	4
Chandler, Wes, San Diego	56	874	15.6	40	4
Brennan, Brian, Cleveland	55	838	15.2	57t	6
Brooks, James, Cincinnati	54	686	12.7	54	4
Hardy, Bruce, Miami	54	430	8.0	18t	5
Reed, Andre, Buffalo	53	739	13.9	55t	7
Paige, Stephone, Kansas City	52	829	15.9	51	11
Walker, Wesley, N.Y. Jets	49	1016	20.7	83t	12
Metzelaars, Pete, Buffalo	49	485	9.9	44t	3
Riddick, Robb, Buffalo	49	468	9.6	31t	1

	No.	Yards	Avg.	Long	TD
McNeil, Freeman, N.Y. Jets	49	410	8.4	26	1
Nathan, Tony, Miami	48	457	9.5	23t	2
Fontenot, Herman, Cleveland	47	559	11.9	72t	1
Abercrombie, Walter, Pittsburgh	47	395	8.4	27	2
Marshall, Henry, Kansas City	46	652	14.2	31	1
Allen, Marcus, L.A. Raiders	46	453	9.8	36	2
Watson, Steve, Denver	45	699	15.5	46	3
Williams, Dokie, L.A. Raiders	43	843	19.6	53	8
Fryar, Irving, New England	43	737	17.1	69t	6
Warner, Curt, Seattle	41	342	8.3	26	0
Slaughter, Webster, Cleveland	40	577	14.4	47t	4
Holman, Rodney, Cincinnati	40	570	14.3	34t	2
Langhorne, Reggie, Cleveland	39	678	17.4	66	1
Newsome, Ozzie, Cleveland	39	417	10.7	31	3
Jackson, Mark, Denver	38	738	19.4	53	1
Lipps, Louis, Pittsburgh	38	590	15.5	48	3
Moore, Nat, Miami	38	431	11.3	38t	7
Baty, Greg, New England	37	331	8.9	22	2
Byner, Earnest, Cleveland	37	328	8.9	40	2
Pinkett, Allen, Houston	35	248	7.1	20	1
Burkett, Chris, Buffalo	34	778	22.9	84t	4
Stallworth, John, Pittsburgh	34	466	13.7	40t	1
Joiner, Charlie, San Diego	34	440	12.9	33	2
McMillan, Randy, Indianapolis	34	289	8.5	45	0
Franklin, Byron, Seattle	33	547	16.6	49	2
Hector, Johnny, N.Y. Jets	33	302	9.2	23	0
Smith, Jeff, Kansas City	33	230	7.0	18	3
Williams, John L., Seattle	33	219	6.6	23	0
Johnson, Vance, Denver	31	363	11.7	34t	2
Johnson, Trumaine, San Diego	30	399	13.3	30	1
Holohan, Pete, San Diego	29	356	12.3	34	1
Woolfolk, Butch, Houston	28	314	11.2	30	2
Mack, Kevin, Cleveland	28	292	10.4	44	0
Erenberg, Rich, Pittsburgh	27	217	8.0	19	3
Winder, Sammy, Denver	26	171	6.6	20t	5
Beach, Pat, Indianapolis	25	265	10.6	26	1
Bentley, Albert, Indianapolis	25	230	9.2	38	0
Hawkins, Frank, L.A. Raiders	25	166	6.6	16	0
Hawthorne, Greg, New England	24	192	8.0	17	0
Rozier, Mike, Houston	24	180	7.5	23	0
Hester, Jessie, L.A. Raiders	23	632	27.5	81t	6
Sewell, Steve, Denver	23	294	12.8	40	1
Moore, Ricky, Buffalo	23	184	8.0	27	0
James, Lionel, San Diego	23	173	7.5	18	0
Mobley, Orson, Denver	22	332	15.1	32	1
Skansi, Paul, Seattle	22	271	12.3	30	0
Boyer, Mark, Indianapolis	22	237	10.8	38	1
Williams, Jamie, Houston	22	227	10.3	33	1
Harmon, Ronnie, Buffalo	22	185	8.4	27	1
Carson, Carlos, Kansas City	21	497	23.7	70t	4
Sweeney, Calvin, Pittsburgh	21	337	16.0	58	1
Sampson, Clinton, Denver	21	259	12.3	43	0
Gothard, Preston, Pittsburgh	21	246	11.7	34	1
Davenport, Ron, Miami	20	177	8.9	27	1
Arnold, Walt, Kansas City	20	169	8.5	27	1
Butler, Raymond, Seattle	19	351	18.5	67t	4
Johnson, Dan, Miami	19	170	8.9	20	4
Green, Boyce, Kansas City	19	137	7.2	17	0
Barksdale, Rod, L.A. Raiders	18	434	24.1	57t	2
Turner, Daryl, Seattle	18	334	18.6	72t	7
Drewrey, Willie, Houston	18	299	16.6	31	0
James, Craig, New England	18	129	7.2	17	0
Paige, Tony, N.Y. Jets	18	121	6.7	18	0
Thompson, Weegie, Pittsburgh	17	191	11.2	20	5
Wallace, Ray, Houston	17	177	10.4	35t	2
Jackson, Earnest, Pittsburgh	17	169	9.9	28	0
Heard, Herman, Kansas City	17	83	4.9	13	0
Starring, Stephen, New England	16	295	18.4	47	2
McGee, Tim, Cincinnati	16	276	17.3	51	1
Wonsley, George, Indianapolis	16	175	10.9	60	0
Gill, Owen, Indianapolis	16	137	8.6	15	0
Butler, Jerry, Buffalo	15	302	20.1	53	2
Pruitt, James, Miami	15	235	15.7	27	2
Kay, Clarence, Denver	15	195	13.0	34	1
Klever, Rocky, N.Y. Jets	15	150	10.0	21	0
Tice, Mike, Seattle	15	150	10.0	25	0
Tatupu, Mosi, New England	15	145	9.7	25	0
Jones, Cedric, New England	14	222	15.9	28	1
Kinnebrew, Larry, Cincinnati	13	136	10.5	31	1
Hudson, Gordon, Seattle	13	131	10.1	30	1
Lang, Gene, Denver	13	105	8.1	26	2
Byrum, Carl, Buffalo	13	104	8.0	17	1
Johnson, Bill, Cincinnati	13	103	7.9	17	0
McCallum, Napoleon, L.A. Raiders	13	103	7.9	22	0
Bell, Greg, Buffalo	12	142	11.8	40t	2
Coffman, Paul, Kansas City	12	75	6.3	10	2
Kattus, Eric, Cincinnati	11	99	9.0	28	1
McGee, Buford, San Diego	10	105	10.5	18	0
Hughes, David, Pittsburgh	10	98	9.8	22	0
Dickey, Curtis, Cleveland	10	78	7.8	12	0
Harry, Emile, Kansas City	9	211	23.4	53	1
Capers, Wayne, Indianapolis	9	118	13.1	27	0
Weathers, Clarence, Cleveland	9	100	11.1	16	0
Moriarty, Larry, Houston-K.C.	9	67	7.4	19	0
Sohn, Kurt, N.Y. Jets	8	129	16.1	24t	2
Wilkins, Gary, Buffalo	8	74	9.3	26	0
Hayes, Jonathan, Kansas City	8	69	8.6	16	0
Pruitt, Mike, Kansas City	8	56	7.0	13	0
Scott, Willie, New England	8	41	5.1	8t	3
Banks, Chuck, Houston	7	71	10.1	17	0
LaFleur, Greg, Indianapolis	7	56	8.0	11	0
Jennings, Stanford, Cincinnati	6	86	14.3	34	0
Moffett, Tim, L.A. Raiders	6	77	12.8	17	0
Teal, Jimmy, Buffalo	6	60	10.0	20	1
Mueller, Vance, L.A. Raiders	6	54	9.0	20	0
Spencer, Tim, San Diego	6	48	8.0	15	0
Kreider, Steve, Cincinnati	5	96	19.2	23	0
Jensen, Jim, Miami	5	50	10.0	20t	1
Barber, Marion, N.Y. Jets	5	36	7.2	16	0
Smith, Tim, Houston	4	72	18.0	25	0
Akiu, Mike, Houston	4	67	16.8	27	0
Hancock, Anthony, Kansas City	4	63	15.8	25	0
Holt, Harry, Cleveland	4	61	15.3	34	1
Rolle, Butch, Buffalo	4	56	14.0	20	0
Harbour, James, Indianapolis	4	46	11.5	28	0
Wilson, Stanley, Cincinnati	4	45	11.3	34	0
Bennett, Woody, Miami	4	33	8.3	13	0
Adams, Curtis, San Diego	4	26	6.5	10	0
Broughton, Walter, Buffalo	3	71	23.7	57	0
Martin, Mike, Cincinnati	3	68	22.7	51	0
Greer, Terry, Cleveland	3	51	17.0	22	0
Richardson, Eric, Buffalo	3	49	16.3	32	0
Hackett, Joey, Denver	3	48	16.0	19	0
Sherwin, Tim, Indianapolis	3	26	8.7	15	1
Lane, Eric, Seattle	3	6	2.0	4	1
Junkin, Trey, L.A. Raiders	2	38	19.0	19	0
Williams, Derwin, New England	2	35	17.5	26	0
Murray, Walter, Indianapolis	2	34	17.0	24	0
Tucker, Travis, Cleveland	2	29	14.5	16	0
Sanders, Chuck, Pittsburgh	2	19	9.5	10	0
Pollard, Frank, Pittsburgh	2	15	7.5	10	0
Sievers, Eric, San Diego	2	14	7.0	9	0
Pattison, Mark, L.A. Raiders	2	12	6.0	6	0
Bell, Ken, Denver	2	10	5.0	7	0
Parker, Andy, L.A. Raiders	2	8	4.0	6	1
Muñoz, Anthony, Cincinnati	2	7	3.5	5t	2
Bligen, Dennis, N.Y. Jets	2	6	3.0	4	0
Reeder, Dan, Pittsburgh	2	4	2.0	3	0
Wilson, Steve, Denver	1	43	43.0	43t	1
Martin, Robbie, Indianapolis	1	41	41.0	41	0
Elway, John, Denver	1	23	23.0	23t	1
Weathers, Robert, New England	1	14	14.0	14	0
Townsell, JoJo, N.Y. Jets	1	11	11.0	11	0
Ware, Timmie, San Diego	1	11	11.0	11	0
McNeil, Gerald, Cleveland	1	9	9.0	9	0
Carter, Joe, Miami	1	6	6.0	6	0
Holloway, Brian, New England	1	5	5.0	5	0
Bailey, Edwin, Seattle	1	3	3.0	3	0
Studdard, Dave, Denver	1	2	2.0	2t	1
Kosar, Bernie, Cleveland	1	1	1.0	1	0
Kenney, Bill, Kansas City	1	0	0.0	0	0
Oliver, Hubert, Houston	1	−2	−2.0	−2	0

t indicates touchdown
Leader based on most passes caught.

NFC Pass Receiving — Individual

	No.	Yards	Avg.	Long	TD
Rice, Jerry, San Francisco	86	1570	18.3	66t	15
Craig, Roger, San Francisco	81	624	7.7	48	0
Smith, J.T., St. Louis	80	1014	12.7	45	6
Walker, Herschel, Dallas	76	837	11.0	84t	2
Clark, Gary, Washington	74	1265	17.1	55	7
Monk, Art, Washington	73	1068	14.6	69	4
Bavaro, Mark, N.Y. Giants	66	1001	15.2	41	4
Lofton, James, Green Bay	64	840	13.1	36	4
Brown, Charlie, Atlanta	63	918	14.6	42	4
Clark, Dwight, San Francisco	61	794	13.0	45t	2
Quick, Mike, Philadelphia	60	939	15.7	75t	9
Jordan, Steve, Minnesota	58	859	14.8	68t	6
Ferrell, Earl, St. Louis	56	434	7.8	30t	3
Jones, James, Detroit	54	334	6.2	21	1
Chadwick, Jeff, Detroit	53	995	18.8	73	5
Nelson, Darrin, Minnesota	53	593	11.2	34	3
Hill, Tony, Dallas	49	770	15.7	63	3
Epps, Phillip, Green Bay	49	612	12.5	53t	4
Jones, Mike, New Orleans	48	625	13.0	45	3
Newsome, Tim, Dallas	48	421	8.8	30	3

	No.	Yards	Avg.	Long	TD
Magee, Calvin, Tampa Bay	45	564	12.5	45	5
Bland, Carl, Detroit	44	511	11.6	34	2
Bryant, Kelvin, Washington	43	449	10.4	40	3
Wilder, James, Tampa Bay	43	326	7.6	25	1
Gault, Willie, Chicago	42	818	19.5	53t	5
Carter, Gerald, Tampa Bay	42	640	15.2	46	2
Dixon, Floyd, Atlanta	42	617	14.7	65	2
Green, Roy, St. Louis	42	517	12.3	48t	6
Sherrard, Mike, Dallas	41	744	18.1	68t	5
Francis, Russ, San Francisco	41	505	12.3	52	1
Tautalatasi, Junior, Philadelphia	41	325	7.9	56	2
Mitchell, Stump, St. Louis	41	276	6.7	24	0
Spagnola, John, Philadelphia	39	397	10.2	38	1
Carter, Anthony, Minnesota	38	686	18.1	60t	7
Martin, Eric, New Orleans	37	675	18.2	84	5
Payton, Walter, Chicago	37	382	10.3	57	3
Giles, Jimmie, Tampa Bay-Detroit	37	376	10.2	30	4
Tice, John, New Orleans	37	330	8.9	29t	3
Stanley, Walter, Green Bay	35	723	20.7	62	2
Cribbs, Joe, San Francisco	35	346	9.9	33	0
Didier, Clint, Washington	34	691	20.3	71t	4
Ellard, Henry, L.A. Rams	34	447	13.1	34t	4
James, Garry, Detroit	34	219	6.4	26	0
Galbreath, Tony, N.Y. Giants	33	268	8.1	19	0
Lewis, Leo, Minnesota	32	600	18.8	76t	2
Johnson, Bobby, N.Y. Giants	31	534	17.2	44t	5
Ivery, Eddie Lee, Green Bay	31	385	12.4	42	1
Jackson, Kenny, Philadelphia	30	506	16.9	49	6
Rice, Allen, Minnesota	30	391	13.0	32t	3
Robinson, Stacy, N.Y. Giants	29	494	17.0	49	2
Jones, Hassan, Minnesota	28	570	20.4	55t	4
Cosbie, Doug, Dallas	28	312	11.1	22t	1
Redden, Barry, L.A. Rams	28	217	7.8	24t	1
Moorehead, Emery, Chicago	26	390	15.0	85	1
Dickerson, Eric, L.A. Rams	26	205	7.9	28	0
Haddix, Michael, Philadelphia	26	150	5.8	29	0
Brown, Ron, L.A. Rams	25	396	15.8	65t	3
Thompson, Leonard, Detroit	25	320	12.8	36t	5
Marsh, Doug, St. Louis	25	313	12.5	27	0
Dorsett, Tony, Dallas	25	267	10.7	36t	1
Hunter, Herman, Detroit	25	218	8.7	18t	1
Cox, Arthur, Atlanta	24	301	12.5	49	1
Ellis, Gerry, Green Bay	24	258	10.8	29	0
Suhey, Matt, Chicago	24	235	9.8	58	0
Springs, Ron, Tampa Bay	24	187	7.8	46	0
Riggs, Gerald, Atlanta	24	136	5.7	11	0
Carruth, Paul Ott, Green Bay	24	134	5.6	19	2
Ortego, Keith, Chicago	23	430	18.7	58t	2
Renfro, Mike, Dallas	22	325	14.8	30t	3
Wrightman, Tim, Chicago	22	241	11.0	29	0
Morris, Joe, N.Y. Giants	21	233	11.1	23	1
Davis, Kenneth, Green Bay	21	142	6.8	18	1
Goodlow, Eugene, New Orleans	20	306	15.3	29t	2
Stamps, Sylvester, Atlanta	20	221	11.1	39t	1
Whisenhunt, Ken, Atlanta	20	184	9.2	23t	3
Warren, Don, Washington	20	164	8.2	20	1
Gentry, Dennis, Chicago	19	238	12.5	41	0
Anderson, Ottis, St. Louis-N.Y.G.	19	137	7.2	19	0
House, Kevin, T.B.-L.A. Rams	18	384	21.3	60t	2
Brenner, Hoby, New Orleans	18	286	15.9	34	0
Banks, Gordon, Dallas	17	202	11.9	23	0
Anderson, Alfred, Minnesota	17	179	10.5	37t	2
Ross, Dan, Green Bay	17	143	8.4	16	1
Hilliard, Dalton, New Orleans	17	107	6.3	17	0
Mayes, Rueben, New Orleans	17	96	5.6	18	0
McConkey, Phil, N.Y. Giants	16	279	17.4	46	1
Carthon, Maurice, N.Y. Giants	16	67	4.2	10	0
Hunter, Tony, L.A. Rams	15	206	13.7	42	0
West, Ed, Green Bay	15	199	13.3	46t	1
Young, Mike, L.A. Rams	15	181	12.1	21	3
Brown, Ted, Minnesota	15	132	8.8	20	0
Sanders, Ricky, Washington	14	286	20.4	71	2
Freeman, Phil., Tampa Bay	14	229	16.4	33t	2
Johnson, Troy, St. Louis	14	203	14.5	39	0
Hill, David, L.A. Rams	14	202	14.4	33	1
Little, David, Philadelphia	14	132	9.4	26	0
Toney, Anthony, Philadelphia	13	177	13.6	47	0
Rathman, Tom, San Francisco	13	121	9.3	14	0
Garrity, Gregg, Philadelphia	12	227	18.9	34	0
Williams, Keith, Atlanta	12	164	13.7	32t	1
Ellerson, Gary, Green Bay	12	130	10.8	32	0
Johnson, Ron, Philadelphia	11	207	18.8	39	1
Manuel, Lionel, N.Y. Giants	11	181	16.5	35	3
Harris, Herbert, New Orleans	11	148	13.5	27	0
Jordan, Buford, New Orleans	11	127	11.5	37	0
Griffin, Keith, Washington	11	110	10.0	28	0
Mularkey, Mike, Minnesota	11	89	8.1	20	2
Byars, Keith, Philadelphia	11	44	4.0	17	0
Allen, Anthony, Atlanta	10	156	15.6	32	2

	No.	Yards	Avg.	Long	TD
Duckworth, Bobby, L.A. Rams-Phil.	10	148	14.8	32	1
Edwards, Kelvin, New Orleans	10	132	13.2	24	0
Bell, Jerry, Tampa Bay	10	120	12.0	25	0
Mowatt, Zeke, N.Y. Giants	10	119	11.9	30	2
Sikahema, Vai, St. Louis	10	99	9.9	27	1
Lewis, David, Detroit	10	88	8.8	16	1
Miller, Solomon, N.Y. Giants	9	144	16.0	32t	2
Wilson, Mike, San Francisco	9	104	11.6	18	1
Guman, Mike, L.A. Rams	9	68	7.6	13	0
Frank, John, San Francisco	9	61	6.8	17	2
Rouson, Lee, N.Y. Giants	8	121	15.1	37t	1
Harmon, Derrick, San Francisco	8	78	9.8	15	0
Wonsley, Nathan, Tampa Bay	8	57	7.1	11	0
Moore, Alvin, Detroit	8	47	5.9	8	0
Jones, Joey, Atlanta	7	141	20.1	41	0
Mandley, Pete, Detroit	7	106	15.1	51	0
Franklin, Pat, Tampa Bay	7	29	4.1	9	1
Smith, Phil, Philadelphia	6	94	15.7	36	0
Williams, David, Tampa Bay	6	91	15.2	25	0
Chandler, Thornton, Dallas	6	57	9.5	15	2
Johnson, Billy, Atlanta	6	57	9.5	27	0
Clark, Jessie, Green Bay	6	41	6.8	12	0
Middleton, Ron, Atlanta	6	31	5.2	8	0
Scott, Chuck, L.A. Rams	5	76	15.2	21	0
Crawford, Derrick, San Francisco	5	70	14.0	42	0
Rubick, Rob, Detroit	5	62	12.4	27	0
Gustafson, Jim, Minnesota	5	61	12.2	18	2
Howard, Bobby, Tampa Bay	5	60	12.0	29	0
Fox, Chas, St. Louis	5	59	11.8	38t	1
Long, Darren, L.A. Rams	5	47	9.4	13	0
Andrews, William, Atlanta	5	35	7.0	14	0
Lavette, Robert, Dallas	5	31	6.2	9	1
Moffitt, Mike, Green Bay	4	87	21.8	34	0
Anderson, Neal, Chicago	4	80	20.0	58t	1
Barnes, Lew, Chicago	4	54	13.5	14	0
Thomas, Calvin, Chicago	4	18	4.5	18	0
Dunn, K.D., Tampa Bay	3	83	27.7	38	0
Harris, Leonard, Tampa Bay	3	52	17.3	23	0
Tilley, Pat, St. Louis	3	51	17.0	18	0
Orr, Terry, Washington	3	45	15.0	22t	1
Heflin, Vince, Tampa Bay	3	42	14.0	15	0
Holman, Scott, St. Louis	3	41	13.7	18	0
Bailey, Stacey, Atlanta	3	39	13.0	21	0
Rhymes, Buster, Minnesota	3	25	8.3	12	0
Rogers, George, Washington	3	24	8.0	13	0
Austin, Cliff, Atlanta	3	21	7.0	9	0
Gray, Mel, New Orleans	2	45	22.5	38	0
Wolfley, Ron, St. Louis	2	32	16.0	28	0
Waters, Mike, Philadelphia	2	27	13.5	19	0
Sanders, Thomas, Chicago	2	18	9.0	18	0
Darby, Byron, Philadelphia	2	16	8.0	13	0
Margerum, Ken, San Francisco	2	12	6.0	6	0
Williams, Scott, Detroit	2	9	4.5	6	0
Lewis, Mark, Green Bay	2	7	3.5	4t	2
Monroe, Carl, San Francisco	2	6	3.0	5	0
Matthews, Aubrey, Atlanta	1	25	25.0	25	0
Fowler, Todd, Dallas	1	19	19.0	19	0
Clack, Darryl, Dallas	1	18	18.0	18	0
Gillespie, Willie, Tampa Bay	1	18	18.0	18	0
Carson, Harry, N.Y. Giants	1	13	13.0	13t	1
Waymer, Dave, New Orleans	1	13	13.0	13	0
Mallory, Rick, Tampa Bay	1	9	9.0	9	0
Tyrrell, Tim, L.A. Rams	1	9	9.0	9	0
Bortz, Mark, Chicago	1	8	8.0	8	0
Ring, Bill, San Francisco	1	8	8.0	8	0
Sargent, Broderick, St. Louis	1	8	8.0	8	0
Franz, Nolan, Green Bay	1	7	7.0	7	0
Holloway, Derek, Washington	1	7	7.0	7	0
White, Charles, L.A. Rams	1	7	7.0	7	0
Williams, John, New Orleans	1	5	5.0	5	0
Novacek, Jay, St. Louis	1	2	2.0	2	0
Hebert, Bobby, New Orleans	1	1	1.0	1	0
Heller, Ron, Tampa Bay	1	1	1.0	1t	1
Wilson, Wayne, New Orleans	1	−3	−3.0	−3	0

t indicates touchdown
Leader based on most passes caught.

Interceptions

Individual Champions

NFC: 10—Ronnie Lott, San Francisco
AFC: 9—Deron Cherry, Kansas City

Most Interceptions, Game

AFC: 3—Leonard Coleman, Indianapolis vs. New Orleans, October 12
3—Lloyd Burruss, Kansas City vs. San Diego, October 19
NFC: 2—By 26 players

Yardage

AFC: 193—Lloyd Burruss, Kansas City
NFC: 150—LeRoy Irvin, Los Angeles Rams

Longest

NFC: 88—Tory Nixon, San Francisco vs. Green Bay, October 26 (TD)

AFC: 80—John Holt, Indianapolis vs. San Diego, November 30

Touchdowns

AFC: 3—Lloyd Burruss, Kansas City

NFC: 2—Tom Holmoe, San Francisco

Team Leaders

AFC: BUFFALO: 4, Charles Romes; CINCINNATI: 7, Louis Breeden; CLEVELAND: 5, Hanford Dixon; DENVER: 6, Mike Harden; HOUSTON: 3, Patrick Allen & Allen Lyday; INDIANAPOLIS: 4, Leonard Coleman; KANSAS CITY: 9, Deron Cherry; LOS ANGELES RAIDERS: 7, Vann McElroy; MIAMI: 2, Glenn Blackwood, William Judson, Don McNeal, & Don Rose; NEW ENGLAND: 8, Ronnie Lippett; NEW YORK JETS: 6, Jerry Holmes; PITTSBURGH: 3, Harvey Clayton, Bryan Hinkle, Lupe Sanchez, Donnie Shell, Eric Williams, & Rick Woods; SAN DIEGO: 5, Gill Byrd; SEATTLE: 5, Dave Brown.

NFC: ATLANTA: 5, Bret Clark; CHICAGO: 7, Mike Richardson; DALLAS: 6, Michael Downs; DETROIT: 5, Devon Mitchell; GREEN BAY: 9, Mark Lee; LOS ANGELES RAMS: 8, Jerry Gray; MINNESOTA: 8, Issiac Holt; NEW ORLEANS: 9, Dave Waymer; NEW YORK GIANTS: 4, Terry Kinard & Perry Williams; PHILADELPHIA: 6, Andre Waters & Roynell Young; ST. LOUIS: 4, Cedric Mack; SAN FRANCISCO: 10, Ronnie Lott; TAMPA BAY: 3, Vito McKeever; WASHINGTON: 5, Darrell Green.

Team Champions

NFC: 39—San Francisco

AFC: 31—Kansas City

AFC Interceptions—Team

	No.	Yards	Avg.	Long	TD
Kansas City	31	567	18.3	72t	4
Los Angeles Raiders	26	275	10.6	32t	1
Seattle	22	216	9.8	25	1
New England	21	312	14.9	69	1
Pittsburgh	20	218	10.9	67t	1
New York Jets	20	164	8.2	29	0
Denver	18	318	17.7	56	2
Cleveland	18	184	10.2	33	0
Cincinnati	17	146	8.6	36t	1
Indianapolis	16	166	10.4	80	0
Houston	16	100	6.3	38	0
San Diego	15	274	18.3	50	1
Miami	13	152	11.7	36	0
Buffalo	10	89	8.9	41	0
AFC Total	263	3,181	—	80	12
AFC Average	18.8	227.2	12.1	—	0.9

NFC Interceptions—Team

	No.	Yards	Avg.	Long	TD
San Francisco	39	578	14.8	88t	5
Chicago	31	370	11.9	58t	1
Los Angeles Rams	28	458	16.4	80t	3
New Orleans	26	235	9.0	43	1
Minnesota	24	319	13.3	59t	2
New York Giants	24	296	12.3	78t	1
Philadelphia	23	124	5.4	21	0
Atlanta	22	294	13.4	41	2
Detroit	22	190	8.6	36	0
Green Bay	20	147	7.4	58t	1
Washington	19	126	6.6	31	0
Dallas	17	183	10.8	34t	1
Tampa Bay	13	128	9.8	57	0
St. Louis	10	121	12.1	35	0
NFC Total	318	3,569	—	88t	17
NFC Average	22.7	254.9	11.2	—	1.2
League Total	581	6,750	—	88t	29
League Average	20.8	241.1	11.6	—	1.0

NFL Top 10 Interceptors

	No.	Yards	Avg.	Long	TD
Lott, Ronnie, San Francisco	10	134	13.4	57t	1
Cherry, Deron, Kansas City	9	150	16.7	49	0
Waymer, Dave, New Orleans	9	48	5.3	17	0
Lee, Mark, Green Bay	9	33	3.7	11	0
Gray, Jerry, L.A. Rams	8	101	12.6	28	0
Lippett, Ronnie, New England	8	76	9.5	43	0
Holt, Issiac, Minnesota	8	54	6.8	27	0
McElroy, Vann, L.A. Raiders	7	105	15.0	28	0
Breeden, Louis, Cincinnati	7	72	10.3	36t	1
Richardson, Mike, Chicago	7	69	9.9	32	0

AFC Interceptions—Individual

	No.	Yards	Avg.	Long	TD
Cherry, Deron, Kansas City	9	150	16.7	49	0
Lippett, Ronnie, New England	8	76	9.5	43	0
McElroy, Vann, L.A. Raiders	7	105	15.0	28	0
Breeden, Louis, Cincinnati	7	72	10.3	36t	1
Harden, Mike, Denver	6	179	29.8	52	2
Holmes, Jerry, N.Y. Jets	6	29	4.8	28	0
Burruss, Lloyd, Kansas City	5	193	38.6	72t	3
Brown, Dave, Seattle	5	58	11.6	24	1
Byrd, Gill, San Diego	5	45	9.0	18	0
Lyles, Lester, N.Y. Jets	5	36	7.2	22	0
Lynn, Johnny, N.Y. Jets	5	36	7.2	26	0
Dixon, Hanford, Cleveland	5	35	7.0	19	0
Dale, Jeffery, San Diego	4	153	38.3	50	0
Ross, Kevin, Kansas City	4	66	16.5	35	0
Robinson, Jerry, L.A. Raiders	4	42	10.5	32t	1
Coleman, Leonard, Indianapolis	4	36	9.0	31	0
Justin, Kerry, Seattle	4	29	7.3	18	0
Romes, Charles, Buffalo	4	23	5.8	23	0
Fulcher, David, Cincinnati	4	20	5.0	15	0
Lewis, Albert, Kansas City	4	18	4.5	13	0
Seale, Sam, L.A. Raiders	4	2	0.5	2	0
Sanchez, Lupe, Pittsburgh	3	71	23.7	67t	1
Hill, Greg, Kansas City	3	64	21.3	26t	1
Wright, Louis, Denver	3	56	18.7	56	0
Williams, Eric, Pittsburgh	3	44	14.7	25	0
Robinson, Eugene, Seattle	3	39	13.0	25	0
Moyer, Paul, Seattle	3	38	12.7	20	0
Wright, Felix, Cleveland	3	33	11.0	33	0
Cocroft, Sherman, Kansas City	3	32	10.7	13	0
Shell, Donnie, Pittsburgh	3	29	9.7	17	0
Woods, Rick, Pittsburgh	3	26	8.7	23	0
Lyday, Allen, Houston	3	24	8.0	24	0
Lilly, Tony, Denver	3	22	7.3	15	0
Allen, Patrick, Houston	3	20	6.7	18	0
Minnifield, Frank, Cleveland	3	20	6.7	20	0
Clayton, Harvey, Pittsburgh	3	18	6.0	14	0
Daniel, Eugene, Indianapolis	3	11	3.7	5	0
Hinkle, Bryan, Pittsburgh	3	7	2.3	6	0
Clayborn, Ray, New England	3	4	1.3	4	0
Rose, Don, Miami	2	63	31.5	36	0
Marion, Fred, New England	2	56	28.0	37t	1
Burroughs, Derrick, Buffalo	2	49	24.5	41	0
McNeal, Don, Miami	2	46	23.0	29	0
McGrew, Larry, New England	2	44	22.0	27	0
Rockins, Chris, Cleveland	2	41	20.5	24	0
Foley, Steve, Denver	2	39	19.5	24	0
James, Roland, New England	2	39	19.5	21	0
Brown, Steve, Houston	2	34	17.0	38	0
Easley, Ken, Seattle	2	34	17.0	24	0
Glenn, Vencie, San Diego	2	31	15.5	31	0
Haynes, Mike, L.A. Raiders	2	28	14.0	22	0
Toran, Stacey, L.A. Raiders	2	28	14.0	19	0
O'Neal, Leslie, San Diego	2	22	11.0	17	1
Nelson, Steve, New England	2	21	10.5	17	0
Eason, Bo, Houston	2	16	8.0	11	0
Hicks, Dwight, Indianapolis	2	16	8.0	16	0
Merriweather, Mike, Pittsburgh	2	14	7.0	11	0
Ellis, Ray, Cleveland	2	12	6.0	7	0
Matthews, Clay, Cleveland	2	12	6.0	8	0
Bickett, Duane, Indianapolis	2	10	5.0	10	0
Blackwood, Glenn, Miami	2	10	5.0	7	0
Scholtz, Bruce, Seattle	2	10	5.0	10	0
Clifton, Kyle, N.Y. Jets	2	8	4.0	7	0
Barker, Leo, Cincinnati	2	7	3.5	7	0
Barnes, Jeff, L.A. Raiders	2	7	3.5	7	0
Hayes, Lester, L.A. Raiders	2	7	3.5	7	0
Johnson, Richard, Houston	2	6	3.0	6	0
Judson, William, Miami	2	0	0.0	0	0
Lyles, Robert, Houston	2	0	0.0	0	0
Taylor, Terry, Seattle	2	0	0.0	0	0
Holt, John, Indianapolis	1	80	80.0	80	0
Rembert, Johnny, New England	1	37	37.0	37	0
Adams, Stefon, L.A. Raiders	1	32	32.0	32	0
Harper, Mark, Cleveland	1	31	31.0	31	0
Hamilton, Harry, N.Y. Jets	1	29	29.0	29	0
Crable, Bob, N.Y. Jets	1	26	26.0	26	0
Spani, Gary, Kansas City	1	24	24.0	24	0
Brown, Donald, San Diego	1	23	23.0	23	0
Hunley, Ricky, Denver	1	22	22.0	22	0
Radecic, Scott, Kansas City	1	20	20.0	20	0
Bussey, Barney, Cincinnati	1	19	19.0	19	0
Zander, Carl, Cincinnati	1	18	18.0	18	0
Martin, Rod, L.A. Raiders	1	15	15.0	15	0
Bellinger, Rodney, Buffalo	1	14	14.0	14	0
Blackwood, Lyle, Miami	1	14	14.0	14	0
Offerdahl, John, Miami	1	14	14.0	14	0
McKenzie, Reggie, L.A. Raiders	1	9	9.0	9	0
Gaines, Greg, Seattle	1	8	8.0	8	0

	No.	Yards	Avg.	Long	TD
Hand, Jon, Indianapolis	1	8	8.0	8	0
Kelly, Joe, Cincinnati	1	6	6.0	6	0
Dennison, Rick, Denver	1	5	5.0	5	0
Armstrong, Harvey, Indianapolis	1	4	4.0	4	0
Horton, Ray, Cincinnati	1	4	4.0	4	0
Brown, Bud, Miami	1	3	3.0	3	0
McSwain, Rod, New England	1	3	3.0	3	0
Smerlas, Fred, Buffalo	1	3	3.0	3	0
Charles, Mike, Miami	1	2	2.0	2	0
Cooks, Johnie, Indianapolis	1	1	1.0	1	0
Bayless, Martin, Buffalo	1	0	0.0	0	0
Bostic, Keith, Houston	1	0	0.0	0	0
Daniel, Kenny, Indianapolis	1	0	0.0	0	0
Donaldson, Jeff, Houston	1	0	0.0	0	0
Freeman, Steve, Buffalo	1	0	0.0	0	0
Hackett, Dino, Kansas City	1	0	0.0	0	0
Kozlowski, Mike, Miami	1	0	0.0	0	0
Smith, Dennis, Denver	1	0	0.0	0	0
Taylor, Ken, San Diego	1	0	0.0	0	0
Wilson, Steve, Denver	1	−5	−5.0	−5	0
Tippett, Andre, New England	0	32	—	32	0
Swain, John, Pittsburgh	0	9	—	9	0

t indicates touchdown
Leader based on most interceptions.

NFC Interceptions—Individual

	No.	Yards	Avg.	Long	TD
Lott, Ronnie, San Francisco	10	134	13.4	57t	1
Waymer, Dave, New Orleans	9	48	5.3	17	0
Lee, Mark, Green Bay	9	33	3.7	11	0
Gray, Jerry, L.A. Rams	8	101	12.6	28	0
Holt, Issiac, Minnesota	8	54	6.8	27	0
Richardson, Mike, Chicago	7	69	9.9	32	0
Irvin, LeRoy, L.A. Rams	6	150	25.0	50t	1
Duerson, Dave, Chicago	6	139	23.2	38	0
Downs, Michael, Dallas	6	54	9.0	31	0
Waters, Andre, Philadelphia	6	39	6.5	21	0
McKyer, Tim, San Francisco	6	33	5.5	21t	1
Young, Roynell, Philadelphia	6	9	1.5	9	0
Cromwell, Nolan, L.A. Rams	5	101	20.2	80t	1
Clark, Bret, Atlanta	5	94	18.8	34	0
Marshall, Wilber, Chicago	5	68	13.6	58t	1
Fellows, Ron, Dallas	5	46	9.2	34t	1
Mitchell, Devon, Detroit	5	41	8.2	17	0
Green, Darrell, Washington	5	9	1.8	7	0
Browner, Joey, Minnesota	4	62	15.5	39t	1
Galloway, Duane, Detroit	4	58	14.5	36	0
Fahnhorst, Jim, San Francisco	4	52	13.0	46	0
Kinard, Terry, N.Y. Giants	4	52	13.0	25	0
Fuller, Jeff, San Francisco	4	44	11.0	26	0
Mack, Cedric, St. Louis	4	42	10.5	24	0
Poe, Johnnie, New Orleans	4	42	10.5	30	0
Case, Scott, Atlanta	4	41	10.3	41	0
Williams, Perry, N.Y. Giants	4	31	7.8	15	0
Cade, Mossy, Green Bay	4	26	6.5	18	0
McNorton, Bruce, Detroit	4	10	2.5	10	0
Holmoe, Tom, San Francisco	3	149	49.7	78t	2
Harris, John, Minnesota	3	69	23.0	28	0
Jordan, Curtis, Washington	3	46	15.3	20	0
Walls, Everson, Dallas	3	46	15.3	24	0
Newsome, Vince, L.A. Rams	3	45	15.0	34	0
Fencik, Gary, Chicago	3	37	12.3	24	0
Wattelet, Frank, New Orleans	3	34	11.3	22	0
Hill, Kenny, N.Y. Giants	3	25	8.3	23	0
Cooper, Evan, Philadelphia	3	20	6.7	20	0
McKeever, Vito, Tampa Bay	3	12	4.0	10	0
Lee, Carl, Minnesota	3	10	3.3	10	0
Johnson, Alonzo, Philadelphia	3	6	2.0	9	0
Williamson, Carlton, San Francisco	3	3	1.0	2	0
Griffin, Don, San Francisco	3	0	0.0	0	0
Jackson, Vestee, Chicago	3	0	0.0	0	0
Nixon, Tory, San Francisco	2	106	53.0	88t	1
Brantley, Scot, Tampa Bay	2	65	32.5	57	0
Gibson, Antonio, New Orleans	2	43	21.5	43	0
Croudip, David, Atlanta	2	35	17.5	29	0
Griffin, James, Detroit	2	34	17.0	21	0
Solomon, Jesse, Minnesota	2	34	17.0	18	0
Milot, Rich, Washington	2	33	16.5	31	0
Wilson, Otis, Chicago	2	31	15.5	21	0
Reasons, Gary, N.Y. Giants	2	28	14.0	18	0
Patterson, Elvis, N.Y. Giants	2	26	13.0	26	0
Sutton, Mickey, L.A. Rams	2	25	12.5	20	0
Jerue, Mark, L.A. Rams	2	23	11.5	22t	1
Welch, Herb, N.Y. Giants	2	22	11.0	16	0
Washington, Lionel, St. Louis	2	19	9.5	19	0
Johnson, Demetrious, Detroit	2	18	9.0	18	0
Williams, Joel, Atlanta	2	18	9.0	14t	1
Maxie, Brett, New Orleans	2	15	7.5	15	0
Wilburn, Barry, Washington	2	14	7.0	14	0
Woodberry, Dennis, Atlanta	2	14	7.0	9	0
Carter, Carl, St. Louis	2	12	6.0	11	0
Williams, Jimmy, Detroit	2	12	6.0	11	0
Wilkes, Reggie, Atlanta	2	11	5.5	10	0
Jakes, Van, New Orleans	2	6	3.0	4	0
Bowles, Todd, Washington	2	0	0.0	0	0
Coffey, Ken, Washington	2	0	0.0	0	0
Curry, Craig, Tampa Bay	2	0	0.0	0	0
Greene, Tiger, Green Bay	2	0	0.0	0	0
Martin, George, N.Y. Giants	1	78	78.0	78t	1
Doleman, Chris, Minnesota	1	59	59.0	59t	1
Stills, Ken, Green Bay	1	58	58.0	58t	1
Smith, Wayne, St. Louis	1	35	35.0	35	0
Butler, Bobby, Atlanta	1	33	33.0	33t	1
Curry, Buddy, Atlanta	1	32	32.0	32	0
Scott, Victor, Dallas	1	31	31.0	31	0
Swoope, Craig, Tampa Bay	1	23	23.0	23	0
Tuiasosopo, Manu, San Francisco	1	22	22.0	22	0
Leopold, Bobby, Green Bay	1	21	21.0	21	0
Carson, Harry, N.Y. Giants	1	20	20.0	20	0
Cousineau, Tom, San Francisco	1	18	18.0	18	0
Hoage, Terry, Philadelphia	1	18	18.0	18	0
Haynes, James, New Orleans	1	17	17.0	17t	1
Millard, Keith, Minnesota	1	17	17.0	17	0
Browner, Keith, Tampa Bay	1	16	16.0	16	0
Johnson, Vaughan, New Orleans	1	15	15.0	15	0
Olkewicz, Neal, Washington	1	15	15.0	15	0
Foules, Elbert, Philadelphia	1	14	14.0	14	0
Gary, Russell, New Orleans	1	14	14.0	14	0
Gayle, Shaun, Chicago	1	13	13.0	13	0
Johnson, Johnnie, L.A. Rams	1	13	13.0	13	0
Johnson, Pepper, N.Y. Giants	1	13	13.0	13	0
Smith, Leonard, St. Louis	1	13	13.0	13	0
Bess, Rufus, Minnesota	1	12	12.0	12	0
Washington, Chris, Tampa Bay	1	12	12.0	12	0
Schulz, Jody, Philadelphia	1	11	11.0	11	0
Cason, Wendell, Atlanta	1	10	10.0	10	0
Turner, Keena, San Francisco	1	9	9.0	9	0
Bostic, John, Detroit	1	8	8.0	8	0
Haley, Charles, San Francisco	1	8	8.0	8	0
Ferguson, Keith, Detroit	1	7	7.0	7	0
Phillips, Reggie, Chicago	1	6	6.0	6	0
Rade, John, Atlanta	1	6	6.0	6	0
Watts, Elbert, Green Bay	1	6	6.0	6	0
Dean, Vernon, Washington	1	5	5.0	5	0
Lockhart, Eugene, Dallas	1	5	5.0	5	0
McMichael, Steve, Chicago	1	5	5.0	5	0
Daniels, Calvin, Washington	1	4	4.0	4	0
Joyner, Seth, Philadelphia	1	4	4.0	4	0
Anderson, John, Green Bay	1	3	3.0	3	0
Cobb, Garry, Philadelphia	1	3	3.0	3	0
Singletary, Mike, Chicago	1	3	3.0	3	0
Studwell, Scott, Minnesota	1	2	2.0	2	0
Williams, Eric, Detroit	1	2	2.0	2	0
Headen, Andy, N.Y. Giants	1	1	1.0	1	0
Holloway, Johnny, Dallas	1	1	1.0	1	0
Jackson, Rickey, New Orleans	1	1	1.0	1	0
Collins, Mark, N.Y. Giants	1	0	0.0	0	0
Davis, Jeff, Tampa Bay	1	0	0.0	0	0
Easmon, Ricky, Tampa Bay	1	0	0.0	0	0
Flynn, Tom, Green Bay	1	0	0.0	0	0
Jones, Rod, Tampa Bay	1	0	0.0	0	0
Lasker, Greg, N.Y. Giants	1	0	0.0	0	0
Marshall, Leonard, N.Y. Giants	1	0	0.0	0	0
Moore, Robert, Atlanta	1	0	0.0	0	0
Wilcher, Mike, L.A. Rams	1	0	0.0	0	0
Bell, Todd, Chicago	1	−1	−1.0	−1	0

t indicates touchdown
Leader based on most interceptions

Punting

Individual Champions
AFC: 45.2 — Rohn Stark, Indianapolis
NFC: 44.8 — Sean Landeta, New York Giants

Net Average
AFC: 37.4 — Reggie Roby, Miami
NFC: 37.1 — Sean Landeta, New York Giants

Longest
AFC: 73 — Reggie Roby, Miami vs. San Francisco, September 28
73 — Reggie Roby, Miami vs. New England, October 5
NFC: 71 — Rick Donnelly, Atlanta vs. New York Jets, November 9

Most Punts
NFC: 108 — John Teltschik, Philadelphia
AFC: 99 — Lewis Colbert, Kansas City

Most Punts, Game

AFC: 11—Vince Gamache, Seattle vs. Kansas City, November 9

NFC: 10—Steve Cox, Washington vs. San Francisco, November 17

10—John Teltschik, Philadelphia vs. Los Angeles Raiders, November 30 [OT]

Team Champions

NFC: 44.8 — New York Giants

AFC: 44.7 — Indianapolis

AFC Punting—Team

	Total Punts	Gross Yards	Long	Gross Avg.	TB	Blk.	Opp. Ret.	Ret. Yards	In 20	Net Avg.
Indianapolis	81	3622	63	44.7	5	0	52	533	22	36.9
Miami	56	2476	73	44.2	9	0	23	200	13	37.4
Cleveland	83	3423	61	41.2	10	0	44	268	21	35.6
Houston	89	3659	66	41.1	9	0	40	303	27	35.7
Kansas City	99	4033	56	40.7	6	0	52	572	23	33.7
New England	92	3746	64	40.7	7	3	60	565	16	33.1
San Diego	79	3193	62	40.4	11	2	43	370	15	32.9
Buffalo	75	3031	57	40.4	9	0	32	260	14	34.5
Los Angeles Raiders	90	3620	64	40.2	11	0	42	357	20	33.8
New York Jets	85	3353	55	39.4	6	0	36	165	27	36.1
Denver	86	3376	57	39.3	9	1	40	362	15	33.0
Pittsburgh	89	3447	64	38.7	11	3	34	364	18	32.2
Seattle	79	3048	55	38.6	7	0	38	298	10	33.0
Cincinnati	59	1996	52	33.8	3	2	19	182	12	29.7
AFC Total	1,142	46,023	73	—	113	11	555	4,799	253	—
AFC Average	81.6	3,287.4	—	40.3	8.1	0.8	39.6	342.8	18.1	34.1

NFC Punting—Team

	Total Punts	Gross Yards	Long	Gross Avg.	TB	Blk.	Opp. Ret.	Ret. Yards	In 20	Net Avg.
New York Giants	79	3539	61	44.8	11	0	41	386	24	37.1
Washington	75	3271	58	43.6	16	0	36	220	21	36.4
Atlanta	79	3421	71	43.3	9	1	47	477	19	35.0
New Orleans	82	3456	66	42.1	11	1	37	234	17	36.6
Philadelphia	111	4547	62	41.0	10	1	63	634	20	33.5
Chicago	70	2850	59	40.7	8	1	23	110	20	36.9
San Francisco	85	3450	62	40.6	8	2	49	373	23	34.3
Dallas	87	3498	58	40.2	10	1	41	301	28	34.4
Tampa Bay	78	3132	60	40.2	8	0	39	414	19	32.8
Minnesota	73	2922	69	40.0	4	1	40	356	15	34.1
Detroit	85	3389	60	39.9	10	2	39	517	18	31.4
Los Angeles Rams	98	3740	57	38.2	5	1	47	416	26	32.9
Green Bay	75	2825	63	37.7	6	5	44	287	8	32.2
St. Louis	92	3411	52	37.1	4	1	44	296	21	33.0
NFC Total	1,169	47,451	71	—	120	17	590	5,021	279	—
NFC Average	83.5	3,389.4	—	40.6	8.6	1.2	42.1	358.6	19.9	34.2
League Total	2311	93,474	73	—	233	28	1,145	9,820	532	—
League Average	82.5	3,338.4	—	40.4	8.3	1.0	40.9	350.7	19.0	34.2

NFL Top 10 Punters

	Net Punts	Gross Yards	Long	Gross Avg.	Total Punts	TB	Blk.	Opp. Ret.	Ret. Yards	In 20	Net Avg.
Stark, Rohn, Indianapolis	76	3432	63	45.2	76	5	0	48	502	22	37.2
Landeta, Sean, N.Y. Giants	79	3539	61	44.8	79	11	0	41	386	24	37.1
Roby, Reggie, Miami	56	2476	73	44.2	56	9	0	23	200	13	37.4
Donnelly, Rick, Atlanta	78	3421	71	43.9	79	9	1	47	477	19	35.0
Cox, Steve, Washington	75	3271	58	43.6	75	16	0	36	220	21	36.4
Hansen, Brian, New Orleans	81	3456	66	42.7	82	11	1	37	234	17	36.6
Camarillo, Rich, New England	89	3746	64	42.1	92	7	3	60	565	16	33.1
Mojsiejenko, Ralf, San Diego	72	3026	62	42.0	74	11	2	42	368	15	32.9
Teltschik, John, Philadelphia	108	4493	62	41.6	109	10	1	62	631	20	33.6
Runager, Max, San Francisco	83	3450	62	41.6	85	8	2	49	373	23	34.3

AFC Punting—Individual

	Net Punts	Gross Yards	Long	Gross Avg.	Total Punts	TB	Blk.	Opp. Ret.	Ret. Yards	In 20	Net Avg.
Stark, Rohn, Indianapolis	76	3432	63	45.2	76	5	0	48	502	22	37.2
Roby, Reggie, Miami	56	2476	73	44.2	56	9	0	23	200	13	37.4
Camarillo, Rich, New England	89	3746	64	42.1	92	7	3	60	565	16	33.1
Mojsiejenko, Ralf, San Diego	72	3026	62	42.0	74	11	2	42	368	15	32.9
Gossett, Jeff, Cleveland	83	3423	61	41.2	83	10	0	44	268	21	35.6
Johnson, Lee, Houston	88	3623	66	41.2	88	9	0	40	303	26	35.7
Colbert, Lewis, Kansas City	99	4033	56	40.7	99	6	0	52	572	23	33.7
Kidd, John, Buffalo	75	3031	57	40.4	75	9	0	32	260	14	34.5
Guy, Ray, L.A. Raiders	90	3620	64	40.2	90	11	0	42	357	20	33.8
Newsome, Harry, Pittsburgh	86	3447	64	40.1	89	11	3	34	364	18	32.2
Jennings, Dave, N.Y. Jets	85	3353	55	39.4	85	6	0	36	165	27	36.1
Gamache, Vince, Seattle	79	3048	55	38.6	79	7	0	38	298	10	33.0
Hayes, Jeff, Cincinnati	56	1965	52	35.1	58	3	2	19	182	11	29.7
Non-Qualifiers											
Weil, Jack, Denver	34	1344	55	39.5	34	3	0	20	169	5	32.8
Norman, Chris, Denver	30	1168	57	38.9	31	4	1	9	94	2	32.1
Horan, Mike, Denver	21	864	50	41.1	21	2	0	11	99	8	34.5
Chandler, Wes, San Diego	5	167	38	33.4	5	0	0	1	2	0	33.0
Kiel, Blair, Indianapolis	5	190	43	38.0	5	0	0	4	31	0	31.8
Esiason, Boomer, Cincinnati	1	31	31	31.0	1	0	0	0	0	1	31.0
Zendejas, Tony, Houston	1	36	36	36.0	1	0	0	0	0	1	36.0

Leader based on gross average, minimum 40 punts.

NFC Punting—Individual

	Net Punts	Gross Yards	Long	Gross Avg.	Total Punts	TB	Blk.	Opp. Ret.	Ret. Yards	In 20	Net Avg.
Landeta, Sean, N.Y. Giants	79	3539	61	44.8	79	11	0	41	386	24	37.1
Donnelly, Rick, Atlanta	78	3421	71	43.9	79	9	1	47	477	19	35.0
Cox, Steve, Washington	75	3271	58	43.6	75	16	0	36	220	21	36.4
Hansen, Brian, New Orleans	81	3456	66	42.7	82	11	1	37	234	17	36.6
Teltschik, John, Philadelphia	108	4493	62	41.6	109	10	1	62	631	20	33.6
Runager, Max, San Francisco	83	3450	62	41.6	85	8	2	49	373	23	34.3
Coleman, Greg, Minnesota	67	2774	69	41.4	67	4	0	39	353	15	34.9
Buford, Maury, Chicago	69	2850	59	41.3	70	8	1	23	110	20	36.9
Saxon, Mike, Dallas	86	3498	58	40.7	87	10	1	41	301	28	34.4
Garcia, Frank, Tampa Bay	77	3089	60	40.1	77	8	0	38	410	19	32.7
Bracken, Don, Green Bay	55	2203	63	40.1	57	5	2	33	235	6	32.8
Black, Mike, Detroit	46	1819	57	39.5	47	5	1	21	250	11	31.3
Hatcher, Dale, L.A. Rams	97	3740	57	38.6	98	5	1	47	416	26	32.9
Cater, Greg, St. Louis	61	2271	52	37.2	62	4	1	24	130	16	33.2
Non-Qualifiers											
Arnold, Jim, Detroit	36	1533	60	42.6	37	4	1	18	267	7	32.1
Arapostathis, Evan, St. Louis	30	1140	50	38.0	30	0	0	20	166	5	32.5
Renner, Bill, Green Bay	15	622	50	41.5	18	1	3	11	52	2	30.6
Nelson, Chuck, Minnesota	3	72	31	24.0	3	0	0	0	0	0	24.0
Cunningham, Randall, Philadelphia	2	54	39	27.0	2	0	0	1	3	0	25.5
Wilson, Wade, Minnesota	2	76	46	38.0	3	0	1	1	3	0	24.3
Murray, Ed, Detroit	1	37	37	37.0	1	1	0	0	0	0	17.0
Springs, Ron, Tampa Bay	1	43	43	43.0	1	0	0	1	4	0	39.0

Leader based on gross average, minimum 40 punts.

Punt Returns

Individual Champions (Average)
AFC: 12.3—Bobby Joe Edmonds, Seattle
NFC: 12.1—Vai Sikahema, St. Louis

Yards
NFC: 522—Vai Sikahema, St. Louis
AFC: 468—Gerald Willhite, Denver

Most Yards, Game
NFC: 145—Vai Sikahema, St. Louis vs. Tampa Bay, December 21 (4 returns)
AFC: 106—James Pruitt, Miami vs. Indianapolis, September 14 (2 returns)
106—Gerald McNeil, Cleveland vs. Detroit, September 28 (4 returns)

Longest
AFC: 84—Gerald McNeil, Cleveland vs. Detroit, September 28 (TD)
NFC: 83—Walter Stanley, Green Bay vs. Detroit, November 27 (TD)

Most Returns
NFC: 57—Lew Barnes, Chicago
AFC: 49—Fulton Walker, Los Angeles Raiders

Most Returns, Game
AFC: 8—Fulton Walker, Los Angeles Raiders vs. Cleveland, November 16 (74 yards)
NFC: 8—Evan Cooper, Philadelphia vs. San Diego, October 26 (28 yards)

Fair Catches
NFC: 18—Don Griffin, San Francisco
AFC: 15—Fulton Walker, Los Angeles Raiders

Touchdowns
NFC: 2—Vai Sikahema, St. Louis
AFC: 1—Bobby Joe Edmonds, Seattle
1—Irving Fryar, New England
1—Mike Harden, Denver
1—Gerald McNeil, Cleveland
1—Ron Pitts, Buffalo
1—James Pruitt, Miami
1—Fulton Walker, Los Angeles Raiders
1—Gerald Willhite, Denver

Team Champions
NFC: 11.73—St. Louis
AFC: 11.72—Seattle

AFC Punt Returns—Team

	No.	FC	Yards	Avg.	Long	TD
Seattle	39	14	457	11.7	75t	1
Denver	48	8	552	11.5	70t	2
New England	42	12	396	9.4	59t	1
San Diego	37	16	334	9.0	30	0
New York Jets	39	9	341	8.7	28	0
Los Angeles Raiders	56	16	484	8.6	70t	1
Pittsburgh	36	13	310	8.6	41	0
Cleveland	41	10	350	8.5	84t	1
Cincinnati	29	17	235	8.1	25	0
Houston	43	15	341	7.9	25	0
Buffalo	32	13	247	7.7	49t	1
Kansas City	35	18	265	7.6	48	0
Miami	40	11	297	7.4	71t	1
Indianapolis	35	13	250	7.1	25	0
AFC Total	552	185	4,859	—	84t	8
AFC Average	39.4	13.2	347.1	8.8	—	0.6

NFC Punt Returns—Team

	No.	FC	Yards	Avg.	Long	TD
St. Louis	45	16	528	11.7	71t	2
Washington	51	20	550	10.8	44	0
Detroit	43	9	420	9.8	81t	1
Green Bay	33	7	316	9.6	83t	1
San Francisco	43	19	397	9.2	76t	1
Los Angeles Rams	42	22	361	8.6	32	0
Philadelphia	44	16	374	8.5	76t	1
Chicago	57	9	482	8.5	35	0
New Orleans	47	15	377	8.0	39	0
New York Giants	41	20	287	7.0	22	0
Minnesota	31	17	215	6.9	15	0
Atlanta	44	12	292	6.6	30	0
Dallas	46	17	252	5.5	28	0
Tampa Bay	26	5	110	4.2	12	0
NFC Total	593	204	4,961	—	83t	6
NFC Average	42.4	14.6	354.4	8.4	—	0.4
League Total	1,145	389	9,820	—	84t	14
League Average	40.9	13.9	350.7	8.6	—	0.5

NFL Top 10 Punt Returners

	No.	FC	Yards	Avg.	Long	TD
Edmonds, Bobby Joe, Seattle	34	14	419	12.3	75t	1
Sikahema, Vai, St. Louis	43	16	522	12.1	71t	2
Willhite, Gerald, Denver	42	8	468	11.1	70t	1
Fryar, Irving, New England	35	10	366	10.5	59t	1
Griffin, Don, San Francisco	38	18	377	9.9	76t	1
Mandley, Pete, Detroit	43	9	420	9.8	81t	1
Jenkins, Ken, Washington	28	11	270	9.6	39	0
Stanley, Walter, Green Bay	33	7	316	9.6	83t	1
Martin, Eric, New Orleans	24	9	227	9.5	39	0
Anderson, Gary, San Diego	25	10	227	9.1	30	0

AFC Punt Returns—Individual

	No.	FC	Yards	Avg.	Long	TD
Edmonds, Bobby Joe, Seattle	34	14	419	12.3	75t	1
Willhite, Gerald, Denver	42	8	468	11.1	70t	1
Fryar, Irving, New England	35	10	366	10.5	59t	1
Anderson, Gary, San Diego	25	10	227	9.1	30	0
Walker, Fulton, L.A. Raiders	49	15	440	9.0	70t	1
Woods, Rick, Pittsburgh	33	12	294	8.9	41	0
McNeil, Gerald, Cleveland	40	10	348	8.7	84t	1
Smith, Jeff, Kansas City	29	11	245	8.4	48	0
Sohn, Kurt, N.Y. Jets	35	8	289	8.3	27	0
Drewrey, Willie, Houston	34	13	262	7.7	25	0
Ellis, Craig, Miami	24	1	149	6.2	17	0
Non-Qualifiers						
Pitts, Ron, Buffalo	18	11	194	10.8	49t	1
Brooks, Bill, Indianapolis	18	7	141	7.8	18	0
Martin, Robbie, Indianapolis	17	5	109	6.4	25	0
Martin, Mike, Cincinnati	13	6	96	7.4	14	0
Broughton, Walter, Buffalo	12	2	53	4.4	13	0
Pruitt, James, Miami	11	1	150	13.6	71t	1
Horton, Ray, Cincinnati	11	3	111	10.1	25	0
James, Lionel, San Diego	9	6	94	10.4	21	0
Givins, Earnest, Houston	8	0	80	10.0	17	0
McCallum, Napoleon, L.A. Raiders	7	1	44	6.3	13	0
Harry, Emile, Kansas City	6	7	20	3.3	7	0
Starring, Stephen, New England	6	0	18	3.0	12	0
Skansi, Paul, Seattle	5	0	38	7.6	14	0
Townsell, JoJo, N.Y. Jets	4	1	52	13.0	28	0
Johnson, Vance, Denver	3	0	36	12.0	19	0
McGee, Tim, Cincinnati	3	4	21	7.0	9	0
Lipps, Louis, Pittsburgh	3	1	16	5.3	10	0
Chandler, Wes, San Diego	3	0	13	4.3	10	0
Jackson, Mark, Denver	2	0	7	3.5	6	0
Simmons, John, Cincinnati	2	4	7	3.5	6	0
Harden, Mike, Denver	1	0	41	41.0	41t	1
Marion, Fred, New England	1	1	12	12.0	12	0
Slaughter, Webster, Cleveland	1	0	2	2.0	2	0
Blackwood, Glenn, Miami	1	0	0	0.0	0	0
Blackwood, Lyle, Miami	1	0	0	0.0	0	0
Clayton, Mark, Miami	1	0	0	0.0	0	0
Hill, Rod, Buffalo	1	0	0	0.0	0	0
Richardson, Eric, Buffalo	1	0	0	0.0	0	0
Thompson, Reyna, Miami	1	0	0	0.0	0	0
Pinkett, Allen, Houston	1	2	−1	−1.0	−1	0
Moore, Nat, Miami	1	6	−2	−2.0	−2	0
Jackson, Victor, Indianapolis	0	1	0	—	0	0
James, Roland, New England	0	1	0	—	0	0
Kozlowski, Mike, Miami	0	3	0	—	0	0

t indicates touchdown
Leader based on average return, minimum 20 returns.

NFC Punt Returns—Individual

	No.	FC	Yards	Avg.	Long	TD
Sikahema, Vai, St. Louis	43	16	522	12.1	71t	2
Griffin, Don, San Francisco	38	18	377	9.9	76t	1
Mandley, Pete, Detroit	43	9	420	9.8	81t	1
Jenkins, Ken, Washington	28	11	270	9.6	39	0
Stanley, Walter, Green Bay	33	7	316	9.6	83t	1
Martin, Eric, New Orleans	24	9	227	9.5	39	0
Barnes, Lew, Chicago	57	9	482	8.5	35	0
Sutton, Mickey, L.A. Rams	28	5	234	8.4	32	0
McConkey, Phil, G.B.-N.Y. Giants	32	12	253	7.9	22	0
Bess, Rufus, Minnesota	23	10	162	7.0	15	0
Banks, Gordon, Dallas	27	14	160	5.9	20	0
Dixon, Floyd, Atlanta	26	3	151	5.8	16	0
Non-Qualifiers						
Lavette, Robert, Dallas	18	3	92	5.1	28	0
Garrity, Gregg, Philadelphia	17	7	187	11.0	76t	1
Cooper, Evan, Philadelphia	16	7	139	8.7	58	0
Ellard, Henry, L.A. Rams	14	10	127	9.1	20	0
Futrell, Bobby, Tampa Bay	14	5	67	4.8	12	0
Green, Darrell, Washington	12	2	120	10.0	23	0
McLemore, Dana, New Orleans	10	3	67	6.7	23	0
Yarber, Eric, Washington	9	4	143	15.9	44	0
Walker, Kevin, Tampa Bay	9	0	27	3.0	10	0

	No.	FC	Yards	Avg.	Long	TD
Johnson, Billy, Atlanta	8	8	87	10.9	30	0
Poe, Johnnie, New Orleans	8	3	71	8.9	17	0
Lewis, Leo, Minnesota	7	4	53	7.6	13	0
Jones, Joey, Atlanta	7	1	36	5.1	14	0
Waters, Mike, Philadelphia	7	1	30	4.3	13	0
Smith, Phil, Philadelphia	4	1	18	4.5	7	0
Crawford, Derrick, San Francisco	4	0	15	3.8	9	0
Manuel, Lionel, N.Y. Giants	3	6	22	7.3	12	0
Harris, Leonard, Tampa Bay	3	0	16	5.3	8	0
Collins, Mark, N.Y. Giants	3	1	11	3.7	6	0
Edwards, Kelvin, New Orleans	3	0	2	0.7	5	0
Galbreath, Tony, N.Y. Giants	3	1	1	0.3	1	0
Allen, Anthony, Atlanta	2	0	10	5.0	9	0
Tullis, Willie, New Orleans	2	0	10	5.0	7	0
Clark, Gary, Washington	1	3	14	14.0	14	0
Stamps, Sylvester, Atlanta	1	0	8	8.0	8	0
Smith, J.T., St. Louis	1	0	6	6.0	6	0
McKyer, Tim, San Francisco	1	1	5	5.0	5	0
Milot, Rich, Washington	1	0	3	3.0	3	0
Carter, Carl, St. Louis	1	0	0	0.0	0	0
Holloway, Johnny, Dallas	1	0	0	0.0	0	0
Rice, Allen, Minnesota	1	0	0	0.0	0	0
Carter, Anthony, Minnesota	0	1	0	—	0	0
Johnson, Johnnie, L.A. Rams	0	7	0	—	0	0
Morrell, Kyle, Minnesota	0	2	0	—	0	0

t indicates touchdown
Leader based on average return, minimum 20 returns.

Kickoff Returns

Individual Champions (Average)
NFC: 28.8—Dennis Gentry, Chicago
AFC: 23.6—Lupe Sanchez, Pittsburgh

Yards
AFC: 1,007—Tim McGee, Cincinnati
NFC: 1,007—Herman Hunter, Detroit

Most Yards, Game
AFC: 234—Bobby Humphery, New York Jets vs. Cincinnati, December 21 (8 returns)
NFC: 186—Mel Gray, New Orleans vs. San Francisco, September 21 (3 returns)

Longest
NFC: 101—Mel Gray, New Orleans vs. San Francisco, September 21 (TD)
AFC: 100—Gerald McNeil, Cleveland vs. Pittsburgh, October 5 (TD)

Most Returns
NFC: 49—Herman Hunter, Detroit
AFC: 47—Gerald McNeil, Cleveland

Most Returns, Game
AFC: 8—Bobby Humphery, New York Jets vs. Cincinnati, December 21 (234 yards)
NFC: 6—Rufus Bess, Minnesota vs. San Francisco, October 12 (168 yards)
6—Rufus Bess, Minnesota vs. Washington, November 2 [OT] (109 yards)
6—Ron Brown, Los Angeles Rams vs. Atlanta, October 12 (122 yards)
6—Herman Hunter, Detroit vs. Green Bay, November 27 (104 yards)
6—Ken Jenkins, Washington vs. Dallas, October 12 (125 yards)

Touchdowns
AFC: 1—Boyce Green, Kansas City
1—Bobby Humphery, New York Jets
1—Gerald McNeil, Cleveland
1—JoJo Townsell, New York Jets
NFC: 1—Lew Barnes, Chicago
1—Mel Gray, New Orleans
1—Dennis Gentry, Chicago

Team Champions
NFC: 24.2—New Orleans
AFC: 22.0—Cincinnati

AFC Kickoff Returns—Team

	No.	Yards	Avg.	Long	TD
Cincinnati	63	1389	22.0	94	0
Seattle	64	1322	20.7	46	0
Denver	53	1094	20.6	42	0
Kansas City	56	1117	19.9	97t	1
New England	58	1147	19.8	52	0
Pittsburgh	66	1304	19.8	64	0
Cleveland	62	1213	19.6	100t	1
Los Angeles Raiders	64	1252	19.6	59	0
Buffalo	55	1074	19.5	49	0
Indianapolis	74	1443	19.5	37	0
Houston	59	1139	19.3	48	0
New York Jets	63	1189	18.9	96t	2
Miami	65	1185	18.2	41	0
San Diego	65	1137	17.5	35	0
AFC Total	867	17,005	—	100t	4
AFC Average	61.9	1,214.6	19.6	—	0.3

NFC Kickoff Returns—Team

	No.	Yards	Avg.	Long	TD
New Orleans	55	1332	24.2	101t	1
Chicago	50	1115	22.3	91t	2
St. Louis	70	1548	22.1	53	0
Minnesota	56	1200	21.4	43	0
Dallas	59	1208	20.5	56	0
Detroit	67	1321	19.7	54	0
Los Angeles Rams	59	1160	19.7	55	0
Washington	60	1175	19.6	37	0
Green Bay	76	1470	19.3	57	0
Atlanta	54	1035	19.2	35	0
San Francisco	42	757	18.0	34	0
Philadelphia	53	945	17.8	51	0
New York Giants	50	868	17.4	30	0
Tampa Bay	75	1302	17.4	33	0
NFC Total	826	16,436	—	101t	3
NFC Average	59.0	1,174.0	19.9	—	0.2
League Total	1,693	33,441	—	101t	7
League Average	60.5	1,194.3	19.8	—	0.3

NFL Top 10 Kickoff Returners

	No.	Yards	Avg.	Long	TD
Gentry, Dennis, Chicago	20	576	28.8	91t	1
Gray, Mel, New Orleans	31	866	27.9	101t	1
Sanchez, Lupe, Pittsburgh	25	591	23.6	64	0
McGee, Tim, Cincinnati	43	1007	23.4	94	0
Humphery, Bobby, N.Y. Jets	28	655	23.4	96t	1
Bell, Ken, Denver	23	531	23.1	42	0
Sikahema, Vai, St. Louis	37	847	22.9	44	0
Lang, Gene, Denver	21	480	22.9	42	0
Bess, Rufus, Minnesota	31	705	22.7	43	0
Edmonds, Bobby Joe, Seattle	34	764	22.5	46	0

AFC Kickoff Returns—Individual

	No.	Yards	Avg.	Long	TD
Sanchez, Lupe, Pittsburgh	25	591	23.6	64	0
McGee, Tim, Cincinnati	43	1007	23.4	94	0
Humphery, Bobby, N.Y. Jets	28	655	23.4	96t	1
Bell, Ken, Denver	23	531	23.1	42	0
Lang, Gene, Denver	21	480	22.9	42	0
Edmonds, Bobby Joe, Seattle	34	764	22.5	46	0
Starring, Stephen, New England	36	802	22.3	52	0
Ellis, Craig, Miami	25	541	21.6	41	0
Bentley, Albert, Indianapolis	32	687	21.5	37	0
Adams, Stefon, L.A. Raiders	27	573	21.2	51	0
McNeil, Gerald, Cleveland	47	997	21.2	100t	1
Morris, Randall, Seattle	23	465	20.2	38	0
Anderson, Gary, San Diego	24	482	20.1	35	0
Drewrey, Willie, Houston	25	500	20.0	32	0
Pinkett, Allen, Houston	26	519	20.0	48	0
Smith, Jeff, Kansas City	29	557	19.2	29	0
Martin, Robbie, Indianapolis	21	385	18.3	27	0
Walker, Fulton, L.A. Raiders	23	368	16.0	27	0
Non-Qualifiers					
Harmon, Ronnie, Buffalo	18	321	17.8	32	0
James, Lionel, San Diego	18	315	17.5	31	0
Davenport, Ron, Miami	16	285	17.8	37	0
Townsell, JoJo, N.Y. Jets	13	322	24.8	93t	1
Jennings, Stanford, Cincinnati	12	257	21.4	41	0
Tasker, Steve, Houston-Buffalo	12	213	17.8	24	0
Broughton, Walter, Buffalo	11	243	22.1	39	0
Green, Boyce, Kansas City	10	254	25.4	97t	1
Fryar, Irving, New England	10	192	19.2	33	0
Hampton, Lorenzo, Miami	9	182	20.2	25	0
Carter, Joe, Miami	9	133	14.8	22	0
Riddick, Robb, Buffalo	8	200	25.0	49	0
McCallum, Napoleon, L.A. Raiders	8	183	22.9	59	0
Sanders, Chuck, Pittsburgh	8	148	18.5	29	0
Brooks, Bill, Indianapolis	8	143	17.9	24	0
Sohn, Kurt, N.Y. Jets	7	124	17.7	36	0
Fontenot, Herman, Cleveland	7	99	14.1	19	0
Harper, Michael, N.Y. Jets	7	71	10.1	19	0
Richardson, Eric, Buffalo	6	123	20.5	28	0
Harry, Emile, Kansas City	6	115	19.2	26	0
Daniel, Kenny, Indianapolis	5	109	21.8	30	0
Adams, Curtis, San Diego	5	100	20.0	25	0
Carson, Carlos, Kansas City	5	88	17.6	29	0
Spencer, Tim, San Diego	5	81	16.2	21	0
Wyatt, Kevin, San Diego	5	74	14.8	23	0
Gill, Owen, Indianapolis	5	73	14.6	28	0
Martin, Mike, Cincinnati	4	83	20.8	21	0
Moriarty, Larry, Kansas City	4	80	20.0	23	0
Jones, Cedric, New England	4	63	15.8	20	0
Langhorne, Reggie, Cleveland	4	57	14.3	20	0
Reeder, Dan, Pittsburgh	4	52	13.0	17	0

	No.	Yards	Avg.	Long	TD
Dupard, Reggie, New England	3	50	16.7	21	0
Johnson, Trumaine, San Diego	3	48	16.0	21	0
Millen, Matt, L.A. Raiders	3	40	13.3	19	0
Hardy, Bruce, Miami	3	39	13.0	16	0
Scholtz, Bruce, Seattle	3	39	13.0	16	0
Willhite, Gerald, Denver	3	35	11.7	23	0
Nicolas, Scott, Cleveland	3	28	9.3	13	0
Rembert, Johnny, New England	3	27	9.0	14	0
Rudolph, Ben, N.Y. Jets	3	17	5.7	10	0
Mueller, Vance, L.A. Raiders	2	73	36.5	46	0
Woolfolk, Butch, Houston	2	38	19.0	21	0
Bellinger, Rodney, Buffalo	2	32	16.0	16	0
Wonsley, George, Indianapolis	2	31	15.5	20	0
Seitz, Warren, Pittsburgh	2	25	12.5	14	0
Simpkins, Ron, Cincinnati	2	24	12.0	15	0
Johnson, Vance, Denver	2	21	10.5	21	0
Riley, Avon, Houston	2	17	8.5	10	0
Hughes, David, Pittsburgh	2	16	8.0	16	0
Hawthorne, Greg, New England	2	13	6.5	13	0
Hunley, Ricky, Denver	2	11	5.5	6	0
Winslow, Kellen, San Diego	2	11	5.5	8	0
Baldwin, Tom, N.Y. Jets	2	3	1.5	4	0
Shuler, Mickey, N.Y. Jets	2	−3	−1.5	0	0
Puzzuoli, Dave, Cleveland	1	32	32.0	32	0
Merriweather, Mike, Pittsburgh	1	27	27.0	27	0
Cocroft, Sherman, Kansas City	1	23	23.0	23	0
Skansi, Paul, Seattle	1	21	21.0	21	0
Holman, Rodney, Cincinnati	1	18	18.0	18	0
Tice, Mike, Seattle	1	17	17.0	17	0
Woods, Rick, Pittsburgh	1	17	17.0	17	0
Jackson, Mark, Denver	1	16	16.0	16	0
Hawkins, Frank, L.A. Raiders	1	15	15.0	15	0
McGee, Buford, San Diego	1	15	15.0	15	0
Williams, Oliver, Indianapolis	1	15	15.0	15	0
Edwards, Randy, Seattle	1	13	13.0	13	0
Chandler, Wes, San Diego	1	11	11.0	11	0
Pitts, Ron, Buffalo	1	7	7.0	7	0
Lee, Larry, Miami	1	5	5.0	5	0
Lane, Eric, Seattle	1	3	3.0	3	0
Rostosky, Pete, Pittsburgh	1	3	3.0	3	0
Johnson, Dan, Miami	1	0	0.0	0	0
Lynn, Johnny, N.Y. Jets	1	0	0.0	0	0
Madsen, Lynn, Houston	1	0	0.0	0	0
Pearson, Aaron, Kansas City	1	0	0.0	0	0
Plummer, Gary, San Diego	1	0	0.0	0	0
Ryan, Jim, Denver	1	0	0.0	0	0
Simmons, John, Cincinnati	1	0	0.0	0	0
Sweeney, Calvin, Pittsburgh	1	0	0.0	0	0
Toth, Tom, Miami	1	0	0.0	0	0

t indicates touchdown
Leader based on average return, minimum 20 returns.

NFC Kickoff Returns—Individual

	No.	Yards	Avg.	Long	TD
Gentry, Dennis, Chicago	20	576	28.8	91t	1
Gray, Mel, New Orleans	31	866	27.9	101t	1
Sikahema, Vai, St. Louis	37	847	22.9	44	0
Bess, Rufus, Minnesota	31	705	22.7	43	0
Brown, Ron, L.A. Rams	36	794	22.1	55	0
Stamps, Sylvester, Atlanta	24	514	21.4	35	0
Hunter, Herman, Detroit	49	1007	20.6	54	0
Jenkins, Ken, Washington	27	554	20.5	37	0
Stanley, Walter, Green Bay	28	559	20.0	55	0
Elder, Donnie, Pittsburgh-Detroit	22	435	19.8	36	0
McConkey, Phil, G.B.-N.Y. Giants	24	471	19.6	27	0
Lavette, Robert, Dallas	36	699	19.4	37	0
Freeman, Phil, Tampa Bay	31	582	18.8	33	0
Crawford, Charles, Philadelphia	27	497	18.4	36	0
Sanders, Thomas, Chicago	22	399	18.1	44	0
Non-Qualifiers					
Clack, Darryl, Dallas	19	421	22.2	51	0
Tautalatasi, Junior, Philadelphia	18	344	19.1	51	0
Crawford, Derrick, San Francisco	15	280	18.7	34	0
Williams, Keith, Atlanta	14	255	18.2	32	0
Verdin, Clarence, Washington	12	240	20.0	29	0
Watts, Elbert, Green Bay	12	239	19.9	40	0
Davis, Kenneth, Green Bay	12	231	19.3	35	0
White, Charles, L.A. Rams	12	216	18.0	28	0
Collins, Mark, N.Y. Giants	11	204	18.5	26	0
Mayes, Rueben, New Orleans	10	213	21.3	34	0
Stills, Ken, Green Bay	10	209	20.9	38	0
Wonsley, Nathan, Tampa Bay	10	208	20.8	29	0
Swanson, Eric, St. Louis	10	206	20.6	40	0
Rhymes, Buster, Minnesota	9	213	23.7	34	0
Griffin, Keith, Washington	8	156	19.5	35	0
Walker, Kevin, Tampa Bay	8	146	18.3	26	0
Monroe, Carl, San Francisco	8	139	17.4	25	0
Ellerson, Gary, Green Bay	7	154	22.0	57	0
Garner, Dwight, Washington	7	142	20.3	26	0
Harris, Herbert, New Orleans	7	122	17.4	22	0
Austin, Cliff, Atlanta	7	120	17.1	25	0
Miller, Solomon, N.Y. Giants	7	111	15.9	23	0
Mitchell, Stump, St. Louis	6	203	33.8	53	0
Fox, Chas, St. Louis	6	161	26.8	38	0
Bland, Carl, Detroit	6	114	19.0	24	0
Futrell, Bobby, Tampa Bay	5	115	23.0	30	0
Griffin, Don, San Francisco	5	97	19.4	28	0
Sutton, Mickey, L.A. Rams	5	91	18.2	22	0
Rice, Allen, Minnesota	5	88	17.6	23	0
Smith, Oscar, Detroit	5	81	16.2	30	0
Hill, Kenny, N.Y. Giants	5	61	12.2	30	0
Harmon, Derrick, San Francisco	4	82	20.5	28	0
Andrews, William, Atlanta	4	71	17.8	22	0
Howard, Bobby, Tampa Bay	4	71	17.8	24	0
Harris, Leonard, Tampa Bay	4	63	15.8	23	0
Carruth, Paul Ott, Green Bay	4	40	10.0	20	0
Anderson, Neal, Chicago	4	26	6.5	13	0
Nelson, Darrin, Minnesota	3	105	35.0	40	0
Barnes, Lew, Chicago	3	94	31.3	85t	1
Graham, William, Detroit	3	72	24.0	27	0
Rathman, Tom, San Francisco	3	66	22.0	22	0
Martin, Eric, New Orleans	3	64	21.3	27	0
Johnson, Troy, St. Louis	3	46	15.3	25	0
Holloway, Derek, Washington	3	44	14.7	18	0
Matthews, Aubrey, Atlanta	3	42	14.0	20	0
Ferrell, Earl, St. Louis	3	41	13.7	27	0
Anderson, Alfred, Minnesota	3	38	12.7	17	0
Franklin, Pat, Tampa Bay	3	23	7.7	18	0
Byars, Keith, Philadelphia	2	47	23.5	31	0
Cooper, Evan, Philadelphia	2	42	21.0	24	0
McLemore, Dana, New Orleans	2	39	19.5	22	0
Mandley, Pete, Detroit	2	37	18.5	37	0
Wilson, Wayne, Minnesota	2	33	16.5	26	0
Newsome, Tim, Dallas	2	32	16.0	18	0
Orr, Terry, Washington	2	31	15.5	16	0
Cherry, Tony, San Francisco	2	29	14.5	17	0
Williams, David, Tampa Bay	2	29	14.5	15	0
Guman, Mike, L.A. Rams	2	28	14.0	16	0
Tullis, Willie, New Orleans	2	28	14.0	19	0
Sargent, Broderick, St. Louis	2	27	13.5	14	0
Frank, John, San Francisco	2	24	12.0	16	0
Carter, Carl, St. Louis	2	21	10.5	14	0
Magee, Calvin, Tampa Bay	2	21	10.5	11	0
Rouson, Lee, N.Y. Giants	2	21	10.5	12	0
Carpenter, Rob, L.A. Rams	2	19	9.5	11	0
Brown, Ted, Minnesota	2	18	9.0	17	0
Quick, Mike, Philadelphia	2	6	3.0	6	0
Banks, Gordon, Dallas	1	56	56.0	56	0
Allen, Greg, Tampa Bay	1	21	21.0	21	0
Epps, Phillip, Green Bay	1	21	21.0	21	0
Croudip, David, Atlanta	1	20	20.0	20	0
Gault, Willie, Chicago	1	20	20.0	20	0
Ellard, Henry, L.A. Rams	1	18	18.0	18	0
Berry, Ed, Green Bay	1	16	16.0	16	0
Heflin, Vince, Tampa Bay	1	15	15.0	15	0
McKyer, Tim, San Francisco	1	15	15.0	15	0
Ring, Bill, San Francisco	1	15	15.0	15	0
Dixon, Floyd, Atlanta	1	13	13.0	13	0
Wilson, Mike, San Francisco	1	10	10.0	10	0
Schulz, Jody, Philadelphia	1	9	9.0	9	0
Krakoski, Joe, Washington	1	8	8.0	8	0
Curry, Craig, Tampa Bay	1	6	6.0	6	0
Boatner, Mack, Tampa Bay	1	2	2.0	2	0
Holmes, Don, St. Louis	1	2	2.0	2	0
Noble, Brian, Green Bay	1	1	1.0	1	0
Dunn, K.D., Tampa Bay	1	0	0.0	0	0
Evans, Leon, Detroit	1	0	0.0	0	0
Irwin, Tim, Minnesota	1	0	0.0	0	0
Lasker, Greg, N.Y. Giants	1	0	0.0	0	0
Randle, Ervin, Tampa Bay	1	0	0.0	0	0
Simmons, Clyde, Philadelphia	1	0	0.0	0	0
Tuinei, Mark, Dallas	1	0	0.0	0	0
Love, Duval, L.A. Rams	1	−6	−6.0	−6	0
Wolfley, Ron, St. Louis	0	−6	—	−6	0

t indicates touchdown
Leader based on average return, minimum 20 returns.

AFC Fumbles—Team

	Fum.	Own Rec.	Fum. *O.B.	TD	Opp. Rec.	Yds.	TD	Tot. Rec.
Denver	24	9	2	0	17	−2	2	26
Kansas City	27	6	4	1	18	1	1	24
New England	27	12	4	0	19	63	2	31
Pittsburgh	27	9	2	0	13	12	0	22
Houston	28	13	3	1	15	105	2	28
San Diego	29	11	2	0	22	22	0	33
Seattle	29	12	4	0	14	1	0	26
Cincinnati	31	11	4	0	11	−21	1	22
Cleveland	31	16	2	2	19	−16	1	35
L.A. Raiders	36	11	1	0	12	4	1	23
N.Y. Jets	37	12	9	0	18	68	0	30
Miami	37	20	3	0	13	−2	0	33
Buffalo	40	17	3	1	8	94	1	25
Indianapolis	41	18	3	0	19	40	0	37

NFC Fumbles—Team

	Fum.	Own Rec.	Fum. *O.B.	TD	Opp. Rec.	Yds.	TD	Tot. Rec.
St. Louis	25	13	2	0	12	0	0	25
Washington	29	19	0	0	9	8	1	28
Detroit	30	13	0	0	19	−2	0	32
Atlanta	31	15	0	0	14	99	2	29
N.Y. Giants	31	18	3	0	19	13	0	37
Minnesota	31	16	1	0	18	−16	0	34
San Francisco	32	22	1	0	10	16	0	32
New Orleans	33	15	0	0	17	31	0	32
Philadelphia	34	18	6	0	13	67	0	31
Green Bay	35	14	3	0	12	−32	0	26
Chicago	36	12	2	0	16	−29	1	28
Tampa Bay	36	15	4	0	19	15	2	34
L.A. Rams	39	15	2	1	15	102	1	30
Dallas	44	23	4	0	18	37	0	41

**indicates fumbled out of bounds*

AFC Fumbles—Individual

	Fum.	Own Rec.	Opp. Rec.	Yds.	Tot. Rec.
Abercrombie, Walter, Pittsburgh	4	0	0	0	0
Abraham, Robert, Houston	0	0	1	0	1
Adams, Curtis, San Diego	3	1	0	0	1
Adams, Stefon, L.A. Raiders	0	0	2	0	2
Allen, Marcus, L.A. Raiders	7	1	0	0	1
Anderson, Gary, San Diego	5	2	0	0	2
Armstrong, Harvey, Indianapolis	0	0	3	0	3
Arnold, Walt, Kansas City	0	2	0	0	2
Baldwin, Tom, N.Y. Jets	1	0	1	0	1
Banks, Chip, Cleveland	0	0	2	0	2
Banks, Chuck, Houston	1	0	0	0	0
Barber, Marion, N.Y. Jets	1	0	0	0	0
Barksdale, Rod, L.A. Raiders	1	1	0	0	1
Barnes, Jeff, L.A. Raiders	1	0	0	0	0
Beach, Pat, Indianapolis	2	1	0	0	1
Bell, Greg, Buffalo	2	2	0	0	2
Bell, Ken, Denver	1	0	0	0	0
Bellinger, Rodney, Buffalo	0	2	2	15	4
Bennett, Woody, Miami	1	0	0	0	0
Benson, Thomas, San Diego	0	0	2	0	2
Bentley, Albert, Indianapolis	2	1	0	9	1
Bickett, Duane, Indianapolis	0	0	1	0	1
Billups, Lewis, Cincinnati	0	0	1	2	1
Bingham, Guy, N.Y. Jets	0	0	1	0	1
Bishop, Keith, Denver	0	1	0	0	1
Blackledge, Todd, Kansas City	5	2	0	−6	2
Blackmon, Don, New England	0	0	2	8	2
Blackwood, Glenn, Miami	2	1	1	0	2
Blackwood, Lyle, Miami	1	1	1	0	2
Bligen, Dennis, N.Y. Jets	2	0	0	0	0
Bostic, Keith, Houston	0	0	1	0	1
Boyer, Mark, Indianapolis	1	0	0	0	0
Brady, Ed, Cincinnati	1	0	0	−7	0
Brennan, Brian, Cleveland	1	1	0	0	1
Brister, Bubby, Pittsburgh	1	0	0	0	0
Brock, Pete, New England	1	1	0	0	1
Brooks, Bill, Indianapolis	2	1	0	0	1
Brooks, James, Cincinnati	2	0	0	0	0
Broughton, Walter, Buffalo	0	0	1	0	1
Broughton, Willie, Indianapolis	5	1	0	0	1
Brown, Bud, Miami	1	2	0	6	2
Brown, Dave, Seattle	0	0	1	0	1
Brown, Donald, San Diego	0	0	2	0	2
Brown, Eddie, Cincinnati	0	2	0	0	2
Brown, Mark, Miami	0	1	3	11	4
Browner, Ross, Cincinnati	0	0	1	0	1
Brudzinski, Bob, Miami	0	0	1	0	1
Burkett, Chris, Buffalo	1	0	0	0	0
Burruss, Lloyd, Kansas City	0	0	1	0	1
Byner, Earnest, Cleveland	1	0	0	0	0
Byrd, Richard, Houston	0	0	1	0	1
Carson, Carlos, Kansas City	1	0	0	0	0
Carter, Joe, Miami	2	0	0	0	0
Carter, Russell, N.Y. Jets	0	0	1	0	1
Chandler, Wes, San Diego	2	0	0	0	0
Cherry, Deron, Kansas City	0	0	2	7	2
Childress, Ray, Houston	0	0	1	0	1
Christensen, Todd, L.A. Raiders	1	0	0	0	0
Clancy, Sam, Cleveland	0	0	1	0	1
Clayborn, Ray, New England	0	0	2	0	2
Clayton, Mark, Miami	1	0	0	0	0
Clifton, Kyle, N.Y. Jets	0	0	1	0	1
Cocroft, Sherman, Kansas City	0	0	1	0	1
Coffman, Paul, Kansas City	1	1	0	0	1
Cofield, Timmy, Kansas City	0	0	1	0	1
Cole, Robin, Pittsburgh	0	0	2	0	2
Coleman, Leonard, Indianapolis	0	0	1	0	1
Collins, Tony, New England	4	1	0	0	1
Collinsworth, Cris, Cincinnati	1	0	0	0	0
Colorito, Tony, Denver	0	0	2	0	2
Comeaux, Darren, Denver	0	0	1	0	1
Cooper, Louis, Kansas City	0	0	1	0	1
Crable, Bob, N.Y. Jets	0	0	3	42	3
Cumby, George, Buffalo	0	0	1	38	1
Daniel, Eugene, Indianapolis	0	0	1	0	1
Daniel, Kenny, Indianapolis	0	0	1	0	1
Davenport, Ron, Miami	4	1	0	0	1
Dickey, Curtis, Cleveland	4	2	0	0	2
Dixon, Hanford, Cleveland	1	1	1	0	2
Doig, Steve, New England	0	0	1	0	1
Donaldson, Jeff, Houston	0	0	2	1	2
Donaldson, Ray, Indianapolis	2	0	0	−4	0
Donnalley, Rick, Kansas City	2	0	0	−27	0
Douglass, Mike, San Diego	0	0	1	0	1
Drewrey, Willie, Houston	3	1	0	0	1
Dunn, Gary, Pittsburgh	0	0	1	0	1
Dupard, Reggie, New England	1	0	0	0	0
Eason, Bo, Houston	1	0	1	0	1
Eason, Tony, New England	4	3	0	0	3
Edmonds, Bobby Joe, Seattle	4	1	0	0	1
Edwards, Eddie, Cincinnati	0	0	2	0	2
Ehin, Chuck, San Diego	0	0	1	0	1
Elder, Donnie, Pittsburgh	1	0	1	0	1
Ellis, Craig, Miami	1	1	0	0	1
Elway, John, Denver	8	1	0	−13	1
Erenberg, Rich, Pittsburgh	1	1	0	0	1
Esiason, Boomer, Cincinnati	12	5	0	−10	5
Everett, Major, Cleveland	0	1	1	0	2
Fike, Danny, Cleveland	0	1	0	0	1
Fletcher, Simon, Denver	0	0	2	0	2
Flick, Tom, San Diego	1	1	0	0	1
Fontenot, Herman, Cleveland	2	0	1	0	1
Foster, Jerome, Miami	0	0	1	0	1
Foster, Roy, Miami	0	2	0	0	2
Fouts, Dan, San Diego	4	2	0	−13	2
Frazier, Guy, Buffalo	0	1	1	0	2
Fryar, Irving, New England	4	1	0	0	1
Frye, David, Miami	0	0	1	0	1
Fulcher, David, Cincinnati	0	0	1	0	1
Gaines, Greg, Seattle	0	0	1	0	1
Gilbert, Gale, Seattle	1	0	0	0	0
Gill, Owen, Indianapolis	4	0	0	0	0
Glasgow, Nesby, Indianapolis	0	0	2	0	2
Glenn, Kerry, N.Y. Jets	0	0	1	0	1
Glenn, Vencie, San Diego	0	0	2	32	2
Golic, Mike, Houston	0	0	2	4	2
Grant, Will, Seattle	0	1	0	0	1
Green. Boyce, Kansas City	3	0	0	0	0
Green, Jacob, Seattle	0	0	1	0	1
Griggs, Anthony, Cleveland	0	0	1	3	1
Grimsley, John, Houston	0	1	1	0	2
Grogan, Steve, New England	2	1	0	0	1
Gross, Al, Cleveland	0	0	1	0	1
Guy, Ray, L.A. Raiders	1	1	0	−18	1
Hackett, Dino, Kansas City	0	0	2	0	2
Hackett, Joey, Denver	0	1	0	0	1
Hairston, Carl, Cleveland	0	0	1	0	1
Hamby, Mike, Buffalo	0	0	1	0	1
Hamilton, Harry, N.Y. Jets	0	0	2	28	2
Hampton, Lorenzo, Miami	4	1	0	0	1
Hand, Jon, Indianapolis	0	0	2	0	2
Hardison, Dee, San Diego	0	0	1	0	1
Hardy, Bruce, Miami	2	0	0	0	0
Harmon, Ronnie, Buffalo	2	0	0	0	0
Harper, Mark, Cleveland	0	0	2	0	2
Harper, Michael, N.Y. Jets	0	1	2	0	3
Harry, Emile, Kansas City	1	0	0	0	0
Hawthorne, Greg, New England	0	1	0	0	1
Hayes, Jeff, Cincinnati	0	1	0	0	1
Hayes, Lester, L.A. Raiders	0	0	2	42	2

	Fum.	Own Rec.	Opp. Rec.	Yds.	Tot. Rec.
Heard, Herman, Kansas City	4	0	0	0	0
Hector, Johnny, N.Y. Jets	2	0	0	0	0
Hellestrae, Dale, Buffalo	1	0	0	−14	0
Henton, Anthony, Pittsburgh	0	0	1	0	1
Herrmann, Mark, San Diego	2	0	0	0	0
Hilger, Rusty, L.A. Raiders	3	1	0	−7	1
Hill, Rod, Buffalo	1	0	0	0	0
Hinkle, Bryan, Pittsburgh	0	0	1	0	1
Hinton, Chris, Indianapolis	0	2	0	0	2
Hogeboom, Gary, Indianapolis	3	2	0	50	2
Holloway, Brian, New England	0	1	0	0	1
Holman, Rodney, Cincinnati	1	0	0	0	0
Holt, John, Indianapolis	0	1	3	0	4
Horan, Mike, Denver	1	1	0	−12	1
Horton, Ray, Cincinnati	2	0	0	0	0
Howard, Carl, N.Y. Jets	0	0	1	4	1
Hudson, Gordon, Seattle	1	0	0	0	0
Hughes, David, Pittsburgh	3	1	0	0	1
Humphery, Bobby, N.Y. Jets	1	1	1	0	2
Hunley, LaMonte, Indianapolis	0	0	1	0	1
Hunley, Ricky, Denver	0	0	1	0	1
Jackson, Earnest, Pittsburgh	3	1	0	0	1
Jackson, Mark, Denver	3	0	0	0	0
Jackson, Michael, Seattle	0	0	1	0	1
James, Craig, New England	5	0	1	0	1
James, Lionel, San Diego	5	1	0	0	1
Jennings, Dave, N.Y. Jets	1	1	0	0	1
Johnson, Bill, Cincinnati	2	0	0	0	0
Johnson, Gregg, Seattle	0	0	1	0	1
Johnson, Mike, Cleveland	0	0	2	0	2
Johnson, Trumaine, San Diego	1	0	0	0	0
Johnson, Vance, Denver	1	0	0	0	0
Jones, Cedric, New England	1	0	0	0	0
Jones, Rulon, Denver	0	0	1	0	1
Justin, Kerry, Seattle	0	0	2	0	2
Kelly, Jim, Buffalo	7	2	0	0	2
Kelly, Joe, Cincinnati	0	0	1	0	1
Kenney, Bill, Kansas City	5	1	0	−6	1
Kidd, John, Buffalo	0	1	0	0	1
King, Emanuel, Cincinnati	0	0	1	1	1
Kinnebrew, Larry, Cincinnati	6	1	0	−2	1
Kolic, Larry, Miami	0	0	1	4	1
Kosar, Bernie, Cleveland	7	3	0	−15	3
Kragen, Greg, Denver	0	0	3	0	3
Krauss, Barry, Indianapolis	0	0	1	0	1
Krieg, Dave, Seattle	10	1	0	−5	1
Krumrie, Tim, Cincinnati	0	0	2	18	2
Lane, Eric, Seattle	0	0	1	0	1
Langhorne, Reggie, Cleveland	2	0	0	0	0
Lankford, Paul, Miami	0	0	1	0	1
Largent, Steve, Seattle	3	0	0	0	0
Lee, Larry, Miami	1	0	0	0	0
Lewis, Albert, Kansas City	0	0	2	0	2
Lipps, Louis, Pittsburgh	2	1	0	0	1
Little, George, Miami	0	0	1	4	1
Long, Howie, L.A. Raiders	0	0	2	0	2
Long, Terry, Pittsburgh	0	1	0	0	1
Lowe, Woodrow, San Diego	0	0	2	0	2
Lyles, Lester, N.Y. Jets	0	0	1	16	1
Lyles, Robert, Houston	0	0	1	93	1
Lyons, Marty, N.Y. Jets	0	0	1	0	1
Maas, Bill, Kansas City	0	0	2	0	2
Macek, Don, San Diego	0	1	0	0	1
Mack, Kevin, Cleveland	6	1	0	0	1
Madsen, Lynn, Houston	1	0	0	0	0
Malone, Mark, Pittsburgh	7	1	0	−8	1
Marino, Dan, Miami	8	4	0	−12	4
Martin, Robbie, Indianapolis	4	1	0	0	1
Matthews, Bruce, Houston	0	1	0	7	1
McCallum, Napoleon, L.A. Raiders	5	1	0	0	1
McElroy, Reggie, N.Y. Jets	0	1	0	−2	1
McGee, Buford, San Diego	4	0	0	−3	0
McGee, Tim, Cincinnati	0	1	0	0	1
McMillan, Randy, Indianapolis	5	2	0	0	2
McMillian, Audrey, Houston	0	0	2	4	2
McNanie, Sean, Buffalo	0	0	1	0	1
McNeil, Freeman, N.Y. Jets	8	0	0	−17	0
McNeil, Gerald, Cleveland	3	0	0	0	0
Meads, Johnny, Houston	0	0	1	0	1
Mecklenburg, Karl, Denver	0	0	1	0	1
Mehl, Lance, N.Y. Jets	0	0	1	0	1
Merriman, Sam, Seattle	0	1	0	0	1
Merriweather, Mike, Pittsburgh	0	0	2	18	2
Metzelaars, Pete, Buffalo	2	1	0	0	1
Millard, Bryan, Seattle	0	1	0	0	1
Minnifield, Frank, Cleveland	0	1	1	0	2
Mobley, Orson, Denver	1	0	0	0	0
Moffett, Tim, L.A. Raiders	0	0	1	0	1
Monger, Matt, N.Y. Jets	0	0	1	0	1
Montoya, Max, Cincinnati	0	1	0	0	1
Moon, Warren, Houston	11	3	0	−4	3
Moore, Ricky, Buffalo	2	0	0	0	0
Moriarty, Larry, Houston-Kansas City	2	0	0	0	0
Morris, Randall, Seattle	2	0	0	0	0
Mosebar, Don, L.A. Raiders	1	1	0	0	1
Mueller, Vance, L.A. Raiders	1	0	0	0	0
Munchak, Mike, Houston	0	1	0	0	1
Nash, Joe, Seattle	0	0	2	0	2
Nelson, Derrie, San Diego	0	0	1	0	1
Nelson, Edmund, Pittsburgh	0	0	2	0	2
Norman, Chris, Denver	1	0	0	0	0
O'Brien, Ken, N.Y. Jets	10	5	0	−3	5
Odom, Cliff, Indianapolis	0	0	2	0	2
O'Neal, Leslie, San Diego	0	0	2	0	2
Pagel, Mike, Cleveland	2	1	0	−4	1
Paige, Tony, N.Y. Jets	2	0	0	0	0
Pennison, Jay, Houston	1	0	0	0	0
Pickel, Bill, L.A. Raiders	0	1	1	0	2
Pinkett, Allen, Houston	2	1	0	0	1
Pitts, Ron, Buffalo	2	2	0	0	2
Plummer, Gary, San Diego	0	0	2	0	2
Plunkett, Jim, L.A. Raiders	4	0	0	−3	0
Pollard, Frank, Pittsburgh	1	0	0	0	0
Pruitt, James, Miami	4	2	0	0	2
Radecic, Scott, Kansas City	0	0	1	0	1
Reed, Andre, Buffalo	2	2	0	2	2
Reich, Frank, Buffalo	1	0	0	0	0
Rembert, Johnny, New England	0	0	3	0	3
Reynolds, Ed, New England	0	0	1	0	1
Richardson, Eric, Buffalo	4	1	0	0	1
Riddick, Robb, Buffalo	8	0	0	0	0
Riley, Avon, Houston	0	0	1	0	1
Rimington, Dave, Cincinnati	2	0	0	−23	0
Risien, Cody, Cleveland	0	2	0	0	2
Ritcher, Jim, Buffalo	0	1	0	0	1
Robbins, Randy, Denver	0	0	2	0	2
Robinson, Eugene, Seattle	0	0	3	6	3
Robinson, Fred, San Diego	0	0	2	0	2
Robinson, Jerry, L.A. Raiders	0	0	2	0	2
Roby, Reggie, Miami	2	2	0	−11	2
Rockins, Chris, Cleveland	1	1	2	0	3
Romes, Charles, Buffalo	0	0	1	6	1
Ross, Kevin, Kansas City	0	0	3	33	3
Rozier, Mike, Houston	6	2	0	0	2
Ruth, Mike, New England	0	1	0	0	1
Sampson, Clinton, Denver	1	0	0	0	0
Sanchez, Lupe, Pittsburgh	2	1	0	0	1
Seale, Sam, L.A. Raiders	0	0	1	0	1
Seitz, Warren, Pittsburgh	0	1	0	0	1
Shipp, Jackie, Miami	0	0	1	0	1
Shuler, Mickey, N.Y. Jets	0	1	0	0	1
Simmons, John, Cincinnati	1	0	0	0	0
Sims, Darryl, Pittsburgh	0	0	1	2	1
Sims, Kenneth, New England	0	0	1	6	1
Skansi, Paul, Seattle	1	0	0	0	0
Slaughter, Webster, Cleveland	1	1	0	0	1
Smith, Billy Ray, San Diego	0	0	1	0	1
Smith, Dennis, Denver	0	0	1	0	1
Smith, Jeff, Kansas City	4	0	0	0	0
Smith, Mike, Miami	0	0	1	0	1
Snipes, Angelo, San Diego	0	0	1	0	1
Sohn, Kurt, N.Y. Jets	3	1	0	0	1
Spencer, Tim, San Diego	2	1	0	0	1
Stark, Rohn, Indianapolis	1	1	0	0	1
Starring, Stephen, New England	4	1	1	−5	2
Steinkuhler, Dean, Houston	0	2	0	0	2
Stephenson, Dwight, Miami	0	1	0	0	1
Still, Art, Kansas City	0	0	2	0	2
Strock, Don, Miami	1	1	0	−4	1
Studdard, Dave, Denver	0	1	0	0	1
Talley, Darryl, Buffalo	0	0	1	47	1
Tatupu, Mosi, New England	1	0	0	0	0
Taylor, Ken, San Diego	0	0	1	0	1
Thompson, Reyna, Miami	1	0	0	0	0
Tice, Mike, Seattle	0	0	1	0	1
Tippett, Andre, New England	0	0	1	0	1
Toon, Al, N.Y. Jets	3	1	0	0	1
Toran, Stacey, L.A. Raiders	0	0	1	0	1
Toth, Tom, Miami	1	0	0	0	0
Townsend, Andre, Denver	0	0	1	7	1
Traynowicz, Mark, Buffalo	0	1	0	0	1
Trudeau, Jack, Indianapolis	13	6	0	−15	6
Tucker, Travis, Cleveland	0	0	1	0	1
Van Pelt, Brad, Cleveland	0	0	1	0	1
Veris, Garin, New England	0	0	2	0	2
Walker, Fulton, L.A. Raiders	3	2	0	0	2

	Fum.	Own Rec.	Opp. Rec.	Yds.	Tot. Rec.
Walker, Wesley, N.Y. Jets	3	0	0	0	0
Wallace, Ray, Houston	1	0	0	0	0
Warner, Curt, Seattle	6	5	0	0	5
Willhite, Gerald, Denver	5	3	0	0	3
Williams, Brent, New England	0	0	4	54	4
Williams, Dokie, L.A. Raiders	2	1	0	0	1
Williams, Eric, Pittsburgh	0	0	1	0	1
Williams, Jamie, Houston	0	1	0	0	1
Williams, John L., Seattle	1	0	0	0	0
Williams, Lee, San Diego	0	0	1	6	1
Williams, Oliver, Indianapolis	1	0	0	0	0
Williams, Reggie, Cincinnati	0	0	1	0	1
Wilson, Marc, L.A. Raiders	6	1	0	−10	1
Wilson, Mike, Seattle	0	2	0	0	2
Wilson, Stanley, Cincinnati	1	0	0	0	0
Winder, Sammy, Denver	2	1	0	0	1
Winslow, Kellen, San Diego	0	2	0	0	2
Winston, Dennis, Pittsburgh	0	0	1	0	1
Wolfley, Craig, Pittsburgh	0	1	0	0	1
Wonsley, George, Indianapolis	1	0	0	0	0
Woodard, Ken, Denver	0	0	1	16	1
Woods, Rick, Pittsburgh	2	0	0	0	0
Wooten, Ron, New England	0	1	0	0	1
Wright, Felix, Cleveland	0	0	1	0	1
Wright, Louis, Denver	0	0	1	0	1
Zander, Carl, Cincinnati	0	0	1	0	1

Yards includes aborted plays, own recoveries, and opponent recoveries.
Touchdowns: Walt Arnold, Kansas City; Rodney Bellinger, Buffalo; Brian Brennan, Cleveland; Jeff Donaldson, Houston; Eddie Edwards, Cincinnati; Al Gross, Cleveland; Lester Hayes, L.A. Raiders; Robert Lyles, Houston; Pete Metzelaars, Buffalo; Mike Munchak, Houston; Johnny Rembert, New England; Kevin Ross, Kansas City; Webster Slaughter, Cleveland; Andre Townsend, Denver; Brent Williams, New England; and Ken Woodard, Denver.
Includes both offensive and defensive recoveries for touchdowns.

NFC Fumbles—Individual

	Fum.	Own Rec.	Opp. Rec.	Yds.	Tot. Rec.
Albritton, Vince, Dallas	0	0	2	0	2
Allen, Anthony, Atlanta	1	1	0	0	1
Anderson, Alfred, Minnesota	3	2	0	0	2
Anderson, Neal, Chicago	1	0	0	0	0
Anderson, Ottis, St. Louis	2	0	0	0	0
Andrews, William, Atlanta	0	1	0	0	1
Archer, David, Atlanta	8	1	0	−3	1
Ard, Billy, N.Y. Giants	0	1	0	1	1
Ashley, Walker, Minnesota	0	0	1	0	1
Austin, Cliff, Atlanta	1	0	1	0	1
Baker, Charles, St. Louis	0	0	1	0	1
Banks, Carl, N.Y. Giants	0	0	2	5	2
Banks, Gordon, Dallas	4	3	0	0	3
Barnes, Lew, Chicago	5	3	0	0	3
Barrows, Scott, Detroit	0	1	0	0	1
Bartkowski, Steve, L.A. Rams	4	2	0	−2	2
Bavaro, Mark, N.Y. Giants	3	1	1	0	2
Berry, Ed, Green Bay	0	1	0	0	1
Bess, Rufus, Minnesota	3	2	1	0	3
Black, Mike, Detroit	1	1	0	0	1
Bland, Carl, Detroit	1	2	0	8	2
Board, Dwaine, San Francisco	0	1	1	16	2
Bostic, Jeff, Washington	0	1	0	1	1
Britt, James, Atlanta	0	0	2	73	2
Brown, Charlie, Atlanta	1	0	0	0	0
Brown, Robert, Green Bay	0	0	1	0	1
Brown, Ron, L.A. Rams	1	2	0	0	2
Browner, Joey, Minnesota	0	0	4	0	4
Browner, Keith, Tampa Bay	0	0	2	0	2
Bryant, Kelvin, Washington	2	1	0	0	1
Buford, Maury, Chicago	1	0	0	0	0
Burt, Jim, N.Y. Giants	0	0	3	1	3
Byars, Keith, Philadelphia	3	2	0	0	2
Cannon, John, Tampa Bay	0	0	2	0	2
Carreker, Alphonso, Green Bay	0	0	2	0	2
Carruth, Paul, Green Bay	1	0	0	0	0
Carson, Harry, N.Y. Giants	0	0	2	0	2
Carter, Anthony, Minnesota	1	0	0	0	0
Carter, Carl, St. Louis	1	1	0	0	1
Carter, Gerald, Tampa Bay	2	0	0	0	0
Carthon, Maurice, N.Y. Giants	1	0	0	0	0
Casillas, Tony, Atlanta	0	0	1	0	1
Cason, Wendell, Atlanta	0	0	1	0	1
Cavanaugh, Matt, Philadelphia	2	0	0	0	0
Chadwick, Jeff, Detroit	1	0	0	0	0
Chandler, Thornton, Dallas	1	0	0	0	0
Cherry, Bill, Green Bay	1	0	0	−23	0
Cherry, Tony, San Francisco	2	2	0	0	2
Chilton, Gene, St. Louis	0	1	0	0	1
Clack, Darryl, Dallas	3	0	0	0	0
Clark, Bret, Altanta	0	0	2	0	2
Clark, Bruce, New Orleans	0	0	3	28	3
Clark, Dwight, San Francisco	0	2	0	0	2
Clark, Gary, Washington	1	1	0	0	1
Clark, Jessie, Green Bay	1	0	0	0	0
Clasby, Bob, St. Louis	0	0	1	0	1
Cobb, Garry, Philadelphia	0	0	1	0	1
Cofer, Mike, Detroit	0	0	3	0	3
Coffey, Ken, Washington	0	0	1	0	1
Collier, Reggie, Dallas	2	0	0	0	0
Collins, Mark, N.Y. Giants	2	2	1	5	3
Contz, Bill, New Orleans	0	2	0	0	2
Conwell, Joe, Philadelphia	0	1	0	0	1
Cooper, Evan, Philadelphia	2	1	0	0	1
Covert, Jimbo, Chicago	0	1	0	0	1
Cox, Arthur, Atlanta	1	2	0	0	2
Craig, Roger, San Francisco	4	1	0	0	1
Crawford, Charles, Philadelphia	1	0	1	0	1
Crawford, Derrick, San Francisco	1	1	0	0	1
Cribbs, Joe, San Francisco	5	1	0	0	1
Cromwell, Nolan, L.A. Rams	0	0	1	0	1
Cross, Randy, San Francisco	0	1	0	0	1
Cunningham, Randall, Philadelphia	7	4	0	0	4
Curry, Buddy, Atlanta	0	0	1	0	1
Davis, Jeff, Tampa Bay	0	0	1	0	1
Davis, Kenneth, Green Bay	2	0	0	0	0
DeBerg, Steve, Tampa Bay	2	1	0	−5	1
Dickerson, Eric, L.A. Rams	12	2	0	0	2
Dils, Steve, L.A. Rams	4	1	0	−6	1
Dixon, Floyd, Atlanta	3	2	0	0	2
Dorsett, Tony, Dallas	5	2	0	0	2
Dorsey, John, Green Bay	0	0	2	0	2
Doss, Reggie, L.A. Rams	0	0	1	0	1
Downs, Michael, Dallas	0	0	1	17	1
Duerson, Dave, Chicago	0	0	2	6	2
Dukes, Jamie, Atlanta	0	1	0	0	1
Edelman, Brad, New Orleans	0	1	0	0	1
Edwards, Kelvin, New Orleans	2	2	0	0	2
Ellard, Henry, L.A. Rams	3	1	0	0	1
Ellerson, Gary, Green Bay	3	0	0	0	0
Ellis, Gerry, Green Bay	4	1	0	0	1
Ellison, Riki, San Francisco	0	0	1	0	1
Everett, Jim, L.A. Rams	2	0	0	−2	0
Fellows, Ron, Dallas	0	0	2	2	2
Fencik, Gary, Chicago	0	0	1	0	1
Ferguson, Joe, Detroit	3	2	0	0	2
Ferguson, Keith, Detroit	1	0	1	0	1
Ferragamo, Vince, Green Bay	3	0	0	−8	0
Ferrell, Earl, St. Louis	6	0	0	0	0
Flutie, Doug, Chicago	3	2	0	−4	2
Foules, Elbert, Philadelphia	0	0	2	0	2
Fowler, Todd, Dallas	1	0	1	0	1
Franklin, Pat, Tampa Bay	1	0	1	0	1
Freeman, Phil, Tampa Bay	1	1	0	0	1
Fuller, Jeff, San Francisco	2	1	0	0	1
Fuller, Steve, Chicago	2	1	0	−3	1
Fusina, Chuck, Green Bay	4	4	0	−1	4
Futrell, Bobby, Tampa Bay	1	1	0	0	1
Galbreath, Tony, N.Y. Giants	3	2	0	0	2
Galloway, David, St. Louis	0	0	2	0	2
Galloway, Duane, Detroit	0	0	1	0	1
Gann, Mike, Atlanta	0	0	3	12	3
Garner, Dwight, Washington	1	0	0	0	0
Gault, Willie, Chicago	1	0	0	0	0
Gay, William, Detroit	0	0	1	0	1
Gayle, Shaun, Chicago	0	0	1	0	1
Geathers, James, New Orleans	0	0	1	0	1
Gibson, Antonio, New Orleans	0	0	1	0	1
Goodlow, Eugene, New Orleans	1	1	0	0	1
Gray, Jerry, L.A. Rams	0	0	1	0	1
Green, Darrell, Washington	1	1	0	0	1
Green, Roy, St. Louis	1	0	0	0	0
Greene, Kevin, L.A. Rams	0	0	1	13	1
Griffin, Don, San Francisco	3	2	0	0	2
Grimm, Russ, Washington	0	2	0	0	2
Guman, Mike, L.A. Rams	1	0	0	0	0
Haddix, Michael, Philadelphia	1	1	0	0	1
Haley, Charles, San Francisco	1	0	2	3	2
Hampton, Dan, Chicago	0	0	2	0	2
Hansen, Brian, New Orleans	1	1	0	0	1
Harmon, Derrick, San Francisco	1	1	0	0	1
Harrell, James, Detroit	0	0	2	0	2
Harris, Herbert, New Orleans	1	0	0	0	0
Harris, Leonard, Tampa Bay	1	0	0	0	0
Harris, Timothy, Green Bay	0	0	1	0	1
Harrison, Dennis, Atlanta	0	0	1	0	1

	Fum.	Own Rec.	Opp. Rec.	Yds.	Tot. Rec.
Haynes, James, New Orleans	0	0	2	7	2
Hebert, Bobby, New Orleans	3	0	0	0	0
Heflin, Vince, Tampa Bay	0	0	1	48	1
Heller, Ron, Tampa Bay	0	1	0	0	1
Hendrix, Manuel, Dallas	0	0	1	0	1
Hilgenberg, Jay, Chicago	1	0	0	−28	0
Hill, David, L.A. Rams	1	2	0	0	2
Hill, Kenny, N.Y. Giants	1	1	2	0	3
Hill, Tony, Dallas	1	0	0	0	0
Hilliard, Dalton, New Orleans	3	0	0	0	0
Hipple, Eric, Detroit	7	2	0	−1	2
Hoage, Terry, Philadelphia	0	0	2	0	2
Holloway, Johnny, Dallas	1	0	0	0	0
Holmes, Ron, Tampa Bay	0	0	1	0	1
Holmoe, Tom, San Francisco	0	1	2	0	3
Holt, Issiac, Minnesota	1	0	0	0	0
Hopkins, Wes, Philadelphia	0	0	1	−4	1
Howard, Bobby, Tampa Bay	1	0	0	0	0
Humphrey, Donnie, Green Bay	0	0	1	0	1
Hunter, Herman, Detroit	1	1	0	0	1
Hunter, Tony, L.A. Rams	2	0	0	0	0
Irvin, LeRoy, L.A. Rams	1	1	2	55	3
Irwin, Tim, Minnesota	0	2	0	0	2
Ivery, Eddie Lee, Green Bay	0	0	1	0	1
Jackson, Rickey, New Orleans	0	0	1	0	1
Jackson, Vestee, Chicago	0	1	1	−7	2
James, Garry, Detroit	3	1	0	0	1
Jaworski, Ron, Philadelphia	4	1	0	0	1
Jeffcoat, Jim, Dallas	0	0	2	8	2
Jenkins, Ken, Washington	4	0	0	0	0
Jerue, Mark, L.A. Rams	1	0	0	0	0
Jiles, Dwayne, Philadelphia	0	1	0	0	1
Johnson, Alonzo, Philadelphia	0	1	0	0	1
Johnson, Bobby, N.Y. Giants	1	0	0	0	0
Johnson, Demetrious, Detroit	0	0	2	2	2
Johnson, Johnnie, L.A. Rams	0	1	1	0	2
Johnson, Ron, Philadelphia	0	0	1	0	1
Johnson, Vaughan, New Orleans	0	0	1	0	1
Jones, Anthony, Washington	0	0	1	0	1
Jones, Ed, Dallas	0	0	3	0	3
Jones, Hassan, Minnesota	1	0	0	0	0
Jones, James, Detroit	6	2	0	0	2
Jones, Mike, New Orleans	2	1	0	0	1
Jones, Rod, Tampa Bay	0	0	1	0	1
Jordan, Buford, New Orleans	2	0	0	0	0
Jordan, Steve, Minnesota	0	1	0	0	1
Junior, E.J., St. Louis	0	0	1	0	1
Kemp, Jeff, San Francisco	3	1	0	−3	1
Kinard, Terry, N.Y. Giants	0	0	2	0	2
Koart, Matt, Green Bay	0	0	1	0	1
Korte, Steve, New Orleans	0	1	0	0	1
Kramer, Tommy, Minnesota	7	3	0	−3	3
Lavette, Robert, Dallas	3	3	0	0	3
Lee, Mark, Green Bay	0	0	1	0	1
Lewis, Leo, Minnesota	3	1	0	0	1
Little, David, Philadelphia	1	0	0	−14	0
Lockhart, Eugene, Dallas	0	0	1	0	1
Lofton, James, Green Bay	3	2	0	8	2
Lomax, Neil, St. Louis	7	6	0	0	6
Long, Chuck, Detroit	1	0	0	0	0
Love, Duval, L.A. Rams	1	0	0	0	0
Mack, Cedric, St. Louis	0	0	1	0	1
Magee, Calvin, Tampa Bay	1	0	0	0	0
Mandley, Pete, Detroit	3	1	0	0	1
Manley, Dexter, Washington	0	0	1	26	1
Marshall, Leonard, N.Y. Giants	0	0	3	0	3
Marshall, Wilber, Chicago	0	0	3	12	3
Martin, Charles, Green Bay	0	0	1	0	1
Martin, Chris, Minnesota	0	0	1	0	1
Martin, Doug, Minnesota	0	0	2	0	2
Martin, Eric, New Orleans	5	0	0	0	0
Martin, George, N.Y. Giants	0	0	1	0	1
Maxie, Brett, New Orleans	0	0	1	0	1
Maxwell, Vernon, Detroit	0	0	4	0	4
May, Mark, Washington	0	1	0	0	1
Mayes, Rueben, New Orleans	4	0	0	0	0
McConkey, Phil, N.Y. Giants	1	1	0	0	1
McKeever, Vito, Tampa Bay	0	1	0	−4	1
McMahon, Jim, Chicago	1	0	0	0	0
McMichael, Steve, Chicago	0	0	2	0	2
McNorton, Bruce, Detroit	0	0	2	0	2
Meisner, Greg, L.A. Rams	0	0	1	15	1
Millard, Keith, Minnesota	0	0	1	3	1
Miller, Brett, Atlanta	0	1	0	0	1
Miller, Shawn, L.A. Rams	0	0	2	29	2
Miller, Solomon, N.Y. Giants	1	4	0	0	4
Mills, Sam, New Orleans	0	0	1	0	1
Milot, Rich, Washington	1	1	1	0	2

	Fum.	Own Rec.	Opp. Rec.	Yds.	Tot. Rec.
Mitchell, Stump, St. Louis	4	1	0	0	1
Monaco, Ron, St. Louis	0	1	0	0	1
Monk, Art, Washington	2	2	0	0	2
Monroe, Carl, San Francisco	1	1	0	0	1
Montana, Joe, San Francisco	3	0	0	0	0
Moore, Alvin, Detroit	2	0	1	−11	1
Moorehead, Emery, Chicago	1	1	0	0	1
Moroski, Mike, San Francisco	3	0	0	0	0
Morris, Joe, N.Y. Giants	6	2	0	0	2
Morrison, Tim, Washington	0	0	1	0	1
Mowatt, Zeke, N.Y. Giants	1	0	1	0	1
Murphy, Kevin, Tampa Bay	0	0	1	0	1
Nelson, Bob, Tampa Bay	0	0	1	0	1
Nelson, Darrin, Minnesota	3	0	0	0	0
Nelson, Karl, N.Y. Giants	0	1	0	0	1
Newberry, Tom, L.A. Rams	0	1	0	0	1
Newsome, Tim, Minnesota	2	1	0	0	1
Newsome, Vince, L.A. Rams	0	0	1	0	1
Newton, Tim, Minnesota	0	0	1	0	1
Nixon, Tory, San Francisco	0	1	1	0	2
Noga, Niko, St. Louis	0	0	2	0	2
Nunn, Freddie Joe, St. Louis	0	0	1	0	1
Oates, Bart, N.Y. Giants	1	0	0	−4	0
Olkewicz, Neal, Washington	0	1	2	0	3
Ortego, Keith, Chicago	1	0	0	0	0
Owens, Mel, L.A. Rams	0	0	1	0	1
Pankey, Irv, L.A. Rams	0	1	0	0	1
Paris, Bubba, San Francisco	0	1	0	0	1
Payton, Walter, Chicago	6	0	0	0	0
Pelluer, Steve, Dallas	9	3	0	0	3
Penn, Jesse, Dallas	0	1	2	12	3
Perry, William, Chicago	1	0	0	0	0
Phillips, Joe, Minnesota	0	0	1	0	1
Pitts, Mike, Atlanta	0	0	2	22	2
Poe, Johnnie, New Orleans	0	0	1	0	1
Quick, Mike, Philadelphia	1	1	0	0	1
Radloff, Wayne, Atlanta	0	1	0	−3	1
Rafferty, Tom, Dallas	0	1	0	0	1
Rains, Dan, Chicago	0	0	1	0	1
Redden, Barry, L.A. Rams	1	0	0	0	0
Reeves, Ken, Philadelphia	0	1	0	0	1
Rice, Allen, Minnesota	5	2	0	0	2
Rice, Jerry, San Francisco	2	3	0	0	3
Richards, Howard, Dallas	0	2	0	0	2
Richardson, Mike, Chicago	3	0	0	−5	0
Riggs, Gerald, Atlanta	6	1	0	0	1
Roberts, Larry, San Francisco	0	0	1	0	1
Robinson, Stacy, N.Y. Giants	1	0	0	0	0
Rogers, George, Washington	7	2	0	0	2
Rohrer, Jeff, Dallas	0	0	1	0	1
Ruettgers, Ken, Green Bay	0	1	0	0	1
Sanders, Thomas, Chicago	2	0	0	0	0
Schonert, Turk, Atlanta	5	1	0	−2	1
Schroeder, Jay, Washington	9	5	0	−19	5
Scott, Randy, Green Bay	0	0	1	0	1
Scully, John, Atlanta	0	2	0	0	2
Sikahema, Vai, St. Louis	2	0	0	0	0
Simms, Phil, N.Y. Giants	9	3	0	−2	3
Singletary, Reggie, Philadelphia	0	0	1	0	1
Smith, J.T., St. Louis	1	3	0	0	3
Smith, Phil, Philadelphia	1	0	0	0	0
Smith, Wayne, St. Louis	0	0	1	0	1
Solomon, Jesse, Minnesota	0	0	2	0	2
Spagnola, John, Philadelphia	2	1	0	0	1
Springs, Ron, Tampa Bay	2	0	0	0	0
Stamps, Sylvester, Atlanta	4	1	0	0	1
Stanley, Walter, Green Bay	1	0	0	0	0
Stills, Ken, Green Bay	1	0	0	0	0
Stoudt, Cliff, St. Louis	1	0	0	0	0
Studwell, Scott, Minnesota	0	0	4	0	4
Suhey, Matt, Chicago	1	0	0	0	0
Sully, Ivory, Tampa Bay	0	0	4	0	4
Sutton, Mickey, L.A. Rams	0	1	0	0	1
Swanke, Karl, Green Bay	3	0	0	−4	0
Swilley, Dennis, Minnesota	1	0	0	−14	0
Swoope, Craig, Tampa Bay	0	0	2	0	2
Tautalatasi, Junior, Philadelphia	6	1	0	0	1
Teltschik, John, Philadelphia	0	1	0	0	1
Thomas, Calvin, Chicago	3	2	0	0	2
Thurman, Dennis, St. Louis	0	0	1	0	1
Tice, John, New Orleans	1	1	0	0	1
Titensor, Glen, Dallas	0	1	0	0	1
Toles, Alvin, New Orleans	0	0	1	0	1
Tomczak, Mike, Chicago	2	0	0	0	0
Tuinei, Mark, Dallas	1	3	0	0	3
Tyler, Wendell, San Francisco	1	0	0	0	0
Tyrrell, Tim, L.A. Rams	1	0	0	0	0
Van Horne, Keith, Chicago	0	1	0	0	1

	Fum.	Own Rec.	Opp. Rec.	Yds.	Tot. Rec.
Vann, Norwood, L.A. Rams	0	0	3	0	3
Veingrad, Alan, Green Bay	0	1	0	0	1
Walker, Herschel, Dallas	5	2	0	0	2
Walker, Kevin, Tampa Bay	1	1	0	0	1
Walter, Mike, San Francisco	0	0	1	0	1
Warren, Don, Washington	1	1	0	0	1
Warren, Frank, New Orleans	0	0	3	0	3
Washington, Chris, Tampa Bay	0	0	2	0	2
Washington, Lionel, St. Louis	0	0	1	0	1
Waters, Andre, Philadelphia	0	0	2	81	2
Waters, Mike, Philadelphia	3	1	0	0	1
Wattelet, Frank, New Orleans	0	0	1	0	1
Waymer, Dave, New Orleans	0	1	0	0	1
Welch, Herb, N.Y. Giants	0	0	1	7	1
West, Ed, Green Bay	0	1	0	0	1
White, Charles, L.A. Rams	2	0	0	0	0
White, Danny, Dallas	6	1	0	−2	1
White, Randy, Dallas	0	0	2	0	2
Wilburn, Barry, Washington	0	0	2	0	2
Wilder, James, Tampa Bay	10	3	0	0	3
Williams, Eric, Detroit	0	0	1	0	1
Williams, Jimmy, Detroit	0	0	1	0	1
Williams, Keith, Atlanta	1	0	0	0	0
Williamson, Carlton, San Francisco	0	0	1	0	1
Wilson, Brenard, Philadelphia	0	0	2	4	2
Wilson, Dave, New Orleans	8	4	0	−4	4
Wilson, Mike, San Francisco	0	1	0	0	1
Wilson, Otis, Chicago	0	0	3	0	3
Wilson, Wade, Minnesota	3	1	0	−2	1
Wonsley, Nathan, Tampa Bay	2	2	0	0	2
Wright, Randy, Green Bay	8	3	0	−4	3
Wrightman, Tim, Chicago	1	0	0	0	0
Young, Mike, L.A. Rams	2	0	0	0	0
Young, Steve, Tampa Bay	11	4	0	−24	4
Zimmerman, Gary, Minnesota	0	2	0	0	2

Yards includes aborted plays, own recoveries, and opponent recoveries.
Touchdowns: James Britt, Atlanta; Pat Franklin, Tampa Bay; Vince Heflin, Tampa Bay; LeRoy Irvin, Los Angeles Rams; Dexter Manley, Washington; Wilber Marshall, Chicago; Tom Newberry, Los Angeles Rams; and Mike Pitts, Atlanta.
Includes both offensive and defensive recoveries for touchdowns.

Sacks

Individual Champions
NFC: 20.5—Lawrence Taylor, New York Giants
AFC: 15.5—Sean Jones, Los Angeles Raiders

Most Sacks, Game
AFC: 5—Leslie O'Neal, San Diego vs. Dallas, November 16
NFC: 4—Garry Cobb, Philadelphia vs. Atlanta, October 5
4—Lawrence Taylor, New York Giants vs. Philadelphia, October 12
4—Reggie White, Philadelphia vs. St. Louis, November 2
4—Reggie White, Philadelphia vs. Los Angeles Raiders, November 30 [OT]
4—Keith Ferguson, Detroit vs. Philadelphia, November 16
4—Rickey Jackson, New Orleans vs. Atlanta, December 14

Team Champions
AFC: 63—Los Angeles Raiders
NFC: 62—Chicago

AFC Sacks—Team

	Sacks	Yards
Los Angeles Raiders	63	463
San Diego	62	440
Denver	49	459
New England	48	346
Seattle	47	306
Kansas City	44	360
Pittsburgh	43	289
Cincinnati	42	368
Buffalo	36	267
Cleveland	35	258
Miami	33	268
Houston	32	201
New York Jets	28	178
Indianapolis	24	194
AFC Total	586	4,397
AFC Average	41.9	314.1

NFC Sacks—Team

	Sacks	Yards
Chicago	62	503
New York Giants	59	414
Washington	55	424
Dallas	53	364
Philadelphia	53	406
San Francisco	51	448
New Orleans	47	343
Detroit	41	290
St. Louis	41	355
Los Angeles Rams	39	292
Minnesota	38	259
Green Bay	28	222
Atlanta	26	177
Tampa Bay	19	153
NFC Total	612	4,650
NFC Average	43.7	332.1
League Total	1,198	9,047
League Average	42.8	323.1

NFL Top 10 Individual Leaders in Sacks

	Total
Taylor, Lawrence, N.Y. Giants	20.5
Manley, Dexter, Washington	18.5
White, Reggie, Philadelphia	18.0
Jones, Sean, L.A. Raiders	15.5
Smith, Bruce, Buffalo	15.0
Williams, Lee, San Diego	15.0
Jeffcoat, Jim, Dallas	14.0
Jones, Rulon, Denver	13.5
O'Neal, Leslie, San Diego	12.5
Haley, Charles, San Francisco	12.0
Marshall, Leonard, N.Y. Giants	12.0
Green, Jacob, Seattle	12.0
Willis, Keith, Pittsburgh	12.0

AFC Sacks—Individual

Jones, Sean, L.A. Raiders	15.5
Smith, Bruce, Buffalo	15.0
Williams, Lee, San Diego	15.0
Jones, Rulon, Denver	13.5
O'Neal, Leslie, San Diego	12.5
Green, Jacob, Seattle	12.0
Willis, Keith, Pittsburgh	12.0
Pickel, Bill, L.A. Raiders	11.5
Townsend, Greg, L.A. Raiders	11.5
Smith, Billy Ray, San Diego	11.0
Veris, Garin, New England	11.0
Still, Art, Kansas City	10.5
Mecklenburg, Karl, Denver	9.5
Tippett, Andre, New England	9.5
Hairston, Carl, Cleveland	9.0
King, Emanuel, Cincinnati	9.0
Blackmon, Don, New England	7.5
Long, Howie, L.A. Raiders	7.5
Camp, Reggie, Cleveland	7.0
Maas, Bill, Kansas City	7.0
Williams, Brent, New England	7.0
Browner, Ross, Cincinnati	6.5
Clancy, Sam, Cleveland	6.5
Edwards, Eddie, Cincinnati	6.5
Gary, Keith, Pittsburgh	6.5
Hardison, Dee, San Diego	6.5
McNanie, Sean, Buffalo	6.5
Merriweather, Mike, Pittsburgh	6.0
Puzzuoli, Dave, Cleveland	6.0
Toran, Stacey, L.A. Raiders	6.0
Young, Fredd, Seattle	6.0
Fletcher, Simon, Denver	5.5
Koch, Pete, Kansas City	5.5
Wilson, Earl, San Diego	5.5
Benson, Thomas, San Diego	5.0
Bickett, Duane, Indianapolis	5.0
Brown, Mark, Miami	5.0
Childress, Ray, Houston	5.0
Cofield, Timmy, Kansas City	5.0
Gaines, Greg, Seattle	5.0
Hand, Jon, Indianapolis	5.0
Martin, Rod, L.A. Raiders	5.0
Nash, Joe, Seattle	5.0
Nelson, Edmund, Pittsburgh	5.0
Banks, Chip, Cleveland	4.5
Cooper, Louis, Kansas City	4.5
Hinkle, Bryan, Pittsburgh	4.5
Williams, Reggie, Cincinnati	4.5
Betters, Doug, Miami	4.0
Bryant, Jeff, Seattle	4.0
Edwards, Randy, Seattle	4.0
Gilbert, Freddie, Denver	4.0
Green, Hugh, Miami	4.0
Humphery, Bobby, N.Y. Jets	4.0
Klecko, Joe, N.Y. Jets	4.0
Little, George, Miami	4.0
Rembert, Johnny, New England	4.0
Robbins, Randy, Denver	4.0
Thompson, Donnell, Indianapolis	4.0
Armstrong, Harvey, Indianapolis	3.5
Bennett, Barry, N.Y. Jets	3.5
Crable, Bob, N.Y. Jets	3.5
Meads, Johnny, Houston	3.5
Williams, Gerald, Pittsburgh	3.5
Zander, Carl, Cincinnati	3.5
Baker, Jesse, Dallas-Houston	3.0
Byrd, Richard, Houston	3.0
Foster, Jerome, Miami	3.0
Lyles, Robert, Houston	3.0
Lyons, Marty, N.Y. Jets	3.0
Robinson, Fred, S.D.-Miami	3.0
Scholtz, Bruce, Seattle	3.0
Skow, Jim, Cincinnati	3.0
Talley, Darryl, Buffalo	3.0
Woodard, Ken, Denver	3.0
Dunn, Gary, Pittsburgh	2.5
Ehin, Chuck, San Diego	2.5
Marve, Eugene, Buffalo	2.5
Plummer, Gary, San Diego	2.5
Townsend, Andre, Denver	2.5
Abraham, Robert, Houston	2.0
Ahrens, Dave, Indianapolis	2.0
Barnes, Jeff, L.A. Raiders	2.0
Bostic, Keith, Houston	2.0
Brudzinski, Bob, Miami	2.0
Fulcher, David, Cincinnati	2.0
Gastineau, Mark, N.Y. Jets	2.0
Griffin, Leonard, Kansas City	2.0
Jackson, Charles, N.Y. Jets	2.0
Merriman, Sam, Seattle	2.0
Offerdahl, John, Miami	2.0
Robinson, Jerry, L.A. Raiders	2.0
Ross, Kevin, Kansas City	2.0
Smerlas, Fred, Buffalo	2.0
Smith, Doug, Houston	2.0
Turner, T.J., Miami	2.0
Donaldson, Jeff, Houston	1.5
Paul, Whitney, Kansas City	1.5
Baldwin, Tom, N.Y. Jets	1.0
Baumhower, Bob, Miami	1.0
Bayless, Martin, Buffalo	1.0
Billups, Lewis, Cincinnati	1.0
Broughton, Willie, Indianapolis	1.0
Brown, Steve, Houston	1.0
Bush, Frank, Houston	1.0
Bussey, Barney, Cincinnati	1.0
Butler, Keith, Seattle	1.0
Cherry, Deron, Kansas City	1.0
Comeaux, Darren, Denver	1.0
Cooks, Johnie, Indianapolis	1.0
Cumby, George, Buffalo	1.0
DeAyala, Kiki, Cincinnati	1.0
Dennison, Rick, Denver	1.0
Drane, Dwight, Buffalo	1.0

Easley, Ken, Seattle 1.0
Ellis, Ray, Cleveland 1.0
Franks, Elvis, N.Y. Jets 1.0
Frazier, Guy, Buffalo 1.0
Fuller, William, Houston 1.0
Golic, Mike, Houston 1.0
Grimsley, John, Houston 1.0
Hamby, Mike, Buffalo 1.0
Hammerstein, Mike, Cincinnati 1.0
Hodge, Milford, New England 1.0
Holle, Eric, Kansas City 1.0
James, Roland, New England 1.0
Johnson, Gregg, Seattle 1.0
Johnson, Richard, Houston 1.0
Kellar, Scott, Indianapolis 1.0
Kelly, Joe, Cincinnati 1.0
Krumrie, Tim, Cincinnati 1.0
Lewis, Albert, Kansas City 1.0
Lilly, Tony, Denver 1.0
Lyles, Lester, N.Y. Jets 1.0
Madsen, Lynn, Houston 1.0
Matthews, Clay, Cleveland 1.0
McAlister, Ken, Kansas City 1.0
McArthur, Kevin, N.Y. Jets 1.0
McGrew, Larry, New England 1.0
McKenzie, Reggie, L.A. Raiders 1.0
Mehl, Lance, N.Y. Jets 1.0
Millen, Matt, L.A. Raiders 1.0
Mitz, Alonzo, Seattle 1.0
Moore, Mack, Miami 1.0
Moyer, Paul, Seattle 1.0
Nelson, Steve, New England 1.0
Odom, Cliff, Indianapolis 1.0
Owens, Dennis, New England 1.0
Pearson, J.C., Kansas City 1.0
Prater, Dean, Buffalo 1.0
Radecic, Scott, Kansas City 1.0
Reynolds, Ed, New England 1.0
Rudolph, Ben, N.Y. Jets 1.0
Ruth, Mike, New England 1.0
Ryan, Jim, Denver 1.0
Sanford, Lucius, Buffalo 1.0
Shipp, Jackie, Miami 1.0
Simmons, John, Cincinnati 1.0
Sims, Darryl, Pittsburgh 1.0
Smith, Dennis, Denver 1.0
Smith, Mike, Miami 1.0
Sochia, Brian, Miami 1.0
Taylor, Malcolm, Houston 1.0
Cole, Robin, Pittsburgh 0.5
Holt, John, Indianapolis 0.5
Hunley, Ricky, Denver 0.5
Jackson, Tom, Denver 0.5
Little, David, Pittsburgh 0.5
Sims, Kenneth, New England 0.5
Unrein, Terry, San Diego 0.5
Williams, Toby, New England 0.5

NFC Sacks—Individual

Taylor, Lawrence, N.Y. Giants 20.5
Manley, Dexter, Washington 18.5
White, Reggie, Philadelphia 18.0
Jeffcoat, Jim, Dallas 14.0
Haley, Charles, San Francisco 12.0
Marshall, Leonard, N.Y. Giants 12.0
Dent, Richard, Chicago 11.5
Stover, Jeff, San Francisco 11.0
Baker, Al, St. Louis 10.5
Millard, Keith, Minnesota 10.5
Hampton, Dan, Chicago 10.0
Mann, Charles, Washington 10.0
Ferguson, Keith, Detroit 9.5
Brown, Greg, Philadelphia 9.0
Geathers, James, New Orleans 9.0
Jackson, Rickey, New Orleans 9.0
Martin, Doug, Minnesota 9.0
Board, Dwaine, San Francisco 8.0
Clarke, Ken, Philadelphia 8.0
Harris, Timothy, Green Bay 8.0
Jeter, Gary, L.A. Rams 8.0
McMichael, Steve, Chicago 8.0
Wilson, Otis, Chicago 8.0
Cofer, Mike, Detroit 7.5
Warren, Frank, New Orleans 7.5
Bryan, Rick, Atlanta 7.0
Duerson, Dave, Chicago 7.0
Greene, Kevin, L.A. Rams 7.0
Nunn, Freddie Joe, St. Louis 7.0
Banks, Carl, N.Y. Giants 6.5
Gay, William, Detroit 6.5
Reed, Doug, L.A. Rams 6.5
White, Randy, Dallas 6.5
Butz, Dave, Washington 6.0
Clark, Bruce, New Orleans 6.0
Cobb, Garry, Philadelphia 6.0
Gann, Mike, Atlanta 5.5
Jones, Ed, Dallas 5.5
Marshall, Wilber, Chicago 5.5
Pitts, Mike, Atlanta 5.5
Roberts, Larry, San Francisco 5.5
Wilcher, Mike, L.A. Rams 5.5
Dutton, John, Dallas 5.0
Lockhart, Eugene, Dallas 5.0
Miller, Shawn, L.A. Rams 5.0
Newton, Tim, Minnesota 5.0
Perry, William, Chicago 5.0
Galloway, David, St. Louis 4.5
Hamilton, Steve, Washington 4.5
Smerek, Don, Dallas 4.5
Bell, Anthony, St. Louis 4.0
Browner, Keith, Tampa Bay 4.0
Owens, Mel, L.A. Rams 4.0
Swilling, Pat, New Orleans 4.0
Washington, Chris, Tampa Bay 4.0
Williams, Eric, Detroit 4.0
Baker, Charles, St. Louis 3.5
Elliott, Tony, New Orleans 3.5
Green, Curtis, Detroit 3.5
Robinson, Gerald, Minnesota 3.5
Sally, Jerome, N.Y. Giants 3.5
Clasby, Bob, St. Louis 3.0
Coleman, Monte, Washington 3.0
Doleman, Chris, Minnesota 3.0
Gibson, Antonio, New Orleans 3.0
Greenwood, David, Green Bay 3.0
Johnson, Ezra, Green Bay 3.0
Kaufman, Mel, Washington 3.0
Martin, George, N.Y. Giants 3.0
Smith, Leonard, St. Louis 3.0
Turner, Keena, San Francisco 3.0
Bates, Bill, Dallas 2.5
Brooks, Kevin, Dallas 2.5
Carreker, Alphonso, Green Bay 2.5
Fuller, Jeff, San Francisco 2.5
Headen, Andy, N.Y. Giants 2.5
Holmes, Ron, Tampa Bay 2.5
Howard, David, Minnesota 2.5
Penn, Jesse, Dallas 2.5
Brown, Robert, Green Bay 2.0
Cannon, John, Tampa Bay 2.0
Carson, Harry, N.Y. Giants 2.0
Carter, Michael, San Francisco 2.0
Costello, Joe, Atlanta 2.0
Grant, Darryl, Washington 2.0
Griffin, James, Detroit 2.0
Harris, Al, Chicago 2.0
Haynes, James, New Orleans 2.0
Howard, Erik, N.Y. Giants 2.0
Jiles, Dwayne, Philadelphia 2.0
Johnson, Pepper, N.Y. Giants 2.0
Joyner, Seth, Philadelphia 2.0
Kellin, Kevin, Tampa Bay 2.0
King, Angelo, Detroit 2.0
Logan, Dave, Tampa Bay 2.0
Lott, Ronnie, San Francisco 2.0
Maxwell, Vernon, Detroit 2.0
McColl, Milt, San Francisco 2.0
Meisner, Greg, L.A. Rams 2.0
Milot, Rich, Washington 2.0
Mullaney, Mark, Minnesota 2.0
Noble, Brian, Green Bay 2.0
Noga, Niko, St. Louis 2.0
Olkewicz, Neal, Washington 2.0
Rohrer, Jeff, Dallas 2.0
Simmons, Clyde, Philadelphia 2.0
Singletary, Mike, Chicago 2.0
Smith, Lance, St. Louis 2.0
Snipes, Angelo, Washington 2.0
Thomas, Ben, N.E.-G.B 2.0
Waters, Andre, Philadelphia 2.0
Williams, Jimmy, Detroit 2.0
Leopold, Bobby, Green Bay 1.5
Young, Lonnie, St. Louis 1.5
Burt, Jim, N.Y. Giants 1.0
Cade, Mossy, Green Bay 1.0
Casillas, Tony, Atlanta 1.0
Clark, Bret, Atlanta 1.0
Cooper, Evan, Philadelphia 1.0
Daniels, Calvin, Washington 1.0
Darby, Byron, Philadelphia 1.0
Downs, Michael, Dallas 1.0
Ekern, Carl, L.A. Rams 1.0
Fahnhorst, Jim, San Francisco 1.0
Fencik, Gary, Chicago 1.0
Greene, Tiger, Green Bay 1.0
Griffin, Don, San Francisco 1.0
Harrison, Dennis, Atlanta 1.0
Hartenstine, Mike, Chicago 1.0
Hegman, Mike, Dallas 1.0
Hill, Kenny, N.Y. Giants 1.0
Johnson, Alonzo, Philadelphia 1.0
Johnson, Vaughan, New Orleans 1.0
Kinard, Terry, N.Y. Giants 1.0
Lasker, Greg, N.Y. Giants 1.0
Martin, Charles, Green Bay 1.0
Moore, Robert, Atlanta 1.0
Nelson, Bob, Tampa Bay 1.0
Poe, Johnnie, New Orleans 1.0
Rade, John, Atlanta 1.0
Rivera, Ron, Chicago 1.0
Scott, Randy, Green Bay 1.0
Singletary, Reggie, Philadelphia 1.0
Stensrud, Mike, Minnesota 1.0
Studwell, Scott, Minnesota 1.0
Swoope, Craig, Tampa Bay 1.0
Walter, Mike, San Francisco 1.0
Walton, Alvin, Washington 1.0
Watts, Elbert, Green Bay 1.0
Wilks, Jim, New Orleans 1.0
Williams, Perry, N.Y. Giants 1.0
Browner, Joey, Minnesota 0.5
Harrell, James, Detroit 0.5
Randle, Ervin, Tampa Bay 0.5
Robinson, Shelton, Detroit 0.5

INSIDE THE NUMBERS

NFL Home/Road Records, Past 5 Seasons

AFC

BUFFALO

	Total	Home	Road	Playoffs
1982	4-5	4-1	0-4	None
1983	8-8	3-5	5-3	None
1984	2-14	2-6	0-8	None
1985	2-14	2-6	0-8	None
1986	4-12	3-5	1-7	None

CINCINNATI

	Total	Home	Road	Playoffs
1982	7-2	4-0	3-2	0-1*
1983	7-9	4-4	3-5	None
1984	8-8	5-3	3-5	None
1985	7-9	5-3	2-6	None
1986	10-6	6-2	4-4	None

*Lost first-round game

CLEVELAND

	Total	Home	Road	Playoffs
1982	4-5	2-2	2-3	0-1*
1983	9-7	6-2	3-5	None
1984	5-11	2-6	3-5	None
1985	8-8	5-3	3-5	0-1**
1986	12-4	6-2	6-2	1-1***

*Lost first-round game
**Lost divisional playoff game
***Lost AFC Championship Game

DENVER

	Total	Home	Road	Playoffs
1982	2-7	1-4	1-3	None
1983	9-7	6-2	3-5	0-1*
1984	13-3	7-1	6-2	0-1**
1985	11-5	6-2	5-3	None
1986	11-5	7-1	4-4	2-1***

*Lost first-round game
**Lost divisional playoff game
***Lost Super Bowl XXI

HOUSTON

	Total	Home	Road	Playoffs
1982	1-8	1-4	0-4	None
1983	2-14	2-6	0-8	None
1984	3-13	2-6	1-7	None
1985	5-11	4-4	1-7	None
1986	5-11	4-4	1-7	None

INDIANAPOLIS/BALTIMORE (1982-83)

	Total	Home	Road	Playoffs
1982	0-8-1	0-3-1	0-5	None
1983	7-9	3-5	4-4	None
1984	4-12	2-6	2-6	None
1985	5-11	4-4	1-7	None
1986	3-13	1-7	2-6	None

KANSAS CITY

	Total	Home	Road	Playoffs
1982	3-6	2-2	1-4	None
1983	6-10	5-3	1-7	None
1984	8-8	5-3	3-5	None
1985	6-10	5-3	1-7	None
1986	10-6	6-2	4-4	0-1*

*Lost first-round game

LOS ANGELES RAIDERS

	Total	Home	Road	Playoffs
1982	8-1	4-0	4-1	1-1*
1983	12-4	6-2	6-2	3-0**
1984	11-5	6-2	5-3	0-1***
1985	12-4	7-1	5-3	0-1#
1986	8-8	3-5	5-3	None

*Lost second-round game
**Won Super Bowl XVIII
***Lost first-round game
#Lost divisional playoff game

MIAMI

	Total	Home	Road	Playoffs
1982	7-2	4-0	3-2	3-1*
1983	12-4	7-1	5-3	0-1**
1984	14-2	7-1	7-1	2-1***
1985	12-4	8-0	4-4	1-1#
1986	8-8	4-4	4-4	None

*Lost Super Bowl XVII
**Lost divisional playoff game
***Lost Super Bowl XIX
#Lost AFC Championship Game

NEW ENGLAND

	Total	Home	Road	Playoffs
1982	5-4	3-1	2-3	0-1*
1983	8-8	5-3	3-5	None
1984	9-7	5-3	4-4	None
1985	11-5	7-1	4-4	3-1**
1986	11-5	4-4	7-1	0-1***

*Lost first-round game
**Lost Super Bowl XX
***Lost divisional playoff game

NEW YORK JETS

	Total	Home	Road	Playoffs
1982	6-3	3-1	3-2	2-1*
1983	7-9	2-6	5-3	None
1984	7-9	3-5	4-4	None
1985	11-5	7-1	4-4	0-1**
1986	10-6	5-3	5-3	1-1***

*Lost AFC Championship Game
**Lost first-round game
***Lost divisional playoff game

PITTSBURGH

	Total	Home	Road	Playoffs
1982	6-3	4-0	2-3	0-1*
1983	10-6	4-4	6-2	0-1**
1984	9-7	6-2	3-5	1-1***
1985	7-9	5-3	2-6	None
1986	6-10	4-4	2-6	None

*Lost first-round game
**Lost first-round game
***Lost AFC Championship Game

SAN DIEGO

	Total	Home	Road	Playoffs
1982	6-3	3-1	3-2	1-1*
1983	6-10	4-4	2-6	None
1984	7-9	4-4	3-5	None
1985	8-8	6-2	2-6	None
1986	4-12	2-6	2-6	None

*Lost second-round game

SEATTLE

	Total	Home	Road	Playoffs
1982	4-5	3-2	1-3	None
1983	9-7	5-3	4-4	2-1*
1984	12-4	7-1	5-3	1-1**
1985	8-8	5-3	3-5	None
1986	10-6	7-1	3-5	None

*Lost AFC Championship Game
**Lost divisional playoff game

NFC

ATLANTA

	Total	Home	Road	Playoffs
1982	5-4	2-3	3-1	0-1*
1983	7-9	4-4	3-5	None
1984	4-12	2-6	2-6	None
1985	4-12	3-5	1-7	None
1986	7-8-1	2-5-1	5-3	None

*Lost first-round game

CHICAGO

	Total	Home	Road	Playoffs
1982	3-6	2-2	1-4	None
1983	8-8	5-3	3-5	None
1984	10-6	6-2	4-4	1-1*
1985	15-1	8-0	7-1	3-0**
1986	14-2	7-1	7-1	0-1***

*Lost NFC Championship Game
**Won Super Bowl XX
***Lost divisional playoff game

DALLAS

	Total	Home	Road	Playoffs
1982	6-3	3-2	3-1	2-1*
1983	12-4	6-2	6-2	0-1**
1984	9-7	5-3	4-4	None
1985	10-6	7-1	3-5	0-1***
1986	7-9	3-5	4-4	None

*Lost NFC Championship Game
**Lost first-round game
***Lost divisional playoff game

DETROIT

	Total	Home	Road	Playoffs
1982	4-5	2-3	2-2	0-1*
1983	9-7	6-2	3-5	0-1**
1984	4-11-1	2-5-1	2-6	None
1985	7-9	6-2	1-7	None
1986	5-11	1-7	4-4	None

*Lost first-round game
**Lost divisional playoff game

GREEN BAY

	Total	Home	Road	Playoffs
1982	5-3-1	3-1	2-2-1	1-1*
1983	8-8	5-3	3-5	None
1984	8-8	5-3	3-5	None
1985	8-8	5-3	3-5	None
1986	4-12	1-7	3-5	None

*Lost second-round game

LOS ANGELES RAMS

	Total	Home	Road	Playoffs
1982	2-7	1-4	1-3	None
1983	9-7	5-3	4-4	1-1*
1984	10-6	5-3	5-3	0-1**
1985	11-5	6-2	5-3	1-1***
1986	10-6	6-2	4-4	0-1#

*Lost divisional playoff game
**Lost first-round game
***Lost NFC Championship Game
#Lost first-round game

MINNESOTA

	Total	Home	Road	Playoffs
1982	5-4	4-1	1-3	1-1*
1983	8-8	3-5	5-3	None
1984	3-13	2-6	1-7	None
1985	7-9	4-4	3-5	None
1986	9-7	5-3	4-4	None

*Lost second-round game

NEW ORLEANS

	Total	Home	Road	Playoffs
1982	4-5	2-3	2-2	None
1983	8-8	5-3	3-5	None
1984	7-9	3-5	4-4	None
1985	5-11	3-5	2-6	None
1986	7-9	4-4	3-5	None

NEW YORK GIANTS

	Total	Home	Road	Playoffs
1982	4-5	2-3	2-2	None
1983	3-12-1	1-7	2-5-1	None
1984	9-7	6-2	3-5	1-1*
1985	10-6	6-2	4-4	1-1**
1986	14-2	8-0	6-2	3-0***

*Lost divisional playoff game
**Lost divisional playoff game
***Won Super Bowl XXI

PHILADELPHIA

	Total	Home	Road	Playoffs
1982	3-6	1-4	2-2	None
1983	5-11	1-7	4-4	None
1984	6-9-1	5-3	1-6-1	None
1985	7-9	4-4	3-5	None
1986	5-10-1	2-5-1	3-5	None

ST. LOUIS

	Total	Home	Road	Playoffs
1982	5-4	1-3	4-1	0-1*
1983	8-7-1	4-3-1	4-4	None
1984	9-7	5-3	4-4	None
1985	5-11	4-4	1-7	None
1986	4-11-1	3-5	1-6-1	None

*Lost first-round game

SAN FRANCISCO

	Total	Home	Road	Playoffs
1982	3-6	0-5	3-1	None
1983	10-6	4-4	6-2	1-1*
1984	15-1	7-1	8-0	3-0**
1985	10-6	5-3	5-3	0-1***
1986	10-5-1	6-2	4-3-1	0-1#

*Lost NFC Championship Game
**Won Super Bowl XIX
***Lost first-round game
#Lost divisional playoff game

TAMPA BAY

	Total	Home	Road	Playoffs
1982	5-4	4-1	1-3	0-1*
1983	2-14	1-7	1-7	None
1984	6-10	6-2	0-8	None
1985	2-14	2-6	0-8	None
1986	2-14	1-7	1-7	None

*Lost first-round game

WASHINGTON

	Total	Home	Road	Playoffs
1982	8-1	3-1	5-0	4-0*
1983	14-2	7-1	7-1	2-1**
1984	11-5	7-1	4-4	0-1***
1985	10-6	5-3	5-3	None
1986	12-4	7-1	5-3	2-1#

*Won Super Bowl XVII
**Lost Super Bowl XVIII
***Lost divisional playoff game
#Lost NFC Championship Game

Records for Each Current NFL Team for Most Points in a Game (Regular Season Only)

Note: When the record has been achieved more than once, only the most recent game is shown; summaries are listed in alphabetical order by conference. Bold face indicates team holding record.

BUFFALO BILLS
September 18, 1966, at Buffalo
Miami . . . . 3 7 0 14 — 24
Buffalo . . . . 21 27 3 7 — 58
TDs: Buff—Bobby Burnett 2, Butch Byrd 2, Jack Spikes 2, Bobby Crockett, Jack Kemp; Mia—Dave Kocourek, Bo Roberson, John Roderick. TD Passes: Buff—Jack Kemp, Daryle Lamonica; Mia—George Wilson 3. FGs: Buff—Booth Lusteg; Mia—Gene Mingo.

CINCINNATI BENGALS
December 17, 1972, at Houston
Cincinnati . . . . 3 13 17 28 — 61
Houston . . . . 3 7 0 7 — 17
TDs: Cin—Doug Dressler 3, Lemar Parrish 2, Ken Anderson, Neal Craig; Hou—Ken Burrough, Fred Willis. TD Passes: Cin—Ken Anderson; Hou—Kent Nix 2. FGs: Cin—Horst Muhlmann 4; Hou—Skip Butler.

CLEVELAND BROWNS
November 7, 1954, at Cleveland
Washington . . . . 0 3 0 0 — 3
Cleveland . . . . 13 14 21 14 — 62
TDs: Clev—Darrell Brewster 2, Mo Bassett, Ken Gorgal, Otto Graham, Dub Jones, Dante Lavelli, Curley Morrison. TD Passes: Clev—George Ratterman 3, Otto Graham. FGs: Clev—Lou Groza 2; Wash—Vic Janowicz.

DENVER BRONCOS
October 6, 1963, at Denver
San Diego . . . . 13 7 0 14 — 34
Denver . . . . 3 14 9 24 — 50
TDs: Den—Lionel Taylor 2, Goose Gonsoulin, Gene Prebola, Donnie Stone; SD—Keith Lincoln 2, Lance Alworth, Paul Lowe, Jacque MacKinnon. TD Passes: Den—John McCormick 3; SD—Tobin Rote 3, John Hadl 2. FGs: Den—Gene Mingo 5.

HOUSTON OILERS
October 14, 1962, at Houston
New York Titans . . . . 3 7 7 0 — 17
Houston . . . . 14 21 14 7 — 56
TDs: Hou—Bill Groman, 2, Bob McLeod 2, Dave Smith 2, Willard Dewveall, Charley Hennigan; NY—Dick Christy, Ed Cooke. TD Passes: Hou—George Blanda 6, Jacky Lee. FGs: NY—Bill Shockley.

INDIANAPOLIS COLTS
December 12, 1976, at Baltimore
Buffalo . . . . 3 3 7 7 — 20
Baltimore Colts . . . . 7 13 28 10 — 58
TDs: Balt—Roger Carr, Raymond Chester, Glenn Doughty, Roosevelt Leaks, Derrel Luce, Lydell Mitchell, Howard Stevens; Buff—Bob Chandler, O.J. Simpson. TD Passes: Balt—Bert Jones 3; Buff—Gary Marangi. FGs: Balt—Toni Linhart 3; Buff—George Jakowenko 2.

KANSAS CITY CHIEFS
September 7, 1963, at Denver
Kansas City . . . . 14 14 21 10 — 59
Denver . . . . 0 7 0 0 — 7
TDs: KC—Chris Burford 2, Frank Jackson 2, Dave Grayson, Abner Haynes, Sherrill Headrick, Curtis McClinton; Den—Lionel Taylor. TD Passes: KC—Len Dawson 4, Curtis McClinton; Den—Mickey Slaughter. FG: KC—Tommy Brooker.

LOS ANGELES RAIDERS
December 22, 1963, at Oakland
Houston . . . . 14 21 14 0 — 49
Oakland Raiders . . . . 7 28 7 10 — 52
TDs: Oak—Art Powell 4, Clem Daniels, Claude Gibson, Ken Herock; Hou—Willard Dewveall 2, Dave Smith 2, Charley Hennigan, Bob McLeod, Charley Tolar. TD Passes: Oak—Tom Flores 6; Hou—George Blanda 5. FG: Oak—Mike Mercer.

MIAMI DOLPHINS
November 24, 1977, at St. Louis
Miami . . . . 14 14 20 7 — 55
St. Louis . . . . 7 0 0 7 — 14
TDs: Mia—Nat Moore 3, Gary Davis, Duriel Harris, Leroy Harris, Benny Malone, Andre Tillman; StL—Ike Harris, Terry Metcalf. TD Passes: Mia—Bob Griese 6; StL—Jim Hart.

NEW ENGLAND PATRIOTS
September 9, 1979, at New England
New York Jets . . . . 3 0 0 0 — 3
New England . . . . 14 21 7 14 — 56
TDs: NE—Harold Jackson 3, Stanley Morgan 2, Allan Clark, Andy Johnson, Don Westbrook. TD Passes: NE—Steve Grogan 5, Tom Owen. FG: NYJ—Pat Leahy.

NEW YORK JETS
November 17, 1985, at New York
Tampa Bay . . . . 14 7 7 0 — 28
New York Jets . . . . 17 24 14 7 — 62
TDs: NYJ—Mickey Shuler 3, Johnny Hector 2, Tony Paige, Al Toon, Wesley Walker; TB—James Wilder 2, Kevin House, Calvin Magee. TD Passes: NYJ—Ken O'Brien 5; TB—Steve DeBerg 2. FGs: NYJ—Pat Leahy 2.

PITTSBURGH STEELERS
November 30, 1952, at Pittsburgh
New York Giants . . . . 0 0 7 0 — 7
Pittsburgh . . . . 14 14 7 28 — 63
TDs: Pitt—Lynn Chandnois 2, Dick Hensley 2, Jack Butler, George Hays, Ray Mathews, Ed Modzelewski, Elbie Nickel; NYG—Bill Stribling. TD Passes: Pitt—Jim Finks 4, Gary Kerkorian; NYG—Tom Landry.

SAN DIEGO CHARGERS
December 22, 1963, at San Diego
Denver . . . . 7 10 3 0 — 20
San Diego . . . . 10 16 10 22 — 58
TDs: SD—Paul Lowe 2, Chuck Allen, Bobby Jackson, Dave Kocourek, Keith Lincoln, Jacque MacKinnon; Den—Billy Joe, Donnie Stone. TD Passes: SD—John Hadl, Tobin Rote; Den—Don Breaux. FGs: SD—George Blair 3; Den—Gene Mingo 2.

SEATTLE SEAHAWKS
October 30, 1977, at Seattle
Buffalo . . . . 3 0 7 7 — 17
Seattle . . . . 14 28 7 7 — 56
TDs: Sea—Steve Largent 2, Duke Fergerson, Al Hunter, David Sims, Sherman Smith, Don Testerman, Jim Zorn; Buff—Joe Ferguson, John Kimbrough. TD Passes: Sea—Jim Zorn 4; Buff—Joe Ferguson. FG: Buff—Carson Long.

ATLANTA FALCONS
September 16, 1973, at New Orleans
Atlanta . . . . 0 24 21 17 — 62
New Orleans . . . . 0 0 7 0 — 7
TDs: Atl—Ken Burrow 2, Eddie Ray 2, Wes Chesson, Tom Hayes, Art Malone, Joe Profit; NO—Bill Butler. TD Passes: Atl—Dick Shiner 3, Bob Lee; NO—Archie Manning. FGs: Atl—Nick Mike-Mayer.

CHICAGO BEARS
December 7, 1980, at Chicago
Green Bay . . . . 0 7 0 0 — 7
Chicago . . . . 0 28 13 20 — 61
TDs: Chi—Walter Payton 3, Brian Baschnagel, Robin Earl, Roland Harper, Willie McClendon, Len Walterscheid, Rickey Watts; GB—James Lofton. TD Passes: Chi—Vince Evans 3; GB—Lynn Dickey.

DALLAS COWBOYS
October 12, 1980, at Dallas
San Francisco . . . . 0 7 0 7 — 14
Dallas . . . . 14 24 14 7 — 59
TDs: Dall—Drew Pearson 3, Ron Springs 2, Tony Dorsett, Billy Joe DuPree, Robert Newhouse; SF—Dwight Clark 2. TD Passes: Dall—Danny White 4; SF—Steve DeBerg 2. FG: Dall—Rafael Septien.

DETROIT LIONS
October 26, 1952, at Green Bay
Detroit . . . . 14 14 14 10 — 52
Green Bay . . . . 7 3 7 0 — 17
TDs: Det—Jug Girard 2, Bob Hoernschemeyer 2, Jack Christiansen, Jim Smith, Bill Swiacki; GB—Billy Howton, Jim Keane. TD Passes: Det—Bobby Layne 3; GB—Babe Parilli, Tobin Rote. FGs: Det—Pat Harder; GB—Bill Reichardt.

GREEN BAY PACKERS
October 7, 1945, at Milwaukee
Detroit . . . . 0 7 7 7 — 21
Green Bay . . . . 0 41 9 7 — 57
TDs: GB—Don Hutson 4, Charley Brock, Irv Comp, Ted Fritsch, Clyde Goodnight; Det—Chuck Fenenbock, John Greene, Bob Westfall. TD Passes: GB—Tex McKay 4, Lou Brock, Irv Comp; Det—Dave Ryan.

LOS ANGELES RAMS
October 22, 1950, at Los Angeles
Baltimore . . . . 13 0 7 7 — 27
Los Angeles . . . . 21 14 14 21 — 70
TDs: LA—Bob Boyd 2, Vitamin T. Smith 2, Tom Fears, Elroy (Crazylegs) Hirsch, Dick Hoerner, Ralph Pasquariello, Dan Towler, Bob Waterfield; Balt—Chet Mutryn 2, Adrian Burk, Billy Stone. TD Passes: LA—Norm Van Brocklin 2, Bob Waterfield 2, Glenn Davis; Balt—Adrian Burk 3.

MINNESOTA VIKINGS
October 18, 1970, at Minnesota
Dallas . . . . 3 3 0 7 — 13
Minnesota . . . . 14 20 17 3 — 54
TDs: Minn—Clint Jones 2, Ed Sharockman 2, John Beasley, Dave Osborn; Dall—Calvin Hill. TD Pass: Minn—Gary Cuozzo. FGs: Minn—Fred Cox 4; Dall—Mike Clark 2.

NEW ORLEANS SAINTS
November 21, 1976, at Seattle
New Orleans . . . . 3 17 28 3 — 51
Seattle . . . . 6 0 7 14 — 27
TDs: NO—Bobby Douglass 2, Tony Galbreath, Chuck Muncie, Tom Myers, Elex Price; Sea—Sherman Smith 2, Steve Largent, Jim Zorn. TD Pass: Sea—Bill Munson. FGs: NO—Rich Szaro 3.

NEW YORK GIANTS
November 26, 1972, at New York
Philadelphia . . . . 3 7 0 0 — 10
New York Giants . . . . 14 24 10 14 — 62
TDs: NYG—Don Herrmann 2, Ron Johnson 2, Bob Tucker 2, Randy Johnson; Phil—Harold Jackson. TD Passes: NYG—Norm Snead 3, Randy Johnson 2; Phil—John Reaves. FGs: NYG—Pete Gogolak 2; Phil—Tom Dempsey.

PHILADELPHIA EAGLES
November 6, 1934, at Philadelphia
Cincinnati Reds . . . . 0 0 0 0 — 0
Philadelphia . . . . 26 6 12 20 — 64
TDs: Phil—Joe Carter 3, Swede Hanson 3, Marvin Ellstrom, Roger Kirkman, Ed Matesic, Ed Storm. TD Passes: Phil—Ed Matesic 2, Albert Weiner 2, Marvin Elstrom.

ST. LOUIS CARDINALS
November 13, 1949, at New York
Chicago Cardinals . . . . . . 7 31 14 13 — 65
New York Bulldogs . . . . 7 0 6 7 — 20
TDs: Chi—Red Cochran 2, Pat Harder 2, Bill Dewell, Mel Kutner, Bob Ravensburg, Vic Schwall, Charlie Trippi; NY—Joe Golding, Frank Muehlheuser, Johnny Rauch. TD Passes: Chi—Paul Christman 3, Jim Hardy 3; NY—Bobby Layne. FG: Chi—Pat Harder.

SAN FRANCISCO 49ERS
September 19, 1965, at San Francisco
Chicago . . . . 3 0 0 21 — 24
San Francisco . . . . 0 24 21 7 — 52
TDs: SF—Bernie Casey 2, John David Crow, Charlie Krueger, Gary Lewis, Dave Parks, Ken Willard; Chi—Charlie Bivins 2, Andy Livingston. TD Passes: SF—John Brodie 4; Chi—Rudy Bukich 2. FGs: SF—Tommy Davis; Chi—Roger LeClerc.

TAMPA BAY BUCCANEERS
December 16, 1984, at Tampa Bay
New York Jets . . . . 0 7 0 14 — 21
Tampa Bay . . . . 10 7 3 21 — 41
TDs: TB—Jerry Bell 2, James Wilder 2, Jay Carroll; NYJ—Glenn Dennison, Johnny Hector, Tony Paige. TD Passes: TB—Steve DeBerg 3; NYJ—Ken O'Brien 2. FGs: TB—Obed Ariri.

WASHINGTON REDSKINS
November 27, 1966, at Washington
New York Giants . . . . 0 14 14 13 — 41
Washington . . . . 13 21 14 24 — 72
TDs: Wash—A. D. Whitfield 3, Brig Owens 2, Charley Taylor 2, Rickie Harris, Joe Don Looney, Bobby Mitchell; NYG—Allen Jacobs, Homer Jones, Dan Lewis, Joe Morrison, Aaron Thomas, Gary Wood. TD Passes: Wash—Sonny Jurgensen 3; NYG—Gary Wood 2, Tom Kennedy. FG: Wash—Charlie Gogolak.

NFL Games In Which a Team Has Scored 60 or More Points

(Home team in capitals)

Regular Season

WASHINGTON 72, New York Giants 41	November 27, 1966
LOS ANGELES RAMS 70, Baltimore 27	October 22, 1950
Chicago Cardinals 65, NEW YORK BULLDOGS 20	November 13, 1949
LOS ANGELES RAMS 65, Detroit 24	October 29, 1950
PHILADELPHIA 64, Cincinnati 0	November 6, 1934
CHICAGO CARDINALS 63, New York Giants 35	October 17, 1948
PITTSBURGH 62, New York Giants 7	November 30, 1952
CLEVELAND 62, New York Giants 14	December 6, 1953
CLEVELAND 62, Washington 3	November 7, 1954
NEW YORK GIANTS 62, Philadelphia 10	November 26, 1972
Atlanta 62, NEW ORLEANS 7	September 16, 1973
NEW YORK JETS 62, Tampa Bay 28	November 17, 1985
CHICAGO 61, San Francisco 20	December 12, 1965
Cincinnati 61, HOUSTON 17	December 17, 1972
CHICAGO 61, Green Bay 7	December 7, 1980
CHICAGO CARDINALS 60, Rochester 0	October 7, 1923

Postseason

Chicago Bears 73, WASHINGTON 0	December 8, 1940

Youngest and Oldest Regular Starters in NFL in 1986

Minimum: 8 Games Started

Five Youngest Regular Starters

	Birthdate	Games Started	Position
John L. Williams, Seattle	11/23/64	16	RB
Brent Williams, New England	10/23/64	16	DE
Webster Slaughter, Cleveland	10/19/64	16	WR
David Fulcher, Cincinnati	9/28/64	16	S
Timothy Harris, Green Bay	9/10/64	10	LB

Five Oldest Regular Starters

	Birthdate	Games Started	Position
Charlie Joiner, San Diego	10/14/47	9	WR
Jim Plunkett, L.A. Raiders	12/5/47	8	QB
Dave Butz, Washington	6/23/50	16	DT
Paul Howard, Denver	9/12/50	13	G
John Dutton, Dallas	2/6/51	16	DT

Youngest and Oldest Regular Starters By Position

Minimum: 8 Games Started

	Youngest	Oldest
Quarterback	11/25/63 Bernie Kosar, Clev.	12/5/47 Jim Plunkett, Raiders
Running back	11/23/64 John L. Williams, Sea.	4/3/54 Mike Pruitt, K.C.
Wide receiver	10/19/64 Webster Slaughter, Clev.	10/14/47 Charlie Joiner, S.D.
Tight end	4/28/63 Mark Bavaro, Giants	4/3/53 Russ Francis, S.F.
Center	3/11/63 Matt Darwin, Phil.	3/18/52 Mike Webster, Pitt.
Guard	5/18/64 Will Wolford, Buff.	9/12/50 Paul Howard, Den.
Tackle	8/8/63 Ron Mattes, Sea.	9/26/51 Henry Lawrence, Raiders
Def. end	10/23/64 Brent Williams, N.E.	2/23/51 Ed Jones, Dall.
Def. tackle	12/31/63 Scott Kellar, Ind.	6/23/50 Dave Butz, Wash.
Linebacker	9/10/64 Timothy Harris, G.B.	4/4/51 Tom Jackson, Den.
Cornerback	3/31/64 Rod Jones, T.B.	1/16/53 Dave Brown, Sea.
Safety	9/28/64 David Fulcher, Cin.	8/26/52 Donnie Shell, Pitt.

Records of Teams on Opening Day, 1933-86

AFC	W	L	T	Pct.	Longest W Strk.	Longest L Strk.	Current Streak
San Diego	18	9	0	.667	6	4	W-3
Denver	16	10	1	.615	3	4	W-1
Indianapolis	20	14	0	.588	8	3	L-3
Cleveland	21	16	0	.568	5	4	L-4
L.A. Raiders	15	12	0	.556	5	5	L-1
Pittsburgh	25	23	4	.521	4	3	L-1
Houston	14	13	0	.519	4	3	W-2
Kansas City	14	13	0	.519	4	4	W-4
Miami	10	10	1	.500	4	3	L-2
Cincinnati	9	10	0	.474	4	4	L-4
N.Y. Jets	12	15	0	.444	3	5	W-1
New England	12	15	0	.444	3	3	W-3
Buffalo	9	18	0	.333	3	5	L-4
Seattle	3	8	0	.273	3	8	W-3

NFC	W	L	T	Pct.	Longest W Strk.	Longest L Strk.	Current Streak
Dallas	22	4	1	.846	17	2	W-4
Atlanta	13	8	0	.619	5	3	W-1
Minnesota	15	10	1	.600	4	2	L-1
N.Y. Giants	29	21	4	.580	3	3	L-1
Detroit	29	23	2	.558	7	4	W-2
L.A. Rams	27	22	0	.551	5	6	W-2
Green Bay	28	23	3	.549	5	6	L-2
Chicago	29	24	1	.547	7	6	W-3
Washington	25	25	4	.500	6	5	W-1
San Francisco	16	20	1	.444	4	3	W-1
St. Louis	23	29	1	.442	6	6	L-1
Philadelphia	20	32	1	.385	5	9	L-3
Tampa Bay	3	8	0	.273	3	5	L-5
New Orleans	3	17	0	.150	1	6	L-3

Note: All tied games occurred prior to 1972, when calculation of ties as half-win, half-loss was begun.

Records of all NFL teams for 1986 in each category of games:

AFC	Status at Halftime: Leading	Tied	Trailing	Status After 3 Quarters: Leading	Tied	Trailing
Buffalo	4-2	0-1	0-9	4-4	0-1	0-7
Cincinnati	9-0	0-1	1-5	8-0	0-0	2-6
Cleveland	7-1	3-0	2-3	9-0	0-0	3-4
Denver	8-0	0-1	3-4	10-0	0-0	1-5
Houston	5-2	0-1	0-8	5-1	0-0	0-10
Indianapolis	0-1	0-1	3-11	0-0	1-0	2-13
Kansas City	6-1	2-1	2-4	8-0	0-0	2-6
L.A. Raiders	5-3	0-1	3-4	7-4	0-0	1-4
Miami	7-0	0-0	1-8	7-1	0-1	1-6
New England	8-2	1-0	2-3	8-2	1-0	2-3
N.Y. Jets	9-1	1-0	0-5	8-0	0-1	2-5
Pittsburgh	4-0	1-1	1-9	5-3	1-0	0-7
San Diego	4-4	0-1	0-7	4-3	0-0	0-9
Seattle	6-0	1-0	3-6	9-0	0-0	1-6

NFC	Halftime: Leading	Tied	Trailing	After 3 Quarters: Leading	Tied	Trailing
Atlanta	5-3	0-0	2-5-1	5-1	0-0	2-7-1
Chicago	10-1	1-0	3-1	11-0	0-1	3-1
Dallas	7-3	0-0	0-6	5-3	0-0	2-6
Detroit	5-1	0-2	0-8	5-2	0-0	0-9
Green Bay	3-2	0-0	1-10	3-1	0-1	1-10
L.A. Rams	9-0	0-1	1-5	7-1	3-0	0-5
Minnesota	8-2	0-0	1-5	8-3	0-0	1-4
New Orleans	6-1	1-1	0-7	7-2	0-0	0-7
N.Y. Giants	11-1	0-0	3-1	12-1	0-0	2-1
Philadelphia	4-3	0-0-1	1-7	3-2	0-0-1	2-8
St. Louis	3-0	0-0-1	1-11	3-0	0-0-1	1-11
San Francisco	8-2-1	1-0	1-3	8-1-1	1-1	1-3
Tampa Bay	2-2	0-0	0-12	2-1	0-1	0-12
Washington	7-1	1-0	4-3	8-0	0-0	4-4

Trailing at Halftime

	1981–86	1986 ONLY
Home Teams	126-363-3 (.259)	14-77-1 (.158)
Road Teams	117-532-1 (.181)	25-93-0 (.212)
All Teams	243-895-4 (.215)	39-170-1 (.188)

Trailing After 3 Quarters

	1981–86	1986 ONLY
Home Teams	101-402-2 (.202)	12-76-1 (.140)
Road Teams	96-576-2 (.144)	24-103-0 (.189)
All Teams	197-978-4 (.169)	36-179-1 (.169)

Walter Payton's Career Rushing vs. Each Opponent

Opponent	Games	Rushes	Yards	Yards Per Rush	Yards Per Game	TD
Atlanta	7	139	503	3.6	71.9	3
Buffalo	1	39	155	4.0	155.0	1
Cincinnati	2	28	129	4.6	64.5	0
Cleveland	2	33	143	4.3	71.5	1
Dallas	6	137	692	5.1	115.3	3
Denver	5	98	538	5.5	107.6	2
Detroit	24	483	1900	3.9	79.2	10
Green Bay	22	514	2413	4.7	109.7	18
Houston	3	58	215	3.7	71.7	1
Indianapolis	3	37	115	3.1	38.3	1
Kansas City	2	54	262	4.9	131.0	3
L.A. Raiders	4	97	359	3.7	89.8	5
L.A. Rams	9	156	646	4.1	71.8	3
Miami	3	45	190	4.2	63.3	1
Minnesota	23	474	2240	4.7	97.4	15
New England	3	39	151	3.9	50.3	0
New Orleans	6	130	792	6.1	132.0	6
N.Y. Giants	1	15	47	3.1	47.0	0
N.Y. Jets	2	48	106	2.2	53.0	0
Philadelphia	5	125	564	4.5	112.8	1
Pittsburgh	2	43	150	3.5	75.0	1
St. Louis	6	130	525	4.0	87.5	6
San Diego	3	76	249	3.3	83.0	2
San Francisco	7	162	774	4.8	110.6	8
Seattle	4	83	448	5.4	112.0	1
Tampa Bay	18	386	1575	4.1	87.5	11
Washington	5	63	312	5.0	62.4	3
Totals	178	3692	16193	4.4	91.0	106

Indianapolis totals include two games vs. Baltimore
L.A. Raiders totals include three games vs. Oakland

Tony Dorsett's Career Rushing vs. Each Opponent

Opponent	Games	Rushes	Yards	Yards Per Rush	Yards Per Game	TD
Atlanta	2	33	176	5.3	88.0	1
Buffalo	2	45	187	4.2	93.5	0
Chicago	5	80	340	4.3	68.0	0
Cincinnati	2	37	183	4.9	91.5	0
Cleveland	3	49	247	5.0	82.3	2
Denver	2	34	112	3.3	56.0	0
Detroit	4	63	282	4.5	70.5	1
Green Bay	3	65	270	4.2	90.0	4
Houston	3	53	278	5.2	92.7	1
Indianapolis	3	69	426	6.2	142.0	0
Kansas City	1	18	108	6.0	108.0	2
L.A. Raiders	3	67	263	3.9	87.7	2
L.A. Rams	6	120	494	4.1	82.3	3
Miami	3	53	229	4.3	76.3	0
Minnesota	5	78	488	6.3	97.6	4
New England	3	53	260	4.9	86.7	1
New Orleans	4	88	461	5.2	115.3	4
N.Y. Giants	18	315	1311	4.2	72.8	8
N.Y. Jets	1	29	121	4.2	121.0	1
Philadelphia	19	333	1377	4.1	72.5	11
Pittsburgh	4	68	289	4.3	72.3	2
St. Louis	16	281	1427	5.1	89.2	11
San Diego	2	31	134	4.3	67.0	0
San Francisco	6	101	323	3.2	53.8	2
Seattle	3	64	283	4.4	94.3	5
Tampa Bay	4	69	292	4.2	73.0	0
Washington	18	329	1219	3.7	67.7	6
Totals	145	2625	11580	4.4	79.9	71

Indianapolis totals include two games vs. Baltimore
L.A. Raiders totals include one game vs. Oakland

Eric Dickerson's Career Rushing vs. Each Opponent

Opponent	Games	Rushes	Yards	Yards Per Rush	Yards Per Game	TD
Atlanta	8	157	772	4.9	96.5	9
Buffalo	1	32	125	3.9	125.0	1
Chicago	3	91	387	4.3	129.0	4
Cincinnati	1	22	89	4.0	89.0	1
Cleveland	1	27	102	3.8	102.0	0
Dallas	2	49	244	5.0	122.0	1
Detroit	2	54	329	6.1	164.5	4
Green Bay	3	76	357	4.7	119.0	2
Houston	1	27	215	8.0	215.0	2
Indianapolis	1	25	121	4.8	121.0	1
Kansas City	1	26	68	2.6	68.0	1
L.A. Raiders	1	25	98	3.9	98.0	0
Miami	2	42	225	5.4	112.5	2
Minnesota	1	25	55	2.2	55.0	1
New England	2	51	196	3.8	98.0	0
New Orleans	8	176	853	4.8	106.6	6
N.Y. Giants	3	77	312	4.1	104.0	1
N.Y. Jets	2	59	299	5.1	149.5	3
Philadelphia	2	45	161	3.6	80.5	0
Pittsburgh	1	23	49	2.1	49.0	0
St. Louis	3	79	525	6.6	175.0	4
San Francisco	8	151	726	4.8	90.8	3
Seattle	1	31	150	4.8	150.0	3
Tampa Bay	3	83	473	5.7	157.7	6
Washington	1	12	37	3.1	37.0	0
Totals	62	1465	6968	4.8	112.4	55

Marcus Allen's Career Rushing vs. Each Opponent

Opponent	Games	Rushes	Yards	Yards Per Rush	Yards Per Game	TD
Atlanta	2	40	212	5.3	106.0	1
Buffalo	1	26	89	3.4	89.0	1
Chicago	1	15	42	2.8	42.0	0
Cincinnati	3	56	182	3.3	60.7	2
Cleveland	2	33	137	4.2	68.5	0
Dallas	2	22	84	3.8	42.0	0
Denver	9	169	762	4.5	84.7	5
Detroit	1	17	56	3.3	56.0	0
Green Bay	1	20	81	4.1	81.0	1
Houston	2	38	177	4.7	88.5	1
Indianapolis	2	28	141	5.0	70.5	0
Kansas City	8	154	564	3.7	70.5	2
L.A. Rams	2	49	216	4.4	108.0	3
Miami	3	63	356	5.7	118.7	5
Minnesota	1	17	54	3.2	54.0	1
New England	1	21	98	4.7	98.0	0
New Orleans	1	28	107	3.8	107.0	2
N.Y. Giants	2	28	104	3.7	52.0	1
N.Y. Jets	1	20	76	3.8	76.0	2
Philadelphia	1	24	59	2.5	59.0	0
Pittsburgh	1	13	38	2.9	38.0	0
St. Louis	1	18	86	4.8	86.0	0
San Diego	9	186	795	4.3	88.3	14
San Francisco	2	35	175	5.0	87.5	1
Seattle	9	146	602	4.1	66.9	7
Washington	2	23	104	4.5	52.0	0
Totals	70	1289	5397	4.2	77.1	49

Records of NFL Divisions in Out-of-Division Games 1978–86

Since 1978, teams in a five-team division have played eight games against out-of-division opponents; teams in a four-team division have played 10 such games. These charts indicate the annual records for each division's teams in games against teams from other divisions:

NFC East

	W	L	T	Pct.	Pos.
1978	21	19	0	.525	2T
1979	23	17	0	.575	3
1980	19	21	0	.475	4
1981	26	14	0	.650	1
1982	13	6	0	.684	1
1983	23	17	0	.575	1
1984	24	15	1	.613	2
1985	22	18	0	.550	2
1986	23	17	0	.575	1T
Totals	194	144	1	.574	2

NFC Central

	W	L	T	Pct.	Pos.
1978	16	24	0	.400	6
1979	14	26	0	.350	5
1980	16	24	0	.400	6
1981	18	22	0	.450	4T
1982	12	12	1	.500	3T
1983	15	25	0	.375	6
1984	11	28	1	.288	6
1985	19	21	0	.475	4
1986	14	26	0	.350	6
Totals	135	208	2	.394	6

NFC West

	W	L	T	Pct.	Pos.
1978	18	22	0	.450	5
1979	13	27	0	.325	6
1980	18	22	0	.450	5
1981	18	22	0	.450	4T
1982	7	15	0	.318	6
1983	22	18	0	.550	2T
1984	24	16	0	.600	3
1985	18	22	0	.450	5
1986	23	17	0	.575	1T
Totals	161	181	0	.471	4

AFC East

	W	L	T	Pct.	Pos.
1978	20	20	0	.500	4
1979	19	21	0	.475	4
1980	20	20	0	.500	3
1981	16	24	0	.400	6
1982	10	10	1	.500	3T
1983	22	18	0	.550	2T
1984	16	24	0	.400	4
1985	21	19	0	.475	3
1986	16	24	0	.400	5
Totals	160	180	1	.471	5

AFC Central

	W	L	T	Pct.	Pos.
1978	24	16	0	.600	1
1979	24	16	0	.600	2
1980	25	15	0	.625	1
1981	20	20	0	.500	3
1982	10	10	0	.500	3T
1983	16	24	0	.400	5
1984	13	27	0	.325	5
1985	15	25	0	.375	6
1986	21	19	0	.525	4
Totals	168	172	0	.494	3

AFC West

	W	L	T	Pct.	Pos.
1978	21	19	0	.525	2T
1979	27	13	0	.675	1
1980	22	18	0	.550	2
1981	22	18	0	.550	2
1982	12	11	0	.522	2
1983	22	18	0	.550	2T
1984	31	9	0	.775	1
1985	25	15	0	.625	1
1986	23	17	0	.575	1T
Totals	205	138	0	.598	1

Composite Standings for Eight Seasons

	W	L	T	Pct.
AFC West	205	138	0	.598
NFC East	194	144	1	.574
AFC Central	168	172	0	.494
NFC West	161	181	0	.471
AFC East	160	180	1	.471
NFC Central	135	208	2	.394

1986 NFL Score by Quarters

AFC Offense	1	2	3	4	OT	PTS
Miami	45	177	102	100	6	430
New England	82	102	99	129	0	412
Cincinnati	69	126	72	139	3	409
Cleveland	82	102	112	86	9	391
Denver	69	131	89	89	0	378
Seattle	69	96	80	121	0	366
N.Y. Jets	54	181	30	93	6	364
Kansas City	67	113	83	95	0	358
San Diego	73	125	48	89	0	335
L.A. Raiders	96	88	90	43	6	323
Pittsburgh	51	83	90	77	6	307
Buffalo	51	87	71	78	0	287
Houston	57	70	71	76	0	274
Indianapolis	51	41	55	82	0	229

NFC Offense	1	2	3	4	OT	PTS
Minnesota	151	85	71	88	3	398
San Francisco	92	123	72	87	0	374
N.Y. Giants	40	130	106	95	0	371
Washington	79	101	92	90	6	368
Chicago	88	84	82	92	6	352
Dallas	61	105	62	118	0	346
L.A. Rams	59	98	72	74	6	309
New Orleans	81	62	47	98	0	288
Atlanta	74	51	64	88	3	280
Detroit	34	82	71	90	0	277
Philadelphia	66	51	48	85	6	256
Green Bay	57	80	65	52	0	254
Tampa Bay	39	74	41	85	0	239
St. Louis	15	79	41	83	0	218

AFC Defense	1	2	3	4	OT	PTS
Seattle	60	103	52	78	0	293
New England	34	83	64	126	0	307
Cleveland	54	98	62	96	0	310
Kansas City	49	121	90	66	0	326
Denver	58	92	61	116	0	327
Houston	37	131	71	81	9	329
Pittsburgh	67	129	54	77	9	336
L.A. Raiders	69	99	92	80	6	346
Buffalo	70	91	69	115	3	348
N.Y. Jets	55	91	95	145	0	386
Cincinnati	113	92	122	67	0	394
San Diego	64	98	101	127	6	396
Indianapolis	123	101	106	70	0	400
Miami	101	127	58	113	6	405

NFC Defense	1	2	3	4	OT	PTS
Chicago	35	36	65	51	0	187
N.Y. Giants	39	84	37	76	0	236
San Francisco	64	61	58	61	3	247
L.A. Rams	46	87	72	56	6	267
Minnesota	60	75	43	89	6	273
Atlanta	34	131	48	67	0	280
New Orleans	64	92	71	60	0	287
Washington	82	77	68	69	0	296
Philadelphia	50	75	86	98	3	312
Detroit	63	100	62	101	0	326
Dallas	44	136	74	83	0	337
St. Louis	82	106	64	99	0	351
Green Bay	124	106	78	110	0	418
Tampa Bay	111	105	103	145	9	473

NFL TOTALS	1	2	3	4	OT	PTS
	1852	2727	2026	2522	66	9193

Team Leaders

Offense	Most Scored	Fewest Scored
1st Quarter	151, Minnesota	15, St. Louis
2nd Quarter	181, N.Y. Jets	41, Indianapolis
3rd Quarter	112, Cleveland	30, N.Y. Jets
4th Quarter	139, Cincinnati	43, L.A. Raiders

Defense	Most Allowed	Fewest Allowed
1st Quarter	124, Green Bay	34, Atlanta 34, New England
2nd Quarter	136, Dallas	36, Chicago
3rd Quarter	122, Cincinnati	37, N.Y. Giants
4th Quarter	145, N.Y. Jets 145, Tampa Bay	51, Chicago

December Records Over Last 10 Years

AFC	1977	1978	1979	1980	1981	1982	1983	1984	1985	1986	Total	Pct.
Miami	2-1	3-0	1-1	2-1	3-0	3-1	3-0	2-1	4-0	2-1	25- 6	.806
Cincinnati	2-1	3-0	1-2	2-1	2-1	3-1	2-1	3-0	2-2	2-1	22-10	.688
L.A. Raiders	2-1	1-2	2-1	3-1	1-2	4-0	2-1	2-1	4-0	0-3	21-12	.636
San Diego	1-2	3-0	2-1	2-1	2-1	4-0	1-2	1-2	3-1	1-2	20-12	.625
Seattle	2-1	2-1	2-1	0-3	2-1	1-3	2-1	1-2	2-2	3-0	17-15	.531
Denver	2-1	2-1	1-2	1-3	2-1	1-3	2-1	2-1	3-1	1-2	17-16	.515
Kansas City	0-3	1-2	2-1	2-1	1-2	1-3	1-2	3-0	2-2	3-0	16-16	.500
Pittsburgh	2-1	3-0	2-1	1-2	0-3	2-2	1-2	2-1	1-3	2-1	16-16	.500
New England	2-1	1-2	1-1	2-1	0-3	2-2	2-1	1-2	3-1	1-2	15-16	.484
N.Y. Jets	1-2	1-2	3-0	1-2	2-1	3-1	1-2	1-2	2-1	0-3	15-16	.484
Cleveland	0-3	1-2	1-2	2-1	0-3	2-2	1-2	1-2	2-2	3-0	13-19	.406
Houston	2-1	1-2	1-2	3-0	2-1	0-4	1-2	1-2	0-4	2-1	13-19	.406
Indianapolis	1-2	0-3	1-2	0-3	1-2	0-3-1	1-2	0-3	2-2	3-0	9-22-1	.297
Buffalo	1-2	1-2	0-3	2-1	2-1	1-3	1-2	1-2	0-4	0-3	9-23	.281

NFC	1977	1978	1979	1980	1981	1982	1983	1984	1985	1986	Total	Pct.
Chicago	3-0	2-1	3-0	2-1	3-0	2-2	2-1	1-2	3-1	3-0	24- 8	.750
Washington	3-0	0-3	2-1	3-0	3-0	3-1	3-0	2-0	3-1	1-2	23- 8	.742
Dallas	3-0	3-0	3-0	2-1	2-1	3-1	1-2	1-2	1-2	0-3	19-12	.613
San Francisco	0-3	1-2	1-2	1-2	3-0	2-2	3-0	3-0	3-1	3-1	20-13	.606
Green Bay	2-1	1-2	1-2	0-3	2-1	2-1-1	2-1	3-0	3-1	1-2	17-14-1	.547
St. Louis	0-3	2-1	2-1	1-2	1-2	3-1	3-0	2-1	1-2	1-1-1	16-14-1	.532
L.A. Rams	2-1	2-1	2-1	2-1	1-2	0-4	1-2	2-1	2-2	1-2	15-17	.469
N.Y. Giants	1-2	1-2	0-3	1-2	3-0	2-2	0-3	1-2	2-2	4-0	15-18	.455
Atlanta	1-2	1-2	2-1	2-1	0-3	3-1	1-2	1-2	2-2	1-2	14-18	.438
Philadelphia	2-1	1-2	2-1	1-2	1-2	2-2	1-2	1-2	1-3	1-1-1	13-18-1	.422
Minnesota	2-1	1-2	1-2	2-1	0-3	2-2	1-2	0-2	2-2	2-1	13-18	.419
Tampa Bay	2-1	0-3	1-2	0-3	2-1	3-1	0-3	2-1	0-4	0-3	10-22	.313
Detroit	1-2	2-1	0-3	2-1	1-2	1-3	2-1	0-3	0-3	0-3	9-22	.290
New Orleans	0-3	2-1	1-2	1-2	0-3	0-4	1-2	1-2	1-3	1-2	8-24	.250

L.A. Raiders totals include Oakland, 1977–81
Indianapolis totals include Baltimore, 1977–83

Retired Uniform Numbers in NFL

AFC

Buffalo:	None	
Cincinnati:	Bob Johnson	54
Cleveland:	Otto Graham	14
	Jim Brown	32
	Ernie Davis	45
	Don Fleming	46
	Lou Groza	76
Denver:	Frank Tripucka	18
	Floyd Little	44
Houston:	Jim Norton	43
	Elvin Bethea	65
Indianapolis:	Johnny Unitas	19
	Buddy Young	22
	Lenny Moore	24
	Art Donovan	70
	Jim Parker	77
	Raymond Berry	82
	Gino Marchetti	89
Kansas City:	Len Dawson	16
	Abner Haynes	28
	Stone Johnson	33
	Mack Lee Hill	36
	Bobby Bell	78
Los Angeles Raiders:	None	
Miami:	Bob Griese	12
New England:	Gino Cappelletti	20
	Jim Hunt	79
	Bob Dee	89
New York Jets:	Joe Namath	12
Pittsburgh:	None	
San Diego:	None	
Seattle:	"Fans/the twelfth man"	12

NFC

Atlanta:	Tommy Nobis	60
Chicago:	Bronko Nagurski	3
	George McAfee	5
	Willie Galimore	28
	Brian Piccolo	41
	Sid Luckman	42
	Bill Hewitt	56
	Bill George	61
	Bulldog Turner	66
	Red Grange	77
Dallas:	None	
Detroit:	Dutch Clark	7
	Bobby Layne	22
	Doak Walker	37
	Joe Schmidt	56
	Chuck Hughes	85
	Charlie Sanders	88
Green Bay:	Tony Canadeo	3
	Don Hutson	14
	Bart Starr	15
	Ray Nitschke	66
Los Angeles Rams:	Bob Waterfield	7
	Merlin Olsen	74
Minnesota:	Fran Tarkenton	10
New Orleans:	Jim Taylor	31
	Doug Atkins	81
New York Giants:	Ray Flaherty	1
	Mel Hein	7
	Y.A. Tittle	14
	Al Blozis	32
	Joe Morrison	40
	Charlie Conerly	42
	Ken Strong	50
Philadelphia:	Steve Van Buren	15
	Tom Brookshier	40
	Pete Retzlaff	44
	Chuck Bednarik	60
	Al Wistert	70
St. Louis:	Larry Wilson	8
	Stan Mauldin	77
	J.V. Cain	88
	Marshall Goldberg	99
San Francisco:	John Brodie	12
	Joe Perry	34
	Jimmy Johnson	37
	Hugh McElhenny	39
	Charlie Krueger	70
	Leo Nomellini	73
Tampa Bay:	Lee Roy Selmon	63
Washington:	Sammy Baugh	33

NFL Players Active in 1986 Who Were Not Drafted by an NFL Team But Have Played at Least 8 Years in NFL

	Yrs.	Pos.	Games	Starts
Woody Bennett, Miami	8	RB	16	14
Rufus Bess, Minnesota	8	CB	16	0
Ken Clarke, Philadelphia	9	NT	16	16
Paul Coffman, Kansas City	9	TE	15	0
Herman Edwards, L.A. Rams-Atlanta	10	CB	7	0
Cleveland Green, Miami	8	T	11	5
Glenn Hyde, Seattle	9	G	3	0
Dave Jennings, N.Y. Jets	13	P	16	0
Pat Leahy, N.Y. Jets	13	K	16	0
Neal Olkewicz, Washington	8	LB	16	16
Jim Ryan, Denver	8	LB	16	14
Donnie Shell, Pittsburgh	13	S	15	15
Doug Smith, L.A. Rams	9	C	16	16
J.T. Smith, St. Louis	9	WR	16	16
Ivory Sully, Tampa Bay	8	S	16	9
Tim Vogler, Buffalo	8	G	9	3
Steve Watson, Denver	8	WR	16	16
Ray Wersching, San Francisco	14	K	16	0
Joel Williams, Atlanta	8	LB	15	14
Brenard Wilson, Philadelphia	8	CB-S	16	0
Steve Wilson, Denver	8	CB	16	0

NFL Players Active in 1986 Who Were Not Drafted by an NFL Team But Have Played in at Least 1 AFC-NFC Pro Bowl

	Yrs.	Pos.	Pro Bowls
Bill Bates, Dallas	4	S	1
Jeff Bostic, Washington	7	C	1
Jim Burt, N.Y. Giants	6	NT	1
Rich Camarillo, New England	6	P	1
Deron Cherry, Kansas City	6	S	4
Paul Coffman, Kansas City	9	TE	3
Jay Hilgenberg, Chicago	6	C	2
Joe Jacoby, Washington	6	T	4
Dave Jennings, N.Y. Jets	13	P	4
Norm Johnson, Seattle	5	K	1
Dave Krieg, Seattle	7	QB	1
Sean Landeta, N.Y. Giants	2	P	1
Nick Lowery, Kansas City	7	K	1
Joe Nash, Seattle	5	NT	1
Donnie Shell, Pittsburgh	13	S	5
Doug Smith, L.A. Rams	9	C	3
J.T. Smith, St. Louis	9	WR	1
Everson Walls, Dallas	6	S	4
Steve Watson, Denver	8	WR	1

Oldest Individual Single-Season or Single-Game Records in NFL Record & Fact Book

Regular Season Records That Have Not Been Surpassed or Tied

Most Points, Game—40, Ernie Nevers, Chi. Cardinals vs. Chi. Bears, Nov. 28, 1929 (6-td, 4-pat)

Most Touchdowns Rushing, Game—6, Ernie Nevers, Chi. Cardinals vs. Chi. Bears, Nov. 28, 1929

Highest Average Gain, Rushing, Season (Qualifiers)—9.94, Beattie Feathers, Chi. Bears, 1934 (101-1,004)

Highest Punting Average, Season (Qualifiers)—51.40, Sammy Baugh, Washington, 1940 (35-1,799)

Highest Punting Average, Game (minimum: 4 punts)—61.75, Bob Cifers, Detroit vs. Chi. Bears, Nov. 24, 1946 (4-247)

Highest Average Gain, Pass Receptions, Season (minimum: 24 receptions)—32.58, Don Currivan, Boston, 1947 (24-782)

Highest Average Gain, Passing, Game (minimum: 20 passes)—18.58, Sammy Baugh, Washington vs. Boston, Oct. 31, 1948 (24-446)

Most Touchdowns, Fumble Recoveries, Game—2, Fred (Dippy) Evans, Chi. Bears vs. Washington, Nov. 28, 1948

Most Yards Gained, Intercepted Passes, Rookie, Season—301, Don Doll, Detroit, 1949

Most Passes Had Intercepted, Game—8, Jim Hardy, Chi. Cardinals vs. Philadelphia, Sept. 24, 1950

Highest Average Gain, Rushing, Game (minimum: 10 attempts)—17.09, Marion Motley, Cleveland vs. Pittsburgh, Oct. 29, 1950 (11-188)

Most Yards Gained, Kickoff Returns, Game—294, Wally Triplett, Detroit vs. Los Angeles, Oct. 29, 1950

Highest Kickoff Return Average, Game (minimum: 3 returns)—73.50, Wally Triplett, Detroit vs. Los Angeles, Oct. 29, 1950 (4-294)

Most Pass Receptions, Game—18, Tom Fears, Los Angeles vs. Green Bay, Dec. 3, 1950

Highest Punt Return Average, Season (Qualifiers)—23.00, Herb Rich, Baltimore, 1950 (12-276)

Highest Punt Return Average, Rookie, Season (Qualifiers)—23.00, Herb Rich, Baltimore, 1950 (12-276)

Most Yards Passing, Game—554, Norm Van Brocklin, Los Angeles vs. N.Y. Yanks, Sept. 28, 1951

Most Touchdowns, Punt Returns, Rookie, Season—4, Jack Christiansen, Detroit, 1951

Most Interceptions By, Season—14, Dick (Night Train) Lane, Los Angeles, 1952

Most Interceptions By, Rookie, Season—14, Dick (Night Train) Lane, Los Angeles, 1952

Highest Average Gain, Passing, Season (Qualifiers)—11.17, Tommy O'Connell, Cleveland, 1957 (110-1,229)

Most Points, Season—176, Paul Hornung, Green Bay, 1960 (15-td, 41-pat, 15-fg)

Highest Pass Rating, Season—110.4, Milt Plum, Cleveland, 1960

Most Yards Gained, Pass Receptions, Rookie, Season—1,473, Bill Groman, Houston, 1960

Records of NFL Teams Since 1970 AFL-NFL Merger

AFC	W- L-T	Pct.	Division Titles	Playoff Berths	Post-season Record	Super Bowl Record
Miami	176- 71-2	.712	9	12	14-10	2-3
L.A. Raiders	169- 74-6	.694	8	12	16-9	3-0
Pittsburgh	154- 94-1	.620	9	11	15-7	4-0
Denver	139-105-5	.569	4	6	4-6	0-2
Cincinnati	131-118-0	.526	3	5	2-5	0-1
Cleveland	126-121-2	.510	4	6	1-6	0-0
New England	122-127-0	.490	2	5	3-5	0-1
Seattle*	78- 87-0	.473	0	2	3-2	0-0
Kansas City	110-134-5	.451	1	2	0-2	0-0
San Diego	110-134-5	.451	3	4	3-4	0-0
N.Y. Jets	108-140-1	.436	0	4	3-4	0-0
Indianapolis	101-146-2	.409	4	5	4-4	1-0
Houston	94-153-2	.381	0	3	4-3	0-0
Buffalo	92-155-2	.373	1	3	1-3	0-0

NFC	W- L-T	Pct.	Division Titles	Playoff Berths	Post-season Record	Super Bowl Record
Dallas	173- 76-0	.695	9	14	19-12	2-3
Washington	160- 88-1	.645	3	9	10-8	1-2
L.A. Rams	157- 88-4	.640	8	12	8-12	0-1
Minnesota	147-100-2	.594	9	10	8-10	0-3
San Francisco	127-119-3	.516	7	8	9-6	2-0
Chicago	123-125-1	.496	3	5	4-4	1-0
St. Louis	112-131-6	.462	2	3	0-3	0-0
Detroit	112-133-4	.458	1	3	0-3	0-0
Atlanta	106-139-4	.433	1	3	1-3	0-0
Philadelphia	104-139-6	.429	1	4	3-4	0-1
Green Bay	103-139-7	.427	1	2	1-2	0-0
N.Y. Giants	103-144-2	.418	1	4	6-3	1-0
New Orleans	78-167-4	.319	0	0	0-0	0-0
Tampa Bay*	48-116-1	.294	2	3	1-3	0-0

*entered NFL in 1976.

Indianapolis totals include Baltimore, 1970-83

L.A. Raiders totals include Oakland, 1970-81

Tie games before 1972 are not calculated in won-lost percentage.

In 1982, due to players' strike, the divisional format was abandoned. (L.A. Raiders and Washington won regular-season conference titles, not included in "Division Titles" totals listed above.)

Longest Current Streaks of Consecutive Starts by Active NFL Players

Walter Payton, Chicago	168
Raymond Clayborn, New England	137
Charles Romes, Buffalo	137
Fred Smerlas, Buffalo	108
Randy White, Dallas	107
Ed Jones, Dallas	105
David Logan, Tampa Bay	103
Jacob Green, Seattle	90
Ray Donaldson, Indianapolis	89
Rickey Jackson, New Orleans	89

By Position

Quarterback	Dan Marino, Miami	48
	Phil Simms, N.Y. Giants	48
Running Back	Walter Payton, Chicago	168
Wide Receiver	Steve Largent, Seattle	50
Tight End	Todd Christensen, L.A. Raiders	73
Offensive Line	Ray Donaldson, Indianapolis	89
Defensive Line	Fred Smerlas, Buffalo	108
Linebacker	Rickey Jackson, New Orleans	89
Defensive Back	Raymond Clayborn, New England	137
	Charles Romes, Buffalo	137

Greatest Comebacks in NFL History (Most Points Overcome To Win Game)

Regular-Season Games

From 28 points behind to win:
December 7, 1980, at San Francisco

New Orleans	14	21	0	0	0 — 35
San Francisco	0	7	14	14	3 — 38

NO —Harris 33 pass from Manning (Ricardo kick)
NO —Childs 21 pass from Manning (Ricardo kick)
NO —Holmes 1 run (Ricardo kick)
SF —Solomon 57 punt return (Wersching kick)
NO —Holmes 1 run (Ricardo kick)
NO —Harris 41 pass from Manning (Ricardo kick)
SF —Montana 1 run (Wersching kick)
SF —Clark 71 pass from Montana (Wersching kick)
SF —Solomon 14 pass from Montana (Wersching kick)
SF —Elliott 7 run (Wersching kick)
SF —FG Wersching 36

	N.O.	S.F.
First Downs	27	24
Total Yards	519	430
Yards Rushing	143	176
Yards Passing	376	254
Turnovers	3	0

From 24 points behind to win:
October 27, 1946, at Washington

Philadelphia	0	0	14	14 — 28
Washington	10	14	0	0 — 24

Wash—Rosato 2 run (Poillon kick)
Wash—FG Poillon 28
Wash—Rosato 4 run (Poillon kick)
Wash—Lapka recovered fumble in end zone (Poillon kick)
Phil —Steele 1 run (Lio kick)
Phil —Pritchard 45 pass from Thompson (Lio kick)
Phil —Steinke 7 pass from Thompson (Lio kick)
Phil —Ferrante 30 pass from Thompson (Lio kick)

	Phil.	Wash.
First Downs	14	8
Total Yards	262	127
Yards Rushing	34	66
Yards Passing	228	61
Turnovers	6	3

From 24 points behind to win:
October 20, 1957, at Detroit

Baltimore	7	14	6	0 — 27
Detroit	0	3	7	21 — 31

Balt —Mutscheller 15 pass from Unitas (Rechichar kick)
Det —FG Martin 47
Balt —Moore 72 pass from Unitas (Rechichar kick)
Balt —Mutscheller 52 pass from Unitas (Rechichar kick)
Balt —Moore 4 pass from Unitas (kick failed)
Det —Junker 14 pass from Rote (Layne kick)
Det —Cassady 26 pass from Layne (Layne kick)
Det —Johnson 1 run (Layne kick)
Det —Cassady 29 pass from Layne (Layne kick)

	Balt.	Det.
First Downs	15	20
Total Yards	322	369
Yards Rushing	117	178
Yards Passing	205	191
Turnovers	6	4

From 24 points behind to win:
October 25, 1959, at Chicago

Philadelphia	0	0	21	7 — 28
Chi. Cardinals	7	10	7	0 — 24

Chi —Crow 10 pass from Roach (Conrad kick)
Chi —J. Hill 77 blocked field goal return (Conrad kick)
Chi —FG Conrad 15
Chi —Lane 37 interception return (Conrad kick)
Phil —Barnes 1 run (Walston kick)
Phil —McDonald 29 pass from Van Brocklin (Walston kick)
Phil —Barnes 2 run (Walston kick)
Phil —McDonald 22 pass from Van Brocklin (Walston kick)

	Phil.	Chi.
First Downs	22	14
Total Yards	399	313
Yards Rushing	168	163
Yards Passing	231	150
Turnovers	2	6

From 24 points behind to win:
October 23, 1960, at Denver

Boston	10	7	7	0 — 24
Denver	0	0	14	17 — 31

Bos —FG Cappelletti 12
Bos —Colclough 10 pass from Songin (Cappelletti kick)
Bos —Wells 6 pass from Songin (Cappelletti kick)
Bos —Miller 47 pass from Songin (Cappelletti kick)
Den—Carmichael 21 pass from Tripucka (Mingo kick)
Den—Jessup 19 pass from Tripucka (Mingo kick)
Den—Carmichael 35 lateral from Taylor, pass from Tripucka (Mingo kick)
Den—Taylor 8 pass from Tripucka (Mingo kick)
Den—FG Mingo 9

	Bos.	Den.
First Downs	19	16
Total Yards	434	326
Yards Rushing	211	65
Yards Passing	223	261
Turnovers	7	4

From 24 points behind to win:
December 15, 1974, at Miami

New England	21	3	0	3 — 27
Miami	0	17	7	10 — 34

NE —Hannah recovered fumble in end zone (J. Smith kick)
NE —Sanders 23 interception return (J. Smith kick)
NE —Herron 4 pass from Plunkett (J. Smith kick)
NE —FG J. Smith 46
Mia—Nottingham 1 run (Yepremian kick)
Mia—Baker 37 pass from Morrall (Yepremian kick)
Mia—FG Yepremian 28
Mia—Baker 46 pass from Morrall (Yepremian kick)
NE —FG J. Smith 34
Mia—Nottingham 2 run (Yepremian kick)
Mia—FG Yepremian 40

	N.E.	Mia.
First Downs	18	18
Total Yards	333	333
Yards Rushing	114	61
Yards Passing	219	272
Turnovers	3	4

From 24 points behind to win:
December 4, 1977, at Minnesota

San Francisco	0	10	14	3 — 27
Minnesota	0	0	7	21 — 28

SF —Delvin Williams 2 run (Wersching kick)
SF —FG Wersching 31
SF —Dave Williams 80 kickoff return (Wersching kick)
SF —Delvin Williams 5 run (Wersching kick)
Minn—McClanahan 15 pass from Lee (Cox kick)
Minn—Rashad 8 pass from Kramer (Cox kick)
Minn—Tucker 9 pass from Kramer (Cox kick)
SF —FG Wersching 31
Minn—S. White 69 pass from Kramer (Cox kick)

	S.F.	Minn.
First Downs	19	18
Total Yards	243	309
Yards Rushing	196	52
Yards Passing	47	257
Turnovers	2	5

From 24 points behind to win:
September 23, 1979, at Denver

Seattle	10	10	14	0 — 34
Denver	0	10	21	6 — 37

Sea—FG Herrera 28
Sea—Doornink 5 run (Herrera kick)
Den—FG Turner 27
Sea—Doornink 5 run (Herrera kick)
Den—Armstrong 2 run (Turner kick)
Sea—FG Herrera 22
Sea—McCullum 13 pass from Zorn (Herrera kick)
Sea—Smith 1 run (Herrera kick)
Den—Studdard 2 pass from Morton (Turner kick)
Den—Moses 11 pass from Morton (Turner kick)
Den—Upchurch 35 pass from Morton (Turner kick)
Den—Lytle 1 run (kick failed)

	Sea.	Den.
First Downs	22	23
Total Yards	350	344
Yards Rushing	153	90
Yards Passing	197	254
Turnovers	4	3

From 24 points behind to win:
September 23, 1979, at Cincinnati

Houston	0	10	17	0	3 — 30
Cincinnati	14	10	0	3	0 — 27

Cin —Johnson 1 run (Bahr kick)
Cin —Alexander 2 run (Bahr kick)
Cin —Johnson 1 run (Bahr kick)
Cin —FG Bahr 52
Hou—Burrough 35 pass from Pastorini (Fritsch kick)
Hou—FG Fritsch 33
Hou—Campbell 8 run (Fritsch kick)
Hou—Caster 22 pass from Pastorini (Fritsch kick)
Hou—FG Fritsch 47
Cin —FG Bahr 55
Hou—FG Fritsch 29

	Hou.	Cin.
First Downs	19	21
Total Yards	361	265
Yards Rushing	177	165
Yards Passing	184	100
Turnovers	3	2

From 24 points behind to win:
November 22, 1982, at Los Angeles

San Diego	10	14	0	0 — 24
L.A. Raiders	0	7	14	7 — 28

SD —FG Benirschke 19
SD —Scales 29 pass from Fouts (Benirschke kick)
SD —Muncie 2 run (Benirschke kick)
SD —Muncie 1 run (Benirschke kick)
Raiders —Christensen 1 pass from Plunkett (Bahr kick)
Raiders —Allen 3 run (Bahr kick)
Raiders —Allen 6 run (Bahr kick)
Raiders —Hawkins 1 run (Bahr kick)

	S.D.	Raiders
First Downs	26	23
Total Yards	411	326
Yards Rushing	72	181
Yards Passing	339	145
Turnovers	4	2

Postseason Games

From 20 points behind to win:
Western Conference Playoff Game
December 22, 1957, at San Francisco

Detroit	0	7	14	10 — 31
San Francisco	14	10	3	0 — 27

SF —Owens 34 pass from Tittle (Soltau kick)
SF —McElhenny 47 pass from Tittle (Soltau kick)
Det—Junker 4 pass from Rote (Martin kick)
SF —Wilson 12 pass from Tittle (Soltau kick)
SF —FG Soltau 25
SF —FG Soltau 10
Det—Tracy 2 run (Martin kick)
Det—Tracy 58 run (Martin kick)
Det—Gedman 3 run (Martin kick)
Det—FG Martin 14

	Det.	S.F.
First Downs	22	20
Total Yards	324	351
Yards Rushing	129	127
Yards Passing	195	224
Turnovers	5	4

From 18 points behind to win:
NFC Divisional Playoff Game
December 23, 1972, at San Francisco

Dallas	3	10	0	17 — 30
San Francisco	7	14	7	0 — 28

SF —Washington 97 kickoff return (Gossett kick)
Dall —FG Fritsch 37
SF —Schreiber 1 run (Gossett kick)
SF —Schreiber 1 run (Gossett kick)
Dall —FG Fritsch 45
Dall —Alworth 28 pass from Morton (Fritsch kick)
SF —Schreiber 1 run (Gossett kick)
Dall —FG Fritsch 27
Dall —Parks 20 pass from Staubach (Fritsch kick)
Dall —Sellers 10 pass from Staubach (Fritsch kick)

	Dall.	S.F.
First Downs	22	13
Total Yards	402	255
Yards Rushing	165	105
Yards Passing	237	150
Turnovers	5	3

From 18 points behind to win:
AFC Divisional Playoff Game
January 4, 1986, at Miami

Cleveland	7	7	7	0 — 21
Miami	3	0	14	7 — 24

Mia —FG Reveiz 51
Clev—Newsome 16 pass from Kosar (Bahr kick)
Clev—Byner 21 run (Bahr kick)
Clev—Byner 66 run (Bahr kick)
Mia —Moore 6 pass from Marino (Reveiz kick)
Mia —Davenport 31 run (Reveiz kick)
Mia —Davenport 1 run (Reveiz kick)

	Clev.	Mia.
First Downs	17	20
Total Yards	313	330
Yards Rushing	251	92
Yards Passing	62	238
Turnovers	1	1

From 14 points behind to win:
NFC Divisional Playoff Game
January 3, 1981, at Philadelphia

Minnesota	7	7	2	0 — 16
Philadelphia	0	7	14	10 — 31

Minn —S. White 30 pass from Kramer (Danmeier kick)
Minn —Brown 1 run (Danmeier kick)
Phil —Carmichael 9 pass from Jaworski (Franklin kick)
Phil —Montgomery 8 run (Franklin kick)
Minn —Safety, Jaworski tackled in end zone by Martin and Blair
Phil —Montgomery 5 run (Franklin kick)
Phil —FG Franklin 33
Phil —Harrington 2 run (Franklin kick)

	Minn.	Phil.
First Downs	14	24
Total Yards	215	305
Yards Rushing	36	126
Yards Passing	179	179
Turnovers	8	3

From 14 points behind to win:
NFC Divisional Playoff Game
January 4, 1981, at Atlanta

Dallas	3	7	0	20 — 30
Atlanta	10	7	7	3 — 27

Atl —FG Mazzetti 38
Atl —Jenkins 60 pass from Bartkowski (Mazzetti kick)
Dall —FG Septien 38
Dall —DuPree 5 pass from D. White (Mazzetti kick)
Atl —Cain 1 run (Mazzetti kick)
Atl —Andrews 5 pass from Bartkowski (Mazzetti kick)
Dall —Newhouse 1 run (Septien kick)
Atl —FG Mazzetti 34
Dall —D. Pearson 14 pass from D. White (Septien kick)
Dall —D. Pearson 23 pass from D. White (pass failed)

	Dall.	Atl.
First Downs	22	18
Total Yards	422	371
Yards Rushing	112	86
Yards Passing	310	283
Turnovers	2	2

NFL Season Records for Receivers on One Team

Most Players, 40 or More Receptions, One Team
6 Dallas 1983
(Ron Springs, 73; Tony Hill, 49; Drew Pearson, 47; Doug Cosbie, 46; Butch Johnson, 41; Tony Dorsett, 40)

Most Players, 50 or More Receptions, One Team
5 Cleveland 1980
(Mike Pruitt, 63; Reggie Rucker, 52; Dave Logan, 51; Ozzie Newsome, 51; Greg Pruitt, 50)

Most Players, 60 or More Receptions, One Team
3 By many teams. (Last time: Miami 1986; San Francisco 1986)

Most Players, 70 or More Receptions, One Team
3 San Diego 1980
(Kellen Winslow, 89; John Jefferson, 82; Charlie Joiner, 71)

Most Players, 80 or More Receptions, One Team
2 San Diego 1980
(Kellen Winslow, 89; John Jefferson, 82)
San Francisco 1980
(Earl Cooper, 83; Dwight Clark, 82)
San Francisco 1986
(Jerry Rice, 86; Roger Craig, 81)

HISTORY

PRO FOOTBALL HALL OF FAME

The Professional Football Hall of Fame is located in Canton, Ohio, site of the organizational meeting on September 17, 1920, from which the National Football League evolved. The NFL recognized Canton as the Hall of Fame site on April 27, 1961. Canton area individuals, foundations, and companies donated almost $400,000 in cash and services to provide funds for the construction of the original two-building complex, which was dedicated on September 7, 1963. The original Hall of Fame complex was almost doubled in size with the completion of a $620,000 expansion project that was dedicated on May 10, 1971. A second expansion project was completed on November 20, 1978. It features three exhibition areas and a theater twice the size of the original one.

The Hall represents the sport of pro football in many ways—through three large and colorful exhibition galleries, in the twin enshrinement halls, with numerous fan-participation electronic devices, a research library, and an NFL gift shop.

In recent years, the Pro Football Hall of Fame has become an extremely popular tourist attraction. At the end of 1986, a total of 4,044,065 fans had visited the Pro Football Hall of Fame.

New members of the Pro Football Hall of Fame are elected annually by a 29-member National Board of Selectors, made up of media representatives from every league city and the president of the Pro Football Writers of America. Between four and seven new members are elected each year. An affirmative vote of approximately 80 percent is needed for election.

Any fan may nominate any eligible player or contributor simply by writing to the Pro Football Hall of Fame. Players must be retired five years to be eligible, while a coach need only to be retired with no time limit specified. Contributors (administrators, owners, *et al.*) may be elected while they are still active.

The charter class of 17 enshrinees was elected in 1963 and the honor roll now stands at 140 with the election of a seven-man class in 1987. That class consists of Larry Csonka, Len Dawson, Joe Greene, John Henry Johnson, Jim Langer, Don Maynard, and Gene Upshaw.

Roster of Members

HERB ADDERLEY
Defensive back. 6-1, 200. Born in Philadelphia, Pennsylvania, June 8, 1939. Michigan State. Inducted in 1980. 1961-69 Green Bay Packers, 1970-72 Dallas Cowboys.

LANCE ALWORTH
Wide receiver. 6-0, 184. Born in Houston, Texas, August 3, 1940. Arkansas. Inducted in 1978. 1962-70 San Diego Chargers, 1971-72 Dallas Cowboys.

DOUG ATKINS
Defensive end. 6-8, 275. Born in Humboldt, Tennessee, May 8, 1930. Tennessee. Inducted in 1982. 1953-54 Cleveland Browns, 1955-66 Chicago Bears, 1967-69 New Orleans Saints.

MORRIS (RED) BADGRO
End. 6-0, 190. Born in Orilla, Washington, December 1, 1902. Southern California. Inducted in 1981. 1927 New York Yankees, 1930-35 New York Giants, 1936 Brooklyn Dodgers.

CLIFF BATTLES
Halfback. 6-1, 201. Born in Akron, Ohio, May 1, 1910. Died April 28, 1981 West Virginia Wesleyan. Inducted in 1968. 1932 Boston Braves, 1933-36 Boston Redskins, 1937 Washington Redskins.

SAMMY BAUGH
Quarterback. 6-2, 180. Born in Temple, Texas, March 17, 1914. Texas Christian. Inducted in 1963. 1937-52 Washington Redskins.

CHUCK BEDNARIK
Center-linebacker. 6-3, 230. Born in Bethlehem, Pennsylvania, May 1, 1925. Pennsylvania. Inducted in 1967. 1949-62 Philadelphia Eagles.

BERT BELL
Commissioner. Team owner. Born in Philadelphia, Pennsylvania, February 25, 1895. Died October 11, 1959. Pennsylvania. Inducted in 1963. 1933-40 Philadelphia Eagles, 1941-42 Pittsburgh Steelers, 1943 Phil-Pitt, 1944-46 Pittsburgh Steelers. Commissioner, 1946-59.

BOBBY BELL
Linebacker. 6-4, 225. Born in Shelby, North Carolina, June 17, 1940. Minnesota. Inducted in 1983. 1963-74 Kansas City Chiefs.

RAYMOND BERRY
End. 6-2, 187. Born in Corpus Christi, Texas, February 27, 1933. Southern Methodist. Inducted in 1973. 1955-67 Baltimore Colts.

CHARLES W. BIDWILL, SR.
Team owner. Born in Chicago, Illinois, September 16, 1895. Died April 19, 1947. Loyola of Chicago. Inducted in 1967. 1933-43 Chicago Cardinals, 1944 Card-Pitt, 1945-47 Chicago Cardinals.

GEORGE BLANDA
Quarterback-kicker. 6-2, 215. Born in Youngwood, Pennsylvania, September 17, 1927. Kentucky. Inducted in 1981. 1949-58 Chicago Bears, 1950 Baltimore Colts, 1960-66 Houston Oilers, 1967-75 Oakland Raiders.

JIM BROWN
Fullback. 6-2, 232. Born in St. Simons, Georgia, February 17, 1936. Syracuse. Inducted in 1971. 1957-65 Cleveland Browns.

PAUL BROWN
Coach. Born in Norwalk, Ohio, September 7, 1908. Miami, Ohio. Inducted in 1967. 1946-49 Cleveland Browns (AAFC), 1950-62 Cleveland Browns, 1968-75 Cincinnati Bengals.

ROOSEVELT BROWN
Offensive tackle. 6-3, 255. Born in Charlottesville, Virginia, October 20, 1932. Morgan State. Inducted in 1975. 1953-65 New York Giants.

WILLIE BROWN
Defensive back. 6-1, 210. Born in Yazoo City, Mississippi, December 2, 1940. Grambling. Inducted in 1984. 1963-66 Denver Broncos, 1967-78 Oakland Raiders.

DICK BUTKUS
Linebacker. 6-3, 245. Born in Chicago, Illinois, December 9, 1942. Illinois. Inducted in 1979. 1965-73 Chicago Bears.

TONY CANADEO
Halfback. 5-11, 195. Born in Chicago, Illinois, May 5, 1919. Gonzaga. Inducted in 1974. 1941-44, 1946-52 Green Bay Packers.

JOE CARR
NFL president. Born in Columbus, Ohio, October 22, 1880. Died May 20, 1939. Did not attend college. Inducted in 1963. President, 1921-39 National Football League.

GUY CHAMBERLIN
End. Coach. 6-2, 210. Born in Blue Springs, Nebraska, January 16, 1894. Died April 4, 1967. Nebraska. Inducted in 1965. 1920 Decatur Staleys, 1921 Chicago Staleys, player-coach 1922-23 Canton Bulldogs, 1924 Cleveland Bulldogs, 1925-26 Frankford Yellow Jackets, 1927 Chicago Cardinals.

JACK CHRISTIANSEN
Defensive back. 6-1, 185. Born in Sublette, Kansas, December 20, 1928. Died June 29, 1986. Colorado State. Inducted in 1970. 1951-58 Detroit Lions.

EARL (DUTCH) CLARK
Quarterback. 6-0, 185. Born in Fowler, Colorado, October 11, 1906. Died August 5, 1978. Colorado College. Inducted in 1963. 1931-32 Portsmouth Spartans, 1934-38 Detroit Lions.

GEORGE CONNOR
Tackle-linebacker. 6-3, 240. Born in Chicago, Illinois, January 21, 1925. Holy Cross, Notre Dame. Inducted in 1975. 1948-55 Chicago Bears.

JIMMY CONZELMAN
Quarterback. Coach. Team owner. 6-0, 180. Born in St. Louis, Missouri, March 6, 1898. Died July 31, 1970. Washington, Missouri. Inducted in 1964. 1920 Decatur Staleys, 1921-22 Rock Island, Ill., Independents, 1923-24 Milwaukee Badgers; owner-coach, 1925-26 Detroit Panthers; player-coach 1927-29, coach 1930 Providence Steamroller; coach, 1940-42 Chicago Cardinals, 1946-48 Chicago Cardinals.

LARRY CSONKA
Fullback. 6-3, 235. Born in Stow, Ohio, December 25, 1946. Syracuse. Inducted in 1987. Miami Dolphins 1968-74, 1979, New York Giants 1976-78.

WILLIE DAVIS
Defensive end. 6-3, 245. Born in Lisbon, Louisiana, July 24, 1934. Grambling. Inducted in 1981. 1958-59 Cleveland Browns, 1960-69 Green Bay Packers.

LEN DAWSON
Quarterback. 6-0, 190. Born in Alliance, Ohio, June 20, 1935. Purdue. Inducted in 1987. Pittsburgh Steelers 1957-59, Cleveland Browns 1960-61, Dallas Texans 1962, Kansas City Chiefs 1963-75.

ART DONOVAN
Defensive tackle. 6-3, 265. Born in Bronx, New York, June 5, 1925. Boston College. Inducted in 1968. 1950 Baltimore Colts, 1951 New York Yanks, 1952 Dallas Texans, 1953-61 Baltimore Colts.

JOHN (PADDY) DRISCOLL
Quarterback. 5-11, 160. Born in Evanston, Illinois, January 11, 1896. Died June 29, 1968. Northwestern. Inducted in 1965. 1920 Decatur Staleys, 1920-25 Chicago Cardinals, 1926-29 Chicago Bears. Coach, 1956-57 Chicago Bears.

BILL DUDLEY
Halfback. 5-10, 176. Born in Bluefield, Virginia, December 24, 1921. Virginia. Inducted in 1966. 1942, 1945-46 Pittsburgh Steelers, 1947-49 Detroit Lions, 1950-51, 1953 Washington Redskins.

GLEN (TURK) EDWARDS
Tackle. 6-2, 260. Born in Mold, Washington, September 28, 1907. Died January 12, 1973. Washington State. Inducted in 1969. 1932 Boston Braves, 1933-36 Boston Redskins, 1937-40 Washington Redskins.

WEEB EWBANK
Coach. Born in Richmond, Indiana, May 6, 1907. Miami, Ohio. Inducted in 1978. 1954-62 Baltimore Colts, 1963-73 New York Jets.

TOM FEARS
End. 6-2, 215. Born in Los Angeles, California, December 3, 1923. Santa Clara, UCLA. Inducted in 1970. 1948-56 Los Angeles Rams.

RAY FLAHERTY
End. Coach. Born in Spokane, Washington, September 1, 1904. Gonzaga. Inducted in 1976. 1926 Los Angeles Wildcats (AFL), 1927-28 New York Yankees, 1928-29, 1931-35 New York Giants. Coach, 1936 Boston Redskins, 1937-42 Washington Redskins, 1946-48 New York Yankees (AAFC), 1949 Chicago Hornets (AAFC).

LEN FORD
End. 6-5, 260. Born in Washington, D.C., February 18, 1926. Died March 14, 1972. Michigan. Inducted in 1976. 1948-49 Los Angeles Dons (AAFC), 1950-57 Cleveland Browns, 1958 Green Bay Packers.

DAN FORTMANN
Guard. 6-0, 207. Born in Pearl River, New York, April 11, 1916. Colgate. Inducted in 1965. 1936-43 Chicago Bears.

FRANK GATSKI
Center. 6-3, 240. Born in Farmington, West Virginia, March 13, 1922. Marshall, Auburn. Inducted in 1985. 1946-49 Cleveland Browns (AAFC), 1950-56 Cleveland Browns, 1957 Detroit Lions.

BILL GEORGE
Linebacker. 6-2, 230. Born in Waynesburg, Pennsylvania, October 27, 1930. Died September 30, 1982. Wake Forest. Inducted in 1974. 1952-

65 Chicago Bears, 1966 Los Angeles Rams.

FRANK GIFFORD
Halfback. 6-1, 195. Born in Santa Monica, California, August 16, 1930. Southern California. Inducted in 1977. 1952-60, 1962-64 New York Giants.

SID GILLMAN
Coach. Born in Minneapolis, Minnesota, October 26, 1911. Ohio State. Inducted in 1983. 1955-59 Los Angeles Rams, 1960 Los Angeles Chargers, 1961-69 San Diego Chargers, 1973-74 Houston Oilers.

OTTO GRAHAM
Quarterback. 6-1, 195. Born in Waukegan, Illinois, December 6, 1921. Northwestern. Inducted in 1965. 1946-49 Cleveland Browns (AAFC), 1950-55 Cleveland Browns.

HAROLD (RED) GRANGE
Halfback. 6-0, 185. Born in Forksville, Pennsylvania, June 13, 1903. Illinois. Inducted in 1963. 1925 Chicago Bears, 1926 New York Yankees (AFL), 1927 New York Yankees, 1929-34 Chicago Bears.

JOE GREENE
Defensive tackle. 6-4, 260. Born in Temple, Texas, September 24, 1946. North Texas State. Inducted in 1987. Pittsburgh Steelers 1969-81.

FORREST GREGG
Tackle. 6-4, 250. Born in Birthright, Texas, October 18, 1933. Southern Methodist. Inducted in 1977. 1956, 1958-70 Green Bay Packers, 1971 Dallas Cowboys.

LOU GROZA
Tackle-kicker. 6-3, 250. Born in Martin's Ferry, Ohio, January 25, 1924. Ohio State. Inducted in 1974. 1946-49 Cleveland Browns (AAFC), 1950-59, 1961-67 Cleveland Browns.

JOE GUYON
Halfback. 6-1, 180. Born in Mahnomen, Minnesota, November 26, 1892. Died November 27, 1971. Carlisle, Georgia Tech. Inducted in 1966. 1920 Canton Bulldogs, 1921 Cleveland Indians, 1922-23 Oorang Indians, 1924 Rock Island, Ill., Independents, 1924-25 Kansas City Cowboys, 1927 New York Giants.

GEORGE HALAS
End. Coach. Team owner. Born in Chicago, Illinois, February 2, 1895. Died October 31, 1983. Illinois. Inducted in 1963. 1920 Decatur Staleys, 1921 Chicago Staleys, 1922-29 Chicago Bears; coach, 1933-42, 1946-55, 1958-67 Chicago Bears.

ED HEALEY
Tackle. 6-3, 220. Born in Indian Orchard, Massachusetts, December 28, 1894. Died December 9, 1978. Dartmouth. Inducted in 1964. 1920-22 Rock Island, Ill., Independents, 1922-27 Chicago Bears.

MEL HEIN
Center. 6-2, 225. Born in Redding, California, August 22, 1909. Washington State. Inducted in 1963. 1931-45 New York Giants.

WILBUR (PETE) HENRY
Tackle. 6-0, 250. Born in Mansfield, Ohio, October 31, 1897. Died February 7, 1952. Washington & Jefferson. Inducted in 1963. 1920-23, 1925-26 Canton Bulldogs, 1927 New York Giants, 1927-28 Pottsville Maroons.

ARNIE HERBER
Quarterback. 6-1, 200. Born in Green Bay, Wisconsin, April 2, 1910. Died October 14, 1969. Wisconsin, Regis College. Inducted in 1966. 1930-40 Green Bay Packers, 1944-45 New York Giants.

BILL HEWITT
End. 5-11, 191. Born in Bay City, Michigan, October 8, 1909. Died January 14, 1947. Michigan. Inducted in 1971. 1932-36 Chicago Bears, 1937-39 Philadelphia Eagles, 1943 Phil-Pitt.

CLARKE HINKLE
Fullback. 5-11, 201. Born in Toronto, Ohio, April 10, 1910. Bucknell. Inducted in 1964. 1932-41 Green Bay Packers.

ELROY (CRAZYLEGS) HIRSCH
Halfback-end. 6-2, 190. Born in Wausau, Wisconsin, June 17, 1923. Wisconsin, Michigan. Inducted in 1968. 1946-48 Chicago Rockets (AAFC), 1949-57 Los Angeles Rams.

PAUL HORNUNG
Halfback. 6-2, 220. Born in Louisville, Kentucky, December 23, 1935. Notre Dame. Inducted in 1986. 1957-62, 1964-66 Green Bay Packers.

KEN HOUSTON
Safety. 6-3, 198. Born in Lufkin, Texas, November 12, 1944. Prairie View A&M. Inducted in 1986. 1967-72 Houston Oilers, 1973-80 Washington Redskins.

CAL HUBBARD
Tackle. 6-5, 250. Born in Keytesville, Missouri, October 11, 1900. Died October 17, 1977. Centenary, Geneva. Inducted in 1963. 1927-28 New York Giants, 1929-33, 1935 Green Bay Packers, 1936 New York Giants, 1936 Pittsburgh Pirates.

SAM HUFF
Linebacker. 6-1, 230. Born in Morgantown, West Virginia, October 4, 1934. West Virginia. Inducted in 1982. 1956-63 New York Giants, 1964-67, 1969 Washington Redskins.

LAMAR HUNT
Team owner. Born in El Dorado, Arkansas, August 2, 1932. Southern Methodist. Inducted in 1972. 1960-62 Dallas Texans, 1963-87 Kansas City Chiefs.

DON HUTSON
End. 6-1, 180. Born in Pine Bluff, Arkansas, January 31, 1913. Alabama. Inducted in 1963. 1935-45 Green Bay Packers.

JOHN HENRY JOHNSON
Fullback. 6-2, 225. Born in Waterproof, Louisiana, November 24, 1929. St. Mary's, Arizona State. Inducted in 1987. San Francisco 49ers 1954-56, Detroit Lions 1957-59, Pittsburgh Steelers 1960-65, Houston Oilers 1966.

DAVID (DEACON) JONES
Defensive end. 6-5, 250. Born in Eatonville, Florida, December 9, 1938. Mississippi Vocational. Inducted in 1980. 1961-71 Los Angeles Rams, 1972-73 San Diego Chargers, 1974 Washington Redskins.

SONNY JURGENSEN
Quarterback. 6-0, 203. Born in Wilmington, North Carolina, August 23, 1934. Duke. Inducted in 1983. 1957-63 Philadelphia Eagles, 1964-74 Washington Redskins.

WALT KIESLING
Guard. Coach. 6-2, 245. Born in St. Paul, Minnesota, March 27, 1903. Died March 2, 1962. St. Thomas (Minnesota). Inducted in 1966. 1926-27 Duluth Eskimos, 1928 Pottsville Maroons, 1929-33 Chicago Cardinals, 1934 Chicago Bears, 1935-36 Green Bay Packers, 1937-38 Pittsburgh Pirates; coach, 1939-42 Pittsburgh Steelers; co-coach, 1943 Phil-Pitt, 1944 Card-Pitt; coach, 1954-56 Pittsburgh Steelers.

FRANK (BRUISER) KINARD
Tackle. 6-1, 210. Born in Pelahatchie, Mississippi, October 23, 1914. Died September 7, 1985. Mississippi. Inducted in 1971. 1938-44 Brooklyn Dodgers-Tigers, 1946-47 New York Yankees (AAFC).

EARL (CURLY) LAMBEAU
Coach. Born in Green Bay, Wisconsin, April 9, 1898. Died June 1, 1965. Notre Dame. Inducted in 1963. 1919-49 Green Bay Packers, 1950-51 Chicago Cardinals, 1952-53 Washington Redskins.

DICK (NIGHT TRAIN) LANE
Defensive back. 6-2, 210. Born in Austin, Texas, April 16, 1928. Scottsbluff Junior College. Inducted in 1974. 1952-53 Los Angeles Rams, 1954-59 Chicago Cardinals, 1960-65 Detroit Lions.

JIM LANGER
Center. 6-2, 255. Born in Little Falls, Minnesota, May 16, 1948. South Dakota State. Inducted in 1987. Miami Dolphins 1970-79, Minnesota Vikings 1980-81.

WILLIE LANIER
Linebacker. 6-1, 245. Born in Clover, Virginia, August 21, 1945. Morgan State. Inducted in 1986. 1967-77 Kansas City Chiefs.

YALE LARY
Defensive back-punter. 5-11, 189. Born in Fort Worth, Texas, November 24, 1930. Texas A&M. Inducted in 1979. 1952-53, 1956-64 Detroit Lions.

DANTE LAVELLI
End. 6-0, 199. Born in Hudson, Ohio, February 23, 1923. Ohio State. Inducted in 1975. 1946-49 Cleveland Browns (AAFC), 1950-56 Cleveland Browns.

BOBBY LAYNE
Quarterback. 6-2, 190. Born in Santa Anna, Texas, December 19, 1926. Died December 1, 1986. Texas. Inducted in 1967. 1948 Chicago Bears, 1949 New York Bulldogs, 1950-58 Detroit Lions, 1958-62 Pittsburgh Steelers.

ALPHONSE (TUFFY) LEEMANS
Fullback. 6-0, 200. Born in Superior, Wisconsin, November 12, 1912. Died January 19, 1979. George Washington. Inducted in 1978. 1936-43 New York Giants.

BOB LILLY
Defensive tackle. 6-5, 260. Born in Olney, Texas, July 26, 1939. Texas Christian. Inducted in 1980. 1961-74 Dallas Cowboys.

VINCE LOMBARDI
Coach. Born in Brooklyn, New York, June 11, 1913. Died September 3, 1970. Fordham. Inducted in 1971. 1959-67 Green Bay Packers, 1969 Washington Redskins.

SID LUCKMAN
Quarterback. 6-0, 195. Born in Brooklyn, New York, November 21, 1916. Columbia. Inducted in 1965. 1939-50 Chicago Bears.

ROY (LINK) LYMAN
Tackle. 6-2, 252. Born in Table Rock, Nebraska, November 30, 1898. Died December 16, 1972. Nebraska. Inducted in 1964. 1922-23, 1925 Canton Bulldogs, 1924 Cleveland Bulldogs, 1925 Frankford Yellow Jackets, 1926-28, 1930-31, 1933-34 Chicago Bears.

TIM MARA
Team owner. Born in New York, New York, July 29, 1887. Died February 17, 1959. Did not attend college. Inducted in 1963. 1925-59 New York Giants.

GINO MARCHETTI
Defensive end. 6-4, 245. Born in Antioch, California, January 2, 1927. San Francisco. Inducted in 1972. 1952 Dallas Texans, 1953-64, 1966 Baltimore Colts.

GEORGE PRESTON MARSHALL
Team owner. Born in Grafton, West Virginia, October 11, 1897. Died August 9, 1969. Randolph-Macon. Inducted in 1963. 1932 Boston Braves, 1933-36 Boston Redskins, 1937-69 Washington Redskins.

OLLIE MATSON
Halfback. 6-2, 220. Born in Trinity, Texas, May 1, 1930. San Francisco. Inducted in 1972. 1952, 1954-58 Chicago Cardinals, 1959-62 Los Angeles Rams, 1963 Detroit Lions, 1964-66 Philadelphia Eagles.

DON MAYNARD
Wide receiver. 6-1, 180. Born in Crosbyton, Texas, January 25, 1937. Texas Western. Inducted in 1987. New York Giants 1958, New York Titans 1960-62, New York Jets 1963-72, St. Louis Cardinals 1973.

GEORGE McAFEE
Halfback. 6-0, 177. Born in Ironton, Ohio, March 13, 1918. Duke. Inducted in 1966. 1940-41, 1945-50 Chicago Bears.

MIKE McCORMACK
Offensive tackle. 6-4, 248. Born in Chicago, Illinois, June 21, 1930. Kansas. Inducted in 1984. 1951 New York Yanks, 1954-62 Cleveland Browns.

HUGH McELHENNY
Halfback. 6-1, 198. Born in Los Angeles, California, December 31, 1928. Washington. Inducted in 1970. 1952-60 San Francisco 49ers, 1961-62 Minnesota Vikings, 1963 New York Giants, 1964 Detroit Lions.

JOHNNY BLOOD (McNALLY)
Halfback. 6-0, 185. Born in New Richmond, Wisconsin, November 27, 1903. Died November 28, 1985. St.

John's (Minnesota). Inducted in 1963. 1925-26 Milwaukee Badgers, 1926-27 Duluth Eskimos, 1928 Pottsville Maroons, 1929-33 Green Bay Packers, 1934 Pittsburgh Pirates, 1935-36 Green Bay Packers; player-coach, 1937-39 Pittsburgh Pirates.

MIKE MICHALSKE
Guard. 6-0, 209. Born in Cleveland, Ohio, April 24, 1903. Died October 26, 1983. Penn State. Inducted in 1964. 1926 New York Yankees (AFL), 1927-28 New York Yankees, 1929-35, 1937 Green Bay Packers.

WAYNE MILLNER
End. 6-0, 191. Born in Roxbury, Massachusetts, January 31, 1913. Died November 19, 1976. Notre Dame. Inducted in 1968. 1936 Boston Redskins, 1937-41, 1945 Washington Redskins.

BOBBY MITCHELL
Running back-wide receiver. 6-0, 195. Born in Hot Springs, Arkansas, June 6, 1935. Illinois. Inducted in 1983. 1958-61 Cleveland Browns, 1962-68 Washington Redskins.

RON MIX
Tackle. 6-4, 250. Born in Los Angeles, California, March 10, 1938. Southern California. Inducted in 1979. 1960 Los Angeles Chargers, 1961-69 San Diego Chargers, 1971 Oakland Raiders.

LENNY MOORE
Back. 6-1, 198. Born in Reading, Pennsylvania, November 25, 1933. Penn State. Inducted in 1975. 1956-67 Baltimore Colts.

MARION MOTLEY
Fullback. 6-1, 238. Born in Leesburg, Georgia, June 5, 1920. South Carolina State, Nevada. Inducted in 1968. 1946-49 Cleveland Browns (AAFC), 1950-53 Cleveland Browns, 1955 Pittsburgh Steelers.

GEORGE MUSSO
Guard-tackle. 6-2, 270. Born in Collinsville, Illinois. April 8, 1910. Millikin. Inducted in 1982. 1933-44 Chicago Bears.

BRONKO NAGURSKI
Fullback. 6-2, 225. Born in Rainy River, Ontario, Canada, November 3, 1908. Minnesota. Inducted in 1963. 1930-37, 1943 Chicago Bears.

JOE NAMATH
Quarterback. 6-2, 200. Born in Beaver Falls, Pennsylvania, May 31, 1943. Alabama. Inducted in 1985. 1965-76 New York Jets, 1977 Los Angeles Rams.

EARLE (GREASY) NEALE
Coach. Born in Parkersburg, West Virginia, November 5, 1891. Died November 2, 1973. West Virginia Wesleyan. Inducted in 1969. 1941-42, 1944-50 Philadelphia Eagles; co-coach, Phil-Pitt 1943.

ERNIE NEVERS
Fullback. 6-1, 205. Born in Willow River, Minnesota, June 11, 1903. Died May 3, 1976. Stanford. Inducted in 1963. 1926-27 Duluth Eskimos, 1929-31 Chicago Cardinals.

RAY NITSCHKE
Linebacker. 6-3, 235. Born in Elmwood Park, Illinois, December 29, 1936. Illinois. Inducted in 1978. 1958-72 Green Bay Packers.

LEO NOMELLINI
Defensive tackle. 6-3, 264. Born in Lucca, Italy, June 19, 1924. Minnesota. Inducted in 1969. 1950-63 San Francisco 49ers.

MERLIN OLSEN
Defensive tackle. 6-5, 270. Born in Logan, Utah, September 15, 1940. Utah State. Inducted in 1982. 1962-76 Los Angeles Rams.

JIM OTTO
Center. 6-2, 255. Born in Wausau, Wisconsin, January 5, 1938. Miami. Inducted in 1980. 1960-74 Oakland Raiders.

STEVE OWEN
Tackle. Coach. 6-0, 235. Born in Cleo Springs, Oklahoma, April 21, 1898. Died May 17, 1964. Phillips. Inducted in 1966. 1924-25 Kansas City Cowboys, 1926-30 New York Giants; coach, 1931-53 New York Giants.

CLARENCE (ACE) PARKER
Quarterback. 5-11, 168. Born in Portsmouth, Virginia, May 17, 1912. Duke. Inducted in 1972. 1937-41 Brooklyn Dodgers, 1945 Boston Yanks, 1946 New York Yankees (AAFC).

JIM PARKER
Guard-tackle. 6-3, 273. Born in Macon, Georgia, April 3, 1934. Ohio State. Inducted in 1973. 1957-67 Baltimore Colts.

JOE PERRY
Fullback. 6-0, 200. Born in Stevens, Arkansas, January 27, 1927. Compton Junior College. Inducted in 1969. 1948-49 San Francisco 49ers (AAFC), 1950-60, 1963 San Francisco 49ers, 1961-62 Baltimore Colts.

PETE PIHOS
End. 6-1, 210. Born in Orlando, Florida, October 22, 1923. Indiana. Inducted in 1970. 1947-55 Philadelphia Eagles.

HUGH (SHORTY) RAY
Supervisor of officials 1938-56. Born in Highland Park, Illinois, September 21, 1884. Died September 16, 1956. Illinois. Inducted in 1966.

DAN REEVES
Team owner. Born in New York, New York, June 30, 1912. Died April 15, 1971. Georgetown. Inducted in 1967. 1941-45 Cleveland Rams, 1946-71 Los Angeles Rams.

JIM RINGO
Center. 6-1, 235. Born in Orange, New Jersey, November 21, 1931. Syracuse. Inducted in 1981. 1953-63 Green Bay Packers, 1964-67 Philadelphia Eagles.

ANDY ROBUSTELLI
Defensive end. 6-0, 230. Born in Stamford, Connecticut, December 6, 1925. Arnold College. Inducted in 1971. 1951-55 Los Angeles Rams, 1956-64 New York Giants.

ART ROONEY
Team owner. Born in Coulterville, Pennsylvania, January 27, 1901. Georgetown, Duquesne. Inducted in 1964. 1933-40 Pittsburgh Pirates, 1941-42, 1949-87 Pittsburgh Steelers, 1943 Phil-Pitt, 1944 Card-Pitt.

PETE ROZELLE
Commissioner. Born in South Gate, California, March 1, 1926. San Francisco. Inducted in 1985. Commissioner 1960-87.

GALE SAYERS
Running back. 6-0, 200. Born in Wichita, Kansas, May 30, 1943. Kansas. Inducted in 1977. 1965-71 Chicago Bears.

JOE SCHMIDT
Linebacker. 6-0, 222. Born in Pittsburgh, Pennsylvania, January 19, 1932. Pittsburgh. Inducted in 1973. 1953-65 Detroit Lions.

O.J. SIMPSON
Running back. 6-1, 212. Born in San Francisco, California, July 9, 1947. Southern California. Inducted in 1985. 1969-77 Buffalo Bills, 1978-79 San Francisco 49ers.

BART STARR
Quarterback. 6-1, 200. Born in Montgomery, Alabama, January 9, 1934. Alabama. Inducted in 1977. 1956-71 Green Bay Packers; coach, 1975-83 Green Bay Packers.

ROGER STAUBACH
Quarterback. 6-3, 202. Born in Cincinnati, Ohio, February 5, 1942. Navy. Inducted in 1985. 1969-79 Dallas Cowboys.

ERNIE STAUTNER
Defensive tackle. 6-2, 235. Born in Prinzing-by-Cham, Bavaria, Germany, April 20, 1925. Boston College. Inducted in 1969. 1950-63 Pittsburgh Steelers.

KEN STRONG
Halfback. 5-11, 210. Born in New Haven, Connecticut, August 6, 1906. Died October 5, 1979. New York University. Inducted in 1967. 1929-32 Staten Island Stapletons, 1933-35, 1939, 1944-47 New York Giants, 1936-37 New York Yanks (AFL).

JOE STYDAHAR
Tackle. 6-4, 230. Born in Kaylor, Pennsylvania, March 3, 1912. Died March 23, 1977. West Virginia. Inducted in 1967. 1936-42, 1945-46 Chicago Bears.

FRAN TARKENTON
Quarterback. 6-0, 185. Born in Richmond, Virginia, February 3, 1940. Georgia. Inducted in 1986. 1961-66, 1972-78 Minnesota Vikings, 1967-71 New York Giants.

CHARLEY TAYLOR
Wide receiver-running back. 6-3, 210. Born in Grand Prairie, Texas, September 28, 1941. Arizona State. Inducted in 1984. 1964-75, 1977 Washington Redskins.

JIM TAYLOR
Fullback. 6-0, 216. Born in Baton Rouge, Louisiana, September 20, 1935. Louisiana State. Inducted in 1976. 1958-66 Green Bay Packers, 1967 New Orleans Saints.

JIM THORPE
Halfback. 6-1, 190. Born in Prague, Oklahoma, May 28, 1888. Died March 28, 1953. Carlisle. Inducted in 1963. 1920 Canton Bulldogs, 1921 Cleveland Indians, 1922-23 Oorang Indians, 1923 Toledo Maroons, 1924 Rock Island, Ill., Independents, 1925 New York Giants, 1926 Canton Bulldogs, 1928 Chicago Cardinals.

Y.A. TITTLE
Quarterback. 6-0, 200. Born in Marshall, Texas, October 24, 1926. Louisiana State. Inducted in 1971. 1948-49 Baltimore Colts (AAFC), 1950 Baltimore Colts, 1951-60 San Francisco 49ers, 1961-64 New York Giants.

GEORGE TRAFTON
Center. 6-2, 235. Born in Chicago, Illinois, December 6, 1896. Died September 5, 1971. Notre Dame. Inducted in 1964. 1920 Decatur Staleys, 1921 Chicago Staleys, 1922-32 Chicago Bears.

CHARLEY TRIPPI
Halfback. 6-0, 185. Born in Pittston, Pennsylvania, December 14, 1922. Georgia. Inducted in 1968. 1947-55 Chicago Cardinals.

EMLEN TUNNELL
Safety. 6-1, 200. Born in Bryn Mawr, Pennsylvania, March 29, 1925. Died July 23, 1975. Toledo, Iowa. Inducted in 1967. 1948-58 New York Giants, 1959-61 Green Bay Packers.

CLYDE (BULLDOG) TURNER
Center. 6-2, 235. Born in Sweetwater, Texas, November 10, 1919. Hardin-Simmons. Inducted in 1966. 1940-52 Chicago Bears.

JOHNNY UNITAS
Quarterback. 6-1, 195. Born in Pittsburgh, Pennsylvania, May 7, 1933. Louisville. Inducted in 1979. 1956-72 Baltimore Colts, 1973 San Diego Chargers.

GENE UPSHAW
Guard. 6-5, 255. Born in Robstown, Texas, August 15, 1945. Texas A & I. Inducted in 1987. Oakland Raiders 1967-81.

NORM VAN BROCKLIN
Quarterback. 6-1, 190. Born in Eagle Butte, South Dakota, March 15, 1926. Died May 2, 1983. Oregon. Inducted in 1971. 1949-57 Los Angeles Rams, 1958-60 Philadelphia Eagles.

STEVE VAN BUREN
Halfback. 6-1, 200. Born in La Ceiba, Honduras, December 28, 1920. Louisiana State. Inducted in 1965. 1944-51 Philadelphia Eagles.

DOAK WALKER
Halfback. 5-10, 172. Born in Dallas, Texas, January 1, 1927. Southern Methodist. Inducted in 1986. 1950-55 Detroit Lions.

PAUL WARFIELD
Wide receiver. 6-0, 188. Born in Warren, Ohio, November 28, 1942. Ohio State. Inducted in 1983. 1964-69, 1976-77 Cleveland Browns, 1970-74 Miami Dolphins.

BOB WATERFIELD
Quarterback. 6-2, 200. Born in Elmira, New York, July 26, 1920. Died March 25, 1983. UCLA. Inducted in 1965. 1945 Cleveland Rams, 1946-52 Los Angeles Rams.

ARNIE WEINMEISTER
Defensive tackle. 6-4, 235. Born in Rhein, Saskatchewan, Canada, March 23, 1923. Washington. Inducted in 1984. 1948-49 New York Yankees (AAFC), 1950-53 New York Giants.

BILL WILLIS
Guard. 6-2, 215. Born in Columbus, Ohio, October 5, 1921. Ohio State. Inducted in 1977. 1946-49 Cleveland Browns (AAFC), 1950-53 Cleveland Browns.

LARRY WILSON
Defensive back. 6-0, 190. Born in Rigby, Idaho, March 24, 1938. Utah. Inducted in 1978. 1960-72 St. Louis Cardinals.

ALEX WOJCIECHOWICZ
Center. 6-0, 235. Born in South River, New Jersey, August 12, 1915. Fordham. Inducted in 1968. 1938-46 Detroit Lions, 1946-50 Philadelphia Eagles.

A CHRONOLOGY OF PROFESSIONAL FOOTBALL

1869 Rutgers and Princeton played a college soccer football game, the first ever, November 6. The game used modified London Football Association rules. During the next seven years, rugby gained favor with the major eastern schools over soccer, and modern football began to develop from rugby.

1876 At the Massasoit convention, the first rules for American football were written. Walter Camp, who would become known as "the father of American football," first became involved with the game.

1892 In an era in which football was a major attraction of local athletic clubs, an intense competition between two Pittsburgh-area clubs, the Allegheny Athletic Association (AAA) and the Pittsburgh Athletic Club (PAC), led to the making of the first professional football player. Former Yale All-America guard William (Pudge) Heffelfinger was paid $500 by the AAA to play in a game against the PAC, becoming the first person to be paid to play football, November 12. The AAA won the game 4-0 when Heffelfinger picked up a PAC fumble and ran 35 yards for a touchdown.

1893 The Pittsburgh Athletic Club signed one of its players, probably halfback Grant Dibert, to the first known pro football contract, which covered all of the PAC's games for the year.

1895 John Brallier became the first football player to openly turn pro, accepting $10 and expenses to play for the Latrobe YMCA against the Jeannette Athletic Club.

1896 The Allegheny Athletic Association team fielded the first completely professional team for its abbreviated two-game season.

1897 The Latrobe Athletic Association football team went entirely professional, becoming the first team to play a full season with only professionals.

1898 A touchdown was changed from four points to five.

1899 Chris O'Brien formed a neighborhood team, which played under the name the Morgan Athletic Club, on the south side of Chicago. The team later became known as the Normals, then the Racine (for a street in Chicago) Cardinals, the Chicago Cardinals, and, in 1960, the St. Louis Cardinals. The team remains the oldest continuing operation in pro football.

1900 William C. Temple took over the team payments for the Duquesne Country and Athletic Club, becoming the first known individual club owner.

1902 Baseball's Philadelphia Athletics, managed by Connie Mack, and the Philadelphia Phillies formed professional football teams, joining the Pittsburgh Stars in the first attempt at a pro football league, named the National Football League. The Athletics won the first night football game ever played, 39-0 over Kanaweola AC at Elmira, New York, November 21.

All three teams claimed the pro championship for the year, but the league president, Dave Berry, named the Stars the champions. Pitcher Rube Waddell was with the Athletics, and pitcher Christy Matthewson was a fullback for Pittsburgh.

The first World Series of pro football, actually a five-team tournament, was played among a team made up of players from both the Athletics and the Phillies, but simply named "New York"; the New York Knickerbockers, the Syracuse AC; the Warlow AC; and the Orange (New Jersey) AC at New York's original Madison Square Garden. New York and Syracuse played the first indoor football game before 3,000, December 28. Syracuse, with Glen (Pop) Warner at guard, won 6-0 and went on to win the tournament.

1903 The Franklin (Pa.) Athletic Club won the second and last World Series of pro football over the Oreos AC of Asbury Park, New Jersey; the Watertown Red and Blacks; and the Orange AC.

Pro football was popularized in Ohio when the Massillon Tigers, a strong amateur team, hired four Pittsburgh pros to play in the season-ending game against Akron. At the same time, pro football declined in the Pittsburgh area, and the emphasis on the pro game moved west from Pennsylvania to Ohio.

1904 A field goal was changed from five points to four.

Ohio had at least seven pro teams, with Massillon winning the Ohio Independent Championship, that is, the pro title. Talk surfaced about forming a state-wide league to end spiraling salaries brought about by constant bidding for players and to write universal rules for the game. The feeble attempt to start the league failed.

Halfback Charles Follis signed a contract with the Shelby AC, making him the first-known black pro football player.

1905 The Canton AC, later to become known as the Bulldogs, became a professional team. Massillon again won the Ohio League championship.

1906 The forward pass was legalized. The first authenticated pass completion in a pro game came on October 27, when George (Peggy) Parratt of Massillon threw a completion to Dan (Bullet) Riley in a victory over a combined Benwood-Moundsville team.

Archrivals Canton and Massillon, the two best pro teams in America, played twice, with Canton winning the first game but Massillon winning the second and the Ohio League championship. A betting scandal and the financial disaster wrought upon the two clubs by paying huge salaries caused a temporary decline in interest in pro football in the two cities and, somewhat, through Ohio.

1909 A field goal dropped from four points to three.

1912 A touchdown was increased from five points to six.

Jack Cusack revived a strong pro team in Canton.

1913 Jim Thorpe, a former football and track star at the Carlisle Indian School (Pa.) and a double gold medal winner at the 1912 Olympics in Stockholm, played for the Pine Village Pros in Indiana.

1915 Massillon again fielded a major team, reviving the old rivalry with Canton. Cusack signed Thorpe to play for Canton for $250 a game.

1916 With Thorpe and former Carlisle teammate Pete Calac starring, Canton went 9-0-1, won the Ohio League championship, and was acclaimed the pro football champion of the world.

1917 Despite an upset by Massillon, Canton again won the Ohio League championship.

1919 Canton again won the Ohio League championship, despite the team having been turned over from Cusack to Ralph Hay. Thorpe and Calac were joined in the backfield by Joe Guyon.

Earl (Curly) Lambeau and George Calhoun organized the Green Bay Packers. Lambeau's employer at the Indian Packing Company provided $500 for equipment and allowed the team to use the company field for practices. The Packers went 10-1.

1920 Pro football was in a state of confusion due to three major problems: dramatically rising salaries; players continually jumping from one team to another following the highest offer; and the use of college players still enrolled in school. A league in which all the members would follow the same rules seemed the answer. An organizational meeting, at which the Akron Pros, Canton Bulldogs, Cleveland Indians, and Dayton Triangles were represented, was held in Canton, Ohio, August 20. This meeting resulted in the formation of the American Professional Football Conference.

A second organizational meeting was held in Canton, September 17. The teams were from four states—Akron, Canton, Cleveland, and Dayton from Ohio; the Hammond Pros and Muncie Flyers from Indiana; the Rochester Jeffersons from New York; and the Rock Island Independents, Decatur Staleys, and Racine Cardinals from Illinois. The name of the league was changed to the American Professional Football Association. Hoping to capitalize on his fame, the members elected Thorpe president; Stanley Cofall of Cleveland was elected vice president. A membership fee of $100 per team was charged to give an appearance of respectability, but no team ever paid it. Scheduling was left up to the teams, and there was a wide variation both in the overall number of games played and in the number played against APFA member teams.

Four other teams—the Buffalo All-Americans, Chicago Tigers, Columbus Panhandles, and Detroit Heralds—joined the league sometime during the year. On September 26, the first game featuring an APFA team was played at Rock Island's Douglas Park. A crowd of 800 watched the Independents defeat the St. Paul Ideals 48-0. A week later, October 3, the first game matching two APFA teams was held. At Triangle Park, Dayton defeated Columbus 14-0, with Lou Partlow of Dayton scoring the first touchdown in a game between association teams. The same day, Rock Island defeated Muncie 45-0.

By the beginning of December, most of the teams in the APFA had abandoned their hopes for a championship, and some of them, including the Chicago Tigers and the Detroit Heralds, had finished their seasons, disbanded, and had their franchises canceled by the Association. Four teams—Akron, Buffalo, Canton, and Decatur—still had championship aspirations, but a series of late-season games among them left Akron as the only undefeated team in the Association. At one of these games, Akron sold tackle Bob Nash to Buffalo for $300 and five percent of the gate receipts—the first APFA player deal.

1921 At the league meeting in Akron, April 30, the championship of the 1920 season was awarded to the Akron Pros. The APFA was reorganized, with Joe Carr of the Columbus Panhandles named president and Carl Storck of Dayton secretary-treasurer. Carr moved the Association's headquarters to Columbus, drafted a league constitution and by-laws, gave teams territorial rights, restricted player movements, developed membership criteria for the franchises, and issued standings for the first time, so that the APFA would have a clear champion.

The Association's membership increased to 22 teams, including the Green Bay Packers, who were awarded to John Clair of the Acme Packing Company.

Thorpe moved from Canton to the Cleveland Indians, but he was hurt early in the season and played very little.

A.E. Staley turned the Decatur Staleys over to player-coach George Halas, who moved the team to Cubs Park in Chicago. Staley paid Halas $5,000 to keep the name "Staleys" for one more year. Halas made halfback Ed (Dutch) Sternaman his partner.

The Staleys claimed the APFA championship with a 9-1-1 record, as did Buffalo at 9-1-2. Carr ruled in favor of the Staleys, giving Halas his first championship.

1922 After admitting the use of players who had college eligibility remaining during the 1921 season, Clair and the Green Bay management withdrew from the APFA, January 28. Curly Lambeau promised to obey league rules and then used $50 of his own money to buy back the franchise. Bad weather and low attendance plagued the Packers, and Lambeau went broke, but local merchants arranged a $2,500 loan for the club. A public non-profit corporation was set up to operate the team, with Lambeau as head coach and manager.

The American Professional Football Association changed its name to the National Football League, June 24. The Chicago Staleys became the Chicago Bears.

The NFL fielded 18 teams, including the new Oorang Indians of Marion, Ohio, an all-Indian team featuring Thorpe, Joe Guyon, and Pete Calac, and sponsored by the Oorang dog kennels.

Canton, led by player-coach Guy Chamberlin and tackles Link Lyman and Wilbur (Pete) Henry, emerged as the league's first true powerhouse, going 10-0-2.

1923 For the first time, all of the franchises considered to be part of the NFL fielded teams. Thorpe played first for Oorang, then for the Toledo Maroons. Against the Bears, Thorpe fumbled, and Halas picked up the ball and returned it 98 yards for a touchdown, a record that would last until 1972.

Canton had its second consecutive undefeated season, going 11-0-1 for the NFL title.

1924 The league had 18 franchises, including new ones in Kansas City, Kenosha, and Frankford, a section of Philadelphia. League champion Canton, successful on the field but not at the box office, was purchased by the owner of the Cleveland franchise, who kept the Canton franchise inactive, while using the best players for his Cleveland team, which he renamed the Bulldogs. Cleveland won the title with a 7-1-1 record.

1925 Five new franchises were admitted to the NFL—the New York Giants, who were awarded to Tim Mara and Billy Gibson for $500; the Detroit Panthers, featuring Jimmy Conzelman as owner, coach, and tailback; the Providence Steam Roller; a new Canton Bulldogs team; and the Pottsville Maroons, who had been perhaps the most successful independent pro team. The NFL established its first player limit, at 16 players.

Late in the season, the NFL made its greatest coup in gaining national recognition. Shortly after the University of Illinois season ended in November, All-America halfback Harold (Red) Grange signed a contract to play with the Chicago Bears. On Thanksgiving Day, a crowd of 36,000—the largest in pro football history—watched Grange and the Bears play the Chicago Cardinals to a scoreless tie at Wrigley Field. At the beginning of December, the Bears left on a barnstorming tour that saw them play eight games in 12 days, in St. Louis, Philadelphia, New York City, Washington, Boston, Pittsburgh, Detroit, and Chicago. A crowd of 73,000 watched the game against the Giants at the Polo Grounds, helping assure the future of the troubled NFL franchise in New York. The Bears then played nine more games in the South and West, including a game in Los Angeles, in which 75,000 fans watched them defeat the Los Angeles Tigers in the Los Angeles Memorial Coliseum.

Pottsville and the Chicago Cardinals were the top contenders for the league title, with Pottsville winning a late-season meeting 21-7. Pottsville scheduled a game against a team of former Notre Dame players for Shibe Park in Philadelphia. Frankford lodged a protest not only because the game was in Frankford's "protected territory," but because it was being played the same day as a Yellow Jackets home game. Carr gave three different notices forbidding Pottsville to play the game, but Pottsville played anyway, December 12. That day, Carr fined the club, suspended it from all rights and privileges (including the right to play for the NFL championship), and returned its franchise to the league. The Cardinals, who ended the season with the best record in the league, were named the 1925 champions.

1926 Grange's manager, C.C. Pyle, told the Bears that Grange wouldn't play for them unless he was paid a five-figure salary and given one-third ownership of the team. The Bears refused. Pyle leased Yankee Stadium in New York City, then petitioned for an NFL franchise. After he was refused, he started the first American Football League. It lasted one season and included Grange's New York Yankees and eight other teams. The AFL champion Philadelphia Quakers played a December game against the New York Giants, seventh in the NFL, and the Giants won 31-0. At the end of the season, the AFL folded.

Halas pushed through a rule that prohibited any team from signing a player whose college class had not graduated.

The NFL grew to 22 teams, including the Duluth Eskimos, who signed All-America fullback Ernie Nevers of Stanford, giving the league a gate attraction to rival Grange. The 15-member Eskimos, dubbed the "Iron Men of the North," played 29 exhibition and league games, 28 on the road, and Nevers played in all but 29 minutes of them.

Frankford edged the Bears for the championship, despite Halas having obtained John (Paddy) Driscoll from the Cardinals. On December 4, the Yellow Jackets scored in the final two minutes to defeat the Bears 7-6 and move ahead of them in the standings.

1927 At a special meeting in Cleveland, April 23, Carr decided to secure the NFL's future by eliminating the financially weaker teams and consolidating the quality players onto a limited number of more successful teams. The new-look NFL dropped to 12 teams, and the center of gravity of the league left the Midwest, where the NFL had started, and began to emerge in the large cities of the East. One of the new teams was Grange's New York Yankees, but Grange suffered a knee injury and the Yankees finished in the middle of the pack. The NFL championship was won by the cross-town rival New York Giants, who posted 10 shutouts in 13 games.

1928 Grange and Nevers both retired from pro football, and Duluth disbanded, as the NFL was reduced to only 10 teams. The Providence Steam Roller of Jimmy Conzelman and Pearce Johnson won the championship, playing in the Cycledrome, a 10,000-seat oval that had been built for bicycle races.

1929 Chris O'Brien sold the Chicago Cardinals to David Jones, July 27. The NFL added a fourth official, the field judge, July 28.

Grange and Nevers returned to the NFL. Nevers scored six rushing touchdowns and four extra points as the Cardinals beat Grange's Bears 40-6, November 28. The 40 points set a record that remains the NFL's oldest.

Providence became the first NFL team to host a game at night under floodlights, against the Cardinals, November 3.

The Packers added back Johnny Blood (McNally), tackle Cal Hubbard, and guard Mike Michalske, and won their first NFL championship, edging the Giants, who featured quarterback Benny Friedman.

1930 Dayton, the last of the NFL's original franchises, was purchased by John Dwyer, moved to Brooklyn, and renamed the Dodgers. The Portsmouth, Ohio, Spartans entered the league.

The Packers edged the Giants for the title, but the most improved team was the Bears. Halas retired as a player and replaced himself as coach of the Bears with Ralph Jones, who refined the T-formation by introducing wide ends and a halfback in motion. Jones also introduced rookie All-America fullback-tackle Bronko Nagurski.

The Giants defeated a team of former Notre Dame players coached by Knute Rockne 22-0 before 55,000 at the Polo Grounds, December 14. The proceeds went to the New York Unemployment Fund to help those suffering because of the Great Depression, and the easy victory helped give the NFL credibility with the press and the public.

1931 The NFL decreased to 10 teams, and halfway through the season the Frankford franchise folded. Carr fined the Bears, Packers, and Portsmouth $1,000 each for using players whose college classes had not graduated.

The Packers won an unprecedented third consecutive title, beating out the Spartans, who were led by rookie backs Earl (Dutch) Clark and Glenn Presnell.

1932 George Preston Marshall, Vincent Bendix, Jay O'Brien, and M. Dorland Doyle were awarded a franchise for Boston, July 9. Despite the presence of two rookies—halfback Cliff Battles and tackle Glen (Turk) Edwards—the new team, named the Braves, lost money and Marshall was left as the sole owner at the end of the year.

NFL membership dropped to eight teams, the lowest in history. Official statistics were kept for the first time. The Bears and the Spartans finished the season in the first-ever tie for first place. After the season finale, the league office arranged for the first playoff game in NFL history. The game was moved indoors to Chicago Stadium because of bitter cold and heavy snow. The arena allowed only an 80-yard field that came right to the walls. The goal posts were moved from the end lines to the goal lines and, for safety, inbounds lines or hashmarks where the ball would be put in play were drawn 10 yards from the walls that butted against the sidelines. The Bears won 9-0, December 18, scoring the winning touchdown on a two-yard pass from Nagurski to Grange. The Spartans claimed Nagurski's pass was thrown from less than five yards behind the line of scrimmage, violating the existing passing rule, but the play stood.

1933 The NFL, which long had followed the rules of college football, made a number of significant changes from the college game for the first time and began to independently develop rules serving its needs and the style of play it preferred. The innovations from the 1932 championship game—inbounds line or hashmarks and goal posts on the goal lines—were adopted. Also the forward pass was legalized from anywhere behind the line of scrimmage, February 25.

Marshall and Halas pushed through a proposal that divided the NFL into two divisions, with the winners to meet in an annual championship game, July 8.

Three new franchises joined the league—the Pittsburgh Pirates of Art Rooney, the Philadelphia Eagles of Bert Bell and Lud Wray, and the Cincinnati Reds. The Staten Island Stapletons suspended operations for a year, but never returned to the league.

Halas bought out Sternaman, became sole owner of the Bears, and reinstated himself as head coach. Marshall changed the name of the Boston Braves to the Redskins. David Jones sold the Chicago Cardinals to Charles W. Bidwill.

In the first NFL Championship Game scheduled before the season, the Western Division champion Bears defeated the Eastern Division champion Giants 23-21 at Wrigley Field, December 17.

1934 G.A. (Dick) Richards purchased the Portsmouth Spartans, moved them to Detroit, and renamed them the Lions.

Professional football gained new prestige when the Bears were matched against the best college football players in the first Chicago College All-Star Game, August 31. The game ended in a scoreless tie before 79,432 at Soldier Field.

The Cincinnati Reds lost their first eight games, then were suspended from the league for defaulting on payments. The St. Louis Gunners, an independent team, joined the NFL by buying the Cincinnati franchise and went 1-2 the last three weeks.

Rookie Beattie Feathers of the Bears became the NFL's first 1,000-yard rusher, gaining 1,004 on 101 carries. The Thanksgiving Day game between the Bears and the Lions became the first NFL game broadcast nationally, with Graham McNamee the announcer for CBS radio.

In the championship game, on an extremely cold and icy day at the Polo Grounds, the Giants trailed the Bears 13-3 in the third quarter before changing to basketball shoes for better footing. The Giants won 30-13 in what has come to be known as the "Sneakers Game," December 9. The player waiver rule was adopted, December 10.

1935 The NFL adopted Bert Bell's proposal to hold an annual draft of college players, to begin in 1936, with teams selecting in an inverse order of finish, May 19. The inbounds line or hashmarks were moved nearer the center of the field, 15 yards from the sidelines.

All-America end Don Hutson of Alabama joined Green Bay. The Lions defeated the Giants 26-7 in the NFL Championship Game, December 15.

1936 There were no franchise transactions for the first year since the formation of the NFL. It also was the first year in which all member teams played the same number of games.

The Eagles made University of Chicago halfback and Heisman Trophy winner Jay Berwanger the first player ever selected in the NFL draft, February 8. The Eagles traded his rights to the Bears, but Berwanger never played pro football. The first player selected to actually sign was the number-two pick, Riley Smith of Alabama, who was selected by Boston.

A rival league was formed, and it became the second to call itself the American Football League. The Boston Shamrocks were its champions.

Due to poor attendance, Marshall, the owner of the host team, moved the Championship Game from Boston to the Polo Grounds in New York. Green Bay defeated the Redskins 21-6, December 13.

1937 Homer Marshman was granted a Cleveland franchise, named the Rams, February 12. Marshall moved the Redskins to Washington, D.C., February 13. The Redskins signed TCU All-America tailback Sammy Baugh, who led them to a 28-21 victory over the Bears in the NFL Championship Game, December 12.

The Los Angeles Bulldogs had an 8-0 record to win the AFL title, but then the two-year-old league folded.

1938 At the suggestion of Halas, Hugh (Shorty) Ray became a technical advisor on rules and officiating to the NFL. A new rule called for a 15-yard penalty for roughing the passer.

Rookie Byron (Whizzer) White of the Pittsburgh Pirates led the NFL in rushing. The Giants defeated the Packers 23-17 for the NFL title, December 11.

Marshall, *Los Angeles Times* sports editor Bill Henry, and promoter Tom Gallery established the Pro Bowl game between the NFL champion and a team of pro all-stars.

1939 The New York Giants defeated the Pro All-Stars 13-10 in the first Pro Bowl, at Wrigley Field, Los Angeles, January 15.

Carr, NFL president since 1921, died in Columbus, May 20. Carl Storck was named acting president, May 25.

An NFL game was televised for the first time when NBC broadcast the Brooklyn Dodgers-Philadelphia Eagles game from Ebbets Field to the approximately 1,000 sets then in New York.

Green Bay defeated New York 27-0 in the NFL Championship Game, December 10 at Milwaukee. NFL attendance exceeded one million in a season for the first time, reaching 1,071,200.

1940 A six-team rival league, the third to call itself the American Football League, was formed, and the Columbus Bullies won its championship.

Halas's Bears, with additional coaching by Clark Shaughnessy of Stanford, defeated the Redskins 73-0 in the NFL Championship Game, December 8. The game, which was the most decisive victory in NFL history, popularized the Bears' T-formation with a man-in-motion. It was the first championship carried on network radio, broadcast by Red Barber to 120 stations of the Mutual Broadcasting System, which paid $2,500 for the rights.

Art Rooney sold the Pittsburgh franchise to Alexis Thompson, December 9, then bought part interest in the Philadelphia Eagles.

1941 Elmer Layden was named the first Commissioner of the NFL, March 1; Storck, the acting president, resigned, April 5. NFL headquarters were moved to Chicago.

Bell and Rooney traded the Eagles to Thompson for the Pirates, then renamed their new team the Steelers. Homer Marshman sold the Rams to Daniel F. Reeves and Fred Levy, Jr.

The league by-laws were revised to provide for playoffs in case there were ties in division races, and sudden-death overtimes in case a playoff game was tied after four quarters. An official *NFL Record Manual* was published for the first time.

Columbus again won the championship of the AFL, but the two-year-old league then folded.

The Bears and the Packers finished in a tie for the Western Division championship, setting up the first divisional playoff game in league history. The Bears won 33-14, then defeated the Giants 37-9 for the NFL championship, December 21.

1942 Players departing for service in World War II depleted the rosters of NFL teams. Halas left the Bears in midseason to join the Navy, and Luke Johnsos and Heartley (Hunk) Anderson served as co-coaches as the Bears went 11-0 in the regular season. The Redskins defeated the Bears 14-6 in the NFL Championship Game, December 13.

1943 The Cleveland Rams, with co-owners Reeves and Levy in the service, were granted permission to suspend operations for one season, April 6. Levy transferred his stock in the team to Reeves, April 16.

The NFL adopted free substitution, April 7. The league also made the wearing of helmets mandatory and approved a 10-game schedule for all teams.

Philadelphia and Pittsburgh were granted permission to merge for one season, June 19. The team, known as Phil-Pitt (and called the Steagles by fans), divided home games between the two cities, and Earle (Greasy) Neale of Philadelphia and Walt Kiesling of Pittsburgh served as co-coaches. The merger automatically dissolved the last day of the season, December 5.

Ted Collins was granted a franchise for Boston, to become active in 1944.

Sammy Baugh led the league in passing, punting, and interceptions. He led the Redskins to a tie with the Giants for the Eastern Division title, and then to a 28-0 victory in a divisional playoff game. The Bears beat the Redskins 41-21 in the NFL Championship Game, December 26.

1944 Collins, who had wanted a franchise in Yankee Stadium in New York, named his new team in Boston the Yanks. Cleveland resumed operations. The Brooklyn Dodgers changed their name to the Tigers.

Coaching from the bench was legalized, April 20.

The Cardinals and the Steelers were granted permission to merge for one year under the name Card-Pitt, April 21. Phil Handler of the Cardinals and Walt Kiesling of the Steelers served as co-coaches. The merger automatically dissolved the last day of the season, December 3.

In the NFL Championship Game, Green Bay defeated the New York Giants 14-7, December 17.

1945 The inbounds lines or hashmarks were moved from 15 yards away from the sidelines to nearer the center of the field—20 yards from the sidelines.

Brooklyn and Boston merged into a team that played home games in both cities and was known simply as "The Yanks." The team was coached by former Boston head coach Herb Kopf. In December, the Brooklyn franchise withdrew from the NFL to join the new All-America Football Conference; all the players on its active and reserve lists were assigned to The Yanks, who once again became the Boston Yanks.

Halas rejoined the Bears late in the season after service with the U.S. Navy. Although Halas took over much of the coaching duties, Anderson and Johnsos remained the coaches of record throughout the season.

Steve Van Buren of Philadelphia led the NFL in rushing, kickoff returns, and scoring.

After the Japanese surrendered ending World War II, a count showed that the NFL service roster, limited to men who had played in league games, totaled 638, 21 of whom had died in action.

Rookie quarterback Bob Waterfield led Cleveland to a 15-14 victory over Washington in the NFL Championship Game, December 16.

1946 The contract of Commissioner Layden was not renewed, and Bert Bell, the co-owner of the Steelers, replaced him, January 11. Bell moved the league headquarters from Chicago to the Philadelphia suburb of Bala Cynwyd.

Free substitution was withdrawn and substitutions were limited to no more than three men at a time. Forward passes were made automatically incomplete upon striking the goal posts, January 11.

The NFL took on a truly national appearance for the first time when Reeves was granted permission by the league to move his NFL champion Rams to Los Angeles.

The rival All-America Football Conference began play with eight teams. The Cleveland Browns, coached by Paul Brown, won the AAFC's first championship, defeating the New York Yankees 14-9.

Bill Dudley of the Steelers led the NFL in rushing, interceptions, and punt returns, and won the league's most valuable player award.

Backs Frank Filchock and Merle Hapes of the Giants were questioned about an attempt by a New York man to fix the championship game with the Bears. Bell suspended Hapes but allowed Filchock to play; he played well, but Chicago won 24-14, December 15.

1947 The NFL added a fifth official, the back judge.

A bonus choice was made for the first time in the NFL draft. One team each year would select the special choice before the first round began. The Chicago Bears won a lottery and the rights to the first choice and drafted back Bob Fenimore of Oklahoma A&M.

The Cleveland Browns again won the AAFC title, defeating the New York Yankees 14-3.

Charles Bidwill, Sr., owner of the Cardinals, died April 19, but his wife and sons retained ownership of the team. On December 28, the Cardinals won the NFL Championship Game 28-21 over the Philadelphia Eagles, who had beaten Pittsburgh 21-0 in a playoff.

1948 Plastic helmets were prohibited. A flexible artificial tee was permitted at the kickoff. Officials other than the referee were equipped with whistles, not horns, January 14.

Fred Mandel sold the Detroit Lions to a syndicate headed by D. Lyle Fife, January 15.

Halfback Fred Gehrke of the Los Angeles Rams painted horns on the Rams' helmets, the first modern helmet emblems in pro football.

The Cleveland Browns won their third straight championship in the AAFC, going 14-0 and then defeating the Buffalo Bills 49-7.

In a blizzard, the Eagles defeated the Cardinals 7-0 in the NFL Championship Game, December 19.

1949 Alexis Thompson sold the champion Eagles to a syndicate headed by James P. Clark, January 15. The Boston Yanks became the New York Bulldogs, sharing the Polo Grounds with the Giants.

Free substitution was adopted for one year, January 20.

The NFL had two 1,000-yard rushers in the same season for the first time—Steve Van Buren of Philadelphia and Tony Canadeo of Green Bay.

The AAFC played its season with a one-division, seven-team format. On December 9, Bell announced a merger agreement in which three AAFC franchises—Cleveland, San Francisco, and Baltimore—would join the NFL in 1950. The Browns won their fourth consecutive AAFC title, defeating the 49ers 21-7, December 11.

In a heavy rain, the Eagles defeated the Rams 14-0 in the NFL Championship Game, December 18.

1950 Unlimited free substitution was restored, opening the way for the era of two platoons and specialization in pro football, January 20.

Curly Lambeau, founder of the franchise and Green Bay's head coach since 1921, resigned under fire, February 1.

The name National Football League was restored after about three months as the National-American Football League. The American and National conferences were created to replace the Eastern and Western divisions, March 3.

The New York Bulldogs became the Yanks and divided the players of the former AAFC Yankees with the Giants. A special allocation draft was held in which the 13 teams drafted the remaining AAFC players, with special consideration for Baltimore, which received 15 choices compared to 10 for other teams.

The Los Angeles Rams became the first NFL team to have all of its games—both home and away—televised. The Washington Redskins followed the Rams in arranging to televise their games; other teams made deals to put selected games on television.

In the first game of the season, former AAFC champion Cleveland defeated NFL champion Philadelphia 35-10. For the first time, deadlocks occurred in both conferences and playoffs were necessary. The Browns defeated the Giants in the American and the Rams defeated the Bears in the National. Cleveland defeated Los Angeles 30-28 in the NFL Championship Game, December 24.

1951 The Pro Bowl game, dormant since 1942, was revived under a new format matching the all-stars of each conference at the Los Angeles Memorial Coliseum. The American Conference defeated the National Conference 28-27, January 14.

Abraham Watner returned the Baltimore franchise and its player contracts back to the NFL for $50,000. Baltimore's former players were made available for drafting at the same time as college players, January 18.

A rule was passed that no tackle, guard, or center would be eligible to catch a forward pass, January 18.

The Rams reversed their television policy and televised only road games.

The NFL Championship Game was televised coast-to-coast for the first time, December 23. The DuMont Network paid $75,000 for the rights to the game, in which the Rams defeated the Browns 24-17.

1952 Ted Collins sold the New York Yanks' franchise back to the NFL, January 19. A new franchise was awarded to a group in Dallas after it purchased the assets of the Yanks, January 24. The new Texans went 1-11, with the owners turning the franchise back to the league in midseason. For the last five games of the season, the commissioner's office operated the Texans as a road team, using Hershey, Pennsylvania, as a home base. At the end of the season the franchise was cancelled, the last time an NFL team failed.

The Pittsburgh Steelers abandoned the Single-Wing for the T-formation, the last pro team to do so.

The Detroit Lions won their first NFL championship in 17 years, defeating the Browns 17-7 in the title game, December 28.

1953 A Baltimore group headed by Carroll Rosenbloom was granted a franchise and was awarded the holdings of the defunct Dallas organization, January 23. The team, named the Colts, put together the largest trade in league history, acquiring 10 players from Cleveland in exchange for five.

The names of the American and National conferences were changed to the Eastern and Western conferences, January 24.

Jim Thorpe died, March 28.

Mickey McBride, founder of the Cleveland Browns, sold the franchise to a syndicate headed by Dave R. Jones, June 10.

The NFL policy of blacking out home games was upheld by Judge Allan K. Grim of the U.S. District Court in Philadelphia, November 12.

The Lions again defeated the Browns in the NFL Championship Game, winning 17-16, December 27.

1954 The Canadian Football League began a series of raids on NFL teams, signing quarterback Eddie LeBaron and defensive end Gene Brito of Washington and defensive tackle Arnie Weinmeister of the Giants, among others.

Fullback Joe Perry of the 49ers became the first player in league history to gain 1,000 yards rushing in consecutive seasons.

Cleveland defeated Detroit 56-10 in the NFL Championship Game, December 26.

1955 The sudden-death overtime rule was used for the first time in a preseason game between the Rams and Giants at Portland, Oregon, August 28. The Rams won 23-17 three minutes into overtime.

A rule change declared the ball dead immediately if the ball carrier touched the ground with any part of his body except his hands or feet while in the grasp of an opponent.

The NFL Players Association was founded.

The Baltimore Colts made an 80-cent phone call to Johnny Unitas and signed him as a free agent. Another quarterback, Otto Graham, played his last game as the Browns defeated the Rams 38-14 in the NFL Championship Game, December 26. Graham had quarterbacked the Browns to 10 championship-game appearances in 10 years.

NBC replaced DuMont as the network for the title game, paying rights fees of $100,000.

1956 Grabbing an opponent's facemask (other than the ball carrier) was made illegal. Using radio receivers to communicate with players on the field was prohibited. A natural leather ball with white end stripes replaced the white ball with black stripes for night games.

The Giants moved from the Polo Grounds to Yankee Stadium.

Halas retired as coach of the Bears, and was replaced by Paddy Driscoll.

CBS became the first network to broadcast some NFL regular-season games to selected television markets across the nation.

The Giants routed the Bears 47-7 in the NFL Championship Game, December 30.

1957 Pete Rozelle was named general manager of the Rams. Anthony J. Morabito, founder and co-owner of the 49ers, died of a heart attack during a game against the Bears at Kezar Stadium, October 28. An NFL-record crowd of 102,368 saw the 49ers-Rams game at the Los Angeles Memorial Coliseum, November 10.

The Lions came from 20 points down to post a 31-27 playoff victory over the 49ers, December 22. Detroit defeated Cleveland 59-14 in the NFL Championship Game, December 29.

1958 The bonus selection in the draft was eliminated, January 29. The last selection was quarterback King Hill of Rice by the Chicago Cardinals.

Halas reinstated himself as coach of the Bears.

Jim Brown of Cleveland gained an NFL record 1,527 yards rushing. In a divisional playoff game, the Giants held Brown to eight yards and defeated Cleveland 10-0.

Baltimore, coached by Weeb Ewbank, defeated the Giants 23-17 in the first sudden-death overtime in an NFL Championship Game, December 28. The game ended when Colts fullback Alan Ameche scored on a one-yard touchdown run after 8:15 of overtime.

1959 Vince Lombardi was named head coach of the Green Bay Packers, January 28. Tim Mara, the co-founder of the Giants, died, February 17.

Lamar Hunt of Dallas announced his intentions to form a second pro football league. The first meeting was held in Chicago, August 14, and consisted of Hunt representing Dallas; Bob Howsam, Denver; K.S. (Bud) Adams, Houston; Barron Hilton, Los Angeles; Max Winter and Bill Boyer, Minneapolis; and Harry Wismer, New York City. They made plans to begin play in 1960.

The new league was named the American Football League, August 22. Buffalo, owned by Ralph Wilson, became the seventh franchise, October 28. Boston, owned by William H. Sullivan, became the eighth team, November 22. The first AFL draft, lasting 33 rounds, was held, November 22. Joe Foss was named AFL Commissioner, November 30. An additional draft of 20 rounds was held by the AFL, December 2.

NFL Commissioner Bert Bell died of a heart attack suffered at Franklin Field, Philadelphia, during the last two minutes of a game between the Eagles and the Steelers, October 11. Treasurer Austin Gunsel was named president in the office of the commissioner, October 14.

The Colts again defeated the Giants in the NFL Championship Game, 31-16, December 27.

1960 Pete Rozelle was elected NFL Commissioner as a compromise choice on the twenty-third ballot, January 26. Rozelle moved the league offices to New York City.

Hunt was elected AFL president for 1960, January 26. Minneapolis withdrew from the AFL, January 27, and the same ownership was given an NFL franchise for Minnesota (to start in 1961), January 28. Dallas received an NFL franchise for 1960, January 28. Oakland received an AFL franchise, January 30.

The AFL adopted the two-point option on points after touchdown, January 28. A "no-tampering" verbal pact, relative to players' contracts, was agreed to between the NFL and AFL, February 9.

The NFL owners voted to allow the transfer of the Chicago Cardinals to St. Louis, March 13.

The AFL signed a five-year television contract with ABC, June 9.

The Boston Patriots defeated the Buffalo Bills 28-7 before 16,000 at Buffalo in the first AFL preseason game, July 30. The Denver Broncos defeated the Patriots 13-10 before 21,597 at Boston in the first AFL regular-season game, September 9.

Philadelphia defeated Green Bay 17-13 in the NFL Championship Game, December 26.

1961 The Houston Oilers defeated the Los Angeles Chargers 24-16 before 32,183 in the first AFL Championship Game, January 1.

Detroit defeated Cleveland 17-16 in the first Playoff Bowl, or Bert Bell Benefit Bowl, between second-place teams in each conference in Miami, January 7.

End Willard Dewveall of the Bears played out his option and joined the Oilers, becoming the first player to deliberately move from one league to the other, January 14.

Ed McGah, Wayne Valley, and Robert Osborne bought out their partners in the ownership of the Raiders, January 17. The Chargers were transferred to San Diego, February 10. Dave R. Jones sold the Browns to a group headed by Arthur B. Modell, March 22. The Howsam brothers sold the Broncos to a group headed by Calvin Kunz and Gerry Phipps, May 26.

NBC was awarded a two-year contract for radio and television rights to the NFL Championship Game for $615,000 annually, $300,000 of which was to go directly into the NFL Player Benefit Plan, April 5.

Canton, Ohio, where the league that became the NFL was formed in 1920, was chosen as the site of the Pro Football Hall of Fame, April 27. Dick McCann, a former Redskins executive, was named executive director.

A bill legalizing single-network television contracts by professional sports leagues was introduced in Congress by Representative Emanuel Celler. It passed the House and Senate and was signed into law by President John F. Kennedy, September 30.

Houston defeated San Diego 10-3 for the AFL championship, December 24. Green Bay won its first NFL championship since 1944, defeating the New York Giants 37-0, December 31.

1962 The Western Division defeated the Eastern Division 47-27 in the first AFL All-Star Game, played before 20,973 in San Diego, January 7.

Both leagues prohibited grabbing any player's facemask. The AFL voted to make the scoreboard clock the official timer of the game.

The NFL entered into a single-network agreement with CBS for telecasting all regular-season games for $4,650,000 annually, January 10.

Judge Roszel Thompson of the U.S. District Court in Baltimore ruled against the AFL in its antitrust suit against the NFL, May 21. The AFL had charged the NFL with monopoly and conspiracy in areas of expansion, television, and player signings. The case lasted two and a half years, the trial two months.

McGah and Valley acquired controlling interest in the Raiders, May 24. The AFL assumed financial responsibility for the New York Titans, November 8. With Commissioner Rozelle as referee, Daniel F. Reeves regained the ownership of the Rams, outbidding his partners in sealed-envelope bidding for the team, November 27.

The Dallas Texans defeated the Oilers 20-17 for the AFL championship at Houston after 17 minutes, 54 seconds of overtime on a 25-yard field goal by Tommy Brooker, December 23. The game lasted a record 77 minutes, 54 seconds.

Judge Edward Weinfeld of the U.S. District Court in New York City upheld the legality of the NFL's television blackout within a 75-mile radius of home games and denied an injunction that would have forced the championship game between the Giants and the Packers to be televised in the New York City area, December 28. The Packers beat the Giants 16-7 for the NFL title, December 30.

1963 The Dallas Texans transferred to Kansas City, becoming the Chiefs, February 8. The New York Titans were sold to a five-man syndicate headed by David (Sonny) Werblin, March 28. Weeb Ewbank became the Titans' new head coach and the team's name was changed to the Jets, April 15. They began play in Shea Stadium.

NFL Properties, Inc., was founded to serve as the licensing arm of the NFL.

Rozelle indefinitely suspended Green Bay halfback Paul Hornung and Detroit defensive tackle Alex Karras for placing bets on their own teams and on other NFL games; he also fined five other Detroit players $2,000 each for betting on one game in which they did not participate, and the Detroit Lions Football Company $2,000 on each of two counts for failure to report information promptly and for lack of sideline supervision.

Paul Brown, head coach of the Browns since their inception, was fired and replaced by Blanton Collier. Don Shula replaced Weeb Ewbank as head coach of the Colts.

The AFL allowed the Jets and Raiders to select players from other franchises in hopes of giving the league more competitive balance, May 11.

NBC was awarded exclusive network broadcasting rights for the 1963 AFL Championship Game for $926,000, May 23.

The Pro Football Hall of Fame was dedicated at Canton, Ohio, September 7.

The U.S. Fourth Circuit Court of Appeals reaffirmed the lower court's finding for the NFL in the $10-million suit brought by the AFL, ending three and a half years of litigation, November 21.

Jim Brown of Cleveland rushed for an NFL single-season record 1,863 yards.

Boston defeated Buffalo 26-8 in the first divisional playoff game in AFL history, December 28. The Chargers defeated the Patriots in the AFL Championship Game, January 5.

The Bears defeated the Giants 14-10 in the NFL Championship Game, a record sixth and last title for Halas in his thirty-sixth season as the Bears' coach, December 29.

1964 The Chargers defeated the Patriots in the AFL Championship Game, January 5.

William Clay Ford, the Lions' president since 1961, purchased the team, January 10. A group representing the late James P. Clark sold the Eagles to a group headed by Jerry Wolman, January 21. Carroll Rosenbloom, the majority owner of the Colts since 1953, acquired complete ownership of the team, January 23.

CBS submitted the winning bid of $14.1 million per year for the NFL regular-season television rights for 1964 and 1965, January 24. CBS acquired the rights to the championship games for 1964 and 1965 for $1.8 million per game, April 17.

The AFL signed a five-year, $36-million television contract with NBC to begin with the 1965 season, assuring each team approximately $900,000 a year from television rights, January 29.

Hornung and Karras were reinstated by Rozelle, March 16.

Pete Gogolak of Cornell signed a contract with Buffalo, becoming the first soccer-style kicker in pro football.

Buffalo defeated San Diego 20-7 in the AFL Championship Game, December 26. Cleveland defeated Baltimore 27-0 in the NFL Championship Game, December 27.

1965 The NFL teams pledged not to sign college seniors until completion of all their games, including bowl games, and empowered the Commissioner to discipline the clubs up to as much as the loss of an entire draft list for a violation of the pledge, February 15.

The NFL added a sixth official, the line judge, February 19. The color of the officials' penalty flags was changed from white to bright gold, April 5.

Atlanta was awarded an NFL franchise for 1966, with Rankin Smith, Sr., as owner, June 30. Miami was awarded an AFL franchise for 1966, with Joe Robbie and Danny Thomas as owners, August 16.

Green Bay defeated Baltimore 13-10 in sudden-death overtime in a Western Conference playoff game. Don Chandler kicked a 25-yard field goal for the Packers after 13 minutes, 39 seconds of overtime, December 26. The Packers then defeated the Browns 23-12 in the NFL Championship Game, January 2.

In the AFL Championship Game, the Bills again defeated the Chargers, 23-0, December 26.

CBS acquired the rights to the NFL regular-season games in 1966 and 1967, with an option for 1968, for $18.8 million per year, December 29.

1966 The AFL-NFL war reached its peak, as the leagues spent a combined $7 million to sign their 1966 draft choices. The NFL signed 75 percent of its 232 draftees, the AFL 46 percent of its 181. Of the 111 common draft choices, 79 signed with the NFL, 28 with the AFL, and 4 went unsigned.

The rights to the 1966 and 1967 NFL Championship Games were sold to CBS for $2 million per game, February 14.

Foss resigned as AFL Commissioner, April 7. Al Davis, the head coach and general manager of the Raiders, was named to replace him, April 8.

Goal posts offset from the goal line, painted bright yellow, and with uprights 20 feet above the crossbar were made standard in the NFL, May 16.

A series of secret meetings regarding a possible AFL-NFL merger were held in the spring between Hunt of Kansas City and Tex Schramm of Dallas. Rozelle announced the merger, June 8. Under the agreement, the two leagues would combine to form an expanded league with 24 teams, to be increased to 26 to 1968 and to 28 by 1970 or soon thereafter. All existing franchises would be retained, and no franchises would be transferred outside their metropolitan areas. While maintaining separate schedules through 1969, the leagues agreed to play an annual AFL-NFL World Championship Game beginning in January, 1967, and to hold a combined draft, also beginning in 1967. Preseason games would be held between teams of each league starting in 1967. Official regular-season play would start in 1970 when the two leagues would officially merge to form one league with two conferences. Rozelle was named Commissioner of the expanded league setup.

Davis rejoined the Raiders, and Milt Woodard was named president of the AFL, July 25.

The St. Louis Cardinals moved into newly constructed Busch Memorial Stadium.

Barron Hilton sold the Chargers to a group headed by Eugene Klein and Sam Schulman, August 25.

Congress approved the AFL-NFL merger, passing legislation exempting the agreement itself from antitrust action, October 21.

New Orleans was awarded an NFL franchise to begin play in 1967, November 1. John Mecom, Jr., of Houston was designated majority stockholder and president of the franchise, December 15.

The NFL was realigned for the 1967-69 seasons into the Capitol and Century Divisions in the Eastern Conference and the Central and Coastal Divisions in the Western Conference, December 2. New Orleans and the New York Giants agreed to switch divisions in 1968 and return to the 1967 alignment in 1969.

The rights to the Super Bowl for four years were sold to CBS and NBC for $9.5 million, December 13.

1967 Green Bay earned the right to represent the NFL in the first AFL-NFL World Championship Game by defeating Dallas 34-27, January 1. The same day, Kansas City defeated Buffalo 31-7 to represent the AFL. The Packers defeated the Chiefs 35-10 before 61,946 fans at the Los Angeles Memorial Coliseum in the first game between AFL and NFL teams, January 15. The winning players' share for the Packers was $15,000 each, and the losing players' share for the Chiefs was $7,500 each. The game was televised by both CBS and NBC.

The "sling-shot" goal post and a six-foot-wide border around the field were made standard in the NFL, February 22.

Baltimore made Bubba Smith, a Michigan State defensive lineman, the first choice in the first combined AFL-NFL draft, March 14.

The AFL awarded a franchise to begin play in 1968 to Cincinnati, May 24. A group with Paul Brown as part owner, general manager, and head coach, was awarded the Cincinnati franchise, September 27.

Arthur B. Modell, the president of the Cleveland Browns, was elected president of the NFL, May 28.

An AFL team defeated an NFL team for the first time, when Denver beat Detroit 13-7 in a preseason game, August 5.

Green Bay defeated Dallas 21-17 for the NFL championship on a last-minute one-yard quarterback sneak by Bart Starr in 13-below-zero temperature at Green Bay, December 31. The same day, Oakland defeated Houston 40-7 for the AFL championship.

1968 Green Bay defeated Oakland 33-14 in Super Bowl II at Miami, January 14. The game had the first $3-million gate in pro football history.

Vince Lombardi resigned as head coach of the Packers, but remained as general manager, January 28.

Werblin sold his shares in the Jets to his partners Don Lillis, Leon Hess, Townsend Martin, and Phil Iselin, May 21. Lillis assumed the presidency of the club, but then died July 23. Iselin was appointed president, August 6.

Halas retired for the fourth and last time as head coach of the Bears, May 27.

The Oilers left Rice Stadium for the Astrodome and became the first NFL team to play its home games in a domed stadium.

The movie "Heidi" became a footnote in sports history when NBC didn't show the last 1:05 of the Jets-Raiders game in order to permit the children's special to begin on time. The Raiders scored two touchdowns in the last 42 seconds to win 43-32, November 17.

Ewbank became the first coach to win titles in both the NFL and AFL when his Jets defeated the Raiders 27-23 for the AFL championship, December 29. The same day, Baltimore defeated Cleveland 34-0.

1969 The AFL established a playoff format for the 1969 season, with the winner in one division playing the runner-up in the other, January 11.

An AFL team won the Super Bowl for the first time, as the Jets defeated the Colts 16-7 at Miami, January 12 in Super Bowl III. The title "Super Bowl" was recognized by the NFL for the first time.

Vince Lombardi became part owner, executive vice-president, and head coach of the Washington Redskins.

Wolman sold the Eagles to Leonard Tose, May 1.

Baltimore, Cleveland, and Pittsburgh agreed to join the AFL teams to form the 13-team American Football Conference of the NFL in 1970, May 17. The NFL also agreed on a playoff format that would include one "wild-card" team per conference—the second-place team with the best record.

Monday Night Football was signed for 1970. ABC acquired the rights to televise 13 NFL regular-season Monday night games in 1970, 1971, and 1972.

George Preston Marshall, president emeritus of the Redskins, died at 72, August 9.

The NFL marked its fiftieth year by the wearing of a special patch by each of the 16 teams.

1970 Kansas City defeated Minnesota 23-7 in Super Bowl IV at New Orleans, January 11. The gross receipts of approximately $3.8 million were the largest ever for a one-day sports event.

Four-year television contracts, under which CBS would televise all NFC games and NBC all AFC games (except Monday night games) and the two would divide televising the Super Bowl and AFC-NFC Pro Bowl games, were announced, January 26.

Art Modell resigned as president of the NFL, March 12. Milt Woodard resigned as president of the AFL, March 13. Lamar Hunt was elected president of the AFC and George Halas was elected president of the NFC, March 19.

The merged 26-team league adopted rules changes putting names on the backs of players' jerseys, making a point after touchdown worth only one point, and making the scoreboard clock the official timing device of the game, March 18.

The Players Negotiating Committee and the NFL Players Association announced a four-year agreement guaranteeing approximately $4,535,000 annually to player pension and insurance benefits, August 3. The owners also agreed to contribute $250,000 annually to improve or implement items such as disability payments, widows' benefits, maternity benefits, and dental benefits. The agreement also provided for increased preseason game and per diem payments, averaging approximately $2.6 million annually.

The Pittsburgh Steelers moved into Three Rivers Stadium. The Cincinnati Bengals moved to Riverfront Stadium.

Lombardi died of cancer at 57, September 3.

Tom Dempsey of New Orleans kicked a game-winning NFL-record 63-yard field goal against Detroit, November 8.

1971 Baltimore defeated Dallas 16-13 on Jim O'Brien's 32-yard field goal with five seconds to go in Super Bowl V at Miami, January 17. The NBC telecast was viewed in an estimated 23,980,000 homes, the largest audience ever for a one-day sports event.

The NFC defeated the AFC 27-6 in the first AFC-NFC Pro Bowl at Los Angeles, January 24.

The Boston Patriots changed their name to the New England Patriots, March 25. Their new stadium, Schaefer Stadium, was dedicated in a 20-14 preseason victory over the Giants.

The Philadelphia Eagles left Franklin Field and played their games at the new Veterans Stadium.

The San Francisco 49ers left Kezar Stadium and moved their games to Candlestick Park.

Daniel F. Reeves, the president and general manager of the Rams, died at 58, April 15.

The Dallas Cowboys moved from

the Cotton Bowl into their new home, Texas Stadium, October 24.

Miami defeated Kansas City 27-24 in sudden-death overtime in an AFC Divisional Playoff Game, December 25. Garo Yepremian kicked a 37-yard field goal for the Dolphins after 22 minutes, 40 seconds of overtime, as the game lasted 82 minutes, 40 seconds overall, making it the longest game in history.

1972 Dallas defeated Miami 24-3 in Super Bowl VI at New Orleans, January 16. The CBS telecast was viewed in an estimated 27,450,000 homes, the top-rated one-day telecast ever.

The inbounds lines or hashmarks were moved nearer the center of the field, 23 yards, 1 foot, 9 inches from the sidelines, March 23. The method of determining won-lost percentage in standings changed. Tie games, previously not counted in the standings, were made equal to a half-game won and a half-game lost, May 24.

Robert Irsay purchased the Los Angeles Rams and transferred ownership of the club to Carroll Rosenbloom in exchange for the Baltimore Colts, July 13.

William V. Bidwill purchased the stock of his brother Charles (Stormy) Bidwill to become the sole owner of the St. Louis Cardinals, September 2.

The National District Attorneys Association endorsed the position of professional leagues in opposing proposed legalization of gambling in professional team sports, September 28.

Franco Harris's "Immaculate Reception" gave the Steelers their first postseason win ever, 13-7 over the Raiders, December 23.

1973 Rozelle announced that all Super Bowl VII tickets were sold and that the game would be telecast in Los Angeles, the site of the game, on an experimental basis, January 3.

Miami defeated Washington 14-7 in Super Bowl VII at Los Angeles, completing a 17-0 season, the first perfect-record regular-season and postseason mark in NFL history, January 14. The NBC telecast was viewed by approximately 75 million people.

The AFC defeated the NFC 33-28 in the Pro Bowl in Dallas, the first time since 1942 that the game was played outside Los Angeles, January 21.

A jersey numbering system was adopted, April 5: 1-19 for quarterbacks and specialists, 20-49 for running backs and defensive backs, 50-59 for centers and linebackers, 60-79 for defensive linemen and interior offensive linemen other than centers, and 80-89 for wide receivers and tight ends. Players who had been in the NFL in 1972 could continue to use old numbers.

NFL Charities, a non-profit organization, was created to derive an income from monies generated from NFL Properties' licensing of NFL trademarks and team names, June 26. NFL Charities was set up to support education and charitable activities and to supply economic support to persons formerly associated with professional football who were no longer able to support themselves.

Congress adopted experimental legislation (for three years) requiring any NFL game that had been declared a sellout 72 hours prior to kickoff to be made available for local televising, September 14. The legislation provided for an annual review to be made by the Federal Communications Commission.

The Buffalo Bills moved their home games from War Memorial Stadium to Rich Stadium in nearby Orchard Park. The Giants tied the Eagles 23-23 in the final game in Yankee Stadium, September 23. The Giants played the rest of their home games at the Yale Bowl in New Haven, Connecticut.

A rival league, the World Football League, was formed and was reported in operation, October 2. It had plans to start play in 1974.

O.J. Simpson of Buffalo became the first player to rush for more than 2,000 yards in a season, gaining 2,003.

1974 Miami defeated Minnesota 24-7 in Super Bowl VIII at Houston, the second consecutive Super Bowl championship for the Dolphins, January 13. The CBS telecast was viewed by approximately 75 million people.

Rozelle was given a 10-year contract effective January 1, 1973, February 27.

Tampa Bay was awarded a franchise to begin operation in 1976, April 24.

Sweeping rules changes were adopted to add action and tempo to games: one sudden-death overtime period was added for preseason and regular-season games; the goal posts were moved from the goal line to the end lines; kickoffs were moved from the 40- to the 35-yard line; after missed field goals from beyond the 20, the ball was to be returned to the line of scrimmage; restrictions were placed on members of the punting team to open up return possibilities; roll-blocking and cutting of wide receivers was eliminated; the extent of downfield contact a defender could have with an eligible receiver was restricted; the penalties for offensive holding, illegal use of the hands, and tripping were reduced from 15 to 10 yards; wide receivers blocking back toward the ball within three yards of the line of scrimmage were prevented from blocking below the waist, April 25.

The Toronto Northmen of the WFL signed Larry Csonka, Jim Kiick, and Paul Warfield of Miami, March 31.

Seattle was awarded an NFL franchise to begin play in 1976, June 4. Lloyd W. Nordstrom, president of the Seattle Seahawks, and Hugh Culverhouse, president of the Tampa Bay Buccaneers, signed franchise agreements, December 5.

The Birmingham Americans defeated the Florida Blazers 22-21 in the WFL World Bowl, winning the league championship, December 5.

1975 Pittsburgh defeated Minnesota 16-6 in Super Bowl IX at New Orleans, the Steelers' first championship since entering the NFL in 1933. The NBC telecast was viewed by approximately 78 million people.

The divisional winners with the highest won-loss percentage were made the home team for the divisional playoffs, and the surviving winners with the highest percentage made home teams for the championship games, June 26.

Referees were equipped with wireless microphones for all preseason, regular-season, and playoff games.

The Lions moved to the new Pontiac Silverdome. The Giants played their home games in Shea Stadium. The Saints moved into the Louisiana Superdome.

The World Football League folded, October 22.

1976 Pittsburgh defeated Dallas 21-17 in Super Bowl X in Miami. The Steelers joined Green Bay and Miami as the only teams to win two Super Bowls; the Cowboys became the first wild-card team to play in the Super Bowl. The CBS telecast was viewed by an estimated 80 million people, the largest television audience in history.

Lloyd Nordstrom, the president of the Seahawks, died at 66, January 20. His brother Elmer succeeded him as majority representative of the team.

The owners awarded Super Bowl XII, to be played on January 15, 1978, to New Orleans. They also adopted the use of two 30-second clocks for all games, visible to both players and fans to note the official time between the ready-for-play signal and snap of the ball, March 16.

A veteran player allocation was held to stock the Seattle and Tampa Bay franchises with 39 players each, March 30-31. In the college draft, Seattle and Tampa Bay each received eight extra choices, April 8-9.

The Giants moved into new Giants Stadium in East Rutherford, New Jersey.

The Steelers defeated the College All-Stars in a storm-shortened Chicago College All-Star Game, the last of the series, July 23. St. Louis defeated San Diego 20-10 in a preseason game before 38,000 in Korakuen Stadium, Tokyo, in the first NFL game outside of North America, August 16.

1977 Oakland defeated Minnesota 32-14 before a record crowd of 100,421 in Super Bowl XI at Pasadena, January 9. The paid attendance was a pro record 103,438. The NBC telecast was viewed by 81.9 million people, the largest ever to view a sports event. The victory was the fifth consecutive for the AFC in the Super Bowl.

The NFL Players Association and the NFL Management Council ratified a collective bargaining agreement extending until 1982, covering five football seasons while continuing the pension plan—including years 1974, 1975, and 1976—with contributions totaling more than $55 million. The total cost of the agreement was estimated at $107 million. The agreement called for a college draft at least through 1986; contained a no-strike, no-suit clause; established a 43-man active player limit; reduced pension vesting to four years; provided for increases in minimum salaries and preseason and postseason pay; improved insurance, medical, and dental benefits; modified previous practices in player movement and control; and reaffirmed the NFL Commissioner's disciplinary authority. Additionally, the agreement called for the NFL member clubs to make payments totaling $16 million the next 10 years to settle various legal disputes, February 25.

The San Francisco 49ers were sold to Edward J. DeBartolo, Jr., March 28.

A 16-game regular season, 4-game preseason was adopted to begin in 1978, March 29. A second wild card team was adopted for the playoffs beginning in 1978, with the wild card teams to play each other and the winners advancing to a round of eight postseason series.

The Seahawks were permanently aligned in the AFC Western Division and the Buccaneers in the NFC Central Division, March 31.

The owners awarded Super Bowl XIII, to be played on January 21, 1979, to Miami to be played in the Orange Bowl; Super Bowl XIV, to be played January 20, 1980, was awarded to Pasadena, to be played in the Rose Bowl, June 14.

Rules changes were adopted to open up the passing game and to cut down on injuries. Defenders were permitted to make contact with eligible receivers only once; the head slap was outlawed; offensive linemen were prohibited from thrusting their hands to an opponent's neck, face, or head; and wide receivers were prohibited from clipping, even in the legal clipping zone.

Rozelle negotiated contracts with the three television networks to televise all NFL regular-season and postseason games, plus selected preseason games, for four years beginning with the 1978 season. ABC was awarded yearly rights to 16 Monday night games, four prime-time games, the AFC-NFC Pro Bowl, and the Hall of Fame games. CBS received the rights to all NFC regular-season and postseason games (except those in the ABC package) and to Super Bowls XIV and XVI. NBC received the rights to all AFC regular-season and postseason games (except those in the ABC package) and to Super Bowls XIII and XV. Industry sources considered it the largest single television package ever negotiated, October.

Chicago's Walter Payton set a single-game rushing record with 275 yards (40 carries) against Minnesota, November 20.

1978 Dallas defeated Denver 27-10 in Super Bowl XII, held indoors for the first time, at the Louisiana Superdome in New Orleans, January 15. The CBS telecast was viewed by more than 102 million people, meaning the game was watched by more viewers than any other show of any kind in the history of television. Dallas's victory was the first for the NFC in six years.

According to a Louis Harris Sports Survey, 70 percent of the nation's sports fans said they followed football, compared to 54 percent who followed baseball. Football increased its lead as the country's favorite, 26 percent to 16 percent for baseball, January 19.

A seventh official, the side judge, was added to the officiating crew, March 14.

The NFL continued a trend toward opening up the game. Rules changes permitted a defender to maintain contact with a receiver within five yards of the line of scrimmage, but restricted contact beyond that point. The pass-blocking rule was interpreted to permit the extending of arms and open hands, March 17.

A study on the use of instant replay as an officiating aid was made during seven nationally televised preseason games.

The NFL played for the first time in Mexico City, with the Saints defeating the Eagles 14-7 in a preseason game, August 5.

Bolstered by the expansion of the

regular-season schedule from 14 to 16 weeks, NFL paid attendance exceeded 12 million (12,771,800) for the first time. The per-game average of 57,017 was the third-highest in league history and the most since 1973.

1979 Pittsburgh defeated Dallas 35-31 in Super Bowl XIII at Miami to become the first team ever to win three Super Bowls, January 21. The NBC telecast was viewed in 35,090,000 homes, by an estimated 96.6 million fans.

The owners awarded three future Super Bowl sites: Super Bowl XV to the Louisiana Superdome in New Orleans, to be played on January 25, 1981; Super Bowl XVI to the Pontiac Silverdome in Pontiac, Michigan, to be played on January 24, 1982; and Super Bowl XVII to Pasadena's Rose Bowl, to be played on January 30, 1983, March 13.

NFL rules changes emphasized additional player safety. The changes prohibited players on the receiving team from blocking below the waist during kickoffs, punts, and field-goal attempts; prohibited the wearing of torn or altered equipment and exposed pads that could be hazardous; extended the zone in which there could be no crackback blocks; and instructed officials to quickly whistle a play dead when a quarterback was clearly in the grasp of a tackler, March 16.

Rosenbloom, the president of the Rams, drowned at 72, April 2. His widow, Georgia, assumed control of the club.

1980 Pittsburgh defeated the Los Angeles Rams 31-19 in Super Bowl XIV at Pasadena to become the first team to win four Super Bowls, January 20. The game was viewed in a record 35,330,000 homes.

The AFC-NFC Pro Bowl, won 37-27 by the NFC, was played before 48,060 fans at Aloha Stadium in Honolulu, Hawaii. It was the first time in the 30-year history of the Pro Bowl that the game was played in a non-NFL city.

Rules changes placed greater restrictions on contact in the area of the head, neck, and face. Under the heading of "personal foul," players were prohibited from directly striking, swinging, or clubbing on the head, neck, or face. Starting in 1980, a penalty could be called for such contact whether or not the initial contact was made below the neck area.

CBS, with a record bid of $12 million, won the national radio rights to 26 NFL regular-season games and all 10 postseason games for the 1980-83 seasons.

The Los Angeles Rams moved their home games to Anaheim Stadium in nearby Orange County, California.

The Oakland Raiders joined the Los Angeles Coliseum Commission's antitrust suit against the NFL. The suit contended the league violated antitrust laws in declining to approve a proposed move by the Raiders from Oakland to Los Angeles.

NFL regular-season attendance of nearly 13.4 million set a record for the third year in a row. The average paid attendance for the 224-game 1980 regular season was 59,787, the highest in the league's 61-year history. NFL games in 1980 were played before 92.4 percent of total stadium capacity.

Television ratings in 1980 were the second-best in NFL history, trailing only the combined ratings of the 1976 season. All three networks posted gains, and NBC's 15.0 rating was its best ever. CBS and ABC had their best ratings since 1977, with 15.3 and 20.8 ratings, respectively. CBS Radio reported a record audience of 7 million for Monday night and special games.

1981 Oakland defeated Philadelphia 27-10 in Super Bowl XV at the Louisiana Superdome in New Orleans, to become the first wild card team to win a Super Bowl, January 25.

Edgar F. Kaiser, Jr., purchased the Denver Broncos from Gerald and Allan Phipps, February 26.

The owners adopted a disaster plan for re-stocking a team should the club be involved in a fatal accident, March 20.

The owners awarded Super Bowl XVIII to Tampa to be played in Tampa Stadium on January 22, 1984, June 3.

A CBS-New York Times poll showed that 48 percent of sports fans preferred football to 31 percent for baseball.

The NFL teams hosted 167 representatives from 44 predominantly black colleges during training camps for a total of 289 days. The program was adopted for renewal during each training camp period.

NFL regular-season attendance—13.6 million for an average of 60,745—set a record for the fourth year in a row. It also was the first time the per-game average exceeded 60,000. NFL games in 1981 were played before 93.8 percent of total stadium capacity.

ABC and CBS set all-time rating highs. ABC finished with a 21.7 rating and CBS with a 17.5 rating. NBC was down slightly to 13.9.

1982 San Francisco defeated Cincinnati 26-21 in Super Bowl XVI at the Pontiac Silverdome, in the first Super Bowl held in the North, January 24. The CBS telecast achieved the highest rating of any televised sports event ever, 49.1 with a 73.0 share. The game was viewed by a record 110.2 million fans. CBS Radio reported a record 14 million listeners for the game.

The NFL signed a five-year contract with the three television networks (ABC, CBS, and NBC) to televise all NFL regular-season and postseason games starting with the 1982 season.

The owners awarded the 1983, 1984, and 1985 AFC-NFC Pro Bowls to Honolulu's Aloha Stadium.

A jury ruled against the NFL in the antitrust trial brought by the Los Angeles Coliseum Commission and the Oakland Raiders, May 7. The verdict cleared the way for the Raiders to move to Los Angeles, where they defeated Green Bay 24-3 in their first preseason game, August 29.

The 1982 season was reduced from a 16-game schedule to 9 as the result of a 57-day players' strike. The strike was called by the NFLPA at 12:00 midnight on Monday, September 20, following the Green Bay at New York Giants game. Play resumed November 21-22 following ratification of the Collective Bargaining Agreement by NFL owners, November 17 in New York.

Under the Collective Bargaining Agreement, which was to run through the 1986 season, the NFL draft was extended through 1992 and the veteran free-agent system was left basically unchanged. A minimum salary schedule for years of experience was established; training camp and postseason pay were increased; players' medical, insurance, and retirement benefits were increased; and a severance-pay system was introduced to aid in career transition, a first in professional sports.

Despite the players' strike, the average paid attendance in 1982 was 58,472, the fifth-highest in league history.

The owners awarded the sites of two Super Bowls, December 14: Super Bowl XIX, to be played on January 25, 1985, to Stanford University Stadium in Palo Alto, California, with San Francisco as host owner; and Super Bowl XX, to be played on January 26, 1986, to the Louisiana Superdome in New Orleans.

1983 Because of the shortened season, the NFL adopted a format of 16 teams competing in a Super Bowl Tournament for the 1982 playoffs. The NFC's number-one seed, Washington, defeated the AFC's number-two seed, Miami, 27-17 in Super Bowl XVII at the Rose Bowl in Pasadena, January 30. The Redskins' victory marked only the second time the NFC had won consecutive Super Bowls.

Super Bowl XVII was the second-highest rated live television program of all time, giving the NFL a sweep of the top 10 live programs in television history. The game was viewed in more than 40 million homes, the largest ever for a live telecast.

Halas, the owner of the Bears and the last surviving member of the NFL's second organizational meeting, died at 88, October 31.

1984 The Los Angeles Raiders defeated Washington 38-9 in Super Bowl XVIII at Tampa Stadium, January 22. The game achieved a 46.4 rating and 71.0 share.

An 11-man group headed by H.R. (Bum) Bright purchased the Dallas Cowboys from Clint Murchison, Jr., March 20. Club president Tex Schramm was designated as managing general partner.

Patrick Bowlen purchased a majority interest in the Denver Broncos from Edgar Kaiser, Jr., March 21.

The Colts relocated to Indianapolis, March 28. Their new home became the Hoosier Dome.

The owners awarded two Super Bowl sites at their May 23-25 meetings: Super Bowl XXI, to be played on January 25, 1987, to the Rose Bowl in Pasadena; and Super Bowl XXII, to be played on January 31, 1988, to San Diego Jack Murphy Stadium.

The New York Jets moved their home games to Giants Stadium in East Rutherford, New Jersey.

Alex G. Spanos purchased a majority interest in the San Diego Chargers from Eugene V. Klein, August 28.

Houston defeated Pittsburgh 23-20 to mark the one-hundredth overtime game in regular-season play since overtime was adopted in 1974, December 2.

On the field, many all-time records were set: Dan Marino of Miami passed for 5,084 yards and 48 touchdowns; Eric Dickerson of the Los Angeles Rams rushed for 2,105 yards; Art Monk of Washington caught 106 passes; and Walter Payton of Chicago broke Jim Brown's career rushing mark, finishing the season with 13,309 yards.

According to a CBS Sports/New York Times survey, 53 percent of the nation's sports fans said they most enjoyed watching football, compared to 18 percent for baseball, December 2-4.

NFL paid attendance exceeded 13 million for the fifth consecutive complete regular season when 13,398,112, an average of 59,813, attended games. The figure was the second-highest in league history. Teams averaged 42.4 points per game, the second-highest total since the 1970 merger.

1985 San Francisco defeated Miami 38-16 in Super Bowl XIX at Stanford Stadium in Palo Alto, California, January 20. The game was viewed on television by more people than any other live event in history. President Ronald Reagan, who took his second oath of office before tossing the coin for the game, was one of 115,936,000 viewers. The game drew a 46.4 rating and a 63.0 share. In addition, 6 million people watched the Super Bowl in the United Kingdom and a similar number in Italy. Super Bowl XIX had a direct economic impact of $113.5 million on the San Francisco Bay area.

NBC Radio and the NFL entered into a two-year agreement granting NBC the radio rights to a 37-game package in each of the 1985-86 seasons, March 6. The package included 27 regular-season games and 10 postseason games.

The owners awarded two Super Bowl sites at their annual meeting, March 10-15: Super Bowl XXIII, to be played on January 22, 1989, to the proposed Dolphins Stadium in Miami; and Super Bowl XXIV, to be played on January 28, 1990, to the Louisiana Superdome in New Orleans.

Norman Braman, in partnership with Edward Leibowitz, bought the Philadelphia Eagles from Leonard Tose, April 29.

Bruce Smith, a Virginia Tech defensive lineman selected by Buffalo, was the first player chosen in the fiftieth NFL draft, April 30.

A group headed by Tom Benson, Jr., was approved to purchase the New Orleans Saints from John W. Mecom, Jr., June 3.

The NFL owners adopted a resolution calling for a series of overseas preseason games, beginning in 1986, with one game to be played in England/Europe and/or one game in Japan each year. The game would be a fifth preseason game for the clubs involved and all arrangements and selection of the clubs would be under the control of the Commissioner, May 23.

The league-wide conversion to videotape from movie film for coaching study was approved.

Commissioner Rozelle was authorized to extend the commitment to Honolulu's Aloha Stadium for the AFC-NFC Pro Bowl for 1988, 1989, and 1990, October 15.

The NFL set a single-weekend paid attendance record when 902,657 tickets were sold for the weekend of October 27-28.

A Louis Harris poll in December revealed that pro football remained the sport most followed by Americans. Fifty-nine percent of those surveyed followed pro football, compared with 54 percent who followed baseball.

The Chicago-Miami Monday game had the highest rating, 29.6, and share, 46.0, of any prime-time game in NFL history, December 2. The game was viewed in more than 25 million homes.

The NFL showed a ratings increase on all three networks for the season, gaining 4 percent on NBC, 10 on CBS, and 16 on ABC.

1986 Chicago defeated New England 46-10 in Super Bowl XX at the Louisiana Superdome, January 26. The Patriots had earned the right to play the Bears by becoming the first wild card team to win three consecutive games on the road. The NBC telecast replaced the final episode of M*A*S*H as the most-viewed television program in history, with an audience of 127 million viewers, according to A.C. Nielsen figures. In addition to drawing a 48.3 rating and a 70 percent share in the United States, Super Bowl XX was televised to 59 foreign countries and beamed via satellite to the QE II. An estimated 300 million Chinese viewed a tape delay of the game in March. NBC Radio figures indicated an audience of 10 million for the game.

Super Bowl XX injected more than $100 million into the New Orleans-area economy, and fans spent $250 per day and a record $17.69 per person on game day.

The owners adopted limited use of instant replay as an officiating aid, prohibited players from wearing or otherwise displaying equipment, apparel, or other items that carry commercial names, names of organizations, or personal messages of any type, March 11.

After an 11-week trial, a jury in U.S. District Court in New York awarded the United States Football League one dollar in its $1.7 billion anti-trust suit against the NFL. The jury rejected all of the USFL's television-related claims, which were the self-proclaimed "heart" of the USFL's case, July 29.

Chicago defeated Dallas 17-6 at Wembley Stadium in London in the first American Bowl. The game drew a sellout crowd of 82,699 and the NBC national telecast in this country produced a 12.4 rating and 36 percent share, making it the second-highest-rated daytime preseason game and highest daytime preseason television audience ever, 10,650,000 viewers, August 3.

Monday Night Football became the longest-running prime-time series in the history of the ABC network.

Instant replay was used to reverse two plays in 31 preseason games. During the regular season, 374 plays were closely reviewed by replay officials, leading to 38 reversals in 224 games. Eighteen plays were closely reviewed by instant replay in 10 postseason games with three reversals.

1987 The New York Giants defeated Denver 39-20 in Super Bowl XXI and captured their first NFL title since 1956. The game, played in Pasadena's Rose Bowl, drew a sellout crowd of 101,063. According to A.C. Nielsen figures, the CBS broadcast of the game was viewed in the U.S. on television by 122,640,000 people, making the telecast the second most watched television show of all-time behind Super Bowl XX. The game was watched live or on tape in 55 foreign countries and NBC Radio's broadcast of the game was heard by a record 10.1 million people.

The NFL set an all-time paid attendance mark of 17,304,463 for all games, including preseason, regular-season, and postseason. Average regular-season game attendance (60,663) exceeded the 60,000 figure for only the second time in league history.

New three-year TV contracts with ABC, CBS, and NBC were announced for 1987-89 at the NFL annual meeting in Maui, Hawaii, March 15. Commissioner Rozelle and Broadcast Committee Chairman Art Modell also announced a three-year contract with ESPN to televise a mini-series of 13 prime-time games. The ESPN contract was the first with a cable network. However, NFL games on ESPN also will be carried on regular television in the city of the visiting team and in the home city if the game is sold out 72 hours in advance.

Owners also voted to continue in effect for one year the instant replay system used during the 1986 season.

Possible sites for Super Bowl XXV were reduced to five locations by the NFL Super Bowl XXV Site Selection Committee: Anaheim Stadium, Los Angeles Memorial Coliseum, Joe Robbie Stadium, San Diego Jack Murphy Stadium, and Tampa Stadium.

NFL and CBS Radio jointly announced agreement granting CBS the radio rights to a 40-game package in each of the next three NFL seasons, 1987-89, April 7.

NFL owners awarded SBXXV, to be played on January 27, 1991, to Tampa Stadium, May 20.

NFL COMMISSIONERS AND PRESIDENTS

1920 . . . . Jim Thorpe, President
1921-39. . . . . Joe Carr, President
1939-41 . . . . . Carl Storck, President
1941-46 . . . . Elmer Layden, Commissioner
1946-59 . . . Bert Bell, Commissioner
1959-60. . . Austin Gunsel, President in the office of the Commissioner
1960-present. . . . . Pete Rozelle, Commissioner

1986

American Conference

Eastern Division

	W	L	T	Pct.	Pts.	OP
New England	11	5	0	.688	412	307
N.Y. Jets*	10	6	0	.625	364	386
Miami	8	8	0	.500	430	405
Buffalo	4	12	0	.250	287	348
Indianapolis	3	13	0	.188	229	400

Central Division

	W	L	T	Pct.	Pts.	OP
Cleveland	12	4	0	.750	391	310
Cincinnati	10	6	0	.625	409	394
Pittsburgh	6	10	0	.375	307	336
Houston	5	11	0	.313	274	329

Western Division

	W	L	T	Pct.	Pts.	OP
Denver	11	5	0	.688	378	327
Kansas City*	10	6	0	.625	358	326
Seattle	10	6	0	.625	366	293
L.A. Raiders	8	8	0	.500	323	346
San Diego	4	12	0	.250	335	396

National Conference

Eastern Division

	W	L	T	Pct.	Pts.	OP
N.Y. Giants	14	2	0	.875	371	236
Washington*	12	4	0	.750	368	296
Dallas	7	9	0	.438	346	337
Philadelphia	5	10	1	.344	256	312
St. Louis	4	11	1	.281	218	351

Central Division

	W	L	T	Pct.	Pts.	OP
Chicago	14	2	0	.875	352	187
Minnesota	9	7	0	.563	398	273
Detroit	5	11	0	.313	277	326
Green Bay	4	12	0	.250	254	418
Tampa Bay	2	14	0	.125	239	473

Western Division

	W	L	T	Pct.	Pts.	OP
San Francisco	10	5	1	.656	374	247
L.A. Rams*	10	6	0	.625	309	267
Atlanta	7	8	1	.469	280	280
New Orleans	7	9	0	.438	288	287

**Wild Card qualifiers for playoffs*

New York Jets gained first AFC Wild Card position on better conference record (8-4) over Kansas City (9-5), Seattle (7-5), and Cincinnati (7-5). Kansas City gained second Wild Card based on better conference record (9-5) over Seattle (7-5) and Cincinnati (7-5).

First round playoff: NEW YORK JETS 35, Kansas City 15
Divisional playoffs: CLEVELAND 23, New York Jets 20 (OT)
DENVER 22, New England 17
AFC championship: Denver 23, CLEVELAND 20 (OT)
First round playoff: WASHINGTON 19, Los Angeles Rams 7
Divisional playoffs: Washington 27, CHICAGO 13
NEW YORK GIANTS 49, San Francisco 3
NFC championship: NEW YORK GIANTS 17, Washington 0
Super Bowl XXI: New York Giants (NFC) 39, Denver (AFC) 20, at Rose Bowl, Pasadena, Calif.

In the Past Standings section, home teams in playoff games are indicated by capital letters.

1985

American Conference

Eastern Division

	W	L	T	Pct.	Pts.	OP
Miami	12	4	0	.750	428	320
N.Y. Jets*	11	5	0	.688	393	264
New England*	11	5	0	.688	362	290
Indianapolis	5	11	0	.313	320	386
Buffalo	2	14	0	.125	200	381

Central Division

	W	L	T	Pct.	Pts.	OP
Cleveland	8	8	0	.500	287	294
Cincinnati	7	9	0	.438	441	437
Pittsburgh	7	9	0	.438	379	355
Houston	5	11	0	.313	284	412

Western Division

	W	L	T	Pct.	Pts.	OP
L.A. Raiders	12	4	0	.750	354	308
Denver	11	5	0	.688	380	329
Seattle	8	8	0	.500	349	303
San Diego	8	8	0	.500	467	435
Kansas City	6	10	0	.375	317	360

National Conference

Eastern Division

	W	L	T	Pct.	Pts.	OP
Dallas	10	6	0	.625	357	333
N.Y. Giants*	10	6	0	.625	399	283
Washington	10	6	0	.625	297	312
Philadelphia	7	9	0	.438	286	310
St. Louis	5	11	0	.313	278	414

Central Division

	W	L	T	Pct.	Pts.	OP
Chicago	15	1	0	.938	456	198
Green Bay	8	8	0	.500	337	355
Minnesota	7	9	0	.438	346	359
Detroit	7	9	0	.438	307	366
Tampa Bay	2	14	0	.125	294	448

Western Division

	W	L	T	Pct.	Pts.	OP
L.A. Rams	11	5	0	.688	340	277
San Francisco*	10	6	0	.625	411	263
New Orleans	5	11	0	.313	294	401
Atlanta	4	12	0	.250	282	452

**Wild Card qualifiers for playoffs*

New York Jets gained first AFC Wild Card position on better conference record (9-3) over New England (8-4) and Denver (8-4). New England gained second AFC Wild Card position based on better record vs. common opponents (4-2) than Denver (3-3). Dallas won NFC Eastern Division title based on better record (3-1) vs. New York Giants (1-3) and Washington (1-3). New York Giants gained first NFC Wild Card position based on better conference record (8-4) over San Francisco (7-5) and Washington (6-6). San Francisco gained second NFC Wild Card position based on head-to-head victory over Washington.

First round playoff: New England 26, NEW YORK JETS 14
Divisional playoffs: MIAMI 24, Cleveland 21;
New England 27, LOS ANGELES RAIDERS 20
AFC championship: New England 31, MIAMI 14
First round playoff: NEW YORK GIANTS 17, San Francisco 3
Divisional playoffs: LOS ANGELES RAMS 20, Dallas 0;
CHICAGO 21, New York Giants 0
NFC championship: CHICAGO 24, Los Angeles Rams 0
Super Bowl XX: Chicago (NFC) 46, New England (AFC) 10, at Louisiana Superdome, New Orleans, La.

1984

American Conference

Eastern Division

	W	L	T	Pct.	Pts.	OP
Miami	14	2	0	.875	513	298
New England	9	7	0	.563	362	352
N.Y. Jets	7	9	0	.438	332	364
Indianapolis	4	12	0	.250	239	414
Buffalo	2	14	0	.125	250	454

Central Division

	W	L	T	Pct.	Pts.	OP
Pittsburgh	9	7	0	.563	387	310
Cincinnati	8	8	0	.500	339	339
Cleveland	5	11	0	.313	250	297
Houston	3	13	0	.188	240	437

Western Division

	W	L	T	Pct.	Pts.	OP
Denver	13	3	0	.813	353	241
Seattle*	12	4	0	.750	418	282
L.A. Raiders*	11	5	0	.688	368	278
Kansas City	8	8	0	.500	314	324
San Diego	7	9	0	.438	394	413

National Conference

Eastern Division

	W	L	T	Pct.	Pts.	OP
Washington	11	5	0	.688	426	310
N.Y. Giants*	9	7	0	.563	299	301
St. Louis	9	7	0	.563	423	345
Dallas	9	7	0	.563	308	308
Philadelphia	6	9	1	.406	278	320

Central Division

	W	L	T	Pct.	Pts.	OP
Chicago	10	6	0	.625	325	248
Green Bay	8	8	0	.500	390	309
Tampa Bay	6	10	0	.375	335	380
Detroit	4	11	1	.281	283	408
Minnesota	3	13	0	.188	276	484

Western Division

	W	L	T	Pct.	Pts.	OP
San Francisco	15	1	0	.938	475	227
L.A. Rams*	10	6	0	.625	346	316
New Orleans	7	9	0	.438	298	361
Atlanta	4	12	0	.250	281	382

**Wild Card qualifiers for playoffs*

New York Giants clinched Wild Card berth based on 3-1 record vs. St. Louis's 2-2 and Dallas's 1-3. St. Louis finished ahead of Dallas based on better division record (5-3 to 3-5).

First round playoff: SEATTLE 13, Los Angeles Raiders 7
Divisional playoffs: MIAMI 31, Seattle 10; Pittsburgh 24, DENVER 17
AFC championship: MIAMI 45, Pittsburgh 28
First round playoff: New York Giants 16, LOS ANGELES RAMS 13
Divisional playoffs: SAN FRANCISCO 21, New York Giants 10;
Chicago 23, WASHINGTON 19
NFC championship: SAN FRANCISCO 23, Chicago 0
Super Bowl XIX: San Francisco (NFC) 38, Miami (AFC) 16, at Stanford Stadium, Stanford, Calif.

1983

American Conference

Eastern Division

	W	L	T	Pct.	Pts.	OP
Miami	12	4	0	.750	389	250
New England	8	8	0	.500	274	289
Buffalo	8	8	0	.500	283	351
Baltimore	7	9	0	.438	264	354
N.Y. Jets	7	9	0	.438	313	331

Central Division

	W	L	T	Pct.	Pts.	OP
Pittsburgh	10	6	0	.625	355	303
Cleveland	9	7	0	.563	356	342
Cincinnati	7	9	0	.438	346	302
Houston	2	14	0	.125	288	460

Western Division

	W	L	T	Pct.	Pts.	OP
L.A. Raiders	12	4	0	.750	442	338
Seattle*	9	7	0	.563	403	397
Denver*	9	7	0	.563	302	327
San Diego	6	10	0	.375	358	462
Kansas City	6	10	0	.375	386	367

National Conference

Eastern Division

	W	L	T	Pct.	Pts.	OP
Washington	14	2	0	.875	541	332
Dallas*	12	4	0	.750	479	360
St. Louis	8	7	1	.531	374	428
Philadelphia	5	11	0	.313	233	322
N.Y. Giants	3	12	1	.219	267	347

Central Division

	W	L	T	Pct.	Pts.	OP
Detroit	9	7	0	.563	347	286
Green Bay	8	8	0	.500	429	439
Chicago	8	8	0	.500	311	301
Minnesota	8	8	0	.500	316	348
Tampa Bay	2	14	0	.125	241	380

Western Division

	W	L	T	Pct.	Pts.	OP
San Francisco	10	6	0	.625	432	293
L.A. Rams*	9	7	0	.563	361	344
New Orleans	8	8	0	.500	319	337
Atlanta	7	9	0	.438	370	389

**Wild Card qualifiers for playoffs*

Seattle and Denver gained Wild Card berths over Cleveland because of their victories over the Browns.

First round playoff: SEATTLE 31, Denver 7
Divisional playoffs: Seattle 27, MIAMI 20; LOS ANGELES RAIDERS 38, Pittsburgh 10
AFC championship: LOS ANGELES RAIDERS 30, Seattle 14
First round playoff: Los Angeles Rams 24, DALLAS 17
Divisional playoffs: SAN FRANCISCO 24, Detroit 23; WASHINGTON 51, L.A. Rams 7
NFC championship: WASHINGTON 24, San Francisco 21
Super Bowl XVIII: Los Angeles Raiders (AFC) 38, Washington (NFC) 9, at Tampa Stadium, Tampa, Fla.

1982

American Conference

	W	L	T	Pct.	Pts.	OP
L.A. Raiders	8	1	0	.889	260	200
Miami	7	2	0	.778	198	131
Cincinnati	7	2	0	.778	232	177
Pittsburgh	6	3	0	.667	204	146
San Diego	6	3	0	.667	288	221
N.Y. Jets	6	3	0	.667	245	166
New England	5	4	0	.556	143	157
Cleveland	4	5	0	.444	140	182
Buffalo	4	5	0	.444	150	154
Seattle	4	5	0	.444	127	147
Kansas City	3	6	0	.333	176	184
Denver	2	7	0	.222	148	226
Houston	1	8	0	.111	136	245
Baltimore	0	8	1	.056	113	236

National Conference

	W	L	T	Pct.	Pts.	OP
Washington	8	1	0	.889	190	128
Dallas	6	3	0	.667	226	145
Green Bay	5	3	1	.611	226	169
Minnesota	5	4	0	.556	187	198
Atlanta	5	4	0	.556	183	199
St. Louis	5	4	0	.556	135	170
Tampa Bay	5	4	0	.556	158	178
Detroit	4	5	0	.444	181	176
New Orleans	4	5	0	.444	129	160
N.Y. Giants	4	5	0	.444	164	160
San Francisco	3	6	0	.333	209	206
Chicago	3	6	0	.333	141	174
Philadelphia	3	6	0	.333	191	195
L.A. Rams	2	7	0	.222	200	250

As the result of a 57-day players' strike, the 1982 NFL regular season schedule was reduced from 16 weeks to 9. At the conclusion of the regular season, the NFL conducted a 16-team postseason Super Bowl Tournament. Eight teams from each conference were seeded 1-8 based on their records during the season.

Miami finished ahead of Cincinnati based on better conference record (6-1 to 6-2). Pittsburgh won common games tie-breaker with San Diego (3-1 to 2-1) after New York Jets were eliminated from three-way tie based on conference record (Pittsburgh and San Diego 5-3 vs. Jets 2-3). Cleveland finished ahead of Buffalo and Seattle based on better conference record (4-3 to 3-3 to 3-5). Minnesota (4-1), Atlanta (4-3), St. Louis (5-4), Tampa Bay (3-3) seeds were determined by best won-lost record in conference games. Detroit finished ahead of New Orleans and the New York Giants based on better conference record (4-4 to 3-5 to 3-5).

First round playoff: MIAMI 28, New England 13
LOS ANGELES RAIDERS 27, Cleveland 10
New York Jets 44, CINCINNATI 17
San Diego 31, PITTSBURGH 28
Second round playoff: New York Jets 17, LOS ANGELES RAIDERS 14
MIAMI 34, San Diego 13
AFC championship: MIAMI 14, New York Jets 0
First round playoff: WASHINGTON 31, Detroit 7
GREEN BAY 41, St. Louis 16
MINNESOTA 30, Atlanta 24
DALLAS 30, Tampa Bay 17
Second round playoff: WASHINGTON 21, Minnesota 7
DALLAS 37, Green Bay 26
NFC championship: WASHINGTON 31, Dallas 17
Super Bowl XVII: Washington (NFC) 27, Miami (AFC) 17, at Rose Bowl, Pasadena, Calif.

1981

American Conference

Eastern Division

	W	L	T	Pct.	Pts.	OP
Miami	11	4	1	.719	345	275
N.Y. Jets*	10	5	1	.656	355	287
Buffalo*	10	6	0	.625	311	276
Baltimore	2	14	0	.125	259	533
New England	2	14	0	.125	322	370

Central Division

	W	L	T	Pct.	Pts.	OP
Cincinnati	12	4	0	.750	421	304
Pittsburgh	8	8	0	.500	356	297
Houston	7	9	0	.438	281	355
Cleveland	5	11	0	.313	276	375

Western Division

	W	L	T	Pct.	Pts.	OP
San Diego	10	6	0	.625	478	390
Denver	10	6	0	.625	321	289
Kansas City	9	7	0	.563	343	290
Oakland	7	9	0	.438	273	343
Seattle	6	10	0	.375	322	388

National Conference

Eastern Division

	W	L	T	Pct.	Pts.	OP
Dallas	12	4	0	.750	367	277
Philadelphia*	10	6	0	.625	368	221
N.Y. Giants*	9	7	0	.563	295	257
Washington	8	8	0	.500	347	349
St. Louis	7	9	0	.438	315	408

Central Division

	W	L	T	Pct.	Pts.	OP
Tampa Bay	9	7	0	.563	315	268
Detroit	8	8	0	.500	397	322
Green Bay	8	8	0	.500	324	361
Minnesota	7	9	0	.438	325	369
Chicago	6	10	0	.375	253	324

Western Division

	W	L	T	Pct.	Pts.	OP
San Francisco	13	3	0	.813	357	250
Atlanta	7	9	0	.438	426	355
Los Angeles	6	10	0	.375	303	351
New Orleans	4	12	0	.250	207	378

**Wild Card qualifiers for playoffs*

San Diego won AFC Western title over Denver on the basis of a better division record (6-2 to 5-3). Buffalo won a Wild Card playoff berth over Denver as the result of a 9-7 victory in head-to-head competition.

First round playoff: Buffalo 31, NEW YORK JETS 27
Divisional playoffs: San Diego 41, MIAMI 38, sudden death overtime; CINCINNATI 28, Buffalo 21
AFC championship: CINCINNATI 27, San Diego 7
First round playoff: New York Giants 27, PHILADELPHIA 21
Divisional playoffs: DALLAS 38, Tampa Bay 0; SAN FRANCISCO 38, New York Giants 24
NFC championship: SAN FRANCISCO 28, Dallas 27
Super Bowl XVI: San Francisco (NFC) 26, Cincinnati (AFC) 21, at Silverdome, Pontiac, Mich.

1980

American Conference

Eastern Division

	W	L	T	Pct.	Pts.	OP
Buffalo	11	5	0	.688	320	260
New England	10	6	0	.625	441	325
Miami	8	8	0	.500	266	305
Baltimore	7	9	0	.438	355	387
N.Y. Jets	4	12	0	.250	302	395

Central Division

	W	L	T	Pct.	Pts.	OP
Cleveland	11	5	0	.688	357	310
Houston*	11	5	0	.688	295	251
Pittsburgh	9	7	0	.563	352	313
Cincinnati	6	10	0	.375	244	312

Western Division

	W	L	T	Pct.	Pts.	OP
San Diego	11	5	0	.688	418	327
Oakland*	11	5	0	.688	364	306
Kansas City	8	8	0	.500	319	336
Denver	8	8	0	.500	310	323
Seattle	4	12	0	.250	291	408

National Conference

Eastern Division

	W	L	T	Pct.	Pts.	OP
Philadelphia	12	4	0	.750	384	222
Dallas*	12	4	0	.750	454	311
Washington	6	10	0	.375	261	293
St. Louis	5	11	0	.313	299	350
N.Y. Giants	4	12	0	.250	249	425

Central Division

	W	L	T	Pct.	Pts.	OP
Minnesota	9	7	0	.563	317	308
Detroit	9	7	0	.563	334	272
Chicago	7	9	0	.438	304	264
Tampa Bay	5	10	1	.344	271	341
Green Bay	5	10	1	.344	231	371

Western Division

	W	L	T	Pct.	Pts.	OP
Atlanta	12	4	0	.750	405	272
Los Angeles*	11	5	0	.688	424	289
San Francisco	6	10	0	.375	320	415
New Orleans	1	15	0	.063	291	487

**Wild Card qualifiers for playoffs*

Philadelphia won division title over Dallas on the basis of best net points in division games (plus 84 net points to plus 50). Minnesota won division title because of a better conference record than Detroit (8-4 to 9-5). Cleveland won division title because of a better conference record than Houston (8-4 to 7-5). San Diego won division title over Oakland on the basis of best net points in division games (plus 60 net points to plus 37).

First round playoff: OAKLAND 27, Houston 7
Divisional playoffs: SAN DIEGO 20, Buffalo 14; Oakland 14, CLEVELAND 12
AFC championship: Oakland 34, SAN DIEGO 27
First round playoff: DALLAS 34, Los Angeles 13
Divisional playoffs: PHILADELPHIA 31, Minnesota 16; Dallas 30, ATLANTA 27
NFC championship: PHILADELPHIA 20, Dallas 7
Super Bowl XV: Oakland (AFC) 27, Philadelphia (NFC) 10, at Louisiana Superdome, New Orleans, La.

1979

American Conference

Eastern Division

	W	L	T	Pct.	Pts.	OP
Miami	10	6	0	.625	341	257
New England	9	7	0	.563	411	326
N.Y. Jets	8	8	0	.500	337	383
Buffalo	7	9	0	.438	268	279
Baltimore	5	11	0	.313	271	351

Central Division

	W	L	T	Pct.	Pts.	OP
Pittsburgh	12	4	0	.750	416	262
Houston*	11	5	0	.688	362	331
Cleveland	9	7	0	.563	359	352
Cincinnati	4	12	0	.250	337	421

Western Division

	W	L	T	Pct.	Pts.	OP
San Diego	12	4	0	.750	411	246
Denver*	10	6	0	.625	289	262
Seattle	9	7	0	.563	378	372
Oakland	9	7	0	.563	365	337
Kansas City	7	9	0	.438	238	262

National Conference

Eastern Division

	W	L	T	Pct.	Pts.	OP
Dallas	11	5	0	.688	371	313
Philadelphia*	11	5	0	.688	339	282
Washington	10	6	0	.625	348	295
N.Y. Giants	6	10	0	.375	237	323
St. Louis	5	11	0	.313	307	358

Central Division

	W	L	T	Pct.	Pts.	OP
Tampa Bay	10	6	0	.625	273	237
Chicago*	10	6	0	.625	306	249
Minnesota	7	9	0	.438	259	337
Green Bay	5	11	0	.313	246	316
Detroit	2	14	0	.125	219	365

Western Division

	W	L	T	Pct.	Pts.	OP
Los Angeles	9	7	0	.563	323	309
New Orleans	8	8	0	.500	370	360
Atlanta	6	10	0	.375	300	388
San Francisco	2	14	0	.125	308	416

**Wild Card qualifiers for playoffs*

Dallas won division title because of a better conference record than Philadelphia (10-2 to 9-3). Tampa Bay won division title because of a better division record than Chicago (6-2 to 5-3). Chicago won a Wild Card berth over Washington on the basis of best net points in all games (plus 57 net points to plus 53).

First round playoff: HOUSTON 13, Denver 7
Divisional playoffs: Houston 17, SAN DIEGO 14; PITTSBURGH 34, Miami 14
AFC championship: PITTSBURGH 27, Houston 13
First round playoff: PHILADELPHIA 27, Chicago 17
Divisional playoffs: TAMPA BAY 24, Philadelphia 17; Los Angeles 21, DALLAS 19
NFC championship: Los Angeles 9, TAMPA BAY 0
Super Bowl XIV: Pittsburgh (AFC) 31, Los Angeles (NFC) 19, at Rose Bowl, Pasadena, Calif.

1978

American Conference

Eastern Division

	W	L	T	Pct.	Pts.	OP
New England	11	5	0	.688	358	286
Miami*	11	5	0	.688	372	254
N.Y. Jets	8	8	0	.500	359	364
Buffalo	5	11	0	.313	302	354
Baltimore	5	11	0	.313	239	421

Central Division

	W	L	T	Pct.	Pts.	OP
Pittsburgh	14	2	0	.875	356	195
Houston*	10	6	0	.625	283	298
Cleveland	8	8	0	.500	334	356
Cincinnati	4	12	0	.250	252	284

Western Division

	W	L	T	Pct.	Pts.	OP
Denver	10	6	0	.625	282	198
Oakland	9	7	0	.563	311	283
Seattle	9	7	0	.563	345	358
San Diego	9	7	0	.563	355	309
Kansas City	4	12	0	.250	243	327

National Conference

Eastern Division

	W	L	T	Pct.	Pts.	OP
Dallas	12	4	0	.750	384	208
Philadelphia*	9	7	0	.563	270	250
Washington	8	8	0	.500	273	283
St. Louis	6	10	0	.375	248	296
N.Y. Giants	6	10	0	.375	264	298

Central Division

	W	L	T	Pct.	Pts.	OP
Minnesota	8	7	1	.531	294	306
Green Bay	8	7	1	.531	249	269
Detroit	7	9	0	.438	290	300
Chicago	7	9	0	.438	253	274
Tampa Bay	5	11	0	.313	241	259

Western Division

	W	L	T	Pct.	Pts.	OP
Los Angeles	12	4	0	.750	316	245
Atlanta*	9	7	0	.563	240	290
New Orleans	7	9	0	.438	281	298
San Francisco	2	14	0	.125	219	350

**Wild Card qualifiers for playoffs*

New England won division title on the basis of a better division record than Miami (6-2 to 5-3). Minnesota won division title because of a better head-to-head record against Green Bay (1-0-1).

First round playoff: Houston 17, MIAMI 9

Divisional playoffs: Houston 31, NEW ENGLAND 14; PITTSBURGH 33, Denver 10

AFC championship: PITTSBURGH 34, Houston 5

First round playoff: ATLANTA 14, Philadelphia 13

Divisional playoffs: DALLAS 27, Atlanta 20; LOS ANGELES 34, Minnesota 10

NFC championship: Dallas 28, LOS ANGELES 0

Super Bowl XIII: Pittsburgh (AFC) 35, Dallas (NFC) 31, at Orange Bowl, Miami, Fla.

1977

American Conference

Eastern Division

	W	L	T	Pct.	Pts.	OP
Baltimore	10	4	0	.714	295	221
Miami	10	4	0	.714	313	197
New England	9	5	0	.643	278	217
N.Y. Jets	3	11	0	.214	191	300
Buffalo	3	11	0	.214	160	313

Central Division

	W	L	T	Pct.	Pts.	OP
Pittsburgh	9	5	0	.643	283	243
Houston	8	6	0	.571	299	230
Cincinnati	8	6	0	.571	238	235
Cleveland	6	8	0	.429	269	267

Western Division

	W	L	T	Pct.	Pts.	OP
Denver	12	2	0	.857	274	148
Oakland*	11	3	0	.786	351	230
San Diego	7	7	0	.500	222	205
Seattle	5	9	0	.357	282	373
Kansas City	2	12	0	.143	225	349

National Conference

Eastern Division

	W	L	T	Pct.	Pts.	OP
Dallas	12	2	0	.857	345	212
Washington	9	5	0	.643	196	189
St. Louis	7	7	0	.500	272	287
Philadelphia	5	9	0	.357	220	207
N.Y. Giants	5	9	0	.357	181	265

Central Division

	W	L	T	Pct.	Pts.	OP
Minnesota	9	5	0	.643	231	227
Chicago*	9	5	0	.643	255	253
Detroit	6	8	0	.429	183	252
Green Bay	4	10	0	.286	134	219
Tampa Bay	2	12	0	.143	103	223

Western Division

	W	L	T	Pct.	Pts.	OP
Los Angeles	10	4	0	.714	302	146
Atlanta	7	7	0	.500	179	129
San Francisco	5	9	0	.357	220	260
New Orleans	3	11	0	.214	232	336

**Wild Card qualifier for playoffs*

Baltimore won division title on the basis of a better conference record than Miami (9-3 to 8-4). Chicago won a Wild Card berth over Washington on the basis of best net points in conference games (plus 48 net points to plus 4).

Divisional playoffs: DENVER 34, Pittsburgh 21; Oakland 37, BALTIMORE 31, sudden death overtime

AFC championship: DENVER 20, Oakland 17

Divisional playoffs: DALLAS 37, Chicago 7; Minnesota 14, LOS ANGELES 7

NFC championship: DALLAS 23, Minnesota 6

Super Bowl XII: Dallas (NFC) 27, Denver (AFC) 10, at Louisiana Superdome, New Orleans, La.

1976

American Conference

Eastern Division

	W	L	T	Pct.	Pts.	OP
Baltimore	11	3	0	.786	417	246
New England*	11	3	0	.786	376	236
Miami	6	8	0	.429	263	264
N.Y. Jets	3	11	0	.214	169	383
Buffalo	2	12	0	.143	245	363

Central Division

	W	L	T	Pct.	Pts.	OP
Pittsburgh	10	4	0	.714	342	138
Cincinnati	10	4	0	.714	335	210
Cleveland	9	5	0	.643	267	287
Houston	5	9	0	.357	222	273

Western Division

	W	L	T	Pct.	Pts.	OP
Oakland	13	1	0	.929	350	237
Denver	9	5	0	.643	315	206
San Diego	6	8	0	.429	248	285
Kansas City	5	9	0	.357	290	376
Tampa Bay	0	14	0	.000	125	412

National Conference

Eastern Division

	W	L	T	Pct.	Pts.	OP
Dallas	11	3	0	.786	296	194
Washington*	10	4	0	.714	291	217
St. Louis	10	4	0	.714	309	267
Philadelphia	4	10	0	.286	165	286
N.Y. Giants	3	11	0	.214	170	250

Central Division

	W	L	T	Pct.	Pts.	OP
Minnesota	11	2	1	.821	305	176
Chicago	7	7	0	.500	253	216
Detroit	6	8	0	.429	262	220
Green Bay	5	9	0	.357	218	299

Western Division

	W	L	T	Pct.	Pts.	OP
Los Angeles	10	3	1	.750	351	190
San Francisco	8	6	0	.571	270	190
Atlanta	4	10	0	.286	172	312
New Orleans	4	10	0	.286	253	346
Seattle	2	12	0	.143	229	429

**Wild Card qualifier for playoffs*

Baltimore won division title on the basis of a better division record than New England (7-1 to 6-2). Pittsburgh won division title because of a two-game sweep over Cincinnati. Washington won Wild Card berth over St. Louis because of a two-game sweep over Cardinals.

Divisional playoffs: OAKLAND 24, New England 21; Pittsburgh 40, BALTIMORE 14

AFC championship: OAKLAND 24, Pittsburgh 7

Divisional playoffs: MINNESOTA 35, Washington 20; Los Angeles 14, DALLAS 12

NFC championship: MINNESOTA 24, Los Angeles 13

Super Bowl XI: Oakland (AFC) 32, Minnesota (NFC) 14, at Rose Bowl, Pasadena, Calif.

1975

American Conference

Eastern Division

	W	L	T	Pct.	Pts.	OP
Baltimore	10	4	0	.714	395	269
Miami	10	4	0	.714	357	222
Buffalo	8	6	0	.571	420	355
New England	3	11	0	.214	258	358
N.Y. Jets	3	11	0	.214	258	433

Central Division

	W	L	T	Pct.	Pts.	OP
Pittsburgh	12	2	0	.857	373	162
Cincinnati*	11	3	0	.786	340	246
Houston	10	4	0	.714	293	226
Cleveland	3	11	0	.214	218	372

Western Division

	W	L	T	Pct.	Pts.	OP
Oakland	11	3	0	.786	375	255
Denver	6	8	0	.429	254	307
Kansas City	5	9	0	.357	282	341
San Diego	2	12	0	.143	189	345

National Conference

Eastern Division

	W	L	T	Pct.	Pts.	OP
St. Louis	11	3	0	.786	356	276
Dallas*	10	4	0	.714	350	268
Washington	8	6	0	.571	325	276
N.Y. Giants	5	9	0	.357	216	306
Philadelphia	4	10	0	.286	225	302

Central Division

	W	L	T	Pct.	Pts.	OP
Minnesota	12	2	0	.857	377	180
Detroit	7	7	0	.500	245	262
Chicago	4	10	0	.286	191	379
Green Bay	4	10	0	.286	226	285

Western Division

	W	L	T	Pct.	Pts.	OP
Los Angeles	12	2	0	.857	312	135
San Francisco	5	9	0	.357	255	286
Atlanta	4	10	0	.286	240	289
New Orleans	2	12	0	.143	165	360

**Wild Card qualifier for playoffs*

Baltimore won division title on the basis of a two-game sweep over Miami.

Divisional playoffs: PITTSBURGH 28, Baltimore 10; OAKLAND 31, Cincinnati 28

AFC championship: PITTSBURGH 16, Oakland 10

Divisional playoffs: LOS ANGELES 35, St. Louis 23; Dallas 17, MINNESOTA 14

NFC championship: Dallas 37, LOS ANGELES 7

Super Bowl X: Pittsburgh (AFC) 21, Dallas (NFC) 17, at Orange Bowl, Miami, Fla.

1974

American Conference

Eastern Division

	W	L	T	Pct.	Pts.	OP
Miami	11	3	0	.786	327	216
Buffalo*	9	5	0	.643	264	244
New England	7	7	0	.500	348	289
N.Y. Jets	7	7	0	.500	279	300
Baltimore	2	12	0	.143	190	329

Central Division

	W	L	T	Pct.	Pts.	OP
Pittsburgh	10	3	1	.750	305	189
Cincinnati	7	7	0	.500	283	259
Houston	7	7	0	.500	236	282
Cleveland	4	10	0	.286	251	344

Western Division

	W	L	T	Pct.	Pts.	OP
Oakland	12	2	0	.857	355	228
Denver	7	6	1	.536	302	294
Kansas City	5	9	0	.357	233	293
San Diego	5	9	0	.357	212	285

National Conference

Eastern Division

	W	L	T	Pct.	Pts.	OP
St. Louis	10	4	0	.714	285	218
Washington*	10	4	0	.714	320	196
Dallas	8	6	0	.571	297	235
Philadelphia	7	7	0	.500	242	217
N.Y. Giants	2	12	0	.143	195	299

Central Division

	W	L	T	Pct.	Pts.	OP
Minnesota	10	4	0	.714	310	195
Detroit	7	7	0	.500	256	270
Green Bay	6	8	0	.429	210	206
Chicago	4	10	0	.286	152	279

Western Division

	W	L	T	Pct.	Pts.	OP
Los Angeles	10	4	0	.714	263	181
San Francisco	6	8	0	.429	226	236
New Orleans	5	9	0	.357	166	263
Atlanta	3	11	0	.214	111	271

**Wild Card qualifier for playoffs*

St. Louis won division title because of a two-game sweep over Washington.

Divisional playoffs: OAKLAND 28, Miami 26; PITTSBURGH 32, Buffalo 14

AFC championship: Pittsburgh 24, OAKLAND 13

Divisional playoffs: MINNESOTA 30, St. Louis 14; LOS ANGELES 19, Washington 10

NFC championship: MINNESOTA 14, Los Angeles 10

Super Bowl IX: Pittsburgh (AFC) 16, Minnesota (NFC) 6, at Tulane Stadium, New Orleans, La

1973

American Conference

Eastern Division

	W	L	T	Pct.	Pts.	OP
Miami	12	2	0	.857	343	150
Buffalo	9	5	0	.643	259	230
New England	5	9	0	.357	258	300
Baltimore	4	10	0	.286	226	341
N.Y. Jets	4	10	0	.286	240	306

Central Division

	W	L	T	Pct.	Pts.	OP
Cincinnati	10	4	0	.714	286	231
Pittsburgh*	10	4	0	.714	347	210
Cleveland	7	5	2	.571	234	255
Houston	1	13	0	.071	199	447

Western Division

	W	L	T	Pct.	Pts.	OP
Oakland	9	4	1	.679	292	175
Denver	7	5	2	.571	354	296
Kansas City	7	5	2	.571	231	192
San Diego	2	11	1	.179	188	386

National Conference

Eastern Division

	W	L	T	Pct.	Pts.	OP
Dallas	10	4	0	.714	382	203
Washington*	10	4	0	.714	325	198
Philadelphia	5	8	1	.393	310	393
St. Louis	4	9	1	.321	286	365
N.Y. Giants	2	11	1	.179	226	362

Central Division

	W	L	T	Pct.	Pts.	OP
Minnesota	12	2	0	.857	296	168
Detroit	6	7	1	.464	271	247
Green Bay	5	7	2	.429	202	259
Chicago	3	11	0	.214	195	334

Western Division

	W	L	T	Pct.	Pts.	OP
Los Angeles	12	2	0	.857	388	178
Atlanta	9	5	0	.643	318	224
New Orleans	5	9	0	.357	163	312
San Francisco	5	9	0	.357	262	319

**Wild Card qualifier for playoffs*

Cincinnati won division title on the basis of a better conference record than Pittsburgh (8-3 to 7-4). Dallas won division title on the basis of a better point differential vs. Washington (net 13 points).

Divisional playoffs: OAKLAND 33, Pittsburgh 14; MIAMI 34, Cincinnati 16

AFC championship: MIAMI 27, Oakland 10

Divisional playoffs: MINNESOTA 27, Washington 20; DALLAS 27, Los Angeles 16

NFC championship: Minnesota 27, DALLAS 10

Super Bowl VIII: Miami (AFC) 24, Minnesota (NFC) 7, at Rice Stadium, Houston, Tex.

1972

American Conference

Eastern Division

	W	L	T	Pct.	Pts.	OP
Miami	14	0	0	1.000	385	171
N.Y. Jets	7	7	0	.500	367	324
Baltimore	5	9	0	.357	235	252
Buffalo	4	9	1	.321	257	377
New England	3	11	0	.214	192	446

Central Division

	W	L	T	Pct.	Pts.	OP
Pittsburgh	11	3	0	.786	343	175
Cleveland*	10	4	0	.714	268	249
Cincinnati	8	6	0	.571	299	229
Houston	1	13	0	.071	164	380

Western Division

	W	L	T	Pct.	Pts.	OP
Oakland	10	3	1	.750	365	248
Kansas City	8	6	0	.571	287	254
Denver	5	9	0	.357	325	350
San Diego	4	9	1	.321	264	344

National Conference

Eastern Division

	W	L	T	Pct.	Pts.	OP
Washington	11	3	0	.786	336	218
Dallas*	10	4	0	.714	319	240
N.Y. Giants	8	6	0	.571	331	247
St. Louis	4	9	1	.321	193	303
Philadelphia	2	11	1	.179	145	352

Central Division

	W	L	T	Pct.	Pts.	OP
Green Bay	10	4	0	.714	304	226
Detroit	8	5	1	.607	339	290
Minnesota	7	7	0	.500	301	252
Chicago	4	9	1	.321	225	275

Western Division

	W	L	T	Pct.	Pts.	OP
San Francisco	8	5	1	.607	353	249
Atlanta	7	7	0	.500	269	274
Los Angeles	6	7	1	.464	291	286
New Orleans	2	11	1	.179	215	361

**Wild Card qualifier for playoffs*

Divisional playoffs: PITTSBURGH 13, Oakland 7; MIAMI 20, Cleveland 14
AFC championship: Miami 21, PITTSBURGH 17
Divisional playoffs: Dallas 30, SAN FRANCISCO 28; WASHINGTON 16, Green Bay 3
NFC championship: WASHINGTON 26, Dallas 3
Super Bowl VII: Miami (AFC) 14, Washington (NFC) 7, at Memorial Coliseum, Los Angeles, Calif.

1971

American Conference

Eastern Division

	W	L	T	Pct.	Pts.	OP
Miami	10	3	1	.769	315	174
Baltimore*	10	4	0	.714	313	140
New England	6	8	0	.429	238	325
N.Y. Jets	6	8	0	.429	212	299
Buffalo	1	13	0	.071	184	394

Central Division

	W	L	T	Pct.	Pts.	OP
Cleveland	9	5	0	.643	285	273
Pittsburgh	6	8	0	.429	246	292
Houston	4	9	1	.308	251	330
Cincinnati	4	10	0	.286	284	265

Western Division

	W	L	T	Pct.	Pts.	OP
Kansas City	10	3	1	.769	302	208
Oakland	8	4	2	.667	344	278
San Diego	6	8	0	.429	311	341
Denver	4	9	1	.308	203	275

National Conference

Eastern Division

	W	L	T	Pct.	Pts.	OP
Dallas	11	3	0	.786	406	222
Washington*	9	4	1	.692	276	190
Philadelphia	6	7	1	.462	221	302
St. Louis	4	9	1	.308	231	279
N.Y. Giants	4	10	0	.286	228	362

Central Division

	W	L	T	Pct.	Pts.	OP
Minnesota	11	3	0	.786	245	139
Detroit	7	6	1	.538	341	286
Chicago	6	8	0	.429	185	276
Green Bay	4	8	2	.333	274	298

Western Division

	W	L	T	Pct.	Pts.	OP
San Francisco	9	5	0	.643	300	216
Los Angeles	8	5	1	.615	313	260
Atlanta	7	6	1	.538	274	277
New Orleans	4	8	2	.333	266	347

**Wild Card qualifier for playoffs*

Divisional playoffs: Miami 27, KANSAS CITY 24, sudden death overtime; Baltimore 20, CLEVELAND 3
AFC championship: MIAMI 21, Baltimore 0
Divisional playoffs: Dallas 20, MINNESOTA 12; SAN FRANCISCO 24, Washington 20
NFC championship: DALLAS 14, San Francisco 3
Super Bowl VI: Dallas (NFC) 24, Miami (AFC) 3, at Tulane Stadium, New Orleans, La.

1970

American Conference

Eastern Division

	W	L	T	Pct.	Pts.	OP
Baltimore	11	2	1	.846	321	234
Miami*	10	4	0	.714	297	228
N.Y. Jets	4	10	0	.286	255	286
Buffalo	3	10	1	.231	204	337
Boston Patriots	2	12	0	.143	149	361

Central Division

	W	L	T	Pct.	Pts.	OP
Cincinnati	8	6	0	.571	312	255
Cleveland	7	7	0	.500	286	265
Pittsburgh	5	9	0	.357	210	272
Houston	3	10	1	.231	217	352

Western Division

	W	L	T	Pct.	Pts.	OP
Oakland	8	4	2	.667	300	293
Kansas City	7	5	2	.583	272	244
San Diego	5	6	3	.455	282	278
Denver	5	8	1	.385	253	264

National Conference

Eastern Division

	W	L	T	Pct.	Pts.	OP
Dallas	10	4	0	.714	299	221
N.Y. Giants	9	5	0	.643	301	270
St. Louis	8	5	1	.615	325	228
Washington	6	8	0	.429	297	314
Philadelphia	3	10	1	.231	241	332

Central Division

	W	L	T	Pct.	Pts.	OP
Minnesota	12	2	0	.857	335	143
Detroit*	10	4	0	.714	347	202
Chicago	6	8	0	.429	256	261
Green Bay	6	8	0	.429	196	293

Western Division

	W	L	T	Pct.	Pts.	OP
San Francisco	10	3	1	.769	352	267
Los Angeles	9	4	1	.692	325	202
Atlanta	4	8	2	.333	206	261
New Orleans	2	11	1	.154	172	347

**Wild Card qualifier for playoffs*

Divisional playoffs: BALTIMORE 17, Cincinnati 0; OAKLAND 21, Miami 14
AFC championship: BALTIMORE 27, Oakland 17
Divisional playoffs: DALLAS 5, Detroit 0; San Francisco 17, MINNESOTA 14
NFC championship: Dallas 17, SAN FRANCISCO 10
Super Bowl V: Baltimore (AFC) 16, Dallas (NFC) 13, at Orange Bowl, Miami, Fla.

1969 NFL

Eastern Conference

Capitol Division

	W	L	T	Pct.	Pts.	OP
Dallas	11	2	1	.846	369	223
Washington	7	5	2	.583	307	319
New Orleans	5	9	0	.357	311	393
Philadelphia	4	9	1	.308	279	377

Century Division

	W	L	T	Pct.	Pts.	OP
Cleveland	10	3	1	.769	351	300
N.Y. Giants	6	8	0	.429	264	298
St. Louis	4	9	1	.308	314	389
Pittsburgh	1	13	0	.071	218	404

Western Conference

Coastal Division

	W	L	T	Pct.	Pts.	OP
Los Angeles	11	3	0	.786	320	243
Baltimore	8	5	1	.615	279	268
Atlanta	6	8	0	.429	276	268
San Francisco	4	8	2	.333	277	319

Central Division

	W	L	T	Pct.	Pts.	OP
Minnesota	12	2	0	.857	379	133
Detroit	9	4	1	.692	259	188
Green Bay	8	6	0	.571	269	221
Chicago	1	13	0	.071	210	339

Conference championships: Cleveland 38, DALLAS 14; MINNESOTA 23, Los Angeles 20
NFL championship: MINNESOTA 27, Cleveland 7
Super Bowl IV: Kansas City (AFL) 23, Minnesota (NFL) 7, at Tulane Stadium, New Orleans, La.

1969 AFL

Eastern Division

	W	L	T	Pct.	Pts.	OP
N.Y. Jets	10	4	0	.714	353	269
Houston	6	6	2	.500	278	279
Boston Patriots	4	10	0	.286	266	316
Buffalo	4	10	0	.286	230	359
Miami	3	10	1	.231	233	332

Western Division

	W	L	T	Pct.	Pts.	OP
Oakland	12	1	1	.923	377	242
Kansas City	11	3	0	.786	359	177
San Diego	8	6	0	.571	288	276
Denver	5	8	1	.385	297	344
Cincinnati	4	9	1	.308	280	367

Divisional Playoffs: Kansas City 13, N.Y. JETS 6; OAKLAND 56, Houston 7
AFL championship: Kansas City 17, OAKLAND 7

1968 NFL

Eastern Conference

Capitol Division

	W	L	T	Pct.	Pts.	OP
Dallas	12	2	0	.857	431	186
N.Y. Giants	7	7	0	.500	294	325
Washington	5	9	0	.357	249	358
Philadelphia	2	12	0	.143	202	351

Century Division

	W	L	T	Pct.	Pts.	OP
Cleveland	10	4	0	.714	394	273
St. Louis	9	4	1	.692	325	289
New Orleans	4	9	1	.308	246	327
Pittsburgh	2	11	1	.154	244	397

Western Conference

Coastal Division

	W	L	T	Pct.	Pts.	OP
Baltimore	13	1	0	.929	402	144
Los Angeles	10	3	1	.769	312	200
San Francisco	7	6	1	.538	303	310
Atlanta	2	12	0	.143	170	389

Central Division

	W	L	T	Pct.	Pts.	OP
Minnesota	8	6	0	.571	282	242
Chicago	7	7	0	.500	250	333
Green Bay	6	7	1	.462	281	227
Detroit	4	8	2	.333	207	241

Conference championships: CLEVELAND 31, Dallas 20; BALTIMORE 24, Minnesota 14
NFL championship: Baltimore 34, CLEVELAND 0
Super Bowl III: N.Y. Jets (AFL) 16, Baltimore (NFL) 7, at Orange Bowl, Miami, Fla.

1968 AFL

Eastern Division

	W	L	T	Pct.	Pts.	OP
N.Y. Jets	11	3	0	.786	419	280
Houston	7	7	0	.500	303	248
Miami	5	8	1	.385	276	355
Boston Patriots	4	10	0	.286	229	406
Buffalo	1	12	1	.077	199	367

Western Division

	W	L	T	Pct.	Pts.	OP
Oakland	12	2	0	.857	453	233
Kansas City	12	2	0	.857	371	170
San Diego	9	5	0	.643	382	310
Denver	5	9	0	.357	255	404
Cincinnati	3	11	0	.214	215	329

Western Division playoff: OAKLAND 41, Kansas City 6
AFL championship: N.Y. JETS 27, Oakland 23

1967 NFL

Eastern Conference

Capitol Division

	W	L	T	Pct.	Pts.	OP
Dallas	9	5	0	.643	342	268
Philadelphia	6	7	1	.462	351	409
Washington	5	6	3	.455	347	353
New Orleans	3	11	0	.214	233	379

Century Division

	W	L	T	Pct.	Pts.	OP
Cleveland	9	5	0	.643	334	297
N.Y. Giants	7	7	0	.500	369	379
St. Louis	6	7	1	.462	333	356
Pittsburgh	4	9	1	.308	281	320

Western Conference

Coastal Division

	W	L	T	Pct.	Pts.	OP
Los Angeles	11	1	2	.917	398	196
Baltimore	11	1	2	.917	394	198
San Francisco	7	7	0	.500	273	337
Atlanta	1	12	1	.077	175	422

Central Division

	W	L	T	Pct.	Pts.	OP
Green Bay	9	4	1	.692	332	209
Chicago	7	6	1	.538	239	218
Detroit	5	7	2	.417	260	259
Minnesota	3	8	3	.273	233	294

Los Angeles won division title on the basis of advantage in points (58-34) in two games vs. Baltimore.

Conference championships: DALLAS 52, Cleveland 14; GREEN BAY 28, Los Angeles 7
NFL championship: GREEN BAY 21, Dallas 17
Super Bowl II: Green Bay (NFL) 33, Oakland (AFL) 14, at Orange Bowl, Miami, Fla.

1967 AFL

Eastern Division

	W	L	T	Pct.	Pts.	OP
Houston	9	4	1	.692	258	199
N.Y. Jets	8	5	1	.615	371	329
Buffalo	4	10	0	.286	237	285
Miami	4	10	0	.286	219	407
Boston Patriots	3	10	1	.231	280	389

Western Division

	W	L	T	Pct.	Pts.	OP
Oakland	13	1	0	.929	468	233
Kansas City	9	5	0	.643	408	254
San Diego	8	5	1	.615	360	352
Denver	3	11	0	.214	256	409

AFL championship: OAKLAND 40, Houston 7

1966 NFL

Eastern Conference

	W	L	T	Pct.	Pts.	OP
Dallas	10	3	1	.769	445	239
Cleveland	9	5	0	.643	403	259
Philadelphia	9	5	0	.643	326	340
St. Louis	8	5	1	.615	264	265
Washington	7	7	0	.500	351	355
Pittsburgh	5	8	1	.385	316	347
Atlanta	3	11	0	.214	204	437
N.Y. Giants	1	12	1	.077	263	501

Western Conference

	W	L	T	Pct.	Pts.	OP
Green Bay	12	2	0	.857	335	163
Baltimore	9	5	0	.643	314	226
Los Angeles	8	6	0	.571	289	212
San Francisco	6	6	2	.500	320	325
Chicago	5	7	2	.417	234	272
Detroit	4	9	1	.308	206	317
Minnesota	4	9	1	.308	292	304

NFL championship: Green Bay 34, DALLAS 27

Super Bowl I: Green Bay (NFL) 35, Kansas City (AFL) 10, at Memorial Coliseum, Los Angeles, Calif.

1966 AFL

Eastern Division

	W	L	T	Pct.	Pts.	OP
Buffalo	9	4	1	.692	358	255
Boston Patriots	8	4	2	.677	315	283
N.Y. Jets	6	6	2	.500	322	312
Houston	3	11	0	.214	335	396
Miami	3	11	0	.214	213	362

Western Division

	W	L	T	Pct.	Pts.	OP
Kansas City	11	2	1	.846	448	276
Oakland	8	5	1	.615	315	288
San Diego	7	6	1	.538	335	284
Denver	4	10	0	.286	196	381

AFL championship: Kansas City 31, BUFFALO 7

1965 NFL

Eastern Conference

	W	L	T	Pct.	Pts.	OP
Cleveland	11	3	0	.786	363	325
Dallas	7	7	0	.500	325	280
N.Y. Giants	7	7	0	.500	270	338
Washington	6	8	0	.429	257	301
Philadelphia	5	9	0	.357	363	359
St. Louis	5	9	0	.357	296	309
Pittsburgh	2	12	0	.143	202	397

Western Conference

	W	L	T	Pct.	Pts.	OP
Green Bay	10	3	1	.769	316	224
Baltimore	10	3	1	.769	389	284
Chicago	9	5	0	.643	409	275
San Francisco	7	6	1	.538	421	402
Minnesota	7	7	0	.500	383	403
Detroit	6	7	1	.462	257	295
Los Angeles	4	10	0	.286	269	328

Western Conference playoff: GREEN BAY 13, Baltimore 10, sudden death overtime

NFL championship: GREEN BAY 23, Cleveland 12

1965 AFL

Eastern Division

	W	L	T	Pct.	Pts.	OP
Buffalo	10	3	1	.769	313	226
N.Y. Jets	5	8	1	.385	285	303
Boston Patriots	4	8	2	.333	244	302
Houston	4	10	0	.286	298	429

Western Division

	W	L	T	Pct.	Pts.	OP
San Diego	9	2	3	.818	340	227
Oakland	8	5	1	.615	298	239
Kansas City	7	5	2	.583	322	285
Denver	4	10	0	.286	303	392

AFL championship: Buffalo 23, SAN DIEGO 0

1964 NFL

Eastern Conference

	W	L	T	Pct.	Pts.	OP
Cleveland	10	3	1	.769	415	293
St. Louis	9	3	2	.750	357	331
Philadelphia	6	8	0	.429	312	313
Washington	6	8	0	.429	307	305
Dallas	5	8	1	.385	250	289
Pittsburgh	5	9	0	.357	253	315
N.Y. Giants	2	10	2	.167	241	399

Western Conference

	W	L	T	Pct.	Pts.	OP
Baltimore	12	2	0	.857	428	225
Green Bay	8	5	1	.615	342	245
Minnesota	8	5	1	.615	355	296
Detroit	7	5	2	.583	280	260
Los Angeles	5	7	2	.417	283	339
Chicago	5	9	0	.357	260	379
San Francisco	4	10	0	.286	236	330

NFL championship: CLEVELAND 27, Baltimore 0

1964 AFL

Eastern Division

	W	L	T	Pct.	Pts.	OP
Buffalo	12	2	0	.857	400	242
Boston Patriots	10	3	1	.769	365	297
N.Y. Jets	5	8	1	.385	278	315
Houston	4	10	0	.286	310	355

Western Division

	W	L	T	Pct.	Pts.	OP
San Diego	8	5	1	.615	341	300
Kansas City	7	7	0	.500	366	306
Oakland	5	7	2	.417	303	350
Denver	2	11	1	.154	240	438

AFL championship: BUFFALO 20, San Diego 7

1963 NFL

Eastern Conference

	W	L	T	Pct.	Pts.	OP
N.Y. Giants	11	3	0	.786	448	280
Cleveland	10	4	0	.714	343	262
St. Louis	9	5	0	.643	341	283
Pittsburgh	7	4	3	.636	321	295
Dallas	4	10	0	.286	305	378
Washington	3	11	0	.214	279	398
Philadelphia	2	10	2	.167	242	381

Western Conference

	W	L	T	Pct.	Pts.	OP
Chicago	11	1	2	.917	301	144
Green Bay	11	2	1	.846	369	206
Baltimore	8	6	0	.571	316	285
Detroit	5	8	1	.385	326	265
Minnesota	5	8	1	.385	309	390
Los Angeles	5	9	0	.357	210	350
San Francisco	2	12	0	.143	198	391

NFL championship: CHICAGO 14, N.Y. Giants 10

1963 AFL

Eastern Division

	W	L	T	Pct.	Pts.	OP
Boston Patriots	7	6	1	.538	317	257
Buffalo	7	6	1	.538	304	291
Houston	6	8	0	.429	302	372
N.Y. Jets	5	8	1	.385	249	399

Western Division

	W	L	T	Pct.	Pts.	OP
San Diego	11	3	0	.786	399	256
Oakland	10	4	0	.714	363	288
Kansas City	5	7	2	.417	347	263
Denver	2	11	1	.154	301	473

Eastern Division playoff: Boston 26, BUFFALO 8

AFL championship: SAN DIEGO 51, Boston 10

1962 NFL

Eastern Conference

	W	L	T	Pct.	Pts.	OP
N.Y. Giants	12	2	0	.857	398	283
Pittsburgh	9	5	0	.643	312	363
Cleveland	7	6	1	.538	291	257
Washington	5	7	2	.417	305	376
Dallas Cowboys	5	8	1	.385	398	402
St. Louis	4	9	1	.308	287	361
Philadelphia	3	10	1	.231	282	356

Western Conference

	W	L	T	Pct.	Pts.	OP
Green Bay	13	1	0	.929	415	148
Detroit	11	3	0	.786	315	177
Chicago	9	5	0	.643	321	287
Baltimore	7	7	0	.500	293	288
San Francisco	6	8	0	.429	282	331
Minnesota	2	11	1	.154	254	410
Los Angeles	1	12	1	.077	220	334

NFL championship: Green Bay 16, N.Y. GIANTS 7

1962 AFL

Eastern Division

	W	L	T	Pct.	Pts.	OP
Houston	11	3	0	.786	387	270
Boston Patriots	9	4	1	.692	346	295
Buffalo	7	6	1	.538	309	272
N.Y. Titans	5	9	0	.357	278	423

Western Division

	W	L	T	Pct.	Pts.	OP
Dallas Texans	11	3	0	.786	389	233
Denver	7	7	0	.500	353	334
San Diego	4	10	0	.286	314	392
Oakland	1	13	0	.071	213	370

AFL championship: Dallas Texans 20, HOUSTON 17, sudden death overtime

1961 NFL

Eastern Conference

	W	L	T	Pct.	Pts.	OP
N.Y. Giants	10	3	1	.769	368	220
Philadelphia	10	4	0	.714	361	297
Cleveland	8	5	1	.615	319	270
St. Louis	7	7	0	.500	279	267
Pittsburgh	6	8	0	.429	295	287
Dallas Cowboys	4	9	1	.308	236	380
Washington	1	12	1	.077	174	392

Western Conference

	W	L	T	Pct.	Pts.	OP
Green Bay	11	3	0	.786	391	223
Detroit	8	5	1	.615	270	258
Baltimore	8	6	0	.571	302	307
Chicago Bears	8	6	0	.571	326	302
San Francisco	7	6	1	.538	346	272
Los Angeles	4	10	0	.286	263	333
Minnesota	3	11	0	.214	285	407

NFL championship: GREEN BAY 37, N.Y. Giants 0

1961 AFL

Eastern Division

	W	L	T	Pct.	Pts.	OP
Houston	10	3	1	.769	513	242
Boston Patriots	9	4	1	.692	413	313
N.Y. Titans	7	7	0	.500	301	390
Buffalo	6	8	0	.429	294	342

Western Division

	W	L	T	Pct.	Pts.	OP
San Diego	12	2	0	.857	396	219
Dallas Texans	6	8	0	.429	334	343
Denver	3	11	0	.214	251	432
Oakland	2	12	0	.143	237	458

AFL championship: Houston 10, SAN DIEGO 3

1960 NFL

Eastern Conference

	W	L	T	Pct.	Pts.	OP
Philadelphia	10	2	0	.833	321	246
Cleveland	8	3	1	.727	362	217
N.Y. Giants	6	4	2	.600	271	261
St. Louis	6	5	1	.545	288	230
Pittsburgh	5	6	1	.455	240	275
Washington	1	9	2	.100	178	309

Western Conference

	W	L	T	Pct.	Pts.	OP
Green Bay	8	4	0	.667	332	209
Detroit	7	5	0	.583	239	212
San Francisco	7	5	0	.583	208	205
Baltimore	6	6	0	.500	288	234
Chicago	5	6	1	.455	194	299
L.A. Rams	4	7	1	.364	265	297
Dallas Cowboys	0	11	1	.000	177	369

NFL championship: PHILADELPHIA 17, Green Bay 13

1960 AFL

Eastern Conference

	W	L	T	Pct.	Pts.	OP
Houston	10	4	0	.714	379	285
N.Y. Titans	7	7	0	.500	382	399
Buffalo	5	8	1	.385	296	303
Boston	5	9	0	.357	286	349

Western Conference

	W	L	T	Pct.	Pts.	OP
L.A. Chargers	10	4	0	.714	373	336
Dallas Texans	8	6	0	.571	362	253
Oakland	6	8	0	.429	319	388
Denver	4	9	1	.308	309	393

AFL championship: HOUSTON 24, L.A. Chargers 16

1959

Eastern Conference

	W	L	T	Pct.	Pts.	OP
N.Y. Giants	10	2	0	.833	284	170
Cleveland	7	5	0	.583	270	214
Philadelphia	7	5	0	.583	268	278
Pittsburgh	6	5	1	.545	257	216
Washington	3	9	0	.250	185	350
Chi. Cardinals	2	10	0	.167	234	324

Western Conference

	W	L	T	Pct.	Pts.	OP
Baltimore	9	3	0	.750	374	251
Chi. Bears	8	4	0	.667	252	196
Green Bay	7	5	0	.583	248	246
San Francisco	7	5	0	.583	255	237
Detroit	3	8	1	.273	203	275
Los Angeles	2	10	0	.167	242	315

NFL championship: BALTIMORE 31, N.Y. Giants 16

1958

Eastern Conference

	W	L	T	Pct.	Pts.	OP
N.Y. Giants	9	3	0	.750	246	183
Cleveland	9	3	0	.750	302	217
Pittsburgh	7	4	1	.636	261	230
Washington	4	7	1	.364	214	268
Chi. Cardinals	2	9	1	.182	261	356
Philadelphia	2	9	1	.182	235	306

Western Conference

	W	L	T	Pct.	Pts.	OP
Baltimore	9	3	0	.750	381	203
Chi. Bears	8	4	0	.667	298	230
Los Angeles	8	4	0	.667	344	278
San Francisco	6	6	0	.500	257	324
Detroit	4	7	1	.364	261	276
Green Bay	1	10	1	.091	193	382

Eastern Conference playoff: N.Y. GIANTS 10, Cleveland 0

NFL championship: Baltimore 23, N.Y. GIANTS 17, sudden death overtime

1957

Eastern Conference

	W	L	T	Pct.	Pts.	OP
Cleveland	9	2	1	.818	269	172
N.Y. Giants	7	5	0	.583	254	211
Pittsburgh	6	6	0	.500	161	178
Washington	5	6	1	.455	251	230
Philadelphia	4	8	0	.333	173	230
Chi. Cardinals	3	9	0	.250	200	299

Western Conference

	W	L	T	Pct.	Pts.	OP
Detroit	8	4	0	.667	251	231
San Francisco	8	4	0	.667	260	264
Baltimore	7	5	0	.583	303	235
Los Angeles	6	6	0	.500	307	278
Chi. Bears	5	7	0	.417	203	211
Green Bay	3	9	0	.250	218	311

Western Conference playoff: Detroit 31, SAN FRANCISCO 27

NFL championship: DETROIT 59, Cleveland 14

1956

Eastern Conference

	W	L	T	Pct.	Pts.	OP
N.Y. Giants	8	3	1	.727	264	197
Chi. Cardinals	7	5	0	.583	240	182
Washington	6	6	0	.500	183	225
Cleveland	5	7	0	.417	167	177
Pittsburgh	5	7	0	.417	217	250
Philadelphia	3	8	1	.273	143	215

Western Conference

	W	L	T	Pct.	Pts.	OP
Chi. Bears	9	2	1	.818	363	246
Detroit	9	3	0	.750	300	188
San Francisco	5	6	1	.455	233	284
Baltimore	5	7	0	.417	270	322
Green Bay	4	8	0	.333	264	342
Los Angeles	4	8	0	.333	291	307

NFL championship: N.Y. GIANTS 47, Chi. Bears 7

1955

Eastern Conference

	W	L	T	Pct.	Pts.	OP
Cleveland	9	2	1	.818	349	218
Washington	8	4	0	.667	246	222
N.Y. Giants	6	5	1	.545	267	223
Chi. Cardinals	4	7	1	.364	224	252
Philadelphia	4	7	1	.364	248	231
Pittsburgh	4	8	0	.333	195	285

Western Conference

	W	L	T	Pct.	Pts.	OP
Los Angeles	8	3	1	.727	260	231
Chi. Bears	8	4	0	.667	294	251
Green Bay	6	6	0	.500	258	276
Baltimore	5	6	1	.455	214	239
San Francisco	4	8	0	.333	216	298
Detroit	3	9	0	.250	230	275

NFL championship: Cleveland 38, LOS ANGELES 14

1954

Eastern Conference

	W	L	T	Pct.	Pts.	OP
Cleveland	9	3	0	.750	336	162
Philadelphia	7	4	1	.636	284	230
N.Y. Giants	7	5	0	.583	293	184
Pittsburgh	5	7	0	.417	219	263
Washington	3	9	0	.250	207	432
Chi. Cardinals	2	10	0	.167	183	347

Western Conference

	W	L	T	Pct.	Pts.	OP
Detroit	9	2	1	.818	337	189
Chi. Bears	8	4	0	.667	301	279
San Francisco	7	4	1	.636	313	251
Los Angeles	6	5	1	.545	314	285
Green Bay	4	8	0	.333	234	251
Baltimore	3	9	0	.250	131	279

NFL championship: CLEVELAND 56, Detroit 10

1953

Eastern Conference

	W	L	T	Pct.	Pts.	OP
Cleveland	11	1	0	.917	348	162
Philadelphia	7	4	1	.636	352	215
Washington	6	5	1	.545	208	215
Pittsburgh	6	6	0	.500	211	263
N.Y. Giants	3	9	0	.250	179	277
Chi. Cardinals	1	10	1	.091	190	337

Western Conference

	W	L	T	Pct.	Pts.	OP
Detroit	10	2	0	.833	271	205
San Francisco	9	3	0	.750	372	237
Los Angeles	8	3	1	.727	366	236
Chi. Bears	3	8	1	.273	218	262
Baltimore	3	9	0	.250	182	350
Green Bay	2	9	1	.182	200	338

NFL championship: DETROIT 17, Cleveland 16

1952

American Conference

	W	L	T	Pct.	Pts.	OP
Cleveland	8	4	0	.667	310	213
N.Y. Giants	7	5	0	.583	234	231
Philadelphia	7	5	0	.583	252	271
Pittsburgh	5	7	0	.417	300	273
Chi. Cardinals	4	8	0	.333	172	221
Washington	4	8	0	.333	240	287

National Conference

	W	L	T	Pct.	Pts.	OP
Detroit	9	3	0	.750	344	192
Los Angeles	9	3	0	.750	349	234
San Francisco	7	5	0	.583	285	221
Green Bay	6	6	0	.500	295	312
Chi. Bears	5	7	0	.417	245	326
Dallas Texans	1	11	0	.083	182	427

National Conference playoff: DETROIT 31, Los Angeles 21
NFL championship: Detroit 17, CLEVELAND 7

1951

American Conference

	W	L	T	Pct.	Pts.	OP
Cleveland	11	1	0	.917	331	152
N.Y. Giants	9	2	1	.818	254	161
Washington	5	7	0	.417	183	296
Pittsburgh	4	7	1	.364	183	235
Philadelphia	4	8	0	.333	234	264
Chi. Cardinals	3	9	0	.250	210	287

National Conference

	W	L	T	Pct.	Pts.	OP
Los Angeles	8	4	0	.667	392	261
Detroit	7	4	1	.636	336	259
San Francisco	7	4	1	.636	255	205
Chi. Bears	7	5	0	.583	286	282
Green Bay	3	9	0	.250	254	375
N.Y. Yanks	1	9	2	.100	241	382

NFL championship: LOS ANGELES 24, Cleveland 17

1950

American Conference

	W	L	T	Pct.	Pts.	OP
Cleveland	10	2	0	.833	310	144
N.Y. Giants	10	2	0	.833	268	150
Philadelphia	6	6	0	.500	254	141
Pittsburgh	6	6	0	.500	180	195
Chi. Cardinals	5	7	0	.417	233	287
Washington	3	9	0	.250	232	326

National Conference

	W	L	T	Pct.	Pts.	OP
Los Angeles	9	3	0	.750	466	309
Chi. Bears	9	3	0	.750	279	207
N.Y. Yanks	7	5	0	.583	366	367
Detroit	6	6	0	.500	321	285
Green Bay	3	9	0	.250	244	406
San Francisco	3	9	0	.250	213	300
Baltimore	1	11	0	.083	213	462

American Conference playoff: CLEVELAND 8, N.Y. Giants 3
National Conference playoff: LOS ANGELES 24, Chi. Bears 14
NFL championship: CLEVELAND 30, Los Angeles 28

1949

Eastern Division

	W	L	T	Pct.	Pts.	OP
Philadelphia	11	1	0	.917	364	134
Pittsburgh	6	5	1	.545	224	214
N.Y. Giants	6	6	0	.500	287	298
Washington	4	7	1	.364	268	339
N.Y. Bulldogs	1	10	1	.091	153	365

Western Division

	W	L	T	Pct.	Pts.	OP
Los Angeles	8	2	2	.800	360	239
Chi. Bears	9	3	0	.750	332	218
Chi. Cardinals	6	5	1	.545	360	301
Detroit	4	8	0	.333	237	259
Green Bay	2	10	0	.167	114	329

NFL championship: Philadelphia 14, LOS ANGELES 0

1948

Eastern Division

	W	L	T	Pct.	Pts.	OP
Philadelphia	9	2	1	.818	376	156
Washington	7	5	0	.583	291	287
N.Y. Giants	4	8	0	.333	297	388
Pittsburgh	4	8	0	.333	200	243
Boston	3	9	0	.250	174	372

Western Division

	W	L	T	Pct.	Pts.	OP
Chi. Cardinals	11	1	0	.917	395	226
Chi. Bears	10	2	0	.833	375	151
Los Angeles	6	5	1	.545	327	269
Green Bay	3	9	0	.250	154	290
Detroit	2	10	0	.167	200	407

NFL championship: PHILADELPHIA 7, Chi. Cardinals 0

1947

Eastern Division

	W	L	T	Pct.	Pts.	OP
Philadelphia	8	4	0	.667	308	242
Pittsburgh	8	4	0	.667	240	259
Boston	4	7	1	.364	168	256
Washington	4	8	0	.333	295	367
N.Y. Giants	2	8	2	.200	190	309

Western Division

	W	L	T	Pct.	Pts.	OP
Chi. Cardinals	9	3	0	.750	306	231
Chi. Bears	8	4	0	.667	363	241
Green Bay	6	5	1	.545	274	210
Los Angeles	6	6	0	.500	259	214
Detroit	3	9	0	.250	231	305

Eastern Division playoff: Philadelphia 21, PITTSBURGH 0
NFL championship: CHI. CARDINALS 28, Philadelphia 21

1946

Eastern Division

	W	L	T	Pct.	Pts.	OP
N.Y. Giants	7	3	1	.700	236	162
Philadelphia	6	5	0	.545	231	220
Washington	5	5	1	.500	171	191
Pittsburgh	5	5	1	.500	136	117
Boston	2	8	1	.200	189	273

Western Division

	W	L	T	Pct.	Pts.	OP
Chi. Bears	8	2	1	.800	289	193
Los Angeles	6	4	1	.600	277	257
Green Bay	6	5	0	.545	148	158
Chi. Cardinals	6	5	0	.545	260	198
Detroit	1	10	0	.091	142	310

NFL championship: Chi. Bears 24, N.Y. GIANTS 14

1945

Eastern Division

	W	L	T	Pct.	Pts.	OP
Washington	8	2	0	.800	209	121
Philadelphia	7	3	0	.700	272	133
N.Y. Giants	3	6	1	.333	179	198
Boston	3	6	1	.333	123	211
Pittsburgh	2	8	0	.200	79	220

Western Division

	W	L	T	Pct.	Pts.	OP
Cleveland	9	1	0	.900	244	136
Detroit	7	3	0	.700	195	194
Green Bay	6	4	0	.600	258	173
Chi. Bears	3	7	0	.300	192	235
Chi. Cardinals	1	9	0	.100	98	228

NFL championship: CLEVELAND 15, Washington 14

1944

Eastern Division

	W	L	T	Pct.	Pts.	OP
N.Y. Giants	8	1	1	.889	206	75
Philadelphia	7	1	2	.875	267	131
Washington	6	3	1	.667	169	180
Boston	2	8	0	.200	82	233
Brooklyn	0	10	0	.000	69	166

Western Division

	W	L	T	Pct.	Pts.	OP
Green Bay	8	2	0	.800	238	141
Chi. Bears	6	3	1	.667	258	172
Detroit	6	3	1	.667	216	151
Cleveland	4	6	0	.400	188	224
Card-Pitt	0	10	0	.000	108	328

NFL championship: Green Bay 14, N.Y. GIANTS 7

1943

Eastern Division

	W	L	T	Pct.	Pts.	OP
Washington	6	3	1	.667	229	137
N.Y. Giants	6	3	1	.667	197	170
Phil-Pitt	5	4	1	.556	225	230
Brooklyn	2	8	0	.200	65	234

Western Division

	W	L	T	Pct.	Pts.	OP
Chi. Bears	8	1	1	.889	303	157
Green Bay	7	2	1	.778	264	172
Detroit	3	6	1	.333	178	218
Chi. Cardinals	0	10	0	.000	95	238

Eastern Division playoff: Washington 28, N.Y. GIANTS 0
NFL championship: CHI. BEARS 41, Washington 21

1942

Eastern Division

	W	L	T	Pct.	Pts.	OP
Washington	10	1	0	.909	227	102
Pittsburgh	7	4	0	.636	167	119
N.Y. Giants	5	5	1	.500	155	139
Brooklyn	3	8	0	.273	100	168
Philadelphia	2	9	0	.182	134	239

Western Division

	W	L	T	Pct.	Pts.	OP
Chi. Bears	11	0	0	1.000	376	84
Green Bay	8	2	1	.800	300	215
Cleveland	5	6	0	.455	150	207
Chi. Cardinals	3	8	0	.273	98	209
Detroit	0	11	0	.000	38	263

NFL championship: WASHINGTON 14, Chi. Bears 6

1941

Eastern Division

	W	L	T	Pct.	Pts.	OP
N.Y. Giants	8	3	0	.727	238	114
Brooklyn	7	4	0	.636	158	127
Washington	6	5	0	.545	176	174
Philadelphia	2	8	1	.200	119	218
Pittsburgh	1	9	1	.100	103	276

Western Division

	W	L	T	Pct.	Pts.	OP
Chi. Bears	10	1	0	.909	396	147
Green Bay	10	1	0	.909	258	120
Detroit	4	6	1	.400	121	195
Chi. Cardinals	3	7	1	.300	127	197
Cleveland	2	9	0	.182	116	244

Western Division playoff: CHI. BEARS 33, Green Bay 14
NFL championship: CHI. BEARS 37, N.Y. Giants 9

1940

Eastern Division

	W	L	T	Pct.	Pts.	OP
Washington	9	2	0	.818	245	142
Brooklyn	8	3	0	.727	186	120
N.Y. Giants	6	4	1	.600	131	133
Pittsburgh	2	7	2	.222	60	178
Philadelphia	1	10	0	.091	111	211

Western Division

	W	L	T	Pct.	Pts.	OP
Chi. Bears	8	3	0	.727	238	152
Green Bay	6	4	1	.600	238	155
Detroit	5	5	1	.500	138	153
Cleveland	4	6	1	.400	171	191
Chi. Cardinals	2	7	2	.222	139	222

NFL championship: Chi. Bears 73, WASHINGTON 0

1939

Eastern Division

	W	L	T	Pct.	Pts.	OP
N.Y. Giants	9	1	1	.900	168	85
Washington	8	2	1	.800	242	94
Brooklyn	4	6	1	.400	108	219
Philadelphia	1	9	1	.100	105	200
Pittsburgh	1	9	1	.100	114	216

Western Division

	W	L	T	Pct.	Pts.	OP
Green Bay	9	2	0	.818	233	153
Chi. Bears	8	3	0	.727	298	157
Detroit	6	5	0	.545	145	150
Cleveland	5	5	1	.500	195	164
Chi. Cardinals	1	10	0	.091	84	254

NFL championship: GREEN BAY 27, N.Y. Giants 0

1938

Eastern Division

	W	L	T	Pct.	Pts.	OP
N.Y. Giants	8	2	1	.800	194	79
Washington	6	3	2	.667	148	154
Brooklyn	4	4	3	.500	131	161
Philadelphia	5	6	0	.455	154	164
Pittsburgh	2	9	0	.182	79	169

Western Division

	W	L	T	Pct.	Pts.	OP
Green Bay	8	3	0	.727	223	118
Detroit	7	4	0	.636	119	108
Chi. Bears	6	5	0	.545	194	148
Cleveland	4	7	0	.364	131	215
Chi. Cardinals	2	9	0	.182	111	168

NFL championship: N.Y. GIANTS 23, Green Bay 17

1937

Eastern Division

	W	L	T	Pct.	Pts.	OP
Washington	8	3	0	.727	195	120
N.Y. Giants	6	3	2	.667	128	109
Pittsburgh	4	7	0	.364	122	145
Brooklyn	3	7	1	.300	82	174
Philadelphia	2	8	1	.200	86	177

Western Division

	W	L	T	Pct.	Pts.	OP
Chi. Bears	9	1	1	.900	201	100
Green Bay	7	4	0	.636	220	122
Detroit	7	4	0	.636	180	105
Chi. Cardinals	5	5	1	.500	135	165
Cleveland	1	10	0	.091	75	207

NFL championship: Washington 28, CHI. BEARS 21

1936

Eastern Division

	W	L	T	Pct.	Pts.	OP
Boston	7	5	0	.583	149	110
Pittsburgh	6	6	0	.500	98	187
N.Y. Giants	5	6	1	.455	115	163
Brooklyn	3	8	1	.273	92	161
Philadelphia	1	11	0	.083	51	206

Western Division

	W	L	T	Pct.	Pts.	OP
Green Bay	10	1	1	.909	248	118
Chi. Bears	9	3	0	.750	222	94
Detroit	8	4	0	.667	235	102
Chi. Cardinals	3	8	1	.273	74	143

NFL championship: Green Bay 21, Boston 6, at Polo Grounds, N.Y.

1935

Eastern Division

	W	L	T	Pct.	Pts.	OP
N. Y. Giants	9	3	0	.750	180	96
Brooklyn	5	6	1	.455	90	141
Pittsburgh	4	8	0	.333	100	209
Boston	2	8	1	.200	65	123
Philadelphia	2	9	0	.182	60	179

Western Division

	W	L	T	Pct.	Pts.	OP
Detroit	7	3	2	.700	191	111
Green Bay	8	4	0	.667	181	96
Chi. Bears	6	4	2	.600	192	106
Chi. Cardinals	6	4	2	.600	99	97

NFL championship: DETROIT 26, N.Y. Giants 7
One game between Boston and Philadelphia was canceled.

1934

Eastern Division

	W	L	T	Pct.	Pts.	OP
N.Y. Giants	8	5	0	.615	147	107
Boston	6	6	0	.500	107	94
Brooklyn	4	7	0	.364	61	153
Philadelphia	4	7	0	.364	127	85
Pittsburgh	2	10	0	.167	51	206

Western Division

	W	L	T	Pct.	Pts.	OP
Chi. Bears	13	0	0	1.000	286	86
Detroit	10	3	0	.769	238	59
Green Bay	7	6	0	.538	156	112
Chi. Cardinals	5	6	0	.455	80	84
St. Louis	1	2	0	.333	27	61
Cincinnati	0	8	0	.000	10	243

NFL championship: N.Y. GIANTS 30, Chi. Bears 13

1933

Eastern Division

	W	L	T	Pct.	Pts.	OP
N.Y. Giants	11	3	0	.786	244	101
Brooklyn	5	4	1	.556	93	54
Boston	5	5	2	.500	103	97
Philadelphia	3	5	1	.375	77	158
Pittsburgh	3	6	2	.333	67	208

Western Division

	W	L	T	Pct.	Pts.	OP
Chi. Bears	10	2	1	.833	133	82
Portsmouth	6	5	0	.545	128	87
Green Bay	5	7	1	.417	170	107
Cincinnati	3	6	1	.333	38	110
Chi. Cardinals	1	9	1	.100	52	101

NFL championship: CHI. BEARS 23, N.Y. Giants 21

1932

	W	L	T	Pct.
Chicago Bears	6	1	6	.857
Portsmouth Spartans	6	1	4	.857
Green Bay Packers	10	3	1	.769
Boston Braves	4	4	2	.500
New York Giants	4	6	2	.400
Brooklyn Dodgers	3	9	0	.250
Chicago Cardinals	2	6	2	.250
Staten Island Stapletons	2	7	3	.222

1931

	W	L	T	Pct.
Green Bay Packers	12	2	0	.857
Portsmouth Spartans	11	3	0	.786
Chicago Bears	8	5	0	.615
Chicago Cardinals	5	4	0	.556
New York Giants	7	6	1	.538
Providence Steam Roller	4	4	3	.500
Staten Island Stapletons	4	6	1	.400
Cleveland Indians	2	8	0	.200
Brooklyn Dodgers	2	12	0	.143
Frankford Yellow Jackets	1	6	1	.143

1930

	W	L	T	Pct.
Green Bay Packers	10	3	1	.769
New York Giants	13	4	0	.765
Chicago Bears	9	4	1	.692
Brooklyn Dodgers	7	4	1	.636
Providence Steam Roller	6	4	1	.600
Staten Island Stapletons	5	5	2	.500
Chicago Cardinals	5	6	2	.455
Portsmouth Spartans	5	6	3	.455
Frankford Yellow Jackets	4	13	1	.222
Minneapolis Red Jackets	1	7	1	.125
Newark Tornadoes	1	10	1	.091

1929

	W	L	T	Pct.
Green Bay Packers	12	0	1	1.000
New York Giants	13	1	1	.929
Frankford Yellow Jackets	9	4	5	.692
Chicago Cardinals	6	6	1	.500
Boston Bulldogs	4	4	0	.500
Orange Tornadoes	3	4	4	.429
Staten Island Stapletons	3	4	3	.429
Providence Steam Roller	4	6	2	.400
Chicago Bears	4	9	2	.308
Buffalo Bisons	1	7	1	.125
Minneapolis Red Jackets	1	9	0	.100
Dayton Triangles	0	6	0	.000

1928

	W	L	T	Pct.
Providence Steam Roller	8	1	2	.889
Frankford Yellow Jackets	11	3	2	.786
Detroit Wolverines	7	2	1	.778
Green Bay Packers	6	4	3	.600
Chicago Bears	7	5	1	.583
New York Giants	4	7	2	.364
New York Yankees	4	8	1	.333
Pottsville Maroons	2	8	0	.200
Chicago Cardinals	1	5	0	.167
Dayton Triangles	0	7	0	.000

1927

	W	L	T	Pct.
New York Giants	11	1	1	.917
Green Bay Packers	7	2	1	.778
Chicago Bears	9	3	2	.750
Cleveland Bulldogs	8	4	1	.667
Providence Steam Roller	8	5	1	.615
New York Yankees	7	8	1	.467
Frankford Yellow Jackets	6	9	3	.400
Pottsville Maroons	5	8	0	.385
Chicago Cardinals	3	7	1	.300
Dayton Triangles	1	6	1	.143
Duluth Eskimos	1	8	0	.111
Buffalo Bisons	0	5	0	.000

1926

	W	L	T	Pct.
Frankford Yellow Jackets	14	1	1	.933
Chicago Bears	12	1	3	.923
Pottsville Maroons	10	2	1	.833
Kansas City Cowboys	8	3	0	.727
Green Bay Packers	7	3	3	.700
Los Angeles Buccaneers	6	3	1	.667
New York Giants	8	4	1	.667
Duluth Eskimos	6	5	3	.545
Buffalo Rangers	4	4	2	.500
Chicago Cardinals	5	6	1	.455
Providence Steam Roller	5	7	1	.417
Detroit Panthers	4	6	2	.400
Hartford Blues	3	7	0	.300
Brooklyn Lions	3	8	0	.273
Milwaukee Badgers	2	7	0	.222
Akron Pros	1	4	3	.200
Dayton Triangles	1	4	1	.200
Racine Tornadoes	1	4	0	.200
Columbus Tigers	1	6	0	.143
Canton Bulldogs	1	9	3	.100
Hammond Pros	0	4	0	.000
Louisville Colonels	0	4	0	.000

1925

	W	L	T	Pct.
Chicago Cardinals	11	2	1	.846
Pottsville Maroons	10	2	0	.833
Detroit Panthers	8	2	2	.800
New York Giants	8	4	0	.667
Akron Indians	4	2	2	.667
Frankford Yellow Jackets	13	7	0	.650
Chicago Bears	9	5	3	.643
Rock Island Independents	5	3	3	.625
Green Bay Packers	8	5	0	.615
Providence Steam Roller	6	5	1	.545
Canton Bulldogs	4	4	0	.500
Cleveland Bulldogs	5	8	1	.385
Kansas City Cowboys	2	5	1	.286
Hammond Pros	1	4	0	.250
Buffalo Bisons	1	6	2	.143
Duluth Kelleys	0	3	0	.000
Rochester Jeffersons	0	6	1	.000
Milwaukee Badgers	0	6	0	.000
Dayton Triangles	0	7	1	.000
Columbus Tigers	0	9	0	.000

1924

	W	L	T	Pct.
Cleveland Bulldogs	7	1	1	.875
Chicago Bears	6	1	4	.857
Frankford Yellow Jackets	11	2	1	.846
Duluth Kelleys	5	1	0	.833
Rock Island Independents	6	2	2	.750
Green Bay Packers	7	4	0	.636
Racine Legion	4	3	3	.571
Chicago Cardinals	5	4	1	.556
Buffalo Bisons	6	5	0	.545
Columbus Tigers	4	4	0	.500
Hammond Pros	2	2	1	.500
Milwaukee Badgers	5	8	0	.385
Akron Indians	2	6	0	.333
Dayton Triangles	2	6	0	.333
Kansas City Blues	2	7	0	.222
Kenosha Maroons	0	5	1	.000
Minneapolis Marines	0	6	0	.000
Rochester Jeffersons	0	7	0	.000

1923

	W	L	T	Pct.
Canton Bulldogs	11	0	1	1.000
Chicago Bears	9	2	1	.818
Green Bay Packers	7	2	1	.778
Milwaukee Badgers	7	2	3	.778
Cleveland Indians	3	1	3	.750
Chicago Cardinals	8	4	0	.667
Duluth Kelleys	4	3	0	.571
Columbus Tigers	5	4	1	.556
Buffalo All-Americans	4	4	3	.500
Racine Legion	4	4	2	.500
Toledo Maroons	2	3	2	.400
Rock Island Independents	2	3	3	.400
Minneapolis Marines	2	5	2	.286
St. Louis All-Stars	1	4	2	.200
Hammond Pros	1	5	1	.167
Dayton Triangles	1	6	1	.143
Akron Indians	1	6	0	.143
Oorang Indians	1	10	0	.091
Rochester Jeffersons	0	2	0	.000
Louisville Brecks	0	3	0	.000

1922

	W	L	T	Pct.
Canton Bulldogs	10	0	2	1.000
Chicago Bears	9	3	0	.750
Chicago Cardinals	8	3	0	.727
Toledo Maroons	5	2	2	.714
Rock Island Independents	4	2	1	.667
Racine Legion	6	4	1	.600
Dayton Triangles	4	3	1	.571
Green Bay Packers	4	3	3	.571
Buffalo All-Americans	5	4	1	.556
Akron Pros	3	5	2	.375
Milwaukee Badgers	2	4	3	.333
Oorang Indians	2	6	0	.250
Minneapolis Marines	1	3	0	.250
Louisville Brecks	1	3	0	.250
Evansville Crimson Giants	0	3	0	.000
Rochester Jeffersons	0	4	1	.000
Hammond Pros	0	5	1	.000
Columbus Panhandles	0	7	0	.000

1921

	W	L	T	Pct.
Chicago Staleys	9	1	1	.900
Buffalo All-Americans	9	1	2	.900
Akron Pros	8	3	1	.727
Canton Bulldogs	5	2	3	.714
Rock Island Independents	4	2	1	.667
Evansville Crimson Giants	3	2	0	.600
Green Bay Packers	3	2	1	.600
Dayton Triangles	4	4	1	.500
Chicago Cardinals	3	3	2	.500
Rochester Jeffersons	2	3	0	.400
Cleveland Indians	3	5	0	.375
Washington Senators	1	2	0	.333
Cincinnati Celts	1	3	0	.250
Hammond Pros	1	3	1	.250
Minneapolis Marines	1	3	1	.250
Detroit Heralds	1	5	1	.167
Columbus Panhandles	1	8	0	.111
Tonawanda Kardex	0	1	0	.000
Muncie Flyers	0	2	0	.000
Louisville Brecks	0	2	0	.000
New York Giants	0	2	0	.000

1920

	W	L	T	Pct.
Akron Pros	8	0	3	1.000
Decatur Staleys	10	1	2	.909
Buffalo All-Americans	9	1	1	.900
Chicago Cardinals	6	2	2	.750
Rock Island Independents	6	2	2	.750
Dayton Triangles	5	2	2	.714
Rochester Jeffersons	6	3	2	.667
Canton Bulldogs	7	4	2	.636
Detroit Heralds	2	3	3	.400
Cleveland Tigers	2	4	2	.333
Chicago Tigers	2	5	1	.286
Hammond Pros	2	5	0	.286
Columbus Panhandles	2	6	2	.250
Muncie Flyers	0	1	0	.000

ALL-TIME TEAM VS. TEAM RESULTS

ATLANTA vs. BUFFALO
Series tied, 2-2
1973—Bills, 17-6 (A)
1977—Bills, 3-0 (B)
1980—Falcons, 30-14 (B)
1983—Falcons, 31-14 (A)
(Points—Falcons 67, Bills 48)
ATLANTA vs. CHICAGO
Falcons lead series, 9-6
1966—Bears, 23-6 (C)
1967—Bears, 23-14 (A)
1968—Falcons, 16-13 (C)
1969—Falcons, 48-31 (A)
1970—Bears, 23-14 (A)
1972—Falcons, 37-21 (C)
1973—Falcons, 46-6 (A)
1974—Falcons, 13-10 (A)
1976—Falcons, 10-0 (C)
1977—Falcons, 16-10 (C)
1978—Bears, 13-7 (C)
1980—Falcons, 28-17 (A)
1983—Falcons, 20-17 (C)
1985—Bears, 36-0 (C)
1986—Bears, 13-10 (A)
(Points—Falcons 285, Bears 256)
ATLANTA vs. CINCINNATI
Bengals lead series, 4-1
1971—Falcons, 9-6 (C)
1975—Bengals, 21-14 (A)
1978—Bengals, 37-7 (C)
1981—Bengals, 30-28 (A)
1984—Bengals, 35-14 (C)
(Points—Bengals 129, Falcons 72)
ATLANTA vs. CLEVELAND
Browns lead series, 6-1
1966—Browns, 49-17 (A)
1968—Browns, 30-7 (C)
1971—Falcons, 31-14 (C)
1976—Browns, 20-17 (A)
1978—Browns, 24-16 (A)
1981—Browns, 28-17 (C)
1984—Browns, 23-7 (A)
(Points—Browns 188, Falcons 112)
ATLANTA vs. DALLAS
Cowboys lead series, 8-2
1966—Cowboys, 47-14 (A)
1967—Cowboys, 37-7 (D)
1969—Cowboys, 24-17 (A)
1970—Cowboys, 13-0 (D)
1974—Cowboys, 24-0 (A)
1976—Falcons, 17-10 (A)
1978—*Cowboys, 27-20 (D)
1980—*Cowboys, 30-27 (A)
1985—Cowboys, 24-10 (D)
1986—Falcons, 37-35 (D)
(Points—Cowboys 271, Falcons 149)
**NFC Divisional Playoff*
ATLANTA vs. DENVER
Series tied, 3-3
1970—Broncos, 24-10 (D)
1972—Falcons, 23-20 (A)
1975—Falcons, 35-21 (A)
1979—Broncos, 20-17 (A) OT
1982—Falcons, 34-27 (D)
1985—Broncos, 44-28 (A)
(Points—Broncos 156, Falcons 147)
ATLANTA vs. DETROIT
Lions lead series, 12-5
1966—Lions, 28-10 (D)
1967—Lions, 24-3 (D)
1968—Lions, 24-7 (A)
1969—Lions, 27-21 (D)
1971—Lions, 41-38 (D)
1972—Lions, 26-23 (A)
1973—Lions, 31-6 (D)
1975—Lions, 17-14 (A)
1976—Lions, 24-10 (D)
1977—Falcons, 17-6 (A)
1978—Falcons, 14-0 (A)
1979—Lions, 24-23 (D)
1980—Falcons, 43-28 (A)
1983—Falcons, 30-14 (D)
1984—Lions, 27-24 (A) OT
1985—Lions, 28-27 (A)
1986—Falcons, 20-6 (D)
(Points—Lions 375, Falcons 330)
ATLANTA vs. GREEN BAY
Packers lead series, 8-6
1966—Packers, 56-3 (Mil)
1967—Packers, 23-0 (Mil)
1968—Packers, 38-7 (A)
1969—Packers, 28-10 (GB)
1970—Packers, 27-24 (GB)
1971—Falcons, 28-21 (A)
1972—Falcons, 10-9 (Mil)
1974—Falcons, 10-3 (A)
1975—Packers, 22-13 (GB)
1976—Packers, 24-20 (A)
1979—Falcons, 25-7 (A)
1981—Falcons, 31-17 (GB)
1982—Packers, 38-7 (A)
1983—Falcons, 47-41 (A) OT
(Points—Packers 354, Falcons 235)
ATLANTA vs. HOUSTON
Falcons lead series, 4-1
1972—Falcons, 20-10 (A)
1976—Oilers, 20-14 (H)
1978—Falcons, 20-14 (A)
1981—Falcons, 31-27 (H)
1984—Falcons, 42-10 (A)
(Points—Falcons 127, Oilers 81)
ATLANTA vs. *INDIANAPOLIS
Colts lead series, 9-0
1966—Colts, 19-7 (A)
1967—Colts, 38-31 (B)
Colts, 49-7 (A)
1968—Colts, 28-20 (A)
Colts, 44-0 (B)
1969—Colts, 21-14 (A)
Colts, 13-6 (B)
1974—Colts, 17-7 (A)
1986—Colts, 28-23 (A)
(Points—Colts 257, Falcons 115)
**Franchise in Baltimore prior to 1984*
ATLANTA vs. KANSAS CITY
Chiefs lead series, 2-0
1972—Chiefs, 17-14 (A)
1985—Chiefs, 38-10 (KC)
(Points—Chiefs 55, Falcons 24)
ATLANTA vs. *L.A. RAIDERS
Raiders lead series, 4-1
1971—Falcons, 24-13 (A)
1975—Raiders, 37-34 (O) OT
1979—Raiders, 50-19 (O)
1982—Raiders, 38-14 (A)
1985—Raiders, 34-24 (A)
(Points—Raiders 172, Falcons 115)
**Franchise in Oakland prior to 1982*
ATLANTA vs. L.A. RAMS
Rams lead series, 29-9-2
1966—Rams, 19-14 (A)
1967—Rams, 31-3 (A)
Rams, 20-3 (LA)
1968—Rams, 27-14 (LA)
Rams, 17-10 (A)
1969—Rams, 17-7 (LA)
Rams, 38-6 (A)
1970—Tie, 10-10 (LA)
Rams, 17-7 (A)
1971—Tie, 20-20 (LA)
Rams, 24-16 (A)
1972—Falcons, 31-3 (A)
Rams, 20-7 (LA)
1973—Rams, 31-0 (LA)
Falcons, 15-13 (A)
1974—Rams, 21-0 (LA)
Rams, 30-7 (A)
1975—Rams, 22-7 (LA)
Rams, 16-7 (A)
1976—Rams, 30-14 (A)
Rams, 59-0 (LA)
1977—Falcons, 17-6 (A)
Rams, 23-7 (LA)
1978—Rams, 10-0 (LA)
Falcons, 15-7 (A)
1979—Rams, 20-14 (LA)
Rams, 34-13 (A)
1980—Falcons, 13-10 (A)
Rams, 20-17 (LA) OT
1981—Rams, 37-35 (A)
Rams, 21-16 (LA)
1982—Falcons, 34-17 (A)
1983—Rams, 27-21 (LA)
Rams, 36-13 (A)
1984—Falcons, 30-28 (LA)
Rams, 24-10 (A)
1985—Rams, 17-6 (LA)
Falcons, 30-14 (A)
1986—Falcons, 26-14 (A)
Rams, 14-7 (LA)
(Points—Rams 864, Falcons 522)
ATLANTA vs. MIAMI
Dolphins lead series, 4-1
1970—Dolphins, 20-7 (A)
1974—Dolphins, 42-7 (M)
1980—Dolphins, 20-17 (A)
1983—Dolphins, 31-24 (M)
1986—Falcons, 20-14 (M)
(Points—Dolphins 127, Falcons 75)
ATLANTA vs. MINNESOTA
Vikings lead series, 9-6
1966—Falcons, 20-13 (M)
1967—Falcons, 21-20 (A)
1968—Vikings, 47-7 (M)
1969—Falcons, 10-3 (A)
1970—Vikings, 37-7 (A)
1971—Vikings, 24-7 (M)
1973—Falcons, 20-14 (A)
1974—Vikings, 23-10 (M)
1975—Vikings, 38-0 (M)
1977—Vikings, 14-7 (A)
1980—Vikings, 24-23 (M)
1981—Falcons, 31-30 (A)
1982—*Vikings, 30-24 (M)
1984—Vikings, 27-20 (M)
1985—Falcons, 14-13 (A)
(Points—Vikings 357, Falcons 221)
**NFC First Round Playoff*
ATLANTA vs. NEW ENGLAND
Patriots lead series, 3-2
1972—Patriots, 21-20 (NE)
1977—Patriots, 16-10 (A)
1980—Falcons, 37-21 (NE)
1983—Falcons, 24-13 (A)
1986—Patriots, 25-17 (NE)
(Points—Falcons 108, Patriots 96)
ATLANTA vs. NEW ORLEANS
Falcons lead series, 24-12
1967—Saints, 27-24 (NO)
1969—Falcons, 45-17 (A)
1970—Falcons, 14-3 (NO)
Falcons, 32-14 (A)
1971—Falcons, 28-6 (A)
Falcons, 24-20 (NO)
1972—Falcons, 21-14 (NO)
Falcons, 36-20 (A)
1973—Falcons, 62-7 (NO)
Falcons, 14-10 (A)
1974—Saints, 14-13 (NO)
Saints, 13-3 (A)
1975—Falcons, 14-7 (A)
Saints, 23-7 (NO)
1976—Saints, 30-0 (NO)
Falcons, 23-20 (A)
1977—Saints, 21-20 (NO)
Falcons, 35-7 (A)
1978—Falcons, 20-17 (NO)
Falcons, 20-17 (A)
1979—Falcons, 40-34 (NO) OT
Saints, 37-6 (A)
1980—Falcons, 41-14 (NO)
Falcons, 31-13 (A)
1981—Falcons, 27-0 (A)
Falcons, 41-10 (NO)
1982—Falcons, 35-0 (A)
Saints, 35-6 (NO)
1983—Saints, 19-17 (A)
Saints, 27-10 (NO)
1984—Falcons, 36-28 (NO)
Saints, 17-13 (A)
1985—Falcons, 31-24 (A)
Falcons, 16-10 (NO)
1986—Falcons, 31-10 (NO)
Saints, 14-9 (A)
(Points—Falcons 845, Saints 599)
ATLANTA vs. N.Y. GIANTS
Falcons lead series, 6-5
1966—Falcons, 27-16 (NY)
1968—Falcons, 24-21 (A)
1971—Giants, 21-17 (A)
1974—Falcons, 14-7 (New Haven)
1977—Falcons, 17-3 (A)
1978—Falcons, 23-20 (A)
1979—Giants, 24-3 (NY)
1981—Giants, 27-24 (A) OT
1982—Falcons, 16-14 (NY)
1983—Giants, 16-13 (A) OT
1984—Giants, 19-7 (A)
(Points—Giants 188, Falcons 185)
ATLANTA vs. N.Y. JETS
Series tied, 2-2
1973—Falcons, 28-20 (NY)
1980—Jets, 14-7 (A)
1983—Falcons, 27-21 (NY)
1986—Jets, 28-14 (A)
(Points—Jets 83, Falcons 76)
ATLANTA vs. PHILADELPHIA
Eagles lead series, 7-6-1
1966—Eagles, 23-10 (P)
1967—Eagles, 38-7 (A)
1969—Falcons, 27-3 (P)
1970—Tie, 13-13 (P)
1973—Falcons, 44-27 (P)
1976—Eagles, 14-13 (A)
1978—*Falcons, 14-13 (A)
1979—Falcons, 14-10 (P)
1980—Falcons, 20-17 (P)
1981—Eagles, 16-13 (P)
1983—Eagles, 28-24 (A)
1984—Falcons, 26-10 (A)
1985—Eagles, 23-17 (P) OT
1986—Eagles, 16-0 (A)
(Points—Eagles 251, Falcons 242)
**NFC First Round Playoff*
ATLANTA vs. PITTSBURGH
Steelers lead series, 6-1
1966—Steelers, 57-33 (A)
1968—Steelers, 41-21 (A)
1970—Falcons, 27-16 (A)
1974—Steelers, 24-17 (P)
1978—Steelers, 31-7 (P)
1981—Steelers, 34-20 (A)
1984—Steelers, 35-10 (P)
(Points—Steelers 238, Falcons 135)
ATLANTA vs. ST. LOUIS
Cardinals lead series, 6-4
1966—Falcons, 16-10 (A)
1968—Cardinals, 17-12 (StL)
1971—Cardinals, 26-9 (A)
1973—Cardinals, 32-10 (A)
1975—Cardinals, 23-20 (StL)
1978—Cardinals, 42-21 (StL)
1980—Falcons, 33-27 (StL) OT
1981—Falcons, 41-20 (A)
1982—Cardinals, 23-20 (A)
1986—Falcons, 33-13 (A)
(Points—Cardinals 233, Falcons 215)
ATLANTA vs. SAN DIEGO
Falcons lead series, 2-0
1973—Falcons, 41-0 (SD)
1979—Falcons, 28-26 (SD)
(Points—Falcons 69, Chargers 26)
ATLANTA vs. SAN FRANCISCO
49ers lead series, 22-17-1
1966—49ers, 44-7 (A)
1967—49ers, 38-7 (SF)
49ers, 34-28 (A)
1968—49ers, 28-13 (SF)
49ers, 14-12 (A)
1969—Falcons, 24-12 (A)
Falcons, 21-7 (SF)
1970—Falcons, 21-20 (A)
49ers, 24-20 (SF)
1971—Falcons, 20-17 (A)
49ers, 24-3 (SF)
1972—49ers, 49-14 (A)
49ers, 20-0 (SF)
1973—49ers, 13-9 (A)
Falcons, 17-3 (SF)
1974—49ers, 16-10 (A)
49ers, 27-0 (SF)
1975—Falcons, 17-3 (SF)
Falcons, 31-9 (A)
1976—49ers, 15-0 (SF)
Falcons, 21-16 (A)
1977—Falcons, 7-0 (SF)
49ers, 10-3 (A)
1978—Falcons, 20-17 (SF)
Falcons, 21-10 (A)
1979—49ers, 20-15 (SF)
Falcons, 31-21 (A)
1980—Falcons, 20-17 (SF)
Falcons, 35-10 (A)
1981—Falcons, 34-17 (A)
49ers, 17-14 (SF)
1982—Falcons, 17-7 (SF)
1983—49ers, 24-20 (SF)
Falcons, 28-24 (A)
1984—49ers, 14-5 (SF)
49ers, 35-17 (A)
1985—49ers, 35-16 (SF)
49ers, 38-17 (A)
1986—Tie, 10-10 (A) OT
49ers, 20-0 (SF)
(Points—49ers 779, Falcons 625)
ATLANTA vs. SEATTLE
Seahawks lead series, 3-0
1976—Seahawks, 30-13 (S)
1979—Seahawks, 31-28 (A)
1985—Seahawks, 30-26 (S)
(Points—Seahawks 91, Falcons 67)
ATLANTA vs. TAMPA BAY
Series tied, 3-3
1977—Falcons, 17-0 (TB)
1978—Buccaneers, 14-9 (TB)
1979—Falcons, 17-14 (A)
1981—Buccaneers, 24-23 (TB)
1984—Buccaneers, 23-6 (TB)
1986—Falcons, 23-20 (TB) OT
(Points—Falcons 95, Buccaneers 95)
ATLANTA vs. WASHINGTON
Redskins lead series, 9-2-1
1966—Redskins, 33-20 (W)
1967—Tie, 20-20 (A)
1969—Redskins, 27-20 (W)
1972—Redskins, 24-13 (W)
1975—Redskins, 30-27 (A)
1977—Redskins, 10-6 (W)
1978—Falcons, 20-17 (A)
1979—Redskins, 16-7 (A)
1980—Falcons, 10-6 (A)
1983—Redskins, 37-21 (W)
1984—Redskins, 27-14 (W)
1985—Redskins, 44-10 (A)
(Points—Redskins 291, Falcons 188)

BUFFALO vs. ATLANTA
Series tied, 2-2;
See Atlanta vs. Buffalo

BUFFALO vs. CHICAGO
Bears lead series, 2-1
1970—Bears, 31-13 (C)
1974—Bills, 16-6 (B)
1979—Bears, 7-0 (B)
(Points—Bears 44, Bills 29)
BUFFALO vs. CINCINNATI
Bengals lead series, 9-5
1968—Bengals, 34-23 (C)
1969—Bills, 16-13 (B)
1970—Bengals, 43-14 (B)
1973—Bengals, 16-13 (B)
1975—Bengals, 33-24 (C)
1978—Bills, 5-0 (B)
1979—Bills, 51-24 (B)
1980—Bills, 14-0 (C)
1981—Bengals, 27-24 (C) OT
*Bengals, 28-21 (C)
1983—Bills, 10-6 (C)
1984—Bengals, 52-21 (C)
1985—Bengals, 23-17 (B)
1986—Bengals, 36-33 (C) OT
(Points—Bengals 335, Bills 286)
AFC Divisional Playoff
BUFFALO vs. CLEVELAND
Browns lead series, 6-2
1972—Browns, 27-10 (C)
1974—Bills, 15-10 (C)
1977—Browns, 27-16 (B)
1978—Browns, 41-20 (C)
1981—Bills, 22-13 (B)
1984—Browns, 13-10 (B)
1985—Browns, 17-7 (C)
1986—Browns, 21-17 (B)
(Points—Browns 169, Bills 117)
BUFFALO vs. DALLAS
Cowboys lead series, 3-1
1971—Cowboys, 49-37 (B)
1976—Cowboys, 17-10 (D)
1981—Cowboys, 27-14 (D)
1984—Bills, 14-3 (B)
(Points—Cowboys 96, Bills 75)
BUFFALO vs. DENVER
Bills lead series, 13-9-1
1960—Broncos, 27-21 (B)
Tie, 38-38 (D)
1961—Broncos, 22-10 (B)
Bills, 23-10 (D)
1962—Broncos, 23-20 (B)
Bills, 45-38 (D)
1963—Bills, 30-28 (D)
Bills, 27-17 (B)
1964—Bills, 30-13 (B)
Bills, 30-19 (D)
1965—Bills, 30-15 (D)
Bills, 31-13 (B)
1966—Bills, 38-21 (B)
1967—Bills, 17-16 (D)
Broncos, 21-20 (B)
1968—Broncos, 34-32 (D)
1969—Bills, 41-28 (B)
1970—Broncos, 25-10 (B)
1975—Bills, 38-14 (B)
1977—Broncos, 26-6 (D)
1979—Broncos, 19-16 (B)
1981—Bills, 9-7 (B)
1984—Broncos, 37-7 (B)
(Points—Bills 569, Broncos 511)
BUFFALO vs. DETROIT
Series tied, 1-1-1
1972—Tie, 21-21 (B)
1976—Lions, 27-14 (D)
1979—Bills, 20-17 (D)
(Points—Lions 65, Bills 55)
BUFFALO vs. GREEN BAY
Bills lead series, 2-1
1974—Bills, 27-7 (GB)
1979—Bills, 19-12 (B)
1982—Packers, 33-21 (Mil)
(Points—Bills 67, Packers 52)
BUFFALO vs. HOUSTON
Oilers lead series, 18-9
1960—Bills, 25-24 (B)
Oilers, 31-23 (H)
1961—Bills, 22-12 (H)
Oilers, 28-16 (B)
1962—Oilers, 28-23 (B)
Oilers, 17-14 (H)
1963—Oilers, 31-20 (B)
Oilers, 28-14 (H)
1964—Bills, 48-17 (H)
Bills, 24-10 (B)
1965—Oilers, 19-17 (B)
Bills, 29-18 (H)
1966—Bills, 27-20 (B)
Bills, 42-20 (H)
1967—Oilers, 20-3 (B)
Oilers, 10-3 (H)
1968—Oilers, 30-7 (B)
Oilers, 35-6 (H)
1969—Oilers, 17-3 (B)
Oilers, 28-14 (H)
1971—Oilers, 20-14 (B)
1974—Oilers, 21-9 (B)
1976—Oilers, 13-3 (B)
1978—Oilers, 17-10 (H)
1983—Bills, 30-13 (B)
1985—Bills, 20-0 (B)
1986—Oilers, 16-7 (H)
(Points—Oilers 543, Bills 473)
BUFFALO vs. *INDIANAPOLIS
Series tied, 16-16-1
1970—Tie, 17-17 (Balt)
Colts, 20-14 (Buff)
1971—Colts, 43-0 (Buff)
Colts, 24-0 (Balt)
1972—Colts, 17-0 (Buff)
Colts, 35-7 (Balt)
1973—Bills, 31-13 (Buff)
Bills, 24-17 (Balt)
1974—Bills, 27-14 (Balt)
Bills, 6-0 (Buff)
1975—Bills, 38-31 (Balt)
Colts, 42-35 (Buff)
1976—Colts, 31-13 (Buff)
Colts, 58-20 (Balt)
1977—Colts, 17-14 (Balt)
Colts, 31-13 (Buff)
1978—Bills, 24-17 (Buff)
Bills, 21-14 (Balt)
1979—Bills, 31-13 (Balt)
Colts, 14-13 (Buff)
1980—Colts, 17-12 (Buff)
Colts, 28-24 (Balt)
1981—Bills, 35-3 (Balt)
Bills, 23-17 (Buff)
1982—Bills, 20-0 (Buff)
1983—Bills, 28-23 (Buff)
Bills, 30-7 (Balt)
1984—Colts, 31-17 (I)
Bills, 21-15 (Buff)
1985—Colts, 49-17 (I)
Bills, 21-9 (Buff)
1986—Bills, 24-13 (Buff)
Colts, 24-14 (I)
(Points—Colts 704, Bills 634)
*Franchise in Baltimore prior to 1984
BUFFALO vs. *KANSAS CITY
Bills lead series, 15-12-1
1960—Texans, 45-28 (B)
Texans, 24-7 (D)
1961—Bills, 27-24 (B)
Bills, 30-20 (D)
1962—Texans, 41-21 (D)
Bills, 23-14 (B)
1963—Tie, 27-27 (B)
Bills, 35-26 (KC)
1964—Bills, 34-17 (B)
Bills, 35-22 (KC)
1965—Bills, 23-7 (KC)
Bills, 34-25 (B)
1966—Chiefs, 42-20 (B)
Bills, 29-14 (KC)
**Chiefs, 31-7 (B)
1967—Chiefs, 23-13 (KC)
1968—Chiefs, 18-7 (B)
1969—Chiefs, 29-7 (B)
Chiefs, 22-19 (KC)
1971—Chiefs, 22-9 (KC)
1973—Bills, 23-14 (B)
1976—Bills, 50-17 (B)
1978—Bills, 28-13 (B)
Chiefs, 14-10 (KC)
1982—Bills, 14-9 (B)
1983—Bills, 14-9 (KC)
1986—Chiefs, 20-17 (B)
Bills, 17-14 (KC)
(Points—Chiefs 608, Bills 603)
Franchise in Dallas prior to 1963 and known as Texans
**AFL Championship*
BUFFALO vs. *L.A. RAIDERS
Raiders lead series, 12-11
1960—Bills, 38-9 (B)
Raiders, 20-7 (O)
1961—Raiders, 31-22 (B)
Bills, 26-21 (O)
1962—Bills, 14-6 (B)
Bills, 10-6 (O)
1963—Raiders, 35-17 (O)
Bills, 12-0 (B)
1964—Bills, 23-20 (B)
Raiders, 16-13 (O)
1965—Bills, 17-12 (B)
Bills, 17-14 (O)
1966—Bills, 31-10 (O)
1967—Raiders, 24-20 (B)
Raiders, 28-21 (O)
1968—Raiders, 48-6 (B)
Raiders, 13-10 (O)
1969—Raiders, 50-21 (O)
1972—Raiders, 28-16 (O)
1974—Bills, 21-20 (B)
1977—Raiders, 34-13 (O)
1980—Bills, 24-7 (B)
1983—Raiders, 27-24 (B)
(Points—Raiders 479, Bills 423)
Franchise in Oakland prior to 1982
BUFFALO vs. L.A. RAMS
Rams lead series, 3-1
1970—Rams, 19-0 (B)
1974—Rams, 19-14 (LA)
1980—Bills, 10-7 (B) OT
1983—Rams, 41-17 (LA)
(Points—Rams 86, Bills 41)
BUFFALO vs. MIAMI
Dolphins lead series, 34-7-1
1966—Bills, 58-24 (B)
Bills, 29-0 (M)
1967—Bills, 35-13 (B)
Dolphins, 17-14 (M)
1968—Tie, 14-14 (M)
Dolphins, 21-17 (B)
1969—Dolphins, 24-6 (M)
Bills, 28-3 (B)
1970—Dolphins, 33-14 (B)
Dolphins, 45-7 (M)
1971—Dolphins, 29-14 (B)
Dolphins, 34-0 (M)
1972—Dolphins, 24-23 (M)
Dolphins, 30-16 (B)
1973—Dolphins, 27-6 (M)
Dolphins, 17-0 (B)
1974—Dolphins, 24-16 (B)
Dolphins, 35-28 (M)
1975—Dolphins, 35-30 (B)
Dolphins, 31-21 (M)
1976—Dolphins, 30-21 (B)
Dolphins, 45-27 (M)
1977—Dolphins, 13-0 (B)
Dolphins, 31-14 (M)
1978—Dolphins, 31-24 (M)
Dolphins, 25-24 (B)
1979—Dolphins, 9-7 (B)
Dolphins, 17-7 (M)
1980—Bills, 17-7 (B)
Dolphins, 17-14 (M)
1981—Bills, 31-21 (B)
Dolphins, 16-6 (M)
1982—Dolphins, 9-7 (B)
Dolphins, 27-10 (M)
1983—Dolphins, 12-0 (B)
Bills, 38-35 (M) OT
1984—Dolphins, 21-17 (B)
Dolphins, 38-7 (M)
1985—Dolphins, 23-14 (B)
Dolphins, 28-0 (M)
1986—Dolphins, 27-14 (M)
Dolphins, 34-24 (B)
(Points—Dolphins 996, Bills 699)
BUFFALO vs. MINNESOTA
Vikings lead series, 4-1
1971—Vikings, 19-0 (M)
1975—Vikings, 35-13 (B)
1979—Vikings, 10-3 (M)
1982—Bills, 23-22 (B)
1985—Vikings, 27-20 (B)
(Points—Vikings 113, Bills 59)
BUFFALO vs. *NEW ENGLAND
Patriots lead series, 30-23-1
1960—Bills, 13-0 (Bos)
Bills, 38-14 (Buff)
1961—Patriots, 23-21 (Buff)
Patriots, 52-21 (Bos)
1962—Tie, 28-28 (Buff)
Patriots, 21-10 (Bos)
1963—Bills, 28-21 (Buff)
Patriots, 17-7 (Bos)
**Patriots, 26-8 (Buff)
1964—Patriots, 36-28 (Buff)
Bills, 24-14 (Bos)
1965—Bills, 24-7 (Buff)
Bills, 23-7 (Bos)
1966—Patriots, 20-10 (Buff)
Patriots, 14-3 (Bos)
1967—Patriots, 23-0 (Buff)
Bills, 44-16 (Bos)
1968—Patriots, 16-7 (Buff)
Patriots, 23-6 (Bos)
1969—Bills, 23-16 (Buff)
Patriots, 35-21 (Bos)
1970—Bills, 45-10 (Bos)
Patriots, 14-10 (Buff)
1971—Patriots, 38-33 (NE)
Bills, 27-20 (Buff)
1972—Bills, 38-14 (Buff)
Bills, 27-24 (NE)
1973—Bills, 31-13 (NE)
Bills, 37-13 (Buff)
1974—Bills, 30-28 (Buff)
Bills, 29-28 (NE)
1975—Bills, 45-31 (Buff)
Bills, 34-14 (NE)
1976—Patriots, 26-22 (Buff)
Patriots, 20-10 (NE)
1977—Bills, 24-14 (NE)
Patriots, 20-7 (Buff)
1978—Patriots, 14-10 (Buff)
Patriots, 26-24 (NE)
1979—Patriots, 26-6 (Buff)
Bills, 16-13 (NE) OT
1980—Bills, 31-13 (Buff)
Patriots, 24-2 (NE)
1981—Bills, 20-17 (Buff)
Bills, 19-10 (NE)
1982—Patriots, 30-19 (NE)
1983—Patriots, 31-0 (Buff)
Patriots, 21-7 (NE)
1984—Patriots, 21-17 (Buff)
Patriots, 38-10 (NE)
1985—Patriots, 17-14 (Buff)
Patriots, 14-3 (NE)
1986—Patriots, 23-3 (Buff)
Patriots, 22-19 (NE)
(Points—Patriots 1,116, Bills 1,056)
*Franchise in Boston prior to 1971
**Division Playoff*
BUFFALO vs. NEW ORLEANS
Bills lead series, 2-1
1973—Saints, 13-0 (NO)
1980—Bills, 35-26 (NO)
1983—Bills, 27-21 (B)
(Points—Bills 62, Saints 60)
BUFFALO vs. N.Y. GIANTS
Giants lead series, 2-1
1970—Giants, 20-6 (NY)
1975—Giants, 17-14 (B)
1978—Bills, 41-17 (B)
(Points—Bills 61, Giants 54)
BUFFALO vs. *N.Y. JETS
Jets lead series, 27-26
1960—Titans, 27-3 (NY)
Titans, 17-13 (B)
1961—Bills, 41-31 (B)
Titans, 21-14 (NY)
1962—Titans, 17-6 (B)
Bills, 20-3 (NY)
1963—Bills, 45-14 (B)
Bills, 19-10 (NY)
1964—Bills, 34-24 (B)
Bills, 20-7 (NY)
1965—Bills, 33-21 (B)
Jets, 14-12 (NY)
1966—Bills, 33-23 (NY)
Bills, 14-3 (B)
1967—Bills, 20-17 (B)
Jets, 20-10 (NY)
1968—Bills, 37-35 (B)
Jets, 25-21 (NY)
1969—Jets, 33-19 (B)
Jets, 16-6 (NY)
1970—Bills, 34-31 (B)
Bills, 10-6 (NY)
1971—Jets, 28-17 (NY)
Jets, 20-7 (B)
1972—Jets, 41-24 (B)
Jets, 41-3 (NY)
1973—Bills, 9-7 (B)
Bills, 34-14 (NY)
1974—Bills, 16-12 (B)
Jets, 20-10 (NY)
1975—Bills, 42-14 (B)
Bills, 24-23 (NY)
1976—Jets, 17-14 (NY)
Jets, 19-14 (B)
1977—Jets, 24-19 (B)
Bills, 14-10 (NY)
1978—Jets, 21-20 (B)
Jets, 45-14 (NY)
1979—Bills, 46-31 (B)
Bills, 14-12 (NY)
1980—Bills, 20-10 (B)
Bills, 31-24 (NY)
1981—Bills, 31-0 (B)
Jets, 33-14 (NY)
**Bills, 31-27 (NY)
1983—Jets, 34-10 (B)
Bills, 24-17 (NY)
1984—Jets, 28-26 (B)
Jets, 21-17 (NY)
1985—Jets, 42-3 (NY)
Jets, 27-7 (B)
1986—Jets, 28-24 (B)
Jets, 14-13 (NY)
(Points—Jets 1,119, Bills 1,056)
*Jets known as Titans prior to 1963
**AFC First Round Playoff*
BUFFALO vs. PHILADELPHIA
Eagles lead series, 3-1
1973—Bills, 27-26 (B)
1981—Eagles, 20-14 (B)
1984—Eagles, 27-17 (B)
1985—Eagles, 21-17 (P)
(Points—Eagles 94, Bills 75)
BUFFALO vs. PITTSBURGH
Steelers lead series, 6-4
1970—Steelers, 23-10 (P)
1972—Steelers, 38-21 (B)
1974—*Steelers, 32-14 (P)
1975—Bills, 30-21 (P)
1978—Steelers, 28-17 (B)
1979—Steelers, 28-0 (P)

1980—Bills, 28-13 (B)
1982—Bills, 13-0 (B)
1985—Steelers, 30-24 (P)
1986—Bills, 16-12 (B)
(Points—Steelers 225, Bills 173)
AFC Divisional Playoff

BUFFALO vs. ST. LOUIS
Cardinals lead series, 3-2
1971—Cardinals, 28-23 (B)
1975—Bills, 32-14 (StL)
1981—Cardinals, 24-0 (StL)
1984—Cardinals, 37-7 (StL)
1986—Bills, 17-10 (B)
(Points—Cardinals 113, Bills 79)

BUFFALO vs. *SAN DIEGO
Chargers lead series, 17-9-2
1960—Chargers, 24-10 (B)
Bills, 32-3 (LA)
1961—Chargers, 19-11 (B)
Chargers, 28-10 (SD)
1962—Bills, 35-10 (B)
Bills, 40-20 (SD)
1963—Chargers, 14-10 (SD)
Chargers, 23-13 (B)
1964—Bills, 30-3 (B)
Bills, 27-24 (SD)
**Bills, 20-7 (B)
1965—Chargers, 34-3 (B)
Tie, 20-20 (SD)
**Bills, 23-0 (SD)
1966—Chargers, 27-7 (SD)
Tie, 17-17 (B)
1967—Chargers, 37-17 (B)
1968—Chargers, 21-6 (B)
1969—Chargers, 45-6 (SD)
1971—Chargers, 20-3 (SD)
1973—Chargers, 34-7 (SD)
1976—Chargers, 34-13 (B)
1979—Chargers, 27-19 (SD)
1980—Bills, 26-24 (SD)
***Chargers, 20-14 (SD)
1981—Bills, 28-27 (SD)
1985—Chargers, 14-9 (B)
Chargers, 40-7 (SD)
(Points—Chargers 616, Bills 463)
**Franchise in Los Angeles prior to 1961*
***AFL Championship*
****AFC Divisional Playoff*

BUFFALO vs. SAN FRANCISCO
Bills lead series, 2-1
1972—Bills, 27-20 (B)
1980—Bills, 18-13 (SF)
1983—49ers, 23-10 (B)
(Points—49ers 56, Bills 55)

BUFFALO vs. SEATTLE
Seahawks lead series, 2-0
1977—Seahawks, 56-17 (S)
1984—Seahawks, 31-28 (S)
(Points—Seahawks 87, Bills 45)

BUFFALO vs. TAMPA BAY
Buccaneers lead series, 3-1
1976—Bills, 14-9 (TB)
1978—Buccaneers, 31-10 (TB)
1982—Buccaneers, 24-23 (TB)
1986—Buccaneers, 34-28 (TB)
(Points—Buccaneers 98, Bills 75)

BUFFALO vs. WASHINGTON
Series tied 2-2
1972—Bills, 24-17 (W)
1977—Redskins, 10-0 (B)
1981—Bills, 21-14 (B)
1984—Redskins, 41-14 (W)
(Points—Redskins 82, Bills 59)

CHICAGO vs. ATLANTA
Falcons lead series, 9-6;
See Atlanta vs. Chicago

CHICAGO vs. BUFFALO
Bears lead series, 2-1;
See Buffalo vs. Chicago

CHICAGO vs. CINCINNATI
Bengals lead series, 2-1
1972—Bengals, 13-3 (Chi)
1980—Bengals, 17-14 (Chi) OT
1986—Bears, 44-7 (Cin)
(Points—Bears 61, Bengals 37)

CHICAGO vs. CLEVELAND
Browns lead series, 6-3
1951—Browns, 42-21 (Cle)
1954—Browns, 39-10 (Chi)
1960—Browns, 42-0 (Cle)
1961—Bears, 17-14 (Chi)
1967—Browns, 24-0 (Cle)
1969—Browns, 28-24 (Chi)
1972—Bears, 17-0 (Cle)
1980—Browns, 27-21 (Cle)
1986—Bears, 41-31 (Chi)
(Points—Browns 247, Bears 151)

CHICAGO vs. DALLAS
Cowboys lead series, 8-5
1960—Bears, 17-7 (C)
1962—Bears, 34-33 (D)
1964—Cowboys, 24-10 (C)
1968—Cowboys, 34-3 (C)
1971—Bears, 23-19 (C)
1973—Cowboys, 20-17 (C)
1976—Cowboys, 31-21 (D)
1977—*Cowboys, 37-7 (D)
1979—Cowboys, 24-20 (D)
1981—Cowboys, 10-9 (D)
1984—Cowboys, 23-14 (C)
1985—Bears, 44-0 (D)
1986—Bears, 24-10 (D)
(Points—Cowboys 272, Bears 243)
**NFC Divisional Playoff*

CHICAGO vs. DENVER
Bears lead series, 4-3
1971—Broncos, 6-3 (D)
1973—Bears, 33-14 (D)
1976—Broncos, 28-14 (C)
1978—Broncos, 16-7 (D)
1981—Bears, 35-24 (C)
1983—Bears, 31-14 (C)
1984—Bears, 27-0 (C)
(Points—Bears 150, Broncos 102)

CHICAGO vs. *DETROIT
Bears lead series, 66-44-5
1930—Spartans, 7-6 (P)
Bears, 14-6 (C)
1931—Bears, 9-6 (C)
Spartans, 3-0 (P)
1932—Tie, 13-13 (C)
Tie, 7-7 (P)
**Bears, 9-0 (C)
1933—Bears, 17-14 (C)
Bears, 17-7 (P)
1934—Bears, 19-16 (D)
Bears, 10-7 (C)
1935—Tie, 20-20 (C)
Lions, 14-2 (D)
1936—Bears, 12-10 (C)
Lions, 13-7 (D)
1937—Bears, 28-20 (C)
Bears, 13-0 (D)
1938—Lions, 13-7 (C)
Lions, 14-7 (D)
1939—Lions, 10-0 (C)
Bears, 23-13 (D)
1940—Bears, 7-0 (C)
Lions, 17-14 (D)
1941—Bears, 49-0 (C)
Bears, 24-7 (D)
1942—Bears, 16-0 (C)
Bears, 42-0 (D)
1943—Bears, 27-21 (D)
Bears, 35-14 (C)
1944—Tie, 21-21 (C)
Lions, 41-21 (D)
1945—Lions, 16-10 (D)
Lions, 35-28 (C)
1946—Bears, 42-6 (C)
Bears, 45-24 (D)
1947—Bears, 33-24 (C)
Bears, 34-14 (D)
1948—Bears, 28-0 (C)
Bears, 42-14 (D)
1949—Bears, 27-24 (C)
Bears, 28-7 (D)
1950—Bears, 35-21 (D)
Bears, 6-3 (C)
1951—Bears, 28-23 (D)
Lions, 41-28 (C)
1952—Bears, 24-23 (C)
Lions, 45-21 (D)
1953—Lions, 20-16 (C)
Lions, 13-7 (D)
1954—Lions, 48-23 (D)
Bears, 28-24 (C)
1955—Bears, 24-14 (D)
Bears, 21-20 (C)
1956—Lions, 42-10 (D)
Bears, 38-21 (C)
1957—Bears, 27-7 (D)
Lions, 21-13 (C)
1958—Bears, 20-7 (D)
Bears, 21-16 (C)
1959—Bears, 24-14 (D)
Bears, 25-14 (C)
1960—Bears, 28-7 (C)
Lions, 36-0 (D)
1961—Bears, 31-17 (D)
Lions, 16-15 (C)
1962—Lions, 11-3 (D)
Bears, 3-0 (C)
1963—Bears, 37-21 (D)
Bears, 24-14 (C)
1964—Lions, 10-0 (C)
Bears, 27-24 (D)
1965—Bears, 38-10 (C)
Bears, 17-10 (D)
1966—Lions, 14-3 (D)
Tie, 10-10 (C)
1967—Bears, 14-3 (C)
Bears, 27-13 (D)
1968—Lions, 42-0 (D)
Lions, 28-10 (C)
1969—Lions, 13-7 (D)
Lions, 20-3 (C)
1970—Lions, 28-14 (D)
Lions, 16-10 (C)
1971—Bears, 28-23 (D)
Lions, 28-3 (C)
1972—Lions, 38-24 (C)
Lions, 14-0 (D)
1973—Lions, 30-7 (C)
Lions, 40-7 (D)
1974—Bears, 17-9 (C)
Lions, 34-17 (D)
1975—Lions, 27-7 (D)
Bears, 25-21 (C)
1976—Bears, 10-3 (C)
Lions, 14-10 (D)
1977—Bears, 30-20 (C)
Bears, 31-14 (D)
1978—Bears, 19-0 (D)
Lions, 21-17 (C)
1979—Bears, 35-7 (C)
Lions, 20-0 (D)
1980—Bears, 24-7 (C)
Bears, 23-17 (D) OT
1981—Lions, 48-17 (D)
Lions, 23-7 (C)
1982—Lions, 17-10 (D)
Bears, 20-17 (C)
1983—Lions, 31-17 (D)
Lions, 38-17 (C)
1984—Bears, 16-14 (C)
Bears, 30-13 (D)
1985—Bears, 24-3 (C)
Bears, 37-17 (D)
1986—Bears, 13-7 (C)
Bears, 16-13 (D)
(Points—Bears 2,131, Lions 1,926)
**Franchise in Portsmouth prior to 1934 and known as the Spartans*
***Championship*

***CHICAGO vs. GREEN BAY**
Bears lead series, 72-55-6
1921—Staleys, 20-0 (C)
1923—Bears, 3-0 (GB)
1924—Bears, 3-0 (C)
1925—Packers, 14-10 (GB)
Bears, 21-0 (C)
1926—Tie, 6-6 (GB)
Bears, 19-13 (C)
Tie, 3-3 (C)
1927—Bears, 7-6 (GB)
Bears, 14-6 (C)
1928—Tie, 12-12 (GB)
Packers, 16-6 (C)
Packers, 6-0 (C)
1929—Packers, 23-0 (GB)
Packers, 14-0 (C)
Packers, 25-0 (C)
1930—Packers, 7-0 (GB)
Packers, 13-12 (C)
Bears, 21-0 (C)
1931—Packers, 7-0 (GB)
Packers, 6-2 (C)
Bears, 7-6 (C)
1932—Tie, 0-0 (GB)
Packers, 2-0 (C)
Bears, 9-0 (C)
1933—Bears, 14-7 (GB)
Bears, 10-7 (C)
Bears, 7-6 (C)
1934—Bears, 24-10 (GB)
Bears, 27-14 (C)
1935—Packers, 7-0 (GB)
Packers, 17-14 (C)
1936—Bears, 30-3 (GB)
Packers, 21-10 (C)
1937—Bears, 14-2 (GB)
Packers, 24-14 (C)
1938—Bears, 2-0 (GB)
Packers, 24-17 (C)
1939—Packers, 21-16 (GB)
Bears, 30-27 (C)
1940—Bears, 41-10 (GB)
Bears, 14-7 (C)
1941—Bears, 25-17 (GB)
Packers, 16-14 (C)
**Bears, 33-14 (C)
1942—Bears, 44-28 (GB)
Bears, 38-7 (C)
1943—Tie, 21-21 (GB)
Bears, 21-7 (C)
1944—Packers, 42-28 (GB)
Bears, 21-0 (C)
1945—Packers, 31-21 (GB)
Bears, 28-24 (C)
1946—Bears, 30-7 (GB)
Bears, 10-7 (C)
1947—Packers, 29-20 (GB)
Bears, 20-17 (C)
1948—Bears, 45-7 (GB)
Bears, 7-6 (C)
1949—Bears, 17-0 (GB)
Bears, 24-3 (C)
1950—Packers, 31-21 (GB)
Bears, 28-14 (C)
1951—Bears, 31-20 (GB)
Bears, 24-13 (C)
1952—Bears, 24-14 (GB)
Packers, 41-28 (C)
1953—Bears, 17-13 (GB)
Tie, 21-21 (C)
1954—Bears, 10-3 (GB)
Bears, 28-23 (C)
1955—Packers, 24-3 (GB)
Bears, 52-31 (C)
1956—Bears, 37-21 (GB)
Bears, 38-14 (C)
1957—Packers, 21-17 (GB)
Bears, 21-14 (C)
1958—Bears, 34-20 (GB)
Bears, 24-10 (C)
1959—Packers, 9-6 (GB)
Bears, 28-17 (C)
1960—Bears, 17-14 (GB)
Packers, 41-13 (C)
1961—Packers, 24-0 (GB)
Packers, 31-28 (C)
1962—Packers, 49-0 (GB)
Packers, 38-7 (C)
1963—Bears, 10-3 (GB)
Bears, 26-7 (C)
1964—Packers, 23-12 (GB)
Packers, 17-3 (C)
1965—Packers, 23-14 (GB)
Bears, 31-10 (C)
1966—Packers, 17-0 (C)
Packers, 13-6 (GB)
1967—Packers, 13-10 (GB)
Packers, 17-13 (C)
1968—Bears, 13-10 (GB)
Packers, 28-27 (C)
1969—Packers, 17-0 (GB)
Packers, 21-3 (C)
1970—Packers, 20-19 (GB)
Bears, 35-17 (C)
1971—Packers, 17-14 (C)
Packers, 31-10 (GB)
1972—Packers, 20-17 (GB)
Packers, 23-17 (C)
1973—Bears, 31-17 (GB)
Packers, 21-0 (C)
1974—Bears, 10-9 (C)
Packers, 20-3 (Mil)
1975—Bears, 27-14 (C)
Packers, 28-7 (GB)
1976—Bears, 24-13 (C)
Bears, 16-10 (GB)
1977—Bears, 26-0 (GB)
Bears, 21-10 (C)
1978—Packers, 24-14 (GB)
Bears, 14-0 (C)
1979—Bears, 6-3 (C)
Bears, 15-14 (GB)
1980—Packers, 12-6 (GB) OT
Bears, 61-7 (C)
1981—Packers, 16-9 (C)
Packers, 21-17 (GB)
1983—Packers, 31-28 (GB)
Bears, 23-21 (C)
1984—Bears, 9-7 (GB)
Packers, 20-14 (C)
1985—Bears, 23-7 (C)
Bears, 16-10 (GB)
1986—Bears, 25-12 (GB)
Bears, 12-10 (C)
(Points—Bears 2,220, Packers 1,950)
**Bears known as Staleys prior to 1922*
***Division Playoff*

CHICAGO vs. HOUSTON
Series tied, 2-2
1973—Bears, 35-14 (C)
1977—Oilers, 47-0 (H)
1980—Oilers, 10-6 (C)
1986—Bears, 20-7 (H)
(Points—Oilers 78, Bears 61)

CHICAGO vs. *INDIANAPOLIS
Colts lead series, 21-14
1953—Colts, 13-9 (B)
Colts, 16-14 (C)
1954—Bears, 28-9 (C)
Bears, 28-13 (B)
1955—Colts, 23-17 (B)
Bears, 38-10 (C)
1956—Colts, 28-21 (B)
Bears, 58-27 (C)
1957—Colts, 21-10 (B)
Colts, 29-14 (C)
1958—Colts, 51-38 (B)
Colts, 17-0 (C)
1959—Bears, 26-21 (B)
Colts, 21-7 (C)
1960—Colts, 42-7 (B)
Colts, 24-20 (C)
1961—Bears, 24-10 (C)
Bears, 21-20 (B)
1962—Bears, 35-15 (C)

Bears, 57-0 (B)
1963—Bears, 10-3 (C)
Bears, 17-7 (B)
1964—Colts, 52-0 (B)
Colts, 40-24 (C)
1965—Colts, 26-21 (C)
Bears, 13-0 (B)
1966—Bears, 27-17 (C)
Colts, 21-16 (B)
1967—Colts, 24-3 (C)
1968—Colts, 28-7 (B)
1969—Colts, 24-21 (C)
1970—Colts, 21-20 (B)
1975—Colts, 35-7 (C)
1983—Colts, 22-19 (B) OT
1985—Bears, 17-10 (C)
(Points—Colts 740, Bears 694)
Franchise in Baltimore prior to 1984

CHICAGO vs. KANSAS CITY
Bears lead series, 2-1
1973—Chiefs, 19-7 (KC)
1977—Bears, 28-27 (C)
1981—Bears, 16-13 (KC) OT
(Points—Chiefs 59, Bears 51)

CHICAGO vs. *L.A. RAIDERS
Raiders lead series, 3-2
1972—Raiders, 28-21 (O)
1976—Raiders, 28-27 (C)
1978—Raiders, 25-19 (C) OT
1981—Bears, 23-6 (O)
1984—Bears, 17-6 (C)
(Points—Bears 107, Raiders 93)
**Franchise in Oakland prior to 1982*

CHICAGO vs. *L.A. RAMS
Bears lead series, 43-28-3
1937—Bears, 20-2 (Clev)
Bears, 15-7 (C)
1938—Rams, 14-7 (C)
Rams, 23-21 (Clev)
1939—Bears, 30-21 (Clev)
Bears, 35-21 (C)
1940—Bears, 21-14 (Clev)
Bears, 47-25 (C)
1941—Bears, 48-21 (Clev)
Bears, 31-13 (C)
1942—Bears, 21-7 (Clev)
Bears, 47-0 (C)
1944—Rams, 19-7 (Clev)
Bears, 28-21 (C)
1945—Rams, 17-0 (Clev)
Rams, 41-21 (C)
1946—Tie, 28-28 (C)
Bears, 27-21 (LA)
1947—Bears, 41-21 (LA)
Rams, 17-14 (C)
1948—Bears, 42-21 (C)
Bears, 21-6 (LA)
1949—Rams, 31-16 (C)
Rams, 27-24 (LA)
1950—Bears, 24-20 (LA)
Bears, 24-14 (C)
**Rams, 24-14 (LA)
1951—Rams, 42-17 (C)
1952—Rams, 31-7 (LA)
Rams, 40-24 (C)
1953—Rams, 38-24 (LA)
Bears, 24-21 (C)
1954—Rams, 42-38 (LA)
Bears, 24-13 (C)
1955—Bears, 31-20 (LA)
Bears, 24-3 (C)
1956—Bears, 35-24 (LA)
Bears, 30-21 (C)
1957—Bears, 34-26 (C)
Bears, 16-10 (LA)
1958—Bears, 31-10 (C)
Rams, 41-35 (LA)
1959—Rams, 28-21 (C)
Bears, 26-21 (LA)
1960—Bears, 34-27 (C)
Tie, 24-24 (LA)
1961—Bears, 21-17 (LA)
Bears, 28-24 (C)
1962—Bears, 27-23 (LA)
Bears, 30-14 (C)
1963—Bears, 52-14 (LA)
Bears, 6-0 (C)
1964—Bears, 38-17 (C)
Bears, 34-24 (LA)
1965—Rams, 30-28 (LA)
Bears, 31-6 (C)
1966—Rams, 31-17 (LA)
Bears, 17-10 (C)
1967—Rams, 28-17 (C)
1968—Bears, 17-16 (LA)
1969—Rams, 9-7 (C)
1971—Rams, 17-3 (LA)
1972—Tie, 13-13 (C)
1973—Rams, 26-0 (C)
1975—Rams, 38-10 (LA)
1976—Rams, 20-12 (LA)
1977—Bears, 24-23 (C)
1979—Bears, 27-23 (C)
1981—Rams, 24-7 (C)
1982—Bears, 34-26 (LA)
1983—Rams, 21-14 (LA)
1984—Rams, 29-13 (LA)
1985—***Bears, 24-0 (C)
1986—Rams, 20-17 (C)
(Points—Bears 1,741, Rams 1,521)
**Franchise in Cleveland prior to 1946*
***Conference Playoff*
****NFC Championship*

CHICAGO vs. MIAMI
Dolphins lead series, 4-0
1971—Dolphins, 34-3 (M)
1975—Dolphins, 46-13 (C)
1979—Dolphins, 31-16 (M)
1985—Dolphins, 38-24 (M)
(Points—Dolphins 149, Bears 56)

CHICAGO vs. MINNESOTA
Vikings lead series, 26-23-2
1961—Vikings, 37-13 (M)
Bears, 52-35 (C)
1962—Bears, 13-0 (M)
Bears, 31-30 (C)
1963—Bears, 28-7 (M)
Tie, 17-17 (C)
1964—Bears, 34-28 (M)
Vikings, 41-14 (C)
1965—Bears, 45-37 (M)
Vikings, 24-17 (C)
1966—Bears, 13-10 (M)
Bears, 41-28 (C)
1967—Bears, 17-7 (M)
Tie, 10-10 (C)
1968—Bears, 27-17 (M)
Bears, 26-24 (C)
1969—Vikings, 31-0 (C)
Vikings, 31-14 (M)
1970—Vikings, 24-0 (C)
Vikings, 16-13 (M)
1971—Bears, 20-17 (M)
Vikings, 27-10 (C)
1972—Bears, 13-10 (C)
Vikings, 23-10 (M)
1973—Vikings, 22-13 (C)
Vikings, 31-13 (M)
1974—Vikings, 11-7 (M)
Vikings, 17-0 (C)
1975—Vikings, 28-3 (M)
Vikings, 13-9 (C)
1976—Vikings, 20-19 (M)
Bears, 14-13 (C)
1977—Vikings, 22-16 (M) OT
Bears, 10-7 (C)
1978—Vikings, 24-20 (C)
Vikings, 17-14 (M)
1979—Bears, 26-7 (C)
Vikings, 30-27 (M)
1980—Vikings, 34-14 (C)
Vikings, 13-7 (M)
1981—Vikings, 24-21 (M)
Bears, 10-9 (C)
1982—Vikings, 35-7 (M)
1983—Vikings, 23-14 (C)
Bears, 19-13 (M)
1984—Bears, 16-7 (C)
Bears, 34-3 (M)
1985—Bears, 33-24 (M)
Bears, 27-9 (C)
1986—Bears, 23-0 (C)
Vikings, 23-7 (M)
(Points—Vikings 1,010, Bears 901)

CHICAGO vs. NEW ENGLAND
Bears lead series, 3-2
1973—Patriots, 13-10 (C)
1979—Patriots, 27-7 (C)
1982—Bears, 26-13 (C)
1985—Bears, 20-7 (C)
*Bears, 46-10 (New Orleans)
(Points—Bears 109, Patriots 70)
**Super Bowl XX*

CHICAGO vs. NEW ORLEANS
Bears lead series, 7-4
1968—Bears, 23-17 (NO)
1970—Bears, 24-3 (NO)
1971—Bears, 35-14 (C)
1973—Saints, 21-16 (NO)
1974—Bears, 24-10 (C)
1975—Bears, 42-17 (NO)
1977—Saints, 42-24 (C)
1980—Bears, 22-3 (C)
1982—Saints, 10-0 (C)
1983—Saints, 34-31 (NO) OT
1984—Bears, 20-7 (C)
(Points—Bears 261, Saints 178)

CHICAGO vs. N.Y. GIANTS
Bears lead series, 27-16-2
1925—Bears, 19-7 (NY)
Giants, 9-0 (C)
1926—Bears, 7-0 (C)
1927—Giants, 13-7 (NY)
1928—Bears, 13-0 (C)
1929—Giants, 26-14 (C)
Giants, 34-0 (NY)
Giants, 14-9 (C)
1930—Giants, 12-0 (C)
Bears, 12-0 (NY)
1931—Bears, 6-0 (C)
Bears, 12-6 (NY)
Giants, 25-6 (C)
1932—Bears, 28-8 (NY)
Bears, 6-0 (C)
1933—Bears, 14-10 (C)
Giants, 3-0 (NY)
*Bears, 23-21 (C)
1934—Bears, 27-7 (C)
Bears, 10-9 (NY)
*Giants, 30-13 (NY)
1935—Bears, 20-3 (NY)
Giants, 3-0 (C)
1936—Bears, 25-7 (NY)
1937—Tie, 3-3 (NY)
1939—Giants, 16-13 (NY)
1940—Bears, 37-21 (NY)
1941—*Bears, 37-9 (C)
1942—Bears, 26-7 (NY)
1943—Bears, 56-7 (NY)
1946—Giants, 14-0 (NY)
*Bears, 24-14 (NY)
1948—Bears, 35-14 (C)
1949—Giants, 35-28 (NY)
1956—Tie, 17-17 (NY)
*Giants, 47-7 (NY)
1962—Giants, 26-24 (C)
1963—*Bears, 14-10 (C)
1965—Bears, 35-14 (NY)
1967—Bears, 34-7 (C)
1969—Giants, 28-24 (NY)
1970—Bears, 24-16 (NY)
1974—Bears, 16-13 (C)
1977—Bears, 12-9 (NY) OT
1985—**Bears, 21-0 (C)
(Points—Bears 758, Giants 574)
**NFL Championship*
***NFC Divisional Playoff*

CHICAGO vs. N.Y. JETS
Bears lead series, 2-1
1974—Jets, 23-21 (C)
1979—Bears, 23-13 (C)
1985—Bears, 19-6 (NY)
(Points—Bears 63, Jets 42)

CHICAGO vs. PHILADELPHIA
Bears lead series, 20-4-1
1933—Tie, 3-3 (P)
1935—Bears, 39-0 (P)
1936—Bears, 17-0 (P)
Bears, 28-7 (P)
1938—Bears, 28-6 (P)
1939—Bears, 27-14 (C)
1941—Bears, 49-14 (P)
1942—Bears, 45-14 (C)
1944—Bears, 28-7 (P)
1946—Bears, 21-14 (C)
1947—Bears, 40-7 (C)
1948—Eagles, 12-7 (P)
1949—Bears, 38-21 (C)
1955—Bears, 17-10 (C)
1961—Eagles, 16-14 (P)
1963—Bears, 16-7 (C)
1968—Bears, 29-16 (P)
1970—Bears, 20-16 (C)
1972—Bears, 21-12 (P)
1975—Bears, 15-13 (C)
1979—*Eagles, 27-17 (P)
1980—Eagles, 17-14 (P)
1983—Bears, 7-6 (P)
Bears, 17-14 (C)
1986—Bears, 13-10 (C) OT
(Points—Bears 570, Eagles 283)
**NFC First Round Playoff*

CHICAGO vs. *PITTSBURGH
Bears lead series, 14-4-1
1934—Bears, 28-0 (P)
1935—Bears, 23-7 (P)
1936—Bears, 27-9 (P)
Bears, 26-6 (C)
1937—Bears, 7-0 (P)
1939—Bears, 32-0 (P)
1941—Bears, 34-7 (C)
1945—Bears, 28-7 (P)
1947—Bears, 49-7 (C)
1949—Bears, 30-21 (C)
1958—Steelers, 24-10 (P)
1959—Bears, 27-21 (C)
1963—Tie, 17-17 (P)
1967—Steelers, 41-13 (P)
1969—Bears, 38-7 (C)
1971—Bears, 17-15 (C)
1975—Steelers, 34-3 (P)
1980—Steelers, 38-3 (P)
1986—Bears, 13-10 (C) OT
(Points—Bears 425, Steelers 271)
**Steelers known as Pirates prior to 1941*

***CHICAGO vs. **ST. LOUIS**
Bears lead series, 50-25-6
(NP denotes Normal Park;
Wr denotes Wrigley Field;
Co denotes Comiskey Park;
So denotes Soldier Field;
all Chicago)
1920—Cardinals, 7-6 (NP)
Staleys, 10-0 (Wr)
1921—Tie, 0-0 (Wr)
1922—Cardinals, 6-0 (Co)
Cardinals, 9-0 (Co)
1923—Bears, 3-0 (Wr)
1924—Bears, 6-0 (Wr)
Bears, 21-0 (Co)
1925—Cardinals, 9-0 (Co)
Tie, 0-0 (Wr)
1926—Bears, 16-0 (Wr)
Bears, 10-0 (So)
Tie, 0-0 (Wr)
1927—Bears, 9-0 (NP)
Cardinals, 3-0 (Wr)
1928—Bears, 15-0 (NP)
Bears, 34-0 (Wr)
1929—Tie, 0-0 (Wr)
Cardinals, 40-6 (Co)
1930—Bears, 32-6 (Co)
Bears, 6-0 (Wr)
1931—Bears, 26-13 (Wr)
Bears, 18-7 (Wr)
1932—Tie, 0-0 (Wr)
Bears, 34-0 (Wr)
1933—Bears, 12-9 (Wr)
Bears, 22-6 (Wr)
1934—Bears, 20-0 (Wr)
Bears, 17-6 (Wr)
1935—Tie, 7-7 (Wr)
Bears, 13-0 (Wr)
1936—Bears, 7-3 (Wr)
Cardinals, 14-7 (Wr)
1937—Bears, 16-7 (Wr)
Bears, 42-28 (Wr)
1938—Bears, 16-13 (So)
Bears, 34-28 (Wr)
1939—Bears, 44-7 (Wr)
Bears, 48-7 (Co)
1940—Cardinals, 21-7 (Co)
Bears, 31-23 (Wr)
1941—Bears, 53-7 (Wr)
Bears, 34-24 (Co)
1942—Bears, 41-14 (Wr)
Bears, 21-7 (Co)
1943—Bears, 20-0 (Wr)
Bears, 35-24 (Co)
1945—Cardinals, 16-7 (Wr)
Bears, 28-20 (Co)
1946—Bears, 34-17 (Co)
Cardinals, 35-28 (Wr)
1947—Cardinals, 31-7 (Co)
Cardinals, 30-21 (Wr)
1948—Bears, 28-17 (Co)
Cardinals, 24-21 (Wr)
1949—Bears, 17-7 (Co)
Bears, 52-21 (Wr)
1950—Bears, 27-6 (Wr)
Cardinals, 20-10 (Co)
1951—Cardinals, 28-14 (Co)
Cardinals, 24-14 (Wr)
1952—Cardinals, 21-10 (Co)
Bears, 10-7 (Wr)
1953—Cardinals, 24-17 (Wr)
1954—Bears, 29-7 (Co)
1955—Cardinals, 53-14 (Co)
1956—Bears, 10-3 (Wr)
1957—Bears, 14-6 (Co)
1958—Bears, 30-14 (Wr)
1959—Bears, 31-7 (So)
1965—Bears, 34-13 (Wr)
1966—Cardinals, 24-17 (StL)
1967—Bears, 30-3 (Wr)
1969—Cardinals, 20-17 (StL)
1972—Bears, 27-10 (StL)
1975—Cardinals, 34-20 (So)
1977—Cardinals, 16-13 (StL)
1978—Bears, 17-10 (So)
1979—Bears, 42-6 (So)
1982—Cardinals, 10-7 (So)
1984—Cardinals, 38-21 (StL)
(Points—Bears 1,517, Cardinals 977)
**Franchise in Decatur prior to 1921; Bears known as Staleys prior to 1922*
***Franchise in Chicago prior to 1960*

CHICAGO vs. SAN DIEGO
Chargers lead series, 4-1
1970—Chargers, 20-7 (C)
1974—Chargers, 28-21 (SD)
1978—Chargers, 40-7 (SD)
1981—Bears, 20-17 (C) OT
1984—Chargers, 20-7 (SD)
(Points—Chargers 125, Bears 62)

CHICAGO vs. SAN FRANCISCO
Bears lead series, 24-23-1
1950—Bears, 32-20 (SF)
Bears, 17-0 (C)
1951—Bears, 13-7 (C)
1952—49ers, 40-16 (C)
Bears, 20-17 (SF)

1953—49ers, 35-28 (C)
49ers, 24-14 (SF)
1954—49ers, 31-24 (C)
Bears, 31-27 (SF)
1955—49ers, 20-19 (C)
Bears, 34-23 (SF)
1956—Bears, 31-7 (C)
Bears, 38-21 (SF)
1957—49ers, 21-17 (C)
49ers, 21-17 (SF)
1958—Bears, 28-6 (C)
Bears, 27-14 (SF)
1959—49ers, 20-17 (SF)
Bears, 14-3 (C)
1960—Bears, 27-10 (C)
49ers, 25-7 (SF)
1961—Bears, 31-0 (C)
49ers, 41-31 (SF)
1962—Bears, 30-14 (SF)
49ers, 34-27 (C)
1963—49ers, 20-14 (SF)
Bears, 27-7 (C)
1964—49ers, 31-21 (SF)
Bears, 23-21 (C)
1965—49ers, 52-24 (SF)
Bears, 61-20 (C)
1966—Tie, 30-30 (C)
49ers, 41-14 (SF)
1967—Bears, 28-14 (SF)
1968—Bears, 27-19 (C)
1969—49ers, 42-21 (SF)
1970—49ers, 37-16 (C)
1971—49ers, 13-0 (SF)
1972—49ers, 34-21 (C)
1974—49ers, 34-0 (C)
1975—49ers, 31-3 (SF)
1976—Bears, 19-12 (SF)
1978—Bears, 16-13 (SF)
1979—Bears, 28-27 (SF)
1981—49ers, 28-17 (SF)
1983—Bears, 13-3 (C)
1984—*49ers, 23-0 (SF)
1985—Bears, 26-10 (SF)
(Points—49ers 1,043, Bears 1,039)
*NFC Championship

CHICAGO vs. SEATTLE
Seahawks lead series, 3-1
1976—Bears, 34-7 (S)
1978—Seahawks, 31-29 (C)
1982—Seahawks, 20-14 (S)
1984—Seahawks, 38-9 (S)
(Points—Seahawks 96, Bears 86)

CHICAGO vs. TAMPA BAY
Bears lead series, 14-4
1977—Bears, 10-0 (TB)
1978—Buccaneers, 33-19 (TB)
Bears, 14-3 (C)
1979—Buccaneers, 17-13 (C)
Bears, 14-0 (TB)
1980—Bears, 23-0 (C)
Bears, 14-13 (TB)
1981—Bears, 28-17 (C)
Buccaneers, 20-10 (TB)
1982—Buccaneers, 26-23 (TB) OT
1983—Bears, 17-10 (C)
Bears, 27-0 (TB)
1984—Bears, 34-14 (C)
Bears, 44-9 (TB)
1985—Bears, 38-28 (C)
Bears, 27-19 (TB)
1986—Bears, 23-3 (TB)
Bears, 48-14 (C)
(Points—Bears 426, Buccaneers 226)

CHICAGO vs. *WASHINGTON
Bears lead series, 20-12-1
1932—Tie, 7-7 (B)
1933—Bears, 7-0 (C)
Redskins, 10-0 (B)
1934—Bears, 21-0 (B)
1935—Bears, 30-14 (B)
1936—Bears, 26-0 (B)
1937—**Redskins, 28-21 (C)
1938—Bears, 31-7 (C)
1940—Redskins, 7-3 (W)
**Bears, 73-0 (W)
1941—Bears, 35-21 (C)
1942—**Redskins, 14-6 (W)
1943—Redskins, 21-7 (W)
**Bears, 41-21 (C)
1945—Redskins, 28-21 (W)
1946—Bears, 24-20 (C)
1947—Bears, 56-20 (W)
1948—Bears, 48-13 (C)
1949—Bears, 31-21 (W)
1951—Bears, 27-0 (W)
1953—Bears, 27-24 (W)
1957—Redskins, 14-3 (C)
1964—Redskins, 27-20 (W)
1968—Redskins, 38-28 (C)
1971—Bears, 16-15 (C)
1974—Redskins, 42-0 (W)
1976—Bears, 33-7 (C)
1978—Bears, 14-10 (W)
1980—Bears, 35-21 (C)
1981—Redskins, 24-7 (C)
1984—***Bears, 23-19 (W)
1985—Bears, 45-10 (C)
1986—***Redskins, 27-13 (C)
(Points—Bears 779, Redskins 530)
*Franchise in Boston prior to 1937 and known as Braves prior to 1933
**NFL Championship
***NFC Divisional Playoff

CINCINNATI vs. ATLANTA
Bengals lead series, 4-1;
See Atlanta vs. Cincinnati

CINCINNATI vs. BUFFALO
Bengals lead series, 9-5;
See Buffalo vs. Cincinnati

CINCINNATI vs. CHICAGO
Bengals lead series, 2-1;
See Chicago vs. Cincinnati

CINCINNATI vs. CLEVELAND
Bengals lead series, 17-16
1970—Browns, 30-27 (Cle)
Bengals, 14-10 (Cin)
1971—Browns, 27-24 (Cin)
Browns, 31-27 (Cle)
1972—Browns, 27-6 (Cle)
Browns, 27-24 (Cin)
1973—Browns, 17-10 (Cle)
Bengals, 34-17 (Cin)
1974—Bengals, 33-7 (Cin)
Bengals, 34-24 (Cle)
1975—Bengals, 24-17 (Cin)
Browns, 35-23 (Cle)
1976—Bengals, 45-24 (Cle)
Bengals, 21-6 (Cin)
1977—Browns, 13-3 (Cin)
Bengals, 10-7 (Cle)
1978—Browns, 13-10 (Cle) OT
Bengals, 48-16 (Cin)
1979—Browns, 28-27 (Cle)
Bengals, 16-12 (Cin)
1980—Browns, 31-7 (Cle)
Browns, 27-24 (Cin)
1981—Browns, 20-17 (Cin)
Bengals, 41-21 (Cle)
1982—Bengals, 23-10 (Cin)
1983—Browns, 17-7 (Clev)
Bengals, 28-21 (Cin)
1984—Bengals, 12-9 (Cin)
Bengals, 20-17 (Clev) OT
1985—Bengals, 27-10 (Cin)
Browns, 24-6 (Clev)
1986—Bengals, 30-13 (Clev)
Browns, 34-3 (Cin)
(Points—Bengals 705, Browns 642)

CINCINNATI vs. DALLAS
Cowboys lead series, 2-1
1973—Cowboys, 38-10 (D)
1979—Cowboys, 38-13 (D)
1985—Bengals, 50-24 (C)
(Points—Cowboys 100, Bengals 73)

CINCINNATI vs. DENVER
Broncos lead series, 9-6
1968—Bengals, 24-10 (C)
Broncos, 10-7 (D)
1969—Broncos, 30-23 (C)
Broncos, 27-16 (D)
1971—Bengals, 24-10 (D)
1972—Bengals, 21-10 (C)
1973—Broncos, 28-10 (D)
1975—Bengals, 17-16 (D)
1976—Bengals, 17-7 (C)
1977—Broncos, 24-13 (C)
1979—Broncos, 10-0 (D)
1981—Bengals, 38-21 (C)
1983—Broncos, 24-17 (D)
1984—Broncos, 20-17 (D)
1986—Broncos, 34-28 (D)
(Points—Broncos 281, Bengals 272)

CINCINNATI vs. DETROIT
Series tied, 2-2
1970—Lions, 38-3 (D)
1974—Lions, 23-19 (C)
1983—Bengals, 17-9 (C)
1986—Bengals, 24-17 (D)
(Points—Lions 87, Bengals 63)

CINCINNATI vs. GREEN BAY
Bengals lead series, 4-2
1971—Packers, 20-17 (GB)
1976—Bengals, 28-7 (C)
1977—Bengals, 17-7 (Mil)
1980—Packers, 14-9 (GB)
1983—Bengals, 34-14 (C)
1986—Bengals, 34-28 (Mil)
(Points—Bengals 139, Packers 90)

CINCINNATI vs. HOUSTON
Bengals lead series, 21-14-1
1968—Oilers, 27-17 (C)
1969—Tie, 31-31 (H)
1970—Oilers, 20-13 (C)
Bengals, 30-20 (H)
1971—Oilers, 10-6 (H)
Bengals, 28-13 (C)
1972—Bengals, 30-7 (C)
Bengals, 61-17 (H)
1973—Bengals, 24-10 (C)
Bengals, 27-24 (H)
1974—Oilers, 34-21 (C)
Oilers, 20-3 (H)
1975—Bengals, 21-19 (H)
Bengals, 23-19 (C)
1976—Bengals, 27-7 (H)
Bengals, 31-27 (C)
1977—Bengals, 13-10 (C) OT
Oilers, 21-16 (H)
1978—Bengals, 28-13 (C)
Oilers, 17-10 (H)
1979—Oilers, 30-27 (C) OT
Oilers, 42-21 (H)
1980—Oilers, 13-10 (C)
Oilers, 23-3 (H)
1981—Oilers, 17-10 (H)
Bengals, 34-21 (C)
1982—Bengals, 27-6 (C)
Bengals, 35-27 (H)
1983—Bengals, 55-14 (H)
Bengals, 38-10 (C)
1984—Bengals, 13-3 (C)
Bengals, 31-13 (H)
1985—Oilers, 44-27 (H)
Bengals, 45-27 (C)
1986—Bengals, 31-28 (C)
Oilers, 32-28 (H)
(Points—Bengals 895, Oilers 716)

CINCINNATI vs.*INDIANAPOLIS
Colts lead series, 5-4
1970—**Colts, 17-0 (B)
1972—Colts, 20-19 (C)
1974—Bengals, 24-14 (B)
1976—Colts, 28-27 (B)
1979—Colts, 38-28 (B)
1980—Bengals, 34-33 (C)
1981—Bengals, 41-19 (B)
1982—Bengals, 20-17 (B)
1983—Colts, 34-31 (C)
(Points—Bengals 224, Colts 220)
*Franchise in Baltimore prior to 1984
**AFC Divisional Playoff

CINCINNATI vs. KANSAS CITY
Chiefs lead series, 9-7
1968—Chiefs, 13-3 (KC)
Chiefs, 16-9 (C)
1969—Bengals, 24-19 (C)
Chiefs, 42-22 (KC)
1970—Chiefs, 27-19 (C)
1972—Bengals, 23-16 (KC)
1973—Bengals, 14-6 (C)
1974—Bengals, 33-6 (C)
1976—Bengals, 27-24 (KC)
1977—Bengals, 27-7 (KC)
1978—Chiefs, 24-23 (C)
1979—Chiefs, 10-7 (C)
1980—Bengals, 20-6 (KC)
1983—Chiefs, 20-15 (KC)
1984—Chiefs, 27-22 (C)
1986—Chiefs, 24-14 (KC)
(Points—Bengals 302, Chiefs 287)

CINCINNATI vs. *L.A. RAIDERS
Raiders lead series, 12-4
1968—Raiders, 31-10 (O)
Raiders, 34-0 (C)
1969—Bengals, 31-17 (C)
Raiders, 37-17 (O)
1970—Bengals, 31-21 (C)
1971—Raiders, 31-27 (O)
1972—Raiders, 20-14 (C)
1974—Raiders, 30-27 (O)
1975—Bengals, 14-10 (C)
**Raiders, 31-28 (O)
1976—Raiders, 35-20 (O)
1978—Raiders, 34-21 (C)
1980—Raiders, 28-17 (O)
1982—Bengals, 31-17 (C)
1983—Raiders, 20-10 (C)
1985—Raiders, 13-6 (LA)
(Points—Raiders 409, Bengals 304)
*Franchise in Oakland prior to 1982
**AFC Divisional Playoff

CINCINNATI vs. L.A. RAMS
Bengals lead series, 3-2
1972—Rams, 15-12 (LA)
1976—Bengals, 20-12 (C)
1978—Bengals, 20-19 (LA)
1981—Bengals, 24-10 (C)
1984—Rams, 24-14 (C)
(Points—Bengals 90, Rams 80)

CINCINNATI vs. MIAMI
Dolphins lead series, 7-3
1968—Dolphins, 24-22 (C)
Bengals, 38-21 (M)
1969—Bengals, 27-21 (C)
1971—Dolphins, 23-13 (C)
1973—*Dolphins, 34-16 (M)
1974—Dolphins, 24-3 (M)
1977—Bengals, 23-17 (C)
1978—Dolphins, 21-0 (M)
1980—Dolphins, 17-16 (M)
1983—Dolphins, 38-14 (M)
(Points—Dolphins 240, Bengals 172)
*AFC Divisional Playoff

CINCINNATI vs. MINNESOTA
Bengals lead series, 3-2
1973—Bengals, 27-0 (C)
1977—Vikings, 42-10 (M)
1980—Bengals, 14-0 (C)
1983—Vikings, 20-14 (M)
1986—Bengals, 24-20 (C)
(Points—Bengals 89, Vikings 82)

CINCINNATI vs. *NEW ENGLAND
Patriots lead series, 6-4
1968—Patriots, 33-14 (B)
1969—Patriots, 25-14 (C)
1970—Bengals, 45-7 (C)
1972—Bengals, 31-7 (NE)
1975—Bengals, 27-10 (C)
1978—Patriots, 10-3 (C)
1979—Patriots, 20-14 (C)
1984—Patriots, 20-14 (NE)
1985—Patriots, 34-23 (NE)
1986—Bengals, 31-7 (NE)
(Points—Bengals 216, Patriots 173)
*Franchise in Boston prior to 1971

CINCINNATI vs. NEW ORLEANS
Bengals lead series 3-2
1970—Bengals, 26-6 (C)
1975—Bengals, 21-0 (NO)
1978—Saints, 20-18 (C)
1981—Saints, 17-7 (NO)
1984—Bengals, 24-21 (NO)
(Points—Bengals 96, Saints 64)

CINCINNATI vs. N.Y. GIANTS
Bengals lead series, 3-0
1972—Bengals, 13-10 (C)
1977—Bengals, 30-13 (C)
1985—Bengals, 35-30 (C)
(Points—Bengals 78, Giants 53)

CINCINNATI vs. N.Y. JETS
Jets lead series, 7-4
1968—Jets, 27-14 (NY)
1969—Jets, 21-7 (C)
Jets, 40-7 (NY)
1971—Jets, 35-21 (NY)
1973—Bengals, 20-14 (C)
1976—Bengals, 42-3 (NY)
1981—Bengals, 31-30 (NY)
1982—*Jets, 44-17 (C)
1984—Jets, 43-23 (NY)
1985—Jets, 29-20 (C)
1986—Bengals, 52-21 (C)
(Points—Jets 307, Bengals 254)
*AFC First Round Playoff

CINCINNATI vs. PHILADELPHIA
Bengals lead series, 4-0
1971—Bengals, 37-14 (C)
1975—Bengals, 31-0 (P)
1979—Bengals, 37-13 (C)
1982—Bengals, 18-14 (P)
(Points—Bengals 123, Eagles 41)

CINCINNATI vs. PITTSBURGH
Steelers lead series, 18-15
1970—Steelers, 21-10 (P)
Bengals, 34-7 (C)
1971—Steelers, 21-10 (P)
Steelers, 21-13 (C)
1972—Bengals, 15-10 (C)
Steelers, 40-17 (P)
1973—Bengals, 19-7 (C)
Steelers, 20-13 (P)
1974—Bengals, 17-10 (C)
Steelers, 27-3 (P)
1975—Steelers, 30-24 (C)
Steelers, 35-14 (P)
1976—Steelers, 23-6 (P)
Steelers, 7-3 (C)
1977—Steelers, 20-14 (P)
Bengals, 17-10 (C)
1978—Steelers, 28-3 (C)
Steelers, 7-6 (P)
1979—Bengals, 34-10 (C)
Steelers, 37-17 (P)
1980—Bengals, 30-28 (C)
Bengals, 17-16 (P)
1981—Bengals, 34-7 (C)
Bengals, 17-10 (P)
1982—Steelers, 26-20 (P) OT
1983—Steelers, 24-14 (C)
Bengals, 23-10 (P)
1984—Steelers, 38-17 (P)
Bengals, 22-20 (C)
1985—Bengals, 37-24 (P)
Bengals, 26-21 (C)
1986—Bengals, 24-22 (C)
Steelers, 30-9 (P)
(Points—Steelers 667, Bengals 579)

CINCINNATI vs. ST. LOUIS
Bengals lead series, 2-1
1973—Bengals, 42-24 (C)
1979—Bengals, 34-28 (C)

1985—Cardinals, 41-27 (StL)
(Points—Bengals 103, Cardinals 93)

CINCINNATI vs. SAN DIEGO
Chargers lead series, 10-7
1968—Chargers, 29-13 (SD)
Chargers, 31-10 (C)
1969—Bengals, 34-20 (C)
Chargers, 21-14 (SD)
1970—Bengals, 17-14 (SD)
1971—Bengals, 31-0 (C)
1973—Bengals, 20-13 (SD)
1974—Chargers, 20-17 (C)
1975—Bengals, 47-17 (C)
1977—Chargers, 24-3 (SD)
1978—Chargers, 22-13 (SD)
1979—Chargers, 26-24 (C)
1980—Chargers, 31-14 (C)
1981—Bengals, 40-17 (SD)
*Bengals, 27-7 (C)
1982—Chargers, 50-34 (SD)
1985—Chargers, 44-41 (C)
(Points—Bengals 399, Chargers 386)
**AFC Championship*

CINCINNATI vs. SAN FRANCISCO
49ers lead series, 4-1
1974—Bengals, 21-3 (SF)
1978—49ers, 28-12 (SF)
1981—49ers, 21-3 (C)
*49ers, 26-21 (Detroit)
1984—49ers, 23-17 (SF)
(Points—49ers 101, Bengals 74)
**Super Bowl XVI*

CINCINNATI vs. SEATTLE
Bengals lead series, 4-2
1977—Bengals, 42-20 (C)
1981—Bengals, 27-21 (C)
1982—Bengals, 24-10 (C)
1984—Seahawks, 26-6 (C)
1985—Seahawks, 28-24 (C)
1986—Bengals, 34-7 (C)
(Points—Bengals 157, Seahawks 112)

CINCINNATI vs. TAMPA BAY
Bengals lead series, 2-1
1976—Bengals, 21-0 (C)
1980—Buccaneers, 17-12 (C)
1983—Bengals, 23-17 (TB)
(Points—Bengals 56, Buccaneers 34)

CINCINNATI vs. WASHINGTON
Redskins lead series, 3-1
1970—Redskins, 20-0 (W)
1974—Bengals, 28-17 (C)
1979—Redskins, 28-14 (W)
1985—Redskins, 27-24 (W)
(Points—Redskins 92, Bengals 66)

CLEVELAND vs. ATLANTA
Browns lead series, 6-1;
See Atlanta vs. Cleveland

CLEVELAND vs. BUFFALO
Browns lead series, 6-2;
See Buffalo vs. Cleveland

CLEVELAND vs. CHICAGO
Browns lead series, 6-3;
See Chicago vs. Cleveland

CLEVELAND vs. CINCINNATI
Bengals lead series, 17-16;
See Cincinnati vs. Cleveland

CLEVELAND vs. DALLAS
Browns lead series, 15-9
1960—Browns, 48-7 (D)
1961—Browns, 25-7 (C)
Browns, 38-17 (D)
1962—Browns, 19-10 (C)
Cowboys, 45-21 (D)
1963—Browns, 41-24 (D)
Browns, 27-17 (C)
1964—Browns, 27-6 (C)
Browns, 20-16 (D)
1965—Browns, 23-17 (C)
Browns, 24-17 (D)
1966—Browns, 30-21 (C)
Cowboys, 26-14 (D)
1967—Cowboys, 21-14 (C)
*Cowboys, 52-14 (D)
1968—Cowboys, 28-7 (C)
*Browns, 31-20 (C)
1969—Browns, 42-10 (C)
*Browns, 38-14 (D)
1970—Cowboys, 6-2 (C)
1974—Cowboys, 41-17 (D)
1979—Browns, 26-7 (C)
1982—Cowboys, 31-14 (D)
1985—Cowboys, 20-7 (D)
(Points—Browns 569, Cowboys 480)
**Conference Championship*

CLEVELAND vs. DENVER
Broncos lead series, 9-3
1970—Browns, 27-13 (D)
1971—Broncos, 27-0 (C)
1972—Browns, 27-20 (D)
1974—Browns, 23-21 (C)
1975—Broncos, 16-15 (D)
1976—Broncos, 44-13 (D)
1978—Broncos, 19-7 (C)
1980—Broncos, 19-16 (C)
1981—Broncos, 23-20 (D) OT
1983—Broncos, 27-6 (D)
1984—Broncos, 24-14 (C)
1986—*Broncos, 23-20 (C) OT
(Points—Broncos 276, Browns 188)
**AFC Championship*

CLEVELAND vs. DETROIT
Lions lead series, 12-4
1952—Lions, 17-6 (D)
*Lions, 17-7 (C)
1953—*Lions, 17-16 (D)
1954—Lions, 14-10 (C)
*Browns, 56-10 (C)
1957—Lions, 20-7 (D)
*Lions, 59-14 (D)
1958—Lions, 30-10 (C)
1963—Lions, 38-10 (D)
1964—Browns, 37-21 (C)
1967—Lions, 31-14 (D)
1969—Lions, 28-21 (C)
1970—Lions, 41-24 (C)
1975—Lions, 21-10 (D)
1983—Browns, 31-26 (D)
1986—Browns, 24-21 (C)
(Points—Lions 411, Browns 297)
**NFL Championship*

CLEVELAND vs. GREEN BAY
Packers lead series, 8-5
1953—Browns, 27-0 (Mil)
1955—Browns, 41-10 (C)
1956—Browns, 24-7 (Mil)
1961—Packers, 49-17 (C)
1964—Packers, 28-21 (Mil)
1965—*Packers, 23-12 (GB)
1966—Packers, 21-20 (C)
1967—Packers, 55-7 (Mil)
1969—Browns, 20-7 (C)
1972—Packers, 26-10 (C)
1980—Browns, 26-21 (C)
1983—Packers, 35-21 (Mil)
1986—Packers, 17-14 (C)
(Points—Packers 299, Browns 260)
**NFL Championship*

CLEVELAND vs. HOUSTON
Browns lead series, 22-11
1970—Browns, 28-14 (C)
Browns, 21-10 (H)
1971—Browns, 31-0 (C)
Browns, 37-24 (H)
1972—Browns, 23-17 (H)
Browns, 20-0 (C)
1973—Browns, 42-13 (C)
Browns, 23-13 (H)
1974—Browns, 20-7 (C)
Oilers, 28-24 (H)
1975—Oilers, 40-10 (C)
Oilers, 21-10 (H)
1976—Browns, 21-7 (H)
Browns, 13-10 (C)
1977—Browns, 24-23 (H)
Oilers, 19-15 (C)
1978—Oilers, 16-13 (C)
Oilers, 14-10 (H)
1979—Oilers, 31-10 (H)
Browns, 14-7 (C)
1980—Oilers, 16-7 (C)
Browns, 17-14 (H)
1981—Oilers, 9-3 (C)
Oilers, 17-13 (H)
1982—Browns, 20-14 (H)
1983—Browns, 25-19 (C) OT
Oilers, 34-27 (H)
1984—Browns, 27-10 (C)
Browns, 27-20 (H)
1985—Browns, 21-6 (H)
Browns, 28-21 (C)
1986—Browns, 23-20 (H)
Browns, 13-10 (C) OT
(Points—Browns 660, Oilers 524)

CLEVELAND vs. *INDIANAPOLIS
Browns lead series, 11-5
1956—Colts, 21-7 (C)
1959—Browns, 38-31 (B)
1962—Colts, 36-14 (C)
1964—**Browns, 27-0 (C)
1968—Browns, 30-20 (B)
**Colts, 34-0 (C)
1971—Browns, 14-13 (B)
***Colts, 20-3 (C)
1973—Browns, 24-14 (C)
1975—Colts, 21-7 (B)
1978—Browns, 45-24 (B)
1979—Browns, 13-10 (C)
1980—Browns, 28-27 (B)
1981—Browns, 42-28 (C)
1983—Browns, 41-23 (C)
1986—Browns, 24-9 (I)
(Points—Browns 357, Colts 331)
**Franchise in Baltimore prior to 1984*
***NFL Championship*
****AFC Divisional Playoff*

CLEVELAND vs. KANSAS CITY
Series tied, 5-5-1
1971—Chiefs, 13-7 (KC)
1972—Chiefs, 31-7 (C)
1973—Tie, 20-20 (KC)
1975—Browns, 40-14 (C)
1976—Chiefs, 39-14 (KC)
1977—Browns, 44-7 (C)
1978—Chiefs, 17-3 (KC)
1979—Browns, 27-24 (KC)
1980—Browns, 20-13 (C)
1984—Chiefs, 10-6 (KC)
1986—Browns, 20-7 (C)
(Points—Browns 208, Chiefs 195)

CLEVELAND vs. *L.A.RAIDERS
Raiders lead series, 10-1
1970—Raiders, 23-20 (O)
1971—Raiders, 34-20 (C)
1973—Browns, 7-3 (O)
1974—Raiders, 40-24 (C)
1975—Raiders, 38-17 (O)
1977—Raiders, 26-10 (C)
1979—Raiders, 19-14 (O)
1980—**Raiders, 14-12 (C)
1982—***Raiders, 27-10 (LA)
1985—Raiders, 21-20 (C)
1986—Raiders, 27-14 (LA)
(Points—Raiders 272, Browns 168)
**Franchise in Oakland prior to 1982*
***AFC Divisional Playoff*
****AFC First Round Playoff*

CLEVELAND vs. L.A. RAMS
Browns lead series, 8-7
1950—*Browns, 30-28 (C)
1951—Browns, 38-23 (LA)
*Rams, 24-17 (LA)
1952—Browns, 37-7 (C)
1955—*Browns, 38-14 (LA)
1957—Browns, 45-31 (C)
1958—Browns, 30-27 (LA)
1963—Browns, 20-6 (C)
1965—Rams, 42-7 (LA)
1968—Rams, 24-6 (C)
1973—Rams, 30-17 (LA)
1977—Rams, 9-0 (C)
1978—Browns, 30-19 (C)
1981—Rams, 27-16 (LA)
1984—Rams, 20-17 (LA)
(Points—Browns 348, Rams 331)
**NFL Championship*

CLEVELAND vs. MIAMI
Browns lead series, 4-3
1970—Browns, 28-0 (M)
1972—*Dolphins, 20-14 (M)
1973—Dolphins, 17-9 (C)
1976—Browns, 17-13 (C)
1979—Browns, 30-24 (C) OT
1985—*Dolphins, 24-21 (M)
1986—Browns, 26-16 (C)
(Points—Browns 145, Dolphins 114)
**AFC Divisional Playoff*

CLEVELAND vs. MINNESOTA
Vikings lead series, 7-2
1965—Vikings, 27-17 (C)
1967—Browns, 14-10 (C)
1969—Vikings, 51-3 (M)
*Vikings, 27-7 (M)
1973—Vikings, 26-3 (M)
1975—Vikings, 42-10 (C)
1980—Vikings, 28-23 (M)
1983—Vikings, 27-21 (C)
1986—Browns, 23-20 (M)
(Points—Vikings 258, Browns 121)
**NFL Championship*

CLEVELAND vs. NEW ENGLAND
Browns lead series, 6-2
1971—Browns, 27-7 (C)
1974—Browns, 21-14 (NE)
1977—Browns, 30-27 (C) OT
1980—Patriots, 34-17 (NE)
1982—Browns, 10-7 (C)
1983—Browns, 30-0 (NE)
1984—Patriots, 17-16 (C)
1985—Browns, 24-20 (C)
(Points—Browns 175, Patriots 126)

CLEVELAND vs. NEW ORLEANS
Browns lead series, 8-1
1967—Browns, 42-7 (NO)
1968—Browns, 24-10 (NO)
Browns, 35-17 (C)
1969—Browns, 27-17 (NO)
1971—Browns, 21-17 (NO)
1975—Browns, 17-16 (C)
1978—Browns, 24-16 (NO)
1981—Browns, 20-17 (C)
1984—Saints 16-14 (C)
(Points—Browns 224, Saints 133)

CLEVELAND vs. N.Y. GIANTS
Browns lead series, 26-16-2
1950—Giants, 6-0 (C)
Giants, 17-13 (NY)
*Browns, 8-3 (C)
1951—Browns, 14-13 (C)
Browns, 10-0 (NY)
1952—Giants, 17-9 (C)
Giants, 37-34 (NY)
1953—Browns, 7-0 (NY)
Browns, 62-14 (C)
1954—Browns, 24-14 (C)
Browns, 16-7 (NY)
1955—Browns, 24-14 (C)
Tie, 35-35 (NY)
1956—Giants, 21-9 (C)
Browns, 24-7 (NY)
1957—Browns, 6-3 (C)
Browns, 34-28 (NY)
1958—Giants, 21-17 (C)
Giants, 13-10 (NY)
*Giants, 10-0 (NY)
1959—Giants, 10-6 (C)
Giants, 48-7 (NY)
1960—Giants, 17-13 (C)
Browns, 48-34 (NY)
1961—Giants, 37-21 (C)
Tie, 7-7 (NY)
1962—Browns, 17-7 (C)
Giants, 17-13 (NY)
1963—Browns, 35-24 (NY)
Giants, 33-6 (C)
1964—Browns, 42-20 (C)
Browns, 52-20 (NY)
1965—Browns, 38-14 (NY)
Browns, 34-21 (C)
1966—Browns, 28-7 (NY)
Browns, 49-40 (C)
1967—Giants, 38-34 (NY)
Browns, 24-14 (C)
1968—Browns, 45-10 (C)
1969—Browns, 28-17 (C)
Giants, 27-14 (NY)
1973—Browns, 12-10 (C)
1977—Browns, 21-7 (NY)
1985—Browns, 35-33 (NY)
(Points—Browns 985, Giants 792)
**Conference Playoff*

CLEVELAND vs. N.Y. JETS
Browns lead series, 8-3
1970—Browns, 31-21 (C)
1972—Browns, 26-10 (NY)
1976—Browns, 38-17 (C)
1978—Browns, 37-34 (C) OT
1979—Browns, 25-22 (NY) OT
1980—Browns, 17-14 (C)
1981—Jets, 14-13 (C)
1983—Browns, 10-7 (C)
1984—Jets, 24-20 (C)
1985—Jets, 37-10 (NY)
1986—*Browns, 23-20 (C) OT
(Points—Browns 250, Jets 220)
**AFC Divisional Playoff*

CLEVELAND vs. PHILADELPHIA
Browns lead series, 29-11-1
1950—Browns, 35-10 (P)
Browns, 13-7 (C)
1951—Browns, 20-17 (C)
Browns, 24-9 (NY)
1952—Browns, 49-7 (P)
Eagles, 28-20 (C)
1953—Browns, 37-13 (C)
Eagles, 42-27 (P)
1954—Eagles, 28-10 (P)
Browns, 6-0 (C)
1955—Browns, 21-17 (C)
Eagles, 33-17 (P)
1956—Browns, 16-0 (P)
Browns, 17-14 (C)
1957—Browns, 24-7 (C)
Eagles, 17-7 (P)
1958—Browns, 28-14 (C)
Browns, 21-14 (P)
1959—Browns, 28-7 (C)
Browns, 28-21 (P)
1960—Browns, 41-24 (P)
Eagles, 31-29 (C)
1961—Eagles, 27-20 (P)
Browns, 45-24 (C)
1962—Eagles, 35-7 (P)
Tie, 14-14 (C)
1963—Browns, 37-7 (C)
Browns, 23-17 (P)
1964—Browns, 28-20 (P)
Browns, 38-24 (C)
1965—Browns, 35-17 (P)
Browns, 38-34 (C)
1966—Browns, 27-7 (C)
Eagles, 33-21 (P)
1967—Eagles, 28-24 (P)
1968—Browns, 47-13 (C)
1969—Browns, 27-20 (P)
1972—Browns, 27-17 (P)
1976—Browns, 24-3 (C)
1979—Browns, 24-19 (P)
1982—Eagles, 24-21 (C)
(Points—Browns 1,045, Eagles 743)

CLEVELAND vs. PITTSBURGH
Browns lead series, 43-31

1950—Browns, 30-17 (P)
Browns, 45-7 (C)
1951—Browns, 17-0 (C)
Browns, 28-0 (P)
1952—Browns, 21-20 (P)
Browns, 29-28 (C)
1953—Browns, 34-16 (C)
Browns, 20-16 (P)
1954—Steelers, 55-27 (P)
Browns, 42-7 (C)
1955—Browns, 41-14 (C)
Browns, 30-7 (P)
1956—Browns, 14-10 (P)
Steelers, 24-16 (C)
1957—Browns, 23-12 (P)
Browns, 24-0 (C)
1958—Browns, 45-12 (P)
Browns, 27-10 (C)
1959—Steelers, 17-7 (P)
Steelers, 21-20 (C)
1960—Browns, 28-20 (C)
Steelers, 14-10 (P)
1961—Browns, 30-28 (P)
Steelers, 17-13 (C)
1962—Browns, 41-14 (P)
Browns, 35-14 (C)
1963—Browns, 35-23 (C)
Steelers, 9-7 (P)
1964—Steelers, 23-7 (C)
Browns, 30-17 (P)
1965—Browns, 24-19 (C)
Browns, 42-21 (P)
1966—Browns, 41-10 (C)
Steelers, 16-6 (P)
1967—Browns, 21-10 (C)
Browns, 34-14 (P)
1968—Browns, 31-24 (C)
Browns, 45-24 (P)
1969—Browns, 42-31 (C)
Browns, 24-3 (P)
1970—Browns, 15-7 (C)
Steelers, 28-9 (P)
1971—Browns, 27-17 (C)
Steelers, 26-9 (P)
1972—Browns, 26-24 (C)
Steelers, 30-0 (P)
1973—Steelers, 33-6 (P)
Browns, 21-16 (C)
1974—Steelers, 20-16 (P)
Steelers, 26-16 (C)
1975—Steelers, 42-6 (C)
Steelers, 31-17 (P)
1976—Steelers, 31-14 (P)
Browns, 18-16 (C)
1977—Steelers, 28-14 (C)
Steelers, 35-31 (P)
1978—Steelers, 15-9 (P) OT
Steelers, 34-14 (C)
1979—Steelers, 51-35 (C)
Steelers, 33-30 (P) OT
1980—Browns, 27-26 (C)
Steelers, 16-13 (P)
1981—Steelers, 13-7 (P)
Steelers, 32-10 (C)
1982—Browns, 10-9 (C)
Steelers, 37-21 (P)
1983—Steelers, 44-17 (P)
Browns, 30-17 (C)
1984—Browns, 20-10 (C)
Steelers, 23-20 (P)
1985—Browns, 17-7 (C)
Steelers, 10-9 (P)
1986—Browns, 27-24 (P)
Browns, 37-31 (C) OT
(Points—Browns 1,684, Steelers 1,486)

CLEVELAND vs. *ST. LOUIS
Browns lead series, 30-10-3
1950—Browns, 34-24 (Cle)
Browns, 10-7 (Chi)
1951—Browns, 34-17 (Chi)
Browns, 49-28 (Cle)
1952—Browns, 28-13 (Cle)
Browns, 10-0 (Chi)
1953—Browns, 27-7 (Chi)
Browns, 27-16 (Cle)
1954—Browns, 31-7 (Cle)
Browns, 35-3 (Chi)
1955—Browns, 26-20 (Chi)
Browns, 35-24 (Cle)
1956—Cardinals, 9-7 (Chi)
Cardinals, 24-7 (Cle)
1957—Browns, 17-7 (Chi)
Browns, 31-0 (Cle)
1958—Browns, 35-28 (Cle)
Browns, 38-24 (Chi)
1959—Browns, 34-7 (Chi)
Browns, 17-7 (Cle)
1960—Browns, 28-27 (Cle)
Tie, 17-17 (StL)
1961—Browns, 20-17 (Cle)
Browns, 21-10 (StL)
1962—Browns, 34-7 (StL)
Browns, 38-14 (Cle)
1963—Cardinals, 20-14 (Cle)
Browns, 24-10 (StL)
1964—Tie, 33-33 (Cle)
Cardinals, 28-19 (StL)
1965—Cardinals, 49-13 (Cle)
Browns, 27-24 (StL)
1966—Cardinals, 34-28 (Cle)
Browns, 38-10 (StL)
1967—Browns, 20-16 (Cle)
Browns, 20-16 (StL)
1968—Cardinals, 27-21 (Cle)
Cardinals, 27-16 (StL)
1969—Tie, 21-21 (Cle)
Browns, 27-21 (StL)
1974—Cardinals, 29-7 (StL)
1979—Browns, 38-20 (StL)
1985—Cardinals, 27-24 (Cle) OT
(Points—Browns 1,080, Cardinals 776)
**Franchise in Chicago prior to 1960*

CLEVELAND vs. SAN DIEGO
Series tied, 5-5-1
1970—Chargers, 27-10 (C)
1972—Browns, 21-17 (SD)
1973—Tie, 16-16 (C)
1974—Chargers, 36-35 (SD)
1976—Browns, 21-17 (C)
1977—Chargers, 37-14 (SD)
1981—Chargers, 44-14 (C)
1982—Chargers, 30-13 (C)
1983—Browns, 30-24 (SD) OT
1985—Browns, 21-7 (SD)
1986—Browns, 47-17 (C)
(Points—Chargers 272, Browns 242)

CLEVELAND vs. SAN FRANCISCO
Browns lead series, 8-4
1950—Browns, 34-14 (C)
1951—49ers, 24-10 (SF)
1953—Browns, 23-21 (C)
1955—Browns, 38-3 (SF)
1959—49ers, 21-20 (C)
1962—Browns, 13-10 (SF)
1968—Browns, 33-21 (SF)
1970—49ers, 34-31 (SF)
1974—Browns, 7-0 (C)
1978—Browns, 24-7 (C)
1981—Browns, 15-12 (SF)
1984—49ers, 41-7 (C)
(Points—Browns 255, 49ers 208)

CLEVELAND vs. SEATTLE
Seahawks lead series, 7-2
1977—Seahawks, 20-19 (S)
1978—Seahawks, 47-24 (S)
1979—Seahawks, 29-24 (C)
1980—Browns, 27-3 (S)
1981—Seahawks, 42-21 (S)
1982—Browns, 21-7 (S)
1983—Seahawks, 24-9 (C)
1984—Seahawks, 33-0 (S)
1985—Seahawks, 31-13 (S)
(Points—Seahawks 236, Browns 158)

CLEVELAND vs. TAMPA BAY
Browns lead series, 3-0
1976—Browns, 24-7 (TB)
1980—Browns, 34-27 (TB)
1983—Browns, 20-0 (C)
(Points—Browns 78, Buccaneers 34)

CLEVELAND vs. WASHINGTON
Browns lead series, 31-8-1
1950—Browns, 20-14 (C)
Browns, 45-21 (W)
1951—Browns, 45-0 (C)
1952—Browns, 19-15 (C)
Browns, 48-24 (W)
1953—Browns, 30-14 (W)
Browns, 27-3 (C)
1954—Browns, 62-3 (C)
Browns, 34-14 (W)
1955—Redskins, 27-17 (C)
Browns, 24-14 (W)
1956—Redskins, 20-9 (W)
Redskins, 20-17 (C)
1957—Browns, 21-17 (C)
Tie, 30-30 (W)
1958—Browns, 20-10 (W)
Browns, 21-14 (C)
1959—Browns, 34-7 (C)
Browns, 31-17 (W)
1960—Browns, 31-10 (W)
Browns, 27-16 (C)
1961—Browns, 31-7 (C)
Browns, 17-6 (W)
1962—Redskins, 17-16 (C)
Redskins, 17-9 (W)
1963—Browns, 37-14 (C)
Browns, 27-20 (W)
1964—Browns, 27-13 (W)
Browns, 34-24 (C)
1965—Browns, 17-7 (W)
Browns, 24-16 (C)
1966—Browns, 38-14 (W)
Browns, 14-3 (C)
1967—Browns, 42-37 (C)
1968—Browns, 24-21 (W)
1969—Browns, 27-23 (C)
1971—Browns, 20-13 (W)
1975—Redskins, 23-7 (C)
1979—Redskins, 13-9 (C)
1985—Redskins, 14-7 (C)
(Points—Browns 1,039, Redskins 612)

DALLAS vs. ATLANTA
Cowboys lead series, 8-2;
See Atlanta vs. Dallas

DALLAS vs. BUFFALO
Cowboys lead series, 3-1;
See Buffalo vs. Dallas

DALLAS vs. CHICAGO
Cowboys lead series, 8-5;
See Chicago vs. Dallas

DALLAS vs. CINCINNATI
Cowboys lead series, 2-1;
See Cincinnati vs. Dallas

DALLAS vs. CLEVELAND
Browns lead series, 15-9;
See Cleveland vs. Dallas

DALLAS vs. DENVER
Cowboys lead series, 3-2
1973—Cowboys, 22-10 (Den)
1977—Cowboys, 14-6 (Dal)
*Cowboys, 27-10 (New Orleans)
1980—Broncos, 41-20 (Den)
1986—Broncos, 29-14 (Den)
(Points—Cowboys 97, Broncos 96)
**Super Bowl XII*

DALLAS vs. DETROIT
Cowboys lead series, 7-3
1960—Lions, 23-14 (Det)
1963—Cowboys, 17-14 (Dal)
1968—Cowboys, 59-13 (Dal)
1970—*Cowboys, 5-0 (Dal)
1972—Cowboys, 28-24 (Dal)
1975—Cowboys, 36-10 (Det)
1977—Cowboys, 37-0 (Dal)
1981—Lions, 27-24 (Det)
1985—Lions, 26-21 (Det)
1986—Cowboys, 31-7 (Det)
(Points—Cowboys 272, Lions 144)
**NFC Divisional Playoff*

DALLAS vs. GREEN BAY
Packers lead series, 8-5
1960—Packers, 41-7 (GB)
1964—Packers, 45-21 (D)
1965—Packers, 13-3 (Mil)
1966—*Packers, 34-27 (D)
1967—*Packers, 21-17 (GB)
1968—Packers, 28-17 (D)
1970—Cowboys, 16-3 (D)
1972—Packers, 16-13 (Mil)
1975—Packers, 19-17 (D)
1978—Cowboys, 42-14 (Mil)
1980—Cowboys, 28-7 (Mil)
1982—**Cowboys, 37-26 (D)
1984—Cowboys, 20-6 (D)
(Points—Packers 273, Cowboys 265)
**NFL Championship*
***NFC Second Round Playoff*

DALLAS vs. HOUSTON
Cowboys lead series, 4-1
1970—Cowboys, 52-10 (D)
1974—Cowboys, 10-0 (H)
1979—Oilers, 30-24 (D)
1982—Cowboys, 37-7 (H)
1985—Cowboys, 17-10 (H)
(Points—Cowboys 140, Oilers 57)

DALLAS vs. *INDIANAPOLIS
Cowboys lead series, 6-3
1960—Colts, 45-7 (D)
1967—Colts, 23-17 (B)
1969—Cowboys, 27-10 (D)
1970—**Colts, 16-13 (Miami)
1972—Cowboys, 21-0 (B)
1976—Cowboys, 30-27 (D)
1978—Cowboys, 38-0 (D)
1981—Cowboys, 37-13 (B)
1984—Cowboys, 22-3 (D)
(Points—Cowboys 212, Colts 137)
**Franchise in Baltimore prior to 1984*
***Super Bowl V*

DALLAS vs. KANSAS CITY
Cowboys lead series, 2-1
1970—Cowboys, 27-16 (KC)
1975—Chiefs, 34-31 (D)
1983—Cowboys, 41-21 (D)
(Points—Cowboys 99, Chiefs 71)

DALLAS vs. *L.A. RAIDERS
Raiders lead series, 3-1
1974—Raiders, 27-23 (O)
1980—Cowboys, 19-13 (O)
1983—Raiders, 40-38 (D)
1986—Raiders, 17-13 (D)
(Points—Raiders 97, Cowboys 93)
**Franchise in Oakland prior to 1982*

DALLAS vs. L.A. RAMS
Rams lead series, 11-10
1960—Rams, 38-13 (D)
1962—Cowboys, 27-17 (LA)
1967—Rams, 35-13 (D)
1969—Rams, 24-23 (LA)
1971—Cowboys, 28-21 (D)
1973—Rams, 37-31 (LA)
*Cowboys, 27-16 (D)
1975—Cowboys, 18-7 (D)
**Cowboys, 37-7 (LA)
1976—*Rams, 14-12 (D)
1978—Rams, 27-14 (LA)
**Cowboys, 28-0 (LA)
1979—Cowboys, 30-6 (D)
*Rams, 21-19 (D)
1980—Rams, 38-14 (LA)
***Cowboys, 34-13 (D)
1981—Cowboys, 29-17 (D)
1983—***Rams, 24-17 (D)
1984—Cowboys, 20-13 (LA)
1985—*Rams, 20-0 (LA)
1986—Rams, 29-10 (LA)
(Points—Cowboys 444, Rams 424)
**NFC Divisional Playoff*
***NFC Championship*
****NFC First Round Playoff*

DALLAS vs. MIAMI
Dolphins lead series, 3-2
1971—*Cowboys, 24-3 (New Orleans)
1973—Dolphins, 14-7 (D)
1978—Dolphins, 23-16 (M)
1981—Cowboys, 28-27 (D)
1984—Dolphins, 28-21 (M)
(Points—Cowboys 96, Dolphins 95)
**Super Bowl VI*

DALLAS vs. MINNESOTA
Cowboys lead series, 10-5
1961—Cowboys, 21-7 (D)
Cowboys, 28-0 (M)
1966—Cowboys, 28-17 (D)
1968—Cowboys, 20-7 (M)
1970—Vikings, 54-13 (M)
1971—*Cowboys, 20-12 (M)
1973—**Vikings, 27-10 (D)
1974—Vikings, 23-21 (D)
1975—*Cowboys, 17-14 (M)
1977—Cowboys, 16-10 (M) OT
**Cowboys, 23-6 (D)
1978—Vikings, 21-10 (D)
1979—Cowboys, 36-20 (M)
1982—Vikings, 31-27 (M)
1983—Cowboys, 37-24 (M)
(Points—Cowboys 327, Vikings 273)
**NFC Divisional Playoff*
***NFC Championship*

DALLAS vs. NEW ENGLAND
Cowboys lead series, 5-0
1971—Cowboys, 44-21 (D)
1975—Cowboys, 34-31 (NE)
1978—Cowboys, 17-10 (D)
1981—Cowboys, 35-21 (NE)
1984—Cowboys, 20-17 (D)
(Points—Cowboys 150, Patriots 100)

DALLAS vs. NEW ORLEANS
Cowboys lead series, 11-1
1967—Cowboys, 14-10 (D)
Cowboys, 27-10 (NO)
1968—Cowboys, 17-3 (NO)
1969—Cowboys, 21-17 (NO)
Cowboys, 33-17 (D)
1971—Saints, 24-14 (NO)
1973—Cowboys, 40-3 (D)
1976—Cowboys, 24-6 (NO)
1978—Cowboys, 27-7 (D)
1982—Cowboys, 21-7 (D)
1983—Cowboys, 21-20 (D)
1984—Cowboys, 30-27 (D) OT
(Points—Cowboys 289, Saints 151)

DALLAS vs. N.Y. GIANTS
Cowboys lead series, 33-14-2
1960—Tie, 31-31 (NY)
1961—Giants, 31-10 (D)
Cowboys, 17-16 (NY)
1962—Giants, 41-10 (D)
Giants, 41-31 (NY)
1963—Giants, 37-21 (NY)
Giants, 34-27 (D)
1964—Tie, 13-13 (D)
Cowboys, 31-21 (NY)
1965—Cowboys, 31-2 (D)
Cowboys, 38-20 (NY)
1966—Cowboys, 52-7 (D)
Cowboys, 17-7 (NY)
1967—Cowboys, 38-24 (D)
1968—Giants, 27-21 (D)
Cowboys, 28-10 (NY)
1969—Cowboys, 25-3 (D)
1970—Cowboys, 28-10 (D)
Giants, 23-20 (NY)
1971—Cowboys, 20-13 (D)
Cowboys, 42-14 (NY)
1972—Cowboys, 23-14 (NY)
Giants, 23-3 (D)
1973—Cowboys, 45-28 (D)
Cowboys, 23-10 (New Haven)
1974—Giants, 14-6 (D)

Cowboys, 21-7 (New Haven)
1975—Cowboys, 13-7 (NY)
Cowboys, 14-3 (D)
1976—Cowboys, 24-14 (NY)
Cowboys, 9-3 (D)
1977—Cowboys, 41-21 (D)
Cowboys, 24-10 (NY)
1978—Cowboys, 34-24 (NY)
Cowboys, 24-3 (D)
1979—Cowboys, 16-14 (NY)
Cowboys, 28-7 (D)
1980—Cowboys, 24-3 (D)
Giants, 38-35 (NY)
1981—Cowboys, 18-10 (D)
Giants, 13-10 (NY) OT
1983—Cowboys, 28-13 (D)
Cowboys, 38-20 (NY)
1984—Giants, 28-7 (NY)
Giants, 19-7 (D)
1985—Cowboys, 30-29 (NY)
Cowboys, 28-21 (D)
1986—Cowboys, 31-28 (D)
Giants, 17-14 (NY)
(Points—Cowboys 1,169, Giants 866)

DALLAS vs. N.Y. JETS
Cowboys lead series, 3-0
1971—Cowboys, 52-10 (D)
1975—Cowboys, 31-21 (NY)
1978—Cowboys, 30-7 (NY)
(Points—Cowboys 113, Jets 38)

DALLAS vs. PHILADELPHIA
Cowboys lead series, 35-18
1960—Eagles, 27-25 (D)
1961—Eagles, 43-7 (D)
Eagles, 35-13 (P)
1962—Cowboys, 41-19 (D)
Eagles, 28-14 (P)
1963—Eagles, 24-21 (P)
Cowboys, 27-20 (D)
1964—Eagles, 17-14 (D)
Eagles, 24-14 (P)
1965—Eagles, 35-24 (D)
Cowboys, 21-19 (P)
1966—Cowboys, 56-7 (D)
Eagles, 24-23 (P)
1967—Eagles, 21-14 (P)
Cowboys, 38-17 (D)
1968—Cowboys, 45-13 (P)
Cowboys, 34-14 (D)
1969—Cowboys, 38-7 (P)
Cowboys, 49-14 (D)
1970—Cowboys, 17-7 (P)
Cowboys, 21-17 (D)
1971—Cowboys, 42-7 (P)
Cowboys, 20-7 (D)
1972—Cowboys, 28-6 (D)
Cowboys, 28-7 (P)
1973—Eagles, 30-16 (P)
Cowboys, 31-10 (D)
1974—Eagles, 13-10 (P)
Cowboys, 31-24 (D)
1975—Cowboys, 20-17 (P)
Cowboys, 27-17 (D)
1976—Cowboys, 27-7 (D)
Cowboys, 26-7 (P)
1977—Cowboys, 16-10 (P)
Cowboys, 24-14 (D)
1978—Cowboys, 14-7 (D)
Cowboys, 31-13 (P)
1979—Eagles, 31-21 (D)
Cowboys, 24-17 (P)
1980—Eagles, 17-10 (P)
Cowboys, 35-27 (D)
*Eagles, 20-7 (P)
1981—Cowboys, 17-14 (P)
Cowboys, 21-10 (D)
1982—Eagles, 24-20 (D)
1983—Cowboys, 37-7 (D)
Cowboys, 27-20 (P)
1984—Cowboys, 23-17 (D)
Cowboys, 26-10 (P)
1985—Eagles, 16-14 (P)
Cowboys, 34-17 (D)
1986—Cowboys, 17-14 (P)
Eagles, 23-21 (D)
(Points—Cowboys 1,301, Eagles 912)
NFC Championship

DALLAS vs. PITTSBURGH
Steelers lead series, 12-11
1960—Steelers, 35-28 (D)
1961—Cowboys, 27-24 (D)
Steelers, 37-7 (P)
1962—Steelers, 30-28 (D)
Cowboys, 42-27 (P)
1963—Steelers, 27-21 (P)
Steelers, 24-19 (D)
1964—Steelers, 23-17 (P)
Cowboys, 17-14 (D)
1965—Steelers, 22-13 (P)
Cowboys, 24-17 (D)
1966—Cowboys, 52-21 (D)
Cowboys, 20-7 (P)
1967—Cowboys, 24-21 (P)
1968—Cowboys, 28-7 (D)
1969—Cowboys, 10-7 (P)
1972—Cowboys, 17-13 (D)
1975—*Steelers, 21-17 (Miami)
1977—Steelers, 28-13 (P)
1978—**Steelers, 35-31 (Miami)
1979—Steelers, 14-3 (P)
1982—Steelers, 36-28 (D)
1985—Cowboys, 27-13 (D)
(Points—Cowboys 513, Steelers 503)
Super Bowl X
***Super Bowl XIII*

DALLAS vs. ST. LOUIS
Cowboys lead series, 31-17-1
1960—Cardinals, 12-10 (StL)
1961—Cardinals, 31-17 (D)
Cardinals, 31-13 (StL)
1962—Cardinals, 28-24 (D)
Cardinals, 52-20 (StL)
1963—Cardinals, 34-7 (D)
Cowboys, 28-24 (StL)
1964—Cardinals, 16-6 (D)
Cowboys, 31-13 (StL)
1965—Cardinals, 20-13 (StL)
Cowboys, 27-13 (D)
1966—Tie, 10-10 (StL)
Cowboys, 31-17 (D)
1967—Cowboys, 46-21 (D)
1968—Cowboys, 27-10 (StL)
1969—Cowboys, 24-3 (D)
1970—Cardinals, 20-7 (StL)
Cardinals, 38-0 (D)
1971—Cowboys, 16-13 (StL)
Cowboys, 31-12 (D)
1972—Cowboys, 33-24 (D)
Cowboys, 27-6 (StL)
1973—Cowboys, 45-10 (D)
Cowboys, 30-3 (StL)
1974—Cardinals, 31-28 (StL)
Cowboys, 17-14 (D)
1975—Cowboys, 37-31 (D) OT
Cardinals, 31-17 (StL)
1976—Cardinals, 21-17 (StL)
Cowboys, 19-14 (D)
1977—Cowboys, 30-24 (StL)
Cardinals, 24-17 (D)
1978—Cowboys, 21-12 (D)
Cowboys, 24-21 (StL) OT
1979—Cowboys, 22-21 (StL)
Cowboys, 22-13 (D)
1980—Cowboys, 27-24 (StL)
Cowboys, 31-21 (D)
1981—Cowboys, 30-17 (D)
Cardinals, 20-17 (StL)
1982—Cowboys, 24-7 (StL)
1983—Cowboys, 34-17 (StL)
Cowboys, 35-17 (D)
1984—Cardinals, 31-20 (D)
Cowboys, 24-17 (StL)
1985—Cardinals, 21-10 (StL)
Cowboys, 35-17 (D)
1986—Cowboys, 31-7 (StL)
Cowboys, 37-6 (D)
(Points—Cowboys 1,149, Cardinals 940)

DALLAS vs. SAN DIEGO
Cowboys lead series, 3-1
1972—Cowboys, 34-28 (SD)
1980—Cowboys, 42-31 (D)
1983—Chargers, 24-23 (SD)
1986—Cowboys, 24-21 (SD)
(Points—Cowboys 123, Chargers 104)

DALLAS vs. SAN FRANCISCO
Series tied, 8-8-1
1960—49ers, 26-14 (D)
1963—49ers, 31-24 (SF)
1965—Cowboys, 39-31 (D)
1967—49ers, 24-16 (SF)
1969—Tie, 24-24 (D)
1970—*Cowboys, 17-10 (SF)
1971—*Cowboys, 14-3 (D)
1972—49ers, 31-10 (D)
**Cowboys, 30-28 (SF)
1974—Cowboys, 20-14 (D)
1977—Cowboys, 42-35 (SF)
1979—Cowboys, 21-13 (SF)
1980—Cowboys, 59-14 (D)
1981—49ers, 45-14 (SF)
*49ers, 28-27 (SF)
1983—49ers, 42-17 (SF)
1985—49ers, 31-16 (SF)
(Points—49ers 430, Cowboys 404)
NFC Championship
***NFC Divisional Playoff*

DALLAS vs. SEATTLE
Cowboys lead series, 3-1
1976—Cowboys, 28-13 (S)
1980—Cowboys, 51-7 (D)
1983—Cowboys, 35-10 (S)
1986—Seahawks, 31-14 (D)
(Points—Cowboys 128, Seahawks 61)

DALLAS vs. TAMPA BAY
Cowboys lead series, 6-0
1977—Cowboys, 23-7 (D)
1980—Cowboys, 28-17 (D)
1981—*Cowboys, 38-0 (D)
1982—Cowboys, 14-9 (D)
**Cowboys, 30-17 (D)
1983—Cowboys, 27-24 (D) OT
(Points—Cowboys 160, Buccaneers 74)
NFC Divisional Playoff
***NFC First Round Playoff*

DALLAS vs. WASHINGTON
Cowboys lead series, 31-21-2
1960—Redskins, 26-14 (W)
1961—Tie, 28-28 (D)
Redskins, 34-24 (W)
1962—Tie, 35-35 (D)
Cowboys, 38-10 (W)
1963—Redskins, 21-17 (W)
Cowboys, 35-20 (D)
1964—Cowboys, 24-18 (D)
Redskins, 28-16 (W)
1965—Cowboys, 27-7 (D)
Redskins, 34-31 (W)
1966—Cowboys, 31-30 (W)
Redskins, 34-31 (D)
1967—Cowboys, 17-14 (W)
Redskins, 27-20 (D)
1968—Cowboys, 44-24 (W)
Cowboys, 29-20 (D)
1969—Cowboys, 41-28 (W)
Cowboys, 20-10 (D)
1970—Cowboys, 45-21 (W)
Cowboys, 34-0 (D)
1971—Redskins, 20-16 (D)
Cowboys, 13-0 (W)
1972—Redskins, 24-20 (W)
Cowboys, 34-24 (D)
*Redskins, 26-3 (W)
1973—Redskins, 14-7 (W)
Cowboys, 27-7 (D)
1974—Redskins, 28-21 (W)
Cowboys, 24-23 (D)
1975—Redskins, 30-24 (W) OT
Cowboys, 31-10 (D)
1976—Cowboys, 20-7 (W)
Redskins, 27-14 (D)
1977—Cowboys, 34-16 (D)
Cowboys, 14-7 (W)
1978—Redskins, 9-5 (W)
Cowboys, 37-10 (D)
1979—Redskins, 34-20 (W)
Cowboys, 35-34 (D)
1980—Cowboys, 17-3 (W)
Cowboys, 14-10 (D)
1981—Cowboys, 26-10 (W)
Cowboys, 24-10 (D)
1982—Cowboys, 24-10 (W)
*Redskins, 31-17 (W)
1983—Cowboys, 31-30 (W)
Redskins, 31-10 (D)
1984—Redskins, 34-14 (W)
Redskins, 30-28 (D)
1985—Cowboys, 44-14 (D)
Cowboys, 13-7 (W)
1986—Cowboys, 30-6 (D)
Redskins, 41-14 (W)
(Points—Cowboys 1,306, Redskins 1,086)
NFC Championship

DENVER vs. ATLANTA
Series tied, 3-3;
See Atlanta vs. Denver

DENVER vs. BUFFALO
Bills lead series, 13-9-1;
See Buffalo vs. Denver

DENVER vs. CHICAGO
Bears lead series, 4-3;
See Chicago vs. Denver

DENVER vs. CINCINNATI
Broncos lead series, 9-6;
See Cincinnati vs. Denver

DENVER vs. CLEVELAND
Broncos lead series, 9-3;
See Cleveland vs. Denver

DENVER vs. DALLAS
Cowboys lead series, 3-2;
See Dallas vs. Denver

DENVER vs. DETROIT
Broncos lead series, 3-2
1971—Lions, 24-20 (Den)
1974—Broncos, 31-27 (Det)
1978—Lions, 17-14 (Det)
1981—Broncos, 27-21 (Den)
1984—Broncos, 28-7 (Det)
(Points—Broncos 120, Lions 96)

DENVER vs. GREEN BAY
Broncos lead series, 3-1
1971—Packers, 34-13 (Mil)
1975—Broncos, 23-13 (D)
1978—Broncos, 16-3 (D)
1984—Broncos, 17-14 (D)
(Points—Broncos 69, Packers 64)

DENVER vs. HOUSTON
Oilers lead series, 18-10-1
1960—Oilers, 45-25 (D)
Oilers, 20-10 (H)
1961—Oilers, 55-14 (D)
Oilers, 45-14 (H)
1962—Broncos, 20-10 (D)
Oilers, 34-17 (H)
1963—Oilers, 20-14 (H)
Oilers, 33-24 (D)
1964—Oilers, 38-17 (D)
Oilers, 34-15 (H)
1965—Broncos, 28-17 (D)
Broncos, 31-21 (H)
1966—Oilers, 45-7 (H)
Broncos, 40-38 (D)
1967—Oilers, 10-6 (H)
Oilers, 20-18 (D)
1968—Oilers, 38-17 (H)
1969—Oilers, 24-21 (H)
Tie, 20-20 (D)
1970—Oilers, 31-21 (H)
1972—Broncos, 30-17 (D)
1973—Broncos, 48-20 (H)
1974—Broncos, 37-14 (D)
1976—Oilers, 17-3 (H)
1977—Broncos, 24-14 (H)
1979—*Oilers, 13-7 (H)
1980—Oilers, 20-16 (D)
1983—Broncos, 26-14 (H)
1985—Broncos, 31-20 (D)
(Points—Oilers 747, Broncos 601)
AFC First Round Playoff

DENVER vs. *INDIANAPOLIS
Broncos lead series, 6-1
1974—Broncos, 17-6 (B)
1977—Broncos, 27-13 (D)
1978—Colts, 7-6 (B)
1981—Broncos, 28-10 (D)
1983—Broncos, 17-10 (B)
Broncos, 21-19 (D)
1985—Broncos, 15-10 (I)
(Points—Broncos 131, Colts 75)
Franchise in Baltimore prior to 1984

DENVER vs. *KANSAS CITY
Chiefs lead series, 34-19
1960—Texans, 17-14 (D)
Texans, 34-7 (Da)
1961—Texans, 19-12 (D)
Texans, 49-21 (Da)
1962—Texans, 24-3 (D)
Texans, 17-10 (Da)
1963—Chiefs, 59-7 (D)
Chiefs, 52-21 (KC)
1964—Broncos, 33-27 (D)
Chiefs, 49-39 (KC)
1965—Chiefs, 31-23 (D)
Chiefs, 45-35 (KC)
1966—Chiefs, 37-10 (KC)
Chiefs, 56-10 (D)
1967—Chiefs, 52-9 (KC)
Chiefs, 38-24 (D)
1968—Chiefs, 34-2 (KC)
Chiefs, 30-7 (D)
1969—Chiefs, 26-13 (D)
Chiefs, 31-17 (KC)
1970—Broncos, 26-13 (D)
Chiefs, 16-0 (KC)
1971—Chiefs, 16-3 (D)
Chiefs, 28-10 (KC)
1972—Chiefs, 45-24 (D)
Chiefs, 24-21 (KC)
1973—Chiefs, 16-14 (KC)
Broncos, 14-10 (D)
1974—Broncos, 17-14 (KC)
Chiefs, 42-34 (D)
1975—Broncos, 37-33 (D)
Chiefs, 26-13 (KC)
1976—Broncos, 35-26 (KC)
Broncos, 17-16 (D)
1977—Broncos, 23-7 (D)
Broncos, 14-7 (KC)
1978—Broncos, 23-17 (KC) OT
Broncos, 24-3 (D)
1979—Broncos, 24-10 (KC)
Broncos, 20-3 (D)
1980—Chiefs, 23-17 (D)
Chiefs, 31-14 (KC)
1981—Chiefs, 28-14 (KC)
Broncos, 16-13 (D)
1982—Chiefs, 37-16 (D)
1983—Broncos, 27-24 (D)
Chiefs, 48-17 (KC)
1984—Broncos, 21-0 (D)
Chiefs, 16-13 (KC)
1985—Broncos, 30-10 (KC)
Broncos, 14-13 (D)
1986—Broncos, 38-17 (D)
Chiefs, 37-10 (KC)
(Points—Chiefs 1,396, Broncos 957)
Franchise in Dallas prior to 1963 and known as Texans

DENVER vs. *L.A. RAIDERS
Raiders lead series, 36-16-2
1960—Broncos, 31-14 (D)
Raiders, 48-10 (O)

1961—Raiders, 33-19 (O)
Broncos, 27-24 (D)
1962—Broncos, 44-7 (D)
Broncos, 23-6 (O)
1963—Raiders, 26-10 (D)
Raiders, 35-31 (O)
1964—Raiders, 40-7 (O)
Tie, 20-20 (D)
1965—Raiders, 28-20 (D)
Raiders, 24-13 (O)
1966—Raiders, 17-3 (D)
Raiders, 28-10 (O)
1967—Raiders, 51-0 (O)
Raiders, 21-17 (D)
1968—Raiders, 43-7 (D)
Raiders, 33-27 (O)
1969—Raiders, 24-14 (D)
Raiders, 41-10 (O)
1970—Raiders, 35-23 (O)
Raiders, 24-19 (D)
1971—Raiders, 27-16 (D)
Raiders, 21-13 (O)
1972—Broncos, 30-23 (O)
Raiders, 37-20 (D)
1973—Tie, 23-23 (D)
Raiders, 21-17 (O)
1974—Raiders, 28-17 (D)
Broncos, 20-17 (O)
1975—Raiders, 42-17 (D)
Raiders, 17-10 (O)
1976—Raiders, 17-10 (D)
Raiders, 19-6 (O)
1977—Broncos, 30-7 (O)
Raiders, 24-14 (D)
**Broncos, 20-17 (D)
1978—Broncos, 14-6 (D)
Broncos, 21-6 (O)
1979—Raiders, 27-3 (O)
Raiders, 14-10 (D)
1980—Raiders, 9-3 (O)
Raiders, 24-21 (D)
1981—Broncos, 9-7 (D)
Broncos, 17-0 (O)
1982—Raiders, 27-10 (LA)
1983—Raiders, 22-7 (D)
Raiders, 22-20 (LA)
1984—Broncos, 16-13 (D)
Broncos, 22-19 (LA) OT
1985—Raiders, 31-28 (LA) OT
Raiders, 17-14 (D) OT
1986—Broncos, 38-36 (D)
Broncos, 21-10 (LA)
(Points—Raiders 1,252, Broncos 922)
Franchise in Oakland prior to 1982
***AFC Championship*

DENVER vs. L.A. RAMS
Rams lead series, 3-2
1972—Broncos, 16-10 (LA)
1974—Rams, 17-10 (D)
1979—Rams, 13-9 (D)
1982—Broncos, 27-24 (LA)
1985—Rams, 20-16 (LA)
(Points—Rams 84, Broncos 78)

DENVER vs. MIAMI
Dolphins lead series, 5-2-1
1966—Dolphins, 24-7 (M)
Broncos, 17-7 (D)
1967—Dolphins, 35-21 (M)
1968—Broncos, 21-14 (D)
1969—Dolphins, 27-24 (M)
1971—Tie, 10-10 (D)
1975—Dolphins, 14-13 (M)
1985—Dolphins, 30-26 (D)
(Points—Dolphins 161, Broncos 139)

DENVER vs. MINNESOTA
Series tied, 2-2
1972—Vikings, 23-20 (D)
1978—Vikings, 12-9 (M) OT
1981—Broncos, 19-17 (D)
1984—Broncos, 42-21 (D)
(Points—Broncos 90, Vikings 73)

DENVER vs. *NEW ENGLAND
Broncos lead series, 13-12
1960—Broncos, 13-10 (B)
Broncos, 31-24 (D)
1961—Patriots, 45-17 (B)
Patriots, 28-24 (D)
1962—Patriots, 41-16 (B)
Patriots, 33-29 (D)
1963—Broncos, 14-10 (D)
Patriots, 40-21 (B)
1964—Patriots, 39-10 (D)
Patriots, 12-7 (B)
1965—Broncos, 27-10 (B)
Patriots, 28-20 (D)
1966—Patriots, 24-10 (D)
Broncos, 17-10 (B)
1967—Broncos, 26-21 (D)
1968—Patriots, 20-17 (D)
Broncos, 35-14 (B)
1969—Broncos, 35-7 (D)
1972—Broncos, 45-21 (D)
1976—Patriots, 38-14 (NE)
1979—Broncos, 45-10 (D)
1980—Patriots, 23-14 (NE)
1984—Broncos, 26-19 (D)
1986—Broncos, 27-20 (D)
**Broncos, 22-17 (D)
(Points—Patriots 564, Broncos 562)
**Franchise in Boston prior to 1971*
***AFC Divisional Playoff*

DENVER vs. NEW ORLEANS
Broncos lead series, 4-0
1970—Broncos, 31-6 (NO)
1974—Broncos, 33-17 (D)
1979—Broncos, 10-3 (D)
1985—Broncos, 34-23 (D)
(Points—Broncos 108, Saints 49)

DENVER vs. N.Y. GIANTS
Giants lead series, 3-2
1972—Giants, 29-17 (NY)
1976—Broncos, 14-13 (D)
1980—Broncos, 14-9 (NY)
1986—Giants, 19-16 (NY)
*Giants, 39-20 (Pasadena)
(Points—Giants 109, Broncos 81)
**Super Bowl XXI*

DENVER vs. *N.Y. JETS
Jets lead series, 11-10-1
1960—Titans, 28-24 (NY)
Titans, 30-27 (D)
1961—Titans, 35-28 (NY)
Broncos, 27-10 (D)
1962—Broncos, 32-10 (NY)
Titans, 46-45 (D)
1963—Tie, 35-35 (NY)
Jets, 14-9 (D)
1964—Jets, 30-6 (NY)
Broncos, 20-16 (D)
1965—Broncos, 16-13 (D)
Jets, 45-10 (NY)
1966—Jets, 16-7 (D)
1967—Jets, 38-24 (D)
Broncos, 33-24 (NY)
1968—Broncos, 21-13 (NY)
1969—Broncos, 21-19 (D)
1973—Broncos, 40-28 (NY)
1976—Broncos, 46-3 (D)
1978—Jets, 31-28 (D)
1980—Broncos, 31-24 (D)
1986—Jets, 22-10 (NY)
(Points—Broncos 540, Jets 530)
**Jets known as Titans prior to 1963*

DENVER vs. PHILADELPHIA
Eagles lead series, 3-2
1971—Eagles, 17-16 (P)
1975—Broncos, 25-10 (D)
1980—Eagles, 27-6 (P)
1983—Eagles, 13-10 (D)
1986—Broncos, 33-7 (P)
(Points—Broncos 90, Eagles 74)

DENVER vs. PITTSBURGH
Broncos lead series, 8-5-1
1970—Broncos, 16-13 (D)
1971—Broncos, 22-10 (P)
1973—Broncos, 23-13 (P)
1974—Tie, 35-35 (D) OT
1975—Steelers, 20-9 (P)
1977—Broncos, 21-7 (D)
*Broncos, 34-21 (D)
1978—Steelers, 21-17 (D)
*Steelers, 33-10 (P)
1979—Steelers, 42-7 (P)
1983—Broncos, 14-10 (P)
1984—*Steelers, 24-17 (D)
1985—Broncos, 31-23 (P)
1986—Broncos, 21-10 (P)
(Points—Steelers 282, Broncos 277)
**AFC Divisional Playoff*

DENVER vs. ST. LOUIS
Broncos lead series, 1-0-1
1973—Tie, 17-17 (StL)
1977—Broncos, 7-0 (D)
(Points—Broncos 24, Cardinals 17)

DENVER vs. *SAN DIEGO
Chargers lead series, 28-25-1
1960—Chargers, 23-19 (D)
Chargers, 41-33 (LA)
1961—Chargers, 37-0 (SD)
Chargers, 19-16 (D)
1962—Broncos, 30-21 (D)
Broncos, 23-20 (SD)
1963—Broncos, 50-34 (D)
Chargers, 58-20 (SD)
1964—Chargers, 42-14 (SD)
Chargers, 31-20 (D)
1965—Chargers, 34-31 (SD)
Chargers, 33-21 (D)
1966—Chargers, 24-17 (SD)
Broncos, 20-17 (D)
1967—Chargers, 38-21 (D)
Chargers, 24-20 (SD)
1968—Chargers, 55-24 (SD)
Chargers, 47-23 (D)
1969—Broncos, 13-0 (D)
Chargers, 45-24 (SD)
1970—Chargers, 24-21 (SD)
Tie, 17-17 (D)
1971—Broncos, 20-16 (D)
Chargers, 45-17 (SD)
1972—Chargers, 37-14 (SD)
Broncos, 38-13 (D)
1973—Broncos, 30-19 (D)
Broncos, 42-28 (SD)
1974—Broncos, 27-7 (D)
Chargers, 17-0 (SD)
1975—Broncos, 27-17 (SD)
Broncos, 13-10 (D) OT
1976—Broncos, 26-0 (D)
Broncos, 17-0 (SD)
1977—Broncos, 17-14 (SD)
Broncos, 17-9 (D)
1978—Broncos, 27-14 (D)
Chargers, 23-0 (SD)
1979—Broncos, 7-0 (D)
Chargers, 17-7 (SD)
1980—Chargers, 30-13 (D)
Broncos, 20-13 (SD)
1981—Broncos, 42-24 (D)
Chargers, 34-17 (SD)
1982—Chargers, 23-3 (D)
Chargers, 30-20 (SD)
1983—Broncos, 14-6 (D)
Chargers, 31-7 (SD)
1984—Broncos, 16-13 (SD)
Broncos, 16-13 (D)
1985—Chargers, 30-10 (SD)
Broncos, 30-24 (D) OT
1986—Broncos, 31-14 (SD)
Chargers, 9-3 (D)
(Points—Chargers 1,264, Broncos 1,065)
**Franchise in Los Angeles prior to 1961*

DENVER vs. SAN FRANCISCO
Broncos lead series, 3-2
1970—49ers, 19-14 (SF)
1973—49ers, 36-34 (D)
1979—Broncos, 38-28 (SF)
1982—Broncos, 24-21 (D)
1985—Broncos, 17-16 (D)
(Points—Broncos 127, 49ers 120)

DENVER vs. SEATTLE
Broncos lead series, 12-8
1977—Broncos, 24-13 (S)
1978—Broncos, 28-7 (D)
Broncos, 20-17 (S) OT
1979—Broncos, 37-34 (D)
Seahawks, 28-23 (S)
1980—Broncos, 36-20 (D)
Broncos, 25-17 (S)
1981—Seahawks, 13-10 (S)
Broncos, 23-13 (D)
1982—Seahawks, 17-10 (D)
Seahawks, 13-11 (S)
1983—Seahawks, 27-19 (S)
Broncos, 38-27 (D)
*Seahawks, 31-7 (S)
1984—Seahawks, 27-24 (D)
Broncos, 31-14 (S)
1985—Broncos, 13-10 (D) OT
Broncos, 27-24 (S)
1986—Broncos, 20-13 (D)
Seahawks, 41-16 (S)
(Points—Broncos 442, Seahawks 406)
**AFC First Round Playoff*

DENVER vs. TAMPA BAY
Broncos lead series, 2-0
1976—Broncos, 48-13 (D)
1981—Broncos, 24-7 (TB)
(Points—Broncos 72, Buccaneers 20)

DENVER vs. WASHINGTON
Series tied, 2-2
1970—Redskins, 19-3 (D)
1974—Redskins, 30-3 (W)
1980—Broncos, 20-17 (D)
1986—Broncos, 31-30 (D)
(Points—Redskins 96, Broncos 57)

DETROIT vs. ATLANTA
Lions lead series, 12-5;
See Atlanta vs. Detroit

DETROIT vs. BUFFALO
Series tied, 1-1-1;
See Buffalo vs. Detroit

DETROIT vs. CHICAGO
Bears lead series, 66-44-5;
See Chicago vs. Detroit

DETROIT vs. CINCINNATI
Series tied, 2-2;
See Cincinnati vs. Detroit

DETROIT vs. CLEVELAND
Lions lead series, 12-4;
See Cleveland vs. Detroit

DETROIT vs. DALLAS
Cowboys lead series, 7-3;
See Dallas vs. Detroit

DETROIT vs. DENVER
Broncos lead series, 3-2;
See Denver vs. Detroit

***DETROIT vs. GREEN BAY**
Packers lead series, 58-48-7
1930—Packers, 47-13 (GB)
Tie, 6-6 (P)
1932—Packers, 15-10 (GB)
Spartans, 19-0 (P)
1933—Packers, 17-0 (GB)
Spartans, 7-0 (P)
1934—Lions, 3-0 (GB)
Packers, 3-0 (D)
1935—Packers, 13-9 (GB)
Packers, 31-7 (GB)
Lions, 20-10 (D)
1936—Packers, 20-18 (GB)
Packers, 26-17 (D)
1937—Packers, 26-6 (GB)
Packers, 14-13 (D)
1938—Lions, 17-7 (GB)
Packers, 28-7 (D)
1939—Packers, 26-7 (GB)
Packers, 12-7 (D)
1940—Lions, 23-14 (GB)
Packers, 50-7 (D)
1941—Packers, 23-0 (GB)
Packers, 24-7 (D)
1942—Packers, 38-7 (Mil)
Packers, 28-7 (D)
1943—Packers, 35-14 (GB)
Packers, 27-6 (D)
1944—Packers, 27-6 (GB)
Packers, 14-0 (D)
1945—Packers, 57-21 (Mil)
Lions, 14-3 (D)
1946—Packers, 10-7 (Mil)
Packers, 9-0 (D)
1947—Packers, 34-17 (GB)
Packers, 35-14 (D)
1948—Packers, 33-21 (GB)
Lions, 24-20 (D)
1949—Packers, 16-14 (GB)
Lions, 21-7 (D)
1950—Lions, 45-7 (GB)
Lions, 24-21 (D)
1951—Lions, 24-17 (GB)
Lions, 52-35 (D)
1952—Lions, 52-17 (GB)
Lions, 48-24 (D)
1953—Lions, 14-7 (GB)
Lions, 34-15 (D)
1954—Lions, 21-17 (GB)
Lions, 28-24 (D)
1955—Packers, 20-17 (GB)
Lions, 24-10 (D)
1956—Lions, 20-16 (GB)
Packers, 24-20 (D)
1957—Lions, 24-14 (GB)
Lions, 18-6 (D)
1958—Tie, 13-13 (GB)
Lions, 24-14 (D)
1959—Packers, 28-10 (GB)
Packers, 24-17 (D)
1960—Packers, 28-9 (GB)
Lions, 23-10 (D)
1961—Lions, 17-13 (Mil)
Packers, 17-9 (D)
1962—Packers, 9-7 (GB)
Lions, 26-14 (D)
1963—Packers, 31-10 (Mil)
Tie, 13-13 (D)
1964—Packers, 14-10 (D)
Packers, 30-7 (GB)
1965—Packers, 31-21 (D)
Lions, 12-7 (GB)
1966—Packers, 23-14 (GB)
Packers, 31-7 (D)
1967—Tie, 17-17 (GB)
Packers, 27-17 (D)
1968—Lions, 23-17 (GB)
Tie, 14-14 (D)
1969—Packers, 28-17 (D)
Lions, 16-10 (GB)
1970—Lions, 40-0 (GB)
Lions, 20-0 (D)
1971—Lions, 31-28 (D)
Tie, 14-14 (Mil)
1972—Packers, 24-23 (D)
Packers, 33-7 (GB)
1973—Tie, 13-13 (GB)
Lions, 34-0 (D)
1974—Packers, 21-19 (Mil)
Lions, 19-17 (D)
1975—Lions, 30-16 (Mil)
Lions, 13-10 (D)
1976—Packers, 24-14 (GB)
Lions, 27-6 (D)
1977—Lions, 10-6 (D)
Packers, 10-9 (GB)
1978—Packers, 13-7 (D)
Packers, 35-14 (Mil)
1979—Packers, 24-16 (Mil)
Packers, 18-13 (D)
1980—Lions, 29-7 (Mil)
Lions, 24-3 (D)

1981—Lions, 31-27 (D)
Packers, 31-17 (GB)
1982—Lions, 30-10 (GB)
Lions, 27-24 (D)
1983—Lions, 38-14 (D)
Lions, 23-20 (Mil) OT
1984—Packers, 41-9 (GB)
Lions, 31-28 (D)
1985—Packers, 43-10 (GB)
Packers, 26-23 (D)
1986—Lions, 21-14 (GB)
Packers, 44-40 (D)
(Points—Packers 2,186, Lions 1,960)
**Franchise in Portsmouth prior to 1934 and known as the Spartans*

DETROIT vs. HOUSTON
Series tied, 2-2
1971—Lions, 31-7 (H)
1975—Oilers, 24-8 (H)
1983—Oilers, 27-17 (H)
1986—Lions, 24-13 (D)
(Points—Lions 80, Oilers 71)

DETROIT vs. *INDIANAPOLIS
Colts lead series, 17-16-2
1953—Lions, 27-17 (B)
Lions, 17-7 (D)
1954—Lions, 35-0 (D)
Lions, 27-3 (B)
1955—Colts, 28-13 (B)
Lions, 24-14 (D)
1956—Lions, 31-14 (B)
Lions, 27-3 (D)
1957—Colts, 34-14 (B)
Lions, 31-27 (D)
1958—Colts, 28-15 (B)
Colts, 40-14 (D)
1959—Colts, 21-9 (B)
Colts, 31-24 (D)
1960—Lions, 30-17 (D)
Lions, 20-15 (B)
1961—Lions, 16-15 (B)
Colts, 17-14 (D)
1962—Lions, 29-20 (B)
Lions, 21-14 (D)
1963—Colts, 25-21 (D)
Colts, 24-21 (B)
1964—Colts, 34-0 (D)
Lions, 31-14 (B)
1965—Colts, 31-7 (B)
Tie, 24-24 (D)
1966—Colts, 45-14 (B)
Lions, 20-14 (D)
1967—Colts, 41-7 (B)
1968—Colts, 27-10 (D)
1969—Tie, 17-17 (B)
1973—Colts, 29-27 (D)
1977—Lions, 13-10 (B)
1980—Colts, 10-9 (D)
1985—Colts, 14-6 (I)
(Points—Colts 724, Lions 665)
**Franchise in Baltimore prior to 1984*

DETROIT vs. KANSAS CITY
Series tied, 2-2
1971—Lions, 32-21 (D)
1975—Chiefs, 24-21 (KC) OT
1980—Chiefs, 20-17 (KC)
1981—Lions, 27-10 (D)
(Points—Lions 97, Chiefs 75)

DETROIT vs. *L.A. RAIDERS
Raiders lead series, 3-2
1970—Lions, 28-14 (D)
1974—Raiders, 35-13 (O)
1978—Raiders, 29-17 (O)
1981—Lions, 16-0 (D)
1984—Raiders, 24-3 (D)
(Points—Raiders 102, Lions 77)
**Franchise in Oakland prior to 1982*

DETROIT vs. *L.A. RAMS
Rams lead series, 37-34-1
1937—Lions, 28-0 (C)
Lions, 27-7 (D)
1938—Rams, 21-17 (C)
Lions, 6-0 (D)
1939—Lions, 15-7 (D)
Rams, 14-3 (C)
1940—Lions, 6-0 (D)
Rams, 24-0 (C)
1941—Lions, 17-7 (D)
Lions, 14-0 (C)
1942—Rams, 14-0 (D)
Rams, 27-7 (C)
1944—Rams, 20-17 (D)
Lions, 26-14 (C)
1945—Rams, 28-21 (D)
1946—Rams, 35-14 (LA)
Rams, 41-20 (D)
1947—Rams, 27-13 (D)
Rams, 28-17 (LA)
1948—Rams, 44-7 (LA)
Rams, 34-27 (D)
1949—Rams, 27-24 (LA)
Rams, 21-10 (D)
1950—Rams, 30-28 (D)
Rams, 65-24 (LA)
1951—Rams, 27-21 (D)
Lions, 24-22 (LA)
1952—Lions, 17-14 (LA)
Lions, 24-16 (D)
**Lions, 31-21 (D)
1953—Rams, 31-19 (D)
Rams, 37-24 (LA)
1954—Lions, 21-3 (D)
Lions, 27-24 (LA)
1955—Rams, 17-10 (D)
Rams, 24-13 (LA)
1956—Lions, 24-21 (D)
Lions, 16-7 (LA)
1957—Lions, 10-7 (D)
Rams, 35-17 (LA)
1958—Rams, 42-28 (D)
Lions, 41-24 (LA)
1959—Lions, 17-7 (LA)
Lions, 23-17 (D)
1960—Rams, 48-35 (LA)
Lions, 12-10 (D)
1961—Lions, 14-13 (D)
Lions, 28-10 (LA)
1962—Lions, 13-10 (D)
Lions, 12-3 (LA)
1963—Lions, 23-2 (LA)
Rams, 28-21 (D)
1964—Tie, 17-17 (LA)
Lions, 37-17 (D)
1965—Lions, 20-0 (D)
Lions, 31-7 (LA)
1966—Rams, 14-7 (D)
Rams, 23-3 (LA)
1967—Rams, 31-7 (D)
1968—Rams, 10-7 (LA)
1969—Lions, 28-0 (D)
1970—Lions, 28-23 (LA)
1971—Rams, 21-13 (D)
1972—Lions, 34-17 (LA)
1974—Rams, 16-13 (LA)
1975—Rams, 20-0 (D)
1976—Rams, 20-17 (D)
1980—Lions, 41-20 (LA)
1981—Rams, 20-13 (LA)
1982—Lions, 19-14 (LA)
1983—Rams, 21-10 (LA)
1986—Rams, 14-10 (LA)
(Points—Rams 1,380, Lions 1,308)
**Franchise in Cleveland prior to 1946*
***Conference Playoff*

DETROIT vs. MIAMI
Dolphins lead series, 2-1
1973—Dolphins, 34-7 (M)
1979—Dolphins, 28-10 (D)
1985—Lions, 31-21 (D)
(Points—Dolphins 83, Lions 48)

DETROIT vs. MINNESOTA
Vikings lead series, 31-18-2
1961—Lions, 37-10 (M)
Lions, 13-7 (D)
1962—Lions, 17-6 (M)
Lions, 37-23 (D)
1963—Lions, 28-10 (D)
Vikings, 34-31 (M)
1964—Lions, 24-20 (M)
Tie, 23-23 (D)
1965—Lions, 31-29 (M)
Vikings, 29-7 (D)
1966—Lions, 32-31 (M)
Vikings, 28-16 (D)
1967—Tie, 10-10 (M)
Lions, 14-3 (D)
1968—Vikings, 24-10 (M)
Vikings, 13-6 (D)
1969—Vikings, 24-10 (M)
Vikings, 27-0 (D)
1970—Vikings, 30-17 (D)
Vikings, 24-20 (M)
1971—Vikings, 16-13 (D)
Vikings, 29-10 (M)
1972—Vikings, 34-10 (D)
Vikings, 16-14 (M)
1973—Vikings, 23-9 (D)
Vikings, 28-7 (M)
1974—Vikings, 7-6 (D)
Lions, 20-16 (M)
1975—Vikings, 25-19 (M)
Lions, 17-10 (D)
1976—Vikings, 10-9 (D)
Vikings, 31-23 (M)
1977—Vikings, 14-7 (M)
Vikings, 30-21 (D)
1978—Vikings, 17-7 (M)
Lions, 45-14 (D)
1979—Vikings, 13-10 (D)
Vikings, 14-7 (M)
1980—Lions, 27-7 (D)
Vikings, 34-0 (M)
1981—Vikings, 26-24 (M)
Lions, 45-7 (D)
1982—Vikings, 34-31 (D)
1983—Vikings, 20-17 (M)
Lions, 13-2 (D)
1984—Vikings, 29-28 (D)
Lions, 16-14 (M)
1985—Vikings, 16-13 (M)
Lions, 41-21 (D)
1986—Lions, 13-10 (M)
Vikings, 24-10 (D)
(Points—Vikings 996, Lions 915)

DETROIT vs. NEW ENGLAND
Series tied, 2-2
1971—Lions, 34-7 (NE)
1976—Lions, 30-10 (D)
1979—Patriots, 24-17 (NE)
1985—Patriots, 23-6 (NE)
(Points—Lions 87, Patriots 64)

DETROIT vs. NEW ORLEANS
Series tied, 4-4-1
1968—Tie, 20-20 (D)
1970—Saints, 19-17 (NO)
1972—Lions, 27-14 (D)
1973—Saints, 20-13 (NO)
1974—Lions, 19-14 (D)
1976—Saints, 17-16 (NO)
1977—Lions, 23-19 (D)
1979—Saints, 17-7 (NO)
1980—Lions, 24-13 (D)
(Points—Lions 166, Saints 153)

***DETROIT vs. N.Y. GIANTS**
Lions lead series, 18-11-1
1930—Giants, 19-6 (P)
1931—Spartans, 14-6 (P)
Giants, 14-0 (NY)
1932—Spartans, 7-0 (P)
Spartans, 6-0 (NY)
1933—Spartans, 17-7 (P)
Giants, 13-10 (NY)
1934—Lions, 9-0 (D)
1935—**Lions, 26-7 (D)
1936—Giants, 14-7 (NY)
Lions, 38-0 (D)
1937—Lions, 17-0 (NY)
1939—Lions, 18-14 (D)
1941—Giants, 20-13 (NY)
1943—Tie, 0-0 (D)
1945—Giants, 35-14 (NY)
1947—Lions, 35-7 (D)
1949—Lions, 45-21 (NY)
1953—Lions, 27-16 (NY)
1955—Giants, 24-19 (D)
1958—Giants, 19-17 (D)
1962—Giants, 17-14 (NY)
1964—Lions, 26-3 (D)
1967—Lions, 30-7 (NY)
1969—Lions, 24-0 (D)
1972—Lions, 30-16 (D)
1974—Lions, 20-19 (D)
1976—Giants, 24-10 (NY)
1982—Giants, 13-6 (D)
1983—Lions, 15-9 (D)
(Points—Lions 520, Giants 344)
**Franchise in Portsmouth prior to 1934 and known as the Spartans*
***NFL Championship*

DETROIT vs. N.Y. JETS
Series tied, 2-2
1972—Lions, 37-20 (D)
1979—Jets, 31-10 (NY)
1982—Jets, 28-13 (D)
1985—Lions, 31-20 (D)
(Points—Jets 99, Lions 91)

***DETROIT vs. PHILADELPHIA**
Lions lead series, 12-9-2
1933—Spartans, 25-0 (P)
1934—Lions, 10-0 (P)
1935—Lions, 35-0 (D)
1936—Lions, 23-0 (P)
1938—Eagles, 21-7 (D)
1940—Lions, 21-0 (P)
1941—Lions, 21-17 (D)
1945—Lions, 28-24 (D)
1948—Eagles, 45-21 (P)
1949—Eagles, 22-14 (D)
1951—Lions, 28-10 (P)
1954—Tie, 13-13 (D)
1957—Lions, 27-16 (P)
1960—Eagles, 28-10 (P)
1961—Eagles, 27-24 (D)
1965—Lions, 35-28 (P)
1968—Eagles, 12-0 (D)
1971—Eagles, 23-20 (D)
1974—Eagles, 28-17 (P)
1977—Lions, 17-13 (D)
1979—Eagles, 44-7 (P)
1984—Tie, 23-23 (D) OT
1986—Lions, 13-11 (P)
(Points—Lions 439, Eagles 405)
**Franchise in Portsmouth prior to 1934 and known as the Spartans*

DETROIT vs. *PITTSBURGH
Lions lead series, 13-9-1
1934—Lions, 40-7 (D)
1936—Lions, 28-3 (D)
1937—Lions, 7-3 (D)
1938—Lions, 16-7 (D)
1940—Pirates, 10-7 (D)
1942—Steelers, 35-7 (D)
1946—Lions, 17-7 (D)
1947—Steelers, 17-10 (P)
1948—Lions, 17-14 (D)
1949—Steelers, 14-7 (P)
1950—Lions, 10-7 (D)
1952—Lions, 31-6 (P)
1953—Lions, 38-21 (D)
1955—Lions, 31-28 (P)
1956—Lions, 45-7 (D)
1959—Tie, 10-10 (P)
1962—Lions, 45-7 (D)
1966—Steelers, 17-3 (P)
1967—Steelers, 24-14 (D)
1969—Steelers, 16-13 (P)
1973—Steelers, 24-10 (P)
1983—Lions, 45-3 (D)
1986—Steelers, 27-17 (P)
(Points—Lions 468, Steelers 314)
**Steelers known as Pirates prior to 1941*

***DETROIT vs. **ST. LOUIS**
Lions lead series, 25-15-5
1930—Tie, 0-0 (P)
Cardinals, 23-0 (C)
1931—Cardinals, 20-19 (C)
1932—Tie, 7-7 (P)
1933—Spartans, 7-6 (P)
1934—Lions, 6-0 (D)
Lions, 17-13 (C)
1935—Tie, 10-10 (D)
Lions, 7-6 (C)
1936 Lions, 39-0 (D)
Lions, 14-7 (C)
1937—Lions, 16-7 (C)
Lions, 16-7 (D)
1938—Lions, 10-0 (D)
Lions, 7-3 (C)
1939—Lions, 21-3 (D)
Lions, 17-3 (C)
1940—Tie, 0-0 (Buffalo)
Lions, 43-14 (C)
1941—Tie, 14-14 (C)
Lions, 21-3 (D)
1942—Cardinals, 13-0 (C)
Cardinals, 7-0 (D)
1943—Lions, 35-17 (D)
Lions, 7-0 (C)
1945—Lions, 10-0 (C)
Lions, 26-0 (D)
1946—Cardinals, 34-14 (C)
Cardinals, 36-14 (D)
1947—Cardinals, 45-21 (C)
Cardinals, 17-7 (D)
1948—Cardinals, 56-20 (C)
Cardinals, 28-14 (D)
1949—Lions, 24-7 (C)
Cardinals, 42-19 (D)
1959—Lions, 45-21 (D)
1961—Lions, 45-14 (StL)
1967—Cardinals, 38-28 (StL)
1969—Lions, 20-0 (D)
1970—Lions, 16-3 (D)
1973—Lions, 20-16 (StL)
1975—Cardinals, 24-13 (D)
1978—Cardinals, 21-14 (StL)
1980—Lions, 20-7 (D)
Cardinals, 24-23 (StL)
(Points—Lions 746, Cardinals 626)
**Franchise in Portsmouth prior to 1934 and known as the Spartans*
***Franchise in Chicago prior to 1960*

DETROIT vs. SAN DIEGO
Lions lead series, 3-2
1972—Lions, 34-20 (D)
1977—Lions, 20-0 (D)
1978—Lions, 31-14 (D)
1981—Chargers, 28-23 (SD)
1984—Chargers, 27-24 (SD)
(Points—Lions 132, Chargers 89)

DETROIT vs. SAN FRANCISCO
Lions lead series, 26-23-1
1950—Lions, 24-7 (D)
49ers, 28-27 (SF)
1951—49ers, 20-10 (D)
49ers, 21-17 (SF)
1952—49ers, 17-3 (SF)
49ers, 28-0 (D)
1953—Lions, 24-21 (D)
Lions, 14-10 (SF)
1954—49ers, 37-31 (SF)
Lions, 48-7 (D)
1955—49ers, 27-24 (D)
49ers, 38-21 (SF)
1956—Lions, 20-17 (D)
Lions, 17-13 (SF)
1957—49ers, 35-31 (SF)
Lions, 31-10 (D)
*Lions, 31-27 (SF)
1958—49ers, 24-21 (SF)
Lions, 35-21 (D)
1959—49ers, 34-13 (D)

49ers, 33-7 (SF)
1960—49ers, 14-10 (D)
Lions, 24-0 (SF)
1961—49ers, 49-0 (D)
Tie, 20-20 (SF)
1962—Lions, 45-24 (D)
Lions, 38-24 (SF)
1963—Lions, 26-3 (D)
Lions, 45-7 (SF)
1964—Lions, 26-17 (SF)
Lions, 24-7 (D)
1965—49ers, 27-21 (D)
49ers, 17-14 (SF)
1966—49ers, 27-24 (SF)
49ers, 41-14 (D)
1967—Lions, 45-3 (SF)
1968—49ers, 14-7 (D)
1969—Lions, 26-14 (SF)
1970—Lions, 28-7 (D)
1971—49ers, 31-27 (SF)
1973—Lions, 30-20 (D)
1974—Lions, 17-13 (D)
1975—Lions, 28-17 (SF)
1977—49ers, 28-7 (SF)
1978—Lions, 33-14 (D)
1980—Lions, 17-13 (D)
1981—Lions, 24-17 (D)
1983—**49ers, 24-23 (SF)
1984—49ers, 30-27 (D)
1985—Lions, 23-21 (D)
(Points—Lions 1,142, 49ers 1,018)
Conference Playoff
**NFC Divisional Playoff*

DETROIT vs. SEATTLE
Seahawks lead series, 2-1
1976—Lions, 41-14 (S)
1978—Seahawks, 28-16 (S)
1984—Seahawks, 38-17 (S)
(Points—Seahawks 80, Lions 74)

DETROIT vs. TAMPA BAY
Lions lead series, 10-8
1977—Lions, 16-7 (D)
1978—Lions, 15-7 (TB)
Lions, 34-23 (D)
1979—Buccaneers, 31-16 (TB)
Buccaneers, 16-14 (D)
1980—Lions, 24-10 (TB)
Lions, 27-14 (D)
1981—Buccaneers, 28-10 (TB)
Buccaneers, 20-17 (D)
1982—Buccaneers, 23-21 (TB)
1983—Lions, 11-0 (TB)
Lions, 23-20 (D)
1984—Buccaneers, 21-17 (TB)
Lions, 13-7 (D) OT
1985—Lions, 30-9 (D)
Buccaneers, 19-16 (TB) OT
1986—Buccaneers, 24-20 (D)
Lions, 38-17 (TB)
(Points—Lions 362, Buccaneers 296)

***DETROIT vs. **WASHINGTON**
Redskins lead series, 19-8
1932—Spartans, 10-0 (P)
1933—Spartans, 13-0 (B)
1934—Lions, 24-0 (D)
1935—Lions, 17-7 (B)
Lions, 14-0 (D)
1938—Redskins, 7-5 (D)
1939—Redskins, 31-7 (W)
1940—Redskins, 20-14 (D)
1942—Redskins, 15-3 (D)
1943—Redskins, 42-20 (W)
1946—Redskins, 17-16 (W)
1947—Lions, 38-21 (D)
1948—Redskins, 46-21 (W)
1951—Lions, 35-17 (D)
1956—Redskins, 18-17 (W)
1965—Lions, 14-10 (D)
1968—Redskins, 14-3 (W)
1970—Redskins, 31-10 (W)
1973—Redskins, 20-0 (D)
1976—Redskins, 20-7 (W)
1978—Redskins, 21-19 (D)
1979—Redskins, 27-24 (D)
1981—Redskins, 33-31 (W)
1982—***Redskins, 31-7 (W)
1983—Redskins, 38-17 (W)
1984—Redskins, 28-14 (W)
1985—Redskins, 24-3 (W)
(Points—Redskins 538, Lions 403)
Franchise in Portsmouth prior to 1934 and known as the Spartans.
**Franchise in Boston prior to 1937*
***NFC First Round Playoff*

GREEN BAY vs. ATLANTA
Packers lead series, 8-6;
See Atlanta vs. Green Bay

GREEN BAY vs. BUFFALO
Bills lead series, 2-1;
See Buffalo vs. Green Bay

GREEN BAY vs. CHICAGO
Bears lead series, 72-55-6;
See Chicago vs. Green Bay

GREEN BAY vs. CINCINNATI
Bengals lead series, 4-2;
See Cincinnati vs. Green Bay

GREEN BAY vs. CLEVELAND
Packers lead series, 8-5;
See Cleveland vs. Green Bay

GREEN BAY vs. DALLAS
Packers lead series, 8-5;
See Dallas vs. Green Bay

GREEN BAY vs. DENVER
Broncos lead series, 3-1;
See Denver vs. Green Bay

GREEN BAY vs. DETROIT
Packers lead series, 58-48-7;
See Detroit vs. Green Bay

GREEN BAY vs. HOUSTON
Oilers lead series, 3-2
1972—Packers, 23-10 (H)
1977—Oilers, 16-10 (GB)
1980—Oilers, 22-3 (GB)
1983—Packers, 41-38 (H) OT
1986—Oilers, 31-3 (GB)
(Points—Oilers 117, Packers 80)

GREEN BAY vs. *INDIANAPOLIS
Packers lead series, 18-17-1
1953—Packers, 37-14 (GB)
Packers, 35-24 (B)
1954—Packers, 7-6 (B)
Packers, 24-13 (Mil)
1955—Colts, 24-20 (Mil)
Colts, 14-10 (B)
1956—Packers, 38-33 (Mil)
Colts, 28-21 (B)
1957—Colts, 45-17 (Mil)
Packers, 24-21 (B)
1958—Colts, 24-17 (Mil)
Colts, 56-0 (B)
1959—Colts, 38-21 (B)
Colts, 28-24 (Mil)
1960—Packers, 35-21 (GB)
Colts, 38-24 (B)
1961—Packers, 45-7 (GB)
Colts, 45-21 (B)
1962—Packers, 17-6 (B)
Packers, 17-13 (GB)
1963—Packers, 31-20 (GB)
Packers, 34-20 (B)
1964—Colts, 21-20 (GB)
Colts, 24-21 (B)
1965—Packers, 20-17 (Mil)
Packers, 42-27 (B)
**Packers, 13-10 (GB) OT
1966—Packers, 24-3 (Mil)
Packers, 14-10 (B)
1967—Colts, 13-10 (B)
1968—Colts, 16-3 (GB)
1969—Colts, 14-6 (B)
1970—Colts, 13-10 (Mil)
1974—Packers, 20-13 (B)
1982—Tie, 20-20 (B) OT
1985—Colts, 37-10 (I)
(Points—Colts 776, Packers 752)
Franchise in Baltimore prior to 1984
**Conference Playoff*

GREEN BAY vs. KANSAS CITY
Series tied, 1-1-1
1966—*Packers, 35-10 (Los Angeles)
1973—Tie, 10-10 (Mil)
1977—Chiefs, 20-10 (KC)
(Points—Packers 55, Chiefs 40)
Super Bowl I

GREEN BAY vs. *L.A. RAIDERS
Raiders lead series, 4-1
1967—**Packers, 33-14 (Miami)
1972—Raiders, 20-14 (GB)
1976—Raiders, 18-14 (O)
1978—Raiders, 28-3 (GB)
1984—Raiders, 28-7 (LA)
(Points—Raiders 108, Packers 71)
Franchise in Oakland prior to 1982
**Super Bowl II*

GREEN BAY vs. *L.A. RAMS
Rams lead series, 39-34-2
1937—Packers, 35-10 (C)
Packers, 35-7 (GB)
1938—Packers, 26-17 (GB)
Packers, 28-7 (C)
1939—Rams, 27-24 (GB)
Packers, 7-6 (C)
1940—Packers, 31-14 (GB)
Tie, 13-13 (C)
1941—Packers, 24-7 (Mil)
Packers, 17-14 (C)
1942—Packers, 45-28 (GB)
Packers, 30-12 (C)
1944—Packers, 30-21 (GB)
Packers, 42-7 (C)
1945—Rams, 27-14 (GB)
Rams, 20-7 (C)
1946—Rams, 21-17 (Mil)
Rams, 38-17 (LA)
1947—Packers, 17-14 (Mil)
Packers, 30-10 (LA)
1948—Packers, 16-0 (GB)
Rams, 24-10 (LA)
1949—Rams, 48-7 (GB)
Rams, 35-7 (LA)
1950—Rams, 45-14 (Mil)
Rams, 51-14 (LA)
1951—Rams, 28-0 (Mil)
Rams, 42-14 (LA)
1952—Rams, 30-28 (Mil)
Rams, 45-27 (LA)
1953—Rams, 38-20 (Mil)
Rams, 33-17 (LA)
1954—Packers, 35-17 (Mil)
Rams, 35-27 (LA)
1955—Packers, 30-28 (Mil)
Rams, 31-17 (LA)
1956—Packers, 42-17 (Mil)
Rams, 49-21 (LA)
1957—Rams, 31-27 (Mil)
Rams, 42-17 (LA)
1958—Rams, 20-7 (GB)
Rams, 34-20 (LA)
1959—Rams, 45-6 (Mil)
Packers, 38-20 (LA)
1960—Rams, 33-31 (Mil)
Packers, 35-2 (LA)
1961—Packers, 35-17 (GB)
Packers, 24-17 (LA)
1962—Packers, 41-10 (Mil)
Packers, 20-17 (LA)
1963—Packers, 42-10 (GB)
Packers, 31-14 (LA)
1964—Rams, 27-17 (Mil)
Tie, 24-24 (LA)
1965—Packers, 6-3 (Mil)
Rams, 21-10 (LA)
1966—Packers, 24-13 (GB)
Packers, 27-23 (LA)
1967—Rams, 27-24 (LA)
**Packers, 28-7 (Mil)
1968—Rams, 16-14 (Mil)
1969—Rams, 34-21 (LA)
1970—Rams, 31-21 (GB)
1971—Rams, 30-13 (LA)
1973—Rams, 24-7 (LA)
1974—Packers, 17-6 (Mil)
1975—Rams, 22-5 (LA)
1977—Rams, 24-6 (Mil)
1978—Rams, 31-14 (LA)
1980—Rams, 51-21 (LA)
1981—Rams, 35-23 (LA)
1982—Packers, 35-23 (Mil)
1983—Packers, 27-24 (Mil)
1984—Packers, 31-6 (Mil)
1985—Rams, 34-17 (LA)
(Points—Rams 1,783, Packers 1,641)
Franchise in Cleveland prior to 1946
**Conference Championship*

GREEN BAY vs. MIAMI
Dolphins lead series, 4-0
1971—Dolphins, 27-6 (Mia)
1975—Dolphins, 31-7 (GB)
1979—Dolphins, 27-7 (Mia)
1985—Dolphins, 34-24 (GB)
(Points—Dolphins 119, Packers 44)

GREEN BAY vs. MINNESOTA
Vikings lead series, 26-24-1
1961—Packers, 33-7 (Minn)
Packers, 28-10 (Mil)
1962—Packers, 34-7 (GB)
Packers, 48-21 (Minn)
1963—Packers, 37-28 (Minn)
Packers, 28-7 (GB)
1964—Vikings, 24-23 (GB)
Packers, 42-13 (Minn)
1965—Packers, 38-13 (Minn)
Packers, 24-19 (GB)
1966—Vikings, 20-17 (GB)
Packers, 28-16 (Minn)
1967—Vikings, 10-7 (Mil)
Packers, 30-27 (Minn)
1968—Vikings, 26-13 (Mil)
Vikings, 14-10 (Minn)
1969—Vikings, 19-7 (Minn)
Vikings, 9-7 (Mil)
1970—Packers, 13-10 (Mil)
Vikings, 10-3 (Minn)
1971—Vikings, 24-13 (GB)
Vikings, 3-0 (Minn)
1972—Vikings, 27-13 (GB)
Packers, 23-7 (Minn)
1973—Vikings, 11-3 (Minn)
Vikings, 31-7 (GB)
1974—Vikings, 32-17 (GB)
Packers, 19-7 (Minn)
1975—Vikings, 28-17 (GB)
Vikings, 24-3 (Minn)
1976—Vikings, 17-10 (Mil)
Vikings, 20-9 (Minn)
1977—Vikings, 19-7 (Minn)
Vikings, 13-6 (GB)
1978—Vikings, 21-7 (Minn)
Tie, 10-10 (GB) OT
1979—Vikings, 27-21 (Minn) OT
Packers, 19-7 (Mil)
1980—Packers, 16-3 (GB)
Packers, 25-13 (Minn)
1981—Vikings, 30-13 (Mil)
Packers, 35-23 (Minn)
1982—Packers, 26-7 (Mil)
1983—Vikings, 20-17 (GB) OT
Packers, 29-21 (Minn)
1984—Packers, 45-17 (Mil)
Packers, 38-14 (Minn)
1985—Packers, 20-17 (Mil)
Packers, 27-17 (Minn)
1986—Vikings, 42-7 (M)
Vikings, 32-6 (GB)
(Points—Packers 978, Vikings 894)

GREEN BAY vs. NEW ENGLAND
Patriots lead series, 2-1
1973—Patriots, 33-24 (NE)
1979—Packers, 27-14 (GB)
1985—Patriots, 26-20 (NE)
(Points—Patriots 73, Packers 71)

GREEN BAY vs. NEW ORLEANS
Packers lead series, 10-3
1968—Packers, 29-7 (Mil)
1971—Saints, 29-21 (Mil)
1972—Packers, 30-20 (NO)
1973—Packers, 30-10 (Mil)
1975—Saints, 20-19 (NO)
1976—Packers, 32-27 (Mil)
1977—Packers, 24-20 (NO)
1978—Packers, 28-17 (Mil)
1979—Packers, 28-19 (Mil)
1981—Packers, 35-7 (NO)
1984—Packers, 23-13 (NO)
1985—Packers, 38-14 (Mil)
1986—Saints, 24-10 (NO)
(Points—Packers 347, Saints 227)

GREEN BAY vs. N.Y. GIANTS
Packers lead series, 25-19-2
1928—Giants, 6-0 (GB)
Packers, 7-0 (NY)
1929—Packers, 20-6 (NY)
1930—Packers, 14-7 (GB)
Giants, 13-6 (NY)
1931—Packers, 27-7 (GB)
Packers, 14-10 (NY)
1932—Packers, 13-0 (GB)
Giants, 6-0 (NY)
1933—Giants, 10-7 (Mil)
Giants, 17-6 (NY)
1934—Packers, 20-6 (Mil)
Giants, 17-3 (NY)
1935—Packers, 16-7 (GB)
1936—Packers, 26-14 (NY)
1937—Giants, 10-0 (NY)
1938—Giants, 15-3 (NY)
*Giants, 23-17 (NY)
1939—*Packers, 27-0 (Mil)
1940—Giants, 7-3 (NY)
1942—Tie, 21-21 (NY)
1943—Packers, 35-21 (NY)
1944—Giants, 24-0 (NY)
*Packers, 14-7 (NY)
1945—Packers, 23-14 (NY)
1947—Tie, 24-24 (NY)
1948—Giants, 49-3 (Mil)
1949—Giants, 30-10 (GB)
1952—Packers, 17-3 (NY)
1957—Giants, 31-17 (GB)
1959—Giants, 20-3 (NY)
1961—Packers, 20-17 (Mil)
*Packers, 37-0 (GB)
1962—*Packers, 16-7 (NY)
1967—Packers, 48-21 (NY)
1969—Packers, 20-10 (Mil)
1971—Giants, 42-40 (GB)
1973—Packers, 16-14 (New Haven)
1975—Packers, 40-14 (Mil)
1980—Giants, 27-21 (NY)
1981—Packers, 27-14 (NY)
Packers, 26-24 (Mil)
1982—Packers, 27-19 (NY)
1983—Giants, 27-3 (NY)
1985—Packers, 23-20 (GB)
1986—Giants, 55-24 (NY)
(Points—Packers 784, Giants 736)
NFL Championship

GREEN BAY vs. N.Y. JETS
Jets lead series, 4-1
1973—Packers, 23-7 (Mil)
1979—Jets, 27-22 (GB)
1981—Jets, 28-3 (NY)
1982—Jets, 15-13 (NY)
1985—Jets, 24-3 (Mil)
(Points—Jets 101, Packers 64)

GREEN BAY vs. PHILADELPHIA
Packers lead series, 17-5
1933—Packers, 35-9 (GB)
Packers, 10-0 (P)
1934—Packers, 19-6 (GB)
1935—Packers, 13-6 (P)

1937—Packers, 37-7 (Mil)
1939—Packers, 23-16 (P)
1940—Packers, 27-20 (GB)
1942—Packers, 7-0 (P)
1946—Packers, 19-7 (P)
1947—Eagles, 28-14 (P)
1951—Packers, 37-24 (GB)
1952—Packers, 12-10 (Mil)
1954—Packers, 37-14 (P)
1958—Packers, 38-35 (GB)
1960—*Eagles, 17-13 (P)
1962—Packers, 49-0 (P)
1968—Packers, 30-13 (GB)
1970—Packers, 30-17 (Mil)
1974—Eagles, 36-14 (P)
1976—Packers, 28-13 (GB)
1978—Eagles, 10-3 (P)
1979—Eagles, 21-10 (GB)
(Points—Packers 505, Eagles 309)
*NFL Championship

GREEN BAY vs. *PITTSBURGH
Packers lead series, 16-11
1933—Packers, 47-0 (GB)
1935—Packers, 27-0 (GB)
Packers, 34-14 (P)
1936—Packers, 42-10 (Mil)
1938—Packers, 20-0 (GB)
1940—Packers, 24-3 (Mil)
1941—Packers, 54-7 (P)
1942—Packers, 24-21 (Mil)
1946—Packers, 17-7 (GB)
1947—Steelers, 18-17 (Mil)
1948—Steelers, 38-7 (P)
1949—Steelers, 30-7 (Mil)
1951—Packers, 35-33 (Mil)
Steelers, 28-7 (P)
1953—Steelers, 31-14 (P)
1954—Steelers, 21-20 (GB)
1957—Packers, 27-10 (P)
1960—Packers, 19-13 (P)
1963—Packers, 33-14 (Mil)
1965—Packers, 41-9 (P)
1967—Steelers, 24-17 (GB)
1969—Packers, 38-34 (P)
1970—Packers, 20-12 (P)
1975—Steelers, 16-13 (Mil)
1980—Steelers, 22-20 (P)
1983—Steelers, 25-21 (GB)
1986—Steelers, 27-3 (P)
(Points—Packers 648, Steelers 467)
*Steelers known as Pirates prior to 1941

GREEN BAY vs. *ST. LOUIS
Packers lead series, 38-21-4
1921—Tie, 3-3 (C)
1922—Cardinals, 16-3 (C)
1924—Cardinals, 3-0 (C)
1925—Cardinals, 9-6 (C)
1926—Cardinals, 13-7 (GB)
Packers, 3-0 (C)
1927—Packers, 13-0 (GB)
Tie, 6-6 (C)
1928—Packers, 20-0 (GB)
1929—Packers, 9-2 (GB)
Packers, 7-6 (C)
Packers, 12-0 (C)
1930—Packers, 14-0 (GB)
Cardinals, 13-6 (C)
1931—Packers, 26-7 (GB)
Cardinals, 21-13 (C)
1932—Packers, 15-7 (GB)
Packers, 19-9 (C)
1933—Packers, 14-6 (C)
1934—Packers, 15-0 (GB)
Cardinals, 9-0 (Mil)
Cardinals, 6-0 (C)
1935—Cardinals, 7-6 (GB)
Cardinals, 3-0 (Mil)
Cardinals, 9-7 (C)
1936—Packers, 10-7 (GB)
Packers, 24-0 (Mil)
Tie, 0-0 (C)
1937—Cardinals, 14-7 (GB)
Packers, 34-13 (Mil)
1938—Packers, 28-7 (Mil)
Packers, 24-22 (Buffalo)
1939—Packers, 14-10 (GB)
Packers, 27-20 (Mil)
1940—Packers, 31-6 (Mil)
Packers, 28-7 (C)
1941—Packers, 14-13 (Mil)
Packers, 17-9 (GB)
1942—Packers, 17-13 (C)
Packers, 55-24 (GB)
1943—Packers, 28-7 (C)
Packers, 35-14 (Mil)
1945—Packers, 33-14 (GB)
1946—Packers, 19-7 (C)
Cardinals, 24-6 (GB)
1947—Cardinals, 14-10 (GB)
Cardinals, 21-20 (C)
1948—Cardinals, 17-7 (Mil)
Cardinals, 42-7 (C)
1949—Cardinals, 39-17 (Mil)
Cardinals, 41-21 (C)
1955—Packers, 31-14 (GB)
1956—Packers, 24-21 (C)
1962—Packers, 17-0 (Mil)
1963—Packers, 30-7 (StL)
1967—Packers, 31-23 (StL)
1969—Packers, 45-28 (GB)
1971—Tie, 16-16 (StL)
1973—Packers, 25-21 (GB)
1976—Cardinals, 29-0 (StL)
1982—**Packers, 41-16 (GB)
1984—Packers, 24-23 (GB)
1985—Cardinals, 43-28 (StL)
(Points—Packers 1,069, Cardinals 801)
*Franchise in Chicago prior to 1960
**NFC First Round Playoff

GREEN BAY vs. SAN DIEGO
Packers lead series, 3-1
1970—Packers, 22-20 (SD)
1974—Packers, 34-0 (GB)
1978—Packers, 24-3 (SD)
1984—Chargers, 34-28 (GB)
(Points—Packers 108, Chargers 57)

GREEN BAY vs. SAN FRANCISCO
49ers lead series, 23-20-1
1950—Packers, 25-21 (GB)
49ers, 30-14 (SF)
1951—49ers, 31-19 (SF)
1952—49ers, 24-14 (SF)
1953—49ers, 37-7 (Mil)
49ers, 48-14 (SF)
1954—49ers, 23-17 (Mil)
49ers, 35-0 (SF)
1955—Packers, 27-21 (Mil)
Packers, 28-7 (SF)
1956—49ers, 17-16 (GB)
49ers, 38-20 (SF)
1957—49ers, 24-14 (Mil)
49ers, 27-20 (SF)
1958—49ers, 33-12 (Mil)
49ers, 48-21 (SF)
1959—Packers, 21-20 (GB)
Packers, 36-14 (SF)
1960—Packers, 41-14 (Mil)
Packers, 13-0 (SF)
1961—Packers, 30-10 (GB)
49ers, 22-21 (SF)
1962—Packers, 31-13 (Mil)
Packers, 31-21 (SF)
1963—Packers, 28-10 (Mil)
Packers, 21-17 (SF)
1964—Packers, 24-14 (Mil)
49ers, 24-14 (SF)
1965—Packers, 27-10 (GB)
Tie, 24-24 (SF)
1966—49ers, 21-20 (SF)
Packers, 20-7 (Mil)
1967—Packers, 13-0 (GB)
1968—49ers, 27-20 (SF)
1969—Packers, 14-7 (Mil)
1970—49ers, 26-10 (SF)
1972—Packers, 34-24 (Mil)
1973—49ers, 20-6 (SF)
1974—49ers, 7-6 (SF)
1976—49ers, 26-14 (GB)
1977—Packers, 16-14 (Mil)
1980—Packers, 23-16 (Mil)
1981—49ers, 13-3 (Mil)
1986—49ers, 31-17 (Mil)
(Points—49ers 916, Packers 846)

GREEN BAY vs. SEATTLE
Packers lead series, 3-1
1976—Packers, 27-20 (Mil)
1978—Packers, 45-28 (Mil)
1981—Packers, 34-24 (GB)
1984—Seahawks, 30-24 (Mil)
(Points—Packers 130, Seahawks 102)

GREEN BAY vs. TAMPA BAY
Packers lead series, 10-6-1
1977—Packers, 13-0 (TB)
1978—Packers, 9-7 (GB)
Packers, 17-7 (TB)
1979—Buccaneers, 21-10 (GB)
Buccaneers, 21-3 (TB)
1980—Tie, 14-14 (TB) OT
Buccaneers, 20-17 (Mil)
1981—Buccaneers, 21-10 (GB)
Buccaneers, 37-3 (TB)
1983—Packers, 55-14 (GB)
Packers, 12-9 (TB) OT
1984—Buccaneers, 30-27 (TB) OT
Packers, 27-14 (GB)
1985—Packers, 21-0 (GB)
Packers, 20-17 (TB)
1986—Packers, 31-7 (Mil)
Packers, 21-7 (TB)
(Points—Packers 310, Buccaneers 246)

GREEN BAY vs. *WASHINGTON
Packers lead series, 14-12-1
1932—Packers, 21-0 (B)
1933—Tie, 7-7 (GB)
Redskins, 20-7 (B)
1934—Packers, 10-0 (B)
1936—Packers, 31-2 (GB)
Packers, 7-3 (B)
**Packers, 21-6 (New York)
1937—Redskins, 14-6 (W)
1939—Packers, 24-14 (Mil)
1941—Packers, 22-17 (W)
1943—Redskins, 33-7 (Mil)
1946—Packers, 20-7 (W)
1947—Packers, 27-10 (Mil)
1948—Redskins, 23-7 (Mil)
1949—Redskins, 30-0 (W)
1950—Packers, 35-21 (Mil)
1952—Packers, 35-20 (Mil)
1958—Redskins, 37-21 (W)
1959—Packers, 21-0 (GB)
1968—Packers, 27-7 (W)
1972—Redskins, 21-16 (W)
***Redskins, 16-3 (W)
1974—Redskins, 17-6 (GB)
1977—Redskins, 10-9 (W)
1979—Redskins, 38-21 (W)
1983—Packers, 48-47 (GB)
1986—Redskins, 16-7 (GB)
(Points—Packers 466, Redskins 436)
*Franchise in Boston prior to 1937 and known as Braves prior to 1933
**NFL Championship
***NFC Divisional Playoff

HOUSTON vs. ATLANTA
Falcons lead series, 4-1;
See Atlanta vs. Houston

HOUSTON vs. BUFFALO
Oilers lead series, 18-9;
See Buffalo vs. Houston

HOUSTON vs. CHICAGO
Series tied, 2-2;
See Chicago vs. Houston

HOUSTON vs. CINCINNATI
Bengals lead series, 21-14-1;
See Cincinnati vs. Houston

HOUSTON vs. CLEVELAND
Browns lead series, 22-11;
See Cleveland vs. Houston

HOUSTON vs. DALLAS
Cowboys lead series, 4-1;
See Dallas vs. Houston

HOUSTON vs. DENVER
Oilers lead series, 18-10-1;
See Denver vs. Houston

HOUSTON vs. DETROIT
Series tied, 2-2;
See Detroit vs. Houston

HOUSTON vs. GREEN BAY
Oilers lead series, 3-2;
See Green Bay vs. Houston

HOUSTON vs. *INDIANAPOLIS
Colts lead series, 5-4
1970—Colts, 24-20 (H)
1973—Oilers, 31-27 (B)
1976—Colts, 38-14 (B)
1979—Oilers, 28-16 (B)
1980—Oilers, 21-16 (H)
1983—Colts, 20-10 (B)
1984—Colts, 35-21 (H)
1985—Colts, 34-16 (I)
1986—Oilers, 31-17 (H)
(Points—Colts 227, Oilers 192)
*Franchise in Baltimore prior to 1984

HOUSTON vs. *KANSAS CITY
Chiefs lead series, 21-12
1960—Oilers, 20-10 (H)
Texans, 24-0 (D)
1961—Texans, 26-21 (D)
Oilers, 38-7 (H)
1962—Texans, 31-7 (H)
Oilers, 14-6 (D)
**Texans, 20-17 (H) OT
1963—Chiefs, 28-7 (KC)
Oilers, 28-7 (H)
1964—Chiefs, 28-7 (KC)
Chiefs, 28-19 (H)
1965—Chiefs, 52-21 (KC)
Oilers, 38-36 (H)
1966—Chiefs, 48-23 (KC)
1967—Chiefs, 25-20 (H)
Oilers, 24-19 (KC)
1968—Chiefs, 26-21 (H)
Chiefs, 24-10 (KC)
1969—Chiefs, 24-0 (KC)
1970—Chiefs, 24-9 (KC)
1971—Chiefs, 20-16 (H)
1973—Chiefs, 38-14 (KC)
1974—Chiefs, 17-7 (H)
1975—Oilers, 17-13 (KC)
1977—Oilers, 34-20 (H)
1978—Oilers, 20-17 (KC)
1979—Oilers, 20-6 (H)
1980—Chiefs, 21-20 (KC)
1981—Chiefs, 23-10 (KC)
1983—Chiefs, 13-10 (H) OT
1984—Oilers, 17-16 (KC)
1985—Oilers, 23-20 (H)
1986—Chiefs, 27-13 (KC)
(Points—Chiefs 744, Oilers 565)
*Franchise in Dallas prior to 1963 and known as Texans
**AFL Championship

HOUSTON vs. *L.A. RAIDERS
Raiders lead series, 22-10
1960—Oilers, 37-22 (O)
Raiders, 14-13 (H)
1961—Oilers, 55-0 (H)
Oilers, 47-16 (O)
1962—Oilers, 28-20 (O)
Oilers, 32-17 (H)
1963—Raiders, 24-13 (H)
Raiders, 52-49 (O)
1964—Oilers, 42-28 (H)
Raiders, 20-10 (O)
1965—Raiders, 21-17 (O)
Raiders, 33-21 (H)
1966—Oilers, 31-0 (H)
Raiders, 38-23 (O)
1967—Raiders, 19-7 (H)
**Raiders, 40-7 (O)
1968—Raiders, 24-15 (H)
1969—Raiders, 21-17 (O)
***Raiders, 56-7 (O)
1971—Raiders, 41-21 (O)
1972—Raiders, 34-0 (H)
1973—Raiders, 17-6 (H)
1975—Oilers, 27-26 (O)
1976—Raiders, 14-13 (H)
1977—Raiders, 34-29 (O)
1978—Raiders, 21-17 (O)
1979—Oilers, 31-17 (H)
1980—****Raiders, 27-7 (O)
1981—Oilers, 17-16 (H)
1983—Raiders, 20-6 (LA)
1984—Raiders, 24-14 (H)
1986—Raiders, 28-17 (H)
(Points—Raiders 784, Oilers 676)
*Franchise in Oakland prior to 1982
**AFL Championship
***Inter-Divisional Playoff
****AFC First Round Playoff

HOUSTON vs. L.A. RAMS
Rams lead series, 3-1
1973—Rams, 31-26 (H)
1978—Rams, 10-6 (H)
1981—Oilers, 27-20 (LA)
1984—Rams, 27-16 (LA)
(Points—Rams 88, Oilers 75)

HOUSTON vs. MIAMI
Series tied, 10-10
1966—Dolphins, 20-13 (H)
Dolphins, 29-28 (M)
1967—Oilers, 17-14 (H)
Oilers, 41-10 (M)
1968—Oilers, 24-10 (M)
Dolphins, 24-7 (H)
1969—Oilers, 22-10 (H)
Oilers, 32-7 (M)
1970—Dolphins, 20-10 (H)
1972—Dolphins, 34-13 (M)
1975—Oilers, 20-19 (H)
1977—Dolphins, 27-7 (M)
1978—Oilers, 35-30 (H)
*Oilers, 17-9 (M)
1979—Oilers, 9-6 (M)
1981—Dolphins, 16-10 (H)
1983—Dolphins, 24-17 (H)
1984—Dolphins, 28-10 (M)
1985—Oilers, 26-23 (H)
1986—Dolphins, 28-7 (M)
(Points—Dolphins 388, Oilers 365)
*AFC First Round Playoff

HOUSTON vs. MINNESOTA
Series tied, 2-2
1974—Vikings, 51-10 (M)
1980—Oilers, 20-16 (H)
1983—Vikings, 34-14 (M)
1986—Oilers, 23-10 (H)
(Points—Vikings 111, Oilers 67)

HOUSTON vs. *NEW ENGLAND
Patriots lead series 14-13-1
1960—Oilers, 24-10 (B)
Oilers, 37-21 (H)
1961—Tie, 31-31 (B)
Oilers, 27-15 (H)
1962—Patriots, 34-21 (B)
Oilers, 21-17 (H)
1963—Patriots, 45-3 (B)
Patriots, 46-28 (H)
1964—Patriots, 25-24 (B)
Patriots, 34-17 (H)
1965—Oilers, 31-10 (H)
Patriots, 42-14 (B)
1966—Patriots, 27-21 (B)
Patriots, 38-14 (H)
1967—Patriots, 18-7 (B)
Oilers, 27-6 (H)
1968—Oilers, 16-0 (B)
Oilers, 45-17 (H)
1969—Patriots, 24-0 (B)

Oilers, 27-23 (H)
1971—Patriots, 28-20 (NE)
1973—Patriots, 32-0 (H)
1975—Oilers, 7-0 (NE)
1978—Oilers, 26-23 (NE)
**Oilers, 31-14 (NE)
1980—Oilers, 38-34 (H)
1981—Patriots, 38-10 (NE)
1982—Patriots, 29-21 (NE)
(Points—Patriots 681, Oilers 588)
Franchise in Boston prior to 1971
***AFC Divisional Playoff*

HOUSTON vs. NEW ORLEANS
Series tied, 2-2-1
1971—Tie, 13-13 (H)
1976—Oilers, 31-26 (NO)
1978—Oilers, 17-12 (NO)
1981—Saints, 27-24 (H)
1984—Saints, 27-10 (H)
(Points—Saints 105, Oilers 95)

HOUSTON vs. N.Y. GIANTS
Giants lead series, 3-0
1973—Giants, 34-14 (NY)
1982—Giants, 17-14 (NY)
1985—Giants, 35-14 (H)
(Points—Giants 86, Oilers 42)

HOUSTON vs. *N.Y. JETS
Oilers lead series, 15-10-1
1960—Oilers, 27-21 (H)
Oilers, 42-28 (NY)
1961—Oilers, 49-13 (H)
Oilers, 48-21 (NY)
1962—Oilers, 56-17 (H)
Oilers, 44-10 (NY)
1963—Jets, 24-17 (NY)
Oilers, 31-27 (H)
1964—Jets, 24-21 (NY)
Oilers, 33-17 (H)
1965—Oilers, 27-21 (H)
Jets, 41-14 (NY)
1966—Jets, 52-13 (NY)
Oilers, 24-0 (H)
1967—Tie, 28-28 (NY)
1968—Jets, 20-14 (H)
Jets, 26-7 (NY)
1969—Jets, 26-17 (NY)
Jets, 34-26 (H)
1972—Oilers, 26-20 (H)
1974—Oilers, 27-22 (NY)
1977—Oilers, 20-0 (H)
1979—Oilers, 27-24 (H) OT
1980—Jets, 31-28 (NY) OT
1981—Jets, 33-17 (NY)
1984—Oilers, 31-20 (H)
(Points—Oilers 714, Jets 600)
Jets known as Titans prior to 1963

HOUSTON vs. PHILADELPHIA
Eagles lead series, 3-0
1972—Eagles, 18-17 (H)
1979—Eagles, 26-20 (H)
1982—Eagles, 35-14 (P)
(Points—Eagles 79, Oilers 51)

HOUSTON vs. PITTSBURGH
Steelers lead series, 26-9
1970—Oilers, 19-7 (P)
Steelers, 7-3 (H)
1971—Steelers, 23-16 (P)
Oilers, 29-3 (H)
1972—Steelers, 24-7 (P)
Steelers, 9-3 (H)
1973—Steelers, 36-7 (H)
Steelers, 33-7 (P)
1974—Steelers, 13-7 (H)
Oilers, 13-10 (P)
1975—Steelers, 24-17 (P)
Steelers, 32-9 (H)
1976—Steelers, 32-16 (P)
Steelers, 21-0 (H)
1977—Oilers, 27-10 (H)
Steelers, 27-10 (P)
1978—Oilers, 24-17 (P)
Steelers, 13-3 (H)
*Steelers, 34-5 (P)
1979—Steelers, 38-7 (P)
Oilers, 20-17 (H)
*Steelers, 27-13 (P)
1980—Steelers, 31-17 (P)
Oilers, 6-0 (H)
1981—Steelers, 26-13 (P)
Oilers, 21-20 (H)
1982—Steelers, 24-10 (H)
1983—Steelers, 40-28 (H)
Steelers, 17-10 (P)
1984—Steelers, 35-7 (P)
Oilers, 23-20 (H) OT
1985—Steelers, 20-0 (P)
Steelers, 30-7 (H)
1986—Steelers, 22-16 (H) OT
Steelers, 21-10 (P)
(Points—Steelers 763, Oilers 430)
**AFC Championship*

HOUSTON vs. ST. LOUIS
Cardinals lead series, 3-1
1970—Cardinals, 44-0 (StL)
1974—Cardinals, 31-27 (H)
1979—Cardinals, 24-17 (H)
1985—Oilers, 20-10 (StL)
(Points—Cardinals 109, Oilers 64)

HOUSTON vs. *SAN DIEGO
Chargers lead series, 17-12-1
1960—Oilers, 38-28 (H)
Chargers, 24-21 (LA)
**Oilers, 24-16 (H)
1961—Chargers, 34-24 (SD)
Oilers, 33-13 (H)
**Oilers, 10-3 (SD)
1962—Oilers, 42-17 (SD)
Oilers, 33-27 (H)
1963—Chargers, 27-0 (SD)
Chargers 20-14 (H)
1964—Chargers, 27-21 (SD)
Chargers, 20-17 (H)
1965—Chargers, 31-14 (SD)
Chargers, 37-26 (H)
1966—Chargers, 28-22 (H)
1967—Chargers, 13-3 (SD)
Oilers, 24-17 (H)
1968—Chargers, 30-14 (SD)
1969—Chargers, 21-17 (H)
1970—Tie, 31-31 (SD)
1971—Oilers, 49-33 (H)
1972—Chargers, 34-20 (SD)
1974—Oilers, 21-14 (H)
1975—Oilers, 33-17 (H)
1976—Chargers, 30-27 (SD)
1978—Chargers, 45-24 (H)
1979—***Oilers, 17-14 (SD)
1984—Chargers, 31-14 (SD)
1985—Oilers, 37-35 (H)
1986—Chargers, 27-0 (SD)
(Points—Chargers 744, Oilers 670)
Franchise in Los Angeles prior to 1961
***AFL Championship*
****AFC Divisional Playoff*

HOUSTON vs. SAN FRANCISCO
49ers lead series, 3-2
1970—49ers, 30-20 (H)
1975—Oilers, 27-13 (SF)
1978—Oilers, 20-19 (H)
1981—49ers, 28-6 (SF)
1984—49ers, 34-21 (H)
(Points—49ers 124, Oilers 94)

HOUSTON vs. SEATTLE
Oilers lead series, 3-2
1977—Oilers, 22-10 (S)
1979—Seahawks, 34-14 (S)
1980—Seahawks, 26-7 (H)
1981—Oilers, 35-17 (H)
1982—Oilers, 23-21 (H)
(Points—Seahawks 108, Oilers 101)

HOUSTON vs. TAMPA BAY
Oilers lead series, 2-1
1976—Oilers, 20-0 (H)
1980—Oilers, 20-14 (H)
1983—Buccaneers, 33-24 (TB)
(Points—Oilers 64, Buccaneers 47)

HOUSTON vs. WASHINGTON
Series tied, 2-2
1971—Redskins, 22-13 (W)
1975—Oilers, 13-10 (H)
1979—Oilers, 29-27 (W)
1985—Redskins, 16-13 (W)
(Points—Redskins 75, Oilers 68)

INDIANAPOLIS vs. ATLANTA
Colts lead series, 9-0;
See Atlanta vs. Indianapolis

INDIANAPOLIS vs. BUFFALO
Series tied, 16-16-1;
See Buffalo vs. Indianapolis

INDIANAPOLIS vs. CHICAGO
Colts lead series, 21-14;
See Chicago vs. Indianapolis

INDIANAPOLIS vs. CINCINNATI
Colts lead series, 5-4;
See Cincinnati vs. Indianapolis

INDIANAPOLIS vs. CLEVELAND
Browns lead series, 11-5;
See Cleveland vs. Indianapolis

INDIANAPOLIS vs. DALLAS
Cowboys lead series, 6-3;
See Dallas vs. Indianapolis

INDIANAPOLIS vs. DENVER
Broncos lead series, 6-1;
See Denver vs. Indianapolis

INDIANAPOLIS vs. DETROIT
Colts lead series, 17-16-2;
See Detroit vs. Indianapolis

INDIANAPOLIS vs. GREEN BAY
Packers lead series, 18-17-1;
See Green Bay vs. Indianapolis

INDIANAPOLIS vs. HOUSTON
Colts lead series, 5-4;
See Houston vs. Indianapolis

***INDIANAPOLIS vs. KANSAS CITY**
Chiefs lead series, 6-3
1970—Chiefs, 44-24 (B)
1972—Chiefs, 24-10 (KC)
1975—Colts, 28-14 (B)
1977—Colts, 17-6 (KC)
1979—Chiefs, 14-0 (KC)
Chiefs, 10-7 (B)
1980—Colts, 31-24 (KC)
Chiefs, 38-28 (B)
1985—Chiefs, 20-7 (KC)
(Points—Chiefs 194, Colts 152)
Franchise in Baltimore prior to 1984

***INDIANAPOLIS vs **L.A. RAIDERS**
Raiders lead series, 4-3
1970—***Colts, 27-17 (B)
1971—Colts, 37-14 (O)
1973—Raiders, 34-21 (B)
1975—Raiders, 31-20 (B)
1977—****Raiders, 37-31 (B) OT
1984—Raiders, 21-7 (LA)
1986—Colts, 30-24 (LA)
(Points—Raiders 178, Colts 173)
Franchise in Baltimore prior to 1984
***Franchise in Oakland prior to 1982*
****AFC Championship*
*****AFC Divisional Playoff*

***INDIANAPOLIS vs. L.A. RAMS**
Colts lead series, 20-15-2
1953—Rams, 21-13 (B)
Rams, 45-2 (LA)
1954—Rams, 48-0 (B)
Colts, 22-21 (LA)
1955—Tie, 17-17 (B)
Rams, 20-14 (LA)
1956—Colts, 56-21 (B)
Rams, 31-7 (LA)
1957—Colts, 31-14 (B)
Rams, 37-21 (LA)
1958—Colts, 34-7 (B)
Rams, 30-28 (LA)
1959—Colts, 35-21 (B)
Colts, 45-26 (LA)
1960—Colts, 31-17 (B)
Rams, 10-3 (LA)
1961—Colts, 27-24 (B)
Rams, 34-17 (LA)
1962—Colts, 30-27 (B)
Colts, 14-2 (LA)
1963—Rams, 17-16 (LA)
Colts, 19-16 (B)
1964—Colts, 35-20 (B)
Colts, 24-7 (LA)
1965—Colts, 35-20 (B)
Colts, 20-17 (LA)
1966—Colts, 17-3 (LA)
Rams, 23-7 (B)
1967—Tie, 24-24 (B)
Rams, 34-10 (LA)
1968—Colts, 27-10 (B)
Colts, 28-24 (LA)
1969—Rams, 27-20 (B)
Colts, 13-7 (LA)
1971—Colts, 24-17 (B)
1975—Rams, 24-13 (LA)
1986—Rams, 24-7 (I)
(Points—Rams 787, Colts 786)
Franchise in Baltimore prior to 1984

***INDIANAPOLIS vs. MIAMI**
Dolphins lead series, 26-9
1970—Colts, 35-0 (B)
Dolphins, 34-17 (M)
1971—Dolphins, 17-14 (M)
Colts, 14-3 (B)
**Dolphins, 21-0 (M)
1972—Dolphins, 23-0 (B)
Dolphins, 16-0 (M)
1973—Dolphins, 44-0 (M)
Colts, 16-3 (B)
1974—Dolphins, 17-7 (M)
Dolphins, 17-16 (B)
1975—Colts, 33-17 (M)
Colts, 10-7 (B) OT
1976—Colts, 28-14 (B)
Colts, 17-16 (M)
1977—Colts, 45-28 (B)
Dolphins, 17-6 (M)
1978—Dolphins, 42-0 (B)
Dolphins, 26-8 (M)
1979—Dolphins, 19-0 (M)
Dolphins, 28-24 (B)
1980—Colts, 30-17 (M)
Dolphins, 24-14 (B)
1981—Dolphins, 31-28 (B)
Dolphins, 27-10 (M)
1982—Dolphins, 24-20 (M)
Dolphins, 34-7 (B)
1983—Dolphins, 21-7 (B)
Dolphins, 37-0 (M)
1984—Dolphins, 44-7 (M)
Dolphins, 35-17 (I)
1985—Dolphins, 30-13 (M)
Dolphins, 34-20 (I)
1986—Dolphins, 30-10 (M)
Dolphins, 17-13 (I)
(Points—Dolphins 814, Colts 486)
Franchise in Baltimore prior to 1984
***AFC Championship*

***INDIANAPOLIS vs. MINNESOTA**
Colts lead series, 12-5-1
1961—Colts, 34-33 (B)
Vikings, 28-20 (M)
1962—Colts, 34-7 (M)
Colts, 42-17 (B)
1963—Colts, 37-34 (M)
Colts, 41-10 (B)
1964—Vikings, 34-24 (M)
Colts, 17-14 (B)
1965—Colts, 35-16 (B)
Colts, 41-21 (M)
1966—Colts, 38-23 (M)
Colts, 20-17 (B)
1967—Tie, 20-20 (M)
1968—Colts, 21-9 (B)
**Colts, 24-14 (B)
1969—Vikings, 52-14 (M)
1971—Vikings, 10-3 (M)
1982—Vikings, 13-10 (M)
(Points—Colts 475, Vikings 372)
Franchise in Baltimore prior to 1984
**Conference Championship*

***INDIANAPOLIS vs. **NEW ENGLAND**
Patriots lead series, 18-15
1970—Colts, 14-6 (Bos)
Colts, 27-3 (Balt)
1971—Colts, 23-3 (NE)
Patriots, 21-17 (Balt)
1972—Colts, 24-17 (NE)
Colts, 31-0 (Balt)
1973—Patriots, 24-16 (NE)
Colts, 18-13 (Balt)
1974—Patriots, 42-3 (NE)
Patriots, 27-17 (Balt)
1975—Patriots, 21-10 (NE)
Colts, 34-21 (Balt)
1976—Colts, 27-13 (NE)
Patriots, 21-14 (Balt)
1977—Patriots, 17-3 (NE)
Colts, 30-24 (Balt)
1978—Colts, 34-27 (NE)
Patriots, 35-14 (Balt)
1979—Colts, 31-26 (Balt)
Patriots, 50-21 (NE)
1980—Patriots, 37-21 (Balt)
Patriots, 47-21 (NE)
1981—Colts, 29-28 (NE)
Colts, 23-21 (Balt)
1982—Patriots, 24-13 (Balt)
1983—Colts, 29-23 (NE) OT
Colts, 12-7 (B)
1984—Patriots, 50-17 (I)
Patriots, 16-10 (NE)
1985—Patriots, 34-15 (NE)
Patriots, 38-31 (I)
1986—Patriots, 33-3 (NE)
Patriots, 30-21 (I)
(Points—Patriots 799, Colts 653)
Franchise in Baltimore prior to 1984
***Franchise in Boston prior to 1971*

***INDIANAPOLIS vs. NEW ORLEANS**
Colts lead series, 3-1
1967—Colts, 30-10 (B)
1969—Colts, 30-10 (NO)
1973—Colts, 14-10 (B)
1986—Saints, 17-14 (I)
(Points—Colts 88, Saints 47)
Franchise in Baltimore prior to 1984

***INDIANAPOLIS vs. N. Y. GIANTS**
Colts lead series, 7-3
1954—Colts, 20-14 (B)
1955—Giants, 17-7 (NY)
1958—Giants, 24-21 (NY)
**Colts, 23-17 (NY) OT
1959—**Colts, 31-16 (B)
1963—Giants, 37-28 (B)
1968—Colts, 26-0 (NY)
1971—Colts, 31-7 (NY)
1975—Colts, 21-0 (NY)
1979—Colts, 31-7 (NY)
(Points—Colts 239, Giants 139)
Franchise in Baltimore prior to 1984
***NFL Championship*

***INDIANAPOLIS vs. N. Y. JETS**
Jets lead series, 18-16
1968—**Jets 16-7 (Miami)
1970—Colts, 29-22 (NY)
Colts, 35-20 (B)
1971—Colts, 22-0 (B)
Colts, 14-13 (NY)
1972—Jets, 44-34 (B)
Jets, 24-20 (NY)
1973—Jets, 34-10 (B)
Jets, 20-17 (NY)
1974—Colts, 35-20 (NY)
Jets, 45-38 (B)
1975—Colts, 45-28 (NY)
Colts, 52-19 (B)
1976—Colts, 20-0 (NY)

Colts, 33-16 (B)
1977—Colts, 20-12 (NY)
Colts, 33-12 (B)
1978—Jets, 33-10 (B)
Jets, 24-16 (NY)
1979—Colts, 10-8 (B)
Jets, 30-17 (NY)
1980—Colts, 17-14 (NY)
Colts, 35-21 (B)
1981—Jets, 41-14 (B)
Jets, 25-0 (NY)
1982—Jets, 37-0 (NY)
1983—Colts, 17-14 (NY)
Jets, 10-6 (B)
1984—Jets, 23-14 (I)
Colts, 9-5 (NY)
1985—Jets, 25-20 (NY)
Jets, 35-17 (I)
1986—Jets, 26-7 (I)
Jets, 31-16 (NY)
(Points—Jets 747, Colts 689)
**Franchise in Baltimore prior to 1984*
***Super Bowl III*

***INDIANAPOLIS vs. PHILADELPHIA**
Series tied, 5-5
1953—Eagles, 45-14 (P)
1965—Colts, 34-24 (B)
1967—Colts, 38-6 (P)
1969—Colts, 24-20 (B)
1970—Colts, 29-10 (B)
1974—Eagles, 30-10 (P)
1978—Eagles, 17-14 (B)
1981—Eagles, 38-13 (P)
1983—Colts, 22-21 (P)
1984—Eagles, 16-7 (P)
(Points—Eagles 227, Colts 205)
**Franchise in Baltimore prior to 1984*

***INDIANAPOLIS vs. PITTSBURGH**
Steelers lead series, 9-4
1957—Steelers, 19-13 (B)
1968—Colts, 41-7 (P)
1971—Colts, 34-21 (B)
1974—Steelers, 30-0 (B)
1975—**Steelers, 28-10 (P)
1976—**Steelers, 40-14 (B)
1977—Colts, 31-21 (B)
1978—Steelers, 35-13 (P)
1979—Steelers, 17-13 (P)
1980—Steelers, 20-17 (B)
1983—Steelers, 24-13 (B)
1984—Colts, 17-16 (I)
1985—Steelers, 45-3 (P)
(Points—Steelers 323, Colts 219)
**Franchise in Baltimore prior to 1984*
***AFC Divisional Playoff*

***INDIANAPOLIS vs. ST. LOUIS**
Cardinals lead series 5-4
1961—Colts, 16-0 (B)
1964—Colts, 47-27 (B)
1968—Colts, 27-0 (B)
1972—Cardinals, 10-3 (B)
1976—Cardinals, 24-17 (StL)
1978—Colts, 30-17 (StL)
1980—Cardinals, 17-10 (B)
1981—Cardinals, 35-24 (B)
1984—Cardinals, 34-33 (I)
(Points—Colts 207, Cardinals 164)
**Franchise in Baltimore prior to 1984*

***INDIANAPOLIS vs. SAN DIEGO**
Chargers lead series, 5-2
1970—Colts, 16-14 (SD)
1972—Chargers, 23-20 (B)
1976—Colts, 37-21 (SD)
1981—Chargers, 43-14 (B)
1982—Chargers, 44-26 (SD)
1984—Chargers, 38-10 (I)
1986—Chargers, 17-3 (I)
(Points—Chargers 200, Colts 126)
**Franchise in Baltimore prior to 1984*

***INDIANAPOLIS vs. SAN FRANCISCO**
Colts lead series, 21-15
1953—49ers, 38-21 (B)
49ers, 45-14 (SF)
1954—Colts, 17-13 (B)
49ers, 10-7 (SF)
1955—Colts, 26-14 (B)
49ers, 35-24 (SF)
1956—49ers, 20-17 (B)
49ers, 30-17 (SF)
1957—Colts, 27-21 (B)
49ers, 17-13 (SF)
1958—Colts, 35-27 (B)
49ers, 21-12 (SF)
1959—Colts, 45-14 (B)
Colts, 34-14 (SF)
1960—49ers, 30-22 (B)
49ers, 34-10 (SF)
1961—Colts, 20-17 (B)
Colts, 27-24 (SF)
1962—49ers, 21-13 (B)
Colts, 22-3 (SF)
1963—Colts, 20-14 (SF)
Colts, 20-3 (B)
1964—Colts, 37-7 (B)
Colts, 14-3 (SF)
1965—Colts, 27-24 (B)
Colts, 34-28 (SF)
1966—Colts, 36-14 (B)
Colts, 30-14 (SF)
1967—Colts, 41-7 (B)
Colts, 26-9 (SF)
1968—Colts, 27-10 (B)
Colts, 42-14 (SF)
1969—49ers, 24-21 (B)
49ers, 20-17 (SF)
1972—49ers, 24-21 (SF)
1986—49ers, 35-14 (SF)
(Points—Colts 850, 49ers 698)
**Franchise in Baltimore prior to 1984*

***INDIANAPOLIS vs. SEATTLE**
Colts lead series, 2-0
1977—Colts, 29-14 (S)
1978—Colts, 17-14 (S)
(Points—Colts 46, Seahawks 28)
**Franchise in Baltimore prior to 1984*

***INDIANAPOLIS vs. TAMPA BAY**
Colts lead series, 2-1
1976—Colts, 42-17 (B)
1979—Buccaneers, 29-26 (B) OT
1985—Colts, 31-23 (TB)
(Points—Colts 99, Buccaneers 69)
**Franchise in Baltimore prior to 1984*

***INDIANAPOLIS vs. WASHINGTON**
Colts lead series, 15-6
1953—Colts, 27-17 (B)
1954—Redskins, 24-21 (W)
1955—Redskins, 14-13 (B)
1956—Colts, 19-17 (B)
1957—Colts, 21-17 (W)
1958—Colts, 35-10 (B)
1959—Redskins, 27-24 (W)
1960—Colts, 20-0 (B)
1961—Colts, 27-6 (W)
1962—Colts, 34-21 (B)
1963—Colts, 36-20 (W)
1964—Colts, 45-17 (B)
1965—Colts, 38-7 (W)
1966—Colts, 37-10 (B)
1967—Colts, 17-13 (W)
1969—Colts, 41-17 (B)
1973—Redskins, 22-14 (W)
1977—Colts, 10-3 (B)
1978—Colts, 21-17 (B)
1981—Redskins, 38-14 (W)
1984—Redskins, 35-7 (I)
(Points—Colts 521, Redskins 352)
**Franchise in Baltimore prior to 1984*

KANSAS CITY vs. ATLANTA
Chiefs lead series, 2-0;
See Atlanta vs. Kansas City

KANSAS CITY vs. BUFFALO
Bills lead series, 15-12-1;
See Buffalo vs. Kansas City

KANSAS CITY vs. CHICAGO
Bears lead series, 2-1;
See Chicago vs. Kansas City

KANSAS CITY vs. CINCINNATI
Chiefs lead series, 9-7;
See Cincinnati vs. Kansas City

KANSAS CITY vs. CLEVELAND
Series tied, 5-5-1;
See Cleveland vs. Kansas City

KANSAS CITY vs. DALLAS
Cowboys lead series, 2-1;
See Dallas vs. Kansas City

KANSAS CITY vs. DENVER
Chiefs lead series, 34-19;
See Denver vs. Kansas City

KANSAS CITY vs. DETROIT
Series tied, 2-2;
See Detroit vs. Kansas City

KANSAS CITY vs. GREEN BAY
Series tied, 1-1-1;
See Green Bay vs. Kansas City

KANSAS CITY vs. HOUSTON
Chiefs lead series, 21-12;
See Houston vs. Kansas City

KANSAS CITY vs. INDIANAPOLIS
Chiefs lead series, 6-3;
See Indianapolis vs. Kansas City

***KANSAS CITY vs. **L.A. RAIDERS**
Raiders lead series, 31-22-2
1960—Texans, 34-16 (O)
Raiders, 20-19 (D)
1961—Texans, 42-35 (O)
Texans, 43-11 (D)
1962—Texans, 26-16 (O)
Texans, 35-7 (D)
1963—Raiders, 10-7 (O)
Raiders, 22-7 (KC)
1964—Chiefs, 21-9 (O)
Chiefs, 42-7 (KC)
1965—Raiders, 37-10 (O)
Chiefs, 14-7 (KC)
1966—Chiefs, 32-10 (O)
Raiders, 34-13 (KC)
1967—Raiders, 23-21 (O)
Raiders, 44-22 (KC)
1968—Chiefs, 24-10 (KC)
Raiders, 38-21 (O)
***Raiders, 41-6 (O)
1969—Raiders, 27-24 (KC)
Raiders, 10-6 (O)
****Chiefs, 17-7 (O)
1970—Tie, 17-17 (KC)
Raiders, 20-6 (O)
1971—Tie, 20-20 (O)
Chiefs, 16-14 (KC)
1972—Chiefs, 27-14 (KC)
Raiders, 26-3 (O)
1973—Chiefs, 16-3 (KC)
Raiders, 37-7 (O)
1974—Raiders, 27-7 (O)
Raiders, 7-6 (KC)
1975—Chiefs, 42-10 (KC)
Raiders, 28-20 (O)
1976—Raiders, 24-21 (KC)
Raiders, 21-10 (O)
1977—Raiders, 37-28 (KC)
Raiders, 21-20 (O)
1978—Raiders, 28-6 (O)
Raiders, 20-10 (KC)
1979—Chiefs, 35-7 (KC)
Chiefs, 24-21 (O)
1980—Raiders, 27-14 (KC)
Chiefs, 31-17 (O)
1981—Chiefs, 27-0 (KC)
Chiefs, 28-17 (O)
1982—Raiders, 21-16 (KC)
1983—Raiders, 21-20 (LA)
Raiders, 28-20 (KC)
1984—Raiders, 22-20 (KC)
Raiders, 17-7 (LA)
1985—Chiefs, 36-20 (KC)
Raiders, 19-10 (LA)
1986—Raiders, 24-17 (KC)
Chiefs, 20-17 (LA)
(Points—Chiefs 1,093, Raiders 1,093)
**Franchise in Dallas prior to 1963 and known as Texans*
***Franchise in Oakland prior to 1982*
****Division Playoff*
*****AFL Championship*

KANSAS CITY vs. L.A. RAMS
Rams lead series, 3-0
1973—Rams, 23-13 (KC)
1982—Rams, 20-14 (LA)
1985—Rams, 16-0 (KC)
(Points—Rams 59, Chiefs 27)

KANSAS CITY vs. MIAMI
Chiefs lead series, 7-6
1966—Chiefs, 34-16 (KC)
Chiefs, 19-18 (M)
1967—Chiefs, 24-0 (M)
Chiefs, 41-0 (KC)
1968—Chiefs, 48-3 (M)
1969—Chiefs, 17-10 (KC)
1971—*Dolphins, 27-24 (KC) OT
1972—Dolphins, 20-10 (KC)
1974—Dolphins, 9-3 (M)
1976—Chiefs, 20-17 (M) OT
1981—Dolphins, 17-7 (KC)
1983—Dolphins, 14-6 (M)
1985—Dolphins, 31-0 (M)
(Points—Chiefs 253, Dolphins 182)
**AFC Divisional Playoff*

KANSAS CITY vs. MINNESOTA
Series tied, 2-2
1969—*Chiefs, 23-7 (New Orleans)
1970—Vikings, 27-10 (M)
1974—Vikings, 35-15 (KC)
1981—Chiefs, 10-6 (M)
(Points—Vikings 75, Chiefs 58)
**Super Bowl IV*

***KANSAS CITY vs. **NEW ENGLAND**
Chiefs lead series, 11-7-3
1960—Patriots, 42-14 (B)
Texans, 34-0 (D)
1961—Patriots, 18-17 (D)
Patriots, 28-21 (B)
1962—Texans, 42-28 (D)
Texans, 27-7 (B)
1963—Tie, 24-24 (B)
Chiefs, 35-3 (KC)
1964—Patriots, 24-7 (B)
Patriots, 31-24 (KC)
1965—Chiefs, 27-17 (KC)
Tie, 10-10 (B)
1966—Chiefs, 43-24 (B)
Tie, 27-27 (KC)
1967—Chiefs, 33-10 (B)
1968—Chiefs, 31-17 (KC)
1969—Chiefs, 31-0 (B)
1970—Chiefs, 23-10 (KC)
1973—Chiefs, 10-7 (NE)
1977—Patriots, 21-17 (NE)
1981—Patriots, 33-17 (NE)
(Points—Chiefs 514, Patriots 381)
**Franchise located in Dallas prior to 1963 and known as Texans*
***Franchise in Boston prior to 1971*

KANSAS CITY vs. NEW ORLEANS
Series tied, 2-2
1972—Chiefs, 20-17 (NO)
1976—Saints, 27-17 (KC)
1982—Saints, 27-17 (NO)
1985—Chiefs, 47-27 (NO)
(Points—Chiefs 101, Saints 98)

KANSAS CITY vs. N.Y. GIANTS
Giants lead series, 4-1
1974—Giants, 33-27 (KC)
1978—Giants, 26-10 (NY)
1979—Giants, 21-17 (KC)
1983—Chiefs, 38-17 (KC)
1984—Giants, 28-27 (NY)
(Points—Giants 125, Chiefs 119)

***KANSAS CITY vs. **N.Y. JETS**
Chiefs lead series, 13-12
1960—Titans, 37-35 (D)
Titans, 41-35 (NY)
1961—Titans, 28-7 (NY)
Texans, 35-24 (D)
1962—Texans, 20-17 (D)
Texans, 52-31 (NY)
1963—Jets, 17-0 (NY)
Chiefs, 48-0 (KC)
1964—Jets, 27-14 (NY)
Chiefs, 24-7 (KC)
1965—Chiefs, 14-10 (NY)
Jets, 13-10 (KC)
1966—Chiefs, 32-24 (NY)
1967—Chiefs, 42-18 (KC)
Chiefs, 21-7 (NY)
1968—Jets, 20-19 (KC)
1969—Chiefs, 34-16 (NY)
***Chiefs, 13-6 (NY)
1971—Jets, 13-10 (NY)
1974—Chiefs, 24-16 (KC)
1975—Jets, 30-24 (KC)
1982—Chiefs, 37-13 (KC)
1984—Jets, 17-16 (KC)
Jets, 28-7 (NY)
1986—****Jets, 35-15 (NY)
(Points—Chiefs 588, Jets 495)
**Franchise in Dallas prior to 1963 and known as Texans*
***Jets known as Titans prior to 1963*
****Inter-Divisional Playoff*
*****AFC First Round Playoff*

KANSAS CITY vs. PHILADELPHIA
Eagles lead series, 1-0
1972—Eagles, 21-20 (KC)

KANSAS CITY vs. PITTSBURGH
Steelers lead series, 9-5
1970—Chiefs, 31-14 (P)
1971—Chiefs, 38-16 (KC)
1972—Steelers, 16-7 (P)
1974—Steelers, 34-24 (KC)
1975—Steelers, 28-3 (P)
1976—Steelers, 45-0 (KC)
1978—Steelers, 27-24 (P)
1979—Steelers, 30-3 (KC)
1980—Steelers, 21-16 (P)
1981—Chiefs, 37-33 (P)
1982—Steelers, 35-14 (P)
1984—Chiefs, 37-27 (P)
1985—Steelers, 36-28 (KC)
1986—Chiefs, 24-19 (P)
(Points—Steelers 381, Chiefs 286)

KANSAS CITY vs. ST. LOUIS
Chiefs lead series, 3-1-1
1970—Tie, 6-6 (KC)
1974—Chiefs, 17-13 (StL)
1980—Chiefs, 21-13 (StL)
1983—Chiefs, 38-14 (KC)
1986—Cardinals, 23-14 (StL)
(Points—Chiefs 96, Cardinals 69)

***KANSAS CITY vs. **SAN DIEGO**
Series tied, 26-26-1
1960—Chargers, 21-20 (LA)
Texans, 17-0 (D)
1961—Chargers, 26-10 (D)
Chargers, 24-14 (SD)
1962—Chargers, 32-28 (SD)
Texans, 26-17 (D)
1963—Chargers, 24-10 (SD)
Chargers, 38-17 (KC)
1964—Chargers, 28-14 (KC)
Chiefs, 49-6 (SD)
1965—Tie, 10-10 (SD)
Chiefs, 31-7 (KC)
1966—Chiefs, 24-14 (KC)
Chiefs, 27-17 (SD)
1967—Chargers, 45-31 (SD)
Chargers, 17-16 (KC)
1968—Chiefs, 27-20 (KC)
Chiefs, 40-3 (SD)
1969—Chiefs, 27-9 (SD)
Chiefs, 27-3 (KC)
1970—Chiefs, 26-14 (KC)
Chargers, 31-13 (SD)

1971—Chargers, 21-14 (SD)
Chiefs, 31-10 (KC)
1972—Chiefs, 26-14 (SD)
Chargers, 27-17 (KC)
1973—Chiefs, 19-0 (SD)
Chiefs, 33-6 (KC)
1974—Chiefs, 24-14 (SD)
Chargers, 14-7 (KC)
1975—Chiefs, 12-10 (SD)
Chargers, 28-20 (KC)
1976—Chargers, 30-16 (KC)
Chiefs, 23-20 (SD)
1977—Chargers, 23-7 (KC)
Chiefs, 21-16 (SD)
1978—Chargers, 29-23 (SD) OT
Chiefs, 23-0 (KC)
1979—Chargers, 20-14 (KC)
Chargers, 28-7 (SD)
1980—Chargers, 24-7 (KC)
Chargers, 20-7 (SD)
1981—Chargers, 42-31 (KC)
Chargers, 22-20 (SD)
1982—Chiefs, 19-12 (KC)
1983—Chargers, 17-14 (KC)
Chargers, 41-38 (SD)
1984—Chiefs, 31-13 (KC)
Chiefs, 42-21 (SD)
1985—Chargers, 31-20 (SD)
Chiefs, 38-34 (KC)
1986—Chiefs, 42-41 (KC)
Chiefs, 24-23 (SD)
(Points—Chiefs 1,174, Chargers 1,057)
Franchise in Dallas prior to 1963 and known as Texans
***Franchise in Los Angeles prior to 1961*

KANSAS CITY vs. SAN FRANCISCO
49ers lead series, 3-1
1971—Chiefs, 26-17 (SF)
1975—49ers, 20-3 (KC)
1982—49ers, 26-13 (KC)
1985—49ers, 31-3 (SF)
(Points—49ers 94, Chiefs 45)

KANSAS CITY vs. SEATTLE
Chiefs lead series, 9-8
1977—Seahawks, 34-31 (KC)
1978—Seahawks, 13-10 (KC)
Seahawks, 23-19 (S)
1979—Chiefs, 24-6 (S)
Chiefs, 37-21 (KC)
1980—Seahawks, 17-16 (KC)
Chiefs, 31-30 (S)
1981—Chiefs, 20-14 (S)
Chiefs, 40-13 (KC)
1983—Chiefs, 17-13 (KC)
Seahawks, 51-48 (S) OT
1984—Seahawks, 45-0 (S)
Chiefs, 34-7 (KC)
1985—Chiefs, 28-7 (KC)
Seahawks, 24-6 (S)
1986—Seahawks, 23-17 (S)
Chiefs, 27-7 (KC)
(Points—Chiefs 405, Seahawks 348)

KANSAS CITY vs. TAMPA BAY
Chiefs lead series, 4-2
1976—Chiefs, 28-19 (TB)
1978—Buccaneers, 30-13 (KC)
1979—Buccaneers, 3-0 (TB)
1981—Chiefs, 19-10 (KC)
1984—Chiefs, 24-20 (KC)
1986—Chiefs, 27-20 (KC)
(Points—Chiefs 111, Buccaneers 102)

KANSAS CITY vs. WASHINGTON
Chiefs lead series, 2-1
1971—Chiefs, 27-20 (KC)
1976—Chiefs, 33-30 (W)
1983—Redskins, 27-12 (W)
(Points—Redskins 77, Chiefs 72)

L.A. RAIDERS vs. ATLANTA
Raiders lead series, 4-1;
See Atlanta vs. L.A. Raiders

L.A. RAIDERS vs. BUFFALO
Raiders lead series, 12-11;
See Buffalo vs. L.A. Raiders

L.A. RAIDERS vs. CHICAGO
Raiders lead series, 3-2;
See Chicago vs. L.A. Raiders

L.A. RAIDERS vs. CINCINNATI
Raiders lead series, 12-4;
See Cincinnati vs. L.A. Raiders

L.A. RAIDERS vs. CLEVELAND
Raiders lead series, 10-1;
See Cleveland vs. L.A. Raiders

L.A. RAIDERS vs. DALLAS
Raiders lead series, 3-1;
See Dallas vs. L.A. Raiders

L.A. RAIDERS vs. DENVER
Raiders lead series, 36-16-2;
See Denver vs. L.A. Raiders

L.A. RAIDERS vs. DETROIT
Raiders lead series, 3-2;
See Detroit vs. L.A. Raiders

L.A. RAIDERS vs. GREEN BAY
Raiders lead series, 4-1;
See Green Bay vs. L.A. Raiders

L.A. RAIDERS vs. HOUSTON
Raiders lead series, 22-10;
See Houston vs. L.A. Raiders

L.A. RAIDERS vs. INDIANAPOLIS
Raiders lead series, 4-3;
See Indianapolis vs. L.A. Raiders

L.A. RAIDERS vs. KANSAS CITY
Raiders lead series, 31-22-2;
See Kansas City vs. L.A. Raiders

***L.A. RAIDERS vs. L.A. RAMS**
Raiders lead series, 4-1
1972—Raiders, 45-17 (O)
1977—Rams, 20-14 (LA)
1979—Raiders, 24-17 (LA)
1982—Raiders, 37-31 (LA Raiders)
1985—Raiders, 16-6 (LA Rams)
(Points—Raiders 136, Rams 91)
**Franchise in Oakland prior to 1982*

***L.A. RAIDERS vs. MIAMI**
Raiders lead series, 15-3-1
1966—Raiders, 23-14 (M)
Raiders, 21-10 (O)
1967—Raiders, 31-17 (O)
1968—Raiders, 47-21 (M)
1969—Raiders, 20-17 (O)
Tie, 20-20 (M)
1970—Dolphins, 20-13 (M)
**Raiders, 21-14 (O)
1973—Raiders, 12-7 (O)
***Dolphins, 27-10 (M)
1974—**Raiders, 28-26 (O)
1975—Raiders, 31-21 (M)
1978—Dolphins, 23-6 (M)
1979—Raiders, 13-3 (O)
1980—Raiders, 16-10 (O)
1981—Raiders, 33-17 (M)
1983—Raiders, 27-14 (LA)
1984—Raiders, 45-34 (M)
1986—Raiders, 30-28 (M)
(Points—Raiders 447, Dolphins 343)
**Franchise in Oakland prior to 1982*
***AFC Divisional Playoff*
****AFC Championship*

***L.A. RAIDERS vs. MINNESOTA**
Raiders lead series, 5-1
1973—Vikings, 24-16 (M)
1976—**Raiders, 32-14 (Pasadena)
1977—Raiders, 35-13 (O)
1978—Raiders, 27-20 (O)
1981—Raiders, 36-10 (M)
1984—Raiders, 23-20 (LA)
(Points—Raiders 169, Vikings 101)
**Franchise in Oakland prior to 1982*
***Super Bowl XI*

***L.A. RAIDERS vs. **NEW ENGLAND**
Series tied, 12-12-1
1960—Raiders, 27-14 (O)
Patriots, 34-28 (B)
1961—Patriots, 20-17 (B)
Patriots, 35-21 (O)
1962—Patriots, 26-16 (B)
Raiders, 20-0 (O)
1963—Patriots, 20-14 (O)
Patriots, 20-14 (B)
1964—Patriots, 17-14 (O)
Tie, 43-43 (B)
1965—Raiders, 24-10 (B)
Raiders, 30-21 (O)
1966—Patriots, 24-21 (B)
1967—Raiders, 35-7 (O)
Raiders, 48-14 (B)
1968—Raiders, 41-10 (O)
1969—Raiders, 38-23 (B)
1971—Patriots, 20-6 (NE)
1974—Raiders, 41-26 (O)
1976—Patriots, 48-17 (NE)
***Raiders, 24-21 (O)
1978—Patriots, 21-14 (O)
1981—Raiders, 27-17 (O)
1985—Raiders, 35-20 (NE)
***Patriots, 27-20 (LA)
(Points—Raiders 635, Patriots 538)
**Franchise in Oakland prior to 1982*
***Franchise in Boston prior to 1971*
****AFC Divisional Playoff*

***L.A. RAIDERS vs. NEW ORLEANS**
Raiders lead series, 3-0-1
1971—Tie, 21-21 (NO)
1975—Raiders, 48-10 (O)
1979—Raiders, 42-35 (NO)
1985—Raiders, 23-13 (LA)
(Points—Raiders 134, Saints 79)
**Franchise in Oakland prior to 1982*

***L.A. RAIDERS vs. N.Y. GIANTS**
Raiders lead series, 3-1
1973—Raiders, 42-0 (O)
1980—Raiders, 33-17 (NY)
1983—Raiders, 27-12 (LA)
1986—Giants, 14-9 (LA)
(Points—Raiders 111, Giants 43)
**Franchise in Oakland prior to 1982*

***L.A. RAIDERS vs. **N.Y. JETS**
Raiders lead series, 12-11-2
1960—Raiders, 28-27 (NY)
Titans, 31-28 (O)
1961—Titans, 14-6 (O)
Titans, 23-12 (NY)
1962—Titans, 28-17 (O)
Titans, 31-21 (NY)
1963—Jets, 10-7 (NY)
Raiders, 49-26 (O)
1964—Jets, 35-13 (NY)
Raiders, 35-26 (O)
1965—Tie, 24-24 (NY)
Raiders, 24-14 (O)
1966—Raiders, 24-21 (NY)
Tie, 28-28 (O)
1967—Jets, 27-14 (NY)
Raiders, 38-29 (O)
1968—Raiders, 43-32 (O)
***Jets, 27-23 (NY)
1969—Raiders, 27-14 (NY)
1970—Raiders, 14-13 (NY)
1972—Raiders, 24-16 (O)
1977—Raiders, 28-27 (NY)
1979—Jets, 28-19 (NY)
1982—****Jets, 17-14 (LA)
1985—Raiders, 31-0 (LA)
(Points—Raiders 591, Jets 568)
**Franchise in Oakland prior to 1982*
***Jets known as Titans prior to 1963*
****AFL Championship*
*****AFC Second Round Playoff*

***L.A. RAIDERS vs. PHILADELPHIA**
Raiders lead series, 3-2
1971—Raiders, 34-10 (O)
1976—Raiders, 26-7 (P)
1980—Eagles, 10-7 (P)
**Raiders, 27-10 (NO)
1986—Eagles, 33-27 (LA) OT
(Points—Raiders 121, Eagles 70)
**Franchise in Oakland prior to 1982*
***Super Bowl XV*

***L.A. RAIDERS vs. PITTSBURGH**
Raiders lead series, 9-6
1970—Raiders, 31-14 (O)
1972—Steelers, 34-28 (P)
**Steelers, 13-7 (P)
1973—Steelers, 17-9 (O)
**Raiders, 33-14 (O)
1974—Raiders, 17-0 (P)
***Steelers, 24-13 (O)
1975—***Steelers, 16-10 (P)
1976—Raiders, 31-28 (O)
***Raiders, 24-7 (O)
1977—Raiders, 16-7 (P)
1980—Raiders, 45-34 (P)
1981—Raiders, 30-27 (O)
1983—**Raiders, 38-10 (LA)
1984—Steelers, 13-7 (LA)
(Points—Raiders 339, Steelers 258)
**Franchise in Oakland prior to 1982*
***AFC Divisional Playoff*
****AFC Championship*

***L.A. RAIDERS vs. ST. LOUIS**
Series tied, 1-1
1973—Raiders, 17-10 (StL)
1983—Cardinals, 34-24 (LA)
(Points—Cardinals 44, Raiders 41)
**Franchise in Oakland prior to 1982*

***L.A. RAIDERS vs. **SAN DIEGO**
Raiders lead series, 35-18-2
1960—Chargers, 52-28 (LA)
Chargers, 41-17 (O)
1961—Chargers, 44-0 (SD)
Chargers, 41-10 (O)
1962—Chargers, 42-33 (O)
Chargers, 31-21 (SD)
1963—Raiders, 34-33 (SD)
Raiders, 41-27 (O)
1964—Chargers, 31-17 (O)
Raiders, 21-20 (SD)
1965—Chargers, 17-6 (O)
Chargers, 24-14 (SD)
1966—Chargers, 29-20 (O)
Raiders, 41-19 (SD)
1967—Raiders, 51-10 (O)
Raiders, 41-21 (SD)
1968—Chargers, 23-14 (O)
Raiders, 34-27 (SD)
1969—Raiders, 24-12 (SD)
Raiders, 21-16 (O)
1970—Tie, 27-27 (SD)
Raiders, 20-17 (O)
1971—Raiders, 34-0 (SD)
Raiders, 34-33 (O)
1972—Tie, 17-17 (O)
Raiders, 21-19 (SD)
1973—Raiders, 27-17 (SD)
Raiders, 31-3 (O)
1974—Raiders, 14-10 (SD)
Raiders, 17-10 (O)
1975—Raiders, 6-0 (SD)
Raiders, 25-0 (O)
1976—Raiders, 27-17 (SD)
Raiders, 24-0 (O)
1977—Raiders, 24-0 (O)
Chargers, 12-7 (SD)
1978—Raiders, 21-20 (SD)
Chargers, 27-23 (O)
1979—Chargers, 30-10 (SD)
Raiders, 45-22 (O)
1980—Chargers, 30-24 (SD) OT
Raiders, 38-24 (O)
***Raiders, 34-27 (SD)
1981—Chargers, 55-21 (O)
Chargers, 23-10 (SD)
1982—Raiders, 28-24 (LA)
Raiders, 41-34 (SD)
1983—Raiders, 42-10 (SD)
Raiders, 30-14 (LA)
1984—Raiders, 33-30 (LA)
Raiders, 44-37 (SD)
1985—Raiders, 34-21 (LA)
Chargers, 40-34 (SD) OT
1986—Raiders, 17-13 (LA)
Raiders, 37-31 (SD) OT
(Points—Raiders 1,409, Chargers 1,254)
**Franchise in Oakland prior to 1982*
***Franchise in Los Angeles prior to 1961*
****AFC Championship*

***L.A. RAIDERS vs. SAN FRANCISCO**
Raiders lead series, 3-2
1970—49ers, 38-7 (O)
1974—Raiders, 35-24 (SF)
1979—Raiders, 23-10 (O)
1982—Raiders, 23-17 (SF)
1985—49ers, 34-10 (LA)
(Points—49ers 123, Raiders 98)
**Franchise in Oakland prior to 1982*

***L.A. RAIDERS vs. SEATTLE**
Series tied, 10-10
1977—Raiders, 44-7 (O)
1978—Seahawks, 27-7 (S)
Seahawks, 17-16 (O)
1979—Seahawks, 27-10 (S)
Seahawks, 29-24 (O)
1980—Raiders, 33-14 (O)
Raiders, 19-17 (S)
1981—Raiders, 20-10 (O)
Raiders, 32-31 (S)
1982—Raiders, 28-23 (LA)
1983—Seahawks, 38-36 (S)
Seahawks, 34-21 (LA)
**Raiders, 30-14 (LA)
1984—Raiders, 28-14 (LA)
Seahawks, 17-14 (S)
***Seahawks, 13-7 (S)
1985—Seahawks, 33-3 (S)
Raiders, 13-3 (LA)
1986—Raiders, 14-10 (LA)
Seahawks, 37-0 (S)
(Points—Seahawks 415, Raiders 399)
**Franchise in Oakland prior to 1982*
***AFC Championship*
****AFC First Round Playoff*

***L.A. RAIDERS vs. TAMPA BAY**
Raiders lead series, 2-0
1976—Raiders, 49-16 (O)
1981—Raiders, 18-16 (O)
(Points—Raiders 67, Buccaneers 32)
**Franchise in Oakland prior to 1982*

***L.A. RAIDERS vs. WASHINGTON**
Raiders lead series, 4-2
1970—Raiders, 34-20 (O)
1975—Raiders, 26-23 (W) OT
1980—Raiders, 24-21 (O)
1983—Redskins, 37-35 (W)
**Raiders, 38-9 (Tampa)
1986—Redskins, 10-6 (W)
(Points—Raiders 163, Redskins 120)
**Franchise in Oakland prior to 1982*
***Super Bowl XVIII*

L.A. RAMS vs. ATLANTA
Rams lead series, 29-9-2;
See Atlanta vs. L.A. Rams

L.A. RAMS vs. BUFFALO
Rams lead series, 3-1;
See Buffalo vs. L.A. Rams

L.A. RAMS vs. CHICAGO
Bears lead series, 43-28-3;
See Chicago vs. L.A. Rams

L.A. RAMS vs. CINCINNATI
Bengals lead series, 3-2;
See Cincinnati vs. L.A. Rams

L.A. RAMS vs. CLEVELAND
Browns lead series, 8-7;
See Cleveland vs. L.A. Rams

L.A. RAMS vs. DALLAS
Rams lead series, 11-10;
See Dallas vs. L.A. Rams

L.A. RAMS vs. DENVER
Rams lead series, 3-2;
See Denver vs. L.A. Rams

L.A. RAMS vs. DETROIT
Rams lead series, 37-34-1;
See Detroit vs. L.A. Rams
L.A. RAMS vs. GREEN BAY
Rams lead series, 39-34-2;
See Green Bay vs. L.A. Rams
L.A. RAMS vs. HOUSTON
Rams lead series, 3-1;
See Houston vs. L.A. Rams
L.A. RAMS vs. INDIANAPOLIS
Colts lead series, 20-15-2;
See Indianapolis vs. L.A. Rams
L.A. RAMS vs. KANSAS CITY
Rams lead series, 3-0;
See Kansas City vs. L.A. Rams
L.A. RAMS VS. L.A. RAIDERS
Raiders lead series, 4-1;
See L.A. Raiders vs. L.A. Rams
L.A. RAMS vs. MIAMI
Dolphins lead series, 4-1
1971—Dolphins, 20-14 (LA)
1976—Rams, 31-28 (M)
1980—Dolphins, 35-14 (LA)
1983—Dolphins, 30-14 (M)
1986—Dolphins 37-31 (LA) OT
(Points—Dolphins 150, Rams 104)
L.A. RAMS vs. MINNESOTA
Vikings lead series, 15-12-2
1961—Rams, 31-17 (LA)
Vikings, 42-21 (M)
1962—Vikings, 38-14 (LA)
Tie, 24-24 (M)
1963—Rams, 27-24 (LA)
Vikings, 21-13 (M)
1964—Rams, 22-13 (LA)
Vikings, 34-13 (M)
1965—Vikings, 38-35 (LA)
Vikings, 24-13 (M)
1966—Vikings, 35-7 (M)
Rams, 21-6 (LA)
1967—Rams, 39-3 (LA)
1968—Rams, 31-3 (M)
1969—Vikings, 20-13 (LA)
*Vikings, 23-20 (M)
1970—Vikings, 13-3 (M)
1972—Vikings, 45-41 (LA)
1973—Vikings, 10-9 (M)
1974—Rams, 20-17 (LA)
**Vikings, 14-10 (M)
1976—Tie, 10-10 (M) OT
**Vikings, 24-13 (M)
1977—Rams, 35-3 (LA)
***Vikings, 14-7 (LA)
1978—Rams, 34-17 (M)
***Rams, 34-10 (LA)
1979—Rams, 27-21 (LA) OT
1985—Rams, 13-10 (LA)
(Points—Rams 600, Vikings 573)
**Conference Championship*
***NFC Championship*
****NFC Divisional Playoff*
L.A. RAMS vs. NEW ENGLAND
Patriots lead series, 3-1
1974—Patriots, 20-14 (NE)
1980—Rams, 17-14 (NE)
1983—Patriots, 21-7 (LA)
1986—Patriots, 30-28 (LA)
(Points—Patriots 85, Rams 66)
L.A. RAMS vs. NEW ORLEANS
Rams lead series, 24-10
1967—Rams 27-13 (NO)
1969—Rams, 36-17 (LA)
1970—Rams, 30-17 (NO)
Rams, 34-16 (LA)
1971—Saints, 24-20 (NO)
Rams, 45-28 (LA)
1972—Rams, 34-14 (LA)
Saints, 19-16 (NO)
1973—Rams, 29-7 (LA)
Rams, 24-13 (NO)
1974—Rams, 24-0 (LA)
Saints, 20-7 (NO)
1975—Rams, 38-14 (LA)
Rams, 14-7 (NO)
1976—Rams, 16-10 (NO)
Rams, 33-14 (LA)
1977—Rams, 14-7 (LA)
Saints, 27-26 (NO)
1978—Rams, 26-20 (NO)
Saints, 10-3 (LA)
1979—Rams, 35-17 (NO)
Saints, 29-14 (LA)
1980—Rams, 45-31 (LA)
Rams, 27-7 (NO)
1981—Saints, 23-17 (NO)
Saints, 21-13 (LA)
1983—Rams, 30-27 (LA)
Rams, 26-24 (NO)
1984—Rams, 28-10 (NO)
Rams, 34-21 (LA)
1985—Rams, 28-10 (LA)
Saints, 29-3 (NO)
1986—Saints, 6-0 (NO)
Rams, 26-13 (LA)
(Points—Rams 822, Saints 565)
***L.A. RAMS vs. N.Y. GIANTS**
Rams lead series, 16-8
1938—Giants, 28-0 (NY)
1940—Rams, 13-0 (NY)
1941—Giants, 49-14 (NY)
1945—Rams, 21-17 (NY)
1946—Rams, 31-21 (NY)
1947—Rams, 34-10 (LA)
1948—Rams, 52-37 (NY)
1953—Rams, 21-7 (LA)
1954—Rams, 17-16 (NY)
1959—Giants, 23-21 (LA)
1961—Giants, 24-14 (NY)
1966—Rams, 55-14 (LA)
1968—Rams, 24-21 (LA)
1970—Rams, 31-3 (NY)
1973—Rams, 40-6 (LA)
1976—Rams, 24-10 (LA)
1978—Rams, 20-17 (NY)
1979—Giants, 20-14 (LA)
1980—Rams, 28-7 (NY)
1981—Giants, 10-7 (NY)
1983—Rams, 16-6 (NY)
1984—Rams, 33-12 (LA)
**Giants, 16-13 (LA)
1985—Giants, 24-19 (NY)
(Points—Rams 562, Giants 398)
**Franchise in Cleveland prior to 1946*
***NFC First Round Playoff*
L.A. RAMS vs. N.Y. JETS
Rams lead series, 3-2
1970—Jets, 31-20 (LA)
1974—Rams, 20-13 (NY)
1980—Rams, 38-13 (LA)
1983—Jets, 27-24 (NY) OT
1986—Rams, 17-3 (NY)
(Points—Rams 119, Jets 87)
***L.A. RAMS vs. PHILADELPHIA**
Rams lead series, 15-10-1
1937—Rams, 21-3 (P)
1939—Rams, 35-13 (Colorado Springs)
1940—Rams, 21-13 (C)
1942—Rams, 24-14 (Akron)
1944—Eagles, 26-13 (P)
1945—Eagles, 28-14 (P)
1946—Eagles, 25-14 (LA)
1947—Eagles, 14-7 (P)
1948—Tie, 28-28 (LA)
1949—Eagles, 38-14 (P)
**Eagles, 14-0 (LA)
1950—Eagles, 56-20 (P)
1955—Rams, 23-21 (P)
1956—Rams, 27-7 (LA)
1957—Rams, 17-13 (LA)
1959—Eagles, 23-20 (P)
1964—Rams, 20-10 (LA)
1967—Rams, 33-17 (LA)
1969—Rams, 23-17 (P)
1972—Rams, 34-3 (P)
1975—Rams, 42-3 (P)
1977—Rams, 20-0 (LA)
1978—Rams, 16-14 (P)
1983—Eagles, 13-9 (P)
1985—Rams, 17-6 (P)
1986—Eagles, 34-20 (P)
(Points—Rams 532, Eagles 453)
**Franchise in Cleveland prior to 1946*
***NFL Championship*
***L.A. RAMS vs. **PITTSBURGH**
Rams lead series, 12-4-2
1938—Rams, 13-7 (New Orleans)
1939—Tie, 14-14 (C)
1941—Rams, 17-14 (Akron)
1947—Rams, 48-7 (P)
1948—Rams, 31-14 (LA)
1949—Tie, 7-7 (P)
1952—Rams, 28-14 (LA)
1955—Rams, 27-26 (LA)
1956—Steelers, 30-13 (P)
1961—Rams, 24-14 (LA)
1964—Rams, 26-14 (P)
1968—Rams, 45-10 (LA)
1971—Rams, 23-14 (P)
1975—Rams, 10-3 (LA)
1978—Rams, 10-7 (LA)
1979—***Steelers, 31-19 (Pasadena)
1981—Steelers, 24-0 (P)
1984—Steelers, 24-14 (P)
(Points—Rams 369, Steelers 274)
**Franchise in Cleveland prior to 1946*
***Steelers known as Pirates prior to 1941*
****Super Bowl XIV*
***L.A. RAMS vs. **ST. LOUIS**
Rams lead series, 21-15-2
1937—Cardinals, 6-0 (Clev)
Cardinals, 13-7 (Chi)
1938—Cardinals, 7-6 (Clev)
Cardinals, 31-17 (Chi)
1939—Rams, 24-0 (Chi)
Rams, 14-0 (Clev)
1940—Rams, 26-14 (Clev)
Cardinals, 17-7 (Chi)
1941—Rams, 10-6 (Clev)
Cardinals, 7-0 (Chi)
1942—Cardinals, 7-0 (Chi)
Rams, 7-3 (Clev)
1945—Rams, 21-0 (Clev)
Rams, 35-21 (Chi)
1946—Cardinals, 34-10 (Chi)
Rams, 17-14 (LA)
1947—Rams, 27-7 (LA)
Cardinals, 17-10 (Chi)
1948—Cardinals, 27-22 (LA)
Cardinals, 27-24 (Chi)
1949—Tie, 28-28 (Chi)
Cardinals, 31-27 (LA)
1951—Rams, 45-21 (LA)
1953—Tie, 24-24 (Chi)
1954—Rams, 28-17 (LA)
1958—Rams, 20-14 (Chi)
1960—Cardinals, 43-21 (LA)
1965—Rams, 27-3 (StL)
1968—Rams, 24-13 (StL)
1970—Rams, 34-13 (LA)
1972—Cardinals, 24-14 (StL)
1975—***Rams, 35-23 (LA)
1976—Cardinals, 30-28 (LA)
1979—Rams, 21-0 (LA)
1980—Rams, 21-13 (StL)
1984—Rams, 16-13 (StL)
1985—Rams, 46-14 (LA)
1986—Rams, 16-10 (StL)
(Points—Rams 759, Cardinals 592)
**Franchise in Cleveland prior to 1946*
***Franchise in Chicago prior to 1960*
****NFC Divisional Playoff*
L.A. RAMS vs. SAN DIEGO
Rams lead series, 2-1
1970—Rams, 37-10 (LA)
1975—Rams, 13-10 (SD) OT
1979—Chargers, 40-16 (LA)
(Points—Rams 66, Chargers 60)
L.A. RAMS vs. SAN FRANCISCO
Rams lead series, 45-27-2
1950—Rams, 35-14 (SF)
Rams, 28-21 (LA)
1951—49ers, 44-17 (SF)
Rams, 23-16 (LA)
1952—Rams, 35-9 (LA)
Rams, 34-21 (SF)
1953—49ers, 31-30 (SF)
49ers, 31-27 (LA)
1954—Tie, 24-24 (LA)
Rams, 42-34 (SF)
1955—Rams, 23-14 (SF)
Rams, 27-14 (LA)
1956—49ers, 33-30 (SF)
Rams, 30-6 (LA)
1957—49ers, 23-20 (SF)
Rams, 37-24 (LA)
1958—Rams, 33-3 (SF)
Rams, 56-7 (LA)
1959—49ers, 34-0 (SF)
49ers, 24-16 (LA)
1960—49ers, 13-9 (SF)
49ers, 23-7 (LA)
1961—49ers, 35-0 (SF)
Rams, 17-7 (LA)
1962—Rams, 28-14 (SF)
49ers, 24-17 (LA)
1963—Rams, 28-21 (LA)
Rams, 21-17 (SF)
1964—Rams, 42-14 (LA)
49ers, 28-7 (SF)
1965—49ers, 45-21 (LA)
49ers, 30-27 (SF)
1966—Rams, 34-3 (LA)
49ers, 21-13 (SF)
1967—49ers, 27-24 (LA)
Rams, 17-7 (SF)
1968—Rams, 24-10 (LA)
Tie, 20-20 (SF)
1969—Rams, 27-21 (SF)
Rams, 41-30 (LA)
1970—49ers, 20-6 (LA)
Rams, 30-13 (SF)
1971—Rams, 20-13 (SF)
Rams, 17-6 (LA)
1972—Rams, 31-7 (LA)
Rams, 26-16 (SF)
1973—Rams, 40-20 (SF)
Rams, 31-13 (LA)
1974—Rams, 37-14 (LA)
Rams, 15-13 (SF)
1975—Rams, 23-14 (SF)
49ers, 24-23 (LA)
1976—49ers, 16-0 (LA)
Rams, 23-3 (SF)
1977—Rams, 34-14 (LA)
Rams, 23-10 (SF)
1978—Rams, 27-10 (LA)
Rams, 31-28 (SF)
1979—Rams, 27-24 (LA)
Rams, 26-20 (SF)
1980—Rams, 48-26 (LA)
Rams, 31-17 (SF)
1981—49ers, 20-17 (SF)
49ers, 33-31 (LA)
1982—49ers, 30-24 (LA)
Rams, 21-20 (SF)
1983—Rams, 10-7 (SF)
49ers, 45-35 (LA)
1984—49ers, 33-0 (LA)
49ers, 19-16 (SF)
1985—49ers, 28-14 (LA)
Rams, 27-20 (SF)
1986—Rams, 16-13 (LA)
49ers, 24-14 (SF)
(Points—Rams 1,785, 49ers 1,470)
L.A. RAMS vs. SEATTLE
Rams lead series, 3-0
1976—Rams, 45-6 (LA)
1979—Rams, 24-0 (S)
1985—Rams, 35-24 (S)
(Points—Rams 104, Seahawks 30)
L.A. RAMS vs. TAMPA BAY
Rams lead series, 6-2
1977—Rams, 31-0 (LA)
1978—Rams, 26-23 (LA)
1979—Buccaneers, 21-6 (TB)
*Rams, 9-0 (TB)
1980—Buccaneers, 10-9 (TB)
1984—Rams, 34-33 (TB)
1985—Rams, 31-27 (TB)
1986—Rams, 26-20 (LA) OT
(Points—Rams 172, Buccaneers 134)
**NFC Championship*
***L.A. RAMS vs. WASHINGTON**
Redskins lead series, 15-5-1
1937—Redskins, 16-7 (C)
1938—Redskins, 37-13 (W)
1941—Redskins, 17-13 (W)
1942—Redskins, 33-14 (W)
1944—Redskins, 14-10 (W)
1945—**Rams, 15-14 (C)
1948—Rams, 41-13 (W)
1949—Rams, 53-27 (LA)
1951—Redskins, 31-21 (W)
1962—Redskins, 20-14 (W)
1963—Redskins, 37-14 (LA)
1967—Tie, 28-28 (LA)
1969—Rams, 24-13 (W)
1971—Redskins, 38-24 (LA)
1974—Redskins, 23-17 (LA)
***Rams, 19-10 (LA)
1977—Redskins, 17-14 (W)
1981—Redskins, 30-7 (LA)
1983—Redskins, 42-20 (LA)
***Redskins, 51-7 (W)
1986—****Redskins, 19-7 (W)
(Points—Redskins 530, Rams 382)
**Franchise in Cleveland prior to 1946*
***NFL Championship*
****NFC Divisional Playoff*
*****NFC First Round Playoff*

MIAMI vs. ATLANTA
Dolphins lead series, 4-1;
See Atlanta vs. Miami
MIAMI vs. BUFFALO
Dolphins lead series, 34-7-1;
See Buffalo vs. Miami
MIAMI vs. CHICAGO
Dolphins lead series, 4-0;
See Chicago vs. Miami
MIAMI vs. CINCINNATI
Dolphins lead series, 7-3;
See Cincinnati vs. Miami
MIAMI vs. CLEVELAND
Browns lead series, 4-3;
See Cleveland vs. Miami
MIAMI vs. DALLAS
Dolphins lead series, 3-2;
See Dallas vs. Miami
MIAMI vs. DENVER
Dolphins lead series, 5-2-1;
See Denver vs. Miami
MIAMI vs. DETROIT
Dolphins lead series, 2-1;
See Detroit vs. Miami
MIAMI vs. GREEN BAY
Dolphins lead series, 4-0;
See Green Bay vs. Miami
MIAMI vs. HOUSTON
Series tied, 10-10;
See Houston vs. Miami
MIAMI vs. INDIANAPOLIS
Dolphins lead series, 26-9;
See Indianapolis vs. Miami
MIAMI vs. KANSAS CITY
Chiefs lead series, 7-6;
See Kansas City vs. Miami
MIAMI vs. L.A. RAIDERS
Raiders lead series, 15-3-1;
See L.A. Raiders vs. Miami
MIAMI vs. L.A. RAMS
Dolphins lead series, 4-1;

See L.A. Rams vs. Miami
MIAMI vs. MINNESOTA
Dolphins lead series, 4-1
1972—Dolphins, 16-14 (Minn)
1973—*Dolphins, 24-7 (Houston)
1976—Vikings, 29-7 (Mia)
1979—Dolphins, 27-12 (Minn)
1982—Dolphins, 22-14 (Mia)
(Points—Dolphins 96, Vikings 76)
Super Bowl VIII
MIAMI vs. *NEW ENGLAND
Dolphins lead series, 25-17
1966—Patriots, 20-14 (M)
1967—Patriots, 41-10 (B)
Dolphins, 41-32 (M)
1968—Dolphins, 34-10 (B)
Dolphins, 38-7 (M)
1969—Dolphins, 17-16 (B)
Patriots, 38-23 (Tampa)
1970—Patriots, 27-14 (B)
Dolphins, 37-20 (M)
1971—Dolphins, 41-3 (M)
Patriots, 34-13 (NE)
1972—Dolphins, 52-0 (M)
Dolphins, 37-21 (NE)
1973—Dolphins, 44-23 (M)
Dolphins, 30-14 (NE)
1974—Patriots, 34-24 (NE)
Dolphins, 34-27 (M)
1975—Dolphins, 22-14 (NE)
Dolphins, 20-7 (M)
1976—Patriots, 30-14 (NE)
Dolphins, 10-3 (M)
1977—Dolphins, 17-5 (M)
Patriots, 14-10 (NE)
1978—Patriots, 33-24 (NE)
Dolphins, 23-3 (M)
1979—Patriots, 28-13 (NE)
Dolphins, 39-24 (M)
1980—Patriots, 34-0 (NE)
Dolphins, 16-13 (M) OT
1981—Dolphins, 30-27 (NE) OT
Dolphins, 24-14 (M)
1982—Patriots, 3-0 (NE)
**Dolphins, 28-13 (M)
1983—Dolphins, 34-24 (M)
Patriots, 17-6 (NE)
1984—Dolphins, 28-7 (M)
Dolphins, 44-24 (NE)
1985—Patriots, 17-13 (NE)
Dolphins, 30-27 (M)
***Patriots, 31-14 (M)
1986—Patriots, 34-7 (NE)
Patriots, 34-27 (M)
(Points—Dolphins 996, Patriots 847)
Franchise in Boston prior to 1971
***AFC First Round Playoff*
****AFC Championship*
MIAMI vs. NEW ORLEANS
Dolphins lead series, 4-1
1970—Dolphins, 21-10 (M)
1974—Dolphins, 21-0 (NO)
1980—Dolphins, 21-16 (M)
1983—Saints, 17-7 (NO)
1986—Dolphins, 31-27 (NO)
(Points—Dolphins 101, Saints 70)
MIAMI vs. N.Y. GIANTS
Dolphins lead series, 1-0
1972—Dolphins, 23-13 (NY)
MIAMI vs. N.Y. JETS
Dolphins lead series, 23-19-1
1966—Jets, 19-14 (M)
Jets, 30-13 (NY)
1967—Jets, 29-7 (NY)
Jets, 33-14 (M)
1968—Jets, 35-17 (NY)
Jets, 31-7 (M)
1969—Jets, 34-31 (NY)
Jets, 27-9 (M)
1970—Dolphins, 20-6 (NY)
Dolphins, 16-10 (M)
1971—Jets, 14-10 (M)
Dolphins, 30-14 (NY)
1972—Dolphins, 27-17 (NY)
Dolphins, 28-24 (M)
1973—Dolphins, 31-3 (M)
Dolphins, 24-14 (NY)
1974—Dolphins, 21-17 (M)
Jets, 17-14 (NY)
1975—Dolphins, 43-0 (NY)
Dolphins, 27-7 (M)
1976—Dolphins, 16-0 (M)
Dolphins, 27-7 (NY)
1977—Dolphins, 21-17 (M)
Dolphins, 14-10 (NY)
1978—Jets, 33-20 (NY)
Jets, 24-13 (M)
1979—Jets, 33-27 (NY)
Jets, 27-24 (M)
1980—Jets, 17-14 (NY)
Jets, 24-17 (M)
1981—Tie, 28-28 (M) OT
Jets, 16-15 (NY)
1982—Dolphins, 45-28 (NY)
Dolphins, 20-19 (M)
*Dolphins, 14-0 (M)
1983—Dolphins, 32-14 (NY)
Dolphins, 34-14 (M)
1984—Dolphins, 31-17 (NY)
Dolphins, 28-17 (M)
1985—Jets, 23-7 (NY)
Dolphins, 21-17 (M)
1986—Jets, 51-45 (NY) OT
Dolphins, 45-3 (M)
(Points—Dolphins 961, Jets 820)
AFC Championship
MIAMI vs. PHILADELPHIA
Dolphins lead series, 3-2
1970—Eagles, 24-17 (P)
1975—Dolphins, 24-16 (M)
1978—Eagles, 17-3 (P)
1981—Dolphins, 13-10 (M)
1984—Dolphins, 24-23 (M)
(Points—Eagles 90, Dolphins 81)
MIAMI vs. PITTSBURGH
Dolphins lead series, 7-3
1971—Dolphins, 24-21 (M)
1972—*Dolphins, 21-17 (P)
1973—Dolphins, 30-26 (M)
1976—Steelers, 14-3 (P)
1979—**Steelers, 34-14 (P)
1980—Steelers, 23-10 (P)
1981—Dolphins, 30-10 (M)
1984—Dolphins, 31-7 (P)
*Dolphins, 45-28 (M)
1985—Dolphins, 24-20 (M)
(Points—Dolphins 232, Steelers 200)
AFC Championship
***AFC Divisional Playoff*
MIAMI vs. ST. LOUIS
Dolphins lead series, 5-0
1972—Dolphins, 31-10 (M)
1977—Dolphins, 55-14 (StL)
1978—Dolphins, 24-10 (M)
1981—Dolphins, 20-7 (StL)
1984—Dolphins, 36-28 (StL)
(Points—Dolphins 166, Cardinals 69)
MIAMI vs. SAN DIEGO
Chargers lead series, 9-5
1966—Chargers, 44-10 (SD)
1967—Chargers, 24-0 (SD)
Dolphins, 41-24 (M)
1968—Chargers, 34-28 (SD)
1969—Chargers, 21-14 (M)
1972—Dolphins, 24-10 (M)
1974—Dolphins, 28-21 (SD)
1977—Chargers, 14-13 (M)
1978—Dolphins, 28-21 (SD)
1980—Chargers, 27-24 (M) OT
1981—*Chargers, 41-38 (M) OT
1982—**Dolphins, 34-13 (M)
1984—Chargers, 34-28 (SD) OT
1986—Chargers, 50-28 (SD)
(Points—Chargers 378, Dolphins 338)
AFC Divisional Playoff
***AFC Second Round Playoff*
MIAMI vs. SAN FRANCISCO
Dolphins lead series, 4-2
1973—Dolphins, 21-13 (M)
1977—Dolphins, 19-15 (SF)
1980—Dolphins, 17-13 (M)
1983—Dolphins, 20-17 (SF)
1984—*49ers, 38-16 (Stanford)
1986—49ers, 31-16 (M)
(Points—49ers 127, Dolphins 109)
Super Bowl XIX
MIAMI vs. SEATTLE
Dolphins lead series, 3-1
1977—Dolphins, 31-13 (M)
1979—Dolphins, 19-10 (M)
1983—*Seahawks, 27-20 (M)
1984—*Dolphins, 31-10 (M)
(Points—Dolphins 101, Seahawks 60)
AFC Divisional Playoff
MIAMI vs. TAMPA BAY
Dolphins lead series, 2-1
1976—Dolphins, 23-20 (TB)
1982—Buccaneers, 23-17 (TB)
1985—Dolphins, 41-38 (M)
(Points—Dolphins 81, Buccaneers 81)
MIAMI vs. WASHINGTON
Dolphins lead series, 4-2
1972—*Dolphins, 14-7 (Los Angeles)
1974—Redskins, 20-17 (W)
1978—Dolphins, 16-0 (W)
1981—Dolphins, 13-10 (M)
1982—**Redskins, 27-17 (Pasadena)
1984—Dolphins, 35-17 (W)
(Points—Dolphins 112, Redskins 81)
Super Bowl VII
***Super Bowl XVII*

MINNESOTA vs. ATLANTA
Vikings lead series, 9-6;
See Atlanta vs. Minnesota
MINNESOTA vs. BUFFALO
Vikings lead series, 4-1;
See Buffalo vs. Minnesota
MINNESOTA vs. CHICAGO
Vikings lead series, 26-23-2;
See Chicago vs. Minnesota
MINNESOTA vs. CINCINNATI
Bengals lead series, 3-2;
See Cincinnati vs. Minnesota
MINNESOTA vs. CLEVELAND
Vikings lead series, 7-2;
See Cleveland vs. Minnesota
MINNESOTA vs. DALLAS
Cowboys lead series, 10-5;
See Dallas vs. Minnesota
MINNESOTA vs. DENVER
Series tied, 2-2;
See Denver vs. Minnesota
MINNESOTA vs. DETROIT
Vikings lead series, 31-18-2;
See Detroit vs. Minnesota
MINNESOTA vs. GREEN BAY
Vikings lead series, 26-24-1;
See Green Bay vs. Minnesota
MINNESOTA vs. HOUSTON
Series tied, 2-2;
See Houston vs. Minnesota
MINNESOTA vs. INDIANAPOLIS
Colts lead series, 12-5-1;
See Indianapolis vs. Minnesota
MINNESOTA vs. KANSAS CITY
Series tied, 2-2;
See Kansas City vs. Minnesota
MINNESOTA vs. L.A. RAIDERS
Raiders lead series, 5-1;
See L.A. Raiders vs. Minnesota
MINNESOTA vs. L.A. RAMS
Vikings lead series, 15-12-2;
See L.A. Rams vs. Minnesota
MINNESOTA vs. MIAMI
Dolphins lead series, 4-1;
See Miami vs. Minnesota
MINNESOTA vs. *NEW ENGLAND
Patriots lead series, 2-1
1970—Vikings, 35-14 (B)
1974—Patriots, 17-14 (M)
1979—Patriots, 27-23 (NE)
(Points—Vikings 72, Patriots 58)
Franchise in Boston prior to 1971
MINNESOTA vs. NEW ORLEANS
Vikings lead series, 9-4
1968—Saints, 20-17 (NO)
1970—Vikings, 26-0 (M)
1971—Vikings, 23-10 (NO)
1972—Vikings, 37-6 (M)
1974—Vikings, 29-9 (M)
1975—Vikings, 20-7 (NO)
1976—Vikings, 40-9 (NO)
1978—Saints, 31-24 (NO)
1980—Vikings, 23-20 (NO)
1981—Vikings, 20-10 (M)
1983—Saints, 17-16 (NO)
1985—Saints, 30-23 (M)
1986—Vikings, 33-17 (M)
(Points—Vikings 331, Saints 186)
MINNESOTA vs. N.Y. GIANTS
Vikings lead series, 6-2
1964—Vikings, 30-21 (NY)
1965—Vikings, 40-14 (M)
1967—Vikings, 27-24 (M)
1969—Giants, 24-23 (NY)
1971—Vikings, 17-10 (NY)
1973—Vikings, 31-7 (New Haven)
1976—Vikings, 24-7 (M)
1986—Giants, 22-20 (M)
(Points—Vikings 212, Giants 129)
MINNESOTA vs. N.Y. JETS
Jets lead series, 3-1
1970—Jets, 20-10 (NY)
1975—Vikings, 29-21 (M)
1979—Jets, 14-7 (NY)
1982—Jets 42-14 (M)
(Points—Jets 97, Vikings 60)
MINNESOTA vs. PHILADELPHIA
Vikings lead series, 9-4
1962—Vikings, 31-21 (M)
1963—Vikings, 34-13 (P)
1968—Vikings, 24-17 (P)
1971—Vikings, 13-0 (P)
1973—Vikings, 28-21 (M)
1976—Vikings, 31-12 (P)
1978—Vikings, 28-27 (M)
1980—Eagles, 42-7 (M)
*Eagles, 31-16 (P)
1981—Vikings, 35-23 (M)
1984—Eagles, 19-17 (P)
1985—Vikings, 28-23 (P)
Eagles, 37-35 (M)
(Points—Vikings 327, Eagles 286)
NFC Divisional Playoff
MINNESOTA vs. PITTSBURGH
Vikings lead series, 6-4
1962—Steelers, 39-31 (P)
1964—Vikings, 30-10 (M)
1967—Vikings, 41-27 (P)
1969—Vikings, 52-14 (M)
1972—Steelers, 23-10 (P)
1974—*Steelers, 16-6 (New Orleans)
1976—Vikings, 17-6 (M)
1980—Steelers, 23-17 (M)
1983—Vikings, 17-14 (P)
1986—Vikings, 31-7 (M)
(Points—Vikings 252, Steelers 179)
Super Bowl IX
MINNESOTA vs. ST. LOUIS
Cardinals lead series, 7-3
1963—Cardinals, 56-14 (M)
1967—Cardinals, 34-24 (M)
1969—Vikings, 27-10 (StL)
1972—Cardinals, 19-17 (M)
1974—Vikings, 28-24 (StL)
*Vikings, 30-14 (M)
1977—Cardinals, 27-7 (M)
1979—Cardinals, 37-7 (StL)
1981—Cardinals, 30-17 (StL)
1983—Cardinals, 41-31 (StL)
(Points—Cardinals 292, Vikings 202)
NFC Divisional Playoff
MINNESOTA vs. SAN DIEGO
Series tied, 3-3
1971—Chargers, 30-14 (SD)
1975—Vikings, 28-13 (M)
1978—Chargers, 13-7 (M)
1981—Vikings, 33-31 (SD)
1984—Chargers, 42-13 (M)
1985—Vikings, 21-17 (M)
(Points—Chargers 146, Vikings 116)
MINNESOTA vs. SAN FRANCISCO
Vikings lead series, 14-12-1
1961—49ers, 38-24 (M)
49ers, 38-28 (SF)
1962—49ers, 21-7 (SF)
49ers, 35-12 (M)
1963—Vikings, 24-20 (SF)
Vikings, 45-14 (M)
1964—Vikings, 27-22 (SF)
Vikings, 24-7 (M)
1965—Vikings, 42-41 (SF)
49ers, 45-24 (M)
1966—Tie, 20-20 (SF)
Vikings, 28-3 (SF)
1967—49ers, 27-21 (M)
1968—Vikings, 30-20 (SF)
1969—Vikings, 10-7 (M)
1970—*49ers, 17-14 (M)
1971—49ers, 13-9 (M)
1972—49ers, 20-17 (SF)
1973—Vikings, 17-13 (SF)
1975—Vikings, 27-17 (M)
1976—49ers, 20-16 (SF)
1977—Vikings, 28-27 (M)
1979—Vikings, 28-22 (M)
1983—49ers, 48-17 (M)
1984—49ers, 51-7 (SF)
1985—Vikings, 28-21 (M)
1986—Vikings, 27-24 (SF) OT
(Points—49ers 651, Vikings 601)
NFC Divisional Playoff
MINNESOTA vs. SEATTLE
Seahawks lead series, 2-1
1976—Vikings, 27-21 (M)
1978—Seahawks, 29-28 (S)
1984—Seahawks, 20-12 (M)
(Points—Seahawks 70, Vikings 67)
MINNESOTA vs. TAMPA BAY
Vikings lead series, 13-5
1977—Vikings, 9-3 (TB)
1978—Buccaneers, 16-10 (M)
Vikings, 24-7 (TB)
1979—Buccaneers, 12-10 (M)
Vikings, 23-22 (TB)
1980—Vikings, 38-30 (M)
Vikings, 21-10 (TB)
1981—Buccaneers, 21-13 (TB)
Vikings, 25-10 (M)
1982—Vikings, 17-10 (M)
1983—Vikings, 19-16 (TB) OT
Buccaneers, 17-12 (M)
1984—Buccaneers, 35-31 (TB)
Vikings, 27-24 (M)
1985—Vikings, 31-16 (TB)
Vikings, 26-7 (M)
1986—Vikings, 23-10 (TB)
Vikings, 45-13 (M)
(Points—Vikings 404, Buccaneers 279)
MINNESOTA vs. WASHINGTON
Series tied, 5-5
1968—Vikings, 27-14 (M)
1970—Vikings, 19-10 (W)
1972—Redskins, 24-21 (M)
1973—*Vikings, 27-20 (M)
1975—Redskins, 31-30 (W)
1976—*Vikings 35-20 (M)
1980—Vikings, 39-14 (W)
1982—**Redskins, 21-7 (W)
1984—Redskins, 31-17 (M)
1986—Redskins, 44-38 (W) OT

(Points—Vikings 260, Redskins 229)
*NFC Divisional Playoff
**NFC Second Round Playoff

NEW ENGLAND vs. ATLANTA
Patriots lead series, 3-2;
See Atlanta vs. New England
NEW ENGLAND vs. BUFFALO
Patriots lead series, 30-23-1;
See Buffalo vs. New England
NEW ENGLAND vs. CHICAGO
Bears lead series, 3-2;
See Chicago vs. New England
NEW ENGLAND vs. CINCINNATI
Patriots lead series, 6-4;
See Cincinnati vs. New England
NEW ENGLAND vs. CLEVELAND
Browns lead series, 6-2;
See Cleveland vs. New England
NEW ENGLAND vs. DALLAS
Cowboys lead series, 5-0;
See Dallas vs. New England
NEW ENGLAND vs. DENVER
Broncos lead series, 13-12;
See Denver vs. New England
NEW ENGLAND vs. DETROIT
Series tied, 2-2;
See Detroit vs. New England
NEW ENGLAND vs. GREEN BAY
Patriots lead series, 2-1;
See Green Bay vs. New England
NEW ENGLAND vs. HOUSTON
Patriots lead series, 14-13-1;
See Houston vs. New England
NEW ENGLAND vs. INDIANAPOLIS
Patriots lead series, 18-15;
See Indianapolis vs. New England
NEW ENGLAND vs. KANSAS CITY
Chiefs lead series, 11-7-3;
See Kansas City vs. New England
NEW ENGLAND vs. L.A. RAIDERS
Series tied, 12-12-1;
See L.A. Raiders vs. New England
NEW ENGLAND vs. L.A. RAMS
Patriots lead series, 3-1;
See L.A. Rams vs. New England
NEW ENGLAND vs. MIAMI
Dolphins lead series, 25-17;
See Miami vs. New England
NEW ENGLAND vs. MINNESOTA
Patriots lead series, 2-1;
See Minnesota vs. New England
NEW ENGLAND vs. NEW ORLEANS
Patriots lead series, 5-0
1972—Patriots, 17-10 (NO)
1976—Patriots, 27-6 (NE)
1980—Patriots, 38-27 (NO)
1983—Patriots, 7-0 (NE)
1986—Patriots, 21-20 (NO)
(Points—Patriots 110, Saints 63)
***NEW ENGLAND vs. N.Y. GIANTS**
Series tied, 1-1
1970—Giants, 16-0 (B)
1974—Patriots, 28-20 (New Haven)
(Points—Giants 36, Patriots 28)
*Franchise in Boston prior to 1971
***NEW ENGLAND vs. **N.Y. JETS**
Jets lead series, 30-23-1
1960—Patriots, 28-24 (NY)
Patriots, 38-21 (B)
1961—Titans, 21-20 (B)
Titans, 37-30 (NY)
1962—Patriots, 43-14 (NY)
Patriots, 24-17 (B)
1963—Patriots, 38-14 (B)
Jets, 31-24 (NY)
1964—Patriots, 26-10 (B)
Jets, 35-14 (NY)
1965—Jets, 30-20 (B)
Patriots, 27-23 (NY)
1966—Tie, 24-24 (B)
Jets, 38-28 (NY)
1967—Jets, 30-23 (NY)
Jets, 29-24 (B)
1968—Jets, 47-31 (Birmingham)
Jets, 48-14 (NY)
1969—Jets, 23-14 (B)
Jets, 23-17 (NY)
1970—Jets, 31-21 (B)
Jets, 17-3 (NY)
1971—Patriots, 20-0 (NE)
Jets, 13-6 (NY)
1972—Jets, 41-13 (NE)
Jets, 34-10 (NY)
1973—Jets, 9-7 (NE)
Jets, 33-13 (NY)
1974—Patriots, 24-0 (NY)
Jets, 21-16 (NE)
1975—Jets, 36-7 (NY)
Jets, 30-28 (NE)
1976—Patriots, 41-7 (NE)
Patriots, 38-24 (NY)
1977—Jets, 30-27 (NY)
Patriots, 24-13 (NE)
1978—Patriots, 55-21 (NE)
Patriots, 19-17 (NY)
1979—Patriots, 56-3 (NE)
Jets, 27-26 (NY)
1980—Patriots, 21-11 (NY)
Patriots, 34-21 (NE)
1981—Jets, 28-24 (NY)
Jets, 17-6 (NE)
1982—Jets, 31-7 (NE)
1983—Patriots, 23-13 (NE)
Jets, 26-3 (NY)
1984—Patriots, 28-21 (NY)
Patriots, 30-20 (NE)
1985—Patriots, 20-13 (NE)
Jets, 16-13 (NY) OT
***Patriots, 26-14 (NY)
1986—Patriots, 20-6 (NY)
Jets, 31-24 (NE)
(Points—Patriots 1,240, Jets 1,214)
*Franchise in Boston prior to 1971
**Jets known as Titans prior to 1963
***AFC First Round Playoff
NEW ENGLAND vs. PHILADELPHIA
Eagles lead series, 3-2
1973—Eagles, 24-23 (P)
1977—Patriots, 14-6 (NE)
1978—Patriots, 24-14 (NE)
1981—Eagles, 13-3 (P)
1984—Eagles, 27-17 (P)
(Points—Eagles 84, Patriots 81)
NEW ENGLAND vs. PITTSBURGH
Steelers lead series, 5-3
1972—Steelers, 33-3 (P)
1974—Steelers, 21-17 (NE)
1976—Patriots, 30-27 (P)
1979—Steelers, 16-13 (NE) OT
1981—Steelers, 27-21 (P) OT
1982—Steelers, 37-14 (P)
1983—Patriots, 28-23 (P)
1986—Patriots, 34-0 (P)
(Points—Steelers 184, Patriots 160)
***NEW ENGLAND vs. ST. LOUIS**
Cardinals lead series, 4-1
1970—Cardinals, 31-0 (StL)
1975—Cardinals, 24-17 (StL)
1978—Patriots, 16-6 (StL)
1981—Cardinals, 27-20 (NE)
1984—Cardinals, 33-10 (NE)
(Points—Cardinals 121, Patriots 63)
*Franchise in Boston prior to 1971
***NEW ENGLAND vs. **SAN DIEGO**
Patriots lead series, 13-12-2
1960—Patriots, 35-0 (LA)
Chargers, 45-16 (B)
1961—Chargers, 38-27 (B)
Patriots, 41-0 (SD)
1962—Patriots, 24-20 (B)
Patriots, 20-14 (SD)
1963—Chargers, 17-13 (SD)
Chargers, 7-6 (B)
***Chargers, 51-10 (SD)
1964—Patriots, 33-28 (SD)
Chargers, 26-17 (B)
1965—Tie, 10-10 (B)
Patriots, 22-6 (SD)
1966—Chargers, 24-0 (SD)
Patriots, 35-17 (B)
1967—Chargers, 28-14 (SD)
Tie, 31-31 (SD)
1968—Chargers, 27-17 (B)
1969—Chargers, 13-10 (B)
Chargers, 28-18 (SD)
1970—Chargers, 16-14 (B)
1973—Patriots, 30-14 (NE)
1975—Patriots, 33-19 (SD)
1977—Patriots, 24-20 (SD)
1978—Patriots, 28-23 (NE)
1979—Patriots, 27-21 (NE)
1983—Patriots, 37-21 (NE)
(Points—Patriots 592, Chargers 564)
*Franchise in Boston prior to 1971
**Franchise in Los Angeles prior to 1961
***AFL Championship
NEW ENGLAND vs. SAN FRANCISCO
49ers lead series, 4-1
1971—49ers, 27-10 (SF)
1975—Patriots, 24-16 (NE)
1980—49ers, 21-17 (SF)
1983—49ers, 33-13 (NE)
1986—49ers, 29-24 (NE)
(Points—49ers 126, Patriots 88)
NEW ENGLAND vs. SEATTLE
Patriots lead series, 5-2
1977—Patriots, 31-0 (NE)
1980—Patriots, 37-31 (S)
1982—Patriots, 16-0 (S)
1983—Seahawks, 24-6 (S)
1984—Patriots, 38-23 (NE)
1985—Patriots, 20-13 (S)
1986—Seahawks, 38-31 (NE)
(Points—Patriots 179, Seahawks 129)
NEW ENGLAND vs. TAMPA BAY
Patriots lead series, 2-0
1976—Patriots, 31-14 (TB)
1985—Patriots, 32-14 (TB)
(Points—Patriots 63, Buccaneers 28)
NEW ENGLAND vs. WASHINGTON
Redskins lead series, 3-1
1972—Patriots, 24-23 (NE)
1978—Redskins, 16-14 (NE)
1981—Redskins, 24-22 (W)
1984—Redskins, 26-10 (NE)
(Points—Redskins 89, Patriots 70)

NEW ORLEANS vs. ATLANTA
Falcons lead series, 24-12;
See Atlanta vs. New Orleans
NEW ORLEANS vs. BUFFALO
Bills lead series, 2-1;
See Buffalo vs. New Orleans
NEW ORLEANS vs. CHICAGO
Bears lead series, 7-4;
See Chicago vs. New Orleans
NEW ORLEANS vs. CINCINNATI
Bengals lead series, 3-2;
See Cincinnati vs. New Orleans
NEW ORLEANS vs. CLEVELAND
Browns lead series, 8-1;
See Cleveland vs. New Orleans
NEW ORLEANS vs. DALLAS
Cowboys lead series, 11-1;
See Dallas vs. New Orleans
NEW ORLEANS vs. DENVER
Broncos lead series, 4-0;
See Denver vs. New Orleans
NEW ORLEANS vs. DETROIT
Series tied, 4-4-1;
See Detroit vs. New Orleans
NEW ORLEANS vs. GREEN BAY
Packers lead series, 10-3;
See Green Bay vs. New Orleans
NEW ORLEANS vs. HOUSTON
Series tied, 2-2-1;
See Houston vs. New Orleans
NEW ORLEANS vs. INDIANAPOLIS
Colts lead series, 3-1;
See Indianapolis vs. New Orleans
NEW ORLEANS vs. KANSAS CITY
Series tied, 2-2;
See Kansas City vs. New Orleans
NEW ORLEANS vs. L.A. RAIDERS
Raiders lead series, 3-0-1;
See L.A. Raiders vs. New Orleans
NEW ORLEANS vs. L.A. RAMS
Rams lead series, 24-10;
See L.A. Rams vs. New Orleans
NEW ORLEANS vs. MIAMI
Dolphins lead series, 4-1;
See Miami vs. New Orleans
NEW ORLEANS vs. MINNESOTA
Vikings lead series, 9-4;
See Minnesota vs. New Orleans
NEW ORLEANS vs. NEW ENGLAND
Patriots lead series, 5-0;
See New England vs. New Orleans
NEW ORLEANS vs. N.Y. GIANTS
Giants lead series, 7-5
1967—Giants, 27-21 (NY)
1968—Giants, 38-21 (NY)
1969—Saints, 25-24 (NY)
1970—Saints, 14-10 (NO)
1972—Giants, 45-21 (NY)
1975—Giants, 28-14 (NY)
1978—Saints, 28-17 (NO)
1979—Saints, 24-14 (NO)
1981—Giants, 20-7 (NY)
1984—Saints, 10-3 (NY)
1985—Giants, 21-13 (NO)
1986—Giants, 20-17 (NY)
(Points—Giants 267, Saints 215)
NEW ORLEANS vs. N.Y. JETS
Jets lead series, 4-1
1972—Jets, 18-17 (NY)
1977—Jets, 16-13 (NO)
1980—Saints, 21-20 (NY)
1983—Jets, 31-28 (NO)
1986—Jets, 28-23 (NY)
(Points—Jets 113, Saints 102)
NEW ORLEANS vs. PHILADELPHIA
Eagles lead series, 8-6
1967—Saints, 31-24 (NO)
Eagles, 48-21 (P)
1968—Eagles, 29-17 (P)
1969—Eagles, 13-10 (P)
Saints, 26-17 (NO)
1972—Saints, 21-3 (NO)
1974—Saints, 14-10 (NO)
1977—Eagles, 28-7 (P)
1978—Eagles, 24-17 (NO)
1979—Eagles, 26-14 (NO)
1980—Eagles, 34-21 (NO)
1981—Eagles, 31-14 (NO)
1983—Saints, 20-17 (P) OT
1985—Saints, 23-21 (NO)
(Points—Eagles 325, Saints 256)
NEW ORLEANS vs. PITTSBURGH
Series tied 4-4
1967—Steelers, 14-10 (NO)
1968—Saints, 16-12 (P)
Saints, 24-14 (NO)
1969—Saints, 27-24 (NO)
1974—Steelers, 28-7 (NO)
1978—Steelers, 20-14 (P)
1981—Steelers, 20-6 (NO)
1984—Saints, 27-24 (NO)
(Points—Steelers 156, Saints 131)
NEW ORLEANS vs. ST. LOUIS
Cardinals lead series, 9-5
1967—Cardinals, 31-20 (StL)
1968—Cardinals, 21-20 (NO)
Cardinals, 31-17 (StL)
1969—Saints, 51-42 (StL)
1970—Cardinals, 24-17 (StL)
1974—Saints, 14-0 (NO)
1977—Cardinals, 49-31 (StL)
1980—Cardinals, 40-7 (NO)
1981—Cardinals, 30-3 (StL)
1982—Cardinals, 21-7 (NO)
1983—Saints, 28-17 (NO)
1984—Saints, 34-24 (NO)
1985—Cardinals, 28-16 (StL)
1986—Saints, 16-7 (StL)
(Points—Cardinals 365, Saints 281)
NEW ORLEANS vs. SAN DIEGO
Chargers lead series, 3-0
1973—Chargers, 17-14 (SD)
1977—Chargers, 14-0 (NO)
1979—Chargers, 35-0 (NO)
(Points—Chargers 66, Saints 14)
NEW ORLEANS vs. SAN FRANCISCO
49ers lead series, 23-10-2
1967—49ers, 27-13 (SF)
1969—Saints, 43-38 (NO)
1970—Tie, 20-20 (SF)
49ers, 38-27 (NO)
1971—49ers, 38-20 (NO)
Saints, 26-20 (SF)
1972—49ers, 37-2 (NO)
Tie, 20-20 (SF)
1973—49ers, 40-0 (SF)
Saints, 16-10 (NO)
1974—49ers, 17-13 (NO)
49ers, 35-21 (SF)
1975—49ers, 35-21 (SF)
49ers, 16-6 (NO)
1976—49ers, 33-3 (SF)
49ers, 27-7 (NO)
1977—49ers, 10-7 (NO) OT
49ers, 20-17 (SF)
1978—Saints, 14-7 (SF)
Saints, 24-13 (NO)
1979—Saints, 30-21 (SF)
Saints, 31-20 (NO)
1980—49ers, 26-23 (NO)
49ers, 38-35 (SF) OT
1981—49ers, 21-14 (SF)
49ers, 21-17 (NO)
1982—Saints, 23-20 (SF)
1983—49ers, 32-13 (NO)
49ers, 27-0 (SF)
1984—49ers, 30-20 (SF)
49ers, 35-3 (NO)
1985—Saints, 20-17 (SF)
49ers, 31-19 (NO)
1986—49ers, 26-17 (SF)
Saints, 23-10 (NO)
(Points—49ers 876, Saints 608)
NEW ORLEANS vs. SEATTLE
Seahawks lead series, 2-1
1976—Saints, 51-27 (S)
1979—Seahawks, 38-24 (S)
1985—Seahawks, 27-3 (NO)
(Points—Seahawks, 92, Saints 78)
NEW ORLEANS vs. TAMPA BAY
Saints lead series, 6-3
1977—Buccaneers, 33-14 (NO)
1978—Saints, 17-10 (TB)
1979—Saints, 42-14 (TB)
1981—Buccaneers, 31-14 (NO)
1982—Buccaneers, 13-10 (NO)
1983—Saints, 24-21 (TB)
1984—Saints, 17-13 (NO)
1985—Saints, 20-13 (NO)
1986—Saints, 38-7 (NO)
(Points—Saints 196, Buccaneers 155)
NEW ORLEANS vs. WASHINGTON
Redskins lead series, 8-4
1967—Redskins, 30-10 (NO)
Saints, 30-14 (W)
1968—Saints, 37-17 (NO)
1969—Redskins, 26-20 (NO)
Redskins, 17-14 (W)
1971—Redskins, 24-14 (W)
1973—Saints, 19-3 (NO)
1975—Redskins, 41-3 (W)
1979—Saints, 14-10 (W)
1980—Redskins, 22-14 (W)

1982—Redskins, 27-10 (NO)
1986—Redskins, 14-6 (NO)
(Points—Redskins 245, Saints 191)

N.Y. GIANTS vs. ATLANTA
Falcons lead series, 6-5;
See Atlanta vs. N.Y. Giants
N.Y. GIANTS vs. BUFFALO
Giants lead series, 2-1;
See Buffalo vs. N.Y. Giants
N.Y. GIANTS vs. CHICAGO
Bears lead series, 27-16-2;
See Chicago vs. N.Y. Giants
N.Y. GIANTS vs. CINCINNATI
Bengals lead series, 3-0;
See Cincinnati vs. N.Y. Giants
N.Y. GIANTS vs. CLEVELAND
Browns lead series, 26-16-2;
See Cleveland vs. N.Y. Giants
N.Y. GIANTS vs. DALLAS
Cowboys lead series, 33-14-2;
See Dallas vs. N.Y. Giants
N.Y. GIANTS vs. DENVER
Giants lead series, 3-2;
See Denver vs. N.Y. Giants
N.Y. GIANTS vs. DETROIT
Lions lead series, 18-11-1;
See Detroit vs. N.Y. Giants
N.Y. GIANTS vs. GREEN BAY
Packers lead series, 25-19-2;
See Green Bay vs. N.Y. Giants
N.Y. GIANTS vs. HOUSTON
Giants lead series, 3-0;
See Houston vs. N.Y. Giants
N.Y. GIANTS vs. INDIANAPOLIS
Colts lead series, 7-3;
See Indianapolis vs. N.Y. Giants
N.Y. GIANTS vs. KANSAS CITY
Giants lead series, 4-1;
See Kansas City vs. N.Y. Giants
N.Y. GIANTS vs. L.A. RAIDERS
Raiders lead series, 3-1;
See L.A. Raiders vs. N.Y. Giants
N.Y. GIANTS vs. L.A. RAMS
Rams lead series, 16-8;
See L.A. Rams vs. N.Y. Giants
N.Y. GIANTS vs. MIAMI
Dolphins lead series, 1-0;
See Miami vs. N.Y. Giants
N.Y. GIANTS vs. MINNESOTA
Vikings lead series, 6-2;
See Minnesota vs. N.Y. Giants
N.Y. GIANTS vs. NEW ENGLAND
Series tied, 1-1;
See New England vs. N.Y. Giants
N.Y. GIANTS vs. NEW ORLEANS
Giants lead series, 7-5;
See New Orleans vs. N.Y. Giants
N.Y. GIANTS vs. N.Y. JETS
Series tied, 2-2
1970—Giants, 22-10 (NYJ)
1974—Jets, 26-20 (New Haven) OT
1981—Jets, 26-7 (NYG)
1984—Giants, 20-10 (NYJ)
(Points—Jets 72, Giants 69)
N.Y. GIANTS vs. PHILADELPHIA
Giants lead series, 58-45-2
1933—Giants, 56-0 (NY)
Giants, 20-14 (P)
1934—Giants, 17-0 (NY)
Eagles, 6-0 (P)
1935—Giants, 10-0 (NY)
Giants, 21-14 (P)
1936—Eagles, 10-7 (P)
Giants, 21-17 (NY)
1937—Giants, 16-7 (P)
Giants, 21-0 (NY)
1938—Eagles, 14-10 (P)
Giants, 17-7 (NY)
1939—Giants, 13-3 (P)
Giants, 27-10 (NY)
1940—Giants, 20-14 (P)
Giants, 17-7 (NY)
1941—Giants, 24-0 (P)
Giants, 16-0 (NY)
1942—Giants, 35-17 (NY)
Giants, 14-0 (P)
1944—Eagles, 24-17 (NY)
Tie, 21-21 (P)
1945—Eagles, 38-17 (P)
Giants, 28-21 (NY)
1946—Eagles, 24-14 (P)
Giants, 45-17 (NY)
1947—Eagles, 23-0 (P)
Eagles, 41-24 (NY)
1948—Eagles, 45-0 (P)
Eagles, 35-14 (NY)
1949—Eagles, 24-3 (NY)
Eagles, 17-3 (P)
1950—Giants, 7-3 (NY)
Giants, 9-7 (P)
1951—Giants, 26-24 (NY)
Giants, 23-7 (P)
1952—Giants, 31-7 (P)
Eagles, 14-10 (NY)
1953—Eagles, 30-7 (P)
Giants, 37-28 (NY)
1954—Giants, 27-14 (NY)
Eagles, 29-14 (P)
1955—Eagles, 27-17 (P)
Giants, 31-7 (NY)
1956—Giants, 20-3 (NY)
Giants, 21-7 (P)
1957—Giants, 24-20 (P)
Giants, 13-0 (NY)
1958—Eagles, 27-24 (P)
Giants, 24-10 (NY)
1959—Eagles, 49-21 (P)
Giants, 24-7 (NY)
1960—Eagles, 17-10 (NY)
Eagles, 31-23 (P)
1961—Giants, 38-21 (NY)
Giants, 28-24 (P)
1962—Giants, 29-13 (P)
Giants, 19-14 (NY)
1963—Giants, 37-14 (P)
Giants, 42-14 (NY)
1964—Eagles, 38-7 (P)
Eagles, 23-17 (NY)
1965—Giants, 16-14 (P)
Giants, 35-27 (NY)
1966—Eagles, 35-17 (P)
Eagles, 31-3 (NY)
1967—Giants, 44-7 (NY)
1968—Giants, 34-25 (P)
Giants, 7-6 (NY)
1969—Eagles, 23-20 (NY)
1970—Giants, 30-23 (NY)
Eagles, 23-20 (P)
1971—Eagles, 23-7 (P)
Eagles, 41-28 (NY)
1972—Giants, 27-12 (P)
Giants, 62-10 (NY)
1973—Tie, 23-23 (NY)
Eagles, 20-16 (P)
1974—Eagles, 35-7 (P)
Eagles, 20-7 (New Haven)
1975—Giants, 23-14 (P)
Eagles, 13-10 (NY)
1976—Eagles, 20-7 (P)
Eagles, 10-0 (NY)
1977—Eagles, 28-10 (NY)
Eagles, 17-14 (P)
1978—Eagles, 19-17 (NY)
Eagles, 20-3 (P)
1979—Eagles, 23-17 (P)
Eagles, 17-13 (NY)
1980—Eagles, 35-3 (P)
Eagles, 31-16 (NY)
1981—Eagles, 24-10 (NY)
Giants, 20-10 (P)
*Giants, 27-21 (P)
1982—Giants, 23-7 (NY)
Giants, 26-24 (P)
1983—Eagles, 17-13 (NY)
Giants, 23-0 (P)
1984—Giants, 28-27 (NY)
Eagles, 24-10 (P)
1985—Giants, 21-0 (NY)
Giants, 16-10 (P) OT
1986—Giants, 35-3 (NY)
Giants, 17-14 (P)
(Points—Giants 2,033, Eagles 1,825)
**NFC First Round Playoff*
N.Y. GIANTS vs. *PITTSBURGH
Giants lead series, 41-26-3
1933—Giants, 23-2 (P)
Giants, 27-3 (NY)
1934—Giants, 14-12 (P)
Giants, 17-7 (NY)
1935—Giants, 42-7 (P)
Giants, 13-0 (NY)
1936—Pirates, 10-7 (P)
1937—Giants, 10-7 (P)
Giants, 17-0 (NY)
1938—Giants, 27-14 (P)
Pirates, 13-10 (NY)
1939—Giants, 14-7 (P)
Giants, 23-7 (NY)
1940—Tie, 10-10 (P)
Giants, 12-0 (NY)
1941—Giants, 37-10 (P)
Giants, 28-7 (NY)
1942—Steelers, 13-10 (P)
Steelers, 17-9 (NY)
1945—Giants, 34-6 (P)
Steelers, 21-7 (NY)
1946—Giants, 17-14 (P)
Giants, 7-0 (NY)
1947—Steelers, 38-21 (NY)
Steelers, 24-7 (P)
1948—Giants, 34-27 (NY)
Steelers, 38-28 (P)
1949—Steelers, 28-7 (P)
Steelers, 21-17 (NY)
1950—Giants, 18-7 (P)
Steelers, 17-6 (NY)
1951—Tie, 13-13 (P)
Giants, 14-0 (NY)
1952—Steelers, 63-7 (P)
1953—Steelers, 24-14 (P)
Steelers, 14-10 (NY)
1954—Giants, 30-6 (P)
Giants, 24-3 (NY)
1955—Steelers, 30-23 (P)
Steelers, 19-17 (NY)
1956—Giants, 38-10 (NY)
Giants, 17-14 (P)
1957—Giants, 35-0 (NY)
Steelers, 21-10 (P)
1958—Giants, 17-6 (NY)
Steelers, 31-10 (P)
1959—Giants, 21-16 (P)
Steelers, 14-9 (NY)
1960—Giants, 19-17 (P)
Giants, 27-24 (NY)
1961—Giants, 17-14 (P)
Giants, 42-21 (NY)
1962—Giants, 31-27 (P)
Steelers, 20-17 (NY)
1963—Steelers, 31-0 (P)
Giants, 33-17 (NY)
1964—Steelers, 27-24 (P)
Steelers, 44-17 (NY)
1965—Giants, 23-13 (P)
Giants, 35-10 (NY)
1966—Tie, 34-34 (P)
Steelers, 47-28 (NY)
1967—Giants, 27-24 (P)
Giants, 28-20 (NY)
1968—Giants, 34-20 (P)
1969—Giants, 10-7 (NY)
Giants, 21-17 (P)
1971—Steelers, 17-13 (P)
1976—Steelers, 27-0 (NY)
1985—Giants, 28-10 (NY)
(Points—Giants 1,370, Steelers 1,159)
**Steelers known as Pirates prior to 1941*
N.Y. GIANTS vs. *ST. LOUIS
Giants lead series, 55-31-2
1926—Giants, 20-0 (NY)
1927—Giants, 28-7 (NY)
1929—Giants, 24-21 (NY)
1930—Giants, 25-12 (NY)
Giants, 13-7 (C)
1935—Cardinals, 14-13 (NY)
1936—Giants, 14-6 (NY)
1938—Giants, 6-0 (NY)
1939—Giants, 17-7 (NY)
1941—Cardinals, 10-7 (NY)
1942—Giants, 21-7 (NY)
1943—Giants, 24-13 (NY)
1946—Giants, 28-24 (NY)
1947—Giants, 35-31 (NY)
1948—Cardinals, 63-35 (NY)
1949—Giants, 41-38 (C)
1950—Cardinals, 17-3 (C)
Giants, 51-21 (NY)
1951—Giants, 28-17 (NY)
Giants, 10-0 (C)
1952—Cardinals, 24-23 (NY)
Giants, 28-6 (C)
1953—Giants, 21-7 (NY)
Giants, 23-20 (C)
1954—Giants, 41-10 (C)
Giants, 31-17 (NY)
1955—Cardinals, 28-17 (C)
Giants, 10-0 (NY)
1956—Cardinals, 35-27 (C)
Giants, 23-10 (NY)
1957—Giants, 27-14 (NY)
Giants, 28-21 (C)
1958—Giants, 37-7 (Buffalo)
Cardinals, 23-6 (NY)
1959—Giants, 9-3 (NY)
Giants, 30-20 (Minn)
1960—Giants, 35-14 (StL)
Cardinals, 20-13 (NY)
1961—Cardinals, 21-10 (NY)
Giants, 24-9 (StL)
1962—Giants, 31-14 (StL)
Giants, 31-28 (NY)
1963—Giants, 38-21 (StL)
Cardinals, 24-17 (NY)
1964—Giants, 34-17 (NY)
Tie, 10-10 (StL)
1965—Giants, 14-10 (NY)
Giants, 28-15 (StL)
1966—Cardinals, 24-19 (StL)
Cardinals, 20-17 (NY)
1967—Giants, 37-20 (StL)
Giants, 37-14 (NY)
1968—Cardinals, 28-21 (NY)
1969—Cardinals, 42-17 (StL)
Giants, 49-6 (NY)
1970—Giants, 35-17 (NY)
Giants, 34-17 (StL)
1971—Giants, 21-20 (StL)
Cardinals, 24-7 (NY)
1972—Giants, 27-21 (NY)
Giants, 13-7 (StL)
1973—Cardinals, 35-27 (StL)
Giants, 24-13 (New Haven)
1974—Cardinals, 23-21 (New Haven)
Cardinals, 26-14 (StL)
1975—Cardinals, 26-14 (StL)
Cardinals, 20-13 (NY)
1976—Cardinals, 27-21 (StL)
Cardinals, 17-14 (NY)
1977—Cardinals, 28-0 (StL)
Giants, 27-7 (NY)
1978—Cardinals, 20-10 (StL)
Giants, 17-0 (NY)
1979—Cardinals, 27-14 (NY)
Cardinals, 29-20 (StL)
1980—Giants, 41-35 (StL)
Cardinals, 23-7 (NY)
1981—Giants, 34-14 (NY)
Giants, 20-10 (StL)
1982—Cardinals, 24-21 (StL)
1983—Tie, 20-20 (StL) OT
Cardinals, 10-6 (NY)
1984—Giants, 16-10 (NY)
Cardinals, 31-21 (StL)
1985—Giants, 27-17 (NY)
Giants, 34-3 (StL)
1986—Giants, 13-6 (StL)
Giants, 27-7 (NY)
(Points—Giants 1,966, Cardinals 1,531)
**Franchise in Chicago prior to 1960*
N.Y. GIANTS vs. SAN DIEGO
Giants lead series, 3-2
1971—Giants, 35-17 (NY)
1975—Giants, 35-24 (NY)
1980—Chargers, 44-7 (SD)
1983—Chargers, 41-34 (NY)
1986—Giants, 20-7 (NY)
(Points—Chargers 133, Giants 131)
N.Y. GIANTS vs. SAN FRANCISCO
Giants lead series, 12-7
1952—Giants, 23-14 (NY)
1956—Giants, 38-21 (SF)
1957—49ers, 27-17 (NY)
1960—Giants, 21-19 (SF)
1963—Giants, 48-14 (NY)
1968—49ers, 26-10 (NY)
1972—Giants, 23-17 (SF)
1975—Giants, 26-23 (SF)
1977—Giants, 20-17 (NY)
1978—Giants, 27-10 (NY)
1979—Giants, 32-16 (NY)
1980—49ers, 12-0 (SF)
1981—49ers, 17-10 (SF)
*49ers, 38-24 (SF)
1984—49ers, 31-10 (NY)
*49ers, 21-10 (SF)
1985—**Giants, 17-3 (NY)
1986—Giants, 21-17 (SF)
*Giants, 49-3 (NY)
(Points—Giants 426, 49ers 346)
**NFC Divisional Playoff*
***NFC First Round Playoff*
N.Y. GIANTS vs. SEATTLE
Giants lead series, 3-2
1976—Giants, 28-16 (NY)
1980—Giants, 27-21 (S)
1981—Giants, 32-0 (S)
1983—Seahawks, 17-12 (NY)
1986—Seahawks, 17-12 (S)
(Points—Giants 111, Seahawks 71)
N.Y. GIANTS vs. TAMPA BAY
Giants lead series, 6-3
1977—Giants, 10-0 (TB)
1978—Giants, 19-13 (TB)
Giants, 17-14 (NY)
1979—Giants, 17-14 (NY)
Buccaneers, 31-3 (TB)
1980—Buccaneers, 30-13 (TB)
1984—Giants, 17-14 (NY)
Buccaneers, 20-17 (TB)
1985—Giants, 22-20 (NY)
(Points—Buccaneers 156, Giants 135)
N.Y. GIANTS vs. *WASHINGTON
Giants lead series, 61-46-3
1932—Braves, 14-6 (B)
Tie, 0-0 (NY)
1933—Redskins, 21-20 (B)
Giants, 7-0 (NY)
1934—Giants, 16-13 (B)
Giants, 3-0 (NY)
1935—Giants, 20-12 (B)
Giants, 17-6 (NY)
1936—Giants, 7-0 (B)
Redskins, 14-0 (NY)
1937—Redskins, 13-3 (W)
Redskins, 49-14 (NY)
1938—Giants, 10-7 (W)
Giants, 36-0 (NY)
1939—Tie, 0-0 (W)
Giants, 9-7 (NY)
1940—Redskins, 21-7 (W)
Giants, 21-7 (NY)

1941—Giants, 17-10 (W)
Giants, 20-13 (NY)
1942—Giants, 14-7 (W)
Redskins, 14-7 (NY)
1943—Giants, 14-10 (NY)
Giants, 31-7 (W)
**Redskins, 28-0 (NY)
1944—Giants, 16-13 (NY)
Giants, 31-0 (W)
1945—Redskins, 24-14 (NY)
Redskins, 17-0 (W)
1946—Redskins, 24-14 (W)
Giants, 31-0 (NY)
1947—Redskins, 28-20 (W)
Giants, 35-10 (NY)
1948—Redskins, 41-10 (W)
Redskins, 28-21 (NY)
1949—Giants, 45-35 (W)
Giants, 23-7 (NY)
1950—Giants, 21-17 (W)
Giants, 24-21 (NY)
1951—Giants, 35-14 (W)
Giants, 28-14 (NY)
1952—Giants, 14-10 (W)
Redskins, 27-17 (NY)
1953—Redskins, 13-9 (W)
Redskins, 24-21 (NY)
1954—Giants, 51-21 (W)
Giants, 24-7 (NY)
1955—Giants, 35-7 (NY)
Giants, 27-20 (W)
1956—Redskins, 33-7 (W)
Giants, 28-14 (NY)
1957—Giants, 24-20 (W)
Redskins, 31-14 (NY)
1958—Giants, 21-14 (W)
Giants, 30-0 (NY)
1959—Giants, 45-14 (NY)
Giants, 24-10 (W)
1960—Tie, 24-24 (NY)
Giants, 17-3 (W)
1961—Giants, 24-21 (W)
Giants, 53-0 (NY)
1962—Giants, 49-34 (NY)
Giants, 42-24 (NY)
1963—Giants, 24-14 (W)
Giants, 44-14 (NY)
1964—Giants, 13-10 (NY)
Redskins, 36-21 (W)
1965—Redskins, 23-7 (NY)
Giants, 27-10 (W)
1966—Giants, 13-10 (NY)
Redskins, 72-41 (W)
1967—Redskins, 38-34 (W)
1968—Giants, 48-21 (NY)
Giants, 13-10 (W)
1969—Redskins, 20-14 (W)
1970—Giants, 35-33 (NY)
Giants, 27-24 (W)
1971—Redskins, 30-3 (NY)
Redskins, 23-7 (W)
1972—Redskins, 23-16 (NY)
Redskins, 27-13 (W)
1973—Redskins, 21-3 (New Haven)
Redskins, 27-24 (W)
1974—Redskins, 13-10 (New Haven)
Redskins, 24-3 (W)
1975—Redskins, 49-13 (W)
Redskins, 21-13 (NY)
1976—Redskins, 19-17 (W)
Giants, 12-9 (NY)
1977—Giants, 20-17 (NY)
Giants, 17-6 (W)
1978—Giants, 17-6 (NY)
Redskins, 16-13 (W) OT
1979—Redskins, 27-0 (W)
Giants, 14-6 (NY)
1980—Redskins, 23-21 (NY)
Redskins, 16-13 (W)
1981—Giants, 17-7 (W)
Redskins, 30-27 (NY) OT
1982—Redskins, 27-17 (NY)
Redskins, 15-14 (W)
1983—Redskins, 33-17 (NY)
Redskins, 31-22 (W)
1984—Redskins, 30-14 (W)
Giants, 37-13 (NY)
1985—Giants, 17-3 (NY)
Redskins, 23-21 (W)
1986—Giants, 27-20 (NY)
Giants, 24-14 (W)
***Giants, 17-0 (NY)
(Points—Giants 2,148, Redskins 1,921)
Franchise in Boston prior to 1937 and known as Braves prior to 1933
***Division Playoff*
****NFC Championship*

N.Y. JETS vs. ATLANTA
Series tied, 2-2;
See Atlanta vs. N.Y. Jets
N.Y. JETS vs. BUFFALO
Jets lead series, 27-26;
See Buffalo vs. N.Y. Jets
N.Y. JETS vs. CHICAGO
Bears lead series, 2-1;
See Chicago vs. N.Y. Jets
N.Y. JETS vs. CINCINNATI
Jets lead series, 7-4;
See Cincinnati vs. N.Y. Jets
N.Y. JETS vs. CLEVELAND
Browns lead series, 8-3;
See Cleveland vs. N.Y. Jets
N.Y. JETS vs. DALLAS
Cowboys lead series, 3-0;
See Dallas vs. N.Y. Jets
N.Y. JETS vs. DENVER
Jets lead series, 11-10-1;
See Denver vs. N.Y. Jets
N.Y. JETS vs. DETROIT
Series tied, 2-2;
See Detroit vs. N.Y. Jets
N.Y. JETS vs. GREEN BAY
Jets lead series, 4-1;
See Green Bay vs. N.Y. Jets
N.Y. JETS vs. HOUSTON
Oilers lead series, 15-10-1;
See Houston vs. N.Y. Jets
N.Y. JETS vs. INDIANAPOLIS
Jets lead series, 18-16;
See Indianapolis vs. N.Y. Jets
N.Y. JETS vs. KANSAS CITY
Chiefs lead series, 13-12;
See Kansas City vs. N.Y. Jets
N.Y. JETS vs. L.A. RAIDERS
Raiders lead series, 12-11-2;
See L.A. Raiders vs. N.Y. Jets
N.Y. JETS vs. L.A. RAMS
Rams lead series, 3-2;
See L.A. Rams vs. N.Y. Jets
N.Y. JETS vs. MIAMI
Dolphins lead series, 23-19-1;
See Miami vs. N.Y. Jets
N.Y. JETS vs. MINNESOTA
Jets lead series, 3-1;
See Minnesota vs. N.Y. Jets
N.Y. JETS vs. NEW ENGLAND
Jets lead series, 30-23-1;
See New England vs. N.Y. Jets
N.Y. JETS vs. NEW ORLEANS
Jets lead series, 4-1;
See New Orleans vs. N.Y. Jets
N.Y. JETS vs. N.Y. GIANTS
Series tied, 2-2;
See N.Y. Giants vs. N.Y. Jets
N.Y. JETS vs. PHILADELPHIA
Eagles lead series, 3-0
1973—Eagles, 24-23 (P)
1977—Eagles, 27-0 (P)
1978—Eagles, 17-9 (P)
(Points—Eagles 68, Jets 32)
N.Y. JETS vs. PITTSBURGH
Steelers lead series, 9-0
1970—Steelers, 21-17 (P)
1973—Steelers, 26-14 (P)
1975—Steelers, 20-7 (NY)
1977—Steelers, 23-20 (NY)
1978—Steelers, 28-17 (NY)
1981—Steelers, 38-10 (P)
1983—Steelers, 34-7 (NY)
1984—Steelers, 23-17 (NY)
1986—Steelers, 45-24 (NY)
(Points—Steelers 258, Jets 133)
N.Y. JETS vs. ST. LOUIS
Cardinals lead series, 2-1
1971—Cardinals, 17-10 (StL)
1975—Cardinals 37-6 (NY)
1978—Jets, 23-10 (NY)
(Points—Cardinals 64, Jets 39)
***N.Y. JETS vs. **SAN DIEGO**
Chargers lead series, 14-7-1
1960—Chargers, 21-7 (NY)
Chargers, 50-43 (LA)
1961—Chargers, 25-10 (NY)
Chargers, 48-13 (SD)
1962—Chargers, 40-14 (SD)
Titans, 23-3 (NY)
1963—Chargers, 24-20 (SD)
Chargers, 53-7 (NY)
1964—Tie, 17-17 (NY)
Chargers, 38-3 (SD)
1965—Chargers, 34-9 (NY)
Chargers, 38-7 (SD)
1966—Jets, 17-16 (NY)
Chargers, 42-27 (SD)
1967—Jets, 42-31 (SD)
1968—Jets, 23-20 (NY)
Jets, 37-15 (SD)
1969—Chargers, 34-27 (SD)
1971—Chargers, 49-21 (SD)
1974—Jets, 27-14 (NY)
1975—Chargers, 24-16 (SD)
1983—Jets, 41-29 (SD)
(Points—Chargers 665, Jets 451)
**Jets known as Titans prior to 1963*
***Franchise in Los Angeles prior to 1961*

N.Y. JETS vs. SAN FRANCISCO
49ers lead series, 4-1
1971—49ers, 24-21 (NY)
1976—49ers, 17-6 (SF)
1980—49ers, 37-27 (NY)
1983—Jets, 27-13 (SF)
1986—49ers, 24-10 (SF)
(Points—49ers 115, Jets 91)
N.Y. JETS vs. SEATTLE
Seahawks lead series, 7-2
1977—Seahawks, 17-0 (NY)
1978—Seahawks, 24-17 (NY)
1979—Seahawks, 30-7 (S)
1980—Seahawks, 27-17 (NY)
1981—Seahawks, 19-3 (NY)
Seahawks, 27-23 (S)
1983—Seahawks, 17-10 (NY)
1985—Jets, 17-14 (NY)
1986—Jets, 38-7 (S)
(Points—Seahawks 182, Jets 132)
N.Y. JETS vs. TAMPA BAY
Jets lead series, 3-1
1976—Jets, 34-0 (NY)
1982—Jets, 32-17 (NY)
1984—Buccaneers, 41-21 (TB)
1985—Jets, 62-28 (NY)
(Points—Jets 149, Buccaneers 86)
N.Y. JETS vs. WASHINGTON
Redskins lead series, 3-0
1972—Redskins, 35-17 (NY)
1976—Redskins, 37-16 (NY)
1978—Redskins, 23-3 (W)
(Points—Redskins 95, Jets 36)

PHILADELPHIA vs. ATLANTA
Eagles lead series, 7-6-1;
See Atlanta vs. Philadelphia
PHILADELPHIA vs. BUFFALO
Eagles lead series, 3-1;
See Buffalo vs. Philadelphia
PHILADELPHIA vs. CHICAGO
Bears lead series, 20-4-1;
See Chicago vs. Philadelphia
PHILADELPHIA vs. CINCINNATI
Bengals lead series, 4-0;
See Cincinnati vs. Philadelphia
PHILADELPHIA vs. CLEVELAND
Browns lead series, 29-11-1;
See Cleveland vs. Philadelphia
PHILADELPHIA vs. DALLAS
Cowboys lead series, 35-18;
See Dallas vs. Philadelphia
PHILADELPHIA vs. DENVER
Eagles lead series, 3-2;
See Denver vs. Philadelphia
PHILADELPHIA vs. DETROIT
Lions lead series, 12-9-2;
See Detroit vs. Philadelphia
PHILADELPHIA vs. GREEN BAY
Packers lead series, 17-5;
See Green Bay vs. Philadelphia
PHILADELPHIA vs. HOUSTON
Eagles lead series, 3-0;
See Houston vs. Philadelphia
PHILADELPHIA vs. INDIANAPOLIS
Series tied, 5-5;
See Indianapolis vs. Philadelphia
PHILADELPHIA vs. KANSAS CITY
Eagles lead series, 1-0;
See Kansas City vs. Philadelphia
PHILADELPHIA vs. L.A. RAIDERS
Raiders lead series, 3-2;
See L.A. Raiders vs. Philadelphia
PHILADELPHIA vs. L.A. RAMS
Rams lead series, 15-10-1;
See L.A. Rams vs. Philadelphia
PHILADELPHIA vs. MIAMI
Dolphins lead series, 3-2;
See Miami vs. Philadelphia
PHILADELPHIA vs. MINNESOTA
Vikings lead series, 9-4;
See Minnesota vs. Philadelphia
PHILADELPHIA vs. NEW ENGLAND
Eagles lead series, 3-2;
See New England vs. Philadelphia
PHILADELPHIA vs. NEW ORLEANS
Eagles lead series, 8-6;
See New Orleans vs. Philadelphia
PHILADELPHIA vs. N.Y. GIANTS
Giants lead series, 58-45-2;
See N.Y. Giants vs. Philadelphia
PHILADELPHIA vs. N.Y. JETS
Eagles lead series, 3-0;
See N.Y. Jets vs. Philadelphia
PHILADELPHIA vs. *PITTSBURGH
Eagles lead series, 42-25-3
1933—Eagles, 25-6 (Phila)
1934—Eagles, 17-0 (Pitt)
Pirates, 9-7 (Phila)
1935—Pirates, 17-7 (Phila)
Eagles, 17-6 (Pitt)
1936—Pirates, 17-0 (Pitt)
Pirates, 6-0 (Johnstown, Pa.)
1937—Pirates, 27-14 (Pitt)
Pirates, 16-7 (Pitt)
1938—Eagles, 27-7 (Buffalo)
Eagles, 14-7 (Charleston, W. Va.)
1939—Eagles, 17-14 (Phila)
Pirates, 24-12 (Pitt)
1940—Pirates, 7-3 (Pitt)
Eagles, 7-0 (Phila)
1941—Eagles, 10-7 (Pitt)
Tie, 7-7 (Phila)
1942—Eagles, 24-14 (Pitt)
Steelers, 14-0 (Phila)
1945—Eagles, 45-3 (Pitt)
Eagles, 30-6 (Phila)
1946—Steelers, 10-7 (Pitt)
Eagles, 10-7 (Phila)
1947—Steelers, 35-24 (Pitt)
Eagles, 21-0 (Phila)
**Eagles, 21-0 (Pitt)
1948—Eagles, 34-7 (Pitt)
Eagles, 17-0 (Phila)
1949—Eagles, 38-7 (Pitt)
Eagles, 34-17 (Phila)
1950—Eagles, 17-10 (Pitt)
Steelers, 9-7 (Phila)
1951—Eagles, 34-13 (Pitt)
Steelers, 17-13 (Phila)
1952—Eagles, 31-25 (Pitt)
Eagles, 26-21 (Phila)
1953—Eagles, 23-17 (Phila)
Eagles, 35-7 (Pitt)
1954—Eagles, 24-22 (Phila)
Steelers, 17-7 (Pitt)
1955—Steelers, 13-7 (Pitt)
Eagles, 24-0 (Phila)
1956—Eagles, 35-21 (Pitt)
Eagles, 14-7 (Phila)
1957—Steelers, 6-0 (Pitt)
Eagles, 7-6 (Phila)
1958—Steelers, 24-3 (Pitt)
Steelers, 31-24 (Phila)
1959—Eagles, 28-24 (Phila)
Steelers, 31-0 (Pitt)
1960—Eagles, 34-7 (Phila)
Steelers, 27-21 (Pitt)
1961—Eagles, 21-16 (Phila)
Eagles, 35-24 (Pitt)
1962—Steelers, 13-7 (Pitt)
Steelers, 26-17 (Phila)
1963—Tie, 21-21 (Phila)
Tie, 20-20 (Pitt)
1964—Eagles, 21-7 (Phila)
Eagles, 34-10 (Pitt)
1965—Steelers, 20-14 (Phila)
Eagles, 47-13 (Pitt)
1966—Eagles, 31-14 (Pitt)
Eagles, 27-23 (Phila)
1967—Eagles, 34-24 (Phila)
1968—Steelers, 6-3 (Pitt)
1969—Eagles, 41-27 (Phila)
1970—Eagles, 30-20 (Phila)
1974—Steelers, 27-0 (Pitt)
1979—Eagles, 17-14 (Phila)
(Points—Eagles 1,330, Steelers 967)
**Steelers known as Pirates prior to 1941*
***Division Playoff*
PHILADELPHIA vs. *ST. LOUIS
Cardinals lead series, 41-34-5
1935—Cardinals, 12-3 (C)
1936—Cardinals, 13-0 (C)
1937—Tie, 6-6 (P)
1938—Eagles, 7-0 (Erie, Pa.)
1941—Eagles, 21-14 (P)
1945—Eagles, 21-6 (P)
1947—Cardinals, 45-21 (P)
**Cardinals, 28-21 (C)
1948—Cardinals, 21-14 (C)
**Eagles, 7-0 (P)
1949—Eagles, 28-3 (P)
1950—Eagles, 45-7 (C)
Cardinals, 14-10 (P)
1951—Eagles, 17-14 (C)
1952—Eagles, 10-7 (P)
Cardinals, 28-22 (C)
1953—Eagles, 56-17 (C)
Eagles, 38-0 (P)
1954—Eagles, 35-16 (C)
Eagles, 30-14 (P)
1955—Tie, 24-24 (C)
Eagles, 27-3 (P)
1956—Cardinals, 20-6 (P)
Cardinals, 28-17 (C)
1957—Eagles, 38-21 (C)
Cardinals, 31-27 (P)
1958—Tie, 21-21 (C)
Eagles, 49-21 (P)
1959—Eagles, 28-24 (Minn)
Eagles, 27-17 (P)
1960—Eagles, 31-27 (P)
Eagles, 20-6 (StL)
1961—Cardinals, 30-27 (P)
Eagles, 20-7 (StL)
1962—Cardinals, 27-21 (P)

Cardinals, 45-35 (StL)
1963—Cardinals, 28-24 (P)
Cardinals, 38-14 (StL)
1964—Cardinals, 38-13 (P)
Cardinals, 36-34 (StL)
1965—Eagles, 34-27 (P)
Eagles, 28-24 (StL)
1966—Cardinals, 16-13 (StL)
Cardinals, 41-10 (P)
1967—Cardinals, 48-14 (StL)
1968—Cardinals, 45-17 (P)
1969—Eagles, 34-30 (StL)
1970—Cardinals, 35-20 (P)
Cardinals, 23-14 (StL)
1971—Eagles, 37-20 (StL)
Eagles, 19-7 (P)
1972—Tie, 6-6 (P)
Cardinals, 24-23 (StL)
1973—Cardinals, 34-23 (P)
Eagles, 27-24 (StL)
1974—Cardinals, 7-3 (StL)
Cardinals, 13-3 (P)
1975—Cardinals, 31-20 (StL)
Cardinals, 24-23 (P)
1976—Cardinals, 33-14 (StL)
Cardinals, 17-14 (P)
1977—Cardinals, 21-17 (P)
Cardinals, 21-16 (StL)
1978—Cardinals, 16-10 (P)
Eagles, 14-10 (StL)
1979—Eagles, 24-20 (StL)
Eagles, 16-13 (P)
1980—Cardinals, 24-14 (StL)
Eagles, 17-3 (P)
1981—Eagles, 52-10 (StL)
Eagles, 38-0 (P)
1982—Cardinals, 23-20 (P)
1983—Cardinals, 14-11 (P)
Cardinals, 31-7 (StL)
1984—Cardinals, 34-14 (P)
Cardinals, 17-16 (StL)
1985—Eagles, 30-7 (P)
Eagles, 24-14 (StL)
1986—Cardinals, 13-10 (StL)
Tie, 10-10 (P) OT
(Points—Eagles 1,671, Cardinals 1,587)
Franchise in Chicago prior to 1960
***NFL Championship*

PHILADELPHIA vs. SAN DIEGO
Series tied, 2-2
1974—Eagles, 13-7 (SD)
1980—Chargers, 22-21 (SD)
1985—Chargers, 20-14 (SD)
1986—Eagles, 23-7 (P)
(Points—Eagles 71, Chargers 56)

PHILADELPHIA vs. SAN FRANCISCO
49ers lead series, 10-4-1
1951—Eagles, 21-14 (P)
1953—49ers, 31-21 (SF)
1956—Tie, 10-10 (P)
1958—49ers, 30-24 (P)
1959—49ers, 24-14 (SF)
1964—49ers, 28-24 (P)
1966—Eagles, 35-34 (SF)
1967—49ers, 28-27 (P)
1969—49ers, 14-13 (SF)
1971—49ers, 31-3 (P)
1973—49ers, 38-28 (SF)
1975—Eagles, 27-17 (P)
1983—Eagles, 22-17 (SF)
1984—49ers, 21-9 (P)
1985—49ers, 24-13 (SF)
(Points—49ers 361, Eagles 291)

PHILADELPHIA vs. SEATTLE
Eagles lead series, 2-1
1976—Eagles, 27-10 (P)
1980—Eagles, 27-20 (S)
1986—Seahawks, 24-20 (S)
(Points—Eagles 74, Seahawks 54)

PHILADELPHIA vs. TAMPA BAY
Eagles lead series, 2-1
1977—Eagles, 13-3 (P)
1979—*Buccaneers, 24-17 (TB)
1981—Eagles, 20-10 (P)
(Points—Eagles 50, Buccaneers 37)
**NFC Divisional Playoff*

PHILADELPHIA vs. *WASHINGTON
Redskins lead series, 59-39-5
1934—Redskins, 6-0 (B)
Redskins, 14-7 (P)
1935—Eagles, 7-6 (B)
1936—Redskins, 26-3 (P)
Redskins, 17-7 (B)
1937—Eagles, 14-0 (W)
Redskins, 10-7 (P)
1938—Redskins, 26-23 (P)
Redskins, 20-14 (W)
1939—Redskins, 7-0 (P)
Redskins, 7-6 (W)
1940—Redskins, 34-17 (P)
Redskins, 13-6 (W)
1941—Redskins, 21-17 (P)
Redskins, 20-14 (W)
1942—Redskins, 14-10 (P)
Redskins, 30-27 (W)
1944—Tie, 31-31 (P)
Eagles, 37-7 (W)
1945—Redskins, 24-14 (W)
Eagles, 16-0 (P)
1946—Eagles, 28-24 (W)
Redskins, 27-10 (P)
1947—Eagles, 45-42 (P)
Eagles, 38-14 (W)
1948—Eagles, 45-0 (W)
Eagles, 42-21 (P)
1949—Eagles, 49-14 (P)
Eagles, 44-21 (W)
1950—Eagles, 35-3 (P)
Eagles, 33-0 (W)
1951—Redskins, 27-23 (P)
Eagles, 35-21 (W)
1952—Eagles, 38-20 (P)
Redskins, 27-21 (W)
1953—Tie, 21-21 (P)
Redskins, 10-0 (W)
1954—Eagles, 49-21 (W)
Eagles, 41-33 (P)
1955—Redskins, 31-30 (P)
Redskins, 34-21 (W)
1956—Eagles, 13-9 (P)
Redskins, 19-17 (W)
1957—Eagles, 21-12 (P)
Redskins, 42-7 (W)
1958—Redskins, 24-14 (P)
Redskins, 20-0 (W)
1959—Eagles, 30-23 (P)
Eagles, 34-14 (W)
1960—Eagles, 19-13 (P)
Eagles, 38-28 (W)
1961—Eagles, 14-7 (P)
Eagles, 27-24 (W)
1962—Redskins, 27-21 (P)
Eagles, 37-14 (W)
1963—Eagles, 37-24 (W)
Redskins, 13-10 (P)
1964—Redskins, 35-20 (W)
Redskins, 21-10 (P)
1965—Redskins, 23-21 (W)
Eagles, 21-14 (P)
1966—Redskins, 27-13 (P)
Eagles, 37-28 (W)
1967—Eagles, 35-24 (P)
Tie, 35-35 (W)
1968—Redskins, 17-14 (W)
Redskins, 16-10 (P)
1969—Tie, 28-28 (W)
Redskins, 34-29 (P)
1970—Redskins, 33-21 (P)
Redskins, 24-6 (W)
1971—Tie, 7-7 (W)
Redskins, 20-13 (P)
1972—Redskins, 14-0 (W)
Redskins, 23-7 (P)
1973—Redskins, 28-7 (P)
Redskins, 38-20 (W)
1974—Redskins, 27-20 (P)
Redskins, 26-7 (W)
1975—Eagles, 26-10 (P)
Eagles, 26-3 (W)
1976—Redskins, 20-17 (P) OT
Redskins, 24-0 (W)
1977—Redskins, 23-17 (W)
Redskins, 17-14 (P)
1978—Redskins, 35-30 (W)
Eagles, 17-10 (P)
1979—Eagles, 28-17 (P)
Redskins, 17-7 (W)
1980—Eagles, 24-14 (P)
Eagles, 24-0 (W)
1981—Eagles, 36-13 (P)
Redskins, 15-13 (W)
1982—Redskins, 37-34 (P) OT
Redskins, 13-9 (W)
1983—Redskins, 23-13 (P)
Redskins, 28-24 (W)
1984—Redskins, 20-0 (W)
Eagles, 16-10 (P)
1985—Eagles, 19-6 (W)
Redskins, 17-12 (P)
1986—Redskins, 41-14 (W)
Redskins, 21-14 (P)
(Points—Eagles 2,079, Redskins 2,033)
**Franchise in Boston prior to 1937*

PITTSBURGH vs. ATLANTA
Steelers lead series, 6-1;
See Atlanta vs. Pittsburgh

PITTSBURGH vs. BUFFALO
Steelers lead series, 6-4;
See Buffalo vs. Pittsburgh

PITTSBURGH vs. CHICAGO
Bears lead series, 14-4-1;
See Chicago vs. Pittsburgh

PITTSBURGH vs. CINCINNATI
Steelers lead series, 18-15;
See Cincinnati vs. Pittsburgh

PITTSBURGH vs. CLEVELAND
Browns lead series, 43-31;
See Cleveland vs. Pittsburgh

PITTSBURGH vs. DALLAS
Steelers lead series, 12-11;
See Dallas vs. Pittsburgh

PITTSBURGH vs. DENVER
Broncos lead series, 8-5-1;
See Denver vs. Pittsburgh

PITTSBURGH vs. DETROIT
Lions lead series, 13-9-1;
See Detroit vs. Pittsburgh

PITTSBURGH vs. GREEN BAY
Packers lead series, 16-11;
See Green Bay vs. Pittsburgh

PITTSBURGH vs. HOUSTON
Steelers lead series, 26-9;
See Houston vs. Pittsburgh

PITTSBURGH vs. INDIANAPOLIS
Steelers lead series, 9-4;
See Indianapolis vs. Pittsburgh

PITTSBURGH vs. KANSAS CITY
Steelers lead series, 9-5;
See Kansas City vs. Pittsburgh

PITTSBURGH vs. L.A. RAIDERS
Raiders lead series, 9-6;
See L.A. Raiders vs. Pittsburgh

PITTSBURGH vs. L.A. RAMS
Rams lead series, 12-4-2;
See L.A. Rams vs. Pittsburgh

PITTSBURGH vs. MIAMI
Dolphins lead series, 7-3;
See Miami vs. Pittsburgh

PITTSBURGH vs. MINNESOTA
Vikings lead series, 6-4;
See Minnesota vs. Pittsburgh

PITTSBURGH vs. NEW ENGLAND
Steelers lead series, 5-3;
See New England vs. Pittsburgh

PITTSBURGH vs. NEW ORLEANS
Series tied, 4-4;
See New Orleans vs. Pittsburgh

PITTSBURGH vs. N.Y. GIANTS
Giants lead series, 41-26-3;
See N.Y. Giants vs. Pittsburgh

PITTSBURGH vs. N.Y. JETS
Steelers lead series, 9-0;
See N.Y. Jets vs. Pittsburgh

PITTSBURGH vs. PHILADELPHIA
Eagles lead series, 42-25-3;
See Philadelphia vs. Pittsburgh

***PITTSBURGH vs. **ST. LOUIS**
Steelers lead series, 29-20-3
1933—Pirates, 14-13 (C)
1935—Pirates, 17-13 (P)
1936—Cardinals, 14-6 (C)
1937—Cardinals, 13-7 (P)
1939—Cardinals, 10-0 (P)
1940—Tie, 7-7 (P)
1942—Steelers, 19-3 (P)
1945—Steelers, 23-0 (P)
1946—Steelers, 14-7 (P)
1948—Cardinals, 24-7 (P)
1950—Steelers, 28-17 (C)
Steelers, 28-7 (P)
1951—Steelers, 28-14 (C)
1952—Steelers, 34-28 (C)
Steelers, 17-14 (P)
1953—Steelers, 31-28 (P)
Steelers, 21-17 (C)
1954—Cardinals, 17-14 (C)
Steelers, 20-17 (P)
1955—Steelers, 14-7 (P)
Cardinals, 27-13 (C)
1956—Steelers, 14-7 (P)
Cardinals, 38-27 (C)
1957—Steelers, 29-20 (P)
Steelers, 27-2 (C)
1958—Steelers, 27-20 (C)
Steelers, 38-21 (P)
1959—Cardinals, 45-24 (C)
Steelers, 35-20 (P)
1960—Steelers, 27-14 (P)
Cardinals, 38-7 (StL)
1961—Steelers, 30-27 (P)
Cardinals, 20-0 (StL)
1962—Steelers, 26-17 (StL)
Steelers, 19-7 (P)
1963—Steelers, 23-10 (P)
Cardinals, 24-23 (StL)
1964—Cardinals, 34-30 (StL)
Cardinals, 21-20 (P)
1965—Cardinals, 20-7 (P)
Cardinals, 21-17 (P)
1966—Steelers, 30-9 (P)
Cardinals, 6-3 (StL)
1967—Cardinals, 28-14 (P)
Tie, 14-14 (StL)
1968—Tie, 28-28 (StL)
Cardinals, 20-10 (P)
1969—Cardinals, 27-14 (P)
Cardinals, 47-10 (StL)
1972—Steelers, 25-19 (StL)
1979—Steelers, 24-21 (StL)
1985—Steelers, 23-10 (P)
(Points—Steelers 1,007, Cardinals 952)
**Steelers known as Pirates prior to 1941*
***Franchise in Chicago prior to 1960*

PITTSBURGH vs. SAN DIEGO
Steelers lead series, 8-4
1971—Steelers, 21-17 (P)
1972—Steelers, 24-2 (SD)
1973—Steelers, 38-21 (P)
1975—Steelers, 37-0 (SD)
1976—Steelers, 23-0 (P)
1977—Steelers, 10-9 (SD)
1979—Chargers, 35-7 (SD)
1980—Chargers, 26-17 (SD)
1982—*Chargers, 31-28 (P)
1983—Steelers, 26-3 (P)
1984—Steelers, 52-24 (P)
1985—Chargers, 54-44 (SD)
(Points—Steelers 327, Chargers 222)
**AFC First Round Playoff*

PITTSBURGH vs. SAN FRANCISCO
Series tied, 6-6
1951—49ers, 28-24 (P)
1952—Steelers, 24-7 (SF)
1954—49ers, 31-3 (SF)
1958—49ers, 23-20 (SF)
1961—Steelers, 20-10 (P)
1965—49ers, 27-17 (SF)
1968—49ers, 45-28 (P)
1973—Steelers, 37-14 (SF)
1977—Steelers, 27-0 (P)
1978—Steelers, 24-7 (SF)
1981—49ers, 17-14 (P)
1984—Steelers, 20-17 (SF)
(Points—Steelers 258, 49ers 226)

PITTSBURGH vs. SEATTLE
Series tied, 3-3
1977—Steelers, 30-20 (P)
1978—Steelers, 21-10 (P)
1981—Seahawks, 24-21 (S)
1982—Seahawks, 16-0 (S)
1983—Steelers, 27-21 (S)
1986—Seahawks, 30-0 (S)
(Points—Seahawks 121, Steelers 99)

PITTSBURGH vs. TAMPA BAY
Steelers lead series, 3-0
1976—Steelers, 42-0 (P)
1980—Steelers, 24-21 (TB)
1983—Steelers, 17-12 (P)
(Points—Steelers 83, Buccaneers 33)

***PITTSBURGH vs. **WASHINGTON**
Redskins lead series, 40-27-3
1933—Redskins, 21-6 (P)
Pirates, 16-14 (B)
1934—Redskins, 7-0 (P)
Redskins, 39-0 (B)
1935—Pirates, 6-0 (P)
Redskins, 13-3 (B)
1936—Pirates, 10-0 (P)
Redskins, 30-0 (B)
1937—Redskins, 34-20 (W)
Pirates, 21-13 (P)
1938—Redskins, 7-0 (P)
Redskins, 15-0 (W)
1939—Redskins, 44-14 (W)
Redskins, 21-14 (P)
1940—Redskins, 40-10 (P)
Redskins, 37-10 (W)
1941—Redskins, 24-20 (P)
Redskins, 23-3 (W)
1942—Redskins, 28-14 (W)
Redskins, 14-0 (P)
1945—Redskins, 14-0 (P)
Redskins, 24-0 (W)
1946—Tie, 14-14 (W)
Steelers, 14-7 (P)
1947—Redskins, 27-26 (W)
Steelers, 21-14 (P)
1948—Redskins, 17-14 (W)
Steelers, 10-7 (P)
1949—Redskins, 27-14 (P)
Redskins, 27-14 (W)
1950—Steelers, 26-7 (W)
Redskins, 24-7 (P)
1951—Redskins, 22-7 (P)
Steelers, 20-10 (W)
1952—Redskins, 28-24 (P)
Steelers, 24-23 (W)
1953—Redskins, 17-9 (P)
Steelers, 14-13 (W)
1954—Steelers, 37-7 (P)
Redskins, 17-14 (W)
1955—Redskins, 23-14 (P)
Redskins, 28-17 (W)
1956—Steelers, 30-13 (P)
Steelers, 23-0 (W)
1957—Steelers, 28-7 (P)
Redskins, 10-3 (W)
1958—Steelers, 24-16 (P)
Tie, 14-14 (W)
1959—Redskins, 23-17 (P)
Steelers, 27-6 (W)

1960—Tie, 27-27 (W)
Steelers, 22-10 (P)
1961—Steelers, 20-0 (P)
Steelers, 30-14 (P)
1962—Steelers, 23-21 (P)
Steelers, 27-24 (W)
1963—Steelers, 38-27 (P)
Steelers, 34-28 (W)
1964—Redskins, 30-0 (P)
Steelers, 14-7 (W)
1965—Redskins, 31-3 (P)
Redskins, 35-14 (W)
1966—Redskins, 33-27 (P)
Redskins, 24-10 (W)
1967—Redskins, 15-10 (P)
1968—Redskins, 16-13 (W)
1969—Redskins, 14-7 (P)
1973—Steelers, 21-16 (P)
1979—Steelers, 38-7 (P)
1985—Redskins, 30-23 (P)
(Points—Redskins 1,319, Steelers 1,074)
Steelers known as Pirates prior to 1941
***Franchise in Boston prior to 1937*

ST. LOUIS vs. ATLANTA
Cardinals lead series, 6-4;
See Atlanta vs. St. Louis
ST. LOUIS vs. BUFFALO
Cardinals lead series, 3-2;
See Buffalo vs. St. Louis
ST. LOUIS vs. CHICAGO
Bears lead series, 50-25-6;
See Chicago vs. St. Louis
ST. LOUIS vs. CINCINNATI
Bengals lead series, 2-1;
See Cincinnati vs. St. Louis
ST. LOUIS vs. CLEVELAND
Browns lead series, 30-10-3;
See Cleveland vs. St. Louis
ST. LOUIS vs. DALLAS
Cowboys lead series, 31-17-1;
See Dallas vs. St. Louis
ST. LOUIS vs. DENVER
Broncos lead series, 1-0-1;
See Denver vs. St. Louis
ST. LOUIS vs. DETROIT
Lions lead series, 25-15-5;
See Detroit vs. St. Louis
ST. LOUIS vs. GREEN BAY
Packers lead series, 38-21-4;
See Green Bay vs. St. Louis
ST. LOUIS vs. HOUSTON
Cardinals lead series, 3-1;
See Houston vs. St. Louis
ST. LOUIS vs. INDIANAPOLIS
Cardinals lead series, 5-4;
See Indianapolis vs. St. Louis
ST. LOUIS vs. KANSAS CITY
Chiefs lead series, 3-1-1;
See Kansas City vs. St. Louis
ST. LOUIS vs. L.A. RAIDERS
Series tied, 1-1;
See L.A. Raiders vs. St. Louis
ST. LOUIS vs. L.A. RAMS
Rams lead series, 21-15-2;
See L.A. Rams vs. St. Louis
ST. LOUIS vs. MIAMI
Dolphins lead series, 5-0;
See Miami vs. St. Louis
ST. LOUIS vs. MINNESOTA
Cardinals lead series, 7-3;
See Minnesota vs. St. Louis
ST. LOUIS vs. NEW ENGLAND
Cardinals lead series, 4-1;
See New England vs. St. Louis
ST. LOUIS vs. NEW ORLEANS
Cardinals lead series, 9-5;
See New Orleans vs. St. Louis
ST. LOUIS vs. N.Y. GIANTS
Giants lead series, 55-31-2;
See N.Y. Giants vs. St. Louis
ST. LOUIS vs. N.Y. JETS
Cardinals lead series, 2-1;
See N.Y. Jets vs. St. Louis
ST. LOUIS vs. PHILADELPHIA
Cardinals lead series, 41-34-5;
See Philadelphia vs. St. Louis
ST. LOUIS vs. PITTSBURGH
Steelers lead series, 29-20-3;
See Pittsburgh vs. St. Louis
ST. LOUIS vs. SAN DIEGO
Chargers lead series, 2-1;
1971—Chargers, 20-17 (SD)
1976—Chargers, 43-24 (SD)
1983—Cardinals, 44-14 (StL)
(Points—Cardinals 85, Chargers 77)
***ST. LOUIS vs. SAN FRANCISCO**
Series tied, 7-7
1951—Cardinals, 27-21 (SF)
1957—Cardinals, 20-10 (SF)
1962—49ers, 24-17 (StL)
1964—Cardinals, 23-13 (SF)
1968—49ers, 35-17 (SF)
1971—49ers, 26-14 (StL)
1974—Cardinals, 34-9 (SF)
1976—Cardinals, 23-20 (StL) OT
1978—Cardinals, 16-10 (SF)
1979—Cardinals, 13-10 (StL)
1980—49ers, 24-21 (SF) OT
1982—49ers, 31-20 (StL)
1983—49ers, 42-27 (StL)
1986—49ers, 43-17 (SF)
(Points—49ers 318, Cardinals 289)
**Team in Chicago prior to 1960*
ST. LOUIS vs. SEATTLE
Cardinals lead series, 2-0
1976—Cardinals, 30-24 (S)
1983—Cardinals, 33-28 (StL)
(Points—Cardinals 63, Seahawks 52)
ST. LOUIS vs. TAMPA BAY
Series tied, 3-3
1977—Buccaneers, 17-7 (TB)
1981—Buccaneers, 20-10 (TB)
1983—Cardinals, 34-27 (TB)
1985—Buccaneers, 16-0 (TB)
1986—Cardinals, 30-19 (TB)
Cardinals, 21-17 (StL)
(Points—Buccaneers 116, Cardinals 102)
***ST. LOUIS vs. **WASHINGTON**
Redskins lead series, 51-32-2
1932—Cardinals, 9-0 (B)
Braves, 8-6 (C)
1933—Redskins, 10-0 (C)
Tie, 0-0 (B)
1934—Redskins, 9-0 (B)
1935—Cardinals, 6-0 (B)
1936—Redskins, 13-10 (B)
1937—Cardinals, 21-14 (W)
1939—Redskins, 28-7 (W)
1940—Redskins, 28-21 (W)
1942—Redskins, 28-0 (W)
1943—Redskins, 13-7 (W)
1945—Redskins, 24-21 (W)
1947—Redskins, 45-21 (W)
1949—Cardinals, 38-7 (C)
1950—Cardinals, 38-28 (W)
1951—Redskins, 7-3 (C)
Redskins, 20-17 (W)
1952—Redskins, 23-7 (C)
Cardinals, 17-6 (W)
1953—Redskins, 24-13 (C)
Redskins, 28-17 (W)
1954—Cardinals, 38-16 (C)
Redskins, 37-20 (W)
1955—Cardinals, 24-10 (W)
Redskins, 31-0 (C)
1956—Cardinals, 31-3 (W)
Redskins, 17-14 (C)
1957—Redskins, 37-14 (C)
Cardinals, 44-14 (W)
1958—Cardinals, 37-10 (C)
Redskins, 45-31 (W)
1959—Cardinals, 49-21 (C)
Redskins, 23-14 (W)
1960—Cardinals, 44-7 (StL)
Cardinals, 26-14 (W)
1961—Cardinals, 24-0 (W)
Cardinals, 38-24 (StL)
1962—Redskins, 24-14 (W)
Tie, 17-17 (StL)
1963—Cardinals, 21-7 (W)
Cardinals, 24-20 (StL)
1964—Cardinals, 23-17 (W)
Cardinals, 38-24 (StL)
1965—Cardinals, 37-16 (W)
Redskins, 24-20 (StL)
1966—Cardinals, 23-7 (StL)
Redskins, 26-20 (W)
1967—Cardinals, 27-21 (W)
1968—Cardinals, 41-14 (StL)
1969—Redskins, 33-17 (W)
1970—Cardinals, 27-17 (StL)
Redskins, 28-27 (W)
1971—Redskins, 24-17 (StL)
Redskins, 20-0 (W)
1972—Redskins, 24-10 (W)
Redskins, 33-3 (StL)
1973—Cardinals, 34-27 (StL)
Redskins, 31-13 (W)
1974—Cardinals, 17-10 (W)
Cardinals, 23-20 (StL)
1975—Redskins, 27-17 (W)
Cardinals, 20-17 (StL) OT
1976—Redskins, 20-10 (W)
Redskins, 16-10 (StL)
1977—Redskins, 24-14 (W)
Redskins, 26-20 (StL)
1978—Redskins, 28-10 (StL)
Cardinals, 27-17 (W)
1979—Redskins, 17-7 (StL)
Redskins, 30-28 (W)
1980—Redskins, 23-0 (W)
Redskins, 31-7 (StL)
1981—Cardinals, 40-30 (StL)
Redskins, 42-21 (W)
1982—Redskins, 12-7 (StL)
Redskins, 28-0 (W)
1983—Redskins, 38-14 (StL)
Redskins, 45-7 (W)
1984—Cardinals, 26-24 (StL)
Redskins, 29-27 (W)
1985—Redskins, 27-10 (W)
Redskins, 27-16 (StL)
1986—Redskins, 28-21 (W)
Redskins, 20-17 (StL)
(Points—Redskins 1,782, Cardinals 1,596)
**Team in Chicago prior to 1960*
***Team in Boston prior to 1937 and known as Braves prior to 1933*

SAN DIEGO vs. ATLANTA
Falcons lead series, 2-0;
See Atlanta vs. San Diego
SAN DIEGO vs. BUFFALO
Chargers lead series, 17-9-2;
See Buffalo vs. San Diego
SAN DIEGO vs. CHICAGO
Chargers lead series, 4-1;
See Chicago vs. San Diego
SAN DIEGO vs. CINCINNATI
Chargers lead series, 10-7;
See Cincinnati vs. San Diego
SAN DIEGO vs. CLEVELAND
Series tied, 5-5-1;
See Cleveland vs. San Diego
SAN DIEGO vs. DALLAS
Cowboys lead series, 3-1;
See Dallas vs. San Diego
SAN DIEGO vs. DENVER
Chargers lead series, 28-25-1;
See Denver vs. San Diego
SAN DIEGO vs. DETROIT
Lions lead series, 3-2;
See Detroit vs. San Diego
SAN DIEGO vs. GREEN BAY
Packers lead series, 3-1;
See Green Bay vs. San Diego
SAN DIEGO vs. HOUSTON
Chargers lead series, 17-12-1;
See Houston vs. San Diego
SAN DIEGO vs. INDIANAPOLIS
Chargers lead series, 5-2;
See Indianapolis vs. San Diego
SAN DIEGO vs. KANSAS CITY
Series tied, 26-26-1;
See Kansas City vs. San Diego
SAN DIEGO vs. L.A. RAIDERS
Raiders lead series, 35-18-2;
See L.A. Raiders vs. San Diego
SAN DIEGO vs. L.A. RAMS
Rams lead series, 2-1;
See L.A. Rams vs. San Diego
SAN DIEGO vs. MIAMI
Chargers lead series, 9-5;
See Miami vs. San Diego
SAN DIEGO vs. MINNESOTA
Series tied, 3-3;
See Minnesota vs. San Diego
SAN DIEGO vs. NEW ENGLAND
Patriots lead series, 13-12-2;
See New England vs. San Diego
SAN DIEGO vs. NEW ORLEANS
Chargers lead series, 3-0;
See New Orleans vs. San Diego
SAN DIEGO vs. N.Y. GIANTS
Giants lead series, 3-2;
See N.Y. Giants vs. San Diego
SAN DIEGO vs. N.Y. JETS
Chargers lead series, 14-7-1;
See N.Y. Jets vs. San Diego
SAN DIEGO vs. PHILADELPHIA
Series tied, 2-2;
See Philadelphia vs. San Diego
SAN DIEGO vs. PITTSBURGH
Steelers lead series, 8-4;
See Pittsburgh vs. San Diego
SAN DIEGO vs. ST. LOUIS
Chargers lead series, 2-1;
See St. Louis vs. San Diego
SAN DIEGO vs. SAN FRANCISCO
Chargers lead series, 3-1
1972—49ers, 34-3 (SF)
1976—Chargers, 13-7 (SD) OT
1979—Chargers, 31-9 (SD)
1982—Chargers, 41-37 (SF)
(Points—Chargers, 88, 49ers 87)
SAN DIEGO vs. SEATTLE
Chargers lead series, 9-8
1977—Chargers, 30-28 (S)
1978—Chargers, 24-20 (S)
Chargers, 37-10 (SD)
1979—Chargers, 33-16 (S)
Chargers, 20-10 (SD)
1980—Chargers, 34-13 (S)
Chargers, 21-14 (SD)
1981—Chargers, 24-10 (SD)
Seahawks, 44-23 (S)
1983—Seahawks, 34-31 (S)
Chargers, 28-21 (SD)
1984—Seahawks, 31-17 (S)
Seahawks, 24-0 (SD)
1985—Seahawks, 49-35 (SD)
Seahawks, 26-21 (S)
1986—Seahawks, 33-7 (S)
Seahawks, 34-24 (SD)
(Points—Seahawks 417, Chargers 409)
SAN DIEGO vs. TAMPA BAY
Chargers lead series, 2-0
1976—Chargers, 23-0 (TB)
1981—Chargers, 24-23 (TB)
(Points—Chargers 47, Buccaneers 23)
SAN DIEGO vs. WASHINGTON
Redskins lead series, 4-0
1973—Redskins, 38-0 (W)
1980—Redskins, 40-17 (W)
1983—Redskins, 27-24 (SD)
1986—Redskins, 30-27 (SD)
(Points—Redskins 135, Chargers 68)

SAN FRANCISCO vs. ATLANTA
49ers lead series, 22-17-1;
See Atlanta vs. San Francisco
SAN FRANCISCO vs. BUFFALO
Bills lead series, 2-1;
See Buffalo vs. San Francisco
SAN FRANCISCO vs. CHICAGO
Bears lead series, 24-23-1;
See Chicago vs. San Francisco
SAN FRANCISCO vs. CINCINNATI
49ers lead series, 4-1;
See Cincinnati vs. San Francisco
SAN FRANCISCO vs. CLEVELAND
Browns lead series, 8-4;
See Cleveland vs. San Francisco
SAN FRANCISCO vs. DALLAS
Series tied, 8-8-1;
See Dallas vs. San Francisco
SAN FRANCISCO vs. DENVER
Broncos lead series, 3-2;
See Denver vs. San Francisco
SAN FRANCISCO vs. DETROIT
Lions lead series, 26-23-1;
See Detroit vs. San Francisco
SAN FRANCISCO vs. GREEN BAY
49ers lead series, 23-20-1;
See Green Bay vs. San Francisco
SAN FRANCISCO vs. HOUSTON
49ers lead series, 3-2;
See Houston vs. San Francisco
SAN FRANCISCO vs. INDIANAPOLIS
Colts lead series, 21-15;
See Indianapolis vs. San Francisco
SAN FRANCISCO vs. KANSAS CITY
49ers lead series, 3-1;
See Kansas City vs. San Francisco
SAN FRANCISCO vs. L.A RAIDERS
Raiders lead series, 3-2;
See L.A. Raiders vs. San Francisco
SAN FRANCISCO vs. L.A. RAMS
Rams lead series, 45-27-2;
See L.A. Rams vs. San Francisco
SAN FRANCISCO vs. MIAMI
Dolphins lead series, 4-2;
See Miami vs. San Francisco
SAN FRANCISCO vs. MINNESOTA
Vikings lead series, 14-12-1;
See Minnesota vs. San Francisco
SAN FRANCISCO vs. NEW ENGLAND
49ers lead series, 4-1;
See New England vs. San Francisco
SAN FRANCISCO vs. NEW ORLEANS
49ers lead series, 23-10-2;
See New Orleans vs. San Francisco
SAN FRANCISCO vs. N.Y. GIANTS
Giants lead series, 12-7;
See N.Y. Giants vs. San Francisco
SAN FRANCISCO vs. N.Y. JETS
49ers lead series, 4-1;
See N.Y. Jets vs. San Francisco
SAN FRANCISCO vs. PHILADELPHIA
49ers lead series, 10-4-1;
See Philadelphia vs. San Francisco
SAN FRANCISCO vs. PITTSBURGH
Series tied, 6-6;
See Pittsburgh vs. San Francisco
SAN FRANCISCO vs. ST. LOUIS
Series tied, 7-7;
See St. Louis vs. San Francisco
SAN FRANCISCO vs. SAN DIEGO
Chargers lead series, 3-1;
See San Diego vs. San Francisco
SAN FRANCISCO vs. SEATTLE
49ers lead series, 2-1
1976—49ers, 37-21 (S)
1979—Seahawks, 35-24 (SF)
1985—49ers, 19-6 (SF)
(Points—49ers 80, Seahawks 62)
SAN FRANCISCO vs. TAMPA BAY
49ers lead series, 6-1
1977—49ers, 20-10 (SF)
1978—49ers, 6-3 (SF)
1979—49ers, 23-7 (SF)

1980—Buccaneers, 24-23 (SF)
1983—49ers, 35-21 (SF)
1984—49ers, 24-17 (SF)
1986—49ers, 31-7 (TB)
(Points—49ers 162, Buccaneers 89)
SAN FRANCISCO vs. WASHINGTON
49ers lead series, 8-7-1
1952—49ers, 23-17 (W)
1954—49ers, 41-7 (SF)
1955—Redskins, 7-0 (W)
1961—49ers, 35-3 (SF)
1967—Redskins, 31-28 (W)
1969—Tie, 17-17 (SF)
1970—49ers, 26-17 (SF)
1971—*49ers, 24-20 (SF)
1973—Redskins, 33-9 (W)
1976—Redskins, 24-21 (SF)
1978—Redskins, 38-20 (W)
1981—49ers, 30-17 (W)
1983—**Redskins, 24-21 (W)
1984—49ers, 37-31 (SF)
1985—49ers, 35-8 (W)
1986—Redskins, 14-6 (W)
(Points—49ers 373, Redskins 308)
**NFC Divisional Playoff*
***NFC Championship*

SEATTLE vs. ATLANTA
Seahawks lead series, 3-0;
See Atlanta vs. Seattle
SEATTLE vs. BUFFALO
Seahawks lead series, 2-0;
See Buffalo vs. Seattle
SEATTLE vs. CHICAGO
Seahawks lead series, 3-1;
See Chicago vs. Seattle
SEATTLE vs. CINCINNATI
Bengals lead series, 4-2;
See Cincinnati vs. Seattle
SEATTLE vs. CLEVELAND
Seahawks lead series, 7-2;
See Cleveland vs. Seattle
SEATTLE vs. DALLAS
Cowboys lead series, 3-1;
See Dallas vs. Seattle
SEATTLE vs. DENVER
Broncos lead series, 12-8;
See Denver vs. Seattle
SEATTLE vs. DETROIT
Seahawks lead series, 2-1;
See Detroit vs. Seattle
SEATTLE vs. GREEN BAY
Packers lead series, 3-1;
See Green Bay vs. Seattle
SEATTLE vs. HOUSTON
Oilers lead series, 3-2;
See Houston vs. Seattle
SEATTLE vs. INDIANAPOLIS
Colts lead series, 2-0;
See Indianapolis vs. Seattle
SEATTLE vs. KANSAS CITY
Chiefs lead series, 9-8;
See Kansas City vs. Seattle
SEATTLE vs. L.A. RAIDERS
Series tied, 10-10;
See L.A. Raiders vs. Seattle
SEATTLE vs. L.A. RAMS
Rams lead series, 3-0;
See L.A. Rams vs. Seattle
SEATTLE vs. MIAMI
Dolphins lead series, 3-1;
See Miami vs. Seattle
SEATTLE vs. MINNESOTA
Seahawks lead series, 2-1;
See Minnesota vs. Seattle
SEATTLE vs. NEW ENGLAND
Patriots lead series, 5-2;
See New England vs. Seattle
SEATTLE vs. NEW ORLEANS
Seahawks lead series, 2-1;
See New Orleans vs. Seattle
SEATTLE vs. N.Y. GIANTS
Giants lead series, 3-2;
See N.Y. Giants vs. Seattle
SEATTLE vs. N.Y. JETS
Seahawks lead series, 7-2;
See N.Y. Jets vs. Seattle
SEATTLE vs. PHILADELPHIA
Eagles lead series, 2-1;
See Philadelphia vs. Seattle
SEATTLE vs. PITTSBURGH
Series tied, 3-3;
See Pittsburgh vs. Seattle
SEATTLE vs. ST. LOUIS
Cardinals lead series, 2-0;
See St. Louis vs. Seattle
SEATTLE vs. SAN DIEGO
Chargers lead series, 9-8;
See San Diego vs. Seattle
SEATTLE vs. SAN FRANCISCO
49ers lead series, 2-1;
See San Francisco vs. Seattle
SEATTLE vs. TAMPA BAY
Seahawks lead series, 2-0
1976—Seahawks, 13-10 (TB)
1977—Seahawks, 30-23 (S)
(Points—Seahawks 43, Buccaneers 33)
SEATTLE vs. WASHINGTON
Redskins lead series, 3-1
1976—Redskins, 31-7 (W)
1980—Seahawks, 14-0 (W)
1983—Redskins, 27-17 (S)
1986—Redskins, 19-14 (W)
(Points—Redskins 77, Seahawks 52)

TAMPA BAY vs. ATLANTA
Series tied, 3-3;
See Atlanta vs. Tampa Bay
TAMPA BAY vs. BUFFALO
Buccaneers lead series, 3-1;
See Buffalo vs. Tampa Bay
TAMPA BAY vs. CHICAGO
Bears lead series, 14-4;
See Chicago vs. Tampa Bay
TAMPA BAY vs. CINCINNATI
Bengals lead series, 2-1;
See Cincinnati vs. Tampa Bay
TAMPA BAY vs. CLEVELAND
Browns lead series, 3-0;
See Cleveland vs. Tampa Bay
TAMPA BAY vs. DALLAS
Cowboys lead series, 6-0;
See Dallas vs. Tampa Bay
TAMPA BAY vs. DENVER
Broncos lead series, 2-0;
See Denver vs. Tampa Bay
TAMPA BAY vs. DETROIT
Lions lead series, 10-8;
See Detroit vs. Tampa Bay
TAMPA BAY vs. GREEN BAY
Packers lead series, 10-6-1;
See Green Bay vs. Tampa Bay
TAMPA BAY vs. HOUSTON
Oilers lead series, 2-1;
See Houston vs. Tampa Bay
TAMPA BAY vs. INDIANAPOLIS
Colts lead series, 2-1;
See Indianapolis vs. Tampa Bay
TAMPA BAY vs. KANSAS CITY
Chiefs lead series, 4-2;
See Kansas City vs. Tampa Bay
TAMPA BAY vs. L.A RAIDERS
Raiders lead series, 2-0;
See L.A. Raiders vs. Tampa Bay
TAMPA BAY vs. L.A. RAMS
Rams lead series, 6-2;
See L.A. Rams vs. Tampa Bay
TAMPA BAY vs. MIAMI
Dolphins lead series, 2-1;
See Miami vs. Tampa Bay
TAMPA BAY vs. MINNESOTA
Vikings lead series, 13-5;
See Minnesota vs. Tampa Bay
TAMPA BAY vs. NEW ENGLAND
Patriots lead series, 2-0;
See New England vs. Tampa Bay
TAMPA BAY vs. NEW ORLEANS
Saints lead series, 6-3;
See New Orleans vs. Tampa Bay
TAMPA BAY vs. N.Y. GIANTS
Giants lead series, 6-3;
See N.Y. Giants vs. Tampa Bay
TAMPA BAY vs. N.Y. JETS
Jets lead series, 3-1;
See N.Y. Jets vs. Tampa Bay
TAMPA BAY vs. PHILADELPHIA
Eagles lead series, 2-1;
See Philadelphia vs. Tampa Bay
TAMPA BAY vs. PITTSBURGH
Steelers lead series, 3-0;
See Pittsburgh vs. Tampa Bay
TAMPA BAY vs. ST. LOUIS
Series tied, 3-3;
See St. Louis vs. Tampa Bay
TAMPA BAY vs. SAN DIEGO
Chargers lead series, 2-0;
See San Diego vs. Tampa Bay
TAMPA BAY vs. SAN FRANCISCO
49ers lead series, 6-1;
See San Francisco vs. Tampa Bay
TAMPA BAY vs. SEATTLE
Seahawks lead series, 2-0;
See Seattle vs. Tampa Bay
TAMPA BAY vs. WASHINGTON
Redskins lead series, 2-0
1977—Redskins, 10-0 (TB)
1982—Redskins, 21-13 (TB)
(Points—Redskins 31, Buccaneers 13)

WASHINGTON vs. ATLANTA
Redskins lead series, 9-2-1;
See Atlanta vs. Washington
WASHINGTON vs. BUFFALO
Series tied 2-2;
See Buffalo vs. Washington
WASHINGTON vs. CHICAGO
Bears lead series, 20-12-1;
See Chicago vs. Washington
WASHINGTON vs. CINCINNATI
Redskins lead series, 3-1;
See Cincinnati vs. Washington
WASHINGTON vs. CLEVELAND
Browns lead series, 31-8-1;
See Cleveland vs. Washington
WASHINGTON vs. DALLAS
Cowboys lead series, 31-21-2;
See Dallas vs. Washington
WASHINGTON vs. DENVER
Series tied, 2-2;
See Denver vs. Washington
WASHINGTON vs. DETROIT
Redskins lead series, 19-8;
See Detroit vs. Washington
WASHINGTON vs. GREEN BAY
Packers lead series, 14-12-1;
See Green Bay vs. Washington
WASHINGTON vs. HOUSTON
Series tied, 2-2;
See Houston vs. Washington
WASHINGTON vs. INDIANAPOLIS
Colts lead series, 15-6;
See Indianapolis vs. Washington
WASHINGTON vs. KANSAS CITY
Chiefs lead series, 2-1;
See Kansas City vs. Washington
WASHINGTON vs. L.A. RAIDERS
Raiders lead series, 4-2;
See L.A. Raiders vs. Washington
WASHINGTON vs. L.A. RAMS
Redskins lead series, 15-5-1;
See L.A. Rams vs. Washington
WASHINGTON vs. MIAMI
Dolphins lead series, 4-2;
See Miami vs. Washington
WASHINGTON vs. MINNESOTA
Series tied, 5-5;
See Minnesota vs. Washington
WASHINGTON vs. NEW ENGLAND
Redskins lead series, 3-1;
See New England vs. Washington
WASHINGTON vs. NEW ORLEANS
Redskins lead series, 8-4;
See New Orleans vs. Washington
WASHINGTON vs. N.Y. GIANTS
Giants lead series, 61-46-3;
See N.Y. Giants vs. Washington
WASHINGTON vs. N.Y. JETS
Redskins lead series, 3-0;
See N.Y. Jets vs. Washington
WASHINGTON vs. PHILADELPHIA
Redskins lead series, 59-39-5;
See Philadelphia vs. Washington
WASHINGTON vs. PITTSBURGH
Redskins lead series, 40-27-3;
See Pittsburgh vs. Washington
WASHINGTON vs. ST. LOUIS
Redskins lead series, 51-32-2;
See St. Louis vs. Washington
WASHINGTON vs. SAN DIEGO
Redskins lead series, 4-0;
See San Diego vs. Washington
WASHINGTON vs. SAN FRANCISCO
49ers lead series, 8-7-1;
See San Francisco vs. Washington
WASHINGTON vs. SEATTLE
Redskins lead series, 3-1;
See Seattle vs. Washington
WASHINGTON vs. TAMPA BAY
Redskins lead series, 2-0;
See Tampa Bay vs. Washington

SUPER BOWL SUMMARIES

Results

Game	Date	Winner	Loser	Site	Attendance
XXI	1-25-87	N.Y. Giants (NFC) 39	Denver (AFC) 20	Pasadena	101,063
XX	1-26-86	Chicago (NFC) 46	New England (AFC) 10	New Orleans	73,818
XIX	1-20-85	San Francisco (NFC) 38	Miami (AFC) 16	Stanford	84,059
XVIII	1-22-84	L.A. Raiders (AFC) 38	Washington (NFC) 9	Tampa	72,920
XVII	1-30-83	Washington (NFC) 27	Miami (AFC) 17	Pasadena	103,667
XVI	1-24-82	San Francisco (NFC) 26	Cincinnati (AFC) 21	Pontiac	81,270
XV	1-25-81	Oakland (AFC) 27	Philadelphia (NFC) 10	New Orleans	76,135
XIV	1-20-80	Pittsburgh (AFC) 31	Los Angeles (NFC) 19	Pasadena	103,985
XIII	1-21-79	Pittsburgh (AFC) 35	Dallas (NFC) 31	Miami	79,484
XII	1-15-78	Dallas (NFC) 27	Denver (AFC) 10	New Orleans	75,583
XI	1- 9-77	Oakland (AFC) 32	Minnesota (NFC) 14	Pasadena	103,438
X	1-18-76	Pittsburgh (AFC) 21	Dallas (NFC) 17	Miami	80,187
IX	1-12-75	Pittsburgh (AFC) 16	Minnesota (NFC) 6	New Orleans	80,997
VIII	1-13-74	Miami (AFC) 24	Minnesota (NFC) 7	Houston	71,882
VII	1-14-73	Miami (AFC) 14	Washington (NFC) 7	Los Angeles	90,182
VI	1-16-72	Dallas (NFC) 24	Miami (AFC) 3	New Orleans	81,023
V	1-17-71	Baltimore (AFC) 16	Dallas (NFC) 13	Miami	79,204
IV	1-11-70	Kansas City (AFL) 23	Minnesota (NFL) 7	New Orleans	80,562
III	1-12-69	N.Y. Jets (AFL) 16	Baltimore (NFL) 7	Miami	75,389
II	1-14-68	Green Bay (NFL) 33	Oakland (AFL) 14	Miami	75,546
I	1-15-67	Green Bay (NFL) 35	Kansas City (AFL) 10	Los Angeles	61,946

Super Bowl Composite Standings

	W	L	Pct	Pts.	OP
Pittsburgh Steelers	4	0	1.000	103	73
Green Bay Packers	2	0	1.000	68	24
San Francisco 49ers	2	0	1.000	64	37
Chicago Bears	1	0	1.000	46	10
New York Giants	1	0	1.000	39	20
New York Jets	1	0	1.000	16	7
Oakland/L.A. Raiders	3	1	.750	111	66
Baltimore Colts	1	1	.500	23	29
Kansas City Chiefs	1	1	.500	33	42
Dallas Cowboys	2	3	.400	112	85
Miami Dolphins	2	3	.400	74	103
Washington Redskins	1	2	.333	43	69
Cincinnati Bengals	0	1	.000	21	26
Los Angeles Rams	0	1	.000	19	31
New England Patriots	0	1	.000	10	46
Philadelphia Eagles	0	1	.000	10	27
Denver Broncos	0	2	.000	30	66
Minnesota Vikings	0	4	.000	34	95

Past Super Bowl Most Valuable Players

(Selected by Sport Magazine)

Super Bowl I — QB Bart Starr, Green Bay
Super Bowl II — QB Bart Starr, Green Bay
Super Bowl III — QB Joe Namath, New York Jets
Super Bowl IV — QB Len Dawson, Kansas City
Super Bowl V — LB Chuck Howley, Dallas
Super Bowl VI — QB Roger Staubach, Dallas
Super Bowl VII — S Jake Scott, Miami
Super Bowl VIII — RB Larry Csonka, Miami
Super Bowl IX — RB Franco Harris, Pittsburgh
Super Bowl X — WR Lynn Swann, Pittsburgh
Super Bowl XI — WR Fred Biletnikoff, Oakland
Super Bowl XII — DT Randy White and DE Harvey Martin, Dallas
Super Bowl XIII — QB Terry Bradshaw, Pittsburgh
Super Bowl XIV — QB Terry Bradshaw, Pittsburgh
Super Bowl XV — QB Jim Plunkett, Oakland
Super Bowl XVI — QB Joe Montana, San Francisco
Super Bowl XVII — RB John Riggins, Washington
Super Bowl XVIII — RB Marcus Allen, Los Angeles Raiders
Super Bowl XIX — QB Joe Montana, San Francisco
Super Bowl XX — DE Richard Dent, Chicago
Super Bowl XXI — QB Phil Simms, New York Giants

Super Bowl XXI

Rose Bowl, Pasadena, California — January 25, 1987
Attendance: 101,063

NEW YORK GIANTS 39, DENVER 20—The NFC champion New York Giants captured their first NFL title since 1956 when they downed the AFC champion Denver Broncos, 39-20, in Super Bowl XXI. The victory marked the NFC's fifth NFL title in the past six seasons. The Broncos, behind the passing of quarterback John Elway, who was 13 of 20 for 187 yards in the first half, held a 10-9 lead at intermission, the narrowest halftime margin in Super Bowl history. Denver's Rich Karlis opened the scoring with a Super Bowl record-tying 48-yard field goal. New York drove 78 yards in nine plays on the next series to take a 7-3 lead on quarterback Phil Simms's six-yard touchdown pass to tight end Zeke Mowatt. The Broncos came right back with a 58-yard scoring drive on six plays capped by Elway's four-yard touchdown run. The only scoring in the second period was the sack of Elway in the end zone by defensive end George Martin for a New York safety. The Giants produced a key defensive stand early in the second quarter when the Broncos had a first down at the New York one-yard line, but failed to score on three running plays and Karlis's 23-yard missed field-goal attempt. The Giants took command of the game in the third period en route to a 30-point second half, the most ever scored in one half of Super Bowl play. New York took the lead for good on tight end Mark Bavaro's 13-yard touchdown catch 4:52 into the third period. The nine-play, 63-yard scoring drive included the successful conversion of a fourth down and one play on the New York 46-yard line. Denver was limited to only two net yards on 10 offensive plays in the third period. Simms set Super Bowl records for most consecutive completions (10) and highest completion percentage (88 percent on 22 completions in 25 attempts). He also passed for 268 yards and three touchdowns and was named the game's most valuable player. New York running back Joe Morris was the game's leading rusher with 20 carries for 67 yards. Denver wide receiver Vance Johnson led all receivers with five catches for 121 yards. The Giants defeated their three playoff opponents by a cumulative total of 82 points (New York 105, opponents 23), the largest such margin by a Super Bowl winner.

Denver (20)	Offense	N.Y. Giants (39)
Vance Johnson	WR	Lionel Manuel
Dave Studdard	LT	Brad Benson
Keith Bishop	LG	Billy Ard
Bill Bryan	C	Bart Oates
Mark Cooper	RG	Chris Godfrey
Ken Lanier	RT	Karl Nelson
Clarence Kay	TE	Mark Bavaro
Steve Watson	WR	Stacy Robinson
John Elway	QB	Phil Simms
Sammy Winder	RB	Joe Morris
Gerald Willhite	RB	Maurice Carthon
	Defense	
Andre Townsend	LE	George Martin
Greg Kragen	NT	Jim Burt
Rulon Jones	RE	Leonard Marshall
Jim Ryan	LOLB	Carl Banks
Karl Mecklenburg	LILB	Gary Reasons
Ricky Hunley	RILB	Harry Carson
Tom Jackson	ROLB	Lawrence Taylor
Louis Wright	LCB	Elvis Patterson
Mike Harden	RCB	Perry Williams
Dennis Smith	SS	Kenny Hill
Steve Foley	FS	Herb Welch

Substitutions

Denver—Offense: K—Rich Karlis. P—Mike Horan. QB—Gary Kubiak. RB—Ken Bell, Gene Lang, Steve Sewell. TE—Joey Hackett, Bobby Micho, Orson Mobley. WR—Mark Jackson, Clint Sampson. G—Mike Freeman. T—Dan Remsberg. Defense: E—Simon Fletcher, Freddie Gilbert. NT—Tony Colorito. LB—Darren Comeaux, Rick Dennison, Ken Woodard. CB—Mark Haynes, Steve Wilson. S—Tony Lilly, Randy Robbins.

N.Y. Giants—Offense: K—Raul Allegre. P—Sean Landeta. QB—Jeff Rutledge. RB—Ottis Anderson, Tony Galbreath, Lee Rouson. TE—Zeke Mowatt. WR—Bobby Johnson, Phil McConkey, Solomon Miller. G—Damian Johnson. T—William Roberts. C—Brian Johnston. Defense: E—Eric Dorsey. NT—Erik Howard, Jerome Sally. LB—Andy Headen, Byron Hunt, Thomas Johnson, Robbie Jones. CB—Mark Collins. S—Tom Flynn, Greg Lasker.

Officials

Referee—Jerry Markbreit. Umpire—Bob Boylston. Line Judge—Bob Beeks. Head Linesman—Terry Gierke. Back Judge—Jim Poole. Field Judge—Pat Mallette. Side Judge—Gil Mace.

Scoring

Denver (AFC)	10	0	0	10	— 20
N.Y. Giants (NFC)	7	2	17	13	— 39

Den —FG Karlis 48
NYG—Mowatt 6 pass from Simms (Allegre kick)
Den —Elway 4 run (Karlis kick)
NYG—Safety, Martin tackled Elway in end zone
NYG—Bavaro 13 pass from Simms (Allegre kick)
NYG—FG Allegre 21
NYG—Morris 1 run (Allegre kick)
NYG—McConkey 6 pass from Simms (Allegre kick)
Den —FG Karlis 28
NYG—Anderson 2 run (kick failed)
Den —V. Johnson 47 pass from Elway (Karlis kick)

Team Statistics

	Denver	N.Y. Giants
Total First Downs	23	24
First Downs Rushing	5	10
First Downs Passing	16	13
First Downs Penalty	2	1
Total Net Yardage	372	399

Total Offensive Plays	64	64
Average Gain per Offensive Play	5.8	6.2
Rushes	19	38
Yards Gained Rushing (net)	52	136
Average Yards per Rush	2.7	3.6
Passes Attempted	41	25
Passes Completed	26	22
Had Intercepted	1	0
Times Tackled Attempting to Pass	4	1
Yards Lost Attempting to Pass	32	5
Yards Gained Passing (net)	320	263
Punts	2	3
Average Distance	41.0	46.0
Punt Returns	1	1
Punt Return Yardage	9	25
Kickoff Returns	5	4
Kickoff Return Yardage	84	53
Interception Return Yardage	0	−7
Total Return Yardage	93	71
Fumbles	2	0
Own Fumbles Recovered	2	0
Opponents Fumbles Recovered	0	0
Penalties	4	6
Yards Penalized	28	48
Total Points Scored	20	39
Touchdowns	2	5
Touchdowns Rushing	1	2
Touchdowns Passing	1	3
Touchdowns Returns	0	0
Extra Points	2	4
Field Goals	2	1
Field Goals Attempted	4	1
Safeties	0	1
Third Down Efficiency	7/14	6/12
Fourth Down Efficiency	0/0	1/2
Time of Possession	25:21	34:39

Individual Statistics

Rushing

Denver	**Att.**	**Yds.**	**LG**	**TD**
Elway	6	27	10	1
Willhite	4	19	11	0
Sewell	3	4	12	0
Lang	2	2	4	0
Winder	4	0	3	0
N.Y. Giants	**Att.**	**Yds.**	**LG**	**TD**
Morris	20	67	11	1
Simms	3	25	22	0
Rouson	3	22	18	0
Galbreath	4	17	7	0
Carthon	3	4	2	0
Anderson	2	1	2t	1
Rutledge	3	0	2	0

Passing

Denver	**Att.**	**Comp.**	**Yds.**	**TD**	**Int.**
Elway	37	22	304	1	1
Kubiak	4	4	48	0	0
N.Y. Giants	**Att.**	**Comp.**	**Yds.**	**TD**	**Int.**
Simms	25	22	268	3	0

Receiving

Denver	**No.**	**Yds.**	**LG**	**TD**
V. Johnson	5	121	54	1
Willhite	5	39	11	0
Winder	4	34	14	0
M. Jackson	3	51	24	0
Watson	2	54	31	0
Sampson	2	20	11	0
Mobley	2	17	11	0
Sewell	2	12	7	0
Lang	1	4	4	0
N.Y. Giants	**No.**	**Yds.**	**LG**	**TD**
Bavaro	4	51	17	1
Morris	4	20	12	0
Carthon	4	13	7	0
Robinson	3	62	36	0
Manuel	3	43	17	0
McConkey	2	50	44	1
Rouson	1	23	23	0
Mowatt	1	6	6t	1

Interceptions

Denver	**No.**	**Yds.**	**LG**	**TD**
None				
N.Y. Giants	**No.**	**Yds.**	**LG**	**TD**
Patterson	1	−7	−7	0

Punting

Denver	**No.**	**Avg.**	**LG**	**Blk.**
Horan	2	41.0	42	0
N.Y. Giants	**No.**	**Avg.**	**LG**	**Blk.**
Landeta	3	46.0	59	0

Punt Returns

Denver	**No.**	**FC**	**Yds.**	**LG**	**TD**
Willhite	1	1	9	9	0
N.Y. Giants	**No.**	**FC**	**Yds.**	**LG**	**TD**
McConkey	1	1	25	25	0

Kickoff Returns

Denver	**No.**	**Yds.**	**LG**	**TD**
Bell	3	48	28	0
Lang	2	36	23	0
N.Y. Giants	**No.**	**Yds.**	**LG**	**TD**
Rouson	3	56	22	0
Flynn	1	−3	−3	0

Super Bowl XX

Louisiana Superdome, New Orleans, Louisiana — January 26, 1986

Attendance: 73,818

CHICAGO 46, NEW ENGLAND 10—The NFC champion Chicago Bears, seeking their first NFL title since 1963, scored a Super Bowl-record 46 points in downing AFC champion New England 46-10 in Super Bowl XX. The previous record for most points in a Super Bowl was 38, shared by San Francisco in XIX and the Los Angeles Raiders in XVIII. The Bears' league-leading defense tied the Super Bowl record for sacks (7) and limited the Patriots to a record-low seven yards rushing. New England took the quickest lead in Super Bowl history when Tony Franklin kicked a 36-yard field goal with 1:19 elapsed in the first period. The score came about because of Larry McGrew's fumble recovery at the Chicago 19-yard line. However, the Bears rebounded for a 23-3 first-half lead, while building a yardage advantage of 236 total yards to New England's minus 19. Running back Matt Suhey rushed eight times for 37 yards, including an 11-yard touchdown run, and caught one pass for 24 yards in the first half. After the Patriots first drive of the second half ended with a punt to the Bears' 4-yard line, Chicago marched 96 yards in nine plays with quarterback Jim McMahon's one-yard scoring run capping the drive. McMahon became the first quarterback in Super Bowl history to rush for a pair of touchdowns. The Bears completed their scoring via a 28-yard interception return by reserve cornerback Reggie Phillips, a one-yard run by defensive tackle/fullback William Perry, and a safety when defensive end Henry Waechter tackled Patriots quarterback Steve Grogan in the end zone. Bears defensive end Richard Dent became the fourth defender to be named the game's most valuable player after contributing 1½ sacks. The Bears' victory margin of 36 points was the largest in Super Bowl history, bettering the previous mark of 29 by the Los Angeles Raiders when they topped Washington 38-9 in Game XVIII. McMahon completed 12 of 20 passes for 256 yards before leaving the game in the fourth period with a wrist injury. The NFL's all-time leading rusher, Bears running back Walter Payton, carried 22 times for 61 yards. Wide receiver Willie Gault caught four passes for 129 yards, the fourth-most receiving yards in a Super Bowl. Chicago coach Mike Ditka became the second man (Tom Flores of Raiders is other) who played in a Super Bowl and coached a team to a victory in the game.

Chicago (NFC)	13	10	21	2	— 46
New England (AFC)	3	0	0	7	— 10

NE—FG Franklin 36
Chi—FG Butler 28
Chi—FG Butler 24
Chi—Suhey 11 run (Butler kick)
Chi—McMahon 2 run (Butler kick)
Chi—FG Butler 24
Chi—McMahon 1 run (Butler kick)
Chi—Phillips 28 interception return (Butler kick)
Chi—Perry 1 run (Butler kick)
NE—Fryar 8 pass from Gorgan (Franklin kick)
Chi—Safety, Waechter tackled Grogan in end zone

Super Bowl XIX

Stanford Stadium, Stanford, California — January 20, 1985

Attendance: 84,059

SAN FRANCISCO 38, MIAMI 16—The San Francisco 49ers captured their second Super Bowl title with a dominating offense and a defense that tamed Miami's explosive passing attack. The Dolphins held a 10-7 lead at the end of the first period, which represented the most points scored by two teams in an opening quarter of a Super Bowl. However, the 49ers used excellent field position in the second period to build a 28-16 halftime lead. Running back Roger Craig set a Super Bowl record by scoring three touchdowns on pass receptions of 8 and 16 yards and a run of 2 yards. San Francisco's Joe Montana was voted the game's most valuable player. He joined Green Bay's Bart Starr and Pittsburgh's Terry Bradshaw as the only two-time Super Bowl most valuable players. Montana completed 24 of 35 passes for a Super Bowl-record 331 yards and three touchdowns, and rushed five times for 59 yards, including a six-yard touchdown. Craig had 58 yards on 15 carries and caught seven passes for 77 yards. Wendell Tyler rushed 13 times for 65 yards and had four catches for 70 yards. Dwight Clark had six receptions for 77 yards, while Russ Francis had five for 60. San Francisco's 537 total net yards bettered the previous Super Bowl record of 429 yards by Oakland in Super Bowl XI. The 49ers also held a time of possession advantage over the Dolphins of 37:11 to 22:49.

Miami (AFC)	10	6	0	0	— 16
San Francisco (NFC)	7	21	10	0	— 38

Mia—FG von Schamann 37
SF—Monroe 33 pass from Montana (Wersching kick)
Mia—D. Johnson 2 pass from Marino (von Schamann kick)
SF—Craig 8 pass from Montana (Wersching kick)
SF—Montana 6 run (Wersching kick)
SF—Craig 2 run (Wersching kick)
Mia—FG von Schamann 31
Mia—FG von Schamann 30
SF—FG Wersching 27
SF—Craig 16 pass from Montana (Wersching kick)

Super Bowl XVIII

Tampa Stadium, Tampa, Florida — January 22, 1984

Attendance: 72,920

LOS ANGELES RAIDERS 38, WASHINGTON 9—The Los Angeles Raiders dominated the Washington Redskins from the beginning in Super Bowl XVIII and achieved the most lopsided victory in Super Bowl history, surpassing Green Bay's 35-10 win over Kansas City in Super Bowl I. The Raiders took a 7-0 lead 4:52 into the game when Derrick Jensen blocked a Jeff Hayes punt and recovered it in the end zone for a touchdown. With 9:14 remaining in the first half, Raiders quarterback Jim Plunkett threw a 12-yard touchdown pass to wide receiver Cliff Branch to complete a three-play, 65-yard drive. Washington cut the Raiders' lead to 14-3 on a 24-yard field goal by Mark Moseley. With seven seconds left in the first half, Raiders linebacker Jack Squirek intercepted a Joe Theismann pass at the Redskins' 5-yard line and ran it in for a touchdown to give Los Angeles a 21-3 halftime lead. In the third period, running back Marcus Allen, who rushed for a Super Bowl record 191 yards on 20 carries, increased the Raiders' lead to 35-3 on touchdown runs of 5 and 74 yards, the latter erasing the previous Super Bowl record of 58 yards set by Baltimore's Tom Matte in Game III. Allen was named the game's most valuable player. The victory over Washington raised Raiders coach Tom Flores' playoff record to 8-1, including a 27-10 win against Philadelphia in Super Bowl XV. The 38 points scored by the Raiders was the highest total by a Super Bowl team. The previous high was 35 points by Green Bay in Game I.

Washington (NFC)	0	3	6	0	— 9
L.A. Raiders (AFC)	7	14	14	3	— 38

Raiders—Jensen recovered blocked punt in end zone (Bahr kick)
Raiders—Branch 12 pass from Plunkett (Bahr kick)
Wash —FG Moseley 24
Raiders—Squirek 5 interception return (Bahr kick)
Wash —Riggins 1 run (kick blocked)
Raiders—Allen 5 run (Bahr kick)
Raiders—Allen 74 run (Bahr kick)
Raiders—FG Bahr 21

Super Bowl XVII

Rose Bowl, Pasadena, California January 30, 1983
Attendance: 103,667

WASHINGTON 27, MIAMI 17—Fullback John Riggins's Super Bowl record 166 yards on 38 carries sparked Washington to a 27-17 victory over AFC champion Miami. It was Riggins's fourth straight 100-yard rushing game during the playoffs, also a record. The win marked Washington's first NFL title since 1942, and was only the second time in Super Bowl history NFC teams scored consecutive victories (Green Bay did it in Super Bowls I and II and San Francisco won Super Bowl XVI). The Redskins, under second-year head coach Joe Gibbs, used a balanced offense that accounted for 400 total yards (a Super Bowl record 276 yards rushing and 124 passing), second in Super Bowl history to 429 yards by Oakland in Super Bowl XI. The Dolphins built a 17-10 halftime lead on a 76-yard touchdown pass from quarterback David Woodley to wide receiver Jimmy Cefalo 6:49 into the first period, a 20-yard field goal by Uwe von Schamann with 6:00 left in the half, and a Super Bowl record 98-yard kickoff return by Fulton Walker with 1:38 remaining. Washington had tied the score at 10-10 with 1:51 left on a four-yard touchdown pass from Joe Theismann to wide receiver Alvin Garrett. Mark Moseley started the Redskins' scoring with a 31-yard field goal late in the first period, and added a 20-yarder midway through the third period to cut the Dolphins' lead to 17-13. Riggins, who was voted the game's most valuable player, gave Washington its first lead of the game with 10:01 left when he ran 43 yards off left tackle for a touchdown on a fourth-and-one situation. Wide receiver Charlie Brown caught a six-yard scoring pass from Theismann with 1:55 left to complete the scoring. The Dolphins managed only 176 yards (142 in first half). Theismann completed 15 of 23 passes for 143 yards, two touchdowns, and had two interceptions. For Miami, Woodley was 4 of 14 for 97 yards, with one touchdown, and one interception. Don Strock was 0 for 3 in relief.

Miami (AFC)	7	10	0	0	— 17
Washington (NFC)	0	10	3	14	— 27

Mia —Cefalo 76 pass from Woodley (von Schamann kick)
Wash—FG Moseley 31
Mia —FG von Schamann 20
Wash—Garrett 4 pass from Theismann (Moseley kick)
Mia —Walker 98 kickoff return (von Schamann kick)
Wash—FG Moseley 20
Wash—Riggins 43 run (Moseley kick)
Wash—Brown 6 pass from Theismann (Moseley kick)

Super Bowl XVI

Pontiac Silverdome, Pontiac, Michigan January 24, 1982
Attendance: 81,270

SAN FRANCISCO 26, CINCINNATI 21—Ray Wersching's Super Bowl record-tying four field goals and Joe Montana's controlled passing helped lift the San Francisco 49ers to their first NFL championship with a 26-21 victory over Cincinnati. The 49ers built a game-record 20-0 halftime lead via Montana's one-yard touchdown run, which capped an 11-play, 68-yard drive; fullback Earl Cooper's 11-yard scoring pass from Montana, which climaxed a Super Bowl record 92-yard drive on 12 plays; and Wersching's 22- and 26-yard field goals. The Bengals rebounded in the second half, closing the gap to 20-14 on quarterback Ken Anderson's five-yard run and Dan Ross's four-yard reception from Anderson, who established Super Bowl passing records for completions (25) and completion percentage (73.5 percent on 25 of 34). Wersching added early fourth-period field goals of 40 and 23 yards to increase the 49ers' lead to 26-14. The Bengals managed to score on an Anderson-to-Ross three-yard pass with only 16 seconds remaining. Ross set a Super Bowl record with 11 receptions for 104 yards. Montana, the game's most valuable player, completed 14 of 22 passes for 157 yards. Cincinnati compiled 356 yards to San Francisco's 275, which marked the first time in Super Bowl history that the team that gained the most yards from scrimmage lost the game.

San Francisco (NFC)	7	13	0	6	— 26
Cincinnati (AFC)	0	0	7	14	— 21

SF —Montana 1 run (Wersching kick)
SF —Cooper 11 pass from Montana (Wersching kick)
SF —FG Wersching 22
SF —FG Wersching 26
Cin—Anderson 5 run (Breech kick)
Cin—Ross 4 pass from Anderson (Breech kick)
SF —FG Wersching 40
SF —FG Wersching 23
Cin—Ross 3 pass from Anderson (Breech kick)

Super Bowl XV

Louisiana Superdome, New Orleans, Louisiana January 25, 1981
Attendance: 76,135

OAKLAND 27, PHILADELPHIA 10—Jim Plunkett threw three touchdown passes, including an 80-yarder to Kenny King, as the Raiders became the first wild card team to win the Super Bowl. Plunkett's touchdown bomb to King—the longest play in Super Bowl history—gave Oakland a decisive 14-0 lead with nine seconds left in the first period. Linebacker Rod Martin had set up Oakland's first touchdown, a two-yard reception by Cliff Branch, with a 16-yard interception return to the Eagles' 32 yard line. The Eagles never recovered from that early deficit, managing only a Tony Franklin field goal (30 yards) and an eight-yard touchdown pass from Ron Jaworski to Keith Krepfle the rest of the game. Plunkett, who became a starter in the sixth game of the season, completed 13 of 21 for 261 yards and was named the game's most valuable player. Oakland won 9 of 11 games with Plunkett starting, but that was good enough only for second place in the AFC West, although they tied division winner San Diego with an 11-5 record. The Raiders, who had previously won Super Bowl XI over Minnesota, had to win three playoff games to get to the championship game. Oakland defeated Houston 27-7 at home followed by road victories over Cleveland, 14-12 and San Diego, 34-27. Oakland's Mark van Eeghen was the game's leading rusher with 80 yards on 19 carries. Philadelphia's Wilbert Montgomery led all receivers with six receptions for 91 yards. Branch had five for 67 and Harold Carmichael of Philadelphia five for 83. Martin finished the game with three interceptions, a Super Bowl record.

Oakland (AFC)	14	0	10	3	— 27
Philadelphia (NFC)	0	3	0	7	— 10

Oak—Branch 2 pass from Plunkett (Bahr kick)
Oak—King 80 pass from Plunkett (Bahr kick)
Phil —FG Franklin 30
Oak—Branch 29 pass from Plunkett (Bahr kick)
Oak—FG Bahr 46
Phil —Krepfle 8 pass from Jaworski (Franklin kick)
Oak—FG Bahr 35

Super Bowl XIV

Rose Bowl, Pasadena, California January 20, 1980
Attendance: 103,985

PITTSBURGH 31, LOS ANGELES 19—Terry Bradshaw completed 14 of 21 passes for 309 yards and set two passing records as the Steelers became the first team to win four Super Bowls. Despite three interceptions by the Rams, Bradshaw kept his poise and brought the Steelers from behind twice in the second half. Trailing 13-10 at halftime, Pittsburgh went ahead 17-13 when Bradshaw hit Lynn Swann with a 47-yard touchdown pass after 2:48 of the third quarter. On the Rams' next possession Vince Ferragamo, who completed 15 of 25 passes for 212 yards, responded with a 50-yard pass to Billy Waddy that moved Los Angeles from its own 26 to the Steelers' 24. On the following play, Lawrence McCutcheon connected with Ron Smith on a halfback option pass that gave the Rams a 19-17 lead. On Pittsburgh's initial possession of the final period, Bradshaw lofted a 73-yard scoring pass to John Stallworth to put the Steelers in front to stay, 24-19. Franco Harris scored on a one-yard run later in the quarter to seal the verdict. A 45-yard pass from Bradshaw to Stallworth was the key play in the drive to Harris's score. Bradshaw, the game's most valuable player for the second straight year, set career Super Bowl records for most touchdown passes (nine) and most passing yards (932). Larry Anderson gave the Steelers excellent field position throughout the game with five kickoff returns for a record 162 yards.

Los Angeles (NFC)	7	6	6	0	— 19
Pittsburgh (AFC)	3	7	7	14	— 31

Pitt—FG Bahr 41
LA —Bryant 1 run (Corral kick)
Pitt—Harris 1 run (Bahr kick)
LA —FG Corral 31
LA —FG Corral 45
Pitt—Swann 47 pass from Bradshaw (Bahr kick)
LA —Smith 24 pass from McCutcheon (kick failed)
Pitt—Stallworth 73 pass from Bradshaw (Bahr kick)
Pitt—Harris 1 run (Bahr kick)

Super Bowl XIII

Orange Bowl, Miami, Florida January 21, 1979
Attendance: 79,484

PITTSBURGH 35, DALLAS 31—Terry Bradshaw threw a record four touchdown passes to lead the Steelers to victory. The Steelers became the first team to win three Super Bowls, mostly because of Bradshaw's accurate arm. Bradshaw, voted the game's most valuable player, completed 17 of 30 passes for 318 yards, a personal high. Three of those passes went for touchdowns—two to John Stallworth and the third, with 26 seconds remaining in the second period, to Rocky Bleier. The Cowboys scored twice before intermission on Roger Staubach's 39-yard pass to Tony Hill and a 37-yard run by linebacker Mike Hegman, who stole the ball from Bradshaw. The Steelers broke open the contest with two touchdowns in a span of 19 seconds midway through the final period. Franco Harris rambled 22 yards up the middle to give the Steelers a 28-17 lead with 7:10 left. Pittsburgh got the ball right back when Randy White fumbled the kickoff and Dennis Winston recovered for the Steelers. On first down, Bradshaw hit Lynn Swann with an 18-yard scoring pass to boost the Steelers' lead to 35-17 with 6:51 to play. The Cowboys refused to let the Steelers run away with the contest. Staubach connected with Billy Joe DuPree on a seven-yard scoring pass with 2:23 left. Then the Cowboys recovered an onside kick and Staubach took them in for another score, passing four yards to Butch Johnson with 22 seconds remaining. Bleier recovered another onside kick with 17 seconds left to seal the victory for the Steelers.

Pittsburgh (AFC)	7	14	0	14	— 35
Dallas (NFC)	7	7	3	14	— 31

Pitt —Stallworth 28 pass from Bradshaw (Gerela kick)
Dall—Hill 39 pass from Staubach (Septien kick)
Dall—Hegman 37 fumble recovery return (Septien kick)

Pitt —Stallworth 75 pass from Bradshaw (Gerela kick)
Pitt —Bleier 7 pass from Bradshaw (Gerela kick)
Dall—FG Septien 27
Pitt —Harris 22 run (Gerela kick)
Pitt —Swann 18 pass from Bradshaw (Gerela kick)
Dall—DuPree 7 pass from Staubach (Septien kick)
Dall—B. Johnson 4 pass from Staubach (Septien kick)

Super Bowl XII

Louisiana Superdome, New Orleans, Louisiana January 15, 1978
Attendance: 75,583

DALLAS 27, DENVER 10—The Cowboys evened their Super Bowl record at 2-2 by defeating Denver before a sellout crowd of 75,583, plus 102,010,000 television viewers, the largest audience ever to watch a sporting event. Dallas converted two interceptions into 10 points and Efren Herrera added a 35-yard field goal for a 13-0 halftime advantage. In the third period Craig Morton engineered a drive to the Cowboys' 30 and Jim Turner's 47-yard field goal made the score 13-3. After an exchange of punts, Butch Johnson made a spectacular diving catch in the end zone to complete a 45-yard pass from Roger Staubach and put the Cowboys ahead 20-3. Following Rick Upchurch's 67-yard kickoff return, Norris Weese guided the Broncos to a touchdown to cut the Dallas lead to 20-10. Dallas clinched the victory when running back Robert Newhouse threw a 29-yard touchdown pass to Golden Richards with 7:04 remaining in the game. It was the first pass thrown by Newhouse since 1975. Harvey Martin and Randy White, who were named co-most valuable players, led the Cowboys' defense, which recovered four fumbles and intercepted four passes.

Dallas (NFC)	10	3	7	7 — 27
Denver (AFC)	0	0	10	0 — 10

Dall—Dorsett 3 run (Herrera kick)
Dall—FG Herrera 35
Dall—FG Herrera 43
Den—FG Turner 47
Dall—Johnson 45 pass from Staubach (Herrera kick)
Den—Lytle 1 run (Turner kick)
Dall—Richards 29 pass from Newhouse (Herrera kick)

Super Bowl XI

Rose Bowl, Pasadena, California January 9, 1977
Attendance: 103,438

OAKLAND 32, MINNESOTA 14—The Raiders won their first NFL championship before a record Super Bowl crowd plus 81 million television viewers, the largest audience ever to watch a sporting event. The Raiders gained a record-breaking 429 yards, including running back Clarence Davis's 137 yards rushing. Wide receiver Fred Biletnikoff made four key receptions, which earned him the game's most valuable player trophy. Oakland scored on three successive possessions in the second quarter to build a 16-0 halftime lead. Errol Mann's 24-yard field goal opened the scoring, then the AFC champions put together drives of 64 and 35 yards, scoring on a one-yard pass from Ken Stabler to Dave Casper and a one-yard run by Pete Banaszak. The Raiders increased their lead to 19-0 on a 40-yard field goal in the third quarter, but Minnesota responded with a 12-play, 58-yard drive late in the period, with Fran Tarkenton passing eight yards to wide receiver Sammy White to cut the deficit to 19-7. Two fourth-quarter interceptions clinched the title for the Raiders. One set up Banaszak's second touchdown run, the other resulted in cornerback Willie Brown's Super Bowl record 75-yard interception return.

Oakland (AFC)	0	16	3	13 — 32
Minnesota (NFC)	0	0	7	7 — 14

Oak —FG Mann 24
Oak —Casper 1 pass from Stabler (Mann kick)
Oak —Banaszak 1 run (kick failed)
Oak —FG Mann 40
Minn—S. White 8 pass from Tarkenton (Cox kick)
Oak —Banaszak 2 run (Mann kick)
Oak —Brown 75 interception return (kick failed)
Minn—Voigt 13 pass from Lee (Cox kick)

Super Bowl X

Orange Bowl, Miami, Florida January 18, 1976
Attendance: 80,187

PITTSBURGH 21, DALLAS 17—The Steelers won the Super Bowl for the second year in a row on Terry Bradshaw's 64-yard touchdown pass to Lynn Swann and an aggressive defense that snuffed out a late rally by the Cowboys with an end-zone interception on the final play of the game. In the fourth quarter, Pittsburgh ran on fourth down and gave up the ball on the Cowboys' 39 with 1:22 to play. Roger Staubach ran and passed for two first downs but his last desperation pass was picked off by Glen Edwards. Dallas's scoring was the result of two touchdown passes by Staubach, one to Drew Pearson for 29 yards and the other to Percy Howard for 34 yards. Toni Fritsch had a 36-yard field goal. The Steelers scored on two touchdown passes by Bradshaw, one to Randy Grossman for seven yards and the long bomb to Swann. Roy Gerela had 36- and 18-yard field goals. Reggie Harrison blocked a punt through the end zone for a safety. Swann set a Super Bowl record by gaining 161 yards on his four receptions.

Dallas (NFC)	7	3	0	7 — 17
Pittsburgh (AFC)	7	0	0	14 — 21

Dall—D. Pearson 29 pass from Staubach (Fritsch kick)
Pitt —Grossman 7 pass from Bradshaw (Gerela kick)
Dall—FG Fritsch 36
Pitt —Safety, Harrison blocked Hoopes's punt through end zone
Pitt —FG Gerela 36
Pitt —FG Gerela 18
Pitt —Swann 64 pass from Bradshaw (kick failed)
Dall—P. Howard 34 pass from Staubach (Fritsch kick)

Super Bowl IX

Tulane Stadium, New Orleans, Louisiana January 12, 1975
Attendance: 80,997

PITTSBURGH 16, MINNESOTA 6—AFC champion Pittsburgh, in its initial Super Bowl appearance, and NFC champion Minnesota, making a third bid for its first Super Bowl title, struggled through a first half in which the only score was produced by the Steelers' defense when Dwight White downed Vikings' quarterback Fran Tarkenton in the end zone for a safety 7:49 into the second period. The Steelers forced another break and took advantage on the second half kickoff when Minnesota's Bill Brown fumbled and Marv Kellum recovered for Pittsburgh on the Vikings' 30. After Rocky Bleier failed to gain on first down, Franco Harris carried three consecutive times for 24 yards, a loss of 3, and a 12-yard touchdown and a 9-0 lead. Though its offense was completely stymied by Pittsburgh's defense, Minnesota managed to move into a threatening position after 4:27 of the final period when Matt Blair blocked Bobby Walden's punt and Terry Brown recovered the ball in the end zone for a touchdown. Fred Cox's kick failed and the Steelers led 9-6. Pittsburgh wasted no time putting the victory away. The Steelers took the ensuing kickoff and marched 66 yards in 11 plays, climaxed by Terry Bradshaw's four-yard scoring pass to Larry Brown with 3:31 left. Pittsburgh's defense permitted Minnesota only 119 yards total offense, including a Super Bowl low of 17 yards rushing. The Steelers, meanwhile, gained 333 yards, including Harris's record 158 yards on 34 carries.

Pittsburgh (AFC)	0	2	7	7 — 16
Minnesota (NFC)	0	0	0	6 — 6

Pitt —Safety, White downed Tarkenton in end zone
Pitt —Harris 12 run (Gerela kick)
Minn—T. Brown recovered blocked punt in end zone (kick failed)
Pitt —L. Brown 4 pass from Bradshaw (Gerela kick)

Super Bowl VIII

Rice Stadium, Houston, Texas January 13, 1974
Attendance: 71,882

MIAMI 24, MINNESOTA 7—The defending NFL champion Dolphins, representing the AFC for the third straight year, scored the first two times they had possession on marches of 62 and 56 yards in the first period while the Miami defense limited the Vikings to only seven plays. Larry Csonka climaxed the initial 10-play drive with a five-yard touchdown bolt through right guard after 5:27 had elapsed. Four plays later, Miami began another 10-play scoring drive, which ended with Jim Kiick bursting one yard through the middle for another touchdown after 13:38 of the period. Garo Yepremian added a 28-yard field goal midway in the second period for a 17-0 Miami lead. Minnesota then drove from its 20 to a second-and-two situation on the Miami 7 yard line with 1:18 left in the half. But on two plays, Miami limited Oscar Reed to one yard. On fourth-and-one from the 6, Reed went over right tackle, but Dolphins middle linebacker Nick Buoniconti jarred the ball loose and Jake Scott recovered for Miami to halt the Minnesota threat. The Vikings were unable to muster enough offense in the second half to threaten the Dolphins. Csonka rushed 33 times for a Super Bowl record 145 yards. Bob Griese of Miami completed six of seven passes for 73 yards.

Minnesota (NFC)	0	0	0	7 — 7
Miami (AFC)	14	3	7	0 — 24

Mia —Csonka 5 run (Yepremian kick)
Mia —Kiick 1 run (Yepremian kick)
Mia —FG Yepremian 28
Mia —Csonka 2 run (Yepremian kick)
Minn—Tarkenton 4 run (Cox kick)

Super Bowl VII

Memorial Coliseum, Los Angeles, California January 14, 1973
Attendance: 90,182

MIAMI 14, WASHINGTON 7—The Dolphins played virtually perfect football in the first half as their defense permitted the Redskins to cross midfield only once and their offense turned good field position into two touchdowns. On its third possession, Miami opened its first scoring drive from the Dolphins' 37 yard line. An 18-yard pass from Bob Griese to Paul Warfield preceded by three plays Griese's 28-yard touchdown pass to Howard Twilley. After Washington moved from its 17 to the Miami 48 with two minutes remaining in the first half, Dolphins linebacker Nick Buoniconti intercepted a Billy Kilmer pass at the Miami 41 and returned it to the Washington 27. Jim Kiick ran for three yards, Larry Csonka for three, Griese passed to Jim Mandich for 19, and Kiick gained one to the 1 yard line. With 18 seconds left until intermission, Kiick scored from the 1. Washington's only touchdown came with 7:07 left in the game and resulted from a misplayed field goal attempt and fumble by Garo Yepremian, with the Redskins' Mike Bass picking the ball out of the air and running 49 yards for the score.

Miami (AFC)	7	7	0	0 — 14
Washington (NFC)	0	0	0	7 — 7

Mia —Twilley 28 pass from Griese (Yepremian kick)
Mia —Kiick 1 run (Yepremian kick)
Wash—Bass 49 fumble recovery return (Knight kick)

Super Bowl VI

Tulane Stadium, New Orleans, Louisiana — January 16, 1972

Attendance: 81,023

DALLAS 24, MIAMI 3—The Cowboys rushed for a record 252 yards and their defense limited the Dolphins to a low of 185 yards while not permitting a touchdown for the first time in Super Bowl history. Dallas converted Chuck Howley's recovery of Larry Csonka's first fumble of the season into a 3-0 advantage and led at halftime 10-3. After Dallas received the second-half kickoff, Duane Thomas led a 71-yard march in eight plays for a 17-3 margin. Howley intercepted Bob Griese's pass at the 50 and returned it to the Miami 9 early in the fourth period, and three plays later Roger Staubach passed seven yards to Mike Ditka for the final touchdown. Thomas rushed for 95 yards and Walt Garrison gained 74. Staubach, voted the game's most valuable player, completed 12 of 19 passes for 119 yards and two touchdowns.

Dallas (NFC)	3	7	7	7	— 24
Miami (AFC)	0	3	0	0	— 3

Dall—FG Clark 9
Dall—Alworth 7 pass from Staubach (Clark kick)
Mia—FG Yepremian 31
Dall—D. Thomas 3 run (Clark kick)
Dall—Ditka 7 pass from Staubach (Clark kick)

Super Bowl V

Orange Bowl, Miami, Florida — January 17, 1971

Attendance: 79,204

BALTIMORE 16, DALLAS 13—A 32-yard field goal by first-year kicker Jim O'Brien brought the Baltimore Colts a victory over the Dallas Cowboys in the final five seconds of Super Bowl V. The game between the champions of the AFC and NFC was played on artificial turf for the first time. Dallas led 13-6 at the half but interceptions by Rick Volk and Mike Curtis set up a Baltimore touchdown and O'Brien's decisive kick in the fourth period. Earl Morrall relieved an injured Johnny Unitas late in the first half, although Unitas completed the Colts' only scoring pass. It caromed off receiver Eddie Hinton's fingertips, off Dallas defensive back Mel Renfro, and finally settled into the grasp of John Mackey, who went 45 yards to score on a 75-yard play.

Baltimore (AFC)	0	6	0	10	— 16
Dallas (NFC)	3	10	0	0	— 13

Dall—FG Clark 14
Dall—FG Clark 30
Balt—Mackey 75 pass from Unitas (kick blocked)
Dall—Thomas 7 pass from Morton (Clark kick)
Balt—Nowatzke 2 run (O'Brien kick)
Balt—FG O'Brien 32

Super Bowl IV

Tulane Stadium, New Orleans, Louisiana — January 11, 1970

Attendance: 80,562

KANSAS CITY 23, MINNESOTA 7—The AFL squared the Super Bowl at two games apiece with the NFL, building a 16-0 halftime lead behind Len Dawson's superb quarterbacking and a powerful defense. Dawson, the fourth consecutive quarterback to be chosen the Super Bowl's top player, called an almost flawless game, completing 12 of 17 passes and hitting Otis Taylor on a 46-yard play for the final Chiefs touchdown. The Kansas City defense limited Minnesota's strong rushing game to 67 yards and had three interceptions and two fumble recoveries. The crowd of 80,562 set a Super Bowl record, as did the gross receipts of $3,817,872.69.

Minnesota (NFL)	0	0	7	0	— 7
Kansas City (AFL)	3	13	7	0	— 23

KC —FG Stenerud 48
KC —FG Stenerud 32
KC —FG Stenerud 25
KC —Garrett 5 run (Stenerud kick)
Minn—Osborn 4 run (Cox kick)
KC —Taylor 46 pass from Dawson (Stenerud kick)

Super Bowl III

Orange Bowl, Miami, Florida — January 12, 1969

Attendance: 75,389

NEW YORK JETS 16, BALTIMORE 7—Jets quarterback Joe Namath "guaranteed" victory on the Thursday before the game, then went out and led the AFL to its first Super Bowl victory over a Baltimore team that had lost only once in 16 games all season. Namath, chosen the outstanding player, completed 17 of 28 passes for 206 yards and directed a steady attack that dominated the NFL champions after the Jets' defense had intercepted Colts quarterback Earl Morrall three times in the first half. The Jets had 337 total yards, including 121 yards rushing by Matt Snell. Johnny Unitas, who had missed most of the season with a sore elbow, came off the bench and led Baltimore to its only touchdown late in the fourth quarter after New York led 16-0.

New York Jets (AFL)	0	7	6	3	— 16
Baltimore (NFL)	0	0	0	7	— 7

NYJ—Snell 4 run (Turner kick)
NYJ—FG Turner 32
NYJ—FG Turner 30
NYJ—FG Turner 9
Balt—Hill 1 run (Michaels kick)

Super Bowl II

Orange Bowl, Miami, Florida — January 14, 1968

Attendance: 75,546

GREEN BAY 33, OAKLAND 14—Green Bay, after winning its third consecutive NFL championship, won the Super Bowl title for the second straight year 33-14 over the AFL champion Raiders in a game that drew the first $3-million gate in football history. Bart Starr again was chosen the game's most valuable player as he completed 13 of 24 passes for 202 yards and one touchdown and directed a Packers attack that was in control all the way after building a 16-7 halftime lead. Don Chandler kicked four field goals and all-pro cornerback Herb Adderley capped the Green Bay scoring with a 60-yard run with an interception. The game marked the last for Vince Lombardi as Packers coach, ending nine years at Green Bay in which he won six Western Conference championships, five NFL championships, and two Super Bowls.

Green Bay (NFL)	3	13	10	7	— 33
Oakland (AFL)	0	7	0	7	— 14

GB —FG Chandler 39
GB —FG Chandler 20
GB —Dowler 62 pass from Starr (Chandler kick)
Oak—Miller 23 pass from Lamonica (Blanda kick)
GB —FG Chandler 43
GB —Anderson 2 run (Chandler kick)
GB —FG Chandler 31
GB —Adderley 60 interception return (Chandler kick)
Oak—Miller 23 pass from Lamonica (Blanda kick)

Super Bowl I

Memorial Coliseum, Los Angeles, California — January 15, 1967

Attendance: 61,946

GREEN BAY 35, KANSAS CITY 10—The Green Bay Packers opened the Super Bowl series by defeating Kansas City's American Football League champions 35-10 behind the passing of Bart Starr, the receiving of Max McGee, and a key interception by all-pro safety Willie Wood. Green Bay broke open the game with three second-half touchdowns, the first of which was set up by Wood's 40-yard return of an interception to the Chiefs' 5 yard line. McGee, filling in for ailing Boyd Dowler after having caught only three passes all season, caught seven from Starr for 138 yards and two touchdowns. Elijah Pitts ran for two other scores. The Chiefs' 10 points came in the second quarter, the only touchdown on a seven-yard pass from Len Dawson to Curtis McClinton. Starr completed 16 of 23 passes for 250 yards and two touchdowns and was chosen the most valuable player. The Packers collected $15,000 per man and the Chiefs $7,500—the largest single-game shares in the history of team sports.

Kansas City (AFL)	0	10	0	0	— 10
Green Bay (NFL)	7	7	14	7	— 35

GB—McGee 37 pass from Starr (Chandler kick)
KC—McClinton 7 pass from Dawson (Mercer kick)
GB—Taylor 14 run (Chandler kick)
KC—FG Mercer 31
GB—Pitts 5 run (Chandler kick)
GB—McGee 13 pass from Starr (Chandler kick)
GB—Pitts 1 run (Chandler kick)

AFC Championship Game

Includes AFL Championship Games (1960-69)

Results

Season	Date	Winner (Share)	Loser (Share)	Score	Site	Attendance
1986	Jan. 11	Denver ($18,000)	Cleveland ($18,000)	23-20*	Cleveland	79,973
1985	Jan. 12	New England ($18,000)	Miami ($18,000)	31-14	Miami	75,662
1984	Jan. 6	Miami ($18,000)	Pittsburgh ($18,000)	45-28	Miami	76,029
1983	Jan. 8	L.A. Raiders ($18,000)	Seattle ($18,000)	30-14	Los Angeles	91,445
1982	Jan. 23	Miami ($18,000)	N.Y. Jets ($18,000)	14-0	Miami	67,396
1981	Jan. 10	Cincinnati ($9,000)	San Diego ($9,000)	27-7	Cincinnati	46,302
1980	Jan. 11	Oakland ($9,000)	San Diego ($9,000)	34-27	San Diego	52,675
1979	Jan. 6	Pittsburgh ($9,000)	Houston ($9,000)	27-13	Pittsburgh	50,475
1978	Jan. 7	Pittsburgh ($9,000)	Houston ($9,000)	34-5	Pittsburgh	50,725
1977	Jan. 1	Denver ($9,000)	Oakland ($9,000)	20-17	Denver	75,044
1976	Dec. 26	Oakland ($8,500)	Pittsburgh ($5,500)	24-7	Oakland	53,821
1975	Jan. 4	Pittsburgh ($8,500)	Oakland ($5,500)	16-10	Pittsburgh	50,609
1974	Dec. 29	Pittsburgh ($8,500)	Oakland ($5,500)	24-13	Oakland	53,800
1973	Dec. 30	Miami ($8,500)	Oakland ($5,500)	27-10	Miami	79,325
1972	Dec. 31	Miami ($8,500)	Pittsburgh ($5,500)	21-17	Pittsburgh	50,845
1971	Jan. 2	Miami ($8,500)	Baltimore ($5,500)	21-0	Miami	76,622
1970	Jan. 3	Baltimore ($8,500)	Oakland ($5,500)	27-17	Baltimore	54,799
1969	Jan. 4	Kansas City ($7,755)	Oakland ($6,252)	17-7	Oakland	53,564
1968	Dec. 29	N.Y. Jets ($7,007)	Oakland ($5,349)	27-23	New York	62,627
1967	Dec. 31	Oakland ($6,321)	Houston ($4,996)	40-7	Oakland	53,330
1966	Jan. 1	Kansas City ($5,309)	Buffalo ($3,799)	31-7	Buffalo	42,080
1965	Dec. 26	Buffalo ($5,189)	San Diego ($3,447)	23-0	San Diego	30,361
1964	Dec. 26	Buffalo ($2,668)	San Diego ($1,738)	20-7	Buffalo	40,242
1963	Jan. 5	San Diego ($2,498)	Boston ($1,596)	51-10	San Diego	30,127
1962	Dec. 23	Dallas ($2,206)	Houston ($1,471)	20-17*	Houston	37,981
1961	Dec. 24	Houston ($1,792)	San Diego ($1,111)	10-3	San Diego	29,556
1960	Jan. 1	Houston ($1,025)	L.A. Chargers ($718)	24-16	Houston	32,183

**Sudden death overtime.*

AFC Championship Game Composite Standings

	W	L	Pct.	Pts.	OP
Kansas City Chiefs*	3	0	1.000	68	31
Denver Broncos	2	0	1.000	43	37
Cincinnati Bengals	1	0	1.000	27	7
Miami Dolphins	5	1	.833	142	86
Buffalo Bills	2	1	.667	50	38
Pittsburgh Steelers	4	3	.571	153	131
Baltimore Colts	1	1	.500	27	38
New England Patriots**	1	1	.500	41	65
New York Jets	1	1	.500	27	37
Oakland/L.A. Raiders	4	7	.364	225	213
Houston Oilers	2	4	.333	76	140
San Diego Chargers***	1	6	.143	111	148
Cleveland Browns	0	1	.000	20	23
Seattle Seahawks	0	1	.000	14	30

**One game played when franchise was in Dallas (Texans). (Won 20-17)*
***One game played when franchise was in Boston. (Lost 51-10)*
****One game played when franchise was in Los Angeles. (Lost 24-16)*

1986 American Football Conference Championship Game

Cleveland Stadium, Cleveland, Ohio — January 11, 1987

Attendance: 79,973

Denver 23, Cleveland 20—The AFC Western Division champion Denver Broncos advanced to their second Super Bowl in franchise history by defeating the Cleveland Browns 23-20 in overtime. Quarterback John Elway capped a 15-play, 98-yard touchdown drive with a five-yard scoring pass to rookie wide receiver Mark Jackson with 37 seconds left in regulation time to tie the game, 20-20. Kicker Rich Karlis added a 33-yard field goal 5:38 into overtime to complete the comeback. Cleveland won the overtime coin toss but the Denver defense held the Browns on four plays. Elway completed a 22-yard pass to rookie tight end Orson Mobley and a 28-yarder to wide receiver Steve Watson to set up Karlis's winning kick. The Browns took an early 7-0 lead, but linebacker Jim Ryan's 26-yard interception return led to Karlis's 19-yard field goal, and Ken Woodard's fumble recovery set up running back Gerald Willhite's one-yard touchdown dive to give the Broncos a 10-7 lead in the second quarter. Following a 26-yard field goal by Karlis, the Browns rallied to take a 20-13 fourth-quarter lead on Mark Moseley's 24-yard field goal and quarterback Bernie Kosar's 48-yard touchdown pass to wide receiver Brian Brennan. Elway completed passes to 10 different receivers to finish with 22 of 38 for 244 yards, with one touchdown and one interception. He also gained 56 yards on four carries. The victory earned the Broncos their first Super Bowl appearance since Super Bowl XII, in which they lost 27-10 to the Dallas Cowboys.

Denver (23)	Offense	Cleveland (20)
Vance Johnson	WR	Reggie Langhorne
Dave Studdard	LT	Rickey Bolden
Keith Bishop	LG	Paul Farren
Bill Bryan	C	Mike Baab
Mark Cooper	RG	Dan Fike
Ken Lanier	RT	Cody Risien
Joey Hackett	TE	Ozzie Newsome
Steve Watson	WR	Webster Slaughter
John Elway	QB	Bernie Kosar
Sammy Winder	RB	Earnest Byner
Orson Mobley	TE-RB	Kevin Mack
	Defense	
Rulon Jones	LE	Reggie Camp
Greg Kragen	NT	Bob Golic
Andre Townsend	RE	Carl Hairston
Jim Ryan	LOLB	Chip Banks
Karl Mecklenburg	LILB	Eddie Johnson
Ricky Hunley	RILB	Anthony Griggs
Tom Jackson	ROLB	Clay Matthews
Louis Wright	LCB	Frank Minnifield
Mike Harden	RCB	Hanford Dixon
Dennis Smith	SS	Ray Ellis
Steve Foley	FS	Chris Rockins

Substitutions

Denver—Offense: K—Rich Karlis. P—Mike Horan. QB—Gary Kubiak. RB—Ken Bell, Gene Lang, Steve Sewell, Gerald Willhite. TE—Clarence Kay, Bobby Micho. WR—Mark Jackson, Clint Sampson. G—Mike Freeman. T—Dan Remsberg. Defense: E—Simon Fletcher, Freddie Gilbert. NT—Tony Colorito. LB—Darren Comeaux, Rick Dennison, Ken Woodard. CB—Steve Wilson. S—Tony Lilly, Randy Robbins. DNP: CB—Mark Haynes.

Cleveland—Offense: K—Mark Moseley. P—Jeff Gossett. RB—Major Everett, Herman Fontenot. TE—Harry Holt, Travis Tucker. WR—Brian Brennan, Gerald McNeil, Clarence Weathers. G—George Lilja, Larry Williams. Defense: E—Sam Clancy. NT—Dave Puzzuoli. LB—Mike Johnson, Scott Nicolas, Brad Van Pelt. CB—Mark Harper, D.D. Hoggard. S—Al Gross, Felix Wright. DNP: QB—Mike Pagel. RB—Curtis Dickey. C—Mark Dennard.

Officials

Referee—Chuck Heberling. Umpire—Gordon Wells. Head Linesman—Ed Marion. Line Judge—Bill Reynolds. Back Judge—Ben Tompkins. Side Judge—Gary Lane. Field Judge—Johnny Grier.

Scoring

Denver	0	10	3	7	3	— 23
Cleveland	7	3	0	10	0	— 20

Clev—Fontenot 6 pass from Kosar (Moseley kick)
Den—FG Karlis 19
Den—Willhite 1 run (Karlis kick)
Clev—FG Moseley 29
Den—FG Karlis 26
Clev—FG Moseley 24
Clev—Brennan 48 pass from Kosar (Moseley kick)
Den—M. Jackson 5 pass from Elway (Karlis kick)
Den—FG Karlis 33

Team Statistics

	Denver	Cleveland
Total First Downs	22	17
First Downs Rushing	6	4
First Downs Passing	13	12
First Downs Penalty	3	1
Total Net Yardage	374	356
Total Offensive Plays	77	66
Average Gain per Offensive Play	4.9	5.4
Rushes	37	33
Yards Gained Rushing (net)	149	100
Average Yards per Rush	4.0	3.0
Passes Attempted	38	32
Passes Completed	22	18
Had Intercepted	1	2
Times Tackled Attempting to Pass	2	1
Yards Lost Attempting to Pass	19	3
Yards Gained Passing (net)	225	256
Punts	7	6
Average Distance	37.6	43.2
Punt Returns	3	3
Punt Return Yardage	10	37
Kickoff Returns	5	6
Kickoff Return Yardage	33	105
Interception Return Yardage	40	0
Total Return Yardage	83	142
Fumbles	1	3
Own Fumbles Recovered	1	2
Opponents Fumbles Recovered	1	0
Penalties	6	9
Yards Penalized	39	76
Total Points Scored	23	20
Touchdowns	2	2
Touchdowns Rushing	1	0
Touchdowns Passing	1	2
Touchdowns Returns	0	0
Extra Points	2	2
Field Goals	3	2
Field Goals Attempted	3	2
Third Down Efficiency	5/18	5/13
Fourth Down Efficiency	1/1	0/0
Time of Possession	34:05	31:43

Individual Statistics

Rushing

Denver	**Att.**	**Yds.**	**LG**	**TD**
Winder	26	83	9	0
Elway	4	56	34	0
Lang	3	9	4	0
Sewell	1	1	1	0
Willhite	3	0	2	1
Cleveland	**Att.**	**Yds.**	**LG**	**TD**
Mack	26	94	15	0
Fontenot	3	3	4	0
Kosar	4	3	3	0

Passing

Denver	**Att.**	**Comp.**	**Yds.**	**TD**	**Int.**
Elway	38	22	244	1	1
Cleveland	**Att.**	**Comp.**	**Yds.**	**TD**	**Int.**
Kosar	32	18	259	2	2

Receiving

Denver	**No.**	**Yds.**	**LG**	**TD**
Watson	3	55	28	0
Sewell	3	47	22	0
Mobley	3	36	22	0
V. Johnson	3	25	14	0
M. Jackson	2	25	20	1
Kay	2	23	15	0
Willhite	2	20	16	0
Winder	2	2	5	0
Sampson	1	10	10	0
Lang	1	1	1	0
Cleveland	**No.**	**Yds.**	**LG**	**TD**
Fontenot	7	66	24	1
Brennan	4	72	48t	1
Langhorne	2	35	22	0
Mack	2	20	12	0
Weathers	1	42	42	0
Slaughter	1	20	20	0
Byner	1	4	4	0

Interceptions

Denver	**No.**	**Yds.**	**LG**	**TD**
Ryan	1	26	26	0
Hunley	1	14	14	0
Cleveland	**No.**	**Yds.**	**LG**	**TD**
Harper	1	0	0	0

Punting

Denver	**No.**	**Avg.**	**LG**	**Blk.**
Horan	6	40.7	48	0
Elway	1	19.0	19	0
Cleveland	**No.**	**Avg.**	**LG**	**Blk.**
Gossett	6	43.2	58	0

Punt Returns

Denver	**No.**	**FC**	**Yds.**	**LG**	**TD**
Willhite	3	1	10	4	0
Cleveland	**No.**	**FC**	**Yds.**	**LG**	**TD**
McNeil	3	1	37	18	0

Kickoff Returns

Denver	**No.**	**Yds.**	**LG**	**TD**
Lang	2	14	14	0
Bell	2	10	10	0
Freeman	1	9	9	0
Cleveland	**No.**	**Yds.**	**LG**	**TD**
McNeil	4	80	30	0
Fontenot	2	25	14	0

NFC Championship Game

Includes NFL Championship Games (1932-69)

Results

Season	Date	Winner (Share)	Loser (Share)	Score	Site	Attendance
1986	Jan. 11	New York Giants ($18,000)	Washington ($18,000)	17-0	New York	76,891
1985	Jan. 12	Chicago ($18,000)	L.A. Rams ($18,000)	24-0	Chicago	66,030
1984	Jan. 6	San Francisco ($18,000)	Chicago ($18,000)	23-0	San Francisco	61,336
1983	Jan. 8	Washington ($18,000)	San Francisco ($18,000)	24-21	Washington	55,363
1982	Jan. 22	Washington ($18,000)	Dallas ($18,000)	31-17	Washington	55,045
1981	Jan. 10	San Francisco ($9,000)	Dallas ($9,000)	28-27	San Francisco	60,525
1980	Jan. 11	Philadelphia ($9,000)	Dallas ($9,000)	20-7	Philadelphia	71,522
1979	Jan. 6	Los Angeles ($9,000)	Tampa Bay ($9,000)	9-0	Tampa Bay	72,033
1978	Jan. 7	Dallas ($9,000)	Los Angeles ($9,000)	28-0	Los Angeles	71,086
1977	Jan. 1	Dallas ($9,000)	Minnesota ($9,000)	23-6	Dallas	64,293
1976	Dec. 26	Minnesota ($8,500)	Los Angeles ($5,500)	24-13	Minnesota	48,379
1975	Jan. 4	Dallas ($8,500)	Los Angeles ($5,500)	37-7	Los Angeles	88,919
1974	Dec. 29	Minnesota ($8,500)	Los Angeles ($5,500)	14-10	Minnesota	48,444
1973	Dec. 30	Minnesota ($8,500)	Dallas ($5,500)	27-10	Dallas	64,422
1972	Dec. 31	Washington ($8,500)	Dallas ($5,500)	26-3	Washington	53,129
1971	Jan. 2	Dallas ($8,500)	San Francisco ($5,500)	14-3	Dallas	63,409
1970	Jan. 3	Dallas ($8,500)	San Francisco ($5,500)	17-10	San Francisco	59,364
1969	Jan. 4	Minnesota ($7,930)	Cleveland ($5,118)	27-7	Minnesota	46,503
1968	Dec. 29	Baltimore ($9,306)	Cleveland ($5,963)	34-0	Cleveland	78,410
1967	Dec. 31	Green Bay ($7,950)	Dallas ($5,299)	21-17	Green Bay	50,861
1966	Jan. 1	Green Bay ($9,813)	Dallas ($6,527)	34-27	Dallas	74,152
1965	Jan. 2	Green Bay ($7,819)	Cleveland ($5,288)	23-12	Green Bay	50,777
1964	Dec. 27	Cleveland ($8,052)	Baltimore ($5,571)	27-0	Cleveland	79,544
1963	Dec. 29	Chicago ($5,899)	New York ($4,218)	14-10	Chicago	45,801
1962	Dec. 30	Green Bay ($5,888)	New York ($4,166)	16-7	New York	64,892
1961	Dec. 31	Green Bay ($5,195)	New York ($3,339)	37-0	Green Bay	39,029
1960	Dec. 26	Philadelphia ($5,116)	Green Bay ($3,105)	17-13	Philadelphia	67,325
1959	Dec. 27	Baltimore ($4,674)	New York ($3,083)	31-16	Baltimore	57,545
1958	Dec. 28	Baltimore ($4,718)	New York ($3,111)	23-17*	New York	64,185
1957	Dec. 29	Detroit ($4,295)	Cleveland ($2,750)	59-14	Detroit	55,263
1956	Dec. 30	New York ($3,779)	Chi. Bears ($2,485)	47-7	New York	56,836
1955	Dec. 26	Cleveland ($3,508)	Los Angeles ($2,316)	38-14	Los Angeles	85,693
1954	Dec. 26	Cleveland ($2,478)	Detroit ($1,585)	56-10	Cleveland	43,827
1953	Dec. 27	Detroit ($2,424)	Cleveland ($1,654)	17-16	Detroit	54,577
1952	Dec. 28	Detroit ($2,274)	Cleveland ($1,712)	17-7	Cleveland	50,934
1951	Dec. 23	Los Angeles ($2,108)	Cleveland ($1,483)	24-17	Los Angeles	57,522
1950	Dec. 24	Cleveland ($1,113)	Los Angeles ($686)	30-28	Cleveland	29,751

1949	Dec. 18	Philadelphia ($1,094)	Los Angeles ($739)	14-0	Los Angeles	27,980
1948	Dec. 19	Philadelphia ($1,540)	Chi. Cardinals ($874)	7-0	Philadelphia	36,309
1947	Dec. 28	Chi. Cardinals ($1,132)	Philadelphia ($754)	28-21	Chicago	30,759
1946	Dec. 15	Chi. Bears ($1,975)	New York ($1,295)	24-14	New York	58,346
1945	Dec. 16	Cleveland ($1,469)	Washington ($902)	15-14	Cleveland	32,178
1944	Dec. 17	Green Bay ($1,449)	New York ($814)	14-7	New York	46,016
1943	Dec. 26	Chi. Bears ($1,146)	Washington ($765)	41-21	Chicago	34,320
1942	Dec. 13	Washington ($965)	Chi. Bears ($637)	14-6	Washington	36,006
1941	Dec. 21	Chi. Bears ($430)	New York ($288)	37-9	Chicago	13,341
1940	Dec. 8	Chi. Bears ($873)	Washington ($606)	73-0	Washington	36,034
1939	Dec. 10	Green Bay ($703.97)	New York ($455.57)	27-0	Milwaukee	32,279
1938	Dec. 11	New York ($504.45)	Green Bay ($368.81)	23-17	New York	48,120
1937	Dec. 12	Washington ($225.90)	Chi. Bears ($127.78)	28-21	Chicago	15,870
1936	Dec. 13	Green Bay ($250)	Boston ($180)	21-6	New York	29,545
1935	Dec. 15	Detroit ($313.35)	New York ($200.20)	26-7	Detroit	15,000
1934	Dec. 9	New York ($621)	Chi. Bears ($414.02)	30-13	New York	35,059
1933	Dec. 17	Chi. Bears ($210.34)	New York ($140.22)	23-21	Chicago	26,000
1932	Dec. 18	Chi. Bears	Portsmouth	9-0	Chicago	11,198

**Sudden death overtime.*

NFC Championship Game Composite Standings

	W	L	Pct.	Pts.	OP
Green Bay Packers	8	2	.800	223	116
Minnesota Vikings	4	1	.800	98	63
Philadelphia Eagles	4	1	.800	79	48
Baltimore Colts	3	1	.750	88	60
Detroit Lions*	4	2	.667	129	109
Chicago Bears	8	5	.615	292	217
Washington Redskins**	5	5	.500	164	235
St. Louis Cardinals***	1	1	.500	28	28
Dallas Cowboys	5	7	.417	227	213
San Francisco 49ers	2	3	.400	85	82
Cleveland Browns	4	7	.364	224	253
Los Angeles Rams****	3	8	.273	120	240
New York Giants	4	11	.267	225	309
Tampa Bay Buccaneers	0	1	.000	0	9

**One game played when franchise was in Portsmouth. (Lost 9-0)*
***One game played when franchise was in Boston. (Lost 21-6)*
****Both games played when franchise was in Chicago. (Won 28-21, lost 7-0)*
*****One game played when franchise was in Cleveland. (Won 15-14)*

1986 National Football Conference Championship Game

Giants Stadium, East Rutherford, New Jersey — January 11, 1987
Attendance: 76,633

New York Giants 17, Washington 0—The NFC Eastern Division champion New York Giants gained the right to try for their first NFL championship since 1956 by blanking the Washington Redskins, 17-0. The game marked the third straight NFC Championship that was won by shutout. The Giants gained the advantage of wind gusts up to 30 miles per hour when they won the coin toss and elected to defend the eastern goal, thus having the wind at their backs the first quarter, when they scored 10 points. The Redskins ran three plays for only four yards and were forced to punt on their first series of the game. New York took over on the Redskins' 47-yard line, and six plays later Raul Allegre kicked a 47-yard field goal 3:22 into the game. After Washington punted on its next series, the Giants again got excellent field position at the Redskins' 38-yard line. On third-and-20 from the Washington 36, wide receiver Lionel Manuel caught a 25-yard pass from Phil Simms for a first down. Three plays later, Simms connected with Manuel in the end zone for an 11-yard completion. Simms threw for 60 yards in the first quarter and ended up with seven completions in 14 attempts for 90 yards. In contrast, Washington quarterback Jay Schroeder was forced to throw 50 times—an NFC Championship Game record. He completed 20 for 195 yards. In the second half, the Giants rushed 27 times and passed only twice. The Redskins passed 34 times and rushed once in the final two periods. New York's final score came on a six-play, 49-yard drive that was sparked by a 30-yard Simms completion to tight end Mark Bavaro to the Washington 17-yard line. Two plays later, running back Joe Morris, who carried 29 times for 87 yards, scored on a one-yard run.

Washington (0)	Offense	N.Y. Giants (17)
Art Monk	WR	Bobby Johnson
Joe Jacoby	LT	Brad Benson
Russ Grimm	LG	Billy Ard
Jeff Bostic	C	Bart Oates
R.C. Thielemann	RG	Chris Godfrey
Mark May	RT	Karl Nelson
Clint Didier	TE	Mark Bavaro
Gary Clark	WR	Stacy Robinson
Jay Schroeder	QB	Phil Simms
George Rogers	RB	Joe Morris
Don Warren	TE-RB	Maurice Carthon

	Defense	
Charles Mann	LE	George Martin
Dave Butz	LT-NT	Jim Burt
Darryl Grant	RT-RE	Leonard Marshall
Dexter Manley	RE-LOLB	Carl Banks
Monte Coleman	LLB-LILB	Gary Reasons
Neal Olkewicz	MLB-RILB	Harry Carson
Rich Milot	RLB-ROLB	Lawrence Taylor
Darrell Green	LCB	Elvis Patterson
Vernon Dean	RCB	Perry Williams
Alvin Walton	SS	Kenny Hill
Curtis Jordan	FS	Herb Welch

Substitutions

Washington—Offense: K—Jess Atkinson. P—Steve Cox. RB—Reggie Branch, Kelvin Bryant, Dwight Garner, Keith Griffin, Rickey Sanders. TE—Terry Orr. WR—Eric Yarber. G—Raleigh McKenzie, Ron Tilton. T—Dan McQuaid. Defense: E—Tom Beasley, Steve Hamilton, Markus Koch. T—Dean Hamel. LB—Calvin Daniels, Shawn Burks. CB—Tim Morrison, Barry Wilburn. S—Todd Bowles, Ken Coffey. DNP: QB—Doug Williams.
N.Y. Giants—Offense: K—Raul Allegre. P—Sean Landeta. QB—Jeff Rutledge. RB—Ottis Anderson, Tony Galbreath, Lee Rouson. TE—Zeke Mowatt. WR—Lionel Manuel, Phil McConkey, Solomon Miller. G—Damian Johnson. T—William Roberts. Defense: E—Eric Dorsey. NT—Erik Howard, Jerome Sally. LB—Andy Headen, Byron Hunt, Pepper Johnson, Robbie Jones. CB—Mark Collins. S—Tom Flynn, Greg Lasker. DNP: C—Brian Johnston.

Officials

Referee: Pat Haggerty. Umpire—Hendi Ancich. Head Linesman—Dale Williams. Line Judge—Jack Johnson. Back Judge—Pete Liske. Side Judge—Gerry Austin. Field Judge—Jack Vaughan.

Scoring

Washington	0	0	0	0	— 0
N.Y. Giants	10	7	0	0	— 17

NYG—FG Allegre 47
NYG—Manuel 11 pass from Simms (Allegre kick)
NYG—Morris 1 run (Allegre kick)

Team Statistics

	Washington	N.Y. Giants
Total First Downs	12	12
First Downs Rushing	2	8
First Downs Passing	7	3
First Downs Penalty	3	1
Total Net Yardage	190	199
Total Offensive Plays	70	61
Average Gain per Offensive Play	2.7	3.7
Rushes	16	46
Yards Gained Rushing (net)	40	117
Average Yards per Rush	2.5	2.5
Passes Attempted	50	14
Passes Completed	20	7
Had Intercepted	1	0
Times Tackled Attempting to Pass	4	1
Yards Lost Attempting to Pass	45	8
Yards Gained Passing (net)	150	82
Punts	9	6
Average Distance	35.6	42.3
Punt Returns	3	5
Punt Return Yardage	19	27
Kickoff Returns	2	0
Kickoff Return Yardage	15	0
Interception Return Yardage	0	15
Total Return Yardage	34	42

Fumbles	3	4
Own Fumbles Recovered	2	1
Opponents Fumbles Recovered	3	1
Penalties	3	6
Yards Penalized	15	48
Total Points Scored	0	17
Touchdowns	0	2
Touchdowns Rushing	0	1
Touchdowns Passing	0	1
Touchdowns Returns	0	0
Extra Points	0	2
Field Goals	0	1
Field Goals Attempted	0	1
Third Down Efficiency	0/14	3/13
Fourth Down Efficiency	0/4	1/2
Time of Possession	26:56	33:04

Individual Statistics

Rushing

Washington	Att.	Yds.	LG	TD
Bryant	6	25	9	0
Rogers	9	15	4	0
Schroeder	1	0	0	0
N.Y. Giants	**Att.**	**Yds.**	**LG**	**TD**
Morris	29	87	22	1
Carthon	7	28	10	0
Anderson	1	3	3	0
Rouson	1	2	2	0
Galbreath	1	−1	−1	0
Simms	7	−2	8	0

Passing

Wash.	Att.	Comp.	Yds.	TD	Int.
Schroeder	50	20	195	0	1
N.Y.G.	**Att.**	**Comp.**	**Yds.**	**TD**	**Int.**
Simms	14	7	90	1	0

Receiving

Washington	No.	Yds.	LG	TD
Monk	8	126	48	0
Bryant	7	45	24	0
Warren	3	9	10	0
Griffin	1	8	8	0
Didier	1	7	7	0
N.Y. Giants	**No.**	**Yds.**	**LG**	**TD**
Carthon	3	18	8	0
Bavaro	2	36	30	0
Manuel	2	36	25	1

Interceptions

Washington	No.	Yds.	LG	TD
None				
N.Y. Giants	**No.**	**Yds.**	**LG**	**TD**
Reasons	1	15	15	0

Punting

Washington	No.	Avg.	LG	Blk.
Cox	9	35.6	46	0
N.Y. Giants	**No.**	**Avg.**	**LG**	**Blk.**
Landeta	6	42.3	46	0

Punt Returns

Washington	No.	FC	Yds.	LG	TD
Yarber	3	0	19	10	0
N.Y. Giants	**No.**	**FC**	**Yds.**	**LG**	**TD**
McConkey	5	0	27	8	0

Kickoff Returns

Washington	No.	Yds.	LG	TD
Orr	1	10	10	0
Branch	1	5	5	0
N.Y. Giants	**No.**	**Yds.**	**LG**	**TD**
None				

AFC Divisional Playoffs

Includes Second-Round Playoff Games (1982), AFL Inter-Divisional Playoff Games (1969), and special playoff games to break ties for AFL Division Championships (1963, 1968)

Results

Season	Date	Winner	Loser	Site	Attendance
1986	Jan. 4	Denver 22	New England 17	Denver	75,262
	Jan. 3	*Cleveland 23	N.Y. Jets 20	Cleveland	79,720
1985	Jan. 5	New England 27	L.A. Raiders 20	Los Angeles	87,163
	Jan. 4	Miami 24	Cleveland 21	Miami	74,667
1984	Dec. 30	Pittsburgh 24	Denver 17	Denver	74,981
	Dec. 29	Miami 31	Seattle 10	Miami	73,469
1983	Jan. 1	L.A. Raiders 38	Pittsburgh 10	Los Angeles	90,380
	Dec. 31	Seattle 27	Miami 20	Miami	74,136
1982	Jan. 16	Miami 34	San Diego 13	Miami	71,383
	Jan. 15	N.Y. Jets 17	L.A. Raiders 14	Los Angeles	90,038
1981	Jan. 3	Cincinnati 28	Buffalo 21	Cincinnati	55,420
	Jan. 2	*San Diego 41	Miami 38	Miami	73,735
1980	Jan. 4	Oakland 14	Cleveland 12	Cleveland	78,245
	Jan. 3	San Diego 20	Buffalo 14	San Diego	52,253
1979	Dec. 30	Pittsburgh 34	Miami 14	Pittsburgh	50,214
	Dec. 29	Houston 17	San Diego 14	San Diego	51,192
1978	Dec. 31	Houston 31	New England 14	New England	60,735
	Dec. 30	Pittsburgh 33	Denver 10	Pittsburgh	50,230
1977	Dec. 24	*Oakland 37	Baltimore 31	Baltimore	59,925
	Dec. 24	Denver 34	Pittsburgh 21	Denver	75,059
1976	Dec. 19	Pittsburgh 40	Baltimore 14	Baltimore	59,296
	Dec. 18	Oakland 24	New England 21	Oakland	53,050
1975	Dec. 28	Oakland 31	Cincinnati 28	Oakland	53,030
	Dec. 27	Pittsburgh 28	Baltimore 10	Pittsburgh	49,557
1974	Dec. 22	Pittsburgh 32	Buffalo 14	Pittsburgh	49,841
	Dec. 21	Oakland 28	Miami 26	Oakland	53,023
1973	Dec. 23	Miami 34	Cincinnati 16	Miami	78,928
	Dec. 22	Oakland 33	Pittsburgh 14	Oakland	52,646
1972	Dec. 24	Miami 20	Cleveland 14	Miami	78,916
	Dec. 23	Pittsburgh 13	Oakland 7	Pittsburgh	50,327
1971	Dec. 26	Baltimore 20	Cleveland 3	Cleveland	70,734
	Dec. 25	*Miami 27	Kansas City 24	Kansas City	45,822
1970	Dec. 27	Oakland 21	Miami 14	Oakland	52,594
	Dec. 26	Baltimore 17	Cincinnati 0	Baltimore	49,694
1969	Dec. 21	Oakland 56	Houston 7	Oakland	53,539
	Dec. 20	Kansas City 13	N.Y. Jets 6	New York	62,977
1968	Dec. 22	Oakland 41	Kansas City 6	Oakland	53,605
1963	Dec. 28	Boston 26	Buffalo 8	Buffalo	33,044

**Sudden death overtime.*

1986 AFC Divisional Playoffs

Cleveland Stadium, Cleveland, Ohio — January 3, 1987
Attendance: 79,720

CLEVELAND 23, NEW YORK JETS 20—Mark Moseley's 27-yard field goal 17:02 into overtime gave the AFC Central champion Browns their first playoff victory since 1969 in the third-longest game in NFL history. Cleveland quarterback Bernie Kosar set NFL postseason passing records for attempts (64), yards (489), and average gain per completion (14.81 yards), and tied another by completing 33 passes to rally the Browns from a 20-10 fourth-quarter deficit. After the Jets took a 10-point lead on Freeman McNeil's 25-yard touchdown run with 4:14 remaining, Kosar drove the Browns 68 yards to set up Kevin Mack's one-yard scoring run with 1:57 left. Cleveland's defense forced New York to punt on the next series. Kosar then completed a 37-yard pass to rookie Webster Slaughter to the Jets' 5-yard line to set up Mark Moseley's 22-yard field goal with seven seconds left in regulation and send the game into overtime. Moseley tied an NFL playoff record by attempting six field goals. Cleveland tight end Ozzie Newsome caught six passes for 114 yards. The Browns' defense held the Jets to 287 total yards and registered a playoff-record nine sacks, including three by defensive end Carl Hairston. The win was Cleveland's club-record thirteenth in 1986. New York's Dave Jennings punted a playoff-record 14 times. Russell Carter's fourth-quarter interception in the end zone snapped Kosar's streak of 133 attempts without an interception.

N.Y. Jets	7	3	3	7	0	0	—20
Cleveland	7	3	0	10	0	3	—23

NYJ—Walker 42 pass from Ryan (Leahy kick)
Clev—Fontenot 37 pass from Kosar (Moseley kick)
Clev—FG Moseley 38
NYJ—FG Leahy 46
NYJ—FG Leahy 37
NYJ—McNeil 25 run (Leahy kick)
Clev—Mack 1 run (Moseley kick)
Clev—FG Moseley 22
Clev—FG Moseley 27

Mile High Stadium, Denver, Colorado January 4, 1987
Attendance: 75,262

DENVER 22, NEW ENGLAND 17—Broncos quarterback John Elway ran for one touchdown and passed for another to lead Denver to its first postseason victory in Mile High Stadium since 1977. Elway threw for a Denver playoff-record 257 yards on 13 of 32 passes. He had a 48-yard touchdown pass to Vance Johnson on the final play of the third quarter to give the Broncos a 20-17 lead they never relinquished. Elway's 22-yard scoring run in the second quarter put Denver ahead 10-7. New England forged a 17-13 lead on Tony Franklin's 28-yard field goal and Tony Eason's 45-yard flea-flicker touchdown pass to Stanley Morgan in the third quarter. Rulon Jones's two sacks included a tackle of Eason in the end zone for a safety with less than two minutes to play. Running back Sammy Winder became the first Denver player ever to rush for over 100 yards in a playoff game with 19 carries for 102 yards. The Broncos' defense set club playoff records for sacks (six), fewest first downs allowed (12), and fewest total yards allowed (271). Morgan caught three passes for 100 yards for the Patriots. Denver's last home playoff win was a 34-21 victory over Pittsburgh in a 1977 divisional playoff game.

New England	0	10	7	0	—17
Denver	3	7	10	2	—22

Den—FG Karlis 27
NE —Morgan 19 pass from Eason (Franklin kick)
Den—Elway 22 run (Karlis kick)
NE —FG Franklin 38
Den—FG Karlis 22
NE —Morgan 45 pass from Eason (Franklin kick)
Den—Johnson 48 pass from Elway (Karlis kick)
Den—Safety, Jones tackled Eason in end zone

NFC Divisional Playoffs

Includes Second-Round Playoff Games (1982), NFL Conference Championship Games (1967-69), and special playoff games to break ties for NFL Division or Conference Championships (1941, 1943, 1947, 1950, 1952, 1957, 1958, 1965)

Results

Season	Date	Winner	Loser	Site	Attendance
1986	Jan. 4	N.Y. Giants 49	San Francisco 3	East Rutherford	75,691
	Jan. 3	Washington 27	Chicago 13	Chicago	65,524
1985	Jan. 5	Chicago 21	N.Y. Giants 0	Chicago	65,670
	Jan. 4	L.A. Rams 20	Dallas 0	Anaheim	66,581
1984	Dec. 30	Chicago 23	Washington 19	Washington	55,431
	Dec. 29	San Francisco 21	N.Y. Giants 10	San Francisco	60,303
1983	Jan. 1	Washington 51	L.A. Rams 7	Washington	54,440
	Dec. 31	San Francisco 24	Detroit 23	San Francisco	59,979
1982	Jan. 16	Dallas 37	Green Bay 26	Dallas	63,972
	Jan. 15	Washington 21	Minnesota 7	Washington	54,593
1981	Jan. 3	San Francisco 38	N.Y. Giants 24	San Francisco	58,360
	Jan. 2	Dallas 38	Tampa Bay 0	Dallas	64,848
1980	Jan. 4	Dallas 30	Atlanta 27	Atlanta	59,793
	Jan. 3	Philadelphia 31	Minnesota 16	Philadelphia	70,178
1979	Dec. 30	Los Angeles 21	Dallas 19	Dallas	64,792
	Dec. 29	Tampa Bay 24	Philadelphia 17	Tampa Bay	71,402
1978	Dec. 31	Los Angeles 34	Minnesota 10	Los Angeles	70,436
	Dec. 30	Dallas 27	Atlanta 20	Dallas	63,406
1977	Dec. 26	Dallas 37	Chicago 7	Dallas	63,260
	Dec. 26	Minnesota 14	Los Angeles 7	Los Angeles	70,203
1976	Dec. 19	Los Angeles 14	Dallas 12	Dallas	63,283
	Dec. 18	Minnesota 35	Washington 20	Minnesota	47,466
1975	Dec. 28	Dallas 17	Minnesota 14	Minnesota	48,050
	Dec. 27	Los Angeles 35	St. Louis 23	Los Angeles	73,459
1974	Dec. 22	Los Angeles 19	Washington 10	Los Angeles	77,925
	Dec. 21	Minnesota 30	St. Louis 14	Minnesota	48,150
1973	Dec. 23	Dallas 27	Los Angeles 16	Dallas	63,272
	Dec. 22	Minnesota 27	Washington 20	Minnesota	48,040
1972	Dec. 24	Washington 16	Green Bay 3	Washington	52,321
	Dec. 23	Dallas 30	San Francisco 28	San Francisco	59,746
1971	Dec. 26	San Francisco 24	Washington 20	San Francisco	45,327
	Dec. 25	Dallas 20	Minnesota 12	Minnesota	47,307
1970	Dec. 27	San Francisco 17	Minnesota 14	Minnesota	45,103
	Dec. 26	Dallas 5	Detroit 0	Dallas	69,613
1969	Dec. 28	Cleveland 38	Dallas 14	Dallas	69,321
	Dec. 27	Minnesota 23	Los Angeles 20	Minnesota	47,900
1968	Dec. 22	Baltimore 24	Minnesota 14	Baltimore	60,238
	Dec. 21	Cleveland 31	Dallas 20	Cleveland	81,497
1967	Dec. 24	Dallas 52	Cleveland 14	Dallas	70,786
	Dec. 23	Green Bay 28	Los Angeles 7	Milwaukee	49,861
1965	Dec. 26	*Green Bay 13	Baltimore 10	Green Bay	50,484
1958	Dec. 21	N.Y. Giants 10	Cleveland 0	New York	61,274
1957	Dec. 22	Detroit 31	San Francisco 27	San Francisco	60,118
1952	Dec. 21	Detroit 31	Los Angeles 21	Detroit	47,645
1950	Dec. 17	Los Angeles 24	Chi. Bears 14	Los Angeles	83,501
	Dec. 17	Cleveland 8	N.Y. Giants 3	Cleveland	33,054
1947	Dec. 21	Philadelphia 21	Pittsburgh 0	Pittsburgh	35,729
1943	Dec. 19	Washington 28	N.Y. Giants 0	New York	42,800
1941	Dec. 14	Chi. Bears 33	Green Bay 14	Chicago	43,425

**Sudden death overtime.*

1986 NFC Divisional Playoffs

Soldier Field, Chicago, Illinois January 3, 1987
Attendance: 65,524

Washington 27, Chicago 13—Washington gained its third NFC Championship Game berth in the past five seasons with a 27-13 victory over the NFC Central and defending NFL champion Chicago. The Redskins became the first Wild Card team to advance to the NFC Championship Game since 1980, when Dallas defeated the Los Angeles Rams and Atlanta before falling to Philadelphia in the title game. Washington took a 14-13 lead on a 23-yard touchdown pass from quarterback Jay Schroeder to wide receiver Art Monk with 7:09 to go in the third period. Monk had opened the Redskins' scoring with a 28-yard catch with 2:15 remaining in the first period. Jess Atkinson connected on 35- and 25-yard field goals late in the fourth quarter to seal the victory. Washington's defense played a major role in the win with two fumble recoveries and two interceptions. The Redskins held Bears running back Walter Payton to 38 yards on 14 carries.

Washington	7	0	7	13	— 27
Chicago	0	13	0	0	— 13

Wash — Monk 28 pass from Schroeder (Atkinson kick)
Chi — Gault 50 pass from Flutie (Butler kick)
Chi — FG Butler 23
Chi — FG Butler 41
Wash — Monk 23 pass from Schroeder (Atkinson kick)
Wash — Rogers 1 run (Atkinson kick)
Wash — FG Atkinson 35
Wash — FG Atkinson 25

Giants Stadium, East Rutherford, New Jersey — January 4, 1987
Attendance: 75,691

New York Giants 49, San Francisco 3—The NFC Eastern Division champion New York Giants advanced to their first NFC Championship Game with a 49-3 win over NFC Western Division titlist San Francisco. The Giants last won the NFL Eastern Conference title in 1963 before losing to Chicago 14-10 in the NFL Championship Game. New York's 46-point margin of victory over the 49ers tied Cleveland's 56-10 win over Detroit in 1954 as the third-largest in NFL playoff history behind Chicago's 73-0 win over Washington in 1940 and Oakland's 56-7 win over Houston in 1969. The Giants compiled 21 first downs to the 49ers' 9 and outgained their opponent 366 yards to 184. New York quarterback Phil Simms tied a club playoff record with four touchdown passes. Giants running back Joe Morris rushed 24 times for 159 yards, and had 45- and 2-yard touchdown runs. New York built a 28-3 halftime lead on two scores with less than a minute to play before halftime. Wide receiver Bobby Johnson caught a 15-yard touchdown pass with 50 seconds left and linebacker Lawrence Taylor's 34-yard interception return for a score with 28 seconds remaining put the game out of reach.

San Francisco	3	0	0	0	— 3
N.Y. Giants	7	21	21	0	— 49

NYG – Bavaro 24 pass from Simms (Allegre kick)
SF – FG Wersching 26
NYG – Morris 45 run (Allegre kick)
NYG – Johnson 15 pass from Simms (Allegre kick)
NYG – Taylor 34 interception return (Allegre kick)
NYG – McConkey 28 pass from Simms (Allegre kick)
NYG – Mowatt 29 pass from Simms (Allegre kick)
NYG – Morris 2 run (Allegre kick)

AFC First-Round Playoff Games

Results

Season	Date	Winner	Loser	Site	Attendance
1986	Dec. 28	N.Y. Jets 35	Kansas City 15	East Rutherford	75,210
1985	Dec. 28	New England 26	N.Y. Jets 14	East Rutherford	75,945
1984	Dec. 22	Seattle 13	L.A. Raiders 7	Seattle	62,049
1983	Dec. 24	Seattle 31	Denver 7	Seattle	64,275
1982	Jan. 9	N.Y. Jets 44	Cincinnati 17	Cincinnati	57,560
	Jan. 9	San Diego 31	Pittsburgh 28	Pittsburgh	53,546
	Jan. 8	L.A. Raiders 27	Cleveland 10	Los Angeles	56,555
	Jan. 8	Miami 28	New England 13	Miami	68,842
1981	Dec. 27	Buffalo 31	N.Y. Jets 27	New York	57,050
1980	Dec. 28	Oakland 27	Houston 7	Oakland	53,333
1979	Dec. 23	Houston 13	Denver 7	Houston	48,776
1978	Dec. 24	Houston 17	Miami 9	Miami	72,445

1986 AFC First-Round Playoff Game

Giants Stadium, East Rutherford, New Jersey — December 28, 1986
Attendance: 75,210

New York Jets 35, Kansas City 15—Jets quarterback Pat Ryan threw three touchdown passes and Freeman McNeil ran for 135 yards to spark the Jets' first home playoff win since a 27-23 decision over the Oakland Raiders on December 29, 1968. Ryan, starting in the first playoff game of his nine-year career, completed 16 of 23 passes for 153 yards. McNeil's one yard touchdown run gave New York a 7-6 first-quarter lead that it never relinquished. McNeil (one yard) and wide receiver Al Toon (11) caught scoring passes from Ryan in the second quarter to give the Jets a 21-6 advantage. New York linebacker Kevin McArthur scored a touchdown on a 21-yard interception return on the first play of the second half to put the game away. It was McNeil's third straight 100-yard game and second-highest playoff total of his career. He gained 202 yards against the Bengals in 1982. Tight end Billy Griggs's six-yard touchdown catch in the fourth quarter was his first NFL reception.

Kansas City	6	0	0	9	— 15
N.Y. Jets	7	14	7	7	— 35

KC —Smith 1 run (kick failed)
NYJ —McNeil 1 run (Leahy kick)
NYJ —McNeil 1 pass from Ryan (Leahy kick)
NYJ —Toon 11 pass from Ryan (Leahy kick)
NYJ —McArthur 21 interception return (Leahy kick)
KC —Lewis recovered blocked punt in end zone (Lowery kick)
NYJ —Griggs 6 pass from Ryan (Leahy kick)
KC —Safety, Jennings ran out of end zone

NFC First-Round Playoff Games

Results

Season	Date	Winner	Loser	Site	Attendance
1986	Dec. 28	Washington 19	L.A. Rams 7	Washington	54,567
1985	Dec. 29	N.Y. Giants 17	San Francisco 3	East Rutherford	75,131
1984	Dec. 23	N.Y. Giants 16	L.A. Rams 13	Anaheim	67,037
1983	Dec. 26	L.A. Rams 24	Dallas 17	Dallas	62,118
1982	Jan. 9	Dallas 30	Tampa Bay 17	Dallas	65,042
	Jan. 9	Minnesota 30	Atlanta 24	Minnesota	60,560
	Jan. 8	Green Bay 41	St. Louis 16	Green Bay	54,282
	Jan. 8	Washington 31	Detroit 7	Washington	55,045
1981	Dec. 27	N.Y. Giants 27	Philadelphia 21	Philadelphia	71,611
1980	Dec. 28	Dallas 34	Los Angeles 13	Dallas	63,052
1979	Dec. 23	Philadelphia 27	Chicago 17	Philadelphia	69,397
1978	Dec. 24	Atlanta 14	Philadelphia 13	Atlanta	59,403

1986 NFC First-Round Playoff Game

Robert F. Kennedy Stadium, Washington, D.C. — December 28, 1986
Attendance: 54,567

Washington 19, Los Angeles Rams 7—The Washington Redskins took advantage of six Los Angeles Rams turnovers (four fumbles and two interceptions) to advance to the NFC Divisional playoffs. The Redskins' Jess Atkinson tied an NFL playoff record by kicking four field goals (25, 20, 38, and 19 yards). Washington held a 36:06 to 23:54 time of possession advantage over Los Angeles. Both teams produced 100-yard rushers in the game. Eric Dickerson of the Rams had 26 carries for 158 yards, and George Rogers of the Redskins rushed 29 times for 115 yards. Los Angeles outgained Washington 324 yards to 228, but was plagued by the turnovers. Quarterback Jay Schroeder connected with running back Kelvin Bryant for a 14-yard touchdown 12:34 into the opening period to give the Redskins a 10-0 lead. Los Angeles's touchdown came on the first play of the fourth period when quarterback Jim Everett completed a 12-yard scoring pass to wide receiver Kevin House.

L.A. Rams	0	0	0	7	— 7
Washington	10	3	3	3	— 19

Wash —FG Atkinson 25
Wash —Bryant 14 pass from Schroeder (Atkinson kick)
Wash —FG Atkinson 20
Wash —FG Atkinson 38
Rams —House 12 pass from Everett (Lansford kick)
Wash —FG Atkinson 19

AFC-NFC PRO BOWL SUMMARIES

NFC leads series, 10-7

Results

Year	Date	Winner	Loser	Site	Attendance
1987	Feb. 1	AFC 10	NFC 6	Honolulu	50,101
1986	Feb. 2	NFC 28	AFC 24	Honolulu	50,101
1985	Jan. 27	AFC 22	NFC 14	Honolulu	50,385
1984	Jan. 29	NFC 45	AFC 3	Honolulu	50,445
1983	Feb. 6	NFC 20	AFC 19	Honolulu	49,883
1982	Jan. 31	AFC 16	NFC 13	Honolulu	50,402
1981	Feb. 1	NFC 21	AFC 7	Honolulu	50,360
1980	Jan. 27	NFC 37	AFC 27	Honolulu	49,800
1979	Jan. 29	NFC 13	AFC 7	Los Angeles	46,281
1978	Jan. 23	NFC 14	AFC 13	Tampa	51,337
1977	Jan. 17	AFC 24	NFC 14	Seattle	64,752
1976	Jan. 26	NFC 23	AFC 20	New Orleans	30,546
1975	Jan. 20	NFC 17	AFC 10	Miami	26,484
1974	Jan. 20	AFC 15	NFC 13	Kansas City	66,918
1973	Jan. 21	AFC 33	NFC 28	Irving	37,091
1972	Jan. 23	AFC 26	NFC 13	Los Angeles	53,647
1971	Jan. 24	NFC 27	AFC 6	Los Angeles	48,222

1987 AFC-NFC Pro Bowl

Aloha Stadium, Honolulu, Hawaii — February 1, 1987

Attendance: 50,101

AFC 10, NFC 6—The AFC defeated the NFC, 10-6, in the lowest-scoring game in AFC-NFC Pro Bowl history. The AFC took a 10-0 halftime lead on Broncos quarterback John Elway's 10-yard touchdown pass to Raiders tight end Todd Christensen and Patriots kicker Tony Franklin's 26-yard field goal. The AFC defense made the lead stand up by forcing the NFC to settle for a pair of field goals from 38 and 19 yards by Saints kicker Morten Andersen after the NFC had first downs at the AFC 31-, 7-, 16-, 15-, 5-, and 7-yard lines. Both AFC scores were set up by fumble recoveries by Seahawks linebacker Fredd Young and Dolphins linebacker John Offerdahl, respectively. Eagles defensive end Reggie White, who tied a Pro Bowl record with four sacks and also contributed seven solo tackles, was voted the game's outstanding player. The AFC victory cut the NFC's lead in the Pro Bowl series to 10-7.

AFC (10)	Offense	NFC (6)
Al Toon (N.Y. Jets)	WR	Jerry Rice (San Francisco)
Anthony Muñoz (Cincinnati)	LT	Jim Covert (Chicago)
Keith Bishop (Denver)	LG	Bill Fralic (Atlanta)
Ray Donaldson (Indianapolis)	C	Jay Hilgenberg (Chicago)
Max Montoya (Cincinnati)	RG	Dennis Harrah (L.A. Rams)
Cody Risien (Cleveland)	RT	Jackie Slater (L.A. Rams)
Todd Christensen (L.A. Raiders)	TE	Mark Bavaro (N.Y. Giants)
Steve Largent (Seattle)	WR	Gary Clark (Washington)
John Elway (Denver)	QB	Tommy Kramer (Minnesota)
James Brooks (Cincinnati)	RB	Eric Dickerson (L.A. Rams)
Earnest Jackson (Pittsburgh)	RB	Walter Payton (Chicago)
	Defense	
Rulon Jones (Denver)	LE	Reggie White (Philadelphia)
Bill Maas (Kansas City)	NT	Steve McMichael (Chicago)
Howie Long (L.A. Raiders)	RE	Dexter Manley (Washington)
Chip Banks (Cleveland)	LOLB	Wilber Marshall (Chicago)
Karl Mecklenburg (Denver)	LILB	Mike Singletary (Chicago)
John Offerdahl (Miami)	RILB	Harry Carson (N.Y. Giants)
Andre Tippett (New England)	ROLB	Lawrence Taylor (N.Y. Giants)
Hanford Dixon (Cleveland)	LCB	Darrell Green (Washington)
Mike Haynes (L.A. Raiders)	RCB	LeRoy Irvin (L.A. Rams)
Dennis Smith (Denver)	SS	Dave Duerson (Chicago)
Deron Cherry (Kansas City)	FS	Ronnie Lott (San Francisco)

Substitutions

AFC—Offense: K—Tony Franklin (New England). P—Rohn Stark (Indianapolis). QB—Boomer Esiason (Cincinnati). RB—Gary Anderson (San Diego), Sammy Winder (Denver). TE—Mickey Shuler (N.Y. Jets). WR—Mark Clayton (Miami), Stanley Morgan (New England). KR—Bobby Joe Edmonds (Seattle). C—Don Mosebar (L.A. Raiders). G—Roy Foster (Miami). T—Chris Hinton (Indianapolis). Defense: E—Jacob Green (Seattle). NT—Bob Golic (Cleveland). LB—Mike Merriweather (Pittsburgh), Fredd Young (Seattle). CB—Raymond Clayborn (New England), Frank Minnifield (Cleveland). S—Lloyd Burruss (Kansas City). ST—Mosi Tatupu (New England).

NFC—Offense: K—Morten Andersen (New Orleans). P—Sean Landeta (N.Y. Giants). QB—Jay Schroeder (Washington). RB—Joe Morris (N.Y. Giants), Gerald Riggs (Atlanta). TE—Steve Jordan (Minnesota). WR—Art Monk (Washington). KR—Vai Sikahema (St. Louis). C—Doug Smith (L.A. Rams). G—Russ Grimm (Washington). T—Brad Benson (N.Y. Giants), Joe Jacoby (Washington). Defense: E—Leonard Marshall (N.Y. Giants). NT—Jim Burt (N.Y. Giants). LB—Carl Ekern (L.A. Rams), Rickey Jackson (New Orleans). CB—Jerry Gray (L.A. Rams). S—Joey Browner (Minnesota). ST—Ron Wolfley (St. Louis). DNP—Mike Quick (Philadelphia).

Head Coaches

AFC—Marty Schottenheimer (Cleveland)
NFC—Joe Gibbs (Washington)

Officials

Referee—Dick Jorgensen. Umpire—Ed Fiffick. Head Linesman—Dale Hamer. Line Judge—Ron DeSouza. Back Judge—Jim Kearney. Side Judge—Dave Hawk. Field Judge—Don Hakes.

Scoring

AFC	7	3	0	0	— 10
NFC	0	0	3	3	— 6

AFC—Christensen 10 pass from Elway (Franklin kick)
AFC—FG Franklin 26
NFC—FG Andersen 38
NFC—FG Andersen 19

Team Statistics

	AFC	NFC
Total First Downs	13	18
First Downs Rushing	4	10
First Downs Passing	8	7
First Downs Penalty	1	1
Total Net Yardage	202	222
Total Offensive Plays	59	63
Average Gain per Offensive Play	3.4	3.5
Rushes	29	29
Yards Gained Rushing (net)	93	105
Average Yards per Rush	3.2	3.6
Passes Attempted	23	30
Passes Completed	10	15
Passes Had Intercepted	1	2
Times Tackled Attempting to Pass	7	4
Yards Lost Attempting to Pass	62	39
Yards Gained Passing (net)	109	117
Punts	9	5
Average Distance	42.0	38.6
Punt Returns	3	7
Punt Return Yardage	11	73
Kickoff Returns	3	3
Kickoff Return Yardage	51	48
Interception Return Yardage	11	23
Total Return Yardage	73	144
Fumbles	0	8
Own Fumbles Recovered	0	5
Opponents Fumbles Recovered	3	0
Penalties	6	4
Yards Penalized	30	30
Total Points Scored	10	6
Touchdowns	1	0
Touchdowns Rushing	0	0
Touchdowns Passing	1	0
Touchdowns Returns	0	0
Extra Points	1	0
Field Goals	1	2
Field Goals Attempted	2	2
Third Down Efficiency	4/16	4/14
Fourth Down Efficiency	1/1	1/1
Time of Possession	28:36	31:24

Individual Statistics

Rushing

AFC	Att.	Yds.	LG	TD
Jackson	7	31	8	0
Brooks	11	23	10	0
Esiason	3	15	10	0
Anderson	3	10	8	0
Winder	3	10	9	0
Elway	1	9	9	0
Largent	1	−5	−5	0
NFC	**Att.**	**Yds.**	**LG**	**TD**
Dickerson	11	33	11	0
Payton	5	24	8	0
Morris	5	20	8	0
Schroeder	2	18	18	0
Riggs	5	16	7	0
Rice	1	−6	−6	0

Passing

AFC	Att.	Comp.	Yds.	TD	Int.
Esiason	12	5	105	0	1
Elway	11	5	66	1	0
NFC	**Att.**	**Comp.**	**Yds.**	**TD**	**Int.**
Schroeder	16	7	83	0	2
Kramer	13	8	73	0	0
Payton	1	0	0	0	0

Receiving

AFC	No.	Yds.	LG	TD
Morgan	2	54	34	0
Brooks	2	36	30	0
Shuler	1	24	24	0
Winder	1	21	21	0
Clayton	1	14	14	0
Largent	1	13	13	0
Christensen	1	10	10t	1
Jackson	1	−1	−1	0
NFC	**No.**	**Yds.**	**LG**	**TD**
Payton	4	24	8	0
Bavaro	3	46	27	0
Clark	3	28	11	0
Dickerson	2	8	7	0
Monk	1	19	19	0
Riggs	1	18	18	0
Rice	1	13	13	0

Interceptions

AFC	No.	Yds.	LG	TD
Haynes	1	11	11	0
Burruss	1	0	0	0
NFC	**No.**	**Yds.**	**LG**	**TD**
Green	1	23	23	0

Punting

AFC	No.	Avg.	LG	Blk.
Stark	9	42.0	48	0
NFC	**No.**	**Avg.**	**LG**	**Blk.**
Landeta	5	38.6	48	0

Punt Returns

AFC	No.	FC	Yds.	LG	TD
Edmonds	3	0	11	5	0
NFC	**No.**	**FC**	**Yds.**	**LG**	**TD**
Sikahema	7	0	73	29	0

Kickoff Returns

AFC	No.	Yds.	LG	TD
Edmonds	2	34	18	0
Anderson	1	17	17	0
NFC	**No.**	**Yds.**	**LG**	**TD**
Sikahema	2	35	25	0
Riggs	1	13	13	0

1986 AFC-NFC Pro Bowl

Aloha Stadium, Honolulu, Hawaii — February 2, 1986

Attendance: 50,101

NFC 28, AFC 24—New York Giants quarterback Phil Simms brought the NFC back from a 24-7 halftime deficit to a 28-24 win over the AFC. Simms, who completed 15 of 27 passes for 212 yards and three touchdowns, was named the most valuable player of the game. The AFC had taken its first-half lead behind a two-yard run by Los Angeles Raiders running back Marcus Allen, who also threw a 51-yard scoring pass to San Diego wide receiver Wes Chandler, an 11-yard touchdown catch by Pittsburgh wide receiver Louis Lipps, and a 34-yard field goal by Steelers kicker Gary Anderson. Minnesota's Joey Browner accounted for the NFC's only score before halftime with a 48-yard touchdown interception return. After intermission, the NFC blanked the AFC while scoring three touchdowns via a 15-yard catch by Washington wide receiver Art Monk, a 2-yard reception by Dallas tight end Doug Cosbie, and a 15-yard catch by Tampa Bay tight end Jimmie Giles with 2:47 remaining in the game. The victory gave the NFC a 10-6 Pro Bowl record vs. the AFC.

NFC	0	7	7	14	— 28
AFC	7	17	0	0	— 24

AFC—Allen 2 run (Anderson kick)
NFC—Browner 48 interception return (Andersen kick)
AFC—Chandler 51 pass from Allen (Anderson kick)
AFC—FG Anderson 34
AFC—Lipps 11 pass from O'Brien (Anderson kick)
NFC—Monk 15 pass from Simms (Andersen kick)
NFC—Cosbie 2 pass from Simms (Andersen kick)
NFC—Giles 15 pass from Simms (Andersen kick)

1985 AFC-NFC Pro Bowl

Aloha Stadium, Honolulu, Hawaii — January 27, 1985

Attendance: 50,385

AFC 22, NFC 14—Defensive end Art Still of the Kansas City Chiefs recovered a fumble and returned it 83 yards for a touchdown to clinch the AFC's victory over the NFC. Still's touchdown came in the fourth period with the AFC trailing 14-12 and was one of several outstanding defensive plays in a Pro Bowl dominated by two record-breaking defenses. Both teams combined for a Pro Bowl-record 17 sacks, including four by New York Jets defensive end Mark Gastineau, who was named the game's outstanding player. The AFC's first score came on a safety when Gastineau tackled running back Eric Dickerson of the Los Angeles Rams in the end zone. The AFC's second score, a six-yard pass from Miami's Dan Marino to Los Angeles Raiders running back Marcus Allen, was set up by a partial block of a punt by Seahawks linebacker Fredd Young.

AFC	0	9	0	13	— 22
NFC	0	0	7	7	— 14

AFC—Safety, Gastineau tackled Dickerson in end zone
AFC—Allen 6 pass from Marino (Johnson kick)
NFC—Lofton 13 pass from Montana (Stenerud kick)
NFC—Payton 1 run (Stenerud kick)
AFC—FG Johnson 33
AFC—Still 83 fumble recovery return (Johnson kick)
AFC—FG Johnson 22

1984 AFC-NFC Pro Bowl

Aloha Stadium, Honolulu, Hawaii — January 29, 1984

Attendance: 50,445

NFC 45, AFC 3—The NFC won its sixth Pro Bowl in the last seven seasons, 45-3 over the AFC. The NFC was led by the passing of most valuable player Joe Theismann of Washington, who completed 21 of 27 passes for 242 yards and three touchdowns. Theismann set Pro Bowl records for completions and touchdown passes. The NFC established Pro Bowl marks for most points scored and fewest points allowed. Running back William Andrews of Atlanta had six carries for 43 yards and caught four passes for 49 yards, including scoring receptions of 16 and 2 yards. Los Angeles Rams rookie Eric Dickerson gained 46 yards on 11 carries, including a 14-yard touchdown run, and had 45 yards on five catches. Rams safety Nolan Cromwell had a 44-yard interception return for a touchdown early in the third period to give the NFC a commanding 24-3 lead. Green Bay wide receiver James Lofton caught an eight-yard touchdown pass, while tight end teammate Paul Coffman had a six-yard scoring catch.

NFC	3	14	14	14	— 45
AFC	0	3	0	0	— 3

NFC—FG Haji-Sheikh 23
NFC—Andrews 16 pass from Theismann (Haji-Sheikh kick)
NFC—Andrews 2 pass from Montana (Haji-Sheikh kick)
AFC—FG Anderson 43
NFC—Cromwell 44 interception return (Haji-Sheikh kick)
NFC—Lofton 8 pass from Theismann (Haji-Sheikh kick)
NFC—Coffman 6 pass from Theismann (Haji-Sheikh kick)
NFC—Dickerson 14 run (Haji-Sheikh kick)

1983 AFC-NFC Pro Bowl

Aloha Stadium, Honolulu, Hawaii — Sunday, February 6, 1983

Attendance: 49,883

NFC 20, AFC 19—Danny White threw an 11-yard touchdown pass to John Jefferson with 35 seconds remaining to give the NFC a 20-19 victory over the AFC. White, who completed 14 of 26 passes for 162 yards, kept the winning 65-yard drive alive with a 14-yard completion to Jefferson on a fourth-and-seven play at the AFC 25. The AFC was ahead 12-10 at halftime and increased the lead to 19-10 in the third period, when Marcus Allen scored on a one-yard run. Dan Fouts, who attempted 30 passes, set Pro Bowl records for most completions (17) and yards (274). John Stallworth was the AFC's leading receiver with seven catches for 67 yards. William Andrews topped the NFC with five receptions for 48 yards. Fouts and Jefferson were voted co-winners of the player of the game award.

AFC	9	3	7	0	— 19
NFC	0	10	0	10	— 20

AFC—Walker 34 pass from Fouts (Benirschke kick)
AFC—Safety, Still tackled Theismann in end zone
NFC—Andrews 3 run (Moseley kick)
NFC—FG Moseley 35
AFC—FG Benirschke 29
AFC—Allen 1 run (Benirschke kick)
NFC—FG Moseley 41
NFC—Jefferson 11 pass from D. White (Moseley kick)

1982 AFC-NFC Pro Bowl

Aloha Stadium, Honolulu, Hawaii — Sunday, January 31, 1982

Attendance: 50,402

AFC 16, NFC 13—Nick Lowery kicked a 23-yard field goal with three seconds remaining to give the AFC a 16-13 victory over the NFC. Lowery's kick climaxed a 69-yard drive directed by quarterback Dan Fouts. The NFC gained a 13-13 tie with 2:43 to go when Tony Dorsett ran four yards for a touchdown. In the drive to the game-winning field goal, Fouts completed three passes, including a 23-yarder to San Diego teammate Kellen Winslow that put the ball on the NFC's 5-yard line. Two plays later, Lowery kicked the field goal. Winslow, who caught six passes for 86 yards, was named co-player of the game along with NFC defensive end Lee Roy Selmon.

NFC	0	6	0	7	— 13
AFC	0	0	13	3	— 16

NFC—Giles 4 pass from Montana (kick blocked)
AFC—Muncie 2 run (kick failed)
AFC—Campbell 1 run (Lowery kick)
NFC—Dorsett 4 run (Septien kick)
AFC—FG Lowery 23

1981 AFC-NFC Pro Bowl

Aloha Stadium, Honolulu, Hawaii — February 1, 1981

Attendance: 50,360

NFC 21, AFC 7—Ed Murray kicked four field goals and Steve Bartkowski fired a 55-yard scoring pass to Alfred Jenkins to lead the NFC to its fourth straight victory over the AFC and a 7-4 edge in the series. Murray was named the game's most valuable player and missed tying Garo Yepremian's Pro Bowl record of five goals when a 37-yard attempt hit the crossbar with 22 seconds remaining. The AFC's only score came on a nine-yard pass from Brian Sipe to Stanley Morgan in the second period. Bartkowski completed 9 of 21 passes for 173 yards, while Sipe connected on 10 of 15 for 142 yards. Ottis Anderson led all rushers with 70 yards on 10 carries. Earl Campbell, the NFL's leading rusher in 1980, was limited to 24 yards on eight attempts.

AFC	0	7	0	0	— 7
NFC	3	6	0	12	— 21

NFC—FG Murray 31
AFC—Morgan 9 pass from Sipe (J. Smith kick)
NFC—FG Murray 31
NFC—FG Murray 34
NFC—Jenkins 55 pass from Bartkowski (Murray kick)
NFC—FG Murray 36
NFC—Safety (Team)

1980 AFC-NFC Pro Bowl

Aloha Stadium, Honolulu, Hawaii — January 27, 1980

Attendance: 49,800

NFC 37, AFC 27—Running back Chuck Muncie ran for two touchdowns and threw a 25-yard option pass for another score to give the NFC its third consecutive victory over the AFC. Muncie, who was selected the game's most valuable player, snapped a 3-3 tie on a one-yard touchdown run at 1:41 of the second quarter, then scored on an 11-yard run in the fourth quarter for the NFC's final touchdown. Two scoring records were set in the game—37 points by the NFC, eclipsing the 33 by the AFC in 1973, and the 64 points by both teams, surpassing the 61 scored in 1973.

NFC	3	20	7	7 — 37
AFC	3	7	10	7 — 27

NFC—FG Moseley 37
AFC—FG Fritsch 19
NFC—Muncie 1 run (Moseley kick)
AFC—Pruitt 1 pass from Bradshaw (Fritsch kick)
NFC—D. Hill 13 pass from Manning (kick failed)
NFC—T. Hill 25 pass from Muncie (Moseley kick)
NFC—Henry 86 punt return (Moseley kick)
AFC—Campbell 2 run (Fritsch kick)
AFC—FG Fritsch 29
NFC—Muncie 11 run (Moseley kick)
AFC—Campbell 1 run (Fritsch kick)

1979 AFC-NFC Pro Bowl

Memorial Coliseum, Los Angeles, California — January 29, 1979
Attendance: 46,281

NFC 13, AFC 7—Roger Staubach completed 9 of 15 passes for 125 yards, including the winning touchdown on a 19-yard strike to Dallas Cowboys teammate Tony Hill in the third period. The winning drive began at the AFC's 45 yard line after a shanked punt. Staubach hit Ahmad Rashad with passes of 15 and 17 yards to set up Hill's decisive catch. The victory gave the NFC a 5-4 advantage in Pro Bowl games. Rashad, who accounted for 89 yards on five receptions, was named the player of the game. The AFC led 7-6 at halftime on Bob Griese's eight-yard scoring toss to Steve Largent late in the second quarter. Largent finished the game with five receptions for 75 yards. The NFC scored first as Archie Manning marched his team 70 yards in 11 plays, capped by Wilbert Montgomery's two-yard touchdown run. The AFC's Earl Campbell was the game's leading rusher with 66 yards on 12 carries.

AFC	0	7	0	0 — 7
NFC	0	6	7	0 — 13

NFC—Montgomery 2 run (kick failed)
AFC—Largent 8 pass from Griese (Yepremian kick)
NFC—T. Hill 19 pass from Staubach (Corral kick)

1978 AFC-NFC Pro Bowl

Tampa Stadium, Tampa, Florida — January 23, 1978
Attendance: 51,337

NFC 14, AFC 13—Walter Payton, the NFL's leading rusher in 1977, sparked a second-half comeback to give the NFC a 14-13 win and tie the series between the two conferences at four victories each. Payton, who was the game's most valuable player, gained 77 yards on 13 carries and scored the tying touchdown on a one-yard burst with 7:37 left in the game. Efren Herrera kicked the winning extra point. The AFC dominated the first half of the game, taking a 13-0 lead on field goals of 21 and 39 yards by Toni Linhart and a 10-yard touchdown pass from Ken Stabler to Oakland teammate Cliff Branch. On the NFC's first possession of the second half, Pat Haden put together the first touchdown drive after Eddie Brown returned Ray Guy's punt to the AFC 46-yard line. Haden connected on all four of his passes on that drive, finally hitting Terry Metcalf with a four-yard scoring toss. The NFC continued to rally and, with Jim Hart at quarterback, moved 63 yards in 12 plays for the go-ahead score. During the winning drive, Hart completed five of six passes for 38 yards and Payton picked up 20 more on the ground.

AFC	3	10	0	0 — 13
NFC	0	0	7	7 — 14

AFC—FG Linhart 21
AFC—Branch 10 pass from Stabler (Linhart kick)
AFC—FG Linhart 39
NFC—Metcalf 4 pass from Haden (Herrera kick)
NFC—Payton 1 run (Herrera kick)

1977 AFC-NFC Pro Bowl

Kingdome, Seattle, Washington — January 17, 1977
Attendance: 64,752

AFC 24, NFC 14—O. J. Simpson's three-yard touchdown burst at 7:03 of the first quarter gave the AFC a lead it would not surrender, the victory breaking a two-game NFC win streak and giving the American Conference stars a 4-3 series lead. The AFC took a 17-7 lead midway through the second period on the first of two Ken Anderson touchdown passes, a 12-yarder to Charlie Joiner. But the NFC mounted a 73-yard drive capped by Lawrence McCutcheon's one-yard touchdown plunge to pull within three of the AFC, 17-14, at the half. Following a scoreless third quarter, player of the game Mel Blount thwarted a possible NFC score when he intercepted Jim Hart's pass in the end zone. Less than three minutes later, Blount again picked off a Hart pass, returning it 16 yards to the NFC 27. That set up Anderson's 27-yard touchdown strike to Cliff Branch for the final score.

NFC	0	14	0	0 — 14
AFC	10	7	0	7 — 24

AFC—Simpson 3 run (Linhart kick)
AFC—FG Linhart 31
NFC—Thomas 15 run (Bakken kick)
AFC—Joiner 12 pass from Anderson (Linhart kick)
NFC—McCutcheon 1 run (Bakken kick)
AFC—Branch 27 pass from Anderson (Linhart kick)

1976 AFC-NFC Pro Bowl

Superdome, New Orleans, Louisiana — January 26, 1976
Attendance: 30,546

NFC 23, AFC 20—Mike Boryla, a late substitute who did not enter the game until 5:39 remained, lifted the National Football Conference to a 23-20 victory over the American Football Conference with two touchdown passes in the final minutes. It was the second straight NFC win, squaring the series at 3-3. Until Boryla started firing the ball the AFC was in control, leading 13-0 at the half. Boryla entered the game after Billy Johnson had raced 90 yards with a punt to make the score 20-9 in favor of the AFC. He floated a 14-yard pass to Terry Metcalf and later fired an eight-yarder to Mel Gray for the winner.

AFC	0	13	0	7 — 20
NFC	0	0	9	14 — 23

AFC—FG Stenerud 20
AFC—FG Stenerud 35
AFC—Burrough 64 pass from Pastorini (Stenerud kick)
NFC—FG Bakken 42
NFC—Foreman 4 pass from Hart (kick blocked)
AFC—Johnson 90 punt return (Stenerud kick)
NFC—Metcalf 14 pass from Boryla (Bakken kick)
NFC—Gray 8 pass from Boryla (Bakken kick)

1975 AFC-NFC Pro Bowl

Orange Bowl, Miami, Florida — January 20, 1975
Attendance: 26,484

NFC 17, AFC 10—Los Angeles quarterback James Harris, who took over the NFC offense after Jim Hart of St. Louis suffered a laceration above his right eye in the second period, threw a pair of touchdown passes early in the fourth period to pace the NFC to its second victory in the five-game Pro Bowl series. The NFC win snapped a three-game AFC victory string. Harris, who was named the player of the game, connected with St. Louis's Mel Gray for an eight-yard touchdown 2:03 into the final period. One minute and 24 seconds later, following a recovery by Washington's Ken Houston of a fumble by Franco Harris of Pittsburgh, Harris tossed another eight-yard scoring pass to Washington's Charley Taylor for the decisive points.

NFC	0	3	0	14 — 17
AFC	0	0	10	0 — 10

NFC—FG Marcol 33
AFC—Warfield 32 pass from Griese (Gerela kick)
AFC—FG Gerela 33
NFC—Gray 8 pass from J. Harris (Marcol kick)
NFC—Taylor 8 pass from J. Harris (Marcol kick)

1974 AFC-NFC Pro Bowl

Arrowhead Stadium, Kansas City, Missouri — January 20, 1974
Attendance: 66,918

AFC 15, NFC 13—Miami's Garo Yepremian kicked his fifth consecutive field goal without a miss from the 42-yard line with 21 seconds remaining to give the AFC its third straight victory since the NFC won the inaugural game following the 1970 season. The field goal by Yepremian, who was voted the game's outstanding player, offset a 21-yard field goal by Atlanta's Nick Mike-Mayer that had given the NFC a 13-12 advantage with 1:41 remaining. The only touchdown in the game was scored by the NFC on a 14-yard pass from Philadelphia's Roman Gabriel to Lawrence McCutcheon of the Los Angeles Rams.

NFC	0	10	0	3 — 13
AFC	3	3	3	6 — 15

AFC—FG Yepremian 16
NFC—FG Mike-Mayer 27
NFC—McCutcheon 14 pass from Gabriel (Mike-Mayer kick)
AFC—FG Yepremian 37
AFC—FG Yepremian 27
AFC—FG Yepremian 41
NFC—FG Mike-Mayer 21
AFC—FG Yepremian 42

1973 AFC-NFC Pro Bowl

Texas Stadium, Irving, Texas — January 21, 1973
Attendance: 37,091

AFC 33, NFC 28—Paced by the rushing and receiving of player of the game O.J. Simpson, the AFC erased a 14-0 first period deficit and built a commanding 33-14 lead midway through the fourth period before the NFC managed two touchdowns in the final minute of play. Simpson rushed for 112 yards and caught three passes for 58 more to gain unanimous recognition in the balloting for player of the game. John Brockington scored three touchdowns for the NFC.

AFC	0	10	10	13 — 33
NFC	14	0	0	14 — 28

NFC—Brockington 1 run (Marcol kick)
NFC—Brockington 3 pass from Kilmer (Marcol kick)
AFC—Simpson 7 run (Gerela kick)
AFC—FG Gerela 18
AFC—FG Gerela 22
AFC—Hubbard 11 run (Gerela kick)
AFC—O. Taylor 5 pass from Lamonica (kick failed)
AFC—Bell 12 interception return (Gerela kick)
NFC—Brockington 1 run (Marcol kick)
NFC—Kwalick 12 pass from Snead (Marcol kick)

1972 AFC-NFC Pro Bowl

Memorial Coliseum, Los Angeles, California January 23, 1972

Attendance: 53,647

AFC 26, NFC 13—Four field goals by Jan Stenerud of Kansas City, including a 6-6 tie-breaker from 48 yards, helped lift the AFC from a 6-0 deficit to a 19-6 advantage early in the fourth period. The AFC defense picked off three interceptions. Stenerud was selected as the outstanding offensive player and his Kansas City teammate, linebacker Willie Lanier, was the game's outstanding defensive player.

AFC	0	3	13	10	— 26
NFC	0	6	0	7	— 13

NFC—Grim 50 pass from Landry (kick failed)
AFC—FG Stenerud 25
AFC—FG Stenerud 23
AFC—FG Stenerud 48
AFC—Morin 5 pass from Dawson (Stenerud kick)
AFC—FG Stenerud 42
NFC—V. Washington 2 run (Knight kick)
AFC—F. Little 6 run (Stenerud kick)

1971 AFC-NFC Pro Bowl

Memorial Coliseum, Los Angeles, California January 24, 1971

Attendance: 48,222

NFC 27, AFC 6—Mel Renfro of Dallas broke open the first meeting between the American Football Conference and National Football Conference all-star teams as he returned a pair of punts 82 and 56 yards for touchdowns in the final period to provide the NFC with a 27-6 victory over the AFC. Renfro was voted the game's outstanding back and linebacker Fred Carr of Green Bay the outstanding lineman.

AFC	0	3	3	0	— 6
NFC	0	3	10	14	— 27

AFC—FG Stenerud 37
NFC—FG Cox 13
NFC—Osborn 23 pass from Brodie (Cox kick)
NFC—FG Cox 35
AFC—FG Stenerud 16
NFC—Renfro 82 punt return (Cox kick)
NFC—Renfro 56 punt return (Cox kick)

Regular Season Interconference Records, 1970-1986

American Football Conference

Eastern Division	W	L	T	Pct.
Miami	45	11	0	.804
New England	26	29	0	.473
New York Jets	24	30	0	.444
Indianapolis	21	28	1	.430
Buffalo	19	31	1	.382
Central Division				
Pittsburgh	36	19	0	.655
Cincinnati	34	22	0	.607
Cleveland	28	29	0	.491
Houston	20	36	1	.360
Western Division				
Los Angeles Raiders	41	16	1	.716
Seattle	19	13	0	.594
Denver	33	26	1	.558
San Diego	25	28	0	.472
Kansas City	20	25	2	.447

National Football Conference

Eastern Division	W	L	T	Pct.
Dallas	39	18	0	.684
Washington	32	22	0	.593
Philadelphia	30	23	0	.566
St. Louis	24	24	2	.500
New York Giants	21	26	0	.447
Central Division				
Minnesota	28	29	0	.491
Detroit	23	30	1	.435
Chicago	23	32	0	.418
Tampa Bay	10	18	0	.357
Green Bay	18	36	2	.339
Western Division				
Los Angeles Rams	33	25	0	.569
San Francisco	30	29	0	.508
Atlanta	20	37	0	.351
New Orleans	12	42	2	.232

Interconference Victories, 1970-1986

Regular Season

	AFC	NFC	Tie
1970	12	27	1
1971	15	23	2
1972	20	19	1
1973	19	19	2
1974	23	17	0
1975	23	17	0
1976	16	12	0
1977	19	9	0
1978	31	21	0
1979	36	16	0
1980	33	19	0
1981	24	28	0
1982	15	14	1
1983	26	26	0
1984	26	26	0
1985	27	25	0
1986	26	26	0
Total	391	344	7

Preseason

	AFC	NFC	Tie
1970	21	28	1
1971	28	28	3
1972	27	25	4
1973	23	35	2
1974	35	25	0
1975	30	26	1
1976	30	31	0
1977	38	25	0
1978	20	19	0
1979	25	18	0
1980	22	20	1
1981	18	19	0
1982	25	16	0
1983	15	24	0
1984	16	19	0
1985	10	22	1
1986	22	17	0
Total	405	397	13

AFC VS. NFC (REGULAR SEASON), 1970-1986

	1970	1971	1972	1973	1974	1975	1976	1977	1978	1979	1980	1981	1982	1983	1984	1985	1986	Totals
Miami	2-1	3-0	3-0	3-0	2-1	3-0	0-2	2-0	3-1	4-0	4-0	3-1	1-1	3-1	4-0	3-1	2-2	45-11
L.A. Raiders	1-2	1-1-1	3-0	2-1	3-0	3-0	3-0	1-1	4-0	4-0	2-2	2-2	3-0	2-2	3-1	3-1	1-3	41-16-1
Pittsburgh	0-3	1-2	2-1	3-0	3-0	2-1	1-1	2-0	3-1	3-1	4-0	3-1	1-0	2-2	3-1	1-3	2-2	36-19
Cincinnati	1-2	1-2	2-1	2-1	2-1	3-0	2-0	2-1	2-2	2-2	2-2	2-2	1-0	3-1	2-2	2-2	3-1	34-22
Denver	2-2	1-3	1-3	0-3-1	2-2	2-1	2-0	1-1	2-2	3-1	3-1	3-1	2-1	0-2	3-1	3-1	3-1	33-26-1
Cleveland	0-3	2-1	1-2	1-2	1-2	1-3	2-0	1-1	4-0	3-1	3-1	3-1	0-2	2-2	1-3	1-3	2-2	28-29
New England	0-3	0-3	3-0	2-1	3-0	1-2	1-1	2-0	2-2	3-1	1-3	0-4	0-1	2-2	0-4	3-1	3-1	26-29
San Diego	1-2	2-1	0-3	1-2	1-2	0-3	2-0	1-1	2-2	3-1	2-2	2-2	1-0	2-2	4-0	1-1	0-4	25-28
N.Y. Jets	2-1	0-3	1-2	0-3	2-1	0-3	0-2	1-1	1-3	3-1	1-3	2-0	4-0	3-1	0-2	2-2	2-2	24-30
Indianapolis	3-0	2-1	0-3	2-1	1-2	2-1	0-2	1-1	2-2	1-1	1-1	0-4	0-1-1	2-0	0-4	3-1	1-3	21-28-1
Houston	0-3	0-2-1	0-3	0-3	0-3	3-0	2-0	2-0	2-2	2-2	4-0	1-3	0-3	1-3	0-4	1-3	2-2	20-36-1
Kansas City	0-2-1	2-1	2-1	1-1-1	1-2	2-1	1-1	1-1	0-2	0-2	2-0	2-2	0-3	2-2	1-1	2-2	1-1	20-25-2
Buffalo	0-3	0-3	2-0-1	2-1	2-1	1-2	0-2	1-1	1-1	2-2	3-1	1-3	1-2	1-3	1-3	0-2	1-1	19-31-1
Seattle								1-0	3-1	3-1	1-3	0-2	1-0	1-3	4-0	2-2	3-1	19-13
Tampa Bay							0-1											0-1
TOTALS	12-27-1	15-23-2	20-19-1	19-19-2	23-17	23-17	16-12	19-9	31-21	36-16	33-19	24-28	15-14-1	26-26	26-26	27-25	26-26	391-344-7

NFC VS. AFC (REGULAR SEASON), 1970-1986

	1970	1971	1972	1973	1974	1975	1976	1977	1978	1979	1980	1981	1982	1983	1984	1985	1986	Totals
Dallas	3-0	3-0	3-0	2-1	2-1	2-1	2-0	1-1	3-1	1-3	3-1	4-0	2-1	2-2	2-2	3-1	1-3	39-18
L.A. Rams	2-1	1-2	1-2	3-0	3-1	3-0	1-1	2-0	2-2	2-2	2-2	1-3	1-2	1-3	3-1	3-1	2-2	33-25
Washington	2-1	1-2	1-2	2-1	2-1	1-2	1-1	1-1	2-2	2-2	1-3	2-2		4-0	3-1	4-0	3-1	32-22
Philadelphia	2-1	1-2	2-1	2-1	2-1	0-3	0-2	1-1	3-1	2-2	3-1	3-1	2-1	1-1	3-1	1-1	2-2	30-23
San Francisco	4-0	2-1	2-1	1-2	0-3	1-2	1-1	0-2	1-3	0-4	2-2	3-1	1-3	2-2	3-1	3-1	4-0	30-29
Minnesota	2-1	2-1	1-2	2-1	2-1	4-0	2-0	1-1	1-3	1-3	1-3	1-3	1-3	4-0	0-4	2-0	1-3	28-29
St. Louis	2-0-1	2-1	1-2	0-2-1	2-1	2-1	1-1	0-2	0-4	1-3	1-1	3-1		3-1	3-1	2-2	1-1	24-24-2
Detroit	3-0	4-0	2-0-1	0-3	1-2	1-2	2-0	2-0	2-2	0-4	0-2	2-2	0-1	1-3	0-4	2-2	1-3	23-20-1
Chicago	1-2	1-2	1-2	2-2	0-3	0-3	0-2	1-1	0-4	2-2	0-4	4-0	1-1	1-1	2-2	3-1	4-0	23-32
N.Y. Giants	3-0	1-2	1-2	1-2	1-2	2-1	0-2	0-2	1-1	1-1	1-3	1-1	1-0	0-4	2-0	2-2	3-1	21-26
Atlanta	1-2	3-0	2-2	2-1	0-3	1-2	0-2	0-2	1-3	1-3	2-2	1-3	1-1	3-1	1-3	0-4	1-3	20-37
Green Bay	2-1	2-1	2-1	1-1-1	2-1	0-3	0-2	0-3	2-2	1-3	1-3	1-1	1-1-1	2-2	0-4	0-4	1-3	18-36-2
New Orleans	0-3	0-1-2	0-3	1-2	0-3	0-3	1-2	0-2	1-3	0-4	1-3	2-2	1-0	1-3	3-1	0-4	1-3	12-42-2
Tampa Bay								0-1	2-0	2-0	1-3	0-4	2-1	1-3	1-1	0-4	1-1	10-18
Seattle							1-0											1-0
TOTALS	27-12-1	23-15-2	19-20-1	19-19-2	17-23	17-23	12-16	9-19	21-31	16-36	19-33	28-24	14-15-1	26-26	26-26	25-27	26-26	344-391-7

1986 Interconference Games

(Home Team in capital letters)

AFC 26, NFC 26

AFC Victories

Houston 31, GREEN BAY 3
Denver 33, PHILADELPHIA 7
BUFFALO 17, St. Louis 10
CLEVELAND 24, Detroit 21
Cincinnati 34, GREEN BAY 28
DENVER 29, Dallas 14
SEATTLE 17, New York Giants 12
Cleveland 23, MINNESOTA 20
NEW YORK JETS 28, New Orleans 23
KANSAS CITY 27, Tampa Bay 20
NEW ENGLAND 25, Atlanta 17
Cincinnati 24, DETROIT 17
PITTSBURGH 27, Green Bay 3
L.A. Raiders 17, DALLAS 13
New York Jets 28, ATLANTA 14
New England 30, L.A. RAMS 28
CINCINNATI 24, Minnesota 20
SEATTLE 24, Philadelphia 20
Seattle 31, DALLAS 14
New England 21, NEW ORLEANS 20
PITTSBURGH 27, Detroit 17
Indianapolis 28, ATLANTA 23
Miami 31, NEW ORLEANS 27
DENVER 31, Washington 30
Miami 37, L.A. RAMS 31 (OT)
HOUSTON 23, Minnesota 10

NFC Victories

CHICAGO 41, Cleveland 31
WASHINGTON 10, L.A. Raiders 6
NEW YORK GIANTS 20, San Diego 7
L.A. Rams 24, INDIANAPOLIS 7
New York Giants 14, L.A. RAIDERS 9
MINNESOTA 31, Pittsburgh 7
Washington 30, SAN DIEGO 27
Chicago 44, CINCINNATI 7
San Francisco 31, MIAMI 16
WASHINGTON 19, Seattle 14
DETROIT 24, Houston 13
SAN FRANCISCO 35, Indianapolis 14
Chicago 20, HOUSTON 7
New Orleans 17, INDIANAPOLIS 14
Green Bay 17, CLEVELAND 14
PHILADELPHIA 23, San Diego 7
TAMPA BAY 34, Buffalo 28
Dallas 24, SAN DIEGO 21
NEW YORK GIANTS 19, Denver 16
ST. LOUIS 23, Kansas City 14
Atlanta 20, MIAMI 14
L.A. Rams 17, NEW YORK JETS 3
Philadelphia 33, L.A. RAIDERS 27 (OT)
CHICAGO 13, Pittsburgh 10 (OT)
SAN FRANCISCO 24, New York Jets 10
San Francisco 29, NEW ENGLAND 24

Monday Night Football, 1970–1986

(Home Team in capitals, games listed in chronological order.)

1986
DALLAS 31, New York Giants 28
Denver 21, PITTSBURGH 10
Chicago 25, GREEN BAY 12
Dallas 31, ST. LOUIS 7
SEATTLE 33, San Diego 7
CINCINNATI 24, Pittsburgh 22
NEW YORK JETS 22, Denver 10
NEW YORK GIANTS 27, Washington 20
Los Angeles Rams 20, CHICAGO 17
CLEVELAND 26, Miami 16
WASHINGTON 14, San Francisco 6
MIAMI 45, New York Jets 3
New York Giants 21, SAN FRANCISCO 17
SEATTLE 37, Los Angeles Raiders 0
Chicago 16, DETROIT 13
New England 34, MIAMI 27

1985
DALLAS 44, Washington 14
CLEVELAND 17, Pittsburgh 7
Los Angeles Rams 35, SEATTLE 24
Cincinnati 37, PITTSBURGH 24
WASHINGTON 27, St. Louis 10
NEW YORK JETS 23, Miami 7
CHICAGO 23, Green Bay 7
LOS ANGELES RAIDERS 34, San Diego 21
ST. LOUIS 21, Dallas 10
DENVER 17, San Francisco 16
WASHINGTON 23, New York Giants 21
SAN FRANCISCO 19, Seattle 6
MIAMI 38, Chicago 24
Los Angeles Rams 27, SAN FRANCISCO 20
MIAMI 30, New England 27
L.A. Raiders 16, L.A. RAMS 6

1984
Dallas 20, LOS ANGELES RAMS 13
SAN FRANCISCO 37, Washington 31
Miami 21, BUFFALO 17
LOS ANGELES RAIDERS 33, San Diego 30
PITTSBURGH 38, Cincinnati 17
San Francisco 31, NEW YORK GIANTS 10
DENVER 17, Green Bay 14
Los Angeles Rams 24, ATLANTA 10
Seattle 24, SAN DIEGO 0
WASHINGTON 27, Atlanta 14
SEATTLE 17, Los Angeles Raiders 14
NEW ORLEANS 27, Pittsburgh 24
MIAMI 28, New York Jets 17
SAN DIEGO 20, Chicago 7
Los Angeles Raiders 24, DETROIT 3
MIAMI 28, Dallas 21

1983
Dallas 31, WASHINGTON 30
San Diego 17, KANSAS CITY 14
LOS ANGELES RAIDERS 27, Miami 14
NEW YORK GIANTS 27, Green Bay 3
New York Jets 34, BUFFALO 10
Pittsburgh 24, CINCINNATI 14
GREEN BAY 48, Washington 47
ST. LOUIS 20, New York Giants 20 (OT)
Washington 27, SAN DIEGO 24
DETROIT 15, New York Giants 9
Los Angeles Rams 36, ATLANTA 13
New York Jets 31, NEW ORLEANS 28
MIAMI 38, Cincinnati 14
DETROIT 13, Minnesota 2
Green Bay 12, TAMPA BAY 9 (OT)
SAN FRANCISCO 42, Dallas 17

1982
Pittsburgh 36, DALLAS 28
Green Bay 27, NEW YORK GIANTS 19
LOS ANGELES RAIDERS 28, San Diego 24
TAMPA BAY 23, Miami 17
New York Jets 28, DETROIT 13
Dallas 37, HOUSTON 7
SAN DIEGO 50, Cincinnati 34
MIAMI 27, Buffalo 10
MINNESOTA 31, Dallas 27

1981
San Diego 44, CLEVELAND 14
Oakland 36, MINNESOTA 10
Dallas 35, NEW ENGLAND 21
Los Angeles 24, CHICAGO 7
PHILADELPHIA 16, Atlanta 13
BUFFALO 31, Miami 21
DETROIT 48, Chicago 17
PITTSBURGH 26, Houston 13
DENVER 19, Minnesota 17
DALLAS 27, Buffalo 14
SEATTLE 44, San Diego 23
ATLANTA 31, Minnesota 30
MIAMI 13, Philadelphia 10
OAKLAND 30, Pittsburgh 27
LOS ANGELES 21, Atlanta 16
SAN DIEGO 23, Oakland 10

1980
Dallas 17, WASHINGTON 3
Houston 16, CLEVELAND 7
PHILADELPHIA 35, New York Giants 3
NEW ENGLAND 23, Denver 14
CHICAGO 23, Tampa Bay 0
DENVER 20, Washington 17
Oakland 45, PITTSBURGH 34
NEW YORK JETS 17, Miami 14
CLEVELAND 27, Chicago 21
HOUSTON 38, New England 34
Oakland 19, SEATTLE 17
Los Angeles 27, NEW ORLEANS 7
OAKLAND 9, Denver 3
MIAMI 16, New England 13 (OT)
LOS ANGELES 38, Dallas 14
SAN DIEGO 26, Pittsburgh 17

1979
Pittsburgh 16, NEW ENGLAND 13 (OT)
Atlanta 14, PHILADELPHIA 10
WASHINGTON 27, New York Giants 0
CLEVELAND 26, Dallas 7
GREEN BAY 27, New England 14
OAKLAND 13, Miami 3
NEW YORK JETS 14, Minnesota 7
PITTSBURGH 42, Denver 7
Seattle 31, ATLANTA 28
Houston 9, MIAMI 6
Philadelphia 31, DALLAS 21
LOS ANGELES 20, Atlanta 14
SEATTLE 30, New York Jets 7
Oakland 42, NEW ORLEANS 35
HOUSTON 20, Pittsburgh 17
SAN DIEGO 17, Denver 7

1978
DALLAS 38, Baltimore 0
MINNESOTA 12, Denver 9 (OT)
Baltimore 34, NEW ENGLAND 27
Minnesota 24, CHICAGO 20
WASHINGTON 9, Dallas 5
MIAMI 21, Cincinnati 0
DENVER 16, Chicago 7
Houston 24, PITTSBURGH 17
ATLANTA 15, Los Angeles 7
BALTIMORE 21, Washington 17
Oakland 34, CINCINNATI 21
HOUSTON 35, Miami 30
Pittsburgh 24, SAN FRANCISCO 7
SAN DIEGO 40, Chicago 7
Cincinnati 20, LOS ANGELES 19
MIAMI 23, New England 3

1977
PITTSBURGH 27, San Francisco 0
CLEVELAND 30, New England 27 (OT)
Oakland 37, KANSAS CITY 28
CHICAGO 24, Los Angeles 23
PITTSBURGH 20, Cincinnati 14
LOS ANGELES 35, Minnesota 3
ST. LOUIS 28, New York Giants 0
BALTIMORE 10, Washington 3
St. Louis 24, DALLAS 17
WASHINGTON 10, Green Bay 9
OAKLAND 34, Buffalo 13
MIAMI 16, Baltimore 6
Dallas 42, SAN FRANCISCO 35

1976
Miami 30, BUFFALO 21
Oakland 24, KANSAS CITY 21
Washington 20, PHILADELPHIA 17 (OT)
MINNESOTA 17, Pittsburgh 6
San Francisco 16, LOS ANGELES 0
NEW ENGLAND 41, New York Jets 7
WASHINGTON 20, St. Louis 10
BALTIMORE 38, Houston 14
CINCINNATI 20, Los Angeles 12
DALLAS 17, Buffalo 10
Baltimore 17, MIAMI 16
SAN FRANCISCO 20, Minnesota 16
OAKLAND 35, Cincinnati 20

1975
Oakland 31, MIAMI 21
DENVER 23, Green Bay 13
Dallas 36, DETROIT 10
WASHINGTON 27, St. Louis 17
New York Giants 17, BUFFALO 14
Minnesota 13, CHICAGO 9
Los Angeles 42, PHILADELPHIA 3
Kansas City 34, DALLAS 31
CINCINNATI 33, Buffalo 24
Pittsburgh 32, HOUSTON 9
MIAMI 20, New England 7
OAKLAND 17, Denver 10
SAN DIEGO 24, New York Jets 16

1974
BUFFALO 21, Oakland 20
PHILADELPHIA 13, Dallas 10
WASHINGTON 30, Denver 3
MIAMI 21, New York Jets 17
DETROIT 17, San Francisco 13
CHICAGO 10, Green Bay 9
PITTSBURGH 24, Atlanta 17
Los Angeles 15, SAN FRANCISCO 13
Minnesota 28, ST. LOUIS 24
Kansas City 42, DENVER 34
Pittsburgh 28, NEW ORLEANS 7
MIAMI 24, Cincinnati 3
Washington 23, LOS ANGELES 17

1973
GREEN BAY 23, New York Jets 7
DALLAS 40, New Orleans 3
DETROIT 31, Atlanta 6
WASHINGTON 14, Dallas 7
Miami 17, CLEVELAND 9
DENVER 23, Oakland 23
BUFFALO 23, Kansas City 14
PITTSBURGH 21, Washington 16
KANSAS CITY 19, Chicago 7
ATLANTA 20, Minnesota 14
SAN FRANCISCO 20, Green Bay 6
MIAMI 30, Pittsburgh 26
LOS ANGELES 40, New York Giants 6

1972
Washington 24, MINNESOTA 21
Kansas City 20, NEW ORLEANS 17
New York Giants 27, PHILADELPHIA 12
Oakland 34, HOUSTON 0
Green Bay 24, DETROIT 23
CHICAGO 13, Minnesota 10
DALLAS 28, Detroit 24
Baltimore 24, NEW ENGLAND 17
Cleveland 21, SAN DIEGO 17
WASHINGTON 24, Atlanta 13
MIAMI 31, St. Louis 10
Los Angeles 26, SAN FRANCISCO 16
OAKLAND 24, New York Jets 16

1971
Minnesota 16, DETROIT 13
ST. LOUIS 17, New York Jets 10
Oakland 34, CLEVELAND 20
DALLAS 20, New York Giants 13
KANSAS CITY 38, Pittsburgh 16
MINNESOTA 10, Baltimore 3
GREEN BAY 14, Detroit 14
BALTIMORE 24, Los Angeles 17
SAN DIEGO 20, St. Louis 17
ATLANTA 28, Green Bay 21
MIAMI 34, Chicago 3
Kansas City 26, SAN FRANCISCO 17
Washington 38, LOS ANGELES 24

1970
CLEVELAND 31, New York Jets 21
Kansas City 44, BALTIMORE 24
DETROIT 28, Chicago 14
Green Bay 22, SAN DIEGO 20
OAKLAND 34, Washington 20
MINNESOTA 13, Los Angeles 3
PITTSBURGH 21, Cincinnati 10
Baltimore 13, GREEN BAY 10
St. Louis 38, DALLAS 0
PHILADELPHIA 23, New York Giants 20
Miami 20, ATLANTA 7
Cleveland 21, HOUSTON 10
Detroit 28, LOS ANGELES 23

Monday Night Won-Loss Records, 1970-1986

	Total	1986	1985	1984	1983	1982	1981	1980	1979	1978	1977	1976	1975	1974	1973	1972	1971	1970
Buffalo	3-9			0-1	0-1	0-1	1-1				0-1	0-2	0-2	1-0	1-0			
Cincinnati	5-10	1-0	1-0	0-1	0-2	0-1				1-2	0-1	1-1	1-0	0-1				0-1
Cleveland	8-4	1-0	1-0				0-1	1-1	1-0		1-0				0-1	1-0	0-1	2-0
Denver	7-9-1	1-1	1-0	1-0			1-0	1-2	0-2	1-1			1-1	0-2	0-0-1			
Houston	6-6					0-1	0-1	2-0	2-0	2-0		0-1	0-1			0-1		0-1
Indianapolis	8-4									2-1	1-1	2-0				1-0	1-1	1-1
Kansas City	7-4				0-1						0-1	0-1	1-0	1-0	1-1	1-0	2-0	1-0
L.A. Raiders	24-4-1	0-1	2-0	2-1	1-0	1-0	2-1	3-0	2-0	1-0	2-0	2-0	2-0	0-1	0-0-1	2-0	1-0	1-0
Miami	22-12	1-2	2-1	3-0	1-1	1-1	1-1	1-1	0-2	2-1	1-0	1-1	1-1	2-0	2-0	1-0	1-0	1-0
New England	3-11	1-0	0-1				0-1	1-2	0-2	0-2	0-1	1-0	0-1			0-1		
New York Jets	7-10	1-1	1-0	0-1	2-0	1-0		1-0	1-1			0-1	0-1	0-1	0-1	0-1	0-1	0-1
Pittsburgh	14-13	0-2	0-2	1-1	1-0	1-0	1-1	0-2	2-1	1-1	2-0	0-1	1-0	2-0	1-1		0-1	1-0
San Diego	10-9	0-1	0-1	1-2	1-1	1-1	2-1	1-0	1-0	1-0			1-0			0-1	1-0	0-1
Seattle	7-3	2-0	0-2	2-0			1-0	0-1	2-0									
Atlanta	5-11			0-2	0-1		1-2		1-2	1-0				0-1	1-1	0-1	1-0	0-1
Chicago	7-13	2-1	1-1	0-1			0-2	1-1		0-3	1-0		0-1	1-0	0-1	1-0	0-1	0-1
Dallas	16-14	2-0	1-1	1-1	1-1	1-2	2-0	1-1	0-2	1-1	1-1	1-0	1-1	0-1	1-1	1-0	1-0	0-1
Detroit	7-7-1	0-1		0-1	2-0	0-1	1-0						0-1	1-0	1-0	0-2	0-1-1	2-0
Green Bay	7-10-1	0-1	0-1	0-1	2-1	1-0			1-0		0-1		0-1	0-1	1-1	1-0	0-1-1	1-1
L.A. Rams	15-12	1-0	2-1	1-1	1-0		2-0	2-0	1-0	0-2	1-1	0-2	1-0	1-1	1-0	1-0	0-2	0-2
Minnesota	9-10				0-1	1-0	0-3		0-1	2-0	0-1	1-1	1-0	1-0	0-1	0-2	2-0	1-0
New Orleans	1-6			1-0	0-1			0-1	0-1					0-1	0-1	0-1		
New York Giants	5-11-1	2-1	0-1	0-1	1-1-1	0-1		0-1	0-1		0-1		1-0		0-1	1-0	0-1	0-1
Philadelphia	5-5						1-1	1-0	1-1			0-1	0-1	1-0		0-1		1-0
St. Louis	5-7-1	0-1	1-1		0-0-1						2-0	0-1	0-1	0-1		0-1	1-1	1-0
San Francisco	7-11	0-2	1-2	2-0	1-0					0-1	0-2	2-0		0-2	1-0	0-1	0-1	
Tampa Bay	1-2				0-1	1-0		0-1										
Washington	17-11	1-1	2-1	1-1	1-2			0-2	1-0	1-1	1-1	2-0	1-0	2-0	1-1	2-0	1-0	0-1

Monday Night Syndrome

1986

Of the 15 winning teams: 10 won the next week; 5 lost the next week; 0 tied the next week

Of the 15 losing teams: 7 won the next week; 8 lost the next week; 0 tied the next week

Of the 30 NFL teams: 17 won the next week; 13 lost the next week; 0 tied the next week

1970-86

Of the 229 winning teams: 128 won the next week; 98 lost the next week; 3 tied the next week

Of the 229 losing teams: 121 won the next week; 107 lost the next week; 1 tied the next week

Of the 6 tying teams: 5 won the next week; 1 lost the next week; 0 tied the next week

Of the 464 NFL teams: 254 won the next week; 206 lost the next week; 4 tied the next week

Thursday-Sunday Night Football, 1974-1986

(Home Team in capitals, games listed in chronological order.)

1986
New England 20, N.Y. JETS 6 (Thur.)
Cincinnati 30, CLEVELAND 13 (Thur.)
L.A. Raiders 37, SAN DIEGO 31 (OT) (Thur.)
L.A. RAMS 29, Dallas 10 (Sun.)
SAN FRANCISCO 24, L.A. Rams 14 (Fri.)

1985
KANSAS CITY 36, L.A. Raiders 20 (Thur.)
Chicago 33, MINNESOTA 24 (Thur.)
Dallas 30, N.Y. GIANTS 29 (Sun.)
SAN DIEGO 54, Pittsburgh 44 (Sun.)
Denver 27, SEATTLE 24 (Fri.)

1984
Pittsburgh 23, NEW YORK JETS 17 (Thur.)
Denver 24, CLEVELAND 14 (Sun.)
DALLAS 30, New Orleans 27 (Sun.)
Washington 31, MINNESOTA 17 (Thur.)
SAN FRANCISCO 19, L.A. Rams 16 (Fri.)

1983
San Francisco 48, MINNESOTA 17 (Thur.)
CLEVELAND 17, Cincinnati 7 (Thur.)
L.A. Raiders 40, DALLAS 38 (Sun.)
L.A. Raiders 42, SAN DIEGO 10 (Thur.)
MIAMI 34, NEW YORK Jets 14 (Fri.)

1982
BUFFALO 23, Minnesota 22 (Thur.)
SAN FRANCISCO 30, L.A. Rams 24 (Thur.)
ATLANTA 17, San Francisco 7 (Sun.)

1981
MIAMI 30, Pittsburgh 10 (Thur.)
Philadelphia 20, BUFFALO 14 (Thur.)
DALLAS 29, Los Angeles 17 (Sun.)
HOUSTON 17, Cleveland 13 (Thur.)

1980
TAMPA BAY 10, Los Angeles 9 (Thur.)
DALLAS 42, San Diego 31 (Sun.)
San Diego 27, MIAMI 24 (OT) (Thur.)
HOUSTON 6, Pittsburgh 0 (Thur.)

1979
Los Angeles 13, DENVER 9 (Thur.)
DALLAS 30, Los Angeles 6 (Sun.)
OAKLAND 45, San Diego 22 (Thur.)
MIAMI 39, New England 24 (Thur.)

1978
New England 21, OAKLAND 14 (Sun.)
Minnesota 21, DALLAS 10 (Thur.)
LOS ANGELES 10, Pittsburgh 7 (Sun.)
Denver 21, OAKLAND 6 (Sun.)

1977
Minnesota 30, DETROIT 21 (Sat.)

1976
Los Angeles 20, DETROIT 17 (Sat.)

1975
LOS ANGELES 10, Pittsburgh 3 (Sat.)

1974
OAKLAND 27, Dallas 23 (Sat.)

History of Overtime Games

Preseason

Aug. 28, 1955	Los Angeles 23, New York Giants 17, at Portland, Oregon
Aug. 24, 1962	Denver 27, Dallas Texans 24, at Fort Worth, Texas
Aug. 10, 1974	San Diego 20, New York Jets 14, at San Diego
Aug. 17, 1974	Pittsburgh 33, Philadelphia 30, at Philadelphia
Aug. 17, 1974	Dallas 19, Houston 13, at Dallas
Aug. 17, 1974	Cincinnati 13, Atlanta 7, at Atlanta
Sept. 6, 1974	Buffalo 23, New York Giants 17, at Buffalo
Aug. 9, 1975	Baltimore 23, Denver 20, at Denver
Aug. 30, 1975	New England 20, Green Bay 17, at Milwaukee
Sept. 13, 1975	Minnesota 14, San Diego 14, at San Diego
Aug. 1, 1976	New England 13, New York Giants 7, at New England
Aug. 2, 1976	Kansas City 9, Houston 3, at Kansas City
Aug. 20, 1976	New Orleans 26, Baltimore 20, at Baltimore
Sept. 4, 1976	Dallas 26, Houston 20, at Dallas
Aug. 13, 1977	Seattle 23, Dallas 17, at Seattle
Aug. 28, 1977	New England 13, Pittsburgh 10, at New England
Aug. 28, 1977	New York Giants 24, Buffalo 21, at East Rutherford, N.J.
Aug. 2, 1979	Seattle 12, Minnesota 9, at Minnesota
Aug. 4, 1979	Los Angeles 20, Oakland 14, at Los Angeles
Aug. 24, 1979	Denver 20, New England 17, at Denver
Aug. 23, 1980	Tampa Bay 20, Cincinnati 14, at Tampa Bay
Aug. 5, 1981	San Francisco 27, Seattle 24, at Seattle
Aug. 29, 1981	New Orleans 20, Detroit 17, at New Orleans
Aug. 28, 1982	Miami 17, Kansas City 17, at Kansas City
Sept. 3, 1982	Miami 16, New York Giants 13, at Miami
Aug. 6, 1983	L.A. Raiders 26, San Francisco 23, at Los Angeles
Aug. 6, 1983	Atlanta 13, Washington 10, at Atlanta
Aug. 13, 1983	St. Louis 27, Chicago 24, at St. Louis
Aug. 18, 1983	New York Jets 20, Cincinnati 17, at Cincinnati
Aug. 27, 1983	Chicago 20, Kansas City 17, at Chicago
Aug. 11, 1984	Pittsburgh 20, Philadelphia 17, at Pittsburgh
Aug. 9, 1985	Buffalo 10, Detroit 10, at Pontiac, Mich.
Aug. 10, 1985	Minnesota 16, Miami 13, at Miami
Aug. 17, 1985	Dallas 27, San Diego 24, at San Diego
Aug. 24, 1985	N.Y. Giants 34, N.Y. Jets 31, at East Rutherford, N.J.
Aug. 15, 1986	Washington 27, Pittsburgh 24, at Washington
Aug. 15, 1986	Detroit 30, Seattle 27, at Detroit
Aug. 23, 1986	Los Angeles Rams 20, San Diego 17, at Anaheim
Aug. 30, 1986	Minnesota 23, Indianapolis 20, at Indianapolis

Regular Season

Sept. 22, 1974—Pittsburgh 35, Denver 35, at Denver; Steelers win toss. Gilliam's pass intercepted and returned by Rowser to Denver's 42. Turner misses 41-yard field goal. Walden punts and Greer returns to Broncos' 39. Van Heusen punts and Edwards returns to Steelers' 16. Game ends with Steelers on own 26.

Nov. 10, 1974—New York Jets 26, New York Giants 20, at New Haven, Conn.; Giants win toss. Gogolak misses 42-yard field goal. Namath passes to Boozer for five yards and touchdown at 6:53.

Sept. 28, 1975—Dallas 37, St. Louis 31, at Dallas; Cardinals win toss. Hart's pass intercepted and returned by Jordan to Cardinals' 37. Staubach passes to DuPree for three yards and touchdown at 7:53.

Oct. 12, 1975—Los Angeles 13, San Diego 10, at San Diego; Chargers win toss. Partee punts to Rams' 14. Dempsey kicks 22-yard field goal at 9:27.

Nov. 2, 1975—Washington 30, Dallas 24, at Washington; Cowboys win toss. Staubach's pass intercepted and returned by Houston to Cowboys' 35. Kilmer runs one yard for touchdown at 6:34.

Nov. 16, 1975—St. Louis 20, Washington 17, at St. Louis; Cardinals win toss. Bakken kicks 37-yard field goal at 7:00.

Nov. 23, 1975—Kansas City 24, Detroit 21, at Kansas City; Lions win toss. Chiefs take over on downs at own 38. Stenerud kicks 26-yard field goal at 6:44.

Nov. 23, 1975—Oakland 26, Washington 23, at Washington; Redskins win toss. Bragg punts to Raiders' 42. Blanda kicks 27-yard field goal at 7:13.

Nov. 30, 1975—Denver 13, San Diego 10, at Denver; Broncos win toss. Turner kicks 25-yard field goal at 4:13.

Nov. 30, 1975—Oakland 37, Atlanta 34, at Oakland; Falcons win toss. James punts to Raiders' 16. Guy punts and Herron returns to Falcons' 41. Nick Mike-Mayer misses 45-yard field goal. Guy punts into Falcons' end zone. James punts to Raiders' 39. Blanda kicks 36-yard field goal at 15:00.

Dec. 14, 1975—Baltimore 10, Miami 7, at Baltimore; Dolphins win toss. Seiple punts to Colts' 4. Linhart kicks 31-yard field goal at 12:44.

Sept. 19, 1976—Minnesota 10, Los Angeles 10, at Minnesota; Vikings win toss. Tarkenton's pass intercepted by Monte Jackson and returned to Minnesota 16. Allen blocks Dempsey's 30-yard field goal attempt, ball rolls into end zone for touchback. Clabo punts and Scribner returns to Rams' 20. Rusty Jackson punts to Vikings' 35. Tarkenton's pass intercepted by Kay at Rams' 1, no return. Game ends with Rams on own 3.

***Sept. 27, 1976—Washington 20, Philadelphia 17,** at Philadelphia; Eagles win toss. Jones punts and E. Brown loses one yard on return to Redskins' 40. Bragg punts 51 yards into end zone for touchback. Jones punts and E. Brown returns to Redskins' 42. Bragg punts and Marshall returns to Eagles' 41. Boryla's pass intercepted by Dusek at Redskins' 37, no return. Bragg punts and Bradley returns. Philadelphia holding penalty moves ball back to Eagles' 8. Boryla pass intercepted by E. Brown and returned to Eagles' 22. Moseley kicks 29-yard field goal at 12:49.

Oct. 17, 1976—Kansas City 20, Miami 17, at Miami; Chiefs win toss. Wilson punts into end zone for touchback. Bulaich fumbles into Kansas City end zone, Collier recovers for touchback. Stenerud kicks 34-yard field goal at 14:48.

Oct. 31, 1976—St. Louis 23, San Francisco 20, at St. Louis; Cardinals win toss. Joyce punts and Leonard fumbles on return, Jones recovers at 49ers' 43. Bakken kicks 21-yard field goal at 6:42.

Dec. 5, 1976—San Diego 13, San Francisco 7, at San Diego; Chargers win toss. Morris runs 13 yards for touchdown at 5:12.

Sept. 18, 1977—Dallas 16, Minnesota 10, at Minnesota; Vikings win toss. Dallas starts on Vikings' 47 after a punt early in the overtime period. Staubach scores seven plays later on a four-yard run at 6:14.

***Sept. 26, 1977—Cleveland 30, New England 27,** at Cleveland; Browns win toss. Sipe throws a 22-yard pass to Logan at Patriots' 19. Cockroft kicks 35-yard field goal at 4:45.

Oct. 16, 1977—Minnesota 22, Chicago 16, at Minnesota; Bears win toss. Parsons punts 53 yards to Vikings' 18. Minnesota drives to Bears' 11. On a first-and-10, Vikings fake a field goal and holder Krause hits Voigt with a touchdown pass at 6:45.

Oct. 30, 1977—Cincinnati 13, Houston 10, at Cincinnati; Bengals win toss. Bahr kicks a 22-yard field goal at 5:51.

Nov. 13, 1977—San Francisco 10, New Orleans 7, at New Orleans; Saints win toss. Saints fail to move ball and Blanchard punts to 49ers' 41. Wersching kicks a 33-yard field goal at 6:33.

Dec. 18, 1977—Chicago 12, New York Giants 9, at East Rutherford, N.J.; Giants win toss. The ball changes hands eight times before Thomas kicks a 28-yard field goal at 14:51.

Sept. 10, 1978—Cleveland 13, Cincinnati 10, at Cleveland; Browns win toss. Collins returns kickoff 41 yards to Browns' 47. Cockroft kicks 27-yard field goal at 4:30.

***Sept. 11, 1978—Minnesota 12, Denver 9,** at Minnesota; Vikings win toss. Danmeier kicks 44-yard field goal at 2:56.

Sept. 24, 1978—Pittsburgh 15, Cleveland 9, at Pittsburgh; Steelers win toss. Cunningham scores on a 37-yard "gadget" pass from Bradshaw at 3:43. Steelers start winning drive on their 21.

Sept. 24, 1978—Denver 23, Kansas City 17, at Kansas City; Broncos win toss. Dilts punts to Kansas City. Chiefs advance to Broncos' 40 where Reed fails to make first down on fourth-and-one situation. Broncos march downfield. Preston scores two-yard touchdown at 10:28.

Oct. 1, 1978—Oakland 25, Chicago 19, at Chicago; Bears win toss. Both teams punt on first possession. On Chicago's second offensive series, Colzie intercepts Avellini's pass and returns it to Bears' 3. Three plays later, Whittington runs two yards for a touchdown at 5:19.

Oct. 15, 1978—Dallas 24, St. Louis 21, at St. Louis; Cowboys win toss. Dallas drives from its 23 into field goal range. Septien kicks 27-yard field goal at 3:28.

Oct. 29, 1978—Denver 20, Seattle 17, at Seattle; Broncos win toss. Ball changes hands four times before Turner kicks 18-yard field goal at 12:59.

Nov. 12, 1978—San Diego 29, Kansas City 23, at San Diego; Chiefs win toss. Fouts hits Jefferson for decisive 14-yard touchdown pass on the last play (15:00) of overtime period.

Nov. 12, 1978—Washington 16, New York Giants 13, at Washington; Redskins win toss. Moseley kicks winning 45-yard field goal at 8:32 after missing first down field goal attempt of 35 yards at 4:50.

Nov. 26, 1978—Green Bay 10, Minnesota 10, at Green Bay; Packers win toss. Both teams have possession of the ball four times.

Dec. 9, 1978—Cleveland 37, New York Jets 34, at Cleveland; Browns win toss. Cockroft kicks 22-yard field goal at 3:07.

Sept. 2, 1979—Atlanta 40, New Orleans 34, at New Orleans; Falcons win toss. Bartkowski's pass intercepted by Myers and returned to Falcons' 46. Erxleben punts to Falcons' 4. James punts to Chandler on Saints' 43. Erxleben punts and Ryckman returns to Falcons' 28. James punts and Chandler returns to Saints' 36. Erxleben retrieves punt snap on Saints' 1 and attempts pass. Mayberry intercepts and returns six yards for touchdown at 8:22.

Sept. 2, 1979—Cleveland 25, New York Jets 22, at New York; Jets win toss. Leahy's 43-yard field goal attempt goes wide right at 4:41. Evans's punt blocked by Dykes is recovered by Newton. Ramsey punts into end zone for touchback. Evans punts and Harper returns to Jets' 24. Robinson's pass intercepted by Davis and returned 33 yards to Jets' 31. Cockroft kicks 27-yard field goal at 14:45.

***Sept. 3, 1979—Pittsburgh 16, New England 13,** at Foxboro; Patriots win toss. Hare punts to Swann at Steelers' 31. Bahr kicks 41-yard field goal at 5:10.

Sept. 9, 1979—Tampa Bay 29, Baltimore 26, at Baltimore; Colts win toss. Landry fumbles, recovered by Kollar at Colts' 14. O'Donoghue kicks 31-yard, first-down field goal at 1:41.

Sept. 16, 1979—Denver 20, Atlanta 17, at Atlanta; Broncos win toss. Broncos march 65 yards to Falcons' 7. Turner kicks 24-yard field goal at 6:15.

Sept. 23, 1979—Houston 30, Cincinnati 27, at Cincinnati; Oilers win toss. Parsley punts and Lusby returns to Bengals' 33. Bahr's 32-yard field goal attempt is wide right at 8:05. Parsley's punt downed on Bengals' 5. McInally punts and Ellender returns to Bengals' 42. Fritsch's third down, 29-yard field goal attempt hits left upright and bounces through at 14:28.

Sept. 23, 1979—Minnesota 27, Green Bay 21, at Minnesota; Vikings win toss. Kramer throws 50-yard touchdown pass to Rashad at 3:18.

Oct. 28, 1979—Houston 27, New York Jets 24, at Houston; Oilers win toss. Oilers march 58 yards to Jets' 18. Fritsch kicks 35-yard field goal at 5:10.

Nov. 18, 1979—Cleveland 30, Miami 24, at Cleveland; Browns win toss. Sipe passes 39 yards to Rucker for touchdown at 1:59.

Nov. 25, 1979—Pittsburgh 33, Cleveland 30, at Pittsburgh; Browns win toss. Sipe's pass intercepted by Blount on Steelers' 4. Bradshaw pass intercepted by Bolton on Browns' 12. Evans punts and Bell returns to Steelers' 17. Bahr kicks 37-yard field goal at 14:51.

Nov. 25, 1979—Buffalo 16, New England 13, at Foxboro; Patriots win toss. Hare's punt downed on Bills' 38. Jackson punts and Morgan returns to Patriots' 20. Grogan's pass intercepted by Haslett and returned to Bills' 42. Ferguson's 51-yard pass to Butler sets up N. Mike-Mayer's 29-yard field goal at 9:15.

Dec. 2, 1979—Los Angeles 27, Minnesota 21, at Los Angeles; Rams win toss. Clark punts and Miller returns to Vikings' 25. Kramer's pass intercepted by Brown and returned to Rams' 40. Cromwell, holding for 22-yard field goal attempt, runs around left end untouched for winning score at 6:53.

*indicates Monday night game
#indicates Thursday night game

Sept. 7, 1980—Green Bay 12, Chicago 6, at Green Bay; Bears win toss. Parsons punts and Nixon returns 16 yards. Five plays later, Marcol returns own blocked field goal attempt 24 yards for touchdown at 6:00.

Sept. 14, 1980—San Diego 30, Oakland 24, at San Diego; Raiders win toss. Pastorini's first-down pass intercepted by Edwards. Millen intercepts Fouts' first-down pass and returns to San Diego 46. Bahr's 50-yard field goal attempt partially blocked by Williams and recovered on Chargers' 32. Eight plays later, Fouts throws 24-yard touchdown pass to Jefferson at 8:09.

Sept. 14, 1980—San Francisco 24, St. Louis 21, at San Francisco; Cardinals win toss. Swider punts and Robinson returns to 49ers' 32. San Francisco drives 52 yards to St. Louis 16, where Wersching kicks 33-yard field goal at 4:12.

Oct. 12, 1980—Green Bay 14, Tampa Bay 14, at Tampa Bay; Packers win toss. Teams trade punts twice. Lee returns second Tampa Bay punt to Green Bay 42. Dickey completes three passes to Buccaneers' 18, where Birney's 36-yard field goal attempt is wide right as time expires.

Nov. 9, 1980—Atlanta 33, St. Louis 27, at St. Louis; Falcons win toss. Strong runs 21 yards for touchdown at 4:20.

#**Nov. 20, 1980—San Diego 27, Miami 24,** at Miami; Chargers win toss. Partridge punts into end zone, Dolphins take over on their own 20. Woodley's pass for Nathan intercepted by Lowe and returned 28 yards to Dolphins' 12. Benirschke kicks 28-yard field goal at 7:14.

Nov. 23, 1980—New York Jets 31, Houston 28, at New York; Jets win toss. Leahy kicks 38-yard field goal at 3:58.

Nov. 27, 1980—Chicago 23, Detroit 17, at Detroit; Bears win toss. Williams returns kickoff 95 yards for touchdown at 0:21.

Dec. 7, 1980—Buffalo 10, Los Angeles 7, at Buffalo; Rams win toss. Corral punts and Hooks returns to Bills' 34. Ferguson's 30-yard pass to Lewis sets up N. Mike-Mayer's 30-yard field goal at 5:14.

Dec. 7, 1980—San Francisco 38, New Orleans 35, at San Francisco; Saints win toss. Erxleben's punt downed by Hardy on 49ers' 27. Wersching kicks 36-yard field goal at 7:40.

*__Dec. 8, 1980—Miami 16, New England 13,__ at Miami; Dolphins win toss. Von Schamann kicks 23-yard field goal at 3:20.

Dec. 14, 1980—Cincinnati 17, Chicago 14, at Chicago; Bengals win toss. Breech kicks 28-yard field goal at 4:23.

Dec. 21, 1980—Los Angeles 20, Atlanta 17, at Los Angeles; Rams win toss. Corral's punt downed at Rams' 37. James punts into end zone for touchback. Corral's punt downed on Falcons' 17. Bartkowski fumbles when hit by Harris, recovered by Delaney. Corral kicks 23-yard field goal on first play of possession at 7:00.

Sept. 27, 1981—Cincinnati 27, Buffalo 24, at Cincinnati; Bills win toss. Cater punts into end zone for touchback. Bengals drive to the Bills' 10 where Breech kicks 28-yard field goal at 9:33.

Sept. 27, 1981—Pittsburgh 27, New England 21, at Pittsburgh; Patriots win toss. Hubach punts and Smith returns five yards to midfield. Four plays later Bradshaw throws 24-yard touchdown pass to Swann at 3:19.

Oct. 4, 1981—Miami 28, New York Jets 28, at Miami; Jets win toss. Teams trade punts twice. Leahy's 48-yard field goal attempt is wide right as time expires.

Oct. 25, 1981—New York Giants 27, Atlanta 24, at Atlanta; Giants win toss. Jennings' punt goes out of bounds at New York 47. Bright returns Atlanta punt to Giants' 14. Woerner fair catches punt at own 28. Andrews fumbles on first play, recovered by Van Pelt. Danelo kicks 40-yard field goal four plays later at 9:20.

Oct. 25, 1981—Chicago 20, San Diego 17, at Chicago; Bears win toss. Teams trade punts. Bears' second punt returned by Brooks to Chargers' 33. Fouts pass intercepted by Fencik and returned 32 yards to San Diego 27. Roveto kicks 27-yard field goal seven plays later at 9:30.

Nov. 8, 1981—Chicago 16, Kansas City 13, at Kansas City; Bears win toss. Teams trade punts. Kansas City takes over on downs on its own 38. Fuller's fumble recovered by Harris on Chicago 36. Roveto's 37-yard field goal wide, but Chiefs penalized for leverage. Roveto's 22-yard field goal attempt three plays later is good at 13:07.

Nov. 8, 1981—Denver 23, Cleveland 20, at Denver; Browns win toss. D. Smith recovers Hill's fumble at Denver 48. Morton's 33-yard pass to Upchurch and six-yard run by Preston set up Steinfort's 30-yard field goal at 4:10.

Nov. 8, 1981—Miami 30, New England 27, at New England; Dolphins win toss. Orosz punts and Morgan returns six yards to New England 26. Grogan's pass intercepted by Brudzinski who returns 19 yards to Patriots' 26. Von Schamann kicks 30-yard field goal on first down at 7:09.

Nov. 15, 1981—Washington 30, New York Giants 27, at New York; Giants win toss. Nelms returns Giants' punt 26 yards to New York 47. Five plays later Moseley kicks 48-yard field goal at 3:44.

Dec. 20, 1981—New York Giants 13, Dallas 10, at New York; Cowboys win toss and kick off. Jennings punts to Dallas 40. Taylor recovers Dorsett's fumble on second down. Danelo's 33-yard field goal attempt hits right upright and bounces back. White's pass for Pearson intercepted by Hunt and returned seven yards to Dallas 24. Four plays later Danelo kicks 35-yard field goal at 6:19.

Sept. 12, 1982—Washington 37, Philadelphia 34, at Philadelphia; Redskins win toss. Theismann completes five passes for 63 yards to set up Moseley's 26-yard field goal at 4:47.

Sept. 19, 1982—Pittsburgh 26, Cincinnati 20, at Pittsburgh; Bengals win toss. Anderson's pass intended for Kreider intercepted by Woodruff and returned 30 yards to Cincinnati 2. Bradshaw completes two-yard touchdown pass to Stallworth on first down at 1:08.

Dec. 19, 1982—Baltimore 20, Green Bay 20, at Baltimore; Packers win toss. K. Anderson intercepts Dickey's first-down pass and returns to Packers' 42. Miller's 44-yard field goal attempt blocked by G. Lewis. Teams trade punts before Stenerud's 47-yard field goal attempt is wide right. Teams trade punts again before time expires in Colts possession.

Jan. 2, 1983—Tampa Bay 26, Chicago 23, at Tampa Bay; Bears win toss. Parsons punts to T. Bell at Buccaneers' 40. Capece kicks 33-yard field goal at 3:14.

Sept. 4, 1983—Baltimore 29, New England 23, at New England; Patriots win toss. Cooks runs 52 yards with fumble recovery three plays into overtime at 0:30.

Sept. 4, 1983—Green Bay 41, Houston 38, at Houston; Packers win toss. Stenerud kicks 42-yard field goal at 5:55.

Sept. 11, 1983—New York Giants 16, Atlanta 13, at Atlanta; Giants win toss. Dennis returns kickoff 54 yards to Atlanta 41. Haji-Sheikh kicks 30-yard field goal at 3:38.

Sept. 18, 1983—New Orleans 34, Chicago 31, at New Orleans; Bears win toss. Parsons punts and Groth returns five yards to New Orleans 34. Stabler pass intercepted by Schmidt at Chicago 47. Parsons punt downed by Gentry at New Orleans 2. Stabler gains 36 yards in four passes; Wilson 38 in six carries. Andersen kicks 41-yard field goal at 10:57.

Sept. 18, 1983—Minnesota 19, Tampa Bay 16, at Tampa; Vikings win toss. Coleman punts and Bell returns eight yards to Tampa Bay 47. Capece's 33-yard field goal attempt sails wide at 7:26. Dils and Young combine for 48-yard gain to Tampa Bay 27. Ricardo kicks 42-yard field goal at 9:27.

Sept. 25, 1983—Baltimore 22, Chicago 19, at Baltimore; Colts win toss. Allegre kicks 33-yard field goal nine plays later at 4:51.

Sept. 25, 1983—Cleveland 30, San Diego 24, at San Diego; Browns win toss. Walker returns kickoff 33 yards to Cleveland 37. Sipe completes 48-yard touchdown pass to Holt four plays later at 1:53.

Sept. 25, 1983—New York Jets 27, Los Angeles Rams 24, at New York; Jets win toss. Ramsey punts to Irvin who returns to 25 but penalty puts Rams on own 13. Holmes 30-yard interception return sets up Leahy's 26-yard field goal at 3:22.

Oct. 9, 1983—Buffalo 38, Miami 35, at Miami; Dolphins win toss. Von Schamann's 52-yard field goal attempt goes wide at 12:36. Cater punts to Clayton who loses 11 to own 13. Von Schamann's 43-yard field goal attempt sails wide at 5:15. Danelo kicks 36-yard field goal nine plays later at 13:58.

Oct. 9, 1983—Dallas 27, Tampa Bay 24, at Dallas; Cowboys win toss. Septien's 51-yard field goal attempt goes wide but Buccaneers penalized for roughing kicker. Septien kicks 42-yard field goal at 4:38.

Oct. 23, 1983—Kansas City 13, Houston 10, at Houston; Chiefs win toss. Lowery kicks 41-yard field goal 13 plays later at 7:41.

Oct. 23, 1983—Minnesota 20, Green Bay 17, at Green Bay; Packers win toss. Scribner's punt downed on Vikings' 42. Ricardo kicks 32-yard field goal eight plays later at 5:05.

*__Oct. 24, 1983—New York Giants 20, St. Louis 20,__ at St. Louis; Cardinals win toss. Teams trade punts before O'Donoghue's 44-yard field goal attempt is wide left. Jennings' punt returned by Bird to St. Louis 21. Lomax pass intercepted by Haynes who loses six yards to New York 33. Jennings' punt downed on St. Louis 17. O'Donoghue's 19-yard field goal attempt is wide right. Rutledge's pass intercepted by L. Washington who returns 25 yards to New York 25. O'Donoghue's 42-yard field goal attempt is wide right. Rutledge's pass intercepted by W. Smith at St. Louis 33 to end game.

Oct. 30, 1983—Cleveland 25, Houston 19, at Cleveland; Oilers win toss. Teams trade punts. Nielsen's pass intercepted by Whitwell who returns to Houston 20. Green runs 20 yards for touchdown on first down at 6:34.

Nov. 20, 1983—Detroit 23, Green Bay 20, at Milwaukee; Packers win toss. Scribner punts and Jenkins returns 14 yards to Green Bay 45. Murray's 33-yard field goal attempt is wide left at 9:32. Whitehurst's pass intercepted by Watkins and returned to Green Bay 27. Murray kicks 37-yard field goal four plays later at 8:30.

Nov. 27, 1983—Atlanta 47, Green Bay 41, at Atlanta; Packers win toss. K. Johnson returns interception 31 yards for touchdown at 2:13.

Nov. 27, 1983—Seattle 51, Kansas City 48, at Seattle; Seahawks win toss. Dixon's 47-yard kickoff return sets up N. Johnson's 42-yard field goal at 1:36.

Dec. 11, 1983—New Orleans 20, Philadelphia 17, at Philadelphia; Eagles win toss. Runager punts to Groth who fair catches on New Orleans 32. Stabler completes two passes for 36 yards to Goodlow to set up Andersen's 50-yard field goal at 5:30.

*__Dec. 12, 1983—Green Bay 12, Tampa Bay 9,__ at Tampa; Packers win toss. Stenerud kicks 23-yard field goal 11 plays later at 4:07.

Sept. 9, 1984—Detroit 27, Atlanta 24, at Atlanta; Lions win toss. Murray kicks 48-yard field goal nine plays later at 5:06.

Sept. 30, 1984—Tampa Bay 30, Green Bay 27, at Tampa; Packers win toss. Scribner punts 44 yards to Tampa Bay 2. Epps returns Garcia's punt three yards to Green Bay 27. Scribner's punt downed on Buccaneers' 33. Ariri kicks 46-yard field goal 11 plays later at 10:32.

Oct. 14, 1984—Detroit 13, Tampa Bay 7, at Detroit; Buccaneers win toss. Tampa Bay drives to Lions' 39 before Wilder fumbles. Five plays later Danielson hits Thompson with 37-yard touchdown pass at 4:34.

Oct. 21, 1984—Dallas 30, New Orleans 27, at Dallas; Cowboys win toss. Septien kicks 41-yard field goal eight plays later at 3:42.

Oct. 28, 1984—Denver 22, Los Angeles Raiders 19, at Los Angeles; Raiders win toss. Hawkins fumble recovered by Foley at Denver 7. Teams trade punts. Karlis' 42-yard field goal attempt is wide left. Teams trade punts. Wilson pass intercepted by R. Jackson at Los Angeles 45, returned 23 yards to Los Angeles 22. Karlis kicks 35-yard field goal two plays later at 15:00.

Nov. 4, 1984—Philadelphia 23, Detroit 23, at Detroit; Lions win toss. Lions drive to Eagles' 3 in eight plays. Murray's 21-yard field goal attempt hits right upright and bounces back. Jaworski's pass intercepted by Watkins at Detroit 5. Teams trade punts. Cooper returns Black's punt five yards to Eagles' 14. Time expires four plays later with Eagles on own 21.

Nov. 18, 1984—San Diego 34, Miami 28, at San Diego; Chargers win toss. McGee scores eight plays later on a 25-yard run at 3:17.

Dec. 2, 1984—Cincinnati 20, Cleveland 17, at Cleveland; Browns win toss. Simmons returns Cox's punt 30 yards to Cleveland 35. Breech kicks 35-yard field goal seven plays later at 4:34.

*indicates Monday night game
#indicates Thursday night game

Dec. 2, 1984—Houston 23, Pittsburgh 20, at Houston; Oilers win toss. Cooper kicks 30-yard field goal 16 plays later at 5:53.

Sept. 8, 1985—St. Louis 27, Cleveland 24, at Cleveland; Cardinals win toss. O'Donoghue kicks 35-yard field goal nine plays later at 5:27.

Sept. 29, 1985—New York Giants 16, Philadelphia 10, at Philadelphia; Eagles win toss. Jaworski's pass tipped by Quick and intercepted by Patterson who returns 29 yards for touchdown at 0:55.

Oct. 20, 1985—Denver 13, Seattle 10, at Denver; Seahawks win toss. Teams trade punts twice. Krieg's pass intercepted by Hunter and returned to Seahawks' 15. Karlis kicks 24-yard field goal four plays later at 9:19.

Nov. 10, 1985—Philadelphia 23, Atlanta 17, at Philadelphia; Falcons win toss. Donnelly's 62-yard punt goes out of bounds at Eagles' 1. Jaworski completes 99-yard touchdown pass to Quick two plays later at 1:49.

Nov. 10, 1985—San Diego 40, Los Angeles Raiders 34, at San Diego; Chargers win toss. James scores on 17-yard run seven plays later at 3:44.

Nov. 17, 1985—Denver 30, San Diego 24, at Denver; Chargers win toss. Thomas' 40-yard field goal attempt blocked by Smith and returned 60 yards by Wright for touchdown at 4:45.

Nov. 24, 1985—New York Jets 16, New England 13, at New York; Jets win toss. Teams trade punts twice. Patriots' second punt returned 46 yards by Sohn to Patriots' 15. Leahy kicks 32-yard field goal one play later at 10:05.

Nov. 24, 1985—Tampa Bay 19, Detroit 16, at Tampa; Lions win toss. Teams trade punts. Lions' punt downed on Buccaneers' 38. Igwebuike kicks 24-yard field goal 11 plays later at 12:31.

Nov. 24, 1985—Los Angeles Raiders 31, Denver 28, at Los Angeles; Raiders win toss. Bahr kicks 32-yard field goal six plays later at 2:42.

Dec. 8, 1985—Los Angeles Raiders 17, Denver 14, at Denver; Broncos win toss. Teams trade punts twice. Elway's fumble recovered by Townsend at Broncos' 8. Bahr kicks 26-yard field goal one play later at 4:55.

Sept. 14, 1986—Chicago 13, Philadelphia 10, at Chicago; Eagles win toss. Crawford's fumble of kickoff recovered by Jackson at Eagles' 35. Butler kicks 23-yard field goal 10 plays later at 5:56.

Sept. 14, 1986—Cincinnati 36, Buffalo 33, at Cincinnati; Bills win toss. Zander intercepts Kelly's first-down pass and returns it to Bills' 17. Breech kicks 20-yard field goal two plays later at 0:56.

Sept. 21, 1986—New York Jets 51, Miami 45, at New York; Jets win toss. O'Brien completes 43-yard touchdown pass to Walker five plays later at 2:35.

Sept. 28, 1986—Pittsburgh 22, Houston 16, at Houston; Oilers win toss. Johnson's punt returned 41 yards by Woods to Oilers' 15. Abercrombie scores on three-yard run three plays later at 2:35.

Sept. 28, 1986—Atlanta 23, Tampa Bay 20, at Tampa; Falcons win toss. Teams trade punts. Luckhurst kicks 34-yard field goal 10 plays later at 12:35.

Oct. 5, 1986—Los Angeles Rams 26, Tampa Bay 20, at Los Angeles; Rams win toss. Dickerson scores four plays later on 42-yard run at 2:16.

Oct. 12, 1986—Minnesota 27, San Francisco 24, at San Francisco; Vikings win toss. C. Nelson kicks 28-yard field goal nine plays later at 4:27.

Oct. 19, 1986—San Francisco 10, Atlanta 10, at Atlanta; Falcons win toss. Teams trade punts twice. Donnelly punts to 49ers' 27. The following play Wilson recovers Rice's fumble at 49ers' 46 as time expires.

Nov. 2, 1986—Washington 44, Minnesota 38, at Washington; Redskins win toss. Schroeder completes 38-yard touchdown pass to Clark four plays later at 1:46.

Nov. 20, 1986—Los Angeles Raiders 37, San Diego 31, at San Diego; Raiders win toss. Teams trade punts. Allen scores five plays later on 28-yard run at 8:33.

Nov. 23, 1986—Cleveland 37, Pittsburgh 31, at Cleveland; Browns win toss. Teams trade punts. Six plays later Kosar hits Slaughter with 36-yard touchdown pass at 6:37.

Nov. 30, 1986—Chicago 13, Pittsburgh 10, at Chicago; Bears win toss and kick off. Newsome's punt returned by Barnes to Chicago 49. Butler kicks 42-yard field goal five plays later at 3:55.

Nov. 30, 1986—Philadelphia 33, Los Angeles Raiders 27, at Los Angeles; Eagles win toss. Teams trade punts. Long recovers Cunningham's fumble at Philadelphia 42. Waters returns Allen's fumble 81 yards to Los Angeles 4. Cunningham scores on one-yard run two plays later at 6:53.

Nov. 30, 1986—Cleveland 13, Houston 10, at Cleveland; Oilers win toss and kick off. Gossett punts to Houston 39. Luck's pass intercepted by Minnifield at Cleveland 21. Gossett punts to Houston 34. Luck's pass intercepted by Minnifield at Cleveland 43 who returns 20 yards to Houston 37. Moseley kicks 29-yard field goal nine plays later at 14:44.

Dec. 7, 1986—St. Louis 10, Philadelphia 10, at Philadelphia; Cardinals win toss. White blocks Schubert's 40-yard field goal attempt. Teams trade punts. McFadden's 43-yard field goal attempt is wide left. Schubert's 37-yard field goal attempt is wide right. Cavanaugh's pass intercepted by Carter and returned to Eagles' 48 to end game.

Dec. 14, 1986—Miami 37, Los Angeles Rams 31, at Los Angeles; Dolphins win toss. Marino completes 20-yard touchdown pass to Duper six plays later at 3:04.

*indicates Monday night game
#indicates Thursday night game

Postseason

Dec. 28, 1958—Baltimore 23, New York Giants 17, at New York; Giants win toss. Maynard returns kickoff to Giants' 20. Chandler punts and Taseff returns one yard to Colts' 20. Colts win at 8:15 on a one-yard run by Ameche.

Dec. 23, 1962—Dallas Texans 20, Houston Oilers 17, at Houston; Texans win toss and kick off. Jancik returns kickoff to Oilers' 33. Norton punts and Jackson makes fair catch on Texans' 22. Wilson punts and Jancik makes fair catch on Oilers' 45. Robinson intercepts Blanda's pass and returns 13 yards to Oilers' 47. Wilson's punt rolls dead at Oilers' 12. Hull intercepts Blanda's pass and returns 23 yards to midfield. Texans win at 17:54 on a 25-yard field goal by Brooker.

Dec. 26, 1965—Green Bay 13, Baltimore 10, at Green Bay; Packers win toss. Moore returns kickoff to Packers' 22. Chandler punts and Haymond returns nine yards to Colts' 41. Gilburg punts and Wood makes fair catch at Packers' 21. Chandler punts and Haymond returns one yard to Colts' 41. Michaels misses 47-yard field goal. Packers win at 13:39 on 25-yard field goal by Chandler.

Dec. 25, 1971—Miami 27, Kansas City 24, at Kansas City; Chiefs win toss. Podolak, after a lateral from Buchanan, returns kickoff to Chiefs' 46. Stenerud's 42-yard field goal is blocked. Seiple punts and Podolak makes fair catch at Chiefs' 17. Wilson punts and Scott returns 18 yards to Dolphins' 39. Yepremian misses 62-yard field goal. Scott intercepts Dawson's pass and returns 13 yards to Dolphins' 46. Seiple punts and Podolak loses one yard to Chiefs' 15. Wilson punts and Scott makes fair catch on Dolphins' 30. Dolphins win at 22:40 on a 37-yard field goal by Yepremian.

Dec. 24, 1977—Oakland 37, Baltimore 31, at Baltimore; Colts win toss. Raiders start on own 42 following a punt late in the first overtime. Oakland works way into a threatening position on Stabler's 19-yard pass to Branch at Colts' 26. Four plays later, on the second play of the second overtime, Stabler hits Casper with a 10-yard touchdown pass at 15:43.

Jan. 2, 1982—San Diego 41, Miami 38, at Miami; Chargers win toss. San Diego drives from its 13 to Miami 8. On second-and-goal, Benirschke misses 27-yard field goal attempt wide left at 9:15. Miami has the ball twice and San Diego twice more before the Dolphins get their third possession. Miami drives from the San Diego 46 to Chargers' 17 and on fourth-and-two, von Schamann's 34-yard field goal attempt is blocked by San Diego's Winslow after 11:27. Fouts then completes four of five passes, including a 29-yarder to Joiner that puts the ball on Dolphins' 10. On first down, Benirschke kicks a 20-yard field goal at 13:52. San Diego's winning drive covered 74 yards in six plays.

Jan. 3, 1987—Cleveland 23, New York Jets 20, at Cleveland; Jets win toss. Jets' punt downed at Browns' 26. Moseley's 23-yard field goal attempt is wide right. Teams trade punts. Jets' second punt downed at Browns' 31. First overtime period expires eight plays later with Browns in possession at Jets' 42. Moseley kicks 27-yard field goal four plays into second overtime at 17:02.

Jan. 11, 1987—Denver 23, Cleveland 20, at Cleveland; Browns win toss. Broncos hold Browns on four downs. Browns' punt returned four yards to Denver's 25. Elway completes 22- and 28-yard passes to set up Karlis's 33-yard field goal nine plays into drive at 5:38.

Overtime Won-Lost Records, 1974-1986 (Regular Season)

	W	L	T
Atlanta	4	7	1
Buffalo	3	2	0
Chicago	6	7	0
Cincinnati	5	3	0
Cleveland	9	5	0
Dallas	5	2	0
Denver	8	3	1
Detroit	3	3	1
Green Bay	3	5	3
Houston	3	7	0
Indianapolis	3	1	1
Kansas City	3	4	0
Los Angeles Raiders	6	4	0
Los Angeles Rams	4	3	1
Miami	3	7	1
Minnesota	6	3	2
New England	0	8	0
New Orleans	2	4	0
New York Giants	4	4	1
New York Jets	5	3	1
Philadelphia	2	5	2
Pittsburgh	6	3	1
St. Louis	3	4	2
San Diego	6	6	0
San Francisco	3	3	1
Seattle	1	2	0
Tampa Bay	4	6	1
Washington	6	2	0

Overtime Games By Year (Regular Season)

1986-16	1979-12
1985-10	1978-11
1984- 9	1977- 6
1983-19	1976- 5
1982- 4	1975- 9
1981-10	1974- 2
1980-13	

Overtime Game Summary—1974-1986

There have been 126 overtime games in regular-season play since the rule was adopted in 1974. A breakdown follows:

86 times both teams had at least one possession (68%)

40 times the team that received after winning the toss drove for winning score (27 FG, 13 TD) (32%)

62 times the team which won the toss won the game (49%)

54 times the team which lost the toss won the game (43%)

78 games were decided by a field goal (62%)
38 games were decided by a touchdown (30%)
10 games ended tied (8%). Last time: St. Louis 10 at Philadelphia 10; 12/7/86
64 times the home team won the game (51%)
52 times the visiting team won the game (49%)

Shortest Overtime Games

0:21 (Chicago 23, Detroit 17; 11/27/80) Initial overtime kickoff return for a touchdown.

0:30 (Baltimore 29, New England 23; 9/4/83)

0:55 (New York Giants 16, Philadelphia 10; 9/29/85)

Longest Overtime Games (all postseason)

22:40 (Miami 27, Kansas City 24; 12/25/71)

17:54 (Dallas Texans 20, Houston 17; 12/13/67)

17:02 (Cleveland 23, New York Jets 20; 1/3/87)

There have been eight postseason overtime games dating back to 1958. In all cases, both teams had at least one possession. Last postseason overtime: Denver 23, Cleveland 20; 1/11/87.

Overtime Scoring Summary

78 were decided by a field goal
16 were decided by a touchdown pass
13 were decided by a touchdown run
3 were decided by interceptions (Atlanta 40, New Orleans 34, 9/2/79; Atlanta 47, Green Bay 41, 11/27/83; New York Giants 16, Philadelphia 10; 9/29/85)
1 was decided by a kickoff return (Chicago 23, Detroit 17; 11/27/80)
1 was decided by a fumble recovery (Baltimore 29, New England 23; 9/4/83)
1 was decided on a fake field goal/touchdown run (Los Angeles Rams 27, Minnesota 21; 12/2/79)
1 was decided on a fake field goal/touchdown pass (Minnesota 22, Chicago 16; 10/16/77)
1 was decided on a blocked field goal (Denver 30, San Diego 24; 11/17/85)
1 was decided on a blocked field goal/recovery by kicker (Green Bay 12, Chicago 6; 9/7/80)
10 ended tied

Overtime Records

Longest Touchdown Pass
99 Yards—Ron Jaworski to Mike Quick, Philadelphia 23, Atlanta 17 (11/10/85)
50 Yards—Tommy Kramer to Ahmad Rashad, Minnesota 27, Green Bay 21 (9/23/79)
48 Yards—Brian Sipe to Harry Holt, Cleveland 30, San Diego 24 (9/23/83)

Longest Touchdown Run
42 Yards—Eric Dickerson, Los Angeles Rams 26, Tampa Bay 20 (10/5/86)
28 Yards—Marcus Allen, Los Angeles Raiders 37, San Diego 31 (11/20/86)
25 Yards—Buford McGee, San Diego 34, Miami 28 (11/18/84)

Longest Field Goal
50 Yards—Morten Andersen, New Orleans 20, Philadelphia 17 (12/11/83)
48 Yards—Eddie Murray, Detroit 27, Atlanta 24 (9/9/84);
Mark Moseley, Washington 30, New York Giants 27 (11/15/81)
46 Yards—Obed Ariri, Tampa Bay 30, Green Bay 27 (9/30/84)

Longest Touchdown Plays
99 Yards—(Pass) Ron Jaworski to Mike Quick, Philadelphia 23, Atlanta 17 (11/10/85)
60 Yards—(Blocked field goal return) Louis Wright, Denver 30, San Diego 24 (11/17/85)
52 Yards—(Fumble recovery) Johnie Cooks, Baltimore 29, New England 23 (9/4/83)

Chicago All-Star Game

Pro teams won 31, lost 19, and tied 2. The game was discontinued after 1976.

Year	Date	Winner	Loser	Attendance
1976	July 23	Pittsburgh 24	All-Stars 0	52,895
1975	Aug. 1	Pittsburgh 21	All-Stars 14	54,103
1974		No game was played		
1973	July 27	Miami 14	All-Stars 3	54,103
1972	July 28	Dallas 20	All-Stars 7	54,162
1971	July 30	Baltimore 24	All-Stars 17	52,289
1970	July 31	Kansas City 24	All-Stars 3	69,940
1969	Aug. 1	N.Y. Jets 26	All-Stars 24	74,208
1968	Aug. 2	Green Bay 34	All-Stars 17	69,917
1967	Aug. 4	Green Bay 27	All-Stars 0	70,934
1966	Aug. 5	Green Bay 38	All-Stars 0	72,000
1965	Aug. 6	Cleveland 24	All-Stars 16	68,000
1964	Aug. 7	Chicago 28	All-Stars 17	65,000
1963	Aug. 2	All-Stars 20	Green Bay 17	65,000
1962	Aug. 3	Green Bay 42	All-Stars 20	65,000
1961	Aug. 4	Philadelphia 28	All-Stars 14	66,000
1960	Aug. 12	Baltimore 32	All-Stars 7	70,000
1959	Aug. 14	Baltimore 29	All-Stars 0	70,000
1958	Aug. 15	All-Stars 35	Detroit 19	70,000
1957	Aug. 9	N.Y. Giants 22	All-Stars 12	75,000
1956	Aug. 10	Cleveland 26	All-Stars 0	75,000
1955	Aug. 12	All-Stars 30	Cleveland 27	75,000
1954	Aug. 13	Detroit 31	All-Stars 6	93,470
1953	Aug. 14	Detroit 24	All-Stars 10	93,818
1952	Aug. 15	Los Angeles 10	All-Stars 7	88,316
1951	Aug. 17	Cleveland 33	All-Stars 0	92,180
1950	Aug. 11	All-Stars 17	Philadelphia 7	88,885
1949	Aug. 12	Philadelphia 38	All-Stars 0	93,780
1948	Aug. 20	Chi. Cardinals 28	All-Stars 0	101,220
1947	Aug. 22	All-Stars 16	Chi. Bears 0	105,840
1946	Aug. 23	All-Stars 16	Los Angeles 0	97,380
1945	Aug. 30	Green Bay 19	All-Stars 7	92,753
1944	Aug. 30	Chi. Bears 24	All-Stars 21	48,769
1943	Aug. 25	All-Stars 27	Washington 7	48,471
1942	Aug. 28	Chi. Bears 21	All-Stars 0	101,100
1941	Aug. 28	Chi. Bears 37	All-Stars 13	98,203
1940	Aug. 29	Green Bay 45	All-Stars 28	84,567
1939	Aug. 30	N.Y. Giants 9	All-Stars 0	81,456
1938	Aug. 31	All-Stars 28	Washington 16	74,250
1937	Sept. 1	All-Stars 6	Green Bay 0	84,560
1936	Sept. 3	All-Stars 7	Detroit 7 (tie)	76,000
1935	Aug. 29	Chi. Bears 5	All-Stars 0	77,450
1934	Aug. 31	Chi. Bears 0	All-Stars 0 (tie)	79,432

NFL Playoff Bowl

Western Conference won 8, Eastern Conference won 2. All games played at Miami's Orange Bowl.

1970	Los Angeles Rams 31, Dallas Cowboys 0
1969	Dallas Cowboys 17, Minnesota Vikings 13
1968	Los Angeles Rams 30, Cleveland Browns 6
1967	Baltimore Colts 20, Philadelphia Eagles 14
1966	Baltimore Colts 35, Dallas Cowboys 3
1965	St. Louis Cardinals 24, Green Bay Packers 17
1964	Green Bay Packers 40, Cleveland Browns 23
1963	Detroit Lions 17, Pittsburgh Steelers 10
1962	Detroit Lions 28, Philadelphia Eagles 10
1961	Detroit Lions 17, Cleveland Browns 16

NUMBER-ONE DRAFT CHOICES

Season	Team	Player	Position	College
1987	Tampa Bay	Vinny Testaverde	QB	Miami
1986	Tampa Bay	Bo Jackson	RB	Auburn
1985	Buffalo	Bruce Smith	DE	Virginia Tech
1984	New England	Irving Fryar	WR	Nebraska
1983	Baltimore	John Elway	QB	Stanford
1982	New England	Kenneth Sims	DT	Texas
1981	New Orleans	George Rogers	RB	South Carolina
1980	Detroit	Billy Sims	RB	Oklahoma
1979	Buffalo	Tom Cousineau	LB	Ohio State
1978	Houston	Earl Campbell	RB	Texas
1977	Tampa Bay	Ricky Bell	RB	Southern California
1976	Tampa Bay	Lee Roy Selmon	DE	Oklahoma
1975	Atlanta	Steve Bartkowski	QB	California
1974	Dallas	Ed Jones	DE	Tennessee State
1973	Houston	John Matuszak	DE	Tampa
1972	Buffalo	Walt Patulski	DE	Notre Dame
1971	New England	Jim Plunkett	QB	Stanford
1970	Pittsburgh	Terry Bradshaw	QB	Louisiana Tech
1969	Buffalo (AFL)	O.J. Simpson	RB	Southern California
1968	Minnesota	Ron Yary	T	Southern California
1967	Baltimore	Bubba Smith	DT	Michigan State
1966	Atlanta	Tommy Nobis	LB	Texas
	Miami (AFL)	Jim Grabowski	FB	Illinois
1965	New York Giants	Tucker Frederickson	HB	Auburn
	Houston (AFL)	Lawrence Elkins	E	Baylor
1964	San Francisco	Dave Parks	E	Texas Tech
	Boston (AFL)	Jack Concannon	QB	Boston College
1963	Los Angeles	Terry Baker	QB	Oregon State
	Kansas City (AFL)	Buck Buchanan	DT	Grambling
1962	Washington	Ernie Davis	HB	Syracuse
	Oakland (AFL)	Roman Gabriel	QB	North Carolina State
1961	Minnesota	Tommy Mason	HB	Tulane
	Buffalo (AFL)	Ken Rice	G	Auburn
1960	Los Angeles Rams	Billy Cannon	HB	Louisiana State
	(AFL had no formal first pick)			
1959	Green Bay	Randy Duncan	QB	Iowa
1958	Chicago Cardinals	King Hill	QB	Rice
1957	Green Bay	Paul Hornung	QB	Notre Dame
1956	Pittsburgh	Gary Glick	DB	Colorado A&M
1955	Baltimore	George Shaw	QB	Oregon
1954	Cleveland	Bobby Garrett	QB	Stanford
1953	San Francisco	Harry Babcock	E	Georgia
1952	Los Angeles	Bill Wade	QB	Vanderbilt
1951	New York Giants	Kyle Rote	HB	Southern Methodist
1950	Detroit	Leon Hart	E	Notre Dame
1949	Philadelphia	Chuck Bednarik	C	Pennsylvania
1948	Washington	Harry Gilmer	QB	Alabama
1947	Chicago Bears	Bob Fenimore	HB	Oklahoma A&M
1946	Boston	Frank Dancewicz	QB	Notre Dame
1945	Chicago Cardinals	Charley Trippi	HB	Georgia
1944	Boston	Angelo Bertelli	QB	Notre Dame
1943	Detroit	Frank Sinkwich	HB	Georgia
1942	Pittsburgh	Bill Dudley	HB	Virginia
1941	Chicago Bears	Tom Harmon	HB	Michigan
1940	Chicago Cardinals	George Cafego	HB	Tennessee
1939	Chicago Cardinals	Ki Aldrich	C	Texas Christian
1938	Cleveland	Corbett Davis	FB	Indiana
1937	Philadelphia	Sam Francis	FB	Nebraska
1936	Philadelphia	Jay Berwanger	HB	Chicago

NFL Paid Attendance

Year	Regular Season		Average	Postseason	Super Bowl
1986	13,588,551 (224 games)		60,663	734,002 (10)	101,063
1985	13,345,047 (224 games)		59,567	710,768 (10)	73,818
1984	13,398,112 (224 games)		59,813	665,194 (10)	84,059
1983	13,277,222 (224 games)		59,273	675,513 (10)	72,932
1982*	7,367,438 (126 games)		58,472	1,033,153 (16)	103,667
1981	13,606,990 (224 games)		60,745	637,763 (10)	81,270
1980	13,392,230 (224 games)		59,787	624,430 (10)	75,500
1979	13,182,039 (224 games)		58,848	630,326 (10)	103,985
1978	12,771,800 (224 games)		57,017	624,388 (10)	79,641
1977	11,018,632 (196 games)		56,218	534,925 (8)	75,804
1976	11,070,543 (196 games)		56,482	492,884 (8)	103,438
1975	10,213,193 (182 games)		56,116	475,919 (8)	80,187
1974	10,236,322 (182 games)		56,244	438,664 (8)	80,997
1973	10,730,933 (182 games)		58,961	525,433 (8)	71,882
1972	10,445,827 (182 games)		57,395	483,345 (8)	90,182
1971	10,076,035 (182 games)		55,363	483,891 (8)	81,023
1970	9,533,333 (182 games)		52,381	458,493 (8)	79,204
1969	6,096,127 (112 games)	NFL	54,430	162,279 (3)	80,562
	2,843,373 (70 games)	AFL	40,620	167,088 (3)	
1968	5,882,313 (112 games)	NFL	52,521	215,902 (3)	75,377
	2,635,004 (70 games)	AFL	37,643	114,438 (2)	
1967	5,938,924 (112 games)	NFL	53,026	166,208 (3)	75,546
	2,295,697 (63 games)	AFL	36,439	53,330 (1)	
1966	5,337,044 (105 games)	NFL	50,829	74,152 (1)	61,946**
	2,160,369 (63 games)	AFL	34,291	42,080 (1)	
1965	4,634,021 (98 games)	NFL	47,286	100,304 (2)	
	1,782,384 (56 games)	AFL	31,828	30,361 (1)	
1964	4,563,049 (98 games)	NFL	46,562	79,544 (1)	
	1,447,875 (56 games)	AFL	25,855	40,242 (1)	
1963	4,163,643 (98 games)	NFL	42,486	45,801 (1)	
	1,208,697 (56 games)	AFL	21,584	63,171 (2)	
1962	4,003,421 (98 games)	NFL	40,851	64,892 (1)	
	1,147,302 (56 games)	AFL	20,487	37,981 (1)	
1961	3,986,159 (98 games)	NFL	40,675	39,029 (1)	
	1,002,657 (56 games)	AFL	17,904	29,556 (1)	
1960	3,128,296 (78 games)	NFL	40,106	67,325 (1)	
	926,156 (56 games)	AFL	16,538	32,183 (1)	
1959	3,140,000 (72 games)		43,617	57,545 (1)	
1958	3,006,124 (72 games)		41,752	123,659 (2)	
1957	2,836,318 (72 games)		39,393	119,579 (2)	
1956	2,551,263 (72 games)		35,434	56,836 (1)	
1955	2,521,836 (72 games)		35,026	85,693 (1)	
1954	2,190,571 (72 games)		30,425	43,827 (1)	
1953	2,164,585 (72 games)		30,064	54,577 (1)	
1952	2,052,126 (72 games)		28,502	97,507 (2)	
1951	1,913,019 (72 games)		26,570	57,522 (1)	
1950	1,977,753 (78 games)		25,356	136,647 (3)	
1949	1,391,735 (60 games)		23,196	27,980 (1)	
1948	1,525,243 (60 games)		25,421	36,309 (1)	
1947	1,837,437 (60 games)		30,624	66,268 (2)	
1946	1,732,135 (55 games)		31,493	58,346 (1)	
1945	1,270,401 (50 games)		25,408	32,178 (1)	
1944	1,019,649 (50 games)		20,393	46,016 (1)	
1943	969,128 (40 games)		24,228	71,315 (2)	
1942	887,920 (55 games)		16,144	36,006 (1)	
1941	1,108,615 (55 games)		20,157	55,870 (2)	
1940	1,063,025 (55 games)		19,328	36,034 (1)	
1939	1,071,200 (55 games)		19,476	32,279 (1)	
1938	937,197 (55 games)		17,040	48,120 (1)	
1937	963,039 (55 games)		17,510	15,878 (1)	
1936	816,007 (54 games)		15,111	29,545 (1)	
1935	638,178 (53 games)		12,041	15,000 (1)	
1934	492,684 (60 games)		8,211	35,059 (1)	

*Players 57-day strike reduced 224-game schedule to 126 games.

**Only Super Bowl that did <u>not</u> sell out.

NFL's 10 Biggest Attendance Weekends

(Paid Count)

Weekend	Games	Attendance
October 27-28, 1985	14	902,128
October 12-13, 1980	14	898,223
September 23-24, 1984	14	894,402
November 11-12, 1979	14	890,972
September 16, 19-20, 1983	14	886,323
November 20, 23-24, 1980	14	885,601
November 9-10, 1986	14	882,762
September 12-13, 1982	14	882,042
November 15-16, 1981	14	881,486
September 5-6-7, 1981	14	881,439

NFL's 10 Highest Scoring Weekends

Point Total	Date	Weekend
761	October 16-17, 1983	7th
732	November 9-10, 1980	10th
725	November 24, 27-28, 1983	13th
710	November 28, December 1-2, 1985	13th
696	October 2-3, 1983	5th
676	September 21-22, 1980	3rd
675	October 23-24, 1983	8th
675	December 19-22, 1986	16th
667	November 22-23, 1981	12th
667	November 22, 25-26, 1984	13th

Top 10 Televised Sports Events

(Based on A.C. Nielsen Figures)

Program	Date	Network	Rating	Share
Super Bowl XVI	1/24/82	CBS	49.1	73.0
Super Bowl XVII	1/30/83	NBC	48.6	69.0
Super Bowl XX	1/26/86	NBC	48.3	70.0
Super Bowl XII	1/15/78	CBS	47.2	67.0
Super Bowl XIII	1/21/79	NBC	47.1	74.0
Super Bowl XVIII	1/22/84	CBS	46.4	71.0
Super Bowl XIX	1/20/85	ABC	46.4	63.0
Super Bowl XIV	1/20/80	CBS	46.3	67.0
Super Bowl XXI	1/25/87	CBS	45.8	66.0
Super Bowl XI	1/9/77	NBC	44.4	73.0

Ten Most Watched TV Programs & Estimated Total Number of Viewers

(Based on A.C. Nielsen Figures)

Program	Date	Network	*Total Viewers
Super Bowl XX	Jan. 26, 1986	NBC	127,000,000
Super Bowl XXI	Jan. 25, 1987	CBS	122,640,000
M*A*S*H (Special)	Feb. 28, 1983	CBS	121,624,000
Super Bowl XIX	Jan. 20, 1985	ABC	115,936,000
Super Bowl XVI	Jan. 24, 1982	CBS	110,230,000
Super Bowl XVII	Jan. 30, 1983	NBC	109,040,000
Super Bowl XII	Jan. 15, 1978	CBS	102,010,000
Roots, Part 8	Jan. 30, 1977	ABC	98,706,000
Super Bowl XIV	Jan. 20, 1980	CBS	97,800,000
Super Bowl XIII	Jan. 21, 1979	NBC	96,640,000

*Watched some portion of the broadcast

RECORDS

ALL-TIME RECORDS

Compiled by Elias Sports Bureau

The following records reflect all available official information on the National Football League from its formation in 1920 to date. Also included are all applicable records from the American Football League, 1960-69.

Individual Records

Service

Most Seasons

26 George Blanda, Chi. Bears, 1949, 1950-58; Baltimore, 1950; Houston, 1960-66; Oakland, 1967-75
21 Earl Morrall, San Francisco, 1956; Pittsburgh, 1957-58; Detroit, 1958-64; N.Y. Giants, 1965-67; Baltimore, 1968-71; Miami, 1972-76
20 Jim Marshall, Cleveland, 1960; Minnesota, 1961-79

Most Seasons, One Club

19 Jim Marshall, Minnesota, 1961-79
18 Jim Hart, St. Louis, 1966-83
Jeff Van Note, Atlanta, 1969-86
17 Lou Groza, Cleveland, 1950-59, 1961-67
Johnny Unitas, Baltimore, 1956-72
John Brodie, San Francisco, 1957-73
Jim Bakken, St. Louis, 1962-78
Mick Tingelhoff, Minnesota, 1962-78

Most Games Played, Career

340 George Blanda, Chi. Bears, 1949, 1950-58; Baltimore, 1950; Houston, 1960-66; Oakland, 1967-75
282 Jim Marshall, Cleveland, 1960; Minnesota, 1961-79
263 Jan Stenerud, Kansas City, 1967-79; Green Bay, 1980-83; Minnesota, 1984-85

Most Consecutive Games Played, Career

282 Jim Marshall, Cleveland, 1960; Minnesota, 1961-79
240 Mick Tingelhoff, Minnesota, 1962-78
234 Jim Bakken, St. Louis, 1962-78

Most Seasons, Coach

40 George Halas, Chi. Bears, 1920-29, 1933-42, 1946-55, 1958-67
33 Earl (Curly) Lambeau, Green Bay, 1921-49; Chi. Cardinals, 1950-51; Washington, 1952-53
27 Tom Landry, Dallas, 1960-86

Scoring

Most Seasons Leading League

5 Don Hutson, Green Bay, 1940-44
Gino Cappelletti, Boston, 1961, 1963-66
3 Earl (Dutch) Clark, Portsmouth, 1932; Detroit, 1935-36
Pat Harder, Chi. Cardinals, 1947-49
Paul Hornung, Green Bay, 1959-61
2 Jack Manders, Chi. Bears, 1934, 1937
Gordy Soltau, San Francisco, 1952-53
Doak Walker, Detroit, 1950, 1955
Gene Mingo, Denver, 1960, 1962
Jim Turner, N.Y. Jets, 1968-69
Fred Cox, Minnesota, 1969-70
Chester Marcol, Green Bay, 1972, 1974
John Smith, New England, 1979-80

Most Consecutive Seasons Leading League

5 Don Hutson, Green Bay, 1940-44
4 Gino Cappelletti, Boston, 1963-66
3 Pat Harder, Chi. Cardinals, 1947-49
Paul Hornung, Green Bay, 1959-61

Points

Most Points, Career

2,002 George Blanda, Chi. Bears, 1949, 1950-58; Baltimore, 1950; Houston, 1960-66; Oakland, 1967-75 (9-td, 943-pat, 335-fg)
1,699 Jan Stenerud, Kansas City, 1967-79; Green Bay, 1980-83; Minnesota, 1984-85 (580-pat, 373-fg)
1,439 Jim Turner, N.Y. Jets, 1964-70; Denver, 1971-79 (1-td, 521-pat, 304-fg)

Most Points, Season

176 Paul Hornung, Green Bay, 1960 (15-td, 41-pat, 15-fg)
161 Mark Moseley, Washington, 1983 (62-pat, 33-fg)
155 Gino Cappelletti, Boston, 1964 (7-td, 38-pat, 25-fg)

Most Points, No Touchdowns, Season

161 Mark Moseley, Washington, 1983 (62-pat, 33-fg)
145 Jim Turner, N.Y. Jets, 1968 (43-pat, 34-fg)
144 Kevin Butler, Chicago, 1985 (51-pat, 31-fg)

Most Seasons, 100 or More Points

7 Jan Stenerud, Kansas City, 1967-71; Green Bay, 1981, 1983
6 Gino Cappelletti, Boston, 1961-66
George Blanda, Houston, 1960-61; Oakland, 1967-69, 1973
Bruce Gossett, Los Angeles, 1966-67, 1969; San Francisco, 1970-71, 1973
5 Lou Michaels, Pittsburgh, 1962; Baltimore, 1964-65, 1967-68
Tony Franklin, Philadelphia, 1979, 1981; New England, 1984-86
Nick Lowery, Kansas City, 1981, 1983-86

Most Points, Rookie, Season

144 Kevin Butler, Chicago, 1985 (51-pat, 31-fg)
132 Gale Sayers, Chicago, 1965 (22-td)
128 Doak Walker, Detroit, 1950 (11-td, 38-pat, 8-fg)
Chester Marcol, Green Bay, 1972 (29-pat, 33-fg)

Most Points, Game

40 Ernie Nevers, Chi. Cardinals vs. Chi. Bears, Nov. 28, 1929 (6-td, 4-pat)
36 Dub Jones, Cleveland vs. Chi. Bears, Nov. 25, 1951 (6-td)
Gale Sayers, Chicago vs. San Francisco, Dec. 12, 1965 (6-td)
33 Paul Hornung, Green Bay vs. Baltimore, Oct. 8, 1961 (4-td, 6-pat, 1-fg)

Most Consecutive Games Scoring

151 Fred Cox, Minnesota, 1963-73
133 Garo Yepremian, Miami, 1970-78; New Orleans, 1979
128 Rafael Septien, Los Angeles, 1977; Dallas, 1978-85

Touchdowns

Most Seasons Leading League

8 Don Hutson, Green Bay, 1935-38, 1941-44
3 Jim Brown, Cleveland, 1958-59, 1963
Lance Alworth, San Diego, 1964-66
2 By many players

Most Consecutive Seasons Leading League

4 Don Hutson, Green Bay, 1935-38, 1941-44
3 Lance Alworth, San Diego, 1964-66
2 By many players

Most Touchdowns, Career

126 Jim Brown, Cleveland, 1957-65 (106-r, 20-p)
120 Walter Payton, Chicago, 1975-86 (106-r, 14-p)
116 John Riggins, N.Y. Jets, 1971-75; Washington, 1976-79, 1981-85 (104-r, 12-p)

Most Touchdowns, Season

24 John Riggins, Washington, 1983 (24-r)
23 O.J. Simpson, Buffalo, 1975 (16-r, 7-p)
22 Gale Sayers, Chicago, 1965 (14-r, 6-p, 2-ret)
Chuck Foreman, Minnesota, 1975 (13-r, 9-p)

Most Touchdowns, Rookie, Season

22 Gale Sayers, Chicago, 1965 (14-r, 6-p, 2-ret)
20 Eric Dickerson, L.A. Rams, 1983 (18-r, 2-p)
16 Billy Sims, Detroit, 1980 (13-r, 3-p)

Most Touchdowns, Game

6 Ernie Nevers, Chi. Cardinals vs. Chi. Bears, Nov. 28, 1929 (6-r)
Dub Jones, Cleveland vs. Chi. Bears, Nov. 25, 1951 (4-r, 2-p)
Gale Sayers, Chicago vs. San Francisco, Dec. 12, 1965 (4-r, 1-p, 1-ret)
5 Bob Shaw, Chi. Cardinals vs. Baltimore, Oct. 2, 1950 (5-p)
Jim Brown, Cleveland vs. Baltimore, Nov. 1, 1959 (5-r)
Abner Haynes, Dall. Texans vs. Oakland, Nov. 26, 1961 (4-r, 1-p)
Billy Cannon, Houston vs. N.Y. Titans, Dec. 10, 1961 (3-r, 2-p)
Cookie Gilchrist, Buffalo vs. N.Y. Jets, Dec. 8, 1963 (5-r)
Paul Hornung, Green Bay vs. Baltimore, Dec. 12, 1965 (3-r, 2-p)
Kellen Winslow, San Diego vs. Oakland, Nov. 22, 1981 (5-p)
4 By many players

Most Consecutive Games Scoring Touchdowns

18 Lenny Moore, Baltimore, 1963-65
14 O.J. Simpson, Buffalo, 1975
13 John Riggins, Washington, 1982-83

Points After Touchdown

Most Seasons Leading League

8 George Blanda, Chi. Bears, 1956; Houston, 1961-62; Oakland, 1967-69, 1972, 1974
4 Bob Waterfield, Cleveland, 1945; Los Angeles, 1946, 1950, 1952
3 Earl (Dutch) Clark, Portsmouth, 1932; Detroit, 1935-36
Jack Manders, Chi. Bears, 1933-35
Don Hutson, Green Bay, 1941-42, 1945

Most Points After Touchdown Attempted, Career

959 George Blanda, Chi. Bears, 1949, 1950-58; Baltimore, 1950; Houston, 1960-66; Oakland, 1967-75
657 Lou Groza, Cleveland, 1950-59, 1961-67
601 Jan Stenerud, Kansas City, 1967-79; Green Bay, 1980-83; Minnesota, 1984-85

Most Points After Touchdown Attempted, Season

70 Uwe von Schamann, Miami, 1984
65 George Blanda, Houston, 1961
63 Mark Moseley, Washington, 1983

Most Points After Touchdown Attempted, Game

10 Charlie Gogolak, Washington vs. N.Y. Giants, Nov. 27, 1966
9 Pat Harder, Chi. Cardinals vs. N.Y. Giants, Oct. 17, 1948; vs. N.Y. Bulldogs, Nov. 13, 1949
Bob Waterfield, Los Angeles vs. Baltimore, Oct. 22, 1950
Bob Thomas, Chicago vs. Green Bay, Dec. 7, 1980
8 By many players

Most Points After Touchdown, Career

943 George Blanda, Chi. Bears, 1949, 1950-58; Baltimore, 1950; Houston, 1960-66; Oakland, 1967-75
641 Lou Groza, Cleveland, 1950-59, 1961-67
580 Jan Stenerud, Kansas City, 1967-79; Green Bay, 1980-83; Minnesota, 1984-85

Most Points After Touchdown, Season

66 Uwe von Schamann, Miami, 1984
64 George Blanda, Houston, 1961
62 Mark Moseley, Washington, 1983

Most Points After Touchdown, Game

9 Pat Harder, Chi. Cardinals vs. N.Y. Giants, Oct. 17, 1948
Bob Waterfield, Los Angeles vs. Baltimore, Oct. 22, 1950
Charlie Gogolak, Washington vs. N.Y. Giants, Nov. 27, 1966
8 By many players

Most Consecutive Points After Touchdown

234 Tommy Davis, San Francisco, 1959-65
221 Jim Turner, N.Y. Jets, 1967-70; Denver, 1971-74
201 George Blanda, Oakland, 1967-71

Highest Points After Touchdown Percentage, Career (200 points after touchdown)

99.43 Tommy Davis, San Francisco, 1959-69 (350-348)
99.22 Nick Lowery, New England, 1978; Kansas City, 1980-86 (257-255)
98.33 George Blanda, Chi. Bears, 1949, 1950-58; Baltimore, 1950; Houston, 1960-66; Oakland, 1967-75 (959-943)

Most Points After Touchdown, No Misses, Season

56 Danny Villanueva, Dallas, 1966
Ray Wersching, San Francisco, 1984
54 Mike Clark, Dallas, 1968
George Blanda, Oakland, 1968
53 Pat Harder, Chi. Cardinals, 1948

Most Points After Touchdown, No Misses, Game

9 Pat Harder, Chi. Cardinals vs. N.Y. Giants, Oct. 17, 1948
Bob Waterfield, Los Angeles vs. Baltimore, Oct. 22, 1950
8 By many players

Field Goals

Most Seasons Leading League

5 Lou Groza, Cleveland, 1950, 1952-54, 1957
4 Jack Manders, Chi. Bears, 1933-34, 1936-37
Ward Cuff, N.Y. Giants, 1938-39, 1943; Green Bay, 1947
Mark Moseley, Washington, 1976-77, 1979, 1982
3 Bob Waterfield, Los Angeles, 1947, 1949, 1951
Gino Cappelletti, Boston, 1961, 1963-64
Fred Cox, Minnesota, 1965, 1969-70
Jan Stenerud, Kansas City, 1967, 1970, 1975

Most Consecutive Seasons Leading League

3 Lou Groza, Cleveland, 1952-54
2 By many players

Most Field Goals Attempted, Career

638 George Blanda, Chi. Bears, 1949, 1950-58; Baltimore, 1950; Houston, 1960-66; Oakland, 1967-75
558 Jan Stenerud, Kansas City, 1967-79; Green Bay, 1980-83; Minnesota, 1984-85
488 Jim Turner, N.Y. Jets, 1964-70; Denver, 1971-79

Most Field Goals Attempted, Season

49 Bruce Gossett, Los Angeles, 1966
Curt Knight, Washington, 1971
48 Chester Marcol, Green Bay, 1972
47 Jim Turner, N.Y. Jets, 1969
David Ray, Los Angeles, 1973
Mark Moseley, Washington, 1983

Most Field Goals Attempted, Game

9 Jim Bakken, St. Louis vs. Pittsburgh, Sept. 24, 1967
8 Lou Michaels, Pittsburgh vs. St. Louis, Dec. 2, 1962
Garo Yepremian, Detroit vs. Minnesota, Nov. 13, 1966
Jim Turner, N.Y. Jets vs. Buffalo, Nov. 3, 1968
7 By many players

Most Field Goals, Career

373 Jan Stenerud, Kansas City, 1967-79; Green Bay, 1980-83; Minnesota, 1984-85
335 George Blanda, Chi. Bears, 1949, 1950-58; Baltimore, 1950; Houston, 1960-66; Oakland, 1967-75
304 Jim Turner, N.Y. Jets, 1964-70; Denver, 1971-79

Most Field Goals, Season

35 Ali Haji-Sheikh, N.Y. Giants, 1983
34 Jim Turner, N.Y. Jets, 1968
33 Chester Marcol, Green Bay, 1972
Mark Moseley, Washington, 1983
Gary Anderson, Pittsburgh, 1985

Most Field Goals, Rookie, Season

35 Ali Haji-Sheikh, N.Y. Giants, 1983
33 Chester Marcol, Green Bay, 1972
31 Kevin Butler, Chicago, 1985

Most Field Goals, Game

7 Jim Bakken, St. Louis vs. Pittsburgh, Sept. 24, 1967
6 Gino Cappelletti, Boston vs. Denver, Oct. 4, 1964
Garo Yepremian, Detroit vs. Minnesota, Nov. 13, 1966
Jim Turner, N.Y. Jets vs. Buffalo, Nov. 3, 1968
Tom Dempsey, Philadelphia vs. Houston, Nov. 12, 1972
Bobby Howfield, N.Y. Jets vs. New Orleans, Dec. 3, 1972
Jim Bakken, St. Louis vs. Atlanta, Dec. 9, 1973
Joe Danelo, N.Y. Giants vs. Seattle, Oct. 18, 1981
Ray Wersching, San Francisco vs. New Orleans, Oct. 16, 1983
5 By many players

Most Field Goals, One Quarter

4 Garo Yepremian, Detroit vs. Minnesota, Nov. 13, 1966 (second quarter)
Curt Knight, Washington vs. N.Y. Giants, Nov. 15, 1970 (second quarter)
3 By many players

Most Consecutive Games Scoring Field Goals

31 Fred Cox, Minnesota, 1968-70
28 Jim Turner, N.Y. Jets, 1970; Denver, 1971-72
21 Bruce Gossett, San Francisco, 1970-72

Most Consecutive Field Goals

23 Mark Moseley, Washington, 1981-82
22 Pat Leahy, N.Y. Jets, 1985-86
20 Garo Yepremian, Miami, 1978; New Orleans, 1979
Morten Andersen, New Orleans, 1985-86

Longest Field Goal

63 Tom Dempsey, New Orleans vs. Detroit, Nov. 8, 1970
60 Steve Cox, Cleveland vs. Cincinnati, Oct. 21, 1984
59 Tony Franklin, Philadelphia vs. Dallas, Nov. 12, 1979

Highest Field Goal Percentage, Career (100 field goals)

77.18 Gary Anderson, Pittsburgh, 1982-86 (149-115)
76.35 Nick Lowery, New England, 1978; Kansas City, 1980-86 (203-155)
74.51 Ed Murray, Detroit, 1980-86 (204-152)

Highest Field Goal Percentage, Season (Qualifiers)

95.24 Mark Moseley, Washington, 1982 (21-20)
91.67 Jan Stenerud, Green Bay, 1981 (24-22)
88.89 Nick Lowery, Kansas City, 1985 (27-24)

Most Field Goals, No Misses, Game

6 Gino Cappelletti, Boston vs. Denver, Oct. 4, 1964
Joe Danelo, N.Y. Giants vs. Seattle, Oct. 18, 1981
Ray Wersching, San Francisco vs. New Orleans, Oct. 16, 1983
5 Roger LeClerc, Chicago vs. Detroit, Dec. 3, 1961
Lou Michaels, Baltimore vs. San Francisco, Sept. 25, 1966
Mac Percival, Chicago vs. Philadelphia, Oct. 20, 1968
Roy Gerela, Houston vs. Miami, Sept. 28, 1969
Jan Stenerud, Kansas City vs. Buffalo, Nov. 2, 1969; vs. Buffalo, Dec. 7, 1969; Minnesota vs. Detroit, Sept. 23, 1984
Horst Muhlmann, Cincinnati vs. Buffalo, Nov. 8, 1970; vs. Pittsburgh, Sept. 24, 1972
Bruce Gossett, San Francisco vs. Denver, Sept. 23, 1973
Nick Mike-Mayer, Atlanta vs. Los Angeles, Nov. 4, 1973
Curt Knight, Washington vs. Baltimore, Nov. 18, 1973
Tim Mazzetti, Atlanta vs. Los Angeles, Oct. 30, 1978
Ed Murray, Detroit vs. Green Bay, Sept. 14, 1980
Rich Karlis, Denver vs. Seattle, Nov. 20, 1983
Pat Leahy, N.Y. Jets vs. Cincinnati, Sept. 16, 1984
Nick Lowery, Kansas City vs. L.A. Raiders, Sept. 12, 1985
Eric Schubert, N.Y. Giants vs. Tampa Bay, Nov. 3, 1985
Gary Anderson, Pittsburgh vs. Kansas City, Nov. 10, 1985
Morten Andersen, New Orleans vs. L.A. Rams, Dec. 1, 1985

Most Field Goals, 50 or More Yards, Career

17 Jan Stenerud, Kansas City, 1967-79; Green Bay, 1980-83; Minnesota, 1984-85
12 Tom Dempsey, New Orleans, 1969-70; Philadelphia, 1971-74; Los Angeles, 1975-76; Houston, 1977; Buffalo, 1978-79
Mark Moseley, Philadelphia, 1970; Houston, 1971-72; Washington, 1974-86; Cleveland, 1986
Nick Lowery, New England, 1978; Kansas City, 1980-86
Ed Murray, Detroit, 1980-86
10 Joe Danelo, Green Bay, 1975; N.Y. Giants, 1976-82; Buffalo, 1983-84

Most Field Goals, 50 or More Yards, Season

5 Fred Steinfort, Denver, 1980
Norm Johnson, Seattle, 1986
4 Horst Muhlmann, Cincinnati, 1970
Mark Moseley, Washington, 1977
Nick Lowery, Kansas City, 1980
Raul Allegre, Baltimore, 1983
3 By many players

Most Field Goals, 50 or More Yards, Game

2 Jim Martin, Detroit vs. Baltimore, Oct. 23, 1960
Tom Dempsey, New Orleans vs. Los Angeles, Dec. 6, 1970
Chris Bahr, Cincinnati vs. Houston, Sept. 23, 1979
Nick Lowery, Kansas City vs. Seattle, Sept. 14, 1980; vs. New Orleans, Sept. 8, 1985
Mark Moseley, Washington vs. New Orleans, Oct. 26, 1980
Fred Steinfort, Denver vs. Seattle, Dec. 21, 1980
Mick Luckhurst, Atlanta vs. Denver, Dec. 5, 1982; vs. L.A. Rams, Oct. 7, 1984
Morten Andersen, New Orleans vs. Philadelphia, Dec. 11, 1983
Paul McFadden, Philadelphia vs. Detroit, Nov. 4, 1984
Pat Leahy, N.Y. Jets vs. New England, Oct. 20, 1985
Tony Zendejas, Houston vs. San Diego, Nov. 24, 1985
Norm Johnson, Seattle vs. L.A. Raiders, Dec. 8, 1986

Safeties

Most Safeties, Career

4 Ted Hendricks, Baltimore, 1969-73; Green Bay, 1974; Oakland, 1975-81; L.A. Raiders, 1982-83
Doug English, Detroit, 1975-79, 1981-85
3 Bill McPeak, Pittsburgh, 1949-57
Charlie Krueger, San Francisco, 1959-73
Ernie Stautner, Pittsburgh, 1950-63
Jim Katcavage, N.Y. Giants, 1956-68
Roger Brown, Detroit, 1960-66; Los Angeles, 1967-69
Bruce Maher, Detroit, 1960-67; N.Y. Giants, 1968-69
Ron McDole, St. Louis, 1961; Houston, 1962; Buffalo, 1963-70; Washington, 1971-78
Alan Page, Minnesota, 1967-78; Chicago, 1979-81
Rulon Jones, Denver, 1980-86
2 By many players

Most Safeties, Season

2 Tom Nash, Green Bay, 1932
Roger Brown, Detroit, 1962
Ron McDole, Buffalo, 1964
Alan Page, Minnesota, 1971
Fred Dryer, Los Angeles, 1973
Benny Barnes, Dallas, 1973
James Young, Houston, 1977
Tom Hannon, Minnesota, 1981
Doug English, Detroit, 1983
Don Blackmon, New England, 1985

Most Safeties, Game

2 Fred Dryer, Los Angeles vs. Green Bay, Oct. 21, 1973

Rushing

Most Seasons Leading League

8 Jim Brown, Cleveland, 1957-61, 1963-65
4 Steve Van Buren, Philadelphia, 1945, 1947-49
O.J. Simpson, Buffalo, 1972-73, 1975-76
3 Earl Campbell, Houston, 1978-80
Eric Dickerson, L.A. Rams, 1983-84, 1986

Most Consecutive Seasons Leading League

5 Jim Brown, Cleveland, 1957-61
3 Steve Van Buren, Philadelphia, 1947-49
Jim Brown, Cleveland, 1963-65
Earl Campbell, Houston, 1978-80
2 Bill Paschal, N.Y. Giants, 1943-44
Joe Perry, San Francisco, 1953-54
Jim Nance, Boston, 1966-67
Leroy Kelly, Cleveland, 1967-68
O.J. Simpson, Buffalo, 1972-73; 1975-76
Eric Dickerson, L.A. Rams, 1983-84

Attempts

Most Seasons Leading League

6 Jim Brown, Cleveland, 1958-59, 1961, 1963-65
4 Steve Van Buren, Philadelphia, 1947-50
Walter Payton, Chicago, 1976-79
3 Cookie Gilchrist, Buffalo, 1963-64; Denver, 1965
Jim Nance, Boston, 1966-67, 1969
O. J. Simpson, Buffalo, 1973-75

Most Consecutive Seasons Leading League

4 Steve Van Buren, Philadelphia, 1947-50
Walter Payton, Chicago, 1976-79
3 Jim Brown, Cleveland, 1963-65
Cookie Gilchrist, Buffalo, 1963-64; Denver, 1965
O.J. Simpson, Buffalo, 1973-75
2 By many players

Most Attempts, Career

3,692 Walter Payton, Chicago, 1975-86
2,949 Franco Harris, Pittsburgh, 1972-83; Seattle, 1984
2,916 John Riggins, N.Y. Jets, 1971-75; Washington, 1976-79, 1981-85

Most Attempts, Season
407 James Wilder, Tampa Bay, 1984
404 Eric Dickerson, L.A. Rams, 1986
397 Gerald Riggs, Atlanta, 1985
Most Attempts, Rookie, Season
390 Eric Dickerson, L.A. Rams, 1983
378 George Rogers, New Orleans, 1981
335 Curt Warner, Seattle, 1983
Most Attempts, Game
43 Butch Woolfolk, N.Y. Giants vs. Philadelphia, Nov. 20, 1983
James Wilder, Tampa Bay vs. Green Bay, Sept. 30, 1984 (OT)
42 James Wilder, Tampa Bay vs. Pittsburgh, Oct. 30, 1983
41 Franco Harris, Pittsburgh vs. Cincinnati, Oct. 17, 1976
Gerald Riggs, Atlanta vs. L.A. Rams, Nov. 17, 1985

Yards Gained
Most Yards Gained, Career
16,193 Walter Payton, Chicago, 1975-86
12,312 Jim Brown, Cleveland, 1957-65
12,120 Franco Harris, Pittsburgh, 1972-83; Seattle, 1984
Most Seasons, 1,000 or More Yards Rushing
10 Walter Payton, Chicago, 1976-81, 1983-86
8 Franco Harris, Pittsburgh, 1972, 1974-79, 1983
Tony Dorsett, Dallas, 1977-81, 1983-85
7 Jim Brown, Cleveland, 1958-61, 1963-65
Most Consecutive Seasons, 1,000 or More Yards Rushing
6 Franco Harris, Pittsburgh, 1974-79
Walter Payton, Chicago, 1976-81
5 Jim Taylor, Green Bay, 1960-64
O.J. Simpson, Buffalo, 1972-76
Tony Dorsett, Dallas, 1977-81
4 Jim Brown, Cleveland, 1958-61
Earl Campbell, Houston, 1978-81
Walter Payton, Chicago, 1983-86
Most Yards Gained, Season
2,105 Eric Dickerson, L.A. Rams, 1984
2,003 O.J. Simpson, Buffalo, 1973
1,934 Earl Campbell, Houston, 1980
Most Yards Gained, Rookie, Season
1,808 Eric Dickerson, L.A. Rams, 1983
1,674 George Rogers, New Orleans, 1981
1,605 Ottis Anderson, St. Louis, 1979
Most Yards Gained, Game
275 Walter Payton, Chicago vs. Minnesota, Nov. 20, 1977
273 O.J. Simpson, Buffalo vs. Detroit, Nov. 25, 1976
250 O.J. Simpson, Buffalo vs. New England, Sept. 16, 1973
Most Games, 200 or More Yards Rushing, Career
6 O.J. Simpson, Buffalo, 1969-77; San Francisco, 1978-79
4 Jim Brown, Cleveland, 1957-65
Earl Campbell, Houston, 1978-84; New Orleans, 1984-85
3 Eric Dickerson, L.A. Rams, 1983-86
Most Games, 200 or More Yards Rushing, Season
4 Earl Campbell, Houston, 1980
3 O.J. Simpson, Buffalo, 1973
2 Jim Brown, Cleveland, 1963
O.J. Simpson, Buffalo, 1976
Walter Payton, Chicago, 1977
Eric Dickerson, L.A. Rams, 1984
Most Consecutive Games, 200 or More Yards Rushing
2 O.J. Simpson, Buffalo, 1973, 1976
Earl Campbell, Houston, 1980
Most Games, 100 or More Yards Rushing, Career
77 Walter Payton, Chicago, 1975-86
58 Jim Brown, Cleveland, 1957-65
47 Franco Harris, Pittsburgh, 1972-83; Seattle, 1984
Most Games, 100 or More Yards Rushing, Season
12 Eric Dickerson, L.A. Rams, 1984
11 O.J. Simpson, Buffalo, 1973
Earl Campbell, Houston, 1979
Marcus Allen, L.A. Raiders, 1985
Eric Dickerson, L.A. Rams, 1986
10 Walter Payton, Chicago, 1977, 1985
Earl Campbell, Houston, 1980
Most Consecutive Games, 100 or More Yards Rushing
11 Marcus Allen, L.A. Raiders, 1985-86
9 Walter Payton, Chicago, 1985
7 O.J. Simpson, Buffalo, 1972-73
Earl Campbell, Houston, 1979
Longest Run From Scrimmage
99 Tony Dorsett, Dallas vs. Minnesota, Jan. 3, 1983 (TD)
97 Andy Uram, Green Bay vs. Chi. Cardinals, Oct. 8, 1939 (TD)
Bob Gage, Pittsburgh vs. Chi. Bears, Dec. 4, 1949 (TD)
96 Jim Spavital, Baltimore vs. Green Bay, Nov. 5, 1950 (TD)
Bob Hoernschemeyer, Detroit vs. N.Y. Yanks, Nov. 23, 1950 (TD)

Average Gain
Highest Average Gain, Career (700 attempts)
5.22 Jim Brown, Cleveland, 1957-65 (2,359-12,312)
5.14 Eugene (Mercury) Morris, Miami, 1969-75; San Diego, 1976 (804-4,133)
5.00 Gale Sayers, Chicago, 1965-71 (991-4,956)
Highest Average Gain, Season (Qualifiers)
9.94 Beattie Feathers, Chi. Bears, 1934 (101-1,004)
6.87 Bobby Douglass, Chicago, 1972 (141-968)
6.78 Dan Towler, Los Angeles, 1951 (126-854)
Highest Average Gain, Game (10 attempts)
17.09 Marion Motley, Cleveland vs. Pittsburgh, Oct. 29, 1950 (11-188)
16.70 Bill Grimes, Green Bay vs. N.Y. Yanks, Oct. 8, 1950 (10-167)
16.57 Bobby Mitchell, Cleveland vs. Washington, Nov. 15, 1959 (14-232)

Touchdowns
Most Seasons Leading League
5 Jim Brown, Cleveland, 1957-59, 1963, 1965
4 Steve Van Buren, Philadelphia, 1945, 1947-49
3 Abner Haynes, Dall. Texans, 1960-62
Cookie Gilchrist, Buffalo, 1962-64
Paul Lowe, L.A. Chargers, 1960; San Diego, 1961, 1965
Leroy Kelly, Cleveland, 1966-68
Most Consecutive Seasons Leading League
3 Steve Van Buren, Philadelphia, 1947-49
Jim Brown, Cleveland, 1957-59
Abner Haynes, Dall. Texans, 1960-62
Cookie Gilchrist, Buffalo, 1962-64
Leroy Kelly, Cleveland, 1966-68
Most Touchdowns, Career
106 Jim Brown, Cleveland, 1957-65
Walter Payton, Chicago, 1975-86
104 John Riggins, N.Y. Jets, 1971-75; Washington, 1976-79, 1981-85
91 Franco Harris, Pittsburgh, 1972-83; Seattle, 1984
Most Touchdowns, Season
24 John Riggins, Washington, 1983
21 Joe Morris, N.Y. Giants, 1985
19 Jim Taylor, Green Bay, 1962
Earl Campbell, Houston, 1979
Chuck Muncie, San Diego, 1981
Most Touchdowns, Rookie, Season
18 Eric Dickerson, L.A. Rams, 1983
14 Gale Sayers, Chicago, 1965
13 Earl Campbell, Houston, 1978
Billy Sims, Detroit, 1980
George Rogers, New Orleans, 1981
Curt Warner, Seattle, 1983
Most Touchdowns, Game
6 Ernie Nevers, Chi. Cardinals vs. Chi. Bears, Nov. 28, 1929
5 Jim Brown, Cleveland vs. Baltimore, Nov. 1, 1959
Cookie Gilchrist, Buffalo vs. N.Y. Jets, Dec. 8, 1963
4 By many players
Most Consecutive Games Rushing for Touchdowns
13 John Riggins, Washington, 1982-83
George Rogers, Washington, 1985-86
11 Lenny Moore, Baltimore, 1963-64
9 Leroy Kelly, Cleveland, 1968

Passing
Most Seasons Leading League
6 Sammy Baugh, Washington, 1937, 1940, 1943, 1945, 1947, 1949
4 Len Dawson, Dall. Texans; 1962; Kansas City, 1964, 1966, 1968
Roger Staubach, Dallas, 1971, 1973, 1978-79
Ken Anderson, Cincinnati, 1974-75, 1981-82
3 Arnie Herber, Green Bay, 1932, 1934, 1936
Norm Van Brocklin, Los Angeles, 1950, 1952, 1954
Bart Starr, Green Bay, 1962, 1964, 1966
Most Consecutive Seasons Leading League
2 Cecil Isbell, Green Bay, 1941-42
Milt Plum, Cleveland, 1960-61
Ken Anderson, Cincinnati, 1974-75, 1981-82
Roger Staubach, Dallas, 1978-79

Pass Rating
Highest Pass Rating, Career (1,500 attempts)
95.2 Dan Marino, Miami, 1983-86
91.2 Joe Montana, San Francisco, 1979-86
84.1 Dave Krieg, Seattle, 1980-86
Highest Pass Rating, Season (Qualifiers)
110.4 Milt Plum, Cleveland, 1960
109.9 Sammy Baugh, Washington, 1945
108.9 Dan Marino, Miami, 1984
Highest Pass Rating, Rookie, Season (Qualifiers)
96.0 Dan Marino, Miami, 1983
88.2 Greg Cook, Cincinnati, 1969
84.0 Charlie Conerly, N.Y. Giants, 1948

Attempts
Most Seasons Leading League
4 Sammy Baugh, Washington, 1937, 1943, 1947-48
Johnny Unitas, Baltimore, 1957, 1959-61
George Blanda, Chi. Bears, 1953; Houston, 1963-65
3 Arnie Herber, Green Bay, 1932, 1934, 1936
Sonny Jurgensen, Washington, 1966-67, 1969
2 By many players
Most Consecutive Seasons Leading League
3 Johnny Unitas, Baltimore, 1959-61
George Blanda, Houston, 1963-65
2 By many players
Most Passes Attempted, Career
6,467 Fran Tarkenton, Minnesota, 1961-66, 1972-78; N.Y. Giants, 1967-71
5,240 Dan Fouts, San Diego, 1973-86
5,186 Johnny Unitas, Baltimore, 1956-72; San Diego, 1973
Most Passes Attempted, Season
623 Dan Marino, Miami, 1986
609 Dan Fouts, San Diego, 1981
605 John Elway, Denver, 1985
Most Passes Attempted, Rookie, Season
439 Jim Zorn, Seattle, 1976
417 Jack Trudeau, Indianapolis, 1986
375 Norm Snead, Washington, 1961
Most Passes Attempted, Game
68 George Blanda, Houston vs. Buffalo, Nov. 1, 1964
62 Joe Namath, N.Y. Jets vs. Baltimore, Oct. 18, 1970
Steve Dils, Minnesota vs. Tampa Bay, Sept. 5, 1981
Phil Simms, N.Y. Giants vs. Cincinnati, Oct. 13, 1985
61 Tommy Kramer, Minnesota vs. Buffalo, Dec. 16, 1979

Completions

Most Seasons Leading League

5 Sammy Baugh, Washington, 1937, 1943, 1945, 1947-48
4 George Blanda, Chi. Bears, 1953; Houston, 1963-65
Sonny Jurgensen, Philadelphia, 1961; Washington, 1966-67, 1969
3 Arnie Herber, Green Bay, 1932, 1934, 1936
Johnny Unitas, Baltimore, 1959-60, 1963
John Brodie, San Francisco, 1965, 1968, 1970
Fran Tarkenton, Minnesota, 1975-76, 1978
Dan Marino, Miami, 1984-86

Most Consecutive Seasons Leading League

3 George Blanda, Houston, 1963-65
Dan Marino, Miami, 1984-86
2 By many players

Most Passes Completed, Career

3,686 Fran Tarkenton, Minnesota, 1961-66, 1972-78; N.Y. Giants, 1967-71
3,091 Dan Fouts, San Diego, 1973-86
2,830 Johnny Unitas, Baltimore, 1956-72; San Diego, 1973

Most Passes Completed, Season

378 Dan Marino, Miami, 1986
362 Dan Marino, Miami, 1984
360 Dan Fouts, San Diego, 1981

Most Passes Completed, Rookie, Season

208 Jim Zorn, Seattle, 1976
204 Jack Trudeau, Indianapolis, 1986
183 Jeff Komlo, Detroit, 1979

Most Passes Completed, Game

42 Richard Todd, N.Y. Jets vs. San Francisco, Sept. 21, 1980
40 Ken Anderson, Cincinnati vs. San Diego, Dec. 20, 1982
Phil Simms, N.Y. Giants vs. Cincinnati, Oct. 13, 1985
39 Dan Marino, Miami vs. Buffalo, Nov. 16, 1986

Most Consecutive Passes Completed

20 Ken Anderson, Cincinnati vs. Houston, Jan. 2, 1983
18 Steve DeBerg, Denver vs. L.A. Rams (17), Dec. 12, 1982; vs. Kansas City (1), Dec. 19, 1982
Lynn Dickey, Green Bay vs. Houston, Sept. 4, 1983
Joe Montana, San Francisco vs. L.A. Rams (13), Oct. 28, 1984; vs. Cincinnati (5), Nov. 4, 1984
17 Bert Jones, Baltimore vs. N.Y. Jets, Dec. 15, 1974
Ken O'Brien, N.Y. Jets vs. Atlanta, Nov. 9, 1986

Completion Percentage

Most Seasons Leading League

8 Len Dawson, Dall. Texans, 1962; Kansas City, 1964-69, 1975
7 Sammy Baugh, Washington, 1940, 1942-43, 1945, 1947-49
4 Bart Starr, Green Bay, 1962, 1966, 1968-69

Most Consecutive Seasons Leading League

6 Len Dawson, Kansas City, 1964-69
3 Sammy Baugh, Washington, 1947-49
Otto Graham, Cleveland, 1953-55
Milt Plum, Cleveland, 1959-61
2 By many players

Highest Completion Percentage, Career (1,500 attempts)

63.17 Joe Montana, San Francisco, 1979-86 (2,878-1,818)
60.93 Dan Marino, Miami, 1983-86 (2,050-1,249)
59.85 Ken Stabler, Oakland, 1970-79; Houston, 1980-81; New Orleans, 1982-84 (3,793-2,270)

Highest Completion Percentage, Season (Qualifiers)

70.55 Ken Anderson, Cincinnati, 1982 (309-218)
70.33 Sammy Baugh, Washington, 1945 (182-128)
67.29 Steve Bartkowski, Atlanta, 1984 (269-181)

Highest Completion Percentage, Rookie, Season (Qualifiers)

58.45 Dan Marino, Miami, 1983 (296-173)
57.14 Jim McMahon, Chicago, 1982 (269-181)
56.07 Fran Tarkenton, Minnesota, 1961 (280-157)

Highest Completion Percentage, Game (20 attempts)

90.91 Ken Anderson, Cincinnati vs. Pittsburgh, Nov. 10, 1974 (22-20)
90.48 Lynn Dickey, Green Bay vs. New Orleans, Dec. 13, 1981 (21-19)
87.50 Danny White, Dallas vs. Philadelphia, Nov. 6, 1983 (24-21)

Yards Gained

Most Seasons Leading League

5 Sonny Jurgensen, Philadelphia, 1961-62; Washington, 1966-67, 1969
4 Sammy Baugh, Washington, 1937, 1940, 1947-48
Johnny Unitas, Baltimore, 1957, 1959-60, 1963
Dan Fouts, San Diego, 1979-82
3 Arnie Herber, Green Bay, 1932, 1934, 1936
Sid Luckman, Chi. Bears, 1943, 1945-46
John Brodie, San Francisco, 1965, 1968, 1970
John Hadl, San Diego, 1965, 1968, 1971
Joe Namath, N.Y. Jets, 1966-67, 1972
Dan Marino, Miami, 1984-86

Most Consecutive Seasons Leading League

4 Dan Fouts, San Diego, 1979-82
3 Dan Marino, Miami, 1984-86
2 By many players

Most Yards Gained, Career

47,003 Fran Tarkenton, Minnesota, 1961-66, 1972-78; N.Y. Giants, 1967-71
40,523 Dan Fouts, San Diego, 1973-86
40,239 Johnny Unitas, Baltimore, 1956-72; San Diego, 1973

Most Seasons, 3,000 or More Yards Passing

6 Dan Fouts, San Diego, 1979-81, 1984-86
5 Sonny Jurgensen, Philadelphia, 1961-62; Washington, 1966-67, 1969
Tommy Kramer, Minnesota, 1979-81, 1985-86
4 Brian Sipe, Cleveland, 1979-81, 1983
Ron Jaworski, Philadelphia, 1980-81, 1983, 1985
Joe Montana, San Francisco, 1981, 1983-85
Danny White, Dallas, 1980-81, 1983, 1985

Most Yards Gained, Season

5,084 Dan Marino, Miami, 1984
4,802 Dan Fouts, San Diego, 1981
4,746 Dan Marino, Miami, 1986

Most Yards Gained, Rookie, Season

2,571 Jim Zorn, Seattle, 1976
2,507 Dennis Shaw, Buffalo, 1970
2,337 Norm Snead, Washington, 1961

Most Yards Gained, Game

554 Norm Van Brocklin, Los Angeles vs. N.Y. Yanks, Sept. 28, 1951
513 Phil Simms, N.Y. Giants vs. Cincinnati, Oct. 13, 1985
509 Vince Ferragamo, L.A. Rams vs. Chicago, Dec. 26, 1982

Most Games, 400 or More Yards Passing, Career

7 Dan Marino, Miami, 1983-86
6 Dan Fouts, San Diego, 1973-86
5 Sonny Jurgensen, Philadelphia, 1957-63; Washington, 1964-74

Most Games, 400 or More Yards Passing, Season

4 Dan Marino, Miami, 1984
3 Dan Marino, Miami, 1986
2 George Blanda, Houston, 1961
Sonny Jurgensen, Philadelphia, 1961
Joe Namath, N.Y. Jets, 1972
Dan Fouts, San Diego, 1982, 1985
Phil Simms, N.Y. Giants, 1985
Ken O'Brien, N.Y. Jets, 1986
Bernie Kosar, Cleveland, 1986

Most Consecutive Games, 400 or More Yards Passing

2 Dan Fouts, San Diego, 1982
Dan Marino, Miami, 1984
Phil Simms, N.Y. Giants, 1985

Most Games, 300 or More Yards Passing, Career

48 Dan Fouts, San Diego, 1973-86
26 Johnny Unitas, Baltimore, 1956-72; San Diego, 1973
25 Sonny Jurgensen, Philadelphia, 1957-63; Washington, 1964-74

Most Games, 300 or More Yards Passing, Season

9 Dan Marino, Miami, 1984
8 Dan Fouts, San Diego, 1980
7 Dan Fouts, San Diego, 1981, 1985
Bill Kenney, Kansas City, 1983
Neil Lomax, St. Louis, 1984

Most Consecutive Games, 300 or More Yards Passing, Season

5 Joe Montana, San Francisco, 1982
4 Dan Fouts, San Diego, 1979
Bill Kenney, Kansas City, 1983
3 By many players

Longest Pass Completion (All TDs except as noted)

99 Frank Filchock (to Farkas), Washington vs. Pittsburgh, Oct. 15, 1939
George Izo (to Mitchell), Washington vs. Cleveland, Sept. 15, 1963
Karl Sweetan (to Studstill), Detroit vs. Baltimore, Oct. 16, 1966
Sonny Jurgensen (to Allen), Washington vs. Chicago, Sept. 15, 1968
Jim Plunkett (to Branch), L.A. Raiders vs. Washington, Oct. 2, 1983
Ron Jaworski (to Quick), Philadelphia vs. Atlanta, Nov. 10, 1985
98 Doug Russell (to Tinsley), Chi. Cardinals vs. Cleveland, Nov. 27, 1938
Ogden Compton (to Lane), Chi. Cardinals vs. Green Bay, Nov. 13, 1955
Bill Wade (to Farrington), Chicago Bears vs. Detroit, Oct. 8, 1961
Jacky Lee (to Dewveall), Houston vs. San Diego, Nov. 25, 1962
Earl Morrall (to Jones), N.Y. Giants vs. Pittsburgh, Sept. 11, 1966
Jim Hart (to Moore), St. Louis vs. Los Angeles, Dec. 10, 1972 (no TD)
97 Pat Coffee (to Tinsley), Chi. Cardinals vs. Chi. Bears, Dec. 5, 1937
Bobby Layne (to Box), Detroit vs. Green Bay, Nov. 26, 1953
George Shaw (to Tarr), Denver vs. Boston, Sept. 21, 1962

Average Gain

Most Seasons Leading League

7 Sid Luckman, Chi. Bears, 1939-43, 1946-47
3 Arnie Herber, Green Bay, 1932, 1934, 1936
Norm Van Brocklin, Los Angeles, 1950, 1952, 1954
Len Dawson, Dall. Texans, 1962; Kansas City, 1966, 1968
Bart Starr, Green Bay, 1966-68

Most Consecutive Seasons Leading League

5 Sid Luckman, Chi. Bears, 1939-43
3 Bart Starr, Green Bay, 1966-68
2 Bernie Masterson, Chi. Bears, 1937-38
Sid Luckman, Chi. Bears, 1946-47
Johnny Unitas, Baltimore, 1964-65
Terry Bradshaw, Pittsburgh, 1977-78
Steve Grogan, New England, 1980-81

Highest Average Gain, Career (1,500 attempts)

8.63 Otto Graham, Cleveland, 1950-55 (1,565-13,499)
8.42 Sid Luckman, Chi. Bears, 1939-50 (1,744-14,686)
8.16 Norm Van Brocklin, Los Angeles, 1949-57; Philadelphia, 1958-60 (2,895-23,611)

Highest Average Gain, Season (Qualifiers)

11.17 Tommy O'Connell, Cleveland, 1957 (110-1,229)
10.86 Sid Luckman, Chi. Bears, 1943 (202-2,194)
10.55 Otto Graham, Cleveland, 1953 (258-2,722)

Highest Average Gain, Rookie, Season (Qualifiers)

9.411 Greg Cook, Cincinnati, 1969 (197-1,854)
9.409 Bob Waterfield, Cleveland, 1945 (171-1,609)
8.36 Zeke Bratkowski, Chi. Bears, 1954 (130-1,087)

Highest Average Gain, Game (20 attempts)

18.58 Sammy Baugh, Washington vs. Boston, Oct. 31, 1948 (24-446)
18.50 Johnny Unitas, Baltimore vs. Atlanta, Nov. 12, 1967 (20-370)
17.71 Joe Namath, N.Y. Jets vs. Baltimore, Sept. 24, 1972 (28-496)

Touchdowns

Most Seasons Leading League

4 Johnny Unitas, Baltimore, 1957-60
Len Dawson, Dall. Texans, 1962; Kansas City, 1963, 1965-66
3 Arnie Herber, Green Bay, 1932, 1934, 1936
Sid Luckman, Chi. Bears, 1943, 1945-46
Y.A. Tittle, San Francisco, 1955; N.Y. Giants, 1962-63
Dan Marino, Miami, 1984-86
2 By many players

Most Consecutive Seasons Leading League

4 Johnny Unitas, Baltimore, 1957-60
3 Dan Marino, Miami, 1984-86
2 By many players

Most Touchdown Passes, Career
342 Fran Tarkenton, Minnesota, 1961-66, 1972-78; N.Y. Giants, 1967-71
290 Johnny Unitas, Baltimore, 1956-72: San Diego, 1973
255 Sonny Jurgensen, Philadelphia, 1957-63; Washington, 1964-74
Most Touchdown Passes, Season
48 Dan Marino, Miami, 1984
44 Dan Marino, Miami, 1986
36 George Blanda, Houston, 1961
Y.A. Tittle, N.Y. Giants, 1963
Most Touchdown Passes, Rookie, Season
22 Charlie Conerly, N.Y. Giants, 1948
20 Dan Marino, Miami, 1983
19 Jim Plunkett, New England, 1971
Most Touchdown Passes, Game
7 Sid Luckman, Chi. Bears vs. N.Y. Giants, Nov. 14, 1943
Adrian Burk, Philadelphia vs. Washington, Oct. 17, 1954
George Blanda, Houston vs. N.Y. Titans, Nov. 19, 1961
Y.A. Tittle, N.Y. Giants vs. Washington, Oct. 28, 1962
Joe Kapp, Minnesota vs. Baltimore, Sept. 28, 1969
6 By many players. Last time: Tommy Kramer, Minnesota vs. Green Bay, Sept. 28, 1986
Most Games, Four or More Touchdown Passes, Career
17 Johnny Unitas, Baltimore, 1956-72; San Diego, 1973
13 George Blanda, Chi. Bears, 1949, 1950-58; Baltimore, 1950; Houston, 1960-66; Oakland, 1967-75
12 Sonny Jurgensen, Philadelphia, 1957-63; Washington, 1964-74
Fran Tarkenton, Minnesota, 1961-66, 1972-78; N.Y. Giants, 1967-71
Dan Fouts, San Diego, 1973-86
Dan Marino, Miami, 1983-86
Most Games, Four or More Touchdown Passes, Season
6 Dan Marino, Miami, 1984
5 Dan Marino, Miami, 1986
4 George Blanda, Houston, 1961
Vince Ferragamo, Los Angeles, 1980
Most Consecutive Games, Four or More Touchdown Passes
4 Dan Marino, Miami, 1984
2 By many players
Most Consecutive Games, Touchdown Passes
47 Johnny Unitas, Baltimore, 1956-60
28 Dave Krieg, Seattle, 1983-85
25 Daryle Lamonica, Oakland, 1968-70

Had Intercepted
Most Consecutive Passes Attempted, None Intercepted
294 Bart Starr, Green Bay, 1964-65
208 Milt Plum, Cleveland, 1959-60
206 Roman Gabriel, Los Angeles, 1968-69
Most Passes Had Intercepted, Career
277 George Blanda, Chi. Bears, 1949, 1950-58; Baltimore, 1950; Houston, 1960-66; Oakland, 1967-75
268 John Hadl, San Diego, 1962-72; Los Angeles, 1973-74; Green Bay, 1974-75; Houston, 1976-77
266 Fran Tarkenton, Minnesota, 1961-66, 1972-78; N.Y. Giants, 1967-71
Most Passes Had Intercepted, Season
42 George Blanda, Houston, 1962
34 Frank Tripucka, Denver, 1960
32 John Hadl, San Diego, 1968
Fran Tarkenton, Minnesota, 1978
Most Passes Had Intercepted, Game
8 Jim Hardy, Chi. Cardinals vs. Philadelphia, Sept. 24, 1950
7 Parker Hall, Cleveland vs. Green Bay, Nov. 8, 1942
Frank Sinkwich, Detroit vs. Green Bay, Oct. 24, 1943
Bob Waterfield, Los Angeles vs. Green Bay, Oct. 17, 1948
Zeke Bratkowski, Chicago vs. Baltimore, Oct. 2, 1960
Tommy Wade, Pittsburgh vs. Philadelphia, Dec. 12, 1965
Ken Stabler, Oakland vs. Denver, Oct. 16, 1977
Steve DeBerg, Tampa Bay vs. San Francisco, Sept. 7, 1986
6 By many players
Most Attempts, No Interceptions, Game
57 Joe Montana, San Francisco vs. Atlanta, Oct. 6, 1985
54 Dan Marino, Miami vs. Buffalo, Nov. 16, 1986
51 Scott Brunner, N.Y. Giants vs. St. Louis, Dec. 26, 1982

Lowest Percentage, Passes Had Intercepted
Most Seasons Leading League, Lowest Percentage, Passes Had Intercepted
5 Sammy Baugh, Washington, 1940, 1942, 1944-45, 1947
3 Charlie Conerly, N.Y. Giants, 1950, 1956, 1959
Bart Starr, Green Bay, 1962, 1964, 1966
Roger Staubach, Dallas, 1971, 1977, 1979
Ken Anderson, Cincinnati, 1972, 1981-82
2 By many players
Lowest Percentage, Passes Had Intercepted, Career (1,500 attempts)
2.64 Joe Montana, San Francisco, 1979-86 (2,878-76)
2.98 Neil Lomax, St. Louis, 1981-86 (2,247-67)
3.27 Dan Marino, Miami, 1983-86 (2,050-67)
Lowest Percentage, Passes Had Intercepted, Season (Qualifiers)
0.66 Joe Ferguson, Buffalo, 1976 (151-1)
1.16 Steve Bartkowski, Atlanta, 1983 (432-5)
1.20 Bart Starr, Green Bay, 1966 (251-3)
Lowest Percentage, Passes Had Intercepted, Rookie, Season (Qualifiers)
2.03 Dan Marino, Miami, 1983 (296-6)
2.10 Gary Wood, N.Y. Giants, 1964 (143-3)
2.82 Bernie Kosar, Cleveland, 1985 (248-7)

Times Sacked
Times Sacked has been compiled since 1963.
Most Times Sacked, Career
483 Fran Tarkenton, Minnesota, 1961-66, 1972-78; N.Y. Giants, 1967-71
405 Craig Morton, Dallas, 1965-74; N.Y. Giants, 1974-76; Denver, 1977-82
398 Ken Anderson, Cincinnati, 1971-86
Most Times Sacked, Season
72 Randall Cunningham, Philadelphia, 1986
62 Ken O'Brien, N.Y. Jets, 1985
61 Neil Lomax, St. Louis, 1985
Most Times Sacked, Game
12 Bert Jones, Baltimore vs. St. Louis, Oct. 26, 1980
Warren Moon, Houston vs. Dallas, Sept. 29, 1985
11 Charley Johnson, St. Louis vs. N.Y. Giants, Nov. 1, 1964
Bart Starr, Green Bay vs. Detroit, Nov. 7, 1965
Jack Kemp, Buffalo vs. Oakland, Oct. 15, 1967
Bob Berry, Atlanta vs. St. Louis, Nov. 24, 1968
Greg Landry, Detroit vs. Dallas, Oct. 6, 1975
Ron Jaworski, Philadelphia vs. St. Louis, Dec. 18, 1983
Paul McDonald, Cleveland vs. Kansas City, Sept. 30, 1984
Archie Manning, Minnesota vs. Chicago, Oct. 28, 1984
Steve Pelluer, Dallas vs. San Diego, Nov. 16, 1986
Randall Cunningham, Philadelphia vs. L.A. Raiders, Nov. 30, 1986 (OT)
10 By many players

Pass Receiving
Most Seasons Leading League
8 Don Hutson, Green Bay, 1936-37, 1939, 1941-45
5 Lionel Taylor, Denver, 1960-63, 1965
3 Tom Fears, Los Angeles, 1948-50
Pete Pihos, Philadelphia, 1953-55
Billy Wilson, San Francisco, 1954, 1956-57
Raymond Berry, Baltimore, 1958-60
Lance Alworth, San Diego, 1966, 1968-69
Most Consecutive Seasons Leading League
5 Don Hutson, Green Bay, 1941-45
4 Lionel Taylor, Denver, 1960-63
3 Tom Fears, Los Angeles, 1948-50
Pete Pihos, Philadelphia, 1953-55
Raymond Berry, Baltimore, 1958-60
Most Pass Receptions, Career
750 Charlie Joiner, Houston, 1969-72; Cincinnati, 1972-75; San Diego, 1976-86
694 Steve Largent, Seattle, 1976-86
649 Charley Taylor, Washington, 1964-75, 1977
Most Seasons, 50 or More Pass Receptions
9 Steve Largent, Seattle, 1976, 1978-81, 1983-86
7 Raymond Berry, Baltimore, 1958-62, 1965-66
Art Powell, N.Y. Titans, 1960-62; Oakland, 1963-66
Lance Alworth, San Diego, 1963-69
Charley Taylor, Washington, 1964, 1966-67, 1969, 1973-75
Charlie Joiner, San Diego, 1976, 1979-81, 1983-85
Wes Chandler, New Orleans, 1979-80; New Orleans-San Diego, 1981; San Diego, 1983-86
Dwight Clark, San Francisco, 1980-86
James Lofton, Green Bay, 1979-81, 1983-86
6 Lionel Taylor, Denver, 1960-65
Bobby Mitchell, Washington, 1962-67
Ahmad Rashad, Minnesota, 1976-81
Ozzie Newsome, Cleveland, 1979-81, 1983-85
Kellen Winslow, San Diego, 1980-84, 1986
Most Pass Receptions, Season
106 Art Monk, Washington, 1984
101 Charley Hennigan, Houston, 1964
100 Lionel Taylor, Denver, 1961
Most Pass Receptions, Rookie, Season
83 Earl Cooper, San Francisco, 1980
72 Bill Groman, Houston, 1960
67 Jack Clancy, Miami, 1967
Cris Collinsworth, Cincinnati, 1981
Most Pass Receptions, Game
18 Tom Fears, Los Angeles vs. Green Bay, Dec. 3, 1950
17 Clark Gaines, N.Y. Jets vs. San Francisco, Sept. 21, 1980
16 Sonny Randle, St. Louis vs. N.Y. Giants, Nov. 4, 1962
Most Consecutive Games, Pass Receptions
139 Steve Largent, Seattle, 1977-86 (current)
127 Harold Carmichael, Philadelphia, 1972-80
121 Mel Gray, St. Louis, 1973-82

Yards Gained
Most Seasons Leading League
7 Don Hutson, Green Bay, 1936, 1938-39, 1941-44
3 Raymond Berry, Baltimore, 1957, 1959-60
Lance Alworth, San Diego, 1965-66, 1968
2 By many players
Most Consecutive Seasons Leading League
4 Don Hutson, Green Bay, 1941-44
2 By many players
Most Yards Gained, Career
12,146 Charlie Joiner, Houston, 1969-72; Cincinnati, 1972-75; San Diego, 1976-86
11,834 Don Maynard, N.Y. Giants, 1958; N.Y. Jets, 1960-72; St. Louis, 1973
11,129 Steve Largent, Seattle, 1976-86
Most Seasons, 1,000 or More Yards, Pass Receiving
8 Steve Largent, Seattle, 1978-81, 1983-86
7 Lance Alworth, San Diego, 1963-69
5 Art Powell, N.Y. Titans, 1960, 1962; Oakland, 1963-64, 1966
Don Maynard, N.Y. Jets, 1960, 1962, 1965, 1967-68
James Lofton, Green Bay, 1980-81, 1983-85
Most Yards Gained, Season
1,746 Charley Hennigan, Houston, 1961
1,602 Lance Alworth, San Diego, 1965
1,570 Jerry Rice, San Francisco, 1986
Most Yards Gained, Rookie, Season
1,473 Bill Groman, Houston, 1960
1,231 Bill Howton, Green Bay, 1952
1,131 Bill Brooks, Indianapolis, 1986
Most Yards Gained, Game
309 Stephone Paige, Kansas City vs. San Diego, Dec. 22, 1985
303 Jim Benton, Cleveland vs. Detroit, Nov. 22, 1945
302 Cloyce Box, Detroit vs. Baltimore, Dec. 3, 1950

Most Games, 200 or More Yards Pass Receiving, Career
5 Lance Alworth, San Diego, 1962-70; Dallas, 1971-72
4 Don Hutson, Green Bay, 1935-45
Charley Hennigan, Houston, 1960-66
3 Don Maynard, N.Y. Giants, 1958; N.Y. Jets, 1960-72; St. Louis, 1973
Wes Chandler, New Orleans, 1978-81; San Diego, 1981-86
Most Games, 200 or More Yards Pass Receiving, Season
3 Charley Hennigan, Houston, 1961
2 Don Hutson, Green Bay, 1942
Gene Roberts, N.Y. Giants, 1949
Lance Alworth, San Diego, 1963
Don Maynard, N.Y. Jets, 1968
Most Games, 100 or More Yards Pass Receiving, Career
50 Don Maynard, N.Y. Giants, 1958; N.Y. Jets, 1960-72; St. Louis, 1973
41 Lance Alworth, San Diego, 1962-70; Dallas, 1971-72
39 Steve Largent, Seattle, 1976-86
Most Games, 100 or More Yards Pass Receiving, Season
10 Charley Hennigan, Houston, 1961
9 Elroy (Crazylegs) Hirsch, Los Angeles, 1951
Bill Groman, Houston, 1960
Lance Alworth, San Diego, 1965
Don Maynard, N.Y. Jets, 1967
Stanley Morgan, New England, 1986
8 Charley Hennigan, Houston, 1964
Lance Alworth, San Diego, 1967
Mark Duper, Miami, 1986
Most Consecutive Games, 100 or More Yards Pass Receiving
7 Charley Hennigan, Houston, 1961
Bill Groman, Houston, 1961
6 Raymond Berry, Baltimore, 1960
Pat Studstill, Detroit, 1966
5 Elroy (Crazylegs) Hirsch, Los Angeles, 1951
Bob Boyd, Los Angeles, 1954
Terry Barr, Detroit, 1963
Lance Alworth, San Diego, 1966
Longest Pass Reception (All TDs except as noted)
99 Andy Farkas (from Filchock), Washington vs. Pittsburgh, Oct. 15, 1939
Bobby Mitchell (from Izo), Washington vs. Cleveland, Sept. 15, 1963
Pat Studstill (from Sweetan), Detroit vs. Baltimore, Oct. 16, 1966
Gerry Allen (from Jurgensen), Washington vs. Chicago, Sept. 15, 1968
Cliff Branch (from Plunkett), L.A. Raiders vs. Washington, Oct. 2, 1983
Mike Quick (from Jaworski), Philadelphia vs. Atlanta, Nov. 10, 1985
98 Gaynell Tinsley (from Russell), Chi. Cardinals vs. Cleveland, Nov. 17, 1938
Dick (Night Train) Lane (from Compton), Chi. Cardinals vs. Green Bay, Nov. 13, 1955
John Farrington (from Wade), Chicago vs. Detroit, Oct. 8, 1961
Willard Dewveall (from Lee), Houston vs. San Diego, Nov. 25, 1962
Homer Jones (from Morrall), N.Y. Giants vs. Pittsburgh, Sept. 11, 1966
Bobby Moore (from Hart), St. Louis vs. Los Angeles, Dec. 10, 1972 (no TD)
97 Gaynell Tinsley (from Coffee), Chi. Cardinals vs. Chi. Bears, Dec. 5, 1937
Cloyce Box (from Layne), Detroit vs. Green Bay, Nov. 26, 1953
Jerry Tarr (from Shaw), Denver vs. Boston, Sept. 21, 1962

Average Gain
Highest Average Gain, Career (200 receptions)
22.26 Homer Jones, N.Y. Giants, 1964-69; Cleveland, 1970 (224-4,986)
20.82 Buddy Dial, Pittsburgh, 1959-63; Dallas, 1964-66 (261-5,436)
20.24 Harlon Hill, Chi. Bears, 1954-61; Pittsburgh, 1962; Detroit, 1962 (233-4,717)
Highest Average Gain, Season (24 receptions)
32.58 Don Currivan, Boston, 1947 (24-782)
31.44 Bucky Pope, Los Angeles, 1964 (25-786)
27.58 Jimmy Orr, Pittsburgh, 1958 (33-910)
Highest Average Gain, Game (3 receptions)
60.67 Bill Groman, Houston vs. Denver, Nov. 20, 1960 (3-182)
Homer Jones, N.Y. Giants vs. Washington, Dec. 12, 1965 (3-182)
60.33 Don Currivan, Boston vs. Washington, Nov. 30, 1947 (3-181)
59.67 Bobby Duckworth, San Diego vs. Chicago, Dec. 3, 1984 (3-179)

Touchdowns
Most Seasons Leading League
9 Don Hutson, Green Bay, 1935-38, 1940-44
3 Lance Alworth, San Diego, 1964-66
2 By many players
Most Consecutive Seasons Leading League
5 Don Hutson, Green Bay, 1940-44
4 Don Hutson, Green Bay, 1935-38
3 Lance Alworth, San Diego, 1964-66
Most Touchdowns, Career
99 Don Hutson, Green Bay, 1935-45
88 Don Maynard, N.Y. Giants, 1958; N.Y. Jets, 1960-72; St. Louis, 1973
87 Steve Largent, Seattle, 1976-86
Most Touchdowns, Season
18 Mark Clayton, Miami, 1984
17 Don Hutson, Green Bay, 1942
Elroy (Crazylegs) Hirsch, Los Angeles, 1951
Bill Groman, Houston, 1961
16 Art Powell, Oakland, 1963
Most Touchdowns, Rookie, Season
13 Bill Howton, Green Bay, 1952
John Jefferson, San Diego, 1979
12 Harlon Hill, Chi. Bears, 1954
Bill Groman, Houston, 1960
Mike Ditka, Chicago, 1961
Bob Hayes, Dallas, 1965
10 Bill Swiacki, N.Y. Giants, 1948
Bucky Pope, Los Angeles, 1964
Sammy White, Minnesota, 1976
Daryl Turner, Seattle, 1984
Most Touchdowns, Game
5 Bob Shaw, Chi. Cardinals vs. Baltimore, Oct. 2, 1950
Kellen Winslow, San Diego vs. Oakland, Nov. 22, 1981
4 By many players. Last time: Wesley Walker, N.Y. Jets vs. Miami, Sept. 21, 1986 (OT)

Most Consecutive Games, Touchdowns
11 Elroy (Crazylegs) Hirsch, Los Angeles, 1950-51
Buddy Dial, Pittsburgh, 1959-60
9 Lance Alworth, San Diego, 1963
8 Bill Groman, Houston, 1961
Dave Parks, San Francisco, 1965

Interceptions By
Most Seasons Leading League
3 Everson Walls, Dallas, 1981-82, 1985
2 Dick (Night Train) Lane, Los Angeles, 1952; Chi. Cardinals, 1954
Jack Christiansen, Detroit, 1953, 1957
Milt Davis, Baltimore, 1957, 1959
Dick Lynch, N.Y. Giants, 1961, 1963
Johnny Robinson, Kansas City, 1966, 1970
Bill Bradley, Philadelphia, 1971-72
Emmitt Thomas, Kansas City, 1969, 1974
Most Interceptions By, Career
81 Paul Krause, Washington, 1964-67; Minnesota, 1968-79
79 Emlen Tunnell, N.Y. Giants, 1948-58; Green Bay, 1959-61
68 Dick (Night Train) Lane, Los Angeles, 1952-53; Chi. Cardinals, 1954-59; Detroit, 1960-65
Most Interceptions By, Season
14 Dick (Night Train) Lane, Los Angeles, 1952
13 Dan Sandifer, Washington, 1948
Orban (Spec) Sanders, N.Y. Yanks, 1950
Lester Hayes, Oakland, 1980
12 By nine players
Most Interceptions By, Rookie, Season
14 Dick (Night Train) Lane, Los Angeles, 1952
13 Dan Sandifer, Washington, 1948
12 Woodley Lewis, Los Angeles, 1950
Paul Krause, Washington, 1964
Most Interceptions By, Game
4 Sammy Baugh, Washington vs. Detroit, Nov. 14, 1943
Dan Sandifer, Washington vs. Boston, Oct. 31, 1948
Don Doll, Detroit vs. Chi. Cardinals, Oct. 23, 1949
Bob Nussbaumer, Chi. Cardinals vs. N.Y. Bulldogs, Nov. 13, 1949
Russ Craft, Philadelphia vs. Chi. Cardinals, Sept. 24, 1950
Bobby Dillon, Green Bay vs. Detroit, Nov. 26, 1953
Jack Butler, Pittsburgh vs. Washington, Dec. 13, 1953
Austin (Goose) Gonsoulin, Denver vs. Buffalo, Sept. 18, 1960
Jerry Norton, St. Louis vs. Washington, Nov. 20, 1960; vs. Pittsburgh, Nov. 26, 1961
Dave Baker, San Francisco vs. L.A. Rams, Dec. 4, 1960
Bobby Ply, Dall. Texans vs. San Diego, Dec. 16, 1962
Bobby Hunt, Kansas City vs. Houston, Oct. 4, 1964
Willie Brown, Denver vs. N.Y. Jets, Nov. 15, 1964
Dick Anderson, Miami vs. Pittsburgh, Dec. 3, 1973
Willie Buchanon, Green Bay vs. San Diego, Sept. 24, 1978
Deron Cherry, Kansas City vs. Seattle, Sept. 29, 1985
Most Consecutive Games, Passes Intercepted By
8 Tom Morrow, Oakland, 1962-63
7 Paul Krause, Washington, 1964
Larry Wilson, St. Louis, 1966
Ben Davis, Cleveland, 1968
6 Dick (Night Train) Lane, Chi. Cardinals, 1954-55
Will Sherman, Los Angeles, 1954-55
Jim Shofner, Cleveland, 1960
Paul Krause, Minnesota, 1968
Willie Williams, N.Y. Giants, 1968
Kermit Alexander, San Francisco, 1968-69
Mel Blount, Pittsburgh, 1975
Eric Harris, Kansas City, 1980
Lester Hayes, Oakland, 1980

Yards Gained
Most Seasons Leading League
2 Dick (Night Train) Lane, Los Angeles, 1952; Chi. Cardinals, 1954
Herb Adderley, Green Bay, 1965, 1969
Dick Anderson, Miami, 1968, 1970
Most Yards Gained, Career
1,282 Emlen Tunnell, N.Y. Giants, 1948-58; Green Bay, 1959-61
1,207 Dick (Night Train) Lane, Los Angeles, 1952-53; Chi. Cardinals, 1954-59; Detroit, 1960-65
1,185 Paul Krause, Washington, 1964-67; Minnesota, 1968-79
Most Yards Gained, Season
349 Charlie McNeil, San Diego, 1961
301 Don Doll, Detroit, 1949
298 Dick (Night Train) Lane, Los Angeles, 1952
Most Yards Gained, Rookie, Season
301 Don Doll, Detroit, 1949
298 Dick (Night Train) Lane, Los Angeles, 1952
275 Woodley Lewis, Los Angeles, 1950
Most Yards Gained, Game
177 Charlie McNeil, San Diego vs. Houston, Sept. 24, 1961
167 Dick Jauron, Detroit vs. Chicago, Nov. 18, 1973
151 Tom Myers, New Orleans vs. Minnesota, Sept. 3, 1978
Mike Haynes, L.A. Raiders vs. Miami, Dec. 2, 1984
Longest Return (All TDs)
102 Bob Smith, Detroit vs. Chi. Bears, Nov. 24, 1949
Erich Barnes, N.Y. Giants vs. Dall. Cowboys, Oct. 22, 1961
Gary Barbaro, Kansas City vs. Seattle, Dec. 11, 1977
Louis Breeden, Cincinnati vs. San Diego, Nov. 8, 1981
101 Richie Petitbon, Chicago vs Los Angeles, Dec. 9, 1962
Henry Carr, N.Y. Giants vs. Los Angeles, Nov. 13, 1966
Tony Greene, Buffalo vs. Kansas City, Oct. 3, 1976
Tom Pridemore, Atlanta vs. San Francisco, Sept. 20, 1981
100 Vern Huffman, Detroit vs. Brooklyn, Oct. 17, 1937
Mike Gaechter, Dall. Cowboys vs. Philadelphia, Oct. 14, 1962
Les (Speedy) Duncan, San Diego vs. Kansas City, Oct. 15, 1967

Tom Janik, Buffalo vs. N.Y. Jets, Sept. 29, 1968
Tim Collier, Kansas City vs. Oakland, Dec. 18, 1977

Touchdowns
Most Touchdowns, Career
9 Ken Houston, Houston, 1967-72; Washington, 1973-80
7 Herb Adderley, Green Bay, 1961-69; Dallas, 1970-72
Erich Barnes, Chi. Bears, 1958-60; N.Y. Giants, 1961-64; Cleveland, 1965-70
Lem Barney, Detroit, 1967-77
6 Tom Janik, Denver, 1963-64; Buffalo, 1965-68; Boston, 1969-70; New England, 1971
Miller Farr, Denver, 1965; San Diego, 1965-66; Houston, 1967-69; St. Louis, 1970-72; Detroit, 1973
Bobby Bell, Kansas City, 1963-74
Most Touchdowns, Season
4 Ken Houston, Houston, 1971
Jim Kearney, Kansas City, 1972
3 Dick Harris, San Diego, 1961
Dick Lynch, N.Y. Giants, 1963
Herb Adderley, Green Bay, 1965
Lem Barney, Detroit, 1967
Miller Farr, Houston, 1967
Monte Jackson, Los Angeles, 1976
Rod Perry, Los Angeles, 1978
Ronnie Lott, San Francisco, 1981
Lloyd Burruss, Kansas City, 1986
2 By many players
Most Touchdowns, Rookie, Season
3 Lem Barney, Detroit, 1967
Ronnie Lott, San Francisco, 1981
2 By many players
Most Touchdowns, Game
2 Bill Blackburn, Chi. Cardinals vs. Boston, Oct. 24, 1948
Dan Sandifer, Washington vs. Boston, Oct. 31, 1948
Bob Franklin, Cleveland vs. Chicago, Dec. 11, 1960
Bill Stacy, St. Louis vs. Dall. Cowboys, Nov. 5, 1961
Jerry Norton, St. Louis vs. Pittsburgh, Nov. 26, 1961
Miller Farr, Houston vs. Buffalo, Dec. 7, 1968
Ken Houston, Houston vs. San Diego, Dec. 19, 1971
Jim Kearney, Kansas City vs. Denver, Oct. 1, 1972
Lemar Parrish, Cincinnati vs. Houston, Dec. 17, 1972
Dick Anderson, Miami vs. Pittsburgh, Dec. 3, 1973
Prentice McCray, New England vs. N.Y. Jets, Nov. 21, 1976
Kenny Johnson, Atlanta vs. Green Bay, Nov. 27, 1983 (OT)
Mike Kozlowski, Miami vs. N.Y. Jets, Dec. 16, 1983
Dave Brown, Seattle vs. Kansas City, Nov. 4, 1984
Lloyd Burruss, Kansas City vs. San Diego, Oct. 19, 1986

Punting
Most Seasons Leading League
4 Sammy Baugh, Washington, 1940-43
Jerrel Wilson, Kansas City, 1965, 1968, 1972-73
3 Yale Lary, Detroit, 1959, 1961, 1963
Jim Fraser, Denver, 1962-64
Ray Guy, Oakland, 1974-75, 1977
Rohn Stark, Baltimore, 1983; Indianapolis, 1985-86
2 By many players
Most Consecutive Seasons Leading League
4 Sammy Baugh, Washington, 1940-43
3 Jim Fraser, Denver, 1962-64
2 By many players

Punts
Most Punts, Career
1,090 Dave Jennings, N.Y. Giants, 1974-84; N.Y. Jets, 1985-86
1,083 John James, Atlanta, 1972-81; Detroit, 1982, Houston, 1982-84
1,072 Jerrel Wilson, Kansas City, 1963-77; New England, 1978
Most Punts, Season
114 Bob Parsons, Chicago, 1981
109 John James, Atlanta, 1978
108 John Teltshick, Philadelphia, 1986
Most Punts, Rookie, Season
108 John Teltshick, Philadelphia, 1986
99 Lewis Colbert, Kansas City, 1986
96 Mike Connell, San Francisco, 1978
Chris Norman, Denver, 1984
Most Punts, Game
14 Dick Nesbitt, Chi. Cardinals vs. Chi. Bears, Nov. 30, 1933
Keith Molesworth, Chi. Bears vs. Green Bay, Dec. 10, 1933
Sammy Baugh, Washington vs. Philadelphia, Nov. 5, 1939
Carl Kinscherf, N.Y. Giants vs. Detroit, Nov. 7, 1943
George Taliaferro, N.Y. Yanks vs. Los Angeles, Sept. 28, 1951
12 Parker Hall, Cleveland vs. Green Bay, Nov. 26, 1939
Beryl Clark, Chi. Cardinals vs. Detroit, Sept. 15, 1940
Len Barnum, Philadelphia vs. Washington, Oct. 4, 1942
Horace Gillom, Cleveland vs. Philadelphia, Dec. 3, 1950
Adrian Burk, Philadelphia vs. Green Bay, Nov. 2, 1952; vs. N.Y. Giants, Dec. 12, 1954
Bob Scarpitto, Denver vs. Oakland, Sept. 10, 1967
Bill Van Heusen, Denver vs. Cincinnati, Oct. 6, 1968
Tom Blanchard, New Orleans vs. Minnesota, Nov. 16, 1975
Rusty Jackson, Los Angeles vs. San Francisco, Nov. 21, 1976
Wilbur Summers, Detroit vs. San Francisco, Oct. 23, 1977
John James, Atlanta vs. Washington, Dec. 10, 1978
Luke Prestridge, Denver vs. Buffalo, Oct. 25, 1981
Greg Coleman, Minnesota vs. Green Bay, Nov. 21, 1982
11 By many players
Longest Punt
98 Steve O'Neal, N.Y. Jets vs. Denver, Sept. 21, 1969
94 Joe Lintzenich, Chi. Bears vs. N.Y. Giants, Nov. 16, 1931
90 Don Chandler, Green Bay vs. San Francisco, Oct. 10, 1965

Average Yardage
Highest Average, Punting, Career (300 punts)
45.16 Rohn Stark, Baltimore, 1982-83; Indianapolis, 1984-86 (389-17, 567)
45.10 Sammy Baugh, Washington, 1937-52 (338-15,245)
44.68 Tommy Davis, San Francisco, 1959-69 (511-22,833)
Highest Average, Punting, Season (Qualifiers)
51.40 Sammy Baugh, Washington, 1940 (35-1,799)
48.94 Yale Lary, Detroit, 1963 (35-1,713)
48.73 Sammy Baugh, Washington, 1941 (30-1,462)
Highest Average, Punting, Rookie, Season (Qualifiers)
46.40 Bobby Walden, Minnesota, 1964 (72-3,341)
46.22 Dave Lewis, Cincinnati, 1970 (79-3,651)
45.92 Frank Sinkwich, Detroit, 1943 (12-551)
Highest Average, Punting, Game (4 punts)
61.75 Bob Cifers, Detroit vs. Chi. Bears, Nov. 24, 1946 (4-247)
61.60 Roy McKay, Green Bay vs. Chi. Cardinals, Oct. 28, 1945 (5-308)
59.40 Sammy Baugh, Washington vs. Detroit, Oct. 27, 1940 (5-297)

Punts Had Blocked
Most Consecutive Punts, None Blocked
623 Dave Jennings, N.Y. Giants, 1976-83
619 Ray Guy, Oakland, 1979-81; L.A. Raiders, 1982-86 (current)
578 Bobby Walden, Minnesota, 1964-67; Pittsburgh, 1968-72
Most Punts Had Blocked, Career
14 Herman Weaver, Detroit, 1970-76; Seattle, 1977-80
12 Jerrel Wilson, Kansas City, 1963-77; New England, 1978
Tom Blanchard, N.Y. Giants, 1971-73; New Orleans, 1974-78; Tampa Bay, 1979-81
11 David Lee, Baltimore, 1966-78

Punt Returns
Most Seasons Leading League
3 Les (Speedy) Duncan, San Diego, 1965-66; Washington, 1971
Rick Upchurch, Denver, 1976, 1978, 1982
2 Dick Christy, N.Y. Titans, 1961-62
Claude Gibson, Oakland, 1963-64
Billy Johnson, Houston, 1975, 1977

Punt Returns
Most Punt Returns, Career
258 Emlen Tunnell, N.Y. Giants, 1948-58; Green Bay, 1959-61
Billy Johnson, Houston, 1974-80; Atlanta, 1982-86
253 Alvin Haymond, Baltimore, 1964-67; Philadelphia, 1968; Los Angeles, 1969-71; Washington, 1972; Houston, 1973
252 Mike Fuller, San Diego, 1975-80; Cincinnati, 1981-82
Most Punt Returns, Season
70 Danny Reece, Tampa Bay, 1979
62 Fulton Walker, Miami-L.A. Raiders, 1985
58 J. T. Smith, Kansas City, 1979
Greg Pruitt, L.A. Raiders, 1983
Most Punt Returns, Rookie, Season
57 Lew Barnes, Chicago, 1986
54 James Jones, Dallas, 1980
53 Louis Lipps, Pittsburgh, 1984
Most Punt Returns, Game
11 Eddie Brown, Washington vs. Tampa Bay, Oct. 9, 1977
10 Theo Bell, Pittsburgh vs. Buffalo, Dec. 16, 1979
Mike Nelms, Washington vs. New Orleans, Dec. 26, 1982
9 Rodger Bird, Oakland vs. Denver, Sept. 10, 1967
Ralph McGill, San Francisco vs. Atlanta, Oct. 29, 1972
Ed Podolak, Kansas City vs. San Diego, Nov. 10, 1974
Anthony Leonard, San Francisco vs. New Orleans, Oct. 17, 1976
Butch Johnson, Dallas vs. Buffalo, Nov. 15, 1976
Larry Marshall, Philadelphia vs. Tampa Bay, Sept. 18, 1977
Nesby Glasgow, Baltimore vs. Kansas City, Sept. 2, 1979
Mike Nelms, Washington vs. St. Louis, Dec. 21, 1980
Leon Bright, N.Y. Giants vs. Philadelphia, Dec. 11, 1982
Pete Shaw, N.Y. Giants vs. Philadelphia, Nov. 20, 1983
Cleotha Montgomery, L.A. Raiders vs. Detroit, Dec. 10, 1984

Fair Catches
Most Fair Catches, Season
24 Ken Graham, San Diego, 1969
22 Lem Barney, Detroit, 1976
21 Ed Podolak, Kansas City, 1970
Steve Schubert, Chicago, 1978
Stanley Morgan, New England, 1979
Most Fair Catches, Game
7 Lem Barney, Detroit vs. Chicago, Nov. 21, 1976
6 Jake Scott, Miami vs. Buffalo, Dec. 20, 1970
Greg Pruitt, L.A. Raiders vs. Seattle, Oct. 7, 1984
5 By many players

Yards Gained
Most Seasons Leading League
3 Alvin Haymond, Baltimore, 1965-66; Los Angeles, 1969
2 Bill Dudley, Pittsburgh, 1942, 1946
Emlen Tunnell, N.Y. Giants, 1951-52
Dick Christy, N.Y. Titans, 1961-62
Claude Gibson, Oakland, 1963-64
Rodger Bird, Oakland, 1966-67
J. T. Smith, Kansas City, 1979-80
Most Yards Gained, Career
3,123 Billy Johnson, Houston, 1974-80; Atlanta, 1982-86
3,008 Rick Upchurch, Denver, 1975-83
2,660 Mike Fuller, San Diego, 1975-80; Cincinnati, 1981-82
Most Yards Gained, Season
692 Fulton Walker, Miami-L.A. Raiders, 1985
666 Greg Pruitt, L.A. Raiders, 1983
656 Louis Lipps, Pittsburgh, 1984

Most Yards Gained, Rookie, Season
656 Louis Lipps, Pittsburgh, 1984
655 Neal Colzie, Oakland, 1975
608 Mike Haynes, New England, 1976
Most Yards Gained, Game
207 LeRoy Irvin, Los Angeles vs. Atlanta, Oct. 11, 1981
205 George Atkinson, Oakland vs. Buffalo, Sept. 15, 1968
184 Tom Watkins, Detroit vs. San Francisco, Oct. 6, 1963
Longest Punt Return (All TDs)
98 Gil LeFebvre, Cincinnati vs. Brooklyn, Dec. 3, 1933
Charlie West, Minnesota vs. Washington, Nov. 3, 1968
Dennis Morgan, Dallas vs. St. Louis, Oct. 13, 1974
97 Greg Pruitt, L.A. Raiders vs. Washington, Oct. 2, 1983
96 Bill Dudley, Washington vs. Pittsburgh, Dec. 3, 1950

Average Yardage
Highest Average, Career (75 returns)
12.87 Henry Ellard, L.A. Rams, 1983-86 (97-1,248)
12.78 George McAfee, Chi. Bears, 1940-41, 1945-50 (112-1,431)
12.75 Jack Christiansen, Detroit, 1951-58 (85-1,084)
Highest Average, Season (Qualifiers)
23.00 Herb Rich, Baltimore, 1950 (12-276)
21.47 Jack Christiansen, Detroit, 1952 (15-322)
21.28 Dick Christy, N.Y. Titans, 1961 (18-383)
Highest Average, Rookie, Season (Qualifiers)
23.00 Herb Rich, Baltimore, 1950 (12-276)
20.88 Jerry Davis, Chi. Cardinals, 1948 (16-334)
20.73 Frank Sinkwich, Detroit, 1943 (11-228)
Highest Average, Game (3 returns)
47.67 Chuck Latourette, St. Louis vs. New Orleans, Sept. 29, 1968 (3-143)
47.33 Johnny Roland, St. Louis vs. Philadelphia, Oct. 2, 1966 (3-142)
45.67 Dick Christy, N.Y. Titans vs. Denver, Sept. 24, 1961 (3-137)

Touchdowns
Most Touchdowns, Career
8 Jack Christiansen, Detroit, 1951-58
Rick Upchurch, Denver, 1975-83
6 Billy Johnson, Houston, 1974-80; Atlanta, 1982-86
5 Emlen Tunnell, N.Y. Giants, 1948-58; Green Bay, 1959-61
Most Touchdowns, Season
4 Jack Christiansen, Detroit, 1951
Rick Upchurch, Denver, 1976
3 Emlen Tunnell, N.Y. Giants, 1951
Billy Johnson, Houston, 1975
LeRoy Irvin, Los Angeles, 1981
2 By many players
Most Touchdowns, Rookie, Season
4 Jack Christiansen, Detroit, 1951
2 By six players
Most Touchdowns, Game
2 Jack Christiansen, Detroit vs. Los Angeles, Oct. 14, 1951; vs. Green Bay, Nov. 22, 1951
Dick Christy, N.Y. Titans vs. Denver, Sept. 24, 1961
Rick Upchurch, Denver vs. Cleveland, Sept. 26, 1976
LeRoy Irvin, Los Angeles vs. Atlanta, Oct. 11, 1981
Vai Sikahema, St. Louis vs. Tampa Bay, Dec. 21, 1986

Kickoff Returns
Most Seasons Leading League
3 Abe Woodson, San Francisco, 1959, 1962-63
2 Lynn Chandnois, Pittsburgh, 1951-52
Bobby Jancik, Houston, 1962-63
Travis Williams, Green Bay, 1967; Los Angeles, 1971

Kickoff Returns
Most Kickoff Returns, Career
275 Ron Smith, Chicago, 1965, 1970-72; Atlanta, 1966-67; Los Angeles, 1968-69; San Diego, 1973; Oakland, 1974
243 Bruce Harper, N.Y. Jets, 1977-84
193 Abe Woodson, San Francisco, 1958-64; St. Louis, 1965-66
Most Kickoff Returns, Season
60 Drew Hill, Los Angeles, 1981
55 Bruce Harper, N.Y. Jets, 1978, 1979
David Turner, Cincinnati, 1979
Stump Mitchell, St. Louis, 1981
53 Eddie Payton, Minnesota, 1980
Buster Rhymes, Minnesota, 1985
Most Kickoff Returns, Rookie, Season
55 Stump Mitchell, St. Louis, 1981
53 Buster Rhymes, Minnesota, 1985
50 Nesby Glasgow, Baltimore, 1979
Dino Hall, Cleveland, 1979
Most Kickoff Returns, Game
9 Noland Smith, Kansas City vs. Oakland, Nov. 23, 1967
Dino Hall, Cleveland vs. Pittsburgh, Oct. 7, 1979
8 George Taliaferro, N.Y. Yanks vs. N.Y. Giants, Dec. 3, 1950
Bobby Jancik, Houston vs. Boston, Dec. 8, 1963; vs. Oakland, Dec. 22, 1963
Mel Renfro, Dallas vs. Green Bay, Nov. 29, 1964
Willie Porter, Boston vs. N.Y. Jets, Sept. 22, 1968
Keith Moody, Buffalo vs. Seattle, Oct. 30, 1977
Brian Baschnagel, Chicago vs. Houston, Nov. 6, 1977
Bruce Harper, N.Y. Jets vs. New England, Oct. 29, 1978; vs. New England, Sept. 9, 1979
Dino Hall, Cleveland vs. Pittsburgh, Nov. 25, 1979
Terry Metcalf, Washington vs. St. Louis, Sept. 20, 1981
Harlan Huckleby, Green Bay vs. Washington, Oct. 17, 1983
Gary Ellerson, Green Bay vs. St. Louis, Sept. 29, 1985
Bobby Humphery, N.Y. Jets vs. Cincinnati, Dec. 21, 1986
7 By many players

Yards Gained
Most Seasons Leading League
3 Bruce Harper, N.Y. Jets, 1977-79
2 Marshall Goldberg, Chi. Cardinals, 1941-42
Woodley Lewis, Los Angeles, 1953-54
Al Carmichael, Green Bay, 1956-57
Timmy Brown, Philadelphia, 1961, 1963
Bobby Jancik, Houston, 1963, 1966
Ron Smith, Atlanta, 1966-67
Most Yards Gained, Career
6,922 Ron Smith, Chicago, 1965, 1970-72; Atlanta, 1966-67; Los Angeles, 1968-69; San Diego, 1973; Oakland, 1974
5,538 Abe Woodson, San Francisco, 1958-64; St. Louis, 1965-66
5,407 Bruce Harper, N.Y. Jets, 1977-84
Most Yards Gained, Season
1,345 Buster Rhymes, Minnesota, 1985
1,317 Bobby Jancik, Houston, 1963
1,314 Dave Hampton, Green Bay, 1971
Most Yards Gained, Rookie, Season
1,345 Buster Rhymes, Minnesota, 1985
1,292 Stump Mitchell, St. Louis, 1981
1,245 Odell Barry, Denver, 1964
Most Yards Gained, Game
294 Wally Triplett, Detroit vs. Los Angeles, Oct. 29, 1950
247 Timmy Brown, Philadelphia vs. Dallas, Nov. 6, 1966
244 Noland Smith, Kansas City vs. San Diego, Oct. 15, 1967
Longest Kickoff Return (All TDs)
106 Al Carmichael, Green Bay vs. Chi. Bears, Oct. 7, 1956
Noland Smith, Kansas City vs. Denver, Dec. 17, 1967
Roy Green, St. Louis vs. Dallas, Oct. 21, 1979
105 Frank Seno, Chi. Cardinals vs. N.Y. Giants, Oct. 20, 1946
Ollie Matson, Chi. Cardinals vs. Washington, Oct. 14, 1956
Abe Woodson, San Francisco vs. Los Angeles, Nov. 8, 1959
Timmy Brown, Philadelphia vs. Cleveland, Sept. 17, 1961
Jon Arnett, Los Angeles vs. Detroit, Oct. 29, 1961
Eugene (Mercury) Morris, Miami vs. Cincinnati, Sept. 14, 1969
Travis Williams, Los Angeles vs. New Orleans, Dec. 5, 1971
104 By many players

Average Yardage
Highest Average, Career (75 returns)
30.56 Gale Sayers, Chicago, 1965-71 (91-2,781)
29.57 Lynn Chandnois, Pittsburgh, 1950-56 (92-2,720)
28.69 Abe Woodson, San Francisco, 1958-64; St. Louis, 1965-66 (193-5,538)
Highest Average, Season (Qualifiers)
41.06 Travis Williams, Green Bay, 1967 (18-739)
37.69 Gale Sayers, Chicago, 1967 (16-603)
35.50 Ollie Matson, Chi. Cardinals, 1958 (14-497)
Highest Average, Rookie, Season (Qualifiers)
41.06 Travis Williams, Green Bay, 1967 (18-739)
33.08 Tom Moore, Green Bay, 1960 (12-397)
32.88 Duriel Harris, Miami, 1976 (17-559)
Highest Average, Game (3 returns)
73.50 Wally Triplett, Detroit vs. Los Angeles, Oct. 29, 1950 (4-294)
67.33 Lenny Lyles, San Francisco vs. Baltimore, Dec. 18, 1960 (3-202)
65.33 Ken Hall, Houston vs. N.Y. Titans, Oct. 23, 1960 (3-196)

Touchdowns
Most Touchdowns, Career
6 Ollie Matson, Chi. Cardinals, 1952, 1954-58; L.A. Rams, 1959-62; Detroit, 1963; Philadelphia, 1964
Gale Sayers, Chicago, 1965-71
Travis Williams, Green Bay, 1967-70; Los Angeles, 1971
5 Bobby Mitchell, Cleveland, 1958-61; Washington, 1962-68
Abe Woodson, San Francisco, 1958-64; St. Louis, 1965-66
Timmy Brown, Green Bay, 1959; Philadelphia, 1960-67; Baltimore, 1968
4 Cecil Turner, Chicago, 1968-73
Most Touchdowns, Season
4 Travis Williams, Green Bay, 1967
Cecil Turner, Chicago, 1970
3 Verda (Vitamin T) Smith, Los Angeles, 1950
Abe Woodson, San Francisco, 1963
Gale Sayers, Chicago, 1967
Raymond Clayborn, New England, 1977
Ron Brown, L.A. Rams, 1985
2 By many players
Most Touchdowns, Rookie, Season
4 Travis Williams, Green Bay, 1967
3 Raymond Clayborn, New England, 1977
2 By six players
Most Touchdowns, Game
2 Timmy Brown, Philadelphia vs. Dallas, Nov. 6, 1966
Travis Williams, Green Bay vs. Cleveland, Nov. 12, 1967
Ron Brown, L.A. Rams vs. Green Bay, Nov. 24, 1985

Combined Kick Returns
Most Combined Kick Returns, Career
510 Ron Smith, Chicago, 1965, 1970-72; Atlanta, 1966-67; Los Angeles, 1968-69; San Diego, 1973; Oakland, 1974 (p-235, k-275)
426 Bruce Harper, N.Y. Jets, 1977-84 (p-183, k-243)
423 Alvin Haymond, Baltimore, 1964-67; Philadelphia, 1968; Los Angeles, 1969-71; Washington, 1972; Houston, 1973 (p-253, k-170)
Most Combined Kick Returns, Season
100 Larry Jones, Washington, 1975 (p-53, k-47)
97 Stump Mitchell, St. Louis, 1981 (p-42, k-55)
94 Nesby Glasgow, Baltimore, 1979 (p-44, k-50)
Most Combined Kick Returns, Game
13 Stump Mitchell, St. Louis vs. Atlanta, Oct. 18, 1981 (p-6, k-7)
12 Mel Renfro, Dallas vs. Green Bay, Nov. 29, 1964 (p-4, k-8)
Larry Jones, Washington vs. Dallas, Dec. 13, 1975 (p-6, k-6)
Eddie Brown, Washington vs. Tampa Bay, Oct. 9, 1977 (p-11, k-1)

Nesby Glasgow, Baltimore vs. Denver, Sept. 2, 1979 (p-9, k-3)
11 By many players

Yards Gained

Most Yards Returned, Career
8,710 Ron Smith, Chicago, 1965, 1970-72; Atlanta, 1966-67; Los Angeles, 1968-69; San Diego, 1973; Oakland, 1974 (p-1,788, k-6,922)
7,191 Bruce Harper, N.Y. Jets, 1977-84 (p-1,784, k-5,407)
6,740 Les (Speedy) Duncan, San Diego, 1964-70; Washington, 1971-74 (p-2,201, k-4,539)
Most Yards Returned, Season
1,737 Stump Mitchell, St. Louis, 1981 (p-445, k-1,292)
1,658 Bruce Harper, N.Y. Jets, 1978 (p-378, k-1,280)
1,591 Mike Nelms, Washington, 1981 (p-492, k-1,099)
Most Yards Returned, Game
294 Wally Triplett, Detroit vs. Los Angeles, Oct. 29, 1950 (k-294)
Woodley Lewis, Los Angeles vs. Detroit, Oct. 18, 1953 (p-120, k-174)
289 Eddie Payton, Detroit vs. Minnesota, Dec. 17, 1977 (p-105, k-184)
282 Les (Speedy) Duncan, San Diego vs. N.Y. Jets, Nov. 24, 1968 (p-102, k-180)

Touchdowns

Most Touchdowns, Career
9 Ollie Matson, Chi. Cardinals, 1952, 1954-58; Los Angeles, 1959-62; Detroit, 1963; Philadelphia, 1964-66 (p-3, k-6)
8 Jack Christiansen, Detroit, 1951-58 (p-8)
Bobby Mitchell, Cleveland, 1958-61; Washington, 1962-68 (p-3, k-5)
Gale Sayers, Chicago, 1965-71 (p-2, k-6)
Rick Upchurch, Denver, 1975-83 (p-8)
Billy Johnson, Houston, 1974-80; Atlanta, 1982-86 (p-6, k-2)
7 Abe Woodson, San Francisco, 1958-64; St. Louis, 1965-66 (p-2, k-5)
Most Touchdowns, Season
4 Jack Christiansen, Detroit, 1951 (p-4)
Emlen Tunnell, N.Y. Giants, 1951 (p-3, k-1)
Gale Sayers, Chicago, 1967 (p-1, k-3)
Travis Williams, Green Bay, 1967 (k-4)
Cecil Turner, Chicago, 1970 (k-4)
Billy Johnson, Houston, 1975 (p-3, k-1)
Rick Upchurch, Denver, 1976 (p-4)
3 Verda (Vitamin T) Smith, Los Angeles, 1950 (k-3)
Abe Woodson, San Francisco, 1963 (k-3)
Raymond Clayborn, New England, 1977 (k-3)
Billy Johnson, Houston, 1977 (p-2, k-1)
LeRoy Irvin, Los Angeles, 1981 (p-3)
Ron Brown, L.A. Rams, 1985 (k-3)
2 By many players
Most Touchdowns, Game
2 Jack Christiansen, Detroit vs. Los Angeles, Oct. 14, 1951 (p-2); vs. Green Bay, Nov. 22, 1951 (p-2)
Jim Patton, N.Y. Giants vs. Washington, Oct. 30, 1955 (p-1, k-1)
Bobby Mitchell, Cleveland vs. Philadelphia, Nov. 23, 1958 (p-1, k-1)
Dick Christy, N.Y. Titans vs. Denver, Sept. 24, 1961 (p-2)
Al Frazier, Denver vs. Boston, Dec. 3, 1961 (p-1, k-1)
Timmy Brown, Philadelphia vs. Dallas, Nov. 6, 1966 (k-2)
Travis Williams, Green Bay vs. Cleveland, Nov. 12, 1967 (k-2); vs. Pittsburgh, Nov. 2, 1969 (p-1, k-1)
Gale Sayers, Chicago vs. San Francisco, Dec. 3, 1967 (p-1, k-1)
Rick Upchurch, Denver vs. Cleveland, Sept. 26, 1976 (p-2)
Eddie Payton, Detroit vs. Minnesota, Dec. 17, 1977 (p-1, k-1)
LeRoy Irvin, Los Angeles vs. Atlanta, Oct. 11, 1981 (p-2)
Ron Brown, L.A. Rams vs. Green Bay, Nov. 24, 1985 (k-2)
Vai Sikahema, St. Louis vs. Tampa Bay, Dec. 21, 1986 (p-2)

Fumbles

Most Fumbles, Career
105 Roman Gabriel, Los Angeles, 1962-72; Philadelphia, 1973-77
96 Dan Fouts, San Diego, 1973-86
95 Johnny Unitas, Baltimore, 1956-72; San Diego, 1973
Most Fumbles, Season
17 Dan Pastorini, Houston, 1973
Warren Moon, Houston, 1984
16 Don Meredith, Dallas, 1964
Joe Cribbs, Buffalo, 1980
Steve Fuller, Kansas City, 1980
Paul McDonald, Cleveland, 1984
Phil Simms, N.Y. Giants, 1985
15 Paul Christman, Chi. Cardinals, 1946
Sammy Baugh, Washington, 1947
Sam Etcheverry, St. Louis, 1961
Len Dawson, Kansas City, 1964
Terry Metcalf, St. Louis, 1976
Steve DeBerg, Tampa Bay, 1984
Most Fumbles, Game
7 Len Dawson, Kansas City vs. San Diego, Nov. 15, 1964
6 Sam Etcheverry, St. Louis vs. N.Y. Giants, Sept. 17, 1961
5 Paul Christman, Chi. Cardinals vs. Green Bay, Nov. 10, 1946
Charlie Conerly, N.Y. Giants vs. San Francisco, Dec. 1, 1957
Jack Kemp, Buffalo vs. Houston, Oct. 29, 1967
Roman Gabriel, Philadelphia vs. Oakland, Nov. 21, 1976
Randall Cunningham, Philadelphia vs. L.A. Raiders, Nov. 30, 1986 (OT)

Fumbles Recovered

Most Fumbles Recovered, Career, Own and Opponents'
43 Fran Tarkenton, Minnesota, 1961-66, 1972-78; N.Y. Giants, 1967-71 (43 own)
38 Jack Kemp, Pittsburgh, 1957; L.A. Chargers, 1960; San Diego, 1961-62; Buffalo, 1962-67, 1969 (38 own)
37 Roman Gabriel, Los Angeles, 1962-72; Philadelphia, 1973-77 (37 own)
Most Fumbles Recovered, Season, Own and Opponents'
9 Don Hultz, Minnesota, 1963 (9 opp)
8 Paul Christman, Chi. Cardinals, 1945 (8 own)
Joe Schmidt, Detroit, 1955 (8 opp)
Bill Butler, Minnesota, 1963 (8 own)
Kermit Alexander, San Francisco, 1965 (4 own, 4 opp)
Jack Lambert, Pittsburgh, 1976 (1 own, 7 opp)
Danny White, Dallas, 1981 (8 own)
7 By many players
Most Fumbles Recovered, Game, Own and Opponents'
4 Otto Graham, Cleveland vs. N.Y. Giants, Oct. 25, 1953 (4 own)
Sam Etcheverry, St. Louis vs. N.Y. Giants, Sept. 17, 1961 (4 own)
Roman Gabriel, Los Angeles vs. San Francisco, Oct. 12, 1969 (4 own)
Joe Ferguson, Buffalo vs. Miami, Sept. 18, 1977 (4 own)
Randall Cunningham, Philadelphia vs. L.A. Raiders, Nov. 30, 1986 (OT) (4 own)
3 By many players

Own Fumbles Recovered

Most Own Fumbles Recovered, Career
43 Fran Tarkenton, Minnesota, 1961-66, 1972-78; N.Y. Giants, 1967-71
38 Jack Kemp, Pittsburgh, 1957; L.A. Chargers, 1960; San Diego, 1961-62; Buffalo, 1962-67, 1969
37 Roman Gabriel, Los Angeles, 1962-72; Philadelphia, 1973-77
Most Own Fumbles Recovered, Season
8 Paul Christman, Chi. Cardinals, 1945
Bill Butler, Minnesota, 1963
Danny White, Dallas, 1981
7 Sammy Baugh, Washington, 1947
Tommy Thompson, Philadelphia, 1947
John Roach, St. Louis, 1960
Jack Larscheid, Oakland, 1960
Gary Huff, Chicago, 1974
Terry Metcalf, St. Louis, 1974
Joe Ferguson, Buffalo, 1977
Fran Tarkenton, Minnesota, 1978
Greg Pruitt, L.A. Raiders, 1983
Warren Moon, Houston, 1984
6 By many players
Most Own Fumbles Recovered, Game
4 Otto Graham, Cleveland vs. N.Y. Giants, Oct. 25, 1953
Sam Etcheverry, St. Louis vs. N.Y. Giants, Sept. 17, 1961
Roman Gabriel, Los Angeles vs. San Francisco, Oct. 12, 1969
Joe Ferguson, Buffalo vs. Miami, Sept. 18, 1977
Randall Cunningham, Philadelphia vs. L.A. Raiders, Nov. 30, 1986 (OT)
3 By many players

Opponents' Fumbles Recovered

Most Opponents' Fumbles Recovered, Career
29 Jim Marshall, Cleveland, 1960; Minnesota, 1961-79
25 Dick Butkus, Chicago, 1965-73
23 Carl Eller, Minnesota, 1964-78; Seattle, 1979
Most Opponents' Fumbles Recovered, Season
9 Don Hultz, Minnesota, 1963
8 Joe Schmidt, Detroit, 1955
7 Alan Page, Minnesota, 1970
Jack Lambert, Pittsburgh, 1976
Most Opponents' Fumbles Recovered, Game
3 Corwin Clatt, Chi. Cardinals vs. Detroit, Nov. 6, 1949
Vic Sears, Philadelphia vs. Green Bay, Nov. 2, 1952
Ed Beatty, San Francisco vs. Los Angeles, Oct. 7, 1956
Ron Carroll, Houston vs. Cincinnati, Oct. 27, 1974
Maurice Spencer, New Orleans vs. Atlanta, Oct. 10, 1976
Steve Nelson, New England vs. Philadelphia, Oct. 8, 1978
Charles Jackson, Kansas City vs. Pittsburgh, Sept. 6, 1981
Willie Buchanon, San Diego vs. Denver, Sept. 27, 1981
Joey Browner, Minnesota vs. San Francisco, Sept. 8, 1985
2 By many players

Yards Returning Fumbles

Longest Fumble Run (All TDs)
104 Jack Tatum, Oakland vs. Green Bay, Sept. 24, 1972 (opp)
98 George Halas, Chi. Bears vs. Oorang Indians, Marion, Ohio, Nov. 4, 1923 (opp)
97 Chuck Howley, Dallas vs. Atlanta, Oct. 2, 1966 (opp)

Touchdowns

Most Touchdowns, Career (Total)
4 Billy Thompson, Denver, 1969-81
3 Ralph Heywood, Detroit, 1947-48; Boston, 1948; N.Y. Bulldogs, 1949
Leo Sugar, Chi. Cardinals, 1954-59; St. Louis, 1960; Philadelphia, 1961; Detroit, 1962
Bud McFadin, Los Angeles, 1952-56; Denver, 1960-63, Houston, 1964-65
Doug Cline, Houston, 1960-66; San Diego, 1966
Bob Lilly, Dall. Cowboys, 1961-74
Chris Hanburger, Washington, 1965-78
Lemar Parrish, Cincinnati, 1970-77; Washington, 1978-81; Buffalo, 1982
Paul Krause, Washington, 1964-67; Minnesota, 1968-79
Brad Dusek, Washington, 1974-81
David Logan, Tampa Bay, 1979-86
Thomas Howard, Kansas City, 1977-83; St. Louis, 1984-85
2 By many players
Most Touchdowns, Season (Total)
2 Harold McPhail, Boston, 1934
Harry Ebding, Detroit, 1937
John Morelli, Boston, 1944
Frank Maznicki, Boston, 1947
Fred (Dippy) Evans, Chi. Bears, 1948
Ralph Heywood, Boston, 1948
Art Tait, N.Y. Yanks, 1951
John Dwyer, Los Angeles, 1952
Leo Sugar, Chi. Cardinals, 1957
Doug Cline, Houston, 1961
Jim Bradshaw, Pittsburgh, 1964
Royce Berry, Cincinnati, 1970
Ahmad Rashad, Buffalo, 1974
Tim Gray, Kansas City, 1977
Charles Phillips, Oakland, 1978
Kenny Johnson, Atlanta, 1981
George Martin, N.Y. Giants, 1981

Del Rodgers, Green Bay, 1982
Mike Douglass, Green Bay, 1983
Shelton Robinson, Seattle, 1983

Most Touchdowns, Career (Own recovered)
2 Ken Kavanaugh, Chi. Bears, 1940-41, 1945-50
Mike Ditka, Chicago, 1961-66; Philadelphia, 1967-68; Dallas, 1969-72
Gail Cogdill, Detroit, 1960-68; Baltimore, 1968; Atlanta, 1969-70
Ahmad Rashad, St. Louis, 1972-73; Buffalo, 1974; Minnesota, 1976-82
Jim Mitchell, Atlanta, 1969-79
Drew Pearson, Dallas, 1973-83
Del Rodgers, Green Bay, 1982, 1984

Most Touchdowns, Season (Own recovered)
2 Ahmad Rashad, Buffalo, 1974
Del Rodgers, Green Bay, 1982
1 By many players

Most Touchdowns, Career (Opponents' recovered)
3 Leo Sugar, Chi. Cardinals, 1954-59; St. Louis, 1960; Philadelphia, 1961; Detroit, 1962
Doug Cline, Houston, 1960-66; San Diego, 1966
Bud McFadin, Los Angeles, 1952-56; Denver, 1960-63; Houston, 1964-65
Bob Lilly, Dall. Cowboys, 1961-74
Chris Hanburger, Washington, 1965-78
Paul Krause, Washington, 1964-67; Minnesota, 1968-79
Lemar Parrish, Cincinnati, 1970-77; Washington, 1978-81; Buffalo, 1982
Bill Thompson, Denver, 1969-81
Brad Dusek, Washington, 1974-81
David Logan, Tampa Bay, 1979-86
Thomas Howard, Kansas City, 1977-83; St. Louis, 1984-85
2 By many players

Most Touchdowns, Season (Opponents' recovered)
2 Harold McPhail, Boston, 1934
Harry Ebding, Detroit, 1937
John Morelli, Boston, 1944
Frank Maznicki, Boston, 1947
Fred (Dippy) Evans, Chi. Bears, 1948
Ralph Heywood, Boston, 1948
Art Tait, N.Y. Yanks, 1951
John Dwyer, Los Angeles, 1952
Leo Sugar, Chi. Cardinals, 1957
Doug Cline, Houston, 1961
Jim Bradshaw, Pittsburgh, 1964
Royce Berry, Cincinnati, 1970
Tim Gray, Kansas City, 1977
Charles Phillips, Oakland, 1978
Kenny Johnson, Atlanta, 1981
George Martin, N.Y. Giants, 1981
Mike Douglass, Green Bay, 1983
Shelton Robinson, Seattle, 1983

Most Touchdowns, Game (Opponents' recovered)
2 Fred (Dippy) Evans, Chi. Bears vs. Washington, Nov. 28, 1948

Combined Net Yards Gained

Rushing, receiving, interception returns, punt returns, kickoff returns, and fumble returns

Most Seasons Leading League
5 Jim Brown, Cleveland, 1958-61, 1964
3 Cliff Battles, Boston, 1932-33; Washington, 1937
Gale Sayers, Chicago, 1965-67
Eric Dickerson, L.A. Rams, 1983-84, 1986
2 By many players

Most Consecutive Seasons Leading League
4 Jim Brown, Cleveland, 1958-61
3 Gale Sayers, Chicago, 1965-67
2 Cliff Battles, Boston, 1932-33
Charley Trippi, Chi. Cardinals, 1948-49
Timmy Brown, Philadelphia, 1962-63
Floyd Little, Denver, 1967-68
James Brooks, San Diego, 1981-82
Eric Dickerson, L.A. Rams, 1983-84

Attempts

Most Attempts, Career
4,189 Walter Payton, Chicago, 1975-86
3,281 Franco Harris, Pittsburgh, 1972-83; Seattle, 1984
3,174 John Riggins, N.Y. Jets, 1971-75; Washington, 1976-79, 1981-85

Most Attempts, Season
496 James Wilder, Tampa Bay, 1984
449 Marcus Allen, L.A. Raiders, 1985
442 Eric Dickerson, L.A. Rams, 1983

Most Attempts, Rookie, Season
442 Eric Dickerson, L.A. Rams, 1983
395 George Rogers, New Orleans, 1981
390 Joe Cribbs, Buffalo, 1980

Most Attempts, Game
48 James Wilder, Tampa Bay vs. Pittsburgh, Oct. 30, 1983
47 James Wilder, Tampa Bay vs. Green Bay, Sept. 30, 1984 (OT)
46 Gerald Riggs, Atlanta vs. L.A. Rams, Nov. 17, 1985

Yards Gained

Most Yards Gained, Career
21,053 Walter Payton, Chicago, 1975-86
15,459 Jim Brown, Cleveland, 1957-65
14,868 Tony Dorsett, Dallas, 1977-86

Most Yards Gained, Season
2,535 Lionel James, San Diego, 1985
2,462 Terry Metcalf, St. Louis, 1975
2,444 Mack Herron, New England, 1974

Most Yards Gained, Rookie, Season
2,272 Gale Sayers, Chicago, 1965
2,212 Eric Dickerson, L.A. Rams, 1983
2,100 Abner Haynes, Dall. Texans, 1960

Most Yards Gained, Game
373 Billy Cannon, Houston vs. N.Y. Titans, Dec. 10, 1961
345 Lionel James, San Diego vs. L.A. Raiders, Nov. 10, 1985 (OT)
341 Timmy Brown, Philadelphia vs. St. Louis, Dec. 16, 1962

Sacks

Sacks have been compiled since 1982.

Most Sacks, Career
64.5 Dexter Manley, Washington, 1982-86
62.5 Mark Gastineau, N.Y. Jets, 1982-86
61.5 Lawrence Taylor, N.Y. Giants, 1982-86

Most Sacks, Season
22 Mark Gastineau, N.Y. Jets, 1984
20.5 Lawrence Taylor, N.Y. Giants, 1986
19 Mark Gastineau, N.Y. Jets, 1983

Most Sacks, Game
6 Fred Dean, San Francisco vs. New Orleans, Nov. 13, 1983
5.5 William Gay, Detroit vs. Tampa Bay, Sept. 4, 1983
5 Howie Long, L.A. Raiders vs. Washington, Oct. 2, 1983
Randy Holloway, Minnesota vs. Atlanta, Sept. 16, 1984
Jim Jeffcoat, Dallas vs. Washington, Nov. 10, 1985
Leslie O'Neal, San Diego vs. Dallas, Nov. 16, 1986

Miscellaneous

Longest Return of Missed Field Goal (All TDs)
101 Al Nelson, Philadelphia vs. Dallas, Sept. 26, 1971
100 Al Nelson, Philadelphia vs. Cleveland, Dec. 11, 1966
Ken Ellis, Green Bay vs. N.Y. Giants, Sept. 19, 1971
99 Jerry Williams, Los Angeles vs. Green Bay, Dec. 16, 1951
Carl Taseff, Baltimore vs. Los Angeles, Dec. 12, 1959
Timmy Brown, Philadelphia vs. St. Louis, Sept. 16, 1962

Team Records

Championships

Most Seasons League Champion
11 Green Bay, 1929-31, 1936, 1939, 1944, 1961-62, 1965-67
9 Chi. Bears, 1921, 1932-33, 1940-41, 1943, 1946, 1963, 1985
5 N.Y. Giants, 1927, 1934, 1938, 1956, 1986

Most Consecutive Seasons League Champion
3 Green Bay, 1929-31, 1965-67
2 Canton, 1922-23
Chi. Bears, 1932-33, 1940-41
Philadelphia, 1948-49
Detroit, 1952-53
Cleveland, 1954-55
Baltimore, 1958-59
Houston, 1960-61
Green Bay, 1961-62
Buffalo, 1964-65
Miami, 1972-73
Pittsburgh, 1974-75, 1978-79

Most Times Finishing First, Regular Season (Since 1933)
16 Clev. Browns, 1950-55, 1957, 1964-65, 1967-69, 1971, 1980, 1985-86
15 Clev./L.A. Rams, 1945, 1949-51, 1955, 1967, 1969, 1973-79, 1985
N.Y. Giants, 1933-35, 1938-39, 1941, 1944, 1946, 1956, 1958-59, 1961-63, 1986
13 Dall. Cowboys, 1966-71, 1973, 1976-79, 1981, 1985
Chi. Bears, 1933-34, 1937, 1940-43, 1946, 1956, 1963, 1984-86

Most Consecutive Times Finishing First, Regular Season (Since 1933)
7 Los Angeles, 1973-79
6 Cleveland, 1950-55
Dallas, 1966-71
Minnesota, 1973-78
Pittsburgh, 1974-79
5 Oakland, 1972-76

Games Won

Most Consecutive Games Won (Incl. postseason games)
18 Chi. Bears, 1933-34, 1941-42
Miami, 1972-73
17 Oakland, 1976-77
14 Washington, 1942-43

Most Consecutive Games Won (Regular season)
17 Chi. Bears, 1933-34
16 Chi. Bears, 1941-42
Miami, 1971-73; 1983-84
15 L.A. Chargers/San Diego, 1960-61

Most Consecutive Games Without Defeat (Incl. postseason games)
24 Canton, 1922-23 (won 21, tied 3)
23 Green Bay, 1928-30 (won 21, tied 2)
18 Chi. Bears, 1933-34 (won 18); 1941-42 (won 18)
Miami, 1972-73 (won 18)

Most Consecutive Games Without Defeat (Regular season)
24 Canton, 1922-23 (won 21, tied 3)
Chi. Bears, 1941-43 (won 23, tied 1)
23 Green Bay, 1928-30 (won 21, tied 2)
17 Chi. Bears, 1933-34 (won 17)

Most Games Won, Season (Incl. postseason games)
18 San Francisco, 1984
Chicago, 1985
17 Miami, 1972
Pittsburgh, 1978
N.Y. Giants, 1986
16 Oakland, 1976
San Francisco, 1981
Washington, 1983
Miami, 1984

Most Games Won, Season (Since 1932)
15 San Francisco, 1984
Chicago, 1985
14 Miami, 1972, 1984
Pittsburgh, 1978
Washington, 1983

Chicago, 1986
N.Y. Giants, 1986
13 Chi. Bears, 1934
Green Bay, 1962
Oakland, 1967, 1976
Baltimore, 1968
San Francisco, 1981
Denver, 1984

Most Consecutive Games Won, Season (Incl. postseason games)
17 Miami, 1972
13 Chi. Bears, 1934
Oakland, 1976
12 Minnesota, 1969
San Francisco, 1984
Chicago, 1985
N.Y. Giants, 1986

Most Consecutive Games Won, Season
14 Miami, 1972
13 Chi. Bears, 1934
12 Minnesota, 1969
Chicago, 1985

Most Consecutive Games Won, Start of Season
14 Miami, 1972, entire season
13 Chi. Bears, 1934, entire season
12 Chicago, 1985

Most Consecutive Games Won, End of Season
14 Miami, 1972, entire season
13 Chi. Bears, 1934, entire season
11 Chi. Bears, 1942, entire season
Cleveland, 1951

Most Consecutive Games Without Defeat, Season (Incl. postseason games)
17 Miami, 1972
13 Chi. Bears, 1926, 1934
Green Bay, 1929
Baltimore, 1967
Oakland, 1976
12 Canton, 1922, 1923
Minnesota, 1969
San Francisco, 1984
Chicago, 1985
N.Y. Giants, 1986

Most Consecutive Games Without Defeat, Season
14 Miami, 1972
13 Chi. Bears, 1926, 1934
Green Bay, 1929
Baltimore, 1967
12 Canton, 1922, 1923
Minnesota, 1969
Chicago, 1985

Most Consecutive Games Without Defeat, Start of Season
14 Miami, 1972, entire season
13 Chi. Bears, 1926, 1934, entire seasons
Green Bay, 1929, entire season
Baltimore, 1967
12 Canton, 1922, 1923, entire seasons
Chicago, 1985

Most Consecutive Games Without Defeat, End of Season
14 Miami, 1972, entire season
13 Green Bay, 1929, entire season
Chi. Bears, 1934, entire season
12 Canton, 1922, 1923, entire seasons

Most Consecutive Home Games Won
27 Miami, 1971-74
20 Green Bay, 1929-32
18 Oakland, 1968-70
Dallas, 1979-81

Most Consecutive Home Games Without Defeat
30 Green Bay, 1928-33 (won 27, tied 3)
27 Miami, 1971-74 (won 27)
18 Chi. Bears, 1932-35 (won 17, tied 1); 1941-44 (won 17, tied 1)
Oakland, 1968-70 (won 18)
Dallas, 1979-81 (won 18)

Most Consecutive Road Games Won
11 L.A. Chargers/San Diego, 1960-61
10 Chi. Bears, 1941-42
Dallas, 1968-69
9 Chi. Bears, 1933-34
Kansas City, 1966-67
Oakland, 1967-68, 1974-75, 1976-77
Pittsburgh, 1974-75
Washington, 1981-83
San Francisco, 1983-84

Most Consecutive Road Games Without Defeat
13 Chi. Bears, 1941-43 (won 12, tied 1)
12 Green Bay, 1928-30 (won 10, tied 2)
11 L.A. Chargers/San Diego, 1960-61 (won 11)
Los Angeles, 1966-68 (won 10, tied 1)

Most Shutout Games Won or Tied, Season (Since 1932)
7 Chi. Bears, 1932 (won 4, tied 3)
Green Bay, 1932 (won 6, tied 1)
Detroit, 1934 (won 7)
5 Chi. Cardinals, 1934 (won 5)
N.Y. Giants, 1944 (won 5)
Pittsburgh, 1976 (won 5)
4 By many teams

Most Consecutive Shutout Games Won or Tied (Since 1932)
7 Detroit, 1934 (won 7)
3 Chi. Bears, 1932 (tied 3)
Green Bay, 1932 (won 3)
New York, 1935 (won 3)
St. Louis, 1970 (won 3)
Pittsburgh, 1976 (won 3)
2 By many teams

Games Lost

Most Consecutive Games Lost
26 Tampa Bay, 1976-77
19 Chi. Cardinals, 1942-43, 1945
Oakland, 1961-62
18 Houston, 1972-73

Most Consecutive Games Without Victory
26 Tampa Bay, 1976-77 (lost 26)
23 Washington, 1960-61 (lost 20, tied 3)

Most Games Lost, Season (Since 1932)
15 New Orleans, 1980
14 Tampa Bay, 1976, 1983, 1985, 1986
San Francisco, 1978, 1979
Detroit, 1979
Baltimore, 1981
New England, 1981
Houston, 1983
Buffalo, 1984, 1985
13 Oakland, 1962
Chicago, 1969
Pittsburgh, 1969
Buffalo, 1971
Houston, 1972, 1973, 1984
Minnesota, 1984
Indianapolis, 1986

Most Consecutive Games Lost, Season
14 Tampa Bay, 1976
New Orleans, 1980
Baltimore, 1981
13 Oakland, 1962
Indianapolis, 1986
12 Tampa Bay, 1977

Most Consecutive Games Lost, Start of Season
14 Tampa Bay, 1976, entire season
New Orleans, 1980
13 Oakland, 1962
Indianapolis, 1986
12 Tampa Bay, 1977

Most Consecutive Games Lost, End of Season
14 Tampa Bay, 1976, entire season
13 Pittsburgh, 1969
11 Philadelphia, 1936
Detroit, 1942, entire season
Houston, 1972

Most Consecutive Games Without Victory, Season
14 Tampa Bay, 1976, entire season
New Orleans, 1980
Baltimore, 1981
13 Washington, 1961
Oakland, 1962
Indianapolis, 1986
12 Dall. Cowboys, 1960, entire season
Tampa Bay, 1977

Most Consecutive Games Without Victory, Start of Season
14 Tampa Bay, 1976, entire season
New Orleans, 1980
13 Washington, 1961
Oakland, 1962
Indianapolis, 1986
12 Dall. Cowboys, 1960, entire season
Tampa Bay, 1977

Most Consecutive Games Without Victory, End of Season
14 Tampa Bay, 1976, entire season
13 Pittsburgh, 1969
12 Dall. Cowboys, 1960, entire season

Most Consecutive Home Games Lost
13 Houston, 1972-73
Tampa Bay, 1976-77
11 Oakland, 1961-62
Los Angeles, 1961-63
10 Pittsburgh, 1937-39
Washington, 1960-61
N.Y. Giants, 1973-75
New Orleans, 1979-80

Most Consecutive Home Games Without Victory
13 Houston, 1972-73 (lost 13)
Tampa Bay, 1976-77 (lost 13)
12 Philadelphia, 1936-38 (lost 11, tied 1)
11 Washington, 1960-61 (lost 10, tied 1)
Oakland, 1961-62 (lost 11)
Los Angeles, 1961-63 (lost 11)

Most Consecutive Road Games Lost
23 Houston, 1981-84
22 Buffalo, 1983-86
19 Tampa Bay, 1983-85

Most Consecutive Road Games Without Victory
23 Houston, 1981-84 (lost 23)
22 Buffalo, 1983-86 (lost 22)
19 Tampa Bay, 1983-85 (lost 19)

Most Shutout Games Lost or Tied, Season (Since 1932)
6 Cincinnati, 1934 (lost 6)
Pittsburgh, 1934 (lost 6)
Philadelphia, 1936 (lost 6)
Tampa Bay, 1977 (lost 6)
5 Boston, 1932 (lost 4, tied 1), 1933 (lost 4, tied 1)
N.Y. Giants, 1932 (lost 4, tied 1)
Cincinnati, 1933 (lost 4, tied 1)
Brooklyn, 1934 (lost 5), 1942 (lost 5)

Detroit, 1942 (lost 5)
Tampa Bay, 1976 (lost 5)
4 By many teams

Most Consecutive Shutout Games Lost or Tied (Since 1932)
6 Brooklyn, 1942-43 (lost 6)
4 Chi. Bears, 1932 (lost 1, tied 3)
Philadelphia, 1936 (lost 4)
3 Chi. Cardinals, 1934 (lost 3), 1938 (lost 3)
Brooklyn, 1935 (lost 3), 1937 (lost 3)
Oakland, 1981 (lost 3)

Tie Games

Most Tie Games, Season
6 Chi. Bears, 1932
5 Frankford, 1929
4 Chi. Bears, 1924
Orange, 1929
Portsmouth, 1929

Most Consecutive Tie Games
3 Chi. Bears, 1932
2 By many teams

Scoring

Most Seasons Leading League
9 Chi. Bears, 1934-35, 1939, 1941-43, 1946-47, 1956
6 Green Bay, 1932, 1936-38, 1961-62
L.A. Rams, 1950-52, 1957, 1967, 1973
5 Oakland, 1967-69, 1974, 1977
Dall. Cowboys, 1966, 1968, 1971, 1978, 1980
San Diego, 1963, 1965, 1981-82, 1985

Most Consecutive Seasons Leading League
3 Green Bay, 1936-38
Chi. Bears, 1941-43
Los Angeles, 1950-52
Oakland, 1967-69

Points

Most Points, Season
541 Washington, 1983
513 Houston, 1961
Miami, 1984
479 Dallas, 1983

Fewest Points, Season (Since 1932)
37 Cincinnati/St. Louis, 1934
38 Cincinnati, 1933
Detroit, 1942
51 Pittsburgh, 1934
Philadelphia, 1936

Most Points, Game
72 Washington vs. N.Y. Giants, Nov. 27, 1966
70 Los Angeles vs. Baltimore, Oct. 22, 1950
65 Chi. Cardinals vs. N.Y. Bulldogs, Nov. 13, 1949
Los Angeles vs. Detroit, Oct. 29, 1950

Most Points, Both Teams, Game
113 Washington (72) vs. N.Y. Giants (41), Nov. 27, 1966
101 Oakland (52) vs. Houston (49), Dec. 22, 1963
99 Seattle (51) vs. Kansas City (48), Nov. 27, 1983 (OT)

Fewest Points, Both Teams, Game
0 In many games. Last time: N.Y. Giants vs. Detroit, Nov. 7, 1943

Most Points, Shutout Victory, Game
64 Philadelphia vs. Cincinnati, Nov. 6, 1934
59 Los Angeles vs. Atlanta, Dec. 4, 1976
57 Chicago vs. Baltimore, Nov. 25, 1962

Fewest Points, Shutout Victory, Game
2 Green Bay vs. Chi. Bears, Oct. 16, 1932
Chi. Bears vs. Green Bay, Sept. 18, 1938

Most Points Overcome to Win Game
28 San Francisco vs. New Orleans, Dec. 7, 1980 (OT) (trailed 7-35, won 38-35)
24 Philadelphia vs. Washington, Oct. 27, 1946 (trailed 0-24, won 28-24)
Detroit vs. Baltimore, Oct. 20, 1957 (trailed 3-27, won 31-27)
Philadelphia vs. Chi. Cardinals, Oct. 25, 1959 (trailed 0-24, won 28-24)
Denver vs. Boston, Oct. 23, 1960 (trailed 0-24, won 31-24)
Miami vs. New England, Dec. 15, 1974 (trailed 0-24, won 34-27)
Minnesota vs. San Francisco, Dec. 4, 1977 (trailed 0-24, won 28-27)
Denver vs. Seattle, Sept. 23, 1979 (trailed 10-34, won 37-34)
Houston vs. Cincinnati, Sept. 23, 1979 (OT) (trailed 0-24, won 30-27)
L.A. Raiders vs. San Diego, Nov. 22, 1982 (trailed 0-24, won 28-24)

Most Points Overcome to Tie Game
31 Denver vs. Buffalo, Nov. 27, 1960 (trailed 7-38, tied 38-38)
28 Los Angeles vs. Philadelphia, Oct. 3, 1948 (trailed 0-28, tied 28-28)

Most Points, Each Half
1st: 49 Green Bay vs. Tampa Bay, Oct. 2, 1983
45 Green Bay vs. Cleveland, Nov. 12, 1967
2nd: 49 Chi. Bears vs. Philadelphia, Nov. 30, 1941
48 Chi. Cardinals vs. Baltimore, Oct. 2, 1950
N.Y. Giants vs. Baltimore, Nov. 19, 1950

Most Points, Both Teams, Each Half
1st: 70 Houston (35) vs. Oakland (35), Dec. 22, 1963
2nd: 65 Washington (38) vs. N.Y. Giants (27), Nov. 27, 1966

Most Points, One Quarter
41 Green Bay vs. Detroit, Oct. 7, 1945 (second quarter)
Los Angeles vs. Detroit, Oct. 29, 1950 (third quarter)
37 Los Angeles vs. Green Bay, Sept. 21, 1980 (second quarter)
35 Chi. Cardinals vs. Boston, Oct. 24, 1948 (third quarter)
Green Bay vs. Cleveland, Nov. 12, 1967 (first quarter); vs. Tampa Bay, Oct. 2, 1983 (second quarter)

Most Points, Both Teams, One Quarter
49 Oakland (28) vs. Houston (21), Dec. 22, 1963 (second quarter)
48 Green Bay (41) vs. Detroit (7), Oct. 7, 1945 (second quarter)
Los Angeles (41) vs. Detroit (7), Oct. 29, 1950 (third quarter)
47 St. Louis (27) vs. Philadelphia (20), Dec. 13, 1964 (second quarter)

Most Points, Each Quarter
1st: 35 Green Bay vs. Cleveland, Nov. 12, 1967
2nd: 41 Green Bay vs. Detroit, Oct. 7, 1945
3rd: 41 Los Angeles vs. Detroit, Oct. 29, 1950
4th: 31 Oakland vs. Denver, Dec. 17, 1960; vs. San Diego, Dec. 8, 1963
Atlanta vs. Green Bay, Sept. 13, 1981

Most Points, Both Teams, Each Quarter
1st: 42 Green Bay (35) vs. Cleveland (7), Nov. 12, 1967
2nd: 49 Oakland (28) vs. Houston (21), Dec. 22, 1963
3rd: 48 Los Angeles (41) vs. Detroit (7), Oct. 29, 1950
4th: 42 Chi. Cardinals (28) vs. Philadelphia (14), Dec. 7, 1947
Green Bay (28) vs. Chi. Bears (14), Nov. 6, 1955
N.Y. Jets (28) vs. Boston (14), Oct. 27, 1968
Pittsburgh (21) vs. Cleveland (21), Oct. 18, 1969

Most Consecutive Games Scoring
274 Cleveland, 1950-71
218 Dallas, 1970-85
217 Oakland, 1966-81

Touchdowns

Most Seasons Leading League, Touchdowns
13 Chi. Bears, 1932, 1934-35, 1939, 1941-44, 1946-48, 1956, 1965
7 Dall. Cowboys, 1966, 1968, 1971, 1973, 1977-78, 1980
6 Oakland, 1967-69, 1972, 1974, 1977
San Diego, 1963, 1965, 1979, 1981-82, 1985

Most Consecutive Seasons Leading League, Touchdowns
4 Chi. Bears, 1941-44
Los Angeles, 1949-52
3 Chi. Bears, 1946-48
Baltimore, 1957-59
Oakland, 1967-69
2 By many teams

Most Touchdowns, Season
70 Miami, 1984
66 Houston, 1961
64 Los Angeles, 1950

Fewest Touchdowns, Season (Since 1932)
3 Cincinnati, 1933
4 Cincinnati/St. Louis, 1934
5 Detroit, 1942

Most Touchdowns, Game
10 Philadelphia vs. Cincinnati, Nov. 6, 1934
Los Angeles vs. Baltimore, Oct. 22, 1950
Washington vs. N.Y. Giants, Nov. 27, 1966
9 Chi. Cardinals vs. Rochester, Oct. 7, 1923; vs. N.Y. Giants, Oct. 17, 1948; vs. N.Y. Bulldogs, Nov. 13, 1949
Los Angeles vs. Detroit, Oct. 29, 1950
Pittsburgh vs. N.Y. Giants, Nov. 30, 1952
Chicago vs. San Francisco, Dec. 12, 1965; vs. Green Bay, Dec. 7, 1980
8 By many teams.

Most Touchdowns, Both Teams, Game
16 Washington (10) vs. N.Y. Giants (6), Nov. 27, 1966
14 Chi. Cardinals (9) vs. N.Y. Giants (5), Oct. 17, 1948
Los Angeles (10) vs. Baltimore (4), Oct. 22, 1950
Houston (7) vs. Oakland (7), Dec. 22, 1963
13 New Orleans (7) vs. St. Louis (6), Nov. 2, 1969
Kansas City (7) vs. Seattle (6), Nov. 27, 1983 (OT)
San Diego (8) vs. Pittsburgh (5), Dec. 8, 1985
N.Y. Jets (7) vs. Miami (6), Sept. 21, 1986 (OT)

Most Consecutive Games Scoring Touchdowns
166 Cleveland, 1957-69
97 Oakland, 1966-73
96 Kansas City, 1963-70

Points After Touchdown

Most Points After Touchdown, Season
66 Miami, 1984
65 Houston, 1961
62 Washington, 1983

Fewest Points After Touchdown, Season
2 Chi. Cardinals, 1933
3 Cincinnati, 1933
Pittsburgh, 1934
4 Cincinnati/St. Louis, 1934

Most Points After Touchdown, Game
10 Los Angeles vs. Baltimore, Oct. 22, 1950
9 Chi. Cardinals vs. N.Y. Giants, Oct. 17, 1948
Pittsburgh vs. N.Y. Giants, Nov. 30, 1952
Washington vs. N.Y. Giants, Nov. 27, 1966
8 By many teams

Most Points After Touchdown, Both Teams, Game
14 Chi. Cardinals (9) vs. N.Y. Giants (5), Oct. 17, 1948
Houston (7) vs. Oakland (7), Dec. 22, 1963
Washington (9) vs. N.Y. Giants (5), Nov. 27, 1966
13 Los Angeles (10) vs. Baltimore (3), Oct. 22, 1950
12 In many games

Field Goals

Most Seasons Leading League, Field Goals
11 Green Bay, 1935-36, 1940-43, 1946-47, 1955, 1972, 1974
7 Washington, 1945, 1956, 1971, 1976-77, 1979, 1982
N.Y. Giants, 1933, 1937, 1939, 1941, 1944, 1959, 1983
5 Portsmouth/Detroit, 1932-33, 1937-38, 1980

Most Consecutive Seasons Leading League, Field Goals
4 Green Bay, 1940-43
3 Cleveland, 1952-54
2 By many teams

Most Field Goals Attempted, Season
49 Los Angeles, 1966
Washington, 1971
48 Green Bay, 1972

47 N.Y. Jets, 1969
Los Angeles, 1973
Washington, 1983

Fewest Field Goals Attempted, Season (Since 1938)
0 Chi. Bears, 1944
2 Cleveland, 1939
Card-Pitt, 1944
Boston, 1946
Chi. Bears, 1947
3 Chi. Bears, 1945
Cleveland, 1945

Most Field Goals Attempted, Game
9 St. Louis vs. Pittsburgh, Sept. 24, 1967
8 Pittsburgh vs. St. Louis, Dec. 2, 1962
Detroit vs. Minnesota, Nov. 13, 1966
N.Y. Jets vs. Buffalo, Nov. 3, 1968
7 By many teams

Most Field Goals Attempted, Both Teams, Game
11 St. Louis (6) vs. Pittsburgh (5), Nov. 13, 1966
Washington (6) vs. Chicago (5), Nov. 14, 1971
Green Bay (6) vs. Detroit (5), Sept. 29, 1974
Washington (6) vs. N.Y. Giants (5), Nov. 14, 1976
10 Denver (5) vs. Boston (5), Nov. 11, 1962
Boston (7) vs. San Diego (3), Sept. 20, 1964
Buffalo (7) vs. Houston (3), Dec. 5, 1965
St. Louis (7) vs. Atlanta (3), Dec. 11, 1966
Boston (7) vs. Buffalo (3), Sept. 24, 1967
Detroit (7) vs. Minnesota (3), Sept. 20, 1971
Washington (7) vs. Houston (3), Oct. 10, 1971
Green Bay (5) vs. St. Louis (5), Dec. 5, 1971
Kansas City (7) vs. Buffalo (3), Dec. 19, 1971
Kansas City (5) vs. San Diego (5), Oct. 29, 1972
Minnesota (6) vs. Chicago (4), Sept. 23, 1973
Cleveland (7) vs. Denver (3), Oct. 19, 1975
Cleveland (5) vs. Denver (5), Oct. 5, 1980
9 In many games

Most Field Goals, Season
35 N.Y. Giants, 1983
34 N.Y. Jets, 1968
33 Green Bay, 1972
Washington, 1983
Pittsburgh, 1985

Fewest Field Goals, Season (Since 1932)
0 Boston, 1932, 1935
Chi. Cardinals, 1932, 1945
Green Bay, 1932, 1944
N.Y. Giants, 1932
Brooklyn, 1944
Card-Pitt, 1944
Chi. Bears, 1944, 1947
Boston, 1946
Baltimore, 1950
Dallas, 1952

Most Field Goals, Game
7 St. Louis vs. Pittsburgh, Sept. 24, 1967
6 Boston vs. Denver, Oct. 4, 1964
Detroit vs. Minnesota, Nov. 13, 1966
N.Y. Jets vs. Buffalo, Nov. 3, 1968; vs. New Orleans, Dec. 3, 1972
Philadelphia vs. Houston, Nov. 12, 1972
St. Louis vs. Atlanta, Dec. 9, 1973
N.Y. Giants vs. Seattle, Oct. 18, 1981
San Francisco vs. New Orleans, Oct. 16, 1983
5 By many teams

Most Field Goals, Both Teams, Game
8 Cleveland (4) vs. St. Louis (4), Sept. 20, 1964
Chicago (5) vs. Philadelphia (3), Oct. 20, 1968
Washington (5) vs. Chicago (3), Nov. 14, 1971
Kansas City (5) vs. Buffalo (3), Dec. 19, 1971
Detroit (4) vs. Green Bay (4), Sept. 29, 1974
Cleveland (5) vs. Denver (3), Oct. 19, 1975
New England (4) vs. San Diego (4), Nov. 9, 1975
San Francisco (6) vs. New Orleans (2), Oct. 16, 1983
7 In many games

Most Consecutive Games Scoring Field Goals
31 Minnesota, 1968-70
21 San Francisco, 1970-72
20 Los Angeles, 1970-71
Miami, 1970-72

Safeties

Most Safeties, Season
4 Detroit, 1962
3 Green Bay, 1932, 1975
Pittsburgh, 1947
N.Y. Yanks, 1950
Detroit, 1960
St. Louis, 1960
Buffalo, 1964
Minnesota, 1965, 1981
Cleveland, 1970
L.A. Rams, 1973, 1984
Houston, 1977
Dallas, 1981
Oakland, 1981
Chicago, 1985
2 By many teams

Most Safeties, Game
3 L.A. Rams vs. N.Y. Giants, Sept. 30, 1984
2 Cincinnati vs. Chi. Cardinals, Nov. 19, 1933
Detroit vs. Brooklyn, Dec. 1, 1935
N.Y. Giants vs. Pittsburgh, Sept. 17, 1950; vs. Washington, Nov. 5, 1961
Chicago vs. Pittsburgh, Nov. 9, 1969
Dallas vs. Philadelphia, Nov. 19, 1972
Los Angeles vs. Green Bay, Oct. 21, 1973
Oakland vs. San Diego, Oct. 26, 1975
Denver vs. Seattle, Jan. 2, 1983

Most Safeties, Both Teams, Game
3 L.A. Rams (3) vs. N.Y. Giants (0), Sept. 30, 1984
2 Chi. Bears (1) vs. San Francisco (1), Oct. 19, 1952
Cincinnati (1) vs. Los Angeles (1), Oct. 22, 1972
Atlanta (1) vs. Detroit (1), Oct. 5, 1980
(Also see previous record)

First Downs

Most Seasons Leading League
9 Chi. Bears, 1935, 1939, 1941, 1943, 1945, 1947-49, 1955
7 San Diego, 1965, 1969, 1980-83, 1985
6 L.A. Rams, 1946, 1950-51, 1954, 1957, 1973

Most Consecutive Seasons Leading League
4 San Diego, 1980-83
3 Chi. Bears, 1947-49
2 By many teams

Most First Downs, Season
387 Miami, 1984
380 San Diego, 1985
379 San Diego, 1981

Fewest First Downs, Season
51 Cincinnati, 1933
64 Pittsburgh, 1935
67 Philadelphia, 1937

Most First Downs, Game
38 Los Angeles vs. N.Y. Giants, Nov. 13, 1966
37 Green Bay vs. Philadelphia, Nov. 11, 1962
36 Pittsburgh vs. Cleveland, Nov. 25, 1979 (OT)

Fewest First Downs, Game
0 N.Y. Giants vs. Green Bay, Oct. 1, 1933; vs. Washington, Sept. 27, 1942
Pittsburgh vs. Boston, Oct. 29, 1933
Philadelphia vs. Detroit, Sept. 20, 1935
Denver vs. Houston, Sept. 3, 1966

Most First Downs, Both Teams, Game
62 San Diego (32) vs. Seattle (30), Sept. 15, 1985
59 Miami (31) vs. Buffalo (28), Oct. 9, 1983 (OT)
Seattle (33) vs. Kansas City (26), Nov. 27, 1983 (OT)
N.Y. Jets (32) vs. Miami (27), Sept. 21, 1986 (OT)
58 Los Angeles (30) vs. Chi. Bears (28), Oct. 24, 1954
Denver (34) vs. Kansas City (24), Nov. 18, 1974
Atlanta (35) vs. New Orleans (23), Sept. 2, 1979 (OT)
Pittsburgh (36) vs. Cleveland (22), Nov. 25, 1979 (OT)
San Diego (34) vs. Miami (24), Nov. 18, 1984 (OT)
Cincinnati (32) vs. San Diego (26), Sept. 22, 1985

Fewest First Downs, Both Teams, Game
5 N.Y. Giants (0) vs. Green Bay (5), Oct. 1, 1933

Most First Downs, Rushing, Season
181 New England, 1978
177 Los Angeles, 1973
176 Chicago, 1985

Fewest First Downs, Rushing, Season
36 Cleveland, 1942
Boston, 1944
39 Brooklyn, 1943
40 Philadelphia, 1940
Detroit, 1945

Most First Downs, Rushing, Game
25 Philadelphia vs. Washington, Dec. 2, 1951
21 Cleveland vs. Philadelphia, Dec. 13, 1959
Los Angeles vs. New Orleans, Nov. 25, 1973
Pittsburgh vs. Kansas City, Nov. 7, 1976
New England vs. Denver, Nov. 28, 1976
Oakland vs. Green Bay, Sept. 17, 1978
20 By eight teams

Fewest First Downs, Rushing, Game
0 By many teams. Last time: New England vs. New Orleans, Nov. 30, 1986

Most First Downs, Passing, Season
259 San Diego, 1985
250 Miami, 1986
244 San Diego, 1980

Fewest First Downs, Passing, Season
18 Pittsburgh, 1941
23 Brooklyn, 1942
N.Y. Giants, 1944
24 N.Y. Giants, 1943

Most First Downs, Passing, Game
29 N.Y. Giants vs. Cincinnati, Oct. 13, 1985
27 San Diego vs. Seattle, Sept. 15, 1985
25 Denver vs. Kansas City, Nov. 18, 1974
N.Y Jets vs. San Francisco, Sept. 21, 1980

Fewest First Downs, Passing, Game
0 By many teams. Last time: Atlanta vs. Chicago, Nov. 24, 1985

Most First Downs, Penalty, Season
41 Denver, 1986
39 Seattle, 1978
38 Buffalo, 1983
Denver, 1983
Buffalo, 1986

Fewest First Downs, Penalty, Season
2 Brooklyn, 1940
4 Chi. Cardinals, 1940
N.Y. Giants, 1942, 1944
Washington, 1944
Cleveland, 1952
Kansas City, 1969
5 Brooklyn, 1939
Chi. Bears, 1939
Detroit, 1953
Los Angeles, 1953
Houston, 1982

Most First Downs, Penalty, Game
11 Denver vs. Houston, Oct. 6, 1985
9 Chi. Bears vs. Cleveland, Nov. 25, 1951
Baltimore vs. Pittsburgh, Oct. 30, 1977
8 Philadelphia vs. Detroit, Dec. 2, 1979
Cincinnati vs. N.Y. Jets, Oct. 6, 1985
Fewest First Downs, Penalty, Game
0 By many teams

Net Yards Gained Rushing and Passing

Most Seasons Leading League
12 Chi. Bears, 1932, 1934-35, 1939, 1941-44, 1947, 1949, 1955-56
7 San Diego, 1963, 1965, 1980-83, 1985
6 L.A. Rams, 1946, 1950-51, 1954, 1957, 1973
Baltimore, 1958-60, 1964, 1967, 1976
Dall. Cowboys, 1966, 1968-69, 1971, 1974, 1977
Most Consecutive Seasons Leading League
4 Chi. Bears, 1941-44
San Diego, 1980-83
3 Baltimore, 1958-60
Houston, 1960-62
Oakland, 1968-70
2 By many teams
Most Yards Gained, Season
6,936 Miami, 1984
6,744 San Diego, 1981
6,535 San Diego, 1985
Fewest Yards Gained, Season
1,150 Cincinnati, 1933
1,443 Chi. Cardinals, 1934
1,486 Chi. Cardinals, 1933
Most Yards Gained, Game
735 Los Angeles vs. N.Y. Yanks, Sept. 28, 1951
683 Pittsburgh vs. Chi. Cardinals, Dec. 13, 1958
682 Chi. Bears vs. N.Y. Giants, Nov. 14, 1943
Fewest Yards Gained, Game
−7 Seattle vs. Los Angeles, Nov. 4, 1979
−5 Denver vs. Oakland, Sept. 10, 1967
14 Chi. Cardinals vs. Detroit, Sept. 15, 1940
Most Yards Gained, Both Teams, Game
1,133 Los Angeles (636) vs. N.Y. Yanks (497), Nov. 19, 1950
1,102 San Diego (661) vs. Cincinnati (441), Dec. 20, 1982
1,087 St. Louis (589) vs. Philadelphia (498), Dec. 16, 1962
Fewest Yards Gained, Both Teams, Game
30 Chi. Cardinals (14) vs. Detroit (16), Sept. 15, 1940
Most Consecutive Games, 400 or More Yards Gained
11 San Diego, 1982-83
6 Houston, 1961-62
San Diego, 1981
5 Chi. Bears, 1947, 1955
Los Angeles, 1950
Philadelphia, 1953
Oakland, 1968
New England, 1981
Cincinnati, 1986
Most Consecutive Games, 300 or More Yards Gained
29 Los Angeles, 1949-51
26 Miami, 1983-85
20 Chi. Bears, 1948-50

Rushing

Most Seasons Leading League
16 Chi. Bears, 1932, 1934-35, 1939-42, 1951, 1955-56, 1968, 1977, 1983-86
6 Cleveland, 1958-59, 1963, 1965-67
5 Buffalo, 1962, 1964, 1973, 1975, 1982
Most Consecutive Seasons Leading League
4 Chi. Bears, 1939-42, 1983-86
3 Detroit, 1936-38
San Francisco, 1952-54
Cleveland, 1965-67
2 By many teams
Most Rushing Attempts, Season
681 Oakland, 1977
674 Chicago, 1984
671 New England, 1978
Fewest Rushing Attempts, Season
211 Philadelphia, 1982
219 San Francisco, 1982
225 Houston, 1982
Most Rushing Attempts, Game
72 Chi. Bears vs. Brooklyn, Oct. 20, 1935
70 Chi. Cardinals vs. Green Bay, Dec. 5, 1948
69 Chi. Cardinals vs. Green Bay, Dec. 6, 1936
Kansas City vs. Cincinnati, Sept. 3, 1978
Fewest Rushing Attempts, Game
6 Chi. Cardinals vs. Boston, Oct. 29, 1933
7 Oakland vs. Buffalo, Oct. 15, 1963
Houston vs. N.Y. Giants, Dec. 8, 1985
8 Denver vs. Oakland, Dec. 17, 1960
Buffalo vs. St. Louis, Sept. 9, 1984
Most Rushing Attempts, Both Teams, Game
108 Chi. Cardinals (70) vs. Green Bay (38), Dec. 5, 1948
105 Oakland (62) vs. Atlanta (43), Nov. 30, 1975 (OT)
103 Kansas City (53) vs. San Diego (50), Nov. 12, 1978 (OT)
Fewest Rushing Attempts, Both Teams, Game
36 Cincinnati (16) vs. Chi. Bears (20), Sept. 30, 1934
37 Atlanta (18) vs. San Francisco (19), Oct. 6, 1985
38 N.Y. Jets (13) vs. Buffalo (25), Nov. 8, 1964

Yards Gained

Most Yards Gained Rushing, Season
3,165 New England, 1978
3,088 Buffalo, 1973
2,986 Kansas City, 1978
Fewest Yards Gained Rushing, Season
298 Philadelphia, 1940
467 Detroit, 1946
471 Boston, 1944
Most Yards Gained Rushing, Game
426 Detroit vs. Pittsburgh, Nov. 4, 1934
423 N.Y. Giants vs. Baltimore, Nov. 19, 1950
420 Boston vs. N.Y. Giants, Oct. 8, 1933
Fewest Yards Gained Rushing, Game
−53 Detroit vs. Chi. Cardinals, Oct. 17, 1943
−36 Philadelphia vs. Chi. Bears, Nov. 19, 1939
−33 Phil-Pitt vs. Brooklyn, Oct. 2, 1943
Most Yards Gained Rushing, Both Teams, Game
595 Los Angeles (371) vs. N.Y. Yanks (224), Nov. 18, 1951
574 Chi. Bears (396) vs. Pittsburgh (178), Oct. 10, 1934
557 Chi. Bears (406) vs. Green Bay (151), Nov. 6, 1955
Fewest Yards Gained Rushing, Both Teams, Game
−15 Detroit (−53) vs. Chi. Cardinals (38), Oct. 17, 1943
4 Detroit (−10) vs. Chi. Cardinals (14), Sept. 15, 1940
63 Chi. Cardinals (−1) vs. N.Y. Giants (64), Oct. 18, 1953

Average Gain

Highest Average Gain, Rushing, Season
5.74 Cleveland, 1963
5.65 San Francisco, 1954
5.56 San Diego, 1963
Lowest Average Gain, Rushing, Season
0.94 Philadelphia, 1940
1.45 Boston, 1944
1.55 Pittsburgh, 1935

Touchdowns

Most Touchdowns, Rushing, Season
36 Green Bay, 1962
33 Pittsburgh, 1976
30 Chi. Bears, 1941
New England, 1978
Washington, 1983
Fewest Touchdowns, Rushing, Season
1 Brooklyn, 1934
2 Chi. Cardinals, 1933
Cincinnati, 1933
Pittsburgh, 1934, 1940
Philadelphia, 1935, 1936, 1937, 1938, 1972
3 By many teams
Most Touchdowns, Rushing, Game
7 Los Angeles vs. Atlanta, Dec. 4, 1976
6 By many teams
Most Touchdowns, Rushing, Both Teams, Game
8 Los Angeles (6) vs. N.Y. Yanks (2), Nov. 18, 1951
Cleveland (6) vs. Los Angeles (2), Nov. 24, 1957
7 In many games

Passing

Attempts

Most Passes Attempted, Season
709 Minnesota, 1981
662 San Diego, 1984
645 Miami, 1986
Fewest Passes Attempted, Season
102 Cincinnati, 1933
106 Boston, 1933
120 Detroit, 1937
Most Passes Attempted, Game
68 Houston vs. Buffalo, Nov. 1, 1964
65 San Diego vs. Kansas City, Oct. 19, 1986
63 Minnesota vs. Tampa Bay, Sept. 5, 1981
Fewest Passes Attempted, Game
0 Green Bay vs. Portsmouth, Oct. 8, 1933
Detroit vs. Cleveland, Sept. 10, 1937
Pittsburgh vs. Brooklyn, Nov. 16, 1941; vs. Los Angeles, Nov. 13, 1949
Cleveland vs. Philadelphia, Dec. 3, 1950
Most Passes Attempted, Both Teams, Game
102 San Francisco (57) vs. Atlanta (45), Oct. 6, 1985
100 Tampa Bay (54) vs. Kansas City (46), Oct. 28, 1984
San Francisco (60) vs. Washington (40), Nov. 17, 1986
98 Minnesota (56) vs. Baltimore (42), Sept. 28, 1969
Fewest Passes Attempted, Both Teams, Game
4 Chi. Cardinals (1) vs. Detroit (3), Nov. 3, 1935
Detroit (0) vs. Cleveland (4), Sept. 10, 1937
6 Chi. Cardinals (2) vs. Detroit (4), Sept. 15, 1940
8 Brooklyn (2) vs. Philadelphia (6), Oct. 1, 1939

Completions

Most Passes Completed, Season
401 San Diego, 1984
392 Miami, 1986
386 San Diego, 1985
Fewest Passes Completed, Season
25 Cincinnati, 1933
33 Boston, 1933
34 Chi. Cardinals, 1934
Detroit, 1934
Most Passes Completed, Game
42 N.Y. Jets vs. San Francisco, Sept. 21, 1980
40 Cincinnati vs. San Diego, Dec. 20, 1982

Dallas vs. Detroit, Sept. 15, 1985
N.Y. Giants vs. Cincinnati, Oct. 13, 1985
39 Miami vs. Buffalo, Nov. 16, 1986

Fewest Passes Completed, Game
0 By many teams. Last time: Buffalo vs. N.Y. Jets, Sept. 29, 1974

Most Passes Completed, Both Teams, Game
68 San Francisco (37) vs. Atlanta (31), Oct. 6, 1985
66 Cincinnati (40) vs. San Diego (26), Dec. 20, 1982
65 San Diego (33) vs. San Francisco (32), Dec. 11, 1982
San Diego (37) vs. Miami (28), Nov. 18, 1984 (OT)

Fewest Passes Completed, Both Teams, Game
1 Chi. Cardinals (0) vs. Philadelphia (1), Nov. 8, 1936
Detroit (0) vs. Cleveland (1), Sept. 10, 1937
Chi. Cardinals (0) vs. Detroit (1), Sept. 15, 1940
Brooklyn (0) vs. Pittsburgh (1), Nov. 29, 1942
2 Chi. Cardinals (0) vs. Detroit (2), Nov. 3, 1935
Buffalo (0) vs. N.Y. Jets (2), Sept. 29, 1974
3 Brooklyn (1) vs. Philadelphia (2), Oct. 1, 1939

Yards Gained

Most Seasons Leading League, Passing Yardage
10 San Diego, 1965, 1968, 1971, 1978-83, 1985
8 Chi. Bears, 1932, 1939, 1941, 1943, 1945, 1949, 1954, 1964
7 Washington, 1938, 1940, 1944, 1947-48, 1967, 1974

Most Consecutive Seasons Leading League, Passing Yardage
6 San Diego, 1978-83
4 Green Bay, 1934-37
2 By many teams

Most Yards Gained, Passing, Season
5,018 Miami, 1984
4,870 San Diego, 1985
4,779 Miami, 1986

Fewest Yards Gained, Passing, Season
302 Chi. Cardinals, 1934
357 Cincinnati, 1933
459 Boston, 1934

Most Yards Gained, Passing, Game
554 Los Angeles vs. N.Y. Yanks, Sept. 28, 1951
530 Minnesota vs. Baltimore, Sept. 28, 1969
506 L.A. Rams vs. Chicago, Dec. 26, 1982

Fewest Yards Gained, Passing, Game
−53 Denver vs. Oakland, Sept. 10, 1967
−52 Cincinnati vs. Houston, Oct. 31, 1971
−39 Atlanta vs. San Francisco, Oct. 23, 1976

Most Yards Gained, Passing, Both Teams, Game
884 N.Y. Jets (449) vs. Miami (435), Sept. 21, 1986 (OT)
883 San Diego (486) vs. Cincinnati (397), Dec. 20, 1982
849 Minnesota (471) vs. Washington (378), Nov. 2, 1986 (OT)

Fewest Yards Gained, Passing, Both Teams, Game
−11 Green Bay (−10) vs. Dallas (−1), Oct. 24, 1965
1 Chi. Cardinals (0) vs. Philadelphia (1), Nov. 8, 1936
7 Brooklyn (0) vs. Pittsburgh (7), Nov. 29, 1942

Times Sacked

Most Seasons Leading League, Fewest Times Sacked
6 Miami, 1973, 1982-86
4 San Diego, 1963-64, 1967-68
San Francisco, 1964-65, 1970-71
3 N.Y. Jets, 1965-66, 1968
Houston, 1961-62, 1978
St. Louis, 1974-76

Most Consecutive Seasons Leading League, Fewest Times Sacked
5 Miami, 1982-86
3 St. Louis, 1974-76
2 By many teams

Most Times Sacked, Season
104 Philadelphia, 1986
70 Atlanta, 1968
69 Atlanta, 1985

Fewest Times Sacked, Season
8 San Francisco, 1970
St. Louis, 1975
9 N.Y. Jets, 1966
10 N.Y. Giants, 1972

Most Times Sacked, Game
12 Pittsburgh vs. Dallas, Nov. 20, 1966
Baltimore vs. St. Louis, Oct. 26, 1980
Detroit vs. Chicago, Dec. 16, 1984
Houston vs. Dallas, Sept. 29, 1985
11 St. Louis vs. N.Y. Giants, Nov. 1, 1964
Los Angeles vs. Baltimore, Nov. 22, 1964
Denver vs. Buffalo, Dec. 13, 1964; vs. Oakland, Nov. 5, 1967
Green Bay vs. Detroit, Nov. 7, 1965
Buffalo vs. Oakland, Oct. 15, 1967
Atlanta vs. St. Louis, Nov. 24, 1968; vs. Cleveland, Nov. 18, 1984
Detroit vs. Dallas, Oct. 6, 1975
Philadelphia vs. St. Louis, Dec. 18, 1983; vs. Detroit, Nov. 16, 1986; vs. L.A. Raiders, Nov. 30, 1986 (OT)
Cleveland vs. Kansas City, Sept. 30, 1984
Minnesota vs. Chicago, Oct. 28, 1984
Dallas vs. San Diego, Nov. 16, 1986
L.A. Raiders vs. Seattle, Dec. 8, 1986
10 By many teams

Most Times Sacked, Both Teams, Game
18 Green Bay (10) vs. San Diego (8), Sept. 24, 1978
17 Buffalo (10) vs. N.Y. Titans (7), Nov. 23, 1961
Pittsburgh (12) vs. Dallas (5), Nov. 20, 1966
Atlanta (9) vs. Philadelphia (8), Dec. 16, 1984
Philadelphia (11) vs. L.A. Raiders (6), Nov. 30, 1986 (OT)
16 Los Angeles (11) vs. Baltimore (5), Nov. 22, 1964
Buffalo (11) vs. Oakland (5), Oct. 15, 1967

Completion Percentage

Most Seasons Leading League, Completion Percentage
11 Washington, 1937, 1939-40, 1942-45, 1947-48, 1969-70
7 Green Bay, 1936, 1941, 1961-62, 1964, 1966, 1968
6 Cleveland, 1951, 1953-55, 1959-60
Dall. Texans/Kansas City, 1962, 1964, 1966-69
San Francisco, 1952, 1957-58, 1965, 1981, 1983

Most Consecutive Seasons Leading League, Completion Percentage
4 Washington, 1942-45
Kansas City, 1966-69
3 Cleveland, 1953-55
2 By many teams

Highest Completion Percentage, Season
70.6 Cincinnati, 1982 (310-219)
64.3 Oakland, 1976 (361-232)
64.2 San Francisco, 1983 (528-339)

Lowest Completion Percentage, Season
22.9 Philadelphia, 1936 (170-39)
24.5 Cincinnati, 1933 (102-25)
25.0 Pittsburgh, 1941 (168-42)

Touchdowns

Most Touchdowns, Passing, Season
49 Miami, 1984
48 Houston, 1961
46 Miami, 1986

Fewest Touchdowns, Passing, Season
0 Cincinnati, 1933
Pittsburgh, 1945
1 Boston, 1932, 1933
Chi. Cardinals, 1934
Cincinnati/St. Louis, 1934
Detroit, 1942
2 Chi. Cardinals, 1932, 1935
Stapleton, 1932
Brooklyn, 1936
Pittsburgh, 1942

Most Touchdowns, Passing, Game
7 Chi. Bears vs. N.Y. Giants, Nov. 14, 1943
Philadelphia vs. Washington, Oct. 17, 1954
Houston vs. N.Y. Titans, Nov. 19, 1961; vs. N.Y. Titans, Oct. 14, 1962
N.Y. Giants vs. Washington, Oct. 28, 1962
Minnesota vs. Baltimore, Sept. 28, 1969
San Diego vs. Oakland, Nov. 22, 1981
6 By many teams.

Most Touchdowns, Passing, Both Teams, Game
12 New Orleans (6) vs. St. Louis (6), Nov. 2, 1969
11 N.Y. Giants (7) vs. Washington (4), Oct. 28, 1962
Oakland (6) vs. Houston (5), Dec. 22, 1963
10 Miami (6) vs. N.Y. Jets (4), Sept. 21, 1986 (OT)

Passes Had Intercepted

Most Passes Had Intercepted, Season
48 Houston, 1962
45 Denver, 1961
41 Card-Pitt, 1944

Fewest Passes Had Intercepted, Season
5 Cleveland, 1960
Green Bay, 1966
6 Green Bay, 1964
St. Louis, 1982
7 Los Angeles, 1969

Most Passes Had Intercepted, Game
9 Detroit vs. Green Bay, Oct. 24, 1943
Pittsburgh vs. Philadelphia, Dec. 12, 1965
8 Green Bay vs. N.Y. Giants, Nov. 21, 1948
Chi. Cardinals vs. Philadelphia, Sept. 24, 1950
N.Y. Yanks vs. N.Y. Giants, Dec. 16, 1951
Denver vs. Houston, Dec. 2, 1962
Chi. Bears vs. Detroit, Sept. 22, 1968
Baltimore vs. N.Y. Jets, Sept. 23, 1973
7 By many teams. Last time: Green Bay vs. New Orleans, Sept. 14, 1986

Most Passes Had Intercepted, Both Teams, Game
13 Denver (8) vs. Houston (5), Dec. 2, 1962
11 Philadelphia (7) vs. Boston (4), Nov. 3, 1935
Boston (6) vs. Pittsburgh (5), Dec. 1, 1935
Cleveland (7) vs. Green Bay (4), Oct. 30, 1938
Green Bay (7) vs. Detroit (4), Oct. 20, 1940
Detroit (7) vs. Chi. Bears (4), Nov. 22, 1942
Detroit (7) vs. Cleveland (4), Nov. 26, 1944
Chi. Cardinals (8) vs. Philadelphia (3), Sept. 24, 1950
Washington (7) vs. N.Y. Giants (4), Dec. 8, 1963
Pittsburgh (9) vs. Philadelphia (2), Dec 12, 1965
10 In many games

Punting

Most Seasons Leading League (Average Distance)
6 Washington, 1940-43, 1945, 1958
Denver, 1962-64, 1966-67, 1982
Kansas City, 1968, 1971-73, 1979, 1984
4 L.A. Rams, 1946, 1949, 1955-56
Baltimore/Indianapolis, 1966, 1969, 1983, 1985
3 Cleveland, 1950-52
San Francisco, 1957, 1962, 1965
N.Y. Giants, 1959, 1980, 1986
Cincinnati, 1970, 1978, 1981
Oakland, 1974, 1975, 1977

Most Consecutive Seasons Leading League (Average Distance)
4 Washington, 1940-43
3 Cleveland, 1950-52
Denver, 1962-64
Kansas City, 1971-73

Most Punts, Season
114 Chicago, 1981
113 Boston, 1934
Brooklyn, 1934
112 Boston, 1935
Fewest Punts, Season
23 San Diego, 1982
31 Cincinnati, 1982
32 Chi. Bears, 1941
Most Punts, Game
17 Chi. Bears vs. Green Bay, Oct. 22, 1933
Cincinnati vs. Pittsburgh, Oct. 22, 1933
16 Cincinnati vs. Portsmouth, Sept. 17, 1933
Chi. Cardinals vs. Chi. Bears, Nov. 30, 1933; vs. Detroit, Sept. 15, 1940
Fewest Punts, Game
0 By many teams. Last time: Miami vs. Buffalo, Oct. 12, 1986
Most Punts, Both Teams, Game
31 Chi. Bears (17) vs. Green Bay (14), Oct. 22, 1933
Cincinnati (17) vs. Pittsburgh (14), Oct. 22, 1933
29 Chi. Cardinals (15) vs. Cincinnati (14), Nov. 12, 1933
Chi. Cardinals (16) vs. Chi. Bears (13), Nov. 30, 1933
Chi. Cardinals (16) vs. Detroit (13), Sept. 15, 1940
Fewest Punts, Both Teams, Game
1 Dall. Cowboys (0) vs. Cleveland (1), Dec. 3, 1961
Chicago (0) vs. Detroit (1), Oct. 1, 1972
San Francisco (0) vs. N.Y. Giants (1), Oct. 15, 1972
Green Bay (0) vs. Buffalo (1), Dec. 5, 1982
Miami (0) vs. Buffalo (1), Oct. 12, 1986
2 In many games

Average Yardage
Highest Average Distance, Punting, Season
47.6 Detroit, 1961 (56-2,664)
47.0 Pittsburgh, 1961 (73-3,431)
46.9 Pittsburgh, 1953 (80-3,752)
Lowest Average Distance, Punting, Season
32.7 Card-Pitt, 1944 (60-1,964)
33.8 Cincinnati, 1986 (59-1,996)
33.9 Detroit, 1969 (74-2,510)

Punt Returns
Most Seasons Leading League (Average Return)
8 Detroit, 1943-45, 1951-52, 1962, 1966, 1969
6 Chi. Cardinals/St. Louis, 1948-49, 1955-56, 1959, 1986
5 Cleveland, 1958, 1960, 1964-65, 1967
Green Bay, 1950, 1953-54, 1961, 1972
Dall. Texans/Kansas City, 1960, 1968, 1970, 1979-80
Most Consecutive Seasons Leading League (Average Return)
3 Detroit, 1943-45
2 By many teams
Most Punt Returns, Season
71 Pittsburgh, 1976
Tampa Bay, 1979
L.A. Raiders, 1985
67 Pittsburgh, 1974
Los Angeles, 1978
L.A. Raiders, 1984
65 San Francisco, 1976
Fewest Punt Returns, Season
12 Baltimore, 1981
San Diego, 1982
14 Los Angeles, 1961
Philadelphia, 1962
Baltimore, 1982
15 Houston, 1960
Washington, 1960
Oakland, 1961
N.Y. Giants, 1969
Philadelphia, 1973
Kansas City, 1982
Most Punt Returns, Game
12 Philadelphia vs. Cleveland, Dec. 3, 1950
11 Chi. Bears vs. Chi. Cardinals, Oct. 8, 1950
Washington vs. Tampa Bay, Oct. 9, 1977
10 Philadelphia vs. N.Y. Giants, Nov. 26, 1950
Philadelphia vs. Tampa Bay, Sept. 18, 1977
Pittsburgh vs. Buffalo, Dec. 16, 1979
Washington vs. New Orleans, Dec. 26, 1982
Most Punt Returns, Both Teams, Game
17 Philadelphia (12) vs. Cleveland (5), Dec. 3, 1950
16 N.Y. Giants (9) vs. Philadelphia (7), Dec. 12, 1954
Washington (11) vs. Tampa Bay (5), Oct. 9, 1977
15 Detroit (8) vs. Cleveland (7), Sept. 27, 1942
Los Angeles (8) vs. Baltimore (7), Nov. 27, 1966
Pittsburgh (8) vs. Houston (7), Dec. 1, 1974
Philadelphia (10) vs. Tampa Bay (5), Sept. 18, 1977
Baltimore (9) vs. Kansas City (6), Sept. 2, 1979
Washington (10) vs. New Orleans (5), Dec. 26, 1982
L.A. Raiders (8) vs. Cleveland (7), Nov. 16, 1986

Fair Catches
Most Fair Catches, Season
34 Baltimore, 1971
32 San Diego, 1969
30 St. Louis, 1967
Minnesota, 1971
Fewest Fair Catches, Season
0 San Diego, 1975
New England, 1976
Tampa Bay, 1976
Pittsburgh, 1977
Dallas, 1982
1 Cleveland, 1974
San Francisco, 1975
Kansas City, 1976
St. Louis, 1976, 1982
San Diego, 1976
L.A. Rams, 1982
Tampa Bay, 1982
2 By many teams
Most Fair Catches, Game
7 Minnesota vs. Dallas, Sept. 25, 1966
Detroit vs. Chicago, Nov. 21, 1976
6 By many teams

Yards Gained
Most Yards, Punt Returns, Season
785 L.A. Raiders, 1985
781 Chi. Bears, 1948
774 Pittsburgh, 1974
Fewest Yards, Punt Returns, Season
27 St. Louis, 1965
35 N.Y. Giants, 1965
37 New England, 1972
Most Yards, Punt Returns, Game
231 Detroit vs. San Francisco, Oct. 6, 1963
225 Oakland vs. Buffalo, Sept. 15, 1968
219 Los Angeles vs. Atlanta, Oct. 11, 1981
Most Yards, Punt Returns, Both Teams, Game
282 Los Angeles (219) vs. Atlanta (63), Oct. 11, 1981
245 Detroit (231) vs. San Francisco (14), Oct. 6, 1963
244 Oakland (225) vs. Buffalo (19), Sept. 15, 1968

Average Yards Returning Punts
Highest Average, Punt Returns, Season
20.2 Chi. Bears, 1941 (27-546)
19.1 Chi. Cardinals, 1948 (35-669)
18.2 Chi. Cardinals, 1949 (30-546)
Lowest Average, Punt Returns, Season
1.2 St. Louis, 1965 (23-27)
1.5 N.Y. Giants, 1965 (24-35)
1.7 Washington, 1970 (27-45)

Touchdowns Returning Punts
Most Touchdowns, Punt Returns, Season
5 Chi. Cardinals, 1959
4 Chi. Cardinals, 1948
Detroit, 1951
N.Y. Giants, 1951
Denver, 1976
3 Washington, 1941
Detroit, 1952
Pittsburgh, 1952
Houston, 1975
Los Angeles, 1981
Most Touchdowns, Punt Returns, Game
2 Detroit vs. Los Angeles, Oct. 14, 1951; vs. Green Bay, Nov. 22, 1951
Chi. Cardinals vs. Pittsburgh, Nov. 1, 1959; vs. N.Y. Giants, Nov. 22, 1959
N.Y. Titans vs. Denver, Sept. 24, 1961
Denver vs. Cleveland, Sept. 26, 1976
Los Angeles vs. Atlanta, Oct. 11, 1981
St. Louis vs. Tampa Bay, Dec. 21, 1986
Most Touchdowns, Punt Returns, Both Teams, Game
2 Philadelphia (1) vs. Washington (1), Nov. 9, 1952
Kansas City (1) vs. Buffalo (1), Sept. 11, 1966
Baltimore (1) vs. New England (1), Nov. 18, 1979
L.A. Raiders (1) vs. Philadelphia (1), Nov. 30, 1986 (OT)
(Also see previous record)

Kickoff Returns
Most Seasons Leading League (Average Return)
7 Washington, 1942, 1947, 1962-63, 1973-74, 1981
6 Chicago Bears, 1943, 1948, 1958, 1966, 1972, 1985
5 N.Y. Giants, 1944, 1946, 1949, 1951, 1953
Most Consecutive Seasons Leading League (Average Return)
3 Denver, 1965-67
2 By many teams
Most Kickoff Returns, Season
88 New Orleans, 1980
86 Minnesota, 1984
84 Baltimore, 1981
Fewest Kickoff Returns, Season
17 N.Y. Giants, 1944
20 N.Y. Giants, 1941, 1943
Chi. Bears, 1942
23 Washington, 1942
Most Kickoff Returns, Game
12 N.Y. Giants vs. Washington, Nov. 27, 1966
10 By many teams
Most Kickoff Returns, Both Teams, Game
19 N.Y. Giants (12) vs. Washington (7), Nov. 27, 1966
18 Houston (10) vs. Oakland (8), Dec. 22, 1963
17 Washington (9) vs. Green Bay (8), Oct. 17, 1983
San Diego (9) vs. Pittsburgh (8), Dec. 8, 1985
Detroit (9) vs. Green Bay (8), Nov. 27, 1986

Yards Gained
Most Yards, Kickoff Returns, Season
1,973 New Orleans, 1980
1,824 Houston, 1963
1,801 Denver, 1963
Fewest Yards, Kickoff Returns, Season
282 N.Y. Giants, 1940
381 Green Bay, 1940
424 Chicago, 1963

Most Yards, Kickoff Returns, Game
362 Detroit vs. Los Angeles, Oct. 29, 1950
304 Chi. Bears vs. Green Bay, Nov. 9, 1952
295 Denver vs. Boston, Oct. 4, 1964
Most Yards, Kickoff Returns, Both Teams, Game
560 Detroit (362) vs. Los Angeles (198), Oct. 29, 1950
453 Washington (236) vs. Philadelphia (217), Sept. 28, 1947
447 N.Y. Giants (236) vs. Cleveland (211), Dec. 4, 1966

Average Yardage
Highest Average, Kickoff Returns, Season
29.4 Chicago, 1972 (52-1,528)
28.9 Pittsburgh, 1952 (39-1,128)
28.2 Washington, 1962 (61-1,720)
Lowest Average, Kickoff Returns, Season
16.3 Chicago, 1963 (26-424)
16.4 Chicago, 1983 (58-953)
16.5 San Diego, 1961 (51-642)

Touchdowns
Most Touchdowns, Kickoff Returns, Season
4 Green Bay, 1967
Chicago, 1970
3 L.A. Rams, 1950, 1985
Chi. Cardinals, 1954
San Francisco, 1963
Denver, 1966
Chicago, 1967
New England, 1977
2 By many teams
Most Touchdowns, Kickoff Returns, Game
2 Chi. Bears vs. Green Bay, Sept. 22, 1940; vs. Green Bay, Nov. 9, 1952
Philadelphia vs. Dallas, Nov. 6, 1966
Green Bay vs. Cleveland, Nov. 12, 1967
L.A. Rams vs. Green Bay, Nov. 24, 1985
Most Touchdowns, Kickoff Returns, Both Teams, Game
2 Washington (1) vs. Philadelphia (1), Nov. 1, 1942
Washington (1) vs. Philadelphia (1), Sept. 28, 1947
Los Angeles (1) vs. Detroit (1), Oct. 29, 1950
N.Y. Yanks (1) vs. N.Y. Giants (1), Nov. 4, 1951 (consecutive)
Baltimore (1) vs. Chi. Bears (1), Oct. 4, 1958
Buffalo (1) vs. Boston (1), Nov. 3, 1962
Pittsburgh (1) vs. Dallas (1), Oct. 30, 1966
St. Louis (1) vs. Washington (1), Sept. 23, 1973 (consecutive)
(Also see previous record)

Fumbles
Most Fumbles, Season
56 Chi. Bears, 1938
San Francisco, 1978
54 Philadelphia, 1946
51 New England, 1973
Fewest Fumbles, Season
8 Cleveland, 1959
11 Green Bay, 1944
12 Brooklyn, 1934
Detroit, 1943
Cincinnati, 1982
Minnesota, 1982
Most Fumbles, Game
10 Phil-Pitt vs. New York, Oct. 9, 1943
Detroit vs. Minnesota, Nov. 12, 1967
Kansas City vs. Houston, Oct. 12, 1969
San Francisco vs. Detroit, Dec. 17, 1978
9 Philadelphia vs. Green Bay, Oct. 13, 1946
Kansas City vs. San Diego, Nov. 15, 1964
N.Y. Giants vs. Buffalo, Oct. 20, 1975
St. Louis vs. Washington, Oct. 25, 1976
San Diego vs. Green Bay, Sept. 24, 1978
Pittsburgh vs. Cincinnati, Oct. 14, 1979
Cleveland vs. Seattle, Dec. 20, 1981
8 By many teams. Last time: Tampa Bay vs. New York Jets, Dec. 12, 1982
Most Fumbles, Both Teams, Game
14 Chi. Bears (7) vs. Cleveland (7), Nov. 24, 1940
St. Louis (8) vs. N.Y. Giants (6), Sept. 17, 1961
Kansas City (10) vs. Houston (4), Oct. 12, 1969
13 Washington (8) vs. Pittsburgh (5), Nov. 14, 1937
Philadelphia (7) vs. Boston (6), Dec. 8, 1946
N.Y. Giants (7) vs. Washington (6), Nov. 5, 1950
Kansas City (9) vs. San Diego (4), Nov. 15, 1964
Buffalo (7) vs. Denver (6), Dec. 13, 1964
N.Y. Jets (7) vs. Houston (6), Sept. 12, 1965
Houston (8) vs. Pittsburgh (5), Dec. 9, 1973
St. Louis (9) vs. Washington (4), Oct. 25, 1976
Cleveland (9) vs. Seattle (4), Dec. 20, 1981
Green Bay (7) vs. Detroit (6), Oct. 6, 1985
12 In many games

Fumbles Lost
Most Fumbles Lost, Season
36 Chi. Cardinals, 1959
31 Green Bay, 1952
29 Chi. Cardinals, 1946
Pittsburgh, 1950
Fewest Fumbles Lost, Season
3 Philadelphia, 1938
Minnesota, 1980
4 San Francisco, 1960
Kansas City, 1982
5 Chi. Cardinals, 1943
Detroit, 1943
N.Y. Giants, 1943
Cleveland, 1959
Minnesota, 1982
Most Fumbles Lost, Game
8 St. Louis vs. Washington, Oct. 25, 1976
7 Cincinnati vs. Buffalo, Nov. 30, 1969
Cleveland vs. Seattle, Dec. 20, 1981
6 By many teams. Last time: L.A. Rams vs. New England, Dec. 11, 1983

Fumbles Recovered
Most Fumbles Recovered, Season, Own and Opponents'
58 Minnesota, 1963 (27 own, 31 opp)
51 Chi. Bears, 1938 (37 own, 14 opp)
San Francisco, 1978 (24 own, 27 opp)
47 Atlanta, 1978 (22 own, 25 opp)
Fewest Fumbles Recovered, Season, Own and Opponents'
9 San Francisco, 1982 (5 own, 4 opp)
11 Cincinnati, 1982 (5 own, 6 opp)
13 Baltimore, 1967 (5 own, 8 opp)
N.Y. Jets, 1967 (7 own, 6 opp)
Philadelphia, 1968 (6 own, 7 opp)
Miami, 1973 (5 own, 8 opp)
Chicago, 1982 (6 own, 7 opp)
Denver, 1982 (6 own, 7 opp)
Miami, 1982 (5 own, 8 opp)
N.Y. Giants, 1982 (7 own, 6 opp)
Most Fumbles Recovered, Game, Own and Opponents'
10 Denver vs. Buffalo, Dec. 13, 1964 (5 own, 5 opp)
Pittsburgh vs. Houston, Dec. 9, 1973 (5 own, 5 opp)
Washington vs. St. Louis, Oct. 25, 1976 (2 own, 8 opp)
9 St. Louis vs. N.Y. Giants, Sept. 17, 1961 (6 own, 3 opp)
Houston vs. Cincinnati, Oct. 27, 1974 (4 own, 5 opp)
Kansas City vs. Dallas, Nov. 10, 1975 (4 own, 5 opp)
Green Bay vs. Detroit, Oct. 6, 1985 (5 own, 4 opp)
8 By many teams
Most Own Fumbles Recovered, Season
37 Chi. Bears, 1938
27 Philadelphia, 1946
Minnesota, 1963
26 Washington, 1940
Pittsburgh, 1948
Fewest Own Fumbles Recovered, Season
2 Washington, 1958
3 Detroit, 1956
Cleveland, 1959
Houston, 1982
4 By many teams
Most Opponents' Fumbles Recovered, Season
31 Minnesota, 1963
29 Cleveland, 1951
28 Green Bay, 1946
Houston, 1977
Seattle, 1983
Fewest Opponents' Fumbles Recovered, Season
3 Los Angeles, 1974
4 Philadelphia, 1944
San Francisco, 1982
5 Baltimore, 1982
Most Opponents' Fumbles Recovered, Game
8 Washington vs. St. Louis, Oct. 25, 1976
7 Buffalo vs. Cincinnati, Nov. 30, 1969
Seattle vs. Cleveland, Dec. 20, 1981
6 By many teams. Last time: New England vs. L.A. Rams, Dec. 11, 1983

Touchdowns
Most Touchdowns, Fumbles Recovered, Season, Own and Opponents'
5 Chi. Bears, 1942 (1 own, 4 opp)
Los Angeles, 1952 (1 own, 4 opp)
San Francisco, 1965 (1 own, 4 opp)
Oakland, 1978 (2 own, 3 opp)
4 Chi. Bears, 1948 (1 own, 3 opp)
Boston, 1948 (4 opp)
Denver, 1979 (1 own, 3 opp), 1984 (4 opp)
Atlanta, 1981 (1 own, 3 opp)
3 By many teams
Most Touchdowns, Own Fumbles Recovered, Season
2 Chi. Bears, 1953
New England, 1973
Buffalo, 1974
Denver, 1975
Oakland, 1978
Green Bay, 1982
New Orleans, 1983
Cleveland, 1986
Most Touchdowns, Opponents' Fumbles Recovered, Season
4 Detroit, 1937
Chi. Bears, 1942
Boston, 1948
Los Angeles, 1952
San Francisco, 1965
Denver, 1984
3 By many teams
Most Touchdowns, Fumbles Recovered, Game, Own and Opponents'
2 Detroit vs. Cleveland, Nov. 7, 1937 (2 opp); vs. Green Bay, Sept. 17, 1950 (1 own, 1 opp); vs. Chi. Cardinals, Dec. 6, 1959 (1 own, 1 opp); vs. Minnesota, Dec. 9, 1962 (1 own, 1 opp)
Philadelphia vs. N.Y. Giants, Sept. 25, 1938 (2 opp); vs. St. Louis, Nov. 21, 1971 (1 own, 1 opp)
Chi. Bears vs. Washington, Nov. 28, 1948 (2 opp)
N.Y. Giants vs. Pittsburgh, Sept. 17, 1950 (2 opp); vs. Green Bay, Sept. 19, 1971 (2 opp)
Cleveland vs. Dall. Cowboys, Dec. 3, 1961 (2 opp); vs. N.Y. Giants, Oct. 25, 1964 (2 opp)
Green Bay vs. Dallas, Nov. 26, 1964 (2 opp)

San Francisco vs. Detroit, Nov. 14, 1965 (2 opp)
Oakland vs. Buffalo, Dec. 24, 1967 (2 opp)
Washington vs. San Diego, Sept. 16, 1973 (2 opp); vs. Minnesota, Nov. 29, 1984 (1 own, 1 opp)
New Orleans vs. San Francisco, Oct. 19, 1975 (2 opp)
Cincinnati vs. Pittsburgh, Oct. 14, 1979 (2 opp)
Atlanta vs. Detroit, Oct. 5, 1980 (2 opp)
Kansas City vs. Oakland, Oct. 5, 1980 (2 opp)
New England vs. Baltimore, Nov. 23, 1980 (2 opp)
Denver vs. Green Bay, Oct. 15, 1984 (2 opp)

Most Touchdowns, Own Fumbles Recovered, Game
1 By many teams

Most Touchdowns, Opponents' Fumbles Recovered, Game
2 Detroit vs. Cleveland, Nov. 7, 1937
Philadelphia vs. N.Y. Giants, Sept. 25, 1938
Chi. Bears vs. Washington, Nov. 28, 1948
N.Y. Giants vs. Pittsburgh, Sept. 17, 1950; vs. Green Bay, Sept. 19, 1971
Cleveland vs. Dall. Cowboys, Dec. 3, 1961; vs. N.Y. Giants, Oct. 25, 1964
Green Bay vs. Dallas, Nov. 26, 1964
San Francisco vs. Detroit, Nov. 14, 1965
Oakland vs. Buffalo, Dec. 24, 1967
Washington vs. San Diego, Sept. 16, 1973
New Orleans vs. San Francisco, Oct. 19, 1975
Cincinnati vs. Pittsburgh, Oct. 14, 1979
Atlanta vs. Detroit, Oct. 5, 1980
Kansas City vs. Oakland, Oct. 5, 1980
New England vs. Baltimore, Nov. 23, 1980
Denver vs. Green Bay, Oct. 15, 1984

Turnovers

(Number of times losing the ball on interceptions and fumbles.)

Most Turnovers, Season
63 San Francisco, 1978
58 Chi. Bears, 1947
Pittsburgh, 1950
N.Y. Giants, 1983
57 Green Bay, 1950
Houston, 1962, 1963
Pittsburgh, 1965

Fewest Turnovers, Season
12 Kansas City, 1982
14 N.Y. Giants, 1943
Cleveland, 1959
16 San Francisco, 1960
Cincinnati, 1982
St. Louis, 1982
Washington, 1982

Most Turnovers, Game
12 Detroit vs. Chi. Bears, Nov. 22, 1942
Chi. Cardinals vs. Philadelphia, Sept. 24, 1950
Pittsburgh vs. Philadelphia, Dec. 12, 1965
11 San Diego vs. Green Bay, Sept. 24, 1978
10 Washington vs. N.Y. Giants, Dec. 4, 1938; vs. N.Y. Giants, Dec. 8, 1963
Pittsburgh vs. Green Bay, Nov. 23, 1941
Detroit vs. Green Bay, Oct. 24, 1943; vs. Denver, Oct. 7, 1984
Chi. Cardinals vs. Green Bay, Nov. 10, 1946; vs. N.Y. Giants, Nov. 2, 1952
Minnesota vs. Detroit, Dec. 9, 1962
Houston vs. Oakland, Sept. 7, 1963
Chicago vs. Detroit, Sept. 22, 1968
St. Louis vs. Washington, Oct. 25, 1976
N.Y. Jets vs. New England, Nov. 21, 1976
San Francisco vs. Dallas, Oct. 12, 1980
Cleveland vs. Seattle, Dec. 20, 1981

Most Turnovers, Both Teams, Game
17 Detroit (12) vs. Chi. Bears (5), Nov. 22, 1942
Boston (9) vs. Philadelphia (8), Dec. 8, 1946
16 Chi. Cardinals (12) vs. Philadelphia (4), Sept. 24, 1950
Chi. Cardinals (8) vs. Chi. Bears (8), Dec. 7, 1958
Minnesota (10) vs. Detroit (6), Dec. 9, 1962
Houston (9) vs. Kansas City (7), Oct. 12, 1969
15 Philadelphia (8) vs. Chi. Cardinals (7), Oct. 3, 1954
Denver (9) vs. Houston (6), Dec. 2, 1962
Washington (10) vs. N.Y. Giants (5), Dec. 8, 1963
St. Louis (9) vs. Kansas City (6), Oct. 2, 1983

Penalties

Most Seasons Leading League, Fewest Penalties
11 Miami, 1968, 1976-84, 1986
9 Pittsburgh, 1946-47, 1950-52, 1954, 1963, 1965, 1968
5 Green Bay, 1955-56, 1966-67, 1974

Most Consecutive Seasons Leading League, Fewest Penalties
9 Miami, 1976-84
3 Pittsburgh, 1950-52
2 By many teams

Most Seasons Leading League, Most Penalties
16 Chi. Bears, 1941-44, 1946-49, 1951, 1959-61, 1963, 1965, 1968, 1976
7 Oakland/L.A. Raiders, 1963, 1966, 1968-69, 1975, 1982, 1984
6 L.A. Rams, 1950, 1952, 1962, 1969, 1978, 1980

Most Consecutive Seasons Leading League, Most Penalties
4 Chi. Bears, 1941-44, 1946-49
3 Chi. Cardinals, 1954-56
Chi. Bears, 1959-61

Fewest Penalties, Season
19 Detroit, 1937
21 Boston, 1935
24 Philadelphia, 1936

Most Penalties, Season
144 Buffalo, 1983
143 L.A. Raiders, 1984
138 Detroit, 1984

Fewest Penalties, Game
0 By many teams. Last time: New Orleans vs. Seattle, Nov. 10, 1985

Most Penalties, Game
22 Brooklyn vs. Green Bay, Sept. 17, 1944
Chi. Bears vs. Philadelphia, Nov. 26, 1944
21 Cleveland vs. Chi. Bears, Nov. 25, 1951
20 Tampa Bay vs. Seattle, Oct. 17, 1976

Fewest Penalties, Both Teams, Game
0 Brooklyn vs. Pittsburgh, Oct. 28, 1934
Brooklyn vs. Boston, Sept. 28, 1936
Cleveland vs. Chi. Bears, Oct. 9, 1938
Pittsburgh vs. Philadelphia, Nov. 10, 1940

Most Penalties, Both Teams, Game
37 Cleveland (21) vs. Chi. Bears (16), Nov. 25, 1951
35 Tampa Bay (20) vs. Seattle (15), Oct. 17, 1976
33 Brooklyn (22) vs. Green Bay (11), Sept. 17, 1944

Yards Penalized

Most Seasons Leading League, Fewest Yards Penalized
11 Miami, 1967-68, 1973, 1977-84
8 Boston/Washington, 1935, 1953-54, 1956-58, 1970, 1985
7 Pittsburgh, 1946-47, 1950, 1952, 1962, 1965, 1968

Most Consecutive Seasons Leading League, Fewest Yards Penalized
8 Miami, 1977-84
3 Washington, 1956-58
Boston, 1964-66
2 By many teams

Most Seasons Leading League, Most Yards Penalized
15 Chi. Bears, 1935, 1937, 1939-44, 1946-47, 1949, 1951, 1961-62, 1968
7 Oakland/L.A. Raiders, 1963-64, 1968-69, 1975, 1982, 1984
6 Buffalo, 1962, 1967, 1970, 1972, 1981, 1983

Most Consecutive Seasons Leading League, Most Yards Penalized
6 Chi. Bears, 1939-44
3 Cleveland, 1976-78
2 By many teams

Fewest Yards Penalized, Season
139 Detroit, 1937
146 Philadelphia, 1937
159 Philadelphia, 1936

Most Yards Penalized, Season
1,274 Oakland, 1969
1,239 Baltimore, 1979
1,209 L.A. Raiders, 1984

Fewest Yards Penalized, Game
0 By many teams. Last time: New Orleans vs. Seattle, Nov. 10, 1985

Most Yards Penalized, Game
209 Cleveland vs. Chi. Bears, Nov. 25, 1951
190 Tampa Bay vs. Seattle, Oct. 17, 1976
189 Houston vs. Buffalo, Oct. 31, 1965

Fewest Yards Penalized, Both Teams, Game
0 Brooklyn vs. Pittsburgh, Oct. 28, 1934
Brooklyn vs. Boston, Sept. 28, 1936
Cleveland vs. Chi. Bears, Oct. 9, 1938
Pittsburgh vs. Philadelphia, Nov. 10, 1940

Most Yards Penalized, Both Teams, Game
374 Cleveland (209) vs. Chi. Bears (165), Nov. 25, 1951
310 Tampa Bay (190) vs. Seattle (120), Oct. 17, 1976
309 Green Bay (184) vs. Boston (125), Oct. 21, 1945

Defense

Scoring

Most Seasons Leading League, Fewest Points Allowed
8 N.Y. Giants, 1935, 1938-39, 1941, 1944, 1958-59, 1961
Chi. Bears, 1932, 1936-37, 1942, 1948, 1963, 1985-86
6 Cleveland, 1951, 1953-57
5 Green Bay, 1935, 1947, 1962, 1965-66

Most Consecutive Seasons Leading League, Fewest Points Allowed
5 Cleveland, 1953-57
3 Buffalo, 1964-66
Minnesota, 1969-71
2 By many teams

Fewest Points Allowed, Season (Since 1932)
44 Chi. Bears, 1932
54 Brooklyn, 1933
59 Detroit, 1934

Most Points Allowed, Season
533 Baltimore, 1981
501 N.Y. Giants, 1966
487 New Orleans, 1980

Fewest Touchdowns Allowed, Season (Since 1932)
6 Chi. Bears, 1932
Brooklyn, 1933
7 Detroit, 1934
8 Green Bay, 1932

Most Touchdowns Allowed, Season
68 Baltimore, 1981
66 N.Y. Giants, 1966
63 Baltimore, 1950

First Downs

Fewest First Downs Allowed Season
77 Detroit, 1935
79 Boston, 1935
82 Washington, 1937

Most First Downs Allowed, Season
406 Baltimore, 1981
371 Seattle, 1981
366 Green Bay, 1983

Fewest First Downs Allowed, Rushing, Season
35 Chi. Bears, 1942
40 Green Bay, 1939
41 Brooklyn, 1944

Most First Downs Allowed, Rushing, Season
179 Detroit, 1985
178 New Orleans, 1980
175 Seattle, 1981
Fewest First Downs Allowed, Passing, Season
33 Chi. Bears, 1943
34 Pittsburgh, 1941
Washington, 1943
35 Detroit, 1940
Philadelphia, 1940, 1944
Most First Downs Allowed, Passing, Season
218 San Diego, 1985
216 San Diego, 1981
N.Y. Jets, 1986
214 Baltimore, 1981
Fewest First Downs Allowed, Penalty, Season
1 Boston, 1944
3 Philadelphia, 1940
Pittsburgh, 1945
Washington, 1957
4 Cleveland, 1940
Green Bay, 1943
N.Y. Giants, 1943
Most First Downs Allowed, Penalty, Season
48 Houston, 1985
46 Houston, 1986
43 L.A. Raiders, 1984

Net Yards Allowed Rushing and Passing
Most Seasons Leading League, Fewest Yards Allowed
8 Chi. Bears, 1942-43, 1948, 1958, 1963, 1984-86
6 N.Y. Giants, 1938, 1940-41, 1951, 1956, 1959
5 Boston/Washington, 1935-37, 1939, 1946
Philadelphia, 1944-45, 1949, 1953, 1981
Most Consecutive Seasons Leading League, Fewest Yards Allowed
3 Boston/Washington, 1935-37
Chicago, 1984-86
2 By many teams
Fewest Yards Allowed, Season
1,539 Chi. Cardinals, 1934
1,703 Chi. Bears, 1942
1,789 Brooklyn, 1933
Most Yards Allowed, Season
6,793 Baltimore, 1981
6,403 Green Bay, 1983
6,352 Minnesota, 1984

Rushing
Most Seasons Leading League, Fewest Yards Allowed
8 Chi. Bears, 1937, 1939, 1942, 1946, 1949, 1963, 1984-85
7 Detroit, 1938, 1950, 1952, 1962, 1970, 1980-81
6 Dallas, 1966-69, 1972, 1978
Most Consecutive Seasons Leading League, Fewest Yards Allowed
4 Dallas, 1966-69
2 By many teams
Fewest Yards Allowed, Rushing, Season
519 Chi. Bears, 1942
558 Philadelphia, 1944
762 Pittsburgh, 1982
Most Yards Allowed, Rushing, Season
3,228 Buffalo, 1978
3,106 New Orleans, 1980
3,010 Baltimore, 1978
Fewest Touchdowns Allowed, Rushing, Season
2 Detroit, 1934
Dallas, 1968
Minnesota, 1971
3 By many teams
Most Touchdowns Allowed, Rushing, Season
36 Oakland, 1961
31 N.Y. Giants, 1980
Tampa Bay, 1986
30 Baltimore, 1981

Passing
Most Seasons Leading League, Fewest Yards Allowed
8 Green Bay, 1947-48, 1962, 1964-68
7 Washington, 1939, 1942, 1945, 1952-53, 1980, 1985
6 Chi. Bears, 1938, 1943-44, 1958, 1960, 1963
Most Consecutive Seasons Leading League, Fewest Yards Allowed
5 Green Bay, 1964-68
2 By many teams
Fewest Yards Allowed, Passing, Season
545 Philadelphia, 1934
558 Portsmouth, 1933
585 Chi. Cardinals, 1934
Most Yards Allowed, Passing, Season
4,389 N.Y. Jets, 1986
4,311 San Diego, 1981
4,293 San Diego, 1985
Fewest Touchdowns Allowed, Passing, Season
1 Portsmouth, 1932
Philadelphia, 1934
2 Brooklyn, 1933
Chi. Bears, 1934
3 Chi. Bears, 1932, 1936
Green Bay, 1932, 1934
N.Y. Giants, 1939, 1944
Most Touchdowns Allowed, Passing, Season
40 Denver, 1963
38 St. Louis, 1969
37 Washington, 1961
Baltimore, 1981

Sacks
Most Seasons Leading League
5 Oakland/L.A. Raiders, 1966-68, 1982, 1986
4 Boston/New England, 1961, 1963, 1977, 1979
Dallas, 1966, 1968-69, 1978
3 Dallas/Kansas City, 1960, 1965, 1969
San Francisco, 1967, 1972, 1976
Most Consecutive Seasons Leading League
3 Oakland, 1966-68
2 Dallas, 1968-69
Most Sacks, Season
72 Chicago, 1984
68 N.Y. Giants, 1985
67 Oakland, 1967
Fewest Sacks, Season
11 Baltimore, 1982
12 Buffalo, 1982
13 Baltimore, 1981
Most Sacks, Game
12 Dallas vs. Pittsburgh, Nov. 20, 1966; vs. Houston, Sept. 29, 1985
St. Louis vs. Baltimore, Oct. 26, 1980
Chicago vs. Detroit, Dec. 16, 1984
11 N.Y. Giants vs. St. Louis, Nov. 1, 1964
Baltimore vs. Los Angeles, Nov. 22, 1964
Buffalo vs. Denver, Dec. 13, 1964
Detroit vs. Green Bay, Nov. 7, 1965; vs. Philadelphia, Nov. 16, 1986
Oakland vs. Buffalo, Oct. 15, 1967; vs. Denver, Nov. 5, 1967
St. Louis vs. Atlanta, Nov. 24, 1968; vs. Philadelphia, Dec. 18, 1983
Dallas vs. Detroit, Oct. 6, 1975
Kansas City vs. Cleveland, Sept. 30, 1984
Chicago vs. Minnesota, Oct. 28, 1984
Cleveland vs. Atlanta, Nov. 18, 1984
San Diego vs. Dallas, Nov. 16, 1986
L.A. Raiders vs. Philadelphia, Nov. 30, 1986 (OT)
Seattle vs. L.A. Raiders, Dec. 8, 1986
10 By many teams
Most Opponents Yards Lost Attempting to Pass, Season
666 Oakland, 1967
583 Chicago, 1984
573 San Francisco, 1976
Fewest Opponents Yards Lost Attempting to Pass, Season
75 Green Bay, 1956
77 N.Y. Bulldogs, 1949
78 Green Bay, 1958

Interceptions By
Most Seasons Leading League
9 N.Y. Giants, 1933, 1937-39, 1944, 1948, 1951, 1954, 1961
8 Green Bay, 1940, 1942-43, 1947, 1955, 1957, 1962, 1965
7 Chi. Bears, 1935-36, 1941-42, 1946, 1963, 1985
Most Consecutive Seasons Leading League
5 Kansas City, 1966-70
3 N.Y. Giants, 1937-39
2 By many teams
Most Passes Intercepted By, Season
49 San Diego, 1961
42 Green Bay, 1943
41 N.Y. Giants, 1951
Fewest Passes Intercepted By, Season
3 Houston, 1982
5 Baltimore, 1982
6 Houston, 1972
St. Louis, 1982
Most Passes Intercepted By, Game
9 Green Bay vs. Detroit, Oct. 24, 1943
Philadelphia vs. Pittsburgh, Dec. 12, 1965
8 N.Y. Giants vs. Green Bay, Nov. 21, 1948; vs. N.Y. Yanks, Dec. 16, 1951
Philadelphia vs. Chi. Cardinals, Sept. 24, 1950
Houston vs. Denver, Dec. 2, 1962
Detroit vs. Chicago, Sept. 22, 1968
N.Y. Jets vs. Baltimore, Sept. 23, 1973
7 By many teams. Last time: New Orleans vs. Green Bay, Sept. 14, 1986
Most Consecutive Games, One or More Interceptions By
46 L.A. Chargers/San Diego, 1960-63
37 Detroit, 1960-63
36 Boston, 1944-47
Washington, 1962-65
Most Yards Returning Interceptions, Season
929 San Diego, 1961
712 Los Angeles, 1952
697 Seattle, 1984
Fewest Yards Returning Interceptions, Season
5 Los Angeles, 1959
42 Philadelphia, 1982
47 Houston, 1982
Most Yards Returning Interceptions, Game
325 Seattle vs. Kansas City, Nov. 4, 1984
314 Los Angeles vs. San Francisco, Oct. 18, 1964
245 Houston vs. N.Y. Jets, Oct. 15, 1967
Most Touchdowns, Returning Interceptions, Season
9 San Diego, 1961
7 Seattle, 1984
6 Cleveland, 1960
Green Bay, 1966
Detroit, 1967
Houston, 1967
Most Touchdowns Returning Interceptions, Game
4 Seattle vs. Kansas City, Nov. 4, 1984
3 Baltimore vs. Green Bay, Nov. 5, 1950
Cleveland vs. Chicago, Dec. 11, 1960

Philadelphia vs. Pittsburgh, Dec. 12, 1965
Baltimore vs. Pittsburgh, Sept. 29, 1968
Buffalo vs. N.Y. Jets, Sept. 29, 1968
Houston vs. San Diego, Dec. 19, 1971
Cincinnati vs. Houston, Dec. 17, 1972
Tampa Bay vs. New Orleans, Dec. 11, 1977
2 By many teams

Most Touchdowns Returning Interceptions, Both Teams, Game
4 Philadelphia (3) vs. Pittsburgh (1), Dec. 12, 1965
Seattle (4) vs. Kansas City (0), Nov. 4, 1984
3 Los Angeles (2) vs. Detroit (1), Nov. 1, 1953
Cleveland (2) vs. N.Y. Giants (1), Dec. 18, 1960
Pittsburgh (2) vs. Cincinnati (1), Oct. 10, 1983
Kansas City (2) vs. San Diego (1), Oct. 19, 1986
(Also see previous record)

Punt Returns

Fewest Opponents Punt Returns, Season
7 Washington, 1962
San Diego, 1982
10 Buffalo, 1982
11 Boston, 1962

Most Opponents Punt Returns, Season
71 Tampa Bay, 1976, 1977
69 N.Y. Giants, 1953
68 Cleveland, 1974

Fewest Yards Allowed, Punt Returns, Season
22 Green Bay, 1967
34 Washington, 1962
39 Cleveland, 1959
Washington, 1972

Most Yards Allowed, Punt Returns, Season
932 Green Bay, 1949
913 Boston, 1947
906 New Orleans, 1974

Lowest Average Allowed, Punt Returns, Season
1.20 Chi. Cardinals, 1954 (46-55)
1.22 Cleveland, 1959 (32-39)
1.55 Chi. Cardinals, 1953 (44-68)

Highest Average Allowed, Punt Returns, Season
18.6 Green Bay, 1949 (50-932)
18.0 Cleveland, 1977 (31-558)
17.9 Boston, 1960 (20-357)

Most Touchdowns Allowed, Punt Returns, Season
4 N.Y. Giants, 1959
3 Green Bay, 1949
Chi. Cardinals, 1951
Los Angeles, 1951
Washington, 1952
Dallas, 1952
Pittsburgh, 1959
N.Y. Jets, 1968
Cleveland, 1977
Atlanta, 1986
Tampa Bay, 1986
2 By many teams

Kickoff Returns

Fewest Opponents Kickoff Returns, Season
10 Brooklyn, 1943
15 Detroit, 1942
Brooklyn, 1944
18 Cleveland, 1941
Boston, 1944

Most Opponents Kickoff Returns, Season
91 Washington, 1983
89 New England, 1980
88 San Diego, 1981

Fewest Yards Allowed, Kickoff Returns, Season
225 Brooklyn, 1943
293 Brooklyn, 1944
361 Seattle, 1982

Most Yards Allowed, Kickoff Returns, Season
2,045 Kansas City, 1966
1,827 Chicago, 1985
1,816 N.Y. Giants, 1963

Lowest Average Allowed, Kickoff Returns, Season
14.3 Cleveland, 1980 (71-1,018)
15.0 Seattle, 1982 (24-361)
15.8 Oakland, 1977 (63-997)

Highest Average Allowed, Kickoff Returns, Season
29.5 N.Y. Jets, 1972 (47-1,386)
29.4 Los Angeles, 1950 (48-1,411)
29.1 New England, 1971 (49-1,427)

Most Touchdowns Allowed, Kickoff Returns, Season
3 Minnesota, 1963, 1970
Dallas, 1966
Detroit, 1980
Pittsburgh, 1986
2 By many teams

Fumbles

Fewest Opponents Fumbles, Season
11 Cleveland, 1956
Baltimore, 1982
13 Los Angeles, 1956
Chicago, 1960
Cleveland, 1963, 1965
Detroit, 1967
San Diego, 1969
14 Baltimore, 1970
Oakland, 1975
Buffalo, 1982
St. Louis, 1982
San Francisco, 1982

Most Opponents Fumbles, Season
50 Minnesota, 1963
San Francisco, 1978
48 N.Y. Giants, 1980
N.Y. Jets, 1986
47 N.Y. Giants, 1977
Seattle, 1984

Turnovers

(Number of times losing the ball on interceptions and fumbles.)

Fewest Opponents Turnovers, Season
11 Baltimore, 1982
13 San Francisco, 1982
15 St. Louis, 1982

Most Opponents Turnovers, Season
66 San Diego, 1961
63 Seattle, 1984
61 Washington, 1983

Most Opponents Turnovers, Game
12 Chi. Bears vs. Detroit, Nov. 22, 1942
Philadelphia vs. Chi. Cardinals, Sept. 24, 1950; vs. Pittsburgh, Dec. 12, 1965
11 Green Bay vs. San Diego, Sept. 24, 1978
10 N.Y. Giants vs. Washington, Dec. 4, 1938; vs. Chi. Cardinals, Nov. 2, 1952; vs. Washington, Dec. 8, 1963
Green Bay vs. Pittsburgh, Nov. 23, 1941; vs. Detroit, Oct. 24, 1943; vs. Chi. Cardinals, Nov. 10, 1946
Detroit vs. Minnesota, Dec. 9, 1962; vs. Chicago, Sept. 22, 1968
Oakland vs. Houston, Sept. 7, 1963
Washington vs. St. Louis, Oct. 25, 1976
New England vs. N.Y. Jets, Nov. 21, 1976
Dallas vs. San Francisco, Oct. 12, 1980
Seattle vs. Cleveland, Dec. 20, 1981
Denver vs. Detroit, Oct. 7, 1984

OUTSTANDING PERFORMERS

1,000 Yards Rushing in a Season

Year	Player, Team	Att.	Yards	Avg.	Long	TD
1986	Eric Dickerson, L.A. Rams[4]	404	1,821	4.5	42	11
	Joe Morris, N.Y. Giants[2]	341	1,516	4.4	54	14
	Curt Warner, Seattle[3]	319	1,481	4.6	60	13
	*Rueben Mayes, New Orleans	286	1,353	4.7	50	8
	Walter Payton, Chicago[10]	321	1,333	4.2	41	8
	Gerald Riggs, Atlanta[3]	343	1,327	3.9	31	9
	George Rogers, Washington[4]	303	1,203	4.0	42	18
	James Brooks, Cincinnati	205	1,087	5.3	56	5
1985	Marcus Allen, L.A. Raiders[3]	390	1,759	4.6	61	11
	Gerald Riggs, Atlanta[2]	397	1,719	4.3	50	10
	Walter Payton, Chicago[9]	324	1,551	4.8	40	9
	Joe Morris, N.Y. Giants	294	1,336	4.5	65	21
	Freeman McNeil, N.Y. Jets[2]	294	1,331	4.5	69	3
	Tony Dorsett, Dallas[8]	305	1,307	4.3	60	7
	James Wilder, Tampa Bay[2]	365	1,300	3.6	28	10
	Eric Dickerson, L.A. Rams[3]	292	1,234	4.2	43	12
	Craig James, New England	263	1,227	4.7	65	5
	*Kevin Mack, Cleveland	222	1,104	5.0	61	7
	Curt Warner, Seattle[2]	291	1,094	3.8	38	8
	George Rogers, Washington[3]	231	1,093	4.7	35	7
	Roger Craig, San Francisco	214	1,050	4.9	62	9
	Earnest Jackson, Philadelphia[2]	282	1,028	3.6	59	5
	Stump Mitchell, St. Louis	183	1,006	5.5	64	7
	Earnest Byner, Cleveland	244	1,002	4.1	36	8
1984	Eric Dickerson, L.A. Rams[2]	379	2,105	5.6	66	14
	Walter Payton, Chicago[8]	381	1,684	4.4	72	11
	James Wilder, Tampa Bay	407	1,544	3.8	37	13
	Gerald Riggs, Atlanta	353	1,486	4.2	57	13
	Wendell Tyler, San Francisco[3]	246	1,262	5.1	40	7
	John Riggins, Washington[5]	327	1,239	3.8	24	14
	Tony Dorsett, Dallas[7]	302	1,189	3.9	31	6
	Earnest Jackson, San Diego	296	1,179	4.0	32	8
	Ottis Anderson, St. Louis[5]	289	1,174	4.1	24	6
	Marcus Allen, L.A. Raiders[2]	275	1,168	4.2	52	13
	Sammy Winder, Denver	296	1,153	3.9	24	4
	*Greg Bell, Buffalo	262	1,100	4.2	85	7
	Freeman McNeil, N.Y. Jets	229	1,070	4.7	53	5
1983	*Eric Dickerson, L.A. Rams	390	1,808	4.6	85	18
	William Andrews, Atlanta[4]	331	1,567	4.7	27	7
	*Curt Warner, Seattle	335	1,449	4.3	60	13
	Walter Payton, Chicago[7]	314	1,421	4.5	49	6
	John Riggins, Washington[4]	375	1,347	3.6	44	24
	Tony Dorsett, Dallas[6]	289	1,321	4.6	77	8
	Earl Campbell, Houston[5]	322	1,301	4.0	42	12
	Ottis Anderson, St. Louis[4]	296	1,270	4.3	43	5
	Mike Pruitt, Cleveland[4]	293	1,184	4.0	27	10
	George Rogers, New Orleans[2]	256	1,144	4.5	76	5
	Joe Cribbs, Buffalo[3]	263	1,131	4.3	45	3
	Curtis Dickey, Baltimore	254	1,122	4.4	56	4
	Tony Collins, New England	219	1,049	4.8	50	10
	Billy Sims, Detroit[3]	220	1,040	4.7	41	7
	Marcus Allen, L.A. Raiders	266	1,014	3.8	19	9
	Franco Harris, Pittsburgh[8]	279	1,007	3.6	19	5
1981	*George Rogers, New Orleans	378	1,674	4.4	79	13
	Tony Dorsett, Dallas[5]	342	1,646	4.8	75	4
	Billy Sims, Detroit[2]	296	1,437	4.9	51	13
	Wilbert Montgomery, Philadelphia[3]	286	1,402	4.9	41	8
	Ottis Anderson, St. Louis[3]	328	1,376	4.2	28	9
	Earl Campbell, Houston[4]	361	1,376	3.8	43	10
	William Andrews, Atlanta[3]	289	1,301	4.5	29	10
	Walter Payton, Chicago[6]	339	1,222	3.6	39	6
	Chuck Muncie, San Diego[2]	251	1,144	4.6	73	19
	*Joe Delaney, Kansas City	234	1,121	4.8	82	3
	Mike Pruitt, Cleveland[3]	247	1,103	4.5	21	7
	Joe Cribbs, Buffalo[2]	257	1,097	4.3	35	3
	Pete Johnson, Cincinnati	274	1,077	3.9	39	12
	Wendell Tyler, Los Angeles[2]	260	1,074	4.1	69	12
	Ted Brown, Minnesota	274	1,063	3.9	34	6
1980	Earl Campbell, Houston[3]	373	1,934	5.2	55	13
	Walter Payton, Chicago[5]	317	1,460	4.6	69	6
	Ottis Anderson, St. Louis[2]	301	1,352	4.5	52	9
	William Andrews, Atlanta[2]	265	1,308	4.9	33	4
	*Billy Sims, Detroit	313	1,303	4.2	52	13
	Tony Dorsett, Dallas[4]	278	1,185	4.3	56	11
	*Joe Cribbs, Buffalo	306	1,185	3.9	48	11
	Mike Pruitt, Cleveland[2]	249	1,034	4.2	56	6
1979	Earl Campbell, Houston[2]	368	1,697	4.6	61	19
	Walter Payton, Chicago[4]	369	1,610	4.4	43	14
	*Ottis Anderson, St. Louis	331	1,605	4.8	76	8
	Wilbert Montgomery, Philadelphia[2]	338	1,512	4.5	62	9
	Mike Pruitt, Cleveland	264	1,294	4.9	77	9
	Ricky Bell, Tampa Bay	283	1,263	4.5	49	7
	Chuck Muncie, New Orleans	238	1,198	5.0	69	11
	Franco Harris, Pittsburgh[7]	267	1,186	4.4	71	11
	John Riggins, Washington[3]	260	1,153	4.4	66	9
	Wendell Tyler, Los Angeles	218	1,109	5.1	63	9
	Tony Dorsett, Dallas[3]	250	1,107	4.4	41	6
	*William Andrews, Atlanta	239	1,023	4.3	23	3
1978	*Earl Campbell, Houston	302	1,450	4.8	81	13
	Walter Payton, Chicago[3]	333	1,395	4.2	76	11
	Tony Dorsett, Dallas[2]	290	1,325	4.6	63	7
	Delvin Williams, Miami[2]	272	1,258	4.6	58	8
	Wilbert Montgomery, Philadelphia	259	1,220	4.7	47	9
	Terdell Middleton, Green Bay	284	1,116	3.9	76	11
	Franco Harris, Pittsburgh[6]	310	1,082	3.5	37	8
	Mark van Eeghen, Oakland[3]	270	1,080	4.0	34	9
	*Terry Miller, Buffalo	238	1,060	4.5	60	7
	Tony Reed, Kansas City	206	1,053	5.1	62	5
	John Riggins, Washington[2]	248	1,014	4.1	31	5
1977	Walter Payton, Chicago[2]	339	1,852	5.5	73	14
	Mark van Eeghen, Oakland[2]	324	1,273	3.9	27	7
	Lawrence McCutcheon, Los Angeles[4]	294	1,238	4.2	48	7
	Franco Harris, Pittsburgh[5]	300	1,162	3.9	61	11
	Lydell Mitchell, Baltimore[3]	301	1,159	3.9	64	3
	Chuck Foreman, Minnesota[3]	270	1,112	4.1	51	6
	Greg Pruitt, Cleveland[3]	236	1,086	4.6	78	3
	Sam Cunningham, New England	270	1,015	3.8	31	4
	*Tony Dorsett, Dallas	208	1,007	4.8	84	12
1976	O.J. Simpson, Buffalo[5]	290	1,503	5.2	75	8
	Walter Payton, Chicago	311	1,390	4.5	60	13
	Delvin Williams, San Francisco	248	1,203	4.9	80	7
	Lydell Mitchell, Baltimore[2]	289	1,200	4.2	43	5
	Lawrence McCutcheon, Los Angeles[3]	291	1,168	4.0	40	9
	Chuck Foreman, Minnesota[2]	278	1,155	4.2	46	13
	Franco Harris, Pittsburgh[4]	289	1,128	3.9	30	14
	Mike Thomas, Washington	254	1,101	4.3	28	5
	Rocky Bleier, Pittsburgh	220	1,036	4.7	28	5
	Mark van Eeghen, Oakland	233	1,012	4.3	21	3
	Otis Armstrong, Denver[2]	247	1,008	4.1	31	5
	Greg Pruitt, Cleveland[2]	209	1,000	4.8	64	4
1975	O.J. Simpson, Buffalo[4]	329	1,817	5.5	88	16
	Franco Harris, Pittsburgh[3]	262	1,246	4.8	36	10
	Lydell Mitchell, Baltimore	289	1,193	4.1	70	11
	Jim Otis, St. Louis	269	1,076	4.0	30	5
	Chuck Foreman, Minnesota	280	1,070	3.8	31	13
	Greg Pruitt, Cleveland	217	1,067	4.9	50	8
	John Riggins, N.Y. Jets	238	1,005	4.2	42	8
	Dave Hampton, Atlanta	250	1,002	4.0	22	5
1974	Otis Armstrong, Denver	263	1,407	5.3	43	9
	*Don Woods, San Diego	227	1,162	5.1	56	7
	O.J. Simpson, Buffalo[3]	270	1,125	4.2	41	3
	Lawrence McCutcheon, Los Angeles[2]	236	1,109	4.7	23	3
	Franco Harris, Pittsburgh[2]	208	1,006	4.8	54	5
1973	O.J. Simpson, Buffalo[2]	332	2,003	6.0	80	12
	John Brockington, Green Bay[3]	265	1,144	4.3	53	3
	Calvin Hill, Dallas[2]	273	1,142	4.2	21	6
	Lawrence McCutcheon, Los Angeles	210	1,097	5.2	37	2
	Larry Csonka, Miami[3]	219	1,003	4.6	25	5
1972	O.J. Simpson, Buffalo	292	1,251	4.3	94	6
	Larry Brown, Washington[2]	285	1,216	4.3	38	8
	Ron Johnson, N.Y. Giants[2]	298	1,182	4.0	35	9
	Larry Csonka, Miami[2]	213	1,117	5.2	45	6
	Marv Hubbard, Oakland	219	1,100	5.0	39	4
	*Franco Harris, Pittsburgh	188	1,055	5.6	75	10
	Calvin Hill, Dallas	245	1,036	4.2	26	6
	Mike Garrett, San Diego[2]	272	1,031	3.8	41	6
	John Brockington, Green Bay[2]	274	1,027	3.7	30	8
	Eugene (Mercury) Morris, Miami	190	1,000	5.3	33	12
1971	Floyd Little, Denver	284	1,133	4.0	40	6
	*John Brockington, Green Bay	216	1,105	5.1	52	4
	Larry Csonka, Miami	195	1,051	5.4	28	7
	Steve Owens, Detroit	246	1,035	4.2	23	8
	Willie Ellison, Los Angeles	211	1,000	4.7	80	4
1970	Larry Brown, Washington	237	1,125	4.7	75	5
	Ron Johnson, N.Y. Giants	263	1,027	3.9	68	8
1969	Gale Sayers, Chicago[2]	236	1,032	4.4	28	8
1968	Leroy Kelly, Cleveland[3]	248	1,239	5.0	65	16
	*Paul Robinson, Cincinnati	238	1,023	4.3	87	8
1967	Jim Nance, Boston[2]	269	1,216	4.5	53	7
	Leroy Kelly, Cleveland[2]	235	1,205	5.1	42	11
	Hoyle Granger, Houston	236	1,194	5.1	67	6
	Mike Garrett, Kansas City	236	1,087	4.6	58	9
1966	Jim Nance, Boston	299	1,458	4.9	65	11
	Gale Sayers, Chicago	229	1,231	5.4	58	8
	Leroy Kelly, Cleveland	209	1,141	5.5	70	15
	Dick Bass, Los Angeles[2]	248	1,090	4.4	50	8
1965	Jim Brown, Cleveland[7]	289	1,544	5.3	67	17
	Paul Lowe, San Diego[2]	222	1,121	5.0	59	7
1964	Jim Brown, Cleveland[6]	280	1,446	5.2	71	7
	Jim Taylor, Green Bay[5]	235	1,169	5.0	84	12
	John Henry Johnson, Pittsburgh[2]	235	1,048	4.5	45	7
1963	Jim Brown, Cleveland[5]	291	1,863	6.4	80	12
	Clem Daniels, Oakland	215	1,099	5.1	74	3
	Jim Taylor, Green Bay[4]	248	1,018	4.1	40	9
	Paul Lowe, San Diego	177	1,010	5.7	66	8
1962	Jim Taylor, Green Bay[3]	272	1,474	5.4	51	19
	John Henry Johnson, Pittsburgh	251	1,141	4.5	40	7
	*Cookie Gilchrist, Buffalo	214	1,096	5.1	44	13
	Abner Haynes, Dall. Texans	221	1,049	4.7	71	13
	Dick Bass, Los Angeles	196	1,033	5.3	57	6
	Charlie Tolar, Houston	244	1,012	4.1	25	7
1961	Jim Brown, Cleveland[4]	305	1,408	4.6	38	8
	Jim Taylor, Green Bay[2]	243	1,307	5.4	53	15
1960	Jim Brown, Cleveland[3]	215	1,257	5.8	71	9
	Jim Taylor, Green Bay	230	1,101	4.8	32	11
	John David Crow, St. Louis	183	1,071	5.9	57	6
1959	Jim Brown, Cleveland[2]	290	1,329	4.6	70	14
	J. D. Smith, San Francisco	207	1,036	5.0	73	10
1958	Jim Brown, Cleveland	257	1,527	5.9	65	17
1956	Rick Casares, Chi. Bears	234	1,126	4.8	68	12
1954	Joe Perry, San Francisco[2]	173	1,049	6.1	58	8
1953	Joe Perry, San Francisco	192	1,018	5.3	51	10
1949	Steve Van Buren, Philadelphia[2]	263	1,146	4.4	41	11
	Tony Canadeo, Green Bay	208	1,052	5.1	54	4

1947	Steve Van Buren, Philadelphia	217	1,008	4.6	45	13
1934	*Beattie Feathers, Chi. Bears	101	1,004	9.9	82	8

**First year in the league.*

200 Yards Rushing in a Game

Date	Player, Team, Opponent	Att.	Yards	TD
Dec. 7, 1986	Rueben Mayes, New Orleans vs. Miami	28	203	2
Oct. 5, 1986	Eric Dickerson, L.A. Rams vs. Tampa Bay (OT)	30	207	2
Dec. 21, 1985	George Rogers, Washington vs. St. Louis	34	206	1
Dec. 21, 1985	Joe Morris, N.Y. Giants vs. Pittsburgh	36	202	3
Dec. 9, 1984	Eric Dickerson, L.A. Rams vs. Houston	27	215	2
Nov. 18, 1984	*Greg Bell, Buffalo vs. Dallas	27	206	1
Nov. 4, 1984	Eric Dickerson, L.A. Rams vs. St. Louis	21	208	0
Sept. 2, 1984	Gerald Riggs, Atlanta vs. New Orleans	35	202	2
Nov. 27, 1983	*Curt Warner, Seattle vs. Kansas City (OT)	32	207	3
Nov. 6, 1983	James Wilder, Tampa Bay vs. Minnesota	31	219	1
Sept. 18, 1983	Tony Collins, New England vs. N.Y. Jets	23	212	3
Sept. 4, 1983	George Rogers, New Orleans vs. St. Louis	24	206	2
Dec. 21, 1980	Earl Campbell, Houston vs. Minnesota	29	203	1
Nov. 16, 1980	Earl Campbell, Houston vs. Chicago	31	206	0
Oct. 26, 1980	Earl Campbell, Houston vs. Cincinnati	27	202	2
Oct. 19, 1980	Earl Campbell, Houston vs. Tampa Bay	33	203	0
Nov. 26, 1978	*Terry Miller, Buffalo vs. N.Y. Giants	21	208	2
Dec. 4, 1977	*Tony Dorsett, Dallas vs. Philadelphia	23	206	2
Nov. 20, 1977	Walter Payton, Chicago vs. Minnesota	40	275	1
Oct. 30, 1977	Walter Payton, Chicago vs. Green Bay	23	205	2
Dec. 5, 1976	O. J. Simpson, Buffalo vs. Miami	24	203	1
Nov. 25, 1976	O. J. Simpson, Buffalo vs. Detroit	29	273	2
Oct. 24, 1976	Chuck Foreman, Minnesota vs. Philadelphia	28	200	2
Dec. 14, 1975	Greg Pruitt, Cleveland vs. Kansas City	26	214	3
Sept. 28, 1975	O. J. Simpson, Buffalo vs. Pittsburgh	28	227	1
Dec. 16, 1973	O. J. Simpson, Buffalo vs. N.Y. Jets	34	200	1
Dec. 9, 1973	O. J. Simpson, Buffalo vs. New England	22	219	1
Sept. 16, 1973	O. J. Simpson, Buffalo vs. New England	29	250	2
Dec. 5, 1971	Willie Ellison, Los Angeles vs. New Orleans	26	247	1
Dec. 20, 1970	John (Frenchy) Fuqua, Pittsburgh vs. Philadelphia	20	218	2
Nov. 3, 1968	Gale Sayers, Chicago vs. Green Bay	24	205	0
Oct. 30, 1966	Jim Nance, Boston vs. Oakland	38	208	2
Oct. 10, 1964	John Henry Johnson, Pittsburgh vs. Cleveland	30	200	3
Dec. 8, 1963	Cookie Gilchrist, Buffalo vs. N.Y. Jets	36	243	5
Nov. 3, 1963	Jim Brown, Cleveland vs. Philadelphia	28	223	1
Oct. 20, 1963	Clem Daniels, Oakland vs. N.Y. Jets	27	200	2
Sept. 22, 1963	Jim Brown, Cleveland vs. Dallas	20	232	2
Dec. 10, 1961	Billy Cannon, Houston vs. N.Y. Titans	25	216	3
Nov. 19, 1961	Jim Brown, Cleveland vs. Philadelphia	34	237	4
Dec. 18, 1960	John David Crow, St. Louis vs. Pittsburgh	24	203	0
Nov. 15, 1959	Bobby Mitchell, Cleveland vs. Washington	14	232	3
Nov. 24, 1957	*Jim Brown, Cleveland vs. Los Angeles	31	237	4
Dec. 16, 1956	*Tom Wilson, Los Angeles vs. Green Bay	23	223	0
Nov. 22, 1953	Dan Towler, Los Angeles vs. Baltimore	14	205	1
Nov. 12, 1950	Gene Roberts, N.Y. Giants vs. Chi. Cardinals	26	218	2
Nov. 27, 1949	Steve Van Buren, Philadelphia vs. Pittsburgh	27	205	0
Oct. 8, 1933	Cliff Battles, Boston vs. N.Y. Giants	16	215	1

**First year in the league.*

Times 200 or More
47 times by 32 players . . . Simpson 6; Brown, Campbell 4; Dickerson 3; Payton, Rogers 2.

4,000 Yards Passing in a Season

Year	Player, Team	Att.	Comp.	Pct.	Yards	TD	Int.
1986	Dan Marino, Miami[3]	623	378	60.7	4,746	44	23
	Jay Schroeder, Washington	541	276	51.0	4,109	22	22
1985	Dan Marino, Miami[2]	567	336	59.3	4,137	30	21
1984	Dan Marino, Miami	564	362	64.2	5,084	48	17
	Neil Lomax, St. Louis	560	345	61.6	4,614	28	16
	Phil Simms, N.Y. Giants	533	286	53.7	4,044	22	18
1983	Lynn Dickey, Green Bay	484	289	59.7	4,458	32	29
	Bill Kenney, Kansas City	603	346	57.4	4,348	24	18
1981	Dan Fouts, San Diego[3]	609	360	59.1	4,802	33	17
1980	Dan Fouts, San Diego[2]	589	348	59.1	4,715	30	24
	Brian Sipe, Cleveland	554	337	60.8	4,132	30	14
1979	Dan Fouts, San Diego	530	332	62.6	4,082	24	24
1967	Joe Namath, N.Y. Jets	491	258	52.5	4,007	26	28

400 Yards Passing in a Game

Date	Player, Team, Opponent	Att.	Comp.	Yards	TD
Dec. 21, 1986	Boomer Esiason, Cincinnati vs. N.Y. Jets	30	23	425	5
Dec. 14, 1986	Dan Marino, Miami vs. L.A. Rams (OT)	46	29	403	5
Nov. 23, 1986	Bernie Kosar, Cleveland vs. Pittsburgh (OT)	46	28	414	2
Nov. 17, 1986	Joe Montana, San Francisco vs. Washington	60	33	441	0
Nov. 16, 1986	Dan Marino, Miami vs. Buffalo	54	39	404	4
Nov. 10, 1986	Bernie Kosar, Cleveland vs. Miami	50	32	401	0
Nov. 2, 1986	Tommy Kramer, Minnesota vs. Washington (OT)	35	20	490	4
Nov. 2, 1986	Ken O'Brien, N.Y. Jets vs. Seattle	32	26	431	4
Oct. 27, 1986	Jay Schroeder, Washington vs. N.Y. Giants	40	22	420	1
Oct. 12, 1986	Steve Grogan, New England vs. N.Y. Jets	42	23	401	3
Sept. 21, 1986	Ken O'Brien, N.Y. Jets vs. Miami (OT)	43	29	479	4
Sept. 21, 1986	Dan Marino, Miami vs. N.Y. Jets (OT)	50	30	448	6
Sept. 21, 1986	Tony Eason, New England vs. Seattle	45	26	414	3
Dec. 20, 1985	John Elway, Denver vs. Seattle	42	24	432	1
Nov. 10, 1985	Dan Fouts, San Diego vs. L.A. Raiders (OT)	41	26	436	4
Oct. 13, 1985	Phil Simms, N.Y. Giants vs. Cincinnati	62	40	513	1
Oct. 13, 1985	Dave Krieg, Seattle vs. Atlanta	51	33	405	4
Oct. 6, 1985	Phil Simms, N.Y. Giants vs. Dallas	36	18	432	3
Oct. 6, 1985	Joe Montana, San Francisco vs. Atlanta	57	37	429	5
Sept. 19, 1985	Tommy Kramer, Minnesota vs. Chicago	55	28	436	3
Sept. 15, 1985	Dan Fouts, San Diego vs. Seattle	43	29	440	4
Dec. 16, 1984	Neil Lomax, St. Louis vs. Washington	46	37	468	2
Dec. 9, 1984	Dan Marino, Miami vs. Indianapolis	41	29	404	4
Dec. 2, 1984	Dan Marino, Miami vs. L.A. Raiders	57	35	470	4
Nov. 25, 1984	Dave Krieg, Seattle vs. Denver	44	30	406	3
Nov. 4, 1984	Dan Marino, Miami vs. N.Y. Jets	42	23	422	2
Oct. 21, 1984	Dan Fouts, San Diego vs. L.A. Raiders	45	24	410	3
Sept. 30, 1984	Dan Marino, Miami vs. St. Louis	36	24	429	3
Sept. 2, 1984	Phil Simms, N.Y. Giants vs. Philadelphia	30	23	409	4
Dec. 11, 1983	Bill Kenney, Kansas City vs. San Diego	41	31	411	4
Nov. 20, 1983	Dave Krieg, Seattle vs. Denver	42	31	418	3
Oct. 9, 1983	Joe Ferguson, Buffalo vs. Miami (OT)	55	38	419	5
Oct. 2, 1983	Joe Theismann, Washington vs. L.A. Raiders	39	23	417	3
Sept. 25, 1983	Richard Todd, N.Y. Jets vs. L.A. Rams (OT)	50	37	446	2
Dec. 26, 1982	Vince Ferragamo, L.A. Rams vs. Chicago	46	30	509	3
Dec. 20, 1982	Dan Fouts, San Diego vs. Cincinnati	40	25	435	1
Dec. 20, 1982	Ken Anderson, Cincinnati vs. San Diego	56	40	416	2
Dec. 11, 1982	Dan Fouts, San Diego vs. San Francisco	48	33	444	5
Nov. 21, 1982	Joe Montana, San Francisco vs. St. Louis	39	26	408	3
Nov. 15, 1981	Steve Bartkowski, Atlanta vs. Pittsburgh	50	33	416	2
Oct. 25, 1981	Brian Sipe, Cleveland vs. Baltimore	41	30	444	4
Oct. 25, 1981	David Woodley, Miami vs. Dallas	37	21	408	3
Oct. 11, 1981	Tommy Kramer, Minnesota vs. San Diego	43	27	444	4
Dec. 14, 1980	Tommy Kramer, Minnesota vs. Cleveland	49	38	456	4
Nov. 16, 1980	Doug Williams, Tampa Bay vs. Minnesota	55	30	486	4
Oct. 19, 1980	Dan Fouts, San Diego vs. N.Y. Giants	41	26	444	3
Oct. 12, 1980	Lynn Dickey, Green Bay vs. Tampa Bay (OT)	51	35	418	1
Sept. 21, 1980	Richard Todd, N.Y. Jets vs. San Francisco	60	42	447	3
Oct. 3, 1976	James Harris, Los Angeles vs. Miami	29	17	436	2
Nov. 17, 1975	Ken Anderson, Cincinnati vs. Buffalo	46	30	447	2
Nov. 18, 1974	Charley Johnson, Denver vs. Kansas City	42	28	445	2
Dec. 11, 1972	Joe Namath, N.Y. Jets vs. Oakland	46	25	403	1
Sept. 24, 1972	Joe Namath, N.Y. Jets vs. Baltimore	28	15	496	6
Dec. 21, 1969	Don Horn, Green Bay vs. St. Louis	31	22	410	5
Sept. 28, 1969	Joe Kapp, Minnesota vs. Baltimore	43	28	449	7
Sept. 9, 1968	Pete Beathard, Houston vs. Kansas City	48	23	413	2
Nov. 26, 1967	Sonny Jurgensen, Washington vs. Cleveland	50	32	418	3
Oct. 1, 1967	Joe Namath, N.Y. Jets vs. Miami	39	23	415	3
Sept. 17, 1967	Johnny Unitas, Baltimore vs. Atlanta	32	22	401	2
Nov. 13, 1966	Don Meredith, Dallas vs. Washington	29	21	406	2
Nov. 28, 1965	Sonny Jurgensen, Washington vs. Dallas	43	26	411	3
Oct. 24, 1965	Fran Tarkenton, Minnesota vs. San Francisco	35	21	407	3
Nov. 1, 1964	Len Dawson, Kansas City vs. Denver	38	23	435	6
Oct. 25, 1964	Cotton Davidson, Oakland vs. Denver	36	23	427	5
Oct. 16, 1964	Babe Parilli, Boston vs. Oakland	47	25	422	4
Dec. 22, 1963	Tom Flores, Oakland vs. Houston	29	17	407	6
Nov. 17, 1963	Norm Snead, Washington vs. Pittsburgh	40	23	424	2
Nov. 10, 1963	Don Meredith, Dallas vs. San Francisco	48	30	460	3
Oct. 13, 1963	Charley Johnson, St. Louis vs. Pittsburgh	41	20	428	2
Dec. 16, 1962	Sonny Jurgensen, Philadelphia vs. St. Louis	34	15	419	5
Nov. 18, 1962	Bill Wade, Chicago vs. Dall. Cowboys	46	28	466	2
Oct. 28, 1962	Y.A. Tittle, N.Y. Giants vs. Washington	39	27	505	7
Sept. 15, 1962	Frank Tripucka, Denver vs. Buffalo	56	29	447	2
Dec. 17, 1961	Sonny Jurgensen, Philadelphia vs. Detroit	42	27	403	3
Nov. 19, 1961	George Blanda, Houston vs. N.Y. Titans	32	20	418	7
Oct. 29, 1961	George Blanda, Houston vs. Buffalo	32	18	464	4
Oct. 29, 1961	Sonny Jurgensen, Philadelphia vs. Washington	41	27	436	3
Oct. 13, 1961	Jacky Lee, Houston vs. Boston	41	27	457	2
Dec. 13, 1958	Bobby Layne, Pittsburgh vs. Chi. Cardinals	49	23	409	2
Nov. 8, 1953	Bobby Thomason, Philadelphia vs. N.Y. Giants	44	22	437	4
Oct. 4, 1952	Otto Graham, Cleveland vs. Pittsburgh	49	21	401	3
Sept. 28, 1951	Norm Van Brocklin, Los Angeles vs. N.Y. Yanks	41	27	554	5
Dec. 11, 1949	Johnny Lujack, Chi. Bears vs. Chi. Cardinals	39	24	468	6
Oct. 31, 1948	Sammy Baugh, Washington vs. Boston	24	17	446	4
Oct. 31, 1948	Jim Hardy, Los Angeles vs. Chi. Cardinals	53	28	406	3
Nov. 14, 1943	Sid Luckman, Chi. Bears vs. N.Y. Giants	32	21	433	7

Times 400 or More
86 times by 53 players . . . Marino 7; Fouts 6; Jurgensen 5; Kramer 4; Krieg, Montana, Namath, Simms 3; Anderson, Blanda, Johnson, Kosar, Meredith, O'Brien, Todd 2.

1,000 Yards Pass Receiving in a Season

Year	Player, Team	No.	Yards	Avg.	Long	TD
1986	Jerry Rice, San Francisco	86	1,570	18.3	66	15
	Stanley Morgan, New England[3]	84	1,491	17.8	44	10
	Mark Duper, Miami[3]	67	1,313	19.6	85	11
	Gary Clark, Washington	74	1,265	17.1	55	7
	Al Toon, N.Y. Jets	85	1,176	13.8	62	8
	Todd Christensen, L.A. Raiders[3]	95	1,153	12.1	35	8
	Mark Clayton, Miami[2]	60	1,150	19.2	68	10
	*Bill Brooks, Indianapolis	65	1,131	17.4	84	8
	Drew Hill, Houston[2]	65	1,112	17.1	81	5
	Steve Largent, Seattle[8]	70	1,070	15.3	38	9
	Art Monk, Washington[3]	73	1,068	14.6	69	4
	*Earnest Givens, Houston	61	1,062	17.4	60	3
	Cris Collinsworth, Cincinnati[4]	62	1,024	16.5	46	10
	Wesley Walker, N.Y. Jets[2]	49	1,016	20.7	83	12
	J. T. Smith, St. Louis	80	1,014	12.7	45	6
	Mark Bavaro, N.Y. Giants	66	1,001	15.2	41	4
1985	Steve Largent, Seattle[7]	79	1,287	16.3	43	6
	Mike Quick, Philadelphia[3]	73	1,247	17.1	99	11
	Art Monk, Washington[2]	91	1,226	13.5	53	2
	Wes Chandler, San Diego[4]	67	1,199	17.9	75	10
	Drew Hill, Houston	64	1,169	18.3	57	9
	James Lofton, Green Bay[5]	69	1,153	16.7	56	4

Year	Player, Team	No.	Yards	Avg.	Long	TD
	Louis Lipps, Pittsburgh	59	1,134	19.2	51	12
	Cris Collinsworth, Cincinnati[3]	65	1,125	17.3	71	5
	Tony Hill, Dallas[3]	74	1,113	15.0	53	7
	Lionel James, San Diego	86	1,027	11.9	67	6
	Roger Craig, San Francisco	92	1,016	11.0	73	6
1984	Roy Green, St. Louis[2]	78	1,555	19.9	83	12
	John Stallworth, Pittsburgh[3]	80	1,395	17.4	51	11
	Mark Clayton, Miami	73	1,389	19.0	65	18
	Art Monk, Washington	106	1,372	12.9	72	7
	James Lofton, Green Bay[4]	62	1,361	22.0	79	7
	Mark Duper, Miami[2]	71	1,306	18.4	80	8
	Steve Watson, Denver[3]	69	1,170	17.0	73	7
	Steve Largent, Seattle[6]	74	1,164	15.7	65	12
	Tim Smith, Houston[2]	69	1,141	16.5	75	4
	Stacey Bailey, Atlanta	67	1,138	17.0	61	6
	Carlos Carson, Kansas City[2]	57	1,078	18.9	57	4
	Mike Quick, Philadelphia[2]	61	1,052	17.2	90	9
	Todd Christensen, L.A. Raiders[2]	80	1,007	12.6	38	7
	Kevin House, Tampa Bay[2]	76	1,005	13.2	55	5
	Ozzie Newsome, Cleveland[2]	89	1,001	11.2	52	5
1983	Mike Quick, Philadelphia	69	1,409	20.4	83	13
	Carlos Carson, Kansas City	80	1,351	16.9	50	7
	James Lofton, Green Bay[3]	58	1,300	22.4	74	8
	Todd Christensen, L.A. Raiders	92	1,247	13.6	45	12
	Roy Green, St. Louis	78	1,227	15.7	71	14
	Charlie Brown, Washington	78	1,225	15.7	75	8
	Tim Smith, Houston	83	1,176	14.2	47	6
	Kellen Winslow, San Diego[3]	88	1,172	13.3	46	8
	Earnest Gray, N.Y. Giants	78	1,139	14.6	62	5
	Steve Watson, Denver[2]	59	1,133	19.2	78	5
	Cris Collinsworth, Cincinnati[2]	66	1,130	17.1	63	5
	Steve Largent, Seattle[5]	72	1,074	14.9	46	11
	Mark Duper, Miami	51	1,003	19.7	85	10
1982	Wes Chandler, San Diego[3]	49	1,032	21.1	66	9
1981	Alfred Jenkins, Atlanta[2]	70	1,358	19.4	67	13
	James Lofton, Green Bay[2]	71	1,294	18.2	75	8
	Frank Lewis, Buffalo[2]	70	1,244	17.8	33	4
	Steve Watson, Denver	60	1,244	20.7	95	13
	Steve Largent, Seattle[4]	75	1,224	16.3	57	9
	Charlie Joiner, San Diego[4]	70	1,188	17.0	57	7
	Kevin House, Tampa Bay	56	1,176	21.0	84	9
	Wes Chandler, N.O.-San Diego[2]	69	1,142	16.6	51	6
	Dwight Clark, San Francisco	85	1,105	13.0	78	4
	John Stallworth, Pittsburgh[2]	63	1,098	17.4	55	5
	Kellen Winslow, San Diego[2]	88	1,075	12.2	67	10
	Pat Tilley, St. Louis	66	1,040	15.8	75	3
	Stanley Morgan, New England[2]	44	1,029	23.4	76	6
	Harold Carmichael, Philadelphia[3]	61	1,028	16.9	85	6
	Freddie Scott, Detroit	53	1,022	19.3	48	5
	*Cris Collinsworth, Cincinnati	67	1,009	15.1	74	8
	Joe Senser, Minnesota	79	1,004	12.7	53	8
	Ozzie Newsome, Cleveland	69	1,002	14.5	62	6
	Sammy White, Minnesota	66	1,001	15.2	53	3
1980	John Jefferson, San Diego[2]	82	1,340	16.3	58	13
	Kellen Winslow, San Diego	89	1,290	14.5	65	9
	James Lofton, Green Bay	71	1,226	17.3	47	4
	Charlie Joiner, San Diego[3]	71	1,132	15.9	51	4
	Ahmad Rashad, Minnesota[2]	69	1,095	15.9	76	5
	Steve Largent, Seattle[3]	66	1,064	16.1	67	6
	Tony Hill, Dallas[2]	60	1,055	17.6	58	8
	Alfred Jenkins, Atlanta	57	1,026	18.0	57	6
1979	Steve Largent, Seattle[2]	66	1,237	18.7	55	9
	John Stallworth, Pittsburgh	70	1,183	16.9	65	8
	Ahmad Rashad, Minnesota	80	1,156	14.5	52	9
	John Jefferson, San Diego[2]	61	1,090	17.9	65	10
	Frank Lewis, Buffalo	54	1,082	20.0	55	2
	Wes Chandler, New Orleans	65	1,069	16.4	85	6
	Tony Hill, Dallas	60	1,062	17.7	75	10
	Drew Pearson, Dallas[2]	55	1,026	18.7	56	8
	Wallace Francis, Atlanta	74	1,013	13.7	42	8
	Harold Jackson, New England[3]	45	1,013	22.5	59	7
	Charlie Joiner, San Diego[2]	72	1,008	14.0	39	4
	Stanley Morgan, New England	44	1,002	22.8	63	12
1978	Wesley Walker, N.Y. Jets	48	1,169	24.4	77	8
	Steve Largent, Seattle	71	1,168	16.5	57	8
	Harold Carmichael, Philadelphia[2]	55	1,072	19.5	56	8
	*John Jefferson, San Diego	56	1,001	17.9	46	13
1976	Roger Carr, Baltimore	43	1,112	25.9	79	11
	Cliff Branch, Oakland[2]	46	1,111	24.2	88	12
	Charlie Joiner, San Diego	50	1,056	21.1	81	7
1975	Ken Burrough, Houston	53	1,063	20.1	77	8
1974	Cliff Branch, Oakland	60	1,092	18.2	67	13
	Drew Pearson, Dallas	62	1,087	17.5	50	2
1973	Harold Carmichael, Philadelphia	67	1,116	16.7	73	9
1972	Harold Jackson, Philadelphia[2]	62	1,048	16.9	77	4
	John Gilliam, Minnesota	47	1,035	22.0	66	7
1971	Otis Taylor, Kansas City[2]	57	1,110	19.5	82	7
1970	Gene Washington, San Francisco	53	1,100	20.8	79	12
	Marlin Briscoe, Buffalo	57	1,036	18.2	48	8
	Dick Gordon, Chicago	71	1,026	14.5	69	13
	Gary Garrison, San Diego[2]	44	1,006	22.9	67	12
1969	Warren Wells, Oakland[2]	47	1,260	26.8	80	14
	Harold Jackson, Philadelphia	65	1,116	17.2	65	9
	Roy Jefferson, Pittsburgh[2]	67	1,079	16.1	63	9
	Dan Abramowicz, New Orleans	73	1,015	13.9	49	7
	Lance Alworth, San Diego[7]	64	1,003	15.7	76	4
1968	Lance Alworth, San Diego[6]	68	1,312	19.3	80	10
	Don Maynard, N.Y. Jets[5]	57	1,297	22.8	87	10
	George Sauer, N.Y. Jets[3]	66	1,141	17.3	43	3
	Warren Wells, Oakland	53	1,137	21.5	94	11
	Gary Garrison, San Diego	52	1,103	21.2	84	10
	Roy Jefferson, Pittsburgh	58	1,074	18.5	62	11
	Paul Warfield, Cleveland	50	1,067	21.3	65	12
	Homer Jones, N.Y. Giants[3]	45	1,057	23.5	84	7
	Fred Biletnikoff, Oakland	61	1,037	17.0	82	6
	Lance Rentzel, Dallas	54	1,009	18.7	65	6
1967	Don Maynard, N.Y. Jets[4]	71	1,434	20.2	75	10
	Ben Hawkins, Philadelphia	59	1,265	21.4	87	10
	Homer Jones, N.Y. Giants[2]	49	1,209	24.7	70	13
	Jackie Smith, St. Louis	56	1,205	21.5	76	9
	George Sauer, N.Y. Jets[2]	75	1,189	15.9	61	6
	Lance Alworth, San Diego[5]	52	1,010	19.4	71	9
1966	Lance Alworth, San Diego[4]	73	1,383	18.9	78	13
	Otis Taylor, Kansas City	58	1,297	22.4	89	8
	Pat Studstill, Detroit	67	1,266	18.9	99	5
	Bob Hayes, Dallas[2]	64	1,232	19.3	95	13
	Charlie Frazier, Houston	57	1,129	19.8	79	12
	Charley Taylor, Washington	72	1,119	15.5	86	12
	George Sauer, N.Y. Jets	63	1,081	17.2	77	5
	Homer Jones, N.Y. Giants	48	1,044	21.8	98	8
	Art Powell, Oakland[5]	53	1,026	19.4	46	11
1965	Lance Alworth, San Diego[3]	69	1,602	23.2	85	14
	Dave Parks, San Francisco	80	1,344	16.8	53	12
	Don Maynard, N.Y. Jets[3]	68	1,218	17.9	56	14
	Pete Retzlaff, Philadelphia	66	1,190	18.0	78	10
	Lionel Taylor, Denver[4]	85	1,131	13.3	63	6
	Tommy McDonald, Los Angeles[3]	67	1,036	15.5	51	9
	*Bob Hayes, Dallas	46	1,003	21.8	82	12
1964	Charley Hennigan, Houston[3]	101	1,546	15.3	53	8
	Art Powell, Oakland[4]	76	1,361	17.9	77	11
	Lance Alworth, San Diego[2]	61	1,235	20.2	82	13
	Johnny Morris, Chicago	93	1,200	12.9	63	10
	Elbert Dubenion, Buffalo	42	1,139	27.1	72	10
	Terry Barr, Detroit[2]	57	1,030	18.1	58	9
1963	Bobby Mitchell, Washington[2]	69	1,436	20.8	99	7
	Art Powell, Oakland[3]	73	1,304	17.9	85	16
	Buddy Dial, Pittsburgh[2]	60	1,295	21.6	83	9
	Lance Alworth, San Diego	61	1,205	19.8	85	11
	Del Shofner, N.Y. Giants[4]	64	1,181	18.5	70	9
	Lionel Taylor, Denver[3]	78	1,101	14.1	72	10
	Terry Barr, Detroit	66	1,086	16.5	75	13
	Charley Hennigan, Houston[2]	61	1,051	17.2	83	10
	Sonny Randle, St. Louis[2]	51	1,014	19.9	68	12
	Bake Turner, N.Y. Jets	71	1,009	14.2	53	6
1962	Bobby Mitchell, Washington	72	1,384	19.2	81	11
	Sonny Randle, St. Louis	63	1,158	18.4	86	7
	Tommy McDonald, Philadelphia[2]	58	1,146	19.8	60	10
	Del Shofner, N.Y. Giants[3]	53	1,133	21.4	69	12
	Art Powell, N.Y. Titans[2]	64	1,130	17.7	80	8
	Frank Clarke, Dall. Cowboys	47	1,043	22.2	66	14
	Don Maynard, N.Y. Titans[2]	56	1,041	18.6	86	8
1961	Charley Hennigan, Houston	82	1,746	21.3	80	12
	Lionel Taylor, Denver[2]	100	1,176	11.8	52	4
	Bill Groman, Houston[2]	50	1,175	23.5	80	17
	Tommy McDonald, Philadelphia	64	1,144	17.9	66	13
	Del Shofner, N.Y. Giants[2]	68	1,125	16.5	46	11
	Jim Phillips, Los Angeles	78	1,092	14.0	69	5
	*Mike Ditka, Chicago	56	1,076	19.2	76	12
	Dave Kocourek, San Diego	55	1,055	19.2	76	4
	Buddy Dial, Pittsburgh	53	1,047	19.8	88	12
	R.C. Owens, San Francisco	55	1,032	18.8	54	5
1960	*Bill Groman, Houston	72	1,473	20.5	92	12
	Raymond Berry, Baltimore	74	1,298	17.5	70	10
	Don Maynard, N.Y. Titans	72	1,265	17.6	65	6
	Lionel Taylor, Denver	92	1,235	13.4	80	12
	Art Powell, N.Y. Titans	69	1,167	16.9	76	14
1958	Del Shofner, Los Angeles	51	1,097	21.5	92	8
1956	Bill Howton, Green Bay[2]	55	1,188	21.6	66	12
	Harlon Hill, Chi. Bears[2]	47	1,128	24.0	79	11
1954	Bob Boyd, Los Angeles	53	1,212	22.9	80	6
	*Harlon Hill, Chi. Bears	45	1,124	25.0	76	12
1953	Pete Pihos, Philadelphia	63	1,049	16.7	59	10
1952	*Bill Howton, Green Bay	53	1,231	23.2	90	13
1951	Elroy (Crazylegs) Hirsch, Los Angeles	66	1,495	22.7	91	17
1950	Tom Fears, Los Angeles[2]	84	1,116	13.3	53	7
	Cloyce Box, Detroit	50	1,009	20.2	82	11
1949	Bob Mann, Detroit	66	1,014	15.4	64	4
	Tom Fears, Los Angeles	77	1,013	13.2	51	9
1945	Jim Benton, Cleveland	45	1,067	23.7	84	8
1942	Don Hutson, Green Bay	74	1,211	16.4	73	17

First year in the league.

250 Yards Pass Receiving in a Game

Date	Player, Team, Opponent	No.	Yards	TD
Dec. 22, 1985	Stephone Paige, Kansas City vs. San Diego	8	309	2
Dec. 20, 1982	Wes Chandler, San Diego vs. Cincinnati	10	260	2
Sept. 23, 1979	*Jerry Butler, Buffalo vs. N.Y. Jets	10	255	4
Nov. 4, 1962	Sonny Randle, St. Louis vs. N.Y. Giants	16	256	1
Oct. 28, 1962	Del Shofner, N.Y. Giants vs. Washington	11	269	1
Oct. 13, 1961	Charley Hennigan, Houston vs. Boston	13	272	1
Oct. 21, 1956	Billy Howton, Green Bay vs. Los Angeles	7	257	2
Dec. 3, 1950	Cloyce Box, Detroit vs. Baltimore	12	302	4
Nov. 22, 1945	Jim Benton, Cleveland vs. Detroit	10	303	1

First year in the league.

2,000 Combined Net Yards Gained in a Season

Year	Player, Team	Rushing Att.-Yds.	Pass Rec.	Punt Ret.	Kickoff Ret.	Fum. Runs	Total Yds.
1986	Eric Dickerson, L.A. Rams	404-1,821	26-205	0-0	0-0	2-0	432-2,026
	Gary Anderson, San Diego	127-442	80-871	25-227	24-482	2-0	258-2,022
1985	Lionel James, San Diego	105-516	86-1,027	25-213	36-779	1-0	253-2,535
	Marcus Allen, L.A. Raiders	380-1,759	67-555	0-0	0-0	2-(−6)	449-2,308
	Roger Craig, San Fran.	214-1,050	92-1,016	0-0	0-0	0-0	306-2,066
	Walter Payton, Chicago	324-1,551	49-483	0-0	0-0	1-0	374-2,034

1984 Eric Dickerson, L.A. Rams	379-2,105	21-139	0-0	0-0	4-15	404-2,259
James Wilder, Tampa Bay	407-1,544	85-685	0-0	0-0	4-0	496-2,229
Walter Payton, Chicago	381-1,684	45-368	0-0	0-0	1-0	427-2,052
1983*Eric Dickerson, L.A. Rams	390-1,808	51-404	0-0	0-0	1-0	442-2,212
William Andrews, Atlanta	331-1,567	59-609	0-0	0-0	2-0	392-2,176
Walter Payton, Chicago	314-1,421	53-607	0-0	0-0	2-0	369-2,028
1981*James Brooks, San Diego	109-525	46-329	22-290	40-949	2-0	219-2,093
William Andrews, Atlanta	289-1,301	81-735	0-0	0-0	0-0	370-2,036
1980 Bruce Harper, N.Y. Jets	45-126	50-634	28-242	49-1,070	3-0	175-2,072
1979 Wilbert Montgomery, Phil.	338-1,512	41-494	0-0	1-6	2-0	382-2,012
1978 Bruce Harper, N.Y. Jets	58-303	13-196	30-378	55-1,280	1-0	157-2,157
1977 Walter Payton, Chicago	339-1,852	27-269	0-0	2-95	5-0	373-2,216
Terry Metcalf, St. Louis	149-739	34-403	14-108	32-772	1-0	230-2,022
1975 Terry Metcalf, St. Louis	165-816	43-378	23-285	35-960	2-23	268-2,462
O.J. Simpson, Buffalo	329-1,817	28-426	0-0	0-0	1-0	358-2,243
1974 Mack Herron, New England	231-824	38-474	35-517	28-629	3-0	335-2,444
Otis Armstrong, Denver	263-1,407	38-405	0-0	16-386	1-0	318-2,198
Terry Metcalf, St. Louis	152-718	50-377	26-340	20-623	7-0	255-2,058
1973 O.J. Simpson, Buffalo	332-2,003	6-70	0-0	0-0	0-0	338-2,073
1966 Gale Sayers, Chicago	229-1,231	34-447	6-44	23-718	3-0	295-2,440
Leroy Kelly, Cleveland	209-1,141	32-366	13-104	19-403	0-0	273-2,014
1965*Gale Sayers, Chicago	166-867	29-507	16-238	21-660	4-0	236-2,272
1963 Timmy Brown, Philadelphia	192-841	36-487	16-152	33-945	2-3	279-2,428
Jim Brown, Cleveland	291-1,863	24-268	0-0	0-0	0-0	315-2,131
1962 Timmy Brown, Philadelphia	137-545	52-849	6-81	30-831	4-0	229-2,306
Dick Christy, N.Y. Titans	114-535	62-538	15-250	38-824	2-0	231-2,147
1961 Billy Cannon, Houston	200-948	43-586	9-70	18-439	2-0	272-2,043
1960*Abner Haynes, Dall. Texans	156-875	55-576	14-215	19-434	4-0	248-2,100

**First year in the league.*

300 Combined Net Yards Gained in a Game

Date	Player, Team, Opponent	No.	Yards	TD
Dec. 22, 1985	Stephone Paige, Kansas City vs. San Diego	8	309	2
Nov. 10, 1985	Lionel James, San Diego vs. L.A. Raiders (OT)	23	345	0
Sept. 22, 1985	Lionel James, San Diego vs. Cincinnati	20	316	2
Dec. 21, 1975	Walter Payton, Chicago vs. New Orleans	32	300	1
Nov. 23, 1975	Greg Pruitt, Cleveland vs. Cincinnati	28	304	2
Nov. 1, 1970	Eugene (Mercury) Morris, Miami vs. Baltimore	17	302	0
Oct. 4, 1970	O. J. Simpson, Buffalo vs. N.Y. Jets	26	303	2
Dec. 6, 1969	Jerry LeVias, Houston vs. N.Y. Jets	18	329	1
Nov. 2, 1969	Travis Williams, Green Bay vs. Pittsburgh	11	314	3
Dec. 18, 1966	Gale Sayers, Chicago vs. Minnesota	20	339	2
Dec. 12, 1965	Gale Sayers, Chicago vs. San Francisco	17	336	6
Nov. 17, 1963	Gary Ballman, Pittsburgh vs. Washington	12	320	2
Dec. 16, 1962	Timmy Brown, Philadelphia vs. St. Louis	19	341	2
Dec. 10, 1961	Billy Cannon, Houston vs. N.Y. Titans	32	373	5
Nov 19, 1961	Jim Brown, Cleveland vs. Philadelphia	38	313	4
Dec. 3, 1950	Cloyce Box, Detroit vs. Baltimore	13	302	4
Oct. 29, 1950	Wally Triplett, Detroit vs. Los Angeles	11	331	1
Nov. 22, 1945	Jim Benton, Cleveland vs. Detroit	10	303	1

Top 10 Scorers

Player	Years	TD	FG	PAT	TP
George Blanda	26	9	335	943	2,002
Jan Stenerud	19	0	373	580	1,699
Jim Turner	16	1	304	521	1,439
Mark Moseley	16	0	300	482	1,382
Jim Bakken	17	0	282	534	1,380
Fred Cox	15	0	282	519	1,365
Lou Groza	17	1	234	641	1,349
Gino Cappelletti	11	42	176	350	1,130
Don Cockroft	13	0	216	432	1,080
Garo Yepremian	14	0	210	444	1,074

Cappelletti's total includes four two-point conversions.

Top 10 Touchdown Scorers

Player	Years	Rush	Pass Rec.	Returns	Total TD
Jim Brown	9	106	20	0	126
Walter Payton	12	106	14	0	120
John Riggins	14	104	12	0	116
Lenny Moore	12	63	48	2	113
Don Hutson	11	3	99	3	105
Franco Harris	13	91	9	0	100
Jim Taylor	10	83	10	0	93
Bobby Mitchell	11	18	65	8	91
Leroy Kelly	10	74	13	3	90
Charley Taylor	13	11	79	0	90

Top 10 Rushers

Player	Years	Att.	Yards	Avg.	Long	TD
Walter Payton	12	3,692	16,193	4.4	76	106
Jim Brown	9	2,359	12,312	5.2	80	106
Franco Harris	13	2,949	12,120	4.1	75	91
Tony Dorsett	10	2,625	11,580	4.4	99	71
John Riggins	14	2,916	11,352	3.9	66	104
O.J. Simpson	11	2,404	11,236	4.7	94	61
Earl Campbell	8	2,187	9,407	4.3	81	74
Jim Taylor	10	1,941	8,597	4.4	84	83
Joe Perry	14	1,737	8,378	4.8	78	53
Larry Csonka	11	1,891	8,081	4.3	54	64

Top 10 Passers

Player	Years	Att.	Comp.	Pct. Comp.	Yards	TD	Pct. TD	Int.	Pct. Int.	Avg. Gain	Rating
Dan Marino	4	2,050	1,249	60.9	16,177	142	6.9	67	3.3	7.89	95.2
Joe Montana	8	2,878	1,818	63.2	21,498	141	4.9	76	2.6	7.47	91.2
Dave Krieg	7	1,822	1,046	57.4	13,677	107	5.9	73	4.0	7.51	84.1
Roger Staubach	11	2,958	1,685	57.0	22,700	153	5.2	109	3.7	7.67	83.4
Danny White	11	2,546	1,517	59.6	19,068	142	5.6	112	4.4	7.49	83.2
Sonny Jurgensen	18	4,262	2,433	57.1	32,224	255	6.0	189	4.4	7.56	82.6
Len Dawson	19	3,741	2,136	57.1	28,711	239	6.4	183	4.9	7.67	82.6
Ken Anderson	16	4,475	2,654	59.3	32,838	197	4.4	160	3.6	7.34	81.9
Dan Fouts	14	5,240	3,091	59.0	40,523	244	4.7	227	4.3	7.73	80.9
Neil Lomax	6	2,247	1,287	57.3	15,989	92	4.1	67	3.0	7.12	80.7

1,500 or more attempts. The passing ratings are based on performance standards established for completion percentage, interception percentage, touchdown percentage, and average gain. Passers are allocated points according to how their marks compare with those standards.

Top 10 Pass Receivers

Player	Years	No.	Yards	Avg.	Long	TD
Charlie Joiner	18	750	12,146	16.2	87	65
Steve Largent	11	694	11,129	16.0	74	87
Charley Taylor	13	649	9,110	14.0	88	79
Don Maynard	15	633	11,834	18.7	87	88
Raymond Berry	13	631	9,275	14.7	70	68
Harold Carmichael	14	590	8,985	15.2	85	79
Fred Biletnikoff	14	589	8,974	15.2	82	76
Harold Jackson	16	579	10,372	17.9	79	76
Lionel Taylor	10	567	7,195	12.7	80	45
Lance Alworth	11	542	10,266	18.9	85	85

Top 10 Interceptors

Player	Years	No.	Yards	Avg.	Long	TD
Paul Krause	16	81	1,185	14.6	81	3
Emlen Tunnell	14	79	1,282	16.2	55	4
Dick (Night Train) Lane	14	68	1,207	17.8	80	5
Ken Riley	15	65	596	9.2	66	5
Dick LeBeau	13	62	762	12.3	70	3
Emmitt Thomas	13	58	937	16.2	73	5
Bobby Boyd	9	57	994	17.4	74	4
Johnny Robinson	12	57	741	13.0	57	1
Mel Blount	14	57	736	12.9	52	2
Lem Barney	11	56	1,077	19.2	71	7
Pat Fischer	17	56	941	16.8	69	4

Top 10 Punters

Player	Years	No.	Yards	Avg.	Long	Blk.
Rohn Stark	5	389	17,567	45.2	72	2
Sammy Baugh	16	338	15,245	45.1	85	9
Tommy Davis	11	511	22,833	44.7	82	2
Yale Lary	11	503	22,279	44.3	74	4
Horace Gillom	7	385	16,872	43.8	80	5
Jerry Norton	11	358	15,671	43.8	78	2
Don Chandler	12	660	28,678	43.5	90	4
Jerrel Wilson	16	1,072	46,139	43.0	72	12
Rich Camarillo	6	406	17,433	42.9	76	3
Norm Van Brocklin	12	523	22,413	42.9	72	3

300 or more punts.

Top 10 Punt Returners

Player	Years	No.	Yards	Avg.	Long	TD
Henry Ellard	4	97	1,248	12.9	83	4
George McAfee	8	112	1,431	12.8	74	2
Jack Christiansen	8	85	1,084	12.8	89	8
Claude Gibson	5	110	1,381	12.6	85	3
Bill Dudley	9	124	1,515	12.2	96	3
Rick Upchurch	9	248	3,008	12.1	92	8
Billy Johnson	12	258	3,123	12.1	87	6
Louis Lipps	3	92	1,109	12.1	76	3
Mack Herron	3	84	982	11.7	66	0
Bill Thompson	13	157	1,814	11.6	60	0

75 or more returns.

Top 10 Kickoff Returners

Player	Years	No.	Yards	Avg.	Long	TD
Gale Sayers	7	91	2,781	30.6	103	6
Lynn Chandnois	7	92	2,720	29.6	93	3
Abe Woodson	9	193	5,538	28.7	105	5
Claude (Buddy) Young	6	90	2,514	27.9	104	2
Travis Williams	5	102	2,801	27.5	105	6
Joe Arenas	7	139	3,798	27.3	96	1
Clarence Davis	8	79	2,140	27.1	76	0
Lenny Lyles	12	81	2,161	26.7	103	3
Steve Van Buren	8	76	2,030	26.7	98	3
Eugene (Mercury) Morris	8	111	2,947	26.5	105	3

75 or more returns.

Top 10 Combined Yards Gained

	Years	Tot.	Rush.	Rec.	Int. Ret.	Punt Ret.	Kickoff Ret.	Fumble
Walter Payton	12	21,053	16,193	4,321	0	0	539	0
Jim Brown	9	15,459	12,312	2,499	0	0	648	0
Tony Dorsett	10	14,868	11,580	3,255	0	0	0	33
Franco Harris	13	14,622	12,120	2,287	0	0	233	−18
O. J. Simpson	11	14,368	11,236	2,142	0	0	990	0
Bobby Mitchell	11	14,078	2,735	7,954	0	699	2,690	0
John Riggins	14	13,435	11,352	2,090	0	0	0	−7
Greg Pruitt	12	13,262	5,672	3,069	0	2,007	2,514	0
Ollie Matson	14	12,884	5,173	3,285	51	595	3,746	34
Tim Brown	10	12,684	3,862	3,399	0	639	4,781	3

YEARLY STATISTICAL LEADERS

Annual Scoring Leaders

Year	Player, Team	TD	FG	PAT	TP
1986	Tony Franklin, New England, AFC	0	32	44	140
	Kevin Butler, Chicago, NFC	0	28	36	120
1985	*Kevin Butler, Chicago, NFC	0	31	51	144
	Gary Anderson, Pittsburgh, AFC	0	33	40	139
1984	Ray Wersching, San Francisco, NFC	0	25	56	131
	Gary Anderson, Pittsburgh, AFC	0	24	45	117
1983	Mark Moseley, Washington, NFC	0	33	62	161
	Gary Anderson, Pittsburgh, AFC	0	27	38	119
1982	*Marcus Allen, L.A. Raiders, AFC	14	0	0	84
	Wendell Tyler, L.A. Rams, NFC	13	0	0	78
1981	Ed Murray, Detroit, NFC	0	25	46	121
	Rafael Septien, Dallas, NFC	0	27	40	121
	Jim Breech, Cincinnati, AFC	0	22	49	115
	Nick Lowery, Kansas City, AFC	0	26	37	115
1980	John Smith, New England, AFC	0	26	51	129
	*Ed Murray, Detroit, NFC	0	27	35	116
1979	John Smith, New England, AFC	0	23	46	115
	Mark Moseley, Washington, NFC	0	25	39	114
1978	*Frank Corral, Los Angeles, NFC	0	29	31	118
	Pat Leahy, N.Y. Jets, AFC	0	22	41	107
1977	Errol Mann, Oakland, AFC	0	20	39	99
	Walter Payton, Chicago, NFC	16	0	0	96
1976	Toni Linhart, Baltimore, AFC	0	20	49	109
	Mark Moseley, Washington, NFC	0	22	31	97
1975	O.J. Simpson, Buffalo, AFC	23	0	0	138
	Chuck Foreman, Minnesota, NFC	22	0	0	132
1974	Chester Marcol, Green Bay, NFC	0	25	19	94
	Roy Gerela, Pittsburgh, AFC	0	20	33	93
1973	David Ray, Los Angeles, NFC	0	30	40	130
	Roy Gerela, Pittsburgh, AFC	0	29	36	123
1972	*Chester Marcol, Green Bay, NFC	0	33	29	128
	Bobby Howfield, N.Y. Jets, AFC	0	27	40	121
1971	Garo Yepremian, Miami, AFC	0	28	33	117
	Curt Knight, Washington, NFC	0	29	27	114
1970	Fred Cox, Minnesota, NFC	0	30	35	125
	Jan Stenerud, Kansas City, AFC	0	30	26	116
1969	Jim Turner, N.Y. Jets, AFL	0	32	33	129
	Fred Cox, Minnesota, NFL	0	26	43	121
1968	Jim Turner, N.Y. Jets, AFL	0	34	43	145
	Leroy Kelly, Cleveland, NFL	20	0	0	120
1967	Jim Bakken, St. Louis, NFL	0	27	36	117
	George Blanda, Oakland, AFL	0	20	56	116
1966	Gino Cappelletti, Boston, AFL	6	16	35	119
	Bruce Gossett, Los Angeles, NFL	0	28	29	113
1965	*Gale Sayers, Chicago, NFL	22	0	0	132
	Gino Cappelletti, Boston, AFL	9	17	27	132
1964	Gino Cappelletti, Boston, AFL	7	25	36	#155
	Lenny Moore, Baltimore, NFL	20	0	0	120
1963	Gino Cappelletti, Boston, AFL	2	22	35	113
	Don Chandler, N.Y. Giants, NFL	0	18	52	106
1962	Gene Mingo, Denver, AFL	4	27	32	137
	Jim Taylor, Green Bay, NFL	19	0	0	114
1961	Gino Cappelletti, Boston, AFL	8	17	48	147
	Paul Hornung, Green Bay, NFL	10	15	41	146
1960	Paul Hornung, Green Bay, NFL	15	15	41	176
	*Gene Mingo, Denver, AFL	6	18	33	123
1959	Paul Hornung, Green Bay	7	7	31	94
1958	Jim Brown, Cleveland	18	0	0	108
1957	Sam Baker, Washington	1	14	29	77
	Lou Groza, Cleveland	0	15	32	77
1956	Bobby Layne, Detroit	5	12	33	99
1955	Doak Walker, Detroit	7	9	27	96
1954	Bobby Walston, Philadelphia	11	4	36	114
1953	Gordy Soltau, San Francisco	6	10	48	114
1952	Gordy Soltau, San Francisco	7	6	34	94
1951	Elroy (Crazylegs) Hirsch, Los Angeles	17	0	0	102
1950	*Doak Walker, Detroit	11	8	38	128
1949	Pat Harder, Chi. Cardinals	8	3	45	102
	Gene Roberts, N.Y. Giants	17	0	0	102
1948	Pat Harder, Chi. Cardinals	6	7	53	110
1947	Pat Harder, Chi. Cardinals	7	7	39	102
1946	Ted Fritsch, Green Bay	10	9	13	100
1945	Steve Van Buren, Philadelphia	18	0	2	110
1944	Don Hutson, Green Bay	9	0	31	85
1943	Don Hutson, Green Bay	12	3	36	117
1942	Don Hutson, Green Bay	17	1	33	138
1941	Don Hutson, Green Bay	12	1	20	95
1940	Don Hutson, Green Bay	7	0	15	57
1939	Andy Farkas, Washington	11	0	2	68
1938	Clarke Hinkle, Green Bay	7	3	7	58
1937	Jack Manders, Chi. Bears	5	8	15	69
1936	Earl (Dutch) Clark, Detroit	7	4	19	73
1935	Earl (Dutch) Clark, Detroit	6	1	16	55
1934	Jack Manders, Chi. Bears	3	10	31	79
1933	Ken Strong, N.Y. Giants	6	5	13	64
	Glenn Presnell, Portsmouth	6	6	10	64
1932	Earl (Dutch) Clark, Portsmouth	6	3	10	55

**First year in the league.*
#Cappelletti's total includes a two-point conversion.

Annual Leaders—Most Field Goals Made

Year	Player, Team	Att.	Made	Pct.
1986	Tony Franklin, New England, AFC	41	32	78.0
	Kevin Butler, Chicago, NFC	41	28	68.3
1985	Gary Anderson, Pittsburgh, AFC	42	33	78.6
	Morten Andersen, New Orleans, NFC	35	31	88.6
	*Kevin Butler, Chicago, NFC	37	31	83.8
1984	*Paul McFadden, Philadelphia, NFC	37	30	81.1
	Gary Anderson, Pittsburgh, AFC	32	24	75.0
	Matt Bahr, Cleveland, AFC	32	24	75.0
1983	*Ali Haji-Sheikh, N.Y. Giants, NFC	42	35	83.3
	*Raul Allegre, Baltimore, AFC	35	30	85.7
1982	Mark Moseley, Washington, NFC	21	20	95.2
	Nick Lowery, Kansas City, AFC	24	19	79.2
1981	Rafael Septien, Dallas, NFC	35	27	77.1
	Nick Lowery, Kansas City, AFC	36	26	72.2
1980	*Ed Murray, Detroit, NFC	42	27	64.3
	John Smith, New England, AFC	34	26	76.5
	Fred Steinfort, Denver, AFC	34	26	76.5
1979	Mark Moseley, Washington, NFC	33	25	75.8
	John Smith, New England, AFC	33	23	69.7
1978	*Frank Corral, Los Angeles, NFC	43	29	67.4
	Pat Leahy, N.Y. Jets, AFC	30	22	73.3
1977	Mark Moseley, Washington, NFC	37	21	56.8
	Errol Mann, Oakland, AFC	28	20	71.4
1976	Mark Moseley, Washington, NFC	34	22	64.7
	Jan Stenerud, Kansas City, AFC	38	21	55.3
1975	Jan Stenerud, Kansas City, AFC	32	22	68.8
	Toni Fritsch, Dallas, NFC	35	22	62.9
1974	Chester Marcol, Green Bay, NFC	39	25	64.1
	Roy Gerela, Pittsburgh, AFC	29	20	69.0
1973	David Ray, Los Angeles, NFC	47	30	63.8
	Roy Gerela, Pittsburgh, AFC	43	29	67.4
1972	*Chester Marcol, Green Bay, NFC	48	33	68.8
	Roy Gerela, Pittsburgh, AFC	41	28	68.3
1971	Curt Knight, Washington, NFC	49	29	59.2
	Garo Yepremian, Miami, AFC	40	28	70.0
1970	Jan Stenerud, Kansas City, AFC	42	30	71.4
	Fred Cox, Minnesota, NFC	46	30	65.2
1969	Jim Turner, N.Y. Jets, AFL	47	32	68.1
	Fred Cox, Minnesota, NFL	37	26	70.3
1968	Jim Turner, N.Y. Jets, AFL	46	34	73.9
	Mac Percival, Chicago, NFL	36	25	69.4
1967	Jim Bakken, St. Louis, NFL	39	27	69.2
	Jan Stenerud, Kansas City, AFL	36	21	58.3
1966	Bruce Gossett, Los Angeles, NFL	49	28	57.1
	Mike Mercer, Oakland-Kansas City, AFL	30	21	70.0
1965	Pete Gogolak, Buffalo, AFL	46	28	60.9
	Fred Cox, Minnesota, NFL	35	23	65.7
1964	Jim Bakken, St. Louis, NFL	38	25	65.8
	Gino Cappelletti, Boston, AFL	39	25	64.1
1963	Jim Martin, Baltimore, NFL	39	24	61.5
	Gino Cappelletti, Boston, AFL	38	22	57.9
1962	Gene Mingo, Denver, AFL	39	27	69.2
	Lou Michaels, Pittsburgh, NFL	42	26	61.9
1961	Steve Myhra, Baltimore, NFL	39	21	53.8
	Gino Cappelletti, Boston, AFL	32	17	53.1
1960	Tommy Davis, San Francisco, NFL	32	19	59.4
	*Gene Mingo, Denver, AFL	28	18	64.3
1959	Pat Summerall, New York Giants	29	20	69.0
1958	Paige Cothren, Los Angeles	25	14	56.0
	*Tom Miner, Pittsburgh	28	14	50.0
1957	Lou Groza, Cleveland	22	15	68.2
1956	Sam Baker, Washington	25	17	68.0
1955	Fred Cone, Green Bay	24	16	66.7
1954	Lou Groza, Cleveland	24	16	66.7
1953	Lou Groza, Cleveland	26	23	88.5
1952	Lou Groza, Cleveland	33	19	57.6
1951	Bob Waterfield, Los Angeles	23	13	56.5
1950	*Lou Groza, Cleveland	19	13	68.4
1949	Cliff Patton, Philadelphia	18	9	50.0
	Bob Waterfield, Los Angeles	16	9	56.3
1948	Cliff Patton, Philadelphia	12	8	66.7
1947	Ward Cuff, Green Bay	16	7	43.8
	Pat Harder, Chi. Cardinals	10	7	70.0
	Bob Waterfield, Los Angeles	16	7	43.8
1946	Ted Fritsch, Green Bay	17	9	52.9
1945	Joe Aguirre, Washington	13	7	53.8
1944	Ken Strong, N.Y. Giants	12	6	50.0
1943	Ward Cuff, N.Y. Giants	9	3	33.3
	Don Hutson, Green Bay	5	3	60.0
1942	Bill Daddio, Chi. Cardinals	10	5	50.0
1941	Clarke Hinkle, Green Bay	14	6	42.9
1940	Clarke Hinkle, Green Bay	14	9	64.3
1939	Ward Cuff, N.Y. Giants	16	7	43.8
1938	Ward Cuff, N.Y. Giants	9	5	55.6
	Ralph Kercheval, Brooklyn	13	5	38.5
1937	Jack Manders, Chi. Bears		8	
1936	Jack Manders, Chi. Bears		7	
	Armand Niccolai, Pittsburgh		7	
1935	Armand Niccolai, Pittsburgh		6	
	Bill Smith, Chi. Cardinals		6	
1934	Jack Manders, Chi. Bears		10	
1933	*Jack Manders, Chi. Bears		6	
	Glenn Presnell, Portsmouth		6	
1932	Earl (Dutch) Clark, Portsmouth		3	

**First year in the league.*

Annual Rushing Leaders

Year	Player, Team	Att.	Yards	Avg.	TD
1986	Eric Dickerson, L.A. Rams, NFC	404	1,821	4.5	11
	Curt Warner, Seattle, AFC	319	1,481	4.6	13
1985	Marcus Allen, L.A. Raiders, AFC	380	1,759	4.6	11
	Gerald Riggs, Atlanta, NFC	397	1,719	4.3	10

1984	Eric Dickerson, L.A. Rams, NFC	379	2,105	5.6	14
	Earnest Jackson, San Diego, AFC	296	1,179	4.0	8
1983	*Eric Dickerson, L.A. Rams, NFC	390	1,808	4.6	18
	*Curt Warner, Seattle, AFC	335	1,449	4.3	13
1982	Freeman McNeil, N.Y. Jets, AFC	151	786	5.2	6
	Tony Dorsett, Dallas, NFC	177	745	4.2	5
1981	*George Rogers, New Orleans, NFC	378	1,674	4.4	13
	Earl Campbell, Houston, AFC	361	1,376	3.8	10
1980	Earl Campbell, Houston, AFC	373	1,934	5.2	13
	Walter Payton, Chicago, NFC	317	1,460	4.6	6
1979	Earl Campbell, Houston, AFC	368	1,697	4.6	19
	Walter Payton, Chicago, NFC	369	1,610	4.4	14
1978	*Earl Campbell, Houston, AFC	302	1,450	4.8	13
	Walter Payton, Chicago, NFC	333	1,395	4.2	11
1977	Walter Payton, Chicago, NFC	339	1,852	5.5	14
	Mark van Eeghen, Oakland, AFC	324	1,273	3.9	7
1976	O.J. Simpson, Buffalo, AFC	290	1,503	5.2	8
	Walter Payton, Chicago, NFC	311	1,390	4.5	13
1975	O.J. Simpson, Buffalo, AFC	329	1,817	5.5	16
	Jim Otis, St. Louis, NFC	269	1,076	4.0	5
1974	Otis Armstrong, Denver, AFC	263	1,407	5.3	9
	Lawrence McCutcheon, Los Angeles, NFC	236	1,109	4.7	3
1973	O.J. Simpson, Buffalo, AFC	332	2,003	6.0	12
	John Brockington, Green Bay, NFC	265	1,144	4.3	3
1972	O.J. Simpson, Buffalo, AFC	292	1,251	4.3	6
	Larry Brown, Washington, NFC	285	1,216	4.3	8
1971	Floyd Little, Denver, AFC	284	1,133	4.0	6
	*John Brockington, Green Bay, NFC	216	1,105	5.1	4
1970	Larry Brown, Washington, NFC	237	1,125	4.7	5
	Floyd Little, Denver, AFC	209	901	4.3	3
1969	Gale Sayers, Chicago, NFL	236	1,032	4.4	8
	Dickie Post, San Diego, AFL	182	873	4.8	6
1968	Leroy Kelly, Cleveland, NFL	248	1,239	5.0	16
	*Paul Robinson, Cincinnati, AFL	238	1,023	4.3	8
1967	Jim Nance, Boston, AFL	269	1,216	4.5	7
	Leroy Kelly, Cleveland, NFL	235	1,205	5.1	11
1966	Jim Nance, Boston, AFL	299	1,458	4.9	11
	Gale Sayers, Chicago, NFL	229	1,231	5.4	8
1965	Jim Brown, Cleveland, NFL	289	1,544	5.3	17
	Paul Lowe, San Diego, AFL	222	1,121	5.0	7
1964	Jim Brown, Cleveland, NFL	280	1,446	5.2	7
	Cookie Gilchrist, Buffalo, AFL	230	981	4.3	6
1963	Jim Brown, Cleveland, NFL	291	1,863	6.4	12
	Clem Daniels, Oakland, AFL	215	1,099	5.1	3
1962	Jim Taylor, Green Bay, NFL	272	1,474	5.4	19
	*Cookie Gilchrist, Buffalo, AFL	214	1,096	5.1	13
1961	Jim Brown, Cleveland, NFL	305	1,408	4.6	8
	Billy Cannon, Houston, AFL	200	948	4.7	6
1960	Jim Brown, Cleveland, NFL	215	1,257	5.8	9
	*Abner Haynes, Dall. Texans, AFL	156	875	5.6	9
1959	Jim Brown, Cleveland	290	1,329	4.6	14
1958	Jim Brown, Cleveland	257	1,527	5.9	17
1957	*Jim Brown, Cleveland	202	942	4.7	9
1956	Rick Casares, Chi. Bears	234	1,126	4.8	12
1955	*Alan Ameche, Baltimore	213	961	4.5	9
1954	Joe Perry, San Francisco	173	1,049	6.1	8
1953	Joe Perry, San Francisco	192	1,018	5.3	10
1952	Dan Towler, Los Angeles	156	894	5.7	10
1951	Eddie Price, N.Y. Giants	271	971	3.6	7
1950	*Marion Motley, Cleveland	140	810	5.8	3
1949	Steve Van Buren, Philadelphia	263	1,146	4.4	11
1948	Steve Van Buren, Philadelphia	201	945	4.7	10
1947	Steve Van Buren, Philadelphia	217	1,008	4.6	13
1946	Bill Dudley, Pittsburgh	146	604	4.1	3
1945	Steve Van Buren, Philadelphia	143	832	5.8	15
1944	Bill Paschal, N.Y. Giants	196	737	3.8	9
1943	*Bill Paschal, N.Y. Giants	147	572	3.9	10
1942	*Bill Dudley, Pittsburgh	162	696	4.3	5
1941	Clarence (Pug) Manders, Brooklyn	111	486	4.4	5
1940	Byron (Whizzer) White, Detroit	146	514	3.5	5
1939	*Bill Osmanski, Chicago	121	699	5.8	7
1938	*Byron (Whizzer) White, Pittsburgh	152	567	3.7	4
1937	Cliff Battles, Washington	216	874	4.0	5
1936	*Alphonse (Tuffy) Leemans, N.Y. Giants	206	830	4.0	2
1935	Doug Russell, Chi. Cardinals	140	499	3.6	0
1934	*Beattie Feathers, Chi. Bears	101	1,004	9.9	8
1933	Jim Musick, Boston	173	809	4.7	5
1932	*Cliff Battles, Boston	148	576	3.9	3

**First year in the league.*

Annual Passing Leaders

Year	Player, Team	Att.	Comp.	Yards	TD	Int.
1986	Tommy Kramer, Minnesota, NFC	372	208	3,000	24	10
	Dan Marino, Miami, AFC	623	378	4,746	44	23
1985	Ken O'Brien, N.Y. Jets, AFC	488	297	3,888	25	8
	Joe Montana, San Francisco, NFC	494	303	3,653	27	13
1984	Dan Marino, Miami, AFC	564	362	5,084	48	17
	Joe Montana, San Francisco, NFC	432	279	3,630	28	10
1983	Steve Bartkowski, Atlanta, NFC	432	274	3,167	22	5
	*Dan Marino, Miami, AFC	296	173	2,210	20	6
1982	Ken Anderson, Cincinnati, AFC	309	218	2,495	12	9
	Joe Theismann, Washington, NFC	252	161	2,033	13	9
1981	Ken Anderson, Cincinnati, AFC	479	300	3,754	29	10
	Joe Montana, San Francisco, NFC	488	311	3,565	19	12
1980	Brian Sipe, Cleveland, AFC	554	337	4,132	30	14
	Ron Jaworski, Philadelphia, NFC	451	257	3,529	27	12
1979	Roger Staubach, Dallas, NFC	461	267	3,586	27	11
	Dan Fouts, San Diego, AFC	530	332	4,082	24	24
1978	Roger Staubach, Dallas, NFC	413	231	3,190	25	16
	Terry Bradshaw, Pittsburgh, AFC	368	207	2,915	28	20
1977	Bob Griese, Miami, AFC	307	180	2,252	22	13
	Roger Staubach, Dallas, NFC	361	210	2,620	18	9
1976	Ken Stabler, Oakland, AFC	291	194	2,737	27	17
	James Harris, Los Angeles, NFC	158	91	1,460	8	6
1975	Ken Anderson, Cincinnati, AFC	377	228	3,169	21	11
	Fran Tarkenton, Minnesota, NFC	425	273	2,994	25	13
1974	Ken Anderson, Cincinnati, AFC	328	213	2,667	18	10
	Sonny Jurgensen, Washington, NFC	167	107	1,185	11	5
1973	Roger Staubach, Dallas, NFC	286	179	2,428	23	15
	Ken Stabler, Oakland, AFC	260	163	1,997	14	10
1972	Norm Snead, N.Y. Giants, NFC	325	196	2,307	17	12
	Earl Morrall, Miami, AFC	150	83	1,360	11	7
1971	Roger Staubach, Dallas, NFC	211	126	1,882	15	4
	Bob Griese, Miami, AFC	263	145	2,089	19	9
1970	John Brodie, San Francisco, NFC	378	223	2,941	24	10
	Daryle Lamonica, Oakland, AFC	356	179	2,516	22	15
1969	Sonny Jurgensen, Washington, NFL	442	274	3,102	22	15
	*Greg Cook, Cincinnati, AFL	197	106	1,854	15	11
1968	Len Dawson, Kansas City, AFL	224	131	2,109	17	9
	Earl Morrall, Baltimore, NFL	317	182	2,909	26	17
1967	Sonny Jurgensen, Washington, NFL	508	288	3,747	31	16
	Daryle Lamonica, Oakland, AFL	425	220	3,228	30	20
1966	Bart Starr, Green Bay, NFL	251	156	2,257	14	3
	Len Dawson, Kansas City, AFL	284	159	2,527	26	10
1965	Rudy Bukich, Chicago, NFL	312	176	2,641	20	9
	John Hadl, San Diego, AFL	348	174	2,798	20	21
1964	Len Dawson, Kansas City, AFL	354	199	2,879	30	18
	Bart Starr, Green Bay, NFL	272	163	2,144	15	4
1963	Y.A. Tittle, N.Y. Giants, NFL	367	221	3,145	36	14
	Tobin Rote, San Diego, AFL	286	170	2,510	20	17
1962	Len Dawson, Dall. Texans, AFL	310	189	2,759	29	17
	Bart Starr, Green Bay, NFL	285	178	2,438	12	9
1961	George Blanda, Houston, AFL	362	187	3,330	36	22
	Milt Plum, Cleveland, NFL	302	177	2,416	18	10
1960	Milt Plum, Cleveland, NFL	250	151	2,297	21	5
	Jack Kemp, L.A. Chargers, AFL	406	211	3,018	20	25
1959	Charlie Conerly, N.Y. Giants	194	113	1,706	14	4
1958	Eddie LeBaron, Washington	145	79	1,365	11	10
1957	Tommy O'Connell, Cleveland	110	63	1,229	9	8
1956	Ed Brown, Chi. Bears	168	96	1,667	11	12
1955	Otto Graham, Cleveland	185	98	1,721	15	8
1954	Norm Van Brocklin, Los Angeles	260	139	2,637	13	21
1953	Otto Graham, Cleveland	258	167	2,722	11	9
1952	Norm Van Brocklin, Los Angeles	205	113	1,736	14	17
1951	Bob Waterfield, Los Angeles	176	88	1,566	13	10
1950	Norm Van Brocklin, Los Angeles	233	127	2,061	18	14
1949	Sammy Baugh, Washington	255	145	1,903	18	14
1948	Tommy Thompson, Philadelphia	246	141	1,965	25	11
1947	Sammy Baugh, Washington	354	210	2,938	25	15
1946	Bob Waterfield, Los Angeles	251	127	1,747	18	17
1945	Sammy Baugh, Washington	182	128	1,669	11	4
	Sid Luckman, Chi. Bears	217	117	1,725	14	10
1944	Frank Filchock, Washington	147	84	1,139	13	9
1943	Sammy Baugh, Washington	239	133	1,754	23	19
1942	Cecil Isbell, Green Bay	268	146	2,021	24	14
1941	Cecil Isbell, Green Bay	206	117	1,479	15	11
1940	Sammy Baugh, Washington	177	111	1,367	12	10
1939	*Parker Hall, Cleveland	208	106	1,227	9	13
1938	Ed Danowski, N.Y. Giants	129	70	848	7	8
1937	*Sammy Baugh, Washington	171	81	1,127	8	14
1936	Arnie Herber, Green Bay	173	77	1,239	11	13
1935	Ed Danowski, N.Y. Giants	113	57	794	10	9
1934	Arnie Herber, Green Bay	115	42	799	8	12
1933	*Harry Newman, N.Y. Giants	136	53	973	11	17
1932	Arnie Herber, Green Bay	101	37	639	9	9

**First year in the league.*

Annual Pass Receiving Leaders

Year	Player, Team	No.	Yards	Avg.	TD
1986	Todd Christensen, L.A. Raiders, AFC	95	1,153	12.1	8
	Jerry Rice, San Francisco, NFC	86	1,570	18.3	15
1985	Roger Craig, San Francisco, NFC	92	1,016	11.0	6
	Lionel James, San Diego, AFC	86	1,027	11.9	6
1984	Art Monk, Washington, NFC	106	1,372	12.9	7
	Ozzie Newsome, Cleveland, AFC	89	1,001	11.2	5
1983	Todd Christensen, L.A. Raiders, AFC	92	1,247	13.6	12
	Roy Green, St. Louis, NFC	78	1,227	15.7	14
	Charlie Brown, Washington, NFC	78	1,225	15.7	8
	Earnest Gray, N.Y. Giants, NFC	78	1,139	14.6	5
1982	Dwight Clark, San Francisco, NFC	60	913	15.2	5
	Kellen Winslow, San Diego, AFC	54	721	13.4	6
1981	Kellen Winslow, San Diego, AFC	88	1,075	12.2	10
	Dwight Clark, San Francisco, NFC	85	1,105	13.0	4
1980	Kellen Winslow, San Diego, AFC	89	1,290	14.5	9
	*Earl Cooper, San Francisco, NFC	83	567	6.8	4
1979	Joe Washington, Baltimore, AFC	82	750	9.1	3
	Ahmad Rashad, Minnesota, NFC	80	1,156	14.5	9
1978	Rickey Young, Minnesota, NFC	88	704	8.0	5
	Steve Largent, Seattle, AFC	71	1,168	16.5	8
1977	Lydell Mitchell, Baltimore, AFC	71	620	8.7	4
	Ahmad Rashad, Minnesota, NFC	51	681	13.4	2
1976	MacArthur Lane, Kansas City, AFC	66	686	10.4	1
	Drew Pearson, Dallas, NFC	58	806	13.9	6
1975	Chuck Foreman, Minnesota, NFC	73	691	9.5	9
	Reggie Rucker, Cleveland, AFC	60	770	12.8	3
	Lydell Mitchell, Baltimore, AFC	60	544	9.1	4
1974	Lydell Mitchell, Baltimore, AFC	72	544	7.6	2
	Charles Young, Philadelphia, NFC	63	696	11.0	3
1973	Harold Carmichael, Philadelphia, NFC	67	1,116	16.7	9
	Fred Willis, Houston, AFC	57	371	6.5	1
1972	Harold Jackson, Philadelphia, NFC	62	1,048	16.9	4
	Fred Biletnikoff, Oakland, AFC	58	802	13.8	7
1971	Fred Biletnikoff, Oakland, AFC	61	929	15.2	9
	Bob Tucker, N.Y. Giants, NFC	59	791	13.4	4
1970	Dick Gordon, Chicago, NFC	71	1,026	14.5	13
	Marlin Briscoe, Buffalo, AFC	57	1,036	18.2	8

1969	Dan Abramowicz, New Orleans, NFL	73	1,015	13.9	7
	Lance Alworth, San Diego, AFL	64	1,003	15.7	4
1968	Clifton McNeil, San Francisco, NFL	71	994	14.0	7
	Lance Alworth, San Diego, AFL	68	1,312	19.3	10
1967	George Sauer, N.Y. Jets, AFL	75	1,189	15.9	6
	Charley Taylor, Washington, NFL	70	990	14.1	9
1966	Lance Alworth, San Diego, AFL	73	1,383	18.9	13
	Charley Taylor, Washington, NFL	72	1,119	15.5	12
1965	Lionel Taylor, Denver, AFL	85	1,131	13.3	6
	Dave Parks, San Francisco, NFL	80	1,344	16.8	12
1964	Charley Hennigan, Houston, AFL	101	1,546	15.3	8
	Johnny Morris, Chicago, NFL	93	1,200	12.9	10
1963	Lionel Taylor, Denver, AFL	78	1,101	14.1	10
	Bobby Joe Conrad, St. Louis, NFL	73	967	13.2	10
1962	Lionel Taylor, Denver, AFL	77	908	11.8	4
	Bobby Mitchell, Washington, NFL	72	1,384	19.2	11
1961	Lionel Taylor, Denver, AFL	100	1,176	11.8	4
	Jim (Red) Phillips, Los Angeles, NFL	78	1,092	14.0	5
1960	Lionel Taylor, Denver, AFL	92	1,235	13.4	12
	Raymond Berry, Baltimore, NFL	74	1,298	17.5	10
1959	Raymond Berry, Baltimore	66	959	14.5	14
1958	Raymond Berry, Baltimore	56	794	14.2	9
	Pete Retzlaff, Philadelphia	56	766	13.7	2
1957	Billy Wilson, San Francisco	52	757	14.6	6
1956	Billy Wilson, San Francisco	60	889	14.8	5
1955	Pete Pihos, Philadelphia	62	864	13.9	7
1954	Pete Pihos, Philadelphia	60	872	14.5	10
	Billy Wilson, San Francisco	60	830	13.8	5
1953	Pete Pihos, Philadelphia	63	1,049	16.7	10
1952	Mac Speedie, Cleveland	62	911	14.7	5
1951	Elroy (Crazylegs) Hirsch, Los Angeles	66	1,495	22.7	17
1950	Tom Fears, Los Angeles	84	1,116	13.3	7
1949	Tom Fears, Los Angeles	77	1,013	13.2	9
1948	*Tom Fears, Los Angeles	51	698	13.7	4
1947	Jim Keane, Chi. Bears	64	910	14.2	10
1946	Jim Benton, Los Angeles	63	981	15.6	6
1945	Don Hutson, Green Bay	47	834	17.7	9
1944	Don Hutson, Green Bay	58	866	14.9	9
1943	Don Hutson, Green Bay	47	776	16.5	11
1942	Don Hutson, Green Bay	74	1,211	16.4	17
1941	Don Hutson, Green Bay	58	738	12.7	10
1940	*Don Looney, Philadelphia	58	707	12.2	4
1939	Don Hutson, Green Bay	34	846	24.9	6
1938	Gaynell Tinsley, Chi. Cardinals	41	516	12.6	1
1937	Don Hutson, Green Bay	41	552	13.5	7
1936	Don Hutson, Green Bay	34	536	15.8	8
1935	*Tod Goodwin, N.Y. Giants	26	432	16.6	4
1934	Joe Carter, Philadelphia	16	238	14.9	4
	Morris (Red) Badgro, N.Y. Giants	16	206	12.9	1
1933	John (Shipwreck) Kelly, Brooklyn	22	246	11.2	3
1932	Ray Flaherty, N.Y. Giants	21	350	16.7	3

First year in the league.

Annual Interception Leaders

Year	Player, Team	No.	Yards	TD
1986	Ronnie Lott, San Francisco, NFC	10	134	1
	Deron Cherry, Kansas City, AFC	9	150	0
1985	Everson Walls, Dallas, NFC	9	31	0
	Albert Lewis, Kansas City, AFC	8	59	0
	Eugene Daniel, Indianapolis, AFC	8	53	0
1984	Ken Easley, Seattle, AFC	10	126	2
	*Tom Flynn, Green Bay, NFC	9	106	0
1983	Mark Murphy, Washington, NFC	9	127	0
	Ken Riley, Cincinnati, AFC	8	89	2
	Vann McElroy, L.A. Raiders, AFC	8	68	0
1982	Everson Walls, Dallas, NFC	7	61	0
	Ken Riley, Cincinnati, AFC	5	88	1
	Bobby Jackson, N.Y. Jets, AFC	5	84	1
	Dwayne Woodruff, Pittsburgh, AFC	5	53	0
	Donnie Shell, Pittsburgh, AFC	5	27	0
1981	*Everson Walls, Dallas, NFC	11	133	0
	John Harris, Seattle, AFC	10	155	2
1980	Lester Hayes, Oakland, AFC	13	273	1
	Nolan Cromwell, Los Angeles, NFC	8	140	1
1979	Mike Reinfeldt, Houston, AFC	12	205	0
	Lemar Parrish, Washington, NFC	9	65	0
1978	Thom Darden, Cleveland, AFC	10	200	0
	Ken Stone, St. Louis, NFC	9	139	0
	Willie Buchanon, Green Bay, NFC	9	93	1
1977	Lyle Blackwood, Baltimore, AFC	10	163	0
	Rolland Lawrence, Atlanta, NFC	7	138	0
1976	Monte Jackson, Los Angeles, NFC	10	173	3
	Ken Riley, Cincinnati, AFC	9	141	1
1975	Mel Blount, Pittsburgh, AFC	11	121	0
	Paul Krause, Minnesota, NFC	10	201	0
1974	Emmitt Thomas, Kansas City, AFC	12	214	2
	Ray Brown, Atlanta, NFC	8	164	1
1973	Dick Anderson, Miami, AFC	8	163	2
	Mike Wagner, Pittsburgh, AFC	8	134	0
	Bobby Bryant, Minnesota, NFC	7	105	1
1972	Bill Bradley, Philadelphia, NFC	9	73	0
	Mike Sensibaugh, Kansas City, AFC	8	65	0
1971	Bill Bradley, Philadelphia, NFC	11	248	0
	Ken Houston, Houston, AFC	9	220	4
1970	Johnny Robinson, Kansas City, AFC	10	155	0
	Dick LeBeau, Detroit, NFC	9	96	0
1969	Mel Renfro, Dallas, NFL	10	118	0
	Emmitt Thomas, Kansas City, AFL	9	146	1
1968	Dave Grayson, Oakland, AFL	10	195	1
	Willie Williams, N.Y. Giants, NFL	10	103	0
1967	Miller Farr, Houston, AFL	10	264	3
	*Lem Barney, Detroit, NFL	10	232	3
	Tom Janik, Buffalo, AFL	10	222	2
	Dave Whitsell, New Orleans, NFL	10	178	2
	Dick Westmoreland, Miami, AFL	10	127	1
1966	Larry Wilson, St. Louis, NFL	10	180	2
	Johnny Robinson, Kansas City, AFL	10	136	1
	Bobby Hunt, Kansas City, AFL	10	113	0
1965	W.K. Hicks, Houston, AFL	9	156	0
	Bobby Boyd, Baltimore, NFL	9	78	1
1964	Dainard Paulson, N.Y. Jets, AFL	12	157	1
	*Paul Krause, Washington, NFL	12	140	1
1963	Fred Glick, Houston, AFL	12	180	1
	Dick Lynch, N.Y. Giants, NFL	9	251	3
	Roosevelt Taylor, Chicago, NFL	9	172	1
1962	Lee Riley, N.Y. Titans, AFL	11	122	0
	Willie Wood, Green Bay, NFL	9	132	0
1961	Billy Atkins, Buffalo, AFL	10	158	0
	Dick Lynch, N.Y. Giants, NFL	9	60	0
1960	*Austin (Goose) Gonsoulin, Denver, AFL	11	98	0
	Dave Baker, San Francisco, NFL	10	96	0
	Jerry Norton, St. Louis, NFL	10	96	0
1959	Dean Derby, Pittsburgh	7	127	0
	Milt Davis, Baltimore	7	119	1
	Don Shinnick, Baltimore	7	70	0
1958	Jim Patton, N.Y. Giants	11	183	0
1957	*Milt Davis, Baltimore	10	219	2
	Jack Christiansen, Detroit	10	137	1
	Jack Butler, Pittsburgh	10	85	0
1956	Lindon Crow, Chi. Cardinals	11	170	0
1955	Will Sherman, Los Angeles	11	101	0
1954	Dick (Night Train) Lane, Chi. Cardinals	10	181	0
1953	Jack Christiansen, Detroit	12	238	1
1952	*Dick (Night Train) Lane, Los Angeles	14	298	2
1951	Otto Schnellbacher, N.Y. Giants	11	194	2
1950	*Orban (Spec) Sanders, N.Y. Yanks	13	199	0
1949	Bob Nussbaumer, Chi. Cardinals	12	157	0
1948	*Dan Sandifer, Washington	13	258	2
1947	Frank Reagan, N.Y. Giants	10	203	0
	Frank Seno, Boston	10	100	0
1946	Bill Dudley, Pittsburgh	10	242	1
1945	Roy Zimmerman, Philadelphia	7	90	0
1944	*Howard Livingston, N.Y. Giants	9	172	1
1943	Sammy Baugh, Washington	11	112	0
1942	Clyde (Bulldog) Turner, Chi. Bears	8	96	1
1941	Marshall Goldberg, Chi. Cardinals	7	54	0
	*Art Jones, Pittsburgh	7	35	0
1940	Clarence (Ace) Parker, Brooklyn	6	146	1
	Kent Ryan, Detroit	6	65	0
	Don Hutson, Green Bay	6	24	0

First year in the league.

Annual Punting Leaders

Year	Player, Team	No.	Avg.	Long
1986	Rohn Stark, Indianapolis, AFC	76	45.2	63
	Sean Landeta, N.Y. Giants, NFC	79	44.8	61
1985	Rohn Stark, Indianapolis, AFC	78	45.9	68
	*Rick Donnelly, Atlanta, NFC	59	43.6	68
1984	Jim Arnold, Kansas City, AFC	98	44.9	63
	*Brian Hansen, New Orleans, NFC	69	43.8	66
1983	Rohn Stark, Baltimore, AFC	91	45.3	68
	*Frank Garcia, Tampa Bay, NFC	95	42.2	64
1982	Luke Prestridge, Denver, AFC	45	45.0	65
	Carl Birdsong, St. Louis, NFC	54	43.8	65
1981	Pat McInally, Cincinnati, AFC	72	45.4	62
	Tom Skladany, Detroit, NFC	64	43.5	74
1980	Dave Jennings, N.Y. Giants, NFC	94	44.8	63
	Luke Prestridge, Denver, AFC	70	43.9	57
1979	*Bob Grupp, Kansas City, AFC	89	43.6	74
	Dave Jennings, N.Y. Giants, NFC	104	42.7	72
1978	Pat McInally, Cincinnati, AFC	91	43.1	65
	*Tom Skladany, Detroit, NFC	86	42.5	63
1977	Ray Guy, Oakland, AFC	59	43.3	74
	Tom Blanchard, New Orleans, NFC	82	42.4	66
1976	Marv Bateman, Buffalo, AFC	86	42.8	78
	John James, Atlanta, NFC	101	42.1	67
1975	Ray Guy, Oakland, AFC	68	43.8	64
	Herman Weaver, Detroit, NFC	80	42.0	61
1974	Ray Guy, Oakland, AFC	74	42.2	66
	Tom Blanchard, New Orleans, NFC	88	42.1	71
1973	Jerrel Wilson, Kansas City, AFC	80	45.5	68
	*Tom Wittum, San Francisco, NFC	79	43.7	62
1972	Jerrel Wilson, Kansas City, AFC	66	44.8	69
	Dave Chapple, Los Angeles, NFC	53	44.2	70
1971	Dave Lewis, Cincinnati, AFC	72	44.8	56
	Tom McNeill, Philadelphia, NFC	73	42.0	64
1970	*Dave Lewis, Cincinnati, AFC	79	46.2	63
	*Julian Fagan, New Orleans, NFC	77	42.5	64
1969	David Lee, Baltimore, NFL	57	45.3	66
	Dennis Partee, San Diego, AFL	71	44.6	62
1968	Jerrel Wilson, Kansas City, AFL	63	45.1	70
	Billy Lothridge, Atlanta, NFL	75	44.3	70
1967	Bob Scarpitto, Denver, AFL	105	44.9	73
	Billy Lothridge, Atlanta, NFL	87	43.7	62
1966	Bob Scarpitto, Denver, AFL	76	45.8	70
	*David Lee, Baltimore, NFL	49	45.6	64
1965	Gary Collins, Cleveland, NFL	65	46.7	71
	Jerrel Wilson, Kansas City, AFL	69	45.4	64
1964	*Bobby Walden, Minnesota, NFL	72	46.4	73
	Jim Fraser, Denver, AFL	73	44.2	67
1963	Yale Lary, Detroit, NFL	35	48.9	73
	Jim Fraser, Denver, AFL	81	44.4	66
1962	Tommy Davis, San Francisco, NFL	48	45.6	82
	Jim Fraser, Denver, AFL	55	43.6	75
1961	Yale Lary, Detroit, NFL	52	48.4	71
	Billy Atkins, Buffalo, AFL	85	44.5	70

1960	Jerry Norton, St. Louis, NFL	39	45.6	62
	*Paul Maguire, L.A. Chargers, AFL	43	40.5	61
1959	Yale Lary, Detroit	45	47.1	67
1958	Sam Baker, Washington	48	45.4	64
1957	Don Chandler, N.Y. Giants	60	44.6	61
1956	Norm Van Brocklin, Los Angeles	48	43.1	72
1955	Norm Van Brocklin, Los Angeles	60	44.6	61
1954	Pat Brady, Pittsburgh	66	43.2	72
1953	Pat Brady, Pittsburgh	80	46.9	64
1952	Horace Gillom, Cleveland	61	45.7	73
1951	Horace Gillom, Cleveland	73	45.5	66
1950	*Fred (Curly) Morrison, Chi. Bears	57	43.3	65
1949	*Mike Boyda, N.Y. Bulldogs	56	44.2	61
1948	Joe Muha, Philadelphia	57	47.3	82
1947	Jack Jacobs, Green Bay	57	43.5	74
1946	Roy McKay, Green Bay	64	42.7	64
1945	Roy McKay, Green Bay	44	41.2	73
1944	Frank Sinkwich, Detroit	45	41.0	73
1943	Sammy Baugh, Washington	50	45.9	81
1942	Sammy Baugh, Washington	37	48.2	74
1941	Sammy Baugh, Washington	30	48.7	75
1940	Sammy Baugh, Washington	35	51.4	85
1939	*Parker Hall, Cleveland	58	40.8	80

**First year in the league.*

Annual Punt Return Leaders

Year	Player, Team	No.	Yards	Avg.	Long	TD
1986	*Bobby Joe Edmonds, Seattle, AFC	34	419	12.3	75	1
	*Vai Sikahema, St. Louis, NFC	43	522	12.1	71	2
1985	Irving Fryar, New England, AFC	37	520	14.1	85	2
	Henry Ellard, L.A. Rams, NFC	37	501	13.5	80	1
1984	Mike Martin, Cincinnati, AFC	24	376	15.7	55	0
	Henry Ellard, L.A. Rams, NFC	30	403	13.4	83	2
1983	*Henry Ellard, L.A. Rams, NFC	16	217	13.6	72	1
	Kirk Springs, N.Y. Jets, AFC	23	287	12.5	76	1
1982	Rick Upchurch, Denver, AFC	15	242	16.1	78	2
	Billy Johnson, Atlanta, NFC	24	273	11.4	71	0
1981	LeRoy Irvin, Los Angeles, NFC	46	615	13.4	84	3
	*James Brooks, San Diego, AFC	22	290	13.2	42	0
1980	J. T. Smith, Kansas City, AFC	40	581	14.5	75	2
	*Kenny Johnson, Atlanta, NFC	23	281	12.2	56	0
1979	John Sciarra, Philadelphia, NFC	16	182	11.4	38	0
	*Tony Nathan, Miami, AFC	28	306	10.9	86	1
1978	Rick Upchurch, Denver, AFC	36	493	13.7	75	1
	Jackie Wallace, Los Angeles, NFC	52	618	11.9	58	0
1977	Billy Johnson, Houston, AFC	35	539	15.4	87	2
	Larry Marshall, Philadelphia, NFC	46	489	10.6	48	0
1976	Rick Upchurch, Denver, AFC	39	536	13.7	92	4
	Eddie Brown, Washington, NFC	48	646	13.5	71	1
1975	Billy Johnson, Houston, AFC	40	612	15.3	83	3
	Terry Metcalf, St. Louis, NFC	23	285	12.4	69	1
1974	Lemar Parrish, Cincinnati, AFC	18	338	18.8	90	2
	Dick Jauron, Detroit, NFC	17	286	16.8	58	0
1973	Bruce Taylor, San Francisco, NFC	15	207	13.8	61	0
	Ron Smith, San Diego, AFC	27	352	13.0	84	2
1972	*Ken Ellis, Green Bay, NFC	14	215	15.4	80	1
	Chris Farasopoulos, N.Y. Jets, AFC	17	179	10.5	65	1
1971	Les (Speedy) Duncan, Washington, NFC	22	233	10.6	33	0
	Leroy Kelly, Cleveland, AFC	30	292	9.7	74	0
1970	Ed Podolak, Kansas City, AFC	23	311	13.5	60	0
	*Bruce Taylor, San Francisco, NFC	43	516	12.0	76	0
1969	Alvin Haymond, Los Angeles, NFL	33	435	13.2	52	0
	*Bill Thompson, Denver, AFL	25	288	11.5	40	0
1968	Bob Hayes, Dallas, NFL	15	312	20.8	90	2
	Noland Smith, Kansas City, AFL	18	270	15.0	80	1
1967	Floyd Little, Denver, AFL	16	270	16.9	72	1
	Ben Davis, Cleveland, NFL	18	229	12.7	52	1
1966	Les (Speedy) Duncan, San Diego, AFL	18	238	13.2	81	1
	Johnny Roland, St. Louis, NFL	20	221	11.1	86	1
1965	Leroy Kelly, Cleveland, NFL	17	265	15.6	67	2
	Les (Speedy) Duncan, San Diego, AFL	30	464	15.5	66	2
1964	Bobby Jancik, Houston, AFL	12	220	18.3	82	1
	Tommy Watkins, Detroit, NFl	16	238	14.9	68	2
1963	Dick James, Washington, NFL	16	214	13.4	39	0
	Claude (Hoot) Gibson, Oakland, AFL	26	307	11.8	85	2
1962	Dick Christy, N.Y. Titans, AFL	15	250	16.7	73	2
	Pat Studstill, Detroit, NFL	29	457	15.8	44	0
1961	Dick Christy, N.Y. Titans, AFL	18	383	21.3	70	2
	Willie Wood, Green Bay, NFL	14	225	16.1	72	2
1960	*Abner Haynes, Dall. Texans, AFL	14	215	15.4	46	0
	Abe Woodson, San Francisco, NFL	13	174	13.4	48	0
1959	Johnny Morris, Chi. Bears	14	171	12.2	78	1
1958	Jon Arnett, Los Angeles	18	223	12.4	58	0
1957	Bert Zagers, Washington	14	217	15.5	76	2
1956	Ken Konz, Cleveland	13	187	14.4	65	1
1955	Ollie Matson, Chi. Cardinals	13	245	18.8	78	2
1954	*Veryl Switzer, Green Bay	24	306	12.8	93	1
1953	Charley Trippi, Chi. Cardinals	21	239	11.4	38	0
1952	Jack Christiansen, Detroit	15	322	21.5	79	2
1951	Claude (Buddy) Young, N.Y. Yanks	12	231	19.3	79	1
1950	*Herb Rich, Baltimore	12	276	23.0	86	1
1949	Verda (Vitamin T) Smith, Los Angeles	27	427	15.8	85	1
1948	George McAfee, Chi. Bears	30	417	13.9	60	1
1947	*Walt Slater, Pittsburgh	28	435	15.5	33	0
1946	Bill Dudley, Pittsburgh	27	385	14.3	52	0
1945	*Dave Ryan, Detroit	15	220	14.7	56	0
1944	*Steve Van Buren, Philadelphia	15	230	15.3	55	1
1943	Andy Farkas, Washington	15	168	11.2	33	0
1942	Merlyn Condit, Brooklyn	21	210	10.0	23	0
1941	Byron (Whizzer) White, Detroit	19	262	13.8	64	0

**First year in the league.*

Annual Kickoff Return Leaders

Year	Player, Team	No.	Yards	Avg.	Long	TD
1986	Dennis Gentry, Chicago, NFC	20	576	28.8	91	1
	*Lupe Sanchez, Pittsburgh, AFC	25	591	23.6	64	0
1985	Ron Brown, L.A. Rams, NFC	28	918	32.8	98	3
	Glen Young, Cleveland, AFC	35	898	25.7	63	0
1984	*Bobby Humphery, N.Y. Jets, AFC	22	675	30.7	97	1
	Barry Redden, L.A. Rams, NFC	23	530	23.0	40	0
1983	Fulton Walker, Miami, AFC	36	962	26.7	78	0
	Darrin Nelson, Minnesota, NFC	18	445	24.7	50	0
1982	*Mike Mosley, Buffalo, AFC	18	487	27.1	66	0
	Alvin Hall, Detroit, NFC	16	426	26.6	96	1
1981	Mike Nelms, Washington, NFC	37	1,099	29.7	84	0
	Carl Roaches, Houston, AFC	28	769	27.5	96	1
1980	Horace Ivory, New England, AFC	36	992	27.6	98	1
	Rich Mauti, New Orleans, NFC	31	798	25.7	52	0
1979	Larry Brunson, Oakland, AFC	17	441	25.9	89	0
	*Jimmy Edwards, Minnesota, NFC	44	1,103	25.1	83	0
1978	Steve Odom, Green Bay, NFC	25	677	27.1	95	1
	*Keith Wright, Cleveland, AFC	30	789	26.3	86	0
1977	*Raymond Clayborn, New England, AFC	28	869	31.0	101	3
	*Wilbert Montgomery, Philadelphia, NFC	23	619	26.9	99	1
1976	*Duriel Harris, Miami, AFC	17	559	32.9	69	0
	Cullen Bryant, Los Angeles, NFC	16	459	28.7	90	1
1975	*Walter Payton, Chicago, NFC	14	444	31.7	70	0
	Harold Hart, Oakland, AFC	17	518	30.5	102	1
1974	Terry Metcalf, St. Louis, NFC	20	623	31.2	94	1
	Greg Pruitt, Cleveland, AFC	22	606	27.5	88	1
1973	Carl Garrett, Chicago, NFC	16	486	30.4	67	0
	*Wallace Francis, Buffalo, AFC	23	687	29.9	101	2
1972	Ron Smith, Chicago, NFC	30	924	30.8	94	1
	*Bruce Laird, Baltimore, AFC	29	843	29.1	73	0
1971	Travis Williams, Los Angeles, NFC	25	743	29.7	105	1
	Eugene (Mercury) Morris, Miami, AFC	15	423	28.2	94	1
1970	Jim Duncan, Baltimore, AFC	20	707	35.4	99	1
	Cecil Turner, Chicago, NFC	23	752	32.7	96	4
1969	Bobby Williams, Detroit, NFL	17	563	33.1	96	1
	*Bill Thompson, Denver, AFL	18	513	28.5	63	0
1968	Preston Pearson, Baltimore, NFL	15	527	35.1	102	2
	*George Atkinson, Oakland, AFL	32	802	25.1	60	0
1967	*Travis Williams, Green Bay, NFL	18	739	41.1	104	4
	*Zeke Moore, Houston, AFL	14	405	28.9	92	1
1966	Gale Sayers, Chicago, NFL	23	718	31.2	93	2
	*Goldie Sellers, Denver, AFL	19	541	28.5	100	2
1965	Tommy Watkins, Detroit, NFL	17	584	34.4	94	0
	Abner Haynes, Denver, AFL	34	901	26.5	60	0
1964	*Clarence Childs, N.Y. Giants, NFL	34	987	29.0	100	1
	Bo Roberson, Oakland, AFL	36	975	27.1	59	0
1963	Abe Woodson, San Francisco, NFL	29	935	32.2	103	3
	Bobby Jancik, Houston, AFL	45	1,317	29.3	53	0
1962	Abe Woodson, San Francisco, NFL	37	1,157	31.3	79	0
	*Bobby Jancik, Houston, AFL	24	826	30.3	61	0
1961	Dick Bass, Los Angeles, NFL	23	698	30.3	64	0
	*Dave Grayson, Dall. Texans, AFL	16	453	28.3	73	0
1960	*Tom Moore, Green Bay, NFL	12	397	33.1	84	0
	Ken Hall, Houston, AFL	19	594	31.3	104	1
1959	Abe Woodson, San Francisco	13	382	29.4	105	1
1958	Ollie Matson, Chi. Cardinals	14	497	35.5	101	2
1957	*Jon Arnett, Los Angeles	18	504	28.0	98	1
1956	*Tom Wilson, Los Angeles	15	477	31.8	103	1
1955	Al Carmichael, Green Bay	14	418	29.9	100	1
1954	Billy Reynolds, Cleveland	14	413	29.5	51	0
1953	Joe Arenas, San Francisco	16	551	34.4	82	0
1952	Lynn Chandnois, Pittsburgh	17	599	35.2	93	2
1951	Lynn Chandnois, Pittsburgh	12	390	32.5	55	0
1950	Verda (Vitamin T) Smith, Los Angeles	22	742	33.7	97	3
1949	*Don Doll, Detroit	21	536	25.5	56	0
1948	*Joe Scott, N.Y. Giants	20	569	28.5	99	1
1947	Eddie Saenz, Washington	29	797	27.5	94	2
1946	Abe Karnofsky, Boston	21	599	28.5	97	1
1945	Steve Van Buren, Philadelphia	13	373	28.7	98	1
1944	Bob Thurbon, Card.-Pitt	12	291	24.3	55	0
1943	Ken Heineman, Brooklyn	16	444	27.8	69	0
1942	Marshall Goldberg, Chi. Cardinals	15	393	26.2	95	1
1941	Marshall Goldberg, Chi. Cardinals	12	290	24.2	41	0

**First year in the league.*

Points Scored

Year	Team	Points
1986	Miami, AFC	430
	Minnesota, NFC	398
1985	San Diego, AFC	467
	Chicago, NFC	456
1984	Miami, AFC	513
	San Francisco, NFC	475
1983	Washington, NFC	541
	L.A. Raiders, AFC	442
1982	San Diego, AFC	288
	Dallas, NFC	226
	Green Bay, NFC	226
1981	San Diego, AFC	478
	Atlanta, NFC	426
1980	Dallas, NFC	454
	New England, AFC	441
1979	Pittsburgh, AFC	416
	Dallas, NFC	371
1978	Dallas, NFC	384
	Miami, AFC	372
1977	Oakland, AFC	351
	Dallas, NFC	345
1976	Baltimore, AFC	417
	Los Angeles, NFC	351
1975	Buffalo, AFC	420
	Minnesota, NFC	377
1974	Oakland, AFC	355
	Washington, NFC	320
1973	Los Angeles, NFC	388
	Denver, AFC	354
1972	Miami, AFC	385
	San Francisco, NFC	353
1971	Dallas, NFC	406
	Oakland, AFC	344
1970	San Francisco, NFC	352
	Baltimore, AFC	321
1969	Minnesota, NFL	379
	Oakland, AFL	377
1968	Oakland, AFL	453
	Dallas, NFL	431
1967	Oakland, AFL	468
	Los Angeles, NFL	398
1966	Kansas City, AFL	448
	Dallas, NFL	445
1965	San Francisco, NFL	421
	San Diego, AFL	340
1964	Baltimore, NFL	428
	Buffalo, AFL	400
1963	N.Y. Giants, NFL	448
	San Diego, AFL	399
1962	Green Bay, NFL	415

Year	Team	Points
	Dall. Texans, AFL	389
1961	Houston, AFL	513
	Green Bay, NFL	391
1960	N.Y. Titans, AFL	382
	Cleveland, NFL	362
1959	Baltimore	374
1958	Baltimore	381
1957	Los Angeles	307
1956	Chi. Bears	363
1955	Cleveland	349
1954	Detroit	337
1953	San Francisco	372
1952	Los Angeles	349
1951	Los Angeles	392
1950	Los Angeles	466
1949	Philadelphia	364
1948	Chi. Cardinals	395
1947	Chi. Bears	363
1946	Chi. Bears	289
1945	Philadelphia	272
1944	Philadelphia	267
1943	Chi. Bears	303
1942	Chi. Bears	376
1941	Chi. Bears	396
1940	Washington	245
1939	Chi. Bears	298
1938	Green Bay	223
1937	Green Bay	220
1936	Green Bay	248
1935	Chi. Bears	192
1934	Chi. Bears	286
1933	N.Y. Giants	244
1932	Green Bay	152

Total Yards Gained

Year	Team	Yards
1986	Cincinnati, AFC	6,490
	San Francisco, NFC	6,082
1985	San Diego, AFC	6,535
	San Francisco, NFC	5,920
1984	Miami, AFC	6,936
	San Francisco, NFC	6,366
1983	San Diego, AFC	6,197
	Green Bay, NFC	6,172
1982	San Diego, AFC	4,048
	San Francisco, NFC	3,242
1981	San Diego, AFC	6,744
	Detroit, NFC	5,933
1980	San Diego, AFC	6,410
	Los Angeles, NFC	6,006
1979	Pittsburgh, AFC	6,258
	Dallas, NFC	5,968
1978	New England, AFC	5,965
	Dallas, NFC	5,959
1977	Dallas, NFC	4,812
	Oakland, AFC	4,736
1976	Baltimore, AFC	5,236
	St. Louis, NFC	5,136
1975	Buffalo, AFC	5,467
	Dallas, NFC	5,025
1974	Dallas, NFC	4,983
	Oakland, AFC	4,718
1973	Los Angeles, NFC	4,906
	Oakland, AFC	4,773
1972	Miami, AFC	5,036
	N.Y. Giants, NFC	4,483
1971	Dallas, NFC	5,035
	San Diego, AFC	4,738
1970	Oakland, AFC	4,829
	San Francisco, NFC	4,503
1969	Dallas, NFL	5,122
	Oakland, AFL	5,036
1968	Oakland, AFL	5,696
	Dallas, NFL	5,117
1967	N.Y. Jets, AFL	5,152
	Baltimore, NFL	5,008
1966	Dallas, NFL	5,145
	Kansas City, AFL	5,114
1965	San Francisco, NFL	5,270
	San Diego, AFL	5,188
1964	Buffalo, AFL	5,206
	Baltimore, NFL	4,779
1963	San Diego, AFL	5,153
	N.Y. Giants, NFL	5,024
1962	N.Y. Giants, NFL	5,005
	Houston, AFL	4,971
1961	Houston, AFL	6,288
	Philadelphia, NFL	5,112
1960	Houston, AFL	4,936
	Baltimore, NFL	4,245
1959	Baltimore	4,458
1958	Baltimore	4,539
1957	Los Angeles	4,143
1956	Chi. Bears	4,537
1955	Chi. Bears	4,316
1954	Los Angeles	5,187
1953	Philadelphia	4,811
1952	Cleveland	4,352
1951	Los Angeles	5,506
1950	Los Angeles	5,420
1949	Chi. Bears	4,873
1948	Chi. Cardinals	4,705
1947	Chi. Bears	5,053
1946	Los Angeles	3,793
1945	Washington	3,549
1944	Chi. Bears	3,239
1943	Chi. Bears	4,045
1942	Chi. Bears	3,900
1941	Chi. Bears	4,265
1940	Green Bay	3,400
1939	Chi. Bears	3,988
1938	Green Bay	3,037
1937	Green Bay	3,201
1936	Detroit	3,703
1935	Chi. Bears	3,454
1934	Chi. Bears	3,900
1933	N.Y. Giants	2,973
1932	Chi. Bears	2,755

Yards Rushing

Year	Team	Yards
1986	Chicago, NFC	2,700
	Cincinnati, AFC	2,533
1985	Chicago, NFC	2,761
	Indianapolis, AFC	2,439
1984	Chicago, NFC	2,974
	N.Y. Jets, AFC	2,189
1983	Chicago, NFC	2,727
	Baltimore, AFC	2,695
1982	Buffalo, AFC	1,371
	Dallas, NFC	1,313
1981	Detroit, NFC	2,795
	Kansas City, AFC	2,633
1980	Los Angeles, NFC	2,799
	Houston, AFC	2,635
1979	N.Y. Jets, AFC	2,646
	St. Louis, NFC	2,582
1978	New England, AFC	3,165
	Dallas, NFC	2,783
1977	Chicago, NFC	2,811
	Oakland, AFC	2,627
1976	Pittsburgh, AFC	2,971
	Los Angeles, NFC	2,528
1975	Buffalo, AFC	2,974
	Dallas, NFC	2,432
1974	Dallas, NFC	2,454
	Pittsburgh, AFC	2,417
1973	Buffalo, AFC	3,088
	Los Angeles, NFC	2,925
1972	Miami, AFC	2,960
	Chicago, NFC	2,360
1971	Miami, AFC	2,429
	Detroit, NFC	2,376
1970	Dallas, NFC	2,300
	Miami, AFC	2,082
1969	Dallas, NFL	2,276
	Kansas City, AFL	2,220
1968	Chicago, NFL	2,377
	Kansas City, AFL	2,227
1967	Cleveland, NFL	2,139
	Houston, AFL	2,122
1966	Kansas City, AFL	2,274
	Cleveland, NFL	2,166
1965	Cleveland, NFL	2,331
	San Diego, AFL	2,085
1964	Green Bay, NFL	2,276
	Buffalo, AFL	2,040
1963	Cleveland, NFL	2,639
	San Diego, AFL	2,203
1962	Buffalo, AFL	2,480
	Green Bay, NFL	2,460
1961	Green Bay, NFL	2,350
	Dall. Texans, AFL	2,189
1960	St. Louis, NFL	2,356
	Oakland, AFL	2,056
1959	Cleveland	2,149
1958	Cleveland	2,526
1957	Los Angeles	2,142
1956	Chi. Bears	2,468
1955	Chi. Bears	2,388
1954	San Francisco	2,498
1953	San Francisco	2,230
1952	San Francisco	1,905
1951	Chi. Bears	2,408
1950	N.Y. Giants	2,336
1949	Philadelphia	2,607
1948	Chi. Cardinals	2,560
1947	Los Angeles	2,171
1946	Green Bay	1,765
1945	Cleveland	1,714
1944	Philadelphia	1,661
1943	Phil-Pitt	1,730
1942	Chi. Bears	1,881
1941	Chi. Bears	2,263
1940	Chi. Bears	1,818
1939	Chi. Bears	2,043
1938	Detroit	1,893
1937	Detroit	2,074
1936	Detroit	2,885
1935	Chi. Bears	2,096
1934	Chi. Bears	2,847
1933	Boston	2,260
1932	Chi. Bears	1,770

Yards Passing

Leadership in this category has been based on net yards since 1952.

Year	Team	Yards
1986	Miami, AFC	4,779
	San Francisco, NFC	4,096
1985	San Diego, AFC	4,870
	Dallas, NFC	3,861
1984	Miami, AFC	5,018
	St. Louis, NFC	4,257
1983	San Diego, AFC	4,661
	Green Bay, NFC	4,365
1982	San Diego, AFC	2,927
	San Francisco, NFC	2,502
1981	San Diego, AFC	4,739
	Minnesota, NFC	4,333
1980	San Diego, AFC	4,531
	Minnesota, NFC	3,688
1979	San Diego, AFC	3,915
	San Francisco, NFC	3,641
1978	San Diego, AFC	3,375
	Minnesota, NFC	3,243
1977	Buffalo, AFC	2,530
	St. Louis, NFC	2,499
1976	Baltimore, AFC	2,933
	Minnesota, NFC	2,855
1975	Cincinnati, AFC	3,241
	Washington, NFC	2,917
1974	Washington, NFC	2,978
	Cincinnati, AFC	2,804
1973	Philadelphia, NFC	2,998
	Denver, AFC	2,519
1972	N.Y. Jets, AFC	2,777
	San Francisco, NFC	2,735
1971	San Diego, AFC	3,134
	Dallas, NFC	2,786
1970	San Francisco, NFC	2,923
	Oakland, AFC	2,865
1969	Oakland, AFL	3,271
	San Francisco, NFL	3,158
1968	San Diego, AFL	3,623
	Dallas, NFL	3,026
1967	N.Y. Jets, AFL	3,845
	Washington, NFL	3,730
1966	N.Y. Jets, AFL	3,464
	Dallas, NFL	3,023
1965	San Francisco, NFL	3,487
	San Diego, AFL	3,103
1964	Houston, AFL	3,527
	Chicago, NFL	2,841
1963	Baltimore, NFL	3,296
	Houston, AFL	3,222
1962	Denver, AFL	3,404
	Philadelphia, NFL	3,385
1961	Houston, AFL	4,392
	Philadelphia, NFL	3,605
1960	Houston, AFL	3,203
	Baltimore, NFL	2,956
1959	Baltimore	2,753
1958	Pittsburgh	2,752
1957	Baltimore	2,388
1956	Los Angeles	2,419
1955	Philadelphia	2,472
1954	Chi. Bears	3,104
1953	Philadelphia	3,089
1952	Cleveland	2,566
1951	Los Angeles	3,296
1950	Los Angeles	3,709
1949	Chi. Bears	3,055
1948	Washington	2,861
1947	Washington	3,336
1946	Los Angeles	2,080
1945	Chi. Bears	1,857
1944	Washington	2,021
1943	Chi. Bears	2,310
1942	Green Bay	2,407
1941	Chi. Bears	2,002
1940	Washington	1,887
1939	Chi. Bears	1,965
1938	Washington	1,536
1937	Green Bay	1,398
1936	Green Bay	1,629
1935	Green Bay	1,449
1934	Green Bay	1,165
1933	N.Y. Giants	1,348
1932	Chi. Bears	1,013

Fewest Points Allowed

Year	Team	Points
1986	Chicago, NFC	187
	Seattle, AFC	293
1985	Chicago, NFC	198
	N.Y. Jets, AFC	264
1984	San Francisco, NFC	227
	Denver, AFC	241
1983	Miami, AFC	250
	Detroit, NFC	286
1982	Washington, NFC	128
	Miami, AFC	131
1981	Philadelphia, NFC	221
	Miami, AFC	275
1980	Philadelphia, NFC	222
	Houston, AFC	251
1979	Tampa Bay, NFC	237
	San Diego, AFC	246
1978	Pittsburgh, AFC	195
	Dallas, NFC	208
1977	Atlanta, NFC	129
	Denver, AFC	148
1976	Pittsburgh, AFC	138
	Minnesota, NFC	176
1975	Los Angeles, NFC	135
	Pittsburgh, AFC	162
1974	Los Angeles, NFC	181
	Pittsburgh, AFC	189
1973	Miami, AFC	150
	Minnesota, NFC	168
1972	Miami, AFC	171
	Washington, NFC	218
1971	Minnesota, NFC	139
	Baltimore, AFC	140
1970	Minnesota, NFC	143
	Miami, AFC	228
1969	Minnesota, NFL	133
	Kansas City, AFL	177
1968	Baltimore, NFL	144
	Kansas City, AFL	170
1967	Los Angeles, NFL	196
	Houston, AFL	199
1966	Green Bay, NFL	163
	Buffalo, AFL	255
1965	Green Bay, NFL	224
	Buffalo, AFL	226
1964	Baltimore, NFL	225
	Buffalo, AFL	242
1963	Chicago, NFL	144
	San Diego, AFL	255
1962	Green Bay, NFL	148
	Dall. Texans, AFL	233
1961	San Diego, AFL	219
	N.Y. Giants, NFL	220
1960	San Francisco, NFL	205
	Dall. Texans, AFL	253
1959	N.Y. Giants	170
1958	N.Y. Giants	183
1957	Cleveland	172
1956	Cleveland	177
1955	Cleveland	218
1954	Cleveland	162
1953	Cleveland	162
1952	Detroit	192
1951	Cleveland	152
1950	Philadelphia	141
1949	Philadelphia	134
1948	Chi. Bears	151
1947	Green Bay	210
1946	Pittsburgh	117
1945	Washington	121
1944	N.Y. Giants	75
1943	Washington	137
1942	Chi. Bears	84
1941	N.Y. Giants	114
1940	Brooklyn	120
1939	N.Y. Giants	85
1938	N.Y. Giants	79
1937	Chi. Bears	100
1936	Chi. Bears	94
1935	Green Bay	96
	N.Y. Giants	96
1934	Detroit	59
1933	Brooklyn	54
1932	Chi. Bears	44

Fewest Total Yards Allowed

Year	Team	Yards
1986	Chicago, NFC	4,130
	L.A. Raiders, AFC	4,804
1985	Chicago, NFC	4,135
	L.A. Raiders, AFC	4,603
1984	Chicago, NFC	3,863
	Cleveland, AFC	4,641
1983	Cincinnati, AFC	4,327
	New Orleans, NFC	4,691
1982	Miami, AFC	2,312
	Tampa Bay, NFC	2,442
1981	Philadelphia, NFC	4,447
	N.Y. Jets, AFC	4,871
1980	Buffalo, AFC	4,101
	Philadelphia, NFC	4,443
1979	Tampa Bay, NFC	3,949
	Pittsburgh, AFC	4,270
1978	Los Angeles, NFC	3,893
	Pittsburgh, AFC	4,168
1977	Dallas, NFC	3,213
	New England, AFC	3,638
1976	Pittsburgh, AFC	3,323
	San Francisco, NFC	3,562
1975	Minnesota, NFC	3,153
	Oakland, AFC	3,629
1974	Pittsburgh, AFC	3,074
	Washington, NFC	3,285
1973	Los Angeles, NFC	2,951
	Oakland, AFC	3,160
1972	Miami, AFC	3,297
	Green Bay, NFC	3,474

Year	Team	Yards
1971	Baltimore, AFC	2,852
	Minnesota, NFC	3,406
1970	Minnesota, NFC	2,803
	N.Y. Jets, AFC	3,655
1969	Minnesota, NFL	2,720
	Kansas City, AFL	3,163
1968	Los Angeles, NFL	3,118
	N.Y. Jets, AFL	3,363
1967	Oakland, AFL	3,294
	Green Bay, NFL	3,300
1966	St. Louis, NFL	3,492
	Oakland, AFL	3,910
1965	San Diego, AFL	3,262
	Detroit, NFL	3,557
1964	Green Bay, NFL	3,179
	Buffalo, AFL	3,878
1963	Chicago, NFL	3,176
	Boston, AFL	3,834
1962	Detroit, NFL	3,217
	Dall. Texans, AFL	3,951
1961	San Diego, AFL	3,726
	Baltimore, NFL	3,782
1960	St. Louis, NFL	3,029
	Buffalo, AFL	3,866
1959	N.Y. Giants	2,843
1958	Chi. Bears	3,066
1957	Pittsburgh	2,791
1956	N.Y. Giants	3,081
1955	Cleveland	2,841
1954	Cleveland	2,658
1953	Philadelphia	2,998
1952	Cleveland	3,075
1951	N.Y. Giants	3,250
1950	Cleveland	3,154
1949	Philadelphia	2,831
1948	Chi. Bears	2,931
1947	Green Bay	3,396
1946	Washington	2,451
1945	Philadelphia	2,073
1944	Philadelphia	1,943
1943	Chi. Bears	2,262
1942	Chi. Bears	1,703
1941	N.Y. Giants	2,368
1940	N.Y. Giants	2,219
1939	Washington	2,116
1938	N.Y. Giants	2,029
1937	Washington	2,123
1936	Boston	2,181
1935	Boston	1,996
1934	Chi. Cardinals	1,539
1933	Brooklyn	1,789

Fewest Yards Rushing Allowed

Year	Team	Yards
1986	N.Y. Giants, NFC	1,284
	Denver, AFC	1,651
1985	Chicago, NFC	1,319
	N.Y. Jets, AFC	1,516
1984	Chicago, NFC	1,377
	Pittsburgh, AFC	1,617
1983	Washington, NFC	1,289
	Cincinnati, AFC	1,499
1982	Pittsburgh, AFC	762
	Detroit, NFC	854
1981	Detroit, NFC	1,623
	Kansas City, AFC	1,747
1980	Detroit, NFC	1,599
	Cincinnati, AFC	1,680
1979	Denver, AFC	1,693
	Tampa Bay, NFC	1,873
1978	Dallas, NFC	1,721
	Pittsburgh, AFC	1,774
1977	Denver, AFC	1,531
	Dallas, NFC	1,651
1976	Pittsburgh, AFC	1,457
	Los Angeles, NFC	1,564
1975	Minnesota, NFC	1,532
	Houston, AFC	1,680
1974	Los Angeles, NFC	1,302
	New England, AFC	1,587
1973	Los Angeles, NFC	1,270
	Oakland, AFC	1,470
1972	Dallas, NFC	1,515
	Miami, AFC	1,548
1971	Baltimore, AFC	1,113
	Dallas, NFC	1,144
1970	Detroit, NFC	1,152
	N.Y. Jets, AFC	1,283
1969	Dallas, NFL	1,050
	Kansas City, AFL	1,091
1968	Dallas, NFL	1,195
	N.Y. Jets, AFL	1,195
1967	Dallas, NFL	1,081
	Oakland, AFL	1,129
1966	Buffalo, AFL	1,051
	Dallas, NFL	1,176
1965	San Diego, AFL	1,094
	Los Angeles, NFL	1,409
1964	Buffalo, AFL	913
	Los Angeles, NFL	1,501
1963	Boston, AFL	1,107
	Chicago, NFL	1,442
1962	Detroit, NFL	1,231
	Dall. Texans, AFL	1,250
1961	Boston, AFL	1,041
	Pittsburgh, NFL	1,463
1960	St. Louis, NFL	1,212
	Dall. Texans, AFL	1,338
1959	N.Y. Giants	1,261
1958	Baltimore	1,291
1957	Baltimore	1,174
1956	N.Y. Giants	1,443
1955	Cleveland	1,189
1954	Cleveland	1,050
1953	Philadelphia	1,117
1952	Detroit	1,145
1951	N.Y. Giants	913
1950	Detroit	1,367
1949	Chi. Bears	1,196
1948	Philadelphia	1,209
1947	Philadelphia	1,329
1946	Chi. Bears	1,060
1945	Philadelphia	817
1944	Philadelphia	558
1943	Phil-Pitt	793
1942	Chi. Bears	519
1941	Washington	1,042
1940	N.Y. Giants	977
1939	Chi. Bears	812
1938	Detroit	1,081
1937	Chi. Bears	933
1936	Boston	1,148
1935	Boston	998
1934	Chi. Cardinals	954
1933	Brooklyn	964

Fewest Yards Passing Allowed

Leadership in this category has been based on net yards since 1952.

Year	Team	Yards
1986	St. Louis, NFC	2,637
	New England, AFC	2,978
1985	Washington, NFC	2,746
	Pittsburgh, AFC	2,783
1984	New Orleans, NFC	2,453
	Cleveland, AFC	2,696
1983	New Orleans, NFC	2,691
	Cincinnati, AFC	2,828
1982	Miami, AFC	1,027
	Tampa Bay, NFC	1,384
1981	Philadelphia, NFC	2,696
	Buffalo, AFC	2,870
1980	Washington, NFC	2,171
	Buffalo, AFC	2,282
1979	Tampa Bay, NFC	2,076
	Buffalo, AFC	2,530
1978	Buffalo, AFC	1,960
	Los Angeles, NFC	2,048
1977	Atlanta, NFC	1,384
	San Diego, AFC	1,725
1976	Minnesota, NFC	1,575
	Cincinnati, AFC	1,758
1975	Minnesota, NFC	1,621
	Cincinnati, AFC	1,729
1974	Pittsburgh, AFC	1,466
	Atlanta, NFC	1,572
1973	Miami, AFC	1,290
	Atlanta, NFC	1,430
1972	Minnesota, NFC	1,699
	Cleveland, AFC	1,736
1971	Atlanta, NFC	1,638
	Baltimore, AFC	1,739
1970	Minnesota, NFC	1,438
	Kansas City, AFC	2,010
1969	Minnesota, NFL	1,631
	Kansas City, AFL	2,072
1968	Houston, AFL	1,671
	Green Bay, NFL	1,796
1967	Green Bay, NFL	1,377
	Buffalo, AFL	1,825
1966	Green Bay, NFL	1,959
	Oakland, AFL	2,118
1965	Green Bay, NFL	1,981
	San Diego, AFL	2,168
1964	Green Bay, NFL	1,647
	San Diego, AFL	2,518
1963	Chicago, NFL	1,734
	Oakland, AFL	2,589
1962	Green Bay, NFL	1,746
	Oakland, AFL	2,306
1961	Baltimore, NFL	1,913
	San Diego, AFL	2,363
1960	Chicago, NFL	1,388
	Buffalo, AFL	2,124
1959	N.Y. Giants	1,582
1958	Chi. Bears	1,769
1957	Cleveland	1,300
1956	Cleveland	1,103
1955	Pittsburgh	1,295
1954	Cleveland	1,608
1953	Washington	1,751
1952	Washington	1,580
1951	Pittsburgh	1,687
1950	Cleveland	1,581
1949	Philadelphia	1,607
1948	Green Bay	1,626
1947	Green Bay	1,790
1946	Pittsburgh	939
1945	Washington	1,121
1944	Chi. Bears	1,052
1943	Chi. Bears	980
1942	Washington	1,093
1941	Pittsburgh	1,168
1940	Philadelphia	1,012
1939	Washington	1,116
1938	Chi. Bears	897
1937	Detroit	804
1936	Philadelphia	853
1935	Chi. Cardinals	793
1934	Philadelphia	545
1933	Portsmouth	558

SUPER BOWL RECORDS

Compiled by Elias Sports Bureau

1967: Super Bowl I	1974: Super Bowl VIII	1981: Super Bowl XV
1968: Super Bowl II	1975: Super Bowl IX	1982: Super Bowl XVI
1969: Super Bowl III	1976: Super Bowl X	1983: Super Bowl XVII
1970: Super Bowl IV	1977: Super Bowl XI	1984: Super Bowl XVIII
1971: Super Bowl V	1978: Super Bowl XII	1985: Super Bowl XIX
1972: Super Bowl VI	1979: Super Bowl XIII	1986: Super Bowl XX
1973: Super Bowl VII	1980: Super Bowl XIV	1987: Super Bowl XXI

Individual Records

Service

Most Games

5 Marv Fleming, Green Bay, 1967-68; Miami, 1972-74
Larry Cole, Dallas, 1971-72, 1976, 1978-79
Cliff Harris, Dallas, 1971-72, 1976, 1978-79
D.D. Lewis, Dallas, 1971-72, 1976, 1978-79
Preston Pearson, Baltimore, 1969; Pittsburgh, 1975; Dallas, 1976, 1978-79
Charlie Waters, Dallas, 1971-72, 1976, 1978-79
Rayfield Wright, Dallas, 1971-72, 1976, 1978-79
4 By many players

Most Games, Winning Team

4 By many players

Most Games, Coach

6 Don Shula, Baltimore, 1969; Miami, 1972-74, 1983, 1985
5 Tom Landry, Dallas, 1971-72, 1976, 1978-79
4 Bud Grant, Minnesota, 1970, 1974-75, 1977
Chuck Noll, Pittsburgh, 1975-76, 1979-80

Most Games, Winning Team, Coach

4 Chuck Noll, Pittsburgh, 1975-76, 1979-80
2 Vince Lombardi, Green Bay, 1967-68
Tom Landry, Dallas, 1972, 1978
Don Shula, Miami, 1973-74
Tom Flores, Oakland, 1981; L.A. Raiders, 1984
Bill Walsh, San Francisco, 1982, 1985

Most Games, Losing Team, Coach

4 Bud Grant, Minnesota, 1970, 1974-75, 1977
Don Shula, Baltimore, 1969; Miami, 1972, 1983, 1985
3 Tom Landry, Dallas, 1971, 1976, 1979

Scoring

Points

Most Points, Career

24 Franco Harris, Pittsburgh, 4 games (4-td)
22 Ray Wersching, San Francisco, 2 games (7-pat, 5-fg)
20 Don Chandler, Green Bay, 2 games (8-pat, 4-fg)

Most Points, Game

18 Roger Craig, San Francisco vs. Miami, 1985 (3-td)
15 Don Chandler, Green Bay vs. Oakland, 1968 (3-pat, 4-fg)
14 Ray Wersching, San Francisco vs. Cincinnati, 1982 (2-pat, 4-fg)
Kevin Butler, Chicago vs. New England, 1986 (5-pat, 3-fg)

Touchdowns

Most Touchdowns, Career

4 Franco Harris, Pittsburgh, 4 games (4-r)
3 John Stallworth, Pittsburgh, 4 games (3-p)
Lynn Swann, Pittsburgh, 4 games (3-p)
Cliff Branch, Oakland-L.A. Raiders, 3 games (3-p)
Roger Craig, San Francisco, 1 game (1-r, 2-p)
2 By many players

Most Touchdowns, Game

3 Roger Craig, San Francisco vs. Miami, 1985 (1-r, 2-p)
2 Max McGee, Green Bay vs. Kansas City, 1967 (2-p)
Elijah Pitts, Green Bay vs. Kansas City, 1967 (2-r)
Bill Miller, Oakland vs. Green Bay, 1968 (2-p)
Larry Csonka, Miami vs. Minnesota, 1974 (2-r)
Pete Banaszak, Oakland vs. Minnesota, 1977 (2-r)
John Stallworth, Pittsburgh vs. Dallas, 1979 (2-p)
Franco Harris, Pittsburgh vs. Los Angeles, 1980 (2-r)
Cliff Branch, Oakland vs. Philadelphia, 1981 (2-p)
Dan Ross, Cincinnati vs. San Francisco, 1982 (2-p)
Marcus Allen, L.A. Raiders vs. Washington, 1984 (2-r)
Jim McMahon, Chicago vs. New England, 1986 (2-r)

Points After Touchdown

Most Points After Touchdown, Career

8 Don Chandler, Green Bay, 2 games (8 att)
Roy Gerela, Pittsburgh, 3 games (9 att)
Chris Bahr, Oakland-L.A. Raiders, 2 games (8 att)
7 Ray Wersching, San Francisco, 2 games (7 att)
5 Garo Yepremian, Miami, 3 games (5 att)
Kevin Butler, Chicago, 1 game (5 att)

Most Points After Touchdown, Game

5 Don Chandler, Green Bay vs. Kansas City, 1967 (5 att)
Roy Gerela, Pittsburgh vs. Dallas, 1979 (5 att)
Chris Bahr, L.A. Raiders vs. Washington, 1984 (5 att)
Ray Wersching, San Francisco vs. Miami, 1985 (5 att)
Kevin Butler, Chicago vs. New England, 1986 (5 att)
4 Rafael Septien, Dallas vs. Pittsburgh, 1979 (4 att)
Matt Bahr, Pittsburgh vs. Los Angeles, 1980 (4 att)
Raul Allegre, N.Y. Giants vs. Denver, 1987, (5 att)

Field Goals

Field Goals Attempted, Career

7 Roy Gerela, Pittsburgh, 3 games
6 Jim Turner, N.Y. Jets-Denver, 2 games
5 Efren Herrera, Dallas, 1 game
Ray Wersching, San Francisco, 2 games

Most Field Goals Attempted, Game

5 Jim Turner, N.Y. Jets vs. Baltimore, 1969
Efren Herrera, Dallas vs. Denver, 1978
4 Don Chandler, Green Bay vs. Oakland, 1968
Roy Gerela, Pittsburgh vs. Dallas, 1976
Ray Wersching, San Francisco vs. Cincinnati, 1982
Rich Karlis, Denver vs. N.Y Giants, 1987

Most Field Goals, Career

5 Ray Wersching, San Francisco, 2 games (5 att)
4 Don Chandler, Green Bay, 2 games (4 att)
Jim Turner, N.Y. Jets-Denver, 2 games (6 att)
Uwe von Schamann, Miami, 2 games (4 att)
3 Mike Clark, Dallas, 2 games (3 att)
Jan Stenerud, Kansas City, 1 game (3 att)
Chris Bahr, Oakland-L.A. Raiders, 2 games (4 att)
Mark Moseley, Washington, 2 games (4 att)
Kevin Butler, Chicago, 1 game (3 att)

Most Field Goals, Game

4 Don Chandler, Green Bay vs. Oakland, 1968
Ray Wersching, San Francisco vs. Cincinnati, 1982
3 Jim Turner, N.Y. Jets vs. Baltimore, 1969
Jan Stenerud, Kansas City vs. Minnesota, 1970
Uwe von Schamann, Miami vs. San Francisco, 1985
Kevin Butler, Chicago vs. New England, 1986

Longest Field Goal

48 Jan Stenerud, Kansas City vs. Minnesota, 1970
Rich Karlis, Denver vs. N.Y. Giants, 1987
47 Jim Turner, Denver vs. Dallas, 1978
46 Chris Bahr, Oakland vs. Philadelphia, 1981

Safeties

Most Safeties, Game

1 Dwight White, Pittsburgh vs. Minnesota, 1975
Reggie Harrison, Pittsburgh vs. Dallas, 1976
Henry Waechter, Chicago vs. New England, 1986
George Martin, N.Y. Giants vs. Denver, 1987

Rushing

Attempts

Most Attempts, Career

101 Franco Harris, Pittsburgh, 4 games
64 John Riggins, Washington, 2 games
57 Larry Csonka, Miami, 3 games

Most Attempts, Game

38 John Riggins, Washington vs. Miami, 1983
34 Franco Harris, Pittsburgh vs. Minnesota, 1975
33 Larry Csonka, Miami vs. Minnesota, 1974

Yards Gained

Most Yards Gained, Career

354 Franco Harris, Pittsburgh, 4 games
297 Larry Csonka, Miami, 3 games
230 John Riggins, Washington, 2 games

Most Yards Gained, Game

191 Marcus Allen, L.A. Raiders vs. Washington, 1984
166 John Riggins, Washington vs. Miami, 1983
158 Franco Harris, Pittsburgh vs. Minnesota, 1975

Longest Run From Scrimmage

74 Marcus Allen, L.A. Raiders vs. Washington, 1984 (TD)
58 Tom Matte, Baltimore vs. N.Y. Jets, 1969
49 Larry Csonka, Miami vs. Washington, 1973

Average Gain

Highest Average Gain, Career (20 attempts)

9.6 Marcus Allen, L.A. Raiders, 1 game (20-191)
5.3 Walt Garrison, Dallas, 2 games (26-139)
5.2 Tony Dorsett, Dallas, 2 games (31-162)

Highest Average Gain, Game (10 attempts)

10.5 Tom Matte, Baltimore vs. N.Y. Jets, 1969 (11-116)
9.6 Marcus Allen, L.A. Raiders vs. Washington, 1984 (20-191)
8.6 Clarence Davis, Oakland vs. Minnesota, 1977 (16-137)

Touchdowns

Most Touchdowns, Career

4 Franco Harris, Pittsburgh, 4 games
2 Elijah Pitts, Green Bay, 1 game
Jim Kiick, Miami, 3 games
Larry Csonka, Miami, 3 games
Pete Banaszak, Oakland, 2 games
Marcus Allen, L.A. Raiders, 1 game
John Riggins, Washington, 2 games
Jim McMahon, Chicago, 1 game

Most Touchdowns, Game

2 Elijah Pitts, Green Bay vs. Kansas City, 1967
Larry Csonka, Miami vs. Minnesota, 1974
Pete Banaszak, Oakland vs. Minnesota, 1977
Franco Harris, Pittsburgh vs. Los Angeles, 1980
Marcus Allen, L.A. Raiders vs. Washington, 1984
Jim McMahon, Chicago vs. New England, 1986

Passing

Attempts

Most Passes Attempted, Career

98 Roger Staubach, Dallas, 4 games
89 Fran Tarkenton, Minnesota, 3 games
84 Terry Bradshaw, Pittsburgh, 4 games

Most Passes Attempted, Game

50 Dan Marino, Miami vs. San Francisco, 1985

38 Ron Jaworski, Philadelphia vs. Oakland, 1981
37 John Elway, Denver vs. N.Y. Giants, 1987

Completions
Most Passes Completed, Career
61 Roger Staubach, Dallas, 4 games
49 Terry Bradshaw, Pittsburgh, 4 games
46 Fran Tarkenton, Minnesota, 3 games
Most Passes Completed, Game
29 Dan Marino, Miami vs. San Francisco, 1985
25 Ken Anderson, Cincinnati vs. San Francisco, 1982
24 Joe Montana, San Francisco vs. Miami, 1985
Most Consecutive Completions, Game
10 Phil Simms, N.Y. Giants vs. Denver, 1987
8 Len Dawson, Kansas City vs. Green Bay, 1967
Joe Theismann, Washington vs. Miami, 1983

Completion Percentage
Highest Completion Percentage, Career (40 attempts)
66.7 Joe Montana, San Francisco, 2 games (57-38)
63.6 Len Dawson, Kansas City, 2 games (44-28)
63.4 Bob Griese, Miami, 3 games (41-26)
Highest Completion Percentage, Game (20 attempts)
88.0 Phil Simms, N.Y. Giants vs. Denver, 1987 (25-22)
73.5 Ken Anderson, Cincinnati vs. San Francisco, 1982 (34-25)
69.6 Bart Starr, Green Bay vs. Kansas City, 1967 (23-16)

Yards Gained
Most Yards Gained, Career
932 Terry Bradshaw, Pittsburgh, 4 games
734 Roger Staubach, Dallas, 4 games
489 Fran Tarkenton, Minnesota, 3 games
Most Yards Gained, Game
331 Joe Montana, San Francisco vs. Miami, 1985
318 Terry Bradshaw, Pittsburgh vs. Dallas, 1979
Dan Marino, Miami vs. San Francisco, 1985
309 Terry Bradshaw, Pittsburgh vs. Los Angeles, 1980
Longest Pass Completion
80 Jim Plunkett (to King), Oakland vs. Philadelphia, 1981 (TD)
76 David Woodley (to Cefalo), Miami vs. Washington, 1983 (TD)
75 Johnny Unitas (to Mackey), Baltimore vs. Dallas, 1971 (TD)
Terry Bradshaw (to Stallworth), Pittsburgh vs. Dallas, 1979 (TD)

Average Gain
Highest Average Gain, Career (40 attempts)
11.10 Terry Bradshaw, Pittsburgh, 4 games (84-932)
9.62 Bart Starr, Green Bay, 2 games (47-452)
9.41 Jim Plunkett, Oakland-L.A. Raiders, 2 games (46-433)
Highest Average Gain, Game (20 attempts)
14.71 Terry Bradshaw, Pittsburgh vs. Los Angeles, 1980 (21-309)
12.80 Jim McMahon, Chicago vs. New England, 1986 (20-256)
12.43 Jim Plunkett, Oakland vs. Philadelphia, 1981 (21-261)

Touchdowns
Most Touchdown Passes, Career
9 Terry Bradshaw, Pittsburgh, 4 games
8 Roger Staubach, Dallas, 4 games
4 Jim Plunkett, Oakland-L.A. Raiders, 2 games
Joe Montana, San Francisco, 2 games
Most Touchdown Passes, Game
4 Terry Bradshaw, Pittsburgh vs. Dallas, 1979
3 Roger Staubach, Dallas vs. Pittsburgh, 1979
Jim Plunkett, Oakland vs. Philadelphia, 1981
Joe Montana, San Francisco vs. Miami, 1985
Phil Simms, N.Y. Giants vs. Denver, 1987
2 By many players

Had Intercepted
Lowest Percentage, Passes Had Intercepted, Career (40 attempts)
0.00 Jim Plunkett, Oakland-L.A. Raiders, 2 games (46-0)
Joe Montana, San Francisco, 2 games (57-0)
2.13 Bart Starr, Green Bay, 2 games (47-1)
4.08 Roger Staubach, Dallas, 4 games (98-4)
Most Attempts, Without Interception, Game
35 Joe Montana, San Francisco vs. Miami, 1985
28 Joe Namath, N.Y. Jets vs. Baltimore, 1969
25 Roger Staubach, Dallas vs. Denver, 1978
Jim Plunkett, L.A. Raiders vs. Washington, 1984
Phil Simms, N.Y. Giants vs. Denver, 1987
Most Passes Had Intercepted, Career
7 Craig Morton, Dallas-Denver, 2 games
6 Fran Tarkenton, Minnesota, 3 games
4 Earl Morrall, Baltimore-Miami, 4 games
Roger Staubach, Dallas, 4 games
Terry Bradshaw, Pittsburgh, 4 games
Joe Theismann, Washington, 2 games
Most Passes Had Intercepted, Game
4 Craig Morton, Denver vs. Dallas, 1978
3 By seven players

Pass Receiving
Receptions
Most Receptions, Career
16 Lynn Swann, Pittsburgh, 4 games
15 Chuck Foreman, Minnesota, 3 games
14 Cliff Branch, Oakland-L.A. Raiders, 3 games
Most Receptions, Game
11 Dan Ross, Cincinnati vs. San Francisco, 1982
10 Tony Nathan, Miami vs. San Francisco, 1985
8 George Sauer, N.Y. Jets vs. Baltimore, 1969

Yards Gained
Most Yards Gained, Career
364 Lynn Swann, Pittsburgh, 4 games
268 John Stallworth, Pittsburgh, 4 games
181 Cliff Branch, Oakland-L.A. Raiders, 3 games
Most Yards Gained, Game
161 Lynn Swann, Pittsburgh vs. Dallas, 1976
138 Max McGee, Green Bay vs. Kansas City, 1967
133 George Sauer, N.Y. Jets vs. Baltimore, 1969
Longest Reception
80 Kenny King (from Plunkett), Oakland vs. Philadelphia, 1981 (TD)
76 Jimmy Cefalo (from Woodley), Miami vs. Washington, 1983 (TD)
75 John Mackey (from Unitas), Baltimore vs. Dallas, 1971 (TD)
John Stallworth (from Bradshaw), Pittsburgh vs. Dallas, 1979 (TD)

Average Gain
Highest Average Gain, Career (8 receptions)
24.4 John Stallworth, Pittsburgh, 4 games (11-268)
22.8 Lynn Swann, Pittsburgh, 4 games (16-364)
17.0 Charlie Brown, Washington, 2 games (9-153)
Highest Average Gain, Game (3 receptions)
40.33 John Stallworth, Pittsburgh vs. Los Angeles, 1980 (3-121)
40.25 Lynn Swann, Pittsburgh vs. Dallas, 1979 (4-161)
38.33 John Stallworth, Pittsburgh vs. Dallas, 1979 (3-115)

Touchdowns
Most Touchdowns, Career
3 John Stallworth, Pittsburgh, 4 games
Lynn Swann, Pittsburgh, 4 games
Cliff Branch, Oakland-L.A. Raiders, 3 games
2 Max McGee, Green Bay, 2 games
Bill Miller, Oakland, 1 game
Butch Johnson, Dallas, 2 games
Dan Ross, Cincinnati, 1 game
Roger Craig, San Francisco, 1 game
Most Touchdowns, Game
2 Max McGee, Green Bay vs. Kansas City, 1967
Bill Miller, Oakland vs. Green Bay, 1968
John Stallworth, Pittsburgh vs. Dallas, 1979
Cliff Branch, Oakland vs. Philadelphia, 1981
Dan Ross, Cincinnati vs. San Francisco, 1982
Roger Craig, San Francisco vs. Miami, 1985

Interceptions By
Most Interceptions By, Career
3 Chuck Howley, Dallas, 2 games
Rod Martin, Oakland-L.A. Raiders, 2 games
2 Randy Beverly, N.Y. Jets, 1 game
Jake Scott, Miami, 3 games
Mike Wagner, Pittsburgh, 3 games
Mel Blount, Pittsburgh, 4 games
Eric Wright, San Francisco, 2 games
Most Interceptions By, Game
3 Rod Martin, Oakland vs. Philadelphia, 1981
2 Randy Beverly, N.Y. Jets vs. Baltimore, 1969
Chuck Howley, Dallas vs. Baltimore, 1971
Jake Scott, Miami vs. Washington, 1973

Yards Gained
Most Yards Gained, Career
75 Willie Brown, Oakland, 2 games
63 Chuck Howley, Dallas, 2 games
Jake Scott, Miami, 3 games
60 Herb Adderley, Green Bay-Dallas, 4 games
Most Yards Gained, Game
75 Willie Brown, Oakland vs. Minnesota, 1977
63 Jake Scott, Miami vs. Washington, 1973
60 Herb Adderley, Green Bay vs. Oakland, 1968
Longest Return
75 Willie Brown, Oakland vs. Minnesota, 1977 (TD)
60 Herb Adderley, Green Bay vs. Oakland, 1968 (TD)
55 Jake Scott, Miami vs. Washington, 1973

Touchdowns
Most Touchdowns, Game
1 Herb Adderley, Green Bay vs. Oakland, 1968
Willie Brown, Oakland vs. Minnesota, 1977
Jack Squirek, L.A. Raiders vs. Washington, 1984
Reggie Phillips, Chicago vs. New England, 1986

Punting
Most Punts, Career
17 Mike Eischeid, Oakland-Minnesota, 3 games
15 Larry Seiple, Miami, 3 games
14 Ron Widby, Dallas, 2 games
Ray Guy, Oakland-L.A. Raiders, 3 games
Most Punts, Game
9 Ron Widby, Dallas vs. Baltimore, 1971
7 By seven players
Longest Punt
62 Rich Camarillo, New England vs. Chicago, 1986
61 Jerrel Wilson, Kansas City vs. Green Bay, 1967
59 Jerrel Wilson, Kansas City vs. Minnesota, 1970
Bobby Walden, Pittsburgh vs. Dallas, 1976
Ken Clark, Los Angeles vs. Pittsburgh, 1980
Sean Landeta, N.Y. Giants vs. Denver, 1987

Average Yardage
Highest Average, Punting, Career (10 punts)
46.5 Jerrel Wilson, Kansas City, 2 games (11-511)
41.9 Ray Guy, Oakland-L.A. Raiders, 3 games (14-587)
41.3 Larry Seiple, Miami, 3 games (15-620)

Highest Average, Punting, Game (4 punts)
48.5 Jerrel Wilson, Kansas City vs. Minnesota, 1970 (4-194)
46.3 Jim Miller, San Francisco vs. Cincinnati, 1982 (4-185)
45.3 Jerrel Wilson, Kansas City vs. Green Bay, 1967 (7-317)

Punt Returns

Most Punt Returns, Career
6 Willie Wood, Green Bay, 2 games
Jake Scott, Miami, 3 games
Theo Bell, Pittsburgh, 2 games
Mike Nelms, Washington, 1 game
5 Dana McLemore, San Francisco, 1 game
4 By seven players

Most Punt Returns, Game
6 Mike Nelms, Washington vs. Miami, 1983
5 Willie Wood, Green Bay vs. Oakland, 1968
Dana McLemore, San Francisco vs. Miami, 1985
4 By six players

Most Fair Catches, Game
3 Ron Gardin, Baltimore vs. Dallas, 1971
Golden Richards, Dallas vs. Pittsburgh, 1976
Greg Pruitt, L.A. Raiders vs. Washington, 1984

Yards Gained

Most Yards Gained, Career
52 Mike Nelms, Washington, 1 game
51 Dana McLemore, San Francisco, 1 game
45 Jake Scott, Miami, 3 games

Most Yards Gained, Game
52 Mike Nelms, Washington vs. Miami, 1983
51 Dana McLemore, San Francisco vs. Miami, 1985
43 Neal Colzie, Oakland vs. Minnesota, 1977

Longest Return
34 Darrell Green, Washington vs. L.A. Raiders, 1984
31 Willie Wood, Green Bay vs. Oakland, 1968
28 Dana McLemore, San Francisco vs. Miami, 1985

Average Yardage

Highest Average, Career (4 returns)
10.8 Neal Colzie, Oakland, 1 game (4-43)
10.2 Dana McLemore, San Francisco, 1 game (5-51)
8.8 Mike Fuller, Cincinnati, 1 game (4-35)

Highest Average, Game (3 returns)
11.3 Lynn Swann, Pittsburgh vs. Minnesota, 1975 (3-34)
10.8 Neal Colzie, Oakland vs. Minnesota, 1977 (4-43)
10.2 Dana McLemore, San Francisco vs. Miami, 1985 (5-51)

Touchdowns

Most Touchdowns, Game
None

Kickoff Returns

Most Kickoff Returns, Career
8 Larry Anderson, Pittsburgh, 2 games
Fulton Walker, Miami, 2 games
7 Preston Pearson, Baltimore-Pittsburgh-Dallas, 5 games
Stephen Starring, New England, 1 game
6 Eugene (Mercury) Morris, Miami, 3 games

Most Kickoff Returns, Game
7 Stephen Starring, New England vs. Chicago, 1986
5 Larry Anderson, Pittsburgh vs. Los Angeles, 1980
Billy Campfield, Philadelphia vs. Oakland, 1981
David Verser, Cincinnati vs. San Francisco, 1982
Alvin Garrett, Washington vs. L.A. Raiders, 1984

Yards Gained

Most Yards Gained, Career
283 Fulton Walker, Miami, 2 games
207 Larry Anderson, Pittsburgh, 2 games
153 Stephen Starring, New England, 1 game

Most Yards Gained, Game
190 Fulton Walker, Miami vs. Washington, 1983
162 Larry Anderson, Pittsburgh vs. Los Angeles, 1980
153 Stephen Starring, New England vs. Chicago, 1986

Longest Return
98 Fulton Walker, Miami vs. Washington, 1983 (TD)
67 Rick Upchurch, Denver vs. Dallas, 1978
48 Thomas Henderson, Dallas vs. Pittsburgh, 1976 (lateral)

Average Yardage

Highest Average, Career (4 returns)
35.4 Fulton Walker, Miami, 2 games (8-283)
25.9 Larry Anderson, Pittsburgh, 2 games (8-207)
22.5 Jim Duncan, Baltimore, 1 game (4-90)

Highest Average, Game (3 returns)
47.5 Fulton Walker, Miami vs. Washington, 1983 (4-190)
32.4 Larry Anderson, Pittsburgh vs. Los Angeles, 1980 (5-162)
31.3 Rick Upchurch, Denver vs. Dallas, 1978 (3-94)

Touchdowns

Most Touchdowns, Game
1 Fulton Walker, Miami vs. Washington, 1983

Fumbles

Most Fumbles, Career
5 Roger Staubach, Dallas, 4 games
3 Franco Harris, Pittsburgh, 4 games
Terry Bradshaw, Pittsburgh, 4 games
2 By five players

Most Fumbles, Game
3 Roger Staubach, Dallas vs. Pittsburgh, 1976
2 Franco Harris, Pittsburgh vs. Minnesota, 1975
Butch Johnson, Dallas vs. Denver, 1978
Terry Bradshaw, Pittsburgh vs. Dallas, 1979

Recoveries

Most Fumbles Recovered, Career
2 Jake Scott, Miami, 3 games (1 own, 1 opp)
Fran Tarkenton, Minnesota, 3 games (2 own)
Franco Harris, Pittsburgh, 4 games (2 own)
Roger Staubach, Dallas, 4 games (2 own)
Bobby Walden, Pittsburgh, 2 games (2 own)
John Fitzgerald, Dallas, 4 games (2 own)
Randy Hughes, Dallas, 3 games (2 opp)
Butch Johnson, Dallas, 2 games (2 own)
Mike Singletary, Chicago, 1 game (2 opp)

Most Fumbles Recovered, Game
2 Jake Scott, Miami vs. Minnesota, 1974 (1 own, 1 opp)
Roger Staubach, Dallas vs. Pittsburgh, 1976 (2 own)
Randy Hughes, Dallas vs. Denver, 1978 (2 opp)
Butch Johnson, Dallas vs. Denver, 1978 (2 own)
Mike Singletary, Chicago vs. New England, 1986 (2 opp)

Yards Gained

Most Yards Gained, Game
49 Mike Bass, Washington vs. Miami, 1973 (opp)
37 Mike Hegman, Dallas vs. Pittsburgh, 1979 (opp)
21 Randy Hughes, Dallas vs. Denver, 1978 (opp)

Longest Return
49 Mike Bass, Washington vs. Miami, 1973 (TD)
37 Mike Hegman, Dallas vs. Pittsburgh, 1979 (TD)
19 Randy Hughes, Dallas vs. Denver, 1978

Touchdowns

Most Touchdowns, Game
1 Mike Bass, Washington vs. Miami, 1973 (opp 49 yds)
Mike Hegman, Dallas vs. Pittsburgh, 1979 (opp 37 yds)

Combined Net Yards Gained

Attempts

Most Attempts, Career
108 Franco Harris, Pittsburgh, 4 games
66 John Riggins, Washington, 2 games
60 Larry Csonka, Miami, 3 games

Most Attempts, Game
39 John Riggins, Washington vs. Miami, 1983
35 Franco Harris, Pittsburgh vs. Minnesota, 1975
34 Matt Snell, N.Y. Jets vs. Baltimore, 1969

Yards Gained

Most Yards Gained, Career
468 Franco Harris, Pittsburgh, 4 games
391 Lynn Swann, Pittsburgh, 4 games
314 Larry Csonka, Miami, 3 games

Most Yards Gained, Game
209 Marcus Allen, L.A. Raiders vs. Washington, 1984
192 Stephen Starring, New England vs. Chicago, 1986
190 Fulton Walker, Miami vs. Washington, 1983

Sacks

Sacks have been compiled since 1983.

Most Sacks, Game
2 Dwaine Board, San Francisco, 1985
Dennis Owens, New England, 1986
Otis Wilson, Chicago, 1986
Leonard Marshall, N.Y. Giants, 1987

Team Records

Games, Victories, Defeats

Most Games
5 Dallas, 1971-72, 1976, 1978-79
Miami, 1972-74, 1983, 1985
4 Minnesota, 1970, 1974-75, 1977
Pittsburgh, 1975-76, 1979-80
Oakland/L.A. Raiders, 1968, 1977, 1981, 1984
3 Washington, 1973, 1983-84

Most Consecutive Games
3 Miami, 1972-74
2 Green Bay, 1967-68
Dallas, 1971-72
Minnesota, 1974-75
Pittsburgh, 1975-76, 1979-80
Washington, 1983-84

Most Games Won
4 Pittsburgh, 1975-76, 1979-80
3 Oakland/L.A. Raiders, 1977, 1981, 1984
2 Green Bay, 1967-68
Miami, 1973-74
Dallas, 1972, 1978
San Francisco, 1982, 1985

Most Consecutive Games Won
2 Green Bay, 1967-68
Miami, 1973-74
Pittsburgh, 1975-76, 1979-80

Most Games Lost
4 Minnesota, 1970, 1974-75, 1977
3 Dallas, 1971, 1976, 1979
Miami, 1972, 1983, 1985
2 Washington, 1973, 1984
Denver, 1978, 1987

Most Consecutive Games Lost
2 Minnesota, 1974-75

Scoring

Most Points, Game
46 Chicago vs. New England, 1986
39 N.Y. Giants vs. Denver, 1987
38 L.A. Raiders vs. Washington, 1984
San Francisco vs. Miami, 1985

Fewest Points, Game
3 Miami vs. Dallas, 1972
6 Minnesota vs. Pittsburgh, 1975
7 By four teams

Most Points, Both Teams, Game
66 Pittsburgh (35) vs. Dallas (31), 1979
59 N.Y. Giants (39) vs. Denver (20), 1987
56 Chicago (46) vs. New England (10), 1986

Fewest Points, Both Teams, Game
21 Washington (7) vs. Miami (14), 1973
22 Minnesota (6) vs. Pittsburgh (16), 1975
23 Baltimore (7) vs. N.Y. Jets (16), 1969

Largest Margin of Victory, Game
36 Chicago vs. New England, 1986 (46-10)
29 L.A. Raiders vs. Washington, 1984 (38-9)
25 Green Bay vs. Kansas City, 1967 (35-10)

Most Points, Each Half
1st: 28 San Francisco vs. Miami, 1985
2nd: 30 N.Y. Giants vs. Denver, 1987

Most Points, Each Quarter
1st: 14 Miami vs. Minnesota, 1974
Oakland vs. Philadelphia, 1981
2nd: 21 San Francisco vs. Miami, 1985
3rd: 21 Chicago vs. New England, 1986
4th: 14 Pittsburgh vs. Dallas, 1976; vs. Dallas, 1979; vs. Los Angeles, 1980
Dallas vs. Pittsburgh, 1979
Cincinnati vs. San Francisco, 1982
Washington vs. Miami, 1983

Most Points, Both Teams, Each Half
1st: 44 San Francisco (28) vs. Miami (16), 1985
2nd: 40 N.Y. Giants (30) vs. Denver (10), 1987

Fewest Points, Both Teams, Each Half
1st: 2 Minnesota (0) vs. Pittsburgh (2), 1975
2nd: 7 Miami (0) vs. Washington (7), 1973

Most Points, Both Teams, Each Quarter
1st: 17 Miami (10) vs. San Francisco (7), 1985
Denver (10) vs. N.Y. Giants (7), 1987
2nd: 27 San Francisco (21) vs. Miami (6), 1985
3rd: 21 Chicago (21) vs. New England (0), 1986
4th: 28 Dallas (14) vs. Pittsburgh (14), 1979

Touchdowns

Most Touchdowns, Game
5 Green Bay vs. Kansas City, 1967
Pittsburgh vs. Dallas, 1979
L.A. Raiders vs. Washington, 1984
San Francisco vs. Miami, 1985
Chicago vs. New England, 1986
N.Y. Giants vs. Denver, 1987
4 Oakland vs. Minnesota, 1977
Dallas vs. Pittsburgh, 1979
Pittsburgh vs. Los Angeles, 1980
3 By many teams

Fewest Touchdowns, Game
0 Miami vs. Dallas, 1972
1 By 13 teams

Most Touchdowns, Both Teams, Game
9 Pittsburgh (5) vs. Dallas (4), 1979
7 N.Y. Giants (5) vs. Denver (2), 1987
6 Green Bay (5) vs. Kansas City (1), 1967
Oakland (4) vs. Minnesota (2), 1977
Pittsburgh (4) vs. Los Angeles (2), 1980
L.A. Raiders (5) vs. Washington (1), 1984
San Francisco (5) vs. Miami (1), 1985
Chicago (5) vs. New England (1), 1986

Fewest Touchdowns, Both Teams, Game
2 Baltimore (1) vs. N.Y. Jets (1), 1969
3 In five games

Points After Touchdown

Most Points After Touchdown, Game
5 Green Bay vs. Kansas City, 1967
Pittsburgh vs. Dallas, 1979
L.A. Raiders vs. Washington, 1984
San Francisco vs. Miami, 1985
Chicago vs. New England, 1986
4 Dallas vs. Pittsburgh, 1979
Pittsburgh vs. Los Angeles, 1980
N.Y. Giants vs. Denver, 1987

Most Points After Touchdown, Both Teams, Game
9 Pittsburgh (5) vs. Dallas (4), 1979
6 Green Bay (5) vs. Kansas City (1), 1967
San Francisco (5) vs. Miami (1), 1985
Chicago (5) vs. New England (1), 1986
N.Y. Giants (4) vs. Denver (2), 1987

Fewest Points After Touchdown, Both Teams, Game
2 Baltimore (1) vs. N.Y. Jets (1), 1969
Baltimore (1) vs. Dallas (1), 1971
Minnesota (0) vs. Pittsburgh (2), 1975

Field Goals

Most Field Goals Attempted, Game
5 N.Y. Jets vs. Baltimore, 1969
Dallas vs. Denver, 1978
4 Green Bay vs. Oakland, 1968
Pittsburgh vs. Dallas, 1976
San Francisco vs. Cincinnati, 1982
Denver vs. N.Y. Giants, 1987

Most Field Goals Attempted, Both Teams, Game
7 N.Y. Jets (5) vs. Baltimore (2), 1969
6 Dallas (5) vs. Denver (1), 1978
5 Green Bay (4) vs. Oakland (1), 1968
Pittsburgh (4) vs. Dallas (1), 1976
Oakland (3) vs. Philadelphia (2), 1981
Denver (4) vs. N.Y. Giants (1), 1987

Fewest Field Goals Attempted, Both Teams, Game
1 Minnesota (0) vs. Miami (1), 1974
2 Green Bay (0) vs. Kansas City (2), 1967
Miami (1) vs. Washington (1), 1973
Dallas (1) vs. Pittsburgh (1), 1979

Most Field Goals, Game
4 Green Bay vs. Oakland, 1968
San Francisco vs. Cincinnati, 1982
3 N.Y. Jets vs. Baltimore, 1969
Kansas City vs. Minnesota, 1970
Miami vs. San Francisco, 1985
Chicago vs. New England, 1986

Most Field Goals, Both Teams, Game
4 Green Bay (4) vs. Oakland (0), 1968
San Francisco (4) vs. Cincinnati (0), 1982
Miami (3) vs. San Francisco (1), 1985
Chicago (3) vs. New England (1), 1986
3 In eight games

Fewest Field Goals, Both Teams, Game
0 Miami vs. Washington, 1973
Pittsburgh vs. Minnesota, 1975
1 Green Bay (0) vs. Kansas City (1), 1967
Minnesota (0) vs. Miami (1), 1974
Pittsburgh (0) vs. Dallas (1), 1979

Safeties

Most Safeties, Game
1 Pittsburgh vs. Minnesota, 1975; vs. Dallas, 1976
Chicago vs. New England, 1986
N.Y. Giants vs. Denver, 1987

First Downs

Most First Downs, Game
31 San Francisco vs. Miami, 1985
24 Cincinnati vs. San Francisco, 1982
Washington vs. Miami, 1983
N.Y. Giants vs. Denver, 1987
23 Dallas vs. Miami, 1972
Denver vs. N.Y. Giants, 1987

Fewest First Downs, Game
9 Minnesota vs. Pittsburgh, 1975
Miami vs. Washington, 1983
10 Dallas vs. Baltimore, 1971
Miami vs. Dallas, 1972
11 Denver vs. Dallas, 1978

Most First Downs, Both Teams, Game
50 San Francisco (31) vs. Miami (19), 1985
47 N.Y. Giants (24) vs. Denver (23), 1987
44 Cincinnati (24) vs. San Francisco (20), 1982

Fewest First Downs, Both Teams, Game
24 Dallas (10) vs. Baltimore (14), 1971
26 Minnesota (9) vs. Pittsburgh (17), 1975
27 Pittsburgh (13) vs. Dallas (14), 1976

Rushing

Most First Downs, Rushing, Game
16 San Francisco vs. Miami, 1985
15 Dallas vs. Miami, 1972
14 Washington vs. Miami, 1983

Fewest First Downs, Rushing, Game
1 New England vs. Chicago, 1986
2 Minnesota vs. Kansas City, 1970; vs. Pittsburgh, 1975; vs. Oakland, 1977
Pittsburgh vs. Dallas, 1979
Miami vs. San Francisco, 1985
3 Miami vs. Dallas, 1972
Philadelphia vs. Oakland, 1981

Most First Downs, Rushing, Both Teams, Game
21 Washington (14) vs. Miami (7), 1983
18 Dallas (15) vs. Miami (3), 1972
Miami (13) vs. Minnesota (5), 1974
San Francisco (16) vs. Miami (2), 1985
17 N.Y. Jets (10) vs. Baltimore (7), 1969

Fewest First Downs, Rushing, Both Teams, Game
8 Baltimore (4) vs. Dallas (4), 1971
Pittsburgh (2) vs. Dallas (6), 1979
9 Philadelphia (3) vs. Oakland (6), 1981
10 Minnesota (2) vs. Kansas City (8), 1970

Passing

Most First Downs, Passing, Game
17 Miami vs. San Francisco, 1985
16 Denver vs. N.Y. Giants, 1987
15 Minnesota vs. Oakland, 1977
Pittsburgh vs. Dallas, 1979
San Francisco vs. Miami, 1985

Fewest First Downs, Passing, Game
1 Denver vs. Dallas, 1978
2 Miami vs. Washington, 1983
4 Miami vs. Minnesota, 1974

Most First Downs, Passing, Both Teams, Game
32 Miami (17) vs. San Francisco (15), 1985
29 Denver (16) vs. N.Y. Giants (13), 1987
28 Pittsburgh (15) vs. Dallas (13), 1979

Fewest First Downs, Passing, Both Teams, Game
9 Denver (1) vs. Dallas (8), 1978

10 Minnesota (5) vs. Pittsburgh (5), 1975
11 Dallas (5) vs. Baltimore (6), 1971
Miami (2) vs. Washington (9), 1983

Penalty

Most First Downs, Penalty, Game
4 Baltimore vs. Dallas, 1971
Miami vs. Minnesota, 1974
Cincinnati vs. San Francisco, 1982
3 Kansas City vs. Minnesota, 1970
Minnesota vs. Oakland, 1977

Most First Downs, Penalty, Both Teams, Game
6 Cincinnati (4) vs. San Francisco (2), 1982
5 Baltimore (4) vs. Dallas (1), 1971
Miami (4) vs. Minnesota (1), 1974
4 Kansas City (3) vs. Minnesota (1), 1970

Fewest First Downs, Penalty, Both Teams, Game
0 Dallas vs. Miami, 1972
Miami vs. Washington, 1973
Dallas vs. Pittsburgh, 1976
Miami vs. San Francisco, 1985
1 Green Bay (0) vs. Kansas City (1), 1967
Miami (0) vs. Washington (1), 1983

Net Yards Gained Rushing and Passing

Most Yards Gained, Game
537 San Francisco vs. Miami, 1985
429 Oakland vs. Minnesota, 1977
408 Chicago vs. New England, 1986

Fewest Yards Gained, Game
119 Minnesota vs. Pittsburgh, 1975
123 New England vs. Chicago, 1986
156 Denver vs. Dallas, 1978

Most Yards Gained, Both Teams, Game
851 San Francisco (537) vs. Miami (314), 1985
782 Oakland (429) vs. Minnesota (353), 1977
771 N.Y. Giants (399) vs. Denver (372), 1987

Fewest Yards Gained, Both Teams, Game
452 Minnesota (119) vs. Pittsburgh (333), 1975
481 Washington (228) vs. Miami (253), 1973
Denver (156) vs. Dallas (325), 1978
497 Minnesota (238) vs. Miami (259), 1974

Rushing

Attempts

Most Attempts, Game
57 Pittsburgh vs. Minnesota, 1975
53 Miami vs. Minnesota, 1974
52 Oakland vs. Minnesota, 1977
Washington vs. Miami, 1983

Fewest Attempts, Game
9 Miami vs. San Francisco, 1985
11 New England vs. Chicago, 1986
19 Kansas City vs. Green Bay, 1967
Minnesota vs. Kansas City, 1970
Denver vs. N.Y. Giants, 1987

Most Attempts, Both Teams, Game
81 Washington (52) vs. Miami (29), 1983
78 Pittsburgh (57) vs. Minnesota (21), 1975
Oakland (52) vs. Minnesota (26), 1977
77 Miami (53) vs. Minnesota (24), 1974
Pittsburgh (46) vs. Dallas (31), 1976

Fewest Attempts, Both Teams, Game
49 Miami (9) vs. San Francisco (40), 1985
52 Kansas City (19) vs. Green Bay (33), 1967
56 Pittsburgh (24) vs. Dallas (32), 1979

Yards Gained

Most Yards Gained, Game
276 Washington vs. Miami, 1983
266 Oakland vs. Minnesota, 1977
252 Dallas vs. Miami, 1972

Fewest Yards Gained, Game
7 New England vs. Chicago, 1986
17 Minnesota vs. Pittsburgh, 1975
25 Miami vs. San Francisco, 1985

Most Yards Gained, Both Teams, Game
372 Washington (276) vs. Miami (96), 1983
337 Oakland (266) vs. Minnesota (71), 1977
332 Dallas (252) vs. Miami (80), 1972

Fewest Yards Gained, Both Teams, Game
171 Baltimore (69) vs. Dallas (102), 1971
174 New England (7) vs. Chicago (167), 1986
186 Philadelphia (69) vs. Oakland (117), 1981

Average Gain

Highest Average Gain, Game
7.00 L.A. Raiders vs. Washington, 1984 (33-231)
6.22 Baltimore vs. N.Y. Jets, 1969 (23-143)
5.35 Oakland vs. Green Bay, 1968 (20-107)

Lowest Average Gain, Game
0.64 New England vs. Chicago, 1986 (11-7)
0.81 Minnesota vs. Pittsburgh, 1975 (21-17)
2.23 Baltimore vs. Dallas, 1971 (31-69)

Touchdowns

Most Touchdowns, Game
4 Chicago vs. New England, 1986
3 Green Bay vs. Kansas City, 1967
Miami vs. Minnesota, 1974
2 Oakland vs. Minnesota, 1977
Pittsburgh vs. Los Angeles, 1980
L.A. Raiders vs. Washington, 1984
San Francisco vs. Miami, 1985
N.Y. Giants vs. Denver, 1987

Fewest Touchdowns, Game
0 By 14 teams

Most Touchdowns, Both Teams, Game
4 Miami (3) vs. Minnesota (1), 1974
Chicago (4) vs. New England (0), 1986
3 Green Bay (3) vs. Kansas City (0), 1967
Pittsburgh (2) vs. Los Angeles (1), 1980
L.A. Raiders (2) vs. Washington (1), 1984
N.Y. Giants (2) vs. Denver (1), 1987

Fewest Touchdowns, Both Teams, Game
0 Pittsburgh vs. Dallas, 1976
Oakland vs. Philadelphia, 1981
1 In seven games

Passing

Attempts

Most Passes Attempted, Game
50 Miami vs. San Francisco, 1985
44 Minnesota vs. Oakland, 1977
41 Baltimore vs. N.Y. Jets, 1969
Denver vs. N.Y. Giants, 1987

Fewest Passes Attempted, Game
7 Miami vs. Minnesota, 1974
11 Miami vs. Washington, 1973
14 Pittsburgh vs. Minnesota, 1975

Most Passes Attempted, Both Teams, Game
85 Miami (50) vs. San Francisco (35), 1985
70 Baltimore (41) vs. N.Y. Jets (29), 1969
66 Denver (41) vs. N.Y. Giants (25), 1987

Fewest Passes Attempted, Both Teams, Game
35 Miami (7) vs. Minnesota (28), 1974
39 Miami (11) vs. Washington (28), 1973
40 Pittsburgh (14) vs. Minnesota (26), 1975
Miami (17) vs. Washington (23), 1983

Completions

Most Passes Completed, Game
29 Miami vs. San Francisco, 1985
26 Denver vs. N.Y. Giants, 1987
25 Cincinnati vs. San Francisco, 1982

Fewest Passes Completed, Game
4 Miami vs. Washington, 1983
6 Miami vs. Minnesota, 1974
8 Miami vs. Washington, 1973
Denver vs. Dallas, 1978

Most Passes Completed, Both Teams, Game
53 Miami (29) vs. San Francisco (24), 1985
48 Denver (26) vs. N.Y. Giants (22), 1987
39 Cincinnati (25) vs. San Francisco (14), 1982

Fewest Passes Completed, Both Teams, Game
19 Miami (4) vs. Washington (15), 1983
20 Pittsburgh (9) vs. Minnesota (11), 1975
22 Miami (8) vs. Washington (14), 1973

Completion Percentage

Highest Completion Percentage, Game (20 attempts)
88.0 N.Y. Giants vs. Denver, 1987 (25-22)
73.5 Cincinnati vs. San Francisco, 1982 (34-25)
68.6 San Francisco vs. Miami, 1985 (35-24)

Lowest Completion Percentage, Game (20 attempts)
32.0 Denver vs. Dallas, 1978 (25-8)
41.5 Baltimore vs. N.Y. Jets, 1969 (41-17)
42.3 Minnesota vs. Pittsburgh, 1975 (26-11)

Yards Gained

Most Yards Gained, Game
326 San Francisco vs. Miami, 1985
320 Denver vs. N.Y. Giants, 1987
309 Pittsburgh vs. Los Angeles, 1980

Fewest Yards Gained, Game
35 Denver vs. Dallas, 1978
63 Miami vs. Minnesota, 1974
69 Miami vs. Washington, 1973

Most Yards Gained, Both Teams, Game
615 San Francisco (326) vs. Miami (289), 1985
583 Denver (320) vs. N.Y. Giants (263), 1987
551 Philadelphia (291) vs. Oakland (260), 1981

Fewest Yards Gained, Both Teams, Game
156 Miami (69) vs. Washington (87), 1973
186 Pittsburgh (84) vs. Minnesota (102), 1975
205 Dallas (100) vs. Miami (105), 1972

Times Sacked

Most Times Sacked, Game
7 Dallas vs. Pittsburgh, 1976
New England vs. Chicago, 1986
6 Kansas City vs. Green Bay, 1967
Washington vs. L.A. Raiders, 1984
5 Dallas vs. Denver, 1978; vs. Pittsburgh, 1979
Cincinnati vs. San Francisco, 1982

Fewest Times Sacked, Game
0 Baltimore vs. N.Y. Jets, 1969; vs. Dallas, 1971
Minnesota vs. Pittsburgh, 1975
Pittsburgh vs. Los Angeles, 1980
Philadelphia vs. Oakland, 1981
1 By eight teams

Most Times Sacked, Both Teams, Game
10 New England (7) vs. Chicago (3), 1986
9 Kansas City (6) vs. Green Bay (3), 1967
Dallas (7) vs. Pittsburgh (2), 1976

Dallas (5) vs. Denver (4), 1978
Dallas (5) vs. Pittsburgh (4), 1979
8 Washington (6) vs. L.A. Raiders (2), 1984

Fewest Times Sacked, Both Teams, Game
1 Philadelphia (0) vs. Oakland (1), 1981
2 Baltimore (0) vs. N.Y. Jets (2), 1969
Baltimore (0) vs. Dallas (2), 1971
Minnesota (0) vs. Pittsburgh (2), 1975
3 In three games

Touchdowns

Most Touchdowns, Game
4 Pittsburgh vs. Dallas, 1979
3 Dallas vs. Pittsburgh, 1979
Oakland vs. Philadelphia, 1981
San Francisco vs. Miami, 1985
N.Y. Giants vs. Denver, 1987
2 By 10 teams

Fewest Touchdowns, Game
0 By 11 teams

Most Touchdowns, Both Teams, Game
7 Pittsburgh (4) vs. Dallas (3), 1979
4 Dallas (2) vs. Pittsburgh (2), 1976
Oakland (3) vs. Philadelphia (1), 1981
San Francisco (3) vs. Miami (1), 1985
N.Y. Giants (3) vs. Denver (1), 1987
3 In six games

Fewest Touchdowns, Both Teams, Game
0 N.Y. Jets vs. Baltimore, 1969
Miami vs. Minnesota, 1974
1 In five games

Interceptions By

Most Interceptions By, Game
4 N.Y. Jets vs. Baltimore, 1969
Dallas vs. Denver, 1978
3 By eight teams

Most Interceptions By, Both Teams, Game
6 Baltimore (3) vs. Dallas (3), 1971
4 In five games

Fewest Interceptions By, Both Teams, Game
1 Oakland (0) vs. Green Bay (1), 1968
Miami (0) vs. Dallas (1), 1972
Minnesota (0) vs. Miami (1), 1974
N.Y. Giants (0) vs. Denver (1), 1987

Yards Gained

Most Yards Gained, Game
95 Miami vs. Washington, 1973
91 Oakland vs. Minnesota, 1977
89 Pittsburgh vs. Dallas, 1976

Most Yards Gained, Both Teams, Game
95 Miami (95) vs. Washington (0), 1973
91 Oakland (91) vs. Minnesota (0), 1977
89 Pittsburgh (89) vs. Dallas (0), 1976

Touchdowns

Most Touchdowns, Game
1 Green Bay vs. Oakland, 1968
Oakland vs. Minnesota, 1977
L.A. Raiders vs. Washington, 1984
Chicago vs. New England, 1986

Punting

Most Punts, Game
9 Dallas vs. Baltimore, 1971
8 Washington vs. L.A. Raiders, 1984
7 By six teams

Fewest Punts, Game
2 Pittsburgh vs. Los Angeles, 1980
Denver vs. N.Y. Giants, 1987
3 By nine teams

Most Punts, Both Teams, Game
15 Washington (8) vs. L.A. Raiders (7), 1984
13 Dallas (9) vs. Baltimore (4), 1971
Pittsburgh (7) vs. Minnesota (6), 1975
12 In three games

Fewest Punts, Both Teams, Game
5 Denver (2) vs. N.Y. Giants (3), 1987
6 Oakland (3) vs. Philadelphia (3), 1981
7 In four games

Average Yardage

Highest Average, Game (4 punts)
48.50 Kansas City vs. Minnesota, 1970 (4-194)
46.25 San Francisco vs. Cincinnati, 1982 (4-185)
45.29 Kansas City vs. Green Bay, 1967 (7-317)

Lowest Average, Game (4 punts)
31.20 Washington vs. Miami, 1973 (5-156)
32.38 Washington vs. L.A. Raiders, 1984 (8-259)
32.40 Oakland vs. Minnesota, 1977 (5-162)

Punt Returns

Most Punt Returns, Game
6 Washington vs. Miami, 1983
5 By five teams

Fewest Punt Returns, Game
0 Minnesota vs. Miami, 1974
1 By 10 teams

Most Punt Returns, Both Teams, Game
9 Pittsburgh (5) vs. Minnesota (4), 1975
8 Green Bay (5) vs. Oakland (3), 1968
Baltimore (5) vs. Dallas (3), 1971
Washington (6) vs. Miami (2), 1983
7 Green Bay (4) vs. Kansas City (3), 1967
Oakland (4) vs. Minnesota (3), 1977
San Francisco (5) vs. Miami (2), 1985

Fewest Punt Returns, Both Teams, Game
2 Dallas (1) vs. Miami (1), 1972
Denver (1) vs. N.Y. Giants (1), 1987
3 Kansas City (1) vs. Minnesota (2), 1970
Minnesota (0) vs. Miami (3), 1974
4 L.A. Raiders (2) vs. Washington (2), 1984
Chicago (2) vs. New England (2), 1986

Yards Gained

Most Yards Gained, Game
52 Washington vs. Miami, 1983
51 San Francisco vs. Miami, 1985
43 Oakland vs. Minnesota, 1977

Fewest Yards Gained, Game
−1 Dallas vs. Miami, 1972
0 By four teams

Most Yards Gained, Both Teams, Game
74 Washington (52) vs. Miami (22), 1983
66 San Francisco (51) vs. Miami (15), 1985
60 Dallas (33) vs. Pittsburgh (27), 1979

Fewest Yards Gained, Both Teams, Game
13 Miami (4) vs. Washington (9), 1973
18 Kansas City (0) vs. Minnesota (18), 1970
20 Dallas (−1) vs. Miami (21), 1972
Minnesota (0) vs. Miami (20), 1974

Average Return

Highest Average, Game (3 returns)
10.8 Oakland vs. Minnesota, 1977 (4-43)
10.2 San Francisco vs. Miami, 1985 (5-51)
8.8 Cincinnati vs. San Francisco, 1982 (4-35)

Touchdowns

Most Touchdowns, Game
None

Kickoff Returns

Most Kickoff Returns, Game
7 Oakland vs. Green Bay, 1968
Minnesota vs. Oakland, 1977
Cincinnati vs. San Francisco, 1982
Washington vs. L.A. Raiders, 1984
Miami vs. San Francisco, 1985
New England vs. Chicago, 1986
6 By six teams

Fewest Kickoff Returns, Game
1 N.Y. Jets vs. Baltimore, 1969
L.A. Raiders vs. Washington, 1984
2 By six teams

Most Kickoff Returns, Both Teams, Game
11 Los Angeles (6) vs. Pittsburgh (5), 1980
Miami (7) vs. San Francisco (4), 1985
New England (7) vs. Chicago (4), 1986
10 Oakland (7) vs. Green Bay (3), 1968
9 In eight games

Fewest Kickoff Returns, Both Teams, Game
5 N.Y. Jets (1) vs. Baltimore (4), 1969
Miami (2) vs. Washington (3), 1973
6 In three games

Yards Gained

Most Yards Gained, Game
222 Miami vs. Washington, 1983
173 Denver vs. Dallas, 1978
162 Pittsburgh vs. Los Angeles, 1980

Fewest Yards Gained, Game
17 L.A. Raiders vs. Washington, 1984
25 N.Y. Jets vs. Baltimore, 1969
32 Pittsburgh vs. Minnesota, 1975

Most Yards Gained, Both Teams, Game
279 Miami (222) vs. Washington (57), 1983
231 Pittsburgh (162) vs. Los Angeles (79), 1980
224 Denver (173) vs. Dallas (51), 1978

Fewest Yards Gained, Both Teams, Game
78 Miami (33) vs. Washington (45), 1973
82 Pittsburgh (32) vs. Minnesota (50), 1975
92 San Francisco (40) vs. Cincinnati (52), 1982

Average Gain

Highest Average, Game (3 returns)
37.0 Miami vs. Washington, 1983 (6-222)
32.4 Pittsburgh vs. Los Angeles, 1980 (5-162)
28.8 Denver vs. Dallas, 1978 (6-173)

Touchdowns

Most Touchdowns, Game
1 Miami vs. Washington, 1983

Penalties

Most Penalties, Game
12 Dallas vs. Denver, 1978
10 Dallas vs. Baltimore, 1971
9 Dallas vs. Pittsburgh, 1979

Fewest Penalties, Game
0 Miami vs. Dallas, 1972
Pittsburgh vs. Dallas, 1976
1 Green Bay vs. Oakland, 1968

Miami vs. Minnesota, 1974; vs. San Francisco, 1985
2 By four teams

Most Penalties, Both Teams, Game
20 Dallas (12) vs. Denver (8), 1978
16 Cincinnati (8) vs. San Francisco (8), 1982
14 Dallas (10) vs. Baltimore (4), 1971
Dallas (9) vs. Pittsburgh (5), 1979

Fewest Penalties, Both Teams, Game
2 Pittsburgh (0) vs. Dallas (2), 1976
3 Miami (0) vs. Dallas (3), 1972
Miami (1) vs. San Francisco (2), 1985
5 Green Bay (1) vs. Oakland (4), 1968

Yards Penalized

Most Yards Penalized, Game
133 Dallas vs. Baltimore, 1971
122 Pittsburgh vs. Minnesota, 1975
94 Dallas vs. Denver, 1978

Fewest Yards Penalized, Game
0 Miami vs. Dallas, 1972
Pittsburgh vs. Dallas, 1976
4 Miami vs. Minnesota, 1974
10 Miami vs. San Francisco, 1985
San Francisco vs. Miami, 1985

Most Yards Penalized, Both Teams, Game
164 Dallas (133) vs. Baltimore (31), 1971
154 Dallas (94) vs. Denver (60), 1978
140 Pittsburgh (122) vs. Minnesota (18), 1975

Fewest Yards Penalized, Both Teams, Game
15 Miami (0) vs. Dallas (15), 1972
20 Pittsburgh (0) vs. Dallas (20), 1976
Miami (10) vs. San Francisco (10), 1985
43 Green Bay (12) vs. Oakland (31), 1968

Fumbles

Most Fumbles, Game
6 Dallas vs. Denver, 1978
5 Baltimore vs. Dallas, 1971
4 In four games

Fewest Fumbles, Game
0 By seven teams

Most Fumbles, Both Teams, Game
10 Dallas (6) vs. Denver (4), 1978
8 Dallas (4) vs. Pittsburgh (4), 1976
7 Pittsburgh (4) vs. Minnesota (3), 1975
New England (4) vs. Chicago (3), 1986

Fewest Fumbles, Both Teams, Game
0 Los Angeles vs. Pittsburgh, 1980
1 Oakland (0) vs. Minnesota (1), 1977
Oakland (0) vs. Philadelphia (1), 1981
2 In four games

Most Fumbles Lost, Game
4 Baltimore vs. Dallas, 1971
Denver vs. Dallas, 1978
New England vs. Chicago, 1986
2 In many games

Most Fumbles Lost, Both Teams, Game
6 Denver (4) vs. Dallas (2), 1978
New England (4) vs. Chicago (2), 1986
5 Baltimore (4) vs. Dallas (1), 1971
4 Minnesota (2) vs. Pittsburgh (2), 1975
Dallas (2) vs. Pittsburgh (2), 1979

Fewest Fumbles Lost, Both Teams, Game
0 Green Bay vs. Kansas City, 1967
Dallas vs. Pittsburgh, 1976
Los Angeles vs. Pittsburgh, 1980
Denver vs. N.Y. Giants, 1987
1 Washington (0) vs. Miami (1), 1973
Miami (0) vs. Minnesota (1), 1974
Oakland (0) vs. Minnesota (1), 1977
Oakland (0) vs. Philadelphia (1), 1981
Washington (0) vs. Miami (1), 1983
2 In four games

Most Fumbles Recovered, Game
8 Dallas vs. Denver, 1978 (4 own, 4 opp)
5 Chicago vs. New England, 1986 (1 own, 4 opp)
4 Pittsburgh vs. Minnesota, 1975 (2 own, 2 opp)
Dallas vs. Pittsburgh, 1976 (4 own)

Turnovers

(Number of times losing the ball on interceptions and fumbles.)

Most Turnovers, Game
8 Denver vs. Dallas, 1978
7 Baltimore vs. Dallas, 1971
6 New England vs. Chicago, 1986

Fewest Turnovers, Game
0 Green Bay vs. Oakland, 1968
Miami vs. Minnesota, 1974
Pittsburgh vs. Dallas, 1976
Oakland vs. Minnesota, 1977; vs. Philadelphia, 1981
N.Y. Giants vs. Denver, 1987
1 By many teams

Most Turnovers, Both Teams, Game
11 Baltimore (7) vs. Dallas (4), 1971
10 Denver (8) vs. Dallas (2), 1978
8 New England (6) vs. Chicago (2), 1986

Fewest Turnovers, Both Teams, Game
1 N.Y. Giants (0) vs. Denver (1), 1987
2 Green Bay (1) vs. Kansas City (1), 1967
Miami (0) vs. Minnesota (2), 1974
3 Green Bay (0) vs. Oakland (3), 1968
Pittsburgh (0) vs. Dallas (3), 1976
Oakland (0) vs. Minnesota (3), 1977

POSTSEASON GAME RECORDS

Compiled by Elias Sports Bureau

Throughout this all-time postseason record section, the following abbreviations are used to indicate various levels of postseason games:

SB — Super Bowl (1966 to date)
AFC — AFC Championship Game (1970 to date) or AFL Championship Game (1960-69)
NFC — NFC Championship Game (1970 to date) or NFL Championship Game (1933-69)
AFC-D — AFC Divisional Playoff Game (1970 to date), AFC Second-Round Playoff Game (1982), AFL Inter-Divisional Playoff Game (1969), or special playoff game to break tie for AFL Division Championship (1963, 1968)
NFC-D — NFC Divisional Playoff Game (1970 to date), NFC Second-Round Playoff Game (1982), NFL Conference Championship Game (1967-69), or special playoff game to break tie for NFL Division or Conference Championship (1941, 1943, 1947, 1950, 1952, 1957, 1958, 1965)
AFC-FR — AFC First-Round Playoff Game (1978 to date)
NFC-FR — NFC First-Round Playoff Game (1978 to date)

Year references are to the season following which the postseason game occurred, even if the game was played in the next calendar year.

Postseason Game Composite Standings

	W	L	Pct.	Pts.	OP
Green Bay Packers	13	5	.722	416	259
Pittsburgh Steelers	15	8	.652	533	447
Los Angeles Raiders*	19	12	.613	761	535
Detroit Lions	6	4	.600	221	208
Seattle Seahawks	3	2	.600	95	95
Miami Dolphins	14	10	.583	535	468
Philadelphia Eagles	7	5	.583	219	173
San Francisco 49ers	9	7	.563	334	337
Dallas Cowboys	20	16	.556	805	640
Kansas City Chiefs**	5	4	.556	159	182
Chicago Bears	11	9	.550	457	375
Baltimore Colts	8	7	.533	264	262
Washington Redskins***	13	12	.520	489	486
Houston Oilers	6	6	.500	168	267
New York Jets	5	5	.500	206	183
Minnesota Vikings	10	12	.455	378	427
Denver Broncos	4	6	.400	170	242
New England Patriots****	4	6	.400	195	258
New York Giants	10	16	.385	430	485
Los Angeles Rams†	11	18	.379	441	619
Buffalo Bills	3	5	.375	138	171
Cleveland Browns	8	15	.348	418	500
San Diego Chargers††	4	8	.333	230	279
Cincinnati Bengals	2	5	.286	137	180
Atlanta Falcons	1	3	.250	85	100
Tampa Bay Buccaneers	1	3	.250	41	94
St. Louis Cardinals†††	1	4	.200	81	134

**24 games played when franchise was in Oakland. (Won 15, lost 9, 587 points scored, 435 points allowed)*
***One game played when franchise was in Dallas (Texans). (Won 20-17)*
****One game played when franchise was in Boston. (Lost 21-6)*
*****Two games played when franchise was in Boston. (Won 26-8, lost 51-10)*
†One game played when franchise was in Cleveland (Won 15-14)
††One game played when franchise was in Los Angeles. (Lost 24-16)
†††Two games played when franchise was in Chicago. (Won 28-21, lost 7-0)

Individual Records

Service

Most Games, Career
27 D. D. Lewis, Dallas (SB-5, NFC-9, NFC-D 12, NFC-FR 1)
26 Larry Cole, Dallas (SB-5, NFC-8, NFC-D-12, NFC-FR 1)
25 Charlie Waters, Dallas (SB-5, NFC-9, NFC-D 10, NFC-FR 1)

Scoring

Points

Most Points, Career
115 George Blanda, Chi. Bears-Houston-Oakland, 19 games (49-pat, 22-fg)
102 Franco Harris, Pittsburgh, 19 games (17-td)
95 Rafael Septien, L.A. Rams-Dallas, 15 games (41-pat, 18-fg)

Most Points, Game
19 Pat Harder, NFC-D: Detroit vs. Los Angeles, 1952 (2-td, 4-pat, 1-fg)
Paul Hornung, NFC: Green Bay vs. N.Y. Giants, 1961 (1-td, 4-pat, 3-fg)
18 By 15 players

Touchdowns

Most Touchdowns, Career
17 Franco Harris, Pittsburgh, 19 games (16-r, 1-p)
12 John Riggins, Washington, 9 games (12-r)
John Stallworth, Pittsburgh, 18 games (12-p)
10 Fred Biletnikoff, Oakland, 19 games (10-p)
Larry Csonka, Miami, 12 games (9-r, 1-p)
Tony Dorsett, Dallas, 17 games (9-r, 1-p)
Marcus Allen, L.A. Raiders, 7 games (8-r, 2-p)

Most Touchdowns, Game
3 Andy Farkas, NFC-D: Washington vs. N.Y. Giants, 1943 (3-r)
Tom Fears, NFC-D: Los Angeles vs. Chi. Bears, 1950 (3-p)
Otto Graham, NFC: Cleveland vs. Detroit, 1954 (3-r)
Gary Collins, NFC: Cleveland vs. Baltimore, 1964 (3-p)
Craig Baynham, NFC-D: Dallas vs. Cleveland, 1967 (2-r, 1-p)
Fred Biletnikoff, AFC-D: Oakland vs. Kansas City, 1968 (3-p)
Tom Matte, NFC: Baltimore vs. Cleveland, 1968 (3-r)
Larry Schreiber, NFC-D: San Francisco vs. Dallas, 1972 (3-r)
Larry Csonka, AFC: Miami vs. Oakland, 1973 (3-r)
Franco Harris, AFC-D: Pittsburgh vs. Buffalo, 1974 (3-r)
Preston Pearson, NFC: Dallas vs. Los Angeles, 1975 (3-p)
Dave Casper, AFC-D: Oakland vs. Baltimore, 1977 (OT) (3-p)
Alvin Garrett, NFC-FR: Washington vs. Detroit, 1982 (3-p)
John Riggins, NFC-D: Washington vs. L.A. Rams, 1983 (3-r)
Roger Craig, SB: San Francisco vs. Miami, 1984 (1-r, 2-p)

Most Consecutive Games Scoring Touchdowns
8 John Stallworth, Pittsburgh, 1978-83
7 John Riggins, Washington, 1982-84
Marcus Allen, L.A. Raiders, 1982-85 (current)
5 Duane Thomas, Dallas, 1970-71
Franco Harris, Pittsburgh, 1974-75
Franco Harris, Pittsburgh, 1977-79

Points After Touchdown

Most Points After Touchdown, Career
49 George Blanda, Chi. Bears-Houston-Oakland, 19 games (49 att)
41 Rafael Septien, L.A. Rams-Dallas, 15 games (41 att)
38 Fred Cox, Minnesota, 18 games (40 att)

Most Points After Touchdown, Game
8 Lou Groza, NFC: Cleveland vs. Detroit, 1954 (8 att)
Jim Martin, NFC: Detroit vs. Cleveland, 1957 (8 att)
George Blanda, AFC-D: Oakland vs. Houston, 1969 (8 att)
7 Danny Villanueva, NFC-D: Dallas vs. Cleveland, 1967 (7 att)
Raul Allegre, NFC-D: N.Y. Giants vs. San Francisco, 1986
6 George Blair, AFC: San Diego vs. Boston, 1963 (6 att)
Mark Moseley, NFC-D: Washington vs. L.A. Rams, 1983 (6 att)
Uwe von Schamann, AFC: Miami vs. Pittsburgh, 1984 (6 att)

Most Points After Touchdown, No Misses, Career
49 George Blanda, Chi. Bears-Houston-Oakland, 19 games
41 Rafael Septien, L.A. Rams-Dallas, 14 games
33 Chris Bahr, Oakland-L.A. Raiders, 11 games

Field Goals

Most Field Goals Attempted, Career
39 George Blanda, Chi. Bears-Houston-Oakland, 19 games
31 Mark Moseley, Washington-Cleveland, 11 games
27 Roy Gerela, Houston-Pittsburgh, 15 games

Most Field Goals Attempted, Game
6 George Blanda, AFC: Oakland vs. Houston, 1967
David Ray, NFC-D: Los Angeles vs. Dallas, 1973
Mark Moseley, AFC-D: Cleveland vs. N.Y. Jets, 1986 (OT)
5 Jerry Kramer, NFC: Green Bay vs. N.Y. Giants, 1962
Gino Cappelletti, AFC-D: Boston vs. Buffalo, 1963
Pete Gogolak, AFC: Buffalo vs. San Diego, 1965
Jan Stenerud, AFC-D: Kansas City vs. N.Y. Jets, 1969
George Blanda, AFC-D: Oakland vs. Pittsburgh, 1973
Ed Murray, NFC-D: Detroit vs. San Francisco, 1983
Mark Moseley, NFC: Washington vs. San Francisco, 1983
Tony Franklin, AFC-FR: New England vs. N.Y. Jets, 1985
4 By many players

Most Field Goals, Career
22 George Blanda, Chi. Bears-Houston-Oakland, 19 games
20 Toni Fritsch, Dallas-Houston, 14 games
18 Rafael Septien, L.A. Rams-Dallas, 15 games

Most Field Goals, Game
4 Gino Cappelletti, AFC-D: Boston vs. Buffalo, 1963
George Blanda, AFC: Oakland vs. Houston, 1967
Don Chandler, SB: Green Bay vs. Oakland, 1967
Curt Knight, NFC: Washington vs. Dallas, 1972
George Blanda, AFC-D: Oakland vs. Pittsburgh, 1973
Ray Wersching, SB: San Francisco vs. Cincinnati, 1981
Tony Franklin, AFC-FR: New England vs. N.Y. Jets, 1985
Jess Atkinson, NFC-FR: Washington vs. L.A. Rams, 1986
3 By many players

Most Consecutive Field Goals
15 Rafael Septien, Dallas, 1978-82

Longest Field Goal
54 Ed Murray, NFC-D: Detroit vs. San Francisco, 1983
52 Lou Groza, NFC: Cleveland vs. Los Angeles, 1951
Curt Knight, NFC-D: Washington vs. Minnesota, 1973
Matt Bahr, AFC-FR: Cleveland vs. L.A. Raiders, 1982
51 Fuad Reveiz, AFC-D: Miami vs. Cleveland, 1985

Highest Field Goal Percentage, Career (10 field goals)
85.7 Rafael Septien, L.A. Rams-Dallas, 15 games (21-18)
80.0 Toni Fritsch, Dallas-Houston, 14 games (25-20)
78.9 Chris Bahr, Oakland-L.A. Raiders, 11 games (19-15)

Safeties

Most Safeties, Game
1 Bill Willis, NFC-D: Cleveland vs. N.Y. Giants, 1950
Carl Eller, NFC-D: Minnesota vs. Los Angeles, 1969
George Andrie, NFC-D: Dallas vs. Detroit, 1970
Alan Page, NFC-D: Minnesota vs. Dallas, 1971
Dwight White, SB: Pittsburgh vs. Minnesota, 1974
Reggie Harrison, SB: Pittsburgh vs. Dallas, 1975
Jim Jensen, NFC-D: Dallas vs. Los Angeles, 1976
Ted Washington, AFC: Houston vs. Pittsburgh, 1978
Randy White, NFC-D: Dallas vs. Los Angeles, 1979
Henry Waechter, SB: Chicago vs. New England, 1985
Rulon Jones, AFC-FR: Denver vs. New England, 1986
George Martin, SB: N.Y. Giants vs. Denver, 1986

Rushing

Attempts

Most Attempts, Career
400 Franco Harris, Pittsburgh, 19 games
302 Tony Dorsett, Dallas, 17 games
251 John Riggins, Washington, 9 games

Most Attempts, Game
38 Ricky Bell, NFC-D: Tampa Bay vs. Philadelphia, 1979
John Riggins, SB: Washington vs. Miami, 1982
37 Lawrence McCutcheon, NFC-D: Los Angeles vs. St. Louis, 1975
John Riggins, NFC-D: Washington vs. Minnesota, 1982
36 John Riggins, NFC: Washington vs. Dallas, 1982
John Riggins, NFC: Washington vs. San Francisco, 1983

Yards Gained

Most Yards Gained, Career
1,556 Franco Harris, Pittsburgh, 19 games
1,383 Tony Dorsett, Dallas, 17 games
996 John Riggins, Washington, 9 games

Most Yards Gained, Game
248 Eric Dickerson, NFC-D: L.A. Rams vs. Dallas, 1985
206 Keith Lincoln, AFC: San Diego vs. Boston, 1963
202 Lawrence McCutcheon, NFC-D: Los Angeles vs. St. Louis, 1975
Freeman McNeil, AFC-FR: N.Y. Jets vs. Cincinnati, 1982

Most Games, 100 or More Yards Rushing, Career
6 John Riggins, Washington, 9 games
5 Franco Harris, Pittsburgh, 19 games
4 Larry Csonka, Miami, 12 games
Chuck Foreman, Minnesota, 13 games
Marcus Allen, L.A. Raiders, 7 games

Most Consecutive Games, 100 or More Yards Rushing
6 John Riggins, Washington, 1982-83
3 Larry Csonka, Miami, 1973-74
Franco Harris, Pittsburgh, 1974-75
Marcus Allen, L.A. Raiders, 1983

Longest Run From Scrimmage
74 Marcus Allen, SB: L.A. Raiders vs. Washington, 1983 (TD)
71 Hugh McElhenny, NFC-D: San Francisco vs. Detroit, 1957
James Lofton, NFC-D: Green Bay vs. Dallas, 1982 (TD)
70 Elmer Angsman, NFC: Chi. Cardinals vs. Philadelphia, 1947 (twice, 2 TDs)

Average Gain

Highest Average Gain, Career (50 attempts)
6.67 Paul Lowe, L.A. Chargers-San Diego, 5 games (57-380)
5.86 Marcus Allen, L.A. Raiders, 7 games (129-756)
5.68 Roger Staubach, Dallas, 20 games (76-432)

Highest Average Gain, Game (10 attempts)
15.90 Elmer Angsman, NFC: Chi. Cardinals vs. Philadelphia, 1947 (10-159)
15.85 Keith Lincoln, AFC: San Diego vs. Boston, 1963 (13-206)
10.90 Bill Osmanski, NFC: Chi. Bears vs. Washington, 1940 (10-109)

Touchdowns

Most Touchdowns, Career
16 Franco Harris, Pittsburgh, 19 games
12 John Riggins, Washington, 9 games
9 Larry Csonka, Miami, 12 games
Tony Dorsett, Dallas, 17 games

Most Touchdowns, Game
3 Andy Farkas, NFC-D: Washington vs. N.Y. Giants, 1943
Otto Graham, NFC: Cleveland vs. Detroit, 1954
Tom Matte, NFC: Baltimore vs. Cleveland, 1968
Larry Schreiber, NFC-D: San Francisco vs. Dallas, 1972
Larry Csonka, AFC: Miami vs. Oakland, 1973
Franco Harris, AFC-D: Pittsburgh vs. Buffalo, 1974
John Riggins, NFC-D: Washington vs. L.A. Rams, 1983

Most Consecutive Games Rushing for Touchdowns
7 John Riggins, Washington, 1982-84
5 Franco Harris, Pittsburgh, 1974-75
Franco Harris, Pittsburgh, 1977-79
3 By many players

Passing

Pass Rating

Highest Pass Rating, Career (100 attempts)
104.8 Bart Starr, Green Bay, 10 games
93.3 Ken Anderson, Cincinnati, 6 games
91.4 Joe Theismann, Washington, 10 games

Attempts

Most Passes Attempted, Career
456 Terry Bradshaw, Pittsburgh, 19 games
410 Roger Staubach, Dallas, 20 games
360 Danny White, Dallas, 18 games

Most Passes Attempted, Game
64 Bernie Kosar, AFC-D: Cleveland vs. N.Y. Jets, 1986 (OT)
53 Dan Fouts, AFC-D: San Diego vs. Miami, 1981 (OT)
Danny White, NFC-FR: Dallas vs. L.A. Rams, 1983
51 Richard Todd, AFC-FR: N.Y. Jets vs. Buffalo, 1981
Neil Lomax, NFC-FR: St. Louis vs. Green Bay, 1982

Completions

Most Passes Completed, Career
261 Terry Bradshaw, Pittsburgh, 19 games
223 Roger Staubach, Dallas, 20 games
206 Danny White, Dallas, 18 games

Most Passes Completed, Game
33 Dan Fouts, AFC-D: San Diego vs. Miami, 1981 (OT)
Bernie Kosar, AFC-D: Cleveland vs. N.Y. Jets, 1986 (OT)
32 Neil Lomax, NFC-FR: St. Louis vs. Green Bay, 1982
Danny White, NFC-FR: Dallas vs. L.A. Rams, 1983
29 Don Strock, AFC-D: Miami vs. San Diego, 1981 (OT)
Dan Marino, SB: Miami vs. San Francisco, 1984

Completion Percentage

Highest Completion Percentage, Career (100 attempts)
66.3 Ken Anderson, Cincinnati, 6 games (166-110)
61.2 Dan Pastorini, Houston, 5 games (116-71)
61.0 Bart Starr, Green Bay, 10 games (213-130)

Highest Completion Percentage, Game (15 completions)
88.0 Phil Simms, SB: N.Y. Giants vs. Denver, 1986 (25-22)
84.2 David Woodley, AFC-FR: Miami vs. New England, 1982 (19-16)
78.9 Norm Van Brocklin, NFC-D: Los Angeles vs. Detroit, 1952 (19-15)

Yards Gained

Most Yards Gained, Career
3,833 Terry Bradshaw, Pittsburgh, 19 games
2,791 Roger Staubach, Dallas, 20 games
2,641 Ken Stabler, Oakland-Houston, 13 games

Most Yards Gained, Game
489 Bernie Kosar, AFC-D: Cleveland vs. N.Y. Jets, 1986 (OT)
433 Dan Fouts, AFC-D: San Diego vs. Miami, 1981 (OT)
421 Dan Marino, AFC: Miami vs. Pittsburgh, 1984

Most Games, 300 or More Yards Passing, Career
5 Dan Fouts, San Diego, 7 games
4 Joe Montana, San Francisco, 10 games
3 Terry Bradshaw, Pittsburgh, 19 games
Danny White, Dallas, 17 games
Dan Marino, Miami, 4 games

Most Consecutive Games, 300 or More Yards Passing
4 Dan Fouts, San Diego, 1979-81
2 Daryle Lamonica, Oakland, 1968
Ken Anderson, Cincinnati, 1981-82 (current)
Terry Bradshaw, Pittsburgh, 1979-82
Joe Montana, San Francisco, 1983-84
Dan Marino, Miami, 1984

Longest Pass Completion
93 Daryle Lamonica (to Dubenion), AFC-D: Buffalo vs. Boston, 1963 (TD)
88 George Blanda (to Cannon), AFC: Houston vs. L.A. Chargers, 1960 (TD)
86 Don Meredith (to Hayes), NFC-D: Dallas vs. Cleveland, 1967 (TD)

Average Gain

Highest Average Gain, Career (100 attempts)
8.45 Joe Theismann, Washington, 10 games (211-1,782)
8.43 Jim Plunkett, Oakland-L.A. Raiders, 10 games (272-2,293)
8.41 Terry Bradshaw, Pittsburgh, 19 games (456-3,833)

Highest Average Gain, Game (20 attempts)
14.71 Terry Bradshaw, SB: Pittsburgh vs. Los Angeles, 1979 (21-309)
13.33 Bob Waterfield, NFC-D: Los Angeles vs. Chi. Bears, 1950 (21-280)
13.16 Dan Marino, AFC: Miami vs. Pittsburgh, 1984 (32-421)

Touchdowns

Most Touchdown Passes, Career
30 Terry Bradshaw, Pittsburgh, 19 games
24 Roger Staubach, Dallas, 20 games
19 Daryle Lamonica, Buffalo-Oakland, 13 games
Ken Stabler, Oakland-Houston, 13 games

Most Touchdown Passes, Game
6 Daryle Lamonica, AFC-D: Oakland vs. Houston, 1969
5 Sid Luckman, NFC: Chi. Bears vs. Washington, 1943
Daryle Lamonica, AFC-D: Oakland vs. Kansas City, 1968
4 Otto Graham, NFC: Cleveland vs. Los Angeles, 1950
Tobin Rote, NFC: Detroit vs. Cleveland, 1957
Bart Starr, NFC: Green Bay vs. Dallas, 1966
Ken Stabler, AFC-D: Oakland vs. Miami, 1974
Roger Staubach, NFC: Dallas vs. Los Angeles, 1975
Terry Bradshaw, SB: Pittsburgh vs. Dallas, 1978
Don Strock, AFC-D: Miami vs. San Diego, 1981 (OT)
Lynn Dickey, NFC-FR: Green Bay vs. St. Louis, 1982
Dan Marino, AFC: Miami vs. Pittsburgh, 1984

Most Consecutive Games, Touchdown Passes
10 Ken Stabler, Oakland, 1973-77
8 Terry Bradshaw, Pittsburgh, 1977-82
Joe Montana, San Francisco, 1981-84
6 Bart Starr, Green Bay, 1965-67
Terry Bradshaw, Pittsburgh, 1972-74
Dan Fouts, San Diego, 1980-82 (current)
Joe Theismann, Washington, 1982-83
Dan Marino, Miami, 1983-85 (current)

Had Intercepted

Lowest Percentage, Passes Had Intercepted, Career (100 attempts)
1.41 Bart Starr, Green Bay, 10 games (213-3)
1.51 Phil Simms, N.Y. Giants, 7 games (199-3)
1.90 Jay Schroeder, Washington, 3 games (105-2)

Most Attempts Without Interception, Game
47 Daryle Lamonica, AFC: Oakland vs. N.Y. Jets, 1968
42 Dan Fouts, AFC-FR: San Diego vs. Pittsburgh, 1982
39 Daryle Lamonica, AFC-D: Oakland vs. Kansas City, 1968
Ron Jaworski, NFC-D: Philadelphia vs. Tampa Bay, 1979
Tommy Kramer, NFC-D: Minnesota vs. Washington, 1982

Most Passes Had Intercepted, Career
26 Terry Bradshaw, Pittsburgh, 19 games
19 Roger Staubach, Dallas, 20 games
17 George Blanda, Chi. Bears-Houston-Oakland, 19 games
Fran Tarkenton, Minnesota, 11 games

Most Passes Had Intercepted, Game
6 Frank Filchock, NFC: N.Y. Giants vs. Chi. Bears, 1946
Bobby Layne, NFC: Detroit vs. Cleveland, 1954
Norm Van Brocklin, NFC: Los Angeles vs. Cleveland, 1955
5 Frank Filchock, NFC: Washington vs. Chi. Bears, 1940
George Blanda, AFC: Houston vs. San Diego, 1961
George Blanda, AFC: Houston vs. Dall. Texans, 1962 (OT)
Y.A. Tittle, NFC: N.Y. Giants vs. Chicago, 1963
Mike Phipps, AFC-D: Cleveland vs. Miami, 1972
Dan Pastorini, AFC: Houston vs. Pittsburgh, 1978
Dan Fouts, AFC-D: San Diego vs. Houston, 1979

Tommy Kramer, NFC-D: Minnesota vs. Philadelphia, 1980
Dan Fouts, AFC-D: San Diego vs. Miami, 1982
Richard Todd, AFC: N.Y. Jets vs Miami, 1982
Gary Danielson, NFC-D: Detroit vs. San Francisco, 1983
4 By many players

Pass Receiving

Receptions

Most Receptions, Career
73 Cliff Branch, Oakland-L.A. Raiders, 22 games
70 Fred Biletnikoff, Oakland, 19 games
67 Drew Pearson, Dallas, 22 games

Most Receptions, Game
13 Kellen Winslow, AFC-D: San Diego vs. Miami, 1981 (OT)
12 Raymond Berry, NFC: Baltimore vs. N.Y. Giants, 1958
11 Dante Lavelli, NFC: Cleveland vs. Los Angeles, 1950
Dan Ross, SB: Cincinnati vs. San Francisco, 1981
Franco Harris, AFC-FR: Pittsburgh vs. San Diego, 1982
Steve Watson, AFC-D: Denver vs. Pittsburgh, 1984

Most Consecutive Games, Pass Receptions
22 Drew Pearson, Dallas, 1973-83
18 Paul Warfield, Cleveland-Miami, 1964-74
Cliff Branch, Oakland-L.A. Raiders, 1974-83
17 John Stallworth, Pittsburgh, 1974-84 (current)

Yards Gained

Most Yards Gained, Career
1,289 Cliff Branch, Oakland-L.A. Raiders, 22 games
1,167 Fred Biletnikoff, Oakland, 19 games
1,121 Paul Warfield, Cleveland-Miami, 18 games

Most Yards Gained, Game
198 Tom Fears, NFC-D: Los Angeles vs. Chi. Bears, 1950
190 Fred Biletnikoff, AFC: Oakland vs. N.Y. Jets, 1968
186 Cliff Branch, AFC: Oakland vs. Pittsburgh, 1974

Most Games, 100 or More Yards Receiving, Career
5 John Stallworth, Pittsburgh, 18 games
4 Fred Biletnikoff, Oakland, 19 games
Dwight Clark, San Francisco, 7 games
3 Tom Fears, L.A. Rams, 6 games
Cliff Branch, Oakland-L.A. Raiders, 22 games
Tony Nathan, Miami, 10 games

Most Consecutive Games, 100 or More Yards Receiving, Career
3 Tom Fears, Los Angeles, 1950-51
2 Lenny Moore, Baltimore, 1958-59
Fred Biletnikoff, Oakland, 1968
Paul Warfield, Miami, 1971
Charlie Joiner, San Diego, 1981
Dwight Clark, San Francisco, 1981
Cris Collinsworth, Cincinnati, 1981-82
John Stallworth, Pittsburgh, 1979-82
Wesley Walker, N.Y. Jets, 1982
Charlie Brown, Washington, 1983

Longest Reception
93 Elbert Dubenion (from Lamonica), AFC-D: Buffalo vs. Boston, 1963 (TD)
88 Billy Cannon (from Blanda), AFC: Houston vs. L.A. Chargers, 1960 (TD)
86 Bob Hayes (from Meredith), NFC: Dallas vs. Cleveland, 1967 (TD)

Average Gain

Highest Average Gain, Career (20 receptions)
22.8 Harold Jackson, L.A. Rams-New England-Minnesota-Seattle, 14 games (24-548)
20.7 Charlie Brown, Washington, 8 games (31-643)
20.5 Frank Lewis, Pittsburgh-Buffalo, 12 games (27-553)

Highest Average Gain, Game (3 receptions)
46.3 Harold Jackson, NFC: Los Angeles vs. Minnesota, 1974 (3-139)
42.7 Billy Cannon, AFC: Houston vs. L.A. Chargers, 1960 (3-128)
42.0 Lenny Moore, NFC: Baltimore vs. N.Y. Giants, 1959 (3-126)

Touchdowns

Most Touchdowns, Career
12 John Stallworth, Pittsburgh, 18 games
10 Fred Biletnikoff, Oakland, 19 games
9 Lynn Swann, Pittsburgh, 16 games

Most Touchdowns, Game
3 Tom Fears, NFC-D: Los Angeles vs. Chi. Bears, 1950
Gary Collins, NFC: Cleveland vs. Baltimore, 1964
Fred Biletnikoff, AFC-D: Oakland vs. Kansas City, 1968
Preston Pearson, NFC: Dallas vs. Los Angeles, 1975
Dave Casper, AFC-D: Oakland vs. Baltimore, 1977 (OT)
Alvin Garrett, NFC-FR: Washington vs. Detroit, 1982

Most Consecutive Games, Touchdown Passes Caught
8 John Stallworth, Pittsburgh, 1978-83
4 Lynn Swann, Pittsburgh, 1978-79
Harold Carmichael, Philadelphia, 1978-80
Fred Solomon, San Francisco, 1983-84
3 By many players

Interceptions By

Most Interceptions, Career
9 Charlie Waters, Dallas, 25 games
Bill Simpson, Los Angeles-Buffalo, 11 games
8 Lester Hayes, Oakland-L.A. Raiders, 13 games
7 Willie Brown, Oakland, 17 games
Dennis Thurman, Dallas, 14 games

Most Interceptions, Game
4 Vernon Perry, AFC-D: Houston vs. San Diego, 1979
3 Joe Laws, NFC: Green Bay vs. N.Y. Giants, 1944
Charlie Waters, NFC-D: Dallas vs. Chicago, 1977
Rod Martin, SB: Oakland vs. Philadelphia, 1980
Dennis Thurman, NFC-D: Dallas vs. Green Bay, 1982
A.J. Duhe, AFC: Miami vs. N.Y. Jets, 1982
2 By many players

Yards Gained

Most Yards Gained, Career
196 Willie Brown, Oakland, 17 games
151 Glen Edwards, Pittsburgh-San Diego, 17 games
149 Bill Simpson, Los Angeles-Buffalo, 11 games
LeRoy Irvin, L.A. Rams, 7 games

Most Yards Gained, Game
98 Darrol Ray, AFC-FR: N.Y. Jets vs. Cincinnati, 1982
94 LeRoy Irvin, NFC-FR: L.A. Rams vs. Dallas, 1983
88 Walt Sumner, NFC-D: Cleveland vs. Dallas, 1969

Longest Return
98 Darrol Ray, AFC-FR: N.Y. Jets vs. Cincinnati, 1982 (TD)
94 LeRoy Irvin, NFC-FR: L.A. Rams vs. Dallas, 1983
88 Walt Sumner, NFC-D: Cleveland vs. Dallas, 1969 (TD)

Touchdowns

Most Touchdowns, Career
3 Willie Brown, Oakland, 17 games
2 Lester Hayes, Oakland-L.A. Raiders, 13 games

Most Touchdowns, Game
1 By 40 players

Punting

Most Punts, Career
111 Ray Guy, Oakland-L.A. Raiders, 22 games
84 Danny White, Dallas, 18 games
73 Mike Eischeid, Oakland-Minnesota, 14 games

Most Punts, Game
14 Dave Jennings, AFC-D: N.Y. Jets vs. Cleveland, 1986 (OT)
12 David Lee, AFC-D: Baltimore vs. Oakland, 1977 (OT)
11 Ken Strong, NFC: N.Y. Giants vs. Chi. Bears, 1933
Jim Norton, AFC: Houston vs. Oakland, 1967
Dale Hatcher, NFC: L.A. Rams vs. Chicago, 1985

Longest Punt
76 Ed Danowski, NFC: N.Y. Giants vs. Detroit, 1935
72 Charlie Conerly, NFC-D: N.Y. Giants vs. Cleveland, 1950
71 Ray Guy, AFC: Oakland vs. San Diego, 1980

Average Yardage

Highest Average, Career (20 punts)
44.5 Rich Camarillo, New England, 6 games (35-1,559)
43.4 Jerrel Wilson, Kansas City-New England, 8 games (43-1,866)
43.1 Don Chandler, N.Y. Giants-Green Bay, 14 games (53-2,282)

Highest Average, Game (4 punts)
56.0 Ray Guy, AFC: Oakland vs. San Diego, 1980 (4-224)
52.5 Sammy Baugh, NFC: Washington vs. Chi. Bears, 1942 (6-315)
51.4 John Hadl, AFC: San Diego vs. Buffalo, 1965 (5-257)

Punt Returns

Most Punt Returns, Career
25 Theo Bell, Pittsburgh-Tampa Bay, 10 games
19 Willie Wood, Green Bay, 10 games
Butch Johnson, Dallas-Denver, 18 games
Phil McConkey, N.Y. Giants, 5 games
18 Neal Colzie, Oakland-Miami-Tampa Bay, 10 games

Most Punt Returns, Game
7 Ron Gardin, AFC-D: Baltimore vs. Cincinnati, 1970
Carl Roaches, AFC-FR: Houston vs. Oakland, 1980
Gerald McNeil, AFC-D: Cleveland vs. N.Y. Jets, 1986 (OT)
Phil McConkey, NFC-D: N.Y. Giants vs. San Francisco, 1986
6 George McAfee, NFC-D: Chi. Bears vs. Los Angeles, 1950
Eddie Brown, NFC-D: Washington vs. Minnesota, 1976
Theo Bell, AFC: Pittsburgh vs. Houston, 1978
Eddie Brown, NFC: Los Angeles vs. Tampa Bay, 1979
John Sciarra, NFC: Philadelphia vs. Dallas, 1980
Kurt Sohn, AFC: N.Y. Jets vs. Miami, 1982
Mike Nelms, SB: Washington vs. Miami, 1982
5 By many players

Yards Gained

Most Yards Gained, Career
221 Neal Colzie, Oakland-Miami-Tampa Bay, 10 games
208 Butch Johnson, Dallas-Denver, 18 games
204 Theo Bell, Pittsburgh-Tampa Bay, 10 games

Most Yards Gained, Game
141 Bob Hayes, NFC-D: Dallas vs. Cleveland, 1967
102 Charley Trippi, NFC: Chi. Cardinals vs. Philadelphia, 1947
101 Bosh Pritchard, NFC-D: Philadelphia vs. Pittsburgh, 1947

Longest Return
81 Hugh Gallarneau, NFC-D: Chi. Bears vs. Green Bay, 1941 (TD)
79 Bosh Pritchard, NFC-D: Philadelphia vs. Pittsburgh, 1947 (TD)
75 Charley Trippi, NFC: Chi. Cardinals vs. Philadelphia, 1947 (TD)

Average Yardage

Highest Average, Career (10 returns)
12.6 Bob Hayes, Dallas, 15 games (12-151)
12.4 Mike Fuller, San Diego-Cincinnati, 7 games (13-161)
12.3 Neal Colzie, Oakland-Miami-Tampa Bay, 10 games (18-221)

Highest Average Gain, Game (3 returns)
47.0 Bob Hayes, NFC-D: Dallas vs. Cleveland, 1967 (3-141)
29.0 George (Butch) Byrd, AFC: Buffalo vs. San Diego, 1965 (3-87)
25.3 Bosh Pritchard, NFC-D: Philadelphia vs. Pittsburgh, 1947 (4-101)

Touchdowns

Most Touchdowns
1 Hugh Gallarneau, NFC-D: Chicago Bears vs. Green Bay, 1941
Bosh Pritchard, NFC-D: Philadelphia vs. Pittsburgh, 1947
Charley Trippi, NFC: Chicago Cardinals vs. Philadelphia, 1947
Verda (Vitamin T) Smith, NFC-D: Los Angeles vs. Detroit, 1952
George (Butch) Byrd, AFC: Buffalo vs. San Diego, 1965
Golden Richards, NFC: Dallas vs. Minnesota, 1973
Wes Chandler, AFC-D: San Diego vs. Miami, 1981 (OT)
Shaun Gayle, NFC-D: Chicago vs. N.Y. Giants, 1985

Kickoff Returns

Most Kickoff Returns, Career

29 Fulton Walker, Miami-L.A. Raiders, 10 games
19 Preston Pearson, Baltimore-Pittsburgh-Dallas, 22 games
18 Charlie West, Minnesota, 9 games

Most Kickoff Returns, Game

7 Don Bingham, NFC: Chi. Bears vs. N.Y. Giants, 1956
Reggie Brown, NFC-FR: Atlanta vs. Minnesota, 1982
David Verser, AFC-FR: Cincinnati vs. N.Y. Jets, 1982
Del Rodgers, NFC-D: Green Bay vs. Dallas, 1982
Henry Ellard, NFC-D: L.A. Rams vs. Washington, 1983
Stephen Starring, SB: New England vs. Chicago, 1985
6 Wallace Francis, AFC-D: Buffalo vs. Pittsburgh, 1974
Eddie Brown, NFC-D: Washington vs. Minnesota, 1976
Eddie Payton, NFC-D: Minnesota vs. Philadelphia, 1980
Alvin Hall, NFC-FR: Detroit vs. Washington, 1982
Fulton Walker, AFC-D: Miami vs. Seattle, 1983
Johnny Hector, AFC-FR: N.Y. Jets vs. New England, 1985
Lorenzo Hampton, AFC: Miami vs. New England, 1985
5 By many players

Yards Gained

Most Yards Gained, Career

677 Fulton Walker, Miami-L.A. Raiders, 10 games
481 Carl Garrett, Oakland, 5 games
458 Cullen Bryant, L.A. Rams-Seattle, 19 games

Most Yards Gained, Game

190 Fulton Walker, SB: Miami vs. Washington, 1982
170 Les (Speedy) Duncan, NFC-D: Washington vs. San Francisco, 1971
169 Carl Garrett, AFC-D: Oakland vs. Baltimore, 1977 (OT)

Longest Return

98 Fulton Walker, SB: Miami vs. Washington, 1982 (TD)
97 Vic Washington, NFC-D: San Francisco vs. Dallas, 1972 (TD)
89 Nat Moore, AFC-D: Miami vs. Oakland, 1974 (TD)
Rod Hill, NFC-D: Dallas vs. Green Bay, 1982

Average Yardage

Highest Average, Career (10 returns)

30.1 Carl Garrett, Oakland, 5 games (16-481)
27.9 George Atkinson, Oakland, 16 games (12-335)
24.2 Larry Anderson, Pittsburgh, 6 games (16-387)

Highest Average, Game (3 returns)

56.7 Les (Speedy) Duncan, NFC-D: Washington vs. San Francisco, 1971 (3-170)
51.3 Ed Podolak, AFC-D: Kansas City vs. Miami, 1971 (OT) (3-154)
49.0 Les (Speedy) Duncan, AFC: San Diego vs. Buffalo, 1964 (3-147)

Touchdowns

Most Touchdowns

1 Vic Washington, NFC-D: San Francisco vs. Dallas, 1972
Nat Moore, AFC-D: Miami vs. Oakland, 1974
Marshall Johnson, AFC-D: Baltimore vs. Oakland, 1977 (OT)
Fulton Walker, SB: Miami vs. Washington, 1982

Fumbles

Most Fumbles, Career

13 Tony Dorsett, Dallas, 17 games
10 Franco Harris, Pittsburgh, 19 games
Terry Bradshaw, Pittsburgh, 19 games
Roger Staubach, Dallas, 20 games
9 Chuck Foreman, Minnesota, 13 games

Most Fumbles, Game

4 Brian Sipe, AFC-D: Cleveland vs. Oakland, 1980
3 Y.A. Tittle, NFC-D: San Francisco vs. Detroit, 1957
Bill Nelsen, AFC-D: Cleveland vs. Baltimore, 1972
Chuck Foreman, NFC: Minnesota vs. Los Angeles, 1974
Lawrence McCutcheon, NFC-D: Los Angeles vs. St. Louis, 1975
Roger Staubach, SB: Dallas vs. Pittsburgh, 1975
Terry Bradshaw, AFC: Pittsburgh vs. Houston, 1978
Earl Campbell, AFC: Houston vs. Pittsburgh, 1978
Franco Harris, AFC: Pittsburgh vs. Houston, 1978
Chuck Muncie, AFC: San Diego vs. Cincinnati, 1981
Andra Franklin, AFC-FR: Miami vs. New England, 1982
Eric Dickerson, NFC-FR: L.A. Rams vs. Washington, 1986
2 By many players

Recoveries

Most Own Fumbles Recovered, Career

5 Roger Staubach, Dallas, 20 games
4 Fran Tarkenton, Minnesota, 11 games
3 Alex Webster, N.Y. Giants, 7 games
Don Meredith, Dallas, 4 games
Franco Harris, Pittsburgh, 19 games
Gerry Mullins, Pittsburgh, 18 games
Ron Jaworski, Los Angeles-Philadelphia, 10 games
Lyle Blackwood, Cincinnati-Baltimore-Miami, 14 games

Most Opponents' Fumbles Recovered, Career

4 Cliff Harris, Dallas, 21 games
Harvey Martin, Dallas, 22 games
Ted Hendricks, Baltimore-Oakland-L.A. Raiders, 21 games
3 Paul Krause, Minnesota, 19 games
Jack Lambert, Pittsburgh, 18 games
Fred Dryer, Los Angeles, 14 games
Charlie Waters, Dallas, 25 games
Jack Ham, Pittsburgh, 16 games
Mike Hegman, Dallas, 16 games
Tom Jackson, Denver, 10 games
Mike Singletary, Chicago, 6 games
Monte Coleman, Washington, 11 games
Darryl Grant, Washington, 11 games
Alvin Walton, Washington, 3 games
2 By many players

Most Fumbles Recovered, Game, Own and Opponents'

3 Jack Lambert, AFC: Pittsburgh vs. Oakland, 1975 (3 opp)
Ron Jaworski, NFC-FR: Philadelphia vs. N.Y. Giants, 1981 (3 own)
2 By many players

Yards Gained

Longest Return

93 Andy Russell, AFC-D: Pittsburgh vs. Baltimore, 1975 (opp, TD)
60 Mike Curtis, NFC-D: Baltimore vs. Minnesota, 1968 (opp, TD)
Hugh Green, NFC-FR: Tampa Bay vs. Dallas, 1982 (opp, TD)
52 Wilber Marshall, NFC: Chicago vs. L.A. Rams, 1985 (opp, TD)

Touchdowns

Most Touchdowns

1 By 22 players

Combined Net Yards Gained

Rushing, receiving, interception returns, punt returns, kickoff returns, and fumble returns.

Attempts

Most Attempts, Career

454 Franco Harris, Pittsburgh, 19 games
350 Tony Dorsett, Dallas, 17 games
275 Chuck Foreman, Minnesota, 13 games

Most Attempts, Game

40 Lawrence McCutcheon, NFC-D: Los Angeles vs. St. Louis, 1975
39 John Riggins, SB: Washington vs. Miami, 1982
38 Ricky Bell, NFC-D: Tampa Bay vs. Philadelphia, 1979
Rob Carpenter, NFC-FR: N.Y. Giants vs. Philadelphia, 1981

Yards Gained

Most Yards Gained, Career

2,060 Franco Harris, Pittsburgh, 19 games
1,786 Tony Dorsett, Dallas, 17 games
1,307 Chuck Foreman, Minnesota, 13 games

Most Yards Gained, Game

350 Ed Podolak, AFC-D: Kansas City vs. Miami, 1971 (OT)
329 Keith Lincoln, AFC: San Diego vs. Boston, 1963
285 Bob Hayes, NFC-D: Dallas vs. Cleveland, 1967

Sacks

Sacks have been compiled since 1982

Most Sacks, Career

9.5 Richard Dent, Chicago, 6 games
7.5 Mark Gastineau, N.Y. Jets, 6 games
6.5 Dwaine Board, San Francisco, 8 games

Most Sacks, Game

3.5 Rich Milot, NFC-D: Washington vs. Chicago, 1984
Richard Dent, NFC-D: Chicago vs. N.Y. Giants, 1985
3 Richard Dent, NFC-D: Chicago vs. Washington, 1984
Garin Veris, AFC-FR: New England vs. N.Y. Jets, 1985
Gary Jeter, NFC-D: L.A. Rams vs. Dallas, 1985
Carl Hairston, AFC-D: Cleveland vs. N.Y. Jets, 1986 (OT)
2.5 Lyle Alzado, AFC-D: L.A. Raiders vs. Pittsburgh, 1983
Jacob Green, AFC-FR: Seattle vs. L.A. Raiders, 1984

Team Records

Games, Victories, Defeats

Most Consecutive Seasons Participating in Postseason Games

9 Dallas, 1975-83
8 Dallas, 1966-73
Pittsburgh, 1972-79
Los Angeles, 1973-80
6 Cleveland, 1950-55
Oakland, 1972-77
Minnesota, 1973-78

Most Games

36 Dallas, 1966-73, 1975-83, 1985
31 Oakland/L. A. Raiders, 1967-70, 1973-77, 1980, 1982-85
29 Cleveland/L. A. Rams, 1945, 1949-52, 1955, 1967, 1969, 1973-80, 1983-86

Most Games Won

20 Dallas, 1967, 1970-73, 1975, 1977-78, 1980-82
19 Oakland/L. A. Raiders, 1967-70, 1973-77, 1980, 1982-83
15 Pittsburgh, 1972, 1974-76, 1978-79, 1984

Most Consecutive Games Won

9 Green Bay, 1961-62, 1965-67
7 Pittsburgh, 1974-76
6 Miami, 1972-73
Pittsburgh, 1978-79
Washington, 1982-83

Most Games Lost

18 L.A. Rams, 1949-50, 1952, 1955, 1967, 1969, 1973-80, 1983-86
16 Dallas, 1966-70, 1972-73, 1975-76, 1978-83, 1985
N. Y. Giants, 1933, 1935, 1939, 1941, 1943-44, 1946, 1950, 1958-59, 1961-63, 1981, 1984-85
15 Cleveland, 1951-53, 1957-58, 1965, 1967-69, 1971-72, 1980, 1982, 1985-86

Most Consecutive Games Lost

6 N.Y. Giants, 1939, 1941, 1943-44, 1946, 1950
Cleveland, 1969, 1971-72, 1980, 1982, 1985
5 N.Y. Giants, 1958-59, 1961-63
Los Angeles, 1952, 1955, 1967, 1969, 1973
Denver, 1977-79, 1983-84
4 Washington, 1972-74, 1976
Baltimore, 1971, 1975-77 (current)
Miami, 1974, 1978-79, 1981
Chi. Cards/St. Louis, 1948, 1974-75, 1982 (current)
Boston/New England, 1963, 1976, 1978, 1982

Scoring

Most Points, Game

73 NFC: Chi. Bears vs. Washington, 1940
59 NFC: Detroit vs. Cleveland, 1957
56 NFC: Cleveland vs. Detroit, 1954

AFC-D: Oakland vs. Houston, 1969

Most Points, Both Teams, Game
79 AFC-D: San Diego (41) vs. Miami (38), 1981 (OT)
73 NFC: Chi. Bears (73) vs. Washington (0), 1940
NFC: Detroit (59) vs. Cleveland (14), 1957
AFC: Miami (45) vs. Pittsburgh (28), 1984
68 AFC-D: Oakland (37) vs. Baltimore (31), 1977 (OT)

Fewest Points, Both Teams, Game
5 NFC-D: Detroit (0) vs. Dallas (5), 1970
7 NFC: Chi. Cardinals (0) vs. Philadelphia (7), 1948
9 NFC: Tampa Bay (0) vs. Los Angeles (9), 1979

Largest Margin of Victory, Game
73 NFC: Chi. Bears vs. Washington, 1940 (73-0)
49 AFC-D: Oakland vs. Houston, 1969 (56-7)
46 NFC: Cleveland vs. Detroit, 1954 (56-10)
NFC-D: N.Y. Giants vs. San Francisco, 1986 (49-3)

Most Points, Shutout Victory, Game
73 NFC: Chi. Bears vs. Washington, 1940
38 NFC-D: Dallas vs. Tampa Bay, 1981
37 NFC: Green Bay vs. N.Y. Giants, 1961

Most Points Overcome to Win Game
20 NFC-D: Detroit vs. San Francisco, 1957 (trailed 7-27, won 31-27)
18 NFC-D: Dallas vs. San Francisco, 1972 (trailed 3-21, won 30-28)
AFC-D: Miami vs. Cleveland, 1985 (trailed 3-21, won 24-21)
14 NFC-D: Philadelphia vs. Minnesota, 1980 (trailed 0-14, won 31-16)
NFC-D: Dallas vs. Atlanta, 1980 (trailed 10-24, won 30-27)

Most Points, Each Half
1st: 38 NFC-D: Washington vs. L.A. Rams, 1983
35 NFC: Cleveland vs. Detroit, 1954
AFC-D: Oakland vs. Houston, 1969
34 NFC: N. Y. Giants vs. Chi. Bears, 1956
2nd: 45 NFC: Chi. Bears vs. Washington, 1940
30 SB: N.Y. Giants vs. Denver, 1986
28 NFC: Chi. Bears vs. N. Y. Giants, 1941
NFC: Detroit vs. Cleveland, 1957
NFC-D: Dallas vs. Cleveland, 1967
NFC-D: Dallas vs. Tampa Bay, 1981

Most Points, Each Quarter
1st: 28 AFC-D: Oakland vs. Houston, 1969
24 AFC-D: San Diego vs. Miami, 1981 (OT)
21 NFC: Chi. Bears vs. Washington, 1940
AFC: San Diego vs. Boston, 1963
AFC-D: Oakland vs. Kansas City, 1968
AFC: Oakland vs. San Diego, 1980
2nd: 26 AFC-D: Pittsburgh vs. Buffalo, 1974
24 NFC-D: Chi. Bears vs. Green Bay, 1941
NFC: Green Bay vs. N. Y. Giants, 1961
21 NFC: Cleveland vs. Detroit, 1954
NFC: N. Y. Giants vs. Chi. Bears, 1956
AFC-D: Houston vs. New England, 1978
NFC-FR: Green Bay vs. St. Louis, 1982
NFC-D: Washington vs. L.A. Rams, 1983
SB: San Francisco vs. Miami, 1984
NFC-D: N.Y. Giants vs. San Francisco, 1986
3rd: 26 NFC: Chi. Bears vs. Washington, 1940
21 NFC-D: Dallas vs. Cleveland, 1967
NFC-D: Dallas vs. Tampa Bay, 1981
AFC-D: L.A. Raiders vs. Pittsburgh, 1983
SB: Chicago vs. New England, 1985
NFC-D: N.Y. Giants vs. San Francisco, 1986
17 NFC: Cleveland vs. Baltimore, 1964
NFC-D: Dallas vs. Chicago, 1977
SB: N.Y. Giants vs. Denver, 1986
4th 27 NFC: N.Y. Giants vs. Chi. Bears, 1934
24 NFC: Baltimore vs. N. Y. Giants, 1959
21 AFC: Pittsburgh vs. Oakland, 1974
NFC: Dallas vs. Los Angeles, 1978
AFC-FR: N. Y. Jets vs. Cincinnati, 1982
NFC: San Francisco vs. Washington, 1983
OT: 6 NFC: Baltimore vs. N.Y. Giants, 1958
AFC-D: Oakland vs. Baltimore, 1977

Touchdowns

Most Touchdowns, Game
11 NFC: Chi. Bears vs. Washington, 1940
8 NFC: Cleveland vs. Detroit, 1954
NFC: Detroit vs. Cleveland, 1957
AFC-D: Oakland vs. Houston, 1969
7 AFC: San Diego vs. Boston, 1963
NFC-D: Dallas vs. Cleveland, 1967
NFC-D: N.Y. Giants vs. San Francisco, 1986

Most Touchdowns, Both Teams, Game
11 NFC: Chi. Bears (11) vs. Washington (0), 1940
10 NFC: Detroit (8) vs. Cleveland (2), 1957
AFC-D: Miami (5) vs. San Diego (5), 1981 (OT)
AFC: Miami (6) vs. Pittsburgh (4), 1984
9 NFC: Chi. Bears (6) vs. Washington (3), 1943
NFC: Cleveland (8) vs. Detroit (1), 1954
NFC-D: Dallas (7) vs. Cleveland (2), 1967
AFC-D: Oakland (8) vs. Houston (1), 1969
AFC-D: Oakland (5) vs. Baltimore (4), 1977 (OT)
SB: Pittsburgh (5) vs. Dallas (4), 1978

Fewest Touchdowns, Both Teams, Game
0 NFC-D: N.Y. Giants vs. Cleveland, 1950
NFC-D: Dallas vs. Detroit, 1970
NFC: Los Angeles vs. Tampa Bay, 1979
1 NFC: Chi. Cardinals (0) vs. Philadelphia (1), 1948
AFC: San Diego (0) vs. Houston (1), 1961
AFC-D: N. Y. Jets (0) vs. Kansas City (1), 1969
NFC-D: Green Bay (0) vs. Washington (1), 1972
2 In many games

Points After Touchdown

Most Points After Touchdown, Game
8 NFC: Cleveland vs. Detroit, 1954
NFC: Detroit vs. Cleveland, 1957
AFC-D: Oakland vs. Houston, 1969
7 NFC: Chi. Bears vs. Washington, 1940
NFC-D: Dallas vs. Cleveland, 1967
NFC-D: N.Y. Giants vs. San Francisco, 1986
6 AFC: San Diego vs. Boston, 1963
NFC-D: Washington vs. L.A. Rams, 1983
AFC: Miami vs. Pittsburgh, 1984

Most Points After Touchdown, Both Teams, Game
10 NFC: Detroit (8) vs. Cleveland (2), 1957
AFC-D: Miami (5) vs. San Diego (5), 1981 (OT)
AFC: Miami (6) vs. Pittsburgh (4), 1984
9 NFC: Cleveland (8) vs. Detroit (1), 1954
NFC-D: Dallas (7) vs. Cleveland (2), 1967
AFC-D: Oakland (8) vs. Houston (1), 1969
8 In many games

Fewest Points After Touchdown, Both Teams, Game
0 NFC-D: N.Y. Giants vs. Cleveland, 1950
NFC-D: Dallas vs. Detroit, 1970
NFC: Los Angeles vs. Tampa Bay, 1979

Field Goals

Most Field Goals, Game
4 AFC-D: Boston vs. Buffalo, 1963
AFC: Oakland vs. Houston, 1967
SB: Green Bay vs. Oakland, 1967
NFC: Washington vs. Dallas, 1972
AFC-D: Oakland vs. Pittsburgh, 1973
SB: San Francisco vs. Cincinnati, 1981
AFC-FR: New England vs. N.Y. Jets, 1985
NFC-FR: Washington vs. L.A. Rams, 1986
3 By many teams

Most Field Goals, Both Teams, Game
5 NFC: Green Bay (3) vs. Cleveland (2), 1965
AFC: Oakland (3) vs. N.Y. Jets (2), 1968
NFC: Washington (4) vs. Dallas (1), 1972
AFC-D: Cincinnati (3) vs. Miami (2), 1973
NFC-D: Los Angeles (3) vs. Dallas (2), 1973
NFC-D: Dallas (3) vs. Green Bay (2), 1982
NFC-FR: N.Y. Giants (3) vs. L.A. Rams (2), 1984
AFC-D: Cleveland (3) vs. N.Y. Jets (2), 1986 (OT)
AFC: Denver (3) vs. Cleveland (2), 1986 (OT)
4 In many games

Most Field Goals Attempted, Game
6 AFC: Oakland vs. Houston, 1967
NFC-D: Los Angeles vs. Dallas, 1973
AFC-D: Cleveland vs. N.Y. Jets, 1986 (OT)
5 By many teams

Most Field Goals Attempted, Both Teams, Game
8 NFC-D: Los Angeles (6) vs. Dallas (2), 1973
NFC-D: Detroit (5) vs. San Francisco (3), 1983
AFC-D: Cleveland (6) vs. N.Y. Jets (2), 1986 (OT)
7 In many games

Safeties

Most Safeties, Game
1 By 16 teams

First Downs

Most First Downs, Game
34 AFC-D: San Diego vs. Miami, 1981 (OT)
33 AFC-D: Cleveland vs. N.Y. Jets, 1986 (OT)
31 SB: San Francisco vs. Miami, 1984

Fewest First Downs, Game
6 NFC: N.Y. Giants vs. Green Bay, 1961
7 NFC: Green Bay vs. Boston, 1936
NFC-D: Pittsburgh vs. Philadelphia, 1947
NFC: Chi. Cardinals vs. Philadelphia, 1948
NFC: Los Angeles vs. Philadelphia, 1949
NFC-D. Cleveland vs. N. Y. Giants, 1958
AFC-D: Cincinnati vs. Baltimore, 1970
NFC-D: Detroit vs. Dallas, 1970
8 By many teams

Most First Downs, Both Teams, Game
59 AFC-D: San Diego (34) vs. Miami (25), 1981 (OT)
55 AFC-FR: San Diego (29) vs. Pittsburgh (26), 1982
50 AFC: Oakland (28) vs. Baltimore (22), 1977 (OT)
NFC-FR: St. Louis (28) vs. Green Bay (22), 1982
AFC-FR: N. Y. Jets (27) vs. Cincinnati (23), 1982
AFC: Miami (28) vs. Pittsburgh (22), 1984
SB: San Francisco (31) vs. Miami (19), 1984

Fewest First Downs, Both Teams, Game
15 NFC: Green Bay (7) vs. Boston (8), 1936
19 NFC: N. Y. Giants (9) vs. Green Bay (10), 1939
NFC: Washington (9) vs. Chi. Bears (10), 1942
20 NFC-D: Cleveland (9) vs. N. Y. Giants (11), 1950

Rushing

Most First Downs, Rushing, Game
19 NFC-FR: Dallas vs. Los Angeles, 1980
18 AFC-D: Miami vs. Cincinnati, 1973
AFC-D: Pittsburgh vs. Buffalo, 1974
16 NFC: Philadelphia vs. Chi. Cardinals, 1948
NFC: Dallas vs. San Francisco, 1970

Fewest First Downs, Rushing, Game
0 NFC: Los Angeles vs. Philadelphia, 1949
AFC-D: Buffalo vs. Boston, 1963
AFC: Oakland vs. Pittsburgh, 1974
1 NFC: N. Y. Giants vs. Green Bay, 1961
AFC-D: Houston vs. Oakland, 1969

NFC: Los Angeles vs. Dallas, 1975
AFC-FR: Cleveland vs. L. A. Raiders, 1982
NFC-D: N.Y. Giants vs. Chicago, 1985
SB: New England vs. Chicago, 1985
2 By many teams

Most First Downs, Rushing, Both Teams, Game
25 NFC-FR: Dallas (19) vs. Los Angeles (6), 1980
23 NFC: Cleveland (15) vs. Detroit (8), 1952
AFC-D: Miami (18) vs. Cincinnati (5), 1973
AFC-D: Pittsburgh (18) vs. Buffalo (5), 1974
22 AFC: Miami (18) vs. Oakland (4), 1973
AFC-D: Buffalo (11) vs. Cincinnati (11), 1981
AFC-D: L.A. Raiders (13) vs. Pittsburgh (9), 1983

Fewest First Downs, Rushing, Both Teams, Game
5 AFC-D: Buffalo (0) vs. Boston (5), 1963
6 NFC: Green Bay (2) vs. Boston (4), 1936
NFC-D: Baltimore (2) vs. Minnesota (4), 1968
AFC-D: Houston (1) vs. Oakland (5), 1969
7 NFC-D: Washington (2) vs. N. Y. Giants (5), 1943
NFC: Baltimore (3) vs. N. Y. Giants (4), 1959
NFC: Washington (3) vs. Dallas (4), 1972
AFC-FR: N. Y. Jets (3) vs. Buffalo (4), 1981

Passing

Most First Downs, Passing, Game
21 AFC-D: Miami vs. San Diego, 1981 (OT)
AFC-D: San Diego vs. Miami, 1981 (OT)
AFC-D: Cleveland vs. N.Y. Jets, 1986 (OT)
20 NFC-FR: Dallas vs. L.A. Rams, 1983
19 NFC-FR: St. Louis vs. Green Bay, 1982
NFC-FR: Dallas vs. Tampa Bay, 1982
AFC-FR: Pittsburgh vs. San Diego, 1982
AFC-FR: San Diego vs. Pittsburgh, 1982
NFC: Dallas vs. Washington, 1982

Fewest First Downs, Passing, Game
0 NFC: Philadelphia vs. Chi. Cardinals, 1948
1 NFC-D: N. Y. Giants vs. Washington, 1943
NFC: Cleveland vs. Detroit, 1953
SB: Denver vs. Dallas, 1977
2 By many teams

Most First Downs, Passing, Both Teams, Game
42 AFC-D: Miami (21) vs. San Diego (21), 1981 (OT)
38 AFC-FR: Pittsburgh (19) vs. San Diego (19), 1982
32 NFC-FR: St. Louis (19) vs. Green Bay (13), 1982
AFC: Miami (18) vs. Pittsburgh (14), 1984
SB: Miami (17) vs. San Francisco (15), 1984

Fewest First Downs, Passing, Both Teams, Game
2 NFC: Philadelphia (0) vs. Chi. Cardinals (2), 1948
4 NFC-D: Cleveland (2) vs. N. Y. Giants (2), 1950
5 NFC: Detroit (2) vs. N. Y. Giants (3), 1935
NFC: Green Bay (2) vs. N. Y. Giants (3), 1939

Penalty

Most First Downs, Penalty, Game
7 AFC-D: New England vs. Oakland, 1976
6 AFC-D: Cleveland vs. N.Y. Jets, 1986 (OT)
5 AFC-FR: Cleveland vs. L. A. Raiders, 1982

Most First Downs, Penalty, Both Teams, Game
9 AFC-D: New England (7) vs. Oakland (2), 1976
8 NFC-FR: Atlanta (4) vs. Minnesota (4), 1982
7 AFC-D: Baltimore (4) vs. Oakland (3), 1977 (OT)

Net Yards Gained Rushing and Passing

Most Yards Gained, Game
610 AFC: San Diego vs. Boston, 1963
569 AFC: Miami vs. Pittsburgh, 1984
564 AFC-D: San Diego vs. Miami, 1981 (OT)

Fewest Yards Gained, Game
86 NFC-D: Cleveland vs. N.Y. Giants, 1958
99 NFC: Chi. Cardinals vs. Philadelphia, 1948
114 NFC-D: N.Y. Giants vs. Washington, 1943

Most Yards Gained, Both Teams, Game
1,036 AFC-D: San Diego (564) vs. Miami (472), 1981 (OT)
1,024 AFC: Miami (569) vs. Pittsburgh (455), 1984
912 AFC-FR: N. Y. Jets (517) vs. Cincinnati (395), 1982

Fewest Yards Gained, Both Teams, Game
331 NFC: Chi. Cardinals (99) vs. Philadelphia (232), 1948
332 NFC-D: N.Y. Giants (150) vs. Cleveland (182), 1950
336 NFC: Boston (116) vs. Green Bay (220), 1936

Rushing

Attempts

Most Attempts, Game
65 NFC: Detroit vs. N.Y. Giants, 1935
61 NFC: Philadelphia vs. Los Angeles, 1949
59 AFC: New England vs. Miami, 1985

Fewest Attempts, Game
9 SB: Miami vs. San Francisco, 1984
11 SB: New England vs. Chicago, 1985
12 AFC-D: Buffalo vs. Boston, 1963

Most Attempts, Both Teams, Game
109 NFC: Detroit (65) vs. N.Y. Giants (44), 1935
97 AFC-D: Baltimore (50) vs. Oakland (47), 1977 (OT)
91 NFC: Philadelphia (57) vs. Chi. Cardinals (34), 1948

Fewest Attempts, Both Teams, Game
45 AFC-FR: N.Y. Jets (22) vs. Buffalo (23), 1981
46 AFC: Buffalo (13) vs. Kansas City (33), 1966
48 AFC-D: Buffalo (12) vs. Boston (36), 1963
AFC: Boston (16) vs. San Diego (32), 1963

Yards Gained

Most Yards Gained, Game
382 NFC: Chi. Bears vs. Washington, 1940
338 NFC-FR: Dallas vs. Los Angeles, 1980
318 AFC: San Diego vs. Boston, 1963

Fewest Yards Gained, Game
7 AFC-D: Buffalo vs. Boston, 1963
SB: New England vs. Chicago, 1985
17 SB: Minnesota vs. Pittsburgh, 1974
21 NFC: Los Angeles vs. Philadelphia, 1949

Most Yards Gained, Both Teams, Game
430 NFC-FR: Dallas (338) vs. Los Angeles (92), 1980
426 NFC: Cleveland (227) vs. Detroit (199), 1952
404 NFC: Chi. Bears (382) vs. Washington (22), 1940

Fewest Yards Gained, Both Teams, Game
90 AFC-D: Buffalo (7) vs. Boston (83), 1963
106 NFC: Boston (39) vs. Green Bay (67), 1936
128 NFC-FR: Philadelphia (53) vs. Atlanta (75), 1978

Average Gain

Highest Average Gain, Game
9.94 AFC: San Diego vs. Boston, 1963 (32-318)
9.29 NFC-D: Green Bay vs. Dallas, 1982 (17-158)
7.35 NFC-FR: Dallas vs. Los Angeles, 1980 (46-338)

Lowest Average Gain, Game
0.58 AFC-D: Buffalo vs. Boston, 1963 (12-7)
0.64 SB: New England vs. Chicago, 1985 (11-7)
0.81 SB: Minnesota vs. Pittsburgh, 1974 (21-17)

Touchdowns

Most Touchdowns, Game
7 NFC: Chi. Bears vs. Washington, 1940
5 NFC: Cleveland vs. Detroit, 1954
4 NFC: Detroit vs. N.Y. Giants, 1935
AFC: San Diego vs. Boston, 1963
NFC-D: Dallas vs. Cleveland, 1967
NFC: Baltimore vs. Cleveland, 1968
NFC-FR: Dallas vs. Los Angeles, 1980
AFC-D: L.A. Raiders vs. Pittsburgh, 1983
SB: Chicago vs. New England, 1985

Most Touchdowns, Both Teams, Game
7 NFC: Chi. Bears (7) vs. Washington (0), 1940
6 NFC: Cleveland (5) vs. Detroit (1), 1954
5 NFC: Chi. Cardinals (3) vs. Philadelphia (2), 1947
AFC: San Diego (4) vs. Boston (1), 1963
AFC-D: Cincinnati (3) vs. Buffalo (2), 1981

Passing

Attempts

Most Attempts, Game
65 AFC-D: Cleveland vs. N.Y. Jets, 1986 (OT)
54 AFC-D: San Diego vs. Miami, 1981 (OT)
53 NFC-FR: Dallas vs. L.A. Rams, 1983

Fewest Attempts, Game
5 NFC: Detroit vs. N.Y. Giants, 1935
6 AFC: Miami vs. Oakland, 1973
7 SB: Miami vs. Minnesota, 1973

Most Attempts, Both Teams, Game
102 AFC-D: San Diego (54) vs. Miami (48), 1981 (OT)
96 AFC: N.Y. Jets (49) vs. Oakland (47), 1968
95 AFC-D: Cleveland (65) vs. N.Y. Jets (30), 1986 (OT)

Fewest Attempts, Both Teams, Game
18 NFC: Detroit (5) vs. N.Y. Giants (13), 1935
21 NFC: Chi. Bears (7) vs. N.Y. Giants (14), 1933
23 NFC: Chi. Cardinals (11) vs. Philadelphia (12), 1948

Completions

Most Completions, Game
34 AFC-D: Cleveland vs. N.Y. Jets, 1986 (OT)
33 AFC-D: San Diego vs. Miami, 1981 (OT)
32 NFC-FR: St. Louis vs. Green Bay, 1982
NFC-FR: Dallas vs. L.A. Rams, 1983

Fewest Completions, Game
2 NFC: Detroit vs. N.Y. Giants, 1935
NFC: Philadelphia vs. Chi. Cardinals, 1948
3 NFC: N.Y. Giants vs. Chi. Bears, 1941
NFC: Green Bay vs. N.Y. Giants, 1944
NFC: Chi. Cardinals vs. Philadelphia, 1947
NFC: Chi. Cardinals vs. Philadelphia, 1948
NFC-D: Cleveland vs. N.Y. Giants, 1950
NFC-D: N.Y. Giants vs. Cleveland, 1950
NFC: Cleveland vs. Detroit, 1953
AFC: Miami vs. Oakland, 1973
4 NFC-D: Dallas vs. Detroit, 1970
AFC: Miami vs. Baltimore, 1971
SB: Miami vs. Washington, 1982
AFC-FR: Seattle vs. L.A. Raiders, 1984

Most Completions, Both Teams, Game
64 AFC-D: San Diego (33) vs. Miami (31), 1981 (OT)
55 AFC-FR: Pittsburgh (28) vs. San Diego (27), 1982
53 SB: Miami (29) vs. San Francisco (24), 1984

Fewest Completions, Both Teams, Game
5 NFC: Philadelphia (2) vs. Chi. Cardinals (3), 1948
6 NFC: Detroit (2) vs. N.Y. Giants (4), 1935
NFC-D: Cleveland (3) vs. N.Y. Giants (3), 1950
11 NFC: Green Bay (3) vs. N.Y. Giants (8), 1944
NFC-D: Dallas (4) vs. Detroit (7), 1970

Completion Percentage

Highest Completion Percentage, Game (20 attempts)
88.0 SB: N.Y. Giants vs. Denver, 1986 (25-22)
80.0 NFC-D: Washington vs. L.A. Rams, 1983 (25-20)
79.2 AFC-D: Pittsburgh vs. Baltimore, 1976 (24-19)

Lowest Completion Percentage, Game (20 attempts)
18.5 NFC: Tampa Bay vs. Los Angeles, 1979 (27-5)
20.0 NFC-D: N.Y. Giants vs. Washington, 1943 (20-4)
25.8 NFC: Chi. Bears vs. Washington, 1937 (31-8)

Yards Gained
Most Yards Gained, Game
483 AFC-D: Cleveland vs. N.Y. Jets, 1986 (OT)
435 AFC: Miami vs. Pittsburgh, 1984
415 AFC-D: San Diego vs. Miami, 1981 (OT)
Fewest Yards Gained, Game
3 NFC: Chi. Cardinals vs. Philadelphia, 1948
7 NFC: Philadelphia vs. Chi. Cardinals, 1948
9 NFC-D: N.Y. Giants vs. Cleveland, 1950
NFC: Cleveland vs. Detroit, 1953
Most Yards Gained, Both Teams, Game
809 AFC-D: San Diego (415) vs. Miami (394), 1981 (OT)
747 AFC: Miami (435) vs. Pittsburgh (312), 1984
666 AFC-D: Cleveland (483) vs. N.Y. Jets (183), 1986 (OT)
Fewest Yards Gained, Both Teams, Game
10 NFC: Chi. Cardinals (3) vs. Philadelphia (7), 1948
38 NFC-D: N.Y. Giants (9) vs. Cleveland (29), 1950
102 NFC-D: Dallas (22) vs. Detroit (80), 1970

Times Sacked
Most Times Sacked, Game
9 AFC: Kansas City vs. Buffalo, 1966
NFC: Chicago vs. San Francisco, 1984
AFC-D: N.Y. Jets vs. Cleveland, 1986 (OT)
8 NFC: Green Bay vs. Dallas, 1967
7 NFC-D: Dallas vs. Los Angeles, 1973
SB: Dallas vs. Pittsburgh, 1975
AFC-FR: Houston vs. Oakland, 1980
NFC-D: Washington vs. Chicago, 1984
SB: New England vs. Chicago, 1985
Most Times Sacked, Both Teams, Game
13 AFC: Kansas City (9) vs. Buffalo (4), 1966
AFC-D: N.Y. Jets (9) vs. Cleveland (4), 1986 (OT)
12 NFC-D: Dallas (7) vs. Los Angeles (5), 1973
NFC-D: Washington (7) vs. Chicago (5), 1984
NFC: Chicago (9) vs. San Francisco (3), 1984
10 AFC-FR: Houston (7) vs. Oakland (3), 1980
NFC-D: N.Y. Giants (6) vs. San Francisco (4), 1984
SB: New England (7) vs. Chicago (3), 1985
Fewest Times Sacked, Both Teams, Game
0 AFC-D: Buffalo vs. Pittsburgh, 1974
AFC-FR: Pittsburgh vs. San Diego, 1982
1 In many games

Touchdowns
Most Touchdowns, Game
6 AFC-D: Oakland vs. Houston, 1969
5 NFC: Chi. Bears vs. Washington, 1943
NFC: Detroit vs. Cleveland, 1957
AFC-D: Oakland vs. Kansas City, 1968
4 NFC: Cleveland vs. Los Angeles, 1950
NFC: Green Bay vs. Dallas, 1966
AFC-D: Oakland vs. Miami, 1974
NFC: Dallas vs. Los Angeles, 1975
SB: Pittsburgh vs. Dallas, 1978
AFC-D: Miami vs. San Diego, 1981 (OT)
NFC-FR: Green Bay vs. St. Louis, 1982
AFC: Miami vs. Pittsburgh, 1984
NFC-D: N.Y. Giants vs. San Francisco, 1986
Most Touchdowns, Both Teams, Game
7 NFC: Chi. Bears (5) vs. Washington (2), 1943
AFC-D: Oakland (6) vs. Houston (1), 1969
SB: Pittsburgh (4) vs. Dallas (3), 1978
AFC-D: Miami (4) vs. San Diego (3), 1981 (OT)
AFC: Miami (4) vs. Pittsburgh (3), 1984
6 NFC-FR: Green Bay (4) vs. St. Louis (2), 1982
5 In many games

Interceptions By
Most Interceptions By, Game
8 NFC: Chi. Bears vs. Washington, 1940
7 NFC: Cleveland vs. Los Angeles, 1955
6 NFC: Green Bay vs. N.Y. Giants, 1939
NFC: Chi. Bears vs. N.Y. Giants, 1946
NFC: Cleveland vs. Detroit, 1954
AFC: San Diego vs. Houston, 1961
Most Interceptions By, Both Teams, Game
10 NFC: Cleveland (7) vs. Los Angeles (3), 1955
AFC: San Diego (6) vs. Houston (4), 1961
9 NFC: Green Bay (6) vs. N.Y. Giants (3), 1939
8 NFC: Chi. Bears (8) vs. Washington (0), 1940
NFC: Chi. Bears (6) vs. N.Y. Giants (2), 1946
NFC: Cleveland (6) vs. Detroit (2), 1954
AFC-FR: Buffalo (4) vs. N.Y. Jets (4), 1981
AFC: Miami (5) vs. N.Y. Jets (3), 1982

Yards Gained
Most Yards Gained, Game
138 AFC-FR: N.Y. Jets vs. Cincinnati, 1982
136 AFC: Dall. Texans vs. Houston, 1962 (OT)
130 NFC-D: Los Angeles vs. St. Louis, 1975
Most Yards Gained, Both Teams, Game
156 NFC: Green Bay (123) vs. N.Y. Giants (33), 1939
149 NFC: Cleveland (103) vs. Los Angeles (46), 1955
141 AFC-FR: Buffalo (79) vs. N.Y. Jets (62), 1981

Touchdowns
Most Touchdowns, Game
3 NFC: Chi. Bears vs. Washington, 1940
2 NFC-D: Los Angeles vs. St. Louis, 1975
1 In many games

Punting
Most Punts, Game
14 AFC-D: N.Y. Jets vs. Cleveland, 1986 (OT)
13 NFC: N.Y. Giants vs. Chi. Bears, 1933
AFC-D: Baltimore vs. Oakland, 1977 (OT)
11 AFC: Houston vs. Oakland, 1967
AFC-D: Houston vs. Oakland, 1969
NFC: L.A. Rams vs. Chicago, 1985
Fewest Punts, Game
0 NFC-FR: St. Louis vs. Green Bay, 1982
AFC-FR: N.Y. Jets vs. Cincinnati, 1982
1 NFC-D: Cleveland vs. Dallas, 1969
AFC: Miami vs. Oakland, 1973
AFC-D: Oakland vs. Cincinnati, 1975
AFC-D: Pittsburgh vs. Baltimore, 1976
AFC: Pittsburgh vs. Houston, 1978
NFC-FR: Green Bay vs. St. Louis, 1982
AFC-FR: Miami vs. New England, 1982
AFC-FR: San Diego vs. Pittsburgh, 1982
2 In many games
Most Punts, Both Teams, Game
23 NFC: N.Y. Giants (13) vs. Chi. Bears (10), 1933
22 AFC-D: N.Y. Jets (14) vs. Cleveland (8), 1986 (OT)
21 AFC-D: Baltimore (13) vs. Oakland (8), 1977 (OT)
NFC: L.A. Rams (11) vs. Chicago (10), 1985
Fewest Punts, Both Teams, Game
1 NFC-FR: St. Louis (0) vs. Green Bay (1), 1982
2 AFC-FR: N.Y. Jets (0) vs. Cincinnati (2), 1982
3 AFC: Miami (1) vs. Oakland (2), 1973
AFC-FR: San Diego (1) vs. Pittsburgh (2), 1982

Average Yardage
Highest Average, Punting, Game (4 punts)
56.0 AFC: Oakland vs. San Diego, 1980
52.5 NFC: Washington vs. Chi. Bears, 1942
51.3 AFC: Pittsburgh vs. Miami, 1972
Lowest Average, Punting, Game (4 punts)
24.9 NFC: Washington vs. Chi. Bears, 1937
25.5 NFC: Green Bay vs. N.Y. Giants, 1962
27.8 AFC-D: San Diego vs. Buffalo, 1980

Punt Returns
Most Punt Returns, Game
8 NFC: Green Bay vs. N.Y. Giants, 1944
7 By eight teams
Most Punt Returns, Both Teams, Game
13 AFC-FR: Houston (7) vs. Oakland (6), 1980
11 NFC: Green Bay (8) vs. N.Y. Giants (3), 1944
NFC-D: Green Bay (6) vs. Baltimore (5), 1965
10 In many games
Fewest Punt Returns, Both Teams, Game
0 NFC: Chi. Bears vs. N.Y. Giants, 1941
AFC: Boston vs. San Diego, 1963
NFC-FR: Green Bay vs. St. Louis, 1982
1 AFC: Miami (0) vs. Pittsburgh (1), 1972
AFC: Cincinnati (0) vs. San Diego (1), 1981
AFC-FR: Cincinnati (0) vs. N.Y. Jets (1), 1982
AFC-FR: San Diego (0) vs. Pittsburgh (1), 1982
NFC-D: Minnesota (0) vs. Washington (1), 1982
AFC: Seattle (0) vs. L.A. Raiders (1), 1983
2 In many games

Yards Gained
Most Yards Gained, Game
155 NFC-D: Dallas vs. Cleveland, 1967
150 NFC: Chi. Cardinals vs. Philadelphia, 1947
112 NFC-D: Philadelphia vs. Pittsburgh, 1947
Fewest Yards Gained, Game
−10 NFC: Green Bay vs. Cleveland, 1965
−9 NFC: Dallas vs. Green Bay, 1966
AFC-D: Kansas City vs. Oakland, 1968
−5 AFC-D: Miami vs. Oakland, 1970
NFC-D: San Francisco vs. Dallas, 1972
NFC: Dallas vs. Washington, 1972
Most Yards Gained, Both Teams, Game
166 NFC-D: Dallas (155) vs. Cleveland (11), 1967
160 NFC: Chi. Cardinals (150) vs. Philadelphia (10), 1947
146 NFC-D: Philadelphia (112) vs. Pittsburgh (34), 1947
Fewest Yards Gained, Both Teams, Game
−9 NFC: Dallas (−9) vs. Green Bay (0), 1966
−6 AFC-D: Miami (−5) vs. Oakland (−1), 1970
−3 NFC-D: San Francisco (−5) vs. Dallas (2), 1972

Touchdowns
Most Touchdowns, Game
1 By eight teams

Kickoff Returns
Most Kickoff Returns, Game
10 NFC-D: L.A. Rams vs. Washington, 1983
9 NFC: Chi. Bears vs. N.Y. Giants, 1956
AFC: Boston vs. San Diego, 1963
AFC: Houston vs. Oakland, 1967
8 By many teams
Most Kickoff Returns, Both Teams, Game
13 NFC-D: Green Bay (7) vs. Dallas (6), 1982
12 AFC: Boston (9) vs. San Diego (3), 1963
NFC: Dallas (6) vs. Green Bay (6), 1966
AFC-D: Baltimore (6) vs. Oakland (6), 1977 (OT)
AFC: Oakland (6) vs. San Diego (6), 1980
AFC-D: Miami (6) vs. San Diego (6), 1981 (OT)

NFC-D: N.Y. Giants (7) vs. San Francisco (5), 1981
AFC-FR: Cincinnati (8) vs. N.Y. Jets (4), 1982
NFC-D: L.A. Rams (10) vs. Washington (2), 1983
11 In many games

Fewest Kickoff Returns, Both Teams, Game
1 NFC: Green Bay (0) vs. Boston (1), 1936
2 NFC-D: Los Angeles (0) vs. Chi. Bears (2), 1950
AFC: Houston (0) vs. San Diego (2), 1961
AFC-D: Oakland (1) vs. Pittsburgh (1), 1972
AFC-D: N.Y. Jets (0) vs. L.A. Raiders (2), 1982
AFC: Miami (1) vs. N.Y. Jets (1), 1982
NFC: N.Y. Giants (0) vs. Washington (2), 1986
3 In many games

Yards Gained

Most Yards Gained, Game
225 NFC: Washington vs. Chi. Bears, 1940
222 SB: Miami vs. Washington, 1982
215 AFC: Houston vs. Oakland, 1967

Most Yards Gained, Both Teams, Game
379 AFC-D: Baltimore (193) vs. Oakland (186), 1977 (OT)
321 NFC-D: Dallas (173) vs. Green Bay (148), 1982
318 AFC-D: Miami (183) vs. Oakland (135), 1974

Fewest Yards Gained, Both Teams, Game
15 NFC: N.Y. Giants (0) vs. Washington (15), 1986
31 NFC-D: Los Angeles (0) vs. Chi. Bears (31), 1950
32 NFC: Green Bay (0) vs. Boston (32), 1936

Touchdowns

Most Touchdowns, Game
1 NFC-D: San Francisco vs. Dallas, 1972
AFC-D: Miami vs. Oakland, 1974
AFC-D: Baltimore vs. Oakland, 1977 (OT)
SB: Miami vs. Washington, 1982

Penalties

Most Penalties, Game
14 AFC-FR: Oakland vs. Houston, 1980
NFC-D: San Francisco vs. N.Y. Giants, 1981
12 NFC-D: Chi. Bears vs. Green Bay, 1941
AFC-D: Pittsburgh vs. Baltimore, 1976
SB: Dallas vs. Denver, 1977
AFC-FR: N.Y. Jets vs. Cincinnati, 1982
11 NFC: N.Y. Giants vs. Green Bay, 1944
AFC-D: Oakland vs. New England, 1976
AFC-D: Pittsburgh vs. Denver, 1978
NFC-FR: Dallas vs. Los Angeles, 1980
NFC-D: San Francisco vs. N.Y. Giants, 1986

Fewest Penalties, Game
0 NFC: Philadelphia vs. Green Bay, 1960
NFC-D: Detroit vs. Dallas, 1970
AFC-D: Miami vs. Oakland, 1970
SB: Miami vs. Dallas, 1971
NFC-D: Washington vs. Minnesota, 1973
SB: Pittsburgh vs. Dallas, 1975
1 By many teams

Most Penalties, Both Teams, Game
22 AFC-FR: Oakland (14) vs. Houston (8), 1980
NFC-D: San Francisco (14) vs. N.Y. Giants (8), 1981
21 AFC-D: Oakland (11) vs. New England (10), 1976
20 SB: Dallas (12) vs. Denver (8), 1977

Fewest Penalties, Both Teams, Game
2 NFC: Washington (1) vs. Chi. Bears (1), 1937
NFC-D: Washington (0) vs. Minnesota (2), 1973
SB: Pittsburgh (0) vs. Dallas (2), 1975
3 AFC: Miami (1) vs. Baltimore (2), 1971
NFC: San Francisco (1) vs. Dallas (2), 1971
SB: Miami (0) vs. Dallas (3), 1971
AFC-D: Pittsburgh (1) vs. Oakland (2), 1972
AFC-D: Miami (1) vs. Cincinnati (2), 1973
SB: Miami (1) vs. San Francisco (2), 1984
4 NFC-D: Cleveland (2) vs. Dallas (2), 1967
NFC-D: Minnesota (1) vs. San Francisco (3), 1970
AFC-D: Miami (0) vs. Oakland (4), 1970
NFC-D: Dallas (2) vs. Minnesota (2), 1971

Yards Penalized

Most Yards Penalized, Game
145 NFC-D: San Francisco vs. N.Y. Giants, 1981
133 SB: Dallas vs. Baltimore, 1970
128 NFC-D: Chi. Bears vs. Green Bay, 1941

Fewest Yards Penalized, Game
0 By six teams

Most Yards Penalized, Both Teams, Game
206 NFC-D: San Francisco (145) vs. N.Y. Giants (61), 1981
192 AFC-D: Denver (104) vs. Pittsburgh (88), 1978
182 NFC-FR: Atlanta (98) vs. Minnesota (84), 1982

Fewest Yards Penalized, Both Teams, Game
9 NFC-D: Washington (0) vs. Minnesota (9), 1973
15 SB: Miami (0) vs. Dallas (15), 1971
20 NFC: Washington (5) vs. Chi. Bears (15), 1937
AFC-D: Pittsburgh (5) vs. Oakland (15), 1972
SB: Pittsburgh (0) vs. Dallas (20), 1975
Miami (10) vs. San Francisco (10), 1984

Fumbles

Most Fumbles, Game
6 By nine teams

Most Fumbles, Both Teams, Game
12 AFC: Houston (6) vs. Pittsburgh (6), 1978
10 NFC: Chi. Bears (5) vs. N.Y. Giants (5), 1934
SB: Dallas (6) vs. Denver (4), 1977
9 NFC-D: San Francisco (6) vs. Detroit (3), 1957
NFC-D: San Francisco (5) vs. Dallas (4), 1972
NFC: Dallas (5) vs. Philadelphia (4), 1980

Most Fumbles Lost, Game
4 NFC: N.Y. Giants vs. Baltimore, 1958 (OT)
AFC: Kansas City vs. Oakland, 1969
SB: Baltimore vs. Dallas, 1970
AFC: Pittsburgh vs. Oakland, 1975
SB: Denver vs. Dallas, 1977
AFC: Houston vs. Pittsburgh, 1978
AFC: Miami vs. New England, 1985
SB: New England vs. Chicago, 1985
NFC-FR: L.A. Rams vs. Washington, 1986
3 By many teams

Fewest Fumbles, Both Teams, Game
0 NFC: Green Bay vs. Cleveland, 1965
AFC: Buffalo vs. San Diego, 1965
AFC-D: Oakland vs. Miami, 1974
AFC-D: Houston vs. San Diego, 1979
NFC-D: Dallas vs. Los Angeles, 1979
SB: Los Angeles vs. Pittsburgh, 1979
AFC-D: Buffalo vs. Cincinnati, 1981
AFC-D: Cleveland vs. N.Y. Jets, 1986 (OT)
AFC-D: Denver vs. New England, 1986
SB: Denver vs. N.Y. Giants, 1986
1 In many games

Recoveries

Most Total Fumbles Recovered, Game
8 SB: Dallas vs. Denver, 1977 (4 own, 4 opp)
7 NFC: Chi. Bears vs. N.Y. Giants, 1934 (5 own, 2 opp)
NFC-D: San Francisco vs. Detroit, 1957 (4 own, 3 opp)
NFC-D: San Francisco vs. Dallas, 1972 (4 own, 3 opp)
AFC: Pittsburgh vs. Houston, 1978 (3 own, 4 opp)
6 AFC: Houston vs. San Diego, 1961 (4 own, 2 opp)
AFC-D: Cleveland vs. Baltimore, 1971 (4 own, 2 opp)
AFC-D: Cleveland vs. Oakland, 1980 (5 own, 1 opp)
NFC: Philadelphia vs. Dallas, 1980 (3 own, 3 opp)

Most Own Fumbles Recovered, Game
5 NFC: Chi. Bears vs. N.Y. Giants, 1934
AFC-D: Cleveland vs. Oakland, 1980
4 By many teams

Turnovers

(Numbers of times losing the ball on interceptions and fumbles.)

Most Turnovers, Game
9 NFC: Washington vs. Chi. Bears, 1940
NFC: Detroit vs. Cleveland, 1954
AFC: Houston vs. Pittsburgh, 1978
8 NFC: N.Y. Giants vs. Chi. Bears, 1946
NFC: Los Angeles vs. Cleveland, 1955
NFC: Cleveland vs. Detroit, 1957
SB: Denver vs. Dallas, 1977
NFC-D: Minnesota vs. Philadelphia, 1980
7 AFC: Houston vs. San Diego, 1961
SB: Baltimore vs. Dallas, 1970
AFC: Pittsburgh vs. Oakland, 1975
NFC-D: Chicago vs. Dallas, 1977
NFC: Los Angeles vs. Dallas, 1978
AFC-D: San Diego vs. Miami, 1982

Fewest Turnovers, Game
0 By many teams

Most Turnovers, Both Teams, Game
14 AFC: Houston (9) vs. Pittsburgh (5), 1978
13 NFC: Detroit (9) vs. Cleveland (4), 1954
AFC: Houston (7) vs. San Diego (6), 1961
12 AFC: Pittsburgh (7) vs. Oakland (5), 1975

Fewest Turnovers, Both Teams, Game
1 AFC-D: Baltimore (0) vs. Cincinnati (1), 1970
AFC-D: Pittsburgh (0) vs. Buffalo (1), 1974
AFC: Oakland (0) vs. Pittsburgh (1), 1976
NFC-D: Minnesota (0) vs. Washington (1), 1982
NFC-D: Chicago (0) vs. N.Y. Giants (1), 1985
SB: N.Y. Giants (0) vs. Denver (1), 1986
2 In many games

AFC-NFC PRO BOWL RECORDS

Compiled by Elias Sports Bureau

Individual Records

Service
Most Games
9 *Ken Houston, Houston, 1971-73; Washington, 1974-79
Joe Greene, Pittsburgh, 1971-77, 1979-80
Jack Lambert, Pittsburgh, 1976-84
Walter Payton, Chicago, 1977-81, 1984-87
8 Tom Mack, Los Angeles, 1971-76, 1978-79
*Franco Harris, Pittsburgh, 1973-76, 1978-81
Lemar Parrish, Cincinnati, 1971-72, 1975-77; Washington, 1978, 1980-81
Art Shell, Oakland, 1973-79, 1981
Ted Hendricks, Baltimore, 1972-74; Green Bay, 1975; Oakland, 1981-82; L.A. Raiders, 1983-84
*John Hannah, New England, 1977, 1979-83, 1985-86
*Randy White, Dallas, 1978, 1980-86
Mike Webster, Pittsburgh, 1979-86
Harry Carson, N.Y. Giants, 1979-80, 1982-87
*Mike Haynes, New England, 1978-81, 1983; L.A. Raiders, 1985-87
7 Ron Yary, Minnesota, 1972-78
Elvin Bethea, Houston, 1972-76, 1979-80
Roger Wehrli, St. Louis, 1971-72, 1975-78, 1980
Jack Youngblood, Los Angeles, 1974-80
Ray Guy, Oakland, 1974-79, 1981
Robert Brazile, Houston, 1977-83
Randy Gradishar, Denver, 1976, 1978-80, 1982-84
James Lofton, Green Bay, 1979, 1981-86
*Also selected, but did not play, in one additional game

Scoring
Points
Most Points, Career
30 Jan Stenerud, Kansas City, 1971-72, 1976; Green Bay, 1985 (6-pat, 8-fg)
18 John Brockington, Green Bay, 1972-74 (3-td)
Earl Campbell, Houston, 1979-82, 1984 (3-td)
Chuck Muncie, New Orleans, 1980; San Diego, 1982-83 (3-td)
William Andrews, Atlanta, 1981-84 (3-td)
Marcus Allen, L.A. Raiders, 1983, 1985-86 (3-td)
16 Garo Yepremian, Miami, 1974, 1979 (1-pat, 5-fg)
Most Points, Game
18 John Brockington, Green Bay, 1973 (3-td)
15 Garo Yepremian, Miami, 1974 (5-fg)
14 Jan Stenerud, Kansas City, 1972 (2-pat, 4-fg)

Touchdowns
Most Touchdowns, Career
3 John Brockington, Green Bay, 1972-74 (2-r, 1-p)
Earl Campbell, Houston, 1979-82, 1984 (3-r)
Chuck Muncie, New Orleans, 1980; San Diego, 1982-83 (3-r)
William Andrews, Atlanta, 1981-84 (1-r, 2-p)
Marcus Allen, L.A. Raiders, 1983, 1985-86 (2-r, 1-p)
2 By 10 players
Most Touchdowns, Game
3 John Brockington, Green Bay, 1973 (2-r, 1-p)
2 Mel Renfro, Dallas, 1971 (2-ret)
Earl Campbell, Houston, 1980 (2-r)
Chuck Muncie, New Orleans, 1980 (2-r)
William Andrews, Atlanta, 1984 (2-p)

Points After Touchdown
Most Points After Touchdown, Career
6 Chester Marcol, Green Bay, 1973, 1975 (6 att)
Mark Moseley, Washington, 1980, 1983 (7 att)
Ali Haji-Sheikh, N.Y. Giants, 1984 (6 att)
Jan Stenerud, Kansas City, 1971-72, 1976; Green Bay, 1985 (6 att)
Most Points After Touchdown, Game
6 Ali Haji-Sheikh, N.Y. Giants, 1984 (6 att)
4 Chester Marcol, Green Bay, 1973 (4 att)
Mark Moseley, Washington, 1980 (5 att)
Morten Andersen, New Orleans, 1986 (4 att)

Field Goals
Most Field Goals Attempted, Career
15 Jan Stenerud, Kansas City, 1971-72, 1976; Green Bay, 1985
7 Garo Yepremian, Miami, 1974, 1979
Mark Moseley, Washington, 1980, 1983
6 Ed Murray, Detroit, 1981
Most Field Goals Attempted, Game
6 Jan Stenerud, Kansas City, 1972
Ed Murray, Detroit, 1981
Mark Moseley, Washington, 1983
5 Garo Yepremian, Miami, 1974
4 Jan Stenerud, Kansas City, 1976
Most Field Goals, Career
8 Jan Stenerud, Kansas City, 1971-72, 1976; Green Bay, 1985
5 Garo Yepremian, Miami, 1974, 1979
4 Ed Murray, Detroit, 1981
Most Field Goals, Game
5 Garo Yepremian, Miami, 1974 (5 att)
4 Jan Stenerud, Kansas City, 1972 (6 att)
Ed Murray, Detroit, 1981 (6 att)
2 By many players
Longest Field Goal
48 Jan Stenerud, Kansas City, 1972
43 Gary Anderson, Pittsburgh, 1984
42 Jim Bakken, St. Louis, 1976

Safeties
Most Safeties, Game
1 Art Still, Kansas City, 1983
Mark Gastineau, N.Y. Jets, 1985

Rushing
Attempts
Most Attempts, Career
81 Walter Payton, Chicago, 1977-81, 1984-87
68 O.J. Simpson, Buffalo, 1973-77
46 Franco Harris, Pittsburgh, 1973-76, 1978-81
Earl Campbell, Houston, 1979-82, 1984
Most Attempts, Game
19 O.J. Simpson, Buffalo, 1974
17 Marv Hubbard, Oakland, 1974
16 O.J. Simpson, Buffalo, 1973
Marcus Allen, L.A. Raiders, 1986

Yards Gained
Most Yards Gained, Career
368 Walter Payton, Chicago, 1977-81, 1984-87
356 O.J. Simpson, Buffalo, 1973-77
220 Earl Campbell, Houston, 1979-82, 1984
Most Yards Gained, Game
112 O. J. Simpson, Buffalo, 1973
104 Marv Hubbard, Oakland, 1974
77 Walter Payton, Chicago, 1978
Longest Run From Scrimmage
41 Lawrence McCutcheon, Los Angeles, 1976
30 O.J. Simpson, Buffalo, 1975
29 Franco Harris, Pittsburgh, 1973

Average Gain
Highest Average Gain, Career (20 attempts)
5.81 Marv Hubbard, Oakland, 1972-74 (36-209)
5.71 Wilbert Montgomery, Philadelphia, 1979-80 (21-120)
5.36 Larry Csonka, Miami, 1971-72, 1975 (22-118)
Highest Average Gain, Game (10 attempts)
7.00 O.J. Simpson, Buffalo, 1973 (16-112)
Ottis Anderson, St. Louis, 1981 (10-70)
6.91 Walter Payton, Chicago, 1985 (11-76)
6.90 Earl Campbell, Houston, 1980 (10-69)

Touchdowns
Most Touchdowns, Career
3 Earl Campbell, Houston, 1979-82, 1984
Chuck Muncie, New Orleans, 1980; San Diego, 1982-83
2 John Brockington, Green Bay, 1972-74
O.J. Simpson, Buffalo, 1973-77
Walter Payton, Chicago, 1977-81, 1984-87
Marcus Allen, L.A. Raiders, 1983, 1985-86
Most Touchdowns, Game
2 John Brockington, Green Bay, 1973
Earl Campbell, Houston, 1980
Chuck Muncie, New Orleans, 1980

Passing
Attempts
Most Attempts, Career
120 Dan Fouts, San Diego, 1980-84, 1986
88 Bob Griese, Miami, 1971-72, 1974-75, 1977, 1979
56 Ken Anderson, Cincinnati, 1976-77, 1982-83
Most Attempts, Game
32 Bill Kenney, Kansas City, 1984
30 Dan Fouts, San Diego, 1983
28 Jim Hart, St. Louis, 1976

Completions
Most Completions, Career
63 Dan Fouts, San Diego, 1980-84, 1986
44 Bob Griese, Miami, 1971-72, 1974-75, 1977, 1979
33 Ken Anderson, Cincinnati, 1976-77, 1982-83
Most Completions, Game
21 Joe Theismann, Washington, 1984
17 Dan Fouts, San Diego, 1983
16 Dan Fouts, San Diego, 1986

Completion Percentage
Highest Completion Percentage, Career (40 attempts)
68.9 Joe Theismann, Washington, 1983-84 (45-31)
58.9 Ken Anderson, Cincinnati, 1976-77, 1982-83 (56-33)
52.5 Dan Fouts, San Diego, 1980-84, 1986 (120-63)
Highest Completion Percentage, Game (10 attempts)
90.0 Archie Manning, New Orleans, 1980 (10-9)
77.8 Joe Theismann, Washington, 1984 (27-21)
71.4 Joe Montana, San Francisco, 1985 (14-10)

Yards Gained
Most Yards Gained, Career
890 Dan Fouts, San Diego, 1980-84, 1986
554 Bob Griese, Miami, 1971-72, 1974-75, 1977, 1979
398 Ken Anderson, Cincinnati, 1976-77, 1982-83
Most Yards Gained, Game
274 Dan Fouts, San Diego, 1983
242 Joe Theismann, Washington, 1984
212 Phil Simms, N.Y. Giants, 1986

Longest Completion
64 Dan Pastorini, Houston (to Burrough, Houston), 1976 (TD)
57 James Harris, Los Angeles (to Gray, St. Louis), 1975
Ken Anderson, Cincinnati (to G. Pruitt, Cleveland), 1977
56 Dan Marino, Miami (to Allen, L.A. Raiders), 1985

Average Gain
Highest Average Gain, Career (40 attempts)
7.64 Joe Theismann, Washington, 1983-84 (45-344)
7.42 Dan Fouts, San Diego, 1980-84, 1986 (120-890)
7.11 Ken Anderson, Cincinnati, 1976-77, 1982-83 (56-398)
Highest Average Gain, Game (10 attempts)
11.40 Ken Anderson, Cincinnati, 1977 (10-114)
11.20 Archie Manning, New Orleans, 1980 (10-112)
11.09 Greg Landry, Detroit, 1972 (11-122)

Touchdowns
Most Touchdowns, Career
3 Joe Theismann, Washington, 1983-84
Joe Montana, San Francisco, 1982, 1984-85
Phil Simms, N.Y. Giants, 1986
2 James Harris, Los Angeles, 1975
Mike Boryla, Philadelphia, 1976
Ken Anderson, Cincinnati, 1976-77, 1982-83
Most Touchdowns, Game
3 Joe Theismann, Washington, 1984
Phil Simms, N.Y. Giants, 1986
2 James Harris, Los Angeles, 1975
Mike Boryla, Philadelphia, 1976
Ken Anderson, Cincinnati, 1977

Had Intercepted
Most Passes Had Intercepted, Career
8 Dan Fouts, San Diego, 1980-84, 1986
6 Jim Hart, St. Louis, 1975-78
5 Ken Stabler, Oakland, 1974-75, 1978
Most Passes Had Intercepted, Game
5 Jim Hart, St. Louis, 1977
4 Ken Stabler, Oakland, 1974
3 Dan Fouts, San Diego, 1986
Most Attempts, Without Interception, Game
27 Joe Theismann, Washington, 1984
Phil Simms, N.Y. Giants, 1986
26 John Brodie, San Francisco, 1971
Danny White, Dallas, 1983
21 Roman Gabriel, Philadelphia, 1974
Dan Marino, Miami, 1985

Percentage, Passes Had Intercepted
Lowest Percentage, Passes Had Intercepted, Career (40 attempts)
0.00 Joe Theismann, Washington, 1983-84 (45-0)
3.41 Bob Griese, Miami, 1971-72, 1974-75, 1977, 1979 (88-3)
5.36 Ken Anderson, Cincinnati, 1976-77, 1982-83 (56-3)

Pass Receiving
Receptions
Most Receptions, Career
18 Walter Payton, Chicago, 1977-81, 1984-87
16 Steve Largent, Seattle, 1979, 1982, 1985-87
14 John Stallworth, Pittsburgh, 1980, 1983, 1985
James Lofton, Green Bay, 1979, 1981-86
Most Receptions, Game
8 Steve Largent, Seattle, 1986
7 John Stallworth, Pittsburgh, 1983
6 John Stallworth, Pittsburgh, 1980
Kellen Winslow, San Diego, 1982

Yards Gained
Most Yards Gained, Career
226 Wes Chandler, New Orleans, 1980; San Diego, 1983-84, 1986
219 Steve Largent, Seattle, 1979, 1982, 1985-87
206 James Lofton, Green Bay, 1979, 1981-86
Most Yards Gained, Game
114 Wes Chandler, San Diego, 1986
96 Ken Burrough, Houston, 1976
91 Alfred Jenkins, Atlanta, 1981
Longest Reception
64 Ken Burrough, Houston (from Pastorini, Houston), 1976 (TD)
57 Mel Gray, St. Louis (from Harris, Los Angeles), 1975
Greg Pruitt, Cleveland (from Anderson, Cincinnati), 1977
56 Marcus Allen, L.A. Raiders (from Marino, Miami), 1985

Touchdowns
Most Touchdowns, Career
2 Mel Gray, St. Louis, 1975-78
Cliff Branch, Oakland, 1975-78
Terry Metcalf, St. Louis, 1975-76, 1978
Tony Hill, Dallas, 1979-80, 1986
William Andrews, Atlanta, 1981-84
James Lofton, Green Bay, 1979, 1981-86
Jimmie Giles, Tampa Bay, 1981-83, 1986
Most Touchdowns, Game
2 William Andrews, Atlanta, 1984

Interceptions By
Most Interceptions, Career
4 Everson Walls, Dallas, 1982-84, 1986
3 Ken Houston, Houston, 1971-73; Washington, 1975-79
Jack Lambert, Pittsburgh, 1976-84
Ted Hendricks, Baltimore, 1972-74; Green Bay, 1975; Oakland, 1981-82; L.A. Raiders, 1983-84
Mike Haynes, New England, 1978-81, 1983; L.A. Raiders, 1985-87
2 By five players

Most Interceptions By, Game
2 Mel Blount, Pittsburgh, 1977
Everson Walls, Dallas, 1982, 1983
LeRoy Irvin, L.A. Rams, 1986

Yards Gained
Most Yards Gained, Career
77 Ted Hendricks, Baltimore, 1972-74; Green Bay, 1975; Oakland, 1981-82; L.A. Raiders, 1983-84
48 Joey Browner, Minnesota, 1986-87
44 Nolan Cromwell, L.A. Rams, 1981-84
Most Yards Gained, Game
65 Ted Hendricks, Baltimore, 1973
48 Joey Browner, Minnesota, 1986
44 Nolan Cromwell, L.A. Rams, 1984
Longest Gain
65 Ted Hendricks, Baltimore, 1973
48 Joey Browner, Minnesota, 1986 (TD)
44 Nolan Cromwell, L.A. Rams, 1984 (TD)

Touchdowns
Most Touchdowns, Game
1 Bobby Bell, Kansas City, 1973
Nolan Cromwell, L.A. Rams, 1984
Joey Browner, Minnesota, 1986

Punting
Most Punts, Career
33 Ray Guy, Oakland, 1974-79, 1981
19 Dave Jennings, N.Y. Giants, 1979-81, 1983
16 Jerrel Wilson, Kansas City, 1971-73
Tom Wittum, San Francisco, 1974-75
Most Punts, Game
10 Reggie Roby, Miami, 1985
9 Tom Wittum, San Francisco, 1974
Rohn Stark, Indianapolis, 1987
8 Jerrel Wilson, Kansas City, 1971
Tom Skladany, Detroit, 1982
Longest Punt
64 Tom Wittum, San Francisco, 1974
61 Reggie Roby, Miami, 1985
60 Ron Widby, Dallas, 1972

Average Yardage
Highest Average, Career (10 punts)
45.25 Jerrel Wilson, Kansas City, 1971-73 (16-724)
44.64 Ray Guy, Oakland, 1974-79, 1981 (33-1,473)
44.63 Tom Wittum, San Francisco, 1974-75 (16-714)
Highest Average, Game (4 punts)
49.00 Ray Guy, Oakland, 1974 (4-196)
47.75 Bob Grupp, Kansas City, 1980 (4-191)
47.40 Ray Guy, Oakland, 1976 (5-237)

Punt Returns
Most Punt Returns, Career
13 Rick Upchurch, Denver, 1977, 1979-80, 1983
10 Mike Nelms, Washington, 1981-83
9 Greg Pruitt, Cleveland, 1974-75, 1977-78; L.A. Raiders, 1984
Most Punt Returns, Game
7 Vai Sikahema, St. Louis, 1987
6 Henry Ellard, L.A. Rams, 1985
5 Rick Upchurch, Denver, 1980
Mike Nelms, Washington, 1981
Carl Roaches, Houston, 1982
Most Fair Catches, Game
2 Jerry Logan, Baltimore, 1971
Dick Anderson, Miami, 1974
Henry Ellard, L.A. Rams, 1985

Yards Gained
Most Yards Gained, Career
183 Billy Johnson, Houston, 1976, 1978; Atlanta, 1984
138 Rick Upchurch, Denver, 1977, 1979-80, 1983
119 Mike Nelms, Washington, 1981-83
Most Yards Gained, Game
159 Billy Johnson, Houston, 1976
138 Mel Renfro, Dallas, 1971
117 Wally Henry, Philadelphia, 1980
Longest Punt Return
90 Billy Johnson, Houston, 1976 (TD)
86 Wally Henry, Philadelphia, 1980 (TD)
82 Mel Renfro, Dallas, 1971 (TD)

Touchdowns
Most Touchdowns, Game
2 Mel Renfro, Dallas, 1971
1 Billy Johnson, Houston, 1976
Wally Henry, Philadelphia, 1980

Kickoff Returns
Most Kickoff Returns, Career
10 Rick Upchurch, Denver, 1977, 1979-80, 1983
Greg Pruitt, Cleveland, 1974-75, 1977-78; L.A. Raiders, 1984
8 Mike Nelms, Washington, 1981-83
6 Terry Metcalf, St. Louis, 1975-76, 1978
Most Kickoff Returns, Game
6 Greg Pruitt, L.A. Raiders, 1984
5 Les (Speedy) Duncan, Washington, 1972
Ron Smith, Chicago, 1973
Herb Mul-Key, Washington, 1974
4 By five players

Yards Gained
Most Yards Gained, Career
309 Greg Pruitt, Cleveland, 1974-75, 1977-78; L.A. Raiders, 1984
222 Rick Upchurch, Denver, 1977, 1979-80, 1983
175 Les (Speedy) Duncan, Washington, 1972
Most Yards Gained, Game
192 Greg Pruitt, L.A. Raiders, 1984
175 Les (Speedy) Duncan, Washington, 1972
152 Ron Smith, Chicago, 1973
Longest Kickoff Return
62 Greg Pruitt, L.A. Raiders, 1984
61 Eugene (Mercury) Morris, Miami, 1972
55 Ron Smith, Chicago, 1973

Touchdowns
Most Touchdowns, Game
None

Fumbles
Most Fumbles, Career
6 Dan Fouts, San Diego, 1980-84, 1986
4 Lawrence McCutcheon, Los Angeles, 1974-78
Franco Harris, Pittsburgh, 1973-76, 1978-81
Jay Schroeder, Washington, 1987
3 O.J. Simpson, Buffalo, 1973-77
William Andrews, Atlanta, 1981-84
Joe Montana, San Francisco, 1982, 1984-85
Walter Payton, Chicago, 1977-81, 1984-87
Vai Sikahema, St. Louis, 1987
Most Fumbles, Game
4 Jay Schroeder, Washington, 1987
3 Dan Fouts, San Diego, 1982
Vai Sikahema, St. Louis, 1987
2 By nine players

Recoveries
Most Fumbles Recovered, Career
3 Harold Jackson, Philadelphia, 1973; Los Angeles, 1974, 1976, 1978 (3-own)
Dan Fouts, San Diego, 1980-84, 1986 (3-own)
Randy White, Dallas, 1978, 1980-86 (3-opp)
2 By many players
Most Fumbles Recovered, Game
2 Dick Anderson, Miami, 1974 (1-own, 1-opp)
Harold Jackson, Los Angeles, 1974 (2-own)
Dan Fouts, San Diego, 1982 (2-own)

Yardage
Longest Fumble Return
83 Art Still, Kansas City, 1985 (TD, opp)
51 Phil Villapiano, Oakland, 1974 (opp)
34 Rick Upchurch, Denver, 1980 (own)

Touchdowns
Most Touchdowns, Game
1 Art Still, Kansas City, 1985

Sacks
Sacks have been compiled since 1983.
Most Sacks, Career
7 Mark Gastineau, N.Y. Jets, 1983-1986
5 Howie Long, L.A. Raiders, 1984-87
4 Lee Roy Selmon, Tampa Bay, 1983-85
Reggie White, Philadelphia, 1987
Most Sacks, Game
4 Mark Gastineau, N.Y. Jets, 1985
Reggie White, Philadelphia, 1987
3 Richard Dent, Chicago, 1985
2 By many players

Team Records

Scoring
Most Points, Game
45 NFC, 1984
Fewest Points, Game
3 AFC, 1984
Most Points, Both Teams, Game
64 NFC (37) vs. AFC (27), 1980
Fewest Points, Both Teams, Game
16 NFC (6) vs. AFC (10), 1987

Touchdowns
Most Touchdowns, Game
6 NFC, 1984
Fewest Touchdowns, Game
0 AFC, 1971, 1974, 1984
NFC, 1987
Most Touchdowns, Both Teams, Game
8 AFC (4) vs. NFC (4), 1973
NFC (5) vs. AFC (3), 1980
Fewest Touchdowns, Both Teams, Game
1 AFC (0) vs. NFC (1), 1974
NFC (0) vs. AFC (1), 1987

Points After Touchdown
Most Points After Touchdown, Game
6 NFC, 1984
Most Points After Touchdown, Both Teams, Game
7 NFC (4) vs. AFC (3), 1973
NFC (4) vs. AFC (3), 1980
NFC (4) vs. AFC (3), 1986

Field Goals
Most Field Goals Attempted, Game
6 AFC, 1972
NFC, 1981, 1983
Most Field Goals Attempted, Both Teams, Game
9 NFC (6) vs. AFC (3), 1983
Most Field Goals, Game
5 AFC, 1974
Most Field Goals, Both Teams, Game
7 AFC (5) vs. NFC (2), 1974

Net Yards Gained Rushing And Passing
Most Yards Gained, Game
466 AFC, 1983
Fewest Yards Gained, Game
146 AFC, 1971
Most Yards Gained, Both Teams, Game
811 AFC (466) vs. NFC (345), 1983
Fewest Yards Gained, Both Teams, Game
424 AFC (202) vs. NFC (222), 1987

Rushing
Attempts
Most Attempts, Game
50 AFC, 1974
Fewest Attempts, Game
18 AFC, 1984
Most Attempts, Both Teams, Game
80 AFC (50) vs. NFC (30), 1974
Fewest Attempts, Both Teams, Game
54 AFC (27) vs. NFC (27), 1983
AFC (18) vs. NFC (36), 1984

Yards Gained
Most Yards Gained, Game
224 NFC, 1976
Fewest Yards Gained, Game
64 NFC, 1974
Most Yards Gained, Both Teams, Game
425 NFC (224) vs. AFC (201), 1976
Fewest Yards Gained, Both Teams, Game
178 AFC (66) vs. NFC (112), 1971

Touchdowns
Most Touchdowns, Game
2 AFC, 1973, 1980, 1982
NFC, 1973, 1977, 1980
Most Touchdowns, Both Teams, Game
4 AFC (2) vs. NFC (2), 1973
AFC (2) vs. NFC (2), 1980

Passing
Attempts
Most Attempts, Game
50 AFC, 1983
Fewest Attempts, Game
17 NFC, 1972
Most Attempts, Both Teams, Game
94 AFC (50) vs. NFC (44), 1983
Fewest Attempts, Both Teams, Game
42 NFC (17) vs. AFC (25), 1972

Completions
Most Completions, Game
31 AFC, 1983
Fewest Completions, Game
7 NFC, 1972, 1982
Most Completions, Both Teams, Game
55 AFC (31) vs. NFC (24), 1983
Fewest Completions, Both Teams, Game
18 NFC (7) vs. AFC (11), 1972

Yards Gained
Most Yards Gained, Game
387 AFC, 1983
Fewest Yards Gained, Game
42 NFC, 1982
Most Yards Gained, Both Teams, Game
608 AFC (387) vs. NFC (221), 1983
Fewest Yards Gained, Both Teams, Game
215 NFC (89) vs. AFC (126), 1972

Times Sacked
Most Times Sacked, Game
9 NFC, 1985
Fewest Times Sacked, Game
0 NFC, 1971
Most Times Sacked, Both Teams, Game
17 NFC (9) vs. AFC (8), 1985
Fewest Times Sacked, Both Teams, Game
4 AFC (2) vs. NFC (2), 1978

Touchdowns
Most Touchdowns, Game
4 NFC, 1984
Most Touchdowns, Both Teams, Game
5 NFC (3) vs. AFC (2), 1986

Interceptions By
Most Interceptions By, Game
6 AFC, 1977

Most Interceptions By, Both Teams, Game
7 AFC (6) vs. NFC (1), 1977

Yards Gained
Most Yards Gained, Game
78 NFC, 1986
Most Yards Gained, Both Teams, Game
99 NFC (64) vs. AFC (35), 1975

Touchdowns
Most Touchdowns, Game
1 AFC, 1973
NFC, 1984, 1986

Punting
Most Punts, Game
10 AFC, 1985
Fewest Punts, Game
2 NFC, 1984
Most Punts, Both Teams, Game
16 AFC (10) vs. NFC (6), 1985
Fewest Punts, Both Teams, Game
6 NFC (2) vs. AFC (4), 1984

Average Yardage
Highest Average, Game
49.00 AFC, 1974 (4-196)

Punt Returns
Most Punt Returns, Game
7 NFC, 1985, 1987
Fewest Punt Returns, Game
0 AFC, 1984
Most Punt Returns, Both Teams, Game
11 NFC (7) vs. AFC (4), 1985
Fewest Punt Returns, Both Teams, Game
3 AFC (0) vs. NFC (3), 1984

Yards Gained
Most Yards Gained, Game
177 AFC, 1976
Fewest Yards Gained, Game
0 AFC, 1984
Most Yards Gained, Both Teams, Game
263 AFC (177) vs. NFC (86), 1976
Fewest Yards Gained, Both Teams, Game
16 AFC (0) vs. NFC (16), 1984

Touchdowns
Most Touchdowns, Game
2 NFC, 1971

Kickoff Returns
Most Kickoff Returns, Game
7 AFC, 1984
Fewest Kickoff Returns, Game
1 NFC, 1971, 1984
Most Kickoff Returns, Both Teams, Game
10 AFC (5) vs. NFC (5), 1976
AFC (5) vs. NFC (5), 1986
Fewest Kickoff Returns, Both Teams, Game
5 NFC (2) vs. AFC (3), 1979

Yards Gained
Most Yards Gained, Game
215 AFC, 1984
Fewest Yards Gained, Game
6 NFC, 1971
Most Yards Gained, Both Teams, Game
293 NFC (200) vs. AFC (93), 1972
Fewest Yards Gained, Both Teams, Game
99 NFC (48) vs. AFC (51), 1987

Touchdowns
Most Touchdowns, Game
None

Fumbles
Most Fumbles, Game
10 NFC, 1974
Most Fumbles, Both Teams, Game
15 NFC (10) vs. AFC (5), 1974

Recoveries
Most Fumbles Recovered, Game
10 NFC, 1974 (6 own, 4 opp)
Most Fumbles Lost, Game
4 AFC, 1974

Yards Gained
Most Yards Gained, Game
87 AFC, 1985

Touchdowns
Most Touchdowns, Game
1 AFC, 1985

Turnovers
(Number of times losing the ball on interceptions and fumbles.)
Most Turnovers, Game
8 AFC, 1974
Fewest Turnovers, Game
1 AFC, 1972, 1976, 1978, 1979, 1985, 1987
NFC, 1976, 1980, 1983
Most Turnovers, Both Teams, Game
12 AFC (8) vs. NFC (4), 1974
Fewest Turnovers, Both Teams, Game
2 AFC (1) vs. NFC (1), 1976

RULES

1987 NFL Roster of Officials

Art McNally, Supervisor of Officials
Jack Reader, Assistant Supervisor of Officials
Nick Skorich, Assistant Supervisor of Officials
Joe Gardi, Assistant Supervisor of Officials
Tony Veteri, Assistant Supervisor of Officials

No.	Name	Position	College
115	Ancich, Hendi	Umpire	Harbor College
81	Anderson, Dave	Head Linesman	Salem College
34	Austin, Gerald	Side Judge	Western Carolina
22	Baetz, Paul	Back Judge	Heidelberg
116	Baker, Bob	Line Judge	East Texas State
55	Barnes, Tom	Back Judge	Minnesota
14	Barth, Gene	Referee	St. Louis
56	Baynes, Ron	Side Judge	Auburn
59	Beeks, Bob	Line Judge	Lincoln
17	Bergman, Jerry	Head Linesman	Duquesne
83	Blum, Ron	Line Judge	Marin College
110	Botchan, Ron	Umpire	Occidental
101	Boylston, Bob	Umpire	Alabama
43	Cashion, Red	Referee	Texas A&M
24	Clymer, Roy	Back Judge	New Mexico State
27	Conway, Al	Umpire	Army
61	Creed, Dick	Side Judge	Louisville
78	Demmas, Art	Umpire	Vanderbilt
45	DeSouza, Ron	Line Judge	Morgan State
74	Dodez, Ray	Line Judge	Wooster
31	Dolack, Dick	Field Judge	Ferris State
6	Dooley, Tom	Referee	VMI
113	Dorkowski, Don	Field Judge	Cal State-L.A.
102	Douglas, Merrill	Side Judge	Utah
12	Dreith, Ben	Referee	Colorado State
39	Fette, Jack	Line Judge	No College
57	Fiffick, Ed	Umpire	Marquette
47	Fincken, Tom	Side Judge	Kansas State
111	Frantz, Earnie	Head Linesman	No College
71	Frederic, Bob	Referee	Colorado
62	Gandy, Duwayne	Side Judge	Tulsa
50	Gereb, Neil	Umpire	California
72	Gierke, Terry	Head Linesman	Portland State
15	Glass, Bama	Line Judge	Colorado
85	Glover, Frank	Head Linesman	Morris Brown
23	Grier, Johnny	Field Judge	D.C. Teachers
75	Habel, Don	Field Judge	Western Oregon
63	Hagerty, Ligouri	Head Linesman	Syracuse
40	Haggerty, Pat	Referee	Colorado State
96	Hakes, Don	Field Judge	Bradley
104	Hamer, Dale	Head Linesman	Calif. Univ., Pa.
42	Hamilton, Dave	Umpire	Utah
105	Hantak, Dick	Referee	Southeast Missouri
66	Hawk, Dave	Side Judge	Southern Methodist
112	Haynes, Joe	Line Judge	Alcorn State
19	Hensley, Tommy	Umpire	Tennessee
54	Johnson, Jack	Line Judge	Pacific Lutheran
114	Johnson, Tom	Head Linesman	Miami, Ohio
97	Jones, Nathan	Side Judge	Lewis & Clark
60	Jorgensen, Dick	Referee	Wisconsin
106	Jury, Al	Back Judge	San Bernardino Valley
107	Kearney, Jim	Back Judge	Pennsylvania
67	Keck, John	Umpire	Cornell College
25	Kelleher, Tom	Back Judge	Holy Cross
108	Kemp, Stan	Side Judge	Michigan
65	Kragseth, Norm	Head Linesman	Northwestern
86	Kukar, Bernie	Field Judge	St. John's
120	Lane, Gary	Side Judge	Missouri
18	Lewis, Bob	Field Judge	No College
21	Liske, Pete	Back Judge	Penn State
90	Mace, Gil	Side Judge	Westminster
82	Mallette, Pat	Field Judge	Nebraska
26	Marion, Ed	Head Linesman	Pennsylvania
9	Markbreit, Jerry	Referee	Illinois
94	Marshall, Vern	Line Judge	Linfield
38	Maurer, Bruce	Side Judge	Ohio State
48	McCarter, Gordon	Referee	Western Reserve
95	McElwee, Bob	Referee	Navy
41	McKenzie, Dick	Line Judge	Ashland
76	Merrifield, Ed	Field Judge	Missouri
35	Miles, Leo	Head Linesman	Virginia State
117	Montgomery, Ben	Umpire	Morehouse
36	Moore, Bob	Back Judge	Dayton
88	Moss, Dave	Umpire	Dartmouth
20	Nemmers, Larry	Side Judge	Upper Iowa
51	Orem, Dale	Line Judge	Louisville
77	Orr, Don	Field Judge	Vanderbilt
64	Parry, Dave	Side Judge	Wabash
10	Phares, Ron	Head Linesman	Virginia Tech
79	Pointer, Aaron	Line Judge	Pacific Lutheran
92	Poole, Jim	Back Judge	San Diego State
58	Quinby, Bill	Side Judge	Iowa State
53	Reynolds, Bill	Line Judge	West Chester State
68	Richard, Louis	Back Judge	Southwest Louisiana
33	Roe, Howard	Line Judge	Wichita State
98	Rosser, Jimmy	Back Judge	Auburn
70	Seeman, Jerry	Referee	Winona State
109	Semon, Sid	Head Linesman	So. California
118	Sifferman, Tom	Back Judge	Seattle
7	Silva, Fred	Referee	San Jose State
73	Skelton, Bobby	Field Judge	Alabama
29	Slavin, Howard	Back Judge	So. California
3	Smith, Boyce	Line Judge	Vanderbilt
119	Spitler, Ron	Field Judge	Panhandle State
91	Stanley, Bill	Field Judge	Redlands
103	Stuart, Rex	Umpire	Appalachian State
37	Toler, Burl	Head Linesman	San Francisco
52	Tompkins, Ben	Back Judge	Texas
32	Tunney, Jim	Referee	Occidental
93	Vaughan, Jack	Field Judge	Mississippi State
100	Wagner, Bob	Umpire	Penn State
28	Wedge, Don	Back Judge	Ohio Wesleyan
87	Weidner, Paul	Head Linesman	Cincinnati
89	Wells, Gordon	Umpire	Occidental
99	Williams, Banks	Back Judge	Houston
8	Williams, Dale	Head Linesman	Cal St.-Northridge
84	Wortman, Bob	Field Judge	Findlay
11	Wyant, Fred	Referee	West Virginia

Numerical Roster

No.	Name	Position
3	Boyce Smith	LJ
6	Tom Dooley	R
7	Fred Silva	R
8	Dale Williams	HL
9	Jerry Markbreit	R
10	Ron Phares	HL
11	Fred Wyant	R
12	Ben Dreith	R
14	Gene Barth	R
15	Bama Glass	LJ
17	Jerry Bergman	HL
18	Bob Lewis	FJ
19	Tommy Hensley	U
20	Larry Nemmers	SJ
21	Pete Liske	BJ
22	Paul Baetz	BJ
23	Johnny Grier	FJ
24	Roy Clymer	BJ
25	Tom Kelleher	BJ
26	Ed Marion	HL
27	Al Conway	U
28	Don Wedge	BJ
29	Howard Slavin	BJ
31	Dick Dolack	FJ
32	Jim Tunney	R
33	Howard Roe	LJ
34	Gerald Austin	SJ
35	Leo Miles	HL
36	Bob Moore	BJ
37	Burl Toler	HL
38	Bruce Maurer	SJ
39	Jack Fette	LJ
40	Pat Haggerty	R
41	Dick McKenzie	LJ
42	Dave Hamilton	U
43	Red Cashion	R
45	Ron DeSouza	LJ
47	Tom Fincken	SJ
48	Gordon McCarter	R
50	Neil Gereb	U
51	Dale Orem	LJ
52	Ben Tompkins	BJ
53	Bill Reynolds	LJ
54	Jack Johnson	LJ
55	Tom Barnes	BJ
56	Ron Baynes	SJ
57	Ed Fiffick	U
58	Bill Quinby	SJ
59	Bob Beeks	LJ
60	Dick Jorgensen	R
61	Dick Creed	SJ
62	Duwayne Gandy	SJ
63	Ligouri Hagerty	HL
64	Dave Parry	SJ
65	Norm Kragseth	HL
66	Dave Hawk	SJ
67	John Keck	U
68	Louis Richard	BJ
70	Jerry Seeman	R
71	Bob Frederic	R
72	Terry Gierke	HL
73	Bobby Skelton	FJ
74	Ray Dodez	LJ
75	Don Habel	FJ
76	Ed Merrifield	FJ
77	Don Orr	FJ
78	Art Demmas	U
79	Aaron Pointer	LJ
81	Dave Anderson	HL
82	Pat Mallette	FJ
83	Ron Blum	LJ
84	Bob Wortman	FJ
85	Frank Glover	HL
86	Bernie Kukar	FJ
87	Paul Weidner	HL
88	Dave Moss	U
89	Gordon Wells	U
90	Gil Mace	SJ
91	Bill Stanley	FJ
92	Jim Poole	BJ
93	Jack Vaughan	FJ
94	Vern Marshall	LJ
95	Bob McElwee	R
96	Don Hakes	FJ
97	Nathan Jones	SJ
98	Jimmy Rosser	BJ
99	Banks Williams	BJ
100	Bob Wagner	U
101	Bob Boylston	U
102	Merrill Douglas	SJ
103	Rex Stuart	U
104	Dale Hamer	HL
105	Dick Hantak	R
106	Al Jury	BJ
107	Jim Kearney	BJ
108	Stan Kemp	SJ
109	Sid Semon	HL
110	Ron Botchan	U
111	Earnie Frantz	HL
112	Joe Haynes	LJ
113	Don Dorkowski	FJ
114	Tom Johnson	HL
115	Hendi Ancich	U
116	Bob Baker	LJ
117	Ben Montgomery	U
118	Tom Sifferman	BJ
119	Ron Spitler	FJ
120	Gary Lane	SJ

1987 Officials at a Glance

Referees

Gene Barth, No. **14,** St. Louis, president, oil company, 17th year.

Red Cashion, No. **43,** Texas A&M, chairman of the board, insurance company, 16th year.

Tom Dooley, No. **6,** VMI, general contractor, 10th year.

Ben Dreith, No. **12,** Colorado State, teacher-counselor, 28th year.

Bob Frederic, No. **71,** Colorado, president, printing and lithographing company, 20th year.

Pat Haggerty, No. **40,** Colorado State, teacher and coach, 23rd year.

Dick Hantak, No. **105,** S.E. Missouri, high school teacher, 10th year.

Dick Jorgensen, No. **60,** Wisconsin, president, commercial bank, 20th year.

Jerry Markbreit, No. **9,** Illinois, trade and barter manager, 12th year.

Gordon McCarter, No. **48,** Western Reserve, regional sales manager, 21st year.

Bob McElwee, No. **95,** U.S. Naval Academy, owner, construction company, 12th year.

Jerry Seeman, No. **70,** Winona State, assistant superintendent, 13th year.

Fred Silva, No. **7,** San Jose State, consultant, 21st year.

Jim Tunney, No. **32,** Occidental, president of motivation company and professional speaker, 28th year.

Fred Wyant, No. **11,** West Virginia, regional sales director, life insurance company, former NFL player, 22nd year.

Umpires

Hendi Ancich, No. **115,** Harbor, longshoreman, 6th year.

Ron Botchan, No. **110,** Occidental, college professor, former AFL player, 8th year.

Bob Boylston, No. **101,** Alabama, stockbroker, 10th year.

Al Conway, No. **27,** Army, national director, industrial sales, 19th year.

Art Demmas, No. **78,** Vanderbilt, investments and financial planning, insurance company, 20th year.

Ed Fiffick, No. **57,** Marquette, podiatric physician, 9th year.

Neil Gereb, No. **50,** California, supervisor, aircraft company, 7th year.

Dave Hamilton, No. **42,** Utah, hospital administrator, 13th year.

Tommy Hensley, No. **19,** Tennessee, owner, land development and management company, 21st year.

John Keck, No. **67,** Cornell, petroleum distributor, 16th year.

Ben Montgomery, No. **117,** Morehouse, school administrator, 6th year.

Dave Moss, No. **88,** Dartmouth, insurance sales, 8th year.

Rex Stuart, No. **103,** Appalachian State, insurance agent, 4th year.

Bob Wagner, No. **100,** Penn State, executive director, 3rd year.

Gordon Wells, No. **89,** Occidental, college professor, physical education, 16th year.

Head Linesmen

Dave Anderson, No. **81,** Salem, senior account executive, health insurance, 4th year.

Jerry Bergman, No. **17,** Duquesne, executive director, pension fund, 21st year.

Earnie Frantz, No. **111,** vice-president and manager, land title company, 7th year.

Terry Gierke, No. **72,** Portland State, real estate broker, 7th year.

Frank Glover, No. **85,** Morris Brown, assistant area superintendent, 16th year.

Ligouri Hagerty, No. **63,** Syracuse, manager, sporting goods company, 12th year.

Dale Hamer, No. **104,** California University, Pa., vice-president equipment finance, 10th year.

Tom Johnson, No. **114,** Miami, Ohio, teacher, vice-president protection service, 6th year.

Norm Kragseth, No. **65,** Northwestern, consultant, 14th year.

Ed Marion, No. **26,** Pennsylvania, regional pension manager, insurance company, 28th year.

Leo Miles, No. **35,** Virginia State, retired university athletic director, former NFL player, 19th year.

Ron Phares, No. **10,** Virginia Tech, vice-president, general contracting firm, 3rd year.

Sid Semon, No. **109,** Southern California, chairman, physical education department, 10th year.

Burl Toler, No. **37,** San Francisco, director of personnel, San Francisco Community College District, 23rd year.

Paul Weidner, No. **87,** Cincinnati, vice-president marketing and administration, major appliances, 2nd year.

Dale Williams, No. **8,** Cal State-Northridge, coordinator, athletic officials, 8th year.

Line Judges

Bob Baker, No. **116,** East Texas State, vocational adjustment coordinator, 1st year.

Bob Beeks, No. **59,** Lincoln, retired law enforcement officer, 20th year.

Ron Blum, No. **83,** Marin College, manager, golf course, 3rd year.

Ron DeSouza, No. **45,** Morgan State, vice-president, student affairs, 8th year.

Ray Dodez, No. **74,** Wooster, communications consultant, 20th year.

Jack Fette, No. **39,** consultant, sporting goods company, 23rd year.

Bama Glass, No. **15,** Colorado, owner, consumer products, 9th year.

Joe Haynes, No. **112,** Alcorn State, public schools deputy superintendent, 4th year.

Jack Johnson, No. **54,** Pacific Lutheran, president, sports promotions, 12th year.

Vern Marshall, No. **94,** Linfield College, counseling, 12th year.

Dick McKenzie, No. **41,** Ashland, school treasurer, 10th year.

Dale Orem, No. **51,** Louisville, mayor, 8th year.

Aaron Pointer, No. **79,** Pacific Lutheran, supervisor of athletics, 1st year.

Bill Reynolds, No. **53,** West Chester State, teacher and athletic director, 13th year.

Howard Roe, No. **33,** Wichita State, manager and administrator, 4th year.

Boyce Smith, No. **3,** Vanderbilt, sales employee benefits and insurance, 7th year.

Back Judges

Paul Baetz, No. **22,** Heidelberg, financial consultant, 10th year.

Tom Barnes, No. **55,** Minnesota, president, manufacturer's representative agency, 21st year.

Roy Clymer, No. **24,** New Mexico State, area manager, gas company, 8th year.

Al Jury, No. **106,** San Bernardino Valley, state traffic officer, 10th year.

Jim Kearney, No. **107,** Pennsylvania, marketing manager, 10th year.

Tom Kelleher, No. **25,** Holy Cross, president, marketing consultant, 28th year.

Pete Liske, No. **21,** Penn State, assistant athletic director, former NFL player, 5th year.

Bob Moore, No. **36,** Dayton, attorney, 4th year.

Jim Poole, No. **92,** San Diego State, college physical education professor, 13th year.

Louis Richard, No. **68,** Southwest Louisiana, sales representative, 2nd year.

Jimmy Rosser, No. **98,** Auburn, president, employee leasing company, 11th year.

Tom Sifferman, No. **118,** Seattle, manufacturer's representative, 2nd year.

Howard Slavin, No. **29,** Southern California, attorney, 1st year.

Ben Tompkins, No. **52,** Texas, attorney, 17th year.

Don Wedge, No. **28,** Ohio Wesleyan, business consultant, 16th year.

Banks Williams, No. **99,** Houston, vice-president sales, concrete company, 10th year.

Side Judges

Gerald Austin, No. **34,** Western Carolina, associate superintendent, county schools, 6th year.

Ron Baynes, No. **56,** Auburn, director and coach, 1st year.

Richard Creed, No. **61,** Louisville, real estate manager, 10th year.

Merrill Douglas, No. **102,** Utah, deputy sheriff, former NFL player, 7th year.

Tom Fincken, No. **47,** Emporia State, high school teacher, 4th year.

Duwayne Gandy, No. **62,** Tulsa, regional sales manager, educational publishing, 7th year.

Dave Hawk, No. **66,** Southern Methodist, co-owner, warehousing company, 16th year.

Nate Jones, No. **97,** Lewis and Clark, high school principal, 11th year.

Stan Kemp, No. **108,** Michigan, vice president, commercial insurance, 2nd year.

Gary Lane, No. **120,** Missouri, executive vice president, former NFL player, 6th year.

Gil Mace, No. **90,** Westminster, national accounts manager, 14th year.

Bruce Maurer, No. **38,** Ohio State, professor, assistant director, 1st year.

Larry Nemmers, No. **20,** Upper Iowa, high school principal, 3rd year.

Dave Parry, No. **64,** Wabash, high school athletic director, 13th year.

Bill Quinby, No. **58,** Iowa, director, personnel services, 10th year.

Field Judges

Dick Dolack, No. **31,** Ferris State, pharmacist, 22nd year.

Don Dorkowski, No. **113,** Los Angeles State, department head/teacher, 2nd year.

Johnny Grier, No. **23,** D.C. Teachers, planning engineer, telephone company, 7th year.

Don Habel, No. **75,** Western Oregon, auto claim superintendent, 4th year.

Don Hakes, No. **96,** Bradley, high school dean of students, 11th year.

Bernie Kukar, No. **86,** St. John's, sales and service, employee benefits, 4th year.

Bob Lewis, No. **18,** management specialist, 12th year.

Pat Mallette, No. **82,** Nebraska, real estate broker, 19th year.

Ed Merrifield, No. **76,** Missouri, sales manager, 13th year.

Don Orr, No. **77,** Vanderbilt, mechanical contractor, 17th year.

Bobby Skelton, No. **73,** Alabama, industrial representative, 3rd year.

Ron Spitler, No. **119,** Panhandle State, vice-president, special services, 6th year.

Bill Stanley, No. **91,** Redlands, college assistant dean, athletic director, 13th year.

Jack Vaughan, No. **93,** Mississippi State, insurance services, 12th year.

Bob Wortman, No. **84,** Findlay, supervisor, college basketball officials, 22nd year.

NFL Digest of Rules

This Digest of Rules of the National Football League has been prepared to aid players, fans, and members of the press, radio, and television media in their understanding of the game.

It is not meant to be a substitute for the official rule book. In any case of conflict between these explanations and the official rules, the rules always have precedence.

In order to make it easier to coordinate the information in this digest the topics discussed generally follow the order of the rule book.

Officials' Jurisdictions, Positions, and Duties

Referee—General oversight and control of game. Gives signals for all fouls and is final authority for rule interpretations. Takes a position in backfield 10 to 12 yards behind line of scrimmage, favors right side (if quarterback is right-handed passer). Determines legality of snap, observes deep back(s) for legal motion. On running play, observes quarterback during and after handoff, remains with him until action has cleared away, then proceeds downfield, checking on runner and contact behind him. When runner is downed, Referee determines forward progress from wing official and if necessary, adjusts final position of ball.

On pass plays, drops back as quarterback begins to fade back, picks up legality of blocks by near linemen. Changes to complete concentration on quarterback as defenders approach. Primarily responsible to rule on possible roughing action on passer and if ball becomes loose, rules whether ball is free on a fumble or dead on an incomplete pass.

During kicking situations, Referee has primary responsibility to rule on kicker's actions and whether or not any subsequent contact by a defender is legal.

Umpire—Primary responsibility to rule on players' equipment, as well as their conduct and actions on scrimmage line. Lines up approximately four to five yards downfield, varying position from in front of weakside tackle to strongside guard. Looks for possible false start by offensive linemen. Observes legality of contact by both offensive linemen while blocking and by defensive players while they attempt to ward off blockers. Is prepared to call rule infractions if they occur on offense or defense. Moves forward to line of scrimmage when pass play develops in order to insure that interior linemen do not move illegally downfield. If offensive linemen indicate screen pass is to be attempted, Umpire shifts his attention toward screen side, picks up potential receiver in order to insure that he will legally be permitted to run his pattern and continues to rule on action of blockers. Umpire is to assist in ruling on incomplete or trapped passes when ball is thrown overhead or short.

Head Linesman—Primarily responsible for ruling on offside, encroachment, and actions pertaining to scrimmage line prior to or at snap. Keys on closest setback on his side of the field. On pass plays, Linesman is responsible to clear this receiver approximately seven yards downfield as he moves to a point five yards beyond the line. Linesman's secondary responsibility is to rule on any illegal action taken by defenders on any delay receiver moving downfield. Has full responsibility for ruling on sideline plays on his side, e.g., pass receiver or runner in or out of bounds. Together with Referee, Linesman is responsible for keeping track of number of downs and is in charge of mechanics of his chain crew in connection with its duties.

Linesman must be prepared to assist in determining forward progress by a runner on play directed toward middle or into his side zone. He, in turn, is to signal Referee or Umpire what forward point ball has reached. Linesman is also responsible to rule on legality of action involving any receiver who approaches his side zone. He is to call pass interference when the infraction occurs and is to rule on legality of blockers and defenders on plays involving ball carriers, whether it is entirely a running play, a combination pass and run, or a play involving a kick.

Line Judge—Straddles line of scrimmage on side of field opposite Linesman. Keeps time of game as a backup for clock operator. Along with Linesman is responsible for offside, encroachment, and actions pertaining to scrimmage line prior to or at snap. Line Judge keys on closest setback on his side of field. Line Judge is to observe his receiver until he moves at least seven yards downfield. He then moves toward backfield side, being especially alert to rule on any back in motion and on flight of ball when pass is made (he must rule whether forward or backward). Line Judge has primary responsibility to rule whether or not passer is behind or beyond line of scrimmage when pass is made. He also assists in observing actions by blockers and defenders who are on his side of field. After pass is thrown, Line Judge directs attention toward activities that occur in back of Umpire. During punting situations, Line Judge remains at line of scrimmage to be sure that only the end men move downfield until kick has been made. He also rules whether or not the kick crossed line and then observes action by members of the kicking team who are moving downfield to cover the kick.

Back Judge—Operates on same side of field as Line Judge, 17 yards deep. Keys on wide receiver on his side. Concentrates on path of end or back, observing legality of his potential block(s) or of actions taken against him. Is prepared to rule from deep position on holding or illegal use of hands by end or back or on defensive infractions committed by player guarding him. Has primary responsibility to make decisions involving sideline on his side of field, e.g., pass receiver or runner in or out of bounds.

Back Judge makes decisions involving catching, recovery, or illegal touching of a loose ball beyond line of scrimmage; rules on plays involving pass receiver, including legality of catch or pass interference; assists in covering actions of runner, including blocks by teammates and that of defenders; calls clipping on punt returns; and, together with Field Judge, rules whether or not field goal attempts are successful.

Side Judge—Operates on same side of field as Linesman, 17 yards deep. Keys on wide receiver on his side. Concentrates on path of end or back, observing legality of his potential block(s) or of actions taken against him. Is prepared to rule from deep position on holding or illegal use of hands by end or back or on defensive infractions committed by player guarding him. Has primary responsibility to make decisions involving sideline on his side of field, e.g., pass receiver or runner in or out of bounds.

Side Judge makes decisions involving catching, recovery, or illegal touching of a loose ball beyond line of scrimmage; rules on plays involving pass receiver, including legality of catch or pass interference; assists in covering actions of runner, including blocks by teammates and that of defenders; and calls clipping on punt returns.

Field Judge—Takes a position 25 yards downfield. In general, favors the tight end's side of field. Keys on tight end, concentrates on his path and observes legality of tight end's potential block(s) or of actions taken against him. Is prepared to rule from deep position on holding or illegal use of hands by end or back or on defensive infractions committed by player guarding him.

Field Judge times interval between plays on 30-second clock plus intermission between two periods of each half; makes decisions involving catching, recovery, or illegal touching of a loose ball beyond line of scrimmage; is responsible to rule on plays involving end line; calls pass interference, fair catch infractions, and clipping on kick returns; and, together with Back Judge, rules whether or not field goals and conversions are successful.

Definitions

1. **Chucking:** Warding off an opponent who is in front of a defender by contacting him with a quick extension of arm or arms, followed by the return of arm(s) to a flexed position, thereby breaking the original contact.
2. **Clipping:** Throwing the body across the back of an opponent's leg or hitting him from the back below the waist while moving up from behind unless the opponent is a runner or the action is in close line play.
3. **Close Line Play:** The area between the positions normally occupied by the offensive tackles, extending three yards on each side of the line of scrimmage.
4. **Crackback:** Eligible receivers who take or move to a position more than two yards outside the tackle may not block an opponent below the waist if they then move back inside to block.
5. **Dead Ball:** Ball not in play.
6. **Double Foul:** A foul by each team during the same down.
7. **Down:** The period of action that starts when the ball is put in play and ends when it is dead.
8. **Encroachment:** When a player enters the neutral zone and makes contact with an opponent before the ball is snapped.
9. **Fair Catch:** An unhindered catch of a kick by a member of the receiving team who must raise one arm a full length above his head while the kick is in flight.
10. **Foul:** Any violation of a playing rule.
11. **Free Kick:** A kickoff, kick after a safety, or kick after a fair catch. It may be a placekick, dropkick, or punt, except a punt may not be used on a kickoff.
12. **Fumble:** The loss of possession of the ball.
13. **Impetus:** The action of a player that gives momentum to the ball.
14. **Live Ball:** A ball legally free kicked or snapped. It continues in play until the down ends.
15. **Loose Ball:** A live ball not in possession of any player.
16. **Muff:** The touching of a loose ball by a player in an unsuccessful attempt to obtain possession.
17. **Neutral Zone:** The space the length of a ball between the two scrimmage lines. The offensive team and defensive team must remain behind their end of the ball.
    Exception: The offensive player who snaps the ball.
18. **Offside:** A player is offside when any part of his body is beyond his scrimmage or free kick line when the ball is snapped.
19. **Own Goal:** The goal a team is guarding.
20. **Pocket Area:** Applies from a point two yards outside of either offensive tackle and includes the tight end if he drops off the line of scrimmage to pass protect. Pocket extends longitudinally behind the line back to offensive team's own end line.
21. **Possession:** When a player controls the ball throughout the act of clearly touching both feet, or any other part of his body other than his hand(s), to the ground inbounds.
22. **Punt:** A kick made when a player drops the ball and kicks it while it is in flight.
23. **Safety:** The situation in which the ball is dead on or behind a team's own goal if the impetus comes from a player on that team. Two points are scored for the opposing team.
24. **Shift:** The movement of two or more offensive players at the same time before the snap.
25. **Striking:** The act of swinging, clubbing, or propelling the arm or forearm in contacting an opponent.
26. **Sudden Death:** The continuation of a tied game into sudden death overtime in which the team scoring first (by safety, field goal, or touchdown) wins.
27. **Touchback:** When a ball is dead on or behind a team's own goal line, provided the impetus came from an opponent and provided it is not a touchdown or a missed field goal.
28. **Touchdown:** When any part of the ball, legally in possession of a player inbounds, is on, above, or over the opponent's goal line, provided it is not a touchback.
29. **Unsportsmanlike Conduct:** Any act contrary to the generally understood principles of sportsmanship.

Summary of Penalties

Automatic First Down

1. Awarded to offensive team on all defensive fouls with these exceptions:
   (a) Offside.
   (b) Encroachment.
   (c) Delay of game.
   (d) Illegal substitution.
   (e) Excessive time out(s).
   (f) Incidental grasp of facemask.
   (g) Prolonged, excessive or premeditated celebrations by individual players or groups of players.

Loss of Down (No yardage)

1. Second forward pass behind the line.
2. Forward pass strikes ground, goal post, or crossbar.
3. Forward pass goes out of bounds.
4. Forward pass is first touched by eligible receiver who has gone out of bounds and returned.
5. Forward pass touches or is caught by an ineligible receiver on or behind line.
6. Forward pass thrown from behind line of scrimmage after ball once crossed the line.

Five Yards

1. Crawling.
2. Defensive holding or illegal use of hands (automatic first down).
3. Delay of game.
4. Encroachment.
5. Too many time outs.
6. False start.
7. Illegal formation.
8. Illegal shift.
9. Illegal motion.
10. Illegal substitution.
11. First onside kickoff out of bounds between goal lines and not touched.
12. Invalid fair catch signal.
13. More than 11 players on the field at snap for either team.
14. Less than seven men on offensive line at snap.
15. Offside.
16. Failure to pause one second after shift or huddle.
17. Running into kicker (automatic first down).
18. More than one man in motion at snap.
19. Grasping facemask of opponent.
20. Player out of bounds at snap.
21. Ineligible member(s) of kicking team going beyond line of scrimmage before ball is kicked.
22. Illegal return.
23. Failure to report change of eligibility.
24. Prolonged, excessive or premeditated celebrations by individual players or groups of players.

10 Yards

1. Offensive pass interference.
2. Ineligible player downfield during passing down.
3. Holding, illegal use of hands, arms or body by offense.
4. Tripping by a member of either team.
5. Helping the runner.
6. Illegal batting or punching a loose ball.
7. Deliberately kicking a loose ball.

15 Yards

1. Chop block.
2. Clipping below the waist.
3. Fair catch interference.
4. Illegal crackback block by offense.
5. Piling on (automatic first down).
6. Roughing the kicker (automatic first down).
7. Roughing the passer (automatic first down).
8. Twisting, turning, or pulling an opponent by the facemask.
9. Unnecessary roughness.
10. Unsportsmanlike conduct.
11. Delay of game at start of either half.
12. Illegal blocking below the waist.
13. A tackler using his helmet to butt, spear, or ram an opponent.
14. Any player who uses the top of his helmet unnecessarily.
15. A punter, placekicker or holder who simulates being roughed by a defensive player.
16. A defender who takes a running start from beyond the line of scrimmage in an attempt to block a field goal or point after touchdown.

Five Yards and Loss of Down

1. Forward pass thrown from beyond line of scrimmage.

10 Yards and Loss of Down

1. Intentional grounding of forward pass (safety if passer is in own end zone). If foul occurs more than 10 yards behind line, play results in loss of down at spot of foul.

15 Yards and Loss of Coin Toss Option

1. Team's late arrival on the field prior to scheduled kickoff.

15 Yards (and disqualification if flagrant)

1. Striking opponent with fist.
2. Kicking or kneeing opponent.
3. Striking opponent on head or neck with forearm, elbow, or hands whether or not the initial contact is made below the neck area.
4. Roughing kicker.
5. Roughing passer.
6. Malicious unnecessary roughness.
7. Unsportsmanlike conduct.
8. Palpably unfair act. (Distance penalty determined by the Referee after consultation with other officials.)

15 Yards and Automatic Disqualification

1. Using a helmet that is not worn as a weapon.

Suspension From Game

1. Illegal equipment. (Player may return after one down when legally equipped.)

Touchdown

1. When Referee determines a palpably unfair act deprived a team of a touchdown. (Example: Player comes off bench and tackles runner apparently en route to touchdown.)

Field

1. Sidelines and end lines are out of bounds. The goal line is actually in the end zone. A player with the ball in his possession scores when the ball is on, above, or over the goal line.
2. The field is rimmed by a white border, a minimum six feet wide, along the sidelines. All of this is out of bounds.
3. The hashmarks (inbound lines) are 70 feet, 9 inches from each sideline.
4. Goal posts must be single-standard type, offset from the end line and painted bright gold. The goal posts must be 18 feet, 6 inches wide and the top face of the crossbar must be 10 feet above the ground. Vertical posts extend at least 30 feet above the crossbar. A ribbon 4 inches by 42 inches long is to be attached to the top of each post. The actual goal is the plane extending indefinitely above the crossbar and between the outer edges of the posts.
5. The field is 360 feet long and 160 feet wide. The end zones are 30 feet deep. The line used in try-for-point plays is two yards out from the goal line.
6. Chain crew members and ball boys must be uniformly identifiable.
7. All clubs must use standardized sideline markers. Pylons must be used for goal line and end line markings.
8. End zone markings and club identification at 50 yard line must be approved by the Commissioner to avoid any confusion as to delineation of goal lines, sidelines, and end lines.

Ball

1. The home club must have 24 balls available for testing by the Referee one hour before game time. In case of bad weather, a playable ball is to be substituted on request of the offensive team captain.

Coin Toss

1. The toss of coin will take place within three minutes of kickoff in center of field. The toss will be called by the visiting captain. The winner may choose one of two privileges and the loser gets the other:
   (a) Receive or kick
   (b) Goal his team will defend
2. Immediately prior to the start of the second half, the captains of both teams must inform the officials of their respective choices. The loser of the original coin toss gets first choice.

Timing

1. The stadium clock is official. In case it stops or is operating incorrectly, the Line Judge takes over the official timing on the field.
2. Each period is 15 minutes. The intermission between the periods is two minutes. Halftime is 15 minutes, unless otherwise specified.
3. On charged team time outs, the Field Judge starts watch and blows whistle after 1 minute 30 seconds, unless it is during the last two minutes of a half when the time is reduced to 60 seconds. However, Referee may allow two minutes for injured player and three minutes for equipment repair.
4. Each team is allowed three time outs each half.
5. Offensive team has 30 seconds to put the ball in play. The time is displayed on two 30-second clocks, which are visible to the players, officials, and fans. Field Judge is to call a delay of game penalty (five yards) when the time limit is exceeded. In case 30-second clocks are not operating, Field Judge takes over the official timing on the field.
6. Clock will start running when ball is snapped following all changes of team possession.

Sudden Death

1. The sudden death system of determining the winner shall prevail when score is tied at the end of the regulation playing time of all NFL games. The team scoring first during overtime play shall be the winner and the game automatically ends upon any score (by safety, field goal, or touchdown) or when a score is awarded by Referee for a palpably unfair act.
2. At the end of regulation time the Referee will immediately toss coin at center of field in accordance with rules pertaining to the usual pregame toss. The captain of the visiting team will call the toss.
3. Following a three-minute intermission after the end of the regulation game, play will be continued in 15-minute periods or until there is a score. There is a two-minute intermission between subsequent periods. The teams change goals at the start of each period. Each team has three time outs and general provisions for play in the last two minutes of a half shall prevail. Disqualified players are not allowed to return.
   Exception: In preseason and regular season games there shall be a maximum of 15 minutes of sudden death with two time outs instead of three. General provisions for play in the last two minutes of a half will be in force.

Timing in Final Two Minutes of Each Half

1. On kickoff, clock does not start until the ball has been legally touched by player of either team in the field of play. (In all other cases, clock starts with kickoff.)

2. A team cannot "buy" an excess time out for a penalty. However, a fourth time out is allowed without penalty for an injured player, who must be removed immediately. A fifth time out or more is allowed for an injury and a five-yard penalty is assessed if the clock was running. Additionally, if the clock was running and the score is tied or the team in possession is losing, the ball cannot be put in play for at least 10 seconds on the fourth or more time out. The half or game can end while those 10 seconds are run off on the clock.
3. If the defensive team is behind in the score and commits a foul when it has no time outs left in the final 30 seconds of either half, the offensive team can decline the penalty for the foul and have the time on the clock expire.

Try-for-Point

1. After a touchdown, the scoring team is allowed a try-for-point during one scrimmage down. The ball may be spotted anywhere between the inbounds lines, two or more yards from the goal line. The successful conversion counts one point, whether by run, kick, or pass.
2. The defensive team never can score on a try-for-point. As soon as defense gets possession, or kick is blocked, ball is dead.
3. Any distance penalty for fouls committed by the defense that prevent the try from being attempted can be enforced on the succeeding kickoff. Any foul committed on a successful try will result in a distance penalty being assessed on the ensuing kickoff.

Players-Substitutions

1. Each team is permitted 11 men on the field at the snap.
2. Unlimited substitution is permitted. However, players may enter the field only when the ball is dead. Players who have been substituted for are not permitted to linger on the field. Such lingering will be interpreted as unsportsmanlike conduct.
3. Players leaving the game must be out of bounds on their own side, clearing the field between the end lines, before a snap or free kick. If player crosses end line leaving field, it is delay of game (five-yard penalty).

Kickoff

1. The kickoff shall be from the kicking team's 35 yard line at the start of each half and after a field goal and try-for-point. A kickoff is one type of free kick.
2. Either a one-, two-, or three-inch tee may be used (no tee permitted for field goal or try-for-point plays). The ball is put in play by a placekick or dropkick.
3. If kickoff clears the opponent's goal posts it is not a field goal.
4. A kickoff is illegal unless it travels 10 yards OR is touched by the receiving team. Once the ball is touched by the receiving team it is a free ball. Receivers may recover and advance. Kicking team may recover but NOT advance UNLESS receiver had possession and lost the ball.
5. When a kickoff goes out of bounds between the goal lines without being touched by the receiving team, the ball belongs to the receivers 30 yards from the spot of the kick or at the out-of-bounds spot unless the ball went out-of-bounds the first time an onside kick was attempted. In this case the kicking team is to be penalized five yards and the ball must be kicked again.
6. When a kickoff goes out of bounds between the goal lines and is touched last by receiving team, it is receiver's ball at out-of-bounds spot.

Free Kick

1. In addition to a kickoff, the other free kicks are a kick after a safety and a kick after a fair catch. In both cases, a dropkick, placekick, or punt may be used (a punt may not be used on a kickoff).
2. On free kick after a fair catch, captain of receiving team has the option to put ball in play by punt, dropkick, or placekick without a tee, or by snap. If the placekick or dropkick goes between the uprights a field goal is scored.
3. On a free kick after a safety, the team scored upon puts ball in play by a punt, dropkick, or placekick without tee. No score can be made on a free kick following a safety, even if a series of penalties places team in position. (A field goal can be scored only on a play from scrimmage or a free kick after a fair catch.)

Field Goal

1. All field goals attempted and missed from scrimmage line beyond the 20 yard line will result in the defensive team taking possession of the ball at the scrimmage line. On any field goal attempted and missed from scrimmage line inside the 20 yard line, ball will revert to defensive team at the 20 yard line.

Safety

1. The important factor in a safety is impetus. Two points are scored for the opposing team when the ball is dead on or behind a team's own goal line if the impetus came from a player on that team.

Examples of Safety:

(a) Blocked punt goes out of kicking team's end zone. Impetus was provided by punting team. The block only changes direction of ball, not impetus.
(b) Ball carrier retreats from field of play into his own end zone and is downed. Ball carrier provides impetus.
(c) Offensive team commits a foul and spot of enforcement is behind its own goal line.
(d) Player on receiving team muffs punt and, trying to get ball, forces or illegally kicks it into end zone where he or a teammate recovers. He has given new impetus to the ball.

Examples of Non-Safety:

(a) Player intercepts a pass and his momentum carries him into his own end zone. Ball is put in play at spot of interception.
(b) Player intercepts a pass in his own end zone and is downed. Impetus came from passing team, not from defense. (Touchback)
(c) Player passes from behind his own goal line. Opponent bats down ball in end zone. (Incomplete pass)

Measuring

1. The forward point of the ball is used when measuring.

Position of Players at Snap

1. Offensive team must have at least seven players on line.
2. Offensive players, not on line, must be at least one yard back at snap. (**Exception:** player who takes snap.)
3. No interior lineman may move after taking or simulating a three-point stance.
4. No player of either team may invade neutral zone before snap.
5. No player of offensive team may charge or move, after assuming set position, in such manner as to lead defense to believe snap has started.
6. If a player changes his eligibility, the Referee must alert the defensive captain after player has reported to him.
7. All players of offensive team must be stationary at snap, except one back who may be in motion parallel to scrimmage line or backward (not forward).
8. After a shift or huddle all players on offensive team must come to an absolute stop for at least one second with no movement of hands, feet, head, or swaying of body.
9. Quarterbacks can be called for a false start penalty (five yards) if their actions are judged to be an obvious attempt to draw an opponent offside.

Use of Hands, Arms, and Body

1. No player on offense may assist a runner except by blocking for him. There shall be no interlocking interference.
2. A runner may ward off opponents with his hands and arms but no other player on offense may use hands or arms to obstruct an opponent by grasping with hands, pushing, or encircling any part of his body during a block.
3. Blocking:
   (a) During a legal block, contact can be made with the head, shoulders, hands and/or outer surface of the forearm, or any other part of the body.
   (b) Hands (open or closed) must be inside the blocker's elbows and can be thrust forward to contact an opponent as long as the contact is inside the opponent's frame. Hands cannot be thrust forward above the frame to contact an opponent on the neck, face or head. **Note:** The frame is defined as that part of the opponent's body below the neck that is presented to the blocker. Hands with extended arms can be thrust forward to contact an opponent within the opponent's frame anywhere on the field.
   (c) As the play develops, a blocker is permitted to work for and maintain position on an opponent as long as he does not push from behind or clip (outside legal clip zone). A blocker lined up more than two yards outside the tackle is subject, also, to the crackback rule and cannot move into the clip zone and push or clip from behind.
   (d) Blocker cannot use his hands or arms to push from behind, hang onto, or encircle an opponent in a manner that restricts his movement as the play develops.
   (e) By use of up and down action of the arm(s), the blocker is permitted to ward off the opponent's attempt to grasp his jersey or arms.
4. A defensive player may not tackle or hold an opponent other than a runner. Otherwise, he may use his hands, arms, or body only:
   (a) To defend or protect himself against an obstructing opponent. **Exception:** An eligible receiver is considered to be an obstructing opponent ONLY to a point five yards beyond the line of scrimmage unless the player who receives the snap clearly demonstrates no further intention to pass the ball. Within this five-yard zone, a defensive player may make contact with an eligible receiver that may be maintained as long as it is continuous and unbroken. The defensive player cannot use his hands or arms to push from behind, hang onto, or encircle an eligible receiver in a manner that restricts movement as the play develops. Beyond this five-yard limitation, a defender may use his hands or arms ONLY to defend or protect himself against impending contact caused by a receiver. In such reaction, the defender may not contact a receiver who attempts to take a path to evade him.
   (b) To push or pull opponent out of the way on line of scrimmage.
   (c) In actual attempt to get at or tackle runner.
   (d) To push or pull opponent out of the way in a legal attempt to recover a loose ball.
   (e) During a legal block on an opponent who is not an eligible pass receiver.
   (f) When legally blocking an eligible pass receiver above the waist. **Exception:** Eligible receivers lined up within two yards of the tackle, whether on or immediately behind the line, may be blocked below the waist at or behind the line of scrimmage. NO eligible receiver may be blocked below the waist after he goes beyond the line. **Note:** Once the quarterback hands off or pitches the ball to a back, or if the quarterback leaves the pocket area, the restrictions on the defensive team relative to the offensive receivers will end, provided the ball is not in the air.
5. A defensive player must not contact an opponent above the shoulders with the palm of his hand except to ward him off on the line. This exception is permitted only if it is not a repeated act against the same opponent during any one contact. In all other cases the palms may be used on head, neck, or face only to ward off or push an opponent in legal attempt to get at the ball.

6. Any offensive player who pretends to possess the ball or to whom a teammate pretends to give the ball may be tackled provided he is crossing his scrimmage line between the ends of a normal tight offensive line.
7. An offensive player who lines up more than two yards outside his own tackle or a player who, at the snap, is in a backfield position and subsequently takes a position more than two yards outside a tackle may not clip an opponent anywhere nor may he contact an opponent below the waist if the blocker is moving toward the ball and if contact is made within an area five yards on either side of the line.
8. A player of either team may block at any time provided it is not pass interference, fair catch interference, or unnecessary roughness.
9. A player may not bat or punch:
   (a) A loose ball (in field of play) toward his opponent's goal line or in any direction in either end zone.
   (b) A ball in player possession or attempt to get possession.
   (c) A pass in flight forward toward opponent's goal line.
   Exception: A forward or backward pass may be batted in any direction at any time by the defense.
10. No player may deliberately kick any ball except as a punt, dropkick, or placekick.

Forward Pass

1. A forward pass may be touched or caught by any eligible receiver. All members of the defensive team are eligible. Eligible receivers on the offensive team are players on either end of line (other than center, guard, or tackle) or players at least one yard behind the line at the snap. A T-formation quarterback is not eligible to receive a forward pass during a play from scrimmage. **Exception:** T-formation quarterback becomes eligible if pass is previously touched by an eligible receiver.
2. An offensive team may make only one forward pass during each play from scrimmage (Loss of down).
3. The passer must be behind his line of scrimmage (Loss of down and five yards, enforced from the spot of pass).
4. Any eligible offensive player may catch a forward pass. If a pass is touched by one offensive player and touched or caught by a second eligible offensive player, pass completion is legal. Further, all offensive players become eligible once a pass is touched by an eligible receiver or any defensive player.
5. The rules concerning a forward pass and ineligible receivers:
   (a) If ball is touched accidentally by an ineligible receiver on or behind his line: loss of down.
   (b) If ineligible receiver is illegally downfield: loss of 10 yards.
   (c) If touched or caught (intentionally or accidentally) by ineligible receiver beyond the line: loss of 10 yards or loss of down.
6. If a forward pass is caught simultaneously by eligible players on opposing teams, possession goes to passing team.
7. Any forward pass becomes incomplete and ball is dead if:
   (a) Pass hits the ground or goes out of bounds.
   (b) Hits the goal post or the crossbar of either team.
   (c) Is caught by offensive player after touching ineligible receiver.
   (d) An illegal pass is caught by the passer.
8. A forward pass is complete when a receiver clearly touches the ground with both feet inbounds while in possession of the ball. If a receiver would have landed inbounds with both feet but is carried or pushed out of bounds while maintaining possession of the ball, pass is complete at the out-of-bounds spot.
9. If an eligible receiver goes out of bounds accidentally or is forced out by a defender and returns to catch a pass, the play is regarded as a pass caught out of bounds. (Loss of down, no yardage.)
10. On a fourth down pass—when the offensive team is inside the opposition's 20 yard line—an incomplete pass results in a loss of down at the line of scrimmage.
11. If a personal foul is committed by the defense prior to the completion of a pass, the penalty is 15 yards from the spot where ball becomes dead.
12. If a personal foul is committed by the offense prior to the completion of a pass, the penalty is 15 yards from the previous line of scrimmage.

Intentional Grounding of Forward Pass

1. Intentional grounding of a forward pass is a foul: loss of down and 10 yards from previous spot if passer is in the field of play or loss of down at the spot of the foul if it occurs more than 10 yards behind the line or safety if passer is in his own end zone when ball is released.
2. It is considered intentional grounding of a forward pass when the ball strikes the ground after the passer throws, tosses, or lobs the ball to prevent a loss of yards by his team.

Protection of Passer

1. By interpretation, a pass begins when the passer—with possession of ball—starts to bring his hand forward. If ball strikes ground after this action has begun, play is ruled an incomplete pass. If passer loses control of ball prior to his bringing his hand forward, play is ruled a fumble.
2. No defensive player may run into a passer of a legal forward pass after the ball has left his hand (15 yards). The Referee must determine whether opponent had a reasonable chance to stop his momentum during an attempt to block the pass or tackle the passer while he still had the ball.
3. Officials are to blow the play dead as soon as the quarterback is clearly in the grasp of any tackler.

Pass Interference

1. There shall be no interference with a forward pass thrown from behind the line. The restriction for the passing team starts with the snap. The restriction on the defensive team starts when the ball leaves the passer's hand. Both restrictions end when the ball is touched by anyone.
2. The penalty for defensive pass interference is an automatic first down at the spot of the foul. If interference is in the end zone, it is first down for the offense on the defense's 1 yard line. If previous spot was inside the defense's 2 yard line, penalty is half the distance to the goal line.
3. The penalty for offensive pass interference is 10 yards from the previous spot.
4. It is pass interference by either team when any player movement beyond the offensive line significantly hinders the progress of an eligible player or such player's opportunity to catch the ball during a legal forward pass. When a player establishes a position to catch the ball in which an opponent cannot reach the ball without first contacting the player in a manner that prevents the player from catching the ball, such action by the opponent shall be considered interference. Provided an eligible player is not interfered with in such a manner, the following exceptions to pass interference will prevail:
   (a) If neither player is looking for the ball and there is incidental contact in the act of moving to the ball that does not materially affect the route of an eligible player, there is no interference. If there is any question whether the incidental contact materially affects the route, the ruling shall be no interference.
   Note: Inadvertent tripping is not a foul in this situation.
   (b) Any eligible player looking for and intent on playing the ball who initiates contact, however severe, while attempting to move to the spot of completion or interception will not be called for interference.
   (c) Any eligible player who makes contact, however severe, with one or more eligible players while looking for and making a genuine attempt to catch or bat a reachable ball, will not be called for interference.
   (d) It must be remembered that defensive players have as much right to the ball as offensive eligible receivers.
   (e) Pass interference by the defense is not to be called when the forward pass is clearly uncatchable.
   (f) Note: There is no defensive pass interference behind the line.

Backward Pass

1. Any pass not forward is regarded as a backward pass or lateral. A pass parallel to the line is a backward pass. A runner may pass backward at any time. Any player on either team may catch the pass or recover the ball after it touches the ground.
2. A backward pass that strikes the ground can be recovered and advanced by offensive team.
3. A backward pass that strikes the ground can be recovered but cannot be advanced by the defensive team.
4. A backward pass caught in the air can be advanced by the defensive team.

Fumble

1. The distinction between a fumble and a muff should be kept in mind in considering rules about fumbles. A fumble is the loss of possession of the ball. A muff is the touching of a loose ball by a player in an unsuccessful attempt to obtain possession.
2. A fumble may be advanced by any player on either team regardless of whether recovered before or after ball hits the ground.
3. A fumble that goes forward and out of bounds will return to the fumbling team at the spot of the fumble unless the ball goes out of bounds in the opponent's end zone. In this case, the defensive team is to take possession at the spot of the fumble.
4. If an offensive player fumbles anywhere on the field during a fourth down play, or if a player fumbles on any down after the two-minute warning in a half, only the fumbling player is permitted to recover and/or advance the ball. If recovered by any other offensive player, the ball is dead at the spot of the fumble unless it is recovered behind the spot of the fumble. In that case, ball is dead at spot of recovery. Any defensive player may recover and/or advance any fumble.
   Exception: The fourth-down fumble rule does not apply if a player touches, but does not possess, a direct snap from center, i.e., a snap in flight as opposed to a hand-to-hand exchange.

Kicks From Scrimmage

1. Any punt or missed field goal that touches a goal post is dead.
2. During a kick from scrimmage, only the end men, as eligible receivers on the line of scrimmage at the time of the snap, are permitted to go beyond the line before the ball is kicked.
   Exception: An eligible receiver who, at the snap, is aligned or in motion behind the line and more than one yard outside the end man on his side of the line, clearly making him the outside receiver, REPLACES that end man as the player eligible to go downfield after the snap. All other members of the kicking team must remain at the line of scrimmage until the ball has been kicked.
3. Any punt that is blocked and does not cross the line of scrimmage can be recovered and advanced by either team. However, if offensive team recovers it must make the yardage necessary for its first down to retain possession if punt was on fourth down.
4. The kicking team may never advance its own kick even though legal recovery is made beyond the line of scrimmage. Possession only.
5. A member of the receiving team may not run into or rough a kicker who kicks from behind his line unless contact is:
   (a) Incidental to and after he had touched ball in flight.
   (b) Caused by kicker's own motions.
   (c) Occurs during a quick kick, or a kick made after a run, or after kicker recovers a loose ball. Ball is loose when kicker muffs snap or snap hits ground.

(d) Defender is blocked into kicker.
The penalty for running into the kicker is 5 yards and an automatic first down. For roughing the kicker: 15 yards and disqualification if flagrant.

6. If a member of the kicking team attempting to down the ball on or inside opponent's 5 yard line carries the ball into the end zone, it is a touchback.
7. Fouls during a punt are enforced from the previous spot (line of scrimmage). **Exception:** Illegal touching, illegal fair catch, invalid fair catch signal, and fouls by the receiving team during loose ball after ball is kicked.
8. While the ball is in the air or rolling on the ground following a punt or field goal attempt and receiving team commits a foul before gaining possession, receiving team will retain possession and will be penalized for its foul.
9. It will be illegal for a defensive player to jump or stand on any player, or be picked up by a teammate or to use a hand or hands on a teammate to gain additional height in an attempt to block a kick (Penalty 15 yards, unsportsmanlike conduct).
10. A punted ball remains a kicked ball until it is declared dead or in possession of either team.
11. Any member of the punting team may down the ball anywhere in the field of play. However, it is illegal touching (Official's time out and receiver's ball at spot of illegal touching). This foul does not offset any foul by receivers during the down.
12. Defensive team may advance all kicks from scrimmage (including unsuccessful field goal) whether or not ball crosses defensive team's goal line. Rules pertaining to kicks from scrimmage apply until defensive team gains possession.

Fair Catch

1. The member of the receiving team must raise one arm a full length above his head and wave it from side to side while kick is in flight. (Failure to give proper sign: receivers' ball five yards behind spot of signal.)
2. No opponent may interfere with the fair catcher, the ball, or his path to the ball. Penalty: 15 yards from spot of foul and fair catch is awarded.
3. A player who signals for a fair catch is not required to catch the ball. However, if a player signals for a fair catch, he may not block or initiate contact with any player on the kicking team until the ball touches a player. Penalty: snap 15 yards behind spot of foul.
4. If ball hits ground or is touched by member of kicking team in flight, fair catch signal is off and all rules for a kicked ball apply.
5. Any undue advance by a fair catch receiver is delay of game. No specific distance is specified for "undue advance" as ball is dead at spot of catch. If player comes to a reasonable stop, no penalty. For violation, five yards.
6. If time expires while ball is in play and a fair catch is awarded, receiving team may choose to extend the period with one free kick down. However, placekicker may not use tee.

Foul on Last Play of Half or Game

1. On a foul by defense on last play of half or game, the down is replayed if penalty is accepted.
2. On a foul by the offense on last play of half or game, the down is not replayed and the play in which the foul is committed is nullified.
Exception: Fair catch interference, foul following change of possession, illegal touching. No score by offense counts.
3. On double foul on last play of half or game, down is replayed.

Spot of Enforcement of Foul

1. There are four basic spots at which a penalty for a foul is enforced:
   (a) Spot of foul: The spot where the foul is committed.
   (b) Previous spot: The spot where the ball was put in play.
   (c) Spot of snap, pass, fumble, return kick, or free kick: The spot where the act connected with the foul occurred.
   (d) Succeeding spot: The spot where the ball next would be put in play if no distance penalty were to be enforced.
   Exception: If foul occurs after a touchdown and before the whistle for a try-for-point, succeeding spot is spot of next kickoff.
2. All fouls committed by offensive team behind the line of scrimmage and in the field of play shall be penalized from the previous spot.
3. When spot of enforcement for fouls involving defensive holding or illegal use of hands by the defense is behind the line of scrimmage, any penalty yardage to be assessed on that play shall be measured from the line if the foul occurred beyond the line.

Double Foul

1. If there is a double foul during a down in which there is a change of possession, the team last gaining possession may keep the ball unless its foul was committed prior to the change of possession.
2. If double foul occurs after a change of possession, the defensive team retains the ball at the spot of its foul or dead ball spot.
3. If one of the fouls of a double foul involves disqualification, that player must be removed, but no penalty yardage is to be assessed.
4. If the kickers foul during a punt before possession changes and the receivers foul after possession changes, penalties will be offset and the down is replayed.

Penalty Enforced on Following Kickoff

1. When a team scores by touchdown, field goal, extra point, or safety and either team commits a personal foul, unsportsmanlike conduct, or obvious unfair act during the down, the penalty will be assessed on the following kickoff.

Official Signals

1

TOUCHDOWN, FIELD GOAL, or SUCCESSFUL TRY
Both arms extended above head.

2

SAFETY
Palms together above head.

3

FIRST DOWN
Arms pointed toward defensive team's goal.

4

DEAD BALL or NEUTRAL ZONE ESTABLISHED
One arm above head with an open hand.
With fist closed: **Fourth Down.**

5

BALL ILLEGALLY TOUCHED, KICKED, OR BATTED
Fingertips tap both shoulders.

6

TIME OUT
Hands crisscrossed above head.
Same signal followed by placing one hand on top of cap: **Referee's Time Out.**
Same signal followed by arm swung at side: **Touchback.**

7

NO TIME OUT or TIME IN WITH WHISTLE
Full arm circled to simulate moving clock.

8

DELAY OF GAME, ILLEGAL SUBSTITUTION OR EXCESS TIME OUT
Folded arms.

9

FALSE START, ILLEGAL SHIFT, ILLEGAL PROCEDURE, ILLEGAL FORMATION, or KICKOFF OR SAFETY KICK OUT OF BOUNDS
Forearms rotated over and over in front of body.

10

PERSONAL FOUL
One wrist striking the other above head.
Same signal followed by swinging leg: **Running Into or Roughing Kicker.**
Same signal followed by raised arm swinging forward: **Running Into or Roughing Passer.**
Same signal followed by hand striking back of calf: **Clipping.**

11

HOLDING
Grasping one wrist, the fist clenched, in front of chest.

12

ILLEGAL USE OF HANDS, ARMS, OR BODY
Grasping one wrist, the hand open and facing forward, in front of chest.

13

PENALTY REFUSED, INCOMPLETE PASS, PLAY OVER or MISSED GOAL
Hands shifted in horizontal plane.

14

PASS JUGGLED INBOUNDS AND CAUGHT OUT OF BOUNDS
Hands up and down in front of chest (following incomplete pass signal).

15

ILLEGAL FORWARD PASS
One hand waved behind back followed by loss of down signal.

16

INTENTIONAL GROUNDING OF PASS
Parallel arms waved in a diag plane across body. Followed by of down signal (23).

17

'ERFERENCE WITH FORWARD PASS or FAIR CATCH
Hands open and extended forward from shoulders with hands vertical.

18

INVALID FAIR CATCH SIGNAL
One hand waved above head.

19

INELIGIBLE RECEIVER or INELIGIBLE MEMBER OF KICKING TEAM DOWNFIELD
Right hand touching top of cap.

20

ILLEGAL CONTACT
One open hand extended forward.

21

FFSIDE or ENCROACHING
Hands on hips.

22

ILLEGAL MOTION AT SNAP
Horizontal arc with one hand.

23

LOSS OF DOWN
Both hands held behind head.

24

CRAWLING, INTERLOCKING INTERFERENCE, PUSHING, or HELPING RUNNER
Pushing movement of hands to front with arms downward.

25

TOUCHING A FORWARD PASS OR SCRIMMAGE KICK
Diagonal motion of one hand across another.

26

UNSPORTSMANLIKE CONDUCT
Arms outstretched, palms down. (Same signal means continuous action fouls are disregarded.) Chop Block.

27

ILLEGAL CUT or BLOCKING BELOW THE WAIST
Hand striking front of thigh preceded by personal foul signal (10).

28

ILLEGAL CRACKBACK
Strike of an open right hand against the right mid thigh preceded by personal foul signal (10).

29

PLAYER DISQUALIFIED
Ejection signal.

30

TRIPPING
Repeated action of right foot in back of left heel.